PROJECT MANAGEMENT

THE MANAGERIAL PROCESS

6th Edition

PROJECT MANAGEMENT

THE MANAGERIAL PROCESS

6th Edition

Clifford F. Gray

Oregon State University

Erik W. Larson

Oregon State University

Gautam V. Desai

S. P. Jain Institute of Management and Research
Mumbai

McGraw Hill Education (India) Private Limited

CHENNAI

McGraw Hill Education Offices

Chennai New York St Louis San Francisco Auckland Bogotá Caracas
Kuala Lumpur Lisbon London Madrid Mexico City Milan Montreal
San Juan Santiago Singapore Sydney Tokyo Toronto

McGraw Hill Education (India) Private Limited

Project Management: The Managerial Process, 6/e

Indian Adaptation done by arrangement with McGraw-Hill Global Education Holdings, LLC, New York.

Sales Territories: India, Pakistan, Nepal, Bangladesh, Sri Lanka and Bhutan

McGraw Hill Education (India) Edition 2014

This edition can be exported from India only by the publishers,
McGraw Hill Education (India) Private Limited.

Print Edition
ISBN (13 digits): 978-93-392-1203-2
ISBN (10 digits): 93-392-1203-7

EBook Edition
ISBN (13 digits): 978-93-392-1204-9
ISBN (10 digits): 93-392-1204-5

Managing Director: *Kaushik Bellani*
Head—Higher Education (Publishing and Marketing): *Vibha Mahajan*
Publishing Manager—SEM & Tech Ed.: *Shalini Jha*
Senior Production Manager: *Manohar Lal*
Junior Production Manager: *Atul Gupta*
Senior Product Specialist: *Navneet Kumar*
General Manager—Production: *Rajender P Ghansela*
Manager—Production: *Reji Kumar*

Published by McGraw Hill Education (India) Private Limited,
444/1, Sri Ekambara Naicker Industrial Estate, Alapakkam, Porur, Chennai 600 116, Tamil Nadu, India.

Typeset at The Composers, 260, C.A. Apt., Paschim Vihar, New Delhi 110 063 and text and cover printed at Magic International Private Limited, Greater Noida 201 306.

Visit us at: www.mheducation.co.in

ABOUT THE AUTHORS

Clifford F. Gray

CLIFFORD F. GRAY is professor emeritus of management at the College of Business, Oregon State University. He continues to teach undergraduate and graduate project management courses overseas and in the United States; he has personally taught more than 100 executive development seminars and workshops. His research and consulting interests have been divided equally between operations management and project management; he has published numerous articles in these areas, plus a text on project management. He has also conducted research with colleagues in the International Project Management Association. Cliff has been a member of the Project Management Institute since 1976 and was one of the founders of the Portland, Oregon, chapter. He was a visiting professor at Kasetsart University in Bangkok, Thailand, in 2005. He was the president of Project Management International, Inc. (a training and consulting firm specializing in project management) 1977–2005. He received his B.A. in economics and management from Millikin University, M.B.A. from Indiana University, and doctorate in operations management from the College of Business, University of Oregon. He is certified Scrum Master.

Erik W. Larson

ERIK W. LARSON is professor of project management at the College of Business, Oregon State University. He teaches executive, graduate, and undergraduate courses on project management and leadership. His research and consulting activities focus on project management. He has published numerous articles on matrix management, product development, and project partnering. He has been honored with teaching awards from both the Oregon State University MBA program and the University of Oregon Executive MBA program. He has been a member of the Portland, Oregon, chapter of the Project Management Institute since 1984. In 1995 he worked as a Fulbright scholar with faculty at the Krakow Academy of Economics on modernizing Polish business education. He was a visiting professor at Chulalongkorn University in Bangkok, Thailand, and at Baden-Wuerttemberg Cooperative State University in Bad Mergentheim, Germany. He received a B.A. in psychology from Claremont McKenna College and a Ph.D. in management from State University of New York at Buffalo. He is a certified project management professional (PMP) and Scrum Master.

Gautam V. Desai

GAUTAM V. DESAI taught project management as consulting faculty (Adjunct Professor) at S.P. Jain Institute of Management & Research from April 2004 to May 2013. He had brilliant academic career and received his B.E. (Electrical) and B.E. (Mechanical) degrees from Gujarat University and M.S. (Mechanical Engineering) from University of Illinois, Urbana, Illinois, where he had been awarded university fellowship. Before taking up teaching in 2004, he had extensive industrial experience (over 40 years) in high-level general management and project management positions. His experience in project management area covered hands-on experience in practically all phases of project management – from conceptualization, feasibility studies and project financing to engineering design, procurement and project construction. He has published a number of articles and cases on project management in reputed Indian journals and magazines.

"Man's mind, once stretched by a new idea, never regains its original dimensions."

OLIVER WENDELL HOLMES, JR.

To my family who have always encircled me with love and encouragement—my parents (Samuel and Charlotte), my wife (Mary), my sons and their wives (Kevin and Dawn, Robert and Sally) and their children (Ryan, Carly, Connor and Lauren).

C.F.G.

"We must not cease from exploration and the end of all exploring will be to arrive where we begin and to know the place for the first time."

T. S. ELIOT

To Ann whose love and support has brought out the best in me. And, to our girls Mary, Rachel, and Tor-Tor for the joy and pride they give me. Finally, to my muse, Neil, for the faith and inspiration he instills.

E.W.L

PREFACE

Our motivation in writing this text continues to be to provide a realistic, socio-technical view of project management. In the past, textbooks on project management focused almost exclusively on the tools and processes used to manage projects and not the human dimension. This baffled us since people not tools complete projects! While we firmly believe that mastering tools and processes is essential to successful project management, we also believe that the effectiveness of these tools and methods is shaped and determined by the prevailing culture of the organization and interpersonal dynamics of the people involved. Thus, we try to provide a holistic view that focuses on both of these dimensions and how they interact to determine the fate of projects.

The role of projects in organizations is receiving increasing attention. Projects are the major tool for implementing and achieving the strategic goals of the organization. In the face of intense, worldwide competition, many organizations have reorganized around a philosophy of innovation, renewal, and organizational learning to survive. This philosophy suggests an organization that is flexible and project driven. Project management has developed to the point where it is a professional discipline having its own body of knowledge and skills. Today it is nearly impossible to imagine anyone at any level in the organization who would not benefit from some degree of expertise in the process of managing projects.

AUDIENCE

This text is written for a wide audience. It covers concepts and skills that are used by managers to propose, plan, secure resources, budget, and lead project teams to successful completions of their projects. The text should prove useful to students and prospective project managers in helping them understand why organizations have developed a formal project management process to gain a competitive advantage. Readers will find the concepts and techniques discussed in enough detail to be immediately useful in new-project situations. Practicing project managers will find the text to be a valuable guide and reference when dealing with typical problems that arise in the course of a project. Managers will also find the text useful in understanding the role of projects in the missions of their organizations. Analysts will find the text useful in helping to explain the data needed for project implementation as well as the operations of inherited or purchased software. Members of the Project Management Institute will find the text is well structured to meet the needs of those wishing to prepare for PMP (Project Management Professional) or CAPM (Certified Associate in Project Management) certification exams. The text has in-depth coverage of the most critical topics found in PMI's *Project Management Body of Knowledge* (PMBOK). People at all levels in the organization assigned to work on projects will find the text useful not only in providing them with a rationale for the use of project management processes but also because of the insights they will gain on how to enhance their contributions to project success.

Our emphasis is not only on how the management process works, but more importantly, on *why* it works. The concepts, principles, and techniques are universally applicable. That is, the text does not specialize by industry type or project scope. Instead, the text is written for the individual who will be required to manage a variety of projects in a variety of different organizational settings. In the case of some small projects, a few of the steps of the techniques can be omitted, but the conceptual framework applies to all organizations in which projects are important to survival. The approach can be used in pure project organizations such as construction, research organizations, and engineering consultancy firms. At the same time, this approach will benefit organizations that carry out many small projects while the daily effort of delivering products or services continues.

CONTENT

In this and other editions we continue to resist the forces that engender scope creep and focus only on essential tools and concepts that are being used in the real world. We have been guided by feedback from practitioners, teachers, and students. Some changes are minor and incremental, designed to clarify and reduce confusion. Other changes are significant. They represent new developments in the field or better ways of teaching project management principles. Below are major changes to the sixth edition.

- Computer exercises and MS Project examples have been updated to MS Project 2010, and 2013 including video tutorials to help students master the basics of MS Project.
- Terms and concepts have been updated to be consistent with the fifth edition of the *Project Management Body of Knowledge* (2013).
- The chapters on Agile Project Management and Careers in Project Management have been expanded.
- Chapter 6 utilizes a new example that clarifies the differences between free and total slack. Chapters 1, 2, 4, 5 and 14 have been updated.
- A description of the Activity on Arrow (AoA) method for calculating networks has been deleted from the text and is now available only in the Instructor's Manual.
- New student exercises and cases have been added to many chapters.
- The Blue Zuma computer exercise in Appendix 2 has been replaced by the new Red Zuma exercise.
- The Snapshot from Practice boxes feature a number of new examples of project management in action as well as new Research Highlights that continue to promote practical application of project management.
- The Instructor's Manual contains a listing of current YouTube videos that correspond to key concepts and Snapshots from Practice.

Overall the text addresses the major questions and issues the authors have encountered over their 60 combined years of teaching project management and consulting with practicing project managers in domestic and foreign environments. The following questions represent the issues and problems practicing project managers find consuming most of their effort: What is the strategic role of projects in contemporary organizations? How are projects prioritized? What organizational and managerial styles will improve chances of project success? How do project managers orchestrate the complex network of relationships involving vendors, subcontractors, project team members, senior management, functional managers, and customers that affect project success? What factors contribute to the development of a high-performance project team? What project management system can be set up to gain some measure of control? How do managers prepare for a new international project in a foreign culture? How does one pursue a career in project management?

Project managers must deal with all these concerns to be effective. All of these issues and problems represent linkages to an integrative project management view. The chapter content of the text has been placed within an overall framework that integrates these topics in a holistic manner. Cases and snapshots are included from the experiences of practicing managers. The future for project managers appears to be promising. Careers will be determined by success in managing projects.

STUDENT LEARNING AIDS

The text website (www.mhhe.com/sie-gray6e) includes study outlines, online quizzes, PowerPoint slides, videos, Microsoft Project Video Tutorials and web links. The trial version of Microsoft Project software can be downloaded from www.project-tutorial.com/microsoft-project-trial.

THIS SPECIAL INDIAN EDTION

The excellent response received by the 4th Special Indian Edition of the book published in 2010 encouraged to come out with this 6th Special Indian Edition (SIE). It includes fourteen additional cases and 12 additional appendices to the corresponding 6th US edition of the book.

An important feature of the cases in this special Indian edition is that they have been prepared in the backdrop of Indian socio-economic, business and industrial conditions, which would be helpful to the Indian reader for internalization of the concepts. In addition, these cases often include detailed step-by-step illustration of some specific project management tools or techniques which the reader can apply to the project-in-hand with ease. We hope that these additional cases would be helpful to the Indian readers.

Another important feature in this special Indian edition is inclusion of appendices integrating the subject topics with the way they have been treated in the latest PMBOK® Guide, 5th Edition. Unlike other books on project management, PMBOK® Guide has identified and defined forty-seven distinct specific processes commonly associated with good project management practices. For each of such identified process, the main activities associated with the process, the necessary inputs and main outputs and the special techniques employed in developing outputs from inputs are listed and described. An important group of Indian students of project management also looks forward to securing Project Management Professional (PMP®) certification from Project Management Institution, U.S.A. (PMI®), which would require passing the test based on the project management concepts presented in PMBOK® Guide. In view of this, it was felt that a single resource book should be prepared that also caters to the need of these aspirants of PMP certification along with a wider discussion of project management topics and, hence, this approach of adding appendices for integration of the main text with the PMBOK ® Guide. These special appendices, attached to the relevant chapters, present the concepts as groups of project management processes, their inputs, outputs and commonly employed techniques as presented in the latest edition of PMBOK® Guide (5th Edition).

The additional appendices and cases for this 6th Special Indian Edition are listed separately after the contents.

Clifford F. Gray

Erik W. Larson

Gautam V. Desai

Publisher's Note

We value your views, comments and suggestions and hence look forward to your communication at *info.india@mheducation.com.* Please feel free to report piracy issues, if any.

ACKNOWLEDGMENTS

Erik W. Larson

Clifford F. Gray

We would like to thank Lacey McNeely for updating the Test Bank and Online Quizzes; Charlie Cook for revising the PowerPoint slides; Oliver F. Lehmann for providing access to PMBOK study questions; and Pinyarat Sirisomboonsuk for accuracy checking the text and Instructor's Resource Manual content.

Next, it is important to note that the text includes contributions from numerous students, colleagues, friends, and managers gleaned from professional conversations. We want them to know we sincerely appreciate their counsel and suggestions. Almost every exercise, case, and example in the text is drawn from a real-world project. Special thanks to managers who graciously shared their current project as ideas for exercises, subjects for cases, and examples for the text. Shlomo Cohen, John A. Drexler, Jim Moran, John Sloan, Pat Taylor, and John Wold, whose work is printed, are gratefully acknowledged. Special gratitude is due Robert Breitbarth of Interact Management, who shared invaluable insights on prioritizing projects. University students and managers deserve special accolades for identifying problems with earlier drafts of the text and exercises.

We are indebted to the reviewers of past editions who shared our commitment to elevating the instruction of project management. The reviewers include Paul S. Allen, Rice University; Denis F. Cioffi, George Washington University; Joseph D. DeVoss, DeVry University; Edward J. Glantz, Pennsylvania State University; Michael Godfrey, University of Wisconsin–Oshkosh; Robert Key, University of Phoenix; Dennis Krumwiede, Idaho State University; Nicholas C. Petruzzi, University of Illinois–Urbana/Champaign; William R. Sherrard, San Diego State University; S. Narayan Bodapati, Southern Illinois University at Edwardsville; Warren J. Boe, University of Iowa; Burton Dean, San Jose State University; Kwasi Amoako-Gyampah, University of North Carolina–Greensboro; Owen P. Hall, Pepperdine University; Bruce C. Hartman, University of Arizona; Richard Irving, York University; Robert T. Jones, DePaul University; Richard L. Luebbe, Miami University of Ohio; William Moylan, Lawrence Technological College of Business; Edward Pascal, University of Ottawa; James H. Patterson, Indiana University; Art Rogers, City University; Christy Strbiak, U.S. Air Force Academy; David A. Vaughan, City University; and Ronald

W. Witzel, Keller Graduate School of Management. Nabil Bedewi, Georgetown University; Scott Bailey, Troy University; Michael Ensby, Clarkson University; Eldon Larsen, Marshall University; Steve Machon, DeVry University–Tinley Park; William Matthews, William Patterson University; Erin Sims, DeVry University–Pomona; Kenneth Solheim, DeVry University–Federal Way; and Oya Tukel, Cleveland State University. Gregory Anderson, Weber State University; Dana Bachman, Colorado Christian University; Alan Cannon, University of Texas, Arlington; Susan Cholette, San Francisco State; Michael Ensby, Clarkson University; Charles Franz, University of Missouri, Columbia; Raouf Ghattas, DeVry University; Robert Groff, Westwood College; Raffael Guidone, New York City College of Technology; George Kenyon, Lamar University; Elias Konwufine, Keiser University; Rafael Landaeta, Old Dominion University; Muhammad Obeidat, Southern Polytechnic State University; Linda Rose, Westwood College; Oya Tukel, Cleveland State University; and Mahmoud Watad, William Paterson University.

In the sixth edition we continue to commit to improving the text content and improving instruction of project management. We are grateful to those reviewers who provided helpful critiques and insights on the fifth edition, which helped us prepare this revision. The reviewers for the sixth edition include Victor Allen, Lawrence Technological University; Mark Angolia, East Carolina University; Alan Cannon, University of Texas at Arlington; Robert Cope, Southeastern Louisiana University; Kenneth DaRin, Clarkson University; Ron Darnell, Amberton University; Jay Goldberg, Marquette University; Mark Huber, University of Georgia; Marshall Issen, Clarkson University; Charles Lesko, East Carolina University; Lacey McNeely, Oregon State University; Donald Smith, Texas A&M University; Peter Sutanto, Prairie View A&M University; Jon Tomlinson, University of Northwestern Ohio. We thank you for your many thoughtful suggestions and for making our book better. Of course we accept responsibility for the final version of the text.

In addition, we would like to thank our colleagues in the College of Business at Oregon State University for their support and help in completing this project. In particular, we recognize Prem Mathew and Ping-Hung Hsieh for their helpful advice and suggestions. We also wish to thank the many students who helped us at different stages of this project, most notably Neil Young, Saajan Patel, Katherine Knox, Dat Nguyen, Lacey McNeely and David Dempsey. Mary Gray deserves special credit for editing and working under tight deadlines on earlier editions. Special thanks go to Pinyarat ("Minkster") Sirisomboonsuk for her help in preparing the last four editions.

Finally, we want to extend our thanks to all the people at McGraw-Hill/Higher Education for their efforts and support. First, we would like to thank Thomas Hayward and Wanda Zeman for providing editorial direction, guidance, and management of the book's development for the sixth edition. And we would also like to thank Jane Mohr, Heather Ervolino, Nichole Birkenholz, Arpana Kumari, and Janean Utley for managing the final production, design, supplement, and media phases of the sixth edition.

Gautam V. Desai

I wish to express, with deep gratitude, my appreciation to S.P. Jain Institute of Management and Research for providing me with an opportunity for teaching project management from April 2004 to May 2013. I am especially thankful to the Dean Dr. Manesh L. Shrikant and the Director Dr. Sesh Aiyer for taking personal interest in my work and giving encouragement.

I am also thankful to The ICFAI University Press for publishing a number of my cases in their prestigious magazine, 'Projects and Profits' and Indian Institute of Industrial Engineering for publishing my papers in their journal.

I also wish to thank my wife, Pauravi, for her active collaboration in reviewing and discussing the cases while I was writing them and making valuable suggestions. I am also thankful to my children Gauravi, Priyadarshi and Shambhavi for their encouragement and support all along.

In the end, I sincerely thank the entire editorial and production team at McGraw Hill Education for their efforts and support. I would like to make here a special mention of *Mr. Tapas Maji, Ms. Surabhi Khare, Mr. Manohar Lal, Ms. Hema Razdan, and Ms. Shalini Negi* for their support and patient coordination without which this work would not have been possible.

NOTE TO STUDENT

You will find the content of this text highly practical, relevant, and current. The concepts discussed are relatively simple and intuitive. As you study each chapter we suggest you try to grasp not only how things work, but why things work. You are encouraged to use the text as a handbook as you move through the three levels of competency:

I know.

I can do.

I can adapt to new situations.

Project management is both people and technical oriented. Project management involves understanding the cause-effect relationships and interactions among the sociotechnical dimensions of projects. Improved competency in these dimensions will greatly enhance your competitive edge as a project manager.

The field of project management is growing in importance and at an exponential rate. It is nearly impossible to imagine a future management career that does not include management of projects. Résumés of managers will soon be primarily a description of the individual's participation in and contributions to projects.

Good luck on your journey through the text and on your future projects.

CHAPTER-BY-CHAPTER REVISIONS FOR THE SIXTH EDITION

Chapter 1: Modern Project Management

- New Snapshot: *Project Management in Action 2013*.
- Makes stronger case for why project management is essential skill set for anyone's career.
- New Snapshot: *A Dozen Examples of Projects Given to Recent College Graduates*.

Chapter 2: Organization Strategy and Project Selection

- New Snapshot: *Does IBM's Watson's Jeopardy Project Represent a Change in Strategy?*
- New Snapshot: *HP's Strategy Revision*.

- Expanded discussion on the importance of project sponsors.
- Revamped description of how project risks are assessed during the proposal phase.
- New case: *Fund Raising Project Selection Case*.

Chapter 3: Organization: Structure and Culture

- New Snapshot: *Google-y*.
- New case: *Horizon Consulting*.

Chapter 4: Defining the Project

- A new central example of a Work Breakdown Structure (WBS).
- Discussion of Process Breakdown Structure (PBS).
- Inclusion of "power/interest" map for assessing stakeholders.

Chapter 5: Estimating Project Times and Costs

- New Snapshot: *Reducing Estimating Error*.
- Introduction to Reference Class Forecasting methodology.
- New case: *Post Graduation Adventure*.

Chapter 6: Developing a Project Schedule

- A new central example that clarifies the differences between free and total slack.
- A description of the Activity on Arrow (AoA) method for calculating networks has been deleted from the text and is now available only in the Instructor's Manual.

Chapter 7: Managing Risk

- New Snapshot: *Playing Soccer in the Desert*.
- New case: *Sustaining Project Risk Management during Implementation*.

Chapter 8 Appendix 1: The Critical–Chain Approach

- New Snapshot: *Critical Chain Applied to Airplane Part Arrivals*.

Chapter 9: Reducing Project Duration

- New Snapshot: *Smartphone Wars*.

Chapter 10: Leadership: Being an Effective Project Manager

- New case: *The Blue Sky Project*.
- New ethical dilemmas mini-case: *Old Princeton Landing*.

Chapter 11: Managing Project Teams

- Expanded discussion on project vision.

Chapter 12: Outsourcing: Managing Interorganizational Relations

- New Snapshot: *The Boeing 787 Dreamliner.*
- New Snapshot: *U.S. Department of Defense's Value Engineering Awards 2013.*
- New case: *Shell Case Fabricators.*

Chapter 15: International Projects

- More extensive discussion of financial risks associated with international projects.
- New Snapshot: *Project X–Namibia, Africa.*
- New exercise assessing relative safety of different countries.

Chapter 17: An Introduction to Agile Project Management

- Elaborates on the role of product owner in Scrum.
- Includes all the principles of Agile Manifesto.
- Introduces the use of Sprint and Release Burndown charts to monitor progress on Agile projects.
- Discusses the use of hybrid models that combine elements of Agile and Waterfall.

Chapter 18: Project Management Career Paths

- New Snapshot: *Ron Parker.*
- Discussion on how to take advantage of opportunities at a university to develop project management skills.
- Expanded discussion of the value of certification.
- New Snapshot: *Grooming the Next Generation at Intel.*

Appendix 2: Computer Project Exercises

- The Blue Zuma computer exercise in Appendix 2 has been replaced by a new Red Zuma exercise.
- A video tutorial that demonstrates step by step how to complete and answer the original Blue Zuma exercise is available online for students.

LIST OF APPENDICES

(For Integration with PMBOK® Guide, Fifth Edition)

Twelve appendices are added to this Sixth Special Indian Edition of the book for facilitating the study of project management for those professionals who wish to prepare for PMP(R) (Project Management Professional) or CAPM (Certified Associate in Project Management) examinations. These examinations conducted by Project Management Institute (PMI) U.S.A. are based on the framework, lexicon and presentation of project management topics according to the format recommended in the latest edition of PMBOK(R) Guide* PMI recommends the presentation of project management concepts in the *Project Management Processes* format with inputs, tools and techniques and outputs for forty-seven project management processes identified by it. These stand-alone appendices comprehensively cover all project management topics closely following the recommendations for framework, lexicon and presentation in the latest (5th Edition) PMBOK Guide.

---

* A Guide to the Project Management Body of Knowledge (PMBOK(R) Guide) – Fifth Edition Published in 2013

LIST OF INDIAN CASES

Fifteen cases illustrating the typical project management situations are included in this Sixth Special Indian Edition. The following cases, included only in this special Indian edition, have two distinctions:

- Most of the project management books authored by western authors are naturally based on the situations arising in the western countries and with a western industrial, economic and cultural backdrop. The cases include in this book are based on project management situations with Indian industrial and cultural backgrounds, which would make internalization of the concepts much easier for Indian professionals.
- Another special feature of the cases in this edition is that they often include detailed step-by-step illustration of some specific project management tool or technique or display a template, which would provide the reader a detailed guidance for applying the technique to the project in hand.

BRIEF CONTENTS

Appendix

CONTENTS

1

MODERN PROJECT MANAGEMENT

All of mankind's greatest accomplishments—from building the great pyramids to discovering a cure for polio to putting a man on the moon—began as a project.

This is a good time to be reading a book about project management. Business leaders and experts have proclaimed that project management is critical to sustainable economic growth. New jobs and competitive advantage are achieved by constant innovation, developing new products and services, and improving both productivity and quality of work. This is the world of project management. Project management provides people with a powerful set of tools that improves their ability to plan, implement, and manage activities to accomplish specific organizational objectives. But project management is more than just a set of tools; it is a results-oriented management style that places a premium on building collaborative relationships among a diverse cast of characters. Exciting opportunities await people skilled in project management.

The project approach has long been the style of doing business in the construction industry, U.S. Department of Defense contracts, and Hollywood as well as big consulting firms. Now project management has spread to all avenues of work. Today, project teams carry out everything from port expansions to hospital restructuring to upgrading information systems. They are creating next generation, fuel efficient vehicles, developing sustainable sources of energy, and exploring the farthest reaches of outer space. The impact of project management is most profound in the electronics industry, where the new folk heroes are young professionals whose Herculean efforts lead to the constant flow of new hardware and software products.

Project management is not limited to the private sector. Project management is also a vehicle for doing good deeds and solving social problems. Endeavors such as providing emergency aid to areas hit by natural disasters, devising a strategy for reducing crime and drug abuse within a city, or organizing a community effort to renovate a public playground would and do benefit from the application of modern project management skills and techniques.

Perhaps the best indicator of demand for project management can be seen in the rapid expansion of the Project Management Institute (PMI), a professional organization for project managers. PMI membership has grown from 93,000 in 2002 to more than 434,000 currently. See the PMI Snapshot from Practice, for information regarding professional certification in project management.

It's nearly impossible to pick up a newspaper or business periodical and not find something about projects. This is no surprise! Approximately $2.5 trillion (about 25 percent of the U.S. gross national product) are spent on projects each year in the United States alone. Other countries are increasingly spending more on projects. Millions of people around the world consider project management the major task in their profession.

Most of the people who excel at managing projects never have the title of project manager. They include accountants, lawyers, administrators, scientists, contractors, public health officials, teachers, and community advocates whose success depends upon being able to lead and manage project work. For some, the very nature of their work is project driven. Projects may be cases for lawyers, audits for accountants, events for artists, and renovations for contractors. For others, projects may be a small, but critical part of their work. For example, a high school teacher who teaches four classes a day is responsible for coaching a group of students to compete in a national debate competition. A store manager who oversees daily operations is charged with developing an employee retention program. A sales account executive is given the additional assignment of team lead to launch daily deals into a new city. A public health official who manages a clinic is also responsible for organizing a Homeless Youth Connect event. For these and others, project management is not a title, but a critical job requirement. It is hard to think of a profession or a career path that would not benefit from being good at managing projects.

Not only is project management critical to most careers, the skill set is transferable across most businesses and professions. At its core, project management fundamentals are universal. The same project management methodology that is used to develop a new product can be adapted to create new services, organize events, refurbish aging operations, and so forth. In a world where it is

SNAPSHOT FROM PRACTICE

The Project Management Institute*

The Project Management Institute (PMI) was founded in 1969 as an international society for project managers. Today PMI has members from more than 180 countries and more than 424,600 members. PMI professionals come from virtually every major industry, including aerospace, automotive, business management, construction, engineering, financial services, information technology, pharmaceuticals, health care, and telecommunications.

PMI provides certification as a *Project Management Professional (PMP)*—someone who has documented sufficient project experience, agreed to follow the PMI code of professional conduct, and demonstrated mastery of the field of project management by passing a comprehensive examination. The number of people earning PMP status has grown dramatically in recent years. In 1996 there were fewer than 3,000 certified project management professionals. By June of 2013 there were more than 537,400 Professional credential holders.

Just as the CPA exam is a standard for accountants, passing the PMP exam may become the standard for project managers. Some companies are requiring that all their project managers be PMP certified. Moreover, many job postings are restricted to PMPs. Job seekers, in general, are finding that being PMP certified is an advantage in the marketplace.

PMI added a certification as a *Certified Associate in Project Management (CAPM)*. CAPM is designed for project team members and entry-level project managers, as well as qualified undergraduate and graduate students who want a credential to recognize their mastery of the project management body of knowledge. CAPM does not require the extensive project management experience associated with the PMP. For more details on PMP and CAPM, "Google" PMI to find the current Web site for the Project Management Institute.

*PMI Today, June 2013, p. 4

estimated that each person is likely to experience three to four career changes, managing projects is a talent worthy of development.

The significance of project management can also be seen in the classroom. Twenty years ago major universities offered one or two classes in project management, primarily for engineers. Today, most universities offer multiple sections of project management classes, with the core group of engineers being supplemented by business students majoring in marketing, management information systems (MIS), and finance, as well as students from other disciplines such as oceanography, health sciences, computer sciences, and liberal arts. These students are finding that their exposure to project management is providing them with distinct advantages when it comes time to look for jobs. More and more employers are looking for graduates with project management skills. See the nearby Snapshot from Practice for examples of projects given to recent college graduates. The logical starting point for developing these skills is understanding the uniqueness of a project and of project managers.

WHAT IS A PROJECT?

What do the following headlines have in common?

Millions watch Olympic Opening Ceremony
Citywide WiFi system set to go live
Hospitals respond to new Health Care Reforms

SNAPSHOT FROM PRACTICE

A Dozen Examples of
Projects Given to Recent
College Graduates

1. Business information: Join a project team charged with installing new data security system.

2. Physical education: Design and develop a new fitness program for senior citizens that combines principles of yoga and aerobics.

3. Marketing: Execute a sales program for new home air purifier.

4. Industrial engineering: Manage a team to create a value chain report for every aspect of key product from design to customer delivery.

5. Chemistry: Develop a quality control program for organization's drug production facilities.

6. Management: Implement a new store layout design.

7. Pre-med neurology student: Join project team linking mind mapping to an imbedded prosthetic that will allow blind people to function near normally.

8. Sports communication: Join Olympic project team that will promote women's sport products for the 2016 Games in Reo de Janeiro, Brazil.

9. Systems engineer: Become a project team member of a project to develop data mining of medical papers and studies related to drug efficacy.

10. Accounting: Work on an audit of a major client.

11. Public health: Research and design a medical marijuana educational program.

12. English: Create a web-based user manual for new electronics product.

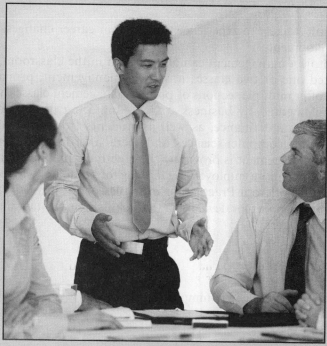

© Troels Graugaard/E1/Getty Images

Apple's new iPhone hits the market

City receives stimulus funds to expand light rail system

All of these events represent projects.

The Project Management Institute provides the following definition of a project:

> A **project** is a temporary endeavor undertaken to create a unique product, service, or result.

Like most organizational effort, the major goal of a project is to satisfy a customer's need. Beyond this fundamental similarity, the characteristics of a project help differentiate it from other endeavors of the organization. The major characteristics of a project are as follows:

1. An established objective.
2. A defined life span with a beginning and an end.
3. Usually, the involvement of several departments and professionals.
4. Typically, doing something that has never been done before.
5. Specific time, cost, and performance requirements.

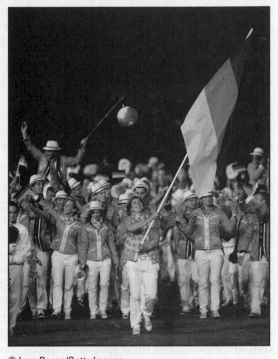

© Lars Baron/Getty Images

First, projects have a defined objective—whether it is constructing a 12-story apartment complex by January 1 or releasing version 2.0 of a specific software package as quickly as possible. This singular purpose is often lacking in daily organizational life in which workers perform repetitive operations each day.

Second, because there is a specified objective, projects have a defined endpoint, which is contrary to the ongoing duties and responsibilities of traditional jobs. In many cases, individuals move from one project to the next as opposed to staying in one job. After helping to install a security system, an IT engineer may be assigned to develop a database for a different client.

Third, unlike much organizational work that is segmented according to functional specialty, projects typically require the combined efforts of a variety of specialists. Instead of working in separate offices under separate managers, project participants, whether they be engineers, financial analysts, marketing professionals, or quality control specialists, work closely together under the guidance of a project manager to complete a project.

The fourth characteristic of a project is that it is nonroutine and has some unique elements. This is not an either/or issue but a matter of degree. Obviously, accomplishing something that has never been done before, such as building a electric automobile or landing two mechanical rovers on Mars, requires solving previously unsolved problems and breakthrough technology. On the other hand, even basic construction projects that involve established sets of routines and procedures require some degree of customization that makes them unique.

Finally, specific time, cost, and performance requirements bind projects. Projects are evaluated according to accomplishment, cost, and time spent. These triple constraints impose a higher degree of accountability than you typically find in most jobs. These three also highlight one of the primary functions of project management, which is balancing the trade-offs between time, cost, and performance while ultimately satisfying the customer.

What a Project Is Not   Projects should not be confused with everyday work. A project is not routine, repetitive work! Ordinary daily work typically requires doing the same or similar work over and over, while a project is done only once; a new product or service exists when the project is completed. Examine the list in Table 1.1 that compares routine, repetitive work and projects. Recognizing the difference is important because too often resources can be used up on daily operations which may not contribute to longer range organization strategies that require innovative new products.

Program versus Project   In practice the terms project and program cause confusion. They are often used synonymously. *A* **program** *is a group of related projects designed to accomplish a common goal over an extended period of time.* Each project within a program has a project manager. The major differences lie in scale and time span.

Program management is the process of *managing* a group of ongoing, inter-dependent, related *projects* in a coordinated way to achieve strategic objectives. For example, a pharmaceutical organization could have a program for curing cancer. The cancer program includes and coordinates *all* cancer projects that continue over an extended time horizon (Gray, 2011). Coordinating all cancer projects under the oversight of a cancer team provides benefits not available from managing them individually. This cancer team also oversees the selection and prioritizing of cancer projects that are included in their special "Cancer" portfolio. Although each project retains its own goals and scope, the project manager and team are also motivated by the higher program goal. Program goals are closely related to broad strategic organization goals.

The Project Life Cycle

Another way of illustrating the unique nature of project work is in terms of the **project life cycle.** Some project managers find it useful to use the project life cycle as the cornerstone for managing projects. The life cycle recognizes that projects have a limited life span and that there are predictable changes in level of effort and focus over the life of the project. There are a number of different life-cycle models in project management literature. Many are unique to a specific industry or type of project. For example, a new software development project may consist of five phases: definition, design, code, integration/test, and maintenance. A generic cycle is depicted in Figure 1.1.

The project life cycle typically passes sequentially through four stages: defining, planning, executing, and delivering. The starting point begins the moment the project is given the go-ahead. Project effort starts slowly, builds to a peak, and then declines to delivery of the project to the customer.

1. **Defining stage:** Specifications of the project are defined; project objectives are established; teams are formed; major responsibilities are assigned.
2. **Planning stage:** The level of effort increases, and plans are developed to determine what the project will entail, when it will be scheduled, whom it will benefit, what quality level should be maintained, and what the budget will be.
3. **Executing stage:** A major portion of the project work takes place—both physical and mental. The physical product is produced (a bridge, a report, a software program). Time, cost, and

TABLE 1.1 ••
Comparison of Routine Work with Projects

Routine, Repetitive Work	Projects
Taking class notes	Writing a term paper
Daily entering sales receipts into the accounting ledger	Setting up a sales kiosk for a professional accounting meeting
Responding to a supply-chain request	Developing a supply-chain information system
Practicing scales on the piano	Writing a new piano piece
Routine manufacture of an Apple iPod	Designing an iPod that is approximately 2×4 inches, interfaces with PC, and stores 10,000 songs
Attaching tags on a manufactured product	Wire-tag projects for GE and Wal-Mart

specification measures are used for control. Is the project on schedule, on budget, and meeting specifications? What are the forecasts of each of these measures? What revisions/changes are necessary?

4. **Closing stage:** Closing includes three activities: delivering the project product to the customer, redeploying project resources, and post-project review. Delivery of the project might include customer training and transferring documents. Redeployment usually involves releasing project equipment/materials to other projects and finding new assignments for team members. Post-project reviews include not only assessing performance but also capturing lessons learned.

In practice, the project life cycle is used by some project groups to depict the timing of major tasks over the life of the project. For example, the design team might plan a major commitment of resources in the defining stage, while the quality team would expect their major effort to increase in the latter stages of the project life cycle. Because most organizations have a portfolio of projects going on concurrently, each at a different stage of each project's life cycle, careful planning and management at the organization and project levels are imperative.

The Project Manager

At first glance project managers perform the same functions as other managers. That is, they plan, schedule, motivate, and control. However, what makes them unique is that they manage temporary, nonrepetitive activities, to complete a fixed life project. Unlike functional managers, who take over existing operations, project managers create a project team and organization where none existed before. They must decide what and how things should be done instead of simply managing set processes. They must meet the challenges of each phase of the project life cycle, and even oversee the dissolution of their operation when the project is completed.

Project managers must work with a diverse troupe of characters to complete projects. They are typically the direct link to the customer and must manage the tension between customer expectations and what is feasible and reasonable. Project managers provide direction, coordination, and integration to the project team, which is often made up of part-time participants loyal to their functional departments. They often must work with a cadre of outsiders—vendors, suppliers, subcontractors—who do not necessarily share their project allegience.

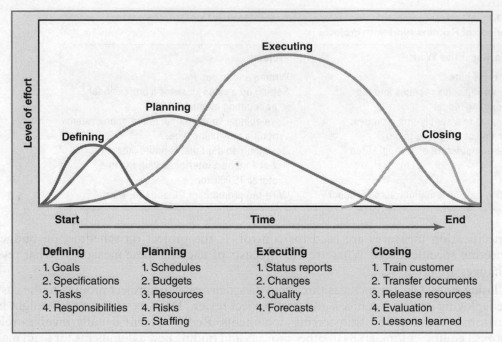

Figure 1.1 *Project Life Cycle*

Project managers are ultimately responsible for performance (frequently with too little authority). They must ensure that appropriate trade-offs are made between the time, cost, and performance requirements of the project. At the same time, unlike their functional counterparts, project managers generally possess only rudimentary technical knowledge to make such decisions. Instead, they must orchestrate the completion of the project by inducing the right people, at the right time, to address the right issues and make the right decisions.

While project management is not for the timid, working on projects can be an extremely rewarding experience. Life on projects is rarely boring; each day is different from the last. Since most projects are directed at solving some tangible problem or pursuing some useful opportunity, project managers find their work personally meaningful and satisfying. They enjoy the act of creating something new and innovative. Project managers and team members can feel immense pride in their accomplishment, whether it is a new bridge, a new product, or needed service. Project managers are often stars in their organization and well compensated.

Good project managers are always in demand. Every industry is looking for effective people who can get the right things done on time. Clearly, project management is a challenging and exciting profession. This text is intended to provide the necessary knowledge, perspective, and tools to enable students to accept the challenge.

Being Part of a Project Team

Most people's first exposure to project management occurs while working as part of a team assigned to complete a specific project. Sometimes this work is full-time, but in most cases, people work part-time on one or more projects. They must learn how to juggle their day-to-day commitments with additional project responsibilities. They may join a team with a long history of working together, in which case roles and norms are firmly established. Alternatively, their team may consist of strangers from different departments and organizations. As such, they endure the growing pains of a group evolving into a team. They need to be a positive force in helping the team coalesce into an effective project team.

Not only are there people issues, but project members are also expected to use project management tools and concepts. They develop or are given a project charter or scope statement that defines the objectives and parameters of the project. They work with others to create a project schedule and budget that will guide project execution. They need to understand project priorities so they can make independent decisions. They must know how to monitor and report project progress. Although much of this book is written from the perspective of a project manager, the tools, concepts, and methods are critical to everyone working on a project. Project members need to know how to avoid the dangers of scope creep, manage the critical path, engage in timely risk management, negotiate, and utilize virtual tools to communicate.

CURRENT DRIVERS OF PROJECT MANAGEMENT

Project management is no longer a special-need management. It is rapidly becoming a standard way of doing business. See Snapshot from Practice: Project Management in Action: 2013. An increasing percentage of the typical firm's effort is being devoted to projects. The future promises an increase in the importance and the role of projects in contributing to the strategic direction of organizations. Several reasons why this is the case are briefly discussed below.

Compression of the Product Life Cycle

One of the most significant driving forces behind the demand for project management is the shortening of the product life cycle. For example, today in high-tech industries the product life cycle is averaging 6 months to 3 years. Only 30 years ago, life cycles of 10 to 15 years were not uncommon. *Time to market* for new products with short life cycles has become increasingly important. A common rule of thumb in the world of high-tech product development is that a six-month project delay can result in a 33 percent loss in product revenue share. Speed, therefore, becomes a competitive advantage; more and more organizations are relying on cross-functional project teams to get new products and services to the market as quickly as possible.

Knowledge Explosion

The growth in new knowledge has increased the complexity of projects because projects encompass the latest advances. For example, building a road 30 years ago was a somewhat simple process. Today, each area has increased in complexity, including materials, specifications, codes, aesthetics, equipment, and required specialists. Similarly, in today's digital, electronic age it is becoming hard to find a new product that does not contain at least one microchip. Product complexity has increased the need to integrate divergent technologies. Project management has emerged as an important discipline for achieving this task.

Triple Bottom Line (planet, people, profit)

The threat of global warming has brought sustainable business practices to the forefront. Businesses can no longer simply focus on maximizing profit to the detriment of the environment

© Frederic J. Brown/AFP/Getty Images

Businesses thrive and survive based on their ability to manage projects that produce products and services that meet market needs. Below is a small sample of projects that are important to their company's future.

ORGANIZATION: PROCTER AND GAMBLE
Project: Global Ordering, Shipping, and Billing Project
The project goal is to improve customer service, processes, and organization structure. The global team relied on virtual communication, while closely managing risk and milestone dates. The new system is designed to allow P&G to make real-time decisions, enabling the company to collect and respond to consumer/retailer feedback to create more compelling promotions to increase sales. The system should also improve efficiencies in supply chains by, for example, identifying the best warehouses to ship products to.
—*PMI Today*, 2012 PMI Project of the Year Finalists, December 2012, p. 7

ORGANIZATION: OAKLAND A'S BASEBALL TEAM
Project: Cisco Stadium
In November 2006, the future of the Oakland A's looked bright as the team announced plans to build a new ballpark in Fremont, CA. Upon announcing plans to build a ballpark, the Oakland A's sold the naming rights to the ballpark to Cisco Systems for $4 million/year over 30 years. The ballpark design mimicked classic ballparks of the past, while combining the most advanced technology in the world. Those plans have since been derailed as opposition increased from major retailers and homeowners near the stadium site. The A's have spent the past five years pursuing other options including building the ballpark in Oakland, near the coliseum, or possibly in San Jose, CA. The A's need the new stadium to turn around lagging attendance, which has been at or near the bottom among major league baseball clubs.
—*Oakland Tribune*, 8/1/12

ORGANIZATION: CHINA SUNERGY CO., LTD
Project: Sanliurfa Solar Park, Turkey
The Chinese company, Sunergy, has entered into a joint agreement with Seul Energy, a leading solar developer, to develop a 500kw solar park in Sanliurfa, Turkey. The plants will incorporate state of the art technology and new types of solar cells. The project is the beginning of an ambitious program designed to meet the expected growth in demand for energy in Central Asia.
—www.prnewswire.com/news-releases/china, accessed 1/5/13

ORGANIZATION: THE WALT DISNEY COMPANY
Project: *Star Wars Episode 7*
Disney spent over $4 billion to purchase Lucasfilm, which included exclusive past and future rights to the popular Star Wars franchise. Preproduction work on the newest Star Wars feature is scheduled to begin in 2013 with a projected release date in 2015. The Star Wars investment is seen by industry experts as an effort by Disney to broaden its pop culture reach and re-establish Disney films in the sci-fi/fantasy genre after the failure of space epic *John Carter* and *Mars Needs Moms*.
—*businessweek.com*, 11/11/12

ORGANIZATION: DISH NETWORK
Project: Hopper
Dish Network made a splash at the 2013 Consumer Electronics Show by showing off the latest generation of Hopper, a whole-home HD DVR system. Hopper includes commercial skipping technology and the ability to move programs onto iPads and other mobile devices. The announcement cemented Dish's position as one of the leaders in the "TV Everywhere" movement in which favorite shows and movies can be accessed from any device at any location. Dish is counting on Hopper and related products to compete against DirecTV and deep-pocketed cable and telecom providers.
—*Ces.cnet.com*, 1/8/13

ORGANIZATION: BILL & MELINDA GATES FOUNDATION
Project: Drought-Tolerant Maize for Africa
The goal of the project is to help farmers in Sub-Saharan Africa living in drought-susceptible areas increase their maize (corn) productivity. Getting the improved maize varieties into the hands of African farmers is the product of over two decades of research and involves a broad coalition of partners, from governments and NGOs to seed dealers and farmers. More than 2 million smallholder farmers in Africa are already realizing the benefits of higher yields. By 2016, the drought-tolerant maize project is expected to boost maize yields by as much as 30%, benefiting up to 40 million people in Africa.
—*gatesfoundation.org*, accessed 1/9/13

ORGANIZATION: FIAT, ITALY
Project: 2013 Fiat 500 EV
Available Spring 2013, the EV is a totally electric version of the popular Fiat 500 line. The EV sports a 100-hp electric motor powered by lithium batteries with 87 miles of electric range. Fiat needs to prove that it is a forward looking company and provide another reason to buy the 500 other than styling or the sales curve will plunge once the cuteness fails. Success will depend upon overcoming customer range anxiety and the risk that governments will stop supporting electric vehicles with attractive subsidies.

—*caranddriver.com*, accessed 1/20/13

ORGANIZATION: SONY, JAPAN
Project: Sony PlayStation 4 (PS4)
It's been seven years since Sony released the highly successful PlayStation 3, and the Internet is buzzing with rumors of a fourth-generation PlayStation. The PS4 reportedly will feature a tablet-style controller and state of the art graphics. At stake is Sony's position in the $10 billion-plus gaming industry.

—*sonyps4.com*, accessed 1/11/13

and society. Efforts to reduce carbon imprint and utilize renewable resources are realized through effective project management. The impact of this movement towards sustainability can be seen in changes in the objectives and techniques used to complete projects. See Snapshot from Practice: Dell Children's Becomes World's First "Green" Hospital.

SNAPSHOT FROM PRACTICE
Dell Children's Becomes World's First "Green" Hospital*

Dateline 1/7/2009, Austin Texas: Dell Children's Medical Center becomes the first hospital in the world to receive platinum LEED (Leadership in Energy & Environmental Design) certification. Platinum certification is the highest award granted by the U.S. Green Building Council.

Dell Children's occupies nearly one-half million square feet on 32 acres that were once part of Austin's old Mueller Airport. Its environmentally sensitive design not only conserves water and electricity, but positively impacts the hospital's clinical environment by improving air quality, making natural sunlight readily available, and reducing a wide range of pollutants.

In order to receive LEED certification, buildings are rated in five key areas: sustainable site development, water savings, energy efficiency, materials selection, and environmental quality. Listed below are some of the accomplishments in each LEED category:

Sustainable Site

- 47,000 tons of Mueller Airport runway material was reused on site.
- About 40 percent fly ash instead of Portland cement in concrete yields a drop in carbon dioxide emissions equivalent to taking 450 cars off the road.
- 925 tons of construction waste was recycled on site.

Water Efficiency and Water Conservation

- Reclaimed water is used for irrigation; xeriscaped landscaping uses native plants, which require less water.
- Low-flow plumbing fixtures.

Energy Efficiency and Energy Conservation

- An on-site natural gas turbine supplies all electricity, which is 75 percent more efficient than coal-fired plants.
- Converted steam energy from a heating/cooling plant supplies all chilled water needs.

Indoor Environment Quality and Lighting

- Most interior spaces are within 32 feet of a window.
- Motion and natural light sensors shut off unneeded lights.

Conservation of Materials and Resources

- Use of local and regional materials saves fuel for shipping.
- Special paints and flooring emit low levels of volatile organic compounds (VOCs).

"Even before the first plans were drawn up, we set our sight on creating a world-class children's hospital, and becoming the first LEED Platinum hospital in the world was definitely part of that," said Robert Bonar, president and CEO, Dell Children's Medical Center of Central Texas. "Our motivation to pursue LEED Platinum was not just environmental. Being a 'green' hospital has profound, measurable effect on healing. What's good for the environment and good for our neighbors is also good for our patients."

* *Austin Business Journal*, 1-11-2009; www.dellchildrens.net/about_us/news/2009/01/08.

Corporate Downsizing

The last decade has seen a dramatic restructuring of organizational life. Downsizing (or rightsizing if you are still employed) and sticking to core competencies have become necessary for survival for many firms. Middle management is a mere skeleton of the past. In today's flatter and leaner organizations, where change is a constant, project management is replacing middle management as a way of ensuring that things get done. Corporate downsizing has also led to a change in the way organizations approach projects. Companies outsource significant segments of project work, and project managers have to manage not only their own people but also their counterparts in different organizations.

Increased Customer Focus

Increased competition has placed a premium on customer satisfaction. Customers no longer simply settle for generic products and services. They want customized products and services that cater to their specific needs. This mandate requires a much closer working relationship between the provider and the receiver. Account executives and sales representatives are assuming more of a project manager's role as they work with their organization to satisfy the unique needs and requests of clients.

Increased customer attention has also prompted the development of customized products and services. For example, 15 years ago buying a set of golf clubs was a relatively simple process: You picked out a set based on price and feel. Today, there are golf clubs for tall players and short players, clubs for players who tend to slice the ball and clubs for those who hook the ball, high-tech clubs with the latest metallurgic discovery guaranteed to add distance, and so forth. Project management is critical both to development of customized products and services and to sustaining lucrative relationships with customers.

Small Projects Represent Big Problems

The velocity of change required to remain competitive or simply keep up has created an organizational climate in which hundreds of projects are implemented concurrently. This climate has created a multiproject environment and a plethora of new problems. Sharing and prioritizing resources across a portfolio of projects is a major challenge for senior management. Many firms have no idea of the problems involved with inefficient management of small projects. Small projects typically carry the same or more risk as do large projects. Small projects are perceived as having little impact on the bottom line because they do not demand large amounts of scarce resources and/or money. Because so many small projects are going on concurrently and because the perception of the inefficiency impact is small, measuring inefficiency is usually nonexistent. Unfortunately, many small projects soon add up to large sums of money. Many customers and millions of dollars are lost each year on small projects in product and service organizations. Small projects can represent hidden costs not measured in the accounting system.

Organizations with many small projects going on concurrently face the most difficult project management problems. A key question becomes one of how to create an organizational environment that supports multiproject management. A process is needed to prioritize and develop a portfolio of small projects that supports the mission of the organization.

In summary, there are a variety of environmental forces interacting in today's business world that contribute to the increased demand for good project management across all industries and sectors. Project management appears to be ideally suited for a business environment requiring accountability, flexibility, innovation, speed, and continuous improvement. These environment and other factors have created the necessity for major oversight of all organization projects.

PROJECT GOVERNANCE

Competing in a global market influenced by rapid change, innovation, and time to market means organizations manage more and more projects. Some means for coordinating and managing projects in this changing environment is needed. Centralization of project management processes and practices has been the practical outcome. For example, Google, Apple, General Electric, and Sony all have over 1,000 projects being implemented concurrently every day of the year across borders and differing cultures. *Questions: How do these organizations oversee the management of all these projects? How were these projects selected? How do they ensure performance measurement and accountability? How can project management continually improve?* Centralization entails governance of all project processes and practices to improve project management.

Governance is designed to improve project management in the whole organization over the long haul. The rationale for integration of project management was to provide senior management with:

- An overview of all project management activities;
- A big picture of how organizational resources are being used;
- An assessment of the risk their portfolio of projects represents;
- A rough metric for measuring the improvement of managing projects relative to others in the industry;
- Linkages of senior management with actual project execution management.

Full insight of all components of the organization is crucial for aligning internal business resources with the requirements of the changing environment. Governance enables management to have greater flexibility and better control of all project management activities.

Operationally, what does project management integration mean? It necessitates combining all of the major dimensions of project management under one umbrella. Each dimension is connected in one seamless, integrated domain. Governance means applying a set of knowledge, skills, tools, and techniques to a collection of projects in order to move the organization toward its strategic goals. This integrative movement represents a major thrust of project driven organizations across all industries. See Figure 1.2, Integrated Management of Projects.

Alignment of Projects with Organizational Strategy

Today, projects are the *modus operandi* for implementing strategy. Yet in some organizations, selection and management of projects often fail to support the strategic plan of the organization. Strategic plans are written by one group of managers, projects selected by another group, and projects implemented by another. These independent decisions by different groups of managers create a set of conditions leading to conflict, confusion, and frequently an unsatisfied customer. Under these conditions, resources of the organization are wasted in non-value-added activities/projects.

Since projects are the modus operandi, strategic alignment of projects is of major importance to conserving and effective use of organization resources. Selection criteria need to ensure each

FIGURE 1.2 *Integrated Management of Projects*

project is prioritized and contributes to strategic goals. Anything less is a waste of scarce organizational resources—people, capital, and equipment. Ensuring alignment requires a selection process that is systematic, open, consistent, and balanced. All of the projects selected become part of a project portfolio that balances the total risk for the organization. Management of the project portfolio ensures that only the most valuable projects are approved and managed across the entire organization.

PROJECT MANAGEMENT TODAY: A SOCIO-TECHNICAL APPROACH

Senior management is often involved in selecting projects but seldom involved in implementing them. Implementing the project is the challenge.

There are two dimensions within the actual execution of projects (see Figure 1.3, The Technical and Sociocultural Dimensions of the Project Management Process). The first dimension is the technical side of the management process, which consists of the formal, disciplined, purely logical parts of the process. This technical dimension includes planning, scheduling, and controlling projects. Clear project scope statements are written to link the project and customer and to facilitate planning and control. Creation of the deliverables and work breakdown structures facilitates planning and monitoring the progress of the project. The work breakdown structure serves as a database that links all levels in the organization, major deliverables, and all work—right down to the tasks in a work package. Effects of project changes are documented and traceable. Thus, any change in one part of the project is traceable to the source by the integrated linkages of the system. This integrated information approach can provide all project managers and the customer with decision information appropriate to their level and needs. A successful project manager will be well trained in the technical side of managing projects.

The second and opposing dimension is the sociocultural side of project management. In contrast to the orderly world of project planning, this dimension involves the much messier, often

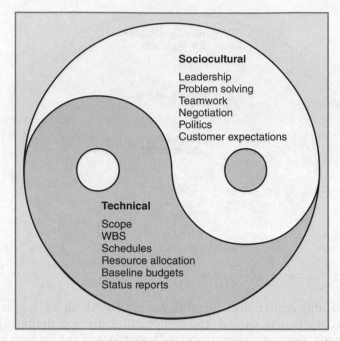

Sociocultural

Leadership
Problem solving
Teamwork
Negotiation
Politics
Customer expectations

Technical

Scope
WBS
Schedules
Resource allocation
Baseline budgets
Status reports

FIGURE 1.3 *The Socio–Technical Dimensions of the Project Management Process*

contradictory and paradoxical world of implementation. It centers on creating a temporary social system within a larger organizational environment that combines the talents of a divergent set of professionals working to complete the project. See Research Highlight: Works Well with Others. Project managers must shape a project culture that stimulates teamwork and high levels of personal motivation as well as a capacity to quickly identify and resolve problems that threaten project work. Things rarely go as planned and project managers must be able to steer the project back on track or alter directions when necessary.

The socio-cultural dimension also involves managing the interface between the project and external environment. Project managers have to assuage and shape expectations of customers, sustain the political support of top management, negotiate with their functional counterparts, monitor subcontractors, and so on. Overall, the manager must build a cooperative social network among a divergent set of allies with different standards, commitments, and perspectives.

Some suggest that the technical dimension represents the "science" of project management while the sociocultural dimension represents the "art" of managing a project. To be successful, a manager must be a master of both. Unfortunately, some project managers become preoccupied with the planning and technical dimension of project management. Often their first real exposure to project management is through project management software, and they become infatuated with network charts, Gantt diagrams, and performance variances; they attempt to manage a project from a distance. Conversely, there are other managers who manage projects by the "seat of their pants," relying heavily on team dynamics and organizational politics to complete a project. Good project managers balance their attention to both the technical and sociocultural aspects of project management.

Research Highlight

WORKS WELL WITH OTHERS*

The phrase "works well with others" has long been a staple on grade school report cards; now, in the IT world, it's the No. 1 criterion for management candidates. In a nationwide survey conducted in 1999, 27 percent of chief information officers (CIOs) cited strong interpersonal skills as the single most important quality for reaching management levels. Advanced technical skills came in second, receiving 23 percent of the response.

The project was sponsored by RHI Consulting, which provides information technology professionals on a project basis. An independent research firm was hired to administer the survey. Over 1,400 CIOs responded to the questionnaire.

Survey respondents were also asked:

In 2005, how frequently will employees in your IT department work on project-based teams with members of other departments throughout the company?

Their responses:		
	Very frequently	57%
	Somewhat frequently	26%
	Somewhat infrequently	10%
	Very infrequently	6%
	Never	1%

Greg Scileppi, RHI Consulting's executive director, recommends that IT professionals develop their interpersonal skills. "The predominance of project teams has created a corresponding need for strong communication and team-player abilities. Technical staff put these skills to test daily as they work with employees at all levels to create and implement IT solutions ranging from simple troubleshooting to corporate web initiatives and system wide upgrades."

* Joanita M. Nellenbach, "People Skills Top Technical Knowledge, CIOs Insist," *PMNetwork* (August 1999), pp. 7–8.

Summary

Project management is a critical skill set in today's world. A project is defined as a nonroutine, one-time effort limited by time, resources, and performance specifications designed to meet customer needs. One of the distinguishing characteristics of project management is that it has both a beginning and an end and typically consists of four phases: defining, planning, executing, and closing. Effective project management begins with selecting and prioritizing projects that support the firm's mission and strategy. Successful implementation requires both technical and social skills. Project managers have to plan and budget projects as well as orchestrate the contributions of others.

Text Overview

This text is written to provide the reader with a comprehensive, integrative understanding of the project management process. The text focuses both on the science of project management and the art of managing projects. Following this introductory chapter, Chapter 2 focuses on how organizations go about evaluating and selecting projects. Special attention is devoted to the importance of aligning project selection to the mission and strategy of the firm. The organizational environment in which projects are implemented is the focus of Chapter 3. The discussion of matrix management and other organizational forms is augmented by a discussion of the role the culture of an organization plays in the implementation of projects.

The next six chapters focus on developing a plan for the project; after all, project success begins with a good plan. Chapter 4 deals with defining the scope of the project and developing a work breakdown structure (WBS). The challenge of formulating cost and time estimates is the subject of Chapter 5. Chapter 6 focuses on utilizing the information from the WBS to create a project plan in the form of a timed and sequenced network of activities.

Risks are a potential threat to every project, and Chapter 7 examines how organizations and managers identify and manage risks associated with project work. Resource allocation is added to the plan in Chapter 8 with special attention devoted to how resource limitations impact the project schedule. After a resource schedule is established, a project time-phased budget is developed. Finally, Chapter 9 examines strategies for reducing ("crashing") project time either prior to the initiation of the project or in response to problems or new demands placed on the project.

Chapters 10 through 12 focus on project implementation and the sociocultural side of project management, beginning with Chapter 10, which focuses on the role of the project manager as a leader and stresses the importance of managing project stakeholders within the organization. Chapter 11 focuses on the core project team; it combines the latest information on team dynamics with leadership skills/techniques for developing a high-performance project team. Chapter 12 continues the theme of managing project stakeholders by discussing how to outsource project work and negotiate with contractors, customers, and suppliers.

Chapter 13 focuses on the kinds of information managers use to monitor project progress, with special attention devoted to the key concept of earned value. The project life cycle is completed with Chapter 14, which covers closing out a project and the important assessment of performance and lessons learned. Four "supplemental" chapters are included to augment the project management core. Implementation of project management in multicultural, international environments is the subject of Chapter 15. Chapter 16 focuses the need for organizational oversight and how it impacts the management of projects. The emergence of agile project management, a more flexible team approach to managing complex projects where requirements cannot be clearly defined before the project begins, is the subject of Chapter 17. Finally, Chapter 18 concludes with coverage of career issues in the field of project management.

Throughout this text you will be exposed to the major aspects of the project management system. However, a true understanding of project management comes not from knowing what a scope statement is, or the critical path, or partnering with contractors, but from comprehending how the different elements of the project management system interact to determine the fate of a project. If, by the end of this text, you come to appreciate and begin to master both the technical and sociocultural dimensions of project management, you should have a distinct competitive advantage over others aspiring to work in the field of project management.

Key Terms

Program
Project

Project life cycle

Project Management
Professional (PMP)

Review Questions

1. Define a project. What are five characteristics that help differentiate projects from other functions carried out in the daily operations of the organization?
2. What are some of the key environmental forces that have changed the way projects are managed? What has been the effect of these forces on the management of projects?
3. Why is the implementation of projects important to strategic planning and the project manager?
4. The technical and sociocultural dimensions of project management are two sides to the same coin. Explain.
5. What is the impact of governance on managing an individual project? Why is this approach important in today's environment?

Exercises

1. Review the front page of your local newspaper, and try to identify all the projects contained in the articles. How many were you able to find?
2. Individually identify what you consider to be the greatest achievements accomplished by mankind in the last five decades. Now share your list with three to five other students in the class, and come up with an expanded list. Review these accomplishments in terms of the definition of a project. What does your review suggest about the importance of project management?
3. Individually identify projects assigned in previous terms. Were both sociocultural and technical elements factors in the success or difficulties in the projects?
4. Check out the Project Management Institute's home page at *www.pmi.org*.
   a. Review general information about PMI as well as membership information.
   b. See if there is a PMI chapter in your state. If not, where is the closest one?
   c. Use the search function at the PMI home page to find information on Project Management Body of Knowledge (PMBOK). What are the major knowledge areas of PMBOK?
   d. Explore other links that PMI provides. What do these links tell you about the nature and future of project management?

   Note: If you have any difficulty accessing any of the Web addresses listed here or elsewhere in the text, you can find up-to-date addresses on the home page of Dr. Erik Larson, coauthor of this text: http://business.oregonstate.edu/faculty-and-staff-bios/erik-larson

References

Ball Parks of Baseball, "Cisco Field," *http://www.ballparksofbaseball.com/future/CiscoField.htm* (accessed June 2, 2009).

Benko, C., and F. W. McFarlan, *Connecting the Dots* (Boston: HBS Press, 2003).

Cohen, D. J., and R. J. Graham, *The Project Manager's MBA* (San Francisco: Jossey-Bass, 2001).

Darnell, R., "The Emerging Role of the Project Manager," *PM Network,* Vol. 11, No. 7 (1997).

Derby, Charles, and Ofer Zwikael, "The Secret of (Defining) Success," *PM Network*, Vol. 26, No. 8, August 2012, pp. 20–22.

Gray, Clifford, "Program Management, A Primer," *PM World Today*, Vol. 13, No. 8, August 2011, pp. 1–7.

Jonas, D., "Empowering Project Portfolio Managers: How Management Involvement Impacts Project Management Performance," *International Journal of Project Management,* Vol. 28, No. 8 (2010), pp. 818–831.

Koh, Aileen, and Lynn Crawford, "Portfolio Management: The Australian Experience," *Project Management Journal,* Vol. 43, No. 6 (2012), pp. 33–41.

Peters, T., *PM Network,* January 2004, Vol. 18, No. 1, p. 19.

Project Management Institute, *Leadership in Project Management Annual* (Newton Square, PA: PMI Publishing, 2006).

Project Management Institute, *A Guide to the Project Management Body of Knowledge (PMBOK),* (Newton Square, PA: PMI Publishing, 2013).

Project Management Institute, *PMI Today,* July 2011, p. 11.

The Standish Group, *CHAOS Summary 2009*, pp. 1–4.

Stewart, T. A., "The Corporate Jungle Spawns a New Species: The Project Manager," *Fortune* (September 1996), pp. 14–15.

APPENDIX 1.1

PART (A)
Definitions and Characteristics of Project, Program, Portfolio and Other Key Terms

One of the aims of the PMBOK® Guide is to promote the use of a common vocabulary for discussing and writing on the subject of project management. In project management literature and some corporate communications, the terms 'project', and 'program' and 'program' and 'portfolio', are often used interchangeably, which introduces ambiguity in the discussion across a much wider audience. Therefore, at the very outset, we shall take up some key definitions.

Project

Project is defined as a temporary endeavor to create a unique product, service or result.
The phrase, *temporary,* emphasizes the specific start and end of the project. The project 'starts' by beginning the specific set of activities to achieve some specific objectives and the project ends when these objectives are achieved or the organization is convinced that achieving the objectives is either not possible or not in the interest of the organization in the light of changed macro-economic or social factors.

Product created by the project is some form of a physical asset. Examples of the product of the project are: a building, a road, a manufacturing facility, a refinery, a new model of motorcycle, etc.

Service created by the project is some form of capability to provide service; it might include some physical assets as well as some technology, trained service personnel, and procedures and methods to serve some specific business or social function. Setting up a telephone or electric power supply network in an area, setting up water and drainage systems, setting up colleges for education, hospitals for healthcare, setting up within a corporate new IT system or new procurement system, and major modifications or enhancements of the governmental services like defense systems are examples of services created by the project.

Result created by the project is some specific outcome within an organization or impacting the environment outside the organization. Within an organization, the outcome like reducing accident level, saving energy usage, developing a new drug or improving quality or productivity in manufacture are instances of results within an organization. While extending the market share, providing the services to a new geographical area or another country, an election campaign, and a military campaign are examples of results of projects, which also impact an environment external to the organization.

The term *'unique'* in the definition lays emphasis on the non-routine nature of the project work and is meant to distinguish a project from a routine operation. The predominantly large part of the work performed in an organization is of operational nature. Manufacturing of products or providing services constitutes the organization's main business. It would be manufacturing of computers for a computer manufacturer, petroleum and LPG for a petroleum refinery, mobile handsets for a handset manufacturer or cloth for a textile mill. Similarly, the operations for banks would be providing financial services, for colleges the education for specific programs, for hospitals medical services and for electric power and telephone companies the supply of electric power or establishing a communication network. In addition, the supporting activities for these main operational works (managing finance, materials procurement, human relations management, quality control, maintenance of operating equipment, etc.) are also parts of routine operations or activities. Both routine ongoing operations and projects require people to carry out work. Both require to be completed within constraints of resources and both require planning, effective execution of the plans and a close monitoring and control to ensure the delivery of planned objectives. However, in case of routine operations, these activities are carried out repetitively all through the year and the procedures, policies, the organization structure, physical assets, technology and materials – all are standardized and pre-set.

Some repetitive operations might be used for creating the product of the project – for example, two projects at different sites and during different period may require use of the same building materials, building trade practices or even the construction teams for constructing a number of buildings. In such situations, though superficial view shows broad overall similarities, an in-depth analysis would reveal a significant variation in details that are necessary for planning, execution and control for effective and efficient management of the projects.

Like many words in general usage, the term project is also often used loosely to designate anything important or special. So, preparing for and going to an important meeting is called "a project". Negotiating a large sales order is called "a project". Manufacturing a standard production order, but with some minor variation in technical specifications is also called "a project". The planned shutdown and repairs in a continuous operation-manufacturing unit (e.g. a petroleum refinery or a blast furnace in a steel plant) is called "a project". Such usage of the term "project" is a trivialization of the term in ordinary usage. Generally, these are instances of routine operations, but sometimes these are managed using the tools and techniques ordinarily employed for project management. At best, they are instances of *management by project*.

Characteristics of a Project

Taking into account the ideas underlying the definition of the project and the nature of the activities constituting the projects, the characteristics of the project can be summarized as follows:

- Temporary endeavor
- Creation of a unique product, service or result
- Vehicle for change – implementing the strategic plans of the organization
- Progressive elaboration of the scope
- Time-bound completion of project work
- Constraints on resources – budget
- Special need for project risk analysis and management

We have already discussed the first two of these project characteristics while discussing the definition of the project. We shall take up discussion of other characteristics after discussing programs and portfolios as defined in PMBOK® Guide.

Program

The term program is applied to a group of related projects managed in a coordinated way to obtain benefits and control, which are not available if managing them individually. Program may include elements of related work outside the scope of the discrete projects in a program.

Let us study the implications in this definition. The projects play the role of instruments of change in implementing the organization's strategic policy. The organization would formulate its strategic plan for long-term and short-term future operations and chalk out a program which would include a number of projects, each with a set of specific objectives to create a unique product, service or result envisioned in the strategic plan. There may be also some common work related to all projects but outside the scope of the individual projects. The program would be managed in such a manner that the quantum and timing of allocating the resources is optimized for most efficient use of resources. The program management also takes into account the interdependence of the products of the projects for delivering the strategic thrust.

As illustrations of the program we can cite the following examples:

- Interconnected highways network – 'golden quadrangle corridors' connecting four metropolitan cities in India is a program; the highways connecting two specific metropolitan cities would be a specific project.

- A nuclear powered submarine would be a program; the nuclear power plant, the submarine structure and operating systems would be different independently controlled projects.
- Electric power supply network based on a hydroelectric power plant would be a program; its constituent projects might be civil construction of the dam, setting up hydraulic turbines and turbo-generators, and transmission system including erection of transmission towers.
- Defense Research Department Organization's Program for defensive missile systems and setting up an on-line airlines or railway booking system are other instances of programs.

Each of these programs would need to set up a number of projects which would be managed in a coordinated way and which would share critical resources for optimized usage.

Portfolio

Term portfolio is applied to a collection of projects and programs that are grouped together for pursuing objectives focused on some specific business strategy.

This definition points out that the scope of portfolio is wider than projects and programs. Unlike the programs, which hold groups of interrelated projects managed in a coordinated way, the portfolio need not be limited to interrelationship. The portfolio of diversified large companies may include projects and programs in the wide spectrum of commercial and industrial activities. For example, the portfolio may include the transportation, industrial equipment and large infrastructure civil construction, or say, setting up and operating a petroleum refinery, operating petrochemicals complexes, textile mills and mobile telephone services. Portfolio management is handled at the highest managerial level; often the owners or entrepreneurs themselves or their close associates look after portfolio management. The focus of portfolio management is on the broad macro-economic and industrial conditions and trends in the nation and how the organization's resources can be augmented and employed for optimum benefits to the organization.

After defining the programs and portfolios and their distinguishing characteristics from projects, we revert to other characteristics of projects.

PLACE OF PROJECTS AS A VEHICLE FOR CHANGE–IMPLEMENTING THE STRATEGIC PLANS OF THE ORGANIZATION

While discussing the characteristics of the project, a reference was made to the place of projects as a vehicle or instrument for change in the organization and for implementing the organization's broad strategic vision. Let us look more closely at this aspect of the project: the very reason for existence of the project, its initiation and authorization.

The Current Operations

All organizations – commercial organizations, not-for-profit social organizations and governmental institutions – are actively engaged in carrying out some function involving day-to-day routine operations in an on-going manner year-after-year.

- A company manufacturing electric motors or lap top computers would keep on producing in its plants electric motors or lap top computers.
- The company providing telecom or banking services would routinely keep providing telecom or banking services.

- Educational institutions would attend to the tasks of providing education, and
- Government departments concerned with defense or environmental administration would attend to tasks cut out for them.

A predominantly large part of the work force of an organization is, therefore, understandably busy with carrying out these routine activities and a predominantly large part of all resources is actively employed in the routine operations.

Need For Creating a New Product Service or Result

While doing these routine operations, from time to time the organizations find the need for some change in their operations for more effective, more efficient, larger scale or improved operation. While doing routine operations, the manufacturing organization may find the need to increase the manufacturing capacity, or to bring out a new product, or to improve the quality of the products, or to employ new technology for saving cost by more efficient use of materials or labour, or, say, setting up facilities for safer routine operations or for meeting the government's environmental regulations. The service organization may feel the need to extend the scope of services, or cover a larger geographical area, or supply a more satisfactory level of service or exploit a new technology to provide an altogether new service. **In other words, the organization might feel *the need for creation of some product, service or result different from the current operations.***

These needs may fall into any of the following categories:

- *Business need*: Setting up a new business, starting a profitable venture for investment, entrepreneurial vision for developing new technology.
- *Market need*: Improving product mix, developing a new product, a customer's requests for some features and others
- *Customer request for project management*: For organizations performing projects on contract – like companies in civil, electrical, HVAC or mechanical and piping construction and project consultancies providing engineering-procurement-construction services
- *Technological push*: developing new technology, making products compatible with new technology and others
- *Organizational structure change,* geographical expansion, recruitment and training campaigns
- *Legal or social requirement, etc*: effluent treatment plant, employees welfare schemes, etc.

Initiating Projects to Provide These New Capabilities to the Organization

However, most *operating organizations* do not have the infrastructure, other resources or people to create new products, services or results, which they need. For managing these changes in the mode of ongoing operations, the organizations embark on projects and commit their resources with the objective of creating these products, services or results. This becomes the scope of the authorized project. The very reason for creation and existence of the project is to manage the project in such a manner that the full scope of the project is accomplished in a cost-effective and timely manner.

The projects are the bridges – which take an organization from current activities (products and services) to new products and services. Project extends the capability of the organization from here-and-now to the visions of future. The projects are thus the vehicles for the changes, which routine operations do not cover. The projects are vehicles for implementing the organization's vision, short- and long-term plans, and business strategy. Peter Drucker once wrote that the primary purpose of the management in an enlightened organization is to introduce innovation – the rest is just routine business. The projects are the instruments for these innovations and in this dynamic business scenario and global competitions era, it is the organizations, which envision the right projects for innovation and implement them effectively and efficiently that will survive and grow.

Progressive Elaboration of Project Scope

Another important characteristic of the project is the progressive elaboration. Projects are involved in activities, which the organization had not handled routinely before. Obviously, the surprises are bound to come, and in order to overcome any unexpected difficulty the project planning must be altered. Less obvious aspect for progressive elaboration springs from the fact that most projects are initiated to implement the vision or broad strategy of the organization. At the very start of the project, the detailed planning is not chalked out. As the project planning is started and pieces of jigsaw puzzle for project planning start falling in place, issues which had remained out of focus at the very initial authorization stage come to light. For meeting the basic objectives underlying the taking up of the project or for effective and efficient project management, some alterations in the project scope are often necessary. That is why, though project managers generally loathe changes and oppose them, all good project managers accept, even look for some minor changes which would optimize the project objectives.

Other Characteristics of Projects

- *Time-bound completion of project work*
  The very definition of the project as a temporary endeavor implies the time bound nature of the project – a definite start and a definite end to carry out the work for meeting the project objectives. But there is additional connotation here to the term 'time bound'. Projects are managed not just to start and complete as a whole according to some schedule, but milestones for end of important project deliverables or key activities are also planned and closely monitored and controlled.
- *Constraints on resources – budget*
  The projects are authorized with a specific quantum of resources – the total cost budgeted for the project or the resources in term of the manpower allocated or permitting the use of existing infrastructure for project work.
- *Special need for project risk analysis and management*
  Unexpected events – risk events or conditions - may occur during routine operations as well as during project work. However, project work might involve undertaking many activities with which the organization may not have prior experience. The need for risk analysis and proactively managing the risks is therefore somewhat greater in project work.

The above three characteristics in a way define the role of a successful project manger. He is supposed to achieve the project objectives with effective coordination of a number of activities; making necessary trade-offs between cost and time and proactively managing the risks, which could adversely impact the project.

PART (B)
Organizational Influences and Project Life Cycle

1. ORGANIZATIONAL INFLUENCE ON PROJECT MANAGEMENT

Projects are conceived and managed within an organization, which in turn operates within a macro-economic and political environment. For managing projects effectively, it is desirable to understand how the organization's established practices influence project management.

1.1 Organizational Culture and Style

The organization's culture implies the unwritten and unspoken values, shared visions, beliefs and expectations, policies and procedures for operating practices, and risk tolerance. It is the all-pervading atmosphere enveloping almost every activity and the basis for formulation of, almost every procedure and every policy. The organization's culture does have an obvious influence on the way the projects are managed; it is an enterprise environmental factor influencing the entire sphere of each aspect of project management.

1.2 Organization's Established Channels of Communications

Organization's established channels for communication play a very important role in project's management. With excellent communication routines and procedures in place, the project manager and his team members would find it easy and convenient for setting of flow of information between the major stakeholders and team members. Electronic communication modes (e-mails, texting, video and web conferencing and others) are very helpful in this. Effective Management Information System (MIS) set up within the organization, and its close relationship with projects, is an important asset for project management.

1.3 Organizational Structure for Project Management

The organizational structure of the entire organization and the role of project management in it have a great influence on the project manager's role, his authority or influencing power and the availability of resources at his disposal for managing the project. It is, therefore, a very important enterprise environmental factor influencing the project success. The choice of organization structure to be adopted by the organization depends on the strategic importance of the project in the organization's overall performance.. Commonly employed organization structures are briefly described below:

(a) Functional Organization   In the organizations with a very strong emphasis on routine operations and where the focus on the projects is diffused, project management is organized as a part of the existing functional organization. Each manager from the group of functional managers plans, schedules and manages the part of project work related to his functional department and the manager having the maximum work part for the project carries out project coordination. Project manager plays a small part-time role and has little or no overall authority on the way the project is managed or the resources are allocated. The merit of such organization structure is that the projects are managed with the existing organizational set-up without any major change and the quality of project work carried out by professionals under the functional organization's hierarchy is relatively superior.

(b) Projectized Organization   In the organizations, where innovation and expansion of diversity and size in its operating activities is very important, or in the organizations performing projects for other organization on a contractual basis (essentially construction industry and other contracted project work); the project management plays a major part in the company's overall success. In a projectized organization, though there may be certain functional departments, the major work force of the company is organized under separate different project managers in-charge of their individual project. Project manager is a full time manager and the staff working for the project manager is entirely devoted to that particular project with full authority to plan and schedule work, prepare and control budget, and deploy manpower. In this set-up, the project manager has a major role to play, full time assignment, and complete responsibility for project management. He has a better availability of resources and superior communication channels including access to top management. The need for reshuffling the organization every time a new major project is taken up, duplication of similar work packages, and inefficiency in deployment of manpower are some of its downside features.

(c) Matrix Organizations   In between the above two extremes are matrix organizations devised from different blends of the functional and projectized organizations. Depending on the degree of authority and managing role assigned to the project manager and committed resources made available to him, the organizations may be classified as strong, weak or balanced matrix organizations. Weak matrix organizations are closest to functional organizations and strong matrix organizations are closest to the projectized organization. When organizations adopt matrix pattern for organization pattern, most organizations develop their own special version of matrix organization.

1.4   Organizational Process Assets

Organizational process assets are defined as the plans, processes, policies and procedures, and knowledge bases specific projects in hand to hand used by the performing organizations. Like organizational environmental factors, organizational process assets are important inputs to most project planning processes. Organizational process assets may be classified into two groups:

(a) Processes and Procedures for Managing Projects   The processes and procedures for managing the projects include the processes for initiating, planning, executing, monitoring and controlling and closing the projects. The policies and procedures for initiation may include the project selection practices and presentations and checking conformance to the organization's human resources policies, health and safety policies, etc. Planning procedures and policies would include the organizational standards and templates and checklists for risk register, standards for quality planning, templates for work breakdown structures and project schedule networks. Procedures and policies in execution phase of the project would include change control procedures, procedures for financial controls, organizational communication networks, and MIS for project management. Policies and procedures at the closing phase of the project would include guidelines for project closing, noting down lessons learnt, archiving important project records, proper handover procedures and final project audits for quality and finance.

(b) Corporate Knowledge Base   The organizations operating in the same or similar technological fields develop special corporate knowledge base, which gives them an edge over others in undertaking, planning and executing projects in these fields. The corporate knowledge base may include technological and financial databases, experience of dealing with suppliers in the industry, project files of previous projects (work breakdown structures, project schedule networks, specifications of critical equipment and their suppliers, etc.)

1.5   Enterprise Environmental Factors

Enterprise Environmental Factors are defined as conditions, not *under the control of the project team,* that influence, constraint or direct the project. Understandably, all realistic project planning has to take into account these factors and hence they are inputs to most project planning processes.

These factors may be related to the specific organization, the industry in which the organization operates or the macro-economic conditions of the country. The factors related to the specific organization would include the existing infrastructure and capital equipment, geographic distribution of the assets, access or expertise in use of specific technology, skilled man-power availability, human resources policies, work authorization and change management practices, established communication channels, project management information system (MIS), risk tolerance, etc. The factors related to the industry in which the organization operates would include industry standards, government regulations for the specific industry, and market conditions. The factors relating to the macro-economic conditions of the country include political climate, economic growth trends and inflation, government policies and standards, legislation related to environmental pollution, health and safety, etc.

2. PROJECT STAKEHOLDERS AND GOVERNANCE

Project Stakeholders

PMBOK® Guide defines a stakeholder as an individual, group or organization who may affect, be affected by, or perceive itself to be affected by a decision, activity or outcome of the project. The stakeholder may be:

- Actively involved with the project activity or internal to the organization (project sponsor, project manager and members of the project team, other internal stakeholders like functional departments and their managers)
- Stakeholders external to the organization (customers and users of the project' s product or service, vendors or contractors supplying product or service for a project, banks and financial institutions, government regulating agencies, project consultants, the residents of a locality of project site, etc.)

PMBOK® Guide, 5th edition, has for the first time identified project stakeholders' management as a separate knowledge area, which includes processes for identifying the stakeholders, planning their management, managing their engagement, and control. The detailed description of the processes is presented along with the descriptions of other project management knowledge areas.

Project Governance

Project Governance essentially provides to the project manager and his team the framework for planning and managing the project in such a manner that the project is aligned with the organization's overall strategy, programs and portfolio. Project governance would help with the rules and procedures for making project decisions, defining roles, tools for planning and executing the project, responsibilities and accountabilities of project team and other participants' for success of project assignments,

Project Management Office (PMO)

When an organization has set it up, it would be able to make valuable contributions in this area. PMO could provide the following elements of project governance:

(a) *Project Management Team Functioning*: Relationship among the project team members (roles, responsibilities and reporting relationships), relationship between the project team and other departments or functions of the organization, relationship between the project team and outside parties; framework for project selection and project planning decisions

(b) *Alignment of Project with Organization's Strategy*: Criteria for project success, delivery acceptance criteria, processes for project communication and progress reports, process for stage gate reviews, processes for identifying, escalating and resolving issues, etc. An elaboration on criteria for project success would be helpful here. The project would be considered a success if the project is completed within the constraints of scope, time, budget, quality, resources and risk as agreed and approved between the project manager and senior management. It is important that these criteria are set in unambiguous terms and objectively measurable metrics. For instance, the description 'not more than 1.3 % defectives' would be a preferred description to 'the best quality' and '93.5 % product yield of IS:xyz material' would be preferred to 'the most efficient production plant.'

3. PROJECT TEAM

The project manager, the project management staff directly involved in managing a project and other groups of individuals who carry out some work (though not necessarily project management) constitute the project team. In this context, project team lead by the project manager includes *project management staff* (members involved with project management activities such as project planning with preparation of work breakdown structure, project schedule network, budget, risk register, project reports and related communication, etc.), *other project staff, customer and his representatives, sellers and their representatives, business partners and their representatives.*

Depending on the project organization structure and the organization culture, the project manager may have different levels of authority over the team members. In case of projectized organization structure with projects recognized as of strategic importance to the organization, the authority of project manager over team members is total and the project team is constituted of full time working dedicated team members. In case of functional organizations, since one of the functional managers acts as a project manager, the project manager's authority over a major part of the project team is total, but due to their other departmental assignments, almost all team members are part time workers. In case of matrix organizations, most of the project team members are part time workers and the project manager has no direct authority over team members. In a matrix organization, the success of project would depend on whether the culture of the organization for project work is properly oriented.

4. NATURE OF PROJECT LIFE CYCLE AND PHASES

Work to be carried out between the start of the project and the close of the project is called the project life cycle. This concept evolves from the fact that the projects have finite life, with a specific start and end; the level and nature of work to be carried out for project between the start and end of most project follows a certain pattern. The project life cycle is constituted of the project phases with the following characteristics:

- *Project phase:* Each phase consists of a set of inter-related activities, generally carried out sequentially, and culminating in completion of one or more deliverables.
- *Pre-planned deliverables or technical hand-offs:* After carrying out the set of activities during a particular phase, the pre-planned deliverables or technical hand-offs are given by the preceding phase to the next phase. The deliverables of the previous phase are pre-requisite for the start of the next phase and it is only after satisfactory hand-off that the next project phase starts. It is like a relay race. The first runner runs his lap and passes on the baton to the next runner. The second runner can start his race part only after receiving the baton in proper order from the first runner.
- *Decision making control gate for project:* The end of one phase and the start of another phase serves as a decision-making control gate for project. At such gates, the project results up to that point are reviewed and given necessary directional inputs.
- *Project termination:* If at any decision making gate at the end of a phase, it becomes clear that the project in its present form cannot meet the desired objectives or that the need for the project objectives no longer exists, the project may be terminated at the gate.
- *Inter-phase relationships:* The relationship between the project phases may be either sequential or overlapping. In case of pure sequential interrelationship between the phases (sometimes described as 'Waterfall Model'), the following phase work starts only after the close and formal hand-offs from the preceding phase. This relationship is helpful in avoiding the uncertainties and risks, but it would require longer total project schedule. In overlapping relationship, the phase may start before completion and formal hand-offs from the previous phase. Like fast tracking technique for schedule compression, this relationship would have greater risk and require more resources. The plus side would be faster delivery of the total project.
- *Predictive, iterative and adaptive life cycles:* In case of traditional repetitive and well-understood projects, life cycle is characterized as *predictive life cycle*; in a predictive project life cycle, the entire life cycle is fully plan-driven from the start and the work is completed according to this detailed plan.

    In case of large and complex projects, when the project objectives need to change as the project phases are completed, *iterative or incremental life cycle* is preferred. In this type of life cycle, the high-level vision of the project objectives is developed at the start and the first iteration is completed with this input. The subsequent iteration takes into account the results or deliverables handed over by the previous iteration.

    The life cycle characterized as *adaptive project life cycle* (or agile method) is essentially change-driven and iterative in development, but the changes are more rapid and frequent.

Such a project life cycle is suitable for projects executed in rapidly changing macro-environment, when it is difficult to set firmly the project objectives in advance.

5. PROJECT LIFE CYCLE CHARACTERISTICS

Depending on the predominant nature of work to be carried out, the project life cycle may be divided into specific stages or generic life cycle structure for good understanding and control of the project during the life cycle. The nomenclature of the project stages given below is according to the 5th Edition of the PMBOK® Guide; it was given slightly differently in the earlier editions.

i. Starting the project (Defining Stage)

In this stage, the project is conceived and very preliminary scope of the project is defined, preliminary estimates of budget and schedule are prepared, and necessary approval or permission from the concerned authorities are obtained (from the customer, top management, or government agencies controlling the industry, etc.) and the approved project is handed over for detailed planning to the project team for the next phase. The typical deliverables or hand-offs from the stage are the project charter (in case of essentially internal projects), firm order from a client or approval (in case of projects performed for other organizations), and necessary permission or license from the governing authority where applicable.

ii. Organizing and preparing the project (Planning Stage)

In this stage, planning is carried out in sufficient detail for all work required to be carried out for project activities. This would include preparing integrated detailed plans for proactively managing all activities related to managing the project: viz. project scope, schedule, budget, quality, communications, project team, risk and procurement. The technical hand-offs from this phase are the detailed plans for project execution.

iii. Carrying out the project work (Executing Stage)

In this stage, most of the actual project work planned during the development phase is carried out using the resources authorized for project work. Project manager and his team monitor and control the quality, technical and performance specifications of work performed, completion of major activities as per set benchmark and within budgeted cost.

iv. Closing the project (Delivering Stage)

In this stage, the project is systematically brought to a close. All deliverables are checked out to ensure that they meet the criteria for project success or agreed specifications. Technical documentation is handed over. The procurement contracts are settled, and the project is handed over to the client or the operating group.

6. CHARACTERISTICS OF PROJECT STAGES

There is considerable variation in the different project stages depending on the industry and nature of the project. However certain general trends do emerge:

- *The work content, staffing and cost are small in the early life cycle* of the project. They pick up and maximum staffing, work and cost expenditure occur during the middle phases and the work content, staffing and cost taper off to zero at the project close.

- *The level of uncertainty or risk to the project success* is the highest near the early stage of the project life cycle. It would gradually taper off as the jigsaw puzzle pieces start falling in place and reduces to a very low level near the close of the project.
- *The ability of stakeholders to influence the project* is the highest during the early stages and preliminary project planning. As the details of project start getting firmed up and executed, the influence of stakeholders decreases and it tapers off to practically no influence near the project close.
- *On the other hand if any correction or change is required to be done, the maximum cost and difficulty occur near the project's later phases,* while it is relatively easy to take care of changes or modifications suggested by different stakeholders at the start of the project.

7. PRODUCT LIFE CYCLE – HOW IT DIFFERS FROM PROJECT LIFE CYCLE

Project life covers the project time span, viz. time during which a specific product, result or service is created by the project. The project creates the product, result or service and hands it over to the operation. The operation then uses the project's product and maintains it till the product's utility is exhausted. At the end of that stage, some modifications or extensive remodeling would be planned and another project would be started for such work. Thus product life cycle is the whole life of the product: from its conception, creation and use till the end. Only a small part of the product life cycle, the part during which such product service or result is created, constitutes project life cycle; in other words, the project life cycle is a sub-set of the product life cycle. So there is life after project's death for a project's product – the period during which the operation uses and maintains the project's product till its useful life.

PART (C)
Project Management Processes and Their Classification

1. USE OF PROJECT MANAGEMENT PROCESSES AS FRAMEWORK FOR PROJECT MANAGEMENT DISCUSSION

Most of the discussion on project management topics in books and technical literature is generally presented as some specific topics of interest, techniques or managerial approaches recommended for efficient and effective project management.

PMBOK® Guide appears to make a radical departure in the framework used for discussion of project management.

i. It starts with defining project management as the application of the knowledge, skills, tools and techniques to project activities to meet the objectives for launching the project.

ii. The next step is introducing the concept of 'project management processes' as the vehicle for application of the project management knowledge or techniques. For this purpose, project management process is defined as a set of inter-related activities performed to create a pre-specified product, service or result. Project management processes are supposed to embody good management practices common to management of almost all projects.

iii. Finally, all project management processes are classified according to the stages in life cycle and knowledge areas into discrete project management processes. A systemic description of each of these individual processes is set down in terms of the inputs, tools and techniques and outputs.

Some detailed discussion on this approach is presented below.

2. PROJECT MANAGEMENT PROCESSES

All work required to be performed in connection with the project is recognized as belonging to two classes or types:

Product-oriented Processes

These processes are actually used in creating the product of the project and they are specific to different industries, technologies and application areas. For example, the product-oriented processes for civil construction would be the design of foundations or structure, preparing and placing reinforced concrete, structural steel fabrication and so forth.

Project Management Processes

From the analysis of the past experience of management of a very large number of projects related to a large variety of industrial and commercial activities, several practices in project management have been identified to be effective as well as efficient. The knowledge, skills and tools and techniques associated with these good project management practices, the desired results or outputs from them and the necessary data or other inputs for using these techniques are collectively identified as project management process. These processes are common to almost all projects and they are concerned with the flow of information throughout the project life and some common generally accepted good tools and techniques for project initiating, planning, executing, monitoring and controlling or closing. The project manager performs his function by judicious application of the necessary project management processes to the project work and achieves the desired project objectives.

Project management is, accordingly, the application of knowledge, skills and tools and techniques to project activities for successfully managing a project. The PMBOK® Guide, 5th Edition, recognizes such 47 discrete project management processes and classifies them into 5 process groups according to the project life cycle stage with which they are associated with and 10 knowledge areas according to the knowledge discipline involved with those processes. PMBOK Guide, 5th edition, has for the first time identified project stakeholders' management as a separate knowledge area resulting in the number of project knowledge areas from 9 to 10. This knowledge area includes processes for identifying the stakeholders, planning stakeholders management, managing stakeholders engagement, and control.

3. DESCRIPTION OF A TYPICAL PROJECT MANAGEMENT PROCESS

Let us take a typical project management process – project cost estimation. Now, there could be inputs to the cost estimation from several different sources. The project scope will provide information for what needs to be accomplished, so the cost estimation has to take that into account. Similarly, the market-availability and prices of products and services required would be another input for cost estimation. There would be different tools and techniques for cost estimation using these inputs based on the purpose for which cost estimate is required: costs based on historical data (Analogous Cost Estimating Technique for preliminary evaluation), cost based on system analysis and parameters (Parametric Cost Estimating Technique for a closer look for project selection stage), cost built up from small project package elements (Bottom-up Cost Estimating Technique for detailed project planning and budgetary control), etc. Using the appropriate technique or tools and corresponding inputs of information, the cost of a project phase or entire project is estimated. The process thus can be visualized as a transforming apparatus, where the inputs are utilized to deliver the outputs using the tools and techniques specific to the process.

4. CLASSIFICATION OF PROJECT MANAGEMENT PROCESSES ACCORDING TO PROJECT LIFE CYCLE

There are similarities among various project management processes and suchcommon features can be used as criteria for classifying the project management processes. These include the flow of information throughout the project life and some common generally accepted good tools and techniques. Analysis also shows that a number of project processes are closely inter-related and are often carried out in close sequence during the specific phase of the project life cycle: PMBOK® Guide, 5th Edition, has identified such 47 project management processes and classified them into five major process groups according to the basic nature of the process and during which part of the life cycle of the project it is predominantly carried out:

1. *Initiating Process Group*: This group of processes defines and authorizes the project or project phase.
2. *Planning Process Group*: This group of processes defines and refines the project objectives and plans detailed course of action for the project activities to attain the project objectives.
3. *Executing Process Group*: This group of processes manages people (own and vendors) and other resources (materials, equipment and technology) to actually carry out the activities as envisaged in the project management plan.
4. *Monitoring & Controlling Process Group:* This group of processes continually measures the performance and monitors the progress against the standards and project objectives so that the corrective action can be taken to keep project on course.
5. *Closing Process Group:* This group of processes formalizes the acceptance of the product, service or result created by the project and brings all project activities to an orderly close.

There is a very strong emphasis on planning function in PMBOK® framework. In the 5th Edition of PMBOK® Guide, out of total 47 project management processes, 24 processes – almost 50 % – belong to planning process group. From the balance 23 project management processes, two belong to initiating process group, eight to executing process group, 11 to monitoring and controlling process group, and two to closing process group.

5. CLASSIFICATION OF PROCESSES ACCORDING TO KNOWLEDGE AREA

Another classification of the project management processes can be made on the basis of the knowledge area with which the processes are primarily concerned. Cost estimating, Budgeting and Cost Control – all three processes are concerned with the cost of resources and their monetary value. So, all these processes are grouped under the knowledge area of Project Cost Management. Similarly, Scope Planning, Scope Definition, Work Breakdown Structure, Scope Verification and Scope Control processes are concerned with the project scope and how it is to be managed, so they are grouped under Project Scope Management knowledge area.

Ten knowledge management areas have thus been identified, which are as follows:

Project Scope Management includes the processes required to ensure that the project includes all the work required to complete the project successfully and only the work required to complete the project successfully. Of total six processes, four are classified as belonging to the planning group (Plan Scope Management, Collect Requirements, Define Scope and Create Work Breakdown Structure) and two are classified as belonging to monitoring and controlling process group (Validate Scope and Control Scope).

Project Time Management includes the processes required for timely completion of the project. Of total seven time management processes, six are classified as belonging to the planning group (Plan Schedule Management, Define Activities, Sequence Activities, Estimate Activity Resources, Estimate Activity Durations, and Develop Schedule) and one process is classified as belonging to monitoring and controlling process group (Control Schedule).

Project Cost Management includes the processes required for estimating the project cost, preparing the project budget and controlling the costs for completion of the project within the approved budget. Of total four cost management processes, three processes are classified as belonging to the planning group (Plan Cost Management, Estimate Costs and Determine Budget) and one process is classified as belonging to monitoring and controlling process group (Control Costs).

Project Quality Management includes the processes required to ensure that all project work conforms to the accepted quality criteria for authorizing the project and that all policies and procedures of the performing organization for quality are followed. Of total three quality management processes, first process is classified as belonging to the planning group (Plan Quality Management), the second process is classified as belonging to executing process group (Perform Quality Assurance) and the third process is classified as belonging to monitoring and controlling process group (Control Quality).

Project Human Resource Management includes the processes required to acquire, organize, train and manage the project team. Of total four human resources management processes, one process is classified as belonging to the planning group (Plan Human Resource Management), other three processes are classified as belonging to executing process group (Acquire Project Team, Develop Project Team, and Manage Project Team).

Project Communication Management includes the processes required to ensure timely generation, collection, distribution and storage of all necessary project information to ensure its availability and satisfy the stakeholders. Of total three communications management processes, one process is classified as belonging to the planning group (Plan Communications Management), the second process is classified as belonging to executing process group (Manage Communications) and the third process is classified as belonging to monitoring and controlling process group (Control Communications).

Project Risk Management includes the processes required to identify the project risks, preparer qualitative and quantitative analysis and prepare suitable risk mitigation plans to ensure that project is completed successfully. Of total six risk management processes, five processes are classified as belonging to the planning group (Plan Risk Management, Identify Risks, Perform Qualitative Risk Analysis, Perform Quantitative Risk Analysis, and Plan Risk Responses) and the sixth process is classified as belonging to monitoring and controlling process group (Control Risks).

Project Procurement Management includes the processes required to acquire materials, products, technologies or services for carrying out the project activities from outsourcing. Of total four procurement management processes, one processes is classified as belonging to the planning group (Plan Procurement Management), the second process is classified as belonging to executing process group (Conduct Procurements), the third is classified as belonging to monitoring and controlling process group (Control Procurements) and the fourth as belonging to the closing process group (Close Procurements).

Project Stakeholder Management includes the processes required to identify the stakeholders (the people, groups or organizations that could impact or could be impacted by the project), analyze their expectations and impact on the project, and develop effective strategies for engaging them and managing their expectations while completing the decisions for execution of key project objectives. Of total four stakeholders management processes, one process is classified as belonging to the initiating process group (Identify Stakeholders), the second process is classified as belonging to the planning process group (Plan Stakeholders Management), the third as belonging to executing process group (Manage Stakeholders Engagement), and the fourth is classified as belonging to monitoring and controlling process group (Control Stakeholders Engagement). This knowledge area is introduced for the first time in the 5th Edition of PMBOK® *Guide*.

Project Integration Management processes are concerned with proactively managing and integrating the project management processes related to the above eight knowledge areas by defining, unifying, coordinating, and making suitable trade-offs. Of total five integration management processes, one process is classified as an initiating process (Develop Project Charter), the second as belonging to the planning group (Develop Project Management Plan), the third is classified as belonging to executing process group (Direct and manage Project Execution), while the two remaining processes are classified as belonging to monitoring and controlling process group (Monitor & Control Project Work and Perform Integrated Change Control) and closing process group (Close Project or Phase) respectively.

In the set of appendices to the relevant chapters in the book, these project management processes would be described in detail (the nature of the process, major inputs, outputs and tools and techniques) according to the knowledge area group they belong to – all cost management processes together, all time management process together, and so on. Along with the individual processes, common concepts and techniques would also be described.

APPENDIX 1.2

Project Integration Management

1. NATURE OF PROJECT INTEGRATION MANAGEMENT

Being in overall charge of the project, the project manager is responsible for all project related decisions and all initiating, planning, executing, monitoring, controlling and closing activities for the project. While doing this, the project manager has to take a holistic view of the entire project and identify and define all project activities, combine and unify them for synergistic effect, and coordinate them for effective and efficient outcomes. When there are conflicting requirements or objectives of different stakeholders, or when constraints force a choice between the one or the other of the project objectives, the project manager and his team would have to decide on the course of trade-offs and devise an optimum solution. It is the project manager and his team that has to manage the stakeholders' expectations, to decide resources allocation, to perform integrated control on all project changes, and to orchestrate all project activities for project success. Resolving the conflicts between the component plans for managing project scope, time, cost, quality and risks and developing and executing a unified project plan is also a part of the project integration management.

PMBOK® Guide, 5th Edition, has classified these general management activities for project work in a group and labeled it as Project Integration Management knowledge area:

One overarching process of the project integration nature is recognized in each project management process group, based on project life cycle, and included in the project integration management knowledge area:

   I. Develop Project Charter (Initiating Process Group)
  II. Develop Project Management Plan (Planning Process Group)
 III. Direct and Manage Project Work (Executing Process Group)
 IV. Monitor and Control Project Work (Monitoring and Controlling Process Group)
  V. Perform Integrated Change Control (Monitoring and Controlling Process Group)
 VI. Close Project or Phase (Closing Process Group)

Monitoring and controlling process group includes an additional process in the project integration management knowledge area, i.e. Perform Integrated Change Control.

2. PROJECT INTEGRATION MANAGEMENT PROCESSES

A brief description of each process, its inputs, outputs and tools and techniques is given here.

2.1 Develop Project Charter (Initiating Process Group)

This process belongs to initiating process group whose output is Project Charter.

PMBOK® Guide defines Project Charter as a document issued by the project initiator or sponsor that formally authorizes the existence of a project (or a project phase) and provides the project manager with the authority to apply organization's resources to project activities.

Project charter is a very important project document and it serves as a reference for making all major decisions during the entire project life cycle – for planning the project details or during the project execution phase. It would include a summary of important details considered while authorizing the project document:

- The business case (justification of the project and its alignment with the organization's business strategy)
- Major project objectives and measurable criteria for judging success
- High level description of the requirements and product of the project
- Overview of project risks
- Constraints and assumptions based on organizational, environmental and external factors.
- Milestones for completion of major project activities
- Project cost estimate and summary budget
- Nomination of project manager and key members of the project team; authority levels and responsibilities
- Name, designation and authority of the project sponsor or the person authorizing the project charter

Inputs

Developing the project charter involves the analysis based on strategic planning, the alignment of the project selected with this strategy and detailed definition of the project – the product or services proposed to be created by the project. The strategic planning, in turn, would start from SWOT analysis: the strengths and weaknesses of the organization and the threats and opportunities present in the macroeconomic and industrial environment. In this context, the important inputs for developing the project charter are:

Project Statement of Work (SOW)   SOW is the narrative description of the products, services, or results to be created by the project. For internal projects, SOW would be derived from the description provided by the project sponsor for the product scope; how the project would align with the organization's strategic plan and the organization's identified business needs. For projects performed for other organizations, SOW would be derived from the bid document prepared by the customer at the initial stage or the contract document executed after the award of project contract.

The Business Case   For internal projects, the project is identified or selected to align with the strategic analysis and meet one of the business needs. The business need may fall into any of the following categories:

- *Business need or opportunity for investment:* Setting up a new business, Setting up new facilities for manufacture or servicing, Expanding production capacity, Backward or forward integration, Starting a profitable venture for diversification of investment, Entrepreneurial vision.
- *Market need*: Offering a suitable product mix to different market segments, Developing a new product, Responding to customer requests for some features, Responding more effectively to the changes in the market in different geographical areas.

- *Technological push*: Developing new technology, Making products compatible with new technology
- Organizational structure change, Geographical expansion, Recruitment and training campaigns
- *Legal or social requirement*: Effluent treatment plant; Employee welfare schemes, Operational safety and health of employees.

Customer Request for Project Management   For organizations performing projects on contract, the project contract provides the main input. The main project contract document would ordinarily provide the scope of work contracted by the parties:

- *Detailed description of the product:* This would include the technical specifications and performance requirements of the product to be created by the project and the scope of vendor's supply (with explicit references to the inclusions and exclusions),
- *Detailed description of the service*: This would include the detailed description of the nature of service, performance acceptance criteria, service level agreements, etc.

This might be supplemented in some cases by including the agreements reached during the contract negotiation and set down in the Memorandum of Understanding (MOU), Minutes of Meetings, e-mails or other correspondence.

Enterprise Environmental Factors   Constraints emanating from the nature of organization's structure, industry practice and marketplace, Legal and environmental standards and Government regulations and legislations are instances of enterprise environmental factors to be taken into account for developing the project charter.

Organizational Process Assets   The Standard Policies and Procedures followed for all projects, experience of the organization during earlier similar projects, The Lessons Learned, and Templates developed, or successful measures used for project planning and execution are examples of some very useful inputs contributed by organizational process assets for developing a project charter.

Tools and Techniques

Expert Judgment   Project Charter is almost like a blueprint for the planning and execution of the project. Developing this very important document requires considerable knowledge, experience and managerial maturity to evaluate a number of factors and resolve conflicts among objectives for charting the course for successful future operations. Expert judgment is the predominantly important technique for this high-level integrative process.

Facilitation Techniques   Developing the charter may be facilitated by techniques based on brainstorming, problem solving, and support from other members of the project team.

Output

Project Charter, described in detail at the start of this section, is the sole output from this process.

2.2   Develop Project Management Plan (Planning Process Group)

The process involves developing project management plan – a single central document defining the basis of all project work and constituent activities. PMBOK® Guide, 5th Edition, defines project management plan as a formal, approved document that defines how project is to be executed, monitored, controlled and closed; it would involve developing an internally self-consistent document integrating all subsidiary plans and other planning documents.

Project Management Plan, an integrated result of all project management planning, is meant to define and refine project objectives and work out in sufficient details the course for effective execution of all project activities. The project management plan takes an holistic view of the whole project and integrates all subsidiary component plans (plans for managing scope, time, cost, quality, human resource, communication, procurement and risks) by unifying and combining the component plans, resolving conflicts and coordinating for efficient execution.

When a project is launched as a part of a program, it needs to be consistent with the program management plan for project governance procedures and policies; sharing of common resources and coordination of schedule with other projects of the program.

A brief description of the inputs, tools and techniques and outputs follows.

Inputs

Project Charter   This is the starting point – what the project has been authorized to accomplish. It is, understandably the single most important input for developing the project management plan.

Outputs from other planning processes   The purpose of this integration processes is to unify, combine and coordinate the subsidiary plans developed separately for addressing the issues related to management of scope, time, cost, quality, communication, human resources, risk procurement and stakeholders. The outputs from these other planning processes become the inputs for development of an integrated plan.

Enterprise Environmental Factors   (organization's infrastructure, existing policies and procedures, industry standards and government regulations) and *Organization's Process Assets* (earlier experience of the organization, lessons learned, policies and procedures for managing a project and the techniques developed for handling time, scope, risk or quality issues, etc.) are other inputs.

Tools and Techniques

Expert Judgment   Expert judgment developed from experience, knowledge, and managerial maturity is necessary to unify, combine and coordinate diverse project component plans, make proper trade-offs, resolve conflicts and develop a project management plan.

Facilitation Techniques   like project team meetings, brainstorming and consultations can also be effective techniques for developing project management plan.

Outputs

Project Management Plan   The output from the process is the document developed by integration of the planning outputs from all planning areas. It would include:

- Subsidiary Plans for management of scope, time, cost, quality, human resources, communication, risk, procurement and stakeholder management,
- Project baselines for managing three core areas – project scope, time and cost
- Overall plan for managing the project through all phases of the project life cycle and change management plan

2.3 Direct and Manage Project Work (Executing Process Group)

During the execution phase, all the work defined in the planning process for accomplishing the project objectives is completed. This would include the project work defined in the original project management plan as well as the changes approved during the project execution. Accordingly, PMBOK® Guide defines 'Direct and Manage Project Work' as the process of leading and performing the work defined in the project management plan and implementing the approved changes to achieve project objectives. All work is completed to the required quality standard by application of the resources (human resources, project funds, infrastructure and technology) and all major stakeholders are kept informed of the project status and the forecasts for project schedule and budget. Direct and Manage Project Work is the overarching execution process integrating the project management processes in the human resources, quality, procurement and communication areas.

Inputs

The inputs for this process are:

- *Project Management Plan*, and *Approved Change Requests,* which define the work to be completed, and
- *Organizational Environmental Factors* and *Organization Process Assets* defining the constraints imposed and facilitation available from the organization while actually carrying out the project work.

The nature and underlying reasons for other inputs mentioned above is self-explanatory, but a brief explanation of Approved Change Requests as an input would be in place here.

Approved Change Requests   The process of defining and refining the details of the activities usually continues throughout the entire project life cycle. This on-going change process is to some extent unavoidable for the project to succeed by meeting the project objectives, since very often some refinements and necessary changes become apparent only after the project has progressed through some planning and execution. The Integrated Change Control process, described hereafter, ensures that the changes are approved only after going through a set of procedural reviews before their approval, so that project resources are not frittered away on changes concerned with outcomes of subsidiary importance. It is the task of the project manager and his team to integrate all such approved change requests and execute them.

Tools and Techniques

Expert Judgment   Effective project execution requires a project manager to be able to work on diverse issues at the same time, manage the expectations of the stakeholders, and be a true leader of the project team. The constant attention to details while keeping the larger picture in view, resolving conflicts and making proper trade offs are other requirements for successful project execution. These traits and project management decisions based on them, which are usually acquired after significant experience of handling diverse project related issues, are summed up under the title 'Expert Judgment' as an input.

Over and above the expert judgment of individual team members or project manager, useful help from sources with expertise on special topics could be availed from outside consultants or other subject matter experts and operating departments specifically dealing with the project work.

Project Management Information Systems These are very helpful in tracking the progress and communicating the status and forecasts of project outcomes to the key stakeholders.

Project Meetings: Conducting project meetings is a very important technique and it plays a crucial role in effective project management during the execution phase. It is during the project meetings that information on different aspects of project is exchanged by the team members. In the process, the individual team member stands to benefit from the collective experience from other members of the team. The project meetings are the best vehicles for keeping the entire team always focused on the overall project objectives and making all members aware of the changing project environment. Meetings should be initiated with well-defined agenda and conducted with precise and focused direction by seeking conflict resolution as and when necessary. Proper record or minutes of the decisions reached in the meeting should be prepared, which should include the activity-specific details – the task, assignment of responsibility to specific members and the available resources and time or budget constraints to be observed for carrying out those project activities.

Outputs

Deliverables Execution process completes the planned project work and produces the project deliverable – 'a unique and verifiable product, service, result or capability to perform' included as one of the project objectives.

Work Performance Data Raw data about the exact performance during project activities is generated from the records maintained during this process. The data would include date-wise work completed, quality checks and tests on the performed work, defects and defects correction, actual costs incurred, issues raised by stakeholders and their resolution, etc. Such raw work performance data is processed to generate the metrics employed for monitoring and controlling the project work according to the subsidiary plans objectives.

Change Requests During the actual execution, some changes from the original plan for more effectively carrying out the work will become apparent. The changing project environment may also necessitate some changes in the originally planned activities.

Change request is a formal proposal to modify any earlier accepted subsidiary plan component. The necessity of a change request may arise for the purpose of *Corrective Action* (re-aligning in project work to objectives set down in the project plan), *Preventive Action* (avoiding the future likely problems), or *Defect Repair* (correcting a defective result from some already executed activity). All change requests would need to go through the formal process of integrated change control (to be described later) before their approval.

Other outputs of this execution process are the updates necessary as the ongoing work necessitates: *Updates In Project Documents* (like project charter, scope statement, risk register, etc.), *Updates in the Component Plans* (for management of scope, time, cost, quality, communication, human resources, risk, procurement and stakeholders) and *Updates in Project Baselines* (for scope, time and cost areas).

2.4 Monitor and Control Project Work (Monitoring and Controlling Process Group)

PMBOK® Guide, 5th Edition, defines this process as the work necessary to track, review and report the progress to meet the performance objectives defined in the project management plan.

The usual feedback control loop employed for process control is also the basis for this process. It starts with the project plan and the details worked out for meeting the project objectives, which serves as the standard for comparison. By the inspection and testing of the deliverables, it is checked if the deliverables meet the objective measurable technical specifications and performance criteria, which the project were set to accomplish. If the deliverables pass the tests successfully, they are formally approved and handed over. If the deliverables fail to meet the tests, the necessary defect repair or correction is initiated. This process thus forms the backbone of the communication with and management of the stakeholders – providing the precise current status of the project, obstacle and risks encountered and steps taken to manage them, and forecasts of the project's schedule, scope and budget.

With this overview of the nature of the process, brief explanation of the inputs, tools and techniques and outputs of this process should be self-explanatory.

Inputs

Project Management Plan along with the *Forecasts for Cost and Schedule* generated from analyzing the work performance and *Performance Reports* are the elements of the feedback control loop for measuring the performance and comparing the result with the desired metric, and, therefore, they form the natural inputs for this process. The control of project activity would have to be tailored to the constraints imposed by the *Enterprise Environmental factors,* and assistance obtained from the Organizational *Process Assets.* They are the other two inputs for this process.

Tools and Techniques

Like for other project integrating processes, *Expert Judgment* (in this case, expertise in the industry practice or technology, which could assist the project manager in interpreting the results and evaluating the work performance data) is the main tool or technique. In the process of evaluation of the work performance outcomes, Certain *Analytical Techniques,* like trends analysis, regression analysis and data from earned value management, could be helpful inputs. *Meetings* (face-to-face discussions in the meetings as well as the minutes of project meetings) and *Project Management Information System* are additional tools for monitoring and controlling project work.

Outputs

Work Performance Reports   This involves collecting information and keeping a record of the actual progress of the work in terms of completing deliverables, the conformance of project work to quality metrics, and actual costs incurred and time taken for individual project activities. They may be in the form of status reports, test results, trend analysis, information conveyed during meetings.

Change Requests   As a part of the inspection and testing for monitoring and controlling the deliverables, the process would issue change requests, when necessary. The change requests might aim to involve a *Corrective Action* (re-aligning the overall project activities with the project objectives), *Defect Repair* (correcting the specific defects of deliverables in progress so that the deliverable would meet the quality standard) or *Preventive Action* (preventing errors or defects in future project activities). Corresponding *Updates in Project Component Plans* and *Updates in Project Documents are* other outputs from this process.

2.5 Perform Integrated Change Control (Monitoring and Controlling Process Group)

This process involves reviewing all change requests, approving the change request after estimating the impacts of the proposed change on project scope, budget or schedule, and incorporating changes and the estimated impacts from the changes in the respective subsidiary project management plans and the forecasts.

This is a very important process and it is at the heart of managing changes to projects –a very necessary and critical aspect of project management. On one hand, the project manager has to ensure that changes to the project are minimal and the resources of the project are not frittered away on peripheral objectives. On the other hand, the project manager must ensure that all changes, originating from thoughtful review of the project work planned or executed up to a point and considered desirable for meeting the basic objectives for which the project was authorized are accepted and implemented.

The change management activities carried out during the process include:

- Ensuring that only the approved changes get implemented and preventing the unapproved changes to slip through the change control process.
- Setting up procedures for proposing changes and for evaluating their impact on project scope, quality, cost and schedule
- Setting up criteria and organization for acceptance of change (Change Control Board or Committee for a major infrastructure project)
- Approving the changes that meet the criteria for acceptance and reject the changes that do not meet the criteria for acceptance
- Incorporating the approved changes into the component plans, project baselines for scope, cost and schedule, and overall project management plan and ensure their execution
- Keeping a record of proposed changes and issues, the summary of evaluation and the acceptance or rejection record and formal acceptance of deliverable based on approved change

With this overview of the nature of the process, brief explanation of the inputs, tools and techniques and outputs of this process should be self-explanatory.

Inputs

The *Change Requests submitted for approval* and Work *Performance Information,* are the primary inputs for this process. The proposed changes are to be evaluated for approval based on their conformance to *Project Management Plan*, Understandably, only those changes are approved and implemented that the constraints imposed by *Enterprise Environmental Factors permit* and *Organizational Project Assets* facilitate.

Tools and Techniques

Expert Judgment (value judgment in assessing proposed changes, guidance from consultants or other experts and stakeholders' views) is again the main technique for this integrative process. *Project Meetings* could also be a useful tool, as it would benefit from collective experience of the group in value judgment of the impact of the proposed change.

Outputs

The decisions taken on the change requests are the main outputs from this essentially decision-making process. The outputs are, therefore, *Approved Change Requests. Change Request Status Updates* (whether a change request is accepted, rejected or under review), *Updates in the Project Management Plan, and most importantly Updates in Project Documents* (to reflect the effect of approved changes on the activity list and sequence, project schedule, project quality and project cost) are other outputs from this process.

2.6   Close Project or Phase (Closing Process Group)

PMBOK® Guide, 5th Edition, defines this process as finalizing all activities across all of the project management process groups to formally complete the project or phase. This process provides the landmark signaling the formal ending of the project and attendant release of the organizational resources for new projects. During the comprehensive review completed during the closing process, the lessons learned from the project become apparent; they are often incorporated into the organization's standard project management procedures, policies or planning templates.

In case of projects completed and closed in a normal manner, the process would include the following activities:

- Reviewing information on all earlier project phases to ensure that all project work is completed to the scope and quality standards set at the project authorization stage
- Closing all project contracts and arranging to disband the project team by reassigning the project team members to their new positions
- Getting formal acceptance of the deliverables (from the operating department or project sponsor in case of internal projects and from the client in case of external project) and handing over the product of the project
- Completing the minor left-out items or taking corrective action and repair of the defects found during the formal acceptance check to facilitate formal acceptance of the project by the client or operating department.
- Preparing a detailed review of the project (formal Project Audit in some case) and record lessons learned from the success and failures in project activities for the organization's knowledge and capability to manage similar projects in future.

In case of a project terminated before its reaching the completion as originally planned, the closing process would involve:

- Preparing a detailed status report of all the project work at the stage at which the project is terminated before its normal completion. Such a record is useful in resolving issues and payments in case of a project performed for a client and re-starting the project in the most effective and efficient manner at a later period, if under changed circumstances restarting the project appears desirable.
- Analyzing the reasons for failure or termination prior to its normal completion and closing.

The inputs, tools and techniques and outputs of the process as described in PMBOK® Guide, 5th Edition, are briefly listed below to make this summary of integration management processes comprehensive. *A detailed and more complete account of the project closing is given in Chapter 14: Project Audit and Closure, under the heading' Project Closure'.*

Inputs

Project Management Plan This input is for the purpose of providing the reference frame for the original scope of project work – what the project was aimed to deliver on completion.

Accepted Deliverables Formal acceptance of deliverables prior to hand over – based on "Verify Scope 'process – provides details of what actually happened and so it is an important input.

Organizational Process Assets The Project closure guidelines of the organization and the procedures for archiving the lessons learnt are other very useful inputs for completing the closing process.

Tools and Techniques

Expert Judgment Experience and proficiency in use of administrative procedures build the expert judgment necessary for closing the project.

Meetings The meetings held for the purpose of formal hand-over of the deliverables to the stakeholders (project sponsor or operating group in case of internal project and customer or other stakeholders in case of external project) and the internal meetings of the project groups for coordination of project deliverables hand-over are useful inputs.

Analytical Techniques The techniques like trend analysis or regression analysis could also be helpful in closing process for projects, which are planned and executed in phases or which are parts of a major program.

Outputs

Transition of Final Product, Service or Result, accomplished during formal acceptance and hand-over of the closing process, is the main output of the process.

Lessons Learned (Updating of the Organizational Process Assets) This is a very important output from the closing process. The increase in the knowledge base of the organization and increased proficiency in managing similar other projects are features that distinguish a progressive dynamic organization from stagnant organizations. Hand-over of suitably organized project files created during project planning and execution of the project, an output from the project at the project closing stage, often provide useful information for using the product or service created by the project. Formal lessons learned reports are useful in planning and managing future projects.

CASE 1.1

A Day in the Life

Rachel, the project manager of a large information systems project, arrives at her office early to get caught up with work before her co-workers and project team arrive. However, as she enters the office she meets Neil, one of her fellow project managers, who also wants to get an early start on the day. Neil has just completed a project overseas. They spend 10 minutes socializing and catching up on personal news.

It takes Rachel 10 minutes to get to her office and settle in. She then checks her voice mail and turns on her computer. She was at her client's site the day before until 7:30 P.M. and has not checked her e-mail or voice mail since 3:30 P.M. the previous day. There are 7 phone messages, 16 e-mails, and 4 notes left on her desk. She spends 15 minutes reviewing her schedule and "to do" lists for the day before responding to messages that require immediate attention.

Rachel spends the next 25 minutes going over project reports and preparing for the weekly status meeting. Her boss, who just arrived at the office, interrupts her. They spend 20 minutes discussing the project. He shares a rumor that a team member is using stimulants on the job. She tells him that she has not seen anything suspicious but will keep an eye on the team member.

The 9:00 A.M. project status meeting starts 15 minutes late because two of the team members have to finish a job for a client. Several people go to the cafeteria to get coffee and doughnuts while others discuss last night's baseball game. The team members arrive, and the remaining 45 minutes of the progress review meeting surface project issues that have to be addressed and assigned for action.

After the meeting Rachel goes down the hallway to meet with Victoria, another IS project manager. They spend 30 minutes reviewing project assignments since the two of them share personnel. Victoria's project is behind schedule and in need of help. They broker a deal that should get Victoria's project back on track.

She returns to her office and makes several phone calls and returns several e-mails before walking downstairs to visit with members of her project team. Her intent is to follow up on an issue that had surfaced in the status report meeting. However, her simple, "Hi guys, how are things going?" elicits a stream of disgruntled responses from the "troops." After listening patiently for over 20 minutes, she realizes that among other things several of the client's managers are beginning to request features that were not in the original project scope statement. She tells her people that she will get on this right away.

Returning to her office she tries to call her counterpart John at the client firm but is told that he is not expected back from lunch for another hour. At this time, Eddie drops by and says, "How about lunch?" Eddie works in the finance office and they spend the next half hour in the company cafeteria gossiping about internal politics. She is surprised to hear that Jonah Johnson, the director of systems projects, may join another firm. Jonah has always been a powerful ally.

She returns to her office, answers a few more e-mails, and finally gets through to John. They spend 30 minutes going over the problem. The conversation ends with John promising to do some investigating and to get back to her as soon as possible.

Rachel puts a "Do not disturb" sign on her door, and lies down in her office. She listens to the third and fourth movement of Ravel's string quartet in F on headphones.

Rachel then takes the elevator down to the third floor and talks to the purchasing agent assigned to her project. They spend the next 30 minutes exploring ways of getting necessary equipment to the project site earlier than planned. She finally authorizes express delivery.

When she returns to her office, her calendar reminds her that she is scheduled to participate in a conference call at 2:30. It takes 15 minutes for everyone to get online. During this time, Rachel catches up on some e-mail. The next hour is spent exchanging information about the technical requirements associated with a new version of a software package they are using on systems projects like hers.

Rachel decides to stretch her legs and goes on a walk down the hallway where she engages in brief conversations with various co-workers. She goes out of her way to thank Chandra for his thoughtful analysis at the status report meeting. She returns to find that John has left a message for her to call him back ASAP. She contacts John, who informs her that, according to his people, her firm's marketing rep had made certain promises about specific features her system would provide. He doesn't know how this communication breakdown occurred, but his people are pretty upset over the situation. Rachel thanks John for the information and immediately takes the stairs to where the marketing group resides.

She asks to see Mary, a senior marketing manager. She waits 10 minutes before being invited into her office. After a heated discussion, she leaves 40 minutes later with Mary agreeing to talk to her people about what was promised and what was not promised.

She goes downstairs to her people to give them an update on what is happening. They spend 30 minutes reviewing the impact the client's requests could have on the project schedule. She also shares with them the schedule changes she and Victoria had agreed to. After she says good night to her team, she heads upstairs to her boss's office and spends 20 minutes updating him on key events of the day. She returns to her office and spends 30 minutes reviewing e-mails and project documents. She logs on to the MS project schedule of her project and spends the next 30 minutes working with "what-if" scenarios. She reviews tomorrow's schedule and writes some personal reminders before starting off on her 30-minute commute home.

1. How effectively do you think Rachel spent her day?
2. What does the case tell you about what it is like to be a project manager?

CASE 1.2

Coal Fired Boilers Project
(An Overview of a Proposal for an Infrastructure Project)

Abstract

Projects play a very important role as instruments of change – as instruments for implementing the organization's business strategy. Judicious selection of projects is, therefore, as important as effective and efficient planning and execution of the projects. Most organizations follow a specific methodology for preparing proposals and decision making for major projects: the type of data to be collected, its presentation and scrutiny for decision making and the availability of necessary supporting details. The executive summary specimen of the case illustrates one such presentation of a proposal for an infrastructure project. It would help to give the readers exposure to some aspects of the modern project planning and management techniques and also serve as a preview of the knowledge, approach and techniques for planning and managing projects presented in the subsequent sections of the book.

CASE TEXT

The whole world is a unified place and the events occurring in one country echo loudly in some distant lands. Altaf Hussein worked as an engineering and maintenance manager in National Mills, an old textile mill in the hinterlands of India. He led a routine work life and hardly ever anything exciting new happened. All this changed suddenly in March 1973, when in an OPEC meeting held in distant Riyadh, the decision was taken to raise the crude prices. The crude oil price was indeed observed to fluctuate or even gradually creep upwards over the years. But the price revision this time was an abrupt upward leap – from U.S. $ 2.73 a barrel to U.S. $ 9.82 a barrel.

The textile mills are heavy users of low pressure steam for their processing departments – dyeing, bleaching and finishing and the cost of steam accounts for a substantial portion of their processing costs. Use of coal as a fuel for raising low-pressure steam would reduce steam costs, but coal is a much unclean and inconvenient fuel compared to oil and so switching over to coal-fired boilers was strongly resisted by the plant management all along. Some textile mills located near the metropolis areas and well-connected by rails had switched over to coal for steam generation, but the procurement and transportation of coal to the hinterland being cumbersome, National Mills had continued to depend on steam generated from oil fired boilers till now. However, with this fourfold increase in the price of oil derived from costly crude, the mill faced dire future. It had to do something about the steam cost or face closure of the entire mill.

Altaf had all along a dislike for use of the old oil-fired boilers with frequent breakdowns and causing unexpected emergencies and workloads on him and his staff, but his proposals for replacing the old boilers with new ones had been rejected twice in the last four years with the argument, "New boilers and the trouble-free continuity in the processing departments is fine, but the investment won't pay for itself." Projection of economic benefits is sometimes difficult to cast into hard cash numbers and Altaf had ultimately lost out on earlier occasions.

Altaf saw in the new situation one more opportunity to push his favourite boiler replacement project – this time with an added twist – new **coal-fired boilers,** which can be justified for economic benefits now hands down. He prepared a brief 3-pages proposal for the new coal fired boilers and sent it to Kamal Nayan Bajaj, Executive Vice-President Friday morning. The proposal was so attractive that Mr.Bajaj summoned Altaf for further discussion that very afternoon. Altaf had projected ₹35 million as the project cost for 80 tonnes/hr capacity boilers and the cost of generated steam to drop from ₹135 per tonne to ₹105 per tonne.

Mr. Bajaj shot a number of questions: "Altaf, the idea is good, but unfortunately, may be, we are late for it. How fast can we execute the project? How sure are you of the viability of the project – the cost of project, saving in operating cost by its generation with coal as fuel? Of course, the most crucial question would be: can we get the boiler on line by February 1974, say latest by March 1974; If your answer to the last question is yes, we can announce in the next annual general meeting in May that the operation cost situation is under control. That would save the day."

"Sir, I am pretty sure of my cost of project and operational cost savings numbers. The project has become now not only just viable but a very attractive investment." enthused Altaf.

"Well, if that is the case, I would be ready to authorize the project right away. You would be the Project Manager and if you deliver the goods, the next promotion to Assistant Vice President is yours! But, remember, you will have to prove your projections first to Mr. Patel, and as the Company Financial Controller, he is as hardnosed as seasoned accountants are. We don't have much time. For a starter, why don't you give me the first thing Monday morning an executive summary of your project proposal, which should include brief project overview? "

Altaf had done his homework well before; so he prepared the executive summary (shown below as an exhibit to this case), which could reassure Mr. Bajaj on all issues raised by him. At Mr. Bajaj's suggestion, Altaf prepared the detailed project proposal, along with a number of documents supporting the figures and projections used in the executive summary:

- Project objectives and criteria for judging project success (particularly the project schedule)
- Financial justification for the project (economic feasibility of the proposal – backed by cash flows based on operating costs and savings, estimated return on investment (ROI) using pay-back period and net present value methods for calculations)
- Scope of the overall work and technical and performance specifications of key deliverables
- Project time frame – milestones for major activities completion
- Preliminary project cost estimate (with breakdown showing major expense heads)
- Key project team members (to be released for working on this project)
- Plan for project communications

After a close scrutiny, Mr. Patel confirmed as realistic the projections in Altaf's proposal and the new **Coal-based Steam Generation Project** was soon authorized.

COAL FIRED BOILERS PROJECT PROPOSAL

Executive Summary

1. Project Scope Statement

Design, procure, install and commission by February 28, 1974 a system for generating 80 tonnes per hour of steam using coal as fuel at a total project cost not exceeding ₹35 million. The minimum return on investment of ₹35 million should be 50% per annum.

2. Project Objectives and Criteria for Project Success

No.	Project Objectives	Criteria for Success
1.	To reduce the cost of production of steam by switching from furnace oil to coal as fuel	Reduce the cost from ₹135/- per tonne to ₹105/- per tonne
2.	To commission the project as early as possible latest by March 31, 1974 so that in the annual general meeting the prospects for improved profitability of the mill's operations could be announced and the market capitalization of the shares can be upgraded	Commission the project latest by March 31, 1974. Announce the results of improved profitability in annual general meeting in May, 1974
3.	To complete the project within estimated budget	Complete the project within +/- 5% of budgeted cost of ₹35 million
4.	To earn adequate ROI	Ensure capability for earning about 50% ROI on investment of ₹35 million

3. Customer/Project Sponsor

There is no external customer; the executive vice-president Kamal Nayan Bajaj is the project sponsor.

4. **Summary of Economic Viability**

Estimated Investment:	₹35 million
Saving in cost of production of steam	₹30/- per tonne

(Based on coal based steam cost of ₹105/ tonne
  Compared to ₹135/ tonne for furnace as fuel)

Annual savings in steam production cost	₹17.7 million

(based on 85 % annual average use of the installed
  Capacity of 80 tonnes/hr at 90 % annual average operating time)

ROI	50.4%

5. **Preliminary Stakeholders Analysis**

Project Sponsor

Kamal Nayan Bajaj, Executive Vice President

Senior Officers of National Mills

Mr. Patel, Company Finance Controller

Heads of operating departments using low pressure steam:

Heads of Dyeing, Bleaching and Finishing Departments

Head of Materials Department for coal procurement, quality testing and storage

Head of Maintenance Department for maintenance and upkeep of the system

Project Team

Project Manager: Altaf Hussein

Key members of the project team: The members deputed to the cross-functional project team (material procurement assistant, senior engineers in charge of civil construction and mechanical and electrical installations

6. **Fit with Current Operations /Similarities to Previous Projects**

- The project has a very close fit to the current operations – generating process steam; only the fuel is planned to be switched. The project would have immediate impact on the entire operations of the mill.
- Some modifications were carried out from time to time in the mill's steam distribution system and piping, but no major installation of the size and scope of the proposed project was undertaken in the last seven years by the company.

7. **Major Deliverables**

Deliverable 1	*System Design:*
	Study the plant's present steam distribution and steam requirements for overall system design
	Equipment layouts in boiler/coal handling areas and piping layouts and detailed construction drawings
Deliverable 2	*Procurement:*
	Procure system components
	Coal-fired boiler and coal handling system
	Structural components for pipe rack
	Piping, valves and other piping components

Deliverable 3   *Project Construction at the site:*
Civil construction for boiler control room, equipment foundations and pipe rack structure
Mechanical installation of boiler, electrical & instrumentation for boiler
Mechanical installation of coal handling system
Installation of steam distribution piping

Deliverable 4   *System commissioning*

Deliverable 5   *Training and handing over the project to operating departments*
Operation and maintenance manuals for boiler, coal handling equipment and special new instrumentation

Deliverable 6   *Project Management:*
Receiving statutory approvals (from Boilers Inspector, Factory Inspector, etc.)
Effective project management to deliver the project on time and within budget

8. Summary Budget (in ₹ million)

Buildings and Structures	3.0
Machinery and Equipment	
Boiler	16.0
Coal handling equipment	6.0
Other equipment	3.0
Installation –materials & labour	3.5
SUB-TOTAL MACHINERY AND EQUPMENT	28.5
Provision for contingency at approx. 10 %	3.5
TOTAL ESTIMATED PROJECT COST	35.0

9. Summary Milestones

The installation of coal-handling system:	January 15, 1974
The installation of the boiler and all systems:	February 1, 1974
The Trial runs for statutory approvals:	February 15, 1974
The performance guarantee runs of entire system:	March 1, 1974
The steam headers and connections to users:	March 15, 1974

10. Assumptions, Risks, and Constraints

SCHEDULE BASED ON FOLLOWING ASSUMPTIONS AND ASSOCIATED RISKS

(a) Authorized Capital Budget Request is received latest by April 1, 1973.

(b) Statutory approvals from The Boiler Inspectorate and Environment Protection Agency for the preliminary proposal for installation of coal fired boiler are approved latest by May 15, 1973.

(c) Engineering consulting company is selected and awarded the contract by April30, 1973.

(d) All key project team members are released to work full time on this project latest by April 30, 1973.

(e) The deliveries at the site for the critical major equipment (coal fired boiler and coal handling equipment) are completed by December 31, 1973 under late delivery penalty purchase order.

SCHEDULE CONSTRAINTS

(a) Two potential key members of the project team are presently working on other urgent projects and their release in the desirable time may be doubtful.

(b) The Boiler Inspectorate is notorious for causing delays in giving approvals for proposals.

(c) Ordinarily boiler delivery period is of the order of 8-9 months minimum, while 6-7 months maximum delivery period is necessary to meet project schedule. (Special efforts to locate a suitable supplier, extra price premium over routine competitive prices and stiff late delivery penalty may be necessary to overcome this.)

(d) The foundation casting must be completed before the expected onset of monsoon, i.e. by June 15.

(e) A large number of holidays would be in August-November period – the expected peak activity period for project construction.

Discussion and Questions

(a) Study the proposal closely. Notice the issues which a major capital expenditure project should address. Compare them with the capital expenditure authorization practice in your organization.

(b) Notice the critical role a major project would play in the organization. For this textile mill, the very existence of the organization depends on coming up with and efficiently managing this major project

(c) Notice the nature of specificity and objective measurable standards included in describing the proposal.

- The inclusion of the technical specifications of the product of the project (Statement of Works or S.O.W.), budget and schedule in the opening project scope statement.

- The project objectives and the objectively measurable criteria for judging the project success for each of those objectives.

- Focus on sponsor or main customer and identifying all major stakeholders; managing the key stakeholders is a major contributor for project success.

- Summary of economic viability analysis, project cost estimate and major milestones for schedule; these figures demarcate the boundaries for project cost and schedule.

- Provision for contingency in project cost and schedule – it is one of the tools for managing project risks.

- Major deliverables – including separately project management as a specific deliverable.

- Analysis of Assumptions, Risks and Constraints. This list is very useful in focusing on major issues and at all later stage reviews of the project for giving it the right direction.

2

ORGANIZATION STRATEGY AND PROJECT SELECTION

*Strategy is implemented through projects. Every project should
have a clear link to the organization's strategy.*

Strategy is fundamentally deciding how the organization will compete. Organizations use projects to convert strategy into new products, services, and processes needed for success. For example, Intel's major strategy is one of differentiation. Its projects target innovation and time to market. Currently, Intel is directing its strategy toward specialty chips for products other than computers, such as autos, security, cell phones, air controls. Another goal is to reduce project cycle times. Intel, NEC, General Electric, and AT&T have reduced their cycle times by 20–50 percent. Projects and project management play the key role in supporting strategic goals. It is vital for project managers to think and act strategically.

Aligning projects with the strategic goals of the organization is crucial for project success. Today's economic climate is unprecedented by rapid changes in technology, global competition, and financial uncertainty. These conditions make strategy/project alignment even more essential for success. Ensuring a strong link between the strategic plan and projects is a difficult task that demands constant attention from top and middle management.

The larger and more diverse an organization, the more difficult it is to create and maintain this strong link. Companies today are under enormous pressure to manage a process that clearly aligns projects to organization strategy. Ample evidence still suggests that many organizations have not developed a process that clearly aligns project selection to the strategic plan. The result is poor utilization of the organization's resources—people, money, equipment, and core competencies. Conversely, organizations that have a coherent link of projects to strategy have more cooperation across the organization, perform better on projects, and have fewer projects.

How can an organization ensure this link and alignment? The answer requires integration of projects with the strategic plan. Integration assumes the existence of a strategic plan and a process for prioritizing projects by their contribution to the plan. A crucial factor to ensure the success of integrating the plan with projects lies in the creation of a process that is open and transparent for all participants to review. This chapter presents an overview of the importance of strategic planning and the process for developing a strategic plan. Typical problems encountered when strategy and projects are not linked are noted. A generic methodology that ensures integration by creating very strong linkages of project selection and priority to the strategic plan is then discussed. The intended outcomes are clear organization focus, best use of scarce organization resources (people, equipment, capital), and improved communication across projects and departments.

Why Project Managers Need to Understand Strategy

Project management historically has been preoccupied solely with the planning and execution of projects. Strategy was considered to be under the purview of senior management. This is old-school thinking. New-school thinking recognizes that project management is at the apex of strategy and operations. Aaron Shenhar speaks to this issue when he states, ". . . it is time to expand the traditional role of the project manager from an operational to a more strategic perspective. In the modern evolving organization, project managers will be focused on business aspects, and their role will expand from getting the job done to achieving the business results and winning in the market place."[1]

---

[1] Shenhar, A., and Dov Dvie, *Reinventing Project Management*, Harvard Business School, 2007, p. 5.

There are two main reasons why project managers need to understand their organization's mission and strategy. The first reason is so they can make appropriate decisions and adjustments. For example, how a project manager would respond to a suggestion to modify the design of a product to enhance performance will vary depending upon whether his company strives to be a product leader through innovation or to achieve operational excellence through low cost solutions. Similarly, how a project manager would respond to delays may vary depending upon strategic concerns. A project manager will authorize overtime if her firm places a premium on getting to the market first. Another project manager will accept the delay if speed is not essential.

The second reason project managers need to understand their organization's strategy is so they can be effective project advocates. Project managers have to be able to demonstrate to senior management how their project contributes to their firm's mission. Protection and continued support come from being aligned with corporate objectives. Project managers also need to be able to explain to team members and other stakeholders why certain project objectives and priorities are critical. This is essential for getting buy-in on contentious trade-off decisions.

For these reasons project managers will find it valuable to have a keen understanding of strategic management and project selection processes, which are discussed next.

THE STRATEGIC MANAGEMENT PROCESS: AN OVERVIEW

Strategic management is the process of assessing "what we are" and deciding and implementing "what we intend to be and how we are going to get there." Strategy describes how an organization intends to compete with the resources available in the existing and perceived future environment.

Two major dimensions of strategic management are responding to changes in the external environment and allocating scarce resources of the firm to improve its competitive position. Constant scanning of the external environment for changes is a major requirement for survival in a dynamic competitive environment. The second dimension is the internal responses to new action programs aimed at enhancing the competitive position of the firm. The nature of the responses depends on the type of business, environment volatility, competition, and the organizational culture.

Strategic management provides the theme and focus of the future direction of the organization. It supports consistency of action at every level of the organization. It encourages integration because effort and resources are committed to common goals and strategies. See Snapshot from Practice: Does IBM's Watson's Jeopardy Project Represent a Change in Strategy? It is a continuous, iterative process aimed at developing an integrated and coordinated long-term plan of action. Strategic management positions the organization to meet the needs and requirements of its customers for the long term. With the long-term position identified, objectives are set, and strategies are developed to achieve objectives and then translated into actions by implementing projects. Strategy can decide the survival of an organization. Most organizations are successful in *formulating* strategies for what course(s) they should pursue. However, the problem in many organizations is *implementing* strategies—that is, making them happen. Integration of strategy formulation and implementation often does not exist.

The components of strategic management are closely linked, and all are directed toward the future success of the organization. Strategic management requires strong links among mission, goals, objectives, strategy, and implementation. The mission gives the general purpose of the organization. Goals give global targets within the mission. Objectives give specific targets to goals.

IBM's investment in artificial intelligence paid off. In February 2010, millions of people were glued to their television sets to watch IBM's Watson outclass two former champion contestants on the Jeopardy quiz show. Watson performed at human expert levels in terms of precision, confidence, and speed during the Jeopardy quiz show.

Does Watson represent a new strategic direction for IBM? Not really. The Watson project is simply a manifestation of the move from computer hardware to a service strategy over a decade ago.

WATSON PROJECT DESCRIPTION

Artificial intelligence has advanced significantly in recent years. Watson goes beyond IBM's chess-playing supercomputer of the late 1990s. Chess is finite, logical, and reduced easily to mathematics. Watson's space is ill-defined and involves dealing with abstraction and the circumstantial nature of language. Since Watson's system can understand natural language, it can extend the way people interact with computers.

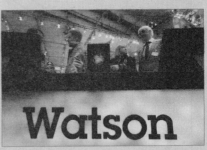

© Sean Gallup/Getty Images

The IBM Watson project took three intense years of research and development by a core team of about 20. Eight university teams working on specific challenge areas augmented these researchers.

Watson depends on over 200 million pages of structured and unstructured data and a program capable of running trillions of operations per second. With this information backup, it attacks a Jeopardy question by parsing the question into small pieces. With the question parsed, the program then searches for relevant data. Using hundreds of decision rules, the program generates possible answers. These answers are assigned a confidence score to decide if Watson should risk offering an answer and how much to bet.

WHAT'S NEXT?

Now that the hype is over, IBM is pursuing their service strategy and the knowledge gained from the Watson project to real business applications. Watson's artificial intelligence design is flexible and suggests a wide variety of opportunities in industries such as finance, medicine, law enforcement, defense. Further extensions to handheld mobile applications that tap into Watson's servers also hold great potential. IBM identified the obvious lowest hanging apples on the tree as providing healthcare solutions and has begun design of such a program.

To create a "doctor's consultant" program would likely follow a design platform similar to Watson's. For example, it would be able to:

- Data mine current medical documents to build a knowledge base
- Integrate individual patient information
- Use system's complex analytics to select relevant data
- Use decision rules to provide physicians with diagnostic options
- Rank options with confidence levels for each option.

Creating a doctor's consultant solution will not replace doctors. Although the system holds tremendous potential, it is manmade and depends on the database, data analytics, and decision rules to select options. Given the doctor's consultant input, a trained doctor makes the final patient diagnosis to supplement physical examination and experience.

The Watson project provides IBM with a flexible component to continue their decade-old strategy, moving IBM from computer hardware to service products.

*Ferrucci, et al. "Building Watson," AI Magazine. vol. 31, no. 3. Fall 2010.

Objectives give rise to formulation of strategies to reach objectives. Finally, strategies require actions and tasks to be implemented. In most cases the actions to be taken represent projects. Figure 2.1 shows a schematic of the **strategic management process** and major activities required.

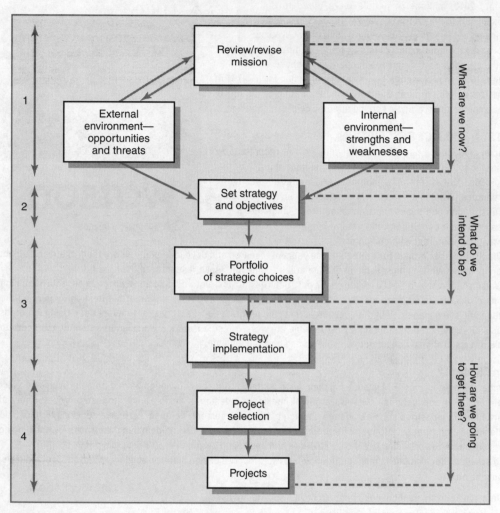

Figure 2.1 *Strategic Management Process*

Four Activities of the Strategic Management Process

The typical sequence of activities of the strategic management process is outlined here; a description of each activity then follows:

1. Review and define the organizational mission.
2. Analyze and formulate strategies.
3. Set objectives to achieve strategy.
4. Implement strategies through projects.

Review and Define the Organizational Mission

The mission identifies "what we want to become," or the raison d'être. Mission statements identify the scope of the organization in terms of its product or service. A written mission statement provides focus for decision making when shared by organizational managers and employees. Everyone in the organization should be keenly aware of the organization's mission. For example, at one large consulting firm, partners who fail to recite the mission statement on demand are required to buy lunch. The mission statement communicates and identifies the purpose of the organization to all stakeholders. Mission statements can be used for evaluating organization performance.

Traditional components found in mission statements are major products and services, target customers and markets, and geographical domain. In addition, statements frequently include organizational philosophy, key technologies, public image, and contribution to society. Including such factors in mission statements relates directly to business success.

Mission statements change infrequently. However, when the nature of the business changes or shifts, revised mission and strategy statements may be required. See Snapshot from Practice: HP's Strategy Revision as an example of a mission and strategy revision.

More specific mission statements tend to give better results because of a tighter focus. Mission statements decrease the chance of false directions by stakeholders. For example, compare the phrasing of the following mission statements:

Provide hospital design services.

Provide data mining and analysis services.

Provide information technology services.

Increase shareholder value.

Provide high-value products to our customer.

Clearly, the first two statements leave less chance for misinterpretation than the others. A rule-of-thumb test for a mission statement is, if the statement can be anybody's mission statement, it will not provide the guidance and focus intended. The mission sets the parameters for developing objectives.

Analyze and Formulate Strategies

Formulating strategy answers the question of *what* needs to be done to reach objectives. Strategy formulation includes determining and evaluating alternatives that support the organization's objectives and selecting the best alternative. The first step is a realistic evaluation of the past and current position of the enterprise. This step typically includes an analysis of "who are the customers" and "what are their needs as they (the *customers*) see them."

The next step is an assessment of the internal and external environments. What are the internal strengths and weaknesses of the enterprise? Examples of internal strengths or weaknesses could be core competencies, such as technology, product quality, management talent, low debt, and dealer networks. Managers can alter internal strengths and weaknesses. Opportunities and threats usually represent external forces for change such as technology, industry structure, and competition. Competitive benchmarking tools are sometimes used here to assess current and future directions. Opportunities and threats are the flip sides of each other. That is, a threat can be perceived as an opportunity, or vice versa. Examples of perceived external threats could be a slowing of the

August 18, 2011, Hewlett Packard announced a dramatic change in strategy. Leo Apotheker, CEO of the world's largest seller of personal computers, decided to exit the low margin PC unit. He wanted to redirect HP to *business software, networking, and storage,* which carry higher margins. Unfortunately, Apotheker failed to communicate the strategic change effectively, lost credibility, and was dismissed. He was replaced by Meg Whitman, while controversy over the company's haphazard direction continued.

THE PC MARKET

Fundamentally, the PC has become a commodity. Although the HP personal computer unit represents nearly a third of total revenue and about 19 percent of HP's profit, growth and profits are slowing. Increased competition from Asia, for example, Lenovo, will continue to erode margins. More importantly, increasing use of smartphones and tablets is already cannibalizing the PC market.

FUTURE MARKETS

In HP's words, their new corporatewide mission *is to provide seamless, secure, context-aware experiences for a connected world.** Business software, networking, and storage can be nicely connected for a grand corporate strategy to meet the new mission.

IBM, Google, Oracle, and Microsoft already dominate the software industry. They and others are all moving to collect and use unstructured data to enhance decision making and/or client requests across numerous industries. All are developing better search engines to sort through any manner of data for information relevant to the search. These dominant players leave HP in a catch-up mode.

HP's plan to compete requires quick action. Executing the software strategy will require purchasing smaller firms or developing collaborative relationships to acquire specific expertise. HP has made two purchases to buttress the new strategy. Autonomy Corporation, UK, will concentrate on mining and searching large structured and unstructured data. Their purchase of Vertica provides an analytics platform for large structured and unstructured data. We can expect to see more purchases that connect software, storage, and networking, which will complement HP's current expertise in the server business.

EXECUTING STRATEGY

HP faces risks. HP has bet the farm on this revised strategy that looks similar to what IBM started over a decade ago. IBM has spent billions and ten years of development to perfect their systems (see previous Watson Snapshot). HP is in a "follower" position. This means gaining market share from tough rivals such as IBM, Apple, Google, Oracle, and Cisco. Can HP afford to go face-to-face with others in stronger cash positions? Can HP sell off its PC division at a reasonable price?

HP must move quickly to catch up. Executing the new mission statement presents numerous leadership challenges. The changes in HP strategies over the last 15 years have caused confusion and a loss of employee loyalty. Additional changes in organizational culture, along with many new mission critical projects, will place further stress on the organization. HP must be vigilant in selecting, prioritizing, and balancing organizational risk for all projects. HP needs to communicate a coherent strategy that can be executed consistently over time.

Although there are outsiders who have praised or criticized the new strategy, we must wait and see how the details unfold. HP's strategic moves will make interesting case studies for years to come.

*HP website, HP newsroom.

economy, a maturing life cycle, exchange rates, or government regulation. Typical opportunities are increasing demand, emerging markets, and demographics. Managers or individual firms have limited opportunities to influence such external environmental factors; however, in recent years notable exceptions have been new technologies such as Apple using the iPod to create a market to sell music. The keys are to attempt to forecast fundamental industry changes and stay in a proactive mode rather than a reactive one. This assessment of the external and internal environments is known as the SWOT analysis (strengths, weaknesses, opportunities, and threats).

From this analysis, critical issues and strategic alternatives are identified. Critical analysis of the strategies includes asking questions: Does the strategy take advantage of our core competencies? Does the strategy exploit our competitive advantage? Does the strategy maximize meeting customers' needs? Does the strategy fit within our acceptable risk range? These strategic alternatives are winnowed down to a critical few that support the basic mission.

Strategy formulation ends with cascading objectives or projects assigned to lower divisions, departments, or individuals. Formulating strategy might range around 20 percent of management's effort, while determining *how* strategy will be implemented might consume 80 percent.

Set Objectives to Achieve Strategies

Objectives translate the organization strategy into specific, concrete, measurable terms. Organizational objectives set targets for all levels of the organization. Objectives pinpoint the direction managers believe the organization should move toward. Objectives answer in detail *where* a firm is headed and *when* it is going to get there. Typically, objectives for the organization cover markets, products, innovation, productivity, quality, finance, profitability, employees, and consumers. In every case, objectives should be as operational as possible. That is, objectives should include a time frame, be measurable, be an identifiable state, and be realistic. Doran created the memory device shown in Exhibit 2.1, which is useful when writing objectives.[2]

Each level below the organizational objectives should support the higher-level objectives in more detail; this is frequently called cascading of objectives. For example, if a firm making leather luggage sets an objective of achieving a 40 percent increase in sales through a research and development strategy, this charge is passed to the marketing, production, and R&D departments. The R&D department accepts the firm's strategy as their objective, and their strategy becomes the design and development of a new "pull-type luggage with hidden retractable wheels." At this point the objective becomes a project to be implemented—to develop the retractable wheel luggage for market within six months within a budget of $200,000. In summary, organizational objectives drive your projects.

EXHIBIT 2.1 •
Characteristics of Objectives

S	Specific	Be specific in targeting an objective
M	Measurable	Establish a measurable indicator(s) of progress
A	Assignable	Make the objective assignable to one person for completion
R	Realistic	State what can realistically be done with available resources
T	Time related	State when the objective can be achieved, that is, duration

[2] Doran, G. T., "There's a Smart Way to Write Management Goals and Objectives," *Management Review,* November 1981, pp. 35–36.

Implement Strategies through Projects

Implementation answers the question of *how* strategies will be realized, given available resources. The conceptual framework for strategy implementation lacks the structure and discipline found in strategy formulation. Implementation requires action and completing tasks; the latter frequently means mission-critical projects. Therefore, implementation must include attention to several key areas.

First, completing tasks requires allocation of resources. Resources typically represent funds, people, management talents, technological skills, and equipment. Frequently, implementation of projects is treated as an "addendum" rather than an integral part of the strategic management process. However, multiple objectives place conflicting demands on organizational resources. Second, implementation requires a formal and informal organization that complements and supports strategy and projects. Authority, responsibility, and performance all depend on organization structure and culture. Third, planning and control systems must be in place to be certain project activities necessary to ensure strategies are effectively performed. Fourth, motivating project contributors will be a major factor for achieving project success. Finally, areas receiving more attention in recent years are portfolio management and prioritizing projects. Although the strategy implementation process is not as clear as strategy formulation, all managers realize that, without implementation, success is impossible. Although the four major steps of strategic management process have not been altered significantly over the years, the view of the time horizon in the strategy formulation process has been altered radically in the last two decades. Global competition and rapid innovation require being highly adaptive to short-run changes while being consistent in the longer run.

THE NEED FOR A PROJECT PORTFOLIO MANAGEMENT SYSTEM

Implementation of projects without a strong **priority system** linked to strategy creates problems. Three of the most obvious problems are discussed below. A **project portfolio** system can go a long way to reduce, or even eliminate, the impact of these problems.

Problem 1: The Implementation Gap

In organizations with short product life cycles, it is interesting to note that frequently participation in strategic planning and implementation includes participants from all levels within the organization. However, in perhaps 80 percent of the remaining product and service organizations, top management pretty much formulates strategy and leaves strategy implementation to functional managers. Within these broad constraints, more detailed strategies and objectives are developed by the functional managers. The fact that these objectives and strategies are made *independently* at different levels by functional groups within the organization hierarchy causes manifold problems.

Some symptoms of organizations struggling with strategy disconnect and unclear priorities are presented here.

- Conflicts frequently occur among functional managers and cause lack of trust.
- Frequent meetings are called to establish or renegotiate priorities.
- People frequently shift from one project to another, depending on current priority. Employees are confused about which projects are important.

- People are working on multiple projects and feel inefficient.
- Resources are not adequate.

Because clear linkages do not exist, the organizational environment becomes dysfunctional, confused, and ripe for ineffective implementation of organization strategy and, thus, of projects. The **implementation gap** refers to the lack of understanding and consensus of organization strategy among top and middle-level managers.

A scenario the authors have seen repeated several times follows. Top management picks their top 20 projects for the next planning period, without priorities. Each functional department—marketing, finance, operations, engineering, information technology, and human resources—selects projects from the list. Unfortunately, independent department priorities across projects are not homogenous. A project that rates first in the IT department can rate 10th in the finance department. Implementation of the projects represents conflicts of interest with animosities developing over organization resources.

If this condition exists, how is it possible to effectively implement strategy? The problem is serious. One study found that only about 25 percent of *Fortune 500* executives believe there is a strong linkage, consistency, and/or agreement between the strategies they formulate and implementation. In another study of Deloitte Consulting, Jeff MacIntyre reports, "Only 23 percent of nearly 150 global executives considered their project portfolios aligned with the core business."[3] Middle managers considered organizational strategy to be under the purview of others or not in their realm of influence. It is the responsibility of senior management to set policies that show a distinct link between organizational strategy and objectives and projects that implement those strategies. The research of Fusco suggests the implementation gap and prioritizing projects are still overlooked by many organizations. He surveyed 280 project managers and found that 24 percent of their organizations did not even publish or circulate their objectives; in addition, 40 percent of the respondents reported that priorities among competing projects were not clear, while only 17 percent reported clear priorities.[4]

Problem 2: Organization Politics

Politics exist in every organization and can have a significant influence on which projects receive funding and high priority. This is especially true when the criteria and process for selecting projects are ill-defined and not aligned with the mission of the firm. Project selection may be based not so much on facts and sound reasoning, but rather on the persuasiveness and power of people advocating projects.

The term **"sacred cow"** is often used to denote a project that a powerful, high-ranking official is advocating. Case in point, a marketing consultant confided that he was once hired by the marketing director of a large firm to conduct an independent, external market analysis for a new product the firm was interested in developing. His extensive research indicated that there was insufficient demand to warrant the financing of this new product. The marketing director chose to bury the report and made the consultant promise never to share this information with anyone. The director explained that this new product was the "pet idea" of the new CEO, who saw it as his legacy to the firm. He went on to describe the CEO's irrational obsession with the project and how he referred to

---

[3] MacIntyre, J., *PM Network,* vol. 20 (11) November 2006, pp. 32–35.

[4] Fusco, J. C., "Better Policies Provide the Key to Implementing Project Management," *Project Management Journal,* vol. 28 (3) 1997, pp. 38–41.

it as his "new baby." Like a parent fiercely protecting his child, the marketing director believed that he would lose his job if such critical information ever became known.

Project sponsors play a significant role in the selection and successful implementation of product innovation projects. Project sponsors are typically high-ranking managers who endorse and lend political support for the completion of a specific project. They are instrumental in winning approval of the project and in protecting the project during the critical development stage. The importance of project sponsors should not be taken lightly. For example, a PMI global survey of over 1,000 project practitioners and leaders over a variety of industries found those organizations having active sponsors on at least 80 percent of their projects/programs have a success rate of 75 percent, eleven percentage points above the survey average of 64 percent. Many promising projects have failed to succeed due to lack of strong sponsorship.[5]

The significance of corporate politics can be seen in the ill-fated ALTO computer project at Xerox during the mid-1970s.[6] The project was a tremendous technological success; it developed the first workable mouse, the first laser printer, the first user-friendly software, and the first local area network. All of these developments were five years ahead of their nearest competitor. Over the next five years this opportunity to dominate the nascent personal computer market was squandered because of internal in-fighting at Xerox and the absence of a strong project sponsor. (Apple's MacIntosh computer was inspired by many of these developments.)

Politics can play a role not only in project selection but also in the aspirations behind projects. Individuals can enhance their power within an organization by managing extraordinary and critical projects. Power and status naturally accrue to successful innovators and risk takers rather than to steady producers. Many ambitious managers pursue high-profile projects as a means for moving quickly up the corporate ladder.

Many would argue that politics and project management should not mix. A more proactive response is that projects and politics invariably mix and that effective project managers recognize that any significant project has political ramifications. Likewise, top management needs to develop a system for identifying and selecting projects that reduces the impact of internal politics and fosters the selection of the best projects for achieving the mission and strategy of the firm.

Problem 3: Resource Conflicts and Multitasking

Most project organizations exist in a multiproject environment. This environment creates the problems of project interdependency and the need to share resources. For example, what would be the impact on the labor resource pool of a construction company if it should win a contract it would like to bid on? Will existing labor be adequate to deal with the new project—given the completion date? Will current projects be delayed? Will subcontracting help? Which projects will have priority? Competition among project managers can be contentious. All project managers seek to have the best people for their projects. The problems of sharing resources and scheduling resources across projects grow exponentially as the number of projects rises. In multiproject environments the stakes are higher and the benefits or penalties for good or bad resource scheduling become even more significant than in most single projects.

Resource sharing also leads to multitasking. Multitasking involves starting and stopping work on one task to go and work on another project, and then returning to the work on the original

[5] PMI, "PMI's Pulse of the Profession," March 2012, Project Management Institute, p. 7.

[6] Smith, D. K., and R. C. Alexander, *Fumbling the Future: How Xerox Invented, Then Ignored the First Personal Computer* (New York: Macmillan, 1988).

task. People working on several tasks concurrently are far less efficient, especially where conceptual or physical shutdown and startup are significant. Multitasking adds to delays and costs. Changing priorities exacerbate the multitasking problems even more. Likewise, multitasking is more evident in organizations that have too many projects for the resources they command.

The number of small and large projects in a portfolio almost always exceeds the available resources (typically by a factor of three to four times the available resources). This capacity overload inevitably leads to confusion and inefficient use of scarce organizational resources. The presence of an implementation gap, of power politics, and of multitasking adds to the problem of which projects are allocated resources first. Employee morale and confidence suffer because it is difficult to make sense of an ambiguous system. A multiproject organization environment faces major problems without a priority system that is clearly linked to the strategic plan.

In essence, to this point we have suggested that many organizations have no meaningful process for addressing the problems we have described. The first and most important change that will go a long way in addressing these and other problems is the development and use of a meaningful project priority process for project selection.

How can the implementation gap be narrowed so that understanding and consensus of organizational strategies run through all levels of management? How can power politics be minimized? Can a process be developed in which projects are consistently prioritized to support organizational strategies? Can the prioritized projects be used to allocate scarce organizational resources—for example, people, equipment? Can the process encourage bottom-up initiation of projects that support clear organizational targets?

What is needed is a set of integrative criteria and a process for evaluating and selecting projects that support higher-level strategies and objectives. A single-project priority system that ranks projects by their contribution to the strategic plan would make life easier. Easily said, but difficult to accomplish in practice. Organizations that managed independent projects and allocated resources ad hoc have shifted focus to selecting the right portfolio of projects to achieve their strategic objectives. This is a quickening trend. The advantages of successful project portfolio systems are becoming well recognized in project-driven organizations. See Exhibit 2.2, which lists a few key benefits; the list could easily be extended.

A project portfolio system is discussed next with emphasis on selection criteria, which is where the power of the portfolio system is established.

EXHIBIT 2.2 ·
Benefits of Project Portfolio Management

- Builds discipline into project selection process.
- Links project selection to strategic metrics.
- Prioritizes project proposals across a common set of criteria, rather than on politics or emotion.
- Allocates resources to projects that align with strategic direction.
- Balances risk across all projects.
- Justifies killing projects that do not support organization strategy.
- Improves communication and supports agreement on project goals.

A PORTFOLIO MANAGEMENT SYSTEM

Succinctly put, the aim of portfolio management is to ensure that projects are aligned with strategic goals and prioritized appropriately. As Foti points out, portfolio management asks "What is strategic to our organization?" (2002) Portfolio management provides information that allows people to make better business decisions. Since projects clamoring for funding and people usually outnumber available resources, it is important to follow a logical and defined process for selecting the projects to implement.

Design of a project portfolio system should include classification of a project, selection criteria depending upon classification, sources of proposals, evaluating proposals, and managing the portfolio of projects.

Classification of the Project

Many organizations find they have three basic kinds of projects in their portfolio: *compliance* (emergency—must do), *operational,* and *strategic* projects. (See Figure 2.2.) Compliance projects are typically those needed to meet regulatory conditions required to operate in a region; hence, they are called "must do" projects. Emergency projects, such as building an auto parts factory destroyed by tsunami, is an example of a must-do project. Compliance and emergency projects usually have penalties if they are not implemented. Operational projects are those that are needed to

FIGURE 2.2   *Portfolio of Projects by Type*

support current operations. These projects are designed to improve efficiency of delivery systems, reduce product costs, and improve performance. Some of these projects, given their limited scope and cost, require only immediate manager approval, while bigger, more expensive projects need extensive review. Choosing to install a new piece of equipment would be an example of the latter while modifying a production process would be an example of the former. Total quality management (TQM) projects are examples of operational projects. Finally, strategic projects are those that directly support the organization's long-run mission. They frequently are directed toward increasing revenue or market share. Examples of strategic projects are new products, research, and development. For a good, complete discussion on classification schemes found in practice, see Crawford, Hobbs, and Turne.

Frequently, these three classifications are further decomposed by product type, organization divisions and functions that will require different criteria for project selection. For example, the same criteria for the finance or legal division would not apply to the IT (information technology) department. This often requires different project selection criteria within the basic three classifications of strategic, operational, and compliance projects.

SELECTION CRITERIA

Although there are many criteria for selecting projects, selection criteria are typically identified as *financial* and *nonfinancial*. A short description of each is given next, followed by a discussion of their use in practice.

Financial Criteria

Financial Models For most managers financial criteria are the preferred method to evaluate projects. These models are appropriate when there is a high level of confidence associated with estimates of future cash flows. Two models and examples are demonstrated here—**payback** and **net present value** (NPV).

Project A has an initial investment of $700,000 and projected cash inflows of $225,000 for 5 years.
Project B has an initial investment of $400,000 and projected cash inflows of $110,000 for 5 years.

1. The payback model measures the time it will take to recover the project investment. Shorter paybacks are more desirable. Payback is the simplest and most widely used model. Payback emphasizes cash flows, a key factor in business. Some managers use the payback model to eliminate unusually risky projects (those with lengthy payback periods). The major limitations of payback are that it ignores the time value of money, assumes cash inflows for the investment period (and not beyond), and does not consider profitability. The payback formula is

$$\text{Payback period (yrs)} = \text{Estimated Project Cost/Annual Savings}$$

Exhibit 2.3 compares the payback for Project A and Project B. The payback for Project A is 3.1 years and for Project B is 3.6 years. Using the payback method both projects are acceptable since both return the initial investment in less than five years and have returns on the investment of 32.1 and 27.5 percent. Payback provides especially useful information for firms concerned with liquidity and having sufficient resources to manage their financial obligations.

Exhibit 2.3 A presents the net present value model.

2. The net present value (NPV) model uses management's minimum desired rate-of-return (discount rate, for example, 20 percent) to compute the present value of all net cash inflows. If the result is positive (the project meets the minimum desired rate of return), it is eligible for further consideration. If the result is negative, the project is rejected. Thus, higher positive NPV's are desirable. Excel uses this formula

$$\text{Project NPV} = I_0 + \sum_{t=1}^{n} \frac{F_t}{(1 + k)^t} \quad \text{where}$$

I_0 = Initial investment (since it is an outflow, the number will be negative)
F_t = Net cash inflow for period t
k = Required rate of return

Exhibit 2.3B presents the NPV model using Microsoft Excel software. The NPV model accepts project A, which has a *positive* NPV of $54,235. Project B is rejected since the NPV is *negative* $31,263. Compare the NPV results with the payback results. The NPV model is more realistic because it considers the time value of money, cash flows, and profitability.

When using the NPV model, the discount rate (return on investment hurdle rate) can differ for different projects. For example, the expected ROI on strategic projects is frequently set higher than operational projects. Similarly, ROI's can differ for riskier versus safer projects. The criteria for setting the ROI hurdle rate should be clear and applied consistently.

EXHIBIT 2.3 ···

Example Comparing Two Projects Using Payback and Net Present Value Method

	A	B	C	D	E	F	G	H	I	J	K	L	M
1							Exhibit 2.3A						
2													
3					Example Comparing Two Projects Using the Payback Method								
4													
5				Project A		Project B				Formulas			
6													
7													
8		Investment		$700,000		$400,000				Project A: Payback = (D8/D9)			
9		Annual savings		$225,000		$110,000				Project B: Payback = (F8/F9)			
10													
11		Payback period*		3.1 years		3.6 years							
12													
13		Rate of return **		32.1%		27.5%				Project A: Rate of return = (D9/D8)			
14										Project B: Rate of return = (F9/F8)			
15	Project A: Accept. Less than 5 years and exceeds 15% desired rate.												
16													
17	Project B: Accept. Less than 5 years and exceeds 15% desired rate.												
18													
19	* Note: Payback does not use the time value of money.												
20	** Note: Rate of return is reciprocal of Payback.												
21													
22													

J3

	A	B	C	D	E	F	G	H	I	J	K	L	M
1													
2						Exhibit 2.3B							
3													
4					Example Comparing Two Projects Using NPV								
5	Project A		Year 0	Year 1	Year 2	Year 3	Year 4	Year 5	Total		Formulas		
6	Required	15%											
7	Outflows		-$700,000						-$700,000				
8	Inflows			$225,000	$225,000	$225,000	$225,000	$225,000	$1,125,000				
9	Net inflows			$225,000	$225,000	$225,000	$225,000	$225,000	$425,000	Project A: =C7+NPV(B6,D9:H9)			
10	NPV	$54,235											
11													
12													
13	Project B												
14	Required	15%											
15	Outflows		-$400,000						-$400,000				
16	Inflows			$110,000	$110,000	$110,000	$110,000	$110,000	$550,000				
17	Net inflows			$110,000	$110,000	$110,000	$110,000	$110,000	$150,000	Project B: =C15+NPV(B14,D17:H17)			
18	NPV	-$31,263											
19													
20													
21													
22	NPV comparison: Accept Project A---NPV is positive.												
23	Reject Project B---NPV is negative.												

Unfortunately, pure financial models fail to include many projects where financial return is impossible to measure and/or other factors are vital to the accept or reject decision. One research study by Foti showed that companies using predominantly financial models to prioritize projects yielded unbalanced portfolios and projects that aren't strategically oriented (2003).

Nonfinancial Criteria

Financial return, while important, does not always reflect strategic importance. The sixties and seventies saw firms become overextended by diversifying too much. Now the prevailing thinking is that long-term survival is dependent upon developing and maintaining core competencies. Companies have to be disciplined in saying no to potentially profitable projects that are outside the realm of their core mission. This requires other criteria be considered beyond direct financial return. For example, a firm may support projects that do not have high profit margins for other strategic reasons including:

To capture larger market share

To make it difficult for competitors to enter the market

To develop an enabler product, which by its introduction will increase sales in more profitable products

To develop core technology that will be used in next-generation products

To reduce dependency on unreliable suppliers

To prevent government intervention and regulation

Less tangible criteria may also apply. Organizations may support projects to restore corporate image or enhance brand recognition. Many organizations are committed to corporate citizenship and support community development projects.

Since no single criterion can reflect strategic significance, portfolio management requires multi-criteria screening models. These models often weight individual criteria so those projects that contribute to the most important strategic objectives are given higher consideration.

Two Multi-Criteria Selection Models

Since no single criterion can reflect strategic significance, portfolio management requires multi-criteria screening models. Two models, the checklist and multi-weighted scoring models, are described next.

Checklist Models   The most frequently used method in selecting projects has been the checklist. This approach basically uses a list of questions to review potential projects and to determine their acceptance or rejection. Several of the typical questions found in practice are listed in Exhibit 2.4. One large, multiproject organization has 250 different questions!

A justification of checklist models is that they allow great flexibility in selecting among many different types of projects and are easily used across different divisions and locations. Although many projects are selected using some variation of the checklist approach, this approach has serious shortcomings. Major shortcomings of this approach are that it fails to answer the relative importance or value of a potential project to the organization and fails to allow for comparison with other potential projects. Each potential project will have a different set of positive and negative answers. How do you compare? Ranking and prioritizing projects by their importance is difficult, if not impossible. This approach also leaves the door open to the potential opportunity for power plays, politics, and other forms of manipulation. To overcome these serious shortcomings experts recommend the use of a multi-weighted scoring model to select projects, which is examined next.

EXHIBIT 2.4 ••
Sample Selection Questions Used in Practice

Topic	Question
Strategy/alignment	What specific organization strategy does this project align with?
Driver	What business problem does the project solve?
Success metrics	How will we measure success?
Sponsorship	Who is the project sponsor?
Risk	What is the impact of not doing this project?
Risk	What is the project risk to our organization?
Risk	Where does the proposed project fit in our risk profile?
Benefits, value, ROI	What is the value of the project to this organization?
Benefits, value, ROI	When will the project show results?
Objectives	What are the project objectives?
Organization culture	Is our organization culture right for this type of project?
Resources	Will internal resources be available for this project?
Approach	Will we build or buy?
Schedule	How long will this project take?
Schedule	Is the time line realistic?
Training/resources	Will staff training be required?
Finance/portfolio	What is the estimated cost of the project?
Portfolio	Is this a new initiative or part of an existing initiative?
Portfolio	How does this project interact with current projects?
Technology	Is the technology available or new?

Multi-Weighted Scoring Models   A weighted scoring model typically uses several weighted selection criteria to evaluate project proposals. Weighted scoring models will generally include qualitative and/or quantitative criteria. Each selection criterion is asssigned a weight. Scores are assigned to each criterion for the project, based on its importance to the project being evaluated. The weights and scores are multiplied to get a total weighted score for the project. Using these multiple screening criteria, projects can then be compared using the weighted score. Projects with higher weighted scores are considered better.

Selection criteria need to mirror the critical success factors of an organization. For example, 3M set a target that 25 percent of the company's sales would come from products fewer than four years old versus the old target of 20 percent. Their priority system for project selection strongly reflects this new target. On the other hand, failure to pick the right factors will render the screening process "useless" in short order. See Snapshot from Practice: Crisis IT.

Figure 2.3 represents a project scoring matrix using some of the factors found in practice. The screening criteria selected are shown across the top of the matrix (e.g., stay within core competencies . . . ROI of 18 percent plus). Management weights each criterion (a value of 0 to a high of, say, 3) by its relative importance to the organization's objectives and strategic plan. Project proposals are then submitted to a project **priority team** or project office.

Each project proposal is then evaluated by its relative contribution/value added to the selected criteria. Values of 0 to a high of 10 are assigned to each criterion for each project. This value represents the project's fit to the specific criterion. For example, project 1 appears to fit well with the strategy of the organization since it is given a value of 8. Conversely, project 1 does nothing to support reducing defects (its value is 0). Finally, this model applies the management weights to

SNAPSHOT FROM PRACTICE
Crisis IT

In May 2007, Frontier Airlines Holdings hired Gerry Coady as chief information officer (CIO). Nearly a year later the airline filed for bankruptcy under Chapter 11. In an interview Coady describes how he managed IT projects during the bankruptcy and recession crisis of 2008–2009.

Fundamentally, Coady faced a situation of too many projects and too few resources. Coady used a strategy of focusing on reducing the number of projects in the portfolio. He put together a steering committee of senior management that reviewed several hundred projects. The end result was a reduction to less than 30 projects remaining in the portfolio.

© PRNewsFoto/Genesis, Inc.

How Can You Get to a Backlog of over 100 Projects?

"There are never enough resources to get everything done." Backlogs build over time. Sacred cow projects get included in the selection system. Projects proposed from people who have left the airline still reside in the project portfolio. Non-value-added projects somehow make their way into the project portfolio. Soon the queue gets longer. With everyone in IT working on too many projects concurrently, project completion and productivity are slow.

Which Projects Remain?

To cut the number of projects, the steering committee used a weighting scheme that reflected the airline's priorities, which were: fly safe, generate revenue, reduce costs, and customer service. The weighting scheme easily weeded out the fluff. Coady noted that "by the time you get to the 20s the margin of differentiation gets narrower and narrower." Of the remaining projects, project sponsors had to have solid justification why their project is important. Reduction of the number of projects places emphasis on high value projects.

What Advice Does Coady Have for Crisis Management?

In times of crisis, it is easier to take bold steps to make changes. But you need to have a clear vision of what you should be focusing on with the resources available. Coady suggests, "It comes back to really having a good idea of what the initial business case for a project is and what resources it is consuming, both people and otherwise."

Source: Worthen, B., "Crisis IT," *The Wall Street Journal*, April 20, 2009, p-R6.

each criterion by importance using a value of 1 to 3. For example, ROI and strategic fit have a weight of 3, while urgency and core competencies have weights of 2. Applying the weight to each criterion, the priority team derives the weighted total points for each project. For example, project 5 has the highest value of $102 [(2 \times 1) + (3 \times 10) + (2 \times 5) + (2.5 \times 10) + (1 \times 0) + (1 \times 8) + (3 \times 9) = 102]$ and project 2 has a low value of 27. If the resources available create a cutoff threshold of 50 points, the priority team would eliminate projects 2 and 4. (Note: Project 4 appears to have some urgency, but it is not classified as a "must" project. Therefore, it is screened with all other proposals.) Project 5 would receive first priority, project *n* second, and so on. In rare cases where resources are severely limited and project proposals are similar in weighted rank, it is prudent to pick the project placing less demand on resources. Weighted multiple criteria models similar to this one are rapidly becoming the dominant choice for prioritizing projects.

Criteria / Weight	Stay within core competencies	Strategic fit	Urgency	25% of sales from new products	Reduce defects to less than 1%	Improve customer loyalty	ROI of 18% plus	Weighted total
	2.0	3.0	2.0	2.5	1.0	1.0	3.0	
Project 1	1	8	2	6	0	6	5	66
Project 2	3	3	2	0	0	5	1	27
Project 3	9	5	2	0	2	2	5	56
Project 4	3	0	10	0	0	6	0	32
Project 5	1	10	5	10	0	8	9	102
Project 6	6	5	0	2	0	2	7	55
⋮								
Project *n*	5	5	7	0	10	10	8	83

FIGURE 2.3 *Project Screening Matrix*

At this point in the discussion it is wise to stop and put things into perspective. While selection models like the one above may yield numerical solutions to project selection decisions, models should not make the final *decisions*—the people using the models should. No model, no matter how sophisticated, can capture the total reality it is meant to represent. Models are tools for guiding the evaluation process so that the decision-makers will consider relevant issues and reach a meeting of the minds as to which projects should be supported and not supported. This is a much more subjective process than calculations suggest.

APPLYING A SELECTION MODEL

Project Classification It is not necessary to have exactly the same criteria for the different types of projects discussed above (strategic and operations). However, experience shows most organizations use similar criteria across all types of projects, with perhaps one or two criteria specific to the type of project—e.g., strategic breakthrough versus operational.

Regardless of criteria differences among different types of projects, the most important criterion for selection is the project's fit to the organization strategy. Therefore, this criterion should be consistent across all types of projects and carry a high priority relative to other criteria. This uniformity across all priority models used can keep departments from suboptimizing the use of organization resources. Anyone generating a project proposal should classify their proposal by type, so the appropriate criteria can be used to evaluate their proposal.

Selecting a Model In the past, financial criteria were used almost to the exclusion of other criteria. However, in the last two decades we have witnessed a dramatic shift to include multiple criteria in project selection. Concisely put, profitability alone is simply not an adequate measure of contribution; however, it is still an important criterion, especially for projects that enhance revenue and market share such as breakthrough R&D projects.

Today, senior management is interested in identifying the potential mix of projects that will yield the best use of human and capital resources to maximize return on investment in the long run. Factors such as researching new technology, public image, ethical position, protection of the environment, core competencies, and strategic fit might be important criteria for selecting projects. Weighted scoring criteria seem the best alternative to meet this need.

Weighted scoring models result in bringing projects to closer alignment with strategic goals. If the scoring model is published and available to everyone in the organization, some discipline and credibility are attached to the selection of projects. The number of wasteful projects using resources is reduced. Politics and "sacred cow" projects are exposed. Project goals are more easily identified and communicated using the selection criteria as corroboration. Finally, using a weighted scoring approach helps project managers understand how their project was selected, how their project contributes to organization goals, and how it compares with other projects. Project selection is one of the most important decisions guiding the future success of an organization.

Criteria for project selection are the area where the power of your portfolio starts to manifest itself. New projects are aligned with the strategic goals of the organization. With a clear method for selecting projects in place, project proposals can be solicited.

Sources and Solicitation of Project Proposals

As you would guess, projects should come from anyone who believes his or her project will add value to the organization. However, many organizations restrict proposals from specific levels or groups within the organization. This could be an opportunity lost. Good ideas are not limited to certain types or classes of organization stakeholders. Encourage and keep solicitations open to all sources—internal and external sponsors.

Figure 2.4A provides an example of a proposal form for an automatic vehicular tracking (Automatic Vehicle Location) public transportation project. Figure 2.4B presents a preliminary risk analysis for a 500-acre wind farm. Many organizations use risk analysis templates to gain a quick insight of a project's inherent risks. Risk factors depend on the organization and type of projects. This information is useful in balancing the project portfolio and identifying major risks when executing the project. Project risk analysis is the subject of Chapter 7.

In some cases organizations will solicit ideas for projects when the knowledge requirements for the project are not available in the organization. Typically, the organization will issue an RFP (Request for Proposal) to contractors/vendors with adequate experience to implement the project. In one example, a hospital published an RFP that asked for a bid to design and build a new operating room that uses the latest technology. Several architecture firms submitted bids to the hospital. The bids for the project were evaluated internally against other potential projects. When the project was accepted as a go, other criteria were used to select the best qualified bidder. See Appendix 2.1 of this chapter for a complete description of requests for proposal (RFP).

Ranking Proposals and Selection of Projects

Culling through so many proposals to identify those that add the most value requires a structured process. Figure 2.5 shows a flow chart of a screening process beginning with the creation of an idea for a project. See template for evaluating contractors in Appendix 2.1.

Project Proposal Form

Date: Jan 22, 2xxx   Proposal # _____ 11 _____   Sponsor _____ J. Moran _____

Project classification?
Strategic_____   Infrastructure __X__   Compliance_____

What business problem does the project solve?
Increase customer satisfaction through kiosk and Web site for bus, streetcar, and fast rail
Enhance driver and traveler safety   Hyperlink to: AVL.tri-met.org

How does this project align with our organization strategy?
Increase customer ridership through better passenger travel planning & scheduling decisions
Faster response to accidents

What are the major deliverables of the project?
GPS vehicle tracking system, Internet access, schedule screen

What is the impact of not doing this project?
Not meeting ridership goals

What are the three major risks for this project?
Cost overruns   Integration of fast rail, bus, and streetcar systems
Hacking system

How will we measure success?   Increased ridership
Customer satisfaction
Meeting budget and schedule

Yes [X] No [ ]   Will this project require internal resources?
Yes [X] No [ ]   Available?

What is the estimated cost of the project? $10 million

How long will this project take? __22__ Weeks

Oversight action: Accept [X]   Return [ ]

Signature _____ XXXXXX _____   Date: Feb. 7, 2xxx

FIGURE 2.4A *A Proposal Form for an Automatic Vehicular Tracking (AVL) Public Transportation Project.*

Data and information are collected to assess the value of the proposed project to the organization and for future backup. If the sponsor decides to pursue the project on the basis of the collected data, it is forwarded to the project priority team (or the project office). Note that the sponsor knows which criteria will be used to accept or reject the project. Given the selection

Brief Risk Assessment

Purpose: To draw attention to apparent project risks that will need management attention.

What are the four major risks of this project?
1. *Government incentives curtailed*
2. *Land use injunction*
3. *Energy price decrease*
4. *New import tax*

Rank risks above by "probability" and "impact" on the chart below by High, Medium or Low.

Risk Intensity Rating

Risk	Probability	Impact
1. *Government incentives curtailed*	*High*	*High*
2. *Land use injunction*	*Medium*	*High*
3. *Energy price decrease*	*Medium*	*Medium*
4. *New import tax*	*Low*	*High*

Check other project risk factors:

Complexity	Low ☐		Average ☒		High ☐
Resource skills	Good ☒		Okay ☐		Lacking ☐
Technology	Low ☐		Average ☒		High ☐

Reviewed by _____*Rachel*_____ Date _____*April 1, 2xxx*_____

FIGURE 2.4B *Risk Analysis for a 500-Acre Wind Farm*

criteria and current portfolio of projects, the priority team rejects or accepts the project. If the project is accepted, the priority team sets implementation in motion.

Figure 2.6 is a partial example of an evaluation form used by a large company to prioritize and select new projects. The form distinguishes between must and want objectives. If a project does not meet designated "must" objectives, it is not considered and removed from consideration. Organization (or division) objectives have been ranked and weighted by their relative importance—for example, "Improve external customer service" carries a relative weight of 83 when compared to other want objectives. The want objectives are directly linked to objectives found in the strategic plan.

Impact definitions represent a further refinement to the screening system. They are developed to gauge the predicted impact a specific project would have on meeting a particular objective. A numeric scheme is created and anchored by defining criteria. To illustrate how this works, let's examine the $5 million in new sales objective. A "0" is assigned if the project will have no impact

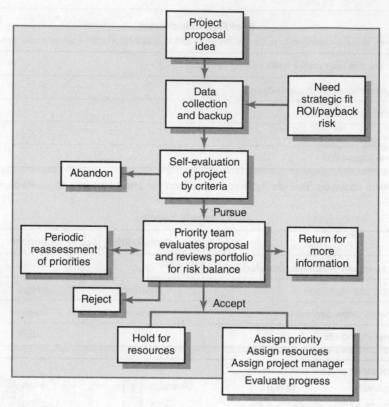

FIGURE 2.5 *Project Screening Process*

on sales or less than $100,000, a "1" is given if predicted sales are more than $100,000 but less than $500,000, a "2" if greater than $500,000. These impact assessments are combined with the relative importance of each objective to determine the predicted overall contribution of a project to strategic objectives. For example, project 26 creates an opportunity to fix field problems, has no effect on sales, and will have major impact on customer service. On these three objectives, project 26 would receive a score of 265 [99 + 0 + (2 × 83)]. Individual weighted scores are totaled for each project and are used to prioritize projects.

Responsibility for Prioritizing

Prioritizing can be an uncomfortable exercise for managers. But prioritizing projects is a major responsibility for senior management. Prioritizing means discipline, accountability, responsibility, constraints, reduced flexibility, and loss of power. Top management commitment means more than giving a blessing to the priority system; it means management will have to rank and weigh, in concrete terms, the objectives and strategies they believe to be most critical to the organization. This public declaration of commitment can be risky if the ranked objectives later prove to be poor choices, but setting the course for the organization is top management's job. The good news is, if management is truly trying to direct the organization to a strong future position, a good project priority system supports their efforts and develops a culture in which everyone is contributing to the goals of the organization.

		Project number			
Must objectives	**Must meet if impacts**	**...26**	**27**	**28**	**29**
All activities meet current legal, safety, and environmental standards	Yes-Meets objective No-Does not meet obj N/A-No impact	n/a			
All new products will have a complete market analysis	Yes-Meets objective No-Does not meet obj N/A-No impact	yes			
Want objectives	**Relative Importance 1-100**	**Single project impact definitions**	Weighted score	Weighted score	Weighted score	Weighted score
Provides immediate response to field problems	99	0 Does not address 1 = Opportunity to fix 2 Urgent problem	99			
Create $5 million in new sales by 20xx	88	0 < $100,000 1 = $100,000–500,000 2 > $500,000	0			
Improve external customer service	83	0 Minor impact 1 = Significant impact 2 Major impact	166			
	↓				
Total weighted score					
Priority					

FIGURE 2.6 *Priority Screening Analysis*

MANAGING THE PORTFOLIO SYSTEM

Managing the portfolio takes the selection system one step higher in that the merits of a particular project are assessed within the context of existing projects. At the same time it involves monitoring and adjusting selection criteria to reflect the strategic focus of the organization. This requires constant effort. The priority system can be managed by a small group of key employees in a small organization. Or, in larger organizations, the priority system can be managed by the project office or a governance team of senior managers.

Senior Management Input

Management of a portfolio system requires two major inputs from senior management. First, senior management must provide guidance in establishing selection criteria that strongly align with the current organization strategies. Second, senior management must annually decide how they wish to balance the available organizational resources (people and capital) among the different types of projects. A preliminary decision of balance must be made by top management (e.g., 20 percent compliance, 50 percent strategic, and 30 percent operational) before project selection takes place, although the balance may be changed when the projects submitted are reviewed. Given these inputs the priority team or project office can carry out its many responsibilities, which include supporting project sponsors and representing the interests of the total organization.

The Governance Team Responsibilities

The governance team, or project office, is responsible for publishing the priority of every project and ensuring the process is open and free of power politics. For example, most organizations using a governance team or project office use an electronic bulletin board to disperse the current portfolio of projects, the current status of each project, and current issues. This open communication discourages power plays. Over time the governance team evaluates the progress of the projects in the portfolio. If this whole process is managed well, it can have a profound impact on the success of an organization.

Constant scanning of the external environment to determine if organizational focus and/or selection criteria need to be changed is imperative! Periodic priority review and changes need to keep current with the changing environment and keep a unified vision of organization focus. Regardless of the criteria used for selection, each project should be evaluated by the same criteria. If projects are classified by must do, operation, and strategic, each project in its class should be evaluated by the same criteria. Enforcing the project priority system is crucial. Keeping the whole system open and aboveboard is important to maintaining the integrity of the system and keeping new, young executives from going around the system. For example, communicating which projects are approved, project ranks, current status of in-process projects, and any changes in priority criteria will discourage people from bypassing the system.

Balancing the Portfolio for Risks and Types of Projects

A major responsibility of the priority team is to balance projects by type, risk, and resource demand. This requires a total organization perspective. Hence, a proposed project that ranks high on most criteria may not be selected because the organization portfolio already includes too many projects with the same characteristics—e.g., project risk level, use of key resources, high cost, nonrevenue producing, long durations. Balancing the portfolio of projects is as important as project selection. Organizations need to evaluate each new project in terms of what it adds to the project mix. Short-term needs need to be balanced with long-term potential. Resource usage needs to be optimized across all projects, not just the most important project.

Two types of risk are associated with projects. First are risks associated with the total portfolio of projects, which should reflect the organization's risk profile. Second are specific project risks that can inhibit the execution of a project, such as schedule, cost, and technical. In this chapter we look only to balancing the organizational risks inherent in the project portfolio, such as market risk, ability to execute, time to market, and technology advances. Project-specific risks will be covered in detail in Chapter 7.

David and Jim Matheson studied R&D organizations and developed a classification scheme that could be used for assessing a project portfolio.[7] They separated projects in terms of degree of difficulty and commercial value and came up with four basic types of projects:

Bread and butter projects are relatively easy to accomplish and produce modest commercial value. They typically involve evolutionary improvements to current products and services. Examples include software upgrades and manufacturing cost reduction efforts.

Pearls are low risk development projects with high commercial payoffs. They represent revolutionary commercial advances using proven technology. Examples include next-generation integrated circuit chip and subsurface imaging to locate oil and gas.

Oysters are high risk, high value projects. These projects involve technological breakthroughs with tremendous, commercial potential. Examples include embryonic DNA treatments and new kinds of metal alloys.

White elephants are projects that at one time showed promise but are no longer viable. Examples include products for a saturated market or a potent energy source with toxic-side-effects.

The Mathesons report that organizations often have too many white elephants and too few pearls and oysters. To maintain strategic advantage they recommend that organizations capitalize on pearls, eliminate or reposition white elephants, and balance resources devoted to bread-and-butter and oyster projects to achieve alignment with overall strategy. Although their research centers on R&D organizations, their observations appear to hold true for all types of project organizations.

Summary

Multiple competing projects, limited skilled resources, dispersed virtual teams, time to market pressures, and limited capital serve as forces for the emergence of project portfolio management that provides the infrastructure for managing multiple projects and linking business strategy with project selection. The most important element of this system is the creation of a ranking system that utilizes multiple criteria that reflect the mission and strategy of the firm. It is critical to communicate priority criteria to all organizational stakeholders so that the criteria can be the source of inspiration for new project ideas.

Every significant project selected should be ranked and the results published. Senior management must take an active role in setting priorities and supporting the priority system. Going around the priority system will destroy its effectiveness. The project governance team needs to consist of seasoned managers who are capable of asking tough questions and distinguishing facts from fiction. Resources (people, equipment, and capital) for major projects must be clearly allocated and not conflict with daily operations or become an overload task.

The governance team needs to scrutinize significant projects in terms of not only their strategic value but also their fit with the portfolio of projects currently being implemented. Highly ranked projects may be deferred or even turned down if they upset the current balance among risks,

---

[7] Matheson, D., and J. Matheson, *The Smart Organization* (Boston: Harvard Business School Press, 1998), pp. 203–209.

resources, and strategic initiatives. Project selection must be based not only on the merits of the specific project but also on what it contributes to the current project portfolio mix. This requires a holistic approach to aligning projects with organizational strategy and resources.

The importance of aligning projects with organization strategy cannot be overstated. We have discussed two types of models found in practice. Checklist models are easy to develop and are justified primarily on the basis of flexibility across different divisions and locations. Unfortunately, questionnaire checklist models do not allow comparison of the relative value (rank) of alternative projects in contributing toward organization strategy. The latter is the major reason the authors prefer multi-weighted scoring models. These models keep project selection highly focused on alignment with organization strategy. Weighted scoring models require major effort in establishing the criteria and weights.

Key Terms

Implementation gap	Priority system	Sacred cow
Net present value	Priority team	Strategic management process
Organization politics	Project portfolio	
Payback	Project screening matrix	

Review Questions

1. Describe the major components of the strategic management process.
2. Explain the role projects play in the strategic management process.
3. How are projects linked to the strategic plan?
4. The portfolio of projects is typically represented by compliance, strategic, and operations projects. What impact can this classification have on project selection?
5. Why does the priority system described in this chapter require that it be open and published? Does the process encourage bottom-up initiation of projects? Does it discourage some projects? Why?
6. Why should an organization not rely only on ROI to select projects?
7. Discuss the pros and cons of the checklist versus the weighted factor method of selecting projects.

Exercises

1. You manage a hotel resort located on the South Beach on the Island of Kauai in Hawaii. You are shifting the focus of your resort from a traditional fun-in-the-sun destination to eco-tourism. (Eco-tourism focuses on environmental awareness and education.) How would you classify the following projects in terms of compliance, strategic, and operational?

a. Convert the pool heating system from electrical to solar power.

b. Build a 4-mile nature hiking trail.

c. Renovate the horse barn.

d. Launch a new promotional campaign with Hawaii Airlines.

e. Convert 12 adjacent acres into a wildlife preserve.

f. Update all the bathrooms in condos that are 10 years old or older.

g. Change hotel brochures to reflect eco-tourism image.

h. Test and revise disaster response plan.

i. Introduce wireless Internet service in café and lounge areas.

How easy was it to classify these projects? What made some projects more difficult than others? What do you think you now know that would be useful for managing projects at the hotel?

2.* Two new software projects are proposed to a young, start-up company. The Alpha project will cost $150,000 to develop and is expected to have annual net cash flow of $40,000. The Beta project will cost $200,000 to develop and is expected to have annual net cash flow of $50,000. The company is very concerned about their cash flow. Using the payback period, which project is better from a cash flow standpoint? Why?

3. A five-year project has a projected net cash flow of $15,000, $25,000, $30,000, $20,000, and $15,000 in the next five years. It will cost $50,000 to implement the project. If the required rate of return is 20 percent, conduct a discounted cash flow calculation to determine the NPV.

4. You work for the 3T company, which expects to earn at least 18 percent on its investments. You have to choose between two similar projects. Below is the cash information for each project. Your analysts predict that inflation rate will be a stable 3 percent over the next 7 years. Which of the two projects would you fund if the decision is based only on financial information? Why?

Omega Year	Inflow	Outflow	Netflow	Alpha Year	Inflow	Outflow	Netflow
Y0	0	$225,000	−225,000	Y0	0	$300,000	−300,000
Y1	0	190,000	−190,000	Y1	$ 50,000	100,000	−50,000
Y2	$ 150,000	0	150,000	Y2	150,000	0	150,000
Y3	220,000	30,000	190,000	Y3	250,000	50,000	200,000
Y4	215,000	0	215,000	Y4	250,000	0	250,000
Y5	205,000	30,000	175,000	Y5	200,000	50,000	150,000
Y6	197,000	0	197,000	Y6	180,000	0	180,000
Y7	100,000	30,000	70,000	Y7	120,000	30,000	90,000
Total	1,087,000	505,000	582,000	Total	1,200,000	530,000	670,000

5.* You are the head of the project selection team at SIMSOX. Your team is considering three different projects. Based on past history, SIMSOX expects at least a rate of return of 20 percent. Your financial advisors predict inflation to remain at 3 percent into the foreseeable future.

---

* The solution to these exercises can be found in Appendix One.

Given the following information for each project, which one should be SIMSOX first priority? Should SIMSOX fund any of the other projects? If so, what should be the order of priority based on return on investment?

Project: **Dust Devils**

Year	Investment	Revenue Stream
0	$500,000	0
1		50,000
2		250,000
3		350,000

Project: **Osprey**

Year	Investment	Revenue Stream
0	$250,000	0
1		75,000
2		75,000
3		75,000
4		50,000

Project: **Voyagers**

Year	Investment	Revenue Stream
0	$75,000	0
1		15,000
2		25,000
3		50,000
4		50,000
5		150,000

6. You are the head of the project selection team at Broken Arrow records. Your team is considering three different recording projects. Based on past history, Broken Arrow expects at least a rate of return of 20 percent. Your financial advisors predict inflation to remain at 2 percent into the foreseeable future.

Given the following information for each project, which one should be Broken Arrow's first priority? Should Broken Arrow fund any of the other projects? If so, what should be the order of priority based on return on investment?

Recording Project: **Time Fades Away**

Year	Investment	Revenue Stream
0	$600,000	0
1		600,000
2		75,000
3		20,000
4		15,000
5		10,000

Recording Project: **On the Beach**

Year	Investment	Revenue Stream
0	$400,000	0
1		400,000
2		100,000
3		25,000
4		20,000
5		10,000

Recording Project: **Tonight's the Night**

Year	Investment	Revenue Stream
0	$200,000	0
1		200,000
2		125,000
3		75,000
4		20,000
5		10,000

7. The Custom Bike Company has set up a weighted scoring matrix for evaluation of potential projects. Below are five projects under consideration.

   a. Using the scoring matrix below, which project would you rate highest? Lowest?

   b. If the weight for "Strong Sponsor" is changed from 2.0 to 5.0, will the project selection change? What are the three highest weighted project scores with this new weight?

   c. Why is it important that the weights mirror critical strategic factors?

Project Screening Matrix

Criteria / Weight	Strong sponsor	Supports business strategy	Urgency	10% of sales from new products	Competition	Fill market gap	Weighted total
	2.0	5.0	4.0	3.0	1.0	3.0	
Project 1	9	5	2	0	2	5	
Project 2	3	7	2	0	5	1	
Project 3	6	8	2	3	6	8	
Project 4	1	0	5	10	6	9	
Project 5	3	10	10	1	8	0	

References

Adler, P. S., et al., "Getting the Most Out of Your Product Development Process," *Harvard Business Review,* vol. 74 (2), pp. 134–52.

Benko, C., and F. W. McFarlan, *Connecting the Dots: Aligning Projects With Objectives in Unpredictable Times* (Boston: Harvard Business School Press, 2003).

Bigelow, D., "Want to Ensure Quality? Think Project Portfolio Management," *PM Network,* vol. 16 (1) April 2002, pp. 16–17.

Bloomberg Businessweek, "IBM Wants to Put Watson in Your Pocket," September 17–23, 2012, pp. 41–42.

Boyer, C., "Make Profit Your Priority," *PM Network,* vol. 15 (10) October 2003, pp. 37–42.

Cohen, D., and R. Graham, *The Project Manager's MBA* (San Francisco: Jossey-Bass, 2001), pp. 58–59.

Crawford, L., B. Hobbs, and J. R. Turne, "Aligning Capability with Strategy: Categorizing of Projects to Do the Right Projects and Do Them Right," *Project Management Journal,* vol. 37 (2) June 2006, pp. 38–50.

Descamps, J. P., "Mastering the Dance of Change: Innovation as a Way of Life," *Prism,* Second Quarter, 1999, pp. 61–67.

Doran, G. T., "There's a Smart Way to Write Management Goals and Objectives," *Management Review,* November 1981, pp. 35–36.

Floyd, S. W., and B. Woolridge, "Managing Strategic Consensus: The Foundation of Effectiveness Implementation," *Academy of Management Executives,* vol. 6 (4) 1992, pp. 27–39.

Foti, R., "Louder Than Words," *PM Network,* December 2002, pp. 22–29. Also see Foti, R., "Make Your Case, Not All Projects Are Equal," *PM Network,* vol. 31(7) 2003, pp. 35–43.

Frank, L., "On Demand," *PM Network,* vol. 18 (4) April 2004, pp. 58–62.

Friedman, Thomas L., *Hot, Flat, and Crowded* (New York: Farrar, Straus, and Giroux, 2008).

Fusco, J. C., "Better Policies Provide the Key to Implementing Project Management," *Project Management Journal,* vol. 28 (3) 1997, pp. 38–41.

Helm, J., and K. Remington, "Effective Project Sponsorship: An Evaluation of the Executive Sponsor in Complex Infrastructure Projects by Senior Project Managers," *Project Management Journal,* vol. 36 (1) September 2005, pp. 51–61.

Hutchens, G., "Doing the Numbers," *PM Network,* vol. 16 (4) March 2002, p. 20.

Johnson, R. E., "Scrap Capital Project Evaluations," *Chief Financial Officer,* May 1998, p. 14.

Kaplan, R. S., and D. P. Norton, "The Balanced Scorecard—Measures That Drive Performance," *Harvard Business Review,* January–February 1992, pp. 73–79. Also see Kaplan, Robert, http://balancedscorecard.org.

Kenny, J., "Effective Project Management for Strategic Innovation and Change in an Organizational Context," *Project Management Journal,* vol. 34 (1) 2003, pp. 45–53.

Kharbanda, O. P., and J. K. Pinto, *What Made Gertie Gallop: Learning from Project Failures* (New York: Van Nostrand Reinhold, 1996), pp. 106–11, 263–83.

Korte, R. F., and T. J. Chermack, "Changing Organizational Culture with Scenario Planning," *Futures,* vol. 39 (6) August 2007, pp. 645–56.

Leifer, R., C. M. McDermott, G. C. O'Connor, L. S. Peters, M. Price, and R. W. Veryzer, *Radical Innovation: How Mature Companies Can Outsmart Upstarts* (Boston: Harvard Business School Press, 2000).

MacIntyre, J., *PM Network,* vol. 20 (11) November 2006, pp. 32–35.

Magretta, Joan, *Understanding Michael Porter: The Essential Guide to Competition and Strategy* (Boston: Harvard Business Press Book, 2011).

Matheson, D., and J. Matheson, *The Smart Organization* (Boston: Harvard Business School Press, 1998), pp. 203–09.

Milosevic, D. Z., and S. Srivannaboon, "A Theoretical Framework for Aligning Project Management with Business Strategy," *Project Management Journal,* vol. 37 (3) August 2006, pp. 98–110.

Morris, P. W., and A. Jamieson, "Moving from Corporate Strategy to Project Strategy," *Project Management Journal,* vol. 36 (4) December 2005, pp. 5–18.

Motta, Silva, and Rogério Hermida Quintella, "Assessment of Non-Financial Criteria in the Selection of Investment Projects for Seed Capital Funding: The Contribution of Scientometrics and Patentometrics," *Journal of Technology Management Innovation,* vol. 7 (3) 2012.

PMI, "PMI's Pulse of the Profession," March 2012, Project Management Institute, p. 7.

Raskin, P., et al., *Great Transitions: The Promise and Lure of the Times Ahead,* retrieved 6-3-08. See *www.gtinitiative.org/documents/Great_Transitions.pdf*

Schwartz, Peter, and Doug Randall, "An Abrupt Climate Change Scenario and its Implications for United States National Security," Global Business Network, Inc., October 2003.

Shenhar, A., "Strategic Project Leadership: Focusing Your Project on Business Success," *Proceedings of the Project Management Institute Annual Seminars & Symposium,* San Antonio, Texas, October 3–10, 2002, CD. Also see Shenhar, Aaron, *Reinventing Project Management* (Harvard Business School, 2007).

Smith, D. K., and R. C. Alexander, *Fumbling the Future: How Xerox Invented, Then Ignored the First Personal Computer* (New York: Macmillan, 1988).

Swanson, S., "All Things Considered," *PM Network,* vol. 25 (2) February 2011, pp. 36–40.

Woodward, H., "Winning in a World of Limited Project Spending," *Proceedings of the Project Management Institute Global Congress North America,* Baltimore, Maryland, September 18–12, 2003, CD.

APPENDIX 2.1

Request for Proposal (RFP)

Once an organization selects a project, the customer or project manager is frequently responsible for developing a request for proposal (RFP) for the project or sections of the project.

The responsible project manager will require input data from all stakeholders connected to the activities covered in the RFP. The RFP will be announced to external contractors/vendors with adequate experience to implement the project. For example, government projects frequently advertise with a "request for proposal" to outside contractors for roads, buildings, airports, military hardware, space vehicles. Similarly, businesses use RFPs to solicit bids for building a clean room, developing a new manufacturing process, delivering software for insurance billing, conducting a market survey. In all of these examples, requirements and features must be in enough detail that contractors have a clear description of the final deliverable that will meet the customer's needs. In most cases the RFP also specifies an expected format for the contractor's bid proposal so the responses of different contractors can be fairly evaluated. Although we typically think of RFPs for external contractors, in some organizations RFPs are used internally; that is, the organization sends out an RFP to different divisions or departments.

The content of the RFP is extremely important. In practice, the most common error is to offer an RFP that lacks sufficient detail. This lack of detail typically results in conflict issues, misunderstandings, often legal claims between the contractor and owner, and, in addition, an unsatisfied customer. All RFPs are different, but the outline in Figure A2.1 is a good starting point for the development of a detailed RFP. Each step is briefly described next.

1. Summary of needs and request for action. The background and a simple description of the final project deliverable are given first. For example, through simulated war games, the U.S. Navy has found their giant warships of the past are too vulnerable against today's technology (an example is the Silkworm antiship missiles). In addition, the Navy's mission has shifted to supporting ground forces and peacekeeping missions, which require getting closer to shore. As a result, the Navy is revamping ships for near-shore duty. The Navy will select three designs for further refine-

1. Summary of needs and request for action
2. Statement of work (SOW) detailing the scope and major deliverables
3. Deliverable specifications/requirements, features, and tasks
4. Responsibilities—vendor and customer
5. Project schedule
6. Costs and payment schedule
7. Type of contract
8. Experience and staffing
9. Evaluation criteria

Figure A2.1   *Request for Proposal*

ment from the responses to its RFP. In general, it is expected that the new ship will be capable of at least 55 knots, measure between 80 and 250 feet in length, and be fitted with radar absorbing panels to thwart guided missiles.

2. Statement of work (SOW) detailing the scope and major deliverables. For example, if the project involves a market research survey, the major deliverables could be design, data collection, data analysis, and providing recommendations by February 21, 2014, for a cost not to exceed $300,000.

3. Deliverable specifications/requirements, features, and tasks. This step should be very comprehensive so bid proposals from contractors can be validated and later used for control. Typical specifications cover physical features such as size, quantity, materials, speed, and color. For example, an IT project might specify requirements for hardware, software, and training in great detail. Tasks required to complete deliverables can be included if they are known.

4. Responsibilities—vendor and customer. Failing to spell out the responsibilities for both parties is notorious for leading to serious problems when the contractor implements the project. For example, who pays for what? (If the contractor is to be on site, will the contractor be required to pay for office space?) What are the limits and exclusions for the contractor? (For example, who will supply test equipment?) What communication plan will be used by the contractor and owner? If escalation of an issue becomes necessary, what process will be used? How will progress be evaluated? Well-defined responsibilities will avoid many unforeseen problems later.

5. Project schedule. This step is concerned with getting a "hard" schedule which can be used for control and evaluating progress. Owners are usually very demanding in meeting the project schedule. In today's business environment, time-to-market is a major "hot button" that influences market share, costs, and profits. The schedule should spell out what, who, and when.

6. Costs and payment schedule. The RFP needs to set out very clearly how, when, and the process for determining costs and conditions for progress payments.

7. Type of contract. Essentially there are two types of contracts—fixed-price and cost-plus. Fixed-price contracts agree on a price or lump sum in advance, and it remains as long as there are no changes to the scope provisions of the agreement. This type is preferred in projects that are well defined with predictable costs and minimal risks. The contractor must exercise care estimating cost because any underestimating of costs will cause the contractor's profit to be reduced. In cost-plus contracts the contractor is reimbursed for all or some of the expenses incurred during performance of the contract. This fee is negotiated in advance and usually involves a percent of total costs. "Time and materials" plus a profit factor are typical of cost-plus contracts. Both types of contracts can include incentive clauses for superior performance in time and cost, or in some cases, penalties—for example, missing the opening date of a new sports stadium.

8. Experience and staffing. The ability of the contractor to implement the project may depend on specific skills; this necessary experience should be specified, along with assurance such staff will be available for this project.

9. Evaluation criteria. The criteria for evaluating and awarding the project contract should be specified. For example, selection criteria frequently include methodology, price, schedule, and experience; in some cases these criteria are weighted. Use of the outline in Figure A2.1 will help to ensure key items in the proposal are not omitted. A well-prepared RFP will provide contractors with sufficient guidelines to prepare a proposal that clearly meets the project and customer's needs.

SELECTION OF CONTRACTOR FROM BID PROPOSALS

Interested contractors respond to project RFPs with a written bid proposal. It is likely that several contractors will submit bid proposals to the customer.

The final step in the RFP process is to select the contractor who best meets the requirements requested in the RFP. The selection criteria given in the RFP are used to evaluate which contractor is awarded the contract to implement the project. Losing contractors should be given an explanation of the key factors that led to the selection of the winning contractor/vendor; appreciation for their participation and effort should be acknowledged. See Figure A2.2, Contractor Evaluation Template, adapted from one used in practice.

Contractor Evaluation Template	Maximum Weight	Proposal 1	Proposal 2	Proposal 3	Proposal 4
Contractor qualifications	Weight = 10				
Technical skills available	Weight = 20				
Understanding of contract and conditions	Weight = 5				
Financial strength to implement project	Weight = 15				
Understanding of proposal specifications	Weight = 10				
Innovativeness and originality of proposal	Weight = 5				
Reputation for delivering on time and budget	Weight = 15				
Price	Weight = 20				
Total	**100**				

Figure A2.2 *Contractor Evaluation Template*

APPENDIX 2.2

Project Selection Methods Based on Financial Criteria for Selection

INTRODUCTION

Organizations embark on projects for a wide array of objectives and use project selection methods particularly suitable for evaluating the individual project or a program or portfolio of projects for achieving those objectives. Thus, a systematic procedure for evaluation of the individual project's contribution in achieving the objectives is developed and used for selecting a project. In this section, we would take a look at the methodology based on financial criteria for selection of projects.

We shall begin with, a brief review of the place of the projects in an organization, the strategic business analysis, the different types of organizational needs revealed by the strategic analysis and non-financial criteria for selection of projects for such needs. This review would help reveal the rationale behind methods for selection for all projects and bring out the role and importance of using the financial criteria for project selection.

1. PLACE OF PROJECTS IN AN ORGANIZATION

(a) The Current Operations
All organizations – commercial organizations, not-for-profit social organizations and governmental institutions – are actively engaged in carrying out some function involving day-to-day routine operations in an on-going manner year-after-year. A predominantly large part of the workforce of an organization is, therefore, understandably busy with carrying out these routine activities and a predominantly large part of all resources are actively employed in the routine operations.

(b) Strategic Analysis of Operations

Identifying the need for creating a new product service or result: While doing these routine operations, from time to time the organizations find the need for some change in their operations for more effective, more efficient, larger scale or improved operation. While doing these routine operations, the manufacturing organization may find the need to increase the capacity for manufacture, or to bring out a new product, or to improve the quality of the products, or to employ new technology for saving cost by more efficient use of materials or labour, or say setting up facilities for safer routine operations or for meeting the government's environmental regulations. The service organization may feel the need to extend the scope of services, or cover a larger geographical area, or supply a more satisfactory level of service or exploit a new technology to provide an altogether new service. In other words, the organization might feel the need for creation of some product, service or result different from the current operations.

These needs may become apparent to the decision makers by intuitive vision, general observation and analysis of the changing external environment (macro-economic conditions, technology trends, industry trends, global influences, etc.) and the assessment of the organization's own innate strengths and resources – core competencies (proficiency in certain technology, expertise in manufacturing or marketing some products, strong brand images, networking and influencing capability, labour management capability, etc.).

Another way would be to carry out a Formal Strategic Planning for identifying the needs for initiating a project. It would involve:

(i) *SWOT Analysis:*
- Assessing the organization's present capabilities or core competencies (The "AS –IS" Scenario– an analysis of its strengths, and weaknesses), and
- Assessing the present state and directions of change in the macro-economic and industrial environment to perceive the opportunities and threats it would present to the organization for its future operations and growth.

(ii) *Formulating the strategy to manage the future operating scenario:* Creating a vision of the way the organization should change to meet the challenges it is likely to face in the future ("SHOULD-BE" Scenario).

(iii) *Developing the program to implement the strategy* (Strategy-based Program for Identification of Project Objectives). Developing the program to implement the strategy and include in the program specific projects – each with an objective to meet the need for creating a new product, service or result envisioned in the strategic program.

(iv) *Initiate individual projects to meet the strategic needs:* Initiating and authorizing individual projects, each addressing a specific part of the organizational strategic program for creating a unique product, service or result.

These needs identified by strategic analysis may fall into any of the following categories:

- *Business need:* Setting up a new business, starting a profitable venture for investment, Entrepreneurial vision, substantial expansion in production or service capacity
- *Market need: Product mix, new product, customer requests for some features,*
- *Customer request for project management (for organizations performing on contract)*
- *Technological push: Developing new technology, making products compatible with new technology*
- *Organizational structure change, Geographical expansion, Recruitment & training campaigns*
- *Legal or social requirement, etc: Effluent treatment plant; Employee welfare schemes.*

The projects can be visualized as the bridges, which take an organization from current activities (products and services) to new products and services. Project extends the capability of the organization from here-and-now to the visions of future. The projects are thus the vehicles for the changes, which routine operations do not cover. The projects are vehicles for implementing the organization's vision, short and long-term plans, and business strategy.

2. PROJECT SELECTION USING NON-NUMERICAL METHODS (METHODS NOT BASED ON FINANCIAL CRITERIA)

Based on the strategic needs of the organization, arrived at either by formal analysis or intuitive vision, the suitable methods for project selection are used. Non-numerical methods, essentially based on non-financial criteria, are used for the projects almost forced on the organization due to operating necessity (manufacturing), competitive necessity (market), legal or social requirements (business continuation) or for pet projects of the power centers in the organization. The projects may be authorized for manufacturing facilities for retaining the competitiveness of the manufacturing operations in the market place, absorbing new technology, saving raw material or energy cost, improving product quality or meeting a legal or social obligations (effluent treatment, operational safety and health of workers, etc.) fall in this operating necessity category. The projects for maintaining the product mix for meeting the changing market pattern, retaining the market share, increasing geographical coverage of services, making products compatible with new technology, meeting specific customer requests or developing a new product fall in competitive necessity category. The projects for reorganization and training of production or sales employees, necessary to remain competitive in the market place, are also the projects forced on the organization due to competitive necessity. The projects executed on behalf of clients by orders do not require any project selection criteria. Like it or not, the similar logic also applies to pet projects of high and mighty in the organization – particularly in entrepreneur-centered organizations.

3. PLACE FOR PROJECT SELECTION BASED ON FINANCIAL CRITERIA

However, for a very large number of projects based on business needs, financial criteria for selection are very important and often resort to casting vote to settle the decision.
For setting up a manufacturing facility, the projects could be for:

- Setting up manufacturing of a new product (a new venture or diversification from existing business lines)
- Carrying out major expansions of existing manufacturing operations
- Carrying out a forward or backward integration of the product already being manufactured

For marketing operations, the projects could be for the following:

- Setting up new warehouses or distribution facilities
- Market expansion in new areas or countries
- Setting up new branch offices
- Setting up IT-based customer service facilities
- For marketing a new product

Large infrastructural projects for public welfare (like building roads and bridges, setting up network for supply of electric power, telephones, water or effluent disposal, etc.) are also often selected based on financial criteria.

4. IMPORTANCE OF RIGOUR IN FINANCIAL CRITERIA FOR SELECTION

The rigour in application of methods based on financial criteria is necessary and important, even though it requires collection and analysis of a large amount of data and complex and time-consuming analytical methods. There are several reasons for such painstaking data collection and analysis:

- The investments involved in many projects are large and thus improper selection of project would misdirect the flow of scarce resources from a critical and important project to a project of peripheral importance. The profitability and growth of the entire organization may be jeopardized with improper selection of the project.
- The investment decisions are irreversible. Most of the projects have a long-term effect on the organization's operations and tend to commit the organization to a path of growth or stagnation.
- The project decisions are for future operations and involve considerable risks. Inadequate financial analysis might expose the organization to large risks. There are instances of many successful organizations going bankrupt after embarking on an improperly selected project.

It must be emphasized here that the methods based on financial criteria (or for that matter any other criteria) only provide a basis for the decision maker. To start with, the numerical analysis carried out in the financial methods is based on the collected data and assumptions for future events. Any error or serious gaps in data for market, project cost, or production costs would reflect in the financial analysis based on them. Secondly, no matter how sophisticated and carefully worked out the assumptions underlying the methods may be, they cannot reflect the reality and all the uncertainties associated with it. In the end, all analysis can take you only so far; it is the flesh and blood decision makers who have to take the decision.

5. METHODS BASED ON FINANCIAL PROJECTIONS AND ANALYSIS

The methods for financial analysis are based on

- making projections for operating results from the product of the project (surplus inward cash flows), and
- comparing the surplus inward cash flows from the project with the investment or outward cash flow using a specific criteria and calculation method to provide a basis for decision making

The project selection methods based on financial criteria are of two types:

- *The methods based on the use of raw future cash flows in the decision making process:* Average Return on Investment (ROI), Payback Period for Investment, and Accounting Rate of Return (ARR) are such methods.
- *The methods, which discount the future cash flows, reflecting the time value of money according to some specific principles and work out a parameter for assisting the investment decision:* Net Present Value (NPV), Internal Rate of Return (IRR) and Profitability Index are this type of methods.

In the subsequent part of this, we shall discuss each of this methods, the calculation procedures, and the merits or limitations of the decisions based on the techniques. However, before doing that, we shall briefly discuss some basic concepts on

(i) *Cash flows, procedures to calculate them, and the assumptions for projections of future cash flows,*

(ii) *Principle underlying discounting of future cash flows*

(iii) *The basis for selecting the factor to be used for discounting – Weighted Average Cost of Capital (WACC)*

5.1 Calculation of Project Cash Flows

5.1.1 Principles for Estimating Project Cash Flows

All investment evaluation methods, which discount the returns from project's earnings in future, use project cash flows as their foundation. Therefore, cash flows should be estimated in conformance with the theoretical construct of the evaluation methods. Without going into the complexities of theoretical basis for the rules, a brief summary of the rules to be used for estimating the cash flows is presented below:

- Interest charges on debt are taken into account in working out the factor used for discounting future cash flows, i.e. Average Weighted Cost of Capital (AWCC). To avoid double accounting, the cash flows are estimated before interest charges.
- Only the incremental value of cash flows directly connected with the project under consideration should be used. In other words, the difference between the cash flows likely with and without the project under consideration should be used.
- There is a common psychological block, which backs financing the project for which some costs have been already incurred. Investment evaluation is concerned with the future benefits or future costs, if the project is undertaken. So, the sunk costs should be ignored.
- Often, the project proposal involves use of resources, which might be available and lying idle. While evaluating the new project, the opportunity costs associated with the use of that resource (the benefits not available due to not being able to put that resource to some alternative use) should be considered.
- The investor is concerned with the net return he can earn from the project after payment of all taxes; if that return is acceptable, the project would be given a go-ahead. So, cash flows should be estimated after making provision for taxes.
- There is a tendency to allocate the overheads based on some factor like sales or occupied area or number of employees. While evaluating the new proposal also, the overheads would be automatically allocated using the same principle, which would give an unnecessary negative bias to the new project. The point likely to be missed out is that existing overheads cannot be wished away if the new project is not accepted. Only the incremental overheads connected with the new projects should be considered while evaluating the proposal for new project.
- Another common pitfall is not making adequate provision for the incremental working capital for the project. The incremental working capital, especially during the increased scale of operation in the later years, is usually not as apparent as the new fixed investment for the project. This pitfall should be avoided.

- Depreciation is a book entry (and not an actual expenditure in cash) permitted as an allowance in lowering the taxable income for calculation of tax liability. The cash flow should be before depreciation charges.
- It is a moot point how the effect of inflation on future costs and prices should be accounted while estimating cash flows. One alternative would be to work out the costs and sales at current prices and project the pro-rata amounts for working out the future cash flows only making the adjustments for operating capacity changes. This alternative assumes that the future sale prices and costs will attain a balance somewhat similar to what exists presently. This is a rational assumption and easier to use for calculations. The alternative would be to assume different inflationary trends for different cost inputs and prices and work out cash flow projections. Since the risks associated with all future events are difficult to project, usually the additional efforts and cost in the exercise are not worthwhile.

Using the above rules, the project operating cash flows, project investment and recovery of residual investment at the end of the economic life of the project are calculated as follows:

5.1.2   Project Operating Cash Flows

1. Estimate the operating capacity and corresponding sales for the future years from the project's operation.
2. Calculate the operating costs, which should include
   - Direct material cost per unit
   - Direct labour cost per unit
   - Direct fuel or energy cost per unit
   - Indirect material cost per period or year (spares and consumables for facilities)
   - Indirect labour cost per period (factory supervision, support functions like maintenance, quality control, warehouse or stores, etc.)
   - Other overheads (rents, taxes, general utilities, etc.)
   - Administrative costs (salary and facility operational costs in office)
   - Selling costs(packing, transportation and distribution charges, sales commissions, advertising, salary of sales and marketing personnel).
3. Calculate interest and depreciation charges
4. Deduct the total operating costs (item 2) and depreciation and interest charges (item 3) from estimated sales (item 1) to work out the taxable income.
5. Calculate tax on the taxable income (item 4) and deduct it from taxable income to work out profit after taxes (PAT).
6. Add back interest and depreciation (item 3) to the profit after tax (PAT, item 5) to arrive at the profit before interest and depreciation but after taxes. This figure is the project's operating cash flows for the year.

5.1.3   Initial Investment Cash Flow

This should include the investment in the new fixed assets and the incremental margins on working capital. A brief explanation is neded in order to provide for margin on working capital. Ordinarily, the organizations avail of short-term loans from the commercial banks against the raw material, goods in process and finished stocks. The banks advance a certain portion of the value of this stock while the organization has to provide finance for the balance or the margin on the working capital. As the operating capacity of the project increases, the working capital requirements also increase; the incremental margins on working capital should thus be provided in the initial and subsequent year investments.

5.1.4 Cash Flow for Recovery of Residual Investment

In case of cash flow for recovery of residual investment at the end of economic life of the project, the recovery of working capital should also be taken into account along with addition to the recovery from the fixed assets.

5.2 Principle Underlying Discounting of Future Cash Flows

Among the methods based on financial criteria for investment, the methods which discount the future cash flows by some pre-determined rate are more authentic.

Why discount the future cash flows and if so in what manner?
'A bird in hand is worth two in the bush' is the age-old wisdom. We all know that money in hand now is worth much more money in future. Putting it the other way, the money expected to be received in future is much less than its face value; so, the value of future cash flow should be suitably reduced or discounted. There are good reasons rooted in human nature and economics for this. The human psychology is to use or consume right away than defer or postpone it to future. The economic reasons are that the money as a resource can be invested to earn more money. On the other hand, in modern times, the inflation reduces the real value of money and the same amount of money, which we did not spend today to buy one kilogram of rice, would be able to buy less than a kilogram of rice after a year due to inflation and consequent erosion of the real value of money.

The correlation of a future cash receipt with its value now is based on the principle of compound interest. It rests on the idea that the principal amount P invested at an $r\%$ per annum interest rate will grow to a value $P(1 + r)$ at the end of one year. If the principal and interest are not returned to the lender, in effect the lender has advanced to the borrower an amount $P(1 + r)$. Using this new principal amount, the value at the end of the second year would be $P(1 + r)^2$. Using the same logic for the subsequent years, we get the general formula expressing the relationship between the principal amount P and its future value P_f after the end of n years as follows:

$$P_f = P(1 + r)^n$$

The factor $(1 + r)^n$ is the relationship between the present value or principal of a single amount and its future value after n years when compounded at $r\%$ per annum. Notice that the factor is always greater than 1; so when an amount is multiplied by it, it increases and when you divide by that factor, the value decreases. If we wish to find the value of the future cash flow from present value, we should multiply by that factor and the amount would grow. If we want to find the present value of a future cash flow, we should divide the future cash flow by that factor and the amount would be reduced or discounted.

If P_v is the present value of future cash flow P_f in the nth year,

$$P_v = P_f/(1 + r)^n \quad \text{and} \quad P_f = P_v \times (1 + r)^n$$

5.3 The Rationale for Selecting the Factor to be Used for Discounting: Weighted Average Cost of Capital (WACC)

For investment decisions, it is quite common to take future cash flows from 5 to 15 years into account. Even relatively small changes in the rate r % per annum, the factor, the value of discounting factor, $(1 + r)^n$ becomes significantly different. For example for a 10-year period, the discounting factor for 8 % per annum rate would be 2.159, while for a 10 % per annum rate, it would be 2.594. The investment decision for comparing two projects with different pattern for future cash flows would depend on the discounting factor selected. So, what should be the rationale for selecting the discounting factor?

One approach would be to use the interest rate offered for bank deposits on long-term fixed deposits or rates offered on similar safe investment outlets. However, most successful business earn more profit (their money grows at a higher rate) than the fixed deposit interest rate. That is precisely the reason that the companies borrow money from the banks and even after paying the principal and interest, they are in a position to retain some surplus. So the discounting rate should be higher than and different from the fixed deposit interest rate.

A somewhat involved and complex finance theory derives this factor to equal the Weighted Average Cost of Capital (WACC), The companies finance a part of the project cost from equity or own funds and a part of the project cost from debts or long-term loans from banks and other financial institutions. Depending on the return expected on equity and its proportion in overall project financing and the interest payable for the debt or long-term loans and its corresponding proportion in financing the project, a composite weighted average can be worked out. This composite discount rate worked out from the ratio of debt to equity in project financing and the corresponding interest rate is called the Weighted Average Cost of Capital (WACC). It is given by the following simple formula to calculate the weighted average:

$$\text{WACC} = (\text{The Proportion of Equity}) \times (\text{Rate at which equity is expected to earn})$$
$$+ (\text{The proportion of debt}) \times (\text{Interest agreed for debt service})$$

To illustrate the method of calculation, if a project is financed by equal proportion of equity and debt (i.e. the equity to debt ratio is 1 : 1), the liability for debt servicing is 10 % per annum and the expectation to earn from equity is 18 % per annum, then

$$\text{WACC} = (0.5 \times 18) + (0.5 \times 10) = 14 \text{ % per annum.}$$

The calculations for rate of return expected from equity are based on market capitalization pattern for a stock of a publicly quoted company. The calculation of rate expected on equity from quoted market value is quite involved and access to that value or the overall equity to debt ratio is limited to the highest echelons in the organizations. For practical purpose, the top management promulgates a discount factor, which is uniformly used for all discounted cash flows calculations for project evaluations. The exact value of the discount rate may vary from one organization to anotherand from time to time. Most commonly used value of the discount factors range from 12% to 16 %. In absence of specific guidance or rule for evaluating projects, discount rate of 14 % or 15 % per annum would generally be a good choice.

6. THE PROJECT SELECTION METHODS BASED ON FINANCIAL CRITERIA

6.1 The Methods Based on the Use of Raw Future Cash Flows (Without discounting)

There are three popular methods based on use of undiscounted future cash flows:

(i) Average Return on Investment (ROI) Method,
(ii) Accounting Rate of Return (ARR) Method, and
(iii) Payback Period Method

We shall take a brief look at these methods in what follows.

6.1.1 Average Return on Investment (ROI) Method

Average rate of return on investment estimates undiscounted or raw values of the profits or returns from investment and expresses them as a ratio or percentage of the incremental investment for the project. Depending on the organizational practice, several variations are prevalent. The numerator, profits or returns from the project may be (a) an estimate of average profit after tax, or (b) profits after tax but before interest, or (c) profits before interest and taxes. The denominator would usually be initial investment for new fixed assets and margin on incremental working capital. The higher the ROI of a project, the more attractive the project investment and hence greater the preference for its selection.

To illustrate the concept, if the average profits before tax and interest for a project investment of ₹1 millions are ₹250,000, the average return on investment (ROI) is 25 %. (Using the convention mentioned in alternative (c) above). Often, the lower or middle operating levels of the organization do not have access to interest and tax positions of the company. For facilitating the decisions on smaller operating level investments, the conventions mentioned in alternatives (b) and (c) above are used.

The merits of the method are that:

- It is easy to understand and simple to apply even for those managers, who have no grounding in accounting.
- The information for calculating ROI would be available with an operating manager required to take a decision on an operational project.

The main disadvantage is that it does not take into account the difference in values of the present and future cash flows. In doing so, it disregards an important basic tenet of economics, which introduces distortion in the realistic economic evaluation of the projects.

6.1.2 Accounting Rate of Return (ARR) Method

As the name suggests, this method follows the principles used in routine accounting reporting. For the future years under consideration, projections are worked out with appropriate assumptions and detailed working for the sales, operating costs, interest, depreciation and taxes and in effect to forecast the effect of project on the profit and loss account of the company. The investment decision is taken by considering in totality the effect of the investment on the organization's profitability.

The merits of the method, as in the earlier ROI case, are the simplicity in the use of the method and acceptance by the businessmen and other managers due to the use of familiar accounting principles. Since it follows the accounting principles in projecting the future profit and loss account, the information for calculation is readily available and easily verifiable from the organization's routine accounting system. The demerit for this method, like the ROI method, is the disregard of the basic economic principle by equating the future cash flows with present values.

6.1.3 Payback Period Method

This method also works out the future cash flows from the project and determines the time required for the project returns to recover the original investment. If a project with an investment of ₹1 million earns cash flows of ₹300,000 in the 1st year, ₹400,000 in the 2nd year and ₹500,000 in the third year, the payback period of the project is 2.6 years (₹700,000 are recovered in the first two years and the balance ₹300,000 would be recovered in the 0.6 part of the third year). If the profitability of the project is high, the period required for recovery of the original project investment will be small and hence preferable to another project with a longer recovery or payback period. Ordinarily, the organizations set the norm of certain maximum payback period and the projects which cannot meet this standard are automatically rejected.

The merits of the method are that it is easy to understand and simple to apply. One additional important advantage is that it would tend to select the projects with high profitability in the short term. In the times, when the macroeconomic conditions are fast changing and the industry is undergoing a major transformation, this method would screen out the more risky late blooming projects. The demerits of the method, like the earlier two methods using undiscounted future cash flows, is not taking into account the time value of money. Another objection is that the method focuses on the project only until the investment is recovered. What happens after that is disregarded. This method would therefore tend to overlook the long-term continued profitability of the project during the selection process.

6.2 The Methods Based on the Use of Discounted Cash Flows

In the recent times, a predominant majority of organizations have been using one of the methods based on discounted cash flows for investment evaluation and project selection. Among the methods depending on financial criteria for project selection using discounted cash flows, two methods are more popular:

- Net Present Value (NPV) Method and its refined version using Benefit to Cost Ratio
- Internal Rate of Return (IRR) Method

We shall briefly discuss each method in what follows.

6.2.1 Net Present Value (NPV)

This is one of the most popular methods. It depends on calculating the net present value (NPV) of all the cash flows from the project. The method consists of summing up the present values of all the project cash flows for the economic life of the project or for a specified period [i.e. the raw estimate of cash flow for the nth year discounted by the corresponding discounting factor, viz. $1/(1 + r)^n$]. The investments are considered negative cash flows and the returns from the project are considered positive cash flows.

If the initial investment (for new fixed assets and margin on incremental working capital) is I, CF_1, CF_2, CF_3 ... and CF_n are the project cash flows respectively at the end of the 1st, 2nd, 3rd and nth year of project operation, and discount rate is r % per annum, then

$$\text{NPV of project} = [CF_1/(1 + r)] + [CF_2/(1 + r)^2] + [CF_3/(1 + r)^3] ... [CF_n/(1 + r)^n\} - I$$

The NPV gives a measure of the benefits a company would get from undertaking a project after fully providing for the cost of capital and the involved time period for receiving the benefits. If this net present value is positive, the project is prima facie acceptable. If the NPV is negative, the project should be rejected. The larger the NPV value, the more profitable and preferable the investment in the project.

It can be seen from the formula above that if the discounting rate r % is increased, the NPV would decrease and if the discount rate r % is decreased, the NPV would increase. The impact of the small changes in the discount rate r is usually quite large on the NPV. The selection of the right discounting rate is, therefore, very important. The discount rate used for NPV calculations is based on the Average Weighted Cost of Capital (AWCC) discussed in 5.3 above. This is a very realistic assumption and since, NPV method is based on the assumption of discounting the future cash flows at that rate, the method is based on sound economic principles and realistic assumptions.

There are some objections against using the NPV method alone. NPV method only gives the value of the total surplus of discounted project cash flows, but it does not relate it to the original investment. Hence the efficiency of the capital for generating NPV is not taken into account. If two projects A and B give equal NPV values, but the investment for project A is much less than investment for project B, project A should be obviously favoured but NPV method as such does not help to distinguish between the two.

6.2.2   Refinement of NPV Method Using Benefits to Cost Ratio

This objection can be overcome by introducing the benefits to cost ratio concept. If the net present value of a project (Project Benefits) is PB and the total incremental investment for the project (Project Cost) is I, then the ratio PB / I is the benefit to cost ratio for a project. This ratio helps to distinguish between the projects with more efficient use of capital. The higher this benefits to cost ratio, the more efficient use of project investment and hence a preferable investment option.

6.2.3   Internal rate of Return (IRR) Method

In the NPV method, the discount rate appears to be chosen somewhat arbitrarily, though the choice of the factor rests on sound economic principles and realistic assumption (average weighted cost of capital). In the IRR method, this objection can also be overcome. IRR is defined as that value of discount rate, which would make the NPV of the project equal to zero. In other words, the NPV of the project cash flows, when discounted at IRR, equals the initial project investment.

If the initial investment (for new fixed assets and margin on incremental working capital) is I, CF_1, CF_2, CF_3 ... and CF_n are the project cash flows respectively at the end of the 1st, 2nd, 3rd and nth year of project operation, and discount rate is r % per annum, then IRR is found by trial and error solution of the following equation:

$$I = [CF_1/(1 + r)] + [CF_2/(1 + r)^2] + [CF_3/(1 + r)^3] ... [CF_n/(1 + r)^n\}$$

If the value of IRR is higher than a certain rate specified by the organization (often called 'hurdle rate'), the project is accepted and if it lower, the project is rejected. If two projects have IRR values higher than the specified hurdle rate, the project with the higher value of IRR is preferred. The hurdle rate, or minimum acceptable IRR value specified by the organization, is usually based on the WACC – weighted average cost of capital. So, if IRR is higher than hurdle rate, a positive NPV would be assured when discount rate used for NPV calculations is WACC

It would be noted that NPV and IRR methods are very close in basic principles – discounting the project cash flows and relating them with the initial investment. Both methods would give similar evaluation (for acceptance or rejection of a project and comparative evaluation of two projects) if the project cash flows follow the conventional pattern of investment in the initial period and positive returns in the subsequent years. If this condition is not satisfied, the IRR method would be subject to serious theoretical objections. There is also another objection based on the theoretical construct of IRR, which assumes that the project cash flows from future years are reinvested into projects which give IRR rate of return. This assumption may not often hold and it can introduce some distortion in the selection metric. Another set of difficulty with the IRR method is of mathematical nature. When the method is applied to projects which do not have steady conventional cash flows but negative as well as positive cash flows for some years, solving the equation gives more than one roots (i.e. more than one values of IRR).

These theoretical objections notwithstanding, IRR has become a very poplar method for evaluating projects – almost as popular as NPV method. The reason lies in the fact that the IRR method does not require use of any 'arbitrary' discount rate for its use. So, it would be possible to calculate IRR merely from the project investment and cash flow data. Since the method gives a value of the time adjusted rate of return on the project, it is very easy for people to compare the IRR rate with the general interest rate for bank loans, inflation rate in the economy, the return on equity and the like for relating it to the external reality of day-to-day experience.

SUMMARY

We discussed a number of techniques for selection of projects based on the financial criteria. Each technique has some special benefits and some likely pitfalls. The organizations usually have a preference for using one or the other method for project selection. Very often, the analysis using different techniques are carried out and the outcomes from them are weighed to come to a conclusion.

The different techniques for financial evaluation of a project provide very valuable guidance to the decision makers. However, the proverbial buck stops on the desk of the decision maker. In the final analysis, the knowledge, experience, risk tolerance, entrepreneurial capability and mature judgment of the decision makers is what plays the role of crucial importance in project selection and related investment decision.

CASE 2.1

Hector Gaming Company

Hector Gaming Company (HGC) is an educational gaming company specializing in young children's educational games. HGC has just completed their fourth year of operation. This year was a banner year for HGC. The company received a large influx of capital for growth by issuing stock privately through an investment banking firm. It appears the return on investment for this past year will be just over 25 percent with zero debt! The growth rate for the last two years has been approximately 80 percent each year. Parents and grandparents of young children have been buying HGC's products almost as fast as they are developed. Every member of the 56-person firm is enthusiastic and looking forward to helping the firm grow to be the largest and best educational gaming company in the world. The founder of the firm, Sally Peters, has been written up in *Young Entrepreneurs* as "the young entrepreneur to watch." She has been able to develop an organization culture in which all stakeholders are committed to innovation, continuous improvement, and organization learning.

Last year, 10 top managers of HGC worked with McKinley Consulting to develop the organization's strategic plan. This year the same 10 managers had a retreat in Aruba to formulate next year's strategic plan using the same process suggested by McKinley Consulting. Most executives seem to have a consensus of where the firm should go in the intermediate and long term. But there is little consensus on how this should be accomplished. Peters, now president of HGC, feels she may be losing control. The frequency of conflicts seems to be increasing. Some individuals are always requested for any new project created. When resource conflicts occur among projects, each project manager believes his or her project is most important. More projects are not meeting deadlines and are coming in over budget. Yesterday's management meeting revealed some top HGC talent have been working on an international business game for college students. This project does not fit the organization vision or market niche. At times it seems everyone is marching to his or her own drummer. Somehow more focus is needed to ensure everyone agrees on *how* strategy should be implemented, given the resources available to the organization.

Yesterday's meeting alarmed Peters. These emerging problems are coming at a bad time. Next week HGC is ramping up the size of the organization, number of new products per year, and marketing efforts. Fifteen new people will join HGC next month. Peters is concerned that policies be in place that will ensure the new people are used most productively. An additional potential problem looms on the horizon. Other gaming companies have noticed the success HGC is having in their niche market; one company tried to hire a key product development employee away from HGC. Peters wants HGC to be ready to meet any potential competition head on and to discourage any new entries into their market. Peters knows HGC is project driven; however, she is not as confident that she has a good handle on how such an organization should be managed—especially with such a fast growth rate and potential competition closer to becoming a reality. The magnitude of emerging problems demands quick attention and resolution.

Peters has hired you as a consultant. She has suggested the following format for your consulting contract. You are free to use another format if it will improve the effectiveness of the consulting engagement.

What is our major problem?

Identify some symptoms of the problem.

What is the major cause of the problem?

Provide a detailed action plan that attacks the problem. Be specific and provide examples that relate to HGC.

CASE 2.2

Film Prioritization

The purpose of this case is to give you experience in using a project priority system that ranks proposed projects by their contribution to the organization's objectives and strategic plan.

COMPANY PROFILE

The company is the film division for a large entertainment conglomerate. The main office is located in Anaheim, California. In addition to the feature film division, the conglomerate includes theme parks, home videos, a television channel, interactive games, and theatrical productions. The company has been enjoying steady growth over the past 10 years. Last year total revenues increased by 12 percent to $21.2 billion. The company is engaged in negotiations to expand its theme park empire to mainland China and Poland. The film division generated $274 million in revenues, which was an increase of 7 percent over the past year. Profit margin was down 3 percent to 16 percent because of the poor response to three of the five major film releases for the year.

COMPANY MISSION

The mission for the firm:

> Our overriding objective is to create shareholder value by continuing to be the world's premier entertainment company from a creative, strategic, and financial standpoint.

The film division supports this mission by producing four to six high-quality, family entertainment films for mass distribution each year. In recent years, the CEO of the company has advocated that the firm take a leadership position in championing environmental concerns.

Company "Must" Objectives

Every project must meet the must objectives as determined by executive management. It is important that selected film projects not violate such objectives of high strategic priority. There are three must objectives:

1. All projects meet current legal, safety, and environmental standards.
2. All film projects should receive a PG or lower advisory rating.
3. All projects should not have an adverse effect on current or planned operations within the larger company.

Company "Want" Objectives

Want objectives are assigned weights for their relative importance. Top management is responsible for formulating, ranking, and weighting objectives to ensure that projects support the company's strategy and mission. The following is a list of the company's want objectives:

1. Be nominated for and win an academy award for Best Animated Feature or Best Picture of the Year.

2. Generate additional merchandise revenue (action figures, dolls, interactive games, music CDs).
3. Raise public consciousness about environmental issues and concerns.
4. Generate profit in excess of 18 percent.
5. Advance the state of the art in film animation, and preserve the firm's reputation.
6. Provide the basis for the development of a new ride at a company-owned theme park.

ASSIGNMENT

You are a member of the priority team in charge of evaluating and selecting film proposals. Use the provided evaluation form to formally evaluate and rank each proposal. Be prepared to report your rankings and justify your decisions.

Assume that all of the projects have passed the estimated hurdle rate of 14 percent ROI. In addition to the brief film synopsis, the proposals include the following financial projections of theater and video sales: 80 percent chance of ROI, 50 percent chance of ROI, and 20 percent chance of ROI.

For example, for proposal #1 (Dalai Lama) there is an 80 percent chance that it will earn at least 8 percent return on investment (ROI), a 50-50 chance the ROI will be 18 percent, and a 20 percent chance that the ROI will be 24 percent.

FILM PROPOSALS

Project Proposal 1: My Life With Dalai Lama

An animated, biographical account of the Dalai Lama's childhood in Tibet based on the popular children's book *Tales from Nepal*. The Lama's life is told through the eyes of "Guoda," a field snake, and other local animals who befriend the Dalai and help him understand the principles of Buddhism.

Probability	80%	50%	20%
ROI	8%	18%	24%

Project Proposal 2: Heidi

A remake of the classic children's story with music written by award-winning composers Syskle and Obert. The big-budget film will feature top-name stars and breathtaking scenery of the Swiss Alps.

Probability	80%	50%	20%
ROI	2%	20%	30%

Project Proposal 3: The Year of The Echo

A low-budget documentary that celebrates the career of one of the most influential bands in rock-and-roll history. The film will be directed by new-wave director Elliot Cznerzy and will combine concert footage and behind-the-scenes interviews spanning the 25-year history of the rock band the Echos. In addition to great music, the film will focus on the death of one of the founding

Project Priority Evaluation Form

Must objectives	Must meet if impacts	1	2	3	4	5	6	7
Meets all safety and environmental standards	Y = yes N = no N/A = not applicable							
PG or G rating	Y = yes N = no N/A = not applicable							
No adverse effect on other operations	Y = yes N = no N/A = not applicable							

Want objectives	Relative Importance 1–100	Single project impact definitions	Weighted Score	Weighted Score	Weighted Score	Weighted Score	Weighted Score	Weighted Score	Weighted Score
Win Best Picture of the Year	70	0 = No potential 1 = Low potential 2 = High potential							
Win Best Animated Feature Film	60	0 = No potential 1 = Low potential 2 = High potential							
Generate additional merchandise	10	0 = No potential 1 = Low potential 2 = High potential							
Raise environmental concerns	55	0 = No potential 1 = Low potential 2 = High potential							
Generate profit greater than 18%	70	0 < 18% 1 = 18–22% 2 > 22%							
Advance state of film animation	40	0 = No impact 1 = Some impact 2 = Great impact							
Provide basis for new theme ride	10	0 = No potential 1 = Low potential 2 = High potential							
Total weighted score									
Priority									

members from a heroin overdose and reveal the underworld of sex, lies, and drugs in the music industry.

Probability	80%	50%	20%
ROI	12%	14%	18%

Project Proposal 4: Escape from Rio Japuni

An animated feature set in the Amazon rainforest. The story centers around Pablo, a young jaguar who attempts to convince warring jungle animals that they must unite and escape the devastation of local clear cutting.

Probability	80%	50%	20%
ROI	15%	20%	24%

Project Proposal 5: Nadia!

The story of Nadia Comaneci, the famous Romanian gymnast who won three gold medals at the 1976 Summer Olympic Games. The low-budget film will document her life as a small child in Romania and how she was chosen by Romanian authorities to join their elite, state-run, athletic program. The film will highlight how Nadia maintained her independent spirit and love for gymnastics despite a harsh, regimented training program.

Probability	80%	50%	20%
ROI	8%	15%	20%

Project Proposal 6: Keiko—One Whale of A Story

The story of Keiko, the famous killer whale, will be told by an imaginary offspring Seiko, who in the distant future is telling her children about their famous grandfather. The big-budget film will integrate actual footage of the whale within a realistic animated environment using state-of-the-art computer imagery. The story will reveal how Keiko responded to his treatment by humans.

Probability	80%	50%	20%
ROI	6%	18%	25%

Project Proposal 7: Grand Island

The true story of a group of junior-high biology students who discover that a fertilizer plant is dumping toxic wastes into a nearby river. The moderate-budget film depicts how students organize a grassroots campaign to fight local bureaucracy and ultimately force the fertilizer plant to restore the local ecosystem.

Probability	80%	50%	20%
ROI	9%	15%	20%

CASE 2.3

Fund Raising Project Selection case

The purpose of this "case exercise" is to provide you with experience in using a project selection process that ranks proposed projects by their contribution to an organization's mission and strategy.

FUND RAISING PROJECT

Assume you are a member of a class on project management. Each student will join a team of 5–7 students who will be responsible for creating, planning and executing a fund raising project for a designated charity. The fund raising project has two goals: (1) raise money for a worthy cause and (2) provide an opportunity for all team members to practice project management skills and techniques.

In addition to completing the project a number of deliverables are required to complete this assignment. These deliverables include:

a) Project Proposal

b) Implementation Plan

c) Risk Management Plan

d) Status Report

e) Project Reflections Presentation

f) Project Retrospective/Audit

Approved projects will receive $250 seed money to be reimbursed upon completion of the project.

"MUST" OBJECTIVES

Every project must meet the "must" objectives as determined by the instructor. There are four must objectives:

1. All projects must be safe, legal and comply with university policies.
2. All projects must be capable of earning at least $500.
3. All projects must be able to be completed within nine weeks.
4. All projects must provide an opportunity for every member of the project team to experience and learn about project management.

Among the factors to consider for the last objective would be the extent there is meaningful work for every member of the team, the degree of coordination required, the extent the team will have to work with external stakeholders, and the complexity of the project.

"WANT" OBJECTIVES

In addition to the must objectives, there are "want" objectives that the instructor would like to achieve. The following is a list of these objectives:

1. Earn more than $500 for a charity
2. Increase public awareness of the charity

3. Provide a resume worthy experience for students
4. Be featured on local TV news
5. Be fun to do

ASSIGNMENT

You are a member of the class priority team in charge of evaluating and approving fund raising projects. Use the provided proposal evaluation form to formally evaluate and rank each proposal. Be prepared to report your rankings and justify your decision. You should assume that these projects would be held at your university or college.

FUND RAISING PROPOSALS

Project Proposal 1: Hoops for Hope

The project is a three-on-three basketball tournament to raise money for the Down Syndrome Association. The tournament will consist of three brackets: Co-ed, Male, and Female teams. There will be a $40 entry fee per team and additional funds will be derived from the sale of commemorative T-shirts ($10). Winning teams will receive gift baskets consisting of donations from local businesses and restaurants. The event will be held at the university recreational center.

Project Proposal 2: Singing for Smiles

The project will hold a karaoke competition with celebrity judges at a popular campus night spot. Funds will be raised by $5 admission at the door and a raffle for prizes donated by local businesses. Funds will be donated to Smile Train, an international organization that performs cleft lip surgery at a cost of $250 per child. The event will feature pictures of children born with cleft lips and with every $50 earned a piece of a picture puzzle will be added until the original picture is covered with a smiling face.

Project Proposal 3: Halo for Heroes

The project will be a Halo video game competition to be held over the weekend utilizing the College's big screen electronic classrooms. Teams of 4 players will play each other in a single elimination tournament with the grand prize being a Sony Play Station 3 donated by a local video game store. Entry fee is 24$ per team and individual players will be able to play in a loser's bracket for 5$. All proceeds will go to the National Military Family Association.

Project Proposal 4: Raffle for Life

Organize a raffle contest. Raffle tickets will be sold for 3$ a piece with the winning ticket worth $300. Each of the six team members will be responsible for selling 50 raffle tickets. All profits will go to the American Cancer Society.

Project Proposal 5: Hold'em for Hunger

Organize a Texas Hold'em poker tournament at a campus dining facility. It will cost 20$ to enter the tournament with a $15 buy-in fee. Prizes include $300, $150, and $50 gift certificates to a large department store. Gift certificates purchased from entry fees. All players will be eligible to win two donated tickets to Men and Women basketball games. Funds raised will go to local county food shelter.

Project Proposal 6: Build Your Own Box

The purpose of this project is to raise awareness of plight of homeless. Students will donate ten dollars to participate in building and living in a cardboard city on the university quad for one night. Building materials will be provided by local recycling centers and hardware stores. Hot soup will be provided by the team at midnight to all participants. Proceeds for go to the local homeless shelter.

Project Priority Evaluation Form

Must objectives	Must meet if impacts	1	2	3	4	5	6	7
Be safe, legal, & comply with University Policies	Y = yes N = no							
Earn at least $500	Y = yes N = no							
Can be completed within 9 weeks	Y = yes N = no							
Opportunity to learn Project Management	Y = yes N = no							

Want objectives	Relative Importance 1–100	Single project impact definitions	1	2	3	4	5	6	7
Earning potential	90	0: 500–750 1: 750–1500 2: >$1500 3: >$2000							
Fun	30	0: None 1: Some fun 2: A lot of fun							
Increase awareness of charity	30	0: No potential 1: Low potential 2: High potential							
Resume worthy	40	0: No potential 1: Low potential 2: High potential							
Be featured on local TV news	40	0: No potential 1: Low potential 2: High potential							
Total weighted score									
Priority									

CASE 2.4

Plant on River Yangtze
(Case Illustrating Application of Techniques for Financial Criteria for Project Selection)

Abstract

The case describes the scenario at the project-conceptualizing phase - right before the start of the formal project life cycle and before developing the Project Charter, which defines and authorizes the project. This stage involves making an assessment for product's market, preparing detailed technical feasibility and economic viability reports for project appraisal, and overview of project risks. The case presents a hypothetical project and some technical aspects under consideration for setting up a manufacturing plant in China. The case includes extracts from the detailed economic viability report of the type financing agencies generally require for their analysis and which the World Bank recommended for submission of applications for projects seeking financial participation. The case is meant to be used as a teaching material in a project management program for illustrating the preparation of the project cash flow statement and calculating the metrics useful for selection of projects according to financial criteria.

CASE TEXT

It was rather late night. Dr. Priyadarshi had been sitting at his desk – sometimes closely poring over some numbers in the tables and doing some mental calculations, sometimes pulling out files and papers from the stack of files spread out in front of him for rechecking data, sometimes just sitting, staring and gazing out of the window concentrating on some train of thoughts. Dr. Priyadarshi was Vice-President - International Operations of the Hercules Refractory Inc. The papers spread out in front of him were the files and reports for the project proposal for setting up in China a plant to manufacture a special refractory product for steel industry: slide type valves for controlling flow of molten steel.

Background

Hercules Refractory was an American multinational company, specializing in manufacture and marketing of very high temperature resistant ceramic products. It had set up collaborative ventures in 40 countries and had on its payroll total 18,000 workers. Under the top management's aggressive leadership, the company had achieved a rapid growth in the last five years and its revenue increased from \$350 millions to \$1.2 billion during this period. Its control slide valves were the standards for the steel industry in controlling the flow of molten steel in thin slab steel casting – the newest technological push achieved in the last decade.

In the early part of the twentieth century, four young technocrat entrepreneurs joined their hands and set up Hercules Refractory. With rapid growth in steel demand during the Second

World War and the economic boom that followed in Europe and U.S.A., the company prospered. The company had from its very beginninglaid emphasis on technical innovation and maintaining a technological lead in the industry. This was continued even in the late 1980s and early 1990s.

With the gradual opening up of the Chinese economy under the leadership of Deng Xiaoping, along with other American companies, Hercules also entered the Chinese market – first with exports, then setting up a 100% owned subsidiary company with an assembly shop using the components imported from the US. This small venture proved highly profitable and senior management of the company began to envisage a very promising opportunity for setting up a major manufacturing facility. Finally near the close of the twentieth century, a strategic planning group collected relevant techno-commercial data for planning a manufacturing facility in China and prepared a project proposal. The project would be for setting up a plant to produce control slide valves. It was this proposal, that Dr. Priyadarshi were to present and discuss the next week with the high powered committee which included the company president, executive vice president, vice–president finance and other senior executives. Priyadarshi started to recapitulate and assimilate the data once more to focus on major issues.

The Project Proposal

The proposal was for setting up in the next 16 months a plant with a capacity to manufacture 100, 000 slide control valves per annum in Eastern part of China with an investment of $ 6 million in fixed assets. The planned capacity would be sufficient to serve about 30 % of the country's current demand, and so the plant can be expected to ramp up to the capacity production level in three years.

Chinese Scenario

The differences between the American and Chinese industrial, organizational, cultural and government operating patterns were the first major issues. Unlike USA, the Chinese market was characterized by a large number of small capacity plants spread all over the country. The manufacturing facilities and technology used in these plants vary considerably from each other. Even otherwise, the industrial statistics always looked suspect to an outsider. Though strategic group should have been expected to do a competent job, however, one cannot be really sure of the extent of demand and growth of steel plant refractory. The extreme sensitiveness of the demand to product price was another issue. There was the fear of losing the formulas for refractory formulations developed over years of R & D if the mix formulation technology was divulged. The interim solution suggested was to set up a program for development of a long storage life pre-mix, which could be prepared in US and exported. The political system in China, its impact on factory organization as well as international trade and the unpredictability in the foreign exchange rates following the dictates in a command economy (as distinguished from market economy in U.S.A,) were some more points to ponder.

Technical Feasibility and Economic Viability

Successful transfer of technology and availability of trained technical personnel was not going to be a problem. Allotment of suitable land, satisfactory logistics for transportation of raw materials or finished products to the plant site, availability of electric power, fuel, water and other utilities was checked out to be satisfactory. The plant did not require disposal of a large quantity of toxic effluents. To what extent the government approvals and organization of construction workers (and later plant production organization) would impact the construction schedule and production volumes introduced uncertainty. The construction cost for the plant and operating production costs were worked out with some contingency investment and time buffers. Exhibit A shows the summary sheet presenting the projection of production volumes, revenues, variable operating costs, fixed overhead costs and cash flows for the five years period.

Once more, Priyadarshi went over the details of the project proposal, which had indeed painted a very rosy picture for return on investment. He tried hard to think of scenarios different from the project report and what uncertainties, if any, could upset this apple cart. He tried hard to think of questions, whose answers he possibly may not have in the project report in front of him, for as the wise Chinese sage Confucius had observed 25 centuries back, "He who knows all the answers has not been asked all the questions ".

EXHIBIT A ....
Production Costs and Cash Flows Summary

(In '000 U.S. Dollars)

	2001	2002	2003	2004	2005
Plant Capacity Utilization, %	45	70	95	95	95
Production Volume, '000 units	45	70	95	95	95
Unit Sales Price, Dollars/unit	100	105	110	115	125
Annual Sales, '000 Dollars	4500	7350	10450	10925	11825
Variable Operating Costs					
Raw materials	1575	2660	3800	4000	4100
Direct labour	675	1260	1900	2000	2050
Electric power, fuel, utilities	450	700	950	1000	1050
Factory supervision & overheads	500	600	800	850	900
Sales & Administrative Expenses	250	350	500	550	600
Gross Profit(PBIDT)	1050	1780	2500	2825	3125
Interest	300	350	400	450	500
Depreciation	600	600	600	600	600
Taxable Profits (PBT)	150	830	1500	1775	2025
Provision for Taxes	50	280	500	590	670
Profits after taxes (PAT)	100	550	1000	1185	1355
Salvage value of investment (@10%)					600
Net Annual Cash flow	700	1150	1600	1785	2555

Basis for cash flow projections:

Plant capacity: 100,000 units/annum

Capacity ramp up: 45 % in 1st year, 70 % in 2nd year, 95 % in 3rd year and onward

Investment in fixed assets: U.S.$ 6 million;

Fixed Asset Financing:	Equity: debt ratio 50:50; loan repayable in 5 annual installments.
Sale Price:	$ 100/unit for first year; Approx 5 % annual escalation
Norms for variable operating cost for 1sr year:	$ 35/unit raw material; $ 15/unit labour, $ 10 per unit electric power, fuel and utilities; approx 5 % escalation for later years
Factory supervision & sales & admin. expenses overheads:	Ad-hoc provision based on judgment
Interest rate:	10 % per annum..
Depreciation:	10 % per annum; straight-line basis for depreciation
Taxation:	33% on taxable profits.
Salvage value of plant	U.S. $ 0.6 million (10 % of initial investment at the end of the plant's economic life of 5 years.)
Weighted Ave. cost of capital:	8 % per annum (discounting factor for future cash flows)

EXHIBIT B ··

Financial Criteria for Project Appraisal (Investor's Perspective)

Pay-back Period: 4.38 years

(Time required for recovering initial cash outlay on the investment from the cash inflows generated by the project. Net cash inflows generated by the project in the first five years are U.S. Dollars 0.7, 1.15, 1.6, 1.785 and 1.955 respectively. Corresponding cumulative cash inflows at the end of 1st to 5th year U.S. $ 0.7, 1.85, 3.45, 5.24 and 7.19 million respectively).

Average Return on Investment: 27.5 % per annum

(ROI)

(Metrics used by different organizations for Return on Investment (ROI) vary widely. One of the more commonly used metric defines ROI as average income after tax, but before interest and tax, expressed as a percentage of initial investment. Average income of the five operating years, before interest and tax, is U.S.$1.65 million, which is 27.5 % return on initial investment of U.S.$ 6 million.

Net Present Value: U.S. $ 0.98 million

(NPV)

(NPV is defined as the net sum of present value of all cash flows – positive as well as negative cash flows expected to occur over the life of the project. Investment is regarded as a negative cash flow and profits after tax but, before interest and depreciation, are regarded as positive cash flows. Salvage value of the initial investment, US $ 0.6 million at 10 % of the initial investment, is also a positive cash flow. Present value of each annual cash flow is worked out by discounting it at the annual discounting factor, which is based on weighted average cost of capital, which is 8 % in this case. It is often referred to as Hurdle Rate).

Internal Rate of Return: 12.1 % per annum

(IRR)

(IRR is defined as that discounting rate at which project's NPV becomes equal to zero. By trial and error calculation with different discounting factors, the IRR for this project works out to be 12.1 % per annum).

Financial Criteria for Project Appraisal   (Lender's or Financial Institution's Perspective)

Equity: Debt ratio: 50: 50

Debt Service Coverage Ratio: 1.11 to 2.00

DSCR
DSCR is defined as the ratio of profit after tax, before interest and depreciation, to the amount required for debt service (interest plus loan repayment). For this project it works out 1.11 for 1st year; from 3rd year onwards, when project reaches capacity utilization, it is approx. 2.0.

Break-even Point (For Capacity Utilization): 57. 5%
In the 3rd year, when the project is expected to reach operating capacity, contribution per unit is $ 40 per piece (sale price -- variable operating cost). The fixed costs (factory supervision, sales and administrative expenses, depreciation and interest) are 2.3 million dollars. The break-even point works out to be 57,500 units (= 2.3 million / 40) or 57.5 % capacity.)

3

ORGANIZATION: STRUCTURE AND CULTURE

Matrix management works, but it sure is difficult at times. All matrix managers must keep up their health and take Stress–Tabs.

—*A Project Manager*

Once management approves a project then the question becomes, how will the project be implemented? This chapter examines three different project management structures used by firms to implement projects: functional organization, dedicated project teams, and matrix structure.

Although not exhaustive, these structures and their variant forms represent the major approaches for organizing projects. The advantages and disadvantages of each of these structures are discussed as well as some of the critical factors that might lead a firm to choose one form over others.

Whether a firm chooses to complete projects within the traditional functional organization or through some form of matrix arrangement is only part of the story. Anyone who has worked for more than one organization realizes that there are often considerable differences in how projects are managed within certain firms even with similar structures. Working in a matrix system at AT&T is different from working in a matrix environment at Hewlett-Packard. Many researchers attribute these differences to the organizational culture at AT&T and Hewlett-Packard. A simple explanation of *organizational culture* is that it reflects the "personality" of an organization. Just as each individual has a unique personality, so each organization has a unique culture. Toward the end of this chapter, we examine in more detail what organizational culture is and the impact that the culture of the parent organization has on organizing and managing projects.

Both the project management structure and the culture of the organization constitute major elements of the enterprise environment in which projects are implemented. It is important for project managers and participants to know the "lay of the land" so that they can avoid obstacles and take advantage of pathways to complete their projects.

PROJECT MANAGEMENT STRUCTURES

A project management system provides a framework for launching and implementing project activities within a parent organization. A good system appropriately balances the needs of both the parent organization and the project by defining the interface between the project and parent organization in terms of authority, allocation of resources, and eventual integration of project outcomes into mainstream operations. With this in mind, we will start the discussion of project management structures.

Organizing Projects within the Functional Organization

One approach to organizing projects is to simply manage them within the existing functional hierarchy of the organization. Once management decides to implement a project, the different segments of the project are delegated to the respective functional units with each unit responsible for completing its segment of the project (see Figure 3.1). Coordination is maintained through normal management channels. For example, a tool manufacturing firm decides to differentiate its product line by offering a series of tools specially designed for left-handed individuals. Top management decides to implement the project, and different segments of the project are distributed to appropriate areas. The industrial design department is responsible for modifying specifications to conform to the needs of left-handed users. The production department is responsible for devising the means for producing new tools according to these new design specifications. The marketing department is responsible for gauging demand and price as well as identifying distribution outlets. The overall project will be managed within the normal hierarchy, with the project being part of the working agenda of top management.

The functional organization is also commonly used when, given the nature of the project, one functional area plays a dominant role in completing the project or has a dominant interest in the success of the project. Under these circumstances, a high-ranking manager in that area is given the responsibility of coordinating the project. For example, the transfer of equipment and personnel to a new office would be managed by a top-ranking manager in the firm's facilities department. Likewise,

Figure 3.1 *Functional Organizations*

a project involving the upgrading of the management information system would be managed by the information systems department. In both cases, most of the project work would be done within the specified department and coordination with other departments would occur through normal channels.

There are advantages and disadvantages for using the existing functional organization to administer and complete projects (Larson, 2004). The major advantages are the following:

1. **No Change.** Projects are completed within the basic functional structure of the parent organization. There is no radical alteration in the design and operation of the parent organization.
2. **Flexibility.** There is maximum flexibility in the use of staff. Appropriate specialists in different functional units can temporarily be assigned to work on the project and then return to their normal work. With a broad base of technical personnel available within each functional department, people can be switched among different projects with relative ease.
3. **In-Depth Expertise.** If the scope of the project is narrow and the proper functional unit is assigned primary responsibility, then in-depth expertise can be brought to bear on the most crucial aspects of the project.
4. **Easy Post-Project Transition.** Normal career paths within a functional division are maintained. While specialists can make significant contributions to projects, their functional field is their professional home and the focus of their professional growth and advancement.

Just as there are advantages for organizing projects within the existing functional organization, there are also disadvantages. These disadvantages are particularly pronounced when the scope of the project is broad and one functional department does not take the dominant technological and managerial lead on the project:

1. **Lack of Focus.** Each functional unit has its own core routine work to do; sometimes project responsibilities get pushed aside to meet primary obligations. This difficulty is compounded

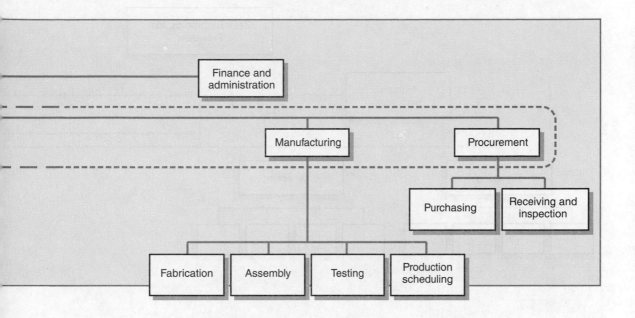

when the project has different priorities for different units. For example, the marketing department may consider the project urgent while the operations people considered it only of secondary importance. Imagine the tension if the marketing people have to wait for the operations people to complete their segment of the project before they proceed.

2. **Poor Integration.** There may be poor integration across functional units. Functional specialists tend to be concerned only with their segment of the project and not with what is best for the total project.

3. **Slow.** It generally takes longer to complete projects through this functional arrangement. This is in part attributable to slow response time—project information and decisions have to be circulated through normal management channels. Furthermore, the lack of horizontal, direct communication among functional groups contributes to rework as specialists realize the implications of others' actions after the fact.

4. **Lack of Ownership.** The motivation of people assigned to the project can be weak. The project may be seen as an additional burden that is not directly linked to their professional development or advancement. Furthermore, because they are working on only a segment of the project, professionals do not identify with the project.

Organizing Projects as Dedicated Teams

At the other end of the structural spectrum is the creation of **dedicated project teams.** These teams operate as separate units from the rest of the parent organization. Usually a full-time project manager is designated to pull together a core group of specialists who work full time on the project. The project manager recruits necessary personnel from both within and outside the parent company. The subsequent team is physically separated from the parent organization and given marching orders to complete the project (see Figure 3.2).

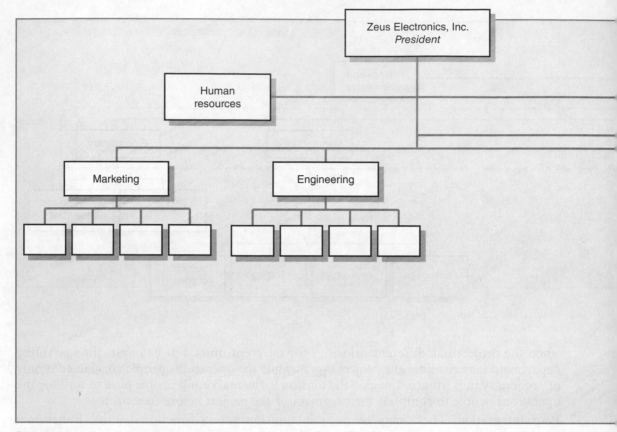

Zeus Electronics, Inc.
President

Human
resources

Marketing

Engineering

FIGURE 3.2 *Dedicated Project Team*

The interface between the parent organization and the project teams will vary. In some cases, the parent organization maintains a tight rein through financial controls. In other cases, firms grant the project manager maximum freedom to get the project done as he sees fit. Lockheed Martin has used this approach to develop next-generation jet airplanes. See Snapshot from Practice: Skunk Works.

In the case of firms where projects are the dominant form of business, such as a construction firm or a consulting firm, the entire organization is designed to support project teams. Instead of one or two special projects, the organization consists of sets of quasi-independent teams working on specific projects. The main responsibility of traditional functional departments is to assist and support these project teams. For example, the marketing department is directed at generating new business that will lead to more projects, while the human resource department is responsible for managing a variety of personnel issues as well as recruiting and training new employees. This type of organization is referred to in the literature as a **Projectized Organization** and is graphically portrayed in Figure 3.3. It is important to note that not all projects are dedicated project teams; personnel can work part-time on several projects.

As in the case of functional organization, the dedicated project team approach has strengths and weaknesses (Larson, 2004). The following are recognized as strengths:

1. **Simple.** Other than taking away resources in the form of specialists assigned to the project, the functional organization remains intact with the project team operating independently.

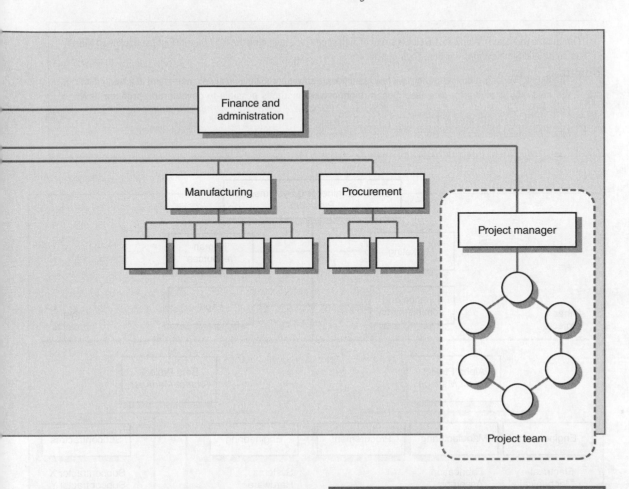

Finance and administration

Manufacturing

Procurement

Project manager

Project team

SNAPSHOT FROM PRACTICE
Skunk Works at Lockheed Martin*

In project management folklore, skunk works is code for a small, dedicated team assigned to a breakthrough project. The first skunk works was created more than a half a century ago by Clarence L. "Kelly" Johnson at Lockheed Aerospace Corporation. Kelly's project had two objectives: 1) to create a jet fighter, the Shooting Star, and 2) to do it as fast as possible. Kelly and a small band of engineering mavericks operated as a dedicated team unencumbered by red tape and the bureaucratic delays of the normal R&D process. The name was coined by team member Irvin Culver after the moonshine brewery deep in the forest in the popular cartoon strip Lil'Abner. The homemade whisky was euphemistically called kickapoo joy juice.

The project was a spectacular success. In just 43 days, Johnson's team of 23 engineers and teams of support personnel put together the first American fighter to fly at more than 500 miles per hour. Lockheed has

© Paul Crock/AFP/Getty Images

continued to use Skunk Works to develop a string of high speed jets, including the F117 Stealth Fighter. Lockheed Martin has an official Skunk Works division. Their charter is:

The Skunk Works is a concentration of a few good people solving problems far in advance—and at a fraction of the cost—by applying the simplest, most straightforward methods possible to develop and produce new products.

* J. Miller, *Lockheed Martin's Skunk Works* (New York: Speciality Publications, 1996).

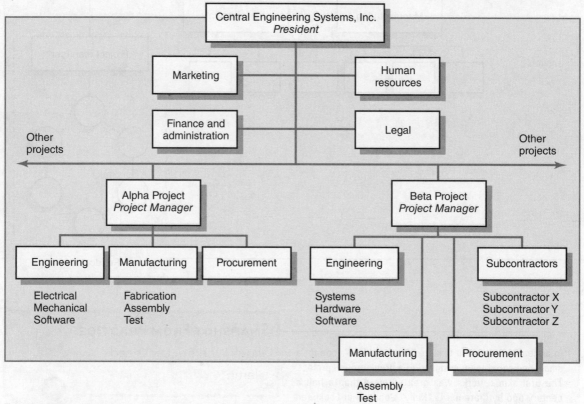

FIGURE 3.3   Projectized Organization Structure

2. **Fast.** Projects tend to get done more quickly when participants devote their full attention to the project and are not distracted by other obligations and duties. Furthermore, response time tends to be quicker under this arrangement because most decisions are made within the team and are not deferred up the hierarchy.

3. **Cohesive.** A high level of motivation and cohesiveness often emerges within the project team. Participants share a common goal and personal responsibility toward the project and the team.

4. **Cross-Functional Integration.** Specialists from different areas work closely together and, with proper guidance, become committed to optimizing the project, not their respective areas of expertise.

In many cases, the project team approach is the optimum approach for completing a project when you view it solely from the standpoint of what is best for completing the project. Its weaknesses become more evident when the needs of the parent organization are taken into account:

1. **Expensive.** Not only have you created a new management position (project manager), but resources are also assigned on a full-time basis. This can result in duplication of efforts across projects and a loss of economies of scale.

2. **Internal Strife.** Sometimes dedicated project teams take on an entity of their own and conflict emerges between the team and the remainder of the organization (see Snapshot from Practice: The Birth of the Mac). This divisiveness can undermine not only the integration of

SNAPSHOT FROM PRACTICE
The Birth of the Mac*

One of the advantages of creating dedicated project teams is that project participants from different functional areas can develop into a highly cohesive work team that is strongly committed to completing the project. While such teams often produce Herculean efforts in pursuit of project completion, there is a negative dimension to this commitment that is often referred to in the literature as **projectitis.** A we–they attitude can emerge between project team members and the rest of the organization. The project team succumbs to *hubris* and develops a holier-than-thou attitude that antagonizes the parent organization. People not assigned to the project become jealous of the attention and prestige being showered on the project team, especially when they believe that it is their hard work that is financing the endeavor. The tendency to assign project teams exotic titles such as "Silver Bullets" and "Tiger Teams," as well as give them special perks, tends to intensify the gap between the project team and the parent organization.

© Apic/Getty Images

Such appears to have been the case with Apple's highly successful Macintosh development team. Steve Jobs, who at the time was both the chairman of Apple and the project manager for the Mac team, pampered his team with perks including at-the-desk massages, coolers stocked with freshly squeezed orange juice, a Bosendorfer grand piano, and first-class plane tickets. No other employees at Apple got to travel first class. Jobs considered his team to be the elite of Apple and had a tendency to refer to everyone else as "Bozos" who "didn't get it." Engineers from the Apple II division, which was the bread and butter of Apple's sales, became incensed with the special treatment their colleagues were getting.

One evening at Ely McFly's, a local watering hole, the tensions between Apple II engineers seated at one table and those of a Mac team at another boiled over. Aaron Goldberg, a long-time industry consultant, watched from his barstool as the squabbling escalated. "The Mac guys were screaming, 'We're the future!' The Apple II guys were screaming, 'We're the money!' Then there was a geek brawl. Pocket protectors and pens were flying. I was waiting for a notebook to drop, so they would stop and pick up the papers."

Although comical from a distance, the discord between the Apple II and Mac groups severely hampered Apple's performance during the 1980s. John Sculley, who replaced Steve Jobs as chairman of Apple, observed that Apple had evolved into two "warring companies" and referred to the street between the Apple II and Macintosh buildings as "the DMZ" (demilitarized zone).

* J. Carlton, *Apple: The Inside Story of Intrigue, Egomania, and Business Blunders* (New York: Random House, 1997), pp. 13–14; J. Sculley, *Odyssey: Pepsi to Apple . . . A Journey of Adventure, Ideas, and the Future* (New York: Harper & Row, 1987), pp. 270–79.

the eventual outcomes of the project into mainstream operations but also the assimilation of project team members back into their functional units once the project is completed.

3. **Limited Technological Expertise.** Creating self-contained teams inhibits maximum technological expertise being brought to bear on problems. Technical expertise is limited somewhat to the talents and experience of the specialists assigned to the project. While nothing prevents specialists from consulting with others in the functional division, the we–they syndrome and the fact that such help is not formally sanctioned by the organization discourage this from happening.

4. **Difficult Post-Project Transition.** Assigning full-time personnel to a project creates the dilemma of what to do with personnel after the project is completed. If other project work is not available, then the transition back to their original functional departments may be difficult because of their prolonged absence and the need to catch up with recent developments in their functional area.

Organizing Projects within a Matrix Arrangement

One of the biggest management innovations to emerge in the past 40 years has been the matrix organization. **Matrix** management is a hybrid organizational form in which a horizontal project

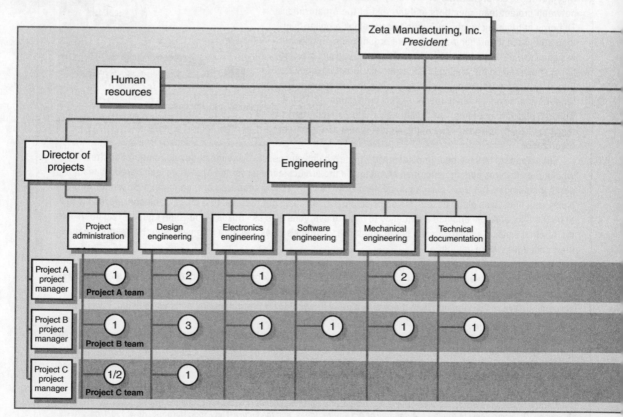

FIGURE 3.4 *Matrix Organization Structure*

management structure is "overlaid" on the normal functional hierarchy. In a matrix system, there are usually two chains of command, one along functional lines and the other along project lines. Instead of delegating segments of a project to different units or creating an autonomous team, project participants report simultaneously to both functional and project managers.

Companies apply this matrix arrangement in a variety of different ways. Some organizations set up temporary matrix systems to deal with specific projects, while "matrix" may be a permanent fixture in other organizations. Let us first look at its general application and then proceed to a more detailed discussion of finer points. Consider Figure 3.4. There are three projects currently under way: A, B, and C. All three project managers (PM A-C) report to a director of project management, who supervises all projects. Each project has an administrative assistant, although the one for project C is only part time.

Project A involves the design and expansion of an existing production line to accommodate new metal alloys. To accomplish this objective, project A has assigned to it 3.5 people from manufacturing and 6 people from engineering. These individuals are assigned to the project on a part-time or full-time basis, depending on the project's needs during various phases of the project. Project B involves the development of a new product that requires the heavy representation of engineering, manufacturing, and marketing. Project C involves forecasting changing needs of an existing customer base. While these three projects, as well as others, are being completed, the functional divisions continue performing their basic, core activities.

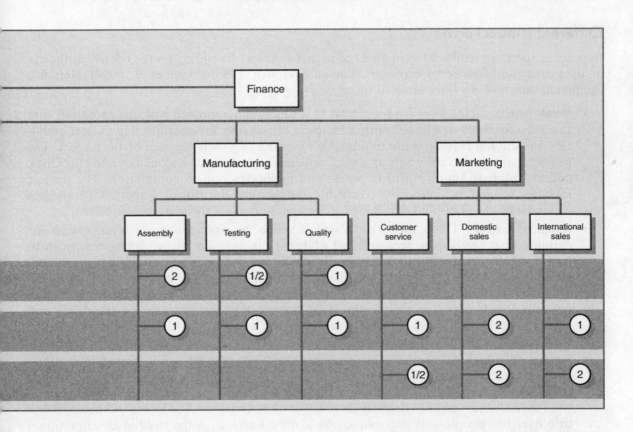

The matrix structure is designed to optimally utilize resources by having individuals work on multiple projects as well as being capable of performing normal functional duties. At the same time, the matrix approach attempts to achieve greater integration by creating and legitimizing the authority of a project manager. In theory, the matrix approach provides a dual focus between functional/technical expertise and project requirements that is missing in either the project team or functional approach to project management. This focus can most easily be seen in the relative input of functional managers and project managers over key project decisions (see Table 3.1).

TABLE 3.1 ···
Division of Project Manager and Functional Manager Responsibilities in a Matrix Structure

Project Manager	Negotiated Issues	Functional Manager
What has to be done?	Who will do the task?	How will it be done?
When should the task be done?	Where will the task be done?	
How much money is available to do the task?	Why will the task be done?	How will the project involvement impact normal functional activities?
How well has the total project been done?	Is the task satisfactorily completed?	How well has the functional input been integrated?

Different Matrix Forms

In practice there are really different kinds of matrix systems, depending on the relative authority of the project and functional managers (Larson & Gobeli, 1985; Bowen et al., 1994). Here is a thumbnail sketch of the three kinds of matrices:

- **Weak matrix**—This form is very similar to a functional approach with the exception that there is a formally designated project manager responsible for coordinating project activities. Functional managers are responsible for managing their segment of the project. The project manager basically acts as a staff assistant who draws the schedules and checklists, collects information on status of work, and facilitates project completion. The project manager has indirect authority to expedite and monitor the project. Functional managers call most of the shots and decide who does what and when the work is completed.

- **Balanced matrix**—This is the classic matrix in which the project manager is responsible for defining what needs to be accomplished while the functional managers are concerned with how it will be accomplished. More specifically, the project manager establishes the overall plan for completing the project, integrates the contribution of the different disciplines, sets schedules, and monitors progress. The functional managers are responsible for assigning personnel and executing their segment of the project according to the standards and schedules set by the project manager. The merger of "what and how" requires both parties to work closely together and jointly approve technical and operational decisions.

- **Strong matrix**—This form attempts to create the "feel" of a project team within a matrix environment. The project manager controls most aspects of the project, including scope trade-offs and assignment of functional personnel. The project manager controls when and what specialists do and has final say on major project decisions. The functional manager has title over her people and is consulted on a need basis. In some situations a functional manager's department may serve as a "subcontractor" for the project, in which case they have more control over specialized work. For example, the development of a new series of laptop computers may require a team of experts from different disciplines working on the basic design and performance requirements within a project matrix arrangement. Once the specifications have been determined, final design and production of certain components (i.e., power source) may be assigned to respective functional groups to complete.

Matrix management both in general and in its specific forms has unique strengths and weaknesses (Larson & Gobeli, 1987). The advantages and disadvantages of matrix organizations in general are noted below, while only briefly highlighting specifics concerning different forms:

1. **Efficient.** Resources can be shared across multiple projects as well as within functional divisions. Individuals can divide their energy across multiple projects on an as-needed basis. This reduces duplication required in a projectized structure.

2. **Strong Project Focus.** A stronger project focus is provided by having a formally designated project manager who is responsible for coordinating and integrating contributions of different units. This helps sustain a holistic approach to problem solving that is often missing in the functional organization.

3. **Easier Post-Project Transition.** Because the project organization is overlaid on the functional divisions, specialists maintain ties with their functional group, so they have a homeport to return to once the project is completed.

4. **Flexible.** Matrix arrangements provide for flexible utilization of resources and expertise within the firm. In some cases functional units may provide individuals who are managed by the project manager. In other cases the contributions are monitored by the functional manager.

The strengths of the matrix structure are considerable. Unfortunately, so are the potential weaknesses. This is due in large part to the fact that a matrix structure is more complicated and the creation of multiple bosses represents a radical departure from the traditional hierarchical authority system.

Furthermore, one does not install a matrix structure overnight. Experts argue that it takes 3–5 years for a matrix system to fully mature. So many of the problems described below represent growing pains.

1. **Dysfunctional Conflict.** The matrix approach is predicated on tension between functional managers and project managers who bring critical expertise and perspectives to the project. Such tension is viewed as a necessary mechanism for achieving an appropriate balance between complex technical issues and unique project requirements. While the intent is noble, the effect is sometimes analogous to opening Pandora's box. Legitimate conflict can spill over to a more personal level, resulting from conflicting agendas and accountabilities. Worthy discussions can degenerate into heated arguments that engender animosity among the managers involved.

2. **Infighting.** Any situation in which equipment, resources, and people are being shared across projects and functional activities lends itself to conflict and competition for scarce resources. Infighting can occur among project managers, who are primarily interested in what is best for their project.

3. **Stressful.** Matrix management violates the management principle of unity of command. Project participants have at least two bosses—their functional head and one or more project

managers. Working in a matrix environment can be extremely stressful. Imagine what it would be like to work in an environment in which you are being told to do three conflicting things by three different managers.

4. **Slow.** In theory, the presence of a project manager to coordinate the project should accelerate the completion of the project. In practice, decision making can get bogged down as agreements have to be forged across multiple functional groups. This is especially true for the balanced matrix.

When the three variant forms of the matrix approach are considered, we can see that advantages and disadvantages are not necessarily true for all three forms of matrix. The Strong matrix is likely to enhance project integration, diminish internal power struggles, and ultimately improve control of project activities and costs. On the downside, technical quality may suffer because functional areas have less control over their contributions. Finally, projectitis may emerge as the members develop a strong team identity.

The Weak matrix is likely to improve technical quality as well as provide a better system for managing conflict across projects because the functional manager assigns personnel to different projects. The problem is that functional control is often maintained at the expense of poor project integration. The Balanced matrix can achieve better balance between technical and project requirements, but it is a very delicate system to manage and is more likely to succumb to many of the problems associated with the matrix approach.

WHAT IS THE RIGHT PROJECT MANAGEMENT STRUCTURE?

There is empirical evidence that project success is directly linked to the amount of autonomy and authority project managers have over their projects (Gray et al., 1990; Larson & Gobeli, 1988; Larson & Gobeli, 1987). However, most of this research is based on what is best for managing specific projects. It is important to remember what was stated in the beginning of the chapter—that the best system balances the needs of the project with those of the parent organization. So what project structure should an organization use? This is a complicated question with no precise answers. A number of issues need to be considered at both the organization and project level.

Organization Considerations

At the organization level, the first question that needs to be asked is how important is project management to the success of the firm? What percentage of core work involves projects? If over 75 percent of work involves projects, then an organization should consider a fully projectized organization. If an organization has both standard products and projects, then a matrix arrangement would appear to be appropriate. If an organization has very few projects, then a less formal arrangement is probably all that is required. Dedicated teams could be created on an as-needed basis and the organization could outsource project work.

A second key question is resource availability. Remember, matrix evolved out of the necessity to share resources across multiple projects and functional domains while at the same time creating legitimate project leadership. For organizations that cannot afford to tie up critical personnel on individual projects, a matrix system would appear to be appropriate. An alternative would be to create a dedicated team but outsource project work when resources are not available internally.

Within the context of the first two questions, an organization needs to assess current practices and what changes are needed to more effectively manage projects. A strong project matrix is not installed overnight. The shift toward a greater emphasis on projects has a host of political implications that need to be worked through, requiring time and strong leadership. For example, we have observed many companies that make the transition from a functional organization to a matrix organization begin with a weak functional matrix. This is due in part to resistance by functional and department managers toward transferring authority to project managers. With time, these matrix structures eventually evolve into a project matrix. Many organizations have created Project Management Offices to support project management efforts. See Snapshot from Practice: POs: Project Offices.

Project Considerations

At the project level, the question is how much autonomy the project needs in order to be successfully completed. Hobbs and Ménard (1993) identify seven factors that should influence the choice of project management structure:

- Size of project.
- Strategic importance.
- Novelty and need for innovation.
- Need for integration (number of departments involved).
- Environmental complexity (number of external interfaces).
- Budget and time constraints.
- Stability of resource requirements.

SNAPSHOT FROM PRACTICE
POs: Project Offices*

Project offices (POs) were originally developed as a response to the poor track record many companies had in completing projects on time, within budget, and according to plan. They were often established to help matrix systems mature into more effective project delivery platforms.

Today, POs come in many different shapes and forms. One interesting way of classifying POs was set forth by Casey and Peck, who describe certain POs in terms of being (1) a weather station, (2) a control tower, or (3) a resource pool. Each of these models performs a very different function for its organization.

- **Weather Station.** The primary function of the weather station PO is to track and monitor project performance. It is typically created to satisfy top management's need to stay on top of the portfolio of projects under way in the firm. Staff provides an independent forecast of project performance. The questions answered for specific projects include:
  - How are our projects progressing? Which ones are on track? Which ones are not?
  - How are we doing in terms of cost? Which projects are over or under budget?
  - What are the major problems confronting projects? Are contingency plans in place? What can the organization do to help the project?
- **Control Tower.** The primary function of the control tower PO is to improve project execution. It considers project management as a profession to be protected and advanced. Staff at the PO identify best practices and standards for project management excellence. They work as consultants and trainers to support project managers and their teams.
- **Resource Pool.** The goal of the resource pool PO is to provide the organization with a cadre of trained project managers and professionals. It operates like an academy for continually upgrading the skills of a firm's project professionals. In addition to training, this kind of PO also serves to elevate the stature of project management within the organization.

* W. Casey and W. Peck, "Choosing the Right PMO Setup," *PM Network*, vol. 15, no. 2(2001), pp. 40–47.

The higher the levels of these seven factors, the more autonomy and authority the project manager and project team need to be successful.[1] This translates into using either a dedicated project team or a project matrix structure. For example, these structures should be used for large projects that are strategically critical and are new to the company, thus requiring much innovation. These structures would also be appropriate for complex, multidisciplinary projects that require input from many departments, as well as for projects that require constant contact with customers to assess their expectations. Dedicated project teams should also be used for urgent projects in which the nature of the work requires people working steadily from beginning to end.

Many firms that are heavily involved in project management have created a flexible management system that organizes projects according to project requirements. For example, Chaparral Steel, a mini-mill that produces steel bars and beams from scrap metal, classifies projects into three categories: advanced development, platform, and incremental. Advanced development projects are high-risk endeavors involving the creation of a breakthrough product or process. Platform projects are medium-risk projects involving system upgrades that yield new products and processes. Incremental projects are low-risk, short-term projects that involve minor adjustments in existing products and processes. At any point in time, Chaparral might have 40–50 projects underway, of which only one or two are advanced, three to five are platform projects, and the remainder are small, incremental projects. The incremental projects are almost all done within a weak matrix with the project manager coordinating the work of functional subgroups. A strong matrix is used to complete the platform projects, while dedicated project teams are typically created to complete the advanced development projects. More and more companies are using this "mix and match" approach to managing projects.

ORGANIZATIONAL CULTURE

The decision for combining a discussion of project management structures and organizational cultures in this chapter can be traced to a conversation we, the authors, had with two project managers who work for a medium-sized information technology firm.

The managers were developing a new operating platform that would be critical to the future success of their company. When they tried to describe how this project was organized, one manager began to sketch out on a napkin a complicated structure involving 52 different teams, each with a project leader and a technical leader! In response to our further probing to understand how this system worked, the manager stopped short and proclaimed, "The key to making this structure work is the culture in our company. This approach would never work at company Y, where I worked before. But because of our culture here we are able to pull it off."

This comment, our observations of other firms, and research suggest there is a strong connection between project management structure, organizational culture, and project success.[2] We have observed organizations successfully manage projects within the traditional functional organization because the culture encouraged cross-functional integration. Conversely we have seen matrix structures break down because the culture of the organization did not support the division of authority between project managers and functional managers. We have also observed companies

---

[1] For a more sophisticated discussion of contingency factors related to managing specific projects see: A. J. Shenhar and D. Dvir, *Reinventing Project Management: The Diamond Approach to Successful Growth and Innovation* (Boston: Harvard Press, 2007).

[2] See, for example: Kerzner, H., *In Search of Excellence in Project Management* (New York: Von Nostrand Reinhold, 1997); Matheson, D., and J. Matheson, *The Smart Organization* (Boston: HBS Press, 1998).

relying on independent project teams because the dominant culture would not support the innovation and speed necessary for success.

What Is Organizational Culture?

Organizational culture refers to a system of shared norms, beliefs, values, and assumptions which binds people together, thereby creating shared meanings (Deal & Kennedy, 1982). This system is manifested by customs and habits that exemplify the values and beliefs of the organization. For example, egalitarianism may be expressed in the informal dress worn at a high-tech firm. Conversely, mandated uniforms at a department store reinforce respect for the hierarchy.

Culture reflects the personality of the organization and, similar to an individual's personality, can enable us to predict attitudes and behaviors of organizational members. Culture is also one of the defining aspects of an organization that sets it apart from other organizations even in the same industry.

Research suggests that there are 10 primary characteristics which, in aggregate, capture the essence of an organization's culture:[3]

1. **Member identity**—the degree to which employees identify with the organization as a whole rather than with their type of job or field of professional expertise.
2. **Team emphasis**—the degree to which work activities are organized around groups rather than individuals.
3. **Management focus**—the degree to which management decisions take into account the effect of outcomes on people within the organization.
4. **Unit integration**—the degree to which units within the organization are encouraged to operate in a coordinated or interdependent manner.
5. **Control**—the degree to which rules, policies, and direct supervision are used to oversee and control employee behavior.
6. **Risk tolerance**—the degree to which employees are encouraged to be aggressive, innovative, and risk seeking.
7. **Reward criteria**—the degree to which rewards such as promotion and salary increases are allocated according to employee performance rather than seniority, favoritism, or other nonperformance factors.
8. **Conflict tolerance**—the degree to which employees are encouraged to air conflicts and criticisms openly.
9. **Means versus end orientation**—the degree to which management focuses on outcomes rather than on techniques and processes used to achieve those results.
10. **Open-systems focus**—the degree to which the organization monitors and responds to changes in the external environment.

As shown in Figure 3.5, each of these dimensions exists on a continuum. Assessing an organization according to these 10 dimensions provides a composite picture of the organization's

---

[3] Harrison, M. T., and J. M. Beyer, *The Culture of Organizations* (Englewood Cliffs, NJ: Prentice Hall, 1993); O'Reilly, C. A., J. Chatman, and D. F. Caldwell, "People and Organizational Culture: A Profile Comparison Approach to Assessing Person-Organization Fit," *Academy of Management Journal*, vol. 34, no. 3. September 1991, pp. 487–516; and Schein, E., *Organizational Culture and Leadership: A Dynamic View* (San Francisco, CA: Jossey-Bass, 2010).

FIGURE 3.5   *Key Dimensions Defining an Organization's Culture*

Job ——— 1. Member identity ——— Organization
Individual ——— 2. Team emphasis ——— Group
Task ——— 3. Management focus ——— People
Independent ——— 4. Unit integration ——— Interdependent
Loose ——— 5. Control ——— Tight
Low ——— 6. Risk tolerance ——— High
Performance ——— 7. Reward criteria ——— Other
Low ——— 8. Conflict tolerance ——— High
Means ——— 9. Means-ends orientation ——— Ends
Internal ——— 10. Open-system focus ——— External

culture. This picture becomes the basis for feelings of shared understanding that the members have about the organization, how things are done, and the way members are supposed to behave.

Culture performs several important functions in organizations. An organization's culture *provides a sense of identity* for its members. The more clearly an organization's shared perceptions and values are stated, the more strongly people can identify with their organization and feel a vital part of it. Identity generates commitment to the organization and reasons for members to devote energy and loyalty to the organization.

A second important function is that culture *helps legitimize the management system* of the organization. Culture helps clarify authority relationships. It provides reasons why people are in a position of authority and why their authority should be respected.

Most importantly, organizational culture *clarifies and reinforces standards of behavior.* Culture helps define what is permissible and inappropriate behavior. These standards span a wide range of behavior from dress code and working hours to challenging the judgment of superiors and collaborating with other departments. Ultimately, culture *helps create social order* within an organization. Imagine what it would be like if members didn't share similar beliefs, values, and assumptions—chaos! The customs, norms, and ideals conveyed by the culture of an organization provide the stability and predictability in behavior that is essential for an effective organization. See Snapshot from Practice: Google-y for an example of this.

Although our discussion of organizational culture may appear to suggest one culture dominates the entire organization, in reality this is rarely the case. "Strong" or "thick" are adjectives used to denote a culture in which the organization's core values and customs are widely shared within the entire organization. Conversely, a "thin" or "weak" culture is one that is not widely shared or practiced within a firm.

Even within a strong organizational culture, there are likely to be subcultures often aligned within specific departments or specialty areas. As noted earlier in our discussion of project management structures, it is not uncommon for norms, values, and customs to develop within a

In 2012 Google Inc. topped *Fortune* magazine's list of best companies to work at for the third time in the past five years. When one enters the 24-hour Googleplex located in Mountain View, California, you feel that you are walking through a new-age college campus rather than the corporate office of a billion-dollar business. The collection of interconnected low-rise buildings with colorful, glass-encased offices feature upscale trappings—free gourmet meals three times a day, free use of an outdoor wave pool, indoor gym and large child care facility, private shuttle bus service to and from San Francisco and other residential areas—that are the envy of workers across the Bay area. These perks and others reflect Google's culture of keeping people happy and thinking in unconventional ways.

© Proehl Studios/Corbis

The importance of corporate culture is no more evident than in the fact that the head of Human Resources, Stacy Savides Sullivan, also has the title of Chief Culture Officer. Her task is to try to preserve the innovative culture of a start-up as Google quickly evolves into a mammoth international corporation. Sullivan characterizes Google culture as "team-oriented, very collaborative and encouraging people to think nontraditionally, different from where they ever worked before— work with integrity and for the good of the company and for the good of the world, which is tied to our overall mission of making information accessible to the world." Google goes to great lengths to screen new employees to not only make sure that they have outstanding technical capabilities but also that they are going to fit Google's culture. Sullivan goes on to define a Google-y employee as somebody who is "flexible, adaptable, and not focusing on titles and hierarchy, and just gets stuff done."

Google's culture is rich with customs and traditions not found in corporate America. For example, project teams typically have daily "stand-up" meetings seven minutes after the hour. Why seven minutes after the hour? Because Google cofounder Sergey Brin once estimated that it took seven minutes to walk across the Google campus. Everybody stands to make sure no one gets too comfortable and no time is wasted during the rapid-fire update. As one manager noted, "The whole concept of the stand-up is to talk through what everyone's doing, so if someone is working on what you're working on, you can discover and collaborate not duplicate."

Another custom is "dogfooding." This is when a project team releases the functional prototype of a future product to Google employees for them to test drive. There is a strong norm within Google to test new products and provide feedback to the developers. The project team receives feedback from thousands of Google-ys. The internal focus group can log bugs or simply comment on design or functionality. Fellow Google-ys do not hold back on their feedback and are quick to point out things they don't like. This often leads to significant product improvements.

* Walters, H., "How Google Got Its New Look," *BusinessWeek,* May 10, 2010; Goo, S. K., "Building a 'Googley' Workforce," *Washington Post,* October 21, 2006; Mills, E., "Meet Google's Culture Czar," *CNET News.com,* April 27, 2007.

specific field or profession such as marketing, finance, or operations. People working in the marketing department may have a different set of norms and values than those working in finance.

Countercultures sometimes emerge within organizations that embody a different set of values, beliefs, and customs—often in direct contradiction with the culture espoused by top management.

How pervasive these subcultures and countercultures are affect the strength of the culture of the organization and the extent to which culture influences members' actions and responses.

Identifying Cultural Characteristics

Deciphering an organization's culture is a highly interpretative, subjective process that requires assessment of both current and past history. The student of culture cannot simply rely on what people report about their culture. The physical environment in which people work, as well as how people act and respond to different events that occur, must be examined. Figure 3.6 contains a worksheet for diagnosing the culture of an organization. Although by no means exhaustive, the checklist often yields clues about the norms, customs, and values of an organization:

1. **Study the physical characteristics of an organization.** What does the external architecture look like? What image does it convey? Is it unique? Are the buildings and offices the same quality for all employees? Or are modern buildings and fancier offices reserved for senior executives or managers from a specific department? What are the customs concerning dress? What symbols does the organization use to signal authority and status within the organization? These physical characteristics can shed light on who has real power within the organization, the extent to which the organization is internally differentiated, and how formal the organization is in its business dealings.

FIGURE 3.6 *Organizational Culture Diagnosis Worksheet*

Power Corp.

I. Physical Characteristics:
Architecture, office layout, décor, attire

Corporate HQ is 20 story modern building—president on top floor. Offices are bigger in the top floors than lower floors. Formal business attire (white shirts, ties, power suits, . . .). Power appears to increase the higher up you are.

II. Public Documents:
Annual reports, internal newsletters, vision statements

At the heart of the Power Corp. way is our vision . . . to be the global energy company most admired for its people, partnership, and performance.

Integrity. We are honest with others and ourselves. We meet the highest ethical standards in all business dealings. We do what we say we will do.

III. Behavior:
Pace, language, meetings, issues discussed, decision-making style, communication patterns, rituals

Hierarchical decision-making, pace brisk but orderly, meetings start on time and end on time, subordinates choose their words very carefully when talking to superiors, people rarely work past 6:00 P.M., president takes top performing unit on a boat cruise each year . . .

IV. Folklore:
Stories, anecdotes, heroines, heroes, villains

Young project manager was fired after going over his boss's head to ask for additional funds.

Stephanie C. considered a hero for taking complete responsibility for a technical error.

Jack S. was labeled a traitor for joining chief competitor after working for Power Corp. for 15 years.

2. **Read about the organization.** Examine annual reports, mission statements, press releases, and internal newsletters. What do they describe? What principles are espoused in these documents? Do the reports emphasize the people who work for the organization and what they do or the financial performance of the firm? Each emphasis reflects a different culture. The first demonstrates concern for the people who make up the company. The second may suggest a concern for results and the bottom line.

3. **Observe how people interact within the organization.** What is their pace—is it slow and methodical or urgent and spontaneous? What rituals exist within the organization? What values do they express? Meetings can often yield insightful information. Who are the people at the meetings? Who does the talking? To whom do they talk? How candid is the conversation? Do people speak for the organization or for the individual department? What is the focus of the meetings? How much time is spent on various issues? Issues that are discussed repeatedly and at length are clues about the values of the organization's culture.

4. **Interpret stories and folklore surrounding the organization.** Look for similarities among stories told by different people. The subjects highlighted in recurring stories often reflect what is important to an organization's culture. For example, many of the stories that are repeated at Versatec, a Xerox subsidiary that makes graphic plotters for computers, involve their flamboyant cofounder, Renn Zaphiropoulos. According to company folklore, one of the very first things Renn did when the company was formed was to assemble the top management team at his home. They then devoted the weekend to handmaking a beautiful teak conference table around which all future decisions would be made. This table came to symbolize the importance of teamwork and maintaining high standards of performance, two essential qualities of the culture at Versatec. Try to identify who the heroes and villains are in the folklore company. What do they suggest about the culture's ideals? Returning to the Versatec story, when the company was eventually purchased by Xerox many employees expressed concern that Versatec's informal, play hard/work hard culture would be overwhelmed by the bureaucracy at Xerox. Renn rallied the employees to superior levels of performance by arguing that if they exceeded Xerox's expectations they would be left alone. Autonomy has remained a fixture of Versatec's culture long after Renn's retirement.

   It is also important to pay close attention to the basis for promotions and rewards. What do people see as the keys to getting ahead within the organization? What contributes to downfalls? These last two questions can yield important insights into the qualities and behaviors which the organization honors as well as the cultural taboos and behavioral land mines that can derail a career. For example, one project manager confided that a former colleague was sent to project management purgatory soon after publicly questioning the validity of a marketing report. From that point on, the project manager was extra careful to privately consult the marketing department whenever she had questions about their data.

With practice an observer can assess how strong the dominant culture of an organization is and the significance of subcultures and countercultures. Furthermore, learners can discern and identify where the culture of an organization stands on the 10 cultural dimensions presented earlier and, in essence, begin to build a cultural profile for a firm. Based on this profile, conclusions can be drawn about specific customs and norms that need to be adhered to as well as those behaviors and actions that violate the norms of a firm.

IMPLICATIONS OF ORGANIZATIONAL CULTURE FOR ORGANIZING PROJECTS

Project managers have to be able to operate in several, potentially diverse, organizational cultures. First, they have to interact with the culture of their parent organization as well as the subcultures of various departments (e.g., marketing, accounting). Second, they have to interact with the project's client or customer organizations. Finally, they have to interact in varying degrees with a host of other organizations connected to the project. These organizations include suppliers and vendors, subcontractors, consulting firms, government and regulatory agencies, and, in many cases, community groups. Many of these organizations are likely to have very different cultures. Project managers have to be able to read and speak the culture they are working in to develop strategies, plans, and responses that are likely to be understood and accepted. Still, the emphasis of this chapter is on the relationship between organizational culture and project management structure, and it is necessary to defer further discussion of these implications until Chapters 10–12, which focus on leadership, team building, and outsourcing.

Earlier we stated that we believe there are strong relationships among project management structure, organizational culture, and successful project management. To explore these relationships further, let us return to the dimensions that can be used to characterize the culture of an organization. When examining these dimensions we could hypothesize that certain aspects of the culture of an organization would support successful project management while other aspects would deter or interfere with effective management. Figure 3.7 attempts to identify which cultural characteristics create an environment conducive to completing most complex projects involving people from different disciplines.

Note that, in many cases, the ideal culture is not at either extreme. For example, a fertile project culture would likely be one in which management balances its focus on the needs of both the task and the people. An optimal culture would balance concern with output (ends) and processes to achieve those outcomes (means). In other cases, the ideal culture would be on one end of a dimension or the other. For example, because most projects require collaboration across disciplines, it would be desirable that the culture of the organization emphasize working in teams and identifying with the organization, not just the professional domain. Likewise, it is important that the culture support a certain degree of risk taking and a tolerance for constructive conflict.

One organization that appears to fit this ideal profile is 3M. 3M has received acclaim for creating an entrepreneurial culture within a large corporate framework. The essence of its culture is captured in phrases that have been chanted

FIGURE 3.7 *Cultural Dimensions of an Organization Supportive of Project Management*

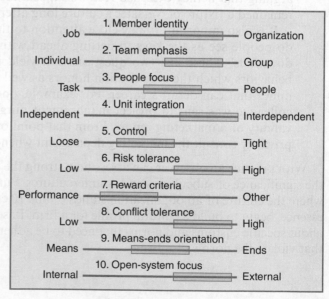

often by 3Mers throughout its history: "Encourage experimental doodling." "Hire good people and leave them alone." "If you put fences around people, you get sheep. Give people the room they need." Freedom and autonomy to experiment are reflected in the "15 percent rule," which encourages technical people to spend up to 15 percent of their time on projects of their own choosing and initiative. This fertile culture has contributed to 3M's branching out into more than 60,000 products and 35 separate business units (Collins & Porras, 1994).

The metaphor we choose to describe the relationship between organizational culture and project management is that of a riverboat trip. Culture is the river and the project is the boat. Organizing and completing projects within an organization in which the culture is conducive to project management is like paddling downstream: much less effort is required. In many cases, the current can be so strong that steering is all that is required. Such is the case for projects that operate in a project-friendly environment where team-work and cross-functional cooperation are the norms, where there is a deep commitment to excellence, and where healthy conflict is voiced and dealt with quickly and effectively.

Conversely, trying to complete a project in a toxic culture is like paddling upstream: much more time, effort, and attention are needed to reach the destination. This would be the situation in cultures that discourage teamwork and cooperation, that have a low tolerance for conflict, and where getting ahead is based less on performance and more on cultivating favorable relationships with superiors. In such cases, the project manager and her people not only have to overcome the natural obstacles of the project but also have to overcome the prevailing negative forces inherent in the culture of the organization.

The implications of this metaphor are important. Greater project authority and time are necessary to complete projects that encounter a strong, negative cultural current. Conversely, less formal authority and fewer dedicated resources are needed to complete projects in which the cultural currents generate behavior and cooperation essential to project success.

The key issue is the degree of interdependency between the parent organization and the project team. In cases where the prevalent organizational culture supports the behaviors essential to project completion, a weaker, more flexible project management structure can be effective. For example, one of the major reasons Chaparral Steel is able to use a functional matrix to successfully complete incremental projects is that its culture contains strong norms for cooperation (Bowen et al., 1994). See the Research Highlight: The Secret of Success for another example of how culture supports successful project management.

When the dominant organization culture inhibits collaboration and innovation, it is advisable to insulate the project team from the dominant culture. Here it becomes necessary to create a self-sufficient project team. If a dedicated project team is impossible because of resource constraints, then at least a project matrix should be used where the project manager has dominant control over the project. In both cases, the managerial strategy is to create a distinct team subculture in which a new set of norms, customs, and values evolve that will be conducive to project completion.

Under extreme circumstances this project culture could even represent a counterculture in that many of the norms and values are the antithesis of the dominant, parent culture. Such was the case when IBM decided to develop their personal computer quickly in 1980 (Smith & Reinertsen, 1995). They knew that the project could get bogged down by the overabundance of computer knowledge and bureaucracy in the company. They also realized that they would have to work closely with suppliers and make use of many non-IBM parts if they were to get to the market quickly. This was not the IBM way at the time, so IBM established the PC project team in a warehouse in Boca Raton, Florida, far from corporate headquarters and other corporate development facilities that existed within the organization.

Research Highlight

THE SECRET OF SUCCESS*

In *The Secret of Success: The Double Helix of Formal and Informal Structures in an R&D Laboratory* Polly Rizova revealed the results of a year-long investigation into the inner workings of a Fortune 500 R&D Lab. Through interviews with key participants and analysis of social networking data, Rizova assessed the efficacy of six high-tech development projects.

Four critical success factors emerged from her research. One element that is crucial to success is a heavy reliance on open and unrestricted patterns of communication, coupled with a low degree of formal reporting. In other words, team members freely interacted with each other regardless of title, experience, or discipline. A second key is having individuals on the project who are highly respected across the laboratory for their exceptional technical skills and experience. Similarly, it is also vital to have individuals involved in the project who are highly respected for their organizational expertise and experience. Having both "technical stars" and "organizational stars" on the project team were essential to success. The final factor is a strong and sustained support for the project from the company's corporate management. What's more, her analysis revealed interactive nature of the four conditions; namely that no one condition was likely to produce successful outcomes on its own, but only when put together in a way in which they reinforce each other. Here the culture of the laboratory was seen as the key catalyst.

Rizova describes a matrix system in which people work on multiple projects simultaneously but with a different wrinkle. Individuals occupy different positions and play different roles depending upon the project. For example, it is common for a senior engineer to be the manager of one project and a researcher on another that is led by his or her subordinate. In essence one must "boss" his or her own boss. At first glance this formal structure should create destructive tensions. However, Rizova argues that the organizational culture of the lab is the glue that keeps things running smoothly.

She described a culture in which the social norms of cooperation, respect, and civility are upheld and reproduced. It is a culture characterized by trust and a strong drive toward superior individual and organizational learning and achievement. The culture is captured in the comments of researchers:

> That is one of the nicest things around here. Your opinions are listened to. Superiors consider our advice. You will find that most of the projects here are a team effort.
>
> What I like most is the positive thinking and the "whatever it takes" attitude. Personality conflicts can be devastating. Here everyone helps you and supports you. There is no "I" in the word team.
>
> Very friendly environment. . . . I met new people and learned a lot from them. They do not mind sharing their expertise.

* Polly S. Rizova, *The Secret of Success: The Double Helix of Formal and Informal Structures in an R&D Laboratory* (Stanford, CA: Stanford University Press, 2007).

Summary

This chapter examined two major characteristics of the parent organization that affect the implementation and completion of projects. The first is the formal structure of the organization and how it chooses to organize and manage projects. Although the individual project manager may have very little say as to how the firm chooses to manage projects, he or she must be able to recognize the options available as well as the inherent strengths and weaknesses of different approaches.

Three basic project management structures were described and assessed as to their weaknesses and strengths. Only under unique circumstances can a case be made for managing a project within the normal functional hierarchy. When thinking only in terms of what is best for the project, the creation of an independent project team is clearly favored. However, the most effective project management system appropriately balances the needs of the project with those of the parent organization. Matrix structures emerged out of the parent organization's need to share personnel and resources across multiple projects and operations while creating legitimate project focus. The matrix approach is a hybrid organizational form that combines elements of both the functional and project team forms in an attempt to realize the advantages of both.

The second major characteristic of the parent organization that was discussed in this chapter is the concept of organizational culture. Organizational culture is the pattern of beliefs and expectations shared by an organization's members. Culture includes the behavioral norms, customs, shared values, and the "rules of the game" for getting along and getting ahead within the organization. It is important for project managers to be "culture sensitive" so that they can develop appropriate strategies and responses and avoid violating key norms that would jeopardize their effectiveness within the organization.

The interaction between project management structure and organizational culture is a complicated one. We have suggested that in certain organizations, culture encourages the implementation of projects. In this environment the project management structure used plays a less decisive role in the success of the project. Conversely, for other organizations in which the culture stresses internal competition and differentiation, just the opposite may be true. The prevailing norms, customs, and attitudes inhibit effective project management, and the project management structure plays a more decisive role in the successful implementation of projects. At a minimum, under adverse cultural conditions, the project manager needs to have significant authority over the project team; under more extreme conditions firms should physically relocate dedicated project teams to complete critical projects. In both cases, the managerial strategy should be to insulate project work from the dominant culture so that a more positive "subculture" can emerge among project participants.

The project management structure of the organization and the culture of the organization are major elements of the environment in which a project is initiated. Subsequent chapters will examine how project managers and professionals work within this environment to successfully complete projects.

Key Terms

Balanced matrix	Organizational culture	Strong matrix
Dedicated project team	Projectized organization	Weak matrix
Matrix	Project office (PO)	

Review Questions

1. What are the relative advantages and disadvantages of the functional, matrix, and dedicated team approaches to managing projects?
2. What distinguishes a weak matrix from a strong matrix?
3. Under what conditions would it be advisable to use a strong matrix instead of a dedicated project team?
4. How can project management offices (POs) support effective project management?
5. Why is it important to assess the culture of an organization before deciding what project management structure should be used to complete a project?
6. Other than culture, what other organizational factors should be used to determine which project management structure should be used?
7. What do you believe is more important for successfully completing a project—the formal project management structure or the culture of the parent organization?

Exercises

1. Going to college is analogous to working in a matrix environment in that most students take more than one class and must distribute their time across multiple classes. What problems does this situation create for you? How does it affect your performance? How could the system be better managed to make your life less difficult and more productive?
2. You work for LL Company, which manufactures high-end optical scopes for hunting rifles. LL Company has been the market leader for the past 20 years and has decided to diversify by applying its technology to develop a top-quality binocular. What kind of project management structure would you recommend they use for this project? What information would you like to have to make this recommendation, and why?
3. You work for Barbata Electronics. Your R&D people believe they have come up with an affordable technology that will double the capacity of existing MP3 players and uses audio format that is superior to MP3. The project is code named KYSO (Knock Your Socks Off). What kind of project management structure would you recommend they use for the KYSO project? What information would you like to have to make this recommendation and why?
4. This chapter discussed the role of values and beliefs in forming an organization's culture. The topic of organization culture is big business on the Internet. Many companies use their Web pages to describe their mission, vision, and corporate values and beliefs. There also are many consulting firms that advertise how they help organizations to change their culture. The purpose of this exercise is for you to obtain information pertaining to the organizational culture for two different companies. You can go about this task by very simply searching on the key words "organizational culture" or "corporate vision and values." This search will identify numerous companies for you to use to answer the following questions. You may want to select companies that you would like to work for in the future.
    a. What are the espoused values and beliefs of the companies?

    b. Use the worksheet in Figure 3.6 to assess the Web page. What does the Web page reveal about the culture of this organization? Would this culture be conducive to effective project management?

5. Use the cultural dimensions listed in Figure 3.5 to assess the culture of your school. Instead of employees, consider students, and instead of management, use faculty. For example, member identity refers to the degree to which students identify with the school as a whole rather than their major or option. Either as individuals or in small groups rate the culture of your school on the 10 dimensions.

    a. What dimensions were easy to evaluate and which ones were not?

    b. How strong is the culture of your school?

    c. What functions does the culture serve for your school?

    d. Do you think the culture of your school is best suited to maximizing your learning? Why or why not?

    e. What kind of projects would be easy to implement in your school and what kind of projects would be difficult given the structure and culture of your school? Explain your answer.

6. You work as an analyst in the marketing department for Springfield International (SI). SI uses a weak matrix to develop new services. Management has created an extremely competitive organizational culture that places an emphasis upon achieving results above everything else. One of the project managers that you have been assigned to help has been pressuring you to make his project your number one priority. He also wants you to expand the scope of your work on his project beyond what your marketing manager believes is necessary or appropriate. The project manager is widely perceived as a rising star within SI. Up to now you have been resisting the project manager's pressure and complying with your marketing manager's directives. However, your most recent interchange with the project manager ended by his saying, "I'm not happy with the level of help I am getting from you and I will remember this when I become VP of Marketing." How would you respond and why?

References

Block, T. R., and J. D. Frame, *The Project Office—A Key to Managing Projects Effectively* (Menlo Park, CA: Crisp Publications, 1998).

Block, T. R., and J. D. Frame, "Today's Project Office: Gauging Attitudes," *PM Network,* August 2001.

Bowen, H. K., K. B. Clark, C. A. Holloway, and S. C. Wheelwright, *The Perpetual Enterprise Machine* (New York: Oxford University Press, 1994).

Brown, S., and K. R. Eisenhardt, "Product Development: Past Research, Present Findings, and Future Directions," *Academy of Management Review,* 20 (2) 1995, pp. 343–78.

Cameron, K. S., and R. E. Quinn, *Diagnosing and Changing Organizational Culture: Based on the Competing Values Framework* (Upper Saddle River, NJ: Prentice Hall, 2011).

Carlton, J., *Apple: The Inside Story of Intrigue, Egomania, and Business Blunders* (New York: Random House, 1997), pp. 13–14.

Casey, W., and W. Peck, "Choosing the Right PMO Setup," *PM Network,* 15 (2) 2001, pp. 40–47.

Collins, J. C., and J. I. Porras, *Built to Last: The Successful Habits of Visionary Companies* (New York: HarperCollins, 1994), pp. 150–58.

Deal, T. E., and A. A. Kennedy, *Corporate Cultures: The Rites and Rituals of Corporate Life* (Reading, MA: Addison-Wesley, 1982).

De Laat, P. B., "Matrix Management of Projects and Power Struggles: A Case Study of an R&D Laboratory," *IEEE Engineering Management Review,* Winter 1995.

Filipczak, B., "Beyond the Gates of Microsoft," *Training,* September 1992, pp. 37–44.

Gallagher, R. S., *The Soul of an Organization: Understanding the Values That Drive Successful Corporate Cultures* (Chicago: Dearborn Trade Publishing, 2002).

Graham, R. J., and R. L. Englund, *Creating an Environment for Successful Projects: The Quest to Manage Project Management* (San Francisco: Jossey-Bass, 1997).

Gray, C., S. Dworatschek, D. H. Gobeli, H. Knoepfel, and E. W. Larson, "International Comparison of Project Organization Structures: Use and Effectiveness," *International Journal of Project Management,* vol. 8, no. 1, February 1990, pp. 26–32.

Harrison, M. T., and J. M. Beyer, *The Culture of Organizations* (Englewood Cliffs, NJ: Prentice Hall, 1993).

Hobbs, B., and P. Ménard, "Organizational Choices for Project Management," in Paul Dinsmore (ed.), *The AMA Handbook of Project Management* (New York: AMACOM, 1993).

Hobday, M., "The Project-Based Organization: An Ideal Form for Managing Complex Products and Systems?" *Research Policy,* vol. 29, no. 17, 2000.

Jassawalla, A. R., and H. C. Sashittal, "Cultures that Support Product-Innovation Processes," *Academy of Management Executive,* 15 (3) 2002, pp. 42–54.

Johnson, C. L., M. Smith, and L. K. Geary, *More Than My Share in All* (Washington, D.C.: Smithsonian Institute Publications, 1990).

Kerzner, H., *In Search of Excellence in Project Management* (New York: Von Nostrand Reinhold, 1997).

Kerzner, H., "Strategic Planning for the Project Office," *Project Management Journal,* 34 (2) 2003, pp. 13–25.

Larson, E. W., "Project Management Structures" in *The Wiley Handbook for Managing Projects,* P. Morris & J. Pinto (eds.) (New York: Wiley, 2004), pp. 48–66.

Larson, E. W., and D. H. Gobeli, "Matrix Management: Contradictions and Insights," *California Management Review,* vol. 29, no. 4, Summer 1987, p. 137.

Larson, E. W., and D. H. Gobeli, "Organizing for Product Development Projects," *Journal of Product Innovation Management,* vol. 5, 1988, pp. 180–90.

Larsson, U. (ed.), *Cultures of Creativity: The Centennial Exhibition of the Nobel Prize* (Canton, MA: Science History Publications, 2001).

Laslo, Z., and A. I. Goldberg, "Matrix Structures and Performance: The Search for Optimal Adjustments to Organizational Objectives?" *IEEE Transactions in Engineering Management,* vol. 48, no. 12, 2001.

Lawrence, P. R., and J. W. Lorsch, *Organization and Environment* (Homewood, IL: Irwin, 1969).

Majchrzak, A., and Q. Wang, "Breaking the Functional Mind-Set in Process Organizations," *Harvard Business Review,* Sept.–Oct. 1996, pp. 93–99.

Miller, J., *Lockheed Martin's Skunk Works* (New York: Speciality Publications, 1996).

Olson, E. M., O. C. Walker, Jr., and R. W. Ruekert, "Organizing for Effective New Product Development: The Moderating Role of Product Innovativeness," *Journal of Marketing,* vol. 59 (January), 1995, pp. 48–62.

O'Reilly, C. A., J. Chatman, and D. F. Caldwell, "People and Organizational Culture: A Profile Comparison Approach to Assessing Person-Organization Fit," *Academy of Management Journal,* vol. 34, no. 3, September 1991, pp. 487–516.

Pettegrew, A. M., "On Studying Organizational Culture," *Administrative Science Quarterly,* vol. 24, no. 4, 1979, pp. 570–81.

Powell, M., and J. Young, "The Project Management Support Office" in *The Wiley Handbook for Managing Projects,* P. Morris and J. Pinto (eds.) (New York: Wiley, 2004), pp. 937–69.

Rebello, K., "Inside Microsoft," *Business Weekly,* July 15, 1996, pp. 56–67.

Rizova, P., *The Secret of Success: The Double Helix of Formal and Informal Structures in an R&D Laboratory* (Stanford, CA: Stanford University Press, 2007).

Schein, E., *Organizational Culture and Leadership: A Dynamic View* (San Francisco, CA: Jossey-Bass, 2010).

Sculley, J., *Odyssey: Pepsi to Apple . . . A Journey of Adventure, Ideas, and the Future* (New York: Harper & Row, 1987), pp. 270–79.

Shenhar, A. J., "From Theory to Practice: Toward a Typology of Project Management Styles," *IEEE Transactions in Engineering Management,* 41 (1) 1998, pp. 33–48.

Shenhar, A. J., D. Dvir, T. Lechler, and M. Poli, "One Size Does Not Fit All—True for Projects, True for Frameworks," *Frontiers of Project Management Research and Application,* Proceedings of PMI Research Conference, Seattle, 2002, pp. 99–106.

Smith, P. G., and D. G. Reinertsen, *Developing Products in Half the Time* (New York: Van Nostrand Reinhold, 1995).

Stuckenbruck, L. C., *Implementation of Project Management* (Upper Darby, PA: Project Management Institute, 1981).

Youker, R., "Organizational Alternatives for Project Management," *Project Management Quarterly,* vol. 8, March 1977, pp. 24–33.

CASE 3.1

Moss and McAdams Accounting Firm

Bruce Palmer had worked for Moss and McAdams (M&M) for six years and was just promoted to account manager. His first assignment was to lead an audit of Johnsonville Trucks. He was quite pleased with the five accountants who had been assigned to his team, especially Zeke Olds. Olds was an Army vet who returned to school to get a double major in accounting and computer sciences. He was on top of the latest developments in financial information systems and had a reputation for coming up with innovative solutions to problems.

M&M was a well-established regional accounting firm with 160 employees located across six offices in Minnesota and Wisconsin. The main office, where Palmer worked, was in Green Bay, Wisconsin. In fact, one of the founding members, Seth Moss, played briefly for the hometown NFL Packers during the late 1950s. M&M's primary services were corporate audits and tax preparation. Over the last two years the partners decided to move more aggressively into the consulting business. M&M projected that consulting would represent 40 percent of their growth over the next five years.

M&M operated within a matrix structure. As new clients were recruited, a manager was assigned to the account. A manager might be assigned to several accounts, depending on the size and scope of the work. This was especially true in the case of tax preparation projects, where it was not uncommon for a manager to be assigned to 8 to 12 clients. Likewise, senior and staff accountants were assigned to multiple account teams. Ruby Sands was the office manager responsible for assigning personnel to different accounts at the Green Bay office. She did her best to assign staff to multiple projects under the same manager. This wasn't always possible, and sometimes accountants had to work on projects led by different managers.

M&M, like most accounting firms, had a tiered promotion system. New CPAs entered as junior or staff accountants. Within two years, their performance was reviewed and they were either asked to leave or promoted to senior accountant. Sometime during their fifth or sixth year, a decision was made to promote them to account manager. Finally, after 10 to 12 years with the firm, the manager was considered for promotion to partner. This was a very competitive position. During the last five years, only 20 percent of account managers at M&M had been promoted to partner. However, once a partner, they were virtually guaranteed the position for life and enjoyed significant increases in salary, benefits, and prestige. M&M had a reputation for being a results-driven organization; partner promotions were based on meeting deadlines, retaining clients, and generating revenue. The promotion team based its decision on the relative performance of the account manager in comparison to his or her cohorts.

One week into the Johnsonville audit, Palmer received a call from Sands to visit her office. There he was introduced to Ken Crosby, who recently joined M&M after working nine years for a Big 5 accounting firm. Crosby was recruited to manage special consulting projects. Sands reported that Crosby had just secured a major consulting project with Springfield Metals. This was a major coup for the firm: M&M had competed against two Big 5 accounting firms for the project. Sands went on to explain that she was working with Crosby to put together his team. Crosby insisted that Zeke Olds be assigned to his team. Sands told him that this would be impossible because Olds was already assigned to work on the Johnsonville audit. Crosby persisted, arguing that Olds's expertise was essential to the Springfield project. Sands decided to work out a compromise and have Olds split time across both projects.

At this time Crosby turned to Palmer and said, "I believe in keeping things simple. Why don't we agree that Olds works for me in the mornings and you in the afternoons. I'm sure we can work out any problems that come up. After all, we both work for the same firm."

SIX WEEKS LATER

Palmer could scream whenever he remembered Crosby's words, "After all, we both work for the same firm." The first sign of trouble came during the first week of the new arrangement when Crosby called, begging to have Olds work all of Thursday on his project. They were conducting an extensive client visit, and Olds was critical to the assessment. After Palmer reluctantly agreed, Crosby said he owed him one. The next week when Palmer called Crosby to request that he return the favor, Crosby flatly refused and said any other time but not this week. Palmer tried again a week later and got the same response.

At first Olds showed up promptly at 1:00 P.M. at Palmer's office to work on the audit. Soon it became a habit to show up 30 to 60 minutes late. There was always a good reason. He was in a meeting in Springfield and couldn't just leave, or an urgent task took longer than planned. One time it was because Crosby took his entire team out to lunch at the new Thai restaurant—Olds was over an hour late because of slow service. In the beginning Olds would usually make up the time by working after hours, but Palmer could tell from conversations he overheard that this was creating tension at home.

What probably bothered Palmer the most were the e-mails and telephone calls Olds received from Crosby and his team members during the afternoons when he was supposed to be working for Palmer. A couple of times Palmer could have sworn that Olds was working on Crosby's project in his (Palmer's) office.

Palmer met with Crosby to talk about the problem and voice his complaints. Crosby acted surprised and even a little bit hurt. He promised things would change, but the pattern continued.

Palmer was becoming paranoid about Crosby. He knew that Crosby played golf with Olds on the weekends and could just imagine him badmouthing the Johnsonville project and pointing out how boring auditing work was. The sad fact was that there probably was some truth to what he was saying. The Johnsonville project was getting bogged down, and the team was slipping behind schedule. One of the contributing factors was Olds's performance. His work was not up to its usual standards. Palmer approached Olds about this, and Olds became defensive. Olds later apologized and confided that he found it difficult switching his thinking from consulting to auditing and then back to consulting. He promised to do better, and there was a slight improvement in his performance.

The last straw came when Olds asked to leave work early on Friday so that he could take his wife and kids to a Milwaukee Brewers baseball game. It turned out Springfield Metals had given Crosby their corporate tickets, and he decided to treat his team with box seats right behind the Brewers dugout. Palmer hated to do it, but he had to refuse the request. He felt guilty when he overheard Olds explaining to his son on the telephone why they couldn't go to the game.

Palmer finally decided to pick up the phone and request an urgent meeting with Sands to resolve the problem. He got up enough nerve and put in the call only to be told that Sands wouldn't be back in the office until next week. As he put the receiver down, he thought maybe things would get better.

TWO WEEKS LATER

Sands showed up unexpectedly at Palmer's office and said they needed to talk about Olds. Palmer was delighted, thinking that now he could tell her what had been going on. But before he had a chance to speak, Sands told him that Olds had come to see her yesterday. She told him that Olds confessed that he was having a hard time working on both Crosby's and Palmer's projects. He was having difficulty concentrating on the auditing work in the afternoon because he was thinking about some of the consulting issues that had emerged during the morning. He was putting in extra hours to try to meet both of the projects' deadlines, and this was creating problems at home. The bottom line was that he was stressed out and couldn't deal with the situation. He asked that he be assigned full-time to Crosby's project. Sands went on to say that Olds didn't blame Palmer, in fact he had a lot of nice things to say about him. He just enjoyed the consulting work more and found it more challenging. Sands concluded by saying, "I told him I understood, and I would talk to you about the situation and see what could be done. Frankly, I think we should pull him from your project and have him work full-time on Crosby's project. What do you think?"

1. If you were Palmer at the end of the case, how would you respond?
2. What, if anything, could Palmer have done to avoid losing Olds?
3. What advantages and disadvantages of a matrix type organization are apparent from this case?
4. What could the management at M&M do to more effectively manage situations like this?

CASE 3.2

Horizon Consulting

Patti Smith looked up at the bright blue Carolina sky before she entered the offices of Horizon Consulting. Today was Friday, which meant she needed to prepare for the weekly status report meeting. Horizon Consulting is a **custom software development company** that offers fully integrated **mobile application services** for **iPhone™, Android™, Windows Mobile®** and **BlackBerry®** platforms. Horizon was founded by James Thrasher, a former Marketing executive, who quickly saw the potential for digital marketing via smartphones. Horizon enjoyed initial success in sports marketing, but quickly expanded to other industries. A key to their success was the decline in cost for developing smartphone applications which expanded the client base. The decline in cost was primarily due to learning curve and ability to build customized solutions on established platforms.

Patti Smith was a late bloomer who went back to college after working in the restaurant business for nine years. She and her former husband had tried unsuccessfully to operate a vegetarian restaurant in Golden, Colorado. After her divorce, she returned to University of Colorado where she majored in Management Information Systems with a minor in Marketing. While she enjoyed her marketing classes much more than her MIS classes, she felt the IT know-how acquired would give her an advantage in the job market. This turned out to be true as Horizon hired her to be an Account Manager soon after graduation.

Patti Smith was hired to replace Stephen Stills who had started the restaurant side of the business at Horizon. Stephen was "let go" according to one Account Manager for being a *prima donna* and hoarding resources. Patti's clients ranged from high-end restaurants to hole in wall Mom and Pop shops. She helped develop smartphone apps that let users make reservations, browse menus, receive alerts on daily specials, provide customer feedback, order take-out and in some cases order delivery. As an Account Manager she worked with clients to assess their needs, develop a plan, and create customized smartphone apps.

Horizon appeared to be a good fit for Patti. She had enough technical training to be able to work with software engineers and help guide them to produce client-ready products. At the same time she could relate to the restaurateurs and enjoyed working with them on web design and digital marketing.

Horizon was organized into three departments: Sales, Software Development, and Graphics, with Account Managers acting as project managers. Account Managers generally came from Sales, and would divide their time between projects and making sales pitches to potential new clients. Horizon employed a core group of software engineers and designers, supplemented by contracted programmers when needed.

The first step in developing a smartphone application involved the Account Manager meeting with the client to define the requirements and vision for the application. The Account Manager would then work with a Graphic User Interface (GUI) designer to come up with a preliminary story board of how the application would function and look. Once the initial concept and requirements were approved the Account Manager was assigned two pairs of software engineers. The first pair (app engineers) would work on the smartphone side of the application while the second pair would work on the client side of the application. Horizon preferred to have software engineers work in tandem so they could check each other's work. The two app engineers would typically work full time on the application until it was completed while the other engineers would work on multiple projects as needed. Likewise, GUI designers would work on the project at certain key stages in the product development cycle when their expertise was needed.

The head of Graphics manages the GUI designers' schedule while the head of Software manages the software engineer assignments. At the end of each project Account Managers submitted performance reviews of their team. The Director of Sales was responsible for the Account Managers' performance reviews based on customer satisfaction, generation of sales, and project performance.

Horizon believed in iterative development and every two to three weeks Account Managers were expected to demonstrate the latest version of applications to clients. This led to useful feedback and in many cases redefining the scope of the project. Often clients wanted to add more functionality to their application once they realized what the software could do. Depending upon the complexity of the application and changes introduced once the project was under way, it typically took Horizon two to four months to deliver a finished product to a client.

Patti was currently working on three projects. One was for Shanghai Wok, a busy Chinese mom and pop restaurant located in downtown Charlotte, North Carolina. The owners of Shanghai Wok wanted Horizon to create a smartphone app that would allow customers to order and pay in advance for meals they would simply pick up at a walk-up window. The second project was for Taste of India that operated in Kannapolis, North Carolina. They wanted Horizon to create a phone app that would allow staff at the nearby bio-tech firms to order food that would be delivered on-site during lunch and dinner hours. The last project was for Nearly Normal, a vegetarian restaurant which wanted to send out e-mail alerts to subscribers that would describe in detail their daily fresh specials.

James Thrasher was an admirer of Google and encouraged a playful but focused environment at work. Employees were allowed to decorate their work spaces, bring pets to work, and play ping pong or pool when they needed a break. Horizon paid its employees well but the big payoff was the annual Christmas bonus. This bonus was based on overall company profits, which were distributed proportionately based on pay grade and performance reviews. It was not uncommon for employees to receive a 10–15 percent boost in pay at the end of the year.

STATUS REPORT MEETING

As was her habit Patti entered the status report meeting room early. David Briggs was in the midst of describing the game-winning catch John Lorsch had made in last night's softball game. Horizon sponsored a co-ed city league softball team which most of the Account Managers played on. Patti had been coaxed to play to ensure that the requisite number of "females" were on the field. She balked at the idea at first; softball wasn't really her sport, but she was glad she did. Not only was it fun, but it gave her a chance to get to know the other managers.

James Thrasher entered the room and everyone settled down to business. He started off as he always did by asking if anybody had important news to bring to everyone's attention. Jackson Browne slowly raised his hand and said, "I am afraid I do. I just received notification from Apple IOS that they have rejected our TAT app." TAT was a phone app that Jackson was the project lead on that allowed subscribers to reserve and see in real time what swimming lanes were available at a prestigious athletic club. This announcement was followed by a collective groan. Before an Apple app could go operational it had to be submitted and approved by Apple. Usually this was not a problem, but lately Apple had been rejecting apps for a variety of reasons. Jackson went on to circulate the list of changes that had to be made before Apple would approve the app. The group studied the list, and in some cases ridiculed the new requirements.

Ultimately, James Thrasher asked Jackson how long it would take to make the necessary changes and resubmit the app for approval. Jackson felt it would probably take two to three weeks at most. Thrasher asked who the engineers that worked on this project were. Patti's heart fell. One of the app engineers who had developed the TAT app was working on her Shanghai Wok project. She knew what was going to happen next. Thrasher announced, "OK everyone, it only makes sense that these engineers are the best ones to finish what they had started so they are all going to have to be reassigned back to the TAT project. Those affected are going to have to get together after this meeting and figure how you are going to replace them." The meeting then proceeded as planned with each account manager reporting the status of their projects, and sharing relevant issues with the group.

POST-MEETING

As everyone filed out, Patti looked around to see who else was in her same boat. There were three other Account Managers as well as Jackson Browne. Resource assignments were a reoccurring issue at Horizon given the nature of their work. Horizon had developed a policy where decisions were made based on project priority. Each project was assigned a Green, Blue or Purple designation based on the company priority. Priority status was based on the extent the project contributed to the mission of the firm. The Shanghai Wok project given its limited size and scope was a Purple project, which was the lowest ranking. The list of available software engineers was displayed on the big screen. Patti was only familiar with a few of the names.

Leigh Taylor who had the only Green project immediately selected Jason Wheeler from the list. She had used him before and was confident in his work. Tom Watson and Samantha Stewart both had Blue Projects and both needed to replace a mobile app engineer. They both immediately jumped on the name of Prem Mathew, claiming he was the best person for their project. After some friendly jousting, Tom said, "OK, Sam, you can have him; I remember when you helped me out on the Argos project; besides my project is just beginning. I'll take Shin Chen." Everyone looked at Patti; she started by saying, "You know, I am only familiar with a few of these names; I guess I'll go with Mike Thu." Jackson interjected, "Hey everyone, I am really sorry this happened, and I am sure Mike is a good programmer, but I recommend you work with Axel Gerthoff. I have used him before, and he is a very quick study and a joy to work with." This was a relief to Patti and she quickly took his advice. They left to submit a report to Thrasher detailing the decisions they each had made and the impact on their project.

1. How successful was the post-meeting?
2. What factors contributed to the success or failure of this meeting?
3. What kind of project management structure does Horizon use? Is it the right structure? Explain.

4

DEFINING THE PROJECT

Select a dream
Use your dream to set a goal
Create a plan
Consider resources

> *E*nhance skills and abilities
> *S*pend time wisely
> *S*tart! Get organized and go
>
> *. . . it is one of those acro-whatevers, said Pooh.* *

Project managers in charge of a single small project can plan and schedule the project tasks without much formal planning and information. However, when the project manager must manage several small projects or a large complex project, a threshold is quickly reached in which the project manager can no longer cope with the detail.

This chapter describes a disciplined, structured method for selectively collecting information to use through all phases of the project life cycle, to meet the needs of all stakeholders (e.g., customer, project manager), and to measure performance against the strategic plan of the organization. The method suggested is a selective outline of the project called the *work breakdown structure*. The early stages of developing the outline serve to ensure that all tasks are identified and that participants of the project have an understanding of what is to be done. Once the outline and its detail are defined, an integrated information system can be developed to schedule work and allocate budgets. This baseline information is later used for control.

In addition, the chapter presents a variant of the work breakdown structure called the *process breakdown structure* as well as responsibility matrices that are used for smaller, less complex projects. With the work of the project defined through the *work breakdown structure,* the chapter concludes with the process of creating a communication plan used to help coordinate project activities and follow progress.

The five generic steps described herein provide a structured approach for collecting the project information necessary for developing a work breakdown structure. These steps and the development of project networks found in the next chapters all take place concurrently, and several iterations are typically required to develop dates and budgets that can be used to manage the project. The old saying "We can control only what we have planned" is true; therefore, defining the project is the first step.

STEP 1: DEFINING THE PROJECT SCOPE

Defining the project scope sets the stage for developing a project plan. Project scope is a definition of the end result or mission of your project—a product or service for your client/customer. The primary purpose is to define as clearly as possible the deliverable(s) for the end user and to focus project plans. As fundamental and essential as scope definition appears, it is frequently overlooked by project leaders of well-managed, large corporations.

Research clearly shows that a poorly defined scope or mission is the most frequently mentioned barrier to project success. In a study involving more than 1,400 project managers in the United States and Canada, Gobeli and Larson (1986) found that approximately 50 percent of the planning problems relate to unclear definition of scope and goals. This and other studies suggest a strong correlation between project success and clear scope definition (cf., Ashley et al., 1987; Pinto and Slevin, 1988; Standish Group, 2009). The scope document directs focus on the project purpose throughout the life of the project for the customer and project participants.

---

* Roger E. Allen and Stephen D. Allen, *Winnie-the-Pooh on Success* (New York: Penguin, 1997), p. 10.

The scope should be developed under the direction of the project manager, customer, and other significant stakeholders. The project manager is responsible for seeing that there is agreement with the owner on project objectives, deliverables at each stage of the project, technical requirements, and so forth. For example, a deliverable in the early stage might be specifications; for the second stage, three prototypes for production; for the third, a sufficient quantity to introduce to market; and finally, marketing promotion and training.

Your project scope definition is a document that will be published and used by the project owner and project participants for planning and measuring project success. *Scope* describes what you expect to deliver to your customer when the project is complete. Your project scope should define the results to be achieved in specific, tangible, and measurable terms.

Employing a Project Scope Checklist

Clearly, project scope is the keystone interlocking all elements of a project plan. To ensure that scope definition is complete, you may wish to use the following checklist:

Project Scope Checklist

1. Project objective
2. Deliverables
3. Milestones
4. Technical requirements
5. Limits and exclusions
6. Reviews with customer
---

1. **Project objective.** The first step of project scope definition is to define the overall objective to meet your customer's need(s). For example, as a result of extensive market research a computer software company decides to develop a program that automatically translates verbal sentences in English to Russian. The project should be completed within three years at a cost not to exceed $1.5 million. Another example is to design and produce a completely portable, hazardous waste, thermal treatment system in 13 months at a cost not to exceed $13 million. The project objective answers the questions of what, when, and how much.

2. **Deliverables.** The next step is to define major deliverables—the expected, measurable outputs over the life of the project. For example, deliverables in the early design phase of a project might be a list of specifications. In the second phase deliverables could be software coding and a technical manual. The next phase could be the prototype. The final phase could be final tests and approved software. Note: Deliverables and requirements are often used interchangeably.

3. **Milestones.** A milestone is a significant event in a project that occurs at a point in time. The milestone schedule shows only major segments of work; it represents first, rough-cut estimates of time, cost, and resources for the project. The milestone schedule is built using the deliverables as a platform to identify major segments of work and an end date—for example, testing complete and finished by July 1 of the same year. Milestones should be natural, important control points in the project. Milestones should be easy for all project participants to recognize.

4. **Technical requirements.** More frequently than not, a product or service will have technical requirements to ensure proper performance. Technical requirements typically clarify either

the deliverables or define the performance specifications. For example, a technical requirement for a personal computer might be the ability to accept 120-volt alternating current or 240-volt direct current without any adapters or user switches. Another well-known example is the ability of 911 emergency systems to identify the caller's phone number and location of the phone. Examples from information systems projects include speed and capacity of database systems and connectivity with alternative systems. For understanding the importance of key requirements, see Snapshot from Practice: Big Bertha.

5. **Limits and exclusions.** The limits of scope should be defined. Failure to do so can lead to false expectations and to expending resources and time on the wrong problem. Examples of limits are: local air transportation to and from base camps will be outsourced; system maintenance and repair will be done only up to one month after final inspection; client will be billed for additional training beyond that prescribed in the contract. Exclusions further define the boundary of the project by stating what is not included. Examples include: data will be collected by the client, not the contractor; a house will be built, but no landscaping or security devices added; software will be installed, but no training given.

6. **Reviews with customer.** Completion of the scope checklist ends with a review with your customer—internal or external. The main concern here is the understanding and agreement of expectations. Is the customer getting what he or she desires in deliverables? Does the project definition identify key accomplishments, budgets, timing, and performance requirements? Are questions of limits and exclusions covered? Clear communication in all these issues is imperative to avoid claims or misunderstanding.

Scope definition should be as brief as possible but complete; one or two pages are typical for small projects. See Snapshot from Practice: Scope Statement as below.

SNAPSHOT FROM PRACTICE
Scope Statement

PROJECT OBJECTIVE

To construct a high-quality, custom home within five months at cost not to exceed $500,000.

DELIVERABLES

- A 2,200-square-foot, 2½-bath, 3-bedroom, finished home.
- A finished garage, insulated and sheetrocked.
- Kitchen appliances to include range, oven, microwave, and dishwasher.
- High-efficiency gas furnace with programmable thermostat.

MILESTONES

1. Permits approved—March 5
2. Foundation poured—March 14
3. Drywall in. Framing, sheathing, plumbing, electrical, and mechanical inspections passed—May 25
4. Final inspection—June 7

TECHNICAL REQUIREMENTS

1. Home must meet local building codes.
2. All windows and doors must pass NFRC class 40 energy ratings.
3. Exterior wall insulation must meet an "R" factor of 21.
4. Ceiling insulation must meet an "R" factor of 38.
5. Floor insulation must meet an "R" factor of 25.
6. Garage will accommodate two large-size cars and one 20-foot Winnebago.
7. Structure must pass seismic stability codes.

LIMITS AND EXCLUSIONS

1. The home will be built to the specifications and design of the original blueprints provided by the customer.
2. Owner is responsible for landscaping.
3. Refrigerator is not included among kitchen appliances.
4. Air conditioning is not included but prewiring is included.
5. Contractor reserves the right to contract out services.
6. Contractor is responsible for subcontracted work.
7. Site work limited to Monday through Friday, 8:00 A.M. to 6:00 P.M.

CUSTOMER REVIEW

John and Joan Smith

The checklist on pages 150–152 is generic. Different industries and companies will develop unique checklists and templates to fit their needs and specific kinds of projects. A few companies engaged in contracted work refer to scope statements as "statements of work" (SOW). Other organizations use the term *project charter*. However, the term **project charter** has emerged to have a special meaning in the world of project management. A project charter refers to a document that authorizes the project manager to initiate and lead the project. This document is issued by upper management and provides the project manager with written authority to use organizational resources for project activities. Often the charter will include a brief scope description as well as such items as risk limits, customer needs, spending limits, and even team composition.

Many projects suffer from **scope creep,** which is the tendency for the project scope to expand over time—usually by changing requirements, specifications, and priorities. Scope creep can be reduced by carefully writing your scope statement. A scope statement that is too broad is an invitation for scope creep. Scope creep can have a positive or negative effect on the project, but in most cases scope creep means added costs and possible project delays. Changes in requirements, specifications, and priorities frequently result in cost overruns and delays. Examples are abundant—Denver airport baggage handling system; Boston's new freeway system ("The Big Dig"); China's fast train in Shanghai; and the list goes on. On software development projects, scope creep is manifested in bloated products in which added functionality undermines ease of use.

If the project scope needs to change, it is critical to have a sound change control process in place that records the change and keeps a log of all project changes. The log identifies the change, impact, and those responsible for accepting or rejecting a proposed change.

Change control is one of the topics of Chapter 7. Project managers in the field constantly suggest that dealing with changing requirements is one of their most challenging problems.

STEP 2: ESTABLISHING PROJECT PRIORITIES

Quality and the ultimate success of a project are traditionally defined as meeting and/or exceeding the expectations of the customer and/or upper management in terms of cost (budget), time (schedule), and performance (scope) of the project (see Figure 4.1). The interrelationship among these criteria varies. For example, sometimes it is necessary to compromise the performance and scope of the project to get the project done quickly or less expensively. Often the longer a project takes, the more expensive it becomes. However, a positive correlation between cost and schedule may not always be true. Other times project costs can be reduced by using cheaper, less efficient labor or equipment that extends the duration of the project. Likewise, as will be seen in Chapter 9, project managers are often forced to expedite or "crash" certain key activities by adding additional labor, thereby raising the original cost of the project.

FIGURE 4.1 *Project Management Trade-offs*

One of the primary jobs of a project manager is to manage the trade-offs among time, cost, and performance. To do so, project managers must define and understand the nature of the priorities of the project. They need to have a candid discussion with the project customer and upper management to establish the relative importance of each criterion. For example, what happens when the customer keeps adding requirements? Or if, midway through the project, a trade-off must be made between cost and expediting, which criterion has priority?

One technique found in practice that is useful for this purpose is completing a **priority matrix** for the project to identify which criterion is constrained, which should be enhanced, and which can be accepted:

Constrain. The original parameter is fixed. The project must meet the completion date, specifications and scope of the project, or budget.

Enhance. Given the scope of the project, which criterion should be optimized? In the case of time and cost, this usually means taking advantage of opportunities to either reduce costs or shorten the schedule. Conversely, with regard to performance, enhancing means adding value to the project.

Accept. For which criterion is it tolerable not to meet the original parameters? When trade-offs have to be made, is it permissible for the schedule to slip, to reduce the scope and performance of the project, or to go over budget?

Figure 4.2 displays the priority matrix for the development of a new wireless modem. Because *time* to market is important to sales, the project manager is instructed to take advantage of every opportunity to reduce completion time. In doing so, going over *budget* is acceptable though not desirable. At the same time, the original *performance* specifications for the modem as well as reliability standards cannot be compromised.

Priorities vary from project to project. For example, for many software projects time to market is critical, and companies like Microsoft may defer original scope requirements to later versions in order to get to the market first. Alternatively, for special event projects (conferences, parades, tournaments) time is constrained once the date has been announced, and if the budget is tight, the project manager will compromise the scope of the project in order to complete the project on time.

Some would argue that all three criteria are always constrained and that good project managers should seek to optimize each criterion. If everything goes well on a project and no major problems or setbacks are encountered, their argument may be valid. However, this situation is rare, and project managers are often forced to make tough decisions that benefit one criterion while compromising the other two. The purpose of this exercise is to define and agree on what the

FIGURE 4.2 *Project Priority Matrix*

priorities and constraints of the project are so that when "push comes to shove," the right decisions can be made.

There are likely to be natural limits to the extent managers can constrain, optimize, or accept any one criterion. It may be acceptable for the project to slip one month behind schedule but no further or to exceed the planned budget by as much as $20,000. Likewise, it may be desirable to finish a project a month early, but after that cost conservation should be the primary goal. Some project managers document these limits as part of creating the priority matrix.

In summary, developing a priority matrix for a project *before the project begins* is a useful exercise. It provides a forum for clearly establishing priorities with customers and top management so as to create shared expectations and avoid misunderstandings. The priority information is essential to the planning process, where adjustments can be made in the scope, schedule, and budget allocation. Finally, the matrix is useful midway in the project for approaching a problem that must be solved.

One caveat must be mentioned; during the course of a project, priorities may change. The customer may suddenly need the project completed one month sooner, or new directives from top management may emphasize cost saving initiatives. The project manager needs to be vigilant in order to anticipate and confirm changes in priorities and make appropriate adjustments.

STEP 3: CREATING THE WORK BREAKDOWN STRUCTURE

Major Groupings Found in a WBS

Once the scope and deliverables have been identified, the work of the project can be successively subdivided into smaller and smaller work elements. The outcome of this hierarchical process is called the **work breakdown structure (WBS).** Use of WBS helps to assure project managers that all products and work elements are identified, to integrate the project with the current organization, and to establish a basis for control. Basically, the WBS is an outline of the project with different levels of detail.

Figure 4.3 shows the major groupings commonly used in the field to develop a hierarchical WBS. The WBS begins with the project as the final deliverable. Major project work deliverables/ systems are identified first; then the subdeliverables necessary to accomplish the larger deliverables

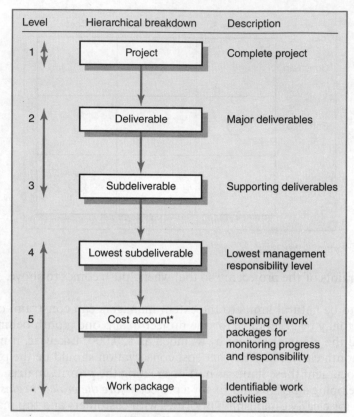

* This breakdown groups work packages by type of work within a deliverable and allows assignment of responsibility to an organizational unit. This extra step facilitates a system for monitoring project progress (discussed in Chapter 13).

FIGURE 4.3 *Hierarchical Breakdown of the WBS*

are defined. The process is repeated until the subdeliverable detail is small enough to be manageable and where one person can be responsible. This subdeliverable is further divided into work packages. Because the lowest subdeliverable usually includes several work packages, the work packages are grouped by type of work—for example, design and testing. These groupings within a subdeliverable are called cost accounts. This grouping facilitates a system for monitoring project progress by work, cost, and responsibility.

How WBS Helps the Project Manager

The WBS defines all the elements of the project in a hierarchical framework and establishes their relationships to the project end item(s). Think of the project as a large work package that is successively broken down into smaller work packages; the total project is the summation of all the smaller work packages. This hierarchical structure facilitates evaluation of cost, time, and technical performance at all levels in the organization over the life of the project. The WBS also provides management with information appropriate to each level. For example, top management deals primarily with major deliverables, while first-line supervisors deal with smaller subdeliverables and work packages.

Each item in the WBS needs a time and cost estimate. With this information it is possible to plan, schedule, and budget your project. The WBS also serves as a framework for tracking cost and work performance.

As the WBS is developed, organizational units and individuals are assigned responsibility for executing work packages. This integrates the work and the organization. In practice, this process is sometimes called the organization breakdown structure (OBS), which will be further discussed later in the chapter.

Use of the WBS provides the opportunity to "roll up" (sum) the budget and actual costs of the smaller work packages into larger work elements so that performance can be measured by organizational units and work accomplishment.

The WBS can also be used to define communication channels and assist in understanding and coordinating many parts of the project. The structure shows the work and organizational units responsible and suggests where written communication should be directed. Problems can be quickly addressed and coordinated because the structure integrates work and responsibility.

A Simple WBS Development

Figure 4.4 shows a simplified WBS to develop a new prototype tablet computer. At the top of the chart (level 1) is the project end item—the E-Slim Tablet x-13 Prototype. The subdeliverables levels (2–5) below level 1 represent further decomposition of work. The levels of the structure can also represent information for different levels of management. For example, level 1 information represents the total project objective and is useful to top management; levels 2, 3, and 4 are suitable for middle management; and level 5 is for first-line managers.

In Figure 4.4 level 2 indicates there are two major deliverables—Hardware and CPU, or central processing unit. (There are likely to be other major deliverables such as software, but for illustrative purposes we are limiting our focus to just two major deliverables.) At level 3, the CPU is connected to three deliverables—Power Supply, Flash ROM, and I/O Controller. The I/O Controller has three subdeliverables at level 4—USB Slots, Internet, and Touch Screen. The many subdeliverables for USB Slots and Internet have not been decomposed. The Touch Screen (shaded) has been decomposed down to level 5 and to the work package level.

Note that level 2, Hardware, skips levels 3 and 4 because the final subdeliverables can be pushed down to the lowest manageable level 5; skipping levels 3 and 4 suggests little coordination is needed and skilled team members are already familiar with the work needed to complete the level 5 subdeliverables. For example, Hardware requires four subdeliverables at level 5—Frame, Cameras, Speakers, and Antenna. Each subdeliverable includes work packages that will be completed by an assigned organizational unit. Observe that the Cameras subdeliverable includes four work packages—WP-C1, 2, 3, and 4. The Back Light, a subdeliverable of Touch Screen, includes three work packages—WP-L 1, 2, and 3.

The lowest level of the WBS is called a **work package.** Work packages are short-duration tasks that have a definite start and stop point, consume resources, and represent cost. Each work package is a control point. A work package manager is responsible for seeing that the package is completed on time, within budget, and according to technical specifications. Practice suggests a work package should not exceed 10 workdays or one reporting period. If a work package has a duration exceeding 10 days, check or monitoring points should be established within the duration, say, every three to five days, so progress and problems can be identified before too much time has passed. Each work package of the WBS should be as independent of other packages of the project as possible. No work package is described in more than one subdeliverable of the WBS.

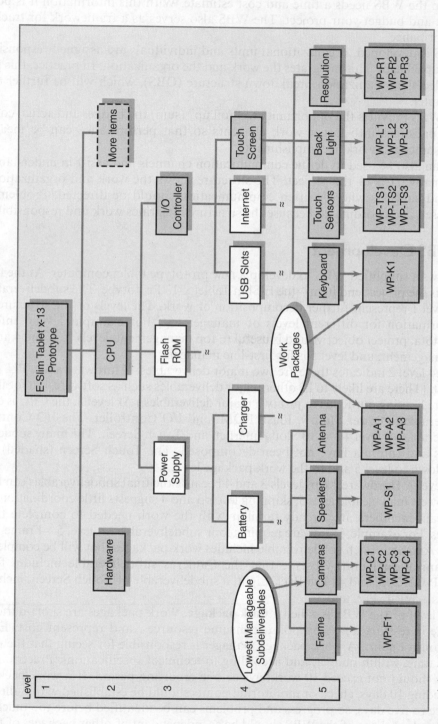

FIGURE 4.4 Work Breakdown Structure

There is an important difference from start to finish between the last work breakdown subdeliverable and a work package. Typically, a work breakdown subdeliverable includes the outcomes of more than one work package from perhaps two or three departments. Therefore, the subdeliverable does not have a duration of its own and does not consume resources or cost money directly. (In a sense, of course, a duration for a particular work breakdown element can be derived from identifying which work package must start first [earliest] and which package will be the latest to finish; the difference from start to finish becomes the duration for the subdeliverable.) The higher elements are used to identify deliverables at different phases in the project and to develop status reports during the execution stage of the project life cycle. Thus, the work package is the basic unit used for planning, scheduling, and controlling the project.

To review, each work package in the WBS

1. Defines work (what).
2. Identifies time to complete a work package (how long).
3. Identifies a time-phased budget to complete a work package (cost).
4. Identifies resources needed to complete a work package (how much).
5. Identifies a single person responsible for units of work (who).
6. Identifies monitoring points for measuring progress (how well).

Creating a WBS from scratch can be a daunting task. Project managers should take advantage of relevant examples from previous projects to begin the process.

WBSs are products of group efforts. If the project is small, the entire project team may be involved breaking down the project into its components. For large, complex projects, the people responsible for the major deliverables are likely to meet to establish the first two levels of deliverables. In turn, further detail would be delegated to the people responsible for the specific work. Collectively this information would be gathered and integrated into a formal WBS by a project support person. The final version would be reviewed by the inner echelon of the project team. Relevant stakeholders (most notably customers) would be consulted to confirm agreement and revise when appropriate.

Project teams developing their first WBS frequently forget that the structure should be end-item, output oriented. First attempts often result in a WBS that follows the organization structure—design, marketing, production, finance. If a WBS follows the organization structure, the focus will be on the organization function and processes rather than the project output or deliverables. In addition, a WBS with a process focus will become an accounting tool that records costs by function rather than a tool for "output" management. Every effort should be made to develop a WBS that is output oriented in order to concentrate on concrete deliverables. See Snapshot from Practice: Creating a WBS.

STEP 4: INTEGRATING THE WBS WITH THE ORGANIZATION

The WBS is used to link the organizational units responsible for performing the work. In practice, the outcome of this process is the **organization breakdown structure (OBS).** The OBS depicts how the firm has organized to discharge work responsibility. The purposes of the OBS are to provide a framework to summarize organization unit work performance, identify organization units responsible for work packages, and tie the organizational unit to cost control accounts. Recall, cost accounts group similar work packages (usually under the purview of a department). The OBS

Figure 4.4 represents the classic WBS in which the project is broken down to the lowest manageable deliverable and subsequent work packages. Many situations do not require this level of detail. This begs the questions of how far you should break down the work.

There is no set answer to this question. However, here are some tips given by project managers:

Break down the work until you can do an estimate that is accurate enough for your purposes. If you are doing a ball-park estimate to see if the project is worthy of serious consideration, you probably do not need to break it down beyond major deliverables. On the other hand, if you are pricing a project to submit a competitive bid, then you are likely to go down to the work package level.

The WBS should conform to how you are going to schedule work. For example, if assignments are made in terms of days, then tasks should be limited as best as possible to one day or more to complete. Conversely, if hours are the smallest unit for scheduling, then work can be broken down to one-hour increments.

© Erik Larson

Final activities should have clearly defined start/end events. Avoid open-ended tasks like "research" or "market analysis." Take it down to the next level in which deliverables/outcomes are more clearly defined. Instead of ending with market analysis include items such as identify market share, list user requirements, or write a problem statement.

If accountability and control are important, then break the work down so that one individual is clearly responsible for the work. For example, instead of stopping at product design, take it to the next level and identify specific components of the design (i.e., electrical schematics, power source, etc.) that different individuals will be responsible for creating.

The bottom line is that the WBS should provide the level of detail needed to manage the specific project successfully.

defines the organization subdeliverables in a hierarchical pattern in successively smaller and smaller units. Frequently, the traditional organization structure can be used. Even if the project is completely performed by a team, it is necessary to break down the team structure for assigning responsibility for budgets, time, and technical performance.

As in the WBS, the OBS assigns the lowest organizational unit the responsibility for work packages within a cost account. Herein lies one major strength of using WBS and OBS; they can be *integrated* as shown in Figure 4.5. The intersection of work packages and the organizational unit creates a project control point **(cost account)** that integrates work and responsibility. For example, at level 5 Touch Sensors has three work packages that have been assigned to the Design, Quality Control Test, and Production departments. The intersection of the WBS and OBS represents the set of work packages necessary to complete the subdeliverable located immediately above and the organizational unit on the left responsible for accomplishing the packages at the intersection. Note that the design department is responsible for five different work packages across the Hardware and Touch Screen deliverables.

Later we will use the intersection as a cost account for management control of projects. For example, the Cameras element requires completion of work packages whose primary responsibility

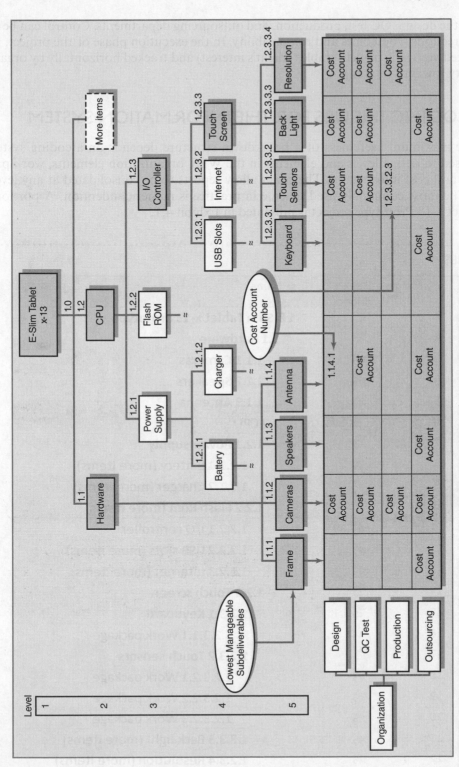

FIGURE 4.5 Integration of WBS and OBS

will include the design, QC test, production, and outsourcing departments. Control can be checked from two directions—outcomes and responsibility. In the execution phase of the project, progress can be tracked vertically on deliverables (client's interest) and tracked horizontally by organization responsibility (owner's interest).

STEP 5: CODING THE WBS FOR THE INFORMATION SYSTEM

Gaining the maximum usefulness of a breakdown structure depends on a coding system. The codes are used to define levels and elements in the WBS, organization elements, work packages, and budget and cost information. The codes allow reports to be consolidated at any level in the structure. The most commonly used scheme in practice is numeric indention. A portion of the E-Slim Tablet x-13 Prototype project is presented in Exhibit 4.1.

EXHIBIT 4.1 ....
Coding the WBS

	ⓘ	Task Mode ▾	Task Name ▾
1			⊟ **1 E-Slim Tablet x-13 Prototype**
2			⊟ **1.1 Hardware**
3			1.1.1 Cameras
4			1.1.2 Speakers
5			1.1.3 Antenna
6			⊟ **1.2 CPU**
7			⊟ **1.2.1 Power supply**
8			1.2.1.1 Battery (more items)
9			1.2.1.2 Charger (more items)
10			⊟ **1.2.2 Flash Rom (more items)**
11			1.2.2.1 I/O controller
12			1.2.2.2 USB slots (more items)
13			1.2.2.3 Internet (more items)
14			⊟ **1.2.3 Touch screen**
15			⊟ **1.2.3.1 Keyboard**
16			1.2.3.1.1 Work package
17			⊟ **1.2.3.2 Touch sensors**
18			1.2.3.2.1 Work package
19			1.2.3.2.2 Work package
20			1.2.3.2.3 Work package
21			1.2.3.3 Back light (more items)
22			1.2.3.4 Resolution (more items)

Note the project identification is 1.0. Each successive indention represents a lower element or work package. Ultimately the numeric scheme reaches down to the work package level, and all tasks and elements in the structure have an identification code. The "cost account" is the focal point because all budgets, work assignments, time, cost, and technical performance come together at this point.

This coding system can be extended to cover large projects. Additional schemes can be added for special reports. For example, adding a "23" after the code could indicate a site location, an elevation, or a special account such as labor. Some letters can be used as special identifiers such as "M" for materials or "E" for engineers. You are not limited to only 10 subdivisions (0–9); you can extend each subdivision to large numbers—for example, $.1 - .99$ or $.1 - .9999$. If the project is small, you can use whole numbers. The following example is from a large, complex project:

$$3R - 237A - P2 - 33.6$$

where 3R identifies the facility, 237A represents elevation and the area, P2 represents pipe two inches wide, and 33.6 represents the work package number. In practice most organizations are creative in combining letters and numbers to minimize the length of WBS codes.

On larger projects, the WBS is further supported with a **WBS dictionary** that provides detailed information about each element in the WBS. The dictionary typically includes the work package level (code), name, and functional description. In some cases the description is supported with specifications. The availability of detailed descriptions has an added benefit of dampening scope creep.

Process Breakdown Structure

The WBS is best suited for design and build projects that have tangible outcomes such as an offshore mining facility or a new car prototype. The project can be decomposed or broken down into major deliverables, subdeliverables, further subdeliverables, and ultimately to work packages. It is more difficult to apply WBS to less tangible, *process-oriented* projects in which the final outcome is a product of a series of steps or phases. Here, the big difference is that the project evolves over time with each phase affecting the next phase. Information systems projects typically fall in this category—for example, creating an extranet website or an internal software database system. Process projects are driven by performance requirements, not by plans/blueprints. Some practitioners choose to utilize what we refer to as a **process breakdown structure (PBS)** instead of the classic WBS.

Figure 4.6 provides an example of a PBS for a software development project. Instead of being organized around deliverables, the project is organized around phases. Each of the five major phases can be broken down into more specific activities until a sufficient level of detail is achieved to communicate what needs to be done to complete that phase. People can be assigned to specific activities, and a complementary OBS can be created just as is done for the WBS. Deliverables are not ignored but are defined as outputs required to move to the next phase. The software industry often refers to PBS as the "waterfall method" since progress flows downward through each phase.[1]

---

[1] The limitations of the waterfall method for software development have led to the emergence of Agile project management methods that are the subject of Chapter 17.

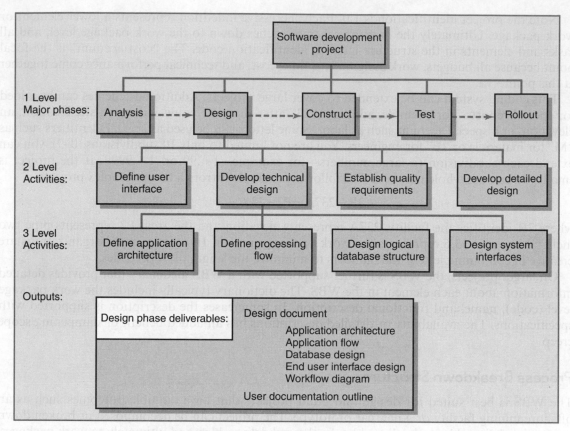

FIGURE 4.6 *PBS for Software Development Project*

Checklists that contain the phase exit requirements are developed to manage project progress. These checklists provide the means to support phase walk-throughs and reviews. Checklists vary depending upon the project and activities involved but typically include the following details:

- Deliverables needed to exit a phase and begin a new one.
- Quality checkpoints to ensure that deliverables are complete and accurate.
- Sign-offs by all responsible stakeholders to indicate that the phase has been successfully completed and that the project should move on to the next phase.

As long as exit requirements are firmly established and deliverables for each phase are well defined, the PBS provides a suitable alternative to the standard WBS for projects that involve extensive development work.

RESPONSIBILITY MATRICES

In many cases, the size and scope of the project do not warrant an elaborate WBS or OBS. One tool that is widely used by project managers and task force leaders of small projects is the

responsibility matrix (RM). The RM (sometimes called a linear responsibility chart) summarizes the tasks to be accomplished and who is responsible for what on a project. In its simplest form an RM consists of a chart listing all the project activities and the participants responsible for each activity. For example, Figure 4.7 illustrates an RM for a market research study. In this matrix the R is used to identify the committee member who is responsible for coordinating the efforts of other team members assigned to the task and making sure that the task is completed. The S is used to identify members of the five-person team who will support and/or assist the individual responsible. Simple RMs like this one are useful not only for organizing and assigning responsibilities for small projects but also for subprojects of large, more complex projects.

	Project Team				
Task	Richard	Dan	Dave	Linda	Elizabeth
Identify target customers	R	S		S	
Develop draft questionnaire	R	S	S		
Pilot-test questionnaire		R		S	
Finalize questionnaire	R	S	S	S	
Print questionnaire					R
Prepare mailing labels					R
Mail questionnaires					R
Receive and monitor returned questionnaires				R	S
Input response data			R		
Analyze results		R	S	S	
Prepare draft of report	S	R	S	S	
Prepare final report	R		S		

R = Responsible
S = Supports/assists

FIGURE 4.7 *Responsibility Matrix for a Market Research Project*

More complex RMs not only identify individual responsibilities but also clarify critical interfaces between units and individuals that require coordination. For example, Figure 4.8 is an RM for a larger, more complex project to develop a new piece of automated equipment. Notice that within each cell a numeric coding scheme is used to define the nature of involvement on that specific task. Such an RM extends the WBS/OBS and provides a clear and concise method for depicting responsibility, authority, and communication channels.

Responsibility matrices provide a means for all participants in a project to view their responsibilities and agree on their assignments. They also help clarify the extent or type of authority exercised by each participant in performing an activity in which two or more parties have overlapping involvement. By using an RM and by defining authority, responsibility, and communications within its framework, the relationship between different organizational units and the work content of the project is made clear.

Deliverables	Design	Development	Documentation	Assembly	Testing	Purchasing	Quality Assur.	Manufacturing
			Organization					
Architectural designs	1	2			2			3
Hardware specifications	2	1				2	3	3
Kernel specifications	1	3						3
Utilities specifications	2	1			3			
Hardware design	1			3		3	3	3
Disk drivers	3	1	2					
Memory management	1	3			3			
Operating system documentation	2	2	1					
Prototypes	5		4	1	3	3	3	4
Integrated acceptance test	5	2	2		1		5	5

1	Responsible
2	Support
3	Consult
4	Notification
5	Approval

Figure 4.8 *Responsibility Matrix for the Conveyor Belt Project*

PROJECT COMMUNICATION PLAN

Once the project deliverables and work are clearly identified, following up with an internal communication plan is vital. Stories abound of poor communication as a major contributor to project failure. Having a robust communications plan can go a long way toward mitigating project problems and can ensure that customers, team members, and other stakeholders have the information to do their jobs.

The communication plan is usually created by the project manager and/or the project team in the early stage of project planning.

Communication is a key component in coordinating and tracking project schedules, issues, and action items. The plan maps out the flow of information to different stakeholders and becomes an integral part of the overall project plan. The purpose of a project communication plan is to express what, who, how, and when information will be transmitted to project stakeholders so schedules, issues, and action items can be tracked.

Project communication plans address the following core questions:

- What information needs to be collected and when?
- Who will receive the information?
- What methods will be used to gather and store information?
- What are the limits, if any, on who has access to certain kinds of information?
- When will the information be communicated?
- How will it be communicated?

Developing a communication plan that answers these questions usually entails the following basic steps:

1. **Stakeholder analysis.** Identify the target groups. Typical groups could be the customer, sponsor, project team, project office, or anyone who needs project information to make decisions and/or contribute to project progress. A common tool found in practice to initially identify and analyze major project stakeholders' communication needs is presented in Figure 4.9.[2] How and what is communicated is influenced by the stakeholder interest and power. Some of these stakeholders may have the power either to block or enhance your project. By identifying stakeholders and prioritizing them on the "Power/Interest" map, you can plan the type and frequency of communications needed. (More on stakeholders will be discussed in Chapter 10.)

FIGURE 4.9 *Stakeholder Communications*

[2] For a more elaborate scheme for assessing stakeholders, see: Lynda Bourne, *Stakeholder Relationship Management* (Farnham, U.K.: Gower Publishing Ltd., 2009).

For example, on a typical project you want to manage closely the professionals doing the work, while you want to satisfy senior management and project sponsor with periodic updates. Unions and operation managers interested in capacity would be someone you would want to keep informed, while you would only need to provide general information to the legal, public relations, and other departments.

2. **Information needs.** What information is pertinent to stakeholders who contribute to the project's progress? The simplest answer to this question can be obtained by asking the different people what information they need and when they need it. For example, top management needs to know how the project is progressing, whether it is encountering critical problems, and the extent to which project goals are being realized. This information is required so that they can make strategic decisions and manage the portfolio of projects. Project team members need to see schedules, task lists, specifications, and the like, so they know what needs to be done next. External groups need to know any changes in the schedule and performance requirements of the components they are providing. Frequent information needs found in communication plans are:

Project status reports	Deliverable issues
Changes in scope	Team status meetings
Gating decisions	Accepted request changes
Action items	Milestone reports

3. **Sources of information.** When the information needs are identified, the next step is to determine the sources of information. That is, where does the information reside? How will it be collected? For example, information relating to the milestone report, team meetings, and project status meetings would be found in the minutes and reports of various groups.

4. **Dissemination modes.** In today's world, traditional status report meetings are being supplemented by e-mail, teleconferencing, SharePoint, and a variety of database sharing programs to circulate information. In particular, many companies are using the Web to create a "virtual project office" to store project information. Project management software feeds information directly to the Web site so that different people have immediate access to relevant project information. In some cases, appropriate information is routed automatically to key stakeholders. Backup paper hardcopy to specific stakeholders is still critical for many project changes and action items.

5. **Responsibility and timing.** Determine who will send out the information. For example, a common practice is to have secretaries of meetings forward the minutes or specific information to the appropriate stakeholders. In some cases the responsibility lies with the project manager or project office. Timing and frequency of distribution appropriate to the information need to be established.

The advantage of establishing a communication plan is that instead of responding to information requests, you are controlling the flow of information. This reduces confusion and unnecessary interruptions, and it can provide project managers greater autonomy. Why? By reporting on a regular basis how things are going and what is happening, you allow senior management to feel more comfortable about letting the team complete the project without interference. See Figure 4.10 for a sample Shale Oil Research Project Communication Plan.

What Information	Target Audience	When?	Method of Communication	Provider
Milestone report	Senior management and project manager	Bimonthly	E-mail and hardcopy	Project office
Project status reports & agendas	Staff and customer	Weekly	E-mail and hardcopy	Project manager
Team status reports	Project manager and project office	Weekly	E-mail	Team recorder
Issues report	Staff and customer	Weekly	E-mail	Team recorder
Escalation reports	Staff and customer	When needed	Meeting and hardcopy	Project manager
Outsourcing performance	Staff and customer	Bimonthly	Meeting	Project manager
Accepted change requests	Project office, senior mgmt., customer, staff, and project mgr.	Anytime	E-mail and hardcopy	Design department
Oversight gate decisions	Senior management and project manager	As required	E-mail meeting report	Oversight group or project office

FIGURE 4.10 *Shale Oil Research Project Communication Plan*

The importance of establishing up-front a plan for communicating important project information cannot be overstated. Many of the problems that plague a project can be traced back to insufficient time devoted to establishing a well-grounded internal communication plan.

Summary

The project scope definition, priorities, and breakdown structure are the keys to nearly every aspect of managing the project. The scope definition provides focus and emphasis on the end item(s) of the project. Establishing project priorities allows managers to make appropriate trade-off decisions. The structure helps ensure all tasks of the project are identified and provides two views of the project—one on deliverables and one on organization responsibility. The WBS avoids having the project driven by organization function or by a finance system. The structure forces attention to realistic requirements of personnel, hardware, and budgets. Use of the structure provides a powerful framework for project control that identifies deviations from plan, identifies responsibility, and spots areas for improved performance. No well-developed project plan or control system is possible without a disciplined, structured approach. The WBS, OBS, and cost account codes provide this discipline. The WBS will serve as the database for developing the project network which establishes the timing of work, people, equipment, and costs.

PBS is often used for process-based projects with ill-defined deliverables. In small projects responsibility matrices may be used to clarify individual responsibility.

Clearly defining your project is the first and most important step in planning. The absence of a clearly defined project plan consistently shows up as the major reason for project failures. Whether you use a WBS, PBS, or responsibility matrix will depend primarily on the size and nature of your project. Whatever method you use, definition of your project should be adequate to allow for good control as the project is being implemented. Follow-up with a clear communication plan for coordinating and tracking project progress will help keep important stakeholders informed and avoid some potential problems.

Key Terms

Cost account	Process breakdown structure	Scope statement
Milestone	(PBS)	WBS dictionary
Organization breakdown	Project charter	Work breakdown structure
structure (OBS)	Responsibility matrix	(WBS)
Priority matrix	Scope creep	Work package

Review Questions

1. What are the six elements of a typical scope statement?
2. What questions does a project objective answer? What would be an example of a good project objective?
3. What does it mean if the priorities of a project include: Time-constrain, Scope-accept, and Cost-enhance?
4. What kinds of information are included in a work package?
5. When would it be appropriate to create a responsibility matrix rather than a full-blown WBS?
6. How does a communication plan benefit management of projects?

Exercises

1. You are in charge of organizing a dinner-dance concert for a local charity. You have reserved a hall that will seat 30 couples and have hired a jazz combo.

   a. Develop a scope statement for this project that contains examples of all the elements. Assume that the event will occur in 4 weeks and provide your best guess estimate of the dates for milestones.

   b. What would the priorities likely be for this project?

2. In small groups, identify real life examples of a project that would fit each of the following priority scenarios:

   a. Time-constrain, Scope-enhance, Cost-accept

   b. Time-accept, Scope-constrain, Cost-accept

   c. Time-constrain, Scope-accept, Cost-enhance

3. Develop a WBS for a project in which you are going to build a bicycle. Try to identify all of the major components and provide three levels of detail.

4. You are the father or mother of a family of four (kids ages 13 and 15) planning a weekend camping trip. Develop a responsibility matrix for the work that needs to be done prior to starting your trip.

5. Develop a WBS for a local stage play. Be sure to identify the deliverables and organizational units (people) responsible. How would you code your system? Give an example of the work packages in one of your cost accounts. Develop a corresponding OBS which identifies who is responsible for what.

6. Use an example of a project you are familiar with or are interested in. Identify the deliverables and organizational units (people) responsible. How would you code your system? Give an example of the work packages in one of your cost accounts.

7. Develop a communication plan for an airport security project. The project entails installing the hardware and software system that (1) scans a passenger's eyes, (2) fingerprints the passenger, and (3) transmits the information to a central location for evaluation.

8. Go to an Internet search engine (e.g., Google) and type in "project communication plan." Check three or four that have ".gov" as their source. How are they similar or dissimilar? What would be your conclusion concerning the importance of an internal communication plan?

9. Your roommate is about to submit a scope statement for a spring concert sponsored by the entertainment council at Western Evergreen State University (WESU). WESU is a residential university with over 22,000 students. This will be the first time in six years since WESU sponsored a spring concert. The entertainment council has budgeted $40,000 for the project. The event is to occur on June 5th. Since your roommate knows you are taking a class on project management she has asked you to review her scope statement and make suggestions for improvement. She considers the concert a resume-building experience and wants to be as professional as possible. Below is a draft of her scope statement. What suggestions would you make and why?

WESU Spring Music Concert

Project Objective

To organize and deliver a 6-hour music concert

Deliverables

- Concert security
- Contact local newspapers and radio stations

- Separate beer garden
- Six hours of musical entertainment
- Design a commemorative concert t-shirt
- Local sponsors
- Food venues
- Event insurance
- Safe environment

Milestones

1. Secure all permissions and approvals
2. Sign big-name artist
3. Contact secondary artists
4. Secure vendor contracts
5. Advertising campaign
6. Plan set-up
7. Concert
8. Clean-up

Technical Requirements

1. Professional sound stage and system
2. At least five performing acts
3. Restroom facilities
4. Parking
5. Compliance with WESU and city requirements/ordinances

Limits and Exclusions

- Seating capacity for 8,000 students.
- Performers are responsible for travel arrangement to and from WESU.
- Performers must provide own liability insurance.
- Performers and security personnel will be provided lunch and dinner on the day of the concert.
- Vendors contribute 25 percent of sales to concert fund.
- Concert must be over at 12:15 A.M.

Customer Review: WESU

References

Ashley, D. B., et al., "Determinants of Construction Project Success," *Project Management Journal,* 18 (2) June 1987, p. 72.

Chilmeran, A. H., "Keeping Costs on Track," *PM Network,* 19 (2) 2004, pp. 45–51.

Gary, L. "Will Project Scope Cost You—Or Create Value?" *Harvard Management Update,* January 2005.

Gobeli, D. H., and E. W. Larson, "Project Management Problems," *Engineering Management Journal,* 2, 1990, pp. 31–36.

Ingebretsen, M., "Taming the Beast," *PM Network,* July 2003, pp. 30–35.

Katz, D. M., "Case Study: Beware 'Scope Creep' on ERP Projects," *CFO.com,* March 27, 2001.

Kerzner, H., *Project Management: A Systems Approach to Planning,* 8th ed. (New York: Van Nostrand Reinhold, 2003).

Lewis, J. P., *Project Planning, Scheduling and Controlling,* 3rd ed. (Burr Ridge, IL: McGraw-Hill, 2000).

Luby, R. E., D. Peel, and W. Swahl, "Component-Based Work Breakdown Structure," *Project Management Journal,* 26 (2) December 1995, pp. 38–44.

Murch, R., *Project Management: Best Practices for IT Professionals* (Upper Darby, NJ: Prentice Hall, 2001).

Pinto, J. K., and D. P. Slevin, "Critical Success Factors Across the Project Life Cycle," *Project Management Journal,* 19 (3) June 1988, p. 72.

Pitagorsky, G., "Realistic Project Planning Promotes Success," *Engineer's Digest,* 29 (1) 2001.

PMI Standards Committee, *Guide to the Project Management Body of Knowledge* (Newton Square, PA: Project Management Institute, 2000).

Posner, B. Z., "What It Takes to Be a Good Project Manager," *Project Management Journal,* 18 (1) March 1987, p. 52.

Raz, T., and S. Globerson, "Effective Sizing and Content Definition of Work Packages," *Project Management Journal,* 29 (4) 1998, pp. 17–23.

The Standish Group, *CHAOS Summary 2009,* pp. 1–4.

Tate, K., and K. Hendrix, "Chartering IT Projects," *Proceedings, 30th Annual, Project Management Institute* (Philadelphia, PA. 1999), CD.

APPENDIX 4.1

Project Scope Management

Definitions of Project and Project Scope

PMBOK® Guide, 5th Edition, defines project as "A *temporary endeavor undertaken to create a unique product, service or result*" and project scope as "*The work that must be performed to deliver a product, service or result with specified features and functions*". These very definitions of project and project scope underscore the importance accorded to scope management processes by PMBOK® Guide. Organizations undertake projects, which act as vehicles of change and instruments for implementing the organization's strategic initiatives, and project scope includes the work to be accomplished for this purpose. Therefore, project scope management is indeed at the heart of planning and execution of the project.

Key Issues in Project Scope Management

PMBOK® Guide defines scope management processes as "*The processes required to ensure that the project includes all the work required and, only the work required, to complete the project successfully.*"

From the nature of project scope and project scope management as defined above, we see that managing the project scope is essentially focusing on defining and controlling what is and what is not included in project. With this sharp focus on inclusion and exclusion of the work in the project scope viewpoint, three important or key issues in project scope management are identified and listed below:

- *Prevent indiscriminate scope creep* – To ensure that the project thrust remains focused and resources are not frittered away.
- *Include all deliverables in project work and complete them satisfactorily* – To ensure that all work planned to be included for meeting the project objectives is completed to the satisfaction of the stakeholders.
- *Use discretion in permitting some scope changes*, which are crucial for meeting the project objectives though they may not have been properly spelt out at the stage of defining scope.

Project Scope Management Processes

PMBOK® Guide identifies six scope management processes, which collectively address the above-mentioned key issues of scope management (see Figure 4.11). Of the six scope management processes, four processes are in the planning group and two are in the monitoring and controlling group.

Planning Group includes four processes:

1. Plan Scope Management
2. Collect Requirements
3. Define Scope, and
4. Create WBS

Monitoring and Controlling Group includes two processes:

1. Validate Scope, and
2. Control Scope

Before we understand how these processes collectively manage to carry out the task of project scope management as defined above, let us first learn more about each process; their Inputs, Tools and Techniques, and Outputs.

1. PLAN SCOPE MANAGEMENT

Plan Scope Management is the process of creating a scope management plan, which documents how the project scope will be defined, validated and controlled. (PMBOK® Guide, 5th Edition).

The process essentially sets down the methodology for how the scope management would be carried out during the entire project life cycle. It is useful in controlling scope creep. During this process, the information included in the project charter and the approved subsidiary project management plans (viz. the subsidiary plans to manage the project schedule, quality, communication, procurement, risk, etc. which include the approved changes) is analyzed. Using this information and the organization's policies and procedures for managing similar projects and the lessons learned from them, the scope management plan is developed.

Inputs

Project Charter and the *Approved Subsidiary Plans of the Project Management Plan* provide the basic inputs for developing the scope management plan. The infrastructure and general management practices of the organization set down the framework within which the project scope is to be managed. These factors, combined, referred to as *Enterprise Environmental Factors* provide another input. These factors include physical infrastructure, availability of technology, skilled personnel and cost management and human resources management practices. The *Organizational Process Assets* – the organization's experience in managing earlier similar projects and the procedures, templates or other helpful practices already developed during managing them – would be other helpful inputs for formulating the project scope management plan.

Tools and Techniques

Expert Judgment and *Project Team Meetings* are the tools for this process. *Expert Judgment* refers to the prior experience with similar projects as well as exposure in developing scope management plans.

Outputs

Scope management Plan and *Requirements Management Plan are the two outputs from this process. Scope Management Plan:* As discussed before, this plan sets down the methodology for scope management processes and it would include:

- Guidelines for preparing detailed *Project Scope Statement* and the procedures for creating and maintaining approved WBS developed from the project scope statement.
- The procedures for validating the scope – the rules and procedures for acceptance of individual deliverables.
- The procedures for incorporating and approving the changes in project scope – linked with integrated change control, these procedures are crucial in avoiding scope creeps.

Requirements Management Plan: A component of the project management plan, this subsidiary plan describes how the requirements would be analyzed, documented and managed. It would generally include:

- Planning, tracking and reporting requirements – particularly taking into account the relationships between project phases.
- Configuration management, covering how the changes in the product would be approved and controlled to continue to meet the stakeholders' requirements.

2. COLLECT REQUIREMENTS

Collect Requirements is the process of determining, documenting and managing the stakeholders needs to meet the project objectives (PMBOK® Guide, 5th Edition).

It is the satisfaction of the needs of key stakeholders (project sponsor within the organization, client for whom the project is performed, or other key stakeholders) that provides the measure for judging the success of a project. The starting point for crystallizing the project objectives, therefore, would be collecting and analyzing the needs of the stakeholders, which a particular project is authorized to meet. No doubt, the primary vision of the project objectives would be captured in the project charter (or similar project-authorizing document) issued at the start of the project. However, often, all necessary details are not visualized at the very start of the project. As the project planning is taken up and the details for project work are mapped out, some important changes in the work necessary to meet the project objective become apparent. The collect requirement process addresses this issue by going back once more to the stakeholders and ensuring that the project scope includes such refinements and the project scope fully reflects the key stakeholders' needs for which the project is authorized.

We will now take a closer look at the major inputs, outputs and tools and techniques for this process.

Inputs

Major approved project planning documents concerning the project scope for meeting key stakeholders' needs are the inputs to this process. They include:

- Scope Management Plan
- Requirements Management Plan
- Stakeholders Management plan
- Project Charter, and
- Stakeholder Register

Tools and Techniques

The techniques for collecting requirements essentially facilitate close interaction with the key stakeholders to unearth their real needs and arrive at common agreed requirements. For this purpose close interaction with the key stakeholders would be accomplished – either on a one-on-one basis or as a group through facilitated workshops:

- *Formal interviews with the stakeholders (including recorded minutes)*
- *Group discussions of key stakeholders*
- *Facilitated workshops, which bring together key stakeholders (often belonging to cross-functional disciplines) and arrive at an agreement for the optimum solution for the requirements, which would provide the foundation for scope planning*
- *Questionnaires and surveys*
- *Inviting reactions on a preliminary scheme or prototype* – For a software project, the proto-typical web pages for key documents and the demonstration of general operating scheme could be very valuable. Similarly a prototype model would be quite useful in visualizing and/or experiencing the user's interaction.

Outputs

Major output of the process is the *Requirements Documentation*. It formally documents how individual requirements set down for the project contribute towards meeting the business needs. The contents of formal documentation of the requirements would include:

- unambiguous complete and consistent statement of the requirements and the criteria for acceptance set down by the key stakeholders,

- stakeholders' communication and reporting requirements,
- the functional and non-functional requirements of the solution, the technology and standards compliance, and
- assumptions, constraints and interdependencies of the requirements.

3. DEFINE SCOPE

Define scope is the process of developing a detailed description of the project and the product of the project (PMBOK® Guide, 5th Edition).

Preparation of detailed scope statement is critical for project success. In this process, detailed description of the project and the product of the project are developed. The project objectives are analyzed to arrive at the major deliverables, which must be created to meet the objectives. The criteria for acceptance of the product and the major deliverables (the performance requirements, technical specifications and criteria for satisfaction of theses work components) are defined and specified. The work excluded from the project scope is explicitly spelled out. The assumptions and constraints taken into account in project planning are listed and analyzed. Finally, preliminary estimates for project cost and schedule are also developed for general guidelines. In this manner, this process provides the blueprint of detailed project planning leading to the next scope management process, (Create Work Breakdown Structure – WBS) which requires more detailed project planning.

The major inputs, tools and techniques and outputs for this process are set down below.

Inputs

Major inputs for defining the scope are the project objectives, major deliverables and criteria for acceptance for the product of the project. *The Scope Management Plan* and Project Charter are good inputs for this purpose. This basic information is elaborated and further refined by the process of direct reference to the *Requirements Documentation* – the output of the Collect Requirements process.

In addition to these three inputs for the process scope contents, *The Organization's Process Assets* (policies and procedures for planning and executing projects, earlier used templates for drafting project scope statement, lessons learnt from earlier similar projects, etc.) are other helpful inputs for defining project scope.

Tools and Techniques

Preparing the project scope statement requires essentially drafting a comprehensive project scope document. Therefore, the techniques and tools employed would depend on:

- *Product Analysis* – the form and nature of the project's product.
- *Identification of Project Execution Approach* – based on evaluation of the available alternatives and selecting the most appropriate for the situation.
- *Expert Judgment* – the expertise developed by the project manager from his experience in handling similar projects earlier.

Output

The output of the process is *Project Scope Statement.* Project scope statement describes the overall scope of the project work (including explicit description of exclusions), major deliverables, and assumptions & constraints. Along with Project Charter, Project Scope Statement forms the basis for all subsequent project decisions, conflict resolution and trade-offs during the execution phase. It also provides the basis for assessing the relevance or importance of the change requests in terms of overall project objectives.

Contents of a typical *Project Scope Statement* would be:

- Project Objectives – a comprehensive statement of the project objectives based on the directives in the project charter document and analyzed and confirmed by collect requirement process.
- Product scope description – characteristics of the product, service or result described in the project charter, including the performance requirements, detailed technical specifications, applicable quality standards and project satisfaction criteria
- Project deliverables and project acceptance criteria – Deliverable is a unique and verifiable product, result or capability that must be produced to complete the project phase or process. It is necessary that deliverables are defined and described in concrete terms and are subject to objectively measurable results or characteristics.
- Project boundaries – It is important to specifically mention of exclusions to avoid misunderstanding at a later stage in the project and preempt unwarranted expectations from the project
- Project Constraints and assumptions taken into account for project planning – The constraints on project planning may include pre-defined budget, imposed dates on completion of specific milestones of project schedule, and contractual agreement terms in case of a project performed for a customer under contract. Taking for granted of certain conditions or factors employed in project planning without pre-verification are called assumptions; project scope statement would includes a list of such assumptions, which are checked for validity during the detailed planning and risk identification,
- Project Management Guidelines
  - Project Cost
  - Major milestones and project schedule
  - Quality aspects and acceptance requirements
  - Project management Team & project organization

Compare the checklist for project scope given in "Snapshot from Practice – Scope Statement for a High Quality Custom Home" in this chapter with the above and observe the close similarities.

4. CREATE WBS

Create WBS is the process of subdividing the project deliverables and project work into smaller and more manageable components. (PMBOK® Guide, 5ᵗʰ Edition).

WBS is defined as "A deliverable oriented hierarchical decomposition of the work to be executed by the project team to accomplish the project objectives and create the required deliverables. It organizes and defines the total scope of the project". Each descending level of WBS represents an increasingly detailed definition of the project work. The WBS is decomposed until meaningful work packages are defined. In this manner, this process ensures that all work necessary for the project is included in the project plan, accurate estimates for resource requirements and time are developed and responsibility is assigned for executing each work package. On completion of all work packages planned in the WBS, the total scope of project work is covered.

The WBS structure includes unique identifiers from the code of accounts and accordingly provides a hierarchical structure for summation of costs, schedules and resource information. As one of the special tools used in project management, its purpose is.

- *To define* solution strategy or general approach, and implementation tactics
- *To support more accurate estimates of project duration and cost* than can be made at the project level
- *To assign the responsibility of each work package* or major component/sub-component to an individual, group, department, or outside agency (Responsibility Assignment Matrix)
- *To provide a basis for estimating project resources* – Departmental or subcontractor support

The Inputs, Outputs and Tools and Techniques for the process are briefly mentioned below.

Inputs

The main inputs for creating the WBS structure are as follows:

- *Scope Management Plan* – providing the methodology for creating WBS
- *The Project Scope Statement* – the document produced from Define Scope process
- *The Requirements Documentation* – the document prepared from the Collect Requirements process
- *Enterprise Environmental Factors* – applicable industry practice or standards, and
- *The Organizational Process Assets* – the organization's past experience of planning and executing similar projects, policies and procedures, templates for creating a WBS and the lessons learnt from earlier projects.

Tools and Techniques

The Decomposition of Deliverables into gradually smaller and better-defined elements till work packages level is reached is the technique. The mode of decomposition would depend on the project's product and the industry practice. It may be based on the phases of the project life cycle or the external agencies or departments employed for project work or the major deliverables consisting of work spread across different life cycle phases and performing agencies.

Expert Judgment: The decomposition of deliverables depends to a good extent on the nature of the project and the industry practice. Expert judgment acquired through a significant experience in the industry and working on similar projects serves as an important tool.

Outputs

Scope Baseline: This is the main output of the process and is constituted of the approved version of the Project Scope Statement, Work Breakdown Structure (WBS), and WBS Dictionary as described below:

- *Approved Project Scope Statement:* It includes the description of the project scope, major deliverables, assumptions and constraints.
- *WBS*: The hierarchical breakdown of the major deliverables into manageable smaller components called work packages, and comprehensively covering the total project work.
- *WBS Dictionary* is an important accompanying document of WBS and contains detailed description of the work and technical documentation of each work package. It is a document that supports WBS and includes all detailed information, which a brief tabular structure of the WBS cannot hold. WBS Dictionary holds code of account identifier, description of work, performance specifications, technical specification (drawings and standards), quality requirements, acceptance criteria, estimated cost, schedule milestones and contract information, and responsibility assignment.

The Contents of a Typical Work Package

A work package should include the following:

- Unique identification from a code of accounts
- Detailed technical or performance specification set down in WBS dictionary
- Estimated / Budgeted Cost
- Estimated time duration or expected milestone
- Preceding and succeeding project activity or work package
- Assigned Responsibility (RAM)
- Applicable standard of acceptance or quality level

Heuristics for Preparing WBS

To know, how far the decomposition of the major deliverable should be carried out is very important. General principle is that such decomposition should be carried out until resulting work package would unambiguously define the total scope of work in the work package. This would cover the technical and performance specifications, the resource requirements and cost, the sequencing of activities with expected start and end times of the activities. Each work package should have its unique identification number for control and it should be possible to assign independent responsibility for the entire work package.

The following guidelines could be helpful in deciding the degree of decomposition of project scope into work packages during 'Create WBS' process:

- Tendency to decompose to a very high degree or leave unduly large work package should be curbed. Work packages should ordinarily not be smaller than 1% to 2 % of the total project scope and not greater than 8–10% of the scope. Generally decomposing the project into 10–20 major deliverables is found satisfactory.

- It should be possible to assign unambiguously responsibility for individual work packages.
- It should be possible to provide complete technical and performance specifications for work included in each work package.
- It should be possible to estimate the time required to carry out the activity for the work package
- It should be possible to estimate the resources required and cost to be incurred for the work package.
- The interface between the sequential work packages should be clearly demarcated and no portion of work should remain outside the WBS.

5. VALIDATE SCOPE

Validate scope is the process of formalizing the acceptance of the completed project deliverables (PMBOK® Guide, 5th Edition).

This process belongs to monitoring and controlling process group and it is meant to ensure that all deliverables and work packages planned in the WBS are completed to the satisfaction of the sponsor or key stakeholders and are formally accepted by the stakeholders. The process requires carrying out inspection and testing to ensure that the deliverables meet the necessary performance and technical specifications.

Inputs

For this process, the major inputs are:

- *Project Management Plan*: It includes Project Scope Statement, WBS and WBS Dictionary
- *Requirements Documentation*
- *Verified Deliverables, and*
- *Work Performance Data*

The first two inputs set down what is required to be done for completing a deliverable and the next two provide documentary proof of the tests and inspection carried out for checking the performance.

Tools and Techniques

Tools and techniques for verification are inspection and testing – activities involving physical inspection, measurement of technical specifications and performance testing to verify that the completed deliverable meets the product satisfaction criteria set down in the project scope.

Outputs

After the testing and inspection, the deliverable is formally accepted to meet the criteria for its acceptance set down in the project scope statement and elaborated in the WBS and WBS Dictionary. If the testing reveals the necessity of adding any more project work, the change requests are originated. Summing up, the outputs from the process are:

- Accepted Deliverables
- *Change Requests* for deliverables not accepted for the first time and requiring some change or defect repair before acceptance
- *Work Performance Information* – from the inspection reports or performance test results

6. CONTROL SCOPE

Control Scope is the process of monitoring the status of the project and product scope and managing changes to the scope baseline. (PMBOK® Guide, 5th Edition)

This process would ensure that all requested changes and recommended corrective actions found during scope verification are suitably processed through policies and procedures set down in *Integrated Change Control Process* – like forms for change requests, authority levels, impact evaluation of suggested change on cost and schedule, etc. Approved changes should be incorporated in the project plan updates (i.e. project planning documents like WBS, Project Schedule, Project Cost and Budget, Quality Plans, etc.)

The Inputs, Outputs and Tools and Techniques for the process are briefly described below:

Inputs

Like the standard feedback control loop, the inputs for the Control Scope process are planned versus actual performance. So, the requirements set down in the components of the *Project Management Plan* (*Scope Baseline* including WBS and WBS Dictionary, Project schedule, quality standards) and Product Requirements documentation included in project plan are one set of inputs specifying the standards with which the deliverable would be compared. The actual *Work Performance Results* found from inspection and testing during Validate Scope process are another set of inputs specifying what is actually accomplished. The comparison would help ascertain whether the work is completed as per the agreed scope.

Tools and Techniques

The technique for Control Scope involves *analyzing the variance* between the standards set down in the project plan documents and actual work performance results from Validate Scope process.

Outputs

The main outputs from this process are:

- *Change Requests* (for including approved corrective or preventive actions to ensure that the deliverable meets the project satisfaction criteria),
- *Project Plan Updates* (for incorporating the approved changes into the Project Plan and revising the cost and time schedule taking into account impacts of the accepted changes on the project budget and project schedule), and
- *Work Performance Measurements* (actual versus planned for communicating to the stakeholders)

HOW SIX SCOPE MANAGEMENT PROCESSES
COLLECTIVELY ADDRESS
KEY ISSUES OF SCOPE MANAGEMENT

Total deliverables as defined in project scope statement (project scope definition process

Work packages, after creation of W.B.S (Create WBS process)

1. **Project Objectives vaguely defined at Project Charter Stage**

2. **Overall project scope defined and documented through Collect Requirements and Define Scope Processes**

3. **Hierarchical decomposition of scope by Create WBS and testing by Verify Scope process to ensure that entire scope is covered.**

4. **Scope Control Procedures and Rules for authorizing changes in project scope (for maintaining integrity of boundary)**

W.P.1 W.P.2 W.P.3 W.P.4 W.P.5 W.P.6 W.P.7 W.P.8 W.P.9 W.P.10 W.P.11 W.P.12 W.P.13 W.P.14 W.P.15

Work from project charter not included in the project scope at the detailed planning stage while preparing project scope statement (Exclusion at scope planning process)

Work not envisioned for inclusion in the project charter, but at the detailed planning stage, it is considered necessary and included in project scope

Project scope – broad objectives & vision articulated in project charter and preliminary scope statement

FIGURE 4.11 *Scope Management Processes*

APPENDIX 4.2

Project Communications Management

Great natural leaders as well as successful corporate managers are usually blessed with distinctly superior skills for all forms for communication – verbal as well as written, formal as well as informal. This natural skill in communication of an experienced general management professional, no doubt, would be an important asset for project communication also. However, it would be possible for most project managers to learn to manage project communication to the satisfaction of all key stakeholders by bearing in mind the special characteristics of project communication.

The logical organization of the project communication involves:

- Identifying the key stakeholders, determining their information needs and formulating the communication plan for desired flow of project information
- Setting up efficient systems for collection, storage, analysis and retrieval of the information for future use
- Collecting and distributing project information and reporting performance in a timely manner.

According to PMBOK® Guide, 5th Edition, Project Communications Management includes the processes required to ensure timely and appropriate planning, collection, creation, distribution, storage, retrieval management control, monitoring and ultimate disposition of project information.

Recasting the section on Project Communication Management by splitting it into two knowledge areas (Project Communications Management and Project Stakeholder Management) is one of the major changes in PMBOK Guide, 5th Edition, from its earlier 4th edition version. Accordingly, some of the processes listed in Project Communications Management in 4th edition have been shifted to Project Stakeholder Management in the 5th edition and a new section is added under the title Project Stakeholder Management as a knowledge area

PMBOK Guide, 5th Edition, lists 3 processes in project communications management:

1. Plan Communications Management   (Planning Process Group)
2. Manage Communications   (Executing Process Group)
3. Control Communications   (Monitoring and Controlling Group)

Let us study these processes, their inputs, tools and techniques and outputs.

1. PLAN COMMUNICATIONS MANAGEMENT (PLANNING PROCESS GROUP)

Plan Communications Management is the process of developing an appropriate approach and plan for project communications based on stakeholders' information needs and requirements and available organizational assets. (PMBOK® Guide, 5th Edition).

Once the stakeholders' needs for communication are determined, the communication plan is formulated. Communications management is planned to identify and document the approach for most effective and efficient communications with the stakeholders. The communications management plan takes into account which stakeholders need what specific information, who is authorized to access what specific information, when do they need it, in what format or details they need it, and the frequency of update and methodology for storage. In most medium and large size projects, communication planning is formally done during the early stages of the project and the reports, the report formats, frequency of reporting, the persons receiving the specific reports, medium of delivery and other details are settled and followed.

Inputs

The Project Management Plan and the *Stakeholder Register* provide the basis for planning project communications management and, therefore, they constitute the main inputs for planning communications management.

Other inputs are *Enterprise Environmental Factors* (organization structure and the project environment and communication technology most suitable for a specific communication) and *Organizational Process Assets* (essentially for lessons learned from the methodology employed and results achieved on earlier projects on communication planning).

Tools and Techniques

The following tools and technologies associated with communication planning should be taken into account:

- *Analysis of Communications Requirement* – The stakeholders' needs for information, based on the Stakeholders Register (output of Identify Stakeholders process) would need to be analyzed in light of the number of communication channels, hierarchical or free form communication channels, organizational structure and whether the stakeholders are internal or external to plan project communications.
- *Communication Technology* – This tool concerns the nature of technology to be used for project communication—verbal or written communication, urgency of communication and availability of suitable technology, project duration and environment.
- *Communication Models* – This part is concerned with understanding the basic communication model and exploiting it for effective and efficient communication and preventing the lapses likely to occur. There are five steps in formal communication model:
  - Encoding – sender transforming project data into information suitable for transmission
  - Message Transmission – sender transmitting the message to the recipient using suitable available technology (verbal or written communication – letter, minutes of meeting, formal reports, e-mails, other project management information system including access to communication content, etc.)
  - Decoding – recipient converting the message into information suitable for his needs
  - Acknowledgment – receipt of communication sent by receiver to the sender
  - Feedback or Response – sent by the receiver to the sender of his understanding of the received message
- *Communication Methods* – The broad classification of whether the communication would be
  - *Interactive communication* (meetings or phone calls) – most effective but most time and effort consuming; desirable or necessary for critical communication to key stakeholders
  - *"Push" Communication* (reports, e-mails, minutes of meetings, etc. sent periodically), which does not check whether the recipient actually received and understood the message; suitable for routine periodic updates to a larger audience of stakeholders, and
  - *"Pull" Communication* (making available access to information) – least expensive and quite suitable for wider circulation of a relatively large volume of information.
- *Meetings* – Face-to-face meeting between project team members and concerned stakeholders is another most commonly employed tool for project communication. Important meetings are planned with a pre-arranged time and place, list of participants, prior circulation of agenda and information relevant for discussion in the meeting. The minutes of meeting, which records salient issues discussed and decisions agreed, are circulated to all participants.

Outputs

The output of the Plan Communication process is the *Communications Management Plan.* It essentially includes detailed account of who needs what specific information (developed from stakeholders register and strategy to mange stakeholders), when do they need it, in what detail do they need it, the frequency of update and the preferred form of receiving the information. Somewhat more detailed discussion on the nature and contents of the project Communications Management Plan is given below.

Nature and Contents of Communications Management Plan

This is a very important planning document for all projects – especially important for the organizations performing projects on a contract basis. Most project managers and senior managers stress the need for effective communications in the project and the communication management plan should address to it by encompassing the entire spectrum of the key stakeholders needs. It should, therefore, include:

- The list of major reports that would be prepared for communication during the project life cycle – Ordinarily, this list should include major project planning documents (project charter, scope statement, cost estimate and budget, Gantt chart for major project milestones, quality plan, risk register, and major technical documentations like facilities design report for an infrastructures project) as well as periodic status reports and phase-gate review reports.
- The format, content and the level of details to be included in these reports – Often, the organizations have some tradition about what these reports should contain, and in that case, it should be followed generally with any specific modification required to suit the needs of the project in hand.
- The list of which stakeholders should receive which reports and the frequency of reporting – To avoid the information overload and distributing an avalanche of project information to all stakeholders, a judicious selection of the recipients of each report should be prepared on the need-to-know basis and the organization hierarchy.
- Methods or technologies used to convey the information – This aspect should cover how the communication would be handled, by issue of formal hard copy reports, formal presentations in meetings, informal memoranda and e-mails, project meetings and minutes of meetings, prints of drawings and technical specifications for review or execution, and
- The person(s) or group responsible for preparing and issue of specific communication

2. MANAGE COMMUNICATIONS (EXECUTING PROCESS GROUP)

Manage Communications is the process of creating, collecting, storing, retrieving, and ultimate disposal of the project information (PMBOK Guide, 5th Edition)

The communication management plan includes the framework for all formal and informal communications during the project: the details of who will get what information in what form and what frequency and the responsibility for generating and distributing the information. As the project is executed, the results of work performance become available in the concrete deliverables form. The physical inspection and performance testing during the Validate Scope process give the actual status of the work. Managing project communications involves interacting with the stakeholders to address their information needs employing suitable communication technology, models and methods. The communications content could comprise performance reports, deliverables status, project cost incurred and progress in schedule and forecasts for project milestones achievement and cost at completion of those milestones. The mode for information distribution – whether formal or informal and whether written or verbal – is also actually determined during the communications planning stage and all that is required to be done during the execution is actual compilation and distribution of the project status information to the stakeholders according to the communication plan reporting scheme.

The inputs, tools and techniques and outputs of the Distribute Information process are as follows:

Inputs

The main inputs for the Manage Communications process are:

- *Communications Management Plan:* This is the prime input; it is the output of the Plan Communications Management process (and a subsidiary of the Project Management Plan), which provides the methodology of managing communications, and
- *Work Performance Reports:* The reports include information to be communicated to the project stakeholders on the project status on the reporting date, including inspection and testing results, and updated forecast for based on the progress so far.
- *Enterprise Environmental Factors:* These constraints are set due to the organization structure and culture, project management information system (Project MIS), and government or industry practices and regulations.
- *Organizational Process Assets:* These essentially include policies and procedures for collecting and disseminating project information, templates for project status reports, and lessons learned from earlier similar projects

Tools and Techniques

The main techniques for managing communications are based on the following:

- *Communications Technology*: The ease with which methods could be available for use for sharing the information among stakeholders is a decisive factor for selecting the technology employed for project communications. These may be participation in project meetings, issue of formal written reports or other written communications (letters, e-mails, faxes, etc.), verbal communications (telephones or videoconferences) or providing access to information based on its confidentiality and needs of the stakeholder.
- *Communication Models:* Formal system for encoding, transmission, decoding, acknowledgment and feedback for project communications ensures that important project information is timely available to the stakeholder and acted upon. The barriers to communication (misunderstanding the message or missing out some critical element) are avoided to ensure smooth and effective communication.
- *Communication Methods:* The communication methods may include interactive communication mode (face-to-face meetings, video-conferences, or telephone calls, etc.), "push" communication mode (written reports, e-mails, minutes of meetings, memos, press releases, etc. distributed periodically without any interaction with the recipient) or "pull"

communication methods (making access to necessary information available through intra-net or similar 'publicly available' project documents).

- *Project Information Management Systems:* Information can be distributed by written or verbal communication. The written documents may be in the form of hard copy reports, electronic communication (e-mails, voice mails, fax, etc.) or in the form of project management software and other intra-net data sharing.

- *Performance Reporting:* Performance reporting is intended to convey to the stakeholders the actual progress made on the date of reporting, the estimated forecast of the project schedule and cost at completion and its comparison with the corresponding values at the original planning stage. This would involve preparing a status report with analysis of work completed during the reporting period and planned to be completed during the next period, schedule and cost forecast based on the progress, current status of risks and issues, major approved change requests and the progress on them.

Outputs

The main outputs of the process are:

- *Project Communications:* Project communications comprise all project information collected, analyzed and communicated to stakeholders. This may include formal project performance reports (periodic status reports, reports for reviewing progress at a specific phase gate, etc.) related to the actual progress in project work, the cost incurred and schedule maintained. Formal written reports are generally issued at specific occasion or according to pre-decided frequency

- *Updates on Project Management Plan* and *Project Documents:* Based on the forecasts in the performance reports, the components of the Project Management Plan (particularly related to management of scope, time and cost) would need to be up-dated. Similarly, some project documents (issue logs, project schedule, funding requirements projections, etc.) would also need to be updated.

- *Updates on Organizational Process Assets (Lessons Learned):* This is an important and special category of information to be distributed. For every project, during the execution phase, some previously unexpected situation occurs. The reasons behind development of such a situation and the remedial measures or the handling technique used for successfully overcoming the problem are very useful part of the organization's learning. The project team should always be vigilant to record such lessons learned, get their details and circulate them throughout the organization for the benefit of other current or future projects.

3. CONTROL COMMUNICATIONS (MONITORING AND CONTROLLING PROCESS GROUP)

Control Communications is the process of monitoring and controlling communications throughout the project life cycle to ensure that the information needs of the stakeholders are met. (PMBOK® Guide, 5th Edition).

This process addresses the key issue of effective and efficient flow of information to all important stakeholders.

Inputs

The inputs for this process are:

- *Project Management Plan:* Some important components of the project management plan that form the basis of the project communication management are: Inputs for Control Communications. Plan Stakeholders' Management, Projects Communications Management Plan, and Scope and Cost Baselines and Project Schedule.
- *Project Communications:* All project communications during the project life cycle, including project status reports and forecasts for project completion date and costs, are inputs to Control communications process.
- *Organizational Process Assets:* Organization's policies and procedures, records storage and retention policies, report templates and similar other organizational process assets provide important inputs.
- *Work Performance data* and *Issue Logs* are other important inputs to the process.

Tools and Techniques

The techniques applicable for this process are:

- *Project Management Information Systems (MIS):* Project MIS provides the standard forms and templates, which are useful in controlling the flow of information to different stakeholders' groups.
- *Expert Judgment:* Assessing the impact of specific communications and type of intervention and timeframe for it requires expert judgment.

Outputs

The main outputs of the process are:

- *Work Performance Information:* This is the main output of the performance reports, which is discussed below in detail separately.
- *Change Requests:* Based on the analysis of work performance reports, change requests may be initiated to bring back the orientation of the project to align with the basic project objectives.
- *Up-dates in Project Management Plan (Component plans)* and *Project Documents:* Essentially, this is for accommodating the Change Requests.
- *Organizational Process Assets Updates* (Essentially lessons learnt in the form of Report Formats and performance analysis technique updates)

Contents of a Typical Performance Report

Performance report summarizes the information on the status of the project and its normative evaluation by comparing the actual performance with the planned values. At the same time, it should summarise the unresolved risks and issues as well as the forecasts for expected time and cost at completion. Accordingly, a typical performance report might include:

- Summary of current status of the project in core areas of scope, time, cost and quality

- Analysis of the performance by comparison with the planned values
- Status of unresolved risks ad issues
- Forecast for project completion (time, budget, any major scope change from original)

Some additional important concepts in project communication deserve special attention:

(i) Communication Channels in Free and Hierarchical Information Flows and Their Suitability for Project Communication

(ii) Written and Verbal Communications

We shall briefly discuss them below:

(i) **Communication Channels in Free and Hierarchical Information Flows and Their Suitability for Project Communication**

Project communication is essentially the flow of information between the people engaged in the project activities. In that context, the communication process can be visualized as a network, where the people involved in the communication are the nodes and the active or permissible channels of communication between any two persons would be the lines joining these nodes.

From a network analysis point of view, there are two basic forms of communication networks:

Hierarchical Information Flow Network: This is the formal communication network in many organizations. The instructions or orders pass down from the higher levels or upper management to the next lower level and feedbacks or site information flow upward from the lower levels to the next higher managerial level and so forth.

The network basically looks like a set of straight lines connecting the nodes representing successively lower managerial levels. The merits of this communication network are that there is a strict accountability for communication and all instructions or orders pass down the command chain and all feedbacks pass up the command chain properly filtered for content and relevance. The drawback in the network is that there is a considerable time delay between the origination of the instruction or command at top management level and its receipt and execution at the lower operating level. Similar time delay occurs also in case of any important feedback passing from the operating level to the top management.

Free and Open Flow Information Network: In this form of communication network, everyone is free to communicate to every one else without any restriction. The network represents the exchanges for information likely in any unstructured assembly or meeting.

The network looks like a star with the straight lines connecting all nodes to each other. For a network with n persons in the communicating network (i.e. n nodes in the diagram), the number of communication channels (i.e. the number of straight lines joining the nodes in the diagram) would be $n(n-1)/2$. For as small a number of people as 10, this network would have 45 channels of communication; it would be really a cacophony in an open meeting, if all people choose to exercise their right to communicate! This type of communication network is ideal for brainstorming and visualizing a vast number of ideas or options for actions, when the situation is fluid and no single source has predominantly superior feedback to give. When a specific time-bound action based on instructions from some superior source of knowledge or skill is required, this form of network is wasteful and delaying the action in a crisis situation.

A combination of both basic forms is generally used for project communications. In a large project organization, the project manager may communicate through assistant project managers or department heads essentially using a hierarchical network, while the assistant project managers or section heads may have among themselves set up a free flow network. The project life cycle stage would also influence the form of communication network to be chosen. During the early planning phase of the project life cycle, it would be preferable to have the free flow and open communication channels for a large number of ideas and options to emerge for consideration. During the execution and monitoring stage, on the other hand, it would be generally preferable to limit the free communication and adopt some restricted form of communication channels.

(ii) Written and Verbal Communication

Sometimes, a project manager wonders whether he should use verbal communication or written. The general rule is to use the written mode for all formal documents:

- The technical feasibility and economic viability reports,
- The Project Charter and Project Scope Statement,
- The Project Plan (along with its subsidiary plans for cost, time, quality and risk management etc.),
- Project design basis and design reports for infrastructure projects,
- Lessons learned reports and Quality or Cost Audits, and
- Monthly or Quarterly Status Reports

This tradition is probably the reason for the humorous apocryphal saying that, "The weight of the paper work for a construction project equals the weight of the concrete cast!" Written communication is slower, impersonal, and takes effort. However, its merits are that accurate, detailed and well thought out presentation of complex ideas and information can be made and a permanent record of the project events is available for later analysis.

The anecdotal and news-of-the-moment communication should be informal, and so preferably, verbal. Where a person-to-person explanation is necessary, verbal communication is, of course, a must. But even when the formal documented communication is used, an informal discussion with the team members or key stakeholders, along with the issue of formal document, lends it a personal touch and helps set up good rapport. Verbal communications are a two-way affair, so the listener has a chance to seek clarifications and receive the full impact of the message conveyed, while the sender can get assurance of message having been properly received and understood. The other obvious advantages of verbal communication (person-to-person talk or telephone calls) are that it takes much less effort and time.

The written communication can be in the form of hard copies of printed/typed reports, e-mails, or intra-net transmittals. E-mail has the facility of being a written record, and yet to the extent that it is usually somewhat informal, permits e-mails to be sent in relatively shorter time and with less effort. Intra-net transmittals, especially of project schedule files of large projects, are very convenient to use; again they could be updated with small effort and short time.

Ability for effective verbal and written communication is an important part of the skill set desired from a project management professional and, thus a conscious effort should be made to hone this skill.

CASE 4.1

Manchester United Soccer Club

Nicolette Larson was loading the dishwasher with her husband, Kevin, and telling him about the first meeting of the Manchester United Tournament Organizing Committee. Nicolette, a self-confessed "soccer mom," had been elected tournament director and was responsible for organizing the club's first summer tournament.

Manchester United Soccer Club (MUSC) located in Manchester, New Hampshire, was formed in 1992 as a way of bringing recreational players to a higher level of competition and preparing them for the State Olympic Development Program and/or high school teams. The club currently has 24 boys and girls (ranging in age from under 9 to 16) on teams affiliated with the Hampshire Soccer Association and the Granite State Girls Soccer League. The club's board of directors decided in the fall to sponsor a summer invitational soccer tournament to generate revenue. Given the boom in youth soccer, hosting summer tournaments has become a popular method for raising funds. MUSC teams regularly compete in three to four tournaments each summer at different locales in New England. These tournaments have been reported to generate between $50,000 and $70,000 for the host club.

MUSC needs additional revenue to refurbish and expand the number of soccer fields at the Rock Rimmon soccer complex. Funds would also be used to augment the club's scholarship program, which provides financial aid to players who cannot afford the $450 annual club dues.

Nicolette gave her husband a blow-by-blow account of what transpired during the first tournament committee meeting that night. She started the meeting by having everyone introduce themselves and by proclaiming how excited she was that the club was going to sponsor its own tournament. She then suggested that the committee brainstorm what needed to be done to pull off the event; she would record their ideas on a flipchart.

What emerged was a free-for-all of ideas and suggestions. One member immediately stressed the importance of having qualified referees and spent several minutes describing in detail how his son's team was robbed in a poorly officiated championship game. This was followed by other stories of injustice on the soccer field. Another member suggested that they needed to quickly contact the local colleges to see if they could use their fields. The committee spent more than 30 minutes talking about how they should screen teams and how much they should charge as an entry fee. An argument broke out over whether they should reward the winning teams in each age bracket with medals or trophies. Many members felt that medals were too cheap, while others thought the trophies would be too expensive. Someone suggested that they seek local corporate sponsors to help fund the tournament. The proposed sale of tournament T-shirts and sweatshirts was followed by a general critique of the different shirts parents had acquired at different tournaments. One member advocated that they recruit an artist he knew to develop a unique silk-screen design for the tournament. The meeting adjourned 30 minutes late with only half of the members remaining until the end. Nicolette drove home with seven sheets of ideas and a headache.

As Kevin poured a glass of water for the two aspirin Nicolette was about to take, he tried to comfort her by saying that organizing this tournament would be a big project not unlike the projects he works on at his engineering and design firm. He offered to sit down with her the next night and help her plan the project. He suggested that the first thing they needed to do was to develop a WBS for the project.

1. Make a list of the major deliverables for the project and use them to develop a draft of the work breakdown structure for the tournament that contains at least three levels of detail. What are the major deliverables associated with hosting an event such as a soccer tournament?
2. How would developing a WBS alleviate some of the problems that occurred during the first meeting and help Nicolette organize and plan the project?
3. Where can Nicolette find additional information to help her develop a WBS for the tournament?
4. How could Nicolette and her task force use the WBS to generate cost estimates for the tournament? Why would this be useful information?

CASE 4.2

Hotel Pulkeshi International

(Case Illustrating Development of Project Scope Statement and Work Breakdown Structure)

Abstract

Project Scope Statement and Work Breakdown Structure (WBS) are the basic project documents for planning the project work. This case focuses on illustrating the technique for preparing Project Scope Statement and WBS for a construction project. The case includes description of the project initiation processes and presents a specimen of the Project Scope Statement modeled on the PMBOK® Guide recommendations. A WBS specimen based on the case details and conforming to the guidelines given in the Practice Standard for Work Breakdown Structure published by PMI is also presented at the end.

CASE TEXT

How would you describe a luxuriously furnished well-appointed conference room in sylvan surroundings, where you can look out of the French window and see a small man-made lake with some lotus in full bloom and a black swan majestically floating? Most people would be tempted to use the cliché "a Five-Star Facility". But in this case it would be an understatement; it was the Head Office Conference Room of the famous *Coronation Hotels* chain – "Seven Star Facility" would be a more appropriate description.

The centre mahogany table spotlessly polished and with a beautiful 51 candles chandelier overhanging above, was surrounded by plush chairs adequate in number to seat at least 20 people. But at the table now were only five people. At the head of the table sat Soli Jamashedji, the aging patriarch and founder of the Coronation Hotels chain. In a side chair, slightly drawn away from the table was a young man in his early thirties with rimless glasses, Padmanabhan Iyer, or Paddy as addressed by most people in the organization. He was one of the top graduates of IIM–Ahmedabad, where he had studied after his basic degree in computer science at IIT- Delhi. Soli used to lean a lot on him for business analysis using modern management analytical techniques, particularly in connection with mergers and acquisitions or setting up hotels at new locations. Other three senior officers at the table were Saurav Chakraborti (Director – Marketing), Satpal Singh (Executive Director – Operations) and Manish Shah (Director – Finance).

The principal agenda for the meeting was taking the decision on the future expansion plans of the Coronation Hotels. After the early pleasantries exchange, Saurav started presenting his findings. He pointed out that, "In view of the increasing emphasis on the development of the tourism industry, the flow of the foreigners and NRIs visiting India in the next five years was expected to increase by 12–15% per annum between 2005–06 and 2010–11 by the Government of India as well as several independent economic survey institutions. Earlier, most foreign tourists used to limit their itinerary to Delhi, Agra and Taj Mahal, some metropolitan cities (Mumbai, Banglore, Mysore), cave sculptures of Khajuraho or Ajanta-Ellora, tiger sanctuaries of Bandhavgarh or Kanha forest and similar well-trodden tourist circuits. However, recently a trend was noticed that an increasing part of these tourists wanted to go for out of the way or unusual destinations. One such cluster of locations could be in the northern Karanatak region – Badami (the capital of the Chalukya dynasty), Bijapur (famous for Chand Bibi who fought emperor Akabar), Vijayanagar Dynasty's Hampi and even Banglore-Mysore nearby."

Saurav spread out a small map of India and pointed out, " Here; here is Badami – now a small sleeping urban town in North Karnataka, but once the capital of the mighty Chalukya Dynasty king Pulkeshi-II, who stopped the emperor Harsh Vardhan's mighty and victorious army on the banks of river Narmada … and .." Before he could complete, Manish stopped him with a friendly banter, "Yes, yes Saurav; we got your point. You suggest that we set up a new hotel nearby? What capacity? What investment? Any preliminary market survey of likely occupancy figures? Apparently, this location would be of interest to the history buffs; so, are there any other well-known or interesting historical sites nearby? How far and convenient is it to visit Badami from the nearest airport?"

Saurav looked back disapprovingly but quietly continued, "Patience, Manish! We have done the preliminary market survey, investment and feasibility analysis in our group and the site looks very promising. Mr. Jamashedji is aware of all this. Now is the time to do some hard nose assessment and even some detailed planning if we generally agree on the proposal".

Satpal Singh chipped in, "Yes, we have also been receiving inquiries from our patrons at Bangalore and Mysore hotels, if they could go to and stay at one of our hotels in Bijapur or Badami; so it may be worth a detailed study".

"O.K; fellows; looks like a good starting point", Jamshedji concluded and then he looked at Paddy and said, " Paddy, start working and get all the details and have all the dope on the proposal for us to take the decision in the next operating committee meeting six weeks from now". The discussion in the meeting shifted to other subjects.

Paddy had under his command Strategic Planning Group, a crack core team of 10 brilliant executives – accountants, engineers, and market research persons. The team collected the necessary data and prepared the base case feasibility report. They also carried out risk analysis and ran some computer simulation based on it (Jamashedji always chided Paddy by remarking whether the computer simulation analytical tool, *Monte Carlo Analysis,* was named so as an implied admission of the gambling nature of the analysis). *Sensitivity Analysis* was carried out for determining the effect on the profitability of the new venture if the real-life scenario in future turned out different from the base case assumptions. They also studied the hotel capacity expansion in phases and carried out the *Decision Tree Analysis* to arrive at the optimum hotel room capacity for the first phase – 100 rooms. Paddy's team found that the new hotel location in the vicinity of Badami would be an attractive investment proposition. Paddy christened the project *Hotel Pulkeshi International* after the famous Chalukya dynasty emperor.

At the next operating committee meeting, Paddy presented the brief technical details of the project (likely optional locations, an architect's impressions of the hotel, general floor lay outs, land and site development cost, construction and furnishing costs, etc.) and the financial projections worked out by his team in cooperation with the finance group (projections of the next five years likely operating results in terms of occupancy, operating cost and profitability and the net cash flows).

Jamashedji felt pleased with the way Paddy and his group worked out the data for decision-making. After some discussions on the project assumptions and the working paper details underlying the summary, the committee gave a green signal for going ahead. "Then gentlemen, we agree to go ahead with *Hotel Pulkeshi International* project at Badami, right? Satpal, you pick out a good project manager for this project, and get him started working on the project". Then after a pause of half a minute, he added, with a wink in his eye, "But before that, Paddy, you prepare the Project Charter and Project Scope Statement like that bald professor of project management used to harp on in the 1-day project management seminar you insisted on me to attend last month". Everybody thought it was a joke and started to smile, when Jamashedji added, "No, I am serious; what he said makes sense".

Attachment 1 shows the Project Scope Statement prepared by Paddy's strategic planning group.

Satpal Singh zeroed in on Ram Prasad as the project manager to be appointed for Hotel Pulkeshi International. Ram Prasad was also an IIT-Kanpur trained civil engineer, who had joined the Coronation Hotels group seven years back. He had an impressive track record of efficient management of civil construction projects before he joined the Coronation Group. In Coronation, he got gradually involved with the entire gamut of the hotel projects and the last project, *Hotel Sabaramati,* which was managed under his independent command, earned him good reputation. There was some unspoken rivalry between Ram Prasad and Paddy. Ram Prasad looked upon numbers churning office engineers as something amiss of their basic profession. Paddy thought that the real business of business was after all the bottom line of the entire operations. Paddy had some latent contempt for these hard-core engineering people. Satpal Singh was somewhat aware of this and decided to exploit the situation for effective management of project Hotel Pulkeshi International.

"Ram, we are happy to select you to be the project manager for our newest hotel project, *Hotel Pulkeshi International*", Satpal told him, and "Here are the market research and project feasibility study data for the project to give you grounding in the overall strategy." Then he pulled out another set of file papers from his folder and said, "These papers contain the Project Charter and Project Scope Statement prepared by the Strategic Planning Group – your good friend Paddy. Paddy appears to nurse the grouse that we engineers are not focused on the overall project objectives and get lost among the trees and miss the forest. I want you to show him what we actually accomplish in bricks and mortars and not just paper projects. But I also want to show that you could be as systematic in your project planning as he himself could ever hope to be. Get the point? Start with preparing a systematic Work Breakdown Structure (WBS) for the project. I understand that is the cornerstone in the modern project planning. Let us discuss it on Monday two weeks from now", then he looked at the calendar and added, "December 19, 3 PM; fine? Anything you want in terms of resources just let me know and you would have them"

Ram Prasad came back to his room and worked day and night with his core project team of seven people (one architect and landscape designer, two civil engineers, one mechanical/utility engineer, one electrical engineer, one accounts manager, one interior designer). He prepared the overall project management plan and an impressive WBS using the guidelines given in the *Practice Standard for Work Breakdown Structure* published by the Project Management Institute (PMI), U.S.A.

Questions for Case Discussion

The Project Scope Statement and Work Breakdown Structures (WBS) presented in the case are based on PMBOK®) Guide recommendations for preparing these documents. They provide good templates as a starting point for developing these documents for other projects.

Using these templates, prepare the Project Scope Statement and Work Breakdown Structure for the last project you worked on.

Attachment 1

PROJECT SCOPE STATEMENT
(Hotel Pulkeshi International)

The Coronation Hotels Group proposes to set up a new hotel in the vicinity of Badami, Karnataka State. The broad parameters of the scope of this project are given below:

The facilities shall conform to the construction, layout, furnishing, and operating standards currently followed at all other Coronation Group locations and would permit the new facility to be classified as a Five Star Facility according to the International Hotel Management Association guidelines.

1. PROJECT OBJECTIVES

The project objectives are:

- To set up a new 100-rooms capacity 5-star hotel in the vicinity of Badami, Karnataka
- To take advantage of the niche group of foreign tourists to southern India
- To maintain Coronation's market share among the premier hotel accommodations
- To earn a net return of 20 % per annum on equity investment

2. GENERAL DESCRIPTION OF FACILITIES

The facilities should conform to the following general requirements:

- The overall layout, the architecture and landscaping of the entire facility should be spacious and give an impression of a luxury five star hotel. The master plan should include a provision for the expansion of the facility to a total 500 rooms hotel in future.
- The initial capacity of the hotel would be 100 air conditioned fully carpeted guest rooms, each with facility for accommodating 2 guests. The rooms shall be furnished according to current Coronation Group hotels standard and should include suitable number of single or double beds, a writing table, two sofa chairs with a small service table, a small fridge, a TV set, outlets for intercom and outside phones, an outlet for internet connection for laptop computers, and other usual amenities.
- Hotel should include three restaurants serving Indian, western and Chinese cuisine; a coffee shop, a bar, and a central kitchen for giving room service to guests.
- A swimming pool and gym facilities for guests
- Two large halls suitable for assembly of 150–200 persons for use in case of some prestigious occasions or receptions
- Four small conference rooms, with capacities to accommodate 20 to 35 guests, for some company meetings or conferences
- Other facilities like a medicines shop, souvenirs and personal needs shop and several shops to be given on a franchise basis to outsiders to set up arts, sculptures, novelties, fancy textiles shops and the like

This description of facilities is not exhaustive and will need to be reviewed and planned during the detailed planning stage.

3. PROJECT ASSUMPTIONS

The basic assumptions for success in meeting project objectives are as follows:

1. The company board formally approves the project latest by January 31, 2007.
2. The statutory approvals necessary for setting up the hotel are received by March 31, 2007
3. Preliminary funding arrangements are in place for the project cash outflows to begin latest by June 1, 2007.
4. The foreign tourist flow and its niche clientele composition materializes as per current projections
5. The occupancy rates of minimum 70 % during the off seasons and full occupancy during the peak periods are maintained.
6. The key persons for the project team are assigned to the project by March 31, 2007.

4. PROJECT DELIVERABLES

The first level project deliverables are:

- Acquisition of land, site development and landscaping
- Necessary statutory approvals for starting the project and on an ongoing basis as needed

- Construction of buildings and structures
- Setting up utilities facilities (water, electricity, firefighting, etc.)
- Furnishing; Main furniture hardware and soft furnishing
- Recruitment and training of staff
- Preliminary marketing
- Project management for on-time and within-budget completion of the project deliverables to meet the project satisfaction criteria

5. PRELIMINARY PROJECT SCHEDULE

Assuming that the basic statutory approvals and financing arrangements are in place for the project construction to start by June 2007, the following milestones are envisaged:

Site selection and acquisition	August 31, 2007
Detailed planning of the facility	September 30, 2007
Award of civil construction contract	October 15, 2007
Start of civil construction at the site	November 1, 2007
Completion of basic buildings and structures	September 30, 2008
Final finishing and furnishing	November 30, 2008
Recruitment of new key staff and training completion	December 15, 2008
Functionally complete in operation to serve guests	January 1, 2009

6. PRELIMINARY COST ESTIMATE

The preliminary cost estimate for the project is ₹145 crore is as follows:

		(₹ in crore)
Land and site development		12.00
Buildings, Structures & Furnishings		
Civil construction	45.00	
Utilities & facilities	15.00	
Furnishings	38.00	
Landscape & gardens	2.00	100.00
Preliminary & pre-operative expenses		18.00
Provision for contingency (@ 10 %, rounded up)		15.00
Total Project Cost		**₹145.00 crores**

WORK BREAKDOWN STRUCTURE (WBS)
(Hotel Pulkeshi International)

1. Confirm needs analysis and refine project planning

   1.1 Confirm the needs for service

   1.2 Confirm the market size, quality of service and hotel capacity

   1.3 Verify the project assumptions

   1.4 Prepare refined cost estimate for the project and check with the preliminary cost estimate

   1.5 Prepare preliminary schedule and check its compatibility with the expected completion

   1.6 Verify the cash flow and project feasibility assumptions

   1.7 Prepare detailed project management plan

2. Acquire land, carry out site development and landscaping

   2.1 Evaluate available sites and select the site

   2.2 Negotiate land acquisition with the suppliers and purchase land

   2.3 Carry out land survey and load bearing tests for soil

   2.4 Carry our site development activities

      2.4.1 Construct approach roads

      2.4.2 Construct boundary wall or fence

      2.4.3 Start overall leveling and fine leveling of the main hotel building area

      2.4.4 Arrange for water supply and electricity

      2.4.5 Plant trees near the outskirts or clear areas

3. Obtain necessary statutory approvals (for project start and on-going basis)

   3.1 Receive approval for building construction plan

   3.2 Receive electricity supply related approvals

      3.2.1 Load sanction and initial connection

      3.2.2 Electricity Inspectorate – approval after construction inspection

   3.3 Receive approvals from water supply authority

      3.3.1 Load sanction and initial connection

   3.4 Receive drainage and effluents connection approvals

   3.5 Receive building completion certificate and occupancy certificate

4. Prepare Master Plan for the premises

   4.1 Select and appoint architect

   4.2 Prepare the master plan for property development (incl. future expansion)

5. Prepare building construction plans

   5.1 Prepare overall floor-wise hotel layout plans

   5.2 Prepare detailed civil engineering designs

      5.2.1 Columns and plinth beams layout and sizing

      5.2.2 Slab designs

5.2.3 Construction details for lintels, staircase, walls, windows and doors

5.2.4 Color scheme and finishes

5.2.5 Specifications for flooring, fittings and fixtures

5.3 Prepare water piping and drainage piping plans

5.4 Prepare electrical cables layouts

5.5 Prepare fire escapes and sprinkler layout plans

5.6 Prepare air conditioning scheme and ducting layouts

5.6 Prepare telephone and intercom network layouts

6. **Carry out construction activities at the site**

6.1 Select road construction contractor and construct internal roads

6.2 Construct the main building

6.2.1 Select the prime contractor for all construction work (civil engineering, electrical, water and drainage, air conditioning, telephones, fire-fighting systems, etc.)

6.2.2 Construct RCC structure (columns, beams, slabs, walls, windows)

6.2.3 Install electric cabling

6.2.4 Install water and drainage piping

6.2.5 Install central AC equipment and distribution ducting

6.2.6 Install telephone network lines

6.2.7 Install sprinklers and fire safety equipment

6.2.8 Finish flooring, ceiling and painting

6.3 Construct ancillary buildings

6.4 Complete landscaping, plant shrubs, bushes and lawns

7. **Furnish the hotel facilities**

7.1 Prepare the Master Plan for interior decoration

7.2 Install entrance lobby and floor lobbies' furniture

7.3 Install room furniture – beds, sofas, tables, fridges, etc.

7.4 Install soft furniture – curtains, mattresses, art works frames, etc.

8. **Recruit and train staff**

8.1 Get key and supervisory staff assigned from other operating locations

8.2 Recruit other supervisory staff and train

8.3 Recruit daily operating workers and train

9. **Manage project effectively and efficiently**

9.1 Acquire project team, communicate the overall scheme and start project work

9.2 Prepare detailed cost estimate and month-wise budget for cash out-flows

9.3 Prepare detailed project activities network and project schedule using MS Projects

9.4 Prepare detailed communication plan.

9.5 Execute, monitor and control the project activities according to project management plan

9.6 Close the contracts

10. **Preliminary commercial activities**

10.1 Keep the central marketing group informed of the project progress

10.2 Invite the Chairman Soli Jamashedji, Executive Director Satpal Singh, other directors and Karnataka Tourism Development Minister for hotel inauguration

CASE 4.3

Process Development at Union Chemicals

(A Case Focusing on Project Communications and Project Stakeholder Management Areas)

Abstract

The project success, no doubt, requires effectively managing the core project management issues of scope, time, cost and quality. In the midst of hectic project activities, a hardworking, conscientious project manager might sometime neglect paying attention to the soft skills of project management: interpersonal skills in leading and managing the team, conflict management, negotiation, and managing project communication for key stakeholders. This case study focuses on a project communication management and especially on the importance of managing the communication needs of the key stakeholders for project success. Failing to manage the communication needs of the key stakeholders, the project manager in the case, though successful in addressing all key project objectives, is forced to quit disgraced.

CASE TEXT

It was Monday, February 1. The siren blew at 5-30 PM and within only a few minutes the staff bus of Union Chemicals began to get filled up with the middle level staff entitled to travel by the company bus. Girish Pandya also stepped in and without exchanging any pleasantry with the colleagues already sitting in the bus he headed straight to the back corner seat, and buried his head in the current copy of the Time magazine as soon as he slumped there.

"Hey Girish, after a long many months, I found you quitting the work on time and coming with us plebeians in this bus. Why, you have already solved all problems of the high pressure alpha-naphthol process or what?" Patankar chided Girish while sliding into the next seat in the bus. "Leave me alone, Sidh! I am really dead tired to-day." said Girish. Though he continued to bury his head into the open pages of the magazine, Girish's mind was not there. He was pondering over the project to develop new process for manufacture of alpha-naphthol which ran the course in the last five months.

History

Girish Pandya was a mechanical engineer with a reasonably bright academic career and had proved a competent shift-in-charge for one of the production departments at Union Chemical's plant. His real strength, however, was his ability think out of the box and the sound grasp of fundamental engineering principles – "engineering fundas" as the students' jargon referred to them. This enabled him to come out now and then with an altogether unconventional solution to production problems, which came up from time to time in the production department and baffled the group.

Union Chemicals was a subsidiary of a U.K. based large multinational company of the same name, with the parent organization having a noteworthy presence in the U.K. The UK Company had been manufacturing and marketing a number of specialty chemicals in the UK. Some of the chemicals, which fell out of favour with the UK parent company due to the concerns raised by the environmentalists and the Green Brigade, were licensed to the Indian subsidiary for manufacture in India and distribution worldwide – especially to South-East Asian countries.

Indian subsidiary of Union Chemicals remained a routine manufacturing operation for a number of chemicals. With the globalization trend, the parent company decided on the strategy of trying to exploit the opportunity of availability of competent low-cost technical personnel in India to shift a part of its research effort to India. A well-equipped laboratory, for such research effort and development department to build and operate pilot plants, was set up for development of a new process or for trying out important modifications in a process step of an already commercially established process. These two departments, staffed with academically highflying PhDs in chemistry or chemical engineering, soon occupied the position of the blue-eyed boys of the top management. Dr. Arnav Patel headed this departmental group. Raman Shah headed four production departments at the plant; each department concerned with one specific chemical. There was an understandable rivalry between Dr. Patel and Mr. Shah and Dr. Patel had started to edge out Raman Shah.

Selection of the Project Manager

In the later part of 2003, there was a buzz that the UK company had landed a big process research contract and that Union Chemical's Indian operations may be given a piece of the cake. Everyone had thought that the assignment will be passed on to Dr. Arnav Patel's group and he would sprint ahead in the race to be the next CEO of Union Chemical's India operations.

On September 18, 2003, Raman Shah called Girish into his office just around 5:20 PM. Irish's first reaction was to get upset at the prospect of missing his regular staff bus travel to home and his impatience showed through his body language. The seasoned manager, that Raman Shah was, did not miss the signal. "Girish, I have called you for something very important. You can afford to miss your staff bus travel today, but you dare not miss the bus of opportunity I want to talk to you about. Our parent company has passed on a part of the high-pressure alpha-naphthol process research project to us in India - **and under my charge**. We need to set up a small pilot plant based on the preliminary chemical process information developed by the head office R & D group. I want you to head that pilot plant effort!"

"But why not Dr.Arnav Patel's group? They have some good Ph.Ds strutting around. And, then of all the people, why me? I haven't got even a Master's degree – I am just a graduate mechanical engineer, not even a chemist!" blurted Girish unbelieving of the great opportunity, which appeared to knock at his door – the opportunity, which he had not even dared to dream.

"Good questions, Girish. I like your practical no-nonsense approach. In fact, that is precisely why I want to choose you for heading the effort. You are highly creative and you have sound knowledge of engineering fundamentals; I have personally seen it in working. The new process for alpha-naphthol will require very high-pressure reaction and separation process steps and so your creativity and sound engineering will be a real asset. And why our department? Because, we do make another naphthalene based intermediate and so our production department has a group of persons quite familiar with the basic raw material. Since you mentioned, let me share with you, off records, of course, my personal opinion of those chemistry Ph.Ds. of Arnav. They are just good at mixing colored solutions in the test tubes; nothing more. Our head office has also found out that they usually have no clue about the engineering aspects of a commercial production process for a chemical plant. That's why they want me to take the lead on this. It will be my baby – the project will be a feather in my cap", Raman would not miss an opportunity to express his low opinion of the work Dr. Arnav Patel and his group did. Then he continued, "And now let me tell you, what's in it for you. Well, if you can swing this process development work, you will be department head jumping four of your seniors in the queue. I have great confidence in your ability to deliver the results. For the time being, you will work at your current level only till the process development succeeds, and work very hard – say 14 hours a day- but the opportunity is really big if you make it. " Girish did not have to think very long to accept the offer, though he asked for a week's time, for thinking over in that evening meeting.

The Project Start

Like proverbial true love, the path of a project is also not strewn with roses.

The first obstacle that Girish faced was getting the sanction for the resources for setting up the pilot plant. For setting up a small pilot plant would require first understanding the basic chemistry of the laboratory scale process developed by the head office. The next step would be to prepare designs of the pilot plant equipment and prepare detailed engineering specifications for procurement. Procuring the equipment, installing them, carrying out trial runs and making suitable modifications in the equipment and processing steps based on trial results were the next project phases. After staying back at the plant and working very late evenings for a whole week, Girish came up with the basic pilot plant scheme and the cost of setting up the project.

"The project will cost ₹6.5 millions and take 6 months", Girish announced the next week Monday morning to Raman.

"What? ₹5 million is the budget sanctioned by the head office. We have to keep project cost within it. And we have to also complete it within 4 months" Raman almost shouted, though in fact the head office had given the outer limit for this work to be 6 months.

Girish leafed back and forth his sheaf of papers with detailed list of items and cost and started to explain his cost estimate basis. Raman just waved him aside and said, "Forget those numbers. Rework them and bring the project cost to total ₹4.9 million. We must meet HO project cost expectations to start with. If the project succeeds, we will run the overrun request after the project completion - nobody will grudge it then."

"But, sir, … " Girish stuttered.

"Do as I say. If you want to be all that truthful and accurate, forget the assignment. I can pull out some other, even more senior engineer, for this assignment."

Girish did not have much choice except to follow Raman's instructions.

Project Execution

Selecting the project team was the next hurdle. The project would require as team members an engineer from the design and drafting department, an engineer for procurement and a chemist for testing the raw materials, in-process streams and final product. "I will get you Shashi Rana from the Materials Department and Sudhakar Joshi from Engineering & Design Department to work with you. At the end of six weeks, we have to submit the first interim report of the project status to HO; Mr. Williams, the Process Development-Head at HO will himself be in the video conference meeting to discuss the report; so just get on the work as fast as you can."

Shashi Rana was a young but very promising engineer and Girish and Shashi started to work on the equipment procurement in real earnest. The process required a high temperature hydrolysis reaction (at over 220 degrees C) in an aqueous medium. The corrosive nature of the reactants and high-pressure requirements called for a special metering pump built with stainless steel 316 L. The reactor and some pipe fittings also required to be special – and not off the shelf items. Shashi and Girish started a close follow-up with the vendors for the special items – discussing and clearing the technical difficulties that vendors brought up from time to time and visiting the shops for inspection and first-hand information.

All this kept Girish so busy that his interim report at the end of the six weeks was a mere 2-page long document. HO had expected a much more elaborate submission from the Indian subsidiary and may be referrals to them for some help or clarifications all along in the 6-week period! Since Girish did not contact HO, Mr. Williams himself started calling India to talk with the project manager and, most of the times, he was told that Girish was visiting the vendor's shop or in the Engineering & Design Department reviewing the drawings. Mr. Williams expressed his displeasure to Raman Shah.

Raman Shah called Girish to his office. Girish was full of enthusiasm for the headway he could make in engineering design and procurement in spite of the heavy odds. Raman Shah threw cold water on his enthusiasm. "What a 2-page rag sheets-like report you submitted for 6-weeks status report! Mr. Williams was furious. He also said you were never available, whenever he called you."

"I and Shashi were at the vendor's shops to test out the components of the metering pump, so that it would surely work…"

"Your job as a project manager is to manage the project – not to test the components. Weren't you telling me that at the project management program, you recently took at that institution, they stressed on the importance of project communication – especially managing the communication needs of the key stakeholders and all that? HO and Mr. Williams are our key stakeholders for the project- understand? Write out a detailed report now … preferably before the end of the next week, submit with an explanation that for some unforeseen problems, you could not submit your formal 6-week report on time, so you chose to send a short interim report to meet dead line. The video conference meeting will follow it in 2-days."

For all the very hard work he had done for the past six weeks and the promise for success, which it showed, this was a bitter pill to swallow for Girish. His 2-page report, if anybody had read closely, would have earned him kudos for the extraordinary work he and his team had put. The HO, and at its prodding now Raman, merely wanted reams of papers rather than concrete results, he felt. For the whole next week, Girish sat at his desk and drafted and redrafted report parts, with elaborate tables and graphs, paying attention to the report language, report format and fonts and color scheme of the graphs! The final 70-page report looked beautiful and for that very reason, Girish hated it and hated himself for being forced to spend time in so unproductive activities.

But Girish's troubles were not over. HO went over the report with a fine comb and had several queries based on the reading. The e-mails between HO and Girish started crossing the continents faster and more furious than ever, when finally Mr. Williams again called Raman Shah and explained that he was quite unhappy with the way the project was managed and he would have to consider sending his engineer, Dr. Rudolph, to India to oversee Girish's work, if the situation does not improve soon.

In the meantime, Girish's problems with his other senior colleagues at the plant also multiplied. The Materials Department Head complained to Raman Shah that Girish had started overloading Shashi Rana so much with this project work that she was unable to manage her other assignments in the department. "Besides, I have no clue about what Girish and Shashi are doing. If it is that important and prestigious project, why am I not in the list of project report recipients? Girish has never even dropped in my office and let me know what is happening in the project or how our department can contribute". Well, so, this was what really hurt the Materials Department Head. "I would have to ask Shashi to pay attention to other projects." He warned.

The Head of Design & Engineering Department was also equally upset about his being in the dark. He told Raman Shah, "Raman, Girish is doing some design & engineering work on that high pressure hydrolysis process. I had worked on similar two process designs earlier. I could have given him some really useful tips on the design and engineering specifications for the components. Girish never even talked with me. He just sits with Sudhakar Joshi, calculates design parameters, prepares some sketches and specifications and runs around. If the things don't work, Girish will blame Sudhakar and CEO will blame me why I did not intervene and help."

Raman gave some lame excuses, but he himself really had not detailed up-to-date information on the project. So, what could he share with the Head – Engineering & Design?

In the meantime, six more weeks passed and all the equipment and components arrived at the site. Begging the maintenance mechanical and electrical supervisors, Girish got them installed even though some work overflowed into the weekends requiring overtime; he got it done, but just as a personal favor to himself! The time came for submission of the second status report. Girish now had to take papers home and work late till early morning three days in a row. His wife remarked, "In the last three months, you have not been at home for more than a few hours to eat and sleep. You haven't got a decent raise in the last three years, so what is all this hard work for? " Girish could not explain her reality he faced; he just stood silent and looked down to avoid her accusing gaze.

Finally the report was ready and it included good news if someone could really read and understand it rather than flip over it. Girish, however, was not lucky in this respect. Raman Shah remarked, "You appear to go out even beyond your own project cost estimate. I won't be able to explain such huge overruns on project cost". CEO passed on to Dr.Arnav Patel a copy of the report for review. He remarked, "Looks like not meticulously designed set of experiments. You see, if Girish had contacted me earlier, I would have helped him with a much better and more economical experiments set using the principles of Design of Experiments (DOE)." But Dr. Ramanathan, in charge of testing laboratory, was somewhat more kind, "Get whatever tests you want done – but during regular working hours – no overtime or weekends, please." Girish again had to use his personal relationships with Dr. Ramanathan's staff and actually got testing done, even during weekends when necessary, to expedite the project.

The first results, though promising, were not adequate for finalizing the design parameters for a commercial process. The main reaction was good, but some side-reactions also occurred, which reduced the overall yield to 84%. At the same time, the product purity was 97.2%. A minimum yield of 90% and product purity of 98.5% were necessary for process commercialization. Girish went through with redesign of some components to permit the operating conditions for a 10 degrees higher temperature and 150 psi higher pressure. By the end of 16 weeks, the redesigned set up was ready for the next set of trial runs. This was when the four months project schedule conveyed by Girish to HO at the start of the project was to come to a close. Mr. Williams was furiously looking for some final results and report as promised by the Indian subsidiary. He decided that the time had come for his more active intervention.

He called Raman Shah, "Look Raman, you have let us down badly. You don't realize but the process development part the India Company is working on is only a small miniscule part. Not even the tip of the iceberg. We cannot allow India Company to jeopardize our multi-million pounds research project contract. I am sending Dr. Rudolph to India; he will be there on February 1. Mind well, it is not too soon; it would be fifteen days beyond the deadline you yourself had scheduled!"

Girish did not see the Republic Day parade on TV on the national holiday. He was doing the final test run on the modified pilot plant. Shashi Rana and Sudhakar Joshi were also there. The test appeared to run quite well and the laboratory results and analysis would be over by January 29. Mahatma Gandhi Assassination Day, January 30, was observed as a holiday at the plant. Girish was at home – the very first time at home in the last five months. He was dead tired – every bone in his body ached; every nerve in his mind had gone numb.

The first phone call he received that day was from Raman Shah. "Dr. Rudolph will reach here day after to-morrow. Are you ready with all the briefings for him? We have already missed the 4-months project schedule dead line. We also would not be able to hide that the project will have large cost overruns. You better prepare some good briefing to win him over. "

The next call he received was from Shashi Rana, " Hey, you are at home? I thought you would also be with us at the laboratory. You should be right here at the plant for celebration! Our last trial run is successful beyond our imagination. We got 98.7% product purity at 91.3% yield. **Did you hear? 98.7% product purity at 91.3% yield**!" Shashi almost shouted while uttering the last sentence.

The third call was again from Raman Shah, "By the way, Girish, who have you arranged to go and receive Dr. Rudolph at the airport? And what about booking his accommodation at Taj Intercontinental Hotel? I hope you would personally go there. You are quite negligent in dealing with some of these crucial issues".

Girish sat stunned after Raman Shah's last call. The entire five months period passed in front of his mind's eyes like a review. He had worked night and day and offered blood and sweat for making the project a success. Now, how will HO hierarchy see it? 'Dr. Rudolph visited India and straightened out the pilot plant project!' 'Yes, very timely intervention by Dr. Williams of HO, who kept a hawk-eye on the entire project.' 'Excellent cooperation and coordination by India plant – particularly Raman Shah! 'Forget the Head Office – even his own superior here in the India plant, Raman Shah- even he did not realize the pains we took to succeed. And while doing the project work, I have surely not made friends with other senior department heads in the plant, nor the seniors in my own department. It is a desperate situation. I have to move out," he concluded, "there is no future for me to continue working here now".

He sat deeply immersed in himself for good one hour. Then he moved over to the phone, dialed Raman Shah and started speaking in as calm a voice as he could keep, "Sir, please arrange for some one else to receive Dr. Rudolph. In fact, please ask some one else to take charge of whatever is left in the project from now onwards. After all, as you explained me on the first day, the project is 'your baby' and 'the feather in your cap'. By the way, the second set of trial runs has succeeded and we could get yield and purity required – Shashti told me on the phone – so my conscience is clear about meeting my commitments. I would hand over my resignation the first thing on February 1 morning." Then, without waiting to listen to the response, he put the phone down.

Epilogue

Union Chemicals, UK, made a grand success of the research project contract and the contribution from the Indian subsidiary in working on a critical research component was not lost sight of. Raman Shah was promoted as the next CEO of Union Chemicals, India.

Questions for Case Discussion

1. In your opinion,
   • Did the project succeed?
   • Did Girish Pandya succeed as a Project Manager?
2. Using the background of this case discuss the project communication management and its importance in successful project management.
3. PMBOK(R) Guide, 5th Edition, lists 3 processes in project communication management:
   • Plan Communications Management
   • Manage Communications and
   • Control Communications
   PMBOK(R) Guide, 5th Edition, also lists 4 processes in project Stakeholder management :
   • Identify Stakeholders
   • Plan Stakeholder Management
   • Manage Stakeholder Management
   • Control Stakeholder Management
   Discuss Girish Pandya's performance in project communications and project stakeholder management areas in context of the above processes.

5

ESTIMATING PROJECT TIMES AND COSTS

*Project estimation is indeed a yardstick for project cost control. And if the yardstick is faulty, you start on the "wrong foot."... we exhort you not to underestimate the estimate.**

Given the urgency to start work on the project, managers sometimes minimize or avoid the effort to follow through on estimating project time and cost. This attitude is a huge mistake and costly. There are important reasons to make the effort and incur the cost of estimating for your project. Exhibit 5.1 summarizes some key reasons.

Exhibit 5.1 •••
Why Estimating Time and Cost are Important

- Estimates are needed to support good decisions.
- Estimates are needed to schedule work.
- Estimates are needed to determine how long the project should take and its cost.
- Estimates are needed to determine whether the project is worth doing.
- Estimates are needed to develop cash flow needs.
- Estimates are needed to determine how well the project is progressing.
- Estimates are needed to develop time-phased budgets and establish the project baseline.

Estimating is the process of forecasting or approximating the time and cost of completing project deliverables. Estimating processes are frequently classified as top-down and bottom-up. Top-down estimates are usually done by senior management. Management will often derive estimates from analogy, group consensus, or mathematical relationships. Bottom-up estimates are typically performed by the people who are doing the work. Their estimates are based on estimates of elements found in the work breakdown structure.

All project stakeholders prefer accurate cost and time estimates, but they also understand the inherent uncertainty in all projects. Inaccurate estimates lead to false expectations and consumer dissatisfaction. Accuracy is improved with greater effort, but is it worth the time and cost— estimating costs money! Project estimating becomes a trade-off, balancing the benefits of better accuracy against the costs for securing increased accuracy.

Cost, time, and budget estimates are the lifeline for control; they serve as the standard for comparison of actual and plan throughout the life of the project. Project status reports depend on reliable estimates as the major input for measuring variances and taking corrective action. Ideally, the project manager, and in most cases the customer, would prefer to have a database of detailed schedule and cost estimates for every work package in the project. Regrettably, such detailed data gathering is not always possible or practical and other methods are used to develop project estimates.

FACTORS INFLUENCING THE QUALITY OF ESTIMATES

A typical statement in the field is the desire to "have a 95 percent probability of meeting time and cost estimates." *Past experience* is a good starting point for developing time and cost estimates. But

---

* O. P. Kharbanda and J. K. Pinto, *What Made Gertie Gallop: Learning from Project Failures* (New York: Van Nostrand Reinhold, 1996), p. 73.

past experience estimates must almost always be refined by other considerations to reach the 95 percent probability level. Factors related to the uniqueness of the project will have a strong influence on the accuracy of estimates. Project, people, and external factors all need to be considered to improve quality of estimates for project times and costs.

Planning Horizon

The quality of the estimate depends on the *planning horizon;* estimates of current events are close to 100 percent accurate but are reduced for more distant events. For example, cost estimates for a party you are organizing this weekend should be much more accurate than the estimates for a wedding that will take place in three months. The accuracy of time and cost estimates should improve as you move from the conceptual phase to the point where individual work packages are defined. Long-duration projects increase the uncertainty in estimates.

Project Duration

Time to implement new *technology* has a habit of expanding in an increasing, nonlinear fashion. Sometimes poorly written scope specifications for new technology result in errors in estimating times and costs.

People

The *people* factor can influence the quality of time and cost estimates. For example, accuracy of estimates depends on the skills of the people making the estimates. How familiar are they with the task they are estimating?

Project Structure and Organization

Which *project structure* is chosen to manage the project will influence time and cost estimates. One of the major advantages of a dedicated project team discussed earlier is the speed gained from concentrated focus and localized project decisions. This speed comes at an additional cost of tying up personnel full time. Conversely, projects operating in a matrix environment may reduce costs by more efficiently sharing personnel across projects but may take longer to complete since attention is divided and coordination demands are higher.

Padding Estimates

In some cases people are inclined to *pad estimates.* For example, if you are asked how long it takes you to drive to the airport, you might give an average time of 30 minutes, assuming a 50/50 chance of getting there in 30 minutes. If you are asked the fastest you could possibly get there, you might reduce the driving time to 20 minutes. Finally, if you are asked how long the drive would take if you absolutely had to be there to meet with the president, it is likely you would increase the estimate to say 50 minutes to ensure not being late. In work situations where you are asked for time and cost estimates, most of us are inclined to add a little padding to increase the probability and reduce the risk of being late. If everyone at all levels of the project adds a little padding to reduce risk, the project duration and cost are seriously overstated. This phenomenon causes some managers or owners to call for a 10–15 percent cut in time and/or cost for the project. Of course the next time the game is played, the person estimating cost and/or time will pad the estimate to 20 percent or more. Clearly such games defeat chances for realistic estimates, which is what is needed to be competitive.

Organization Culture

Organization culture can significantly influence project estimates. In some organizations padding estimates is tolerated and even privately encouraged. Other organizations place a premium on accuracy and strongly discourage estimating gamesmanship. Organizations vary in the importance they attach to estimates. The prevailing belief in some organizations is that detailed estimating takes too much time and is not worth the effort or that it's impossible to predict the future. Other organizations subscribe to the belief that accurate estimates are the bedrock of effective project management. Organization culture shapes every dimension of project management; estimating is not immune to this influence.

Other Factors

Finally, *nonproject factors* can impact time and cost estimates. For example, equipment down-time can alter time estimates. National holidays, vacations, and legal limits can influence project estimates. Project priority can influence resource assignment and impact time and cost.

Project estimating is a complex process. The quality of time and cost estimates can be improved when these variables are considered in making the estimates. Estimates of time and cost together allow the manager to develop a time-phased budget, which is imperative for project control. Before discussing macro and micro estimating methods for times and costs, a review of estimating guidelines will remind us of some of the important "rules of the game" that can improve estimating.

ESTIMATING GUIDELINES FOR TIMES, COSTS, AND RESOURCES

Managers recognize time, cost, and resource estimates must be accurate if project planning, scheduling, and controlling are to be effective. However, there is substantial evidence suggesting poor estimates are a major contributor to projects that have failed. Therefore, every effort should be made to see that initial estimates are as accurate as possible since the choice of no estimates leaves a great deal to luck and is not palatable to serious project managers. Even though a project has never been done before, a manager can follow seven guidelines to develop useful work package estimates.

1. **Responsibility.** At the work package level, estimates should be made by the person(s) most familiar with the task. Draw on their expertise! Except for supertechnical tasks, those responsible for getting the job done on schedule and within budget are usually first-line supervisors or technicians who are experienced and familiar with the type of work involved. These people will not have some preconceived, imposed duration for a deliverable in mind. They will give an estimate based on experience and best judgment. A secondary benefit of using those responsible is the hope they will "buy in" to seeing that the estimate materializes when they implement the work package. If those involved are not consulted, it will be difficult to hold them responsible for failure to achieve the estimated time. Finally, drawing on the expertise of team members who will be responsible helps to build communication channels early.

2. **Use several people to estimate.** It is well known that a cost or time estimate usually has a better chance of being reasonable and realistic when several people with relevant experience and/

or knowledge of the task are used (sometimes called "crowdsourcing"). True, people bring different biases based on their experience. But discussion of the individual differences in their estimate leads to consensus and tends to eliminate extreme estimate errors.

3. **Normal conditions.** When task time, cost, and resource estimates are determined, they are based on certain assumptions. *Estimates should be based on normal conditions, efficient methods, and a normal level of resources.* Normal conditions are sometimes difficult to discern, but it is necessary to have a consensus in the organization as to what normal conditions mean in this project. If the normal workday is eight hours, the time estimate should be based on an eight-hour day. Similarly, if the normal workday is two shifts, the time estimate should be based on a two-shift workday. Any time estimate should reflect efficient methods for the resources normally available. The time estimate should represent the normal level of resources—people or equipment. For example, if three programmers are available for coding or two road graders are available for road construction, time and cost estimates should be based on these normal levels of resources unless it is anticipated the project will change what is currently viewed as "normal." In addition, possible conflicts in demand for resources on parallel or concurrent activities should not be considered at this stage. The need for adding resources will be examined when resource scheduling is discussed in a later chapter.

4. **Time units.** Specific time units to use should be selected early in the development phase of the project network. *All task time estimates need consistent time units.* Estimates of time must consider whether normal time is represented by calendar days, workdays, workweeks, person days, single shift, hours, minutes, etc. In practice the use of workdays is the dominant choice for expressing task duration. However, in projects such as a heart transplant operation, minutes probably would be more appropriate as a time unit. One such project that used minutes as the time unit was the movement of patients from an old hospital to an elegant new one across town. Since there were several life-endangering moves, minutes were used to ensure patient safety so proper emergency life-support systems would be available if needed. The point is, network analysis requires a standard unit of time. When computer programs allow more than one option, some notation should be made of any variance from the standard unit of time. If the standard unit of time is a five-day workweek and the estimated activity duration is in calendar days, it must be converted to the normal workweek.

5. **Independence.** Estimators should treat each task as independent of other tasks that might be integrated by the WBS. Use of first-line managers usually results in considering tasks independently; this is good. Top managers are prone to aggregate many tasks into one time estimate and then deductively make the individual task time estimates add to the total. If tasks are in a chain and performed by the same group or department, it is best not to ask for all the time estimates in the sequence at once to avoid the tendency for a planner or a supervisor to look at the whole path and try to adjust individual task times in the sequence to meet an arbitrary imposed schedule or some rough "guesstimate" of the total time for the whole path or segment of the project. This tendency does not reflect the uncertainties of individual activities and generally results in optimistic task time estimates. In summary, each task time estimate should be considered independently of other activities.

6. **Contingencies.** *Work package estimates should not include allowances for contingencies.* The estimate should assume normal or average conditions even though every work package will not materialize as planned. For this reason top management needs to create an extra fund for contingencies that can be used to cover unforeseen events.

7. **Adding risk assessment to the estimate helps to avoid surprises to stakeholders.** It is obvious some tasks carry more time and cost risks than others. For example, a new technology usually carries more time and cost risks than a proven process. Simply identifying the degree of risk lets stakeholders consider alternative methods and alter process decisions. A simple breakdown by optimistic, most likely, and pessimistic for task time could provide valuable information regarding time and cost. See Chapter 7 for further discussion of project risk.

Where applicable, these guidelines will greatly help to avoid many of the pitfalls found so often in practice. See Snapshot from Practice: Reducing Estimating Errors for a similar set of guidelines.

SNAPSHOT FROM PRACTICE
Reducing Estimating Errors*

Complexity is the major source of estimating error, says Kerry Wills, Project Management Sr. Director at the healthcare services organization Cigna, in Hartford, Connecticut. "Project managers cannot possibly be experts in all areas and therefore need to rely on the stakeholders for their expertise when estimating," Willis notes. To minimize errors he recommends treating estimating as a living process and not a one-time event.

He follows the same approach on all of his projects:

1. **Identify all of the stakeholders** based on the scope of the project and organizational history.
2. **Involve the stakeholders when creating the estimates.** "You can't hold people accountable for estimates they didn't help create," Willis says.
3. **Aggregate the estimates by comparing several models** (resource based, parametric, etc.).
4. **Manage the project against the estimates.** This includes making adjustments based on changes in project scope.
5. **Track projects closely** using tools such as earned value to gauge progress toward estimates.
6. **Track actual costs and time at a granular level** to recalibrate the model for future projects.

"The initial estimate could be perfect, but if it is not managed, then the end result will be bad and people will point to the estimating process," Wills argues.

*S. Swanson, "Estimating Errors," *PMNetwork*, October 2011, pp. 62–66.

TOP-DOWN VERSUS BOTTOM-UP ESTIMATING

Since estimating efforts cost money, the time and detail devoted to estimating is an important decision. Yet, when estimating is considered, you as a project manager may hear statements such as these:

Rough order of magnitude is good enough. Spending time on detailed estimating wastes money.
*Time is everything; our survival depends on getting there first! Time and cost
accuracy is not an issue.*
The project is internal. We don't need to worry about cost.
The project is so small, we don't need to bother with estimates. Just do it.

TABLE 5.1 •

Conditions for Preferring Top–Down or Bottom–Up Time and Cost Estimates

Condition	Top-Down Estimates	Bottom-Up Estimates
Strategic decision making	X	
Cost and time important		X
High uncertainty	X	
Internal, small project	X	
Fixed-price contract		X
Customer wants details		X
Unstable scope	X	

However, there are sound reasons for using top-down or bottom-up estimates. Table 5.1 depicts conditions that suggest when one approach is preferred over another.

Top-down estimates usually are derived from someone who uses experience and/or information to determine the project duration and total cost. However, these estimates are sometimes made by top managers who have very little knowledge of the component activities used to complete the project. For example, a mayor of a major city making a speech noted that a new law building would be constructed at a cost of $23 million and would be ready for occupancy in two and one-half years. Although the mayor probably asked for an estimate from someone, the estimate could have come from a luncheon meeting with a local contractor who wrote an estimate (guesstimate) on a napkin. This is an extreme example, but in a relative sense this scenario is frequently played out in practice. See Snapshot from Practice: Council Fumes, for another example of this. The question actually is, *do these estimates represent low-cost, efficient methods*? Seldom. The fact that the estimate came from the top can influence people responsible to "do what it takes to make the estimate."

If possible and practical, you want to push the estimating process down to the work package level for bottom-up estimates that establish low-cost, efficient methods. This process can take place after the project has been defined in detail. Good sense suggests project estimates should come from the people most knowledgeable about the estimate needed. The use of several people with relevant experience with the task can improve the time and cost estimate. The **bottom-up** approach at the work package level can serve as a check on cost elements in the WBS by rolling up the work packages and associated cost accounts to major deliverables. Similarly, resource requirements can be checked. Later, the time, resource, and cost estimates from the work packages can be consolidated into time-phased networks, resource schedules, and budgets that are used for control.

The bottom-up approach also provides the customer with an opportunity to compare the low-cost, efficient method approach with any imposed restrictions. For example, if the project completion duration is imposed at two years and your bottom-up analysis tells you the project will take two and one-half years, the client can now consider the trade-off of the low-cost method versus compressing the project to two years—or in rare cases canceling the project. Similar trade-offs can be compared for different levels of resources or increases in technical performance. The assumption is any movement away from the low-cost, efficient method will increase costs—e.g., overtime. The preferred approach in defining the project is to make rough top-down estimates, develop the WBS/OBS, make bottom-up estimates, develop schedules and budgets, and reconcile differences between top-down and bottom-up estimates. Hopefully, these steps will be done *before* final negotiation with either an internal or external customer. In conclusion, the ideal approach is

Portland, Oregon's, Willamette riverfront development has exploded with seven condominium towers and a new health sciences center under construction. The health science complex is to be linked with Oregon Health Sciences University (OHSU), which is high on a nearby hill, with an aerial cable tram.

The aerial tram linking the waterfront district to OHSU is to support the university expansion, to increase biotechnology research, and to become Portland's icon equivalent to Seattle's Space Needle. All of the hype turned south when news from a hearing suggested that the real budget for the tram construction, originally estimated at $15 million, is going to be about $55–$60 million, nearly triple the original estimate. The estimate could even go higher. Commissioners want to find out why city staff knowingly relied on flawed estimates. Mike Lindberg, president of the nonprofit Aerial Transportation Inc., acknowledged "the $15 million number was not a good number. It was simply a guesstimate." Commissioner Erik Sten said, "Those numbers were presented as much more firm than they appear to have been. . . . It appears the actual design wasn't costed out. That's pretty shoddy."

© Cliff Gray

* *The Oregonian,* January 13, 2006, by Frank Ryan, pages A1 and A14, and April 2, 2006, page A1.

for the project manager to allow enough time for both the top-down and bottom-up estimates to be worked out so a complete plan based on reliable estimates can be offered to the customer. In this way false expectations are minimized for all stakeholders and negotiation is reduced.

METHODS FOR ESTIMATING PROJECT TIMES AND COSTS

Top–Down Approaches for Estimating Project Times and Costs

At the strategic level top-down estimating methods are used to evaluate the project proposal. Sometimes much of the information needed to derive accurate time and cost estimates is not available in the initial phase of the project—for example, design is not finalized. In these situations top-down estimates are used until the tasks in the WBS are clearly defined.

Consensus Methods

This method simply uses the pooled experience of senior and/or middle managers to estimate the total project duration and cost. This typically involves a meeting where experts discuss, argue, and ultimately reach a decision as to their best guess estimate. Firms seeking greater rigor will use the Delphi Method to make these macro estimates. See Snapshot from Practice: The Delphi Method.

SNAPSHOT FROM PRACTICE
The Delphi Method

Originally developed by the RAND Corporation in 1969 for technological forecasting, the **Delphi Method** is a group decision process about the likelihood that certain events will occur. The Delphi Method makes use of a panel of experts familiar with the kind of project in question. The notion is that well-informed individuals, calling on their insights and experience, are better equipped to estimate project costs/times than theoretical approaches or statistical methods. Their responses to estimate questionnaires are anonymous, and they are provided with a summary of opinions.

Experts are then encouraged to reconsider, and if appropriate, to change their previous estimate in light of the replies of other experts. After two or three rounds it is believed that the group will converge toward the "best" response through this consensus process. The midpoint of responses is statistically categorized by the median score. In each succeeding round of questionnaires, the range of responses by the panelists will presumably decrease and the median will move toward what is deemed to be the "correct" estimate.

One distinct advantage of the Delphi Method is that the experts never need to be brought together physically. The process also does not require complete agreement by all panelists, since the majority opinion is represented by the median. Since the responses are anonymous, the pitfalls of ego, domineering personalities, and the "bandwagon or halo effect" in responses are all avoided. On the other hand, future developments are not always predicted correctly by iterative consensus nor by experts, but at times by creative, "off the wall" thinking.

It is important to recognize that these first top-down estimates are only a rough cut and typically occur in the "conceptual" stage of the project. The top-down estimates are helpful in initial development of a complete plan. However, such estimates are sometimes significantly off the mark because little detailed information is gathered. At this level individual work items are not identified. Or, in a few cases, the top-down estimates are not realistic because top management "wants the project." Nevertheless, the initial top-down estimates are helpful in determining whether the project warrants more formal planning, which would include more detailed estimates. Be careful that macro estimates made by senior managers are not dictated to lower level managers who might feel compelled to accept the estimates even if they believe resources are inadequate.

Although your authors prefer to avoid the top-down approach if possible, we have witnessed surprising accuracy in estimating project duration and cost in isolated cases. Some examples are building a manufacturing plant, building a distribution warehouse, developing air control for skyscraper buildings, and road construction. However, we have also witnessed some horrendous miscalculations, usually in areas where the technology is new and unproven. Top-down methods can be useful if experience and judgment have been accurate in the past.

Ratio Methods

Top-down methods (sometimes called parametric) usually use ratios, or surrogates, to estimate project times or costs. Top-down approaches are often used in the concept or "need" phase of a project to get an initial duration and cost estimate for the project. For example, contractors frequently use number of square feet to estimate the cost and time to build a house; that is, a house of 2,700 square feet might cost $160 per square foot (2,700 feet × $160 per foot equals $432,000). Likewise, knowing the square feet and dollars per square foot, experience suggests it should take approximately 100 days to complete. Two other common examples of top-down cost estimates are the cost for a new plant estimated by capacity size, or a software product estimated by features and complexity.

Apportion Methods

This method is an extension to the ratio method. **Apportionment** is used when projects closely follow past projects in features and costs. Given good historical data, estimates can be made quickly with little effort and reasonable accuracy. This method is very common in projects that are relatively standard but have some small variation or customization.

Anyone who has borrowed money from a bank to build a house has been exposed to this process. Given an estimated total cost for the house, banks and the FHA (Federal Housing Authority) authorize pay to the contractor by completion of specific segments of the house. For example, foundation might represent 3 percent of the total loan, framing 25 percent, electric, plumbing and heating 15 percent, etc. Payments are made as these items are completed. An analogous process is used by some companies that apportion costs to deliverables in the WBS— given average cost percentages from past projects. Figure 5.1 presents an example similar to one found in practice. Assuming the total project cost is estimated, using a top-down estimate, to be $500,000, the costs are apportioned as a percentage of the total cost. For example, the costs apportioned to the "Document" deliverable are 5 percent of the total, or $25,000. The subdeliverables "Doc-1 and Doc-2" are allocated 2 and 3 percent of the total—$10,000 and $15,000, respectively.

FIGURE 5.1 *Apportion Method of Allocating Project Costs Using the Work Breakdown Structure*

Function Point Methods for Software and System Projects

In the software industry, software development projects are frequently estimated using weighted macro variables called **"function points"** or major parameters such as number of inputs, number of outputs, number of inquiries, number of data files, and number of interfaces. These weighted variables are adjusted for a complexity factor and added. The total adjusted count provides the basis for estimating the labor effort and cost for a project (usually using a regression formula derived from data of past projects). This latter method assumes adequate historical data by type of software project for the industry—for example, MIS systems. In the U.S. software industry, one-person month represents on average five function points. A person working one month can generate on average (across all types of software projects) about five function points. Of course each organization needs to develop its own average for its specific type of work. Such historical data provide a basis for estimating the project duration. Variations of this top-down approach are used by companies such as IBM, Bank of America, Sears Roebuck, HP, AT&T, Ford Motors, GE, DuPont and many others. See Table 5.2 and Table 5.3 for a simplified example of function point count methodology.

TABLE 5.2

Simplified Basic Function Point Count Process for a Prospective Project or Deliverable

| Element | Complexity Weighting | | | |
	Low	Average	High	Total
Number of *inputs*	_____ × 2 +	_____ × 3 +	_____ × 4	= _____
Number of *outputs*	_____ × 3 +	_____ × 6 +	_____ × 9	= _____
Number of *inquiries*	_____ × 2 +	_____ × 4 +	_____ × 6	= _____
Number of *files*	_____ × 5 +	_____ × 8 +	_____ × 12	= _____
Number of *interfaces*	_____ × 5 +	_____ × 10 +	_____ × 15	= _____

TABLE 5.3

Example: Function Point Count Method

Software Project 13: Patient Admitting and Billing			
15	Inputs	Rated complexity as low	(2)
5	Outputs	Rated complexity as average	(6)
10	Inquiries	Rated complexity as average	(4)
30	Files	Rated complexity as high	(12)
20	Interfaces	Rated complexity as average	(10)

Application of Complexity Factor				
Element	Count	Low	Average	High	Total
---	---	---	---	---	---
Inputs	15	× 2			= 30
Outputs	5		× 6		= 30
Inquiries	10		× 4		= 40
Files	30			× 12	= 360
Interfaces	20		× 10		= 200
				Total	660

From historical data the organization developed the weighting scheme for complexity found in Table 5.2. Function points are derived from multiplying the number of kinds of elements by weighted complexity.

Table 5.3 shows the data collected for a specific task or deliverable: Patient Admitting and Billing—the number of inputs, outputs, inquiries, files, and interfaces along with the expected complexity rating. Finally, the application of the element count is applied and the function point count total is 660. Given this count and the fact that one-person month has historically been equal to 5 function points, the job will require 132 person months (660/5 = 132). Assuming you have 10 programmers who can work on this task, the duration would be approximately 13 months. The cost is easily derived by multiplying the labor rate per month times 132 person months. For example, if the monthly programmer rate is $4,000, then the estimated cost would be $528,000 (132 × 4,000). Although function point metrics are useful, their accuracy depends on adequate historical data, currency of data, and relevancy of the project/deliverable to past averages.

Learning Curves

Some projects require that the same task, group of tasks, or product be repeated several times. Managers know intuitively that the time to perform a task improves with repetition. This phenomenon is especially true of tasks that are labor intensive. In these circumstances the pattern of improvement phenomenon can be used to predict the reduction in time to perform the task. From empirical evidence across *all* industries, the pattern of this improvement has been quantified in the **learning curve** (also known as improvement curve, experience curve, and industrial progress curve), which is described by the following relationship:

Each time the output quantity doubles, the unit labor hours are reduced at a constant rate.

In practice the improvement ratio may vary from 60 percent, representing very large improvement, to 100 percent, representing no improvement at all. Generally, as the difficulty of the work decreases the expected improvement also decreases and the improvement ratio that is used becomes greater. One significant factor to consider is the proportion of labor in the task in relation to machine-paced work. Obviously, a lower percentage of improvement can occur only in operations with high labor content. Appendix 5.1 at the end of the chapter provides a detailed example of how the improvement phenomenon can be used to estimate time and cost for repetitive tasks.

The main disadvantage of top-down approaches to estimating is simply that the time and cost for a specific task are not considered. Grouping many tasks into a common basket encourages errors of omission and the use of imposed times and costs.

Micro estimating methods are usually more accurate than macro methods.

Bottom-Up Approaches for Estimating Project Times and Costs

Template Methods

If the project is similar to past projects, the costs from past projects can be used as a starting point for the new project. Differences in the new project can be noted and past times and costs adjusted to reflect these differences. For example, a ship repair drydock firm has a set of standard repair projects (i.e., templates for overhaul, electrical, mechanical) that are used as starting points for estimating the cost and duration of any new project. Differences from the appropriate standardized project are noted (for times, costs, and resources) and changes are made. This approach enables the firm to develop a potential schedule, estimate costs, and develop a budget in a very short time span. Development of such templates in a database can quickly reduce estimate errors.

Parametric Procedures Applied to Specific Tasks

Just as parametric techniques such as cost per square foot can be the source of top-down estimates, the same technique can be applied to specific tasks. For example, as part of an MS Office conversion project, 36 different computer workstations needed to be converted. Based on past conversion projects, the project manager determined that on average one person could convert three workstations per day. Therefore the task of converting the 36 workstations would take three technicians four days [(36/3)/3]. Similarly, to estimate the wallpapering allowance on a house remodel, the contractor figured a cost of $5 per square yard of wallpaper and $2 per yard to install it, for a total cost of $7. By measuring the length and height of all the walls she was able to calculate the total area in square yards and multiply it by $7.

Range Estimating

When do you use range estimating? **Range estimating** works best when work packages have significant uncertainty associated with the time or cost to complete. If the work package is routine and carries little uncertainty, using a person most familiar with the work package is usually the best approach. They know from experience or know where to find the information to estimate work package durations and costs. However, when work packages have significant uncertainty associated with the time or cost to complete, it is a prudent policy to require three time estimates—low, average, and high (borrowed off of PERT methodology that uses probability distributions). The low to high give a range within which the average estimate will fall. Determining the low and high estimates for the activity is influenced by factors such as complexity, technology, newness, familiarity.

How do you get the estimates? Since range estimating works best for work packages that have significant uncertainty, having a group determine the low, average, and high cost or duration gives best results. Group estimating tends to refine extremes by bringing more evaluative judgments to the estimate and potential risks. The judgment of others in a group helps to moderate extreme perceived risks associated with a time or cost estimate. Involving others in making activity estimates gains buy in and credibility to the estimate.

Figure 5.2 presents an abridged estimating template using three time estimates for work packages developed by a cross functional group(s) of project stakeholders. The group estimates show the low, average, and high for each work package. The Risk Level column is the group's independent assessment of the degree of confidence that the actual time will be very close to the estimate. In a sense this number represents the group's evaluation of many factors (e.g., complexity, technology) that might impact the average time estimate. In our example, the group feels work packages 104, 108, 110, 111, and 114 have a high chance that the average time may vary from expected. Likewise, the group's confidence feels the risk of work packages 102, 105 and 112 not materializing as expected is low.

How do you use the estimate? Group range estimating gives the project manager and owner an opportunity to assess the confidence associated with project times (and/or costs). For example, a contractor responsible for building a high rise apartment building can tell the owner that the project will cost between 3.5 and 4.1 million dollars and take between six and nine months to complete. The approach helps to reduce surprises as the project progresses. The range estimating method also provides a basis for assessing risk, managing resources, and determining the project contingency fund. (See Chapter 7 for a discussion of contingency funds.) Range estimating is popular in software and new product projects where up-front

	A	B	C	D	E	F	G	H
1	Project number: 18				Project Manager: Dawn O'Connor			
2	Project description:	New Organic Wine Launch			Date: 2/17/2xxx			
3			Organic Wine Launch Project					
4			Range Estimates					
5								
6	WBS	Description	Low	Average	High	Range	Risk	
7	ID		Estimate	Estimate	Estimate		Level	
8			Days	Days	Days	Days		
9								
10	102	Approval	1	1	3	2	low	
11	103	Design packaging	4	7	12	8	medium	
12	104	ID potential customers	14	21	35	21	high	
13	105	Design bottle logo	5	7	10	5	low	
14	106	Contract kiosk space	8	10	15	7	medium	
15	107	Construct kiosk	4	4	8	4	medium	
16	108	Design fair brochure	6	7	12	6	high	
17	109	Trade journal advertising	10	12	15	5	medium	
18	110	Production test	10	14	20	10	high	
19	111	Produce to inventory	5	5	10	5	high	
20	112	Business card scanner hookup	1	2	3	2	low	
21	113	Video hook up	2	2	4	2	medium	
22	114	Event rehearsal	2	2	5	3	high	

FIGURE 5.2 *Range Estimating Template*

requirements are fuzzy and not well known. Group range estimating is often used with phase estimating, which is discussed next.

A Hybrid: Phase Estimating

This approach begins with a top-down estimate for the project and then refines estimates for phases of the project as it is implemented. Some projects by their nature cannot be rigorously defined because of the uncertainty of design or the final product. Although rare, such projects do exist. These projects are often found in aerospace projects, IT projects, new technology projects, and construction projects where design is incomplete. In these projects, phase or life-cycle estimating is frequently used.

Phase estimating is used when an unusual amount of uncertainty surrounds a project and it is impractical to estimate times and costs for the entire project. Phase estimating uses a two-estimate system over the life of the project. A detailed estimate is developed for the immediate phase and a macro estimate is made for the remaining phases of the project. Figure 5.3 depicts the phases of a project and the progression of estimates over its life.

For example, when the project need is determined, a macro estimate of the project cost and duration is made so analysis and decisions can be made. Simultaneously a detailed estimate is made for deriving project specifications and a macro estimate for the remainder of the project. As the project progresses and specifications are solidified, a detailed estimate for design is made and a macro estimate for the remainder of the project is computed. Clearly, as the project progresses through its life cycle and more information is available, the reliability of the estimates should be improving. See Snapshot from Practice: Estimating Accuracy.

Phase estimating is preferred by those working on projects where the final product is not known and the uncertainty is very large—for example, the integration of wireless phones and computers. The commitment to cost and schedule is only necessary over the next phase of the project and commitment to unrealistic future schedules and costs based on poor information is avoided. This

FIGURE 5.3 *Phase Estimating over Project Life Cycle*

SNAPSHOT FROM PRACTICE
Estimate Accuracy

The smaller the element of a work package, the more accurate the overall estimate is likely to be. The extent of this improvement varies by type of project. The table below is developed to reflect this observation. For example, information technology projects that determine their time and cost estimates in the conceptual stage can expect their "actuals" to err up to 200 percent over cost and duration and, perhaps, as much as 30 percent under estimates. Conversely, estimates for buildings, roads, etc., made after the work packages are clearly defined, have a smaller error in actual costs and times of 15 percent over estimate and 5 percent less than estimate. Although these estimates vary by project, they can serve as ballpark numbers for project stakeholders selecting how project time and cost estimates will be derived.

Time and Cost Estimate Accuracy by Type of Project

	Bricks and Mortar	Information Technology
Conceptual stage	+60% to −30%	+200% to −30%
Deliverables defined	+30% to −15%	+100% to −15%
Work packages defined	+15% to −5%	+50% to −5%

progressive macro/micro method provides a stronger basis for using schedule and cost estimates to manage progress during the next phase.

Unfortunately your customer—internal or external—will want an accurate estimate of schedule and cost the moment the decision is made to implement the project. Additionally, the customer who is paying for the project often perceives phase estimating as a blank check because costs and schedules are not firm over most of the project life cycle. Even though the reasons for phase estimating are sound and legitimate, most customers have to be sold on its legitimacy. A major advantage for the customer is the opportunity to change features, re-evaluate, or even cancel the project in each new phase. In conclusion, phase estimating is very useful in projects that possess huge uncertainties concerning the final nature (shape, size, features) of the project.

Top-Down Estimates	Bottom-Up Estimates
Intended Use	**Intended Use**
Feasibility/conceptual phase Rough time/cost estimate Fund requirements Resource capacity planning	Budgeting Scheduling Resource requirements Fund timing
Preparation Cost	**Preparation Cost**
1/10 to 3/10 of a percent of total project cost	3/10 of a percent to 1.0 percent of total project cost
Accuracy	**Accuracy**
Minus 20%, to plus 60%	Minus 10%, to plus 30%
Method	**Method**
Consensus Ratio Apportion Function point Learning curves	Template Parametric WBS packages Range estimates

FIGURE 5.4 *Top-Down and Bottom-Up Estimates*

See Figure 5.4 for a summary of the differences between top-down and bottom-up estimates.

Obtaining accurate estimates is a challenge. Committed organizations accept the challenge of coming up with meaningful estimates and invest heavily in developing their capacity to do so. Accurate estimates reduce uncertainty and support a discipline for effectively managing projects.

LEVEL OF DETAIL

Level of detail is different for different levels of management. At any level the detail should be no more than is necessary and sufficient. Top management interests usually center on the total project and major milestone events that mark major accomplishments—e.g., "Build Oil Platform in the North Sea" or "Complete Prototype." Middle management might center on one segment of the project or one milestone. First-line managers' interests may be limited to one task or work package. One of the beauties of WBS is the ability to aggregate network information so each level of management can have the kind of information necessary to make decisions.

Getting the level of detail in the WBS to match management needs for effective implementation is crucial, but the delicate balance is difficult to find. See Snapshot from Practice: Level of Detail. The level of detail in the WBS varies with the complexity of the project; the need for control; the project size, cost, duration; and other factors. If the structure reflects excessive detail, there is a tendency to break the work effort into department assignments. This tendency can become a barrier to success, since the emphasis will be on departmental outcomes rather than on deliverable outcomes. Excessive detail also means more unproductive paperwork. Note that if the level of the WBS is increased by one, the number of cost accounts may increase geometrically. On the other hand, if the level of detail is not adequate, an organization unit may find the structure falls short

Practicing project managers advocate keeping the level of detail to a minimum. But there are limits to this suggestion. One of the most frequent errors of new project managers is to forget that the task time estimate will be used to control schedule and cost performance. A frequent rule of thumb used by practicing project managers says that a task duration should not exceed 5 workdays or at the most 10 workdays, if workdays are the time units used for the project. Such a rule probably will result in a more detailed network, but the additional detail pays off in controlling schedule and cost as the project progresses.

Suppose the task is "build prototype computer-controlled conveyor belt," the time estimate is 40 workdays, and the budget $300,000. It may be better to divide the task into seven or eight smaller tasks for control purposes. If one of the smaller tasks gets behind because of problems or a poor time estimate, it will be possible to take corrective action quickly and avoid delaying successive tasks and the project. If the single task of 40 workdays is used, it is possible that no corrective action would be taken until day 40, since many people have a tendency to "wait and see" or avoid admitting they are behind or passing on bad news; the result may mean far more than 5 days behind schedule.

The 5- to 10-day rule of thumb applies to cost and performance goals. If using the rule of thumb suggested above results in too many network tasks, an alternative is available, but it has conditions. The activity time can be extended beyond the 5- to 10-day rule only *IF* control monitoring checkpoints for segments of the task can be established so clear measures of progress can be identified by a specific percent complete.

This information is invaluable to the control process of measuring schedule and cost performance—for example, payments for contract work are paid on "percent complete" basis. Defining a task with clear definable start and end points and intermediate points enhances the chances of early detection of problems, corrective action, and on-time project completion.

of meeting its needs. Fortunately, the WBS has built-in flexibility. Participating organization units may expand their portion of the structure to meet their special needs. For example, the engineering department may wish to further break their work on a deliverable into smaller packages by electrical, civil, and mechanical. Similarly, the marketing department may wish to break their new product promotion into TV, radio, periodicals, and newspapers.

TYPES OF COSTS

Assuming work packages are defined, detailed cost estimates can be made. Here are typical kinds of costs found in a project:

1. Direct costs
   a. Labor
   b. Materials
   c. Equipment
   d. Other
2. Direct project overhead costs
3. General and administrative (G&A) overhead costs

The total project cost estimate is broken down in this fashion to sharpen the control process and improve decision making.

Direct Costs

These costs are clearly chargeable to a specific work package. **Direct costs** can be influenced by the project manager, project team, and individuals implementing the work package. These costs represent real cash outflows and must be paid as the project progresses; therefore, direct costs are usually separated from overhead costs. Lower-level project rollups frequently include only direct costs.

Direct Project Overhead Costs

Direct overhead rates more closely pinpoint which resources of the organization are being used in the project. Direct project **overhead costs** can be tied to project deliverables or work packages. Examples include the salary of the project manager and temporary rental space for the project team. Although overhead is not an immediate out-of-pocket expense, it is *real* and must be covered in the long run if the firm is to remain viable. These rates are usually a ratio of the dollar value of the resources used—e.g., direct labor, materials, equipment. For example, a direct labor burden rate of 20 percent would add a direct overhead charge of 20 percent to the direct labor cost estimate. A direct charge rate of 50 percent for materials would carry an additional 50 percent charge to the material cost estimate. Selective direct overhead charges provide a more accurate project (job or work package) cost, rather than using a blanket overhead rate for the whole project.

General and Administrative (G&A) Overhead Costs

These represent organization costs that are not directly linked to a specific project. These costs are carried for the duration of the project. Examples include organization costs across all products and projects such as advertising, accounting, and senior management above the project level. Allocation of G&A costs varies from organization to organization. However, G&A costs are usually allocated as a percent of total direct cost, or a percent of the total of a specific direct cost such as labor, materials, or equipment.

Given the totals of direct and overhead costs for individual work packages, it is possible to cumulate the costs for any deliverable or for the entire project. A percentage can be added for profit if you are a contractor. A breakdown of costs for a proposed contract bid is presented in Figure 5.5.

Direct costs	$80,000
Direct overhead	$20,000
Total direct costs	$100,000
G&A overhead (20%)	$20,000
Total costs	$120,000
Profit (20%)	$24,000
Total bid	$144,000

FIGURE 5.5 *Contract Bid Summary Costs*

Perceptions of costs and budgets vary depending on their users. The project manager must be very aware of these differences when setting up the project budget and when communicating these differences to others. Figure 5.6 depicts these different perceptions. The project manager can commit costs months before the resource is used. This information is useful to the financial officer of the organization in forecasting future cash outflows. The project manager is interested in when the budgeted cost is expected to occur, and when the budgeted cost actually is charged (earned); the respective timings of these two cost figures are used to measure project schedule and cost variances.

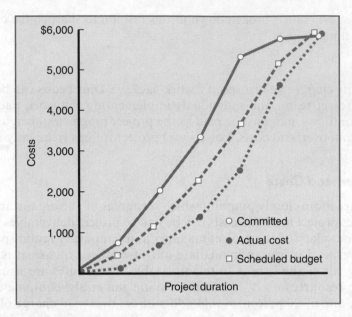

FIGURE 5.6 *Three Views of Cost*

REFINING ESTIMATES

As described earlier in Chapter 4, detailed work package estimates are aggregated and "rolled up" by deliverable to estimate the total direct cost of the project. Similarly, estimated durations are entered into the project network to establish the project schedule and determine the overall duration of the project. Experience tells us that for many projects the total estimates do not materialize and the actual costs and schedule of some projects significantly exceed original work package–based estimates. In order to compensate for the problem of actual cost and schedule exceeding estimates, some project managers adjust total costs by some multiplier (i.e., total estimated costs × 1.20).

The practice of adjusting original estimates by 20 or even 100 percent begs the question of why, after investing so much time and energy on detailed estimates, could the numbers be so far off? There are a number of reasons for this, most of which can be traced to the estimating process and the inherent uncertainty of predicting the future. Some of these reasons are discussed below.

- **Interaction costs are hidden in estimates.** According to the guidelines, each task estimate is supposed to be done independently. However, tasks are rarely completed in a vacuum. Work on one task is dependent upon prior tasks, and the hand-offs between tasks require time and attention. For example, people working on prototype development need to interact with design engineers after the design is completed, whether to simply ask clarifying questions or to make adjustments in the original design. Similarly, the time necessary to coordinate activities is typically not reflected in independent estimates. Coordination is reflected in meetings and briefings as well as time necessary to resolve disconnects between tasks. Time, and therefore cost, devoted to managing interactions rises exponentially as the number of people and different disciplines involved increases on a project.

- **Normal conditions do not apply.** Estimates are supposed to be based on normal conditions. While this is a good starting point, it rarely holds true in real life. This is especially true when it comes to the availability of resources. Resource shortages, whether in the form of people, equipment, or materials, can extend original estimates. For example, under normal conditions four bulldozers are typically used to clear a certain site size in five days, but the availability of only three bulldozers would extend the task duration to eight days. Similarly, the decision to outsource certain tasks can increase costs as well as extend task durations since time is added to acclimating outsiders to the particulars of the project and the culture of the organization.

- **Things go wrong on projects.** Design flaws are revealed after the fact, extreme weather conditions occur, accidents happen, and so forth. Although you shouldn't plan for these risks to happen when estimating a particular task, the likelihood and impact of such events need to be considered.

- **Changes in project scope and plans.** As one gets further and further into the project, a manager obtains a better understanding of what needs to be done to accomplish the project. This may lead to major changes in project plans and costs. Likewise, if the project is a commercial project, changes often have to be made midstream to respond to new demands by the customer and/or competition. Unstable project scopes are a major source of cost overruns. While every effort should be made up front to nail down the project scope, it is becoming increasingly difficult to do so in our rapidly changing world.

- **Overly optimistic.** There is solid research indicating that there is a tendency in people to overestimate how quickly they can get things done and underestimate how long it will take them to complete tasks. This would be especially true in organizational cultures where padding is not the norm. See Snapshot from Practice: Mega Projects: A Special Case.

- **Strategic misrepresentation.** There is growing evidence that some project promoters underestimate the costs of projects and overestimate project benefits in order to win approval. This appears to be particularly true for large-scale public works projects which have a notorious habit of coming in way over budget (remember the earlier Council Fumes Snapshot).

The reality is that for many projects not all of the information needed to make accurate estimates is available, and it is impossible to predict the future. The challenge is further compounded by human nature and the political dynamics associated with gaining project approval. The dilemma is that without solid estimates, the credibility of the project plan is eroded. Deadlines become meaningless, budgets become rubbery, and accountability becomes problematic.

Challenges similar to those described above will influence the final time and cost estimates. Even with the best estimating efforts, it may be necessary to revise estimates based on relevant information *prior* to establishing a baseline schedule and budget.

Effective organizations adjust estimates of specific tasks once risks, resources, and particulars of the situation have been more clearly defined. They recognize that the rolled up estimates generated from a detailed estimate based on the WBS are just the starting point. As they delve further into the project-planning process, they make appropriate revisions both in the time and cost of specific activities. They factor the final assignment of resources into the project budget and schedule. For

Research Highlight

MEGA PROJECTS: A SPECIAL CASE

The record of cost estimates for mega projects is not stellar. Popular examples of large cost overruns include the Sydney Opera House, the Chunnel connecting England and France, and Boston's artery/tunnel "Big Dig." In a study of government-approved infrastructure projects, Bent Flyvbjerg found costs for bridges and tunnels, for road, and for rail to be underestimated 33.8%, 20.4%, and 44.7%, respectively, from initial baseline estimates to reality.[1]

Flyvbjerg suggested "… government officials should not trust cost estimates presented by project promoters whose main ambition is to build a project for their private or political gain. These estimates tend to be overly optimistic. Advocates know that high costs reduce the likelihood of funding." The issue comes down to how to mitigate these influences in our estimates.

One approach lies in using an "external view" based on actual outcomes of similar projects completed in the past. It is called **Reference Class Forecasting** (RCF) and uses Flyvbjerg's research approach.

© Michael Dwyer/Alamy

REFERENCE CLASS FORECASTING METHODOLOGY

Fundamentally, his method is simple and straightforward and involves three major steps:

1. *Select a reference class of projects similar to your potential project,* for example, cargo ships or bridges.
2. *Collect and arrange outcome data as a distribution.* Create a distribution of cost overruns as a percent of original project estimate (low to high).
3. *Use the distribution data to arrive at a realistic forecast.* Compare the original cost estimate for the project with the reference class projects. (For example, ask advocate what strong evidence do you have that your project will not follow the projects in the reference class?)

APPLICATION

Flyvbjerg's seminal studies served as an impetus for the use of Reference Class Forecasting. For example, the UK Department for Transport and HM Treasury employs the method as part of project appraisal for large transportation projects under their jurisdiction. The American Planning Association (APA) recommends the RCF method and strongly suggests planners should never rely solely on conventional forecasting techniques when making forecasts. The AACE International (the Association for the Advancement of Cost Engineering) recommends the use of RCF as a validation of cost estimates. Reference class forecasting can easily be applied to projects such as sport events, research and development, information technology systems, power plants and dams, construction, sport arenas, movies, energy exploration, space exploration, and many more classes.[2]

BENEFITS

The benefits of reference class forecasting are compelling:

• Outside empirical data mitigates human bias.
• Political, strategic, and promoter forces have difficulty ignoring outside reference class forecast information.
• Serves as reality check for funding large projects.

- Helps executives avoid unsound optimism.
- Leads to improved accountability.
- Provides basis for project contingency funds.

FUTURE APPLICATION BEYOND INFRASTRUCTURE

Given cost overruns in nine out of ten mega projects, inaccuracies have to be reduced to improve chances of funding. The use of Reference Class Forecasting is increasing as governments and organizations require the method be used to temper project advocate estimates and reduce inaccuracies.

[1] See for example: Lovallo, D., and D. Kahneman, "Delusions of Success: How Optimism Undermines Executives' Decisions," *Harvard Business Review,* July 2003, pp. 56–63; Buehler, R., D. Griffen, and M. Ross,
"Exploring the 'Planning Fallacy': Why People Underestimate Their Task Completion Times," *Journal of Personality and Social Psychology,* 67 (3), pp. 366–381.

[2] Flyvbjerg, Bent, "From Nobel Prize to Project Management: Getting Risks Right," *Project Management Journal,* August 2006, pp. 5–15.

example, when they realize that only three instead of four bulldozers are available to clear a site, they adjust both the time and cost of that activity. They adjust estimates to account for specific actions to mitigate potential risks on the project. For example, to reduce the chances of design code errors, they would add the cost of independent testers to the schedule and budget. Finally, organizations adjust estimates to take into account abnormal conditions. For example, if soil samples reveal excessive ground water, then they adjust foundation costs and times.

There will always be some mistakes, omissions, and adjustments that will require additional changes in estimates. Fortunately every project should have a change management system in place to accommodate these situations and any impact on the project baseline. Change management and contingency funds will be discussed later in Chapter 7.

CREATING A DATABASE FOR ESTIMATING

The best way to improve estimates is to collect and archive data on past project estimates and actuals. Saving historical data—estimates and actuals—provides a knowledge base for improving project time and cost estimating. Creating an estimating database is a "best practice" among leading project management organizations.

Some organizations have large estimating departments of professional estimators—e.g., Boeing, IBM—that have developed large **time and cost databases.** Others collect these data through the project office. This database approach allows the project estimator to select a specific work package item from the database for inclusion. The estimator then makes any necessary adjustments concerning the materials, labor, and equipment. Of course any items not found in the database can be added to the project—and ultimately to the database if desired. Again, the quality of the database estimates depends on the experience of the estimators, but over time the data quality should improve. Such structured databases serve as feedback for estimators and as benchmarks for cost and time for each project. In addition, comparison of estimate and actual for different projects can suggest the degree of risk inherent in estimates. See Figure 5.7 for the structure of a database similar to those found in practice.

FIGURE 5.7 *Estimating Database Templates*

Summary

Quality time and cost estimates are the bedrock of project control. Past experience is the best starting point for these estimates. The quality of estimates is influenced by other factors such as people, technology, and downtimes. The key for getting estimates that represent realistic average times and costs is to have an organization culture that allows errors in estimates without incriminations. If times represent average time, we should expect that 50 percent will be less than the estimate and 50 percent will exceed the estimate. The use of teams that are highly motivated can help in keeping task times and costs near the average. For this reason, it is crucial to get the team to buy into time and cost estimates.

Using top-down estimates is good for initial and strategic decision making or in situations where the costs associated with developing better estimates have little benefit. However, in most cases the bottom-up approach to estimating is preferred and more reliable because it assesses each work package, rather than the whole project, section, or deliverable of a project. Estimating time and costs for each work package facilitates development of the project schedule and a time-phased budget, which are needed to control the project as it is implemented. Using the estimating guidelines will help eliminate many common mistakes made by those unacquainted with estimating times and costs for project control. Establishing a time and cost estimating database fits well with the learning organization philosophy.

The level of time and cost detail should follow the old saying of "no more than is necessary and sufficient." Managers must remember to differentiate between committed outlays, actual costs, and scheduled costs. It is well known that up-front efforts in clearly defining project objectives, scope, and specifications vastly improve time and cost estimate accuracy.

Finally, how estimates are gathered and how they are used can affect their usefulness for planning and control. The team climate, organization culture, and organization structure can strongly influence the importance attached to time and cost estimates and how they are used in managing projects.

Key Terms

Apportionment	Learning curves	Ratio methods
Bottom-up estimates	Overhead costs	Reference Class Forecasting
Delphi Method	Padding estimates	Template method
Direct costs	Phase estimating	Time and cost databases
Function points	Range estimating	Top-down estimates

Review Questions

1. Why are accurate estimates critical to effective project management?
2. How does the culture of an organization influence the quality of estimates?
3. What are the differences between bottom-up and top-down estimating approaches? Under what conditions would you prefer one over the other?
4. What are the major types of costs? Which costs are controllable by the project manager?

Exercises

1. Calculate the direct cost of labor for a project team member using the following data:

   Hourly rate: $40/hr

   Hours needed: 80

   Overhead rate: 40%

2. Mrs. Tolstoy and her husband, Serge, are planning their dream house. The lot for the house sits high on a hill with a beautiful view of the Appalachian Mountains. The plans show the size of the house to be 2,900 square feet. The average price for a lot and house similar to this one has been $120 per square foot. Fortunately, Serge is a retired plumber and feels he can save money by installing the plumbing himself. Mrs. Tolstoy feels she can take care of the interior decorating.

   The following average cost information is available from a local bank that makes loans to local contractors and disperses progress payments to contractors when specific tasks are verified as complete.

24%	Excavation and framing complete
8%	Roof and fireplace complete
3%	Wiring roughed in

6%	Plumbing roughed in
5%	Siding on
17%	Windows, insulation, walks, plaster, and garage complete
9%	Furnace installed
4%	Plumbing fixtures installed
10%	Exterior paint, light fixtures installed, finish hardware installed
6%	Carpet and trim installed
4%	Interior decorating
4%	Floors laid and finished

a. What is the estimated cost for the Tolstoy's house if they use contractors to complete all of the house?

b. Estimate what the cost of the house would be if the Tolstoys use their talents to do some of the work themselves.

3. Below is a project WBS with cost apportioned by percents. If the total project cost is estimated to be $600,000, what are the estimated costs for the following deliverables?
a. Design?
b. Programming?
c. In-house testing?

What weaknesses are inherent in this estimating approach?

4. Firewall Project XT. Using the "complexity weighting" scheme shown in Exercise 5.3 and the function point complexity weighted table shown below, estimate the total function point count. Assume historical data suggest five function points equal one person a month and six people can work on the project.

Complexity Weight Table		
Number of inputs	10	Rated complexity low
Number of outputs	20	Rated complexity average
Number of inquiries	10	Rated complexity average
Number of files	30	Rated complexity high
Number of interfaces	50	Rated complexity high

a. What is the estimated project duration?
b. If 20 people are available for the project, what is the estimated project duration?
c. If the project must be completed in six months, how many people will be needed for the project?

References

Buehler, R., D. Griffen, and M. Ross, "Exploring the 'Planning Fallacy': Why People Underestimate Their Task Completion Times," *Journal of Personality and Social Psychology,* vol. 67 (3), pp. 366–381.

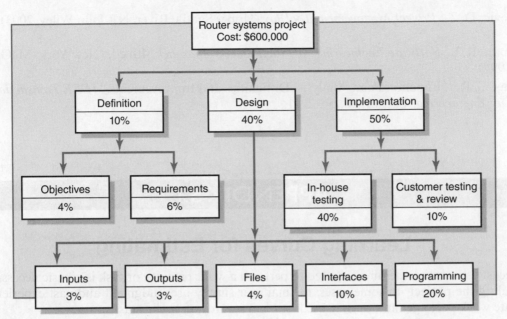

EXERCISE 5.3 *WBS Figure*

Dalkey, N. C., D. L. Rourke, R. Lewis, and D. Snyder, *Studies in the Quality of Life: Delphi and Decision Making* (Lexington, MA: Lexington Books, 1972).

Flyvbjerg, Bent, "From Nobel Prize to Project Management: Getting Risks Right," *Project Management Journal,* August 2006, pp. 5–15; Flyvbjerg, Bent, "Curbing Optimism Bias and Strategic Misrepresentation in Planning: Reference Class Forecasting in Practice," *European Planning Studies,* vol. 16, No. 1 (January 2008), pp. 3–21; and Flyvbjerg, Bent, N. Bruzelius, and W. Rothengatter, *Mega Projects and Risk: An Anatomy of Ambition* (Cambridge Press, 2003).

Gray, N. S., "Secrets to Creating the Elusive 'Accurate Estimate,'" *PM Network,* 15 (8) August 2001, p. 56.

Jeffery, R., G. C. Low, and M. Barnes, "A Comparison of Function Point Counting Techniques," *IEEE Transactions on Software Engineering,* 19 (5) 1993, pp. 529–32.

Jones, C., *Applied Software Measurement* (New York: McGraw-Hill, 1991).

Jones, C., *Estimating Software Costs* (New York: McGraw-Hill, 1998).

Kharbanda, O. P., and J. K. Pinto, *What Made Gertie Gallop: Learning from Project Failures* (New York: Van Nostrand Reinhold, 1996).

Lovallo, D., and D. Kahneman, "Delusions of Success: How Optimism Undermines Executives' Decisions," *Harvard Business Review,* July 2003, pp. 56–63.

Magne, E., K. Emhjellenm, and P. Osmundsen, "Cost Estimation Overruns in the North Sea," *Project Management Journal* 34 (1) 2003, pp. 23–29.

McLeod, G., and D. Smith, *Managing Information Technology Projects* (Cambridge, MA: Course Technology, 1996).

Milosevic, D. Z., *Project Management ToolBox* (Upper Saddle River, NJ: John Wiley, 2003), p. 229.

Pressman, R. S., *Software Engineering: A Practitioner's Approach,* 4th ed. (New York: McGraw-Hill, 1997).

Symons, C. R., "Function Point Analysis: Difficulties and Improvements," *IEEE Transactions on Software Engineering,* 14 (1) 1988, pp. 2–11.

APPENDIX 5.1

Learning Curves for Estimating

A forecast estimate of the time required to perform a work package or task is a basic necessity for scheduling the project. In some cases, the manager simply uses judgment and past experience to estimate work package time, or may use historical records of similar tasks.

Most managers and workers intuitively know that improvement in the amount of time required to perform a task or group of tasks occurs with repetition. A worker can perform a task better/quicker the second time and each succeeding time she/he performs it (without any technological change). It is this pattern of improvement that is important to the project manager and project scheduler.

This improvement from repetition generally results in a reduction of labor hours for the accomplishment of tasks and results in lower project costs. From empirical evidence across *all* industries, the pattern of this improvement has been quantified in the *learning curve* (also known as improvement curve, experience curve, and industrial progress curve), which is described by the following relationship:

Each time the output quantity doubles, the unit labor hours are reduced at a constant rate.

For example, assume that a manufacturer has a new contract for 16 prototype units and a total of 800 labor hours were required for the first unit. Past experience has indicated that on similar types of units the improvement rate was 80 percent. This relationship of improvement in labor hours is shown below:

Unit		Labor Hours
1		800
2	800 × .80 =	640
4	640 × .80 =	512
8	512 × .80 =	410
16	410 × .80 =	328

By using Table A5.1 unit values, similar labor hours per unit can be determined. Looking across the 16 unit level and down the 80 percent column, we find a ratio of .4096. By multiplying this ratio times the labor hours for the first unit, we obtained the per unit value:

$$.4096 \times 800 = 328 \text{ hours or } 327.68$$

TABLE A5.1 ....
Learning Curves Unit Values

Units	60%	65%	70%	75%	80%	85%	90%	95%
1	1.0000	1.0000	1.0000	1.0000	1.0000	1.0000	1.0000	1.0000
2	.6000	.6500	.7000	.7500	.8000	.8500	.9000	.9500
3	.4450	.5052	.5682	.6338	.7021	.7729	.8462	.9219
4	.3600	.4225	.4900	.5625	.6400	.7225	.8100	.9025
5	.3054	.3678	.4368	.5127	.5956	.6857	.7830	.8877
6	.2670	.3284	.3977	.4754	.5617	.6570	.7616	.8758
7	.2383	.2984	.3674	.4459	.5345	.6337	.7439	.8659
8	.2160	.2746	.3430	.4219	.5120	.6141	.7290	.8574
9	.1980	.2552	.3228	.4017	.4930	.5974	.7161	.8499
10	.1832	.2391	.3058	.3846	.4765	.5828	.7047	.8433
12	.1602	.2135	.2784	.3565	.4493	.5584	.6854	.8320
14	.1430	.1940	.2572	.3344	.4276	.5386	.6696	.8226
16	.1296	.1785	.2401	.3164	.4096	.5220	.6561	.8145
18	.1188	.1659	.2260	.3013	.3944	.5078	.6445	.8074
20	.1099	.1554	.2141	.2884	.3812	.4954	.6342	.8012
22	.1025	.1465	.2038	.2772	.3697	.4844	.6251	.7955
24	.0961	.1387	.1949	.2674	.3595	.4747	.6169	.7904
25	.0933	.1353	.1908	.2629	.3548	.4701	.6131	.7880
30	.0815	.1208	.1737	.2437	.3346	.4505	.5963	.7775
35	.0728	.1097	.1605	.2286	.3184	.4345	.5825	.7687
40	.0660	.1010	.1498	.2163	.3050	.4211	.5708	.7611
45	.0605	.0939	.1410	.2060	.2936	.4096	.5607	.7545
50	.0560	.0879	.1336	.1972	.2838	.3996	.5518	.7486
60	.0489	.0785	.1216	.1828	.2676	.3829	.5367	.7386
70	.0437	.0713	.1123	.1715	.2547	.3693	.5243	.7302
80	.0396	.0657	.1049	.1622	.2440	.3579	.5137	.7231
90	.0363	.0610	.0987	.1545	.2349	.3482	.5046	.7168
100	.0336	.0572	.0935	.1479	.2271	.3397	.4966	.7112
120	.0294	.0510	.0851	.1371	.2141	.3255	.4830	.7017
140	.0262	.0464	.0786	.1287	.2038	.3139	.4718	.6937
160	.0237	.0427	.0734	.1217	.1952	.3042	.4623	.6869
180	.0218	.0397	.0691	.1159	.1879	.2959	.4541	.6809
200	.0201	.0371	.0655	.1109	.1816	.2887	.4469	.6757
250	.0171	.0323	.0584	.1011	.1691	.2740	.4320	.6646
300	.0149	.0289	.0531	.0937	.1594	.2625	.4202	.5557
350	.0133	.0262	.0491	.0879	.1517	.2532	.4105	.6482
400	.0121	.0241	.0458	.0832	.1453	.2454	.4022	.6419
450	.0111	.0224	.0431	.0792	.1399	.2387	.3951	.6363
500	.0103	.0210	.0408	.0758	.1352	.2329	.3888	.6314
600	.0090	.0188	.0372	.0703	.1275	.2232	.3782	.6229
700	.0080	.0171	.0344	.0659	.1214	.2152	.3694	.6158
800	.0073	.0157	.0321	.0624	.1163	.2086	.3620	.6098
900	.0067	.0146	.0302	.0594	.1119	.2029	.3556	.6045
1,000	.0062	.0137	.0286	.0569	.1082	.1980	.3499	.5998
1,200	.0054	.0122	.0260	.0527	.1020	.1897	.3404	.5918
1,400	.0048	.0111	.0240	.0495	.0971	.1830	.3325	.5850
1,600	.0044	.0102	.0225	.0468	.0930	.1773	.3258	.5793
1,800	.0040	.0095	.0211	.0446	.0895	.1725	.3200	.5743
2,000	.0037	.0089	.0200	.0427	.0866	.1683	.3149	.5698
2,500	.0031	.0077	.0178	.0389	.0606	.1597	.3044	.5605
3,000	.0027	.0069	.0162	.0360	.0760	.1530	.2961	.5530

That is, the 16th unit should require close to 328 labor hours, assuming an 80 percent improvement ratio.

Obviously, a project manager may need more than a single unit value for estimating the time for some work packages. The cumulative values in Table A5.2 provide factors for computing the cumulative total labor hours of all units. In the previous example, for the first 16 units, the total labor hours required would be

$$800 \times 8.920 = 7,136 \text{ hours}$$

By dividing the total cumulative hours (7,136) by the units, the average unit labor hours can be obtained:

$$7,136 \text{ labor hours/16 units} = 446 \text{ average labor hours per unit}$$

Note how the labor hours for the 16th unit (328) differs from the average for all 16 units (446). The project manager, knowing the average labor costs and processing costs, could estimate the total prototype costs. (The mathematical derivation of factors found in Tables A5.1 and A5.2 can be found in Jelen, F. C., and J. H. Black, *Cost and Optimization Engineering,* 2nd ed. (New York: McGraw-Hill, 1983.)

FOLLOW-ON CONTRACT EXAMPLE

Assume the project manager gets a follow-on order of 74 units; how should she estimate labor hours and cost? Going to the cumulative Table A5.2 we find at the 80 percent ratio and 90 total units intersection—a 30.35 ratio.

$800 \times 30.35 =$	24,280 labor hours for 90 units
Less previous 16 units =	7,136
Total follow-on order =	17,144 labor hours
17,144/74 equals 232 average labor hours per unit	

Labor hours for the 90th unit can be obtained from Table A5.1: $.2349 \times 800 = 187.9$ labor hours. (For ratios between given values, simply estimate.)

Exercise A5.1

Norwegian Satellite Development Company
Cost Estimates
for
World Satellite Telephone Exchange Project

NSDC has a contract to produce eight satellites to support a worldwide telephone system (for Alaska Telecom, Inc.) that allows individuals to use a single, portable telephone in any location on earth to call in and out. NSDC will develop and produce the eight units. NSDC has estimated that the R&D costs will be NOK (Norwegian Krone) 12,000,000. Material costs are expected to be NOK 6,000,000. They have estimated the design and production of the first satellite will require 100,000 labor hours and an 80 percent improvement curve is expected. Skilled labor cost is NOK 300 per hour. Desired profit for all projects is 25 percent of total costs.

Learning Curves Cumulative Values

Units	60%	65%	70%	75%	80%	85%	90%	95%
1	1.000	1.000	1.000	1.000	1.000	1.000	1.000	1.000
2	1.600	1.650	1.700	1.750	1.800	1.850	1.900	1.950
3	2.045	2.155	2.268	2.384	2.502	2.623	2.746	2.872
4	2.405	2.578	2.758	2.946	3.142	3.345	3.556	3.774
5	2.710	2.946	3.195	3.459	3.738	4.031	4.339	4.662
6	2.977	3.274	3.593	3.934	4.299	4.688	5.101	5.538
7	3.216	3.572	3.960	4.380	4.834	5.322	5.845	6.404
8	3.432	3.847	4.303	4.802	5.346	5.936	6.574	7.261
9	3.630	4.102	4.626	5.204	5.839	6.533	7.290	8.111
10	3.813	4.341	4.931	5.589	6.315	7.116	7.994	8.955
12	4.144	4.780	5.501	6.315	7.227	8.244	9.374	10.62
14	4.438	5.177	6.026	6.994	8.092	9.331	10.72	12.27
16	4.704	5.541	6.514	7.635	8.920	10.38	12.04	13.91
18	4.946	5.879	6.972	8.245	9.716	11.41	13.33	15.52
20	5.171	6.195	7.407	8.828	10.48	12.40	14.64	17.13
22	5.379	6.492	7.819	9.388	11.23	13.38	15.86	18.72
24	5.574	6.773	8.213	9.928	11.95	14.33	17.10	20.31
25	5.668	6.909	8.404	10.19	12.31	14.80	17.71	21.10
30	6.097	7.540	9.305	11.45	14.02	17.09	20.73	25.00
35	6.478	8.109	10.13	12.72	15.64	19.29	23.67	28.86
40	6.821	8.631	10.90	13.72	17.19	21.43	26.54	32.68
45	7.134	9.114	11.62	14.77	18.68	23.50	29.37	36.47
50	7.422	9.565	12.31	15.78	20.12	25.51	32.14	40.22
60	7.941	10.39	13.57	17.67	22.87	29.41	37.57	47.65
70	8.401	11.13	14.74	19.43	25.47	33.17	42.87	54.99
80	8.814	11.82	15.82	21.09	27.96	36.80	48.05	62.25
90	9.191	12.45	16.83	22.67	30.35	40.32	53.14	69.45
100	9.539	13.03	17.79	24.18	32.65	43.75	58.14	76.59
120	10.16	14.16	19.57	27.02	37.05	50.39	67.93	90.71
140	10.72	15.08	21.20	29.67	41.22	56.78	77.46	104.7
160	11.21	15.97	22.72	32.17	45.20	62.95	86.80	118.5
180	11.67	16.79	24.14	34.54	49.03	68.95	95.96	132.1
200	12.09	17.55	25.48	36.80	52.72	74.79	105.0	145.7
250	13.01	19.28	28.56	42.08	61.47	88.83	126.9	179.2
300	13.81	20.81	31.34	46.94	69.66	102.2	148.2	212.2
350	14.51	22.18	33.89	51.48	77.43	115.1	169.0	244.8
400	15.14	23.44	36.26	55.75	84.85	127.6	189.3	277.0
450	15.72	24.60	38.48	59.80	91.97	139.7	209.2	309.0
500	16.26	25.68	40.58	63.68	98.85	151.5	228.8	340.6
600	17.21	27.67	44.47	70.97	112.0	174.2	267.1	403.3
700	18.06	29.45	48.04	77.77	124.4	196.1	304.5	465.3
800	18.82	31.09	51.36	84.18	136.3	217.3	341.0	526.5
900	19.51	32.60	54.46	90.26	147.7	237.9	376.9	587.2
1,000	20.15	34.01	57.40	96.07	158.7	257.9	412.2	647.4
1,200	21.30	36.59	62.85	107.0	179.7	296.6	481.2	766.6
1,400	22.32	38.92	67.85	117.2	199.6	333.9	548.4	884.2
1,600	23.23	41.04	72.49	126.8	218.6	369.9	614.2	1001.
1,800	24.06	43.00	76.85	135.9	236.8	404.9	678.8	1116.
2,000	24.83	44.84	80.96	144.7	254.4	438.9	742.3	1230.
2,500	26.53	48.97	90.39	165.0	296.1	520.8	897.0	1513.
3,000	27.99	52.62	98.90	183.7	335.2	598.9	1047.	1791.

A. How many labor hours should the eighth satellite require?
B. How many labor hours for the whole project of eight satellites?
C. What price would you ask for the project? Why?
D. Midway through the project your design and production people realize that a 75 percent improvement curve is more appropriate. What impact does this have on the project?
E. Near the end of the project Deutsch Telefon AG has requested a cost estimate for four satellites identical to those you have already produced. What price will you quote them? Justify your price.

APPENDIX 5.2

Project Cost Management

1. NATURE OF PROJECT COST MANAGEMENT

Project Cost Management involves managing the processes for planning, estimating, budgeting, financing, funding, managing and controlling project costs in order to complete all project activities included in the project within the approved budget.

The cornerstones of project management are managing the project scope, time and cost. For successful project management, these triple constraints need to be managed effectively and simultaneously. However, often, the project cost management performance turns out to be more crucial than performance in other areas for the following reasons:

• First, most organizations always find themselves short of the resources they need for their operation and strategic growth. Hence, any cost overrun on a major project would put severe strains on the company's resources and operations.

• Secondly, the project cost is likely to leave a life-long impact on the viability of the project and may be the entire organization.

Hence, project managers need to pay close attention to all aspects of cost management.

2. COST MANAGEMENT PROCESSES

PMBOK® Guide, 5th Edition, includes in project cost management total 4 processes – three processes of planning process group and one process of monitoring and controlling process group:

1. *Plan Cost Management* (Planning Process Group): Process for establishing the policies, procedures, and documentation for planning, managing, expending, and controlling project costs.

2. *Estimate Costs* (Planning Process Group): Process for developing an approximation of the monetary resources needed to complete project activities.

3. *Determine Budget* (Planning Process Group): Process for aggregating the estimated costs of individual project activities according to the project network and developing an authorized cost baseline – the time-phased outflow of funds for project work.
4. *Control Costs* (Monitoring and Controlling Process Group): Process for monitoring the status of project to update the project costs and managing changes to the cost baseline.

3. PLAN COST MANAGEMENT

This process "establishes the policies, procedures, and documentation for planning, managing, expending, and controlling project costs". (PMBOK® Guide, 5th Edition)

The process provides the overall methodology to be employed for the project cost management processes throughout the project life cycle. The output from the process is *Cost Management Plan* (described in detail in later part of this section), which sets down the rules for preparing cost estimates, preparing the budget (time-phased outflow of funds for project work), rules for measuring cost management performance and application for Earned Value Management, and setting up linkage of the project costs to organizational cost accounting procedures (by providing framework and rules for setting up control accounts). The inputs, tools and techniques, and outputs of the process are described below.

Inputs

Project Management Plan: Essentially, this document includes the project work to be completed (scope baseline) and the time frame for its completion (schedule baseline), which form the basis for developing the cost estimate. Other important details included in the project management component plans relate to costs for managing quality, risk and communications.

Project Charter: Project Charter provides the overview of the entire project – its strategic importance, deliverables, budgeted cost and schedules, and assumptions and constraints, which can influence the project costs.

Enterprise Environmental Factors: There are several very important environmental factors, which have a serious bearing on project costs:

- Prices of products, and services to be procured from the market for project work
- Organization culture for the quality of project work and project management practices
- Macroeconomic conditions in the industry and the entire country (growth rate of industry, inflation rates, etc.)
- Global trends and exchange rates, if imported products or services need to be used for project work
- Published commercial information database for standard costs of materials, services, wage rates for skilled work, etc.

Organizational Process Assets: While planning project cost management, the following organizational assets can be helpful:

- The established policies and procedures for project cost management in the organization
- for estimating costs, preparing budgets for project cash flows, and project cost accounting rules

- Lessons learned from earlier projects
- Financial control procedures and available databases

Tools and Techniques

- *Expert Judgment:* Expertise developed by a project manager from knowledge and experience of managing projects and particularly expertise or experience in the application area and industry for which the project is planned.
- *Financial Techniques:* Different modes of financing the project cash flows (from equity, cash accruals from current operations, suppliers' credit, leasing the equipments, etc.) would have important bearing on developing project cost management plan.
- *Project Team Meetings*

Outputs

The output from the process is an important project document. It is described below in detail.

Cost Management Plan

Cost Management Plan is the overarching document in the project cost management, which sets the framework, basic policies and procedures for the other three cost management processes. It is a component of the integrated *project management plan*. The document would address the issues like:

- Specifying the precision level and the policies and procedures for preparing project cost estimates and control documents
- In some cases, the project team does not have access to actual costs in monetary terms; cost management plan could provide basis for substituting the monetary values by some other suitable measure for resource costs (man-hours or man-days for labour and some valuable material quantity units like reinforcing steels in tones or cement bags for civil construction).
- Providing linkage to the organization's accounting practices and codes for recording and reporting project costs
- Specifying formats for reports for cost estimates, budgets, variance reports, earned value management and other project cost related reporting

4. ESTIMATE COSTS

The cost estimating is the process for developing an approximation of the monetary resources needed to complete project activities (PMBOK® Guide, 5th Edition)

The keywords to note here are "monetary resources required to complete (all) project activities" 'in monetary terms' and 'approximate'. Firstly, the cost estimates are usually expressed in monetary units; however, sometimes the project manager or project team does not have access to certain cost elements. In such cases, a suitable comparable unit for a measure of resource could be substituted, e.g. the number of man-hours for software or engineering consultancy industry, or number of cement bags for construction industry. Secondly, depending on the details worked out in project planning, the availability of resource cost, and the rigor employed in developing the cost estimates, the accuracy of cost estimate would vary, but it would always remain approximate till the last cost element is accounted for.

Background Concepts and Information on Project Cost Estimating Practices

It would be helpful if some important background information and concepts on project cost estimating are discussed before starting the discussion on inputs, tools and techniques and outputs according to the framework set down in the PMBOK® Guide. The topics presented for this purpose are as follows:

A. Need for different cost estimates during the project life cycle
B. Classification of cost estimates based on approaches for developing cost estimates
C. Classification of cost estimates based on the accuracy of estimates
D. Different techniques for developing cost estimates.

For cost estimates desired during the different phases of the project life cycle, the degree of reliability of the cost estimate, the management levels participating in the estimating process, and the time and cost involved in preparing the estimates would be different. Similarly, the tools and techniques employed for developing the cost estimates would also be different. The subsequent sections discuss these issues.

A. Needs for Different Types of Cost Estimates during the Project Life Cycle

Cost estimating is not a one-time activity during the project life cycle. Cost estimates may need to be developed

- before formal initiation of the project during the project selection phase,
- during the project-initiation stage for setting the preliminary project cost boundary,
- during the planning stage with gradual and successive refinements as the project planning matures to develop detailed project budget for use in project monitoring and control, and
- during the monitoring and controlling phase for devising alternative cost influencing plans for cost control.

The rigor and degree of the reliability or accuracy of the cost estimate required at different phases of the project are distinctly different and, therefore, different types of cost estimates are developed to suit project needs. **Figure A1 shows a process flow diagram,** *which presents the type of cost estimate desired at different stages in the selection phase of the project life cycle and the cost estimating technique associated with preparing such estimates.*

Keeping in view its business strategy, an organization would think of a project idea. It would need to decide whether the project as conceived is within the reach of the resources the organization can raise. It would need at this first decision-making gate an order of magnitude cost estimate, which does not necessarily have high accuracy (say, +40%). The estimates would be prepared with minimal efforts and time expenditure, under almost direct supervision and direction of the top management. The estimates are based on expert judgment and historical project cost data of some similar projects from the company's archives or published data–using an analogous cost estimating technique, one of the top-down cost estimating techniques.

If the investment estimate is within reach of the organization, or alternatively if the project's characteristics (capacity, technology, sophistication, etc.) can be modified to bring the investment within the resources which the organization can raise, the company would like to refine its cost estimate to work out the technical feasibility and economic viability of the project. The accuracy

FIGURE A1 *Place of Cost Estimating Techniques in Project Life Cycle*

and rigor demanded from the project cost estimate at this decision making gate is somewhat higher (say, ± 30%). Though the estimate is worked out using a top-down estimating technique, *parametric cost estimating technique*, project details are worked out to specify the major deliverables or major systems and the quantity of the parameter influencing the system cost is determined. For example, for an infrastructure project, the parameter for site development cost would be area of plot, parameter for building cost would be floor area of buildings, parameter for material handling system would be the tonnage capacity (tons/hr or cubic meter per day, etc.), parameter for electrical system would be the KVA rating of distributed power, etc. The *Function Points Analysis* would provide similar parameter for software project cost estimation. Along with the project cost estimate, the operating costs are also worked out. With these details, the technical feasibility of the project and economic viability of the project can be worked out. If the project is technically feasible and return on capital employed meets the norms set by the organization for project acceptance, the second decision-making gate for project selection is cleared.

Since the organization may be considering at a point of time several alternative proposals for investment, it might commit more resources for working out the project details, including the total project cost to the next higher level of accuracy, say ±15 to 20%, which would be adequate for final selection and formal authorization of the project. The cost estimating technique employed at this stage would be one of the bottom-up cost estimating techniques, based on working out adequate project details to enable a far more reliable cost boundary for formal initiation of the project. At this stage, the middle and operating managerial levels would also be involved. The project would be analyzed into specific deliverables and sub-deliverables up to work package stage and well-defined technical parameters and associated cost would be worked out. Rolling these cost elements up, the total project cost, investment, and schedule of capital expenditure would be ready for the formal initiation of the project.

Once the project is formally launched, the project team would set down the major and minor deliverables and prepare a work breakdown structure up to work packages and major project activities, for which reliable cost estimates would be available. The cost estimating technique would be essentially one of the bottom-up cost estimating techniques and the accuracy of the cost estimate would depend on the details worked out in project planning, say ±10% to ±5%.

It is not necessary that all organizations need to go through each of the above decision-making gates as described above. However, the above description illustrates the need for developing different types of cost estimates during the life cycle of the project and the different techniques employed for developing these estimates. In the next two sections, different types of cost estimates and different types of cost estimating techniques are discussed.

As described in the preceding section, the type of project cost estimates desired to meet the project needs would determine:

- The accuracy or overall dependability of the estimate
- Type of detailed information worked out to develop the estimate
- Tools and techniques used for developing the estimate
- Effort, time and cost associated with development of the estimates
- The managerial level at which the major estimating work is carried out or directed.

B. Classification of Estimates Based on Cost Estimating Approach

One classification of the project cost estimates is based on the cost estimating technique used and associated nature of information flow during the estimate preparation and the degree of details worked out during the cost estimating process. When the cost estimates are developed at the top management level without working out project details and passed down to the operating level, the estimates are called top-down type of an estimate and the technique is called top-down cost estimating technique. On the other hand, when the cost estimates are developed at lower or operating levels after working out adequate project details and sent up to top management for approval or decision-making, the estimates are called bottom-up type of an estimate and the technique is called bottom-up cost estimating technique.

Top-Down Cost Estimates

The top management plays a predominant role in developing the Top-Down Cost Estimate. Such estimates are prepared by the top management for taking a broad overview and are meant to serve as the first decision-making gate for the project. The estimates are prepared without detailed project information, in a relatively short time span and without involvement of middle or operating managerial levels. The merits of such estimates are that these require less effort and time, and reflect the top management's experience and judgment in taking a comprehensive overview without getting bogged down into the details. Their main disadvantage is less accuracy (as they are developed without working out adequate project details) and some possible resistance in their willing acceptance at the operating-level later.

Bottom-Up Cost Estimates

On the other hand, Bottom-Up Cost Estimates are developed at operating or middle management levels after working out sufficient project details. They are prepared at the detailed project planning stage and are intended for budgetary control during the project execution phase. Work break down structure for the project is prepared up to individual work packages and costs for the work packages or major activities are estimated. These individual cost elements are rolled up to come up with the total project cost. Understandably, Bottom-Up estimates require much greater effort, cost and time to prepare. The plus point is the increased accuracy and its full acceptance by the operating group during execution.

A Composite of Top-Down and Bottom-Up Estimates

Frequently, a combination of the Top-Down and Bottom-Up techniques is practiced by most organizations using an iterative mode. After the preliminary approval by the top management accompanied by a Top-Down budget for the project, the middle and operating levels develop detailed planning and work break-down structure, work out the costs, and roll them up to develop the Bottom-Up Cost Estimate for its review and approval by the top management. After the review by the top management, discussions and necessary revisions, the approved project cost estimate is passed down for project budgeting.

C. Classification Based on the Degree of Accuracy of the Cost Estimate (ASCE Classification)

The American Society of Cost Engineers (ASCE) has developed a classification of the types of project cost estimates essentially based on the degree of accuracy of the cost estimates. The descriptive name of the cost estimate gives a general idea of the accuracy, rigor, availability of supporting details, techniques used for developing the estimate and similar information. For example, order of magnitude or ball park estimate by its very name suggests the estimate to be rough and ready estimate, developed at a short notice, with little effort and availability and scant details. On the other hand, definitive or detailed estimate by its name implies much greater accuracy of the estimate, developed after working out considerable details and with large effort.

Different organizations use different nomenclatures for indicating the type of estimate, its accuracy and project phase for which it is meant. Table A1 gives the nomenclature used by ASCE for classifying cost estimates into five categories. The table also gives associated accuracy, effort levels ordinarily spent, nature and degree of supporting details, managerial level at which the estimating work is done and the tools and techniques ordinarily employed to develop the estimate

D. Techniques for Developing Cost Estimates

Technique employed for developing the project cost estimate would be geared to the type of cost estimate desired to meet the organization's need at a particular phase of the project life cycle. Ordinarily, at the project selection stage, one of the top-down cost estimating techniques (Analogous or Parametric cost estimating) is used. For detailed project planning and setting the project budget for monitoring and control, the technique used is some variation of the Bottom-up cost estimating techniques (Definitive or Detailed Cost Estimating techniques based on work packages and corresponding cost elements, or resource rates and corresponding requirements of resources worked out in detail). Table A2 presents at a glance the purpose, necessary inputs, typical process steps in the technique, characteristics of the output and expected accuracy from these techniques. Also, a detailed illustration of the analogous, parametric and definitive cost estimating techniques is presented in the **Case 5.1, National Acetylene Company** at the end of this section.

Analogous Cost Estimating Technique

This is one of the Top-Down types of cost estimating techniques and it is essentially used at the project selection stage by the top management. As the name suggests, the technique is based on using the actual historical costs of similar previous projects (analogues) as the basis for estimating the cost of the project in hand. The degree of similarity between the analogues selected for basis and the expert judgment of the estimator play a critical role in the accuracy of the estimate developed. In general, the analogous estimates are not supposed to be very accurate and could be off by as much as +/–40%, if the analogous projects used for reference are not closely similar the proposed project.

The technique starts with collection of actual historical data of costs of similar projects and any readily available project details like the year of analogue project construction, location, capacity, technology employed, etc. either from organization's own earlier projects files or from published technical or commercial data. From this data, the cost of the proposed plant is deduced, which may require expert judgment to make allowances as far as available information would permit for differences between the selected analogous project and the proposed project for the following aspects:

- The differences in the general price levels between projects construction years
- The project capacities
- Other project details in terms of product quality requirements, feedstock, and degree of automation or sophistication desired, etc.

The merits of the technique are that it would require relatively less effort, cost and time to develop the estimate; the chief disadvantage is low level of accuracy or reliability.

Parametric Cost Estimating Technique

This is also a Top-Down type of cost estimating techniques and often used at the project selection stage by the top management; however, the technique is based on quantitative analysis of the important factors or parameters, which influence cost and hence it accuracy or reliability is higher (say, ±30% or better) than analogous cost estimating.

The principle underlying the technique is that the cost of a project is predominantly influenced by the value of a few important parameters, like the tonnage in structural steel construction, code lines or functional point value for a software project, storage capacity for a system of tankages, square foot area in case of building, man-hours in case of certain labour contracts, kilowatt rating for electric power distribution system, etc. Generally, the correlation between these parameters and costs is readily available (say ₹4,000 per square feet, or ₹300 per man-hour) from the organization's project archives or published material in industry and trade literature. Statistical methods (Regression Analysis) can be used for analyzing the cost data and influencing parameter from project archives if relationship is not available readily.

The first step in the technique is the analysis of the project in terms of main deliverables and sub-deliverables (in some cases, systems and sub-systems), identifying the cost influencing parameters with those deliverables or systems and estimating their values. Then using the generally known cost-parameter relationships, the costs of different deliverables can be estimated and rolling them up, the total cost of the project can be estimated. Depending upon the degree of details and sophistication used in the project analysis and the reliability of the relationship correlating project parameter and cost, reasonably accurate estimates can be developed.

Like analogous cost estimating, the fact that this technique would require relatively less effort, cost and time than most bottom-up estimating techniques is the main merit of the technique. The low level of accuracy or reliability is the disadvantage. Compared to analogous estimating, the technique is more reliable; on the other hand, it would require more inputs in terms of effort, cost and time.

Bottom-Up Estimating Techniques

A variety of bottom-up techniques are used for detailed project planning or project control. Definitive or detailed cost estimates are prepared at the detailed planning stage or while setting up project cost budgets for cost control use. These techniques based on bottom-up cost estimating require the project team to work out the details that commensurate with the desired overall accuracy of the estimate (say ±5 to ±10% in detailed planning or project cost control phases).

The general procedure for the technique involves developing a work breakdown structure detailed enough to arrive at the level of work packages for which the cost data can be estimated. If work breakdown structure has enough details, the accuracy of the overall estimate would be high, even if the accuracy of individual packages is not very high. The underlying reason is that the overestimates of some work packages would cancel out the underestimates of other work packages and the overall total project cost estimate would be reasonably accurate. Understandably, the effort, cost and time required to develop a bottom-up cost estimate are high and would depend on the degree of details of the project analysis. The project management team has to use discretion to work out details to such a degree as would be adequate for practical project management and control.

Determining Resource Cost Rates

This technique is one of the bottom-up techniques of cost estimating and it relies on the analysis of organization's historical cost data (accounting data). Generally, this technique is more commonly used by the organizations working on contracting for outsiders' projects – providing products or services (civil construction projects, piping or electrical work contracts, consulting contracts, software development projects, general business process outsourcing type of project, etc). This technique can enable development of sufficiently accurate cost estimates (say, from ±5% to ±15%) depending upon the degree of details and sophistication used in the project analysis.

From the analysis of its books of accounts, the contracting organization works out and keeps ready for use the resource costs rates (for example, ₹10,000 per ton fabrication labor, ₹1000 per man-day for software coding work, ₹200,000/- deployment charge and ₹30,000 per day hiring charges for a crane, etc.). For working out the resource rates, the costs are sorted into costs directly related to the use of the resource and indirect or overhead costs. The indirect costs are then apportioned or allocated to different resource rates using some rationale for allocation. The composite resource rates for use in the estimates for bidding on contracts are worked out by adding the direct costs and the corresponding allocated cost per unit of resource rate.

The project on hand is analyzed into the major deliverables and sub-deliverables and the corresponding use of resources for the deliverables is worked out. Using the composite resource rates and the quantity of resources required for deliverables, the cost for each major deliverable, and in turn the total cost of the project, is estimated. This cost is suitably modified by providing the margin or reserve necessary to manage the project risks and operating profits to arrive at the contract bid price. Quotations from vendors or published information in trade or industry literature may also be useful for working out resource rates, for works which the organization may need to outsource.

Inputs, Tools and Techniques and Outputs of Cost Estimating Process

After our slight diversion to discuss the background concepts and information on project cost estimating practices, we revert to the inputs, tools and techniques and outputs for the cost estimating process according to PMBOK® Guide, 5th Edition.

Inputs

Basically, for estimating the cost of work package or activity, we would need

- the purpose for developing the cost estimate and during what phase of the project life cycle,
- the direct cost for materials, labor and services required to complete the project deliverables, and
- the charges for use of the infrastructure and technology required to carry out the work.

As discussed in detail in earlier part of this section, the type of the cost estimate and the technique used for preparing the estimate would determine the exact nature of inputs. The following rather long list of process inputs listed in the PMBOK® Guide, 5th Edition under *Project Management Plan*, should be understood keeping these basic requirements in focus:

Cost Management Plan   This input is to ensure that the cost estimate is prepared with conformance to rules and guidelines set down in project cost management plan.

Human Resources Management Plan   This input would be useful in assessing the project staffing requirements (in skill and numbers) and corresponding cost.

Scope Baseline   This input specifies the deliverables and the specific project work. The following parts of the project scope baseline would impact the cost estimate.

- *Project Scope Statement* describes the business need and justification for the project and hence it provides the broad perspective of what detailed planning project work should include.

- *Work Breakdown Structure (WBS)* and accompanying document WBS Dictionary provide the breakdown of the major deliverables into individual components, for which suitable technical or functional details can be specified and the corresponding costs determined.
- WBS Dictionary used for detailed description, specifications and drawings for work to be carried out.

Project Schedule   The type and quantum of resources required (type of equipment, materials, skilled and unskilled labor, etc.) depend to a great extent on the project schedule, hence this input.

Risk Register   This input is to account for the effect of the nature of risks and the risk management response on project costs

Enterprise Environment Factors   This input influences the monetary value of the resources required to complete the project deliverables activities. Some important enterprise environment factors are listed below:

- Under what commercial terms and prices the materials, products and services are available in the market for completing the project's deliverables
- Prices of products and services to be procured from the market for project work; this data may be available from the published database or from specific enquiries and quotations for major special equipment or items
- Organization culture for the quality of project work and project management practices
- Macroeconomic conditions in the industry and the entire country (growth rate of industry, inflation rates, etc.)
- Global trends and exchange rates, if imported products or services need to be used for project work
- Published commercial information database for standard costs of materials, services, wage rates for skilled work, etc.

Organizational Process Assets   This input would facilitate preparing the cost estimate by making available

- The organization's knowledge database (historical information of costs on earlier projects and data archived in project files)
- The organization's own cost estimating procedures (cost estimating templates, cost estimating policies, quality or safety standards used for products and services, etc.)
- The organization's financial control procedures

Tools and Techniques

The tools and techniques are essentially concerned with how the input data is processed to turn out the desired outputs. As discussed in earlier section, depending on the project life cycle phase and project needs, different techniques are employed. They require different levels of rigor and development of details are employed for project cost estimating.

Analogous and parametric cost estimating techniques are generally used at the project selection stage or early life cycle of the project. Bottom-up estimating is used for detailed project planning and developing the project budgets. When an organization is engaged in executing a number of projects on contractual basis for other companies using a common pool of resources, the project costs are worked out from the quantum of resource requirements and the resource cost rates based on historical (accounting) information.

Accordingly, the comprehensive list of tools and techniques for estimating costs includes:

1. *Expert Judgment:* This input refers to the experience of the project team having worked on projects of similar nature and in related industries and familiarity with the project cost estimating work.

2. *Analogous Estimating Technique:* This technique uses historical data of past project costs with suitable broad adjustments made for the differences between the project-on-hand and the earlier project, for which cost data is available.

3. *Parametric Estimating Technique:* This technique uses a preliminary analysis of the project deliverables and the key parameters that determine the deliverables cost.

4. *Determining Resource Cost Rates:* This technique is useful for estimating the cost of projects, which use the common resource pool for the project work. The technique is often used for organizations providing contractual services for projects for initial bid preparation as well as cost control during execution.

5. *Bottom-up Estimating:* This technique involves working out the costs of individual work packages constituting the major deliverables and then aggregating the costs by trolling up the cost elements to arrive at the total project cost. For detailed project planning, budgeting and cost control during execution phase, the numbers worked out by this technique are generally used. This technique usually yields very reliable cost estimates; for in the first place, the technique is based on focusing on detailed analysis, and secondly, if sufficient number of activities are included in the total project cost, the pluses and minuses in the errors would tend to cancel each other out to enable increased overall accuracy.

6. *Three-Point Estimating:* By its very nature, there are uncertainties associated with all cost elements employed in preparing a cost estimate. Three-Point Estimate is a technique aimed at reducing the uncertainty and improving the reliability of the cost estimate. In this technique, three separate estimates are developed (a) Most likely, (b) Optimistic, and (c) Pessimistic estimates.

   Depending on the distribution assumed for the elements cost, the more reliable version of the cost estimate can be worked out using a suitable formula.

   For assumed triangular distribution,
   Estimated Cost = (Optimistic Cost + Pessimistic Cost + Most Likely Cost)/3}
   Alternatively, for assumed Beta distribution,
   Estimated Cost = (Optimistic Cost + 4 Most Likely Cost + Pessimistic Cost)/6

7. *Vendor Bid Analysis:* The use of this technique is helpful when historical data or commercial database is not available for the combination of products and services constituting the work package, specific products or services. In this situation, the offers received from vendors against requests for proposals for specific work packages are used for estimating the costs.

8. *Reserve Analysis:* To provide some reserve in the cost estimate is necessary for making an allowance for contingency to allow for uncertainty in cost estimates due to either some minor changes in scope of work packages or escalation in the cost of material or service rates. The usual practice is to provide a reserve of a certain percent (say, 5 to 10%) of the subtotal of estimated cost of all other cost elements.

9. *Cost of Quality:* This should be factored in while preparing the cost estimate. It would include the cost associated with attaining the desired level of quality in the project work. It would be the sum total of the cost of conformance (cost for building into the product quality and testing) and the cost of non-conformance (cost of rework, scrap and cost related to warranties and product liability).

10. *Project Management Software:* This is useful in systematically collecting and collating the cost data. In addition, some special software based on Monte Carlo simulation technique can help in developing the probabilistic values of cost estimate taking into account the risk factors according to input data.

Outputs

Activity Cost Estimate: This is the obvious output of the cost estimating process. However, two necessary important outputs from the cost estimating technique, which are sometimes not obvious, are discussed in detail below.

Supporting Details for Activity Cost Estimates: It is not just enough that the cost estimator provides some number representing the estimated cost of the project activity or the entire project. Other project stakeholders, who have not been involved in the estimating process themselves, would find it difficult to fully grasp the impact of the cost estimate in absence of some of the supporting details. Therefore, it is highly desirable for a cost estimate to be accompanied by the following supporting details:

- The basis and modus operandi used for developing the cost estimate
- The degree of in-depth analysis carried out to develop the cost and which should reflect in terms of the indicated accuracy or reliability of the cost estimate (±10% or ±30%?)
- Documentation of major assumptions and constraints forming the estimate basis
- Cost of important parameter (say, the cost of steel and cement for a construction project, expected price escalation on a yearly basis for long duration projects, etc.)
- Preliminary vendor bid for critical major cost element

Requested Changes and Update of Cost Management Plan: The very process of estimating cost of activities and the accompanying activity analysis may throw up other alternatives and more economical approaches for planning and executing the project. If some of the alternatives are distinctly favorable to the project, the change request would originate from the cost management processes (say, change in the intermediate product or service specifications, grouping of activities, etc.). There would be corresponding update of the cost management plan.

TABLE A1
Classification of Estimates American Association of Cost Engineers (AACE)

	Order of Magnitude	"Ball Park" Study Estimates	Preliminary Cost Estimate	Definitive Cost Estimate	Detailed Cost Estimate
Purpose	As the first decision Making gate for project Initiation	As the second decision making gate for project initiation	Authorization of Preliminary budget	Authorization of Project Budget	Cost data to be used for detailed project planning and accountable budgetary controls
Basis	Scale-up ratios or cost escalation factors from known cost of similar plants No process flow sheets No system designs No equipment details No technology details	Basic technology or Process flow identified But incomplete information on details	Well defined engineering Or technology information with Flow sheets List of equipments Preliminary specifications	A detailed scope of all project deliverables, including: The flow sheets, Equipment lists with specifications, Preliminary lay-outs, and Budgetary quotes for critical equipment	A thorough list of work packages With detailed technical work contents and cost elements details
Accuracy	±40%	±30%	±20%	±10%	±5%
Efforts/Costs	Minimal level efforts	Low effort level	Medium level efforts	Somewhat extensive efforts and costs depending on the nature of the project	Extensive efforts and associated costs
Duration Required	Very brief	Brief	A time-bound short duration program	Somewhat extensive duration	As necessary for detailed project planning
Organization Level	Top management	Top and Middle management	Upper middle level Management	Upper middle level and lower middle management	Operating level for project activity – and supervised by middle upper management

TABLE A2
Cost Estimating Tools and Techniques

	Analogous Estimating	Parametric Estimating	Bottom-Up Estimating	Resource Cost Rate Estimating
Purpose	Preparing an Order of Magnitude estimate at the project selection stage for estimating project investment – first decision making gate for project selection	Preparing Ballpark or Study Estimate for determining the technical feasibility and economic viability of the project – second decision making gate for project selection	Preparing Detailed Cost Estimate to serve as: • The final decision making gate at project selection for ranking the alternative projects, or • Detailed project-planning tool; for working out cost baseline and budget for monitoring and controlling the project.	Useful to an organization for developing cost of projects requiring use of a different mix of certain common resources (materials, equipment, labor). Especially useful for a contracting organization working on job-work projects (construction work, software projects, consultancy etc.)
Inputs	Actual historical cost data of a previous similar project (Analogue) and any available additional useful details (capacity, technology, process, etc.)	• Preliminary boundaries for the project size, schedule, degree of sophistication • Analysis of proposed project into top level systems or deliverables and system parameters influencing costs • Cost data of projects with similar cost influencing parameters.	• Project charter and Project scope statement • Work Breakdown structure • Enterprise environmental factors • Organizational process assets • Risk Analysis, reserve Analysis, Quality requirements	• Work breakdown structure up to work packages level and further the analysis of the resources requirements (material, labor, infrastructure equipment use, etc.) • Resources rates worked out from the company's historical costs and projections based on them
Technique	Estimate the cost of the proposed project by allowing for the differences in the analogue and proposed projects using expert judgment for: • Different times and locations • Different capacities • Different quality requirements • Degree of sophistication	Analyze the proposed project into major systems and deliverables Work out system's parameters influencing the cost From comparison of the system parameters and costs of other projects, deduce the costs of major deliverables or systems and roll up these elements to work out total project cost	• Analyze the project charter, project scope statement and work breakdown structure up to work packages level • Estimate the cost of individual work packages from the cost elements involved in the work package to serve as budget • Roll up the cost estimates of the work packages to develop the total project cost	• Apply the projected resource cost rates worked out from historical data (accounts) to individual work package • Estimate the cost of work packages to serve as budget for detailed planning and monitoring and controlling • Roll up the cost of work packages to develop the total project cost
Output and Characteristics	• Top-Down Estimating Technique • Generally used at top managerial level • Requires less effort, cost and time for preparation • Accuracy very low (+40%)	• Top-Down Estimating Technique • Generally used at top or high middle managerial levels • Effort, cost and time for preparation more than analogous but less than detailed • Accuracy low (±30%)	• Bottom–up cost estimating • Generally used at middle and operating levels • Considerable, effort, cost and time required for such estimate • Accuracy depends on the rigor and details – from +10 to ±5%	• Bottom–up cost estimating • Generally used at middle and operating levels • Considerable, effort, cost and time required for such estimate • Accuracy depends on the rigor and details – from ±10 to ±5%

5. DETERMINE BUDGET

Project budgeting is the process of adding up the cost estimates of the individual project activities or work packages to develop a time-phased cost baseline for measuring project cost performance. It would serve as a standard for monitoring and controlling the project during the execution phase of the project. The project budget, after its formal approval, represents the organization's commitment of the resources allocated to the project during the budget period. At the same time, the budget also serves as a standard for measuring the project cost performance and thus it also functions as a valuable instrument for project cost control.

Nature of Project Budgets (Time-Phased Cash Outflows) and Process for Developing Project Budgets

Before we discuss the inputs, Tools and Techniques and Outputs of the process following the framework presented in PMBOK ® Guide, 5th Edition, a brief review of the nature of project budget and the process of developing project budget would be helpful.

Since the project budget is a time-phased aggregation of the cost estimates for the individual activities or work packages, for developing the project budget, we must know not only the cost estimate for individual activities or work packages, but also when they will be needed. Accordingly, the process of developing project budget would involve the following steps:

1. Develop cost estimates of individual activities or work packages (the outputs of earlier cost estimating process)
2. Set down the precedence or succession order of the activities to develop the project network and in turn the project schedule (the output of project schedule process).
3. Allocate to different budgetary time periods the cost of work packages according to the project schedule.
4. For each budgetary period, aggregate the costs to be incurred during the period for all work packages scheduled during that period.
5. The individual budgetary period costs give the cash outflows for each period and the cumulative cost would give the project cost baseline.

The following simple illustration will clarify the steps described above. The illustration is focused on developing project budget for 3 project work packages with the cost estimates and precedence-succession given in the following table:

Work Package	Estimated Total Cost	Estimated Time Required	Preceding Work Package	Succeeding Work Package
A	₹10,000`	1 month	Start	B and C
B	₹40,000	2 months	A	D
C	₹90,000	3 months	A	E (not included here)
D	₹7000	1 month	B	F (not included here)

Based on this simple network portion and estimated costs, the project budget for the first four months would be as follows:

Work Package	Estimated Total Cost	Estimated Time Required	1st Month	2nd Month	3rd Month	4th Month
A	₹10,000˙	1 month	₹10,000	—	—	—
B	₹40,000	2 months	—	₹20,000	₹20,000	—
C	₹90,000	3 months	—	₹30,000	₹30,000	₹30,000
D	₹7000	1 month	—	—	—	₹ 7,000
Month-wise Project Budget			₹10,000	₹50,000	₹50,000	₹37,000

Inputs, Tools and Techniques and Outputs of Determine Budget Process

The inputs, tools and techniques and outputs for the cost budgeting process according to PMBOK® Guide, 5th Edition, are as follows:

Inputs

Cost budgeting would require, as inputs, data on the activity or project costs on one hand and the time during which these costs are to be incurred. With this basic process mapping and taking into account the overall project constraints, the following inputs, as enumerated by PMI in its PMBOK Guide, can be identified:

Cost Management Plan: This input is to ensure that the project budget is prepared with conformance to rules and guidelines set down in project cost management plan.

Scope Baseline: This input specifies the deliverables and the specific project work. The following parts of the project scope baseline would impact the cost estimate and in turn the project budget.

• *Project Scope Statement* describes the business need and justification for the project and hence it provides the broad perspective of what detailed planning project work should include.

• *Work Breakdown Structure (WBS)* and accompanying document WBS Dictionary provide the breakdown of the major deliverables into individual components, for which suitable technical or functional details can be specified and the corresponding costs determined.

• *WBS Dictionary* for detailed description, specifications and drawings for work to be carried out

Activity Cost Estimates and Activity Cost Estimate Support Details (outputs of the cost estimating process) give the actual costs to be incurred.

Project Schedule: The type and quantum of resources required (type of equipment, materials, skilled and unskilled labor, etc.) depends to a great extent on the project schedule, hence this input.

Resource Calendars give the time periods in which the costs on the activities are to be incurred.

Risk Register: This input is to account for the effect of the nature of risks and the risk management response on project costs

Contractual Obligations give the constraints on account of payment terms for products or services to be procured.

Organizational Process Assets: This input refers to the organization's policy for developing project budgets, reporting procedures, etc.

Tools and Techniques

The basic technique for preparing project budgets and cot base line is aggregating costs of different activities or work packages during specific calendar time periods keeping in view the project schedule for carrying out these expenses. However, when such detailed analysis of cost of activities and project schedule is not done in case of some projects (either because they are too small or simple or they are quite similar to the other projects routinely executed by the organization), parametric estimating of costs and working out cost base line directly could be a practical and viable option for budgeting technique. Finally, the expenditure on project has to be within the funding limits of the organization and hence reconciliation with the funding limits is also an essential tool for determining project budget.

With this perspective, the list of tools and techniques listed in PMBOK® Guide, 5th Edition, are presented below:

Cost Aggregation: The project schedule is reviewed and the cost of all project activities planned to be completed in the particular calendar period are summed up to develop the preliminary project budget.
It is subjected to some of the following analysis before formally adopting it.

Reserve Analysis: The contingency and management reserve are included in the preliminary budget.

Expert Judgment: The preliminary budget is reviewed in terms of the expertise acquired in the light of similar other projects by availing the expert judgment of consultants and other experts if necessary.

Historical Relationships: The total cost of the project is compared with the historical data of similar projects using parametric or analogous costing.

Funding Limits Reconciliation: Finally the project schedule and budget are adjusted to comply with the funds which could be released for the project in specific periods.

Outputs

The budgeting process develops time-phased estimates for individual project activity and the overall project cost baseline from cumulative rolling up of these costs. With that background, the following outputs are listed in PMBOK® Guide, 5th Edition, are presented below:

Cost Baseline: It is the approved version of the cumulative time-phased budget for project activities and the entire project, against which the project performance would be measured during the execution phase for monitoring and control.

Project Funding Requirements: From period-wise expenditure worked out in the budget, the project funding requirements are developed.

Update of Cost Management Plan and Origin of Change Request: The funding constraints may impose changes in the project plan to execute work in a manner that can be satisfactorily funded by the organization from the resources available at its command The change request originated from the budgeting process and the corresponding update in project cost management plan are other outputs from the budgeting process.

6. CONTROL COSTS

Control Costs is the process of monitoring the status of the project to update the project costs and managing changes to the cost baseline. (PMBOK® Guide, 5th Edition)

The classic feedback control loop is the model for Control Cost process. The standard for cost performance expected from the project is given by the project cost baseline (output of the cost budgeting process). The actual cost performance of the project is available from the actual work carried out at a specific stage and the cost incurred for completing the work at that stage. The difference between the two, *the cost variance*, provides the project manager a directional map for identifying factors impacting the cost should be influenced for improved cost control.

The first part of the process, monitoring the project costs, requires the project manager's constant focus on the actual progress of the project activities, their monetary value and comparison with the values in approved project cost base line. From the cost variance data generated from this analysis, project manager gets directions for how he should go about for proactively managing the factors that influence the project costs. Sophisticated analytical techniques, like Earned Value Management, are developed for this.

Second part of the process, managing changes to the cost baseline, requires influencing the factors that impact the cost baseline and getting approval for such project changes. The reason for this possibility arises from the fact that the cost of carrying out any activity would depend on the precise specifications for the work to be done and the time frame in which it is to be carried out. Usually there is some leeway in the precise specifications or the time frame for its execution – for example, whether a premium price should be paid for a particular product or service for the project and similarly whether premium for earlier delivery should be paid (which might justify, in turn, overtime payments, permit overuse of other resources, etc.).

In light of the above nature of the process, the inputs, tools and techniques and outputs for the cost controlling process according to PMBOK® Guide, 5th Edition, are listed below. The first two inputs listed in PMBOK Guide provide the standards against which the actual cost performance on the project is to be measured; the next two inputs listed provide the details of the actual project cost performance

Inputs

Project Management Plan It includes the following two important documents.

- *Cost Baseline:* Cost baseline provides the time-phased budget for individual work package or activity and also for the entire project; hence, it provides the standard for measuring the cost performance of the project for the purpose of monitoring and controlling.
- *Cost management Plan:* This provides the methodology for Control Cost Process, particularly the rules for carrying out Earned Value Analysis.

Project Funding Requirements: Depending on the constraints and convenience of the organizing the fund flows for project work, some modification in the final budget document might have been incorporated. Cost Control needs to take into account project funding requirement as an input.

Work Performance Data: This data may be somewhat more comprehensive than periodic performance reports mentioned above. These may also include status and cost of the work packages or activities during the execution, a review of the completed and balance work and the forecast for completion in terms of time and cost.

Organizational Process Assets: The policies and procedures set down by the organization for cost control, reporting formats for cost reports, and similar organizational tools would provide additional helpful inputs.

Tools and Techniques

Techniques for cost control aim at the following:

- Analysis of the cost performance on the project by comparing the actual performance against the budgetary standards and cost baseline (cost variance)
- Forecasting the project performance (estimated time and cost to complete the total project)

Accordingly the main tools and techniques for cost control are:

Earned Value Management (EVM): This cost control technique has recently become popular. It aims at an integrated control of the scope, cost and schedule performance of the project. In view of the importance gained by this technique, a detailed discussion on it is also presented separately.

Forecasting: Forecasting the values of time and cost Estimates at Completion (EAC) is another important tool used during the process. Ordinarily, use of this technique is integrated with EVM as one of its parts.

Project Performance Reviews: This more traditional tool involves carrying out Cost Variance Analysis, based on the calculation of variance from the budget or cost baseline. Use of the company's proprietary Project Management Software may be helpful in such an analysis.

Outputs

Three primary outputs of the cost control process are:

Work Performance Information: The variances from the budget in traditional cost control and Cost Performance Index (CPI), Schedule Performance Index (SPI) and other metrics developed from EVM technique.

Cost Forecasts: The estimated time and cost for project completion, again either calculated in the traditional way or calculated using the EVM technique

Change Requests: The changes to be incorporated to influence the factors, which would impact the cost performance in the desired direction.

Updates in Cost Estimate (as a part of forecasting performance), *Updates in Project Management Plan* (as a part of the integration for cost baseline and cost management plan) and Updates in *Organizational Process Assets* (Lessons learned from cost control, financial database, etc.) are other secondary outputs from the process.

CASE 5.1

Sharp Printing, AG

Three years ago the Sharp Printing (SP) strategic management group set a goal of having a color laser printer available for the consumer and small business market for less than $200. A few months later the senior management met off-site to discuss the new product. The results of this meeting were a set of general technical specifications along with major deliverables, a product launch date, and a cost estimate based on prior experience.

Shortly afterward, a meeting was arranged for middle management explaining the project goals, major responsibilities, the project start date, and importance of meeting the product launch date within the cost estimate. Members of all departments involved attended the meeting. Excitement was high. Although everyone saw the risks as high, the promised rewards for the company and the personnel were emblazoned in their minds. A few participants questioned the legitimacy of the project duration and cost estimates. A couple of R&D people were worried about the technology required to produce the high-quality product for less than $200. But given the excitement of the moment, everyone agreed the project was worth doing and doable. The color laser printer project was to have the highest project priority in the company.

Lauren was selected to be the project manager. She had 15 years of experience in printer design and manufacture, which included successful management of several projects related to printers for commercial markets. Since she was one of those uncomfortable with the project cost and time estimates, she felt getting good bottom-up time and cost estimates for the deliverables was her first concern. She quickly had a meeting with the significant stakeholders to create a WBS identifying the work packages and organizational unit responsible for implementing the work packages. Lauren stressed she wanted time and cost estimates from those who would do the work or were the most knowledgeable, if possible. Getting estimates from more than one source was encouraged. Estimates were due in two weeks.

The compiled estimates were placed in the WBS/OBS. The corresponding cost estimate seemed to be in error. The cost estimate was $1,250,000 over the senior management estimate; this represents about a 20 percent overrun! The time estimate from the developed project network was only four months over the top management time estimate. Another meeting was scheduled with the significant stakeholders to check the estimates and to brainstorm for alternative solutions; the cost and time estimates appeared to be reasonable. Some of the suggestions for the brainstorming session are listed below.

- Change scope.
- Outsource technology design.
- Use the priority matrix (found in Chapter 4) to get top management to clarify their priorities.

- Partner with another organization or build a research consortium to share costs and to share the newly developed technology and production methods.
- Cancel the project.
- Commission a break-even study for the laser printer.

Very little in the way of concrete savings was identified, although there was consensus that time could be compressed to the market launch date, but at additional costs.

Lauren met with the marketing (Connor), production (Kim), and design (Gage) managers who yielded some ideas for cutting costs, but nothing significant enough to have a large impact. Gage remarked, "I wouldn't want to be the one to deliver the message to top management that their cost estimate is $1,250,000 off! Good luck, Lauren."

1. At this point, what would you do if you were the project manager?
2. Was top management acting correctly in developing an estimate?
3. What estimating techniques should be used for a mission critical project such as this?

CASE 5.2

Post Graduation Adventure

Josh and Mike met each other as roommates during freshmen year at MacAlister College in St. Paul, Minnesota. Despite a rocky start they became best friends. They are planning on going on a two week adventure together to celebrate their graduation in June. Josh has never been to Europe and wants to visit France or Spain. Mike spent a semester abroad in Aarhus, Denmark, and traveled extensively in Northern Europe. Even though he never went to France or Spain, Mike wants to go to some place more exotic like South Africa or Vietnam. For the past week they have been arguing back and forth over where they should go. Josh argues that it will cost too much to fly to South Africa or Vietnam, while Mike counters that it will be much cheaper to travel in Vietnam or South Africa once they are there. Each of them agreed that they can spend no more than $3,500 each on the trip and could be gone for only two weeks.

One evening when they were arguing with each other over beers with friends, Sara said, "Why don't you use what you learned in your project management class to decide what to do?" Josh and Mike looked at each other and agreed that made perfect sense.

1. Assume you are either Mike or Josh; how would you go about making a decision using project management methodology?
2. Looking first at only cost, what decision would you make?
3. After cost, what other factors should be considered before making a decision?

CASE 5.3

National Acetylene Company

(Project Cost Estimation for a Manufacturing Facility Using Analogous, Parametric and Detailed Cost-Estimating Techniques)

Abstract

It may be necessary to develop cost estimates for project selection, the initiation phase of the project for project authorization, and finally for development of detailed budgeted costs used for monitoring and controlling project cost. The need for accuracy in developing such estimates, the constraints on time and effort available for developing the estimates, and the rigour for the methodology used for estimation vary according to the purpose for which the cost estimate is to be developed. The case presents scenarios for application of three common cost estimating techniques (analogous, parametric and detailed cost-estimating techniques) and associated rigour and accuracy of the estimate.

CASE TEXT

In January 1992, Vishnu Mhatre, General Manager – Strategic Business Planning at National Acetylene Company, sat at his table poring over the several investment proposals for setting up manufacturing facilities for the company's diversification plan. Suddenly, there was a flash in his mind and he was surprised at why he had overlooked the obvious option for his company's diversification plan: setting up a calcium carbide unit with backward integration of the company's current operation! Of course, it was true that setting up a reasonable sized calcium carbide plant needed a substantial investment and National Acetylene did not have that kind of funds available for investment earlier. But the company was doing rather well in the two years. Only the other day, while he was chatting with Mr. Padhye, Director – Finance, Padhye had mentioned that the company may be in a position to consider investment proposals for around ₹25 crore. Mhatre wondered whether that kind of investment would be adequate for setting up an economically viable calcium carbide manufacturing plant. He decided to act fast and wanted to keep on hand at least a preliminary investment proposal for discussion at the quarterly directors' meeting scheduled next week, if the opportunity was within reach available resources.

National Acetylene Company (NAC) was one of the reputed suppliers of bottled acetylene gas for oxy-acetylene type welding processes in the Pune area. It purchased calcium carbide from a supplier located in a different state and generated acetylene by hydrolyzing it in its plant. Acetylene generated from hydrolysis of calcium carbide is absorbed in the acetone and filled in the gas cylinders supplied to the customers. Acetylene being a highly explosive gas, the plant for generating and filling acetylene in the cylinders required expertise in the design of the plant, which required minute attention to a number of details. In view of these technological barriers and somewhat higher capital investment, the entry by new entrants would not be easy. Considering the rapidly growing market for bottled acetylene in the area with the increased steel fabrication activity, NAC decided to expand its scale of operation. The top management also wanted to look at the opportunity for backward integration to set up a captive facility for production of 10,000 tonnes calcium carbide.

The plant for production of calcium carbide required a large capital investment and consequently arranging for institutional finance from a development bank (for setting up the production facility) was inevitable. The viability of the project depended to a great extent on the accuracy of the estimate for the capital cost of the project. Mhatre would have to head the efforts for the detailed feasibility report. He knew that he would have to be very careful not only in estimating the cost for setting up the plant, but also in preparing its presentation, which would be acceptable to the financial institution without much hassle.

Mhatre realized that before the final commitment to go ahead, he would need to develop a fairly reliable estimate for the calcium carbide plant cost. However, for the preliminary consideration, it would be sufficient for him to check out if the opportunity would be within reach. There was not much time for detailed cost estimate, which could be used for a firm investment decision; but surely he would have to come up with a "ball park" figure for the investment.

He called his assistant, Avinash Rane and explained to him that he wanted to develop a rough estimate for the cost of setting up calcium carbide plant with an annual production capacity of 10,000 tonnes per annum "The technical literature from U.S mentions the economically viable plant's size to be at least 50,000 tonnes; but that may be too big for us in India. Besides, I suspect that investment for that size plant may also be out of our reach. "Mhatre explained the idea underlying his choice of capacity.

"I entirely agree with you, Sir. I will start work right away. By the way, when do you need this?" Avinash asked.

"Yesterday, my friend! Drop everything else on your hand; just concentrate on this one. The board meeting is next Thursday and I want to have a preliminary discussion on the proposal in that meeting if the cost looks right. So you have 3 days to come up with this number."

"But, you know the kind of information we process and the details we work into our investment proposals; how can we ..." Avinash left the sentence unfinished.

"I understand, Avinash, that you do not like to prepare proposals without reliable investment, operating costs and market size figures. I admire your professional approach and I would prefer to take that myself if the situation permitted. In fact, we will do precisely that, if we get a go-ahead signal in the next week meeting. But right now, we just don't have more time. If we miss this quarterly meeting, we will simply lose 3 months; that is plain and simple. What I want is some idea of cost ..."

"How much accuracy would be good enough for this exercise?" Avinash interrupted

"If I say ±40 %?"

"Well, then let me tell you how I plan to proceed. I will look up the investment figures of calcium carbide plants in the last few years, so that we can have a look at them and prepare our guestimate for preliminary discussions. I would also carry out rough and ready preliminary plant design and work out the important parameters on which the plant cost would depend and their current costs. Based on this data, I will prepare my cost estimates for your review in the next three days. If you find them acceptable and the investment outlay within our reach and interest, we can use some consultant's service for developing a definitive cost estimate for taking the final investment decision."

Avinash moved towards the cabin door. Before stepping out, however, he just held the door half-open and added, "And you will have to relax your deadline for my vinyl acetate operating cost report for a week" before stepping out.

What Avinash presented for discussion after two days is shown in Exhibit 1. The investment estimates thrown up from the data looked encouraging and Metallurgical Consultants, a reputed company for metallurgical projects, was commissioned to prepare a Definitive Cost Estimate. The executive summary of the consultant's report included the project cost details briefly extracted in Exhibit 2.

EXHIBIT 1 ··
Data Collected for Developing Cost Estimate for a 10,000 Tonnes Capacity Calcium Carbide Plant

1. Data for developing a cost estimate from the historical information:
(Data for application of Analogous Cost Estimating technique)
In 1982, Raymond Carbide set up a plant for production of calcium carbide. It was similar in scope – a stand-alone calcium carbide manufacturing plant and not connected with any other manufacturing facility.

The source of data: Raymond Carbide's Annual Shareholders' Report, 1983.
- The Production capacity of the plant: 20,000 tonnes per annum on 3-shifts continuous basis.
- Project location: Jadughoda, Bihar
- Cost of project: ₹24 crores
- Reserve Bank Wholesale Price Index for Materials for 1982: 282
- Reserve Bank Wholesale Price Index for Materials for 1992: 340
- Relative costs of construction labour in Bihar/ Maharashtra :75 :100
- Breakdown of project cost into materials and labour: 90% cost for purchased equipment and construction materials; 10 % cost for construction labour at the site.

2. Basic design parameters for 10,000 TPA capacity calcium carbide plant and available current cost data for the parameters
(Data for application of Parametric Cost estimating technique)
Based on the preliminary plant design calculations, the following parameters having an important bearing on the plant cost have been identified and worked out.. The current estimated cost for these parameters have been also collected and presented in the table below.

(Costs in ₹ crore)

	Available Cost Data	Parameter Unit Value	Requirements for 10,000 TPA Project
Plant site land area, sq.m	₹200,000/-	1000 sq.m	40,000 sq.m
Site development	₹20,000	1000 sq.m	40,000 sq.m
Plant buildings	Rs ₹8,000/-	1.0 sq. m	3,000 sq.m
Warehouses for Storage	₹ 5,000	1.0 sq. m	3,000 sq.m
Raw Material Handling System	₹40 lakh	2.0 T/hr	10.0 T/hr
Electric Furnace	₹5 crore	40 T/batch	80 T/batch
Product Handling System	₹50 lakh	2.0 T/hr	10.0 T/hr
Electric Sub-station	₹1.6 crore	1.0 MW	2.5 MW

EXHIBIT 2 ··
Definitive Cost Estimate (Bottom–up Detailed Cost Estimating Technique)

Mr. Mhatre commissioned Metallurgical Consultants for preparing a detailed feasibility report for the project. The report submitted by Metallurgical Consultants had about 300 pages and contained a 20 pages chapter on the project cost estimate supported by budgetary quotations for critical or major equipment or sub-systems.

A section on the project cost estimate from the executive summary of the report is extracted and presented below:

Extract from Metallurgical Consultants Project Report
The cost of **New Fixed Investment** for the project to set up a plant for an annual production of 10,000 tonnes calcium carbide from purchased calcium carbonate and petroleum coke at Pune is estimated at ₹24.20 crore ±10%. The

estimate is valid for the plant construction to start latest by September 1992 and the construction to be completed in the next 18- month period. The breakdown of the cost (**at WBS Level 1**) follows:

(Cost in ₹lakh)

Land and site development	78.50
Buildings	
• Warehouses for raw materials storage	98.00
• Main production plant building	320.00
• Warehouse for finished product	45.00
• Ancillary buildings (workshop, etc.)	28.00
• Plant office and Quality Test Laboratory	16.00
• Sub-total buildings	507.00
Plant & Machinery	
• Purchased equipment at the site	956.50
• Installation expenses	137.00
• Auxiliary equipment	282.00
Sub-total plant and machinery	1375.50
Lump sum Technical Know-how fees	75.00
Detailed Engineering & Site Construction Supervision	92.00
Miscellaneous Fixed Assets	72.00
Sub-total	2200.00
Provision for Contingency	220.00
Total cost for New Fixed Investment	2420.00

Basis for the Cost Estimate

• The cost for land is taken from the offers for land prices available in the Pune industrial belt. The site development costs for earthwork have been based on the database available with the company from earlier project.

• The preliminary layout and sizing of the plant is carried out to determine the size and the type of construction for the proposed production unit. The requirements for storage of raw materials and finished products (providing for 6 weeks storage Capacity) have also been worked out for preliminary sizing of these buildings. Again, the building costs have been estimated using parametric costing for similar constructions from our database. For this estimate, the price of structural steel is taken at ₹15,800 per tonne, reinforcing steel at ₹14,300 per tonne and cement at ₹2200 per tonne.

• Preliminary flow sheet for the production process was prepared and the list of all major production equipment was finalized. Preliminary brief specifications for inviting budgetary quotations from equipment suppliers were worked out, the quotations were invited (some on telephones) and used for this estimate. The installation expenses include the civil foundations, mechanical erection at the site and electric power cabling and earthing. The provision for auxiliary equipment (laboratory and fire fighting equipment) and miscellaneous fixed assets (office equipment, telecom equipment, cars and trucks) is based on our experience for similar recent projects. Provision for technical know-how fees is according to the draft technical collaboration agreement made available by National Acetylene.

• The total provision for contingency is made at 10 per cent – 5 % to take care of for scope changes necessary during detailed project planning and execution and 5 % for price escalations.

Questions for Discussion

1. Develop
   - The 'Order of Magnitude' cost estimate using the data in the first part of Exhibit 1 using analogous cost estimating technique.
   - The 'Ball Park' cost estimate using the data in the second part of Exhibit 1 using parametric cost estimating technique.
2. The Definitive Cost Estimate is the most reliable or accurate; why did Mhatre go through the exercise of developing the cost estimate using other techniques successively? Explain why the Definitive Cost Estimate report includes a substantial amount of supporting details.

CASE 5.4

Infotech Corporation

(Case Illustrating Application of Resource Rate Technique for Estimating Cost for a Software Project)

Abstract

The case presents scenario and data necessary for application of resource rate technique generally used for estimating costs for software projects, for engineering consulting projects, and projects in construction contracting sector. The technique involves working out lump sum rates for use of a unit of a particular resource based on the analysis of both the direct costs and allocated overheads from earlier periods or earlier projects' cost data and experience (Lessons learned). These rates are applied to the estimated quantities of the resources to work out the estimated cost. The technique is easy, fairly reliable and popular with most software and project consulting companies.

CASE TEXT

Infotech Corporation (Infotech) is specialized in providing special business solutions to the customers. For this purpose, Infotech adopted the commercially available software to facilitate the client's special business needs by designing the proper interface between the available ready software packages and the customer's requirements; design special forms and short commands for simple user-friendly operations. This process required system design, code writing, testing and technical write-up for training and operating manuals. The company employed 10 system **designers,**

30 software-coding persons, 5 testers and 2 technical writers. It also included another 15 people in the supervisory, management and support function categories.

Infotech had a good reputation in the industry and could retain skilled professionals with its lucrative pay scales and liberal leave plans. The average salary of Infotech's employee was ₹45,000 per month for system designers, ₹20,000 per month for coding department, ₹20,000 per month for testers and ₹25,000 per month for technical writers. The company also offered all its employees two weeks paid vacation, 11 days paid public holidays, 7 days sick leave and 7 days casual leave. The company required each employee to work 40 hours per week on a regular basis with Saturdays and Sundays off. The company's policy was to understaff its operation to some extent, which required some overtime-working routine for most employees, but with liberal overtime payment scales (overtime payment at 50% over regular rates), the employees generally accepted the work culture.

Before 2001, Infotech could get away with its bids based on "Dollar Economy" pricing and providing arbitrary 450% overheads on its direct costs. But gradually the competition increased and Infotech found it necessary to develop a reliable costing system for the job bids based on realistic overhead costs and profit margins.

In August 2002, Mr. Vasudevan, Sales Manager, visited the office of one of its regular clients, Sundaram Computers, and met their outsourcing manager, Ms Vidyalaksmi. Infotech had established a relationship of trust with Sundaram Computers and whenever Sundaram found itself shorthanded to complete some critical assignments on time, it outsourced some modules from Infotech. Vidyalakshmi told Vasudevan that they wanted to outsource some database development work to Infotech, if it could adhere to a rather tight delivery schedule and she passed on to him the Database Schema, Entity Relations Diagrams and the summary of functionalities expected by the client from the preliminary work carried out by Sundaram. Vidyalaksmi emphasized that Sundaram wanted a firm fixed price contract offer for the assignment and delivery time would be the essence of the contract. Vasudevan returned to his office and immediately assigned the project cell to complete on an urgent basis a study of the work involved and the estimate of man-hours. He also asked the project department to check out if the December 15 delivery can be met in light of the on-going jobs in the regular course and if not what would be the extent of overtime work required. The project cell completed the study in the next two days and sent to Vasudevan the summary of the man-hours estimate for Sundaram Project. **Exhibit 1** lists a brief summary of the company's expenses on different heads during the earlier accounting year and **Exhibit 2** shows the man-hours estimated by the project cell for the project enquiry sent by Mr. Vasudevan.

Based on this data, Vasudevan proposed to quote ₹18.5 lakh for a firm fixed price contract and sent the following note to Infotech's Executive Vice President for getting his approval:

August 14, 2002

From : G. Vasudevan

To: M. Vishvamohan

Subject: Making an FFP Contract Offer to Sundaram Computers

Sundaram Computers have approached us for making an FFP contract offer for two database related modules; a part of their contracted offer to their client. On the basis of the technical specifications studied by the project cell their total estimate is 1600 man-hours for the job.

I have worked out our offer based on the following:

- Estimate of category-wise man-hours prepared by the project cell and the man-hour rate worked for each category from our current salary scale
- Provision of 20% overtime work taking into account the required delivery and our current work-load
- The allocation of overhead expenses based on our annual budget for 2002
- Provision of 15% contingency on the project cost worked out as above.
- A mark-up of about 30% on our project cost.

Accordingly, I propose to quote ₹18.5 lakh for FFP contract. The relevant work papers are enclosed.

Request your approval

Vasudevan

EXHIBIT 1 ··

Summary of Annual Operating Costs Budget for 2002

(All expenses in ₹lakh)

Salaries and Wages		
• System Designers	54.0	
• Coders	72.0	
• Testers	12.0	
• Technical writers	6.0	
• Supervisory and managerial staff	166.0	
• Supporting subordinate staff	40.0	
Sub-total salaries and wages		**350.0**
Other staff related expenses		
• Professional Meetings	12.0	
• Travel	48.0	
• Training	10.0	
Sub-total other staff related expenses		**70.0**
Other Office Overheads		
• Rent	20.0	
• Insurance	12.0	
• Electricity charges	24.0	
• Telephones	36.0	
• Stationery	8.0	
Sub-total other office overheads		100.0
Equipment Depreciation		**12.0**
Interest payments on loans		**48.0**
TOTAL ANNUAL EXPENSES		**580.0**

Exhibit 2 ···
Man-hours Estimate for Sundaram Computers

Estimate Summary

Total 1600 man-hours are estimated to be required for Sundaram Computers project with the breakdown given in Table 1 below:

Basis for Estimate

1. A preliminary Function Point Analysis was carried out to estimate the man-hours. The numbers for man-hours from Function Point Analysis were compared with the actual man-hours spent by us for a somewhat similar database assignment for ICICI in October 2001 and they matched well.
2. The estimates are based on normal working man-hours. Since this is a high-pressure job with the project to be completed by December 15 and we have some prior commitments, .we should provide for doing at least 20% of the work on this project overtime.
3. The estimate provided is for only the direct man-hours. All supporting service man-hours and organizational overheads would have to be accounted separately.

Table 1 ··

Category-wise Estimate of Man-hours for Sundaram Computers

Task	Skill-set Required	Man-hours
Preliminary Study and Overall Scheme	System Designer	40
Plan System Architecture	System Designer	360
Design (Detailed Code-writing)		
Module (a)	Programmers (C ++ platform)	330
Module (b)	Programmers (Oracle platform)	470
Writing Test Specification and Testing	Program Testers	200
Preparing Instruction Manual	Technical Writers	50
Project Management	Project Leads	150
(@ 10 % of above sub-total)		
Total Estimated Man-hours		**1600**

On receiving Vishvamohan's approval, Vasudevan promptly approached Sundaram Computers with their offer. Two days later, Vidyalakshmi called Vasudevan "You appear to have padded up your offer a lot. We can't pay you that price. We appreciate the quality of your work and your reliability in meeting deadlines. So, we would be quite happy to outsource this work to you but not at that price; we just don't have that kind of margin on this job. Let me make you a fair counteroffer. If you would be ready to accept ₹13.50 lakhs total for a firm fixed price contract, the job is yours. In that case, collect the purchase order and the balance technical details and start the work right away."

Vasudevan was reasonably confident of Vishvamohan accepting whatever recommendation he would make concerning Sundaram's counteroffer. He knew that Infotech order backlog was not heavy. He sat down studying the papers and thinking out what course of action Infotech should take.

Questions for Discussion

This case requires application of 'Resource Rate' technique, which is generally employed by organizations executing projects for clients as contract work (like engineering contractors, software companies, etc.).

1. Develop the cost of project for Sundarm Computers based on the available data.
2. Should Infotech accept the Sundaram's counter offer?

CASE 5.5

Priyadarshi Melamine Company

(Application of Monte Carlo Simulation Technique for Managing Risk in Project Cost Estimate due to Variability of the Cost Elements)

Abstract

The phase of final approval and sanction of budget for a major project usually involves preparing a techno-economic feasibility report with somewhat detailed project cost estimate. Traditionally, the cost estimates prepared are built-up by Bottom-Up cost estimating technique from preliminary planning data but based on somewhat detailed cost estimate with major deliverables suitably decomposed into manageable size work packages. The cost estimates are 'definitive' in nature – a single value estimate based on the best guess from available data and details. From its very nature, this methodology does not address the issue of uncertainties due to the variability in the costs likely during actual execution.

With the availability of large capacity high-speed computers, it has become possible to build complex models for project cost elements and include in them the variability of individual cost elements. Monte Carlo technique is one of such very useful quantitative techniques for making available at the project planning stage a clearer picture of the risks and uncertainties in the cost for completing the project. The output of Monte Carlo simulation presents in a graphical form a range of project cost estimates and the corresponding chance or probability associated with any individual estimate. In the last decade, major international corporations are taking increasing interest in this technique for decision making, planning and managing major projects and programs.

*This case explains the application of Monte Carlo technique for project cost. The technique is illustrated by taking the case of a typical project scenario of estimating project cost for setting up a manufacturing facility. **Using standard Excel® software, Monte Carlo simulation is developed for***

working out total project cost while taking into account variability in the individual cost elements.
The step-wise description of the application is in sufficient details (including cell entries for building
the simulation) to enable an interested project professional to pick up fine nuances in the application
and use the technique for some specific project on his hand, or as an aid for self-study or as a case to
be used for classroom teaching.

CASE TEXT

1. INTRODUCTION

Cost estimating process involves developing an approximate estimate in monetary terms for the
resources required to complete satisfactorily all project activities. During different phases of the
project life cycle, the reliability of the cost estimates, degree of attention to project activity details
for working out the costs, the time and expenses involved in preparing the cost estimates, and
management levels participating in the cost estimating exercise need to be different.

Top-Down Cost Estimating Techniques for Initial Conceptualization Phase of Project:
During the project conceptualization and initiating phases of the project life cycles, emphasis is on
the big picture and not on fine details. At that stage, the management would want to take a decision
on the economic viability of the project and the order of magnitude of the resources necessary to
undertake the project compared to the organization's financial capability. There is no time then for
working out the fine details; there is no need for spending efforts for working out fine details and
spending money. Therefore, at that stage, the cost estimating techniques employed are generally
"Top Down" in nature. At this stage, *Analogous Cost Estimating* or *Parametric Cost Estimating* –
two popular Top Down cost-estimating techniques are most often employed. For Analogous cost
estimation, the management relies on historical project cost data – from its own project files or
from published literature – for different projects of similar nature and uses an expert judgment in
arriving at the rough, order of magnitude cost, for the project under consideration. In case of
Parametric Cost Estimating, somewhat more attention to details is given. The project is first
analyzed in terms of major deliverables and the requirements of the system parameters to meet
these deliverables. The cost estimates for the constituent systems are worked out based on the
nature and quantity of the critical parameters influencing the cost of the systems. Both these Top
Down estimating techniques can be helpful in developing preliminary or order of magnitude cost
estimates useful at the conceptualization stage.

Bottom-up Cost Estimating Techniques for Detailed Project Planning and Contract-based Project
Executions:
Once the economic viability of the project is established and the project appears to be able to meet
the strategic goals of the organization adequately, the organization would want to define the
project details more clearly and develop far more reliable cost estimate of the resources for a final
review before formally launching the project. *Bottom-Up* cost estimating techniques are employed
to arrive at a far more reliable estimate of project cost at this stage. With the formal launch of the
project, the project team would work out the major and minor deliverables and develop them by
further subdivision – hierarchical decomposition – into work packages. These work packages
would have well defined technical and performance specifications, the estimates for resources and
time required for completing the activities included in the work package activities and
corresponding costs.

Application of Simulation Techniques for Managing Risks in Project Cost Estimation: (Developing Probabilistic Estimates of Cost)

As the above description of the cost estimating techniques suggests, the estimates of the costs for project activities are *definitive* in nature. The uncertainty or risk inherent in all future activities and the possible impact of these uncertainties on the project cost is not taken into account in developing the cost estimate. In case of small projects or internal projects for the organization's own benefits, this may not be considered a significant handicap. However, when projects are to be executed for other organizations, with predetermined specific cost or price in terms of the contract, the management would want to arrive at a better estimate of the uncertainty or risk involved in undertaking the project contract. Also, when the projects are large in comparison with the organization's current financial capability and when the necessity of completing the project without major overruns even in face of some adverse risks is paramount, the organization would prefer to have a *probabilistic estimate of cost,* which would attempt to take into account the future uncertainties and their impact on project costs. In such a probabilistic cost estimate, essentially, in place of one definitive cost estimate, the probabilities associated with different likely costs based on assessed future scenarios and corresponding variability are developed. The outcome of a probabilistic estimate would give an array of different cost estimates and the corresponding probability of meeting that estimate. To illustrate this: the probabilistic cost estimate would provide the probabilities corresponding to a range of project costs. For instance, from the graphical output of the simulation, it would be possible to state," The probability of completing this project in ₹30 millions cost is 50%; the probability of completing the project in ₹35 million is 70%; the probability of completing the project in ₹40 million is 95% ... " and so on.

Illustration of Monte Carlo Simulation Technique for Developing Probabilistic Project Cost Estimates

This case presents the underlying principles and general methodology of applying Monte Carlo simulation technique. Then it goes on to illustrate the application of this technique to project cost estimation. The article explains the general methodology for application of the technique using standard Excel® software by taking a hypothetical case study of developing project cost for setting up a manufacturing facility. The illustration is detailed enough to give step-wise instructions for applying the technique, which would enable a project management professional to grasp the operational details and apply it to his/her own project: input details, simulation steps, and results output with analysis.

2. PRIYADARSHI MELAMINE COMPANY

The large mahogany table was slightly off centre in the well-appointed office with maroon colored carpet and fully paneled walls with darkly polished veneer. Except for small in-out trays in a side corner, the tabletop was almost clear. At the table sat Siddharth Mehta, Director Projects, Indian Investment Bank. He was a tall bespectacled man in his late forties. While he was shuffling the neatly stacked papers in the folder in front of him, there was a knock at the door and Ms Moha Desai entered. Mehta indicated her to take a seat and started discussion immediately without any preliminaries. "I was looking at the executive summary page of the cost estimate of Priyadarshi Melamine Company project, which we would be appraising with a view to sanction a term loan for the project. I saw the project feasibility report prepared by Chemicals Project Consultancy and back-up working papers prepared by you." Then he once more turned over the pages and added while scanning the papers, "The project appears to have been planned well and project cost estimate includes adequate provision for all project work. Your back up working papers, along with details in the feasibility report, properly justifies estimates for all cost items. For unexpected change in scope and price escalation you have made a provision for contingency at 10%, which should also be ordinarily sufficient for a project of this type and size." There was a silence for over a minute.

Then Siddharth folded up the papers, looked at Moha and said, "You know, there is one nagging doubt bothering me all these years about our basic cost estimating procedure and the manner in which it addresses the issue of managing risk in estimating total project cost. I just mentioned to you that 10% contingency provision should adequately take care of unforeseen project expenditure. But, really what is the logical basis for our taking that 10% figure? Why not less - why not more? What are our realistic chances for managing to complete the project within the estimated cost? Contingency provision is just used as a tool for managing the project cost risk, an arbitrarily guessed number without any logical and factual back up. We don't know how effective or appropriate our guess would turn out. I wonder, if there is a procedure or methodology to allow us to be more aware of the risk elements influencing actual project cost and to what degree of confidence we can estimate the costs."

"Very true, sir", Moha responded. Then after a pause she added, "The defense for that arbitrary percentage would be its successful application in scores of projects in the last three years – sort of empirical evidence!" and smiled.

"Well, in absence of any better measure, we can continue to use that figure" Siddharth conceded, "But I always have some nagging doubt about this traditional mode of managing project cost risk. I always felt that some better procedure for arriving at the contingency figure should be developed."

Moha thought for a while and then whispered a suggestion, "Sir, one month back, I had attended at IIM a 1-week seminar on 'Application of Quantitative Techniques in Project Risk Management'. There Prof. Shah discussed a simulation technique, which would actually permit to simulate through a computer program the nature of variability of different cost items and the total impact these random variations would have on the total cost of the project. This modeling technique, called Monte Carlo Simulation, would permit to carry out hundreds of such simulations, which our high-speed large capacity computers can churn out in a few hours. The output would be in the form of a graph showing cumulative probability corresponding to any specific total project cost. For example, from such a graph, you can read out that there is say, 50% chance for completing this project in ₹100 million, or that in order to have confidence level of 80%, the provision for project cost should be, say ₹120 million and for 95% confidence level, the estimate for total project cost should be pegged at ₹130 million, etc. The arbitrary contingency percentage need not be used. The seasoned manager could take into account the nature of the project and the degree of detailed work that went into building the cost estimate, the general trends in the industry, macro-economic conditions in the country, etc. and take a *calculated risk* for deciding on a total project cost estimate. Of course, the arbitrariness element is not entirely eliminated with this technique also, but in my opinion, it surely is a more logical and justifiable way for project cost risk management." Siddharth thought over that for a while and then turned to Moha, "Moha, would you like to try out that technique on this Priyadarshi Melamine project? From what you say, the technique does look interesting and promising."

For the next two weeks, Moha was busy building the Monte Carlo simulation for the project. **Exhibit 1** presents **The Definitive Project Cost Estimate** (extracted from *'The Executive Summary of the Techno-economical Feasibility Report'* prepared by Chemical Projects Consultancy).

Exhibit 1 ···
Priyadarshi Melamine Company

Definitive Project Cost Estimate

[Priyadarshi Melamine Company had commissioned Chemical Projects Consultants to prepare the techno-economic feasibility report for the project. The report submitted by Chemical Projects Consultants had about 300 pages and contained a 45-pages chapter on the project cost estimate. The supporting details included overall manufacturing facility planning for identifying cost centers: master plan for plant layout showing major civil constructions, list and preliminary specifications of major equipments, and budgetary quotations for critical or major equipment or sub-systems. *A section on the project cost estimate from the Executive Summary of the report is extracted and presented below.*]

The cost of **New Fixed Investment** for the project to set up a plant near Mehsana, Gujarat, for an annual production of 10,000 tons technical grade melamine from purchased urea is estimated at ₹930 million ±10%. It is based on a process developed by Inventa A.G., W.Germany for manufacture of melamine from urea. The estimate is valid for the plant construction to start latest by September 2011 and the construction to be completed in the next 18 months period. The breakdown of the cost **(at WBS Level 1)** follows:

(Cost in ₹ Millions)

Land and site development		**18.00**
Buildings		
• Warehouses for raw materials storage	21.00	
• Main production plant building	78.00	
• Warehouse for finished product	45.00	
• Ancillary buildings (workshop, etc.)	28.00	
• Plant office and Quality Test Laboratory	16.00	
Sub-total buildings	**188.00**	**188.00**
Plant and Machinery		
• Purchased equipment at the site	325.00	
• Installation expenses	87.00	
• Auxiliary equipment	68.00	
Sub-total plant and machinery	**480.00**	**480.00**
Lump sum Technical Know-how fees		35.00
Detailed Engineering, procurement and Site Construction Supervision		55.00
Miscellaneous Fixed Assets		42.00
Pre-operative Expenses		22.00
(Sub-total up to above: 840.00)		
Provision for Contingency		90.00
(@ approx. 10%, rounded to the next 10 million)		
TOTAL NEW FIXED INVESTMENT		₹930.00 million

Basis for the Cost Estimate:
• *Land:* The cost for land is taken from the offers for land prices available in the Mehsana industrial belt. The site development costs for earthwork have been based on the database available with the company from earlier project.

- *Buildings:* The preliminary layout and sizing of the plant buildings is carried out to determine the size and the type of construction for the proposed production unit. The requirements for storage of raw materials and finished products (providing for 6 weeks storage capacity) have also been worked out for preliminary sizing of these buildings. Again, the building costs have been estimated using parametric costing for similar constructions from our database. For this estimate, the price of structural steel is taken at ₹49,500 per ton, reinforcing steel at ₹47,300 per ton and cement at ₹5,400 per ton.
- *Major Equipment & Installation Costs:* Preliminary flow sheet for the production process was prepared and the list of all major production equipment was finalized. Preliminary brief specifications for inviting budgetary quotations from equipment suppliers were worked out, the quotations were invited (some on telephones) and used for this estimate. The installation expenses include the civil foundations, mechanical erection at the site and electric power cabling and earthing. The provision for auxiliary equipment (laboratory and firefighting equipment) and miscellaneous fixed assets (office equipment, telecom equipment, cars and trucks) is based on our experience for similar recent projects.
- *Technical Know-how Fees:* Provision for technical knowhow fees is made according to the terms of the draft technical collaboration agreement made available by Priyadarshi Melamine.
- *Pre-operative Expenses:* Pre-operative expenses include hiring and training expenses for key personnel and cost of trial runs for 4 weeks (including raw materials, utilities and salaries)
- *Provision for Contingency:* The total provision for contingency is made at 10 per cent: 5% to take care of for scope changes necessary during detailed project planning and execution and 5% for price escalations.

3. DEVELOPING THE SPREADSHEET MODEL

3.1   Inputs and Simulation Variables

The Definitive Project Cost Estimate, presented in Exhibit 1, is the basic source of information for inputs for simulation. Exhibit 1 gives single-value estimates of different cost centers like Land and Site Development, Buildings, Plant and Machinery, Technical Know-how Fees, etc. However, it does not give any indication of the variability likely to be associated with the cost estimated for any cost center. Additional work is carried out at this stage to determine the nature of variability and the variability defining parameters. For normal distributions, variability is defined by providing the pessimistic and optimistic estimates of each cost center in addition to the mean value already given in the Exhibit 1. For discrete distributions, discrete values and corresponding probabilities for discrete values are estimated and provided. In Attachment A, Part 1, these details and the cell entry details for building this variability into the simulation model are tabulated.

3.2   Spread Sheet Entries (Attachment A, Parts 1 and 2)

The Excel® spread sheet entries are in two groups:

Data Entry for Variability of Cost Centers, mentioned in 3.1 above, is given in table on Attachment A, Part 1. It should be noted that the Provision for Contingency, arbitrarily made at 10 % of the total of the rest of the cost centers, is only an ad-hoc provision for risk management. In this model simulation, different scenarios for each cost center are separately worked out and the total cost is arrived at by adding these individual costs; hence the provision for contingency is omitted.

Cell Entries for Monte Carlo Iterations are presented in the table on Attachment A, Part 2, according to the following rationale and methodology:

- For normal distributions, the pessimistic and optimistic estimates are taken as the 3-standard deviation limits around the mean, and accordingly, the standard deviation is calculated as 1/6 of the difference between the pessimistic and optimistic values. In case of discrete distributions, the cumulative probabilities are calculated and used as the table for VLOOKUP function for iterations.

- The formulae used for the first iteration of the simulation are entered as shown. For the next 99 iterations, the formula in first iteration is copied and *formula is pasted*. The printout presented in this paper includes only the first 25 iterations to economize on space.

- Since the random numbers put out in the spread sheet table would keep on changing with every re-opening of the table, the values need to be 'fixed' for a particular study-set by "copying and pasting values". The table containing the "fixed values" of first 25 of the total 100 entries is shown in the print out.

- The estimate for total cost for each iteration is worked out by summing up the estimate for individual cost centers for each iteration. The Mean and Standard Deviation of the total estimated cost are calculated using standard Excel® formulae.

- The Data Analysis tool of the Excel® software is used to analyze the results and plot the cumulative frequency histogram.

- The Confidence Interval for the Mean (Standard Error of Mean) is calculated by the formula: 95% Confidence Interval for the Mean = 1.96 x Std. Deviation/ (Sq. Root of iteration numbers)

- The provision for contingency for each iteration is calculated by the difference by which the total estimated cost for the iteration exceeds the estimated total cost excluding contingency provision (₹840 million in this case). If the total estimated cost for any iteration works out to be below ₹840 million, the contingency provision required is taken as zero.

- The provision for contingency in percentage terms is calculated from the contingency necessary for an iteration expressed as a percent of total cost (₹840 million in this case).

3.3 Spread Sheet Output and Summary (Attachment B, Part 1)

- The specimen of spreadsheet developed using the data and methodology set down in 3.2 above is presented in Attachment B. The simulation is carried out with 100 iterations; however, the print out of Attachment B attached with this paper includes only the first 25 iterations to economize on space.

- The Data Analysis tool of Excel® is used to plot the Cumulative Frequency Diagram included in the Attachment B. From that diagram, the total cost estimate corresponding to any desired degree of confidence (cumulative probability) can be read.

- Summary of estimated cost for this particular case simulation (based on 100 iterations) is as follows:

Estimated total cost, (₹ in million)

Maximum Value	= 927
Minimum Value	= 779

Mean Value = 851
Standard Deviation = 38
Standard Error of Mean = 4
95% Confidence Interval
for Mean Value = 851 ± 8 or 843 to 859 Million Rupees

Provision for Contingency:
For this particular simulation, the maximum value of estimated cost from 100 iterations is ₹927 million. The total estimated cost excluding contingency provision is ₹840 million and 10.4% provision for contingency would be necessary to cover this extreme scenario. Considering that extreme case scenario has very low probability (less than 2.5%, since the value is 2.3 standard deviations away from the mean value), the standard 10% contingency provision appears reasonable for variations visualized in this case.

4.0 CONCLUSIONS

This case illustrates application of Monte Carlo model simulation technique for analyzing and managing risks in project cost estimation. The Monte Carlo technique for simulation modeling illustrated in this article provides quantitative assessment of the risks, in terms of cumulative probability in achieving a particular value of total cost estimate, when the individual constituent cost centers have different variability. With very detailed step-wise illustration of the technique, it should be possible to imbibe from this article the essentials of this technique to a degree that can help to apply the technique for some similar project.

Ordinarily, the risk in project cost estimation is managed by provision of contingency. The provision of contingency is arbitrarily taken as some percent of the sum of known and identified costs. To what extent this ad hoc contingency provision covers the actual risk is not known. Monte Carlo simulation provides an alternative approach in which the degree of confidence can be judged. From the Cumulative Frequency Diagram developed with this technique, the confidence level associated with any specific cost estimate can be determined and vice versa.

Another merit in building such models is that it would be possible to visualize the effect of unusual larger variation in the individual constituent cost centers – say civil construction costs or equipment procurement cost, etc. – and its effect on total project cost. From the basic simulation model, sensitivity analysis of "What If?" nature studies can be carried out by tweaking the specific Excel input cells.

It would bear to repeat once more the caution in using these quantitative techniques. Sometimes, the precise numerical metrics worked out by such techniques might give an unwarranted sense of assurance and confidence in decision-making. All modeling techniques have their own limitations and unpredictability of future cannot be wished away by use of any technique. This simulation would not do away with the importance of mature judgment and feeling the pulse of the project cost, which the seasoned project managers acquire over the years. The meticulous attention to the details for collecting and analyzing the data for formulating the model parameters is another very important prerequisite for meaningful application of the technique. But after taking these caveats into account, the technique should definitely help to bring the project decision maker one step closer in a more focused and objective evaluation of the project cost.

Attachment A: Part 1

Priyadarshi Melamine Company
Cell Entry Details Table for Monte Carlo Simulation For Project Cost
1. Data Entry: Variability of Cost Centers

Description	Cell No.	Cell Entry
Land and Site Development	B7:D7 (Merged)	Land & Site Development
Type of Distribution Variability	D8	Discrete
Probability for 1st discrete value	C10	0.5
1st Discrete Value, Cost (₹ Million)	D10	10.00
Probability for 2nd discrete value	C11	0.5
2nd Discrete Value, Cost (Rest Million)	D11	30.00
Raw Materials Warehouse	B15:D15 (Merged)	Raw Materials Warehouse
Type of Distribution Variability	D16	Normal
Mean value (₹ Million)	D17	21.00
Optimistic value (₹ Million)	D18	16.00
Pessimistic value (₹ Million)	D19	25.00
Std. Deviation	D20	=(D21-D20)/6
Description	Cell No.	Cell Entry
Main Production Plant Building	B23:D23 (Merged)	Main Production Plant Building
Type of Distribution Variability	D24	Normal
Mean value (₹ Million)	D25	78.00
Optimistic value (₹ Million)	D26	70.00
Pessimistic value (₹ million)	D27	100.00
Std. Deviation	D28	=(D27-D26)/6
Finished Products Warehouse	B37:D37(Merged)	Finished Products Warehouse
Type of Distribution Variability	D38	Normal
Mean value (₹ Million)	D39	45.00
Optimistic value (₹ Million)	D40	40.00
Pessimistic value (₹ million)	D41	50.00
Std. Deviation	D42	=(D41-D40)/6
Ancillary Buildings	B45:D45 (Merged)	Ancillary Buildings
Type of Distribution Variability	D46	Normal
Mean value (₹ Million)	D47	28.00
Optimistic value (₹ Million)	D48	20.00
Pessimistic value (₹ million)	D49	36.00
Std. Deviation	D50	=(D49-D48)/6

Attachment A: Part 1 (*Contd.*)

Description	Cell No.	Cell Entry
Office and Q.C. Buildings	B53:D53 (Merged)	Office and Q.C. Buildings
Type of Distribution Variability	D54	Normal
Mean value (₹ Million)	D55	16.00
Optimistic value (₹ Million)	D56	15.00
Pessimistic value (₹ Million)	D57	25.00
Std. Deviation	D58	=(D57-D56)/6
Purchased Equipment at Site	F7:H7 (Merged)	Purchased Equipment at Site
Type of Distribution Variability	H8	Discrete
Probability for 1st discrete value	G10	0.4
1st Discrete Value, Cost (₹ Million)	H10	300.00
Probability for 2nd discrete value	G11	0.3
2nd Discrete Value, Cost (₹ Million)	H11	320.00
Probability for 3rd discrete value	G12	0.3
3rd Discrete Value, Cost (₹ Million)	H12	370.00
Installation Expenses	F15:H15 (Merged)	Installation Expenses
Type of Distribution Variability	H16	Normal
Mean value (₹ Million)	H17	87.00
Optimistic value (₹ Million)	H18	75.00
Pessimistic value (₹ million)	H19	100.00
Std. Deviation	H20	=(H19-H18)/6
Auxiliary Equipment	F23:H23 (Merged)	Auxiliary Equipment
Type of Distribution Variability	H24	Normal
Mean value (₹ Million)	H25	68.00
Optimistic value (₹ Million)	H26	56.00
Pessimistic value (₹ million)	H27	80.00
Std. Deviation	H28	=
Technical Know-how Fees	J7:L7 (Merged)	Technical Know-how Fees
Type of Distribution Variability	L8	Constant
Constant value (₹ Million)	L9	35.00
Det. Egg, Procurement & Const. Supervision at Site	J14:L14 & J15:L15 (Merged)	Det. Engg, Procurement and Const. Sup at Site
Type of Distribution Variability	L16	Discrete
Probability for 1st discrete value	K18	0.25

Attachment A: Part 1 (*Contd.*)

Description	Cell No.	Cell Entry
1st Discrete Value, Cost (₹ Million)	L18	30.00
Probability for 2nd discrete value	K19	0.50
2nd Discrete Value, Cost (₹ Million)	L19	55.00
Probability for 3rd discrete value	K20	0.25
3rd Discrete Value, Cost (₹ Million)	L20	95.00
Miscellaneous Fixed Assets	J23:L23(Merged)	Miscellaneous Fixed Assets
Type of Distribution Variability	J24	Normal
Mean value (₹ Million)	J25	42.00
Optimistic value (₹ Million)	J26	35.00
Pessimistic value (₹ Million)	J27	50.00
Std. Deviation	J28	=(J27-J26)/6
Pre-operative Expenses	J37:L37(Merged)	Pre-operative Expenses
Type of Distribution Variability	L38	Normal
Mean value (₹ Million)	L39	22.00
Optimistic value (₹ Million)	L40	10.00
Pessimistic value (₹ Million)	L41	40.00
Std. Deviation	L42	=(L41-L40)/6

Attachment A: Part 2

Priyadarshi Melamine Company
Cell Entry Details Table for Monte Carlo Simulation for Project Cost
2. Cell Entries for Monte Carlo Iterations

Description	Cell No.	Cell Entry
	B69	Iteration No.
	B70:B94	Iteration Identification No's 1 to 25
Land and Site Development	C69	Land and Site Development
Iteration No. 1	C70	=ROUND(VLOOKUP(RAND(), $B$10:$D$11,3),0)
Iteration No. 2 to N (N=25)	C71:C94	Copy and Paste Formula Cell C70
Raw Material Warehouse	E69	Raw Malt. Warehouse
Iteration No. 1	E70	=Round (Norminv(RAND(), ,$D$17,$D$20),1)
Iteration No. 2 to N (N=25)	E71:E94	Copy and Paste Formula Cell E70
Main Production Plant Building	F69	Production Building
Iteration No. 1	F70	=Round (Norminv(RAND(),$D$25,$D$28),1)
Iteration No. 2 to N (N=25)	F71:F94	Copy and Paste Formula Cell F70
Finished Products Warehouse	G69	Fin. Prod. Warehouse
Iteration No. 1	G70	=Round (Norminv(RAND(), $D$39,$D$42),1)
Iteration No. 2 to N (N=25)	G71:G94	Copy and Paste Formula Cell G70
Ancillary Building	H69	Ancillary Building
Iteration No. 1	H70	=Round (Norminv(RAND(), $D$47,$D$50),1)
Iteration No. 2 to N (N=25)	H71:H94	Copy and Paste Formula Cell H70
Office and Q.C. Building	I69	Office and Q.C. Build.
Iteration No. 1	I70	=Round (Norminv(RAND(), $D$55,$D$58),1)
Iteration No. 2 to N (N=25)	I71:I94	Copy and Paste Formula Cell I70
Sub-total Buildings	J69	Sub-total Buildings
Iteration No. 1	J70	=(E70+F70+G70+H70+I70)
Iteration No. 2 to N (N=25)	J71:J94	Copy and Paste Formula Cell J70
Purchased Equipment at Site	C99	Purchased Eqpt. at Site
Iteration No. 1	C100	=ROUND(VLOOKUP(RAND(), $F$10:$H$12,3),0)
Iteration No. 2 to N (N=25)	C101:C124	Copy and Paste Formula Cell C100
Installation Expenses	D99	Installation Expenses
Iteration No. 1	D100	=Round (Norminv(RAND(), $H$17,$H$20),1)
Iteration No. 2 to N (N=25)	D101:D124	Copy and Paste Formula Cell D100
Auxiliary Equipment	E99	Auxiliary Equipment

Attachment A: Part 2 (*Contd.*)

Description	Cell No.	Cell Entry
Iteration No. 1	E100	=Round (Norminv(RAND(), $H$25,$H$28),1)
Iteration No. 2 to N (N=25)	E101:E124	Copy and Paste Formula Cell E100
Sub-total Plant and Machinery	F99	Sub-total Plant and Machinery
Iteration No. 1	F100	=(C100+D100+E100)
Iteration No. 2 to N (N=25)	F101:F124	Copy and Paste Formula Cell F100
Technical Know-how fees	H99	Technical Knowhow
Iteration No. 1	H100	=L9
Iteration No. 2 to N (N=25)	H101:H124	Copy and Paste Formula Cell H100
Detailed Engg. and Constn Supvn	I99	Det. Engg and Constn Supvn
Iteration No. 1	I100	=ROUND(VLOOKUP(RAND(), $J$18:$L$20,3),0)
Miscellaneous Fixed Assets	J99	Misc. Fixed Assets
Iteration No. 2 to N (N=25)	J101:J124	Copy and Paste Formula Cell J100
Pre-operative Expenses	K99	Pre-oper. Expenses
Iteration No. 1	K100	=Round (Norminv(RAND(), $J$25,$J$28),1)
Iteration No. 2 to N (N=25)	K101:K124	Copy and Paste Formula Cell K100
TOTAL NEW FIXED ASSETS	L99	TOTAL NEW FIXED ASSETS
Iteration No. 1	L100	=(C70+J70+F100+H100+I100+J100+K100)
Iteration No. 2 to N (N=25)	L101:L124	Copy and Paste Formula Cell L100
Contingency Provision Required	M99	Contingency Provision Required
Iteration No. 1	M100	= MAX((L100-840),0)
Iteration No. 2 to N (N=25)	M101:M124	Copy and Paste Formula Cell M100
Contingency Provision as Per Cent	N99	Contingency Provision Per Cent
Iteration No. 1	N100	=ROUND((M100/840)*100,1)
Iteration No. 2 to N (N=25)	N101:N124	Copy and Paste Formula Cell N100
	C127	Max(L100:L124)
Maximum Cost	AA127:B127 (Merged)	Maximum Cost
	C128	Min(L100:L124)
Minimum Cost	AA128:B128 (Merged)	Minimum Cost

PROJECT COST ESTIMATE : PRIYADARSHI MELAMINE COMPANY

Attachment B – Part 1

Cost in Rs Million

Land and Site Development

Distribution		Discrete
Cum. Prob.	Probability	Cost
0.00	0.50	10.00
0.500	0.50	30.00

Purchased Equipment at Site

Distribution		Discrete
Cum. Prob.	Probability	Cost
0.00	0.4	300.00
0.40	0.3	320.00
0.70	0.3	370.00

Purchased Equipment at Site

Distribution	Constant
Value	35.00

Raw Materials Warehouse

Distribution	Normal
Mean	21.00
Optimistic	16.00
Pessimistic	25.00
Std. Devn.	1.50

Installation Expenses

Distribution	Normal
Mean	87.00
Optimistic	75.00
Pessimistic	100.00
Std. Devn.	4.17

Detailed Engineering, Procurement & Construction Supervision at Site

Distribution		Discrete
Cum. Prob.	Probability	Cost
0.00	0.25	30.00
0.25	0.50	55.00
0.75	0.25	95.00

Main Production Plant Building

Distribution	Normal
Mean	78.00
Optimistic	70.00
Pessimistic	100.00
Std. Devn.	5.00

Auxiliary Equipment

Distribution	Normal
Mean	68.00
Optimistic	56.00
Pessimistic	80.00
Std. Devn.	4.00

Miscellaneous Fixed Assets

Distribution	Normal
Mean	42.00
Optimistic	35.00
Pessimistic	50.00
Std. Devn.	2.50

G.V.Desai

PROJECT COST ESTIMATE : PRIYADARSHI MELAMINE COMPANY — Attachment B – Part 2

Cost in Rs Million

Finished Products Warehouse

Distribution	Discrete
Mean	45.00
Optimistic	40.00
Pessimistic	50.00
Std. Devn.	1.67

Pre-operative Expenses

Distribution	Constant
Mean	22.00
Optimistic	10.00
Pessimistic	40.00
Std. Devn.	5.00

Ancilliary Buildings

Distribution	Normal
Mean	28.00
Optimistic	20.00
Pessimistic	36.00
Std. Devn.	2.67

Officer and Q. C. Lab

Distribution	Normal
Mean	16.00
Optimistic	15.00
Pessimistic	25.00
Std. Devn.	1.67

G.V.Desai

Attachment B – Part 3

PROJECT COST ESTIMATE : PRIYADARSHI MELAMINE COMPANY

Monte Carlo Simulation (The first 25 entries out of total 100 iterations shown here)

Iteration No	Land & Site Dev.	Raw Malt Warehouse	Production Building	Fin. Prod. Warehouse	Ancillary Building	Office & Q.C.Buld.	Sub-total Buildings
1	30	23	80	47	28	16	194
2	10	22	86	45	31	16	200
3	10	23	80	46	25	14	188
4	10	22	81	44	28	18	193
5	10	22	76	44	31	16	189
6	30	21	79	46	30	14	190
7	30	22	79	45	25	16	187
8	10	17	80	45	27	20	189
9	30	21	72	44	26	15	178
10	30	19	71	46	28	16	180
11	10	18	71	46	30	13	178
12	10	21	75	46	30	16	188
13	10	24	80	43	28	17	192
14	30	20	78	48	33	16	195
15	10	19	71	45	32	15	182
16	10	20	85	43	30	17	195
17	30	20	74	46	29	14	183
18	30	23	70	43	30	16	182
19	30	21	84	44	28	19	196
20	10	23	75	44	30	18	190
21	30	24	86	41	26	21	198
22	10	22	76	46	30	15	189
23	10	24	80	45	29	17	195
24	10	22	77	45	24	14	182
25	10	23	82	44	26	14	189

PROJECT COST ESTIMATE : PRIYADARSHI MELAMINE COMPANY

Attachment B – Part 4

Monte Carlo Simulation (The first 25 entries out of total 100 iterations shown here)

Iteration No.	Purchased Eqpt. At site	Installation Expenses	Auxiliary Equipment	Sub-total Plant and Machinery	Technical Knowhow	Det. Engg. and Constn Supvn.	Misc. Fixed Assets	Pre-oper. Expenses	Total New Fixed Assets	Contingency Provision Required	Contingency Provision Per cent
1	370	89	69	528	35	55	41	23	874	34	4
2	300	82	68	450	35	30	40	23	759	0	0
3	370	96	67	533	35	55	45	27	893	53	6.3
4	300	83	74	457	35	30	44	23	805	0	0
5	300	88	68	456	35	55	44	28	842	2	0.2
6	320	84	61	465	35	95	40	15	866	26	3.1
7	370	87	71	528	35	55	38	25	898	58	6.9
8	300	86	68	454	35	30	44	19	799	0	0
9	300	93	67	460	35	55	43	26	807	0	0
10	320	89	74	483	35	55	38	16	844	4	0.5
11	300	87	67	454	35	55	40	20	819	0	0
12	300	94	62	456	35	55	47	25	824	0	0
13	300	88	72	460	35	55	39	23	820	0	0
14	300	92	70	462	35	55	40	20	838	0	0
15	300	85	73	458	35	95	41	28	883	43	5.1
16	320	83	77	480	35	55	44	23	838	0	0
17	320	91	69	480	35	95	44	25	908	68	8.1
18	300	82	72	454	35	55	45	16	809	0	0
19	370	85	66	521	35	55	39	29	887	47	5.6
20	320	90	68	478	35	30	40	21	806	0	0
21	300	91	67	458	35	55	43	16	821	0	0
22	300	87	68	455	35	95	46	8	834	0	0
23	300	86	66	452	35	95	41	32	857	17	2
24	320	89	74	483	35	55	44	23	843	3	0.4
25	300	85	57	442	35	95	44	17	857	17	2

PROJECT COST ESTIMATE : PRIYADARSHI MELAMINE COMPANY

Attachment B – Part 5

Monte Carlo Simulation (The first 25 entries out of total 100 iterations shown here)

Maximum Cost	₹ 927 million
Minimum Cost	₹ 779 million
Bin interval	₹ 10 million
Max. Contingency,%	10.4
Min. Contingency %	0
Average ,%	2.7

Bin	Frequency	Cumulative %
750	0	0.00%
760	0	0.00%
770	0	0.00%

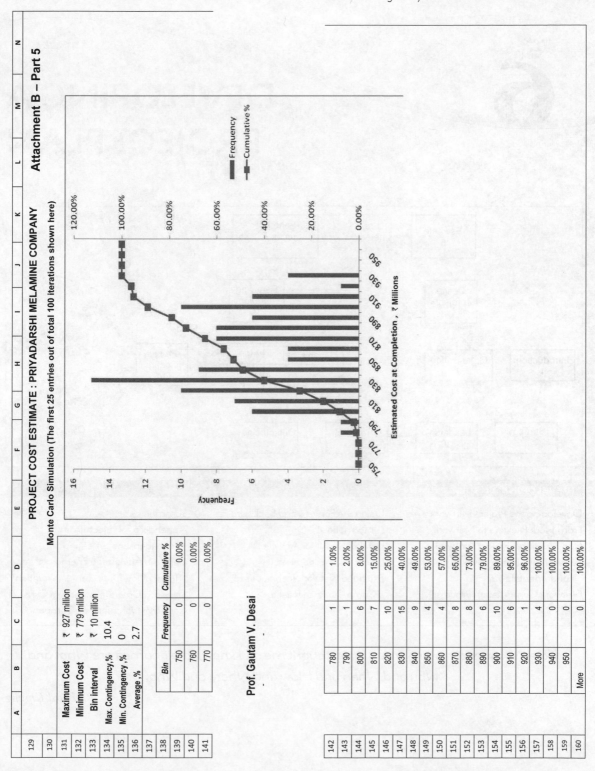

Bin	Frequency	Cumulative %
780	1	1.00%
790	1	2.00%
800	6	8.00%
810	7	15.00%
820	10	25.00%
830	15	40.00%
840	9	49.00%
850	4	53.00%
860	4	57.00%
870	8	65.00%
880	8	73.00%
890	6	79.00%
900	10	89.00%
910	6	95.00%
920	1	96.00%
930	4	100.00%
940	0	100.00%
950	0	100.00%
More	0	100.00%

Prof. Gautam V. Desai

6

DEVELOPING A PROJECT PLAN

I keep six honest serving–men (they taught me all I knew); their names are What and Why and When and How and Where and Who.

Rudyard Kipling

DEVELOPING THE PROJECT NETWORK

The project network is the tool used for planning, scheduling, and monitoring project progress. The network is developed from the information collected for the WBS and is a graphic flow chart of the project job plan. The network depicts the project activities that must be completed, the logical sequences, the interdependencies of the activities to be completed, and in most cases the times for the activities to start and finish along with the longest path(s) through the network—the *critical path*. The network is the framework for the project information system that will be used by the project managers to make decisions concerning project time, cost, and performance.

Developing the project networks takes time for someone or some group to develop; therefore, they cost money! Are networks really worth the struggle? The answer is definitely yes, except in cases where the project is considered trivial or very short in duration.[1] The network is easily understood by others because the network presents a graphic display of the flow and sequence of work through the project. Once the network is developed, it is very easy to modify or change when unexpected events occur as the project progresses. For example, if materials for an activity are delayed, the impact can be quickly assessed and the whole project revised in only a few minutes with the computer. These revisions can be communicated to all project participants quickly (for example, via e-mail or project website).

The project network provides other invaluable information and insights. It provides the basis for scheduling labor and equipment. It enhances communication that melds all managers and groups together in meeting the time, cost, and performance objectives of the project. It provides an estimate of project duration rather than picking a project completion date from a hat or someone's preferred date. The network gives the times when activities can start and finish and when they can be delayed. It provides the basis for budgeting the cash flow of the project. It identifies which activities are "critical" and, therefore, should not be delayed if the project is to be completed as planned. It highlights which activities to consider if the project needs to be compressed to meet a deadline.

There are other reasons project networks are worth their weight in gold. Basically, project networks minimize surprises by getting the plan out early and allowing corrective feedback. A commonly heard statement from practitioners is that the project network represents three-quarters of the planning process. Perhaps this is an exaggeration, but it signals the perceived importance of the network to project managers in the field.

FROM WORK PACKAGE TO NETWORK

Project networks are developed from the WBS. The project network is a visual flow diagram of the sequence, interrelationships, and dependencies of all the activities that must be accomplished to complete the project. *An **activity** is an element in the project that consumes time—for example, work or waiting.* Work packages from the WBS are used to build the activities found in the project network. An activity can include one or more work packages. The activities are placed in a sequence that provides for orderly completion of the project. Networks are built using nodes (boxes) and arrows (lines).

Integrating the work packages and the network represents a point where the management process often fails in practice. The primary explanations for this failure are that (1) different groups

---

[1] This process could be clarified and improved by using a simple responsibility matrix (see Chapter 3).

(people) are used to define work packages and activities and (2) the WBS is poorly constructed and not deliverable/output oriented. Integration of the WBS and project network is crucial to effective project management. The project manager must be careful to guarantee continuity by having some of the same people who defined the WBS and work packages develop the network activities.

Networks provide the project schedule by identifying dependencies, sequencing, and timing of activities, which the WBS is not designed to do. The primary inputs for developing a project network plan are work packages. Remember, a work package is defined independently of other work packages, has definite start and finish points, requires specific resources, includes technical specifications, and has cost estimates for the package. However, dependency, sequencing, and timing of each of these factors are not included in the work package. A network activity can include one or more work packages.

Figure 6.1 shows a segment of the WBS example and how the information is used to develop a project network. The lowest level deliverable in Figure 6.1 is "circuit board." The cost accounts (design, production, test, software) denote project work, organization unit responsible, and time-phased budgets for the work packages. Each cost account represents one or more work packages. For example, the design cost account has two work packages (D-1-1 and D-1-2)—specifications and documentation. The software and production accounts also have two work packages. Developing a network requires sequencing tasks from all work packages that have measurable work.

Figure 6.1 traces how work packages are used to develop a project network. You can trace the use of work packages by the coding scheme. For example, activity A uses work packages D-1-1 and D-1-2 (specifications and documentation), while activity C uses work package S-22-1. This methodology of selecting work packages to describe activities is used to develop the project network, which sequences and times project activities. Care must be taken to include all work packages. *The manager derives activity time estimates from the task times in the work package.* For example, activity B (proto 1) requires five weeks to complete; activity K (test) requires three weeks to complete. After computing the activity **early and late times,** the manager can schedule resources and time-phase budgets (with dates).

CONSTRUCTING A PROJECT NETWORK

Terminology

Every field has its jargon that allows colleagues to communicate comfortably with each other about the techniques they use. Project managers are no exception. Here are some terms used in building project networks.

Activity. For project managers, an *activity* is an element of the project that requires time. It may or may not require resources. Typically an activity consumes time—either while people work or while people wait. Examples of the latter are time waiting for contracts to be signed, materials to arrive, drug approval by the government, budget clearance, etc. Activities usually represent one or more tasks from a work package. Descriptions of activities should use a verb/noun format: for example, develop product specifications.

Merge activity. This is an activity that has more than one activity immediately preceding it (more than one dependency arrow flowing to it).

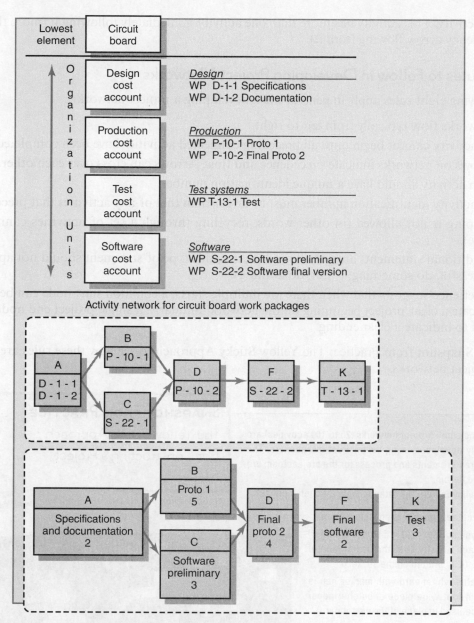

FIGURE 6.1 *WBS/Work Packages to Network*

Parallel activities. These are activities that can take place at the same time, if the manager wishes. However, the manager may choose to have parallel activities *not* occur simultaneously.

Path. A sequence of connected, dependent activities.

Critical path. When this term is used, it means the path(s) with the longest duration through the network; if an activity on the path is delayed, the project is delayed the same amount of time.

Burst activity. This activity has more than one activity immediately following it (more than one dependency arrow flowing from it).

Basic Rules to Follow in Developing Project Networks

The following eight rules apply in general when developing a project network:

1. Networks flow typically from left to right.
2. An activity cannot begin until all preceding connected activities have been completed.
3. Arrows on networks indicate precedence and flow. Arrows can cross over each other.
4. Each activity should have a unique identification number.
5. An activity identification number must be larger than that of any activities that precede it.
6. Looping is not allowed (in other words, recycling through a set of activities cannot take place).
7. Conditional statements are not allowed (that is, this type of statement should not appear: If successful, do something; if not, do nothing).
8. Experience suggests that when there are multiple starts, a common start node can be used to indicate a clear project beginning on the network. Similarly, a single project end node can be used to indicate a clear ending.

Read the Snapshot from Practice: The Yellow Sticky Approach to see how these rules are used to create project networks.

In practice small project networks (25 to 100 activities) are frequently developed using yellow Post-it® stickers. The meeting requirements and process for the project team are described herein.

The following are the requirements for such a project:

1. Project team members and a facilitator.
2. One yellow sticker (3 × 4 inches or larger) for each activity with the description of the activity printed on the sticker.
3. Erasable whiteboard with marker pen (a long, 4-foot-wide piece of butcher paper can be used in place of the whiteboard).

All of the yellow stickers are placed in easy view of all team members. The team begins by identifying those activity stickers that have no predecessors. Each of these activity stickers is then attached to the whiteboard. A start node is drawn, and a dependency arrow is connected to each activity.

© Erik Larson

Given the initial network start activities, each activity is examined for immediate successor activities. These activities are attached to the whiteboard and dependency arrows drawn. This process is continued until all of the yellow stickers are attached to the whiteboard with dependency arrows. (Note: The process can be reversed, beginning with those activities that have no successor activities and connecting them to a project end node. The predecessor activities are selected for each activity and attached to the whiteboard with dependency arrows marked.)

When the process is complete, the dependencies are recorded in the project software, which develops a computer-designed network along with the critical path(s) and early, late, and slack times. This methodology sensitizes team members early to the interdependencies among activities of the project. But more importantly, the methodology empowers team members by giving them input to the important decisions that they must implement later.

ACTIVITY-ON-NODE (AON) FUNDAMENTALS

Historically, two methods have been used to develop project networks: **activity-on-node (AON)** and **activity-on-arrow (AOA).** Over time the availability of advanced computer graphics improved the clarity and visual appeal of the AON method. Today, the activity-on-node method has come to dominate nearly all project network plans. For this reason, we have limited our discussion to AON methods. Figure 6.2 shows a few typical uses of building blocks for the AON network construction. An **activity** is represented by a *node* (box). The node can take many forms, but in recent years the node represented as a rectangle (box) has dominated. The dependencies among activities are depicted by *arrows* between the rectangles (boxes) on the AON network. The arrows indicate how the activities are related and the sequence in which things must be accomplished. The length and slope of the arrow are arbitrary and set for convenience of drawing the network. The letters in the boxes serve here to identify the activities while you learn the fundamentals of network construction and analysis. In practice, activities have identification numbers and descriptions.

There are three basic relationships that must be established for activities included in a project network. The relationships can be found by answering the following three questions for each activity:

1. Which activities must be completed immediately *before* this activity? These activities are called *predecessor* activities.
2. Which activities must immediately *follow* this activity? These activities are called *successor* activities.
3. Which activities can occur *while* this activity is taking place? This is known as a *concurrent* or *parallel* relationship.

Sometimes a manager can use only questions 1 and 3 to establish relationships. This information allows the network analyst to construct a graphic flow chart of the sequence and logical interdependencies of project activities.

Figure 6.2A is analogous to a list of things to do where you complete the task at the top of the list first and then move to the second task, etc. This figure tells the project manager that activity A must be completed before activity B can begin, and activity B must be completed before activity C can begin.

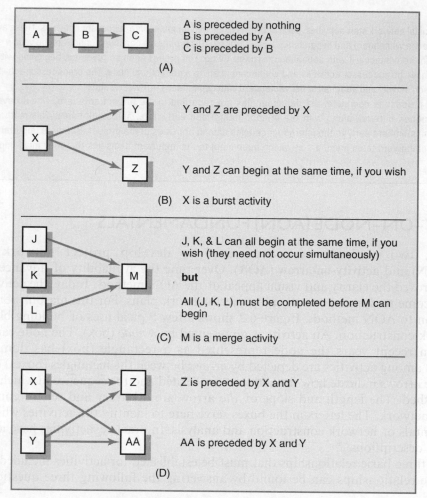

FIGURE 6.2 *Activity–on–Node Network Fundamentals*

Figure 6.2B tells us that activities Y and Z cannot begin until activity X is completed. This figure also indicates that activities Y and Z can occur concurrently or simultaneously if the project manager wishes; however, it is not a necessary condition. For example, pouring a concrete driveway (activity Y) can take place while landscape planting (activity Z) is being accomplished, but land clearing (activity X) must be completed before activities Y and Z can start. Activities Y and Z are considered *parallel* activities. Parallel paths allow concurrent effort, which may shorten time to do a series of activities. Activity X is sometimes referred to as a *burst* activity because more than one arrow bursts from the node. The number of arrows indicates how many activities immediately follow activity X.

Figure 6.2C shows us activities J, K, and L can occur simultaneously if desired, and activity M cannot begin until activities J, K, and L are all completed. Activities J, K, and L are parallel activities. Activity M is called a *merge* activity because more than one activity must be completed before M can begin. Activity M could also be called a milestone—a significant accomplishment.

In Figure 6.2D, activities X and Y are parallel activities that can take place at the same time; activities Z and AA are also parallel activities. But activities Z and AA cannot begin until activities X and Y are both completed. Given these fundamentals of AON, we can practice developing a simple network. Remember, the arrows can cross over each other (e.g., Figure 6.2D), be bent, or be any length or slope. Neatness is not a criterion for a valid, useful network—only accurate inclusion of all project activities, their dependencies, and time estimates.

Information for a simplified project network is given in Table 6.1. This project represents a new automated warehouse system for picking frozen food package orders and moving them to a staging area for delivery to stores.

TABLE 6.1 ••

Network Information

AUTOMATED WAREHOUSE Order Picking System		
Activity	**Description**	**Preceding Activity**
A	Define Requirements	None
B	Assign Team	A
C	Design Hardware	A
D	Code Software	B
E	Build and Test Hardware	C
F	Develop Patent Request	C
G	Test Software	D
H	Integrate Systems	E, F, G

Figure 6.3 shows the first steps in constructing the AON project network from the information in Table 6.1. We see that activity A (define requirements) has nothing preceding it; therefore, it is the first node to be drawn. Next, we note that activities B and C (assign team and design hardware) are both preceded by activity A. We draw two arrows and connect them to activities B and C. This segment shows the project manager that activity A must be completed before activities B and C can begin. After A is completed, B and C can take place concurrently, if desired. Figure 6.4 shows the completed network with all of the activities sequences and dependencies.

The information in Figure 6.4 is tremendously valuable to those managing the project. However, estimating the duration for each activity will further increase the value of the network. A realistic project plan and schedule require reliable time estimates for project activities. The addition of time to the network

FIGURE 6.3 *Automated Warehouse— Partial Network*

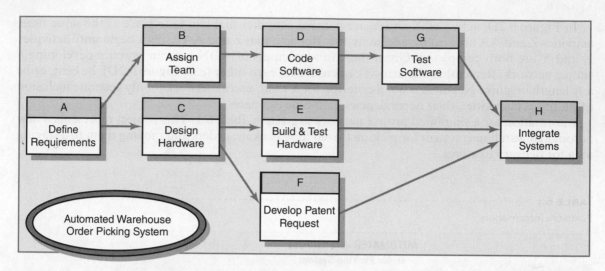

FIGURE 6.4   *Automated Warehouse—Completed Network*

allows us to estimate how long the project will take. When activities can or must start, when resources must be available, which activities can be delayed, and when the project is estimated to be complete are all determined from the times assigned. Deriving an activity time estimate necessitates early assessment of resource needs in terms of material, equipment, and people. In essence the project network with activity time estimates links planning, scheduling, and controlling of projects.

NETWORK COMPUTATION PROCESS

Drawing the project network places the activities in the right sequence for computing start and finish times of activities. Activity time estimates are taken from the task times in the work package and added to the network (review Figure 6.2). Performing a few simple computations allows the project manager to complete a process known as the forward and backward pass. Completion of the *forward and backward pass* will answer the following questions:

Forward Pass—Earliest Times

1. How soon can the activity start? (early start—ES)
2. How soon can the activity finish? (early finish—EF)
3. How soon can the project be finished? (expected time—TE)

Backward Pass—Latest Times

1. How late can the activity start? (late start—LS)
2. How late can the activity finish? (late finish—LF)
3. Which activities represent the critical path (CP)? This is the longest path in the network which, when delayed, will delay the project.
4. How long can the activity be delayed? (slack or float—SL)

The terms in parentheses represent the acronyms used in most texts and computer programs and by project managers. The forward and backward pass process is presented next.

Forward Pass—Earliest Times

The forward pass starts with the first project activity(ies) and traces each path (chain of sequential activities) through the network to the last project activity(ies). As you trace along the path, you *add* the activity times. The longest path denotes the project completion time for the plan and is called the critical path (CP). Table 6.2 lists the activity times in workdays for the Automated Warehouse project example we used for drawing a network.

TABLE 6.2
Network Information

AUTOMATED WAREHOUSE Order Picking System			
Activity	**Description**	**Preceding Activity**	**Activity Time**
A	Define Requirements	None	10 workdays
B	Assign Team	A	5
C	Design Hardware	A	25
D	Code Software	B	20
E	Build and Test Hardware	C	50
F	Develop Patent Request	C	15
G	Test Software	D	35
H	Integrate Systems	E, F, G	15

Figure 6.5 shows the network with the activity time estimate found in the node (see "DUR" for duration in the legend). For example, activity A (define requirements) has an activity duration of 10 workdays, and activity E (build and test hardware) has a duration of 50 days. The forward pass begins with the project start time, which is usually time zero. (Note: Calendar times can be computed for the project later in the planning phase.)

In our Automated Warehouse example, the early start time for the first activity (activity A) is zero. This time is found in the upper left corner of the activity A node in Figure 6.6. The early finish for activity A is 10 days (EF = ES + DUR or 0 + 10 = 10). Next, we see that activity A is the predecessor for activities B (assign team) and C (design hardware). Therefore, the earliest activities B and C can begin is the instant in time when activity A is completed; this time is 10 days. You can now see in Figure 6.6 that activities B and C have an early start (ES) of 10 days. Using the formula EF = ES + DUR, the early finish (EF) times for activities B and C are 15 and 35 days. Following the same process of moving along each network path, the early start and finish times for selected activities are shown here:

Activity D: ES = 15 EF = 15 + 20 = 35   Activity F: ES = 35 EF = 35 + 15 = 50

Activity E: ES = 35 EF = 35 + 50 = 85   Activity G: ES = 35 EF = 35 + 35 = 70

FIGURE 6.5   *Activity–on–Node Network*

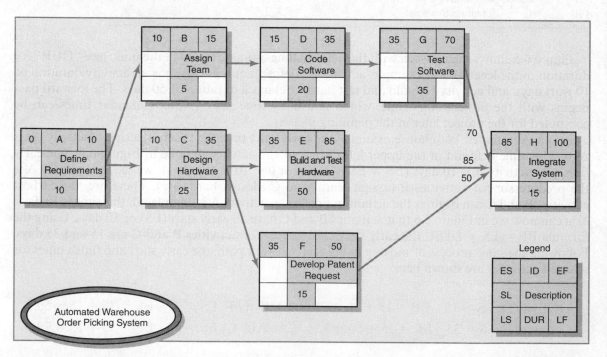

FIGURE 6.6   *Activity–on–Node Network Forward Pass*

Activity H (integrate system) is a merge activity because it is preceded by more than one activity. The early start (ES) of a merge activity depends on the early finish (EF) of all activities that merge to it. In this project activity H is preceded by activities E, F, and G. Which activity controls the ES of activity H? The answer is activity E. In Figure 6.6 the EF times are 85, 50, and 70. Since 85 days is the largest EF time, activity E controls the ES for Activity H, which is 85. If activity E is delayed, activity H will be delayed. The early finish for activity H or the project is 100 days (EF = ES + DUR or 85 + 15 = 100).

The forward pass requires that you remember just three things when computing early activity times:

1. You *add* activity times along each path in the network (ES + DUR = EF).
2. You carry the early finish (EF) to the next activity where it becomes its early start (ES), *unless*
3. If the next succeeding activity is a *merge* activity, you select the *largest* early finish number (EF) of *all* its immediate predecessor activities.

The three questions derived from the forward pass have been answered; that is, early start (ES), early finish (EF), and the project expected duration (TE) times have been computed. The backward pass is the next process to learn.

Backward Pass—Latest Times

The backward pass starts with the last project activity(ies) on the network. You trace backward on each path *subtracting* activity times to find the late start (LS) and late finish (LF) times for each activity. Before the backward pass can be computed, the late finish for the last project activity(ies) must be selected. In early planning stages, this time is usually set equal to the early finish (EF) of the last project activity (or in the case of multiple finish activities, the activity with the largest EF). In some cases an imposed project duration deadline exists, and this date will be used. Let us assume for planning purposes we can accept the EF project duration (TE) equal to 100 workdays. The LF for activity H becomes 100 days (EF = LF) (see Figure 6.7).

The backward pass is similar to the forward pass; you need to remember three things:

1. You *subtract* activity times along each path starting with the project end activity (LF − DUR = LS).
2. You carry the LS to the next preceding activity to establish its LF, *unless*
3. If the next preceding activity is a *burst* activity; in this case you select the *smallest* LS of all its immediate successor activities to establish its LF.

Let's apply these rules to our Automated Warehouse example. Beginning with activity H (integrate systems) and a LF of 100 workdays, the LS for activity H is 85 days (LF − DUR = LS or 100 − 15 = 85). The LS for activity H becomes the LF for activities E, F, and G. Moving backward on the network the late starts for E, F, and G are shown here (LS = LF − DUR):

Activity E: LS = 85−50 = 35   Activity G: 85−35 = 50

Activity F: LS = 85−15 = 70

At this point we see that activity C is a *burst* activity that ties to (precedes) activities E and F. The late finish for activity C is controlled by the LS of activities E and F. The *smallest* LS of activities

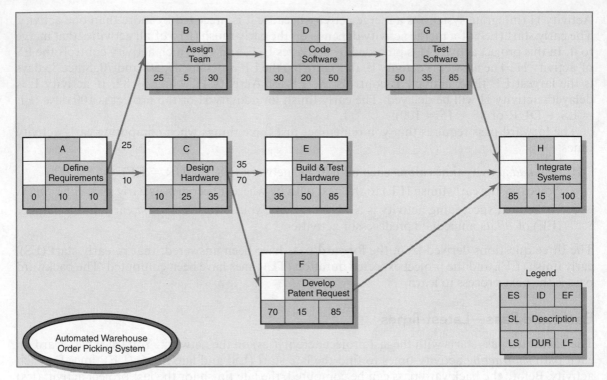

FIGURE 6.7 *Activity–on–Node Network Backward Pass*

E and F (LS's = 35 and 70) is activity E. This establishes the LF for activity C. The LS for activity C becomes 10. Moving backward to the first project activity, we note it is also a *burst* activity that links to activities B and C. The LF of activity A is controlled by activity C that has the smallest LS of 10 days. Given a LF of 10 days, the LS for activity is time period zero (LS = 10 − 10 = 0). The backward pass is complete, and the latest activity times are known. Figure 6.8 shows the completed network with all the early, late, and slack times included. Slack can be important to managing your project.

Determining Slack (or Float)

Total Slack

When the forward and backward passes have been computed, it is possible to determine which activities can be delayed by computing "slack" or "float." **Total slack** *tells us the amount of time an activity can be delayed and not delay the project.* Stated differently, *total slack is the amount of time an activity can exceed its early finish date without affecting the project end date or an imposed completion date.*

Total slack or float for an activity is simply the difference between the LS and ES (LS − ES = SL) or between LF and EF (LF − EF = SL). For example, in Figure 6.8 the total slack for activity D is 15 workdays, for activity F is 35 days, and for activity E is zero. If total slack of one activity in a path is used, the ES for all activities that follow in the chain will be delayed and their slack

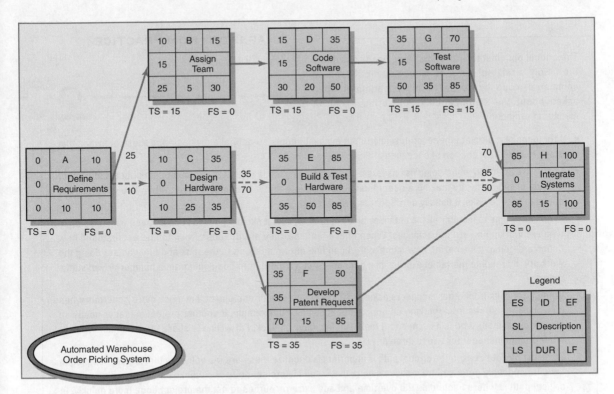

FIGURE 6.8 *Forward and Backward Passes Completed with Slack Times*

reduced. Use of total slack *must be coordinated* with all participants in the activities that follow in the chain.

After slack for each activity is computed, the critical path(s) is (are) easily identified. When the LF = EF for the end project activity, the critical path can be identified as those activities that also have LF = EF or a slack of zero (LF − EF = 0 or LS − ES = 0). *The critical path is the network path(s) that has(have) the least slack in common.* This awkward arrangement of words is necessary because a problem arises when the project finish activity has a LF that differs from the EF found in the forward pass—for example, an imposed duration date. If this is the case, the slack on the critical path will *not* be zero; it will be the difference between the project EF and the imposed LF of the last project activity. For example, if the EF for the project is 100 days, but the imposed LF or target date is set at 95 days, all activities on the critical path would have a slack of minus 5 days. Of course, this would result in a late start 5 days for the first project activity—a good trick if the project is to start now. Negative slack occurs in practice when the critical path is delayed.

In Figure 6.8 the critical path is marked with dashed arrows—activities A, C, E, and H. Delay of any of these activities will delay the total project by the same number of days. Since actual projects may have many critical activities with numerous preceding dependencies, coordination among those responsible for critical activities is crucial. Critical activities typically represent about 10 percent of the activities of the project. Therefore, project managers pay close attention to the critical path activities to be sure they are not delayed. See Snapshot from Practice: The Critical Path.

The critical path method (CPM) has long been considered the "Holy Grail" of project management. Here are comments made by veteran project managers when asked about the significance of the critical path in managing projects:

- I try to make it a point whenever possible to put my best people on critical activities or on those activities that stand the greatest chance of becoming critical.

- I pay extra attention when doing risk assessment to identifying those risks that can impact the critical path, either directly or indirectly, by making a noncritical activity so late that it becomes critical. When I've got money to spend to reduce risks, it usually gets spent on critical tasks.

- I don't have time to monitor all the activities on a big project, but I make it a point to keep in touch with the people who are working on critical activities. When I have the time, they are the ones I visit to find out firsthand how things are going. It's amazing how much more I can find out from talking to the rank and file who are doing the work and by reading the facial expressions of people—much more than I can gain from a number-driven status report.

- When I get calls from other managers asking to "borrow" people or equipment, I'm much more generous when it involves resources from working on noncritical activities. For example, if another project manager needs an electrical engineer who is assigned to a task with five days of slack, I'm willing to share that engineer with another project manager for two to three days.

- The most obvious reason the critical path is important is because these are the activities that impact completion time. If I suddenly get a call from above saying they need my project done two weeks earlier than planned, the critical path is where I schedule the overtime and add extra resources to get the project done more quickly. In the same way, if the project schedule begins to slip, it's the critical activities I focus on to get back on schedule.

We use the term **sensitivity** to reflect the likelihood the original critical path(s) will change once the project is initiated. Sensitivity is a function of the number of critical or near-critical paths. A network schedule that has only one critical path and noncritical activities that enjoy significant slack would be labeled insensitive. Conversely, a sensitive network would be one with more than one critical path and/or noncritical activities with very little slack. Under these circumstances the original critical path is much more likely to change once work gets under way on the project. How sensitive is the Automated Warehouse schedule? Not very, since there is only one critical path and the two other noncritical paths have 15 and 35 days of slack, which suggests considerable flexibility. Project managers assess the sensitivity of their network schedules to determine how much attention they should devote to managing the critical path.

Free Slack (Float)

Free slack (FS) is unique. *It is the amount of time an activity can be delayed without delaying any immediately following (successor) activity. Or, free slack is the amount of time an activity can exceed its early finish date without affecting the early start date of any successor(s).* Free slack can never be negative. Only activities that occur at the end of a chain of activities, where you have a merge activity, can have free slack. See Figure 6.8, the Automated Warehouse project.

In Figure 6.8 activity G has free slack of 15 days, while activities B and D do not. In this case, activity G is the last activity in the upper path, and it merges to activity H. Hence, to delay activity G up to 15 days *does not delay any following activities and requires no coordination with managers of other activities.* Conversely, if either activity B or D is delayed, the managers of following activities need to be notified that the slack has been used so they can adjust their start schedules. For example, if activity B is delayed 5 days, the manager of activity B should notify those in charge of the following activities (D and G) their slack has been reduced to 10 time units and their early start will be delayed 5 days. In this example, activity D cannot then start until day 20, which reduces activity D slack to 10 days (LS − ES = SL or 30 − 20 = 10). Free slack for activity G is also reduced to 10 days.

Free slack occurs at the last activity in a chain of activities. In some situations the "chain" has only one link. Activity F in Figure 6.8 is an example. It has free slack of 35 days. Note that it needs no coordination with other activities—unless a delay exceeds the free slack of 35 days. (Note: The moment you exceed all free slack available, you delay the project and must coordinate with others who are impacted.)

The distinction between free and total slack at first glance seems trivial, but in reality it is very important. When you are responsible for a late activity that has zero free slack you impact the schedules of subsequent activities. You should notify the managers of the remaining activities in the chain that you will be late. Again, note that total slack is shared across the whole path. Alternatively, if you are responsible for an activity that has free slack when you start, you do not need to notify anyone as long as your work does not absorb all of the slack!

USING THE FORWARD AND BACKWARD PASS INFORMATION

Returning to the Automated Warehouse project network in Figure 6.8, what does a slack of 35 days for activity F (develop patent request) mean for the project manager? In this specific case it means activity F can be delayed 35 days. In a larger sense the project manager soon learns that free slack is important because it allows flexibility in scheduling scarce project resources—personnel and equipment—that are used on more than one parallel activity or another project.

Knowing the four activity times of ES, LS, EF, and LF is invaluable for the planning, scheduling, and controlling phases of the project. The ES and LF tell the project manager the time interval in which the activity should be completed. For example, activity G (test software) must be completed within the time interval 35 and 85 days; the activity can start as early as day 35 or finish as late as day 85. Conversely, activity C (design hardware), must start on day 10, or the project will be delayed.

When the critical path is known, it is possible to tightly manage the resources of the activities on the critical path so no mistakes are made that will result in delays. In addition, if for some reason the project must be expedited to meet an earlier date, it is possible to select those activities, or combination of activities, that will cost the least to shorten the project. Similarly, if the critical path is delayed and the time must be made up by shortening some activity or activities on the critical path to make up any negative slack, it is possible to identify the activities on the critical path that cost the least to shorten. If there are other paths with very little slack, it may be necessary to shorten activities on those paths also.

LEVEL OF DETAIL FOR ACTIVITIES

Time-phasing work and budgets of the project mandate careful definition of the activities that make up the project network. Typically an activity represents one or more tasks from a work package. How many tasks you include in each activity sets the level of detail. In some cases it is possible to end up with too much information to manage, and this can result in increased overhead costs. Managers of small projects have been able to minimize the level of detail by eliminating some of the preliminary steps to drawing networks. Larger firms also recognize the cost of information overload and are working to cut down the level of detail in networks and in most other dimensions of the project.

PRACTICAL CONSIDERATIONS

Network Logic Errors

Project network techniques have certain logic rules that must be followed. One rule is that conditional statements such as "if test successful build proto, if failure redesign" are not permitted. The network is not a decision tree; it is a project plan that we assume will materialize. If conditional statements were allowed, the forward and backward pass would make little sense. Although in reality a plan seldom materializes as we expect in every detail, it is a reasonable initial assumption. You shall see that once a network plan is developed, it is an easy step to make revisions to accommodate changes.

Another rule that defeats the project network and computation process is *looping*. Looping is an attempt by the planner to return to an earlier activity. Recall that the activity identification numbers should always be higher for the activities following an activity in question; this rule helps to avoid the illogical precedence relationships among the activities. An activity should only occur once; if it is to occur again, the activity should have a new name and identification number and should be placed in the right sequence on the network. Figure 6.9 shows an illogical loop. If this loop were allowed to exist, this path would perpetually repeat itself. Many computer programs catch this type of logic error.

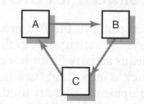

FIGURE 6.9   *Illogical Loop*

Activity Numbering

Each activity needs a unique identification code—a letter or a number. In practice very elegant schemes exist. Most schemes number activities in ascending order, that is, each succeeding activity has a larger number so that the flow of the project activities is toward project completion. It is customary to leave gaps between numbers (1, 5, 10, 15 . . .). Gaps are desirable so you can add missing or new activities later. Because it is nearly impossible to draw a project network perfectly, numbering networks is frequently not done until after the network is complete.

In practice you will find computer programs that accept numeric, alphabetic, or a combination of activity designations. Combination designations are often used to identify cost, work skill, departments, and locations. As a general rule, activity numbering systems should be ascending and as simple as possible. The intent is to make it as easy as you can for project participants to follow work through the network and locate specific activities.

Use of Computers to Develop Networks

All of the tools and techniques discussed in this chapter can be used with computer software currently available. Two examples are shown in Figures 6.10 and 6.11. Figure 6.10 presents a generic AON computer output for the Automated Warehouse Picking System project. Observe that these computer outputs use numbers to identify activities. The critical path is identified by the nodes (activities) 2, 4, 6, and 9. The activity description is shown on the top line of the activity node. The activity start time and identification are on the second line. The finish time and duration are on the third line of the node. The project starts on January 1 and is planned to finish May 20. Note this sample computer network has included non-work days of holidays and weekends.

Figure 6.11 presents an early start **Gantt chart.**[2] Bar charts are popular because they present an easy-to-understand, clear picture on a time-scaled horizon. They are used during planning, resource scheduling, and status reporting. The format is a two-dimensional representation of the project schedule, with activities down the rows and time across the horizontal axis. In this computer output the shaded bars represent the activity durations. The extended lines from the bars represent slack. For example, "test software" (ID # 8) has a duration of 35 days (shaded area of the bar) and 15 days slack (represented by the extended line). The bar also indicates test software has an early start of February 19 and would finish April 8, but can finish as late as April 29 because it has 15 days of slack. When calendar dates are used on the time axis, Gantt charts provide a clear overview of the project schedule and can often be found posted on the walls of project offices. Unfortunately, when projects have many dependency relationships, the dependency lines soon become overwhelming and defeat the simplicity of the Gantt chart.

Project management software can be a tremendous help in the hands of those who understand and are familiar with the tools and techniques discussed in this text. However, there is nothing more dangerous than someone using the software with little or no knowledge of how the software derives its output. Mistakes in input are very common and require someone skilled in the concepts, tools, and information system to recognize that errors exist so false actions are avoided.

Calendar Dates

Ultimately you will want to assign calendar dates to your project activities. If a computer program is not used, dates are assigned manually. Lay out a calendar of workdays (exclude non-workdays), and number them. Then relate the calendar workdays to the workdays on your project network. Most computer programs will assign calendar dates automatically after you identify start dates, time units, non-workdays, and other information.

Multiple Starts and Multiple Projects

Some computer programs require a common start and finish event in the form of a node—usually a circle or rectangle—for a project network. Even if this is not a requirement, it is a good idea because it avoids "dangler" paths. Dangler paths give the impression that the project does not have a clear beginning or ending. If a project has more than one activity that can begin when the project is to start, each path is a dangler path. The same is true if a project network ends with more than one activity; these unconnected paths are also called danglers. Danglers can be avoided by tying dangler activities to a common project start or finish node.

---

[2] Gantt charts were introduced over 100 years ago by Henry Gantt.

FIGURE 6.10 *Automated Warehouse Order Picking System Network*

Automated Warehouse
Order Picking System Network Diagram

FIGURE 6.11 *Automated Order Warehouse Picking System Bar Chart*

			Automated Warehouse Order Picking System Bar Chart						
						Automated Warehouse Order Picking System Schedule Table			
ID	Duration	Task Name	Start	Finish	Late Start	Late Finish	Total Slack	Free Slack	
2	10	Define Req.s	Tue 1/1	Mon 1/14	Tue 1/1	Tue 1/15	0 days	0 days	
3	5	Assign Team	Tue 1/15	Mon 1/21	Tue 2/5	Mon 2/11	15 days	0 days	
4	25	Design Hardware	Tue 1/15	Mon 2/18	Tue 1/15	Mon 2/18	0 days	0 days	
5	20	Code Software	Tue 1/22	Mon 2/18	Tue 2/12	Mon 3/11	15 days	0 days	
6	50	Build and Test HW	Tue 2/19	Mon 4/29	Tue 2/19	Mon 4/29	0 days	0 days	
7	15	Dev. Patent Request	Tue 2/19	Mon 3/11	Tue 4/9	Mon 4/29	35 days	35 days	
8	35	Test Software	Tue 2/19	Mon 4/8	Tue 3/12	Mon 4/29	15 days	15 days	
9	15	Integrate Systems	Tue 4/30	Mon 5/20	Tue 4/30	Mon 5/20	0 days	0 days	

When several projects are tied together in an organization, using a common start and end node helps to identify the total planning period of all projects. Use of pseudo or dummy wait activities from the common start node allows different start dates for each project.

EXTENDED NETWORK TECHNIQUES TO COME CLOSER TO REALITY

The method for showing relationships among activities in the last section is called the finish-to-start relationship because it assumes all immediate preceding connected activities must be completed before the next activity can begin. In an effort to come closer to the realities of projects, some useful extensions have been added. The use of *laddering* was the first obvious extension practitioners found very useful.

Laddering

The assumption that all immediate preceding activities must be 100 percent complete is too restrictive for some situations found in practice. This restriction occurs most frequently when one activity overlaps the start of another and has a long duration. Under the standard finish-to-start relationship, when an activity has a long duration and will delay the start of an activity immediately following it, the activity can be broken into segments and the network drawn using a *laddering* approach so the following activity can begin sooner and not delay the work. This segmenting of the larger activity gives the appearance of steps on a ladder on the network, thus the name. The classic example used in many texts and articles is laying pipe, because it is easy to visualize. The trench must be dug, pipe laid, and the trench refilled. If the pipeline is one mile long, it is not necessary to dig one mile of trench before the laying of pipe can begin or to lay one mile of pipe before refill can begin. Figure 6.12 shows how these overlapping activities might appear in an AON network using the standard finish-to-start approach.

FIGURE 6.12 *Example of Laddering Using Finish–to–Start Relationship*

Use of Lags to Reduce Schedule Detail and Project Duration

The use of *lags* has been developed to offer greater flexibility in network construction. *A lag is the minimum amount of time a dependent activity must be delayed to begin or end*. The use of lags in project networks occurs for two primary reasons:

1. When activities of long duration delay the start or finish of successor activities, the network designer normally breaks the activity into smaller activities to avoid the long delay of the successor activity. Use of lags can avoid such delays and reduce network detail.
2. Lags can be used to constrain the start and finish of an activity.

The most commonly used relationship extensions are start-to-start, finish-to-finish, and combinations of these two. These relationship patterns are discussed in this section.

Finish–to–Start Relationship

The finish-to-start relationship represents the typical, generic network style used in the early part of the chapter. However, there are situations in which the next activity in a sequence must be delayed even when the preceding activity is complete. For example, removing concrete forms cannot begin until the poured cement has cured for two time units. Figure 6.13 shows this **lag relationship** for AON networks. Finish-to-start lags are frequently used when ordering materials. For example, it may take 1 day to place

FIGURE 6.13 *Finish–to–Start Relationship*

orders but take 19 days to receive the goods. The use of finish-to-start allows the activity duration to be only 1 day and the lag 19 days. This approach ensures the activity cost is tied to placing the order only rather than charging the activity for 20 days of work. This same finish-to-start lag relationship is useful to depict transportation, legal, and mail lags.

The use of finish-to-start lags should be carefully checked to ensure their validity. Conservative project managers or those responsible for completion of activities have been known to use lags as a means of building in a "slush" factor to reduce the risk of being late. A simple rule to follow is that the use of finish-to-start lags must be justified and approved by someone responsible for a large section of the project. The legitimacy of lags is not usually difficult to discern. The legitimate use of the additional relationship shown can greatly enhance the network by more closely representing the realities of the project.

Start–to–Start Relationship

An alternative to segmenting the activities as we did earlier is to use a start-to-start relationship. Typical start-to-start relationships are shown in Figure 6.14. Figure 6.14A shows the start-to-start relationship with zero lag, while Figure 6.14B shows the same relationship with a lag of five time units. It is important to note that the relationship may be used with or without a lag. If time is assigned, it is usually shown on the dependency arrow of an AON network.

In Figure 6.14B, activity Q cannot begin until five time units after activity P begins. This type of relationship typically depicts a situation in which you can perform a portion of one activity and begin a following activity before completing the first. This relationship can be used on the pipe-laying project. Figure 6.15 shows the project using an AON network. The start-to-start relationship reduces network detail and project delays by using lag relationships.

It is possible to find compression opportunities by changing finish-to-start relations to start-to-start relationships. A review of finish-to-start critical activities may point out opportunities that can be revised to be parallel by using start-to-start relationships. For example, in place of a finish-to-start activity "design house, then build foundation," a start-to-start relationship could be used in which the foundation can be started, say, five days (lag) after design has started—assuming the

FIGURE 6.14   *Start–to–Start Relationship*

FIGURE 6.15   *Use of Lags to Reduce Project Duration*

design of the foundation is the first part of the total design activity. This start-to-start relationship with a small lag allows a sequential activity to be worked on in parallel and to compress the duration of the critical path. This same concept is frequently found in projects in which concurrent engineering is used to speed completion of a project. **Concurrent engineering,** which is highlighted in the Snapshot from Practice: Concurrent Engineering, basically breaks activities into smaller segments so that work can be done in parallel and the project expedited (Turtle, 1994). Start-to-start relationships can depict the concurrent engineering conditions and reduce network detail. Of course, the same result can be accomplished by breaking an activity into small packages that can be implemented in parallel, but this latter approach increases the network and tracking detail significantly.

Finish–to–Finish Relationship

This relationship is found in Figure 6.16. The finish of one activity depends on the finish of another activity. For example, testing cannot be completed any earlier than four days after the prototype is complete. Note that this is not a finish-to-start relationship because the testing of subcomponents can begin before the prototype is completed, but four days of "system" testing is required after the prototype is finished.

FIGURE 6.16   *Finish–to–Finish Relationship*

Start–to–Finish Relationship

This relationship represents situations in which the finish of an activity depends on the start of another activity. For example, system documentation cannot end until three days after testing has started (see Figure 6.17). Here all the relevant information to complete the system documentation is produced after the first three days of testing.

FIGURE 6.17   *Start–to–Finish Relationship*

In the old days, when a new product development project was initiated by a firm, it would start its sequential journey in the research and development department. Concepts and ideas would be worked out and the results passed to the engineering department, which sometimes reworked the whole product. This result would be passed to manufacturing, where it might be reworked once more in order to ensure the product could be manufactured using existing machinery and operations. Quality improvements were initiated after the fact once defects and improvement opportunities were discovered during production. This sequential approach to product development required a great deal of time, and it was not uncommon for the final product to be totally unrecognizable when compared to original specifications.

Given the emphasis on speed to the market, companies have abandoned the sequential approach to product development and have adopted a more holistic approach titled concurrent engineering. In a nutshell, *concurrent engineering* entails the active involvement of all the relevant specialty areas throughout the design and development process. The traditional chainlike sequence of finish-to-start relationships is replaced by a series of start-to-start lag relationships as soon as meaningful work can be initiated for the next phase. Figure 6.18 summarizes the dramatic gains in time to market achieved by this approach.

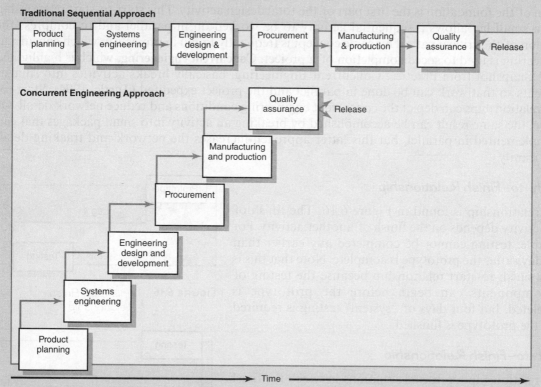

FIGURE 6.18 *New Product Development Process*

Within the world of project management this approach is also called *Fast Tracking*. General Motors used this approach to design the very first American hybrid car, the Chevy Volt. From the very beginning specialists from marketing, engineering, design, manufacturing, quality assurance, and other relevant departments were involved in every stage of the project. Not only did the project meet all of its objectives, it was completed ahead of schedule.

*"Chevrolet Volt Hits Road, Ahead of Schedule," *The New York Times*, June 25, 2009; retrieved online June 2, 2011.

Combinations of Lag Relationships

More than one lag relationship can be attached to an activity. These relationships are usually start-to-start and finish-to-finish combinations tied to two activities. For example, debug cannot begin until two time units after coding has started. Coding must be finished four days before debug can be finished (see Figure 6.19).

FIGURE 6.19 *Combination Relationships*

An Example Using Lag Relationships—The Forward and Backward Pass

The forward and backward pass procedures are the same as explained earlier in the chapter for finish-to-start relationships (without lags). The modifying technique lies in the need to check each new relationship to see if it alters the start or finish time of another activity.

An example of the outcome of the forward and backward pass is shown in Figure 6.20. Order hardware depends upon the design of the system (start-to-start). Three days into the design of the system (activity A), it is possible to order the required hardware (activity B). It takes four days after the order is placed (activity B) for the hardware to arrive so it can begin to be installed (activity C). After two days of installing the software system (activity D), the testing of the system can begin

FIGURE 6.20 *Network Using Lags*

(activity E). System testing (activity E) can be completed two days after the software is installed (activity D). Preparing system documentation (activity F) can begin once the design is completed (activity A), but it cannot be completed until two days after testing the system (activity E). This final relationship is an example of a finish-to-finish lag.

Note how an activity can have a critical finish and/or start. Activities E and F have critical finishes (zero slack), but their activity starts have 4 and 12 days of slack. It is only the finish of activities E and F that are critical. Conversely, activity A has zero slack to start but has five days of slack to finish. The critical path follows activity start and finish constraints that occur due to the use of the additional relationships available and the imposed lags. You can identify the critical path in Figure 6.20 by following the dashed line on the network.

If a lag relationship exists, each activity must be checked to see if the start or finish is constrained. For example, in the forward pass the EF of activity E (test system) (18) is controlled by the finish of activity D (install software) and the lag of two time units (16 + lag 2 = 18). Finally, in the backward pass, the LS of activity A (design system) is controlled by activity B (order hardware) and the lag relationship to activity A (3 − 3 = 0).

Hammock Activities

Another of the extended techniques uses a **hammock activity.** This type of activity derives its name because it spans over a segment of a project. The hammock activity duration is determined *after* the network plan is drawn. Hammock activities are frequently used to identify the use of fixed resources or costs over a segment of the project. Typical examples of hammock activities are inspection services, consultants, or construction management services. A hammock activity derives its duration from the time span between other activities. For example, a special color copy machine is needed for a segment of a tradeshow publication project. A hammock activity can be used to indicate the need for this resource and to apply costs over this segment of the project. This hammock is linked from the start of the first activity in the segment that uses the color copy machine to the end of the last activity that uses it. The hammock duration is simply the difference between the EF for the last activity and the ES of the first activity. The duration is computed after the forward pass and hence has no influence on other activity times. Figure 6.21 provides an example of a hammock activity used in a network. The duration for the hammock activity is derived from the early start of activity B and the early finish of activity F; that is, the difference between 13 and 5, or 8 time units. The hammock duration will change if any ES or EF in the chain-sequence changes. Hammock activities are very useful in assigning and controlling indirect project costs.[3]

Another major use of hammock activities is to aggregate sections of a project. This is similar to developing a subnetwork, but the precedence is still preserved. This approach is sometimes used to present a "macro network" for upper management levels. Using a hammock activity to group activities can facilitate getting the right level of detail for specific sections of a project.

---

[3] In order to designate G as a Hammock activity in MS Project 2012 you would copy and paste for activity G the start date of activity B and the finish date for activity F (http://support.microsoft.com/kb/141733).

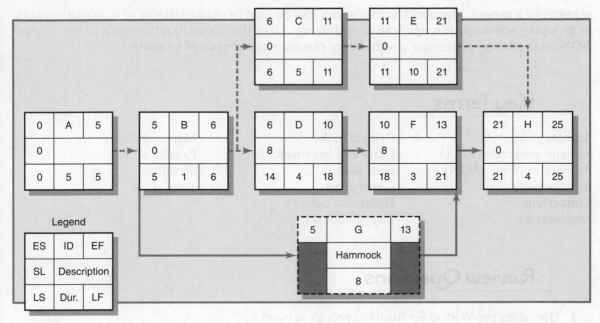

FIGURE 6.21   *Hammock Activity Example*

Summary

Many project managers feel the project network is their most valuable exercise and planning document. Project networks sequence and time-phase the project work, resources, and budgets. Work package tasks are used to develop activities for networks. Every project manager should feel comfortable working in an AON environment. The AON method uses nodes (boxes) for activities and arrows for dependencies. The forward and backward passes establish early and late times for activities. Although most project managers use computers to generate networks and activity times, they find a keen understanding of network development and the ability to compute activity times is invaluable in the field. Computers break down; input errors give false information; some decisions must be made without computer "what if" analysis. Project managers who are well acquainted with network development and AON methods and who are able to compute activity times will encounter fewer problems than project managers less well acquainted. Project networks help to ensure there are no surprises.

Several extensions and modifications have been appended to the original AON method. Lags allow the project planner to more closely replicate the actual conditions found in practice. The use of lags can result in the start or finish of an activity becoming critical. Some computer software simply calls the whole activity critical rather than identifying the start or finish as being critical. Caution should be taken to ensure that lags are not used as a buffer for possible errors in estimating time. Finally, hammock activities are useful in tracking costs of resources used for a particular segment of a project. Hammock activities can also be used to reduce the size of a project network by grouping activities for simplification and clarity. All of the discussed refinements to the original AON methodology contribute toward better planning and control of projects.

Key Terms

Activity	Critical path	Merge activity
Activity-on-arrow (AOA)	Early and late times	Parallel activity
Activity-on-node (AON)	Free slack	Sensitivity
Burst activity	Gantt chart	Total slack
Concurrent	Hammock activity	
engineering	Lag relationship	

Review Questions

1. How does the WBS differ from the project network?
2. How are WBS and project networks linked?
3. Why bother creating a WBS? Why not go straight to a project network and forget the WBS?
4. Why is slack important to the project manager?
5. What is the difference between free slack and total slack?
6. Why are lags used in developing project networks?
7. What is a hammock activity, and when is it used?

Exercises

Creating a Project Network

1. Here is a partial work breakdown structure for a wedding. Use the method described in the Snapshot from Practice: The Yellow Sticky Approach to create a network for this project.

Note: Do not include summary tasks in the network (i.e., 1.3, Ceremony, is a summary task; 1.2, Marriage license, is not a summary task). Do not consider who would be doing the task in building the network. For example, do not arrange "hiring a band" to occur after "florist" because the same person is responsible for doing both tasks. Focus only on technical dependencies between tasks.

Hint: Start with the last activity (wedding reception), and work your way back to the start of the project. Build the logical sequence of tasks by asking the following question: In order to have or do this, what must be accomplished immediately before this? Once completed, check forward in time by asking this question: Is this task(s) the only thing that is needed immediately before the start of the next task?

Work Breakdown Structure

1. Wedding project
   1.1 Decide on date
   1.2 Marriage license
   1.3 Ceremony
       1.3.1 Rent church
       1.3.2 Florist
       1.3.3 Create/print programs
       1.3.4 Hire photographer
       1.3.5 Wedding ceremony
   1.4 Guests
       1.4.1 Develop guest list
       1.4.2 Order invitations
       1.4.3 Address and mail invitations
       1.4.4 Track RSVPs
   1.5 Reception
       1.5.1 Reserve reception hall
       1.5.2 Food and beverage
       1.5.2.1 Choose caterer
       1.5.2.2 Decide on menu
       1.5.2.3 Make final order
       1.5.3 Hire band
       1.5.4 Decorate reception hall
       1.5.5 Wedding reception

Drawing AON Networks

2. Draw a project network from the following information. What activity(s) is a burst activity? What activity(s) is a merge activity?

ID	Description	Predecessor
A	Survey site	None
B	Install drainage	A
C	Install power lines	A
D	Excavate site	B, C
E	Pour foundation	D

3.*Draw a project network from the following information. What activity(s) is a burst activity? What activity(s) is a merge activity?

---

* The solution to this exercise can be found in Appendix One.

ID	Description	Predecessor
A	Identify topic	None
B	Research topic	A
C	Draft paper	B
D	Edit paper	C
E	Create graphics	C
F	References	C
G	Final draft	D, E, F

4. Draw a project network from the following information. What activity(s) is a burst activity? What activity(s) is a merge activity?

ID	Description	Predecessor
A	Contract signed	None
B	Survey designed	A
C	Target market identified	B
D	Data collection	B, C
E	Develop presentation	B
F	Analyze results	D
G	Demographics	C
H	Presentation	E, F, G

5. Draw a project network from the following information. What activity(s) is a burst activity? What activity(s) is a merge activity?

ID	Description	Predecessor
A	Order review	None
B	Order standard parts	A
C	Produce standard parts	A
D	Design custom parts	A
E	Software development	A
F	Manufacture custom parts	C, D
G	Assemble	B, F
H	Test	E, G

AON Network Times

6. From the following information, develop an AON project network. Complete the forward and backward pass, compute activity slack, and identify the critical path. How many days will the project take?

ID	Description	Predecessor	Time
A	Survey site	None	2
B	Install drainage	A	5
C	Install power lines	A	3
D	Excavate site	B, C	4
E	Pour foundation	D	3

7. The project information for the custom order project of the Air Control Company is presented here. Draw a project network for this project. Compute the early and late activity times and the slack times. Identify the critical path.

ID	Activity	Predecessor	Time
A	Order review	None	2
B	Order standard parts	A	15
C	Produce standard parts	A	10
D	Design custom parts	A	13
E	Software development	A	18
F	Manufacture custom hardware	C, D	15
G	Assemble	B, F	10
H	Test	E, G	5

8. You have signed a contract to build a garage for the Simpsons. You will receive a $500 bonus for completing the project within 15 working days. The contract also contains a penalty clause in which you will lose $100 for each day the project takes longer than 15 working days.

   Draw a project network given the information below. Complete the forward and backward pass, compute the activity slack, and identify the critical path. Do you expect to receive a bonus or a penalty on this project?

ID	Description	Predecessor	Time (days)
A	Pour foundation	None	3
B	Erect frame	A	4
C	Roof	B	4
D	Windows	B	1
E	Doors	B	1
F	Electrical	B	3
G	Rough-in frame	C, D, E, F	2
H	Door opener	E, F	1
I	Paint	G, H	2
J	Cleanup	I	1

9. You are creating a customer database for the Modesto Nuts minor league baseball team. Draw a project network given the information below. Complete the forward and backward pass, compute activity slack, and identify the critical path.

   How long will this project take? How sensitive is the network schedule? Calculate the free slack and total slack for all noncritical activities.

ID	Description	Predecessor	Time (days)
A	Systems design	None	2
B	Subsystem A design	A	1
C	Subsystem B design	A	1
D	Subsystem C design	A	1
E	Program A	B	2
F	Program B	C	2
G	Program C	D	2
H	Subsystem A test	E	1
I	Subsystem B test	F	1
J	Subsystem C test	G	1
K	Integration	H, I, J	2
L	Integration test	K	1

10. J. Wold, project manager of Print Software, Inc., wants you to prepare a project network; compute the early, late, and slack activity times; determine the planned project duration; and identify the critical path. His assistant has collected the following information for the Color Printer Drivers Software Project:

ID	Description	Predecessor	Time
A	External specifications	None	8
B	Review design features	A	2
C	Document new features	A	3
D	Write software	A	60
E	Program and test	B	60
F	Edit and publish notes	C	2
G	Review manual	D	2
H	Alpha site	E, F	20
I	Print manual	G	10
J	Beta site	H, I	10
K	Manufacture	J	12
L	Release and ship	K	3

11. *A large eastern city is requesting federal funding for a park-and-ride project. One of the requirements in the request application is a network plan for the design phase of the project. Catherine Walker, the chief engineer, wants you to develop a project network plan to meet this requirement. She has gathered the activity time estimates and their dependencies shown here. Show your project network with the activity early, late, and slack times. Mark the critical path.

---

* The solution to this exercise can be found in Appendix One.

ID	Description	Predecessor	Time
A	Survey	None	5
B	Soils report	A	20
C	Traffic design	A	30
D	Lot layout	A	5
E	Approve design	B, C, D	80
F	Illumination	E	15
G	Drainage	E	30
H	Landscape	E	25
I	Signing	E	20
J	Bid proposal	F, G, H, I	10

12. You are creating a customer database for the Winston-Salem Warthogs minor league baseball team. Draw a project network given the information below. Complete the forward and backward pass, compute activity slack, and identify the critical path.

    How long will this project take? How sensitive is the network schedule? Calculate the free slack and total slack for all noncritical activities.

ID	Description	Predecessor	Time (days)
A	Systems design	None	2
B	Subsystem A design	A	1
C	Subsystem B design	A	2
D	Subsystem C design	A	1
E	Program A	B	2
F	Program B	C	10
G	Program C	D	2
H	Subsystem A test	E	1
I	Subsystem B test	F	1
J	Subsystem C test	G	1
K	Integration	H, I, J	2
L	Integration test	K	1

13.* You are completing a group term paper. Given the project network that follows, complete the forward and backward pass, compute activity slack, and identify the critical path. Use this information to create a Gantt chart for the project. Be sure to show slack for noncritical activities.

---

* The solution to this exercise can be found in Appendix One.

14. You are conducting a market research project for FUN Inc. Given the project network that follows, complete the forward and backward pass, compute activity slack, and identify the critical path. Use this information to create a Gantt chart for the project. Be sure to show slack for noncritical activities.

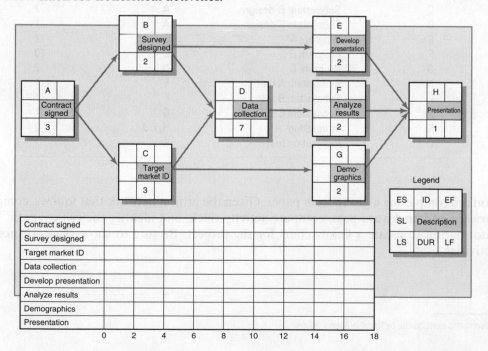

Computer Exercises

15. The planning department of an electronics firm has set up the activities for developing and production of a new MP3 Player. Given the information below, develop a project network using Microsoft Project. Assume a five-day workweek and the project starts on January 4, 2013.

Activity ID	Description	Activity Predecessor	Activity Time (weeks)
1	Staff	None	2
2	Develop market program	1	3
3	Select channels of distribution	1	8
4	Patent	1	12
5	Pilot production	1	4
6	Test market	5	4
7	Ad promotion	2	4
8	Set up for production	4, 6	16

The project team has requested that you create a network for the project, and determine if the project can be completed in 45 weeks.

16. Using Microsoft Project, set up the network and determine the critical path for Phase 1 of the project. The project workweek will be 5 days (M—F).

Whistler Ski Resort Project

Given the fact that the number of skiing visitors to Whistler, B.C., Canada has been increasing at an exciting rate, thanks to the 2010 Winter Olympics, the Whistler Ski Association has been considering construction of another ski lodge and ski complex. The results of an economic feasibility study just completed by members of the staff show that a winter resort complex near the base of Whistler Mountain could be a very profitable venture. The area is accessible by car, bus, train, and air. The board of directors has voted to build the ten-million dollar complex recommended in the study. Unfortunately, due to the short summer season, the complex will have to be built in stages. The first stage (year 1) will contain a day lodge, chair lift, rope tow, generator house (for electricity), and a parking lot designed to accommodate 400 cars and 30 buses. The second and third stages will include a hotel, ice rink, pool, shops, two additional chair lifts, and other attractions. The board has decided that stage one should begin no later than April 1 and be completed by October 1, in time for the next skiing season. You have been assigned the task of project manager, and it is your job to coordinate the ordering of materials and construction activities to ensure the project's completion by the required date.

After looking into the possible sources of materials, you are confronted with the following time estimates. Materials for the chair lift and rope tow will take 30 days and 12 days, respectively, to arrive once the order is submitted. Lumber for the day lodge, generator hut, and foundations will take 9 days to arrive. The electrical and plumbing materials for the day lodge will take 12 days to arrive. The generator will take 12 days to arrive. Before actual construction can begin on the various facilities, a road to the site must be built; this will take 6 days. As soon as the road is in, clearing can begin concurrently on the sites of the day lodge, generator house, chair lift, and rope tow. It is estimated that the clearing task at each site will take 6 days, 3 days, 36 days, and 6 days, respectively. The clearing of the main ski slopes can begin after the area for the chair lift has been cleared; this will take 84 days.

The foundation for the day lodge will take 12 days to complete. Construction of the main framework will take an additional 18 days. After the framework is completed, electrical wiring and plumbing can be installed concurrently. These should take 24 and 30 days, respectively. Finally, the finishing construction on the day lodge can begin; this will take 36 days.

Installation of the chair lift towers (67 days) can begin once the site is cleared, lumber delivered, and the foundation completed (6 days). Also, when the chair lift site has been cleared, construction of a permanent road to the upper towers can be started; this will take 24 days. While the towers are being installed, the electric motor to drive the chair lift can be installed; the motor can be installed in 24 days. Once the towers are completed and the motor installed, it will take 3 days to install the cable and an additional 12 days to install the chairs.

Installation of the towers for the rope tow can begin once the site is cleared and the foundation is built and poured; it takes 4 days to build the foundation, pour the concrete and let it cure, and 20 days to install the towers for the rope tow. While the towers are being erected, installation of the electric motor to drive the rope tow can begin; this activity will take 24 days. After the towers and motor are installed, the rope tow can be strung in 1 day. The parking lot can be cleared once the rope tow is finished; this task will take 18 days.

The foundation for the generator house can begin at the same time as the foundation for the lodge; this will take 6 days. The main framework for the generator house can begin once the foundation is completed; framing will take 12 days. After the house is framed, the diesel generator can be installed in 18 days. Finishing construction on the generator house can now begin and will take 12 more days.

Assignment:
1. Identify the critical path on your network.
2. Can the project be completed by October 1?

Optical Disk Preinstallation Project

17. The optical disk project team has started gathering the information necessary to develop the project network—predecessor activities and activity times in weeks. The results of their meeting are found in the following table.

Activity	Description	Duration	Predecessor
1	Define scope	6	None
2	Define customer problems	3	1
3	Define data records and relationships	5	1
4	Mass storage requirements	5	2, 3
5	Consultant needs analysis	10	2, 3
6	Prepare installation network	3	4, 5
7	Estimate costs and budget	2	4, 5
8	Design section "point" system	1	4, 5
9	Write request proposal	5	4, 5
10	Compile vendor list	3	4, 5
11	Prepare mgmt. control system	5	6, 7
12	Prepare comparison report	5	9, 10
13	Compare system "philosophies"	3	8, 12
14	Compare total installation	2	8, 12
15	Compare cost of support	3	8, 12
16	Compare customer satisfaction level	10	8, 12
17	Assign philosophies points	1	13
18	Assign installation cost	1	14
19	Assign support cost	1	15
20	Assign customer satisfaction points	1	16
21	Select best system	1	11, 17, 18, 19, 20
22	Order system	1	21

The project team has requested that you create a network for the project, and determine if the project can be completed in 45 weeks.

Lag Exercises

18. From the following information, draw the project network. Compute the early, late, and slack times for each activity. Identify the critical path. (Hint: Draw the finish-to-start relationships first.)

ID	Duration	Finish-to-Start Predecessor	Finish-to-Start Lag	Additional Lag Relationships	Lag
A	5	None	0	None	0
B	10	A	0	None	0
C	15	A	0	Start-finish C to D	20
D	5	B	5	Start-start D to E	5
				Finish-finish D to E	25
E	20	B	0	Finish-finish E to F	0
F	15	D	0	None	0
G	10	C	10	Finish-finish G to F	10
H	20	F	0	None	0

19. Given the following information, draw the project network. Compute the early, late, and slack times for the project network. Which activities on the critical path have only the start or finish of the activity on the critical path?

ID	Duration	Finish-to-Start Predecessor	Finish-to-Start Lag	Additional Lag Relationships	Lag
A	2	None	0	None	0
B	4	A	0	None	0
C	6	A	0	Finish-finish C to F	7
D	8	A	0	None	0
E	18	B	0	Finish-finish E to G	9
		C	10		
F	2	D	0	None	0
G	5	F	0	Start-start G to H	10
H	5	None	0	None	0
I	14	E	0	Finish-finish I to J	5
J	15	G, H	0	None	0

20.* Given the information in the following lag exercises, compute the early, late, and slack times for the project network. Which activities on the critical path have only the start or finish of the activity on the critical path?

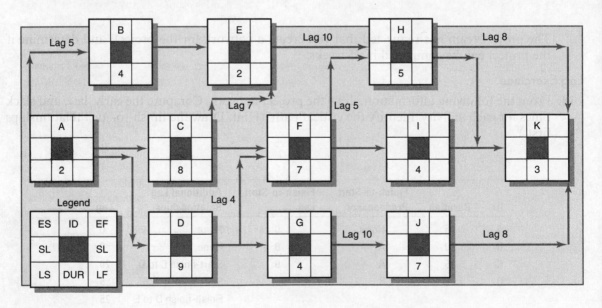

---

* The solution to this exercise can be found in Appendix One.

21. Given the network below, compute the early, late, and slack time for each activity.

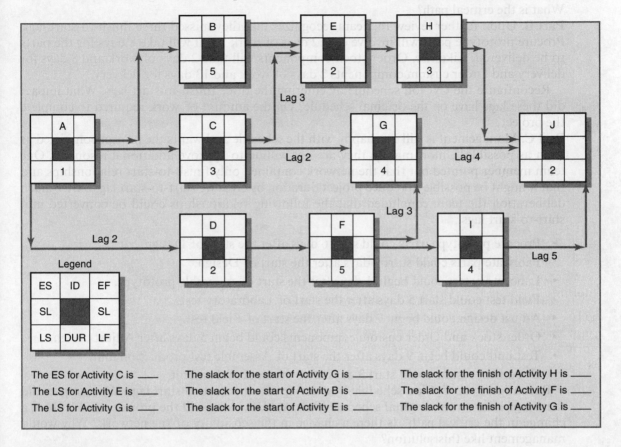

The ES for Activity C is _____
The LS for Activity E is _____
The LS for Activity G is _____

The slack for the start of Activity G is _____
The slack for the start of Activity B is _____
The slack for the start of Activity E is _____

The slack for the finish of Activity H is _____
The slack for the finish of Activity F is _____
The slack for the finish of Activity G is _____

CyClon Project

22. The CyClon project team has started gathering information necessary to develop a project network-predecessor activities and activity time in days. The results of their meeting are found in the following table:

Activity	Description	Duration	Predecessor
1	**CyClon Project**		
2	Design	10	
3	Procure prototype parts	10	2
4	Fabricate parts	8	2
5	Assemble prototype	4	3, 4
6	Laboratory test	7	5
7	Field test	10	6
8	Adjust design	6	7
9	Order stock components	10	8
10	Order custom components	15	8
11	Assemble test production unit	10	9, 10
12	Test unit	5	11
13	Document results	3	12

Part A. Create a network based on the above information. How long will the project take? What is the critical path?

Part B. Upon further review the team recognizes that they missed three finish-to-start lags. Procure prototype parts will involve only 2 days of work but it will take 8 days for the parts to be delivered. Likewise, Order stock components will take 2 days of work and 8 days for delivery and Order custom components 2 days of work and 13 days for delivery.

Reconfigure the CyClon schedule by entering the three finish-to-start lags. What impact did these lags have on the original schedule? On the amount of work required to complete the project?

Part C. Management is still not happy with the schedule and wants the project completed as soon as possible. Unfortunately, they are not willing to approve additional resources. One team member pointed out that the network contained only finish-to-start relationships and that it might be possible to reduce project duration by creating start-to-start lags. After much deliberation the team concluded that the following relationships could be converted into start-to-start lags:

- Procure prototype parts could start 6 days after the start of Design.
- Fabricate parts could start 9 days after the start of Design.
- Laboratory test could begin 1 day after the start of Assemble prototype.
- Field test could start 5 days after the start of Laboratory test.
- Adjust design could begin 7 days after the start of Field test.
- Order stock and Order custom components could begin 5 days after Adjust design.
- Test unit could begin 9 days after the start of Assemble test production unit.
- Document results could start 3 days after the start of Test unit.

Reconfigure the CyClon schedule by entering all nine start-to-start lags. What impact did these lags have on the original schedule (Part A)? How long will the project take? Is there a change in the critical path? Is there a change in the sensitivity of the network? Why would management like this solution?

References

Gantt, H. L., *Work, Wages and Profit*, published by *The Engineering Magazine*, New York, 1910; republished as *Work, Wages and Profits* (Easton, PA: Hive Publishing Company, 1974).

Kelly, J. E., "Critical Path Planning and Scheduling: Mathematical Basis," *Operations Research,* 9 (3) May–June 1961, pp. 296–321.

Levy, F. K., G. L. Thompson, and J. D. West, "The ABCs of the Critical Path Method," *Harvard Business Review,* 41 (5) 1963, pp. 98–108.

Rosenblatt, A., and G. Watson, "Concurrent Engineering," *IEEE Spectrum,* July 1991, pp. 22–37.

Turtle, Q. C., *Implementing Concurrent Project Management* (Englewood Cliffs, NJ: Prentice Hall), 1994.

APPENDIX 6.1

Project Time Management

1. INTRODUCTION

1.1 Importance of Time Management

Project time management, along with project scope and project cost management, is one of the three core areas of project management. The reason for importance of time management is rooted in three factors:

- *Essential Nature of Projects*: By definition, the projects are *temporary* endeavours to create a unique product, service or result. They are authorized with definite starting dates and definite completion dates to accomplish the objectives and these essential constraints for project must be observed during the entire project work. Often, the windows of opportunity for exploiting the value of the product of the project are open for only a small specific time slot – like timing for introduction of a new product, for developing a new technology or a product complying with a new technology, for release of large volume of production to the customers or consumers at opportune times, etc. If the projects do not deliver the project objectives in the schedule earmarked for them, their value to the organization is greatly diminished and sometimes the time, effort and resources spent on a project delayed may turn out to be just entirely wasteful. The cliché, "Time is money", is literally very true for projects and project management.

- *Incremental Costs Associated with Schedule Delay*: Again, often, the project delay results in the loss of focus by the project team and sometimes even by the entire organization. With loss of momentum and enthusiasm, which invariably accompany project delays, the focus on quality gets diffused, the effort level slackens and the period costs associated with the time mount up. The analysis of a vast number of projects confirms the conclusion, that projects with delayed schedule are invariably associated with large cost overruns.

- *Irreversible Recovery of Time Delays*: The project manager and his team must attend to effective time management right from the start, as the lost time cannot be recovered at any cost. If the work done for project deliverable does not meet quality standards or criteria for project success, with extra efforts and costs, some recovery might be possible. It may be possible to compensate the overruns of some project activities by cost economy in some others. But, in case of unacceptable project delays and missing the opportunities, there is no such safety net.

Therefore, all project methodology lay strong emphasis on managing project schedule.

1.2 Key Issues in Time management

The superstructure for effective management of time rests on three pillars:

1.2.1 Well prepared project plans
1.2.2 Vigilant monitoring of progress and prompt corrective actions
1.2.3 Proactive integrated schedule management

We shall briefly discuss these principles below before taking up discussion on the time management processes described in PMBOK® Guide and the inputs, tools and techniques and outputs for them.

1.2.1 Well-Prepared Project Plans

The effective management of project time begins with a well-prepared project plan, which essentially involves following the logical process steps mentioned below:

i. *Identification and definition of activities:* A thorough review of the work packages developed in work breakdown structure is carried out and all activities necessary for accomplishing the work packages are identified and listed. In order to compile this list, the project team must have access to the knowledge or expertise in the industry practice and knowledge of the project's product or service characteristics for understanding the project scope and the nature of work involved in project activities. This exercise has to be carried out very patiently and thoroughly (particularly for projects new to the organization), so that no activity necessary for project work slips between the tables.

   The next step is focusing on each activity and determining the nature, quality standard and performance requirements and the quantum of work for completing each activity. With these two steps, a comprehensive list of well-defined activities would be available with the project team.

ii. *Sequencing the activities:* Sequencing the activities from the list is the next logical step in planning. Often, the sequencing of activities is natural and follows a logical approach and conformance to physical requirements for carrying out the work (like casting the foundation and columns before building the superstructure). However, there is a pitfall to watch out for. Sometimes the dependency of an activity on completion of another activity is not mandatory but a specific activity sequence is adopted only due to traditional practice in the industry. It is desirable to question the dependency of each activity on the prior activity and spot opportunities for good planning (by fast tracking and parallel paths for network).

iii. *Estimating resources and time required for each activity:* In most project work, the availability of resources to the organization or resources released for a particular project is a constraint and the time required for an activity often depends on the quality and availability of resources. Therefore, it is often necessary to decide on the resources available for carrying out an activity and the estimated time for an activity simultaneously. While doing this, it is important to keep in mind this relationship, so that if there is a need to rework the project schedule at a later stage to crash activity duration, the project team would be able to take an informed decision.

iv. *Develop Project Network and Project Schedule:* Using the list of defined activities arranged in a sequence showing the precedence and succession connections between them, the project network is mapped out. Note that except the project start and project end, every activity should have one or more activities preceding it and one or more activities succeeding it. The forward path and backward path analysis of project network would reveal a critical path, which would determine the minimum time for project duration from the start and all activities on the critical path which must be completed for completing the project.

v. *Tailoring the schedule to project constraints or sponsor's requirements:* If the project schedule resulting from this network plan meets the project sponsor's requirements, there would be no further work necessary planning project schedule. More often, the sponsor's needs would necessitate a shorter project schedule than the first pass on the critical path for the network would come out with. This would start another round of review of the project network activities with a view to cut down the project schedule. This could be done by carrying out fast tracking of activities (some activities originally planned to be carried out sequentially are taken up simultaneously or in parallel) or activities crashing (making additional resources available at additional cost to reduce the activity duration). This network tweaking process is continued till the overall schedule meets the project sponsor's requirements.

The modern project planning software are a great help in project planning. The project planning software (like Microsoft Project ® , Prima Vera® or other proprietary software) are very helpful in the steps of activities listing and orderly arranging the list, developing the project network and project schedule, and going through the iterative modification rounds necessary to develop a satisfactory project schedule.

1.2.2 Vigilant Monitoring of Progress and Prompt Corrective Actions

Once an effective planning is accomplished, it needs to be vigilantly followed to ensure that project is completed in the planned schedule. A planning approach that involves carrying out a risk analysis for schedule delays and preparing plans to go into action if the risk occurs could be helpful. A more proactive approach would be to watch out for risk triggers and take the steps envisaged in the risk management plan as soon as the trigger is pressed.

The first necessity for schedule control is close monitoring of the performance. Once the variance between the planned schedule and actual performance is noted, the schedule compression techniques should be deployed.

Frequently, the culprit of the piece turns out to be inadequately controlled scope changes. Scope creep has a tendency to cause cost overruns as well as schedule delays. Effective integrated change control procedures and scope control measures would contribute significantly to schedule control also.

Another useful technique is to take a calculated risk for rework or repair and apply suitable leads or lags between the preceding and succeeding activities. In this approach, as soon as the preceding activity is completed to a degree sufficient to permit availability of information or set up physical condition suitable to start the succeeding activity, it should be taken up for execution without waiting for the preceding activity to reach its proper completion.

1.2.3 Proactive Integrated Schedule Management

Understanding and applying the principles based on relationships between project scope, quality, cost and time can be useful for project schedule management. The classical representation of this relationship visualizes the scope, time and cost as the sides of a triangle; change in any one-side length is likely to change the lengths of other sides. As every project manager knows, the activity durations and project schedule are not absolute unchangeable quantities. It would be possible to reduce some part of the scope or relax a quality standard in order to save time. It might also be possible to use more expensive resources or larger quantum of resources to crash an activity time at the risk of cost overrun. It might be possible to take a chance and take a short cut to compress the activity duration with activities executed in parallel network paths. All these decisions require a project manager to understand thoroughly the effect the variation in parameters would have on the set of activities and project under management. The project manager should also have clear conception of the project sponsor's requirements and priorities so that the right trade-off among the available options could be chosen (for example, whether scope should be reduced or quality standard should be relaxed for cutting down activity duration or whether preventing a minor delay in schedule is worth the risk of significant cost overrun, or adding a feature considered valuable by the sponsor, etc.).

2.0 PROJECT TIME MANAGEMENT PROCESSES

After completing the brief discussion on the importance of time management and the key issues in project time management, we now revert to discussing project time management following the framework presented in PMBOK® Guide, 5th Edition.

PMBOK® Guide, 5th Edition, recommends total seven processes to cover project time management. Six time management processes are in the planning group and one process is in the monitoring and controlling group.

Planning Process Group

1. Plan Schedule Management
2. Define Activities
3. Sequence Activities
4. Estimate Activity Resources
5. Estimate Activity Durations
6. Develop Schedule

Monitoring and Controlling Process Group

1. Control Schedule

The inputs, techniques and tools and outputs for these processes are briefly described below.

2.1 PLAN SCHEDULE MANAGEMENT

Plan Schedule Management is the process of establishing the policies, procedures and documentation for planning, developing, managing, executing, and controlling the project schedule. (PMBOK® Guide, 5th Edition)

This process sets down the methodology for managing project schedule throughout the project life cycle. The output of this process is Schedule Management Plan, which is one of the components of the Project Management Plan and a major input to the process Develop Project Management Plan.

The inputs, tools and techniques, and outputs of the process are described below.

Inputs

Project Management Plan – Scope Baseline (The Project Scope Statement, Work Breakdown Structure, and WBS Dictionary) and relevant information from other component plans for management of cost, risk, communications and quality included in the Project Management Plan provide inputs for developing plan for schedule management.

Project Charter – Summary project milestones and Assumptions and Constraints included in the Project Charter provide inputs.

Enterprise Environmental Factors – Organization structure and culture, availability of resources (infrastructure, technology and skilled manpower), share of resources allocated to the project, and organization's work authorization and cost control systems are inputs for developing Schedule Management Plan.

Organizational Process Assets – Existing policies and procedures for development and control of project schedule, tools available with the organization for development of project schedule and project management software for development and control of project schedule, change control policies and procedures and lessons learned on similar earlier project for schedule management would be used as inputs..

Tools and Techniques

Expert Judgment – This refers to expertise developed from managing project schedule for similar earlier projects and experience with use of materials and services available from vendors in the industry.

Analytical Techniques – Analytical techniques for evaluation of options for fast tracking or project activities crashing, project simulation techniques for evaluating risks associated with options, etc. could be valuable tools.

Meetings – This would include meetings of project team members and meetings with the project sponsor and key stakeholders

Outputs

Schedule Management Plan is the output of this process. A somewhat more detailed discussion on it is presented below.

Schedule Management Plan
This is an important component of the Project Management Plan. It sets down the methodology, policies and procedures for managing the project schedule during the project life cycle. The important contents of this document would include:

- *Scheduling methodology* to be used for all schedule management processes
- *Level of accuracy* in activity duration estimates
- *Units of measures* for activity attributes
- *Project schedule maintenance* – for up-dating status of project schedule and records
- *Rules for performance measurement* for reporting activities completion status
- *Reporting formats for schedule progress*

2.2 DEFINE ACTIVITIES

Defining Activities is the process of identifying and documenting the specific actions to be performed to produce the project deliverables. (PMBOK® Guide, 5th Edition)

This process is involved with identifying the activities to complete a specific work package or deliverable, define the activity attributes and develop a comprehensive list of all activities necessary for meeting the project objectives. The decomposition carried out at the WBS stage is taken one step further and the work package is decomposed into one or more better-defined and more manageable activities in order to come up with a list of activities with activity identification code. The difference in decomposition degree is for bringing out the actual attributes of the activity.

Ordinarily, while defining activities, the project team would be interested in the following attributes of the activities, which would be helpful in developing the overall project activities network:

- The actual work to be carried out
- Determining predecessor and successor activities
- Resource requirements
- Assumptions and Constraints
- Leads and lags possibilities.

Imposed or planned milestones for completion of critical activities are worked out and flagged.

Inputs

Schedule Management Plan – This input provides the methodology (rules) for defining the activities and describing their attributes.

Scope Baseline – This is the next input. Work packages included in the WBS part of the baseline and their technical and performance specifications included in the WBS Dictionary provide the starting point. The work packages are further decomposed as explained above to prepare the activities list.

Enterprise environmental Factors – Project Management Information System and other specific activity listing and definition practices of the organization are inputs in this category.

Organizational Process Assets – Activity lists and templates for activity lists in the earlier similar projects are some of the organizational process assets useful as inputs for defining activities.

Tools and Techniques

Decomposition – Decomposition of work packages into one or more actual activity to be carried out is the first step in defining activities.

Templates – Use of activity lists from similar projects is a useful practical technique.

Expert Judgment – This is reference to expertise based on knowledge and experience of similar earlier projects.

Rolling Wave Planning – This technique requires special mention and explanation. When the project is likely to extend for a long period (over one or two years) or when the nature of the project activities cannot be chalked out accurately in advance (such conditions are likely in project requiring application of new technology, development of a new product or a research project), the rolling wave planning technique is very relevant. The technique is based on carrying out detailed planning for only the near future phase of the project about which sufficient details can be worked out. The planning for the more distant or less clearly visualized future phase of the project is left at only high level of planning and without detailed activity lists and attributes. When the project work to be carried out in the next phase becomes clear enough, the detailed planning of that phase for activity lists and attributes is taken up.

Outputs

Activity Lists – A comprehensive list of all activities, with identification code, obtained by sufficient decomposition of work packages

Activity Attributes – The actual work to be carried out, predecessor and successor activities, and nature of resource requirements, assumptions and constraints, leads and lags possibilities

Milestones List – Mandatory or planned completion dates worked out for critical activities are outputs from the process. Milestones are like regular schedule activities but they have zero duration, since they refer to only a specific moment of time.

2.3   SEQUENCE ACTIVITIES

Sequence Activities is the process of identifying and documenting the relationships among the project activities.   (PMBOK® Guide, 5th Edition)

As the name suggests, the process involves determining and recording the precedence or succession relationship between the project activities and their attributes (identified in the earlier process). The logical relationship among the activities is the basis for sequencing. Every activity, except the start and end of the project, would have some precedent or succeeding activity.

While developing the network diagram, the nature of dependency between the activities (whether mandatory, discretionary or external) and the precise relationships between the start and finish of preceding and succeeding activities (Finish-to-Start, Finish-to-Finish, Start-to-Start and Start-to-Finish)   should be is examined.

PMBOK® Guide, 5th Edition, includes the following inputs, tools and techniques and outputs for the process.

Inputs

Schedule Management Plan – This input provides the methodology for sequencing the activities.

Activity list, Activity Attributes, and Milestones List – These three outputs of the earlier defined activities process, are natural logical inputs for this process.

Other inputs are *Enterprise Environmental Factors* (Project Management Information System, Project Management Software used as Scheduling Tool, and Organization's Work Authorization Systems) *Organizational Process Assets* (data from networks of project files for similar projects) and *Project Scope Statement* (as a double check to ensure that no material deliverable or performance requirement from the original scope is missed out while preparing the WBS and WBS Dictionary).

Tools and Techniques

The techniques required to develop the network diagram from the activities list involves:

- Determining the nature of dependencies
- Employing a suitable diagrammatic method
- Applying suitable leads and lags between closely related activities

These are described in detail and illustrated in the main chapter text. Here only brief listing is done for the sake of comprehensive coverage.

Determining the Nature of Dependencies

The dependencies could be:

- Mandatory Dependencies (dependencies in the inherent nature of the work or contractual requirements)
- Discretionary Dependencies (dependencies adopted from the industry or organization practices by tradition; these dependencies could be challenged and altered for network development, if the project team desires)
- External Dependencies (when activities are dependent on some external agency outside the close control of the project team, e.g. statutory approvals for project work, delivery of critical components by a monopoly supplier, etc.)

Diagrammatic Method (Precedence Diagrammatic Method or PDM Method)

By systematic application of the network diagrammatic methods, the project network is developed. PMBOK® Guide, 5th Edition, lists only one technique: Precedence Diagramming Method or 'Activities-on-Nodes' (AON) method. This method is more commonly employed by proprietary project network software. The earlier edition also listed another technique, 'Activities-on-Arrows' (AOA) method.

The diagrammatic technique requires the dependencies to be classified according to whether the relationship between the activities is:

- Finish-to-Start (The preceding activity must be completed before the succeeding activity can start. This is the most common relationship for mandatory dependencies)
- Finish-to-Finish (The succeeding activity cannot be completed unless the preceding activity is completed)
- Start-to-Start (The succeeding activity can be started only after the start of the preceding activity)
- Start-to-Finish (The preceding activity can be finished only after the start of the succeeding activity)

Applying Suitable Leads and Lags Between Closely Related Activities

Often, the succeeding activity need not wait for the completion of the preceding activity fully. The preceding activity would need to be completed only partly before the necessary information or physical working condition suitable for start of the succeeding activity may be set up. For example, for installing a 3-kilometer long underground piping, the pipe fabrication and installation need not wait till the entire 3 km stretch is excavated. The pipe laying activity can be started with providing a lag of a few days after the start of excavation. Spotting the possibility of such suitable leads and lags can lead to an improved project schedule.

Organizational Process Assets – Use of templates for project networks of similar projects from archives) is also an effort and time saving technique.

Outputs

Project Schedule Network Diagram – This is the output of the process. This diagram shows only all activities and the interrelationship between the activities. It does not include estimates for activity duration and so the time estimate for completion of the project or even the groups of activities for the project cannot be determined from the network at this stage.

2.4 ESTIMATE ACTIVITY RESOURCES

Estimating Activity Resources is the process of estimating the type and quantum of materials, human resources, equipment, (technology), and supplies required to carry out each activity. (PMBOK® Guide, 5th Edition)

Estimate of resource for activities necessary to actually carry out the work for completing the project deliverable is a very important process from the point of actual project execution. *The planning necessary for execution of the project activities has to be based on the knowledge and experience with the industry and the 'product oriented processes', so that requirements of technology, equipment, materials and supplies, and man-power for actually carrying out the project work can be estimated realistically.* The project manager and project team's success very much depends on how knowledgeable or experienced the team is with the industry and project nature.

Inputs

Activity List and *Activity Attributes* are the logical starting points and basic inputs for this process. Other inputs for this process are:

Schedule Management Plan – It provides the methodology – particularly the level of accuracy and units of measurements for estimating the resource quantities.

Resource Calendar – While determining the resource requirement, it is also necessary to ensure from the resources calendar that the resources estimated during this process are available at the time frames desired from project schedule network requirements.

Enterprise Environmental Factors (the quality and availability of resources in the market place and the organization) and *Organizational Process Assets* (organization's policies and procedures for recruiting, compensation and working conditions for employees and for contractual work, etc.), and inputs from *Risk register* and *Activity Cost Estimates* are other logical inputs for this process.

Tools and Techniques

Expert Judgment – As discussed in the introductory part of this process the project activities for any specific industry or specific product would require use of *product-oriented processes*. In turn, to estimate the requirement of the resources for these product oriented processes (equipment, technology, materials or skilled manpower) would require the knowledge of these industries. This is where the expert judgment comes in.

Alternative Methods – Looking for and evaluating for more efficient use of resources could be a very useful tool

Industry Practice Data from Published Sources and *Bottom – Up Estimating* (if ready-made estimates for exactly the same work are not available but the estimates can be built from component for which the estimates might be available) suggest themselves as tools.

Project Management Software – Software (like Microsoft Project® or Prima Vera ®) could be a useful tool.

Outputs

The output from the process would be essentially the *Activity Resources Requirements*, the equipment, materials & supplies, and personnel (with skill levels) required for carrying out an activity. *Up-dates of Project Documents,* such as Activity Lists, Activity Attributes, and Resource Calendars, is another output.

2.5 ESTIMATE ACTIVITY DURATIONS

The process involves "estimating the number of work periods required for completing the individual activity with the estimated (identified as available) resources."

(PMBOK® Guide, 5th Edition)

From the scope of work for the activity and the quality and available quantity of resources, the duration can be estimated for individual activity.

Inputs

Schedule Management Plan – Like for all other time management processes, this document provides the methodology

Activity List, *Activity Attributes, and Activity Resource Requirements* – These three basic inputs suggest themselves.

Resource Availability Calendar – This is another important input for converting the network from the number of days to working project calendar.

In addition, estimating the activity duration requires weighing in the likely impact of a number of other factors from different project documents (Project Scope Statement, Risk Register, Resource Breakdown Structure, Resource Calendar, Lessons Learned on earlier projects, and others.)

Tools and Techniques

Expert Judgment – Expertise based on prior experience with similar projects
The estimating techniques for activity duration follow the general pattern of estimations:

Analogous Estimation: The estimator compares the activity to be planned with a similar activity carried out for a similar project in the past and the time taken for the activity. Applying adjustment factors to reflect the differences in quality standards and sizes of the present and comparable past activity, the duration estimate is worked out.

Parametric Estimation – In this technique, a parameter critical for estimating the duration is defined and from the earlier duration data for a unit value of the identified parameter (the weld length per day or excavation cubic meters per day, etc.) an estimate for activity duration is developed.

Three-point Estimate – This method is based on Beta type statistical distribution theory as applied to PERT (Program Evaluation & Review Technique) applied for network evaluations Three estimates are developed for the activity duration: The most likely (T_{lik}), Optimistic (T_{opt}) and Pessimistic (T_{pess}). From these three estimates, the expected value of the activity duration (T_{exp}) is calculated by the following formula:

$$T_{exp} = (T_{opt} + 4\,T_{lik} + T_{pess})/6$$

Reserve Analysis – This input addresses the provision for contingency or time buffer added to activity duration for managing risk.

Outputs

Activity Duration Estimates – It is the main output of the process. These estimates provide the activity durations in working time periods. They often include the likely range and the probability indications also.

2.6 DEVELOP SCHEDULE

This is the process of analyzing activity sequences, durations, resource requirements, and schedule constraints to create the project schedule model. (PMBOK® Guide, 5th Edition)

This process carries out the integration of all information for planning and managing project time acquired from the earlier mentioned time management processes. The process helps the project manager to take an overview of all project activities and develop the project schedule by unifying and analyzing the outputs from all other schedule-planning processes as well as from some other relevant project documents (project scope statement, risk register, etc.). From its integrative nature, this process is iterative. The milestones determined from the first iteration of project schedule are developed and their compliance to the milestones preferred by key stakeholders is compared. Necessary changes are carried out and compromises to manage the conflicting goals are smoothed out for developing the next iteration. Often such two or three iterations are required before satisfactory project schedule is developed and approved.

The steps involved in developing the project schedule are as follows:

i. Start with the project network, the output of the Sequence Activities process.

ii. Fill in the activity duration estimate for individual activity in the network – an output of Estimate Activity Duration process.

iii. Make the forward and backward pass exercises for the network and develop the schedule for the entire project and the critical path for the project (the path through all activities having no slack between the latest permissible and earliest possible start for each activity)

iv. If the project schedule developed this way is acceptable to the project sponsor or client, the schedule is firmed up.

v. Often, the schedule worked out this way does not meet the desired project schedule. In that case, the activities on the critical path would be reviewed and techniques for schedule compression (activity time crashing and fast tracking) would be applied.

vi. The iteration is continued till a satisfactory project plan and corresponding project schedule are developed.

It is important to note that project management software play a very important part in this process. For any but the simplest project, the manual exercise is almost impossible – very tedious, time consuming and error-prone. For a medium to large-size project, use of project management software is almost mandatory. When a number of iterations are necessary for developing a satisfactory project plan, the project management software proves its value. Secondly, the schedule developed on the software is also very convenient for periodic review during the monitoring and controlling phase.

With this overview and understanding of the process, we describe here the inputs, tools and techniques and outputs of the process as set down in the PMBOK® Guide, 5th Edition.

Inputs

Schedule Management Plan – It provides the rules and procedures for developing the project schedule.

Outputs of Other Schedule Planning Processes – The following planning data developed as outputs of other schedule management planning processes are used as inputs for developing the schedule:

- *Activity List* and *Activity Attributes* (outputs of Define Activity process)
- *Project Schedule Network Diagrams* (output of Sequence Activity process)
- *Activity Resource Requirements* (output of Estimate Activity Resources)
- *Resource Calendars* (Output of Acquire Project Teams Process)
- *Activity Duration Estimates* (output of Estimate Activity Duration process)

The other inputs essentially map project schedule to the project constraints and project success criteria:

- *Project Scope Statement* (Assumptions, constraints and criteria for project success)
- *Risk Register Outputs*
- *Enterprise Environmental Factors* (External environmental constraints)
- *Organizational Process Assets* (The lessons learned and all the help which the organization's knowledge base and project archives can offer)

Tools and Techniques

The technique involved is essentially unifying and analyzing the time-related data for activities and their network relationship to develop the project schedule. Once the first-cut project schedule is ready, it would be necessary to go through the necessary iterations applying schedule compression techniques till satisfactory project schedule is developed.

The list of techniques given in PMBOK® Guide includes two types of techniques:

1. Unifying and analyzing the time data and network

- Schedule Network Analysis (Developing the first cut schedule from analysis and unification of various time data and network from earlier processes)
- Use of *project management software* for developing schedule
- *Modeling Techniques* – Application of *Simulation Technique* and *What-if scenario Analysis*

2. Optimizing the project schedule to Meet Project Objectives

- *Critical Path Method* and *Critical Chain Method* (The analytical techniques for developing optimum schedule from the first schedule developed from unified network)
- *Applying Leads and Lags* (Optimizing the schedule)
- *Schedule Compression* (Modifying the schedule to meet objectives set for project success)
- *Resource Leveling* (Optimizing the overall project plan taking into account resource availability and resource calendar)

Outputs

Of the six outputs of the process listed in PMBOK® Guide, two main outputs are Schedule Baseline and Project Schedule.

Schedule Baseline – It is the management-approved version of the schedule model that can be changed only through formal change control procedures and is used as the basis of comparison of actual project performance. It forms the component part of the project management plan.

Project Schedule – A brief description of the nature of project schedule and its contents would be in place here.

Project Schedule is the complete or comprehensive document for project time management. It shows the planned start date, planned completion date and duration of each activity. Summary milestones for start and completion of a group of activities for a project phase and the entire project are also readily available. When some proprietary software for project managements are used, their special features would enable the project team to include into the project schedule document additional useful project planning details like resource calendar, resource requirements, resource costs, assumptions and constraints for individual activity. The project schedule can be presented in tabular form or any of the following graphical formats:

- *Gantt Charts*: A bar chart with horizontal bars representing important activities labeled and placed in a series of rows and the corresponding horizontal bar lengths on the date line showing the milestones for start and finish of the activities. Strictly speaking, a Gantt Chart is not supposed to show the dependency relationships or leads and lags among the activities, but Gantt Charts for Project Schedule generally include these details.
- *Project Schedule Network Diagrams*: These diagrams show the project network, the activities, the precedence or succeeding dependency relationship of the activities and the critical path for the network. Each activity is represented by a rectangular block and the block labeled to show the activity code, activity duration, scheduled start and completion dates, the slack between the earliest and latest start dates and whether it lies on the critical path for the project.

Proprietary project management software would have several additional features, which would include provisions for activity attributes notes, resource calendars and resource assignments to activities, resource costs and even earned value management calculations. In addition, tracking the project status for monitoring and controlling the project schedule in graphical forms could also be facilitated by the software.

Other outputs of the process are *Schedule Data, Project Calendars*, and *Up-dates of Project Management Plan* and *Project Documents*. The nature of other outputs is self-explanatory; *Schedule Data* is described below.

Schedule Data: This would include besides the basic milestones for project activities, activity list, activity attributes, activity duration estimates, resource requirements, assumptions and constraints in developing the schedule, and provision of contingency reserve or time buffer to manage schedule.

2.7 CONTROL SCHEDULE

Control Schedule is the process of monitoring the status of the project and managing changes to the project schedule baseline to achieve the plan. (PMBOK® Guide, 5th Edition)

Control Schedule is the seventh of the time management processes and the only one in the monitoring and controlling group. It involves tracking the actual status of the project activities and ensuring that the project activities adhere to the planned project schedule.

The typical activities carried out for this process include:

- Tracking the progress of all project activities
- Determining the schedule variance and taking corrective steps when the actual work performance lags behind the planned schedule (using fast tracking or activity crashing techniques)
- Anticipate schedule delays and proactively manage the project changes and risks to keep the project schedule on the track
- Forecasting the milestones for completion of the critical activities and the whole project

Inputs

Like all monitoring and controlling processes, the inputs for the process are the planned standard for comparison (*Project Management Plan* and *Project Schedule* in this case) and the actual status on the control date (*Work Performance Data* in this case). The existing formal and informal procedures and practices for controlling project schedule (a part of *Organizational Process Assets*) are a helpful input.

Tools and Techniques

There are three types of tools are necessary for Control Schedule Process: tracking the project status and finding the variances, taking proactive measures to keep and bring the project schedule on track and the project management software to facilitate the data record and its graphical presentation. These three types of tools are briefly described below:

- *Schedule Variance Analysis* and *Performance Reviews* are tools related to data handling and helping to know the exact schedule status and assess the need for corrective action.

Performance reviews measure, compare and analyze the schedule performance with the schedule base line. Various techniques are used for analyzing performance, which include:

- Trend Analysis
- Critical path Method
- Critical Chain Method
- Earned Value management

- *Resource Leveling, Adjusting Leads and Lags*, and *Schedule Compression Techniques* form the project manager's arsenal for pro-active correction measures for controlling schedule.
- *Project Management Software* – (proprietary software) would help to facilitate recording schedule data and its graphical representation.
- *Simulation, What-if-Analysis and similar modeling techniques* can also be applied for Schedule Control.

Outputs

Work Performance Information – The schedule variance and schedule variance index (using the Earned Value Management technique) is the important output.

Schedule Forecasts – They are developed from the analysis of data acquired for work performance.

Change Requests – Based on forecasts developed from schedule variance analysis, change request may be originated to bring back the project schedule on track.

Updates of Project Documents (particularly the schedule and cost baselines) and *Forecast for Project Completion* are other outputs from the process.

CASE 6.1

Advantage Energy Technology Data Center Migration*

Brian Smith, network administrator at Advanced Energy Technology (AET), has been given the responsibility of implementing the migration of a large data center to a new office location. Careful planning is needed because AET operates in the highly competitive petroleum industry. AET is one of five national software companies that provide an accounting and business management package for oil jobbers and gasoline distributors. A few years ago, AET jumped into the "application service provider" world. Their large data center provides clients with remote access to AET's complete suite of application software systems. Traditionally, one of AET's primary competitive advantages has been the company's trademark IT reliability. Due to the complexity of this project, Brian will have to use a parallel method of implementation. Although this will increase project costs, a parallel approach is essential if reliability is not to be compromised.

---

* Prepared by James Moran, a project management instructor at the College of Business, Oregon State University.

Currently, AET's data center is located on the second floor of a renovated old bank building in downtown Corvallis, Oregon. The company is moving to a new, one-level building located in the recently developed industrial complex at the Corvallis International Airport. On February 1, Brian is formally assigned the task by the Vice-President of Operations, Dan Whitmore, with the following guidelines:

- From start to finish, it is anticipated the entire project will take three to four months to complete.
- It is essential that AET's 235 clients suffer no downtime.

Whitmore advises Brian to come back to the Executive Committee on February 15, with a presentation on the scope of the project that includes costs, "first-cut" timeline, and proposed project team members.

Brian had some preliminary discussions with some of AET's managers and directors from each of the functional departments and then arranged for a full-day scope meeting on February 4 with a few of the managers and technical representatives from operations, systems, facilities, and applications. The scope team determined the following:

- Three to four months is a feasible project timeline and first-cut cost estimate is $80,000–$90,000 (this includes the infrastructure upgrade of the new site).
- Critical to the "no-downtime" requirement is the need to completely rely on AET's remote disaster recovery "hot" site for full functionality.
- Brian will serve as project manager of a team consisting of one team member each from facilities, operations/systems, operations/telecommunications, systems & applications, and customer service.

Brian's Executive Committee report was positively received and, after a few modifications and recommendations, he was formally charged with responsibility for the project. Brian recruited his team and scheduled their first team meeting (March 1) as the initial task of his project planning process.

Once the initial meeting is conducted Brian can hire the contractors to renovate the new data center. During this time Brian will figure out how to design the network. Brian estimates that screening and hiring a contractor will take about one week and that the network design will take about two weeks. The new center requires a new ventilation system. The manufacturer's requirements include an ambient temperature of 67 degrees to keep all of the data servers running at optimal speeds. The ventilation system has a lead time of three weeks. Brian will also need to order new racks to hold the servers, switches, and other network devices. The racks have a two-week delivery time.

The data center supervisor requested that Brian replace all of the old power supplies and data cables. Brian will need to order these as well. Because Brian has a great relationship with the vendor, they guarantee that it will take only one week lead time for the power supplies and the data cables. Once the new ventilation system and racks arrive, Brian can begin installing them. It will take one week to install the ventilation system and three weeks to install the racks. The renovation of the new data center can begin as soon as the contractors have been hired. The contractors tell Brian that construction will take 20 days. Once the construction begins and after Brian installs the ventilation system and racks, the city inspector must approve the construction of the raised floor.

The city inspector will take two days to approve the infrastructure. After the city inspection and after the new power supplies and cables have arrived, Brian can install the power supplies and run the cables. Brian estimates that it will take five days to install the power supplies and one week to run all of the data cables. Before Brian can assign an actual date for taking the network off line and switching to the hot remote site, he must get approval from each of the functional units ("Switchover Approval"). Meetings with each of the functional units will require one week. During this time he can initiate a power check to ensure that each of the racks has sufficient voltage. This will require only one day.

Upon completion of the power check, he can take one week to install his test servers. The test servers will test all of the primary network functions and act as a safeguard before the network is taken off line. The batteries must be charged, ventilation installed, and test servers up and running before management can be assured that the new infrastructure is safe, which will take two days. Then they will sign off the Primary Systems check, taking one day of intense meetings. They will also set an official date for the network move.

Brian is happy that everything has gone well thus far and is convinced that the move will go just as smoothly. Now that an official date is set, the network will be shut down for a day. Brian must move all of the network components to the new data center. Brian will do the move over the weekend—two days—when user traffic is at low point.

ASSIGNMENT

1. Generate a priority matrix for AET's system move.
2. Develop a WBS for Brian's project. Include duration (days) and predecessors.
3. Using a project planning tool, generate a network diagram for this project.

   Note: Base your plan on the following guidelines: eight-hour days, five-day weeks except for when Brian moves the network components over a weekend, no holiday breaks, March 1, 2010, is the project start date. Ordering Ventilation System, New Racks, and Power Supplies/Cables takes only one actual day of work. The remaining days are the time necessary for the vendors to fill and ship the order to Brian. So use Finish to Start lags here. Assume that five days after the start of the Renovation of the Data Center that the raised floor will be ready for inspection (a Start-to-Start lag).

CASE 6.2

Greendale Stadium Case

The G&E Company is preparing a bid to build the new 47,000 seat Greendale baseball stadium. The construction must start July 1, 2011, and be completed in time for the start of the 2014 season. A penalty clause of $100,000 per day of delay beyond May 20, 2014, is written into the contract.

Ben Keith, the president of the company, expressed optimism at obtaining the contract and revealed that the company could net as much as $2 million on the project. He also said if they are successful, the prospects for future projects are quite good since there is a projected renaissance in building classic ball parks with modern luxury boxes.

ASSIGNMENT

Given the information provided in Table 6.3, construct a network schedule for the stadium project and answer the following questions:

1. Will the project be able to be completed by the May 20 deadline? How long will it take?
2. What is the critical path for the project?
3. Based on the schedule would you recommend that G&E pursue this contact? Why? Include a one-page Gantt chart for the stadium schedule.

CASE APPENDIX: TECHNICAL DETAILS OF THE GREENDALE BASEBALL STADIUM

TABLE 6.3 ··
Greendale Stadium Case

ID	Activity	Duration	Predecessor(s)
1	*Baseball Stadium*		
2	Clear stadium site	70 days	—
3	Demolish building	30 days	2
4	Set up construction site	70 days	3
5	Drive support piling	120 days	2
6	Pour lower concrete bowl	120 days	5
7	Pour main concourse	120 days	3,6
8	Install playing field	90 days	3,6
9	Construct upper steel bowl	120 days	3,6
10	Install seats	140 days	7,9
11	Build luxury boxes	90 days	7,9
12	Install jumbotron	30 days	7,9
13	Stadium infrastructure	120 days	7,9
14	Construct steel canopy	75 days	10
15	Light installation	30 days	14
16	Build roof supports	90 days	6
17	Construct roof	180 days	16
18	Install roof tracks	90 days	16
19	Install roof	90 days	17,18
20	Inspection	20 days	8,11,13,15,19

The baseball stadium is an outdoor structure with a retractable roof. The project begins with clearing the site, an activity that lasts 70 days. Once the site is clear, work can start simultaneously on the structure itself and demolishing an adjacent building site. This demolition is necessary to create a construction stage for storing materials and equipment. It will take 30 days to demolish the buildings and another 70 days to set up the construction site.

The work on the stadium begins by driving 160 support pilings, which will take 120 days. Next comes the pouring of the lower concrete bowl (120 days). Once this is done and the construction site has been set up, then the pouring of the main concourse (120 days), the installation of the playing field (90 days), and the construction of the upper steel bowl can occur (120 days).

Once the concourse and upper bowl are completed, work can start simultaneously on building the luxury boxes (90 days), installing the seats (140 days), installing the jumbotron (30 days), and installing stadium infrastructure (120 days) which includes: bathrooms, lockers, restaurants, etc. Once the seats are installed then the steel canopy can be constructed (75 days) followed by the installation of the lights (30 days).

The retractable roof represents the most significant technical challenge to the project. Building the roof track supports (90 days) can begin after the lower concrete bowl is constructed. At this time the dimensions of the roof can be finalized and the construction of the roof at a separate site can begin (180 days). After the roof supports are completed then the roof tracks can be installed (90 days). Once the tracks and the roof are completed then the roof can be installed and made operational (90 days). Once all activities are completed it will take 20 days to inspect the stadium.

For purposes of this case assume the following:

1. The following holidays are observed: January 1, Memorial Day (last Monday in May), July 4th, Labor Day (first Monday in September), Thanksgiving Day (4th Thursday in November), December 25 and 26.
2. If a holiday falls on a Saturday then Friday will be given as an extra day off, and if it falls on a Sunday then Monday will be given as a day off.
3. The construction crew work Monday through Friday.

7

MANAGING RISK

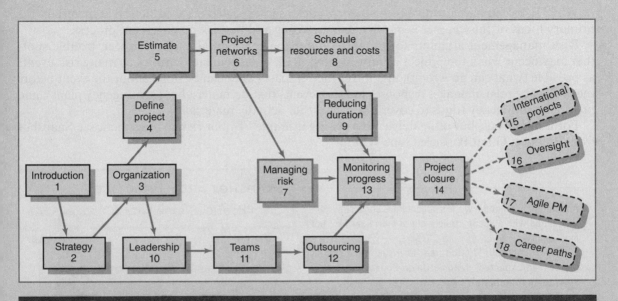

MANAGING RISK

You've got to go out on a limb sometimes because that's where the fruit is.

Will Rogers

Every project manager understands risks are inherent in projects. No amount of planning can overcome *risk,* or the inability to control chance events. In the context of projects, **risk** is an uncertain event or condition that, if it occurs, has a positive or negative effect on project objectives. A risk has a cause and, if it occurs, a consequence. For example, a cause may be a flu virus or change in scope requirements. The event is that team members get stricken with the flu or the product has to be redesigned. If either of these uncertain events occurs, it will impact the cost, schedule, and quality of the project.

Some potential risk events can be identified before the project starts—such as equipment malfunction or change in technical requirements. Risks can be anticipated consequences, like schedule slippages or cost overruns. Risks can be beyond imagination like the 2008 financial meltdown.

While risks can have positive consequences such as unexpected price reduction in materials, the primary focus of this chapter is on what can go wrong and the risk management process.

Risk management attempts to recognize and manage potential and unforeseen trouble spots that may occur when the project is implemented. Risk management identifies as many risk events as possible (what can go wrong), minimizes their impact (what can be done about the event before the project begins), manages responses to those events that do materialize (contingency plans), and provides contingency funds to cover risk events that actually materialize.

For a humorous, but ultimately embarrassing example of poor risk management see Snapshot from Practice: Giant Popsicle Gone Wrong.

SNAPSHOT FROM PRACTICE
Giant Popsicle Gone Wrong*

An attempt to erect the world's largest Popsicle in New York City ended with a scene straight out of a disaster film, but much stickier.

The 25-foot-tall, $17\frac{1}{2}$-ton treat of frozen juice melted faster than expected, flooding Union Square in downtown Manhattan with kiwi-strawberry–flavored fluid.

Bicyclists wiped out in the stream of goo. Pedestrians slipped. Traffic was, well, frozen. Firefighters closed off several streets and used hoses to wash away the thick, sweet slime.

The Snapple Company, a leading maker of soft beverages, had been trying to promote a new line of frozen treats by setting a record for the world's largest Popsicle, but called off the stunt before the frozen giant was pulled fully upright by a construction crane.

Authorities said they were worried the $2\frac{1}{2}$-story popsicle would collapse.

© Brian Smith/Zuma Press, Inc.

Organizers were not sure why it melted so quickly. "We planned for it. We just didn't expect for it to happen so fast," said Snapple spokeswoman Lauren Radcliffe. She said the company would offer to pay the city for the clean-up costs.

* Associated Press, June 23, 2005.

RISK MANAGEMENT PROCESS

Figure 7.1 presents a graphic model of the risk management challenge. The chances of a risk event occurring (e.g., an error in time estimates, cost estimates, or design technology) are greatest during the early stages of a project. This is when uncertainty is highest and many questions remain unanswered. As the project progresses toward completion, risk declines as the answers to critical issues (Will the technology work? Is the timeline feasible?) are resolved. The cost impact of a risk event, however, increases over the life of the project. For example, the risk event of a design flaw occurring after a prototype has been made has a greater cost or time impact than if the flaw were discovered during the planning phase of the project.

The cost of mismanaged risk control early on in the project is exemplified by the ill-fated 1999 NASA Mars Climate Orbiter. Investigations revealed that Lockheed Martin botched the design of critical navigation software. While flight computers on the ground did calculations based on pounds of thrust per second, the spacecraft's computer software used metric units called newtons. A check to see if the values were compatible was never done.

"Our check and balances processes did not catch an error like this that should have been caught," said Ed Weiler, NASA's associate administrator for space science. "That is the bottom line" (*Orlando Sentinel,* 1999). If the error had been discovered early the correction would have been relatively simple and inexpensive. Instead the error was never discovered, and after the nine-month journey to the Red Planet, the $125-million probe approached Mars at too low an altitude and burned up in the planet's atmosphere. Following the 1999 debacle, NASA instituted a more robust risk management system which has produced a string of successful missions to Mars, including the dramatic landing of the *Curiosity* rover in August 2012.[1]

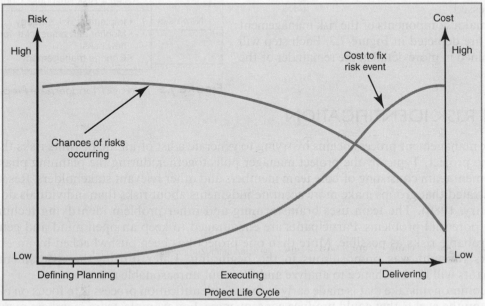

FIGURE 7.1 *Risk Event Graph*

---

[1] E. Landau, "Mars Landing Went 'Flawlessly,' Scientists Say," *CNN.com,* accessed August 14, 2012.

Risk management is a proactive approach rather than reactive. It is a preventive process designed to ensure that surprises are reduced and that negative consequences associated with undesirable events are minimized. It also prepares the project manager to take action when a time, cost, and/or technical advantage is possible. Successful management of project risk gives the project manager better control over the future and can significantly improve chances of reaching project objectives on time, within budget, and meeting required technical (functional) performance.

The sources of project risks are unlimited. There are sources external to the organization, such as inflation, market acceptance, exchange rates, and government regulations. In practice, these risk events are often referred to as "threats" to differentiate them from those that are not within the project manager's or team's responsibility area. (Later we will see budgets for such risk events are placed in a "management reserve" contingency budget.) Since such external risks are usually considered before the decision to go ahead with the project, they will be excluded from the discussion of project risks. However, external risks are extremely important and must be addressed.

The major components of the risk management process are depicted in Figure 7.2. Each step will be examined in more detail in the remainder of the chapter.

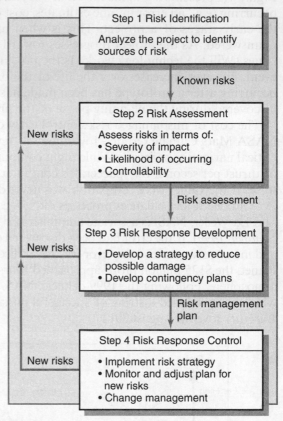

FIGURE 7.2 *The Risk Management Process*

STEP 1: RISK IDENTIFICATION

The risk management process begins by trying to generate a list of all the possible risks that could affect the project. Typically the project manager pulls together, during the planning phase, a risk management team consisting of core team members and other relevant stakeholders. Research has demonstrated that groups make more accurate judgments about risks than individuals do (Snizek and Henry, 1980). The team uses brainstorming and other problem identifying techniques to identify potential problems. Participants are encouraged to keep an open mind and generate as many probable risks as possible. More than one project has been bushwhacked by an event that members thought was preposterous in the beginning. Later during the assessment phase, participants will have a chance to analyze and filter out unreasonable risks.

One common mistake that is made early in the risk identification process is to focus on objectives and not on the events that could produce consequences. For example, team members may identify failing to meet schedule as a major risk. What they need to focus on are the events that could cause this to happen (i.e., poor estimates, adverse weather, shipping delays, etc.). Only by focusing on actual events can potential solutions be found.

Organizations use **risk breakdown structures** (RBSs) in conjunction with work breakdown structures (WBSs) to help management teams identify and eventually analyze risks. Figure 7.3 provides a generic example of an RBS. The focus at the beginning should be on risks that can affect the whole project as opposed to a specific section of the project or network. For example, the discussion of funding may lead the team to identify the possibility of the project budget being cut after the project has started as a significant risk event. Likewise, when discussing the market the team may identify responding to new product releases by competitors as a risk event.

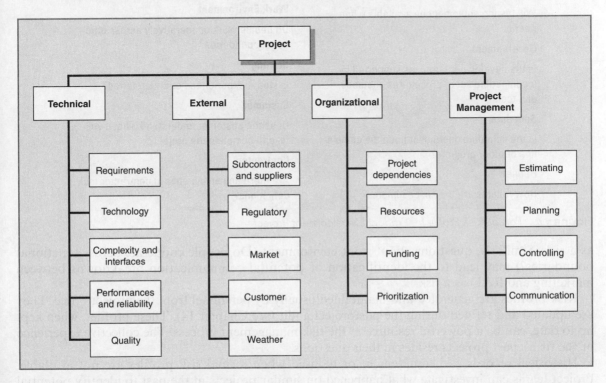

FIGURE 7.3 *The Risk Breakdown Structure (RBS)*

After the macro risks have been identified, specific areas can be checked. An effective tool for identifying specific risks is the work breakdown structure. Use of the RBS reduces the chance a risk event will be missed. On large projects multiple risk teams are organized around specific deliverables and submit their risk management reports to the project manager.

A risk profile is another useful tool. A **risk profile** is a list of questions that address traditional areas of uncertainty on a project. These questions have been developed and refined from previous, similar projects. Figure 7.4 provides a partial example of a risk profile.

Good risk profiles, like RBSs, are tailored to the type of project in question. For example, building an information system is different from building a new car. They are organization specific. Risk profiles recognize the unique strengths and weaknesses of the firm. Finally, risk profiles address both technical and management risks. For example, the profile shown in Figure 7.4 asks questions about design such as, Does the design depend upon unrealistic assumptions? The questions may lead the team to identify that the technology will not work under extreme conditions

Technical Requirements	**Quality**
Are the requirements stable?	Are quality considerations built into the design?
Design	
Does the design depend on unrealistic or optimistic assumptions?	**Management**
	Do people know who has authority for what?
Testing	
Will testing equipment be available when needed?	**Work Environment**
	Do people work cooperatively across functional boundaries?
Development	
Is the development process supported by a compatible set of procedures, methods, and tools?	**Staffing**
	Is staff inexperienced or understaffed?
	Customer
Schedule	Does the customer understand what it will take to complete the project?
Is the schedule dependent upon the completion of other projects?	
	Contractors
Budget	Are there any ambiguities in contractor task definitions?
How reliable are the cost estimates?	

FIGURE 7.4   *Partial Risk Profile for Product Development Project*

as a risk. Similarly, questions about work environment (Do people cooperate across functional boundaries?) may lead to the identification of potential communication breakdowns between marketing and R&D as a risk.

Risk profiles are generated and maintained usually by personnel from the project office. They are updated and refined during the postproject audit (see Chapter 14). These profiles, when kept up to date, can be a powerful resource in the risk management process. The collective experience of the firm's past projects resides in their questions.

Historical records can complement or be used when formal risk profiles are not available. Project teams can investigate what happened on similar projects in the past to identify potential risks. For example, a project manager can check the on-time performance of selected vendors to gauge the threat of shipping delays. IT project managers can access "best practices" papers detailing other companies' experiences converting software systems. Inquiries should not be limited to recorded data. Savvy project managers tap the wisdom of others by seeking the advice of veteran project managers.

The risk identification process should not be limited to just the core team. Input from customers, sponsors, subcontractors, vendors, and other stakeholders should be solicited. Relevant stakeholders can be formally interviewed or included on the risk management team. Not only do these players have a valuable perspective, but by involving them in the risk management process they also become more committed to project success.[2]

One of the keys to success in risk identification is attitude. While a "can do" attitude is essential during implementation, project managers have to encourage critical thinking when it comes to risk identification. The goal is to find potential problems before they happen.

---

[2] The Delphi Method (see p. 136) is a popular technique for involving stakeholders.

The RBS and risk profiles are useful tools for making sure no stones are left unturned. At the same time, when done well the number of risks identified can be overwhelming and a bit discouraging. Initial optimism can be replaced with griping and cries of "what have we gotten ourselves into?" It is important that project managers set the right tone and complete the risk management process so members regain confidence in themselves and the project.

STEP 2: RISK ASSESSMENT

Step 1 produces a list of potential risks. Not all of these risks deserve attention. Some are trivial and can be ignored, while others pose serious threats to the welfare of the project. Managers have to develop methods for sifting through the list of risks, eliminating inconsequential or redundant ones and stratifying worthy ones in terms of importance and need for attention.

Scenario analysis is the easiest and most commonly used technique for analyzing risks. Team members assess the significance of each risk event in terms of:

- Probability of the event.
- Impact of the event.

Simply stated, risks need to be evaluated in terms of the likelihood the event is going to occur and the impact or consequences of its occurrence. The risk of a project manager being struck by lightning at a work site would have major negative impact on the project, but the likelihood is so low it is not worthy of consideration. Conversely, people do change jobs, so an event like the loss of key project personnel would have not only an adverse impact but also a high likelihood of occurring in some organizations. If so, then it would be wise for that organization to be proactive and mitigate this risk by developing incentive schemes for retaining specialists and/or engaging in cross-training to reduce the impact of turnover.

The quality and credibility of the risk analysis process requires that different levels of risk probabilities and impacts be defined. These definitions vary and should be tailored to the specific nature and needs of the project. For example, a relatively simple scale ranging from "very unlikely" to "almost certainly" may suffice for one project, whereas another project may use more precise numerical probabilities (e.g., 0.1, 0.3, 0.5, . . .).

Impact scales can be a bit more problematic since adverse risks affect project objectives differently. For example, a component failure may cause only a slight delay in project schedule but a major increase in project cost. If controlling cost is a high priority, then the impact would be severe. If, on the other hand, time is more critical than cost, then the impact would be minor.

Because impact ultimately needs to be assessed in terms of project priorities, different kinds of impact scales are used. Some scales may simply use rank-order descriptors, such as "low," "moderate," "high," and "very high," whereas others use numeric weights (e.g., 1–10). Some may focus on the project in general while others focus on specific project objectives. The risk management team needs to establish up front what distinguishes a 1 from a 3 or "moderate" impact from "severe" impact. Figure 7.5 provides an example of how impact scales could be defined given the project objectives of cost, time, scope, and quality.

Documentation of scenario analyses can be seen in various risk assessment forms used by companies. Figure 7.6 is a partial example of a risk assessment form used on an IS project involving the upgrade from Windows 7 to Windows 8.

Relative or Numerical Scale					
Project Objective	1 Very Low	2 Low	3 Moderate	4 High	5 Very High
Cost	Insignificant cost increase	< 10% cost increase	10–20% cost increase	20–40% cost increase	> 40% cost increase
Time	Insignificant time increase	< 5% time increase	5–10% time increase	10–20% time increase	> 20% time increase
Scope	Scope decrease barely noticeable	Minor areas of scope affected	Major areas of scope affected	Scope reduction unacceptable to sponsor	Project end item is effectively useless
Quality	Quality degradation barely noticeable	Only very demanding applications are affected	Quality reduction requires sponsor approval	Quality reduction unacceptable to sponsor	Project end item is effectively useless

FIGURE 7.5 *Defined Conditions for Impact Scales of a Risk on Major Project Objectives (Examples for negative impacts only)*

Risk Event	Likelihood	Impact	Detection Difficulty	When
Interface problems	4	4	4	Conversion
System freezing	2	5	5	Start-up
User backlash	4	3	3	Postinstallation
Hardware malfunctioning	1	5	5	Installation

FIGURE 7.6 *Risk Assessment Form*

Notice that in addition to evaluating the severity and probablity of risk events the team also assesses when the event might occur and its detection difficulty. Detection difficulty is a measure of how easy it would be to detect that the event was going to occur in time to take mitigating action, that is, how much warning would we have? So in the Windows 8 conversion example, the detection scale would range from 5 = no warning to 1 = lots of time to react.

Often organizations find it useful to categorize the severity of different risks into some form of risk assessment matrix. The matrix is typically structured around the impact and likelihood of the risk event. For example, the risk matrix presented in Figure 7.7 consists of a 5 × 5 array of elements with each element representing a different set of impact and likelihood values.

FIGURE 7.7 *Risk Severity Matrix*

The matrix is divided into red, yellow, and green zones representing major, moderate, and minor risks, respectively. The red zone is centered on the top right corner of the matrix (high impact/high likelihood), while the green zone is centered on the bottom left corner (low impact/low likelihood). The moderate risk, yellow zone extends down the middle of the matrix. Since impact is generally considered more important than likelihood (a 10 percent chance of losing $1,000,000 is usually considered a more severe risk than a 90 percent chance of losing $1,000), the red zone (major risk) extends farther down the high impact column.

Using the Windows 8 project again as an example, interface problems and system freezing would be placed in the red zone (major risk), while user backlash and hardware malfunctioning would be placed in the yellow zone (moderate risk).

The **risk severity matrix** provides a basis for prioritizing which risks to address. Red zone risks receive first priority followed by yellow zone risks. Green zone risks are typically considered inconsequential and ignored unless their status changes.

Failure Mode and Effects Analysis (FMEA) extends the risk severity matrix by including ease of detection in the equation:

$$\text{Impact} \times \text{Probability} \times \text{Detection} = \text{Risk Value}$$

Each of the three dimensions is rated according to a five-point scale. For example, detection is defined as the ability of the project team to discern that the risk event is imminent. A score of 1 would be given if even a chimpanzee could spot the risk coming. The highest detection score of 5 would be given to events that could only be discovered after it is too late (i.e., system freezing). Similar anchored scales would be applied for severity of impact and the probability of the event occurring. The weighting of the risks is then based on their overall score. For example, a risk with an impact in the "1" zone with a very low probability and an easy detection score might score a 1 ($1 \times 1 \times 1 = 1$). Conversely, a high-impact risk with a high probability and impossible to detect would score 125 ($5 \times 5 \times 5 = 125$). This broad range of numerical scores allows for easy stratification of risk according to overall significance.

No assessment scheme is absolutely foolproof. For example, the weakness of the FMEA approach is that a risk event rated Impact = 1, Probability = 5, and Detection = 5 would receive the same weighted score as an event rated Impact = 5, Probability = 5, and Detection = 1! This underscores the importance of *not* treating risk assessment as simply an exercise in mathematics. There is no substitute for thoughtful discussion of key risk events.

Probability Analysis

There are many statistical techniques available to the project manager that can assist in assessing project risk. Decision trees have been used to assess alternative courses of action using expected values. Statistical variations of net present value (NPV) have been used to assess cash flow risks in projects. Correlations between past projects' cash flow and S-curves (cumulative project cost curve—baseline—over the life of the project) have been used to assess cash flow risks.

PERT (program evaluation and review technique) and PERT simulation can be used to review activity and project risk. PERT and related techniques take a more macro perspective by looking at overall cost and schedule risks. Here the focus is not on individual events but on the likelihood the project will be completed on time and within budget. These methods are useful in assessing the overall risk of the project and the need for such things as contingency funds, resources, and time. The use of PERT simulation is increasing because it uses the same data required for PERT, and software to perform the simulation is readily available.

Basically PERT simulation assumes a statistical distribution (range between optimistic and pessimistic) for each activity duration; it then simulates the network (perhaps over 1,000 simulations) using a random number generator. The outcome is the relative probability, called a criticality index, of an activity becoming critical under the many different, possible activity durations for each activity. PERT simulation also provides a list of potential critical paths and their respective probabilities of occurring. Having this information available can greatly facilitate identifying and assessing schedule risk. (See Appendix 7.1 at the end of this chapter for a more detailed description and discussion.)

STEP 3: RISK RESPONSE DEVELOPMENT

When a risk event is identified and assessed, a decision must be made concerning which response is appropriate for the specific event. Responses to risk can be classified as mitigating, avoiding, transferring, sharing, or retaining.

Mitigating Risk

Reducing risk is usually the first alternative considered. There are basically two strategies for mitigating risk: (1) reduce the likelihood that the event will occur and/or (2) reduce the impact that the adverse event would have on the project. Most risk teams focus first on reducing the likelihood of risk events since, if successful, this may eliminate the need to consider the potentially costly second strategy.

Testing and prototyping are frequently used to prevent problems from surfacing later in a project. An example of testing can be found in an information systems project. The project team was responsible for installing a new operating system in their parent company. Before implementing the project, the team tested the new system on a smaller isolated network. By doing so they discovered a variety of problems and were able to come up with solutions prior to implementation. The team still encountered problems with the installation but the number and severity were greatly reduced.

Often identifying the root causes of an event is useful. For example, the fear that a vendor will be unable to supply customized components on time may be attributable to (1) poor vendor relationships, (2) design miscommunication, and (3) lack of motivation. As a result of this analysis the project manager may decide to take his counterpart to lunch to clear the air, invite the vendor to attend design meetings, and restructure the contract to include incentives for on-time delivery.

Other examples of reducing the probability of risks occurring are scheduling outdoor work during the summer months, investing in up-front safety training, and choosing high-quality materials and equipment.

When the concerns are that duration and costs have been underestimated, managers will augment estimates to compensate for the uncertainties. It is common to use a ratio between old and new project to adjust time or cost. The ratio typically serves as a constant. For example, if past projects have taken 10 minutes per line of computer code, a constant of 1.10 (which represents a 10 percent increase) would be used for the proposed project time estimates because the new project is more difficult than prior projects.

An alternative mitigation strategy is to reduce the impact of the risk if it occurs. For example, a bridge-building project illustrates risk reduction. A new bridge project for a coastal port was to use an innovative, continuous cement-pouring process developed by an Australian firm to save large sums of money and time. The major risk was that the continuous pouring process for each major section of the bridge could not be interrupted. Any interruption would require that the whole cement section (hundreds of cubic yards) be torn down and started over. An assessment of possible risks centered on delivery of the cement from the cement factory. Trucks could be delayed, or the factory could break down. Such risks would result in tremendous rework costs and delays. Risk was reduced by having two additional portable cement plants built nearby on different highways within 20 miles of the bridge project in case the main factory supply was interrupted. These two portable plants carried raw materials for a whole bridge section, and extra trucks were on immediate standby each time continuous pouring was required. Similar risk reduction scenarios are apparent in system and software development projects where parallel innovation processes are used in case one fails.

The Dome to Dust Snapshot from Practice details the steps Controlled Demolition took to minimize damage when they imploded the Seattle Kingdome.

Avoiding Risk

Risk avoidance is changing the project plan to eliminate the risk or condition. Although it is impossible to eliminate all risk events, some specific risks may be avoided before you launch the

On March 26, 2000, the largest concrete domed structure in the world was reduced to a pile of rubble in a dramatic implosion lasting less than 20 seconds. According to Mark Loizeaux, whose Maryland-based Controlled Demolition Inc. was hired to bring the 24-year-old Seattle Kingdome down, "We don't blow things up. We use explosives as an engine, but gravity is the catalyst that will bring it down."

Destroying the Kingdome was the most complicated of the 7,000 demolitions Loizeaux's company has undertaken. Nearly three months of preparations were needed to implode the dome at a total cost of $9 million. The Kingdome was considered to be one of the strongest structures in the world containing over 25,000 tons of concrete with each of its 40 vaulted ribs incorporating seven lengths of two-and-one-quarter-inch reinforcing steel bar.

Strands of orange detonating cord—basically dynamite in a string that explodes at the lightning pace of 24,000 feet per second— connected six pielike divisions of the Kingdome to a nearby control center.

© Tim Matsui/Getty Images

Throughout each section, Controlled Demolition workers drilled nearly 1,000 holes and packed them with high-velocity gelatin explosives the size of hot dogs. Large charges were placed about one-third of the way up each dome rib, smaller charges were put farther up the ribs. When the detonation button was pushed, blasting caps set off a chain reaction of explosions in each section reducing the stadium to rubble.

While the actual implosion was a technical tour-de-force, risk management was a critical part of the project's success. To minimize damage to surrounding buildings, the explosive charges were wrapped in a layer of chain-link fencing covered with thick sheets of geotextile polypropylene fabric to contain flying concrete. Nearby buildings were protected in various manners depending on the structure and proximity to the Dome. Measures included sealing air-handling units, taping seams on doors and windows, covering floors and windows with plywood and draping reinforced polyethylene sheeting around the outside.

To help absorb the impact, air-conditioning units removed from the interior were stacked with other material to create a barrier around the perimeter of the work area.

Hundreds of police officers and security personnel were used to cordon off an area extending roughly 1,000 feet from the Dome from overzealous spectators. Traffic was closed for a larger area. Accommodations were provided for people and pets who lived within the restricted zone.

Eight water trucks, eight sweeper units, and more than 100 workers were deployed immediately after the blast to control dust and begin the cleanup.

As a side note, one-third of the concrete will be crushed and used in the foundation of a new $430 million outdoor football stadium which is being built in its place. The rest of the concrete will be carted away and used in roadbeds and foundations throughout the Seattle area.

* *New York Times*—Sunday Magazine (March 19, 2000); *Seattle Times* (March 27, 2000) website.

project. For example, adopting proven technology instead of experimental technology can eliminate technical failure. Choosing an Australian supplier as opposed to an Indonesian supplier would virtually eliminate the chance that political unrest would disrupt the supply of critical materials. Likewise, one could eliminate the risk of choosing the wrong software by developing web applications using both ASAP.NET and PHP. Choosing to move a concert indoors would eliminate the threat of inclement weather.

Transferring Risk

Passing risk to another party is common; this transfer does not change risk. Passing risk to another party almost always results in paying a premium for this exemption. Fixed-price contracts are the classic example of transferring risk from an owner to a contractor. The contractor understands his or her firm will pay for any risk event that materializes; therefore, a monetary risk factor is added to the contract bid price. Before deciding to transfer risk, the owner should decide which party can best control activities that would lead to the risk occurring. Also, is the contractor capable of absorbing the risk? Clearly identifying and documenting responsibility for absorbing risk is imperative.

Another more obvious way to transfer risk is insurance. However, in most cases this is impractical because defining the project risk event and conditions to an insurance broker who is unfamiliar with the project is difficult and usually expensive. Of course, low-probability and high-consequence risk events such as acts of God are more easily defined and insured. Performance bonds, warranties, and guarantees are other financial instruments used to transfer risk.

On large, international construction projects like petrochemical plants and oil refineries, host countries are insisting on contracts that enforce Build-Own-Operate-Transfer (BOOT) provisions. Here the prime project organization is expected not only to build the facility, but also to take over ownership until its operation capacity has been proven and all the debugging has occurred before final transfer of ownership to the client. In such cases, the host country has transferred financial risk of ownership until the project has been completed and capabilities proven.

Retaining Risk

In some cases a conscious decision is made to accept the risk of an event occurring. Some risks are so large it is not feasible to consider transferring or reducing the event (e.g., an earthquake or flood). The project owner assumes the risk because the chance of such an event occurring is slim. In other cases risks identified in the budget reserve can simply be absorbed if they materialize. The risk is retained by developing a contingency plan to implement if the risk materializes. In a few cases a risk event can be ignored and a cost overrun accepted should the risk event occur.

The more effort given to risk response before the project begins, the better the chances are for minimizing project surprises. Knowing that the response to a risk event will be retained, transferred, or mitigated greatly reduces stress and uncertainty. Again, control is possible with this structured approach.

CONTINGENCY PLANNING

A **contingency plan** is an alternative plan that will be used if a possible foreseen risk event becomes a reality. The contingency plan represents actions that will reduce or mitigate the negative impact of the risk event. A key distinction between a risk response and a contingency plan is that a response is part of the actual implementation plan and action is taken before the risk can materialize, while a contingency plan is not part of the initial implementation plan and only goes into effect after the risk is recognized.

Like all plans, the contingency plan answers the questions of what, where, when, and how much action will take place. The absence of a contingency plan, when a risk event occurs, can cause a manager to delay or postpone the decision to implement a remedy. This postponement can lead to panic, and acceptance of the first remedy suggested. Such after-the-event decision making under pressure can be potentially dangerous and costly. Contingency planning evaluates alternative remedies for possible foreseen events before the risk event occurs and selects the best plan among alternatives. This early contingency planning facilitates a smooth transition to the remedy or work-around plan. The availability of a contingency plan can significantly increase the chances for project success.

Conditions for activating the implementation of the contingency plan should be decided and clearly documented. The plan should include a cost estimate and identify the source of funding. All parties affected should agree to the contingency plan and have authority to make commitments. Because implementation of a contingency plan embodies disruption in the sequence of work, all contingency plans should be communicated to team members so that surprise and resistance are minimized.

Here is an example: A high-tech niche computer company intends to introduce a new "platform" product at a very specific target date. The project's 47 teams all agree delays will not be acceptable. Their contingency plans for two large component suppliers demonstrate how seriously risk management is viewed. One supplier's plant sits on the San Andreas Fault, which is prone to earthquakes. The contingency plan has an alternative supplier, who is constantly updated, producing a replica of the component in another plant. Another key supplier in Toronto, Canada, presents a delivery risk on their due date because of potential bad weather. This contingency plan calls for a chartered plane (already contracted to be on standby) if overland transportation presents a delay problem. To outsiders these plans must seem a bit extreme, but in high-tech industries where time to market is king, risks of identified events are taken seriously.

Risk response matrices such as the one shown in Figure 7.8 are useful for summarizing how the project team plans to manage risks that have been identified. Again, the Windows 8 project is used

Risk Event	Response	Contingency Plan	Trigger	Who is Responsible
Interface problems	Mitigate: Test prototype	Work around until help comes	Not solved within 24 hours	Nils
System freezing	Mitigate: Test prototype	Reinstall OS	Still frozen after one hour	Emmylou
User backlash	Mitigate: Prototype demonstration	Increase staff support	Call from top management	Eddie
Equipment malfunctions	Mitigate: Select reliable vendor Transfer: Warranty	Order replacement	Equipment fails	Jim

FIGURE 7.8 *Risk Response Matrix*

to illustrate this kind of matrix. The first step is to identify whether to reduce, share, transfer, or accept the risk. The team decided to reduce the chances of the system freezing by experimenting with a prototype of the system. Prototype experimentation not only allows them to identify and fix conversion "bugs" before the actual installation, but it also yields information that could be useful in enhancing acceptance by end-users. The project team is then able to identify and document changes between the old and new system that will be incorporated in the training the users receive. The risk of equipment malfunctioning is transferred by choosing a reliable supplier with a strong warranty program.

The next step is to identify contingency plans in case the risk still occurs. For example, if interface problems prove insurmountable, then the team would attempt a work-around until vendor experts arrived to help solve the problem. If the system freezes after installation, the team will first try to reinstall the software. If user dissatisfaction is high, then the IS department will provide more staff support. If the team is unable to get reliable equipment from the original supplier, then it will order a different brand from a second dealer. The team also needs to discuss and agree what would "trigger" implementation of the contingency plan. In the case of the system freezing, the trigger is not being able to unfreeze the system within one hour or, in the case of user backlash, an angry call from top management. Finally, the individual responsible for monitoring the potential risk and initiating the contingency plan needs to be assigned. Smart project managers establish protocols for contingency responses before they are needed. For an example of the importance of establishing protocols see the Risk Management at the Top of the World Snapshot from Practice.

Some of the most common methods for handling risk are discussed here.

SNAPSHOT FROM PRACTICE
Risk Management at the Top of the World*

Into Thin Air, Jon Krakauer's gripping account of an ill-fated attempt to climb Mount Everest in which six climbers died, provides testimony to the risks of extreme mountain climbing. Thirteen days after the tragedy, David Breashears successfully led a film crew to the summit. Their footage can be seen in the spectacular IMAX film, *Everest.*

Accounts of Mount Everest expeditions provide insights into project risk management. First, most climbers spend more than three weeks acclimating their bodies to high-altitude conditions. Native Sherpas are used extensively to carry supplies and set up each of the four base camps that will be used during the final stages of the climb. To reduce the impact of hypoxia, lightheadness, and disorientation caused by shortage of oxygen, most climbers use oxygen masks and bottles during the final ascent. If lucky enough not to be one of the first expeditions of the season, the path to the summit should be staked out and roped by previous climbers. Climbing guides receive last-minute weather reports by radio to confirm whether the weather conditions warrant the risk. Finally, for added insurance, most climbers join their Sherpas in an elaborate *puja* ritual intended to summon the divine support of the gods before beginning their ascent.

All of these efforts pale next to the sheer physical and mental rigors of making the final climb from base camp IV to the summit. This is what climbers refer to as the "death zone" because beyond 26,000 feet the mind and body begin to quickly

© Bobby Model/National Geographic Stock/Getty Images

deteriorate despite supplemental oxygen. Under fair conditions it takes around 18 hours to make the round-trip to the top and back to the base camp. Climbers leave as early as 1:00 A.M. in order to make it back before night falls and total exhaustion sets in.

The greatest danger in climbing Mount Everest is not reaching the summit but making it back to the base camp. One out of every five climbers who make it to the summit dies during their descent. The key is establishing a contingency plan in case the climbers encounter hard going or the weather changes. Guides establish a predetermined turnaround time (i.e., 2:00 P.M.) to ensure a safe return no matter how close the climbers are to the summit. Accepting the time takes tremendous discipline. One who was caught up by time was solo climber Goran Krupp. He turned back 1,000 feet from the top after bicycling 8,000 miles from Stockholm to Katmandu!

Many lives have been lost by failing to adhere to the turnback time and pushing forward to the summit. As one climber put it, "With enough determination, any bloody idiot can get up the hill. The trick is to get back down alive."

* Jon Krakauer, *Into Thin Air* (New York: Doubleday, 1997), p. 190; Broughton Coburn, *Everest: Mountain without Mercy* (New York: National Geographic Society, 1997).

Technical Risks

Technical risks are problematic; they can often be the kind that cause the project to be shut down. What if the system or process does not work? Contingency or backup plans are made for those possibilities that are foreseen. For example, Carrier Transicold was involved in developing a new Phoenix refrigeration unit for truck-trailer applications. This new unit was to use rounded panels made of bonded metals, which at the time was new technology for Transicold. Furthermore, one of its competitors had tried unsuccessfully to incorporate similar bonded metals in their products. The project team was eager to make the new technology work, but it wasn't until the very end of the project that they were able to get the new adhesives to bond adequately to complete the project. Throughout the project, the team maintained a welded-panel fabrication approach just in case they were unsuccessful. If this contingency approach had been needed, it would have increased production costs, but the project still would have been completed on time.

In addition to backup strategies, project managers need to develop methods to quickly assess whether technical uncertainties can be resolved. The use of sophisticated CAD programs has greatly helped resolve design problems. At the same time, Smith and Reinertsen (1995), in their book *Developing Products in Half the Time,* argue that there is no substitute for making something and seeing how it works, feels, or looks. They suggest that one should first identify the high-risk technical areas, then build models or design experiments to resolve the risk as quickly as possible. By isolating and testing the key technical questions early on in a project, project feasibility can be quickly determined and necessary adjustments made such as reworking the process or in some cases closing down the project.[3]

To read how this approach was critical to securing the 2022 World Cup bid, see the Snapshot from Practice: Playing Soccer in the Desert.

Schedule Risks

Often organizations will defer the threat of a project coming in late until it surfaces. Here contingency funds are set aside to expedite or "crash" the project to get it back on track. Crashing,

[3] This is a key principle of Agile project management, which is discussed in Chapter 17.

or reducing project duration, is accomplished by shortening (compressing) one or more activities on the critical path. This comes with additional costs and risk. Techniques for managing this situation are discussed in Chapter 9. Some contingency plans can avoid costly procedures. For example, schedules can be altered by working activities in parallel or using start-to-start lag relationships. Also, using the best people for high-risk tasks can relieve or lessen the chance of some risk events occurring.

Cost Risks

Projects of long duration need some contingency for price changes—which are usually upward. The important point to remember when reviewing price is to avoid the trap of using one lump sum to cover price risks. For example, if inflation has been running about 3 percent, some managers add 3 percent for all resources used in the project. This lump-sum approach does not address exactly where price protection is needed and fails to provide for tracking and control. On cost sensitive projects, price risks should be evaluated item by item. Some purchases and contracts will not change over the life of the project. Those that may change should be identified and estimates made of the magnitude of change. This approach ensures control of the contingency funds as the project is implemented.

Funding Risks

What if the funding for the project is cut by 25 percent or completion projections indicate that costs will greatly exceed available funds? What are the chances of the project being canceled before completion? Seasoned project managers recognize that a complete risk assessment must include an evaluation of funding supply. This is especially true for publicly funded projects. Case in point was the ill-fated ARH-70 Arapaho helicopter which was being developed for the U.S. Army by BellAircraft. Over 300 million dollars had been invested to develop a new age combat and reconnaissance helicopter, when in October 2008, the Defense Department recommended that the project be canceled. The cancellation reflected a need to cut costs and a switch toward using unmanned aircraft for surveillance as well as attack missions.

Just as government projects are subject to changes in strategy and political agenda, business firms frequently undergo changes in priorities and top management. The pet projects of the new CEO replace the pet projects of the former CEO. Resources become tight and one way to fund new projects is to cancel other projects.

Severe budget cuts or lack of adequate funding can have a devastating effect on a project. Typically, when such a fate occurs, there is a need to scale back the scope of the project to what is possible. "All-or-nothing projects" are ripe targets to budget cutters. This was the case of the Arapaho helicopter once the decision was made to move away from manned reconnaissance aircraft. Here the "chunkability" of the project can be an advantage. For example, freeway projects can fall short of the original intentions but still add value for each mile completed.

On a much smaller scale, similar funding risks may exist for more mundane projects. For example, a building contractor may find that due to a sudden downturn in the stock market the owners can no longer afford to build their dream house. Or an IS consulting firm may be left empty handed when a client files for bankruptcy. In the former case the contractor may have as a contingency selling the house on the open market, while unfortunately the consulting firm will have to join the long line of creditors.

OPPORTUNITY MANAGEMENT

For the sake of brevity, this chapter has focused on negative risks—what can go wrong on a project. There is a flip side—what could go right on a project? This is commonly referred to as a positive risk or opportunity. An **opportunity** is an event that can have a positive impact on project objectives. For example, unusually favorable weather can accelerate construction work, or a drop in fuel prices may create savings that could be used to add value to a project. Essentially the same process that is used to manage negative risks is applied to positive risks. Opportunities are identified, assessed in terms of likelihood and impact, responses are determined, and even contingency plans and funds can be established to take advantage of the opportunity if it occurs.

---

[4] PMBOK, 5th ed. (Newton Square, PA: PMI, 2013), pp. 345–6.

The major exception between managing negative risks and opportunity is in the responses. The project management profession has identified four different types of response to an opportunity:[4]

Exploit. This tactic seeks to eliminate the uncertainty associated with an opportunity to ensure that it definitely happens. Examples include assigning your best personnel to a critical burst activity to reduce the time to completion or revising a design to enable a component to be purchased rather than developed internally.

Share. This strategy involves allocating some or all of the ownership of an opportunity to another party who is best able to capture the opportunity for the benefit of the project. Examples include establishing continuous improvement incentives for external contractors or joint ventures.

Enhance. Enhance is the opposite of mitigation in that action is taken to increase the probability and/or the positive impact of an opportunity. Examples include choosing site location based on favorable weather patterns or choosing raw materials that are likely to decline in price.

Accept. Accepting an opportunity is being willing to take advantage of it if it occurs, but not taking action to pursue it.

While it is only natural to focus on negative risks, it is sound practice to engage in active opportunity management as well.

CONTINGENCY FUNDING AND TIME BUFFERS

Contingency funds are established to cover project risks—identified and unknown. When, where, and how much money will be spent is not known until the risk event occurs. Project "owners" are often reluctant to set up project contingency funds that seem to imply the project plan might be a poor one. Some perceive the contingency fund as an add-on slush fund. Others say they will face the risk when it materializes. Usually such reluctance to establish contingency reserves can be overcome with documented risk identification, assessment, contingency plans, and plans for when and how funds will be disbursed.

The size and amount of contingency reserves depend on uncertainty inherent in the project. Uncertainty is reflected in the "newness" of the project, inaccurate time and cost estimates, technical unknowns, unstable scope, and problems not anticipated. In practice, contingencies run from 1 to 10 percent in projects similar to past projects. However, in unique and high-technology projects it is not uncommon to find contingencies running in the 20 to 60 percent range. Use and rate of consumption of reserves must be closely monitored and controlled. Simply picking a percentage of the baseline, say, 5 percent, and calling it the contingency reserve is not a sound approach. Also, adding up all the identified contingency allotments and throwing them into one pot is not conducive to sound control of the reserve fund.

In practice, the contingency reserve fund is typically divided into budget and management reserve funds for control purposes. Budget reserves are set up to cover identified risks; these reserves are those allocated to specific segments or deliverables of the project. Management reserves are set up to cover unidentified risks and are allocated to risks associated with the total project. The risks are separated because their use requires approval from different levels of project authority. Because all risks are probabilistic, the reserves are not included in the baseline for each work package or activity; they are only activated when a risk occurs. If an identified risk does not occur and its chance of occurring is past, the fund allocated to the risk should be deducted from the budget reserve. (This removes the temptation to use budget reserves for other issues or problems.) Of course if the risk does occur, funds are removed from the reserve and added to the cost baseline.

It is important that contingency allowances be independent of the original time and cost estimates. These allowances need to be clearly distinguished to avoid time and budget game playing.

Budget Reserves

These reserves are identified for specific work packages or segments of a project found in the baseline budget or work breakdown structure. For example, a reserve amount might be added to "computer coding" to cover the risk of "testing" showing a coding problem. The reserve amount is determined by costing out the accepted contingency or recovery plan. The budget reserve should be communicated to the project team. This openness suggests trust and encourages good cost performance. However, distributing budget reserves should be the responsibility of both the project manager and the team members responsible for implementing the specific segment of the project. If the risk does not materialize, the funds are removed from the budget reserve. Thus, budget reserves decrease as the project progresses.

Management Reserves

These reserve funds are needed to cover major unforeseen risks and, hence, are applied to the total project. For example, a major scope change may appear necessary midway in the project. Because this change was not anticipated or identified, it is covered from the management reserve. Management reserves are established *after* budget reserves are identified and funds established. These reserves are independent of budget reserves and are controlled by the project manager and the "owner" of the project. The "owner" can be internal (top management) or external to the project organization. Most management reserves are set using historical data and judgments concerning the uniqueness and complexity of the project.

Placing technical contingencies in the management reserve is a special case. Identifying possible technical (functional) risks is often associated with a new, untried, innovative process or product. Because there is a chance the innovation may not work out, a fallback plan is necessary. This type of risk is beyond the control of the project manager. Hence, technical reserves are held in the management reserve and controlled by the owner or top management. The owner and project manager decide when the contingency plan will be implemented and the reserve funds used. It is assumed there is a high probability these funds will never be used.

Table 7.1 shows the development of a contingency fund estimate for a hypothetical project. Note how budget and management reserves are kept separate; control is easily tracked using this format.

Time Buffers

Just as contingency funds are established to absorb unplanned costs, managers use time buffers to cushion against potential delays in the project. And like contingency funds, the amount of time is dependent upon the inherent uncertainty of the project. The more uncertain the project the more

TABLE 7.1 ···

Contingency Fund Estimate (Thousands of Dollars)

Activity	Budget Baseline	Budget Reserve	Project Budget
Design	$500	$15	$515
Code	900	80	980
Test	20	2	22
Subtotal	$1,420	$97	$1,517
Management reserve	—	—	50
Total	$1,420	$97	$1,567

time should be reserved for the schedule. The strategy is to assign extra time at critical moments in the project. For example, buffers are added to

A. activities with severe risks.

B. merge activities that are prone to delays due to one or more preceding activities being late.

C. noncritical activities to reduce the likelihood that they will create another critical path.

D. activities that require scarce resources to ensure that the resources are available when needed.

In the face of overall schedule uncertainty, buffers are sometimes added to the end of the project. For example, a 300-working-day project may have a 30-day project buffer. While the extra 30 days would not appear on the schedule, it is available if needed. Like management reserves, this buffer typically requires the authorization of top management. A more systematic approach to buffer management is discussed in the Chapter 8 Appendix on critical chain project management.

STEP 4: RISK RESPONSE CONTROL

Typically the results of the first three steps of the risk management process are summarized in a formal document often called the risk register. A **risk register** details all identified risks, including descriptions, category, and probability of occurring, impact, responses, contingency plans, owners, and current status. The register is the backbone for the last step in the risk management process: risk control. Risk control involves executing the risk response strategy, monitoring triggering events, initiating contingency plans, and watching for new risks. Establishing a change management system to deal with events that require formal changes in the scope, budget, and/or schedule of the project is an essential element of risk control.

Project managers need to monitor risks just like they track project progress. Risk assessment and updating needs to be part of every status meeting and progress report system. The project team needs to be on constant alert for new, unforeseen risks. Management needs to be sensitive that others may not be forthright in acknowledging new risks and problems. Admitting that there might be a bug in the design code or that different components are not compatible reflects poorly on individual performance. If the prevailing organizational culture is one where mistakes are punished severely, then it is only human nature to protect oneself. Similarly, if bad news is greeted harshly and there is a propensity to "kill the messenger," then participants will be reluctant to speak freely. The tendency to suppress bad news is compounded when individual responsibility is vague and the project team is under extreme pressure from top management to get the project done quickly.

Project managers need to establish an environment in which participants feel comfortable raising concerns and admitting mistakes. The norm should be that mistakes are acceptable, hiding mistakes is intolerable. Problems should be embraced not denied. Participants should be encouraged to identify problems and new risks. Here a positive attitude by the project manager toward risks is a key.

On large, complex projects it may be prudent to repeat the risk identification/assessment exercise with fresh information. Risk profiles should be reviewed to test to see if the original responses held true. Relevant stakeholders should be brought into the discussion and the risk register needs to be updated. While this may not be practical on an ongoing basis, project managers should touch base with them on a regular basis or hold special stakeholder meetings to review the status of risks on the project.

A second key for controlling the cost of risks is documenting responsibility. This can be problematic in projects involving multiple organizations and contractors. Responsibility for risk is frequently passed on to others with the statement, "That is not my worry." This mentality is dangerous. Each identified risk should be assigned (or shared) by mutual agreement of the owner, project manager, and the contractor or person having line responsibility for the work package or segment of the project. It is best to have the line person responsible approve the use of budget reserve funds and monitor their rate of usage. If management reserve funds are required, the line person should play an active role in estimating additional costs and funds needed to complete the project. Having line personnel participate in the process focuses attention on the management reserve, control of its rate of usage, and early warning of potential risk events. If risk management is not formalized, responsibility and responses to risk will be ignored—*it is not my area.*

The bottom line is that project managers and team members need to be vigilant in monitoring potential risks and identify new land mines that could derail a project. Risk assessment has to be part of the working agenda of status meetings and when new risks emerge they need to be analyzed and incorporated into the risk management process.

CHANGE CONTROL MANAGEMENT

A major element of the risk control process is change management. Every detail of a project plan will not materialize as expected. Coping with and controlling project changes present a formidable challenge for most project managers. Changes come from many sources such as the project customer, owner, project manager, team members, and occurrence of risk events. Most changes easily fall into three categories:

1. Scope changes in the form of design or additions represent big changes; for example, customer requests for a new feature or a redesign that will improve the product.
2. Implementation of contingency plans, when risk events occur, represent changes in baseline costs and schedules.
3. Improvement changes suggested by project team members represent another category.

Because change is inevitable, a well-defined change review and control process should be set up early in the project planning cycle.

Change management systems involve reporting, controlling, and recording changes to the project baseline. (Note: Some organizations consider change control systems part of configuration management.) In practice most change management systems are designed to accomplish the following:

1. Identify proposed changes.
2. List expected effects of proposed change(s) on schedule and budget.
3. Review, evaluate, and approve or disapprove changes formally.
4. Negotiate and resolve conflicts of change, conditions, and cost.
5. Communicate changes to parties affected.
6. Assign responsibility for implementing change.
7. Adjust master schedule and budget.
8. Track all changes that are to be implemented.

As part of the project communication plan, stakeholders define up front the communication and decision-making process that will be used to evaluate and accept changes. The process can be captured in a flow diagram like the one presented in Figure 7.9. On small projects this process may simply entail approval of a small group of stakeholders. On larger projects more elaborate decision-making processes are established, with different processes being used for different kinds of change. For example, changes in performance requirements may require multiple sign-offs, including the project sponsor and client, while switching suppliers may be authorized by the project manager. Regardless of the nature of the project, the goal is to establish the process for introducing necessary changes in the project in a timely and effective manner.

Of particular importance is assessing the impact of the change on the project. Often solutions to immediate problems have adverse consequences on other aspects of a project. For example, in overcoming a problem with the exhaust system for a hybrid automobile, the design engineers contributed to the prototype exceeding weight parameters. It is important that the implications of changes are assessed by people with appropriate expertise and perspective. On construction projects this is often the responsibility of the architecture firm, while "software architects" perform a similar function on software development efforts.

Organizations use change request forms and logs to track proposed changes. An example of a simplified change request form is depicted in Figure 7.10. Typically change request forms include a description of the change, the impact of not approving the change, the impact of the change on project scope/schedule/cost, and defined signature paths for review as well as a tracking log number.

An abridged version of a change request log for a construction project is presented in Figure 7.11. These logs are used to monitor change requests. They typically summarize the status of all outstanding change requests and include such useful information as source and date of the change, document codes for related information, cost estimates, and the current status of the request.

FIGURE 7.9 *Change Control Process*

Project name   _Irish/Chinese culture exchange_   Project sponsor   _Irish embassy_

Request number   _12_   Date   _June 6, 2xxx_

Originator _Jennifer McDonald_   Change
                                                    requested by   _Chinese culture office_

Description of requested change

1. _Request river dancers to replace small Irish dance group._
2. _Request one combination dance with river dancers and China ballet group._

Reason for change

River dancers will enhance stature of event. The group is well known and loved by Chinese people.

Areas of impact of proposed change—describe each on separate sheet

[X] Scope   [X] Cost   [ ] Other _____

[ ] Schedule   [ ] Risk

Disposition	Priority	Funding Source
[ ] Approve	[ ] Emergency	[ ] Mgmt. reserve
[X] Approve as amended	[X] Urgent	[ ] Budget reserve
[ ] Disapprove	[ ] Low	[X] Customer
[ ] Deferred		[ ] Other

Sign-off Approvals

Project manager _William O'Mally_   Date _June 12, 2xxx_

Project sponsor _Kenneth Thompson_   Date _June 13, 2xxx_

Project customer _Hong Lee_   Date _June 18, 2xxx_

Other _____   Date _____

FIGURE 7.10   _Sample Change Request_

Every approved change must be identified and integrated into the plan of record through changes in the project WBS and baseline schedule. The plan of record is the current official plan for the project in terms of scope, budget, and schedule. The plan of record serves as a change management benchmark for future change requests as well as the baseline for evaluating project progress.

Figure 7.11   *Change Request Log*

Owner Requested Change Status Report—Open Items							OSU—Weatherford
		Reference	**Dates**				
Rc#	**Description**	**Document**	**Date Rec'd**	**Date Submit**	**Amount**	**Status**	**Comments**
51	Sewer work offset				−188,129	OPEN	FUNDING FROM OTHER SOURCE
52	Stainless Plates at restroom Shower Valves	ASI 56	1/5/2013	3/30/2013	9,308	APPROVED	
53	Waterproofing Options	ASI 77	1/13/2013		169,386	OPEN	
54	Change Electrical floor box spec change	RFI 113	12/5/2013	3/29/2013	2,544	SUBMIT	
55	VE Option for Style and rail doors	Door samples	1/14/2013		−20,000	ROM	
56	Pressure Wash C tower	Owner request	3/15/2013	3/30/2013	14,861	SUBMIT	
57	Fire Lite glass in stairs	Owner request			8,000	QUOTE	ROM BASED ON FIRELITE NT
58	Cyber Café added tele/OFOI equipment	ASI 65	1/30/2013	3/29/2013	4,628	APPROVED	
59	Additional Dampers in C wing	ASI 68	2/4/2013	3/29/2013	1,085	SUBMIT	
60	Revise Corridor ceilings	ASI 72	2/13/2013	3/31/2013	−3,755	SUBMIT	

OPEN—Requires estimate   SUBMIT—RC letter submitted   ASI—Architect's supplemental instructions
ROM—Rough order magnitude   APPROVED—RC letter approved   RFI—Request for information
QUOTE—Subcontractor quotes   REVISE—RC letter to be reviewed

If the change control system is not integrated with the WBS and baseline, project plans and control will soon self-destruct. Thus, one of the keys to a successful change control process is document, document, document! The benefits derived from change control systems are the following:

1. Inconsequential changes are discouraged by the formal process.
2. Costs of changes are maintained in a log.
3. Integrity of the WBS and performance measures is maintained.
4. Allocation and use of budget and management reserve funds are tracked.
5. Responsibility for implementation is clarified.
6. Effect of changes is visible to all parties involved.
7. Implementation of change is monitored.
8. Scope changes will be quickly reflected in baseline and performance measures.

Clearly, change control is important and requires that someone or some group be responsible for approving changes, keeping the process updated, and communicating changes to the project team and relevant stakeholders. Project control depends heavily on keeping the change control process current. This historical record can be used for satisfying customer inquiries, identifying problems in post-project audits, and estimating future project costs.

Summary

To put the processes discussed in this chapter in proper perspective one should recognize that the essence of project management is risk management. Every technique in this book is really a risk management technique. Each in its own way tries to prevent something bad from happening. Project selection systems try to reduce the likelihood that projects will not contribute to the mission of the firm. Project scope statements, among other things, are designed to avoid costly misunderstandings and reduce scope creep. Work breakdown structures reduce the likelihood that some vital part of the project will be omitted or that the budget estimates are unrealistic. Teambuilding reduces the likelihood of dysfunctional conflict and breakdowns in coordination. All of the techniques try to increase stakeholder satisfaction and increase the chances of project success.

From this perspective managers engage in risk management activities to compensate for the uncertainty inherent in project management and that things never go according to plan. Risk management is proactive not reactive. It reduces the number of surprises and leads to a better understanding of the most likely outcomes of negative events.

Although many managers believe that in the final analysis, risk assessment and contingency depend on subjective judgment, some standard method for identifying, assessing, and responding to risks should be included in all projects. The very process of identifying project risks forces some discipline at all levels of project management and improves project performance.

Contingency plans increase the chance that the project can be completed on time and within budget. Contingency plans can be simple "work-arounds" or elaborate detailed plans. Responsibility for risks should be clearly identified and documented. It is desirable and prudent to keep a reserve as a hedge against project risks. Budget reserves are linked to the WBS and should be communicated to the project team. Control of management reserves should remain with the owner, project manager, and line person responsible. Use of contingency reserves should be closely monitored, controlled, and reviewed throughout the project life cycle.

Experience clearly indicates that using a formal, structured process to handle possible foreseen and unforeseen project risk events minimizes surprises, costs, delays, stress, and misunderstandings. Risk management is an iterative process that occurs throughout the lifespan of the project. When risk events occur or changes are necessary, using an effective change control process to quickly approve and record changes will facilitate measuring performance against schedule and cost. Ultimately successful risk management requires a culture in which threats are embraced not denied and problems are identified not hidden.

Key Terms

Avoiding risk

Budget reserve

Change management system

Contingency plan

Management reserve

Mitigating risk

Opportunity

Retaining risk

Risk

Risk breakdown structure
 (RBS)

Risk profile

Risk register

Risk severity matrix

Scenario analysis

Time buffer

Transferring risk

Review Questions

1. Project risks can/cannot be eliminated if the project is carefully planned. Explain.
2. The chances of risk events occurring and their respective costs increasing change over the project life cycle. What is the significance of this phenomenon to a project manager?
3. What is the difference between avoiding a risk and accepting a risk?
4. What is the difference between mitigating a risk and contingency planning?
5. Explain the difference between budget reserves and management reserves.
6. How are the work breakdown structure and change control connected?
7. What are the likely outcomes if a change control process is not used? Why?
8. What are the major differences between managing negative risks versus positive risks (opportunities)?

Exercises

1. Gather a small team of students. Think of a project most students would understand; the kinds of tasks involved should also be familiar. Identify and assess major and minor risks inherent to the project. Decide on a response type. Develop a contingency plan for two to four identified risks. Estimate costs. Assign contingency reserves. How much reserve would your team estimate for the whole project? Justify your choices and estimates.
2. You have been assigned to a project risk team of five members. Because this is the first time your organization has formally set up a risk team for a project, it is hoped that your team will develop a process that can be used on all future projects. Your first team meeting is next Monday morning. Each team member has been asked to prepare for the meeting by developing, in as much detail as possible, an outline that describes how you believe the team should proceed in handling project risks. Each team member will hand out their proposed outline at the beginning of the meeting. Your outline should include but not be limited to the following information:
   a. Team objectives.
   b. Process for handling risk events.

    c. Team activities.

    d. Team outputs.

3. The Manchester United Soccer Tournament project team (review the Manchester United case at the end of Chapter 4) has identified the following potential risks to their project:

    a. Referees failing to show up at designated games.

    b. Fighting between teams.

    c. Pivotal error committed by a referee that determines the outcome of a game.

    d. Abusive behavior along the sidelines by parents.

    e. Inadequate parking.

    f. Not enough teams sign up for different age brackets.

    g. Serious injury.

    How would you recommend that they respond (i.e., avoid, accept, . . .) to these risks and why?

4. Search the World Wide Web (WWW) using the key words: "best practices, project management." What did you find? How might this information be useful to a project manager?

References

Atkinson, W., "Beyond the Basics," *PM Network,* May 2003, pp. 38–43.

Baker, B., and R. Menon, "Politics and Project Performance: The Fourth Dimension of Project Management," *PM Network,* 9 (11) November 1995, pp. 16–21.

Carr, M. J., S. L. Konda, I. Monarch, F. C. Ulrich, and C. F. Walker, "Taxonomy-Based Risk Identification," *Technical Report CMU/SEI-93-TR 6, Software Engineering Institute,* Carnegie Mellon University, Pittsburgh, 1993.

Ford, E. C., J. Duncan, A. G. Bedeian, P. M. Ginter, M. D. Rousculp, and A. M. Adams, "Mitigating Risks, Visible Hands, Inevitable Disasters, and Soft Variables: Management Research that Matters to Managers," *Academy of Management Executive,* 19 (4) November 2005, pp. 24–38.

Gray, C. F., and R. Reinman, "PERT Simulation: A Dynamic Approach to the PERT Technique," *Journal of Systems Management,* March 1969, pp. 18–23.

Hamburger, D. H., "The Project Manager: Risk Taker and Contingency Planner," *Project Management Journal,* 21 (4) 1990, pp. 11–16.

Hulett, D. T., "Project Schedule Risk Assessment," *Project Management Journal,* 26 (1) 1995, pp. 21–31.

Ingebretson, M., "In No Uncertain Terms," *PM Network,* 2002, pp. 28–32.

"Math Mistake Proved Fatal to Mars Orbiter," *The Orlando Sentinel,* November 23, 1999.

Meyer, A. D., C. H. Loch, and M. T. Pich, "Managing Project Uncertainty: From Variation to Chaos," *MIT Sloan Management Review,* Winter 2002, pp. 60–67.

Pavlik, A., "Project Troubleshooting: Tiger Teams for Reactive Risk Management," *Project Management Journal,* 35 (4) December 2004, pp. 5–14.

Pinto, J. K., *Project Management: Achieving Competitive Advantage* (Upper Saddle River, NJ: Pearson, 2007).

Project Management Body of Knowledge (Newton Square, PA: Project Management Institute, 2013).

Schuler, J. R., "Decision Analysis in Projects: Monte Carlo Simulation," *PM Network,* 7 (1) January 1994, pp. 30–36.

Smith, P. G., and G. M. Merritt, *Proactive Risk Management: Controlling Uncertainty in Product Development* (New York: Productivity Press, 2002).

Smith, P. G., and D. G. Reinertsen, *Developing Products in Half the Time* (New York: Van Nostrand Reinhold, 1995).

Snizek, J. A., and R. A. Henry, "Accuracy and Confidence in Group Judgment," *Organizational Behavior and Human Decision Processes,* 4 (3) 1989, pp. 1–28.

APPENDIX 7.1

PERT and PERT Simulation

PERT—PROGRAM EVALUATION AND REVIEW TECHNIQUE

In 1958 the Special Office of the Navy and the Booze, Allen, and Hamilton consulting firm developed PERT (program evaluation and review technique) to schedule the more than 3,300 contractors of the Polaris submarine project and to cover uncertainty of activity time estimates.

PERT is almost identical to the critical path method (CPM) technique except it assumes each activity duration has a range that follows a statistical distribution. PERT uses three time estimates for each activity. Basically, this means each activity duration can range from an optimistic time to a pessimistic time, and a weighted average can be computed for each activity. Because project activities usually represent work, and because work tends to stay behind once it gets behind, the PERT developers chose an approximation of the *beta distribution* to represent activity durations. This distribution is known to be flexible and can accommodate empirical data that do not follow a normal distribution. The activity durations can be skewed more toward the high or low end of the data range. Figure A7.1A depicts a *beta distribution* for activity durations that is skewed toward the right and is representative of work that tends to stay late once it is behind. The distribution for the project duration is represented by a normal (symmetrical) distribution shown in Figure A7.1B. The project distribution represents the sum of the weighted averages of the activities on the critical path(s).

Knowing the weighted average and variances for each activity allows the project planner to compute the probability of meeting different project durations. Follow the steps described in the hypothetical example given next. (The jargon is difficult for those not familiar with statistics, but the process is relatively simple after working through a couple of examples.)

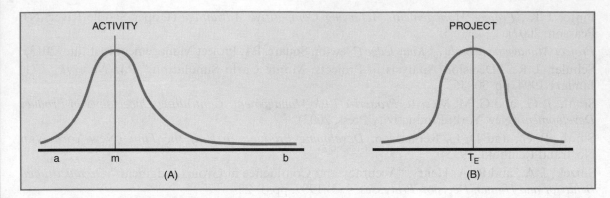

Figure A7.1 *Activity and Project Frequency Distributions*

The weighted average activity time is computed by the following formula:

$$t_e = \frac{a + 4m + b}{6}$$ (7.1)

where t_e = weighted average activity time

a = optimistic activity time (1 chance in 100 of completing the activity earlier under *normal* conditions)

b = pessimistic activity time (1 chance in 100 of completing the activity later under *normal* conditions)

m = most likely activity time

When the three time estimates have been specified, this equation is used to compute the weighted average duration for each activity. The average (deterministic) value is placed on the project network as in the CPM method and the early, late, slack, and project completion times are computed as they are in the CPM method.

The variability in the activity time estimates is approximated by the following equations: Equation 7.2 represents the standard deviation for the *activity*. Equation 7.3 represents the standard deviation for the *project*. Note the standard deviation of the activity is squared in this equation; this is also called variance. This sum includes only activities on the critical path(s) or path being reviewed.

$$\sigma_{t_e} = \left(\frac{b - a}{6}\right)$$ (7.2)

$$\sigma_{T_E} = \sqrt{\Sigma \sigma_{t_e}^2}$$ (7.3)

Finally, the average project duration (T_E) is the sum of all the average activity times along the critical path (sum of t_e), and it follows a normal distribution.

Knowing the average project duration and the variances of activities allows the probability of completing the project (or segment of the project) by a specific time to be computed using standard statistical tables. The equation below (Equation 7.4) is used to compute the "Z" value found in statistical tables (Z = number of standard deviations from the mean), which, in turn, tells the probability of completing the project in the time specified.

$$Z = \frac{T_S - T_E}{\sqrt{\Sigma \sigma_{t_e}^2}}$$

(7.4)

where T_E = critical path duration
T_S = scheduled project duration
Z = probability (of meeting scheduled duration) found in statistical Table A7.2

A HYPOTHETICAL EXAMPLE USING THE PERT TECHNIQUE

The activity times and variances are given in Table A7.1. The project network is presented in Figure A7.2. This figure shows the project network as AOA and AON. The AON network is presented as a reminder that PERT can use AON networks as well as AOA.

TABLE A7.1
Activity Times and Variances

Activity	a	m	b	t_e	$[(b-a)/6]^2$
1–2	17	29	47	30	25
2–3	6	12	24	13	9
2–4	16	19	28	20	4
3–5	13	16	19	16	1
4–5	2	5	14	6	4
5–6	2	5	8	5	1

The expected project duration (T_E) is 64 time units; the critical path is 1-2-3-5-6. With this information, the probability of completing the project by a specific date can easily be computed using standard statistical methods. For example, what is the probability the project will be completed before a scheduled time (T_S) of 67? The normal curve for the project would appear as shown in Figure A7.3.

Using the formula for the Z value, the probability can be computed as follows:

$$Z = \frac{T_S - T_E}{\sqrt{\Sigma \sigma_{t_e}^2}}$$

$$= \frac{67 - 64}{\sqrt{25 + 9 + 1 + 1}}$$

$$= \frac{+3}{\sqrt{36}}$$

$$= +0.50$$

$$P = 0.69$$

FIGURE A7.2   *Hypothetical Network*

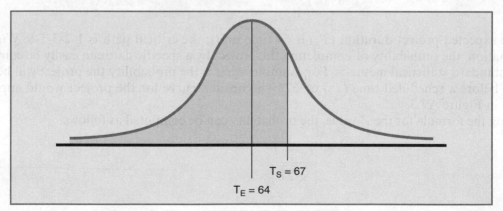

FIGURE A7.3   *Possible Project Durations*

Reading from Table A7.2, a *Z* value of +0.5 gives a probability of 0.69, which is interpreted to mean there is a 69 percent chance of completing the project on or before 67 time units.

Conversely, the probability of completing the project by time period 60 is computed as follows:

$$Z = \frac{60 - 64}{\sqrt{25 + 9 + 1 + 1}}$$

$$= \frac{-4}{\sqrt{36}}$$

$$= -0.67$$

$$P \approx 0.26$$

From Table A7.2, a Z value of -0.67 gives an approximate probability of 0.26, which is interpreted to mean there is about a 26 percent chance of completing the project on or before 60 time units. Note that this same type of calculation can be made for any path or segment of a path in the network.

TABLE A7.2 . . . .
Z Values and Probabilities

Z Value	Probability	Z Value	Probability
−3.0	.001	+0.0	.500
−2.8	.003	+0.2	.579
−2.6	.005	+0.4	.655
−2.4	.008	+0.6	.726
−2.2	.014	+0.8	.788
−2.0	.023	+1.0	.841
−1.8	.036	+1.2	.885
−1.6	.055	+1.4	.919
−1.4	.081	+1.6	.945
−1.2	.115	+1.8	.964
−1.0	.159	+2.0	.977
−0.8	.212	+2.2	.986
−0.6	.274	+2.4	.992
−0.4	.345	+2.6	.995
−0.2	.421	+2.8	.997

When such probabilities are available to management, trade-off decisions can be made to accept or reduce the risk associated with a particular project duration. For example, if the project manager wishes to improve the chances of completing the project by 64 time units, at least two choices are available. First, management can spend money up front to change conditions that will reduce the duration of one or more activities on the critical path. A more prudent, second alternative would be to allocate money to a contingency fund and wait to see how the project is progressing as it is implemented.

EXERCISES

1. Given the project information below, what is the probability of completing the National Holiday Toy project in 93 time units?

Act. ID	Description	Predecessor	Optm. (a)	Most likely (m)	Pess. (b)	Act time t_e	Variance $[(b-a)/6]^2$	Critical
1	Design package	None	6	12	24			
2	Design product	1	16	19	28			
3	Build package	1	4	7	10			
4	Secure patent	2	21	30	39			
5	Build product	2	17	29	47			
6	Paint	3, 4, 5	4	7	10			
7	Test market	6	13	16	19			

2. The Global Tea and Organic Juice companies have merged.

The following information has been collected for the "Consolidation Project."

Activity	Description	Predecessor	a opt	m ml	b pess
1	Codify accounts	None	16	19	28
2	File articles of unification	None	30	30	30
3	Unify price and credit policy	None	60	72	90
4	Unify personnel policies	None	18	27	30
5	Unify data processing	1	17	29	47
6	Train accounting staff	1	4	7	10
7	Pilot run data processing	5	12	15	18
8	Calculate P & L and balance sheet	6, 7	6	12	24
9	Transfer real property	2	18	27	30
10	Train salesforce	3	20	35	50
11	Negotiate with unions	4	40	55	100
12	Determine capital needs	8	11	20	29
13	Explain personnel policies	11	14	23	26
14	Secure line of credit	9, 12	13	16	19
15	End	10, 13, 14	0	0	0

1. Compute the expected time for each activity.
2. Compute the variance for each activity.
3. Compute the expected project duration.
4. What is the probability of completing the project by day 112? Within 116 days?
5. What is the probability of completing "Negotiate with Unions" by day 90?

3. The expected times and variances for the project activities are given below. What is the probability of completing the project in 25 periods?

ID	Description	Predecessor	t_e	Variance $[(b-a)/6]^2$
1	Pilot production	None	6	3
2	Select channels of distrib.	None	7	4
3	Develop mktg. program	None	4	2
4	Test market	1	4	2
5	Patent	1	10	5
6	Full production	4	16	10
7	Ad promotion	3	3	2
8	Release	2,5,6,7	2	1

APPENDIX 7.2

Project Risk Management

1. GENERAL PERCEPTION OF RISKS AND PROJECT RISKS

According to general perception, risk is an uncertain event (i.e. the event having unknown probability of its occurrence) having an unexpected and undesirable impact on some desired objectives or plans. In this sense, the risk is inherently present in all future plans and actions – and all business related decisions, whether they are in the course of routine day-to-day work or operation on one hand or unique and specific task as in the case of a project.

(PMBOKI®' Guide's definition of risk and approach to risk management are somewhat different; they are described from Section 3 onwards in this Appendix.)

Distinction between risk management for operations and projects
However, there are some important distinctions between the risks occurring during routine operations and the risks associated with the projects.

- Firstly, the projects require carrying out activities, which are not routinely carried out within the organization or which involve interactions with external agencies, which are not necessary for routine operations. Therefore, unless conscious effort to think through the project risks is made, these risks do not become apparent and if a plan to manage the risks is not prepared in advance and made ready for going into action, prompt effective and efficient measures for management of the risk would not be available for implementation.

- Secondly, the project decisions taken during implementing major capital projects are irreversible and some of them would leave a very significant effect on the organization over a long period of time. Some crucial decisions taken during the project life cycle significantly affect the operating mode, efficiency and economic viability of the organization. The successful projects set the organizations on path of growth and prosperity and all inadequately handled risks or lapses in project management haunt the organization's operations for years. Managing the risks for a major project is, therefore, important for long-term health of the organization – over and beyond managing the health of the project in hand.

Risk categories

Risks are generally classified into three categories:

- *Known Risks:* These risks have occurred in some of the projects in past, and are already known to the project team. These are readily identifiable and some tried and tested suitable strategy for handling them is usually available. Though, it is not necessary that they would occur on the project in hand nor is it predictable as to when they are very likely to occur; planning in advance to handle such risks is strongly recommended. Building a high plinth level building in flood-prone area or resignation of some key project team member during the project life cycle are risks of this nature.

- *Known–Unknown risks:* These types of risks are an instance of risks which have occurred in the past but their probability of recurrence is low as well as quite unknown and the project team probably may not have handled similar risks before. Therefore, the advantage of 'tried and proven track record of risk handling strategy' may not be available. Building in an earthquake prone zone is an instance of this. The project team's skill in analyzing and planning to handle risks is put to test for handling such risks.

- Unknown-Unknown Risks: These are the types of risks, which no one in the project team is able to foresee and no risk planning is possible. Striking of Tsunami on Tamil Nadu coastline a few years back was a risk of this nature.

Project Risks during Different Phases of the Project Life Cycle

Risk management processes need to be actively used by the project team for the entire project life cycle, since future events are unpredictable and risks could occur during any project phase. However, the severity and frequency of common risks to projects keep on getting smaller as the project moves from initiating and planning to closing phase of the project life cycle. Therefore, ordinarily, major effort for risk identification, analysis and response plans is required at the initiation and planning phases.

2. PROACTIVE MANAGEMENT OF PROJECT RISKS

2.1 Importance of Proactive Risk Management

In earlier eras an approach towards formal planning for risk management was reflected in the stance taken by some hard-boiled off-the-cuff managing project managers: "No necessity of all that plan, we will cross the bridge when we reach it." Or that "I don't want my team to think of all those negative thoughts associated with risk planning." The answer to this approach can be summed up in a witty repartee made in defense of preventive maintenance program: "You can pay for the maintenance now or later – later it would be much more."

This off-the-cuff risk management approach has been now mostly replaced by proactive approach, which analyses the project risks and maps out in advance the strategy for mitigating the risk in case it arose. So much so, that risk management is considered now one of the prime responsibilities of a project manager. The risk analysis does not ensure that the project would be free from all risks, but the preparation in advance for managing the risk if it occurred would definitely reduce the negative impact and bring the exposure from project risk to the organization's risk tolerance level. Also, we may recall that risk is not just a crisis or an accident waiting to happen; it could as well be some opportunity and the risk planning process would keep project team geared up to profit from some windfall opportunity, if good fortune smiles.

2.2 The Steps in Proactive Risk Management

The steps involved in proactive risk management may be summed up as follows:

Phase I: Risk Identification:
This phase of risk management is concerned with collecting data, such as:

- Identifying the likely risk events and their probability,
- Identification of the risk drivers (conditions which might increase or decrease the probability of the risk event)
- Impacts of risk events on scope, time, cost, and quality
- Identification of impact drivers (factors which might increase or decrease the degree of impact of the risk event, if it occurred, on scope, time, cost, and quality)

All this is much easier said than done. Methods have been suggested for making this process more amenable to application – use of techniques like Delphi Technique, Brainstorming, and Checklists developed on the basis of earlier project experiences, etc. All the same, the experience and expertise of the project team is of prime importance in this phase of project risk management.

Phase II: Risk Analysis – Qualitative and Quantitative Approaches
This phase is concerned with analyzing the risk data collected in the earlier phase, which would include:

- Calculating the expected value of negative impact on outcome for each risk event from the probability of risk event and impact if occurred
- Ranking the risk events for prioritization according to the expected value and preparing a Risk Table or Risk Map
- Carrying out further detailed analysis of some selected and prioritized risks using sophisticated quantitative techniques like Sensitivity Analysis, Decision Trees and Monte Carlo Simulation

Once the data for risk analysis is collected, its analysis for prioritization or sophisticated quantitative analysis for more informed direction for managing the risk are straight forward as far as their techniques of application go.

Phase III: Formulating Risk Management Strategies
This phase is concerned with formulating plans to proactively manage the prioritized risks. It should be remembered that there could be several causes for a single risk and that a risk event, if it occurred, could impact negatively several project objectives. The risk management strategy should take this into consideration. The roles and responsibilities of the persons or organizations assigned to manage specific risks and the risk triggers are also documented. The strategies commonly used for handling negative risks are:

- Avoidance – Modifying the project plan to bye-pass the risk-associated activity or replace it with another, which would not be subject to the identified risk.

- *Transfer* – Transferring the risk management to a third party at a known cost for risk management
- *Mitigating the negative impact* – Reducing the negative impact of the risk, in case the risk did occur
- *Acceptance* – Accepting the risk, either if there is no practical way to avoid, transfer or mitigate the risk or that it would not be economically viable to undertake managing that risk proactively.

Phase IV Control and Documentation – Developing and Maintaining Risk Register
The final step in risk management is developing a comprehensive document with the detailed risk management plans, activities for monitoring and controlling the risk, and recording the outcomes and residual risks after main risk event is over. The record might include.

- List of identified risk events with risk-event drivers, likely impacts of consequences and impact drivers
- Planned response for each major risk event
- Responsibility for managing each risk
- Identification of the trigger to activate risk response action
- Recording in the Risk Register the risk management activities and their outcomes with impacts on project objectives of scope, time, cost and quality
- Residual risk after the main event and any new risks on the horizon

3. RISK MANAGEMENT PROCESSES RECOMMENDED IN PMBOK® GUIDE, 5TH EDITION

Risk Definition: *Risk is defined as an uncertain event or condition that, if occurs, has a positive or negative effect on the project's objectives.*

There is an important distinction between this definition of risk and the general concept of risk. PMI's definition includes "positive as well as negative effects" and therefore connotes both good as well as bad effects, *while the common perception of risk is associated with only bad effects or harmful events.* Risk management according to PMI®, therefore, encompasses measures to minimize the negative impacts and to leverage the positive impacts on project objectives (scope, time, cost and quality).

Risk Management Processes
Six processes have been identified for project risk management in PMBOK® Guide, 5th Edition; five risk management processes are in the planning process group and one process is in the monitoring and controlling group. The general approach for project risk management follows the proactive risk management described in the earlier section.

1. *Plan Risk Management (Planning Process Group):* This process sets down the guideline and procedures for how the project risk management activities would be carried out. This would include policies and procedures for identification and analysis of risks, developing plan for managing the prioritized risks and implementing the plan for the tracking the risk management process through out the project life cycle.

2. *Identify Risks (Planning Process Group):* This process involves determining which risks may affect the project outcomes and recording their characteristics and impacts on project outcomes.

3. *Perform Qualitative Risk Analysis (Planning Process Group):* This process aims at prioritizing the identified risks by assessing the probability of risk occurrence, the value of impact if the risk event occurred and calculating the expected value of impact from theses assessments.

4. *Perform Quantitative Risk Analysis (Planning Process Group):* The process of numerical analysis of the major or prioritized risks to arrive at the probabilistic estimate for different likely outcomes.

5. *Plan Risk Responses (Planning Process Group):* This process examines each of the prioritized risks and plans the strategy for managing them (avoiding, transferring, mitigating the impact or accepting the risk), the identification of triggers for risks and the primary responsibility for managing the risk if it occurs.

6. *Control Risks (Monitoring and Controlling Process Group):* This is the process of implementing the risk response plans, tracking identified risks, monitoring residual risks and identifying new risks throughout the project life cycle.

In the rest of this section, we will briefly describe these risk management processes and their inputs, tools and techniques and outputs.

3.1   Plan Risk Management

Plan Risk management is the process of defining how to conduct the risk management activities for a project. (PMBOK® Guide, 5th Edition)

The guidelines and procedures developed during this process are set down in The *Risk Management Plan*, a document, which describes methodology for:

- identifying and listing the risk events and determining and describing the main attributes of the risk,

- carrying out qualitative and quantitative risk analysis to prioritize the risks and develop numerical probabilistic estimate for different risk exposures if risks occurred,

- planning the strategy for managing the prioritized risks, including the approach, identification of risk trigger and assigning the primary responsibility of managing the risk, and

- implementing the risk response plans.

By its very nature, since this process would provide the basic guidelines for the entire risk management efforts, it needs to start at the very early stage of the project planning and should be completed as early as practicable during the planning phase.

Inputs

Components of project management plan – The first set of important inputs for risk planning come from the *project management plan* components. By closely analyzing the tasks involved for the work packages and WBS, the perception of risks associated with the tasks can be obtained. The degree of variation or range in the cost estimates and time duration estimates, similarly point out the degree of uncertainty in the activity cost and activity time duration and hence the corresponding nature of risks. Analysis of quality management plan would reveal the likely pitfalls and risks in attaining the desired quality in product of the project. Analysis and challenging of the assumptions and constraints in the project scope statement would give a sense of the risk arising out of the assumptions not working out.

Project Charter – This would provide the inputs for risk management plan by overviewing the high-level project description and high-level requirements. In addition, by a close review of the assumptions and constraints that are taken into account while conceiving the project and setting down project objectives, the guidance for formulating the risk management plan can become apparent.

Risk Tolerance of the Stakeholders – This input is very critical from a standpoint of practical aspect of risk management in a specific organization. Usually, the *Stakeholder Register* would include in its records enough hints for assessing this aspect.

Enterprise environmental factors – Risk planning also requires looking at what is happening outside the project environment and how the uncertainties in the external environment (in the other divisions of the organization, the industry trends and overall macroeconomic factors) would pose risks to the project. The risk tolerance of the project sponsors and other key stakeholders is also important in the approach to be taken for risk planning.

Organizational process assets – The lessons learned on earlier similar projects, particularly the nature of risks faced and the risk management techniques successfully used, can provide good insight into risk planning process.

Tools and Techniques

Analytical Techniques – The latest trend in project risk management involves use of sophisticated analytical techniques based on Simulation (particularly, *Monte Carlo Simulation Technique*), Sensitivity Analysis, Decision Tree Analysis and others. These techniques aim at understanding and defining the quantum and nature of overall risk to project cost or project schedule and probabilistic values of project's overall cost or schedule, taking into account the risk assessment data. The extensive data input from various sources for risk planning mentioned above requires thorough analysis to provide the basis for preparing the risk management plan. Three cases included in this edition provide step-wise illustration of Monte Carlo and Decision Tree Analysis techniques to enable their application to the project in hand.

Expert Judgment – Expert Judgment refers to the expertise and experience gained by the project team in handling a similar project earlier. It is in untested waters that the leadership of the captain of the ship makes the difference.

Meetings with project team members and stakeholders – Being an uncharted territory, the collective wisdom of knowledgeable team members and stakeholders is a very useful resource for perceiving and planning for risk events.

Outputs

Output of the process is the Risk Management Plan – This is the basic document which will guide planning for all subsequent risk management activities. The contents of Risk Management Plan might include the following:

- *How to identify risk, and analyze and prioritize it? (Methodology)* – It includes identification of sources for risk identification, probability estimating procedures, risk categories, methods assessing the impacts, and methods for performing qualitative and quantitative analysis.

- *Who will do risk management?* – The assignment of risk management tasks to different project team members with well-defined roles and responsibilities.
- *To manage risk at what cost?* – This would cover the provision of contingency funds in the project budget in the cost management plan and provision in the project plan for some specific expenses for measures for avoiding or mitigating risks.
- *What Category of risk?* – (Risk Breakdown Structure) A risk categorization formal structure, called Risk Breakdown Structure, is developed from the experience on earlier projects also useful in risk planning (shown in this chapter)
- *How much risk exposure would be tolerated by stakeholders* – From the analysis of stakeholders risk tolerance, guidelines for risk management can be formulated. Stakeholders might have distinctly different degrees for tolerance of risks in project schedule and project cost.
- *How to define risk probability and impacts based on risk tolerance?* – Clarity in applying uniform and rational methods for estimating the risk probabilities and their classification into relative seriousness or importance is the backbone of sound qualitative and quantitative analysis of risks. Risk management plan gives the desired definitions.
- *How to report?* – Finally, the risk management plan provides the formats and templates for risk management report – the risk register.

3.2 Identify Risk

"Identify Risks is the process of determining which risks may affect the project outcomes and recording their characteristics" (and impacts on project outcomes). (PMBOK® Guide, 5th Edition)

The general description of the process is described in the "Step 1: Risk Identification" of this chapter as well as in discussing proactive risk management in this appendix and so it is not repeated here. However, for the sake of making comprehensive coverage of the treatment of this subject and this process in PMBOK® Guide, 5th Edition, the inputs, tools and techniques and outputs are briefly enumerated below:

Inputs

Risk Management Plan – This is the most important and distinctive input for the process. Provision for risk management activities in the budget and schedule, the responsibility and roles assigned for risk management, risk breakdown structure and definitions of risk probability and impact described in the Risk Management Plan are important inputs.

Project Management Plan – Important components of Project Management Plan, such as Cost Management Plan, Schedule Management Plan, Quality Management Plan, and Human Resources Management Plan also provide valuable inputs in identifying risks.

Project Documents – In addition, a number of inputs for Risk Identify process and Plan Risk Management process are common. Activity Cost Estimate and Activity Duration Estimate, Scope Baseline, Stakeholders 'Register, Risk tolerance profiles of the stakeholders, are among such project documents.

Organizational Process Assets – The templates and risk management techniques and the Lessons Learned from the project files could be mentioned as useful organizational process assets inputs.

Tools and Techniques

Review and Analysis of project planning documents – Review of project documents like *Project Charter, Project Scope Statement, Assumptions and Constraints, Major Contracts, Quality Plan* and *other earlier projects files* - would be an important tool.

Checklist Analysis – Risk Checklist from earlier projects and Risk breakdown structure is another important input. Near the end of this section, a specimen of the checklist for risk identification is given.

Two techniques depend on benefiting from the collective wisdom of project team members (Brainstorming) and for reaching a consensus among experts about the perceived risks *(Delphi Technique)*. They are more useful for projects with unusual technical processes or project activities.

Analysis – Analytical techniques like *SWOT Analysis* and *Cause-and-Effect Diagrams* can also be used as tools.

Expert Judgment – It could be seen from the wide range of inputs and other techniques that expert judgment developed from experience could be of immense value as a tool.

Output

Risk Register – The primary output from the process is Risk Register. It is also a primary out put from other risk management processes described later in this section. Risk Register is defined in PMBOK® Guide as a document containing the results of the qualitative risk analysis, quantitative risk analysis and risk response planning. The Risk Register details all identified risks, including description, category, cause, probability of occurring, impact(s) on objectives, proposed responses, owners, and current status.

Risk Register is a comprehensive reference document concerned with almost all risk management processes. It evolves into its finished final form as the successive risk management processes are carried out. In view of its great importance as a risk management document, a detailed note on Risk Register is provided separately below in this section.

3.3   Perform Qualitative Risk Analysis

Perform Qualitative Risk Analysis is the process of prioritizing risks for further analysis by assessing and combining the probability of occurrence and impact.   *(PMBOK® Guide, 5th Edition)*

This process aims at assessing the importance of managing a particular identified risks by assessing the probability of risk occurrence, the value of impact if the risk event occurred and calculating the risk value or risk exposure. This risk exposure or risk value is calculated by multiplying the assessed probability and impact identified in the Risk Register developed in the earlier process.

Inputs

The list of risks identified and recorded into the *Risk Register* and the definitions for assessing the probability and impact of the risk in the *Risk Management Plan* are the two main inputs. The *Project Scope Statement* and *Scope Baseline* and *Risk database information* from earlier projects (Organizational Process Assets) are other two inputs.

Tools and Techniques

Assessment of Probability and Impacts of Identified Risks
Qualitative Risk Analysis involves the assessment of the probability and impact of the risk on important project outcomes. At this stage (viz. qualitative analysis stage), the assessment is essentially based on meetings of the project team members and expert stakeholders, expert judgment essentially based on experience of handling risks in some similar projects earlier.

Once theses values are assessed, the expected value of the risk (also called 'risk value' or 'risk exposure') is calculated by the product of risk probability and impact if the risk occurred:

Expected Value of Risk = (Risk Probability) × (Impact of risk on scope, cost or time)

The risks are prioritized based on the expected value off the risk – the higher the expected value, the greater the priority for risk planning and management. In Step 2: Risk Assessment" in this chapter, an illustration of the definitions of risk probability and impact, risk value, and risk severity matrix developed from the risk value are described in detail.

Probability and Impact Matrix
Another technique to prioritize risks would be to construct a probability and risk matrix (tabular form) using the probability and impact assessed as described earlier. Certain limiting probability values and impact values could be set down as the boundaries separating the risks according to their assessed priorities (high priority, moderate priority, low priority, etc.)

Risk Categorization
The risks can also be categorized according to the sources of risk (using the Risk Breakdown Structure described earlier), the part of project life cycle, or the affected deliverables, etc.

Expert Judgment
As mentioned earlier, in the absence of quantitative data for the risk under consideration, assessment of probability of risk occurrence, the impacts on different project objectives (Schedule, cost, scope or quality), and finally prioritization criteria also are based on expert judgment.

Outputs

Risk Register Updates: The output from qualitative analysis of risks is a further refinement of the risk register document already created during the 'Identify Risk process'. The updates would include the assessment of the risk values and the prioritization of risks based on the risk values, classification of risks into categories and any general trends spotted during the qualitative analysis process. As mentioned while discussing the output of Identify Risk process, a detailed note on Risk Register is provided separately in this section.

3.4   Perform Quantitative Risk Analysis

Perform Quantitative Risk Analysis is the process of numerically analyzing the effect of identified risks on overall project objectives. *(PMBOK® Guide, 5th Edition)*

The main activity carried out during the process is of numerical analysis of the major or prioritized risks listed in the risk register document after its updating to reflect qualitative risk analysis conclusions. The quantitative risk analysis aims at working out a probabilistic estimate for different likely outcomes using some specialized analytical techniques. The analysis based on some complex techniques permit assessment of probability associated with the impact of risk on a specific project outcome, which could be very helpful in decision-making. However, in turn, the techniques require collection of extensive data to be as reliable in reality as the precision of the numerical values would tend to convey. If such high quality data is not used for analysis, the technique could give a false impression about its reliability.

Three techniques for quantitative risk analysis are popular and common:

1. *Monte Carlo Simulation*, This technique for quantitative risk analysis is based on building a model and carrying out simulation for the project outcomes based on the individual data point generated to correspond to its probability. The final output would be a plot of the cumulative probability of occurrence plotted against project cost or project schedule. From this graph, it would be possible to read out the probability of any selected project cost or project schedule.

   To illustrate the nature of output from Monte Carlo simulation, it would be possible read out from the plot the probability of occurrence of a specific cost chosen from the entire range of possible project costs (e.g. 'The probability would be 75% for the project to be completed in some specific project cost, say ₹30 crores,' or say 'For the project to be completed at the cost of ₹38 crore, the probability is 95%', etc.). Similarly, from the Monte Carlo simulation for project network, the probability for some specific project schedule from the entire range of likely project completion times could be read out. (e.g. The probability for completing the project in 45 weeks is 75% or that the probability would be 90% for the project to be completed in say, 54 weeks, etc.).

   The application of this technique for estimating the project cost estimate, and project schedule are illustrated using hypothetical data in the cases appended to this chapter.

2. *The Sensitivity Analysis* focuses on estimating the relative variation in the project outcomes of interest (cost or time) when a unit variation occurs in one of the variables while keeping all other variables constant. It is useful in examining the impact of individual risk factors on the overall project risk and, thus, it can help select the critical factors for focusing.

   Decision Tree Analysis (Expected Monetary Value Analysis) technique helps to analyze the risks and benefits associated with investment decision strategy, when the investments could be made in phases. A case illustrating this technique is presented in the cases appended to this chapter.

Inputs

Risk Management Plan and *Risk Register* (its updated version after qualitative analysis) provide one set of inputs. *Cost Management Plan* and *Schedule Management Plan* provide another set of data. As mentioned earlier, over and above the data collected for routine risk register documentation, these techniques require collection and assessment of exhaustive additional data inputs. With this dataset, the quantitative analysis is carried out using some of the above-described techniques.

Tools and Techniques

Three important techniques for quantitative risk analysis have been discussed briefly above. In the cases appended to this chapter, two cases illustrate the application of Monte Carlo Simulation

Technique in step-wise details; the details are adequate for an interested person to be able to follow and apply them to a project on his/her hand. One case illustrates in a similar way the Decision Tree Analysis.

Outputs

Probabilistic Analysis of the Project Cost Estimate and Project Schedule – Unlike traditional cost estimate, which presents one single best guess value of the project cost or project duration, the Monte Carlo simulations would show the probability associated with any specific estimate of project cost. Similarly, if the technique is applied to project schedule, the probability associated with any specific estimate of project duration would be obtained.

Up-date of Risk Register – The output from the process is a further update of Risk Register. As mentioned while discussing the output of Identify Risk process, a detailed note on Risk Register is provided separately below in this section.

List of Risks Prioritized According to Quantitative Analysis – The results of quantitative risk analysis can also be used for prioritizing risks. In fact, it would be afar more reliable list than the corresponding list based on qualitative risk analysis.

3.5 Plan Risk Response

Plan Risk Responses is the process of developing the options and action to enhance opportunities to reduce threats to project objectives. (PMBOK® Guide, 5th Edition)

In this process, the project team (i) studies the alternative plans or options for responses for managing the risks in a way that would reduce the threats to project outcomes from negative risks and enhance the opportunities from the positive risks, and (ii) selecting the strategy for optimum results from the options developed. The process involves:

- Analyzing the data in the risk register (the list of prioritized risks from qualitative analysis and the results and trends spotted from quantitative risk analysis) and the methodology and responsibility assignments in the Risk Management Plan
- Developing options for individual risks and selecting the strategy from the available options of risk handling (avoiding, transferring, mitigating and accepting)
- Developing risk response plan for incorporation as an update into the risk register (selected strategy for each prioritized risk, assigning the risk management responsibility, and identifying the triggers)
- Calculating contingency reserves position

Inputs

Risk Register (including its updates from qualitative and quantitative analysis) and *Risk Management Plan* (for methodology, responsibility assignments and risk tolerance thresholds of key stakeholders) provide the main inputs.

Tools and Techniques

PMBOK® Guide makes distinction between the strategies for handling positive and negative risks. The strategies for negative risk include avoiding, transferring, mitigating and accepting the risk.

The strategies for handling opportunities (or positive risks) include exploiting, sharing, enhancing and accepting. These techniques for responding to the risks described earlier while discussing pro-active risk management of this chapter ((vide 2.2, "Steps in Pro-active Risk Management", phase (iii)). For the sake of completeness of this discussion on a stand-alone basis, they are listed below:

Strategies for Negative Risks or Threats

- Avoidance
- Transfer
- Mitigate
- Accept

Strategies for Positive Risks or Opportunities

- Exploit
- Enhance
- Share
- Accept

Contingent Response Strategies

Unlike the firmly planned strategies for positive or negative risks, which form part of the project management plan, the contingent response strategies come into play (and form the part of project activities) only if certain risks occur or triggers for risks occur.

Expert Judgment – Like other risk planning processes, expert judgment is an important technique for this process also.

Outputs

Risk Register Updates – The output of the process is a detailed plan of actions for prioritized risks, which is incorporated as an update in the risk register. The updates would include:

- The risk of prioritized risks and recommended strategy for handling it
- The provision of budget for risk management activities
- Provision of time required for risk management activity in the project schedule
- The assignment of roles and responsibilities for handling risks
- The residual and secondary risks

Updates of project plan components and *Updates of Project Documents* in light of risk response plan are the other outputs. Project Plan components requiring up-dates would include *Schedule Management Plan*, *Cost Management Plan*, *Quality Management Plan*, *Procurement Management Plan*, and *Human Resources Management Plan*. Project Documents requiring updates would include *Scope Baseline*, *Schedule Baseline*, and *Cost Baseline*.

3.6   Control Risks

Control Risks is the process of implementing risk response plans, tracking identified risks, monitoring residual risks, identifying new risks, and evaluating risk process effectiveness throughout the project.

(PMBOK® Guide, 5th Edition)

The process involves of implementing all the planning for risk management carried out in the earlier five risk planning processes. Specifically, it includes:

- Tracking identified and prioritized risks
- Watching out for risk triggers and putting into action the measures planned for handling the risks
- Monitoring the residual risks and identifying the new risks after handling the main risk is over, and
- Evaluating the effectiveness of risk management throughout the project life cycle
- Adjusting the contingency reserves in project budget and time buffers in light of the current position

Inputs

Like all monitoring and controlling processes, the inputs for this process are:

- *Risk Register* and *Project Management Plan* as the desired outcome or standard to be achieved, and
- *Work Performance Data* and *Work Performance Reports* as the actual results obtained.

Tools and Techniques

Variance Analysis – By comparing the variance between what is actually achieved with what was planned to be achieved, the degree and effectiveness of risk management is assessed and the direction for corrective measures for further risk management is set.

Risk Audits – This is another technique, like quality audits, of getting an independent assessment of how the risk management for the project is handled

Reassessment of risk scenario – The process requires continuously reassessing the risk scenario and its reassessment.

Outputs

The outputs of the process are Work Performance Information, Risk Register Updates (outcomes of actual risk handling activities and risk audit conclusions), and updates in the Project Plan and updates in the project documents (technical documentation and assumptions). Change Requests is another output, found necessary for managing some risks, particularly when risk trigger event occurs and contingent risk management is considered necessary.

4.0 RISK REGISTER

(Its gradual development during carrying out risk management planning processes)

While discussing Project Risk Management, PMBOK® Guide, 5th Edition, introduces the concept of Risk Register, a document comprehensively dealing with all project risk issues.

4.1 Risk Register Definition

Risk Register is defined as a document in which the results of risk analysis and risk response planning are recorded. (PMBOK® Guide, 5th Edition)

It contains the results of the qualitative risk analysis, quantitative risk analysis and risk response planning. The Risk Register details all identified risks, including description, category, cause, probability of occurring, impact(s) on project objectives, proposed responses, owners, and current status.

4.2 Development of Risk Register

Risk Register is a comprehensive reference document concerned with almost all risk management processes described in PMBOK® Guide. It evolves into its finished final form as the successive risk management processes are carried out. To start with, it would be important to note that PMBOK's definition of Risk has slightly different connotations from the generally accepted idea. **PMBOK defines risk as "An uncertain event or condition that, if it occurs, has a *positive or negative effect* on project's objectives (viz. scope, schedule, cost and quality)".** The term risk is used in general parlance to refer to only negative or unfavorable aspect of the uncertain event or condition, while PMBOK includes in the term also favorable aspect and possibility of exploiting the opportunity.

The initiation of Risk Register and its progressive elaboration proceeds during the risk management processes as follows:

4.2.1 Identify Risk

Risk Register comes into existence with the process "Identify Risk". Risk Register is the output of this process and includes entries of all risks identified at that stage; as additional risks are identified at the later planning or executing stage, the entries for them are made in the register. At this stage the Risk Register includes just two data sets:

- *List of Identified Risk:* This would include the risk identification, its brief description, the causes for the risk and the likely impact on project objectives (scope, schedule, cost or quality)
- *Attributes of the Identified Risks:* After listing the identified risks, attributes of the individual risk are analysed and included. It should cover:
  - *Probability of Occurrence* of Risk
  - *The Estimate of Impact* of Risk on project cost and project schedule
  - *Risk Event Drivers* – the factors which will influence the probability of occurrence of risk
  - *Risk Impact Drivers* – the factors which will influence the severity of impact of the risk on the cost or schedule
  - *Risk Mitigation Measures* – a preliminary overview of risk mitigation options
- *List of potential responses:* The preliminary analysis of the risk and the likely response to manage the risk

4.2.2 Perform Qualitative Risk Analysis

During this process, teach of the identified risk from the risk register list is analyzed to assess the probability of the risk event to occur and the impact it would have if the risk occurred on project scope, cost, schedule or quality. Using this data, the expected value of the risk impact is evaluated (Expected value of impact = probability of risk × the impact in event of risk occurrence). Once these assessments are worked out, a relative ranking of the risk can be carried out to prioritize further analysis and response planning. So, at this stage of risk management process, the risk

Register includes three additional data for each identified list entry, i.e. Probability, Impact on Occurrence, and Expected Value of Impact. The ranking based expected value of impact would be the basis for qualitative analysis.

4.2.3 Perform Quantitative Risk Analysis

A detailed quantitative risk analysis may be carried out for selected risks based on the prioritization derived from qualitative analysis of risk. Quantitative analysis would require collection of data for more reliable estimate of probability and impacts on outcome and the use of quantitative techniques like Monte Carlo simulation, Decision Tree Analysis and Sensitivity Analysis. Quantitative analysis of risk is therefore far more refined and reliable and comes out with the probabilistic analysis of achieving the time and cost objectives even in the event of risk occurrence. At this stage, therefore, in the Risk Register, the results from quantitative risk analysis are added against the specific entries.

4.2.4 Plan Risk Response

From the prioritized list of risks from the qualitative or quantitative risk analysis, the suitable responses are devised from the four available strategies for risk management. These strategies include:

- *Avoiding Risk:* Change project plan suitably to prevent risk arising by eliminating the work likely to involve risk
- *Transferring Risk:* Transfer the risk to an agent more experienced or capable of handling the work associated with the risk (Outsourcing) or transfer the consequence of risk to a third party (insurance)
- *Mitigating Risk:* Adopt such measures in project plan and execution, which would decrease the probability of occurrence of risk or reduce the impact of risk in case it occurred
- *Accepting Risk:* It is sometimes physically impossible or economically unviable to manage a risk and accepting it in case it occurs is the only way left

After this risk management process, the Risk Register would be further updated to include the planned response to the identified risk entries. At this stage, the main agency or person responsible for managing the risk, if it occurred, and the risk trigger give advance warning of the increased likelihood of risk occurrence.

4.2.5 Control Risk

During this process, the Risk Register is periodically reviewed and updated to current status of the project. The retired risks are removed from the active list of Risk Register and some new risks arising out of mitigation measures taken for managing some risks outcome are added. At the end of the project, Risk Register would provide a very valuable record of lessons learned for how a similar project in future can be planned and executed more effectively.

4.3 The Contents of Risk Register

The contents of Risk Register, after undergoing all updating from sequential risk management processes, would be as listed below. An Excel® format worksheet may be prepared and used with suitable columns to include these contents. These attributes, as evident from the above description of risk management processes, are sequentially added in developing the Risk Register and not at a one go.

List of Identified Risks (Identify Risk)
Attributes against Each Risk Entry

- Description risk event – including causes, impact on which specific objectives (Identify Risk)
- Probability of risk occurrence (Perform Qualitative Risk Analysis)
- Impact in event the risk event occurred (Perform Qualitative Risk Analysis)
- Expected value of risk event (Perform Qualitative Risk Analysis)
- Prioritized ranking or ordering of the list entries (Perform Qualitative Risk Analysis)
- Probabilistic assessment of risk event (Perform Quantitative Risk Analysis)
- Description of strategies for risk management (Plan Risk Response)
- Responsibility assigned for managing risk (Plan Risk Response)
- Description of risk trigger (Plan Risk Response)

The Risk Register would be periodically reviewed and updated during monitoring and controlling phase.

4.4 Specimen for Risk Register (Template)

A tabular template for the Risk Register is presented in the accompanying figure. The columns ordinarily included in the Risk Register template and some guidance on how to complete the risk analysis and update the risk register document are briefly described below:

i. *Risk Event*

   Care should be exercised to clearly articulate the event and not confuse with the impact on project outcome if the risk occurs. So "Cost Overrun" is not a correct articulation of risk; it is the negative impact of some risk. The risk itself may be inflation and price rise of materials, inadequately understood and agree requirements, overtime, etc.

ii. *Risk event drivers*

   Financial Risks, Technical Risks, Commercial risks, Project Planning and Execution Risks, Contractual or Legal Risks

iii. *Probability of each risk event driver*

iv. *Likely negative impact on project objectives outcomes*
   - Scope
   - Cost
   - Schedule
   - Quality

v. *Impact Drivers in case the risk does occur*

   e.g. High tides timings, heavy rains, the cleanliness of drains, evacuation plans vulnerable population in low-lying areas, readiness of emergency assistance services, communications are impact drivers in case of risk analysis for flooding of Mumbai roads during monsoon

vi. *Planned response for each major risk event / event driver*

   Avoidance / Transfer / Sharing Risk/Impact mitigation /Acceptance or retaining risk

vii. *Risk Response Plan for each major risk*
   - Responsibility for risk management (risk owners)
   - Agreed risk response planned

- Trigger
- Residual risks
- Budget for risk response

viii *Contingency provision for risk management in*
Project cost
Project schedule

5.0 CHECK-LIST FOR RISK IDENTIFICATION

Financial Risks (Financial Viability) – exposure to loss due to

- Huge project cost overruns
- Unexpectedly large delay in project implementation
- Total failure in development or use of new technology or material
- Acts of God
- Delayed returns from project
- Returns not up to expectation
- Project failing in meeting all objectives

Technical Risks (Technical Feasibility) – due to

- Requirement for use of unproven technology
- Unavailability of skilled personnel for use of the technology
- Use of an operation previously not used
- Use of new materials

Commercial Risks (Business Plan Failure) – due to

- Total market development not up to expectation
- Failure in capturing planned market share (quality/price constraints)
- Project delay and corresponding delayed cash inflows
- Product pricing and cost unfavourable compared to projections

Project Planning and Execution Risks – due to

- Failure in meeting criteria for project success (scope management)
- Project cost overruns (cost management)
- Schedule delay (time management)

Contractual or Legal Risk – due to

- Discrepancy between estimated and contracted cost
- Project late delivery penalty
- Third party litigations
- Failure in meeting environmental or other legal requirements for communities around the project sites

CASE 7.1

Alaska Fly–Fishing Expedition*

You are sitting around the fire at a lodge in Dillingham, Alaska, discussing a fishing expedition you are planning with your colleagues at Great Alaska Adventures (GAA). Earlier in the day you received a fax from the president of BlueNote, Inc. The president wants to reward her top management team by taking them on an all-expense-paid fly-fishing adventure in Alaska. She would like GAA to organize and lead the expedition.

You have just finished a preliminary scope statement for the project (see below). You are now brainstorming potential risks associated with the project.

1. Brainstorm potential risks associated with this project. Try to come up with at least five different risks.
2. Use a risk assessment form similar to Figure 7.6 to analyze identified risks.
3. Develop a risk response matrix similar to Figure 7.8 to outline how you would deal with each of the risks.

PROJECT SCOPE STATEMENT

Project Objective

To organize and lead a five-day fly-fishing expedition down the Tikchik River system in Alaska from June 21 to 25 at a cost not to exceed $35,000.

Deliverables

- Provide air transportation from Dillingham, Alaska, to Camp I and from Camp II back to Dillingham.
- Provide river transportation consisting of two eight-man drift boats with outboard motors.
- Provide three meals a day for the five days spent on the river.
- Provide four hours fly-fishing instruction.
- Provide overnight accommodations at the Dillingham lodge plus three four-man tents with cots, bedding, and lanterns.
- Provide four experienced river guides who are also fly fishermen.
- Provide fishing licenses for all guests.

Milestones

1. Contract signed January 22.
2. Guests arrive in Dillingham June 20.

---

* This case was prepared with the assistance of Stuart Morigeau.

3. Depart by plane to Base Camp I June 21.
4. Depart by plane from Base Camp II to Dillingham June 25.

Technical Requirements

1. Fly in air transportation to and from base camps.
2. Boat transportation within the Tikchik River system.
3. Digital cellular communication devices.
4. Camps and fishing conform to state of Alaska requirements.

Limits and Exclusions

1. Guests are responsible for travel arrangements to and from Dillingham, Alaska.
2. Guests are responsible for their own fly-fishing equipment and clothing.
3. Local air transportation to and from base camps will be outsourced.
4. Tour guides are not responsible for the number of King Salmon caught by guests.

Customer Review

The president of BlueNote, Inc.

CASE 7.2

Silver Fiddle Construction

You are the president of Silver Fiddle Construction (SFC), which specializes in building high-quality, customized homes in the Grand Junction, Colorado, area. You have just been hired by the Czopeks to build their dream home. You operate as a general contractor and employ only a part-time bookkeeper. You subcontract work to local trade professionals. Housing construction in Grand Junction is booming. You are tentatively scheduled to complete 11 houses this year. You have promised the Czopeks that the final costs will range from $450,000 to $500,000 and that it will take five months to complete the house once groundbreaking has begun. The Czopeks are willing to have the project delayed in order to save costs.

You have just finished a preliminary scope statement for the project (see below). You are now brainstorming potential risks associated with the project.

1. Identify potential risks associated with this project. Try to come up with at least five different risks.
2. Use a risk assessment form similar to Figure 7.6 to analyze identified risks.
3. Develop a risk response matrix similar to Figure 7.8 to outline how you would deal with each of the risks.

PROJECT SCOPE STATEMENT

Project Objective

To construct a high-quality, custom home within five months at a cost not to exceed $500,000.

Deliverables

- A 2,500-square-foot, 2½-bath, 3-bedroom, finished home.
- A finished garage, insulated and sheetrocked.
- Kitchen appliances to include range, oven, microwave, and dishwasher.
- High-efficiency gas furnace with programmable thermostat.

Milestones

1. Permits approved July 5.
2. Foundation poured July 12.
3. "Dry in"—framing, sheathing, plumbing, electrical, and mechanical inspections—passed September 25.
4. Final inspection November 7.

Technical Requirements

1. Home must meet local building codes.
2. All windows and doors must pass NFRC class 40 energy ratings.
3. Exterior wall insulation must meet an "R" factor of 21.
4. Ceiling insulation must meet an "R" factor of 38.
5. Floor insulation must meet an "R" factor of 25.
6. Garage will accommodate two cars and one 28-foot-long Winnebago.
7. Structure must pass seismic stability codes.

Limits and Exclusions

1. The home will be built to the specifications and design of the original blueprints provided by the customer.
2. Owner is responsible for landscaping.
3. Refrigerator is not included among kitchen appliances.
4. Air conditioning is not included, but house is prewired for it.
5. SFC reserves the right to contract out services.

Customer Review

"Bolo" and Izabella Czopek.

CASE 7.3

Trans LAN Project

Trans Systems is a small, information systems consulting firm located in Meridian, Louisiana. Trans has just been hired to design and install a local area network (LAN) for the city of Meridian's social welfare agency. You are the manager for the project, which includes one Trans professional and two interns from a local university. You have just finished a preliminary scope statement for the project (see below). You are now brainstorming potential risks associated with the project.

1. Identify potential risks associated with this project. Try to come up with at least five different risks.
2. Use a risk assessment form similar to Figure 7.6 to analyze identified risks.
3. Develop a risk response matrix similar to Figure 7.8 to outline how you would deal with each of the risks.

PROJECT SCOPE STATEMENT

Project Objective

To design and install a new local area network (LAN) within one month with a budget not to exceed $90,000 for the Meridian Social Service Agency with minimum disruption to ongoing operations.

Deliverables

- Twenty workstations and twenty laptop computers.
- Server with dual-core processors.
- Two color laser printers.
- Windows R2 server and workstation operating system (Windows 7).
- Migration of existing databases and programs to new system.
- Four hours of introduction training for client's personnel.
- Sixteen hours of training for client network administrator.
- Fully operational LAN system.

Milestones

1. Hardware January 22.
2. Setting users' priority and authorization January 26.
3. In-house whole network test completed February 1.
4. Client site test completed February 2.
5. Training completed February 16.

Technical Requirements

1. Workstations with 17-inch flat panel monitors, dual-core processors, 4 GB RAM, 8X DVD+RW, wireless card, Ethernet card, 500 GB hard drive.
2. Laptops with 12-inch display monitor, dual-core processors, 2GB RAM, 8X DVD+RW, wireless card, Ethernet card, 500 GB hard drive and weigh less than 4½ lbs.
3. Wireless network interface cards and Ethernet connections.
4. System must support Windows Vista/Windows 7 platforms.
5. System must provide secure external access for field workers.

Limits and Exclusions

1. On-site work to be done after 8:00 P.M. and before 7:00 A.M. Monday through Saturday.
2. System maintenance and repair only up to one month after final inspection.
3. Warranties transferred to client.
4. Only responsible for installing software designated by the client two weeks before the start of the project.
5. Client will be billed for additional training beyond that prescribed in the contract.

Customer Review

Director of the city of Meridian's Social Service Agency.

CASE 7.4

XSU Spring Concert

You are a member of the X State University (XSU) student body entertainment committee. Your committee has agreed to sponsor a spring concert. The motive behind this concert is to offer a safe alternative to Hasta Weekend. Hasta Weekend is a spring event in which students from XSU rent houseboats and engage in heavy partying. Traditionally this occurs during the last weekend in May. Unfortunately, the partying has a long history of getting out of hand, sometimes leading to fatal accidents. After one such tragedy last spring, your committee wants to offer an alternative experience for those who are eager to celebrate the change in weather and the pending end of the school year.

You have just finished a preliminary scope statement for the project (see below). You are now brainstorming potential risks associated with the project.

1. Identify potential risks associated with this project. Try to come up with at least five different risks.
2. Use a risk assessment form similar to Figure 7.6 to analyze identified risks.
3. Develop a risk response matrix similar to Figure 7.8 to outline how you would deal with each of the risks.

PROJECT SCOPE STATEMENT

Project Objective

To organize and deliver an eight-hour concert at Wahoo Stadium at a cost not to exceed $50,000 on the last Saturday in May.

Deliverables

- Local advertising.
- Concert security.
- Separate Beer Garden.
- Eight hours of music and entertainment.
- Food venues.
- Souvenir concert t-shirts.
- Secure all licenses and approvals.
- Secure sponsors.

Milestones

1. Secure all permissions and approvals by January 15.
2. Sign big-name artist by February 15.
3. Complete artist roster by April 1.
4. Secure vendor contracts by April 15.
5. Setup completed on May 27.
6. Concert on May 28.
7. Cleanup completed by May 31.

Technical Requirements

1. Professional sound stage and system.
2. At least one big-name artist.
3. At least seven performing acts.
4. Restroom facilities for 10,000 people.
5. Parking available for 1,000 cars.
6. Compliance with XSU and city requirements/ordinances.

Limits and Exclusions

1. Performers responsible for travel arrangements to and from XSU.
2. Vendors contribute a set percentage of sales.
3. Concert must be over by 11:30 P.M.

Customer Review

The president of XSU student body.

CASE 7.5

Sustaining Project Risk Management during Implementation

BACKGROUND

Bill (Senior VP of product development): Carlos [project manager], we have to talk. I am concerned about the way we manage project risk here at Futuronics. I just came from an international "Future Mote Devices" meeting at UC Berkeley. [Note: A *mote* is a very small [e.g., 2–3mm square], wireless sensing pod that may be placed on land or in water to measure and communicate data.] The project management sessions receiving most attention addressed risk in product development projects. They described our management of project risk to the letter—failure to sustain risk management *after the project gets rolling*. It seems someone has to get burned before risk management is taken seriously.

Much to my surprise, almost every project manager there admitted their firms have a problem sustaining team members' interest in managing risk after the project is on its way. The old saying, "If you don't manage risk, you pay the price later," generated horror stories from a few who paid the price. We spent some time brainstorming ways to handle the problem at the project level, but there were very few concrete suggestions. The meeting gave me a wakeup call. Carlos, we need to tackle this problem or some new or known risk event could put us both out of a job. The similarities between their horror stories and some of our past mistakes are scary.

Since here at Futuronics we only develop new products that are at least seven years beyond anything on the market, the level of both "known risk events and unknown risk" is far higher than in most other organizations. Managing project risk is important to every project, but here at Futuronics every new product project is loaded with risks. Carlos, I'm willing to work with you to improve our management of project risk at Futuronics.

Carlos: Bill, I am aware of the problem. The PMI Roundtables I attend also talk to the difficulty of keeping teams and other stakeholders willing to revisit risk once the project is on its way. [PMI Roundtables are monthly meetings of practicing PMs across industries designed to address project management problems.] I also heard war stories at a recent project management roundtable meeting. I have some notes from the meeting right here.

It all started with the leader's question: "How many project managers actually manage risk over the complete project life cycle?"

PM 1: We all work through the risk management process well before the project begins. We have the process template of risk identification, assessment, response, control, risk register, and contingency down pat. We just don't follow through after the project begins. I think interest dies. Have you ever tried to get project stakeholders to come to a risk meeting when the project is moving relatively well?

PM 2: A recent e-mail from one of our stakeholders said, "We'll deal with it [risk] when it happens."

PM 3: I agree. Interest seems to move from future oriented to reactionary. Also, risk management seems to degenerate into issue (concerns and problems) management versus real risk management.

PM 4: I ask team members, "What is the risk of not managing risk over the life of the project?" Sometimes this question nudges a few to respond positively, especially if risks have changed or new ones are perceived. I use a failed project where a solid risk management process would have avoided the project failure. I explain all of the risk management processes that would have helped to improve the risk elements—risk identification, triggers, responsibility, transfer, accept, etc.

PM 5: Risk is not a line item in the budget or schedule. Maybe it is in the contingency budget to cover "unknowns of unknowns." I have to watch that management doesn't try to squeeze out the contingency budget for something else.

Carlos continued to share with his boss that there were many more comments, but very few gave much guidance. Carlos then shared his idea:

Carlos: Colette is our best trainer, especially in transition management, and she would be a great choice for following through on this problem. Her training classes on upfront risk management are excellent. Should we ask her to present a session?

Bill: You are right, Carlos, Collette is ideal. She is smart and a great team motivator. Ask her, but give her some kind of direction for focus.

A few days later, Carlos sent out a memo:

Colette, this is to follow up on our lunch conversation yesterday discussing sustaining risk management after the project is on its way. Given the nature of our futuristic company, we should stress the point that our product development projects carry many more inherent risks than do traditional projects. I suggest the training classes should drill down on concrete actions and policies that will encourage interest of team members and other project stakeholders in sustaining risk management practices during project execution.

Colette, we appreciate your taking on this project. When you have developed your training session, please give me a copy so I can schedule and support your efforts.

Regards, Carlos

CHALLENGE

Divide the class into teams of three or more participants.

Colette needs your help to develop her training program. You may wish to consider the questions listed below to initiate ideas.

- Why do project stakeholders lose interest in project risk after the project is underway?
- What are the dangers of not keeping on top of risk management during implementation?
- What kind of business is Futuronics in?

Brainstorm specific actions that will encourage project stakeholders to continue to scan and track the project environment for risk events. Suggest three concrete actions or scenarios that will encourage project stakeholders to change their behavior and truly support risk management while projects are being implemented. The following outline headings may be helpful in developing possible actions that would improve/enhance stakeholder support.

- Improving the risk management process

- Organization actions
- Motivating participation

CASE 7.6

International Capital, Inc.—Part A

International Capital, Inc. (IC), is a small investment banking firm that specializes in securing funds for small- to medium-sized firms. IC is able to use a standardized project format for each engagement. Only activity times and unusual circumstances change the standard network. Beth Brown has been assigned to this client as project manager partner and has compiled the network information and activity times for the latest client as follows:

Activity	Description	Immediate Predecessor
A	Start story draft using template	—
B	Research client firm	—
C	Create "due diligence" rough draft	A, B
D	Coordinate needs proposal with client	C
E	Estimate future demand and cash flows	C
F	Draft future plans for client company	E
G	Create and approve legal documents	C
H	Integrate all drafts into first-draft proposal	D, F, G
I	Line up potential sources of capital	G, F
J	Check, approve, and print final legal proposal	H
K	Sign contracts and transfer funds	I, J

	Time in Workdays		
Activity	Optimistic	Most Likely	Pessimistic
A	4	7	10
B	2	4	8
C	2	5	8
D	16	19	28
E	6	9	24
F	1	7	13
G	4	10	28
H	2	5	14
I	5	8	17
J	2	5	8
K	17	29	45

MANAGERIAL REPORT

Brown and other broker partners have a policy of passing their plan through a project review committee of colleagues. This committee traditionally checks that all details are covered, times are realistic, and resources are available. Brown wishes you to develop a report that presents a planned schedule and expected project completion time in workdays. Include a project network in your report. The average duration for a sourcing capital project is 70 workdays. IC partners have agreed it is good business to set up projects with a 95 percent chance of attaining the plan. How does this project stack up with the average project? What would the average have to be to ensure a 95 percent chance of completing the project in 70 workdays?

CASE 7.7

Advantage Energy Technology Data Center Migration—Part B

In Chapter 6, Brian Smith, network administrator at Advanced Energy Technology (AET), was given the responsibility of implementing the migration of a large data center to a new office location.

Careful planning was needed because AET operates in the highly competitive petroleum industry. AET is one of five national software companies that provide an accounting and business management package for oil jobbers and gasoline distributors. A few years ago, AET jumped into the "application service provider" world. Their large data center provides clients with remote access to AET's complete suite of application software systems. Traditionally, one of AET's primary competitive advantages has been the company's trademark IT reliability. Due to the complexity of this project, the Executive Committee insisted that preliminary analysis of the anticipated completion date be conducted.

Brian compiled the following information, in preparation for some PERT analysis:

1. Based on these estimates and the resultant expected project duration of 69 days, the executive committee wants to know what is the probability of completing the project before a scheduled time (T_S) of 68 days?

2. The significance of this project has the executive committee very concerned. The committee has decided that more analysis of the duration of each activity is needed. Prior to conducting that effort, they asked Brian to calculate what the expected project duration would have to be to ensure a 93 percent chance of completion within 68 days.

ADVANTAGE ENERGY TECHNOLOGY (AET)— ACCOUNTS PAYABLE SYSTEM

The AET sales department has been concerned about a new start-up company that is about to release an accounts payable system. Their investigation indicates that this new package will

		Time in Workdays			
Task Name	Optimistic Dur.	Most Likely Dur.	Pessimistic Dur.	Immediate Predecessor	Critical Path
1 **AET DATA CENTER MIGRATION**	54	68	92		
2 Team meeting	0.5	1	1.5		✓
3 Hire contractors	6	7	8	2	
4 Network design	12	14	16	2	
5 **Ventilation system**	—	—	—	—	
6 Order ventilation system	18	21	30	2	
7 Install ventilation system	5	7	9	6	
8 **New racks**	—	—	—	—	
9 Order new racks	13	14	21	2	✓
10 Install racks	17	21	25	9	✓
11 **Power supplies and cables**	—	—	—	—	
12 Order power supplies & cables	6	7	8	2	
13 Install power supplies	5	5	11	12, 16	
14 Install cables	6	8	10	12, 16	✓
15 Renovation of data center	19	20	27	3, 4	
16 City inspection	1	2	3	3, 7, 10	✓
17 **Switchover Meetings**	—	—	—	—	
18 Facilities	7	8	9	14	
19 Operations/systems	5	7	9	14	
20 Operations/telecommunications	6	7	8	14	
21 Systems and applications	7	7	13	14	
22 Customer service	5	6	13	14	✓
23 Power check	0.5	1	1.5	13, 14, 15	✓
24 Install test servers	5	7	9	18, 19, 20, 21, 22, 23	✓
25 Management safety check	1	2	3	7, 23, 24	✓
26 Primary systems check	1.5	2	2.5	25	✓
27 Set date for move	1	1	1	26	✓
28 Complete move	1	2	3	27	✓

provide features which will seriously compete with AET's current Accounts Payable system and some cases, exceed what AET offers.

Tom Wright, senior applications developer at AET, has been given the responsibility of analyzing, designing, developing, and delivering a new accounts payable system (A/P) for AET customers.

Complicating the issue is the concern of the sales department about AET's recent inability to meet promised delivery dates. They have convinced CEO (Larry Martain) that a significant marketing effort will have to be expended to convince the clients they should wait for the AET product rather than jump to a package provided by a new entry to the petroleum software business. Companion to this effort is the importance of the performance of the software development group.

Consequently, Tom has decided to take the following action: tighten up the estimating effort by his developers; incorporate some new estimating procedures; and use some PERT techniques to generate probabilities associated with his delivery dates.

		Time in Workdays				
	Task Name	Optimistic Dur.	Most Likely Dur.	Pessimistic Dur.	Immediate Predecessor	Critical Path
1	**ACCOUNTS PAYABLE SYSTEM**					
2	Planning meeting	1	1	2		✓
3	Team assignments	3	4	5	2	✓
4	**Program specification**					
5	Customer requirements	8	10	12	3	✓
6	Feasibility study	3	5	7	5	
7	Systems analysis	6	8	10	5	✓
8	Prelim budget & schedule	1	2	3	7	✓
9	Functional specification	3	5	7	7	✓
10	Prelim design	10	12	14	9	✓
11	Configuration and perf needs	3	4	5	10	✓
12	Hardware requirements	4	6	8	11	✓
13	System specification	5	7	9	10	
14	Detailed design	12	14	16	12, 13	✓
15	Program specification	8	10	12	14	✓
16	Programming—first phase	27	32	37	15	✓
17	Documentation	14	16	18	10	
18	**Prototype**					
19	Development	5	7	9	16	✓
20	User testing & feedback	12	14	16	19	✓
21	Programming—second phase	10	12	14	16	
22	Beta testing	18	20	22	21	
23	Final documentation pkg	9	10	11	17, 20	✓
24	Training pkg	4	5	6	21SS, 23	✓
25	Product release	3	5	7	22, 23, 24	✓

SS = Start to Start lag

Tom's planning team made a first-cut at the set of activities and associated durations:

3. Based on these estimates and the critical path, the project duration is estimated at 149 days. But, an AET salesperson in the Southeast Region has discovered that the competing A/P package (with significant improvements) is scheduled for delivery in approximately 145 days. The sales force is very anxious to beat that delivery time. The executive committee asks Tom for an estimated probability of reducing his expected project duration by two days.

4. The executive committee is advised by Tom that after all the estimating was completed, he determined that one of his two critical systems analysts might have to move out of the area for critical family reasons. Tom is still very confident that with some staff rearrangements, assistance from a subcontractor, and some "hands on" activities on his part he can still meet the original delivery date, based on 149 days.

This news is very disconcerting to the committee and the sales staff. At this point, the committee decides that based on the most recent delivery performance of AET, a modified, comfortable delivery date should be communicated to AET clients—one that Tom and his staff are very likely to meet. Consequently, Tom is asked to calculate what the expected project duration would have to be to ensure a 98 percent chance of completion within 160 days—that is a "published, drop dead date" that can be communicated to the clients.

CASE 7.8

Venugopal's Dilemma

(Illustration of Monte Carlo Simulation: A Technique for Quantitative Risk Analysis)

Abstract

Quantitative risk analysis techniques find application for projects of large scope, cost and associated risks. The case here describes a project situation, where a popular quantitative risk analysis technique, Monte Carlo Simulation, is effectively applied. The idea underlying this case presentation is to bring awareness about (i) what a simulation based quantitative risk analysis can accomplish, (ii) the general framework and nature of input data required for carrying out the analysis and (iii) the type of inferences which this technique would develop – the graphical output of the cumulative probability for different likely project outcomes suitable for taking calculated risks. The details of actual simulation technique – 'Monte Carlo simulation' – are available from the textbooks on quantitative analytical methods; they are also illustrated in detail in some other cases in this book. The quantitative techniques themselves are sound in concept and relatively straightforward in application, however, for their meaningful application, the input data would need to be collected with great care and judgment.

CASE TEXT

When Ram Kumar Sharma returned from his U.S. visit, he was just thrilled and eager to display the goldmine opportunity he discovered during the trip. On a routine call to one of his company's customers, where their team of twelve programmers was working on a review of the Y2K impact on the software already used by the customer for over a decade, he happened to meet the outsourcing director of the client. From the discussion over a dinner in the evening, Sharma learnt about the client's plan to invite a tender for a good size business solution IT project. The project appeared to have a potential for attractive margins and so he extended his stay there for two days more and collected the details of the tender and the competitors likely to participate in the tendering process.

Sharma was bubbling with enthusiasm and pride while talking about the opportunity that he had discovered. Vice President, Venugopal was, however, not that enthused. He could see some of the project risks and their likely impacts. All the same, the opportunity was too attractive to be by-passed without a second look.

Venugopal could see that if they landed the contract, it would be indeed a very attractive opportunity of earning over ₹700 to 950 million. But the competition was also strong and his company would have to spend up front a good sum even to prepare the bid. With over ₹300,000 per day cost of a team of hundred workers, who were likely to be involved for bid preparation, and assuming that the team might require eight weeks for the work involved in preparing the details for making the bid, the minimum up-front cost of developing the bid was ₹12 million – not small for his company. The cost could even swell up to ₹24 million. Moreover, there were certain risk elements in the cost for bid preparation, which were subject to variation in a range. *Obtaining the estimate for the cost of bid preparation with a known degree of certainty or confidence was crucial in deciding whether or not his company should undertake the exercise and spend the money in bid preparation.*

The bid was to be prepared for a medium- sized IT system consisting of two mainframe computer installations supporting 80 workstations. The software would consist of the off-the-shelf applications as well as some customization and integration. The system was to be installed (hardware part also) and the users were to be trained. Part of the bid was also for full hardware and software support for 10 years after the system was installed. All this information was obtained by Sharma from the discussion with the client, but the specific requirements, especially the identity of the software application would not be known till the tender was formally issued.

With his vast experience, Venugopal could easily take an overview of the bid preparation activities and break them down into main six or seven work packages. The next step he took was to mull over the likely contents of the work packages and make a very rough estimate of the work effort and corresponding costs for each work package. This six-hour exercise helped to clarify some issues, but Venugopal still did not feel comfortable about the element of risk involved in preparing the bid. Sharma kept on reassuring Venugopal that the client was very happy with the quality of outsourcing work carried out by them for the client so far and that they would have a high chance of winning the tender if they came out with a technically sound and cost effective proposal. This encouraged Venugopal to take a chance for preparing the bid, but before he could decide on that course, he needed some degree of confidence on the exact outlay he would have to be ready to commit for bidding. Venugopal decided to discuss this with Dr. Shesha Iyanger, one of his brilliant new associate, who had a good grounding in quantitative techniques for estimation.

Over a cup of coffee, Venugopal gave Dr. Shesha the essential details of the situation and summarized with a remark, " I would be ready to commit a specific sum for preparing bid, but I would like to know how much chance I have in being able to prepare the bid in that budget. In other words, I would want to *take a calculated risk;* I would like to know the answers to the questions like:

- What are the chances of my preparing the bid within a budget of, say ₹12 million?, or
- What budget I must be prepare to sanction if I want to have the confidence of over 90% in completing preparation of bid within that budget? or, for that matter,
- What would be the most likely (50% confidence level) cost for preparing the bid?"

Dr. Sesha said, "Well, you have rightly described it as a gambling situation, but there are certain simulation modeling techniques for quantitative risk analysis, which could give you the answers you are looking for. The analysis could tell you the degree of confidence you can have on preparing the bid within a certain budget. For example, the analysis could give you an inference that the probability of your preparing the bid within a certain budget, say ₹12 million, is 60 % or 70 %. Or that if you want to have a degree of confidence to be around 95 %, you must be prepared to sanction a higher budget, say ₹16 million. Interestingly, the technique is called *Monte Carlo* simulation – probably an implicit admission of the nature of gambling uncertainty in the tool and reminding me of an old James Bond movie, *Casino Royal,* where he was shown sitting at a gaming table at Monte Carlo.

The technique consists of *creating a scenario by picking at random one of the likely outcomes (*say, cost or time duration*) of each of the elements constituting the total work and working out from these individual estimates the total outcome (say, cost or time for the entire project).* The computer would carry out this exercise for the desired number of scenarios (say 100 or 500) and give you the total cost or time for the project for each scenario. The cumulative frequency distribution of the resulting total cost or time period is plotted against the total project cost or time. From this graph, you could read the degree of confidence, which you can associate with any particular value of total project cost or project schedule. *The technique is statistically sound in concept, but as you realize, the quality of the output would depend on the quality and reliability of the input data.*

Also, let me assure you. This would not take too much work or time. Our new age computers and the available standard software available, say Excel, could be used to work out such quantitative risk analysis in a day at the most. Just give me an idea of the nature of distribution, which the cost of individual packages would take, their minimum and maximum likely values, and I will work out a Monte Carlo simulation model, from which you can gauge the degree of confidence that can be associated with any specific budget you may be prepared to sanction."

Venugopal found the technique interesting and worth exploring. He sat down and worked out the details necessary for the data required to give to Dr. Shesha (Exhibit 1).

Two days later, Dr. Shesh came back to Venugopal and showed him the graph of the cumulative probability of completing the bid versus the bid budget (Exhibit 2).

Venugopal was quite impressed by what he saw. He kept on mulling over studying the graph, drawing the inferences, which could be drawn from it and to what extent the data he gave for the analysis was trustworthy and if the data could be refined for greater reliability.

Well, the quantitative risk analysis could take it just so far. It was now left to Venugopal to keep simmering within and looking at various of issues for decision making: the overall company strategy, financial position of the company, the likely market scenario in the next 12 months, the risk tolerance of the other board members at this stage, and the risks and pay-offs from the successful or unsuccessful outcomes of the bid.

Identification of Activities for Bid Preparation

Venugopal identified seven activities to be the parts of preparing a bid. The corresponding work packages are described below:

Project Management	This work package covers compiling the final documentation for the bid and the cost of project management for preparing the bid.
System Design	This work package covers preparing the overall specifications of the system, design of system architecture, and technical specifications of component products required to build the system. Estimating the cost of man-hours for system design.
Purchased Software	This work package covers identifying the suppliers for proprietary software included in the system design; obtain technical specifications and quotes for provision within the bid. Prepare proposal text describing the software features and how they meet the client's tender specifications.
Software Development	This work package covers:
	(a) Defining the requirements for software to be developed; integrating tasks departmentally and developing the estimate of time and cost

(b) Estimating the time and cost for integration of the departmentally developed software with the overall system.

Installation
This work package covers estimating the time and cost of installing the hardware, proprietary software and departmentally developed software for building the system to meet the functional requirements and the desired features.

Training and Initial Support
This work package covers estimating the training requirements, the cost of preparing and compiling the training manual, the time and cost of personal training of key operating staff of the client, and describing the scope of training offered in the proposal.

Post-installation Support
This work package covers estimating the cost of post-installation support and including its description in the proposal.

EXHIBIT 1 ···
Summary of Work Packages Cost Estimates for Quantitative Risk Analysis

Work Package   Estimated Cost in ₹ lakhs

(Effort in Man-days)	Minimum	Likely	Maximum
Project Management	30.0 (100)	34.5 (115)	36.0 (120)
System Design	42.0 (140)	54.0 (180)	60.0 (200)
Purchased Software	4.5	7.5	9.0
Software Development and Integration tasks	21.0 (70)	24.0 (80)	30.0 (100)
Installation	4.5 (15)	6.0 (20)	9.0 (30)
Training and Initial Support	4.5 (15)	6.0 (20)	9.0 (30)
Post-installation Support	2.5 (8)	4.0 (10)	5.0 (13)
TOTAL COST IN ₹ LAKH	109	136	158
(₹ million)	(10.9)	(13.6)	(15.8)
Total Effort in Man-days	(348)	(425)	(493)

Basis for Estimates: 1. Man-days estimated from references to the project archives for similar projects and confirmed by preliminary function points analysis
2. Average cost of man-days taken at ₹3,000/- per man-day, (salary and allocated overheads) based on the current year budgeted costs.

THE CUMULATIVE PROBABILITY VERSUS BID COST (₹ LAKH)

Tabular Data and Graph (Worked out By Dr. Shesha Iyanger)

From Exhibit 2, Venugopal can get the inferences he desired from the quantitative risk analysis. These are:

1. The probability of completing the bid within the budgeted cost of ₹12 millions is less than 5%. In other words the degree of confidence for completing the bid within ₹12-million budget is less than 5%.

2. For the degree of confidence to be 90%, the budget to be sanctioned for bid preparation must be ₹14.2 million.

3. The most likely cost (50% confidence level) for the bid preparation would be ₹13.4 million.

VENUGOPAL'S DILEMMA (Cumulative Probability vs Bid Cost (₹ Lakhs)

Data Table

Cumulative Probability	Bid Cost (₹ Lakh)
0	118
2	120
2	122
8	124
12	126
20	128
30	130
40	132
52	134
70	136
80	138
88	140
94	142
98	144
100	146

Bid cost vs Cumulative Probability

CASE 7.9

Supercomp Systems Manufacturing
(Qualitative Risk Analysis Technique for Managing Project Risk)

Abstract

Qualitative Risk analysis is an important risk management process used for prioritizing risks. The technique requires developing a cause–effect diagram linking the risk event drivers and risk impact drivers with the impact on the cost or schedule if the risk event occurred. From the probability of the risk event and the corresponding impact on the project cost or schedule, the expected value of the risk is estimated. This expected value is used for prioritizing risks and developing the risk management plan. The case below describes a scenario of qualitative risk management for a project for a manufacturing organization.

CASE TEXT

At the conference room table of Supercomp Systems Manufacturing Ltd. sat four executives with intense facial expressions. The group had been closely working together on a project to develop and market a new slim laptop computer, which would be a kilogram lighter than the models available in the market. Their project brief included developing the prototype, setting up the production line and overseeing for the first three months the production operation for the smooth transfer of the project to the manufacturing group.

The project group had burnt mid-night oil and devised ingenious ways to develop the prototype. Lenovo, the Chinese computer giant considered introducing in the U.S the laptop computer under development by Supercomp as one of its low-cost models in the product line. Lenovo contracted with Supecomp to bankroll the cost of development for the prototype and agreed to purchase at the contracted price about 25,000 units to be supplied in the first three months for seed marketing. Lenovo indicated to Supercomp that if the product was well accepted in the U.S., they expected the market to grow up to 15,000 units per week within a year and, accordingly, suggested Supercomp to set up the manufacturing line with a capacity for at least 5000 units per week to start with.

One look at the prototype model and Nimish Mehta, The Executive Vice-President, realized that Supercomp had a real winner with this product. To reap the full benefits from the new product, he mused, 'it was crucial to ramp-up the production and establish the brand and the position as a pioneer before the competitors came up with their 'me-too'' imitations. "You have done very well so far", Nimish addressed Mahesh, who was the leader of the cross-functional product development team, "How set you guys are in meeting the first quarter's quota for supplying to Lenovo and hand over the project facilities to our manufacturing group for regular production?" The ramp-up of the production line was indeed the final and crucial acid test, which the project group had to pass.

Mahesh had called this meeting for a review and analysis of the risks in meeting the project's ramp-up objectives. The other members of the team were Asutosh Kejarival, an accountant, B. Subramaniam, a senior engineer from production department and Raman Seth, a bright MBA leading a newly set-up supply chain management group in the materials department.

"Sixteen months efforts of our group are now coming to a close and we must pass the test of successfully ramping up the production and win recognition. What problems or risks do we foresee and what can we do about them?" Mahesh opened the discussion, "You know that Lenovo has to be supplied for the first three months 5,000, 7,500 and 12,000 units respectively."

"Well, our assembly line capacity is supposed to be 5,000 units per week on a 3-shifts basis or over 20,000 units in a month. So, it would look that we need not expect any problems in meeting the first 3-month quota before we hand over the facilities. But, before handing over the facility to manufacturing, we need to establish that the production capacity of the assembly line is 5,000 units per week. We may have a problem there. My experience from all these years is that we do face problems in ramping up production. I expect the production rate in the first three months to be about 10,000 units, say 40-45% of the required monthly output. Use only 45% of the sales forecast to be met in the first three months; that is the bitter truth. So we will have a problem in demonstrating the production capacity of the assembly line before handing it over to the manufacturing", Subramaniam explained.

"Do you mean every time the manufacturing ramp-up is launched, the output is a meager, that is, less than half, capacity in the first quarter? We would lose a gross margin of several million dollars – wait a minute, I will calculate the exact number and come back." Kejarival was surprised.

"Not every time, but most times – say seven times out of ten!" Subbu shot back.

The euphoria of the project team, which developed a new winning product in a record time, sank. There was a silence for a minute, while Kejarival flipped his papers back and forth, noted down some numbers and punched in his calculator. "Over U.S Dollars six and a half millions", he announced looking up from the calculator, "Dollars 6,505,191 to be precise. That is the loss in gross revenue if we fail to meet the first quarter's production targets."

"How do you get all these funny accuracy in your numbers – right down to a Rupee?" Subbu asked teasingly.

"It is elementary Dr. Watson!" Kejarival mimicked the famous Sherlock Holmes quote, "Our sale price to Lenovo is U.S. $ 995/- per piece and the cost of goods sold (COGS) is projected to be U.S. $ 512.24 cents per unit. Now, using these sales price and COGS numbers, if we fail to supply 55% of the projected requirement, we stand to lose US $ six and a half million five thousand one hundred and ninety one." Kejarival paused for the impact, "Work it out yourself!"

"That is a big risk. This would top all the ten risks in our list in terms of exposure." Mahesh took charge of the situation, "This is the risk we should take up first for our analysis and try all that we can do to minimize the exposure. Here, look at this table and chart. This is where this risk and exposure would fall on this graph." He pointed out on the graph sheet.

"Mahesh, you are talking of our assembly line capacity. But have you considered the capacity of Tandon Printed Circuit Boards? He won't be able to supply new PCBs to our design at the rate we need." Subbu came out with the first possible hitch in ramping up.

"Don't worry about Tandon." Raman Seth interjected, "While I considered the possible suppliers for the PCBs, I did have preliminary evaluation of Tandon's production capacity. Managing that supply chain is my responsibility and I will work with Tandon to make sure that he supplies as many PCBs as we need for the first quarter. We are still six months before the launch. I will visit his shop and we will re-assess the capacity and then help him augment his capacity with assurances for guaranteed off take of the production or something like that. But, you have a point here, Subbu. For a long-term strategy, I should start to develop an alternative supplier of PCBs also."

" That would go a long way, Raman" Mahesh observed, " Do work with Tandon to make sure that we get the PCBs we want.", then turning towards Subbu, he asked," Tell me, if our assembly line capacity is 5,000 per week, why can't we get that output at that rate in the first three months? "

"These are new machines. New control panels. New assembly jigs. No one in our plant has operated or maintained these types of machines. There is something like *'Learning Curve Principle'* – *for a new operation, each time the output is doubled, the worker hours per unit decrease by a fixed percentage of the previous value.* People take some time to get used to new machines and new methods. They need to be trained." Subbu explained.

"Well, then, since this is the first priority risk in our project, let us manage this risk actively" Mahesh suggested, "We have still a few months to go before the launch. Let us have an intensive training program for the selected work force."

"We must do that if we want to meet the targets. While we are doing that, let us give special attention to the third shift crew. They are the ones who are usually the greatest defaulters on the production targets." Subbu suggested.

"Well, it is not my field of expertise, but I would like to venture here a thought" Raman spoke out slowly. He was the youngest of the group and was understandably circumspect in putting forth such ideas before his senior and more experienced colleagues. "The sale price is fixed and the sales department has booked orders at these prices. So probably not much we can do. But, Asutosh, how did you work out the cost of goods sold per unit with accuracy down to naya paise?"

"Raman, the cost of goods sold (COGS) includes all direct costs of raw materials and labour, all indirect materials and indirect labour, other factory overheads, and provision for depreciation for the new assembly line machinery. Most of the data input is from our group members here; all I have done is simple arithmetic using the proper accounting procedures. " Kejarival replied.

"But then, it looks to me like there could be a leeway in saving something from the direct material & labour costs." Raman ventured again.

Mahesh saw the merit in Raman's idea and immediately supported it, "Yes, I think let us form a production cost review team looking with a magnifying glass all operating costs. We can definitely form a small section of our project team to do that." After a short pause, he added, "Well, let us do it right away. I would christen the team as the Super Lenovo Team. Let us make the list of people to work in it."

"Before we make some big ramp-up plans and commit expenses, Mahesh, please get a confirmation from the sales that indeed they will sell those units to Lenovo. I have noticed that many times the sales projections promise you the moon before the product is in hand. Once the product is available, all kinds of rationalizations are offered for not being able to sell – the high price, the competitor's product features, sales personnel training… a Long list they come up with" Kejarival butted in.

"I will surely get a firm commitment from them", Mahesh assured, before the meeting dispersed.

Discussion Questions and Assignment

1. Identify event drivers and impact drivers for the risk event and construct a cause–effect diagram for the risk event.
2. Estimate expected values of impact for different risk events and prioritize the risks for developing a risk register.

CASE 7.10

Specialty Chemicals Company

(Decision Tree Analysis Technique for Managing Risk for a Project Implemented in Phases)

Abstract

Decision Tree Technique is a useful tool for planning and evaluating the options for a project (or an extended operation) wherein it would be possible to implement the overall business strategy through a sequence of decisions; while each decision may have different chance outcomes associated with it at successive stages. In this manner, this quantitative technique provides a useful alternative for risk management for overall investment strategy underlying the project justification. The technique permits objective evaluation of data collected for different scenarios in a simple and easily understandable context. The graphical presentation is particularly useful for grasping the differences between the available options and risks or benefits associated with them. The case presents an application of the technique to a project for setting up manufacturing facility based on new technology development. The case attempts to illustrate the technique in a manner that could be useful in providing insights into the underlying principles general methodology, data required for applying the technique and merits and limitations of the technique.

CASE TEXT

1. BACKGROUND

Specialty Chemicals Company, set up by Dr. Deshpande, had carved out a niche in the market for textile and plastic colorants as a high quality and reliable supplier of special dyes. Dr. Deshpande was a technocrat-entrepreneur who believed in 'hands on' management. After completing his doctorate from Heidelberg University in Germany, he worked in a small dye-manufacturing company in Dusseldorf and learnt the finer techniques of developing the processes for manufacturing aromatic chemicals based dyes. On his return to India, he set up a small factory in small leasehold shed in an industrial estate. His company flourished rapidly, as the companies from Germany and other Western countries began outsourcing so-called 'polluting chemicals' from developing countries when they faced difficulties in coping with stricter environmental pollution control regulations in their own countries. In the subsequent three years, Specialty Chemicals earned enough profits, which enabled the company it to expand its set up and operations by acquiring a plot of land. Having established a reputable local and foreign clientele and a small, dedicated team for manufacture and marketing, the company was now ready for the great leap forward from small-scale to medium-sized operation.

Just when such an opportunity appeared to be knocking at the door, a series of successful developmental runs were completed in the laboratory for manufacture of phthalocyanine green, an organic dye molecule. Due to its property of being stable and tendency of not migrating, phthalocyanine green was a preferred pigment in formulation of printing inks, certain plastics and coatings. Moreover, very small quantity of pigment being required for formulation of the finished product, the price of the pigment had negligible cost impact on the total finished products cost; thus permitting much higher margins for a supplier of a high quality pigment.

Dr. Deshpande started pondering on different options which he could avail to exploit the opportunity. Though laboratory trials were successful, it would be necessary to tackle some process glitches before smooth regular operation would start. Setting up a small pilot plant with, say, 50 tonnes per annum capacity, would help in this and that too with a much smaller investment, but it would delay setting up the main production plant with around 500 tonnes per annum capacity. If the market developed as fast as expected now, Specialty Chemicals would miss out on the opportunity of high margins and a secure position of the first entrant in the market, if it waited for pilot plant results. On the other hand, if the market developed sluggishly, the pilot plant itself could be used as a small-scale supply operation; helping establish an entry in the market and collect operational experience useful for planning the larger plant later. Also, the investment risk would be reduced by an order of magnitude.

It would be possible also to set up the larger full-scale operation without going through the pilot plant step as Dr. Deshpande was confident of managing the operational risk of solving the technical problems in the full-scale plant. This leapfrog approach of skipping the pilot plant step would give him a lead-time of over a year for marketing his product at a price set as a monopoly supplier. The downside was that if the demand did not pick up as expected, the top-heavy plant investment would remain a millstone in the company's neck for years.

Dr. Deshpande could conceive that he would need to think through a plan which could minimize project risks and maximize the benefits accruing from the new venture and it would involve:

- Evaluating the likely outcome from taking a sequence of decisions over a period – say the next 2 years, and
- Taking into account the reality that future could unfold in a number of scenarios, each with different likelihood or probability.

2. DECISION TREE ANALYSIS TECHNIQUE

Dr. Deshpande had been aware from talks with his friends at the university that an analytic technique, called Decision Tree Analysis, could be helpful in thinking through such a situation. Essentially, Decision Tree Analysis is a technique of presenting, in a tree-shaped graphical form, the information necessary for recording and analyzing the data relevant for making a sequence of decisions that have a bearing on a project or an extended operation. Decision Trees is generally constructed like a process flow chart starting at the left side and proceeding towards right for subsequent parts of scenario and it includes in the presentation the following information:

- *The decisions to be taken in a sequence (Decision Nodes)* – square shaped nodes are generally used for their representation.
- *The chance event outcomes associated with each decision (Event Nodes)* – circular shaped nodes are used for their representation.
- *The costs/benefits associated with each set of decision and chance event (Branches)* – straight lines connecting the decision nodes and chance event nodes represent the different likely sce-

narios. The pay-offs (cost/benefit) associated with each chance event outcomes and corresponding probability of their occurrence are also represented as Branches emanating from chance event nodes.

Decision Trees Analysis proceeds from evaluation of the Expected Value of Outcome of each branch, starting from the right side (the latest event node with pay-offs and probabilities) and going to left side of diagram by "folding back each branch" till reaching the starting decision. The analysis will highlight optimum choice among the set of sequential decisions, corresponding chance outcomes and expected value of pay-off for the optimum decisions set. Understandably, the tool is very useful as a visual and easy-to-understand presentation of the choices of sequential decisions and chance events likely to impact each of them. Its real value for arriving at an optimum decision sequence would depend on the quality of data collected for cost/benefits or pay-offs and the judgment in estimating the probabilities associated with the pay-offs for each chance event.

3. DATA COLLECTED FOR CONSTRUCTING DECISION TREES DIAGRAM

Dr. Deshpande collected the following data for constructing a Decision Tree Diagram:

Decision Nodes
Dr. Deshpande noted that the first decision he would need to take is whether to build a pilot plant or not.

Once it was decided not to build the pilot plant, the next decision would be:

* Whether to drop altogether the idea of building a production plant for the product, or
* Go ahead right away and build the large-scale production plant

Similarly, after building the pilot plant, if that decision route is taken, the options would be:

* Whether to postpone building the large-scale plant till the pilot plant operation is stabilized and initial market testing is in place using the pilot plant, or
* Proceed with building the large-scale production plant.

The cost of building the pilot plant with 50 tonnes/annum capacity was estimated at ₹6 million. The cost of building a 500 tonnes per annum capacity production plant would be around ₹50 million.

Event Nodes
Dr. Deshpande realized that the success or failure of the entire venture would depend on how the market for locally produced phthalocyanine green pigment developed. This, in turn, would depend on the pricing of the product. The product pricing would also impact the profit margins accruing from the new venture. Therefore, theoretically speaking, there would be innumerable scenarios of demands, prices, and corresponding profit margins – the typical demand-supply curves for markets. In order to avoid complications and keep the data collection and generation to a practical level, he decided to focus on two likely scenarios:

* High consumer acceptance with product demand of, say, 400 tonnes per annum, and corresponding profit of ₹160 million, and
* Low consumer acceptance with product demand of the order of, say 150 tonnes per annum, and corresponding profit of ₹60 million.

Chance Event Outcomes and Corresponding Probabilities

If Specialty Chemicals decided to take the plunge directly with the full-scale production plant, it should reckon on 50% chance for both high consumer acceptance and low consumer acceptance scenarios.

On the other hand, if it decided to take the option of building the 50 tonnes capacity pilot plant and wait out for the future market demand to play out before building the larger plant, there would be 40% chance of earning ₹20 million (in case of high consumer acceptance for the local product) and 60% chance of earning ₹10 million (in case of low consumer acceptance for the local product).

Finally, if Specialty Chemicals proceeded with building the large plant right after completing the pilot plant trials, there would be 90% chance of earning ₹160 million (in case of high consumer acceptance for the local product) and 10% chance of earning ₹60 million (in case of low consumer acceptance for the local product).

4. CONSTRUCTION AND ANALYSIS OF DECISION TREE DIAGRAM

4.1 Decision Tree Diagram

Exhibit 1 presents a Decision Tree Diagram constructed using the available data. Looking at the diagram, the following seven scenarios and four decision-sets are seen:

Nodes A-B-M: This decision sequence is for dropping altogether the idea of developing and producing the new product – hence building neither the pilot plant nor the production plant. This is the base case with zero cost and zero profit.

Nodes A-B-D-N: This decision sequence represents the scenario for not building the pilot plant, but plunging right away into building the main production plant. The anticipated outcome is optimistic – high consumer acceptance and high profit (₹160 million) with 50% chance.

Nodes A-B-D-O: This decision sequence represents the scenario for not building the pilot plant, but plunging right away into building the main production plant. The anticipated outcome is pessimistic – low consumer acceptance and low profit (₹60 million) with 50% chance.

Nodes A-C-E-P: This decision sequence represents the scenario for first building the pilot plant and waiting for the market to play out and not building the main production plant immediately. The anticipated outcome is optimistic – high consumer acceptance and high profit (₹20 million) with 40% chance.

Nodes A-C-E-Q: This decision sequence represents the scenario for not building the pilot plant, but plunging right away into building the main production plant. The anticipated outcome is pessimistic – low consumer acceptance and low profit (₹10 million) with 60% chance.

Nodes A-C-F-R: This decision sequence represents the scenario for not building the pilot plant, but plunging right away into building the main production plant. The anticipated outcome is optimistic – high consumer acceptance and high profit (₹160 million) with 90% chance.

Nodes A-C-F-S: This decision sequence represents the scenario for not building the pilot plant, but plunging right away into building the main production plant. The anticipated outcome is pessimistic – low consumer acceptance and low profit (₹60 million) with 10% chance.

Exhibit 1
Decision Tree for Specialty Chemicals

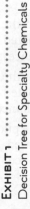

4.2   Analysis of Decision Tree Diagram

Expected value of each branch is calculated and folded back to the starting decision as follows. Expected value of branches at a node = Σ probability × corresponding chance outcome

1. Scenario of (a) not building pilot plant, and (b) not building production plant (Nodes A-B-M)

    Value of branch MB = 0; Value of branch BA = 0;
    Value of scenario at Node A = 0

2. Scenario of (a) not building pilot plant, but (b) building production plant (Nodes A-B-D)

    Value of branch DN = + ₹80 million; Value of branch DO = +₹30 million;
    Value at Node D = +₹110 million Value of branch BD = –₹50 million;
    Value at Node B = +₹60 million Value of branch AB= 0;
    Value of scenario at Node A = +₹60 million

3. Scenario of (a) building pilot plant, but (b) not immediately building production plant (Nodes A-C-E)

    Value of branch EP = + ₹8 million; Value of branch EQ = +₹6 million;
    Value at Node E = +₹14 million Value of branch CE = 0
    Value at Node C = + ₹14 million
    Value of branch AC = –₹8 million Value of scenario at Node A = +₹6 million

4. Scenario of (a) building pilot plant, and (b) building production plant (Nodes A-C-F)

    Value of branch FR = + ₹144 million; Value of branch FS = +₹6 million;
    Value at Node E = +₹150 million Value of branch CF = –₹50 million
    Value at Node C = +₹100 million Value of branch AC= –₹8 million
    Value of scenario at Node A = +₹92 million

In common business language terms, the summary of analysis could be restated as follows:

- The entirely passive approach, Scenario 1, (building neither a pilot plant nor a production unit later) is essentially meant to serve only as the datum line for comparing the decision options.

- The cautious approach, Scenario 2, (building the pilot plant and immediately later building the production unit based on the operational experience) is the most attractive. Underlying basis is the high probability of making profit (90% probability in high consumer acceptance case) by fully exploiting the benefits from high consumer acceptance based on the pilot plant operating experience being already under the belt. With total investment of ₹56 million for building both the pilot plant and production plant, there is a potential of making ₹92 million profit.

- The extremely cautious approach, Scenario 3, (building the pilot plant and postponing to build the production plant till much later) is the least attractive. Though yielding a nominal surplus of ₹6 million, it would also require investment of ₹6 million for the pilot plant – not the right way to go for a dynamic organization. In fact, even the entirely passive approach (Scenario 1) of bypassing this opportunity and not bothering with the new product would be preferable to this extremely cautious approach, since the passive approach at least does not involve any investment risk.

- The aggressive approach, Scenario 4, (Proceeding right away to build the full-scale production unit) appears less attractive than Scenario 2 essentially because of uncertainty in making high profit (low probability, 50%, anticipated for high consumer acceptance). In a way, the difference between Scenario 2 and Scenario 4 reflects the risk associated with aggressive approach of going ahead full blast without testing waters.

5. CONCLUSION

i. Decision Tree Technique is a useful tool for planning and evaluating the options for a project or an extended operation when it would be possible to implement the overall business strategy through a sequence of decisions and when each decision may have different chance outcomes associated with them at successive stages. In this manner, it provides a useful alternative for risk management for overall investment strategy underlying the project justification.

ii. The technique permits objective evaluation of data collected for different scenarios in a simple and easily understandable context. The graphical presentation is particularly useful for grasping the differences between the available options and risks or benefits associated with them.

iii. Like all quantitative techniques, the caveat concerning the sanctity of data and managerial judgment in evaluating the final options applies to this technique also. The expected value, after all, projects only a statistical concept of what would be most likely in case of a large number of trials. What could happen in any company's individual specific case at a point of time would depend on a number of factors – including some characteristics and culture of the company's organization. Decision Tree Analysis is just one more tool to assist the management – it cannot substitute mature judgment and visionary leadership for managing project risk in an optimum way.

8

SCHEDULING RESOURCES AND COSTS

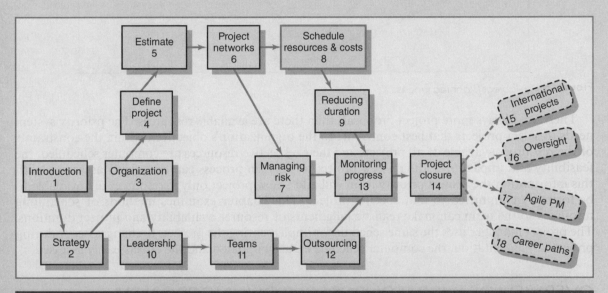

Project network times are not a schedule until resources have been assigned. Cost estimates are not a budget until they have been time-phased.

We have consistently stressed that up-front planning results in big payoffs. For those who have diligently worked through the earlier planning processes chapters, you are nearly ready to launch your project. This chapter completes the final two planning tasks that become the master plan for your project—resource and cost scheduling. (See Figure 8.1.) This process uses the resource schedule to assign **time-phased** costs that provide the project budget *baseline*. Given this time-phased baseline, comparisons can be made with actual and planned schedule and costs. This chapter first discusses the process for developing the project resource schedule. This resource schedule will be used to assign the time-phased budgeted values to create a project budget baseline.

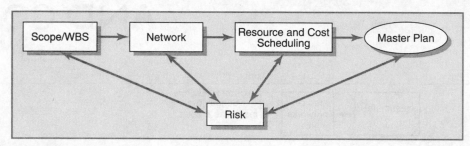

FIGURE 8.1   *Project Planning Process*

There are always more project proposals than there are available resources. The priority system needs to select projects that best contribute to the organization's objectives, within the constraints of the resources available. If all projects and their respective resources are computer scheduled, the feasibility and impact of adding a new project to those in process can be quickly assessed. With this information the project priority team will add a new project only if resources are available to be formally committed to that specific project. This chapter examines methods of scheduling resources so the team can make realistic judgments of resource availability and project durations. The project manager uses the same schedule for implementing the project. If changes occur during project implementation, the computer schedule is easily updated and the effects easily assessed.

OVERVIEW OF THE RESOURCE SCHEDULING PROBLEM

After staff and other resources were assigned to her project, a project manager listed the following questions that still needed to be addressed:

- Will the assigned labor and/or equipment be adequate and available to deal with my project?
- Will outside contractors have to be used?
- Do unforeseen resource dependencies exist? Is there a new critical path?
- How much flexibility do we have in using resources?
- Is the original deadline realistic?

Clearly, this project manager has a good understanding of the problems she is facing. Any project scheduling system should facilitate finding quick, easy answers to these questions.

The planned network and activity project duration times found in previous chapters fail to deal with resource usage and availability. The time estimates for the work packages and network times were made independently with the implicit assumption that resources would be available. This may or may not be the case.

If resources are adequate but the demand varies widely over the life of the project, it may be desirable to even out resource demand by delaying noncritical activities (using slack) to lower peak demand and, thus, increase resource utilization. This process is called **resource smoothing.**

On the other hand, if resources are not adequate to meet peak demands, the late start of some activities must be delayed, and the duration of the project may be increased. This process is called *resource-constrained scheduling.* One research study of more than 50 projects by Woodworth and Willie (1975) found that planned project network durations were increased 38 percent when resources were scheduled.

The consequences of failing to schedule limited resources are costly and project delays usually manifest themselves midway in the project when quick corrective action is difficult. An additional consequence of failing to schedule resources is ignoring the peaks and valleys of resource usage over the duration of the project. Because project resources are usually overcommitted and because resources seldom line up by availability and need, procedures are needed to deal with these problems. This chapter addresses methods available to project managers for dealing with resource utilization and availability through resource leveling and resource-constrained scheduling.

Up to now the start and sequence of activities has been based solely on technical or logical considerations. For example, a project network for framing a house might show three activities in a sequence: (1) pour foundation, (2) build frame, and (3) cover roof. A network for a new software project could place the activities in the network, as a sequence of (1) design, (2) code, and (3) test. In other words, you cannot logically perform activity 2 until 1 is completed, and so on. The project network depicts technical constraints (see Figure 8.2A). The network assumes the personnel and equipment are available to perform the required work. This is often not the case!

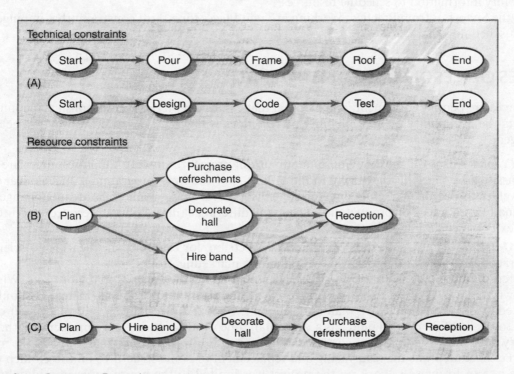

FIGURE 8.2   *Constraint Examples*

The absence or shortage of resources can drastically alter technical constraints. A project network planner may assume adequate resources and show activities occurring in parallel. However, parallel activities hold potential for resource conflicts. For example, assume you are planning a wedding reception that includes four activities—(1) plan, (2) hire band, (3) decorate hall, and (4) purchase refreshments. Each activity takes one day. Activities 2, 3, and 4 could be done in parallel by different people. There is no technical reason or dependency of one on another (see Figure 8.2B). However, if one person must perform all activities, the resource constraint requires the activities be performed in sequence or series. Clearly the consequence is a delay of these activities and a very different set of network relationships (see Figure 8.2C). Note that the resource dependency takes priority over the technological dependency but *does not violate the technological dependency;* that is, hire, decorate, and purchase may now have to take place in sequence rather than concurrently, but they must all be completed before the reception can take place.

The interrelationships and interactions among time and resource constraints are complex for even small project networks. Some effort to examine these interactions before the project begins frequently uncovers surprising problems. Project managers who do not consider resource availability in moderately complex projects usually learn of the problem when it is too late to correct. A deficit of resources can significantly alter project dependency relationships, completion dates, and project costs. Project managers must be careful to schedule resources to ensure availability in the right quantities and at the right time. Fortunately, there are computer software programs that can identify resource problems during the early project planning phase when corrective changes can be considered. These programs only require activity resource needs and availability information to schedule resources.

See the Snapshot from Practice: Working in Tight Places for a third constraint that impinges on project schedules.

TYPES OF RESOURCE CONSTRAINTS

Resources are people, equipment, and material that can be drawn on to accomplish something. In projects the availability or unavailability of resources will often influence the way projects are managed.

1. People. This is the most obvious and important project resource. Human resources are usually classified by the skills they bring to the project—for example, programmer, mechanical engineer, welder, inspector, marketing director, supervisor. In rare cases some skills are interchangeable, but usually with a loss of productivity. The many differing skills of human resources add to the complexity of scheduling projects.

2. Materials. Project materials cover a large spectrum: for example, chemicals for a scientific project, concrete for a road project, survey data for a marketing project.

Material availability and shortages have been blamed for the delay of many projects. When it is known that a lack of availability of materials is important and probable, materials should be included in the project network plan and schedule. For example, delivery and placement of an oil rig tower in a Siberian oil field has a very small time window during one summer month. Any delivery delay means a one-year, costly delay. Another example in which material was the major resource scheduled was the resurfacing and replacement of some structures on the Golden Gate Bridge in San Francisco. Work on the project was limited to the hours between midnight and

In rare situations, physical factors cause activities that would normally occur in parallel to be constrained by contractual or environmental conditions. For example, in theory the renovation of a sailboat compartment might involve four to five tasks that can be done independently. However, since space allows only one person to work at one time, all tasks have to be performed sequentially. Likewise, on a mining project it may be physically possible for only two miners to work in a shaft at a time. Another example would be the erection of a communication tower and nearby groundwork. For safety considerations, the contract prohibits groundwork within 2,000 feet of the tower construction.

The procedures for handling physical factors are similar to those used for resource constraints.

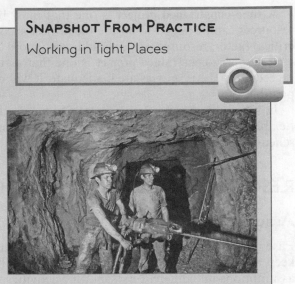

© Digital Vision/PunchStock

5:00 A.M. with a penalty of $1,000 per minute for any work taking place after 5:00 A.M. Scheduling the arrival of replacement structures was an extremely important part of managing the five-hour work-time window of the project. Scheduling materials has also become important in developing products where time-to-market can result in loss of market share.

3. Equipment. Equipment is usually presented by type, size, and quantity. In some cases equipment can be interchanged to improve schedules, but this is not typical. Equipment is often overlooked as a constraint. The most common oversight is to assume the resource pool is more than adequate for the project. For example, if a project needs one earthmoving tractor six months from now and the organization owns four, it is common to assume the resource will not delay the pending project. However, when the earthmoving tractor is due on-site in six months, all four machines in the pool might be occupied on other projects. In multiproject environments it is prudent to use a common resource pool for all projects. This approach forces a check of resource availability across all projects and reserves the equipment for specific project needs in the future. Recognition of equipment constraints before the project begins can avoid high crashing or delay costs.

CLASSIFICATION OF A SCHEDULING PROBLEM

Most of the scheduling methods available today require the project manager to classify the project as either *time constrained* or *resource constrained*. Project managers need to consult their priority matrix (see Figure 4.2) to determine which case fits their project. One simple test to determine if the project is time or resource constrained is to ask, "If the critical path is delayed, will resources be added to get back on schedule?" If the answer is yes, assume the project is time constrained; if no, assume the project is resource constrained.

A **time-constrained project** is one that must be completed by an imposed date. If required, resources can be added to ensure the project is completed by a specific date. Although time is the critical factor, resource usage should be no more than is necessary and sufficient.

A **resource-constrained project** is one that assumes the level of resources available cannot be exceeded. If the resources are inadequate, it will be acceptable to delay the project, but as little as possible.

In scheduling terms, time constrained means time (project duration) is fixed and resources are flexible, while resource constrained means resources are fixed and time is flexible. Methods for scheduling these projects are presented in the next section.

RESOURCE ALLOCATION METHODS

Assumptions

Ease of demonstrating the allocation methods available requires some limiting assumptions to keep attention on the heart of the problem. The rest of the chapter depends entirely on the assumptions noted here. First, splitting activities will not be allowed. This means once an activity is placed in the schedule, assume it will be worked on continuously until it is finished; hence, an activity cannot be started, stopped for a period of time, and then finished. Second, the level of resources used for an activity cannot be changed. These limiting assumptions do not exist in practice, but simplify learning. It is easy for new project managers to deal with the reality of splitting activities and changing the level of resources when they meet them on the job.

Time–Constrained Projects: Smoothing Resource Demand

Scheduling time-constrained projects focuses on resource *utilization.* When demand for a specific resource type is erratic, it is difficult to manage, and utilization may be very poor. Practitioners have attacked the utilization problem using resource leveling techniques that balance demand for a resource. Basically, all **leveling** techniques delay noncritical activities by using positive slack to reduce peak demand and fill in the valleys for the resources. An example will demonstrate the basic procedure for a time-constrained project. See Figure 8.3.

For the purpose of demonstration, the Botanical Garden project uses only one resource (backhoes); all backhoes are interchangeable. The top bar chart shows the activities on a time scale. The dependencies are shown with the vertical connecting arrows. The horizontal arrows following activities represent activity slack (for example, irrigation requires six days to complete and has six days slack). The number of backhoes needed for each task is shown in the shaded activity duration block (rectangle). After the land has been scarified and the plan laid out, work can begin on the walkways, irrigation, and fencing and retaining walls simultaneously. The middle chart shows the resource profile for the backhoes. For periods 4 through 10, four backhoes are needed.

Because this project is declared time constrained, the goal will be to reduce the peak requirement for the resource and thereby increase the utilization of the resource. A quick examination of the ES (early start) resource load chart suggests only two activities have slack that can be used to reduce the peak—fence and walls provide the best choice for smoothing the resource needs. Another choice could be irrigation, but it would result in an up and down resource profile. The choice will probably center on the activity that is perceived as having the least risk of being late.

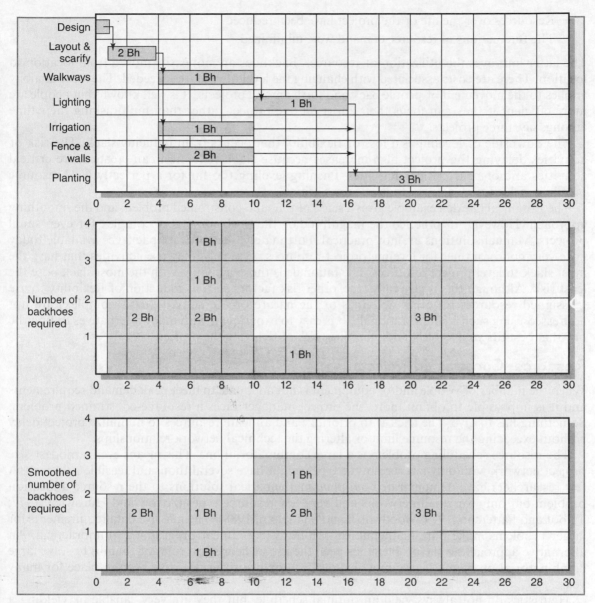

FIGURE 8.3 *Botanical Garden*

The smoothed resource loading chart shows the results of delaying the fence and walls activity. Note the differences in the resource profiles. The important point is the resources needed over the life of the project have been reduced from four to three (25 percent). In addition the profile has been smoothed, which should be easier to manage.

The Botanical Garden project schedule reached the three goals of smoothing:

• The peak of demand for the resource was reduced.

- Resources over the life of the project have been reduced.
- The fluctuations in resource demand were minimized.

The latter improves the utilization of resources. Backhoes are not easily moved from location to location. There are costs associated with changing the level of resources needed. The same analogy applies to the movement of people back and forth among projects. It is well known that people are more efficient if they can focus their effort on one project rather than multitasking their time among, say, three projects.

The downside of leveling is a loss of flexibility that occurs from reducing slack. The risk of activities delaying the project also increases because slack reduction can create more critical activities and/or near-critical activities. Pushing leveling too far for a perfectly level resource profile is risky. Every activity then becomes critical.

The Botanical Garden example gives a sense of the time-constrained problem and the smoothing approach. However, in practice the magnitude of the problem is very complex for even small projects. Manual solutions are not practical. Fortunately, the software packages available today have very good routines for leveling project resources. Typically, they use activities that have the most slack to level project resources. The rationale is those activities with the most slack pose the least risk. Although this is generally true, other risk factors such as reduction of flexibility to use reassigned resources on other activities or the nature of the activity (easy, complex) are not addressed using such a simple rationale. It is easy to experiment with many alternatives to find the one that best fits your project and minimizes risk of delaying the project.

Resource–Constrained Projects

When the number of people and/or equipment is not adequate to meet peak demand requirements and it is impossible to obtain more, the project manager faces a resource-constrained problem. Something has to give. The trick is to prioritize and allocate resources to minimize project delay without exceeding the resource limit or altering the technical network relationships.

The resource scheduling problem is a large combinatorial one. This means even a modest-size project network with only a few resource types might have several thousand feasible solutions. A few researchers have demonstrated *optimum* mathematical solutions to the resource allocation problem but only for small networks and very few resource types (Arrow and Hurowicz, 1977; Talbot and Patterson, 1979; Woodworth and Shanahan, 1988). The massive data requirements for larger problems make pure mathematical solutions (e.g., linear programming) impractical. An alternative approach to the problem has been the use of **heuristics** (rules of thumb) to solve large combinatorial problems. These practical decision or priority rules have been in place for many years.

Heuristics do not always yield an optimal schedule, but they are very capable of yielding a "good" schedule for very complex networks with many types of resources. The efficiency of different rules and combinations of rules has been well documented (Pascoe, 1965; Fendly, 1968). However, because each project is unique, it is wise to test several sets of heuristics on a network to determine the priority allocation rules that minimize project delay. The computer software available today makes it very easy for the project manager to create a good resource schedule for the project. A simple example of the heuristic approach is illustrated here.

Heuristics allocate resources to activities to minimize project delay; that is, heuristics prioritize which activities are allocated resources and which activities are delayed when resources are not adequate.

The parallel method is the most widely used approach to apply heuristics, which have been found to consistently minimize project delay over a large variety of projects. The parallel method is an iterative process that starts from the beginning of project time and, when resources needed exceed the resources available, retains activities first by the priority rules:

1. Minimum slack.
2. Smallest duration.
3. Lowest activity identification number.

The Parallel Method:

Period	Action
	See Figure 8.4
0–1	Only activity 1 is eligible. It requires 2 programmers.
	Load activity 1 into schedule.
1–2	No activities are eligible to be scheduled.
2–3	Activities 2, 3, and 4 are eligible to be scheduled. Activity 3 has the least slack (0)— apply rule 1.
	Load Activity 3 into schedule.
	Activity 2 is next with slack of 2; however, activity 2 requires 2 programmers and only 1 is available.
	Delay activity 2. Update: ES = 3, slack = 1.
	The next eligible activity is activity 4, since it only requires 1 programmer.
	Load activity 4 into schedule.
	See Figure 8.5
3–4	Activity 2 is eligible but exceeds limit of 3 programmers in pool.
	Delay activity 2. Update: ES = 4, slack = 0.
4–5	Activity 2 is eligible but exceeds limit of 3 programmers in pool.
	Delay activity 2. Update: ES = 5, LF = 11, slack = −1.
	Delay activity 7. Update: ES = 11, LF = 13, slack = −1.
5–6	Activity 2 is eligible but exceeds limit of 3 programmers in pool.
	Delay activity 2. Update: ES = 6, LF = 12, slack = −2.
	Delay activity 7. Update: ES = 12, LF = 14, slack = −2.
6–7	Activities 2, 5, and 6 are eligible with slack of −2, 2, and 0, respectively.
	Load activity 2 into schedule (rule 1).
	Because activity 6 has 0 slack, it is the next eligible activity.
	Load activity 6 into schedule (rule 1).
	The programmer limit of 3 is reached.
	Delay activity 5. Update: ES = 7, slack = 1.
7–8	Limit is reached. No programmers available.
	Delay activity 5. Update: ES = 8, slack = 0.
8–9	Limit is reached. No programmers available.
	Delay activity 5. Update: ES = 9, LF = 11, slack = −1.
9–10	Limit is reached. No programmers available.
	Delay activity 5. Update: ES = 10, LF = 12, slack = −2.
10–11	Activity 5 is eligible.
	Load activity 5 into schedule.
	(Note: Activity 6 does not have slack because there are no programmers available— 3 maximum.)
11–12	No eligible activities.
12–13	Activity 7 is eligible.
	Load activity 7 into schedule.

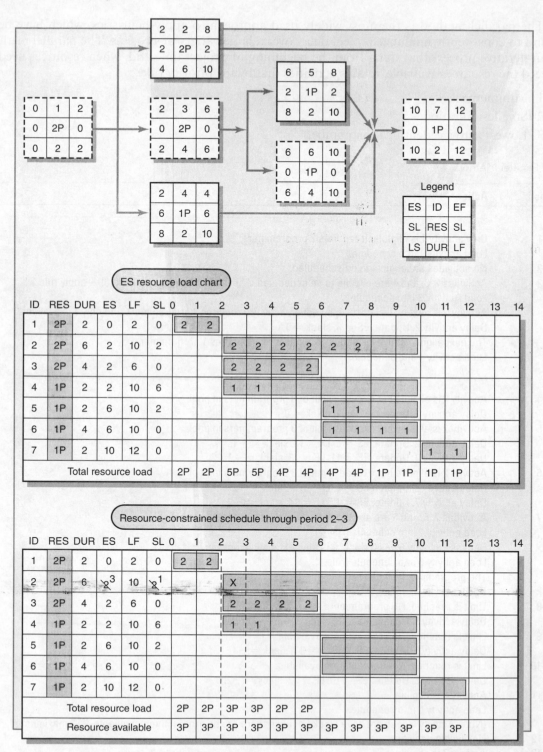

FIGURE 8.4 *Resource–Constrained Schedule through Period 2–3*

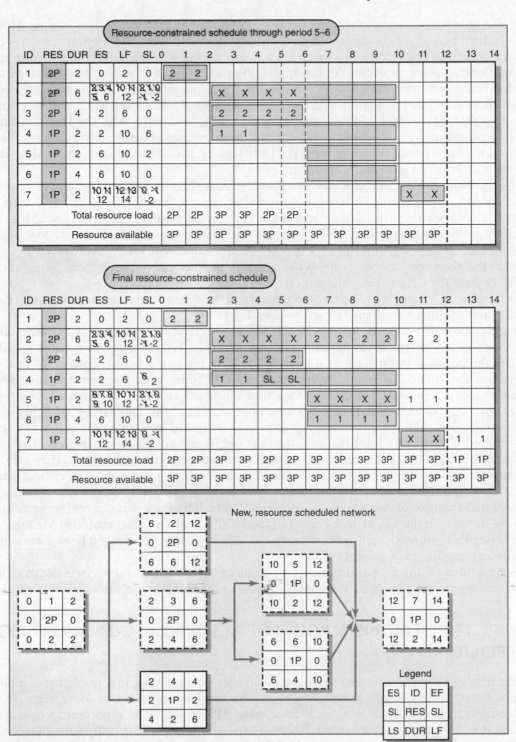

Figure 8.5   *Resource–Constrained Schedule through Period 5–6*

Those not able to be scheduled without delaying others are pushed out farther in time. However, do not attempt to move activities that have already started. When considering activities not to delay, consider the resources each activity uses. In any period when two or more activities require the same resource, the priority rules are applied. For example, if in period 5 three activities are eligible to start (i.e., have the same ES) and require the same resource, the first activity placed in the schedule would be the activity with the least slack (rule 1). However, if all activities have the same slack, the next rule would be invoked (rule 2), and the activity with the smallest duration would be placed in the schedule first. In very rare cases, when all eligible activities have the same slack and the same duration, the tie is broken by the lowest activity identification number (rule 3), since each activity has a unique ID number.

When a resource limit has been reached, the early start (ES) for succeeding activities not yet in the schedule will be delayed (and all successor activities not having free slack) and their slack reduced. In subsequent periods the procedure is repeated until the project is scheduled. The procedure is demonstrated next; see Figure 8.4. The shaded areas in the resource loading chart represent the "scheduling interval" of the *time-constrained* schedule (ES through LF). You can schedule the resource any place *within* the interval and not delay the project. Scheduling the activity beyond the LF will delay the project.

The programmers are limited to three. Follow the actions described in Figures 8.4 and 8.5. Note how the limit of three programmers starts to delay the project.

Observe how it is necessary to update each period to reflect changes in activity early start and slack times so the heuristics can reflect changing priorities. When using the parallel scheduling method, the network in Figure 8.5 on page 261 reflects the new schedule date of 14 time units, rather than the time-constrained project duration of 12 time units. The network has also been revised to reflect new start, finish, and slack times for each activity. Note that activity 6 is still critical and has a slack of 0 time units because no resources are available (they are being used on activities 2 and 5). Compare the slack for each activity found in Figures 8.4 and 8.5; slack has been reduced significantly. Note that activity 4 has only 2 units of slack rather than what appears to be 6 slack units. This occurs because only three programmers are available, and they are needed to satisfy the resource requirements of activities 2 and 5. Note that the number of critical activities (1, 2, 3, 5, 6, 7) has increased from four to six.

This small example demonstrates the scenario of scheduling resources in real projects and the resulting increase in the risk of being late. In practice this is not a trivial problem! Managers who fail to schedule resources usually encounter this scheduling risk when it is too late to work around the problem, resulting in a project delay.

Since manually using the parallel method is impractical on real-world projects because of size, project managers will depend on software programs to schedule project resources.

COMPUTER DEMONSTRATION OF RESOURCE–CONSTRAINED SCHEDULING

Fortunately, project management software is capable of assessing and resolving complicated resource-constrained schedules using heuristics similar to what was described above. We will use the EMR project to demonstrate how this is done using MS Project. It is important to note that the software is not "managing" the project. The software is simply a tool the project manager uses to view the project from different perspectives and conditions. See the Snapshot from Practice: Assessing Resource Allocation on page 269 for more tips on assessing resource problems.

EMR is the name given to the development of a handheld electronic medical reference guide to be used by emergency medical technicians and paramedics. Figure 8.6 contains a time-limited network for the design phase of the project. For the purpose of this example, we assume that only design engineers are required for the tasks and that the design engineers are interchangeable. The number of engineers required to perform each task is noted in the network, where 500 percent means five design engineers are needed for the activity. For example, activity 5, feature specs, requires four design engineers (400 percent).

The project begins January 1, and ends February 14, a duration of 45 workdays. The calendar for the project has been set up to work seven days a week so the reader can trace and more easily see the results and impacts of resources—similar to manual solutions present in chapter exercises. The time-limited (constrained) bar chart for the project is shown in Figure 8.7. This bar chart incorporates the same information used to develop the project network, but presents the project in the form of a bar chart along a time line.

Finally, a resource usage chart is presented for a segment of the project—January 15 to January 23; see Figure 8.8A. Observe that the time-limited project requires 21 design engineers on January 18 and 19 (168 hrs/8 hrs per engineer = 21 engineers). This segment represents the peak requirement for design engineers for the project. However, due to the shortage of design engineers and commitments to other projects, only eight engineers can be assigned to the project. This creates overallocation problems more clearly detailed in Figure 8.8B, which is a resource loading chart for design engineers. Notice that the peak is 21 engineers and the limit of 8 engineers is shown by the gray shaded area.

To resolve this problem we use the "leveling" tool within the software and first try to solve the problem by leveling only within slack. This solution would preserve the original finish date. However, as expected, this does not solve all of the allocation problems. The next option is to allow the software to apply scheduling heuristics and level outside of slack. The new schedule is contained in the revised, resource-limited network chart presented in Figure 8.9. The resource-limited project network indicates the project duration has now been extended to 2/26, or 57 workdays (versus 45 days time limited). The critical path is now 2, 3, 9, 13.

Figure 8.10 presents the project bar chart and the results of leveling the project schedule to reflect the availability of only eight design engineers. The application of the heuristics can be seen in the scheduling of the internal, external, and feature specification activities. All three activities were originally scheduled to start immediately after activity 1, architectural decisions.

This is impossible, since the three activities collectively require 14 engineers. The software chooses to schedule activity 5 first because this activity is on the original critical path and has zero slack (heuristic rule # 1). Next, and concurrently, activity 4 is chosen over activity 3 because activity 4 has a shorter duration (heuristic rule # 2); internal specs, activity 3, is delayed due to the limitation of 8 design engineers. Notice that the original critical path no longer applies because of the resource dependencies created by having only eight design engineers. See Figure 8.9 for the original planned critical path.

Compare the bar chart in Figure 8.10 with the time-limited bar chart in Figure 8.7. For example, note the different start dates for activity 8 (screen). In the time-limited plan (Figure 8.7), the start date for activity 8 is 1/18, while the start date in the resource limited schedule (Figure 8.10) is 2/16, almost a month later!

While resource bar graphs are commonly used to illustrate overallocation problems, we prefer to view resource usage tables like the one presented in Figure 8.8A. This table tells you when you have an overallocation problem and identifies activities that are causing the overallocation.

FIGURE 8.6 *EMR Project Network View Schedule before Resources Leveled*

ID	Task Name	Start	Finish	Late Start	Late Finish	Free Slack	Total Slack
1	**EMR project**	**Tue 1/1**	**Thu 2/14**	**Tue 1/1**	**Thu 2/14**	**0 days**	**0 days**
2	Architectural decisions	Tue 1/1	Sat 1/5	Tue 1/1	Sat 1/5	0 days	0 days
3	Internal specs	Sun 1/6	Thu 1/17	Sat 1/19	Wed 1/30	0 days	13 days
4	External specs	Sun 1/6	Sat 1/12	Thu 1/24	Wed 1/30	5 days	18 days
5	Feature specs	Sun 1/6	Tue 1/15	Sun 1/6	Tue 1/15	0 days	0 days
6	Voice recognition SW	Fri 1/18	Sun 1/27	Thu 1/31	Sat 2/9	13 days	13 days
7	Case	Fri 1/18	Mon 1/21	Wed 2/6	Sat 2/9	19 days	19 days
8	Screen	Fri 1/18	Sat 1/19	Fri 2/8	Sat 2/9	21 days	21 days
9	Database	Wed 1/16	Sat 2/9	Wed 1/16	Sat 2/9	0 days	0 days
10	Microphone-soundcard	Wed 1/16	Sun 1/20	Tue 2/5	Sat 2/9	20 days	20 days
11	Digital devices	Wed 1/16	Tue 1/22	Sun 2/3	Sat 2/9	18 days	18 days
12	Computer I/O	Wed 1/16	Sun 1/20	Tue 2/5	Sat 2/9	20 days	20 days
13	Review design	Sun 2/10	Thu 2/14	Sun 2/10	Thu 2/14	0 days	0 days

FIGURE 8.7   *EMR Project before Resources Added*

FIGURE 8.8A   *EMR Project—Time–Constrained Resource Usage View, January 15–23*

Resource Name	Work	Jan 15						Jan 21		
		T	W	T	F	S	S	M	T	W
Design engineers	**3,024 hrs**	72h	136h	136h	168h	168h	144h	104h	88h	64h
Architectural decisions	200 hrs									
Internal specs	480 hrs	40h	40h	40h						
External specs	224 hrs									
Feature specs	320 hrs	32h								
Voice recognition SW	320 hrs				32h	32h	32h	32h	32h	32h
Case	64 hrs				16h	16h	16h	16h		
Screen	48 hrs				24h	24h				
Database	800 hrs		32h	32h	32h	32h	32h	32h	32h	32h
Microphone-soundcard	80 hrs		16h	16h	16h	16h	16h			
Digital devices	168 hrs		24h	24h	24h	24h	24h	24h	24h	
Computer I/O	120 hrs		24h	24h	24h	24h	24h			
Review design	200 hrs									

| Peak Units | 900% | 1,700% | 1,700% | 2,100% | 2,100% | 1,800% | 1,300% | 1,100% | 800% |

Design Engineers   Overallocated: ▭   Allocated: ▭

FIGURE 8.8B   *Resource Loading Chart for EMR Project, January 15–23*

The Impacts of Resource–Constrained Scheduling

Like leveling schedules, the limited resource schedule usually reduces slack, reduces flexibility by using slack to ensure delay is minimized, and increases the number of critical and near-critical activities. Scheduling complexity is increased because resource constraints are added to technical constraints; start times may now have two constraints. The traditional critical path concept of sequential activities from the start to the end of the project is no longer meaningful. The resource constraints can break the sequence and leave the network with a set of disjointed critical activities. Conversely, parallel activities can become sequential. Activities with slack on a time-constrained network can change from critical to noncritical.

FIGURE 8.9   *EMR Project Network View Schedule after Resources Leveled*

FIGURE 8.10 *EMR Project Resources Leveled*

SPLITTING ACTIVITIES

Splitting tasks is a scheduling technique used to get a better project schedule and/or to increase resource utilization. A planner splits the continuous work included in an activity by interrupting the work and sending the resource to another activity for a period of time and then having the resource resume work on the original activity. Splitting can be a useful tool if the work involved does not include large start-up or shutdown costs—for example, moving equipment from one activity location to another. The most common error is to interrupt "people work," where there are high conceptual start-up and shutdown costs. For example, having a bridge designer take time off to work on the design problem of another project may cause this individual to lose four days shifting conceptual gears in and out of two activities. The cost may be hidden, but it is real. Figure 8.11 depicts the nature of the splitting problem. The original activity has been split into three separate activities: A, B, and C. The shutdown and start-up times lengthen the time for the original activity.

FIGURE 8.11 *Splitting Activities*

Some have argued that the propensity to deal with resource shortages by splitting is a major reason why projects fail to meet schedule (c.f., Goldratt, 1997; Newbold, 1997). We agree. Planners should avoid the use of splitting as much as possible, except in situations where splitting costs are known to be small or when there is no alternative for resolving the resource problem. Computer software offers the splitting option for each activity; use it sparingly. See Snapshot from Practice: Assessing Resource Allocation.

One of the strengths of today's project management software is the ability to identify and provide options for resolving resource allocation problems. A project manager who uses MS Project to plan projects shared with us the following checklist for dealing with resource conflicts after preliminary assignment of resources has been made.

1. Assess whether you have overallocation problems (see *Red* in the resource sheet view).
2. Identify where and when conflicts occur by examining the resource usage view.
3. Resolve the problem by
   a. Replacing overallocated resources with appropriate resources that are available. Then ask if this solves the problem.
   If not:
   b. Use the leveling tool and choose the level within slack option.
      i Does this solve the problem? (Are resources still overallocated?)
      ii Check the sensitivity of the network and ask if this is acceptable.
   If not:
   c. Consider splitting tasks.
      i Make sure to readjust task durations to take into account additional start-up and shutdown time.
4. If 3 does not work then either:
   a. Use level tool default option and ask if you can live with the new completion date.
   If not:
   b. Negotiate for additional resources to complete the project. If not possible
   c. Consider reducing project scope to meet deadline.

While this checklist makes specific references to MS Project, the same steps can be used with most project management software.

BENEFITS OF SCHEDULING RESOURCES

It is important to remember that, if resources are truly limited and activity time estimates are accurate, the resource-constrained schedule *will* materialize as the project is implemented—*not* the time-constrained schedule! Therefore, failure to schedule limited resources can lead to serious problems for a project manager. The benefit of creating this schedule *before* the project begins leaves time for considering reasonable alternatives. If the scheduled delay is unacceptable or the risk of being delayed too high, the assumption of being resource constrained can be reassessed. Cost-time trade-offs can be considered. In some cases priorities may be changed. See Snapshot from Practice: U.S. Forest Service Resource Shortage.

Resource schedules provide the information needed to prepare time-phased work package budgets with dates. Once established, they provide a quick means for a project manager to gauge the impact of unforeseen events such as turnover, equipment breakdowns, or transfer of project personnel. Resource schedules also allow project managers to assess how much flexibility they

A major segment of work in managing U.S. Forest Service (USFS) forests is selling mature timber to logging companies that harvest the timber under contract conditions monitored by the Service. The proceeds are returned to the federal government. The budget allocated to each forest depends on the two-year plan submitted to the U.S. Department of Agriculture.

Olympic Forest headquarters in Olympia, Washington, was developing a two-year plan as a basis for funding. All of the districts in the forest submitted their timber sale projects (numbering more than 50) to headquarters, where they were compiled and aggregated into a project plan for the whole forest. The first computer run was reviewed by a small group of senior managers to determine if the plan was reasonable and "doable." Management was pleased and relieved to note all projects appeared to be doable in the two-year time frame until a question was raised concerning the computer printout. "Why are all the columns in these projects labeled 'RESOURCE' blank?" The response from an engineer was, "We don't use that part of the program."

The discussion that ensued recognized the importance of resources in completing the two-year plan and ended with a request to "try the program with resources included." The new output was startling. The two-year program turned into a three-and-a-half-year plan because of the shortage of specific labor skills such as road engineer and environmental impact specialist. Analysis showed that adding only three skilled people would allow the two-year plan to be completed on time. In addition, further analysis showed hiring only a few more skilled people, beyond the three, would allow an extra year of projects to also be compressed into the two-year plan. This would result in additional revenue of more than $3 million. The Department of Agriculture quickly approved the requested extra dollars for additional staff to generate the extra revenue.

have over certain resources. This is useful when they receive requests from other managers to borrow or share resources. Honoring such requests creates goodwill and an "IOU" that can be cashed in during a time of need.

ASSIGNING PROJECT WORK

When making individual assignments, project managers should match, as best they can, the demands and requirements of specific work with the qualifications and experience of available participants. In doing so, there is a natural tendency to assign the best people the most difficult tasks. Project managers need to be careful not to overdo this. Over time these people may grow to resent the fact that they are always given the toughest assignments. At the same time, less experienced participants may resent the fact that they are never given the opportunity to expand their skill/knowledge base. Project managers need to balance task performance with the need to develop the talents of people assigned to the project.

Project managers not only need to decide who does what but who works with whom. A number of factors need to be considered in deciding who should work together. First, to minimize unnecessary tension, managers should pick people with compatible work habits and personalities but who complement each other (i.e., one person's weakness is the other person's strength). For example, one person may be brilliant at solving complex problems but sloppy at documenting his or her progress. It would be wise to pair this person with an individual who is good at paying attention to details. Experience is another factor. Veterans should be teamed up with new hires—not only so they can

SNAPSHOT FROM PRACTICE

Managing Geeks*

Eric Schmidt, after a successful career at Sun Microsystems, took over struggling Novell, Inc., and helped turn it around within two years. Four years later he became the CEO of Google. One of the keys to his success is his ability to manage the technical wizards who develop the sophisticated systems, hardware, and software that are the backbone of electronically driven companies. He uses the term "geek" (and he can, since he is one, with a Ph.D. in computer science) to describe this group of technologists who rule the cyberworld.

Schmidt has some interesting ideas about assigning geeks to projects. He believes that putting geeks together in project teams with other geeks creates productive peer pressure. Geeks care a great deal about how other geeks perceive them. They are good at judging the quality of technical work and are quick to praise as well as criticize each other's work. Some geeks can be unbearably arrogant, but Schmidt claims that having them work together on projects is the best way to control them—by letting them control each other.

At the same time, Schmidt argues that too many geeks spoil the soup. By this he means that, when there are too many geeks on a development team, there is a tendency for intense technical navel gazing. Members lose sight of deadlines, and delays are inevitable. To combat this tendency, he recommends using geeks only in small groups. He urges breaking up large projects into smaller, more manageable projects so that small teams of geeks can be assigned to them. This keeps the project on time and makes the teams responsible to each other.

* Russ Mitchel, "How to Manage Geeks," *Fast Company* (May 31, 1999), pp. 175–80.

share their experience but also to help socialize the newcomers to the customs and norms of the organization. Finally, future needs should be considered. If managers have some people who have never worked together before but who have to later on in the project, they may be wise to take advantage of opportunities to have these people work together early on so that they can become familiar with each other. Finally, see the Snapshot in Practice: Managing Geeks for some interesting thoughts about how Novell, Inc., puts together teams.

MULTIPROJECT RESOURCE SCHEDULES

For clarity we have discussed key resource allocation issues within the context of a single project. In reality resource allocation generally occurs in a multiproject environment where the demands of one project have to be reconciled with the needs of other projects. Organizations must develop and manage systems for efficiently allocating and scheduling resources across several projects with different priorities, resource requirements, sets of activities, and risks. The system must be dynamic and capable of accommodating new projects as well as reallocating resources once project work is completed. While the same resource issues and principles that apply to a single project also apply to this multiproject environment, application and solutions are more complex, given the interdependency among projects.

The following lists three of the more common problems encountered in managing multiproject resource schedules. Note that these are macro manifestations of single-project problems that are now magnified in a multiproject environment:

1. **Overall schedule slippage.** Because projects often share resources, delays in one project can have a ripple effect and delay other projects. For example, work on one software development project can grind to a halt because the coders scheduled for the next critical task are late in completing their work on another development project.

2. **Inefficient resource utilization.** Because projects have different schedules and requirements, there are peaks and valleys in overall resource demands. For example, a firm may have a staff of 10 electricians to meet peak demands when, under normal conditions, only 5 electricians are required.

3. **Resource bottlenecks.** Delays and schedules are extended as a result of shortages of critical resources that are required by multiple projects. For example, at one Lattice Semiconductor facility, project schedules were delayed because of competition over access to test equipment necessary to debug programs. Likewise, several projects at a U.S. forest area were extended because there was only one silviculturist on the staff.

To deal with these problems, more and more companies create project offices or departments to oversee the scheduling of resources across multiple projects. One approach to multiple project resource scheduling is to use a first come–first served rule. A project queue system is created in which projects currently underway take precedence over new projects. New project schedules are based on the projected availability of resources. This queuing tends to lead to more reliable completion estimates and is preferred on contracted projects that have stiff penalties for being late. The disadvantages of this deceptively simple approach are that it does not optimally utilize resources or take into account the priority of the project. See the Snapshot from Practice: Multiple Project Resource Scheduling.

Many companies utilize more elaborate processes for scheduling resources to increase the capacity of the organization to initiate projects. Most of these methods approach the problem by treating individual projects as part of one big project and adapting the scheduling heuristics previously introduced to this "megaproject." Project schedulers monitor resource usage and provide updated schedules based on progress and resource availability across all projects. One major improvement in project management software in recent years is the ability to prioritize resource allocation to specific projects. Projects can be prioritized in ascending order (e.g., 1, 2, 3, 4, . . .), and these priorities will override scheduling heuristics so that resources go to the project highest on the priority list. (Note: This improvement fits perfectly with organizations that use project priority models similar to those described in Chapter 2.) Centralized project scheduling also makes it easier to identify resource bottlenecks that stifle progress on projects. Once identified, the impact of the bottlenecks can be documented and used to justify acquiring additional equipment, recruiting critical personnel, or delaying the project.

Finally, many companies are using outsourcing as a means for dealing with their resource allocation problems. In some cases, a company will reduce the number of projects they have to manage internally to only core projects and outsource noncritical projects to contractors and consulting firms. In other cases, specific segments of projects are outsourced to overcome resource deficiencies and scheduling problems. Companies may hire temporary workers to expedite certain activities that are falling behind schedule or contract project work during peak periods when there are insufficient internal resources to meet the demands of all projects. The ability to more efficiently manage the ebbs and flows of project work is one of the major driving forces behind outsourcing today.

The case for a central source to oversee project resource scheduling is well known by practitioners. Here is a synopsis of a conversation with one middle manager.

Interviewer: Congratulations on acceptance of your multi-project scheduling proposal. Everyone tells me you were very convincing.

Middle Manager: Thanks. Gaining acceptance was easy this time. The board quickly recognized we have no choice if we are to keep ahead of competition by placing our resources on the right projects.

Interviewer: Have you presented this to the board before?

Middle Manager: Yes, but not this company. I presented the same spiel to the firm I worked for two years ago. For their annual review meeting I was charged to present a proposal suggesting the need and benefits of central capacity resource planning for managing the projects of the firm.

I tried to build a case for bringing projects under one umbrella to standardize practices and to forecast and assign key people to mission critical projects. I explained how benefits such as resource demands would be aligned with mission critical projects, proactive resource planning, and a tool for catching resource bottlenecks and resolving conflicts.

Almost everyone agreed the idea was a good one. I felt good about the presentation and felt confident something was going to happen. But the idea never really got off the ground; it just faded into the sunset.

With hindsight, managers really did not trust colleagues in other departments, so they only gave half-hearted support to central resource planning. Managers wanted to protect their turf and ensure that they would not have to give up power. The culture there was simply too inflexible for the world we live in today. They are still struggling with constant conflicts among projects.

I'm glad I made the switch to this firm. The culture here is much more team-oriented. Management is committed to improving performance.

USING THE RESOURCE SCHEDULE TO DEVELOP A PROJECT COST BASELINE

Once resource assignments have been finalized we are able to develop a baseline budget schedule for the project. Using your project schedule, you can *time-phase* work packages and assign them to their respective scheduled activities to develop a budget schedule over the life of your project. Understanding the reason for time-phasing your budget is very important. Without a time-phased budget good project schedule and cost control are impossible.

Why a Time–Phased Budget Baseline Is Needed

The need for a time-phased budget baseline is demonstrated in the following scenario. The development of a new product is to be completed in 10 weeks at an estimated cost of $400,000 per week for a total cost of $4 million. Management wants a status report at the end of five weeks. The following information has been collected:

- Planned costs for the first five weeks are $2,000,000.
- Actual costs for the first five weeks are $2,400,000.

How are we doing? It would be easy to draw the conclusion there is a $400,000 cost overrun. But we really have no way of knowing. The $400,000 may represent money spent to move the project ahead of schedule. Assume another set of data at the end of five weeks:

* Planned costs for the first five weeks are $2,000,000.
* Actual costs for the first five weeks are $1,700,000.

Is the project costing $300,000 less than we expected? Perhaps. But the $300,000 may represent the fact that the project is behind schedule and work has not started. Could it be the project is behind schedule and over cost? We cannot tell from these data. The many systems found in the real world that use only planned funds (a constant burn rate) and actual costs can provide false and misleading information. There is no way to be certain how much of the physical work has been accomplished. *These systems do not measure how much work was accomplished for the money spent! Hence, without time-phasing cost to match your project schedule, it is impossible to have reliable information for control purposes.*

Creating a Time-Phased Budget

By using information from your WBS and resource schedule, you can create a time-phased cost baseline. Remember from the WBS for the PC Project in Chapters 4 and 5 we integrated the WBS and OBS organization breakdown structure so the work packages could be tracked by deliverable and organization responsible. See Figure 8.12 for an example of the PC Prototype Project arranged by deliverable and organization unit responsible. For each intersection point of the WBS/OBS matrix, you see work package budgets and the total cost. The total cost at each intersection is called a cost or control account. For example, at the intersection of the Read/write head deliverable and the Production department we see there are three work packages with a total budget of $200,000. The sum of all cost accounts in a column should represent the total costs for the deliverable. Conversely, the sum of the cost accounts in a row should represent the costs or budget for the organizational unit responsible to accomplish the work. You can continue to "roll up" costs on the WBS/OBS to total project costs. This WBS provides the information you can use to time phase work packages and assign them to their respective scheduled activities over the life of the project.

Recall, from the development of your work breakdown structure for each work package, the following information needed to be developed:

1. Define work (what).
2. Identify time to complete a work package (how long).
3. Identify a time-phased budget to complete a work package (cost).
4. Identify resources needed to complete a work package (how much).
5. Identify a single person responsible for units of work (who).
6. Identify monitoring points for measuring progress (how well).

Number three, time-phasing the work package, is critical for the final step of creating your budget baseline. The process of time-phasing work packages, which is illustrated next, is demonstrated in Figure 8.13. The work package has a duration of three weeks. Assuming labor, materials, and equipment are tracked separately, the work package costs for labor are distributed over the three weeks as they are expected to occur—$40,000, $30,000, and $50,000 for each week, respectively.

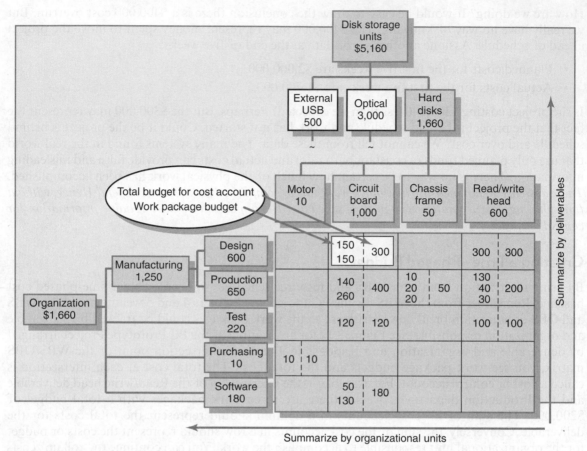

FIGURE 8.12 *Direct Labor Budget Rollup ($000)*

| Time-Phased Work Package Budget Labor cost only | | | | | | | | |

Work Package Description ___Test___   Page ___1___ of ___1___

Work Package ID ___1.1.3.2.3___   Project ___PC Prototype___

Deliverable ___Circuit board___   Date ___3/24/xx___

Responsible organization unit ___Test___   Estimator ___CEG___

Work Package Duration ___3___ weeks   Total labor cost ___$120,000___

Time-Phased Labor Budget ($000)

Work Package	Resource	Labor rate	Work Periods–Weeks					
			1	2	3	4	5	Total
Code 1.1.3.2.3	Quality testers	$xxxx/ week	$40	$30	$50			$120

FIGURE 8.13 *Time–Phased Work Package Budget (labor cost only)*

When the three-week work package is placed in the network schedule, the costs are distributed to the time-phased budget for the same three scheduled weeks. Fortunately, most single WPs become an activity and the process of distributing costs is relatively simple. That is, the relationship is one-for-one. Such budget timing is directly from the work package to the activity.

In a few instances an activity will include more than one work package, where the packages are assigned to *one responsible person or department and deliverable*. In this case the work packages are consolidated into one activity. As seen in Figure 8.14, this activity includes two WPs. The first, WP-1.1.3.2.4.1 (Code), is distributed over the first three weeks. The second, WP-1.1.3.2.4.2 (Integration), is sequenced over weeks 3 and 4. The activity duration is four weeks. When the activity is placed in the schedule, the costs are distributed starting with the schedule start—$20,000, $15,000, $75,000, and $70,000, respectively.

**Time-Phased Work Package Budget
Labor cost only**

Work Package Description __Software__   Page __1__ of __1__

Work Package ID **1.1.3.2.4.1 and 1.1.3.2.4.2**   Project ___PC Prototype___

Deliverable ___Circuit board___   Date ___3/24/xx___

Responsible organization unit _Software_   Estimator ___LGG___

Work Package Duration __4__ weeks   Total labor cost _$180,000_

Time-Phased Labor Budget ($000)

Work Package	Resource	Labor rate	1	2	3	4	5	Total
Code 1.1.3.2.4.1	Program'rs	$2,000/ week	$20	$15	$15			$50
Integration 1.1.3.2.4.2	System/ program'rs	$2,500/ week			$60	$70		$130
Total			$20	$15	$75	$70		$180

FIGURE 8.14 *Two Time–Phased Work Packages (labor cost only)*

These time-phased budgets for work packages are lifted from your WBS and are placed in your project schedule as they are expected to occur over the life of the project. The outcome of these budget allocations is the project *cost* baseline (also called **planned value**—PV), which is used to determine cost and schedule variances as the project is implemented.

Figure 8.15 shows the Patient Entry Project network schedule, which is used to place the time-phased work packages' budgets in the baseline. Figure 8.16 presents the project time-phased budget for the Patient Entry Project and the cumulative graph of the project budget baseline. In this figure you can see how the time-phased work package costs were placed into the network and how the cumulative project budget graph for a project is developed. Notice that costs do not have to be distributed linearly, but the costs should be placed as you expect them to occur.

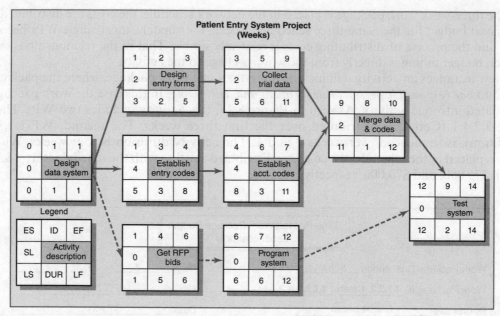

FIGURE 8.15 *Patient Entry Project Network*

ID	Dur.	Task	Budget	($000) Week

ID	Dur.	Task	Budget 0	1	2	3	4	5	6	7	8	9	10	11	12	13	14
1	1	Design data system	5	5													
2	2	Design entry forms	4		2	2											
3	3	Establish entry codes	6		2	2	2										
4	5	Get RFP bids	3		2				1								
5	6	Collect trial data	6			1	1	1	1	1	1						
6	3	Establish account codes	5				2	2	1								
7	6	Program system	12							2		4	2		4		
8	1	Merge data & codes	4									4					
9	2	Test system	7													4	3
		Week total	52	5	6	4	3	3	4	4	1	5	6	0	4	4	3
		Cumulative		5	11	15	18	21	25	29	30	35	41	41	45	49	52

Cumulative Baseline Budget (PV)

FIGURE 8.16 *Patient Entry Time–Phased Work Packages Assigned*

You have now developed complete time and cost plans for your project. These project baselines will be used to compare planned schedule and costs using an integrative system called *earned value*. The application and use of project baselines to measure performance are discussed in detail in Chapter 13. With your project budget baseline established, you are also able to generate cash flow statements for your project like the one presented in Figure 8.17. Such statements prepare the firm to cover costs over the lifespan of the project. Finally, with resource assignments finalized you are able to generate resource usage schedules for your project (see Figure 8.18). These schedules map out the full deployment of personnel and equipment and can be used to generate individual work schedules.

FIGURE 8.17 *CEBOO Project Monthly Cash Flow Statement*

	January	February	March	April	May	June	July
CEBOO Project							
Hardware							
Hardware specifications	$11,480.00	$24,840.00	$3,360.00				
Hardware design			$23,120.00	$29,920.00	$14,960.00		
Hardware documentation					$14,080.00	$24,320.00	
Prototypes							
Order GXs							
Assemble preproduction models							
Operating system							
Kernel specifications	$5,320.00	$9,880.00					
Drivers							
OC drivers				$3,360.00	$12,320.00	$11,760.00	$12,880.00
Serial VO drivers							
Memory management							
Operating system documentation		$10,240.00	$21,760.00				
Network interface							
Utilities							
Utilities specifications				$8,400.00			
Routine utilities				$5,760.00	$21,120.00	$20,160.00	$10,560.00
Complex utilities							
Utilities documentation				$7,680.00	$17,920.00		
Shell							
System integration							
Architectural decisions	$20,400.00						
Integration first phase							
System H/S test							
Project documentation							
Integration acceptance test							
Total	$37,200.00	$44,960.00	$48,240.00	$55,120.00	$80,400.00	$56,240.00	$23,440.00

FIGURE 8.18   *CEBOO Project Weekly Resource Usage Schedule*

	12/30	1/6	1/13	1/20	1/27	2/03
I. Suzuki	24 hrs	40 hrs	40 hrs	40 hrs	40 hrs	40 hrs
Hardware specifications				24 hrs	40 hrs	40 hrs
Hardware design						
Hardware documentation						
Operating system documentation						
Utilities documentation						
Architectural decisions	24 hrs	40 hrs	40 hrs	16 hrs		
J. Lopez	24 hrs	40 hrs	40 hrs	40 hrs	40 hrs	40 hrs
Hardware specifications				12 hrs	20 hrs	20 hrs
Hardware design						
Prototypes						
Kernel specifications				12 hrs	20 hrs	20 hrs
Utilities specifications						
Architectural decisions	24 hrs	40 hrs	40 hrs	16 hrs		
Integration first phase						
J.J. Putz				24 hrs	40 hrs	40 hrs
Hardware documentation						
Kernel specifications				24 hrs	40 hrs	40 hrs
Operating system documentation						
Utilities documentation						
Project documentation						
R. Sexon				24 hrs	40 hrs	40 hrs
Hardware specifications				24 hrs	40 hrs	40 hrs
Prototypes						
Assemble preproduction models						
OC drivers						
Complex utilities						
Integration first phase						
System H/S test						
Integration acceptance test						

Summary

Usage and availability of resources are major problem areas for project managers. Attention to these areas in developing a project schedule can point out resource bottlenecks before the project begins. Project managers should understand the ramifications of failing to schedule resources. The results of resource scheduling are frequently significantly different from the results of the standard CPM method.

With the rapid changes in technology and emphasis on time-to-market, catching resource usage and availability problems before the project starts can save the costs of crashing project activities later. Any resource deviations from plan and schedule that occur when the project is being implemented can be quickly recorded and the effect noted. Without this immediate update capability, the real negative effect of a change may not be known until it happens. Tying resource availability to a multiproject, multiresource system supports a project priority process that selects projects by their contribution to the organization's objectives and strategic plan.

Assignment of individuals to projects may not fit well with those assigned by computer software routines. In these cases overriding the computer solution to accommodate individual differences and skills is almost always the best choice.

The project resource schedule is important because it serves as your time baseline, which is used for measuring time differences between plan and actual. The resource schedule serves as the basis for developing your time-phased project cost budget baseline. The baseline (planned value, PV) is the sum of the cost accounts, and each cost account is the sum of the work packages in the cost account. Remember, if your budgeted costs are not time-phased, you really have no reliable way to measure performance. Although there are several types of project costs, the cost baseline is usually limited to direct costs (such as labor, materials, equipment) that are under the control of the project manager; other indirect costs can be added to project costs separately.

Key Terms

Heuristic	Resource-constrained projects	Time-constrained projects
Leveling	Resource smoothing	Time-phased budget baseline
Planned value (PV)	Splitting	

Review Questions

1. How does resource scheduling tie to project priority?
2. How does resource scheduling reduce flexibility in managing projects?
3. Present six reasons scheduling resources is an important task.
4. How can outsourcing project work alleviate the three most common problems associated with multiproject resource scheduling?
5. Explain the risks associated with leveling resources, compressing or crashing projects, and imposed durations or "catch-up" as the project is being implemented.
6. Why is it critical to develop a time-phased baseline?

Exercises

1. Given the network plan that follows, compute the early, late, and slack times. What is the project duration? Using any approach you wish (e.g., trial and error), develop a loading chart for resources, Electrical Engineers (EE), and resource, Mechanical Engineers (ME). Assume only one of each resource exists. Given your resource schedule, compute the early, late, and slack times for your project. Which activities are now critical? What is the project duration now? Could something like this happen in real projects?

Develop a loading schedule for each resource below. (Figure 8.3)

Fill in the times below for a resource activity schedule.

2. Given the network plan that follows, compute the early, late, and slack times. What is the project duration? Using any approach you wish (e.g., trial and error), develop a loading chart for resources Carpenters (C) and Electricians (E). Assume only one Carpenter is available and two Electricians are available. Given your resource schedule, compute the early, late, and slack times for your project. Which activities are now critical? What is the project duration now?

Develop a loading schedule for each resource below.

Carpenter

Electrician

0   1   2   3   4   5   6   7   8   9   10   11   12   13   14

Fill in the times below for a resource activity schedule.

ID/RES	ES	LS	EF	LF	SL
1-C					
2-C					
3-C					
4-E					
5-2-E					
6-C					

Legend

ES	ID	EF
SL		SL
LS	DUR	LF

Resource

3. Compute the early, late, and slack times for the activities in the network that follows, assuming a time-constrained network. Which activities are critical? What is the time-constrained project duration?

Note: Recall, in the schedule resource load chart the *time-constrained* scheduling interval (ES through LF) has been shaded. Any resource scheduled beyond the shaded area will delay the project.

Assume you have only three resources and you are using a computer that uses software that schedules projects by the parallel method and following heuristics. Schedule only one period at a time!

Minimum slack

Smallest duration

Lowest identification number

Keep a log of each activity change and update you make each period—e.g., period 0–1, 1–2, 2–3, etc. (Use a format similar to the one on page 259.) The log should include any changes or updates in ES and slack times each period, activities scheduled, and activities delayed. (Hint: Remember to maintain the technical dependencies of the network.) Use the resource load chart to assist you in scheduling (see pages 260–261—Figures 8.4 and 8.5).

List the order in which you scheduled the activities of the project. Which activities of your schedule are now critical?

Recompute your slack for each activity given your new schedule. What is the slack for activity 1? 4? 5?

4.*You have prepared the following schedule for a project in which the key resources is a tractor. There are three tractors available to the project. Activities A and D require one tractor to complete while activities B, C, E and F require 2 tractors.

---

*The solution to this exercise can be found in Appendix 1.

Develop a resource-constrained schedule in the loading chart that follows. Use the parallel method and heuristics given. Be sure to update each period as the computer would do. Record the carly start (ES), late finish (LF) and slack (SL) for the new schedule.

5. Develop a resource schedule in the loading chart that follows. Use the parallel method and heuristics given. Be sure to update each period as the computer would do. Note: activities 2, 3, 5, and 6 use two of the resource skills. Three of the resource skills are available. How has slack changed for each activity? Has the risk of being late changed? How?

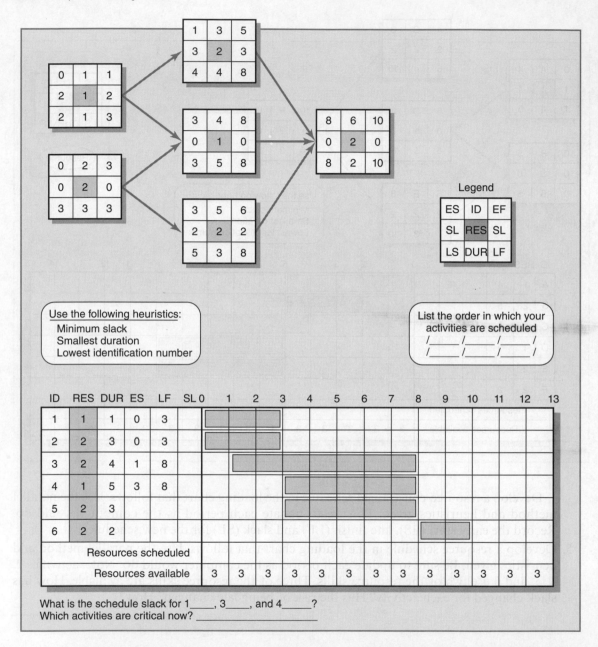

What is the schedule slack for 1_____, 3_____, and 4_____?
Which activities are critical now? _____

6. You have prepared the following schedule for a project in which the key resource is a backhoe. This schedule is contingent on having 3 backhoes. You receive a call from your partner, Brooker, who desperately needs 1 of your backhoes. You tell Brooker you would be willing to let him have the backhoe if you are still able to complete your project in 11 months.

Develop a resource schedule in the loading chart that follows to see if it is possible to complete the project in 11 months with only 2 backhoes. Be sure to record the order in which you schedule the activities using scheduling heuristics. Activities 5 and 6 require 2 backhoes, while activities 1, 2, 3, and 4 require 1 backhoe. No splitting of activities is possible. Can you say yes to Brooker's request?

7.*You are one of three carpenters assigned to complete a short construction project. Right before the start of the project, one of your fellow carpenters was hospitalized and will not be available to work on the project.

Develop a resource-constrained schedule in the loading chart that follows to see how long the project will take with only 2 carpenters. Be sure to record the order in which you schedule the activities using the scheduling heuristics. Activities A, B, C, D, E, G, and H require 2 carpenters to complete. Activity F requires only 1 carpenter. No splitting of activities is possible.

*The solution to this exercise can be found in Appendix 1.

You will receive a bonus if the project is completed within 15 days. Should you start planning how you will spend your bonus?

8. Given the time-phased work packages, complete the baseline budget form for the project.

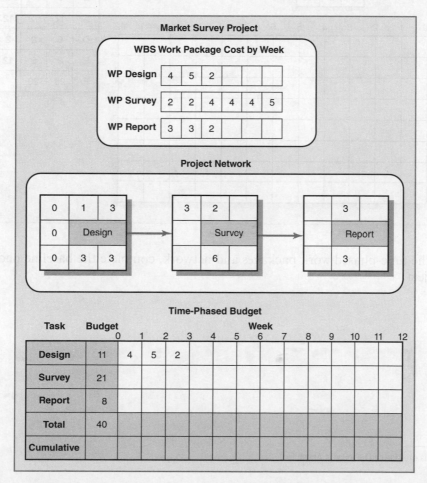

Time-phased budget ($ 000)

Task	Budget	0	1	2	3	4	5	6	7	8	9	10
Activity 1	4	4										
Activity 2	6		1	3	2							
Activity 3	10		2	4	2	2						
Activity 4	8							2	3	3		
Activity 5	3										2	1
Total	31											
Cumulative												

9. Given the time-phased work packages and network, complete the baseline budget form for the project.

Market Survey Project

WBS Work Package Cost by Week

WP Design	4	5	2			
WP Survey	2	2	4	4	4	5
WP Report	3	3	2			

Project Network: Design → Survey → Report

Time-Phased Budget

Task	Budget	0	1	2	3	4	5	6	7	8	9	10	11	12
Design	11	4	5	2										
Survey	21													
Report	8													
Total	40													
Cumulative														

10.*Given the time-phased work packages and network, complete the baseline budget form for the project.

11. Given the time-phased work packages and network, complete the baseline budget form for the project.

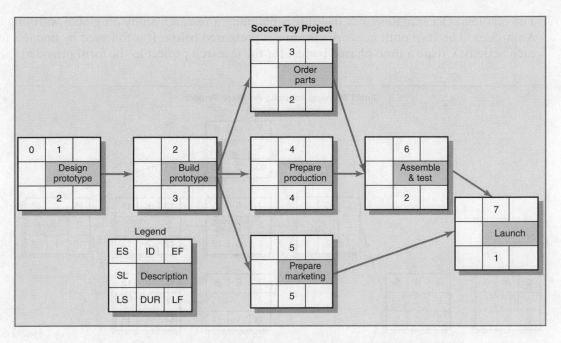

Soccer Toy Project

Cost by Week ($000)

	←1	←2	←3	←4	←5
Design prototype	12	12			
Build prototype	10	10	10		
Order parts	5	5			
Prepare production	16	10	22	16	
Prepare marketing	6	6	0	6	12
Assemble & test	18	18			
Launch	12				

Time-phased Budget ($000)

Week

	Budget	0	1	2	3	4	5	6	7	8	9	10	11	12	13
Design prototype	24														
Build prototype	30														
Order parts	10														
Prepare prod'n	64														
Prepare market'g	30														
Assemble & test	36														
Launch	12														
Total	206														
Cumulative															

12. The National Oceanic Research Institute is planning a research study on global warming in Antarctica. The 16-month network schedule is presented below. It is followed by budgets for each activity. Create a time-phased budget for the research project in the form provided.

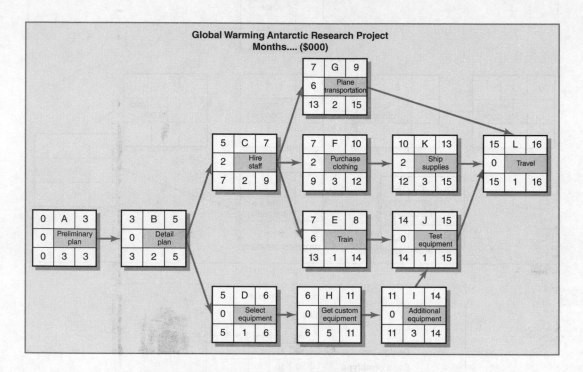

Global Warming Antarctic Research Project
Activity Time Phased Work Packages by Month ($000)

	Task	Duration	Budget	0	1	2	3	4	5	6
A	Preliminary plan	3	3	1	1	1				
B	Detail plan	2	2	1	1					
C	Hire staff	2	4	4						
D	Select equipment	1	5	5						
E	Train	1	3	3						
F	Purchase clothing	3	9	3	0	6				
G	Plane transportation	2	60	5	55					
H	Get custom equipment	5	36	5	5	10	10	6		
I	Additional equipment	3	20	10	5	5				
J	Test equipment	1	6	6						
K	Ship all supplies	5	15	3	3	0	0	9		
L	Travel	1	9	9						
	Total budget		172							

References

Arrow, K. J., and L. Hurowicz, *Studies in Resource Allocation Process* (New York: Cambridge University Press, 1997).

Brucker, P., A. Drexl, R. Mohring, L. Newmann, and E. Pesch, "Resource-constrained Project Scheduling: Notation, Classification, Models and Methods," *European Journal of Operational Research,* Vol. 112, 1999, pp. 3–42.

Burgess, A. R., and J. B. Kellebrew, "Variations in Activity Level on Cyclical Arrow Diagrams," *Journal of Industrial Engineering,* Vol. 13, March–April 1962, pp. 76–83.

Charnes, A., and W. W. Cooper, "A Network Interpretation and Direct Sub Dual Algorithm for Critical Path Scheduling," *Journal of Industrial Engineering,* July–August 1962.

Demeulemeester, E. L., and W. S. Herroelen, *Project Scheduling: A Research Handbook* (Norwell, Mass: Kluwer Academic Publishers, 2002).

Fendly, L. G., "Towards the Development of a Complete Multi Project Scheduling System," *Journal of Industrial Engineering,* Vol. 19, 1968, pp. 505–15.

Goldratt, E., *Critical Chain* (Great Barrington, MA: North River Press, 1997).

Newbold, R. C., "Leveraging Project Resources: Tools for the Next Century," *Proceedings of 28th Annual Project Management Institute, 1997 Seminars and Symposium* (Newtown, PA: Project Management Institute, 1997), pp. 417–21.

Pascoe, T. L., "An Experimental Comparison of Heuristic Methods for Allocating Resources," Ph.D. dissertation, University of Cambridge, United Kingdom, 1965.

Reinersten, D., "Is It Always a Bad Idea to Add Resources to a Late Project?" *Electric Design,* October 30, 2000, pp. 17–18.

Talbot, B. F., and J. H. Patterson, "Optimal Methods for Scheduling Under Resource Constraints," *Project Management Journal,* December 1979.

Wiest, J. D., "A Heuristic Model for Scheduling Large Projects with Unlimited Resources," *Management Science,* Vol. 18, February 1967, pp. 359–77.

Woodworth, B. M., and C. J. Willie, "A Heuristic Algorithm for Resource Leveling in Multiproject, Multiresource Scheduling," *Decision Sciences,* Vol. 6, July 1975, pp. 525–40.

Woodworth, B. M., and S. Shanahan, "Identifying the Critical Sequence in a Resource Constrained Project," *International Journal of Project Management,* Vol. 6, 1988, pp. 89–96.

APPENDIX 8.1

The Critical-Chain Approach

In practice, project managers carefully manage slack on sensitive resource-limited projects. If possible, they will add slack at the end of the project by committing to a completion date that goes beyond the scheduled date. For example, the plans say the project should be completed on April 1, although the official completion date is May 1. Other managers take a more aggressive approach to managing slack within the schedule. They use an early start schedule and prohibit use of slack on any activity or work package to be used unless authorized by the project manager. Progress by percent complete and by remaining time are carefully monitored. Activities that are beating estimated completion times are reported so that succeeding activities can start ahead of schedule. This ensures that the time gained is used to start a succeeding activity earlier and time is not wasted. The overall intent is to create and save slack as a time buffer to complete the project early or to cover delay problems that may creep up on critical activities or paths.

Eliyahu Goldratt, who championed the "theory of constraints" in his popular book *The Goal*, advocates an alternative approach to managing slack.[1] He has coined the term "critical-chain" to recognize that the project network may be constrained by both resource and technical dependencies. Each type of constraint can create task dependencies, and in the case of resource constraints, new task dependencies can be created! Remember how resource constraints shifted the critical path? If not, visit Figure 8.5 again. The critical chain refers to the longest string of dependencies that exist on the project. Chain is used instead of path, since the latter tends to be associated with just technical dependencies not resource dependencies. Goldratt uses the critical chain concept to develop strategies for accelerating the completion of projects. These strategies are based on his observations about time estimates of individual activities.

TIME ESTIMATES

Goldratt argues that there is a natural tendency for people to add safety (just-in-case) time to their estimations. It is believed that those who estimate activity times provide an estimate that has about an 80 to 90 percent chance of being completed on or before the estimated time. Hence, the median time (50/50 chance) is overestimated by approximately 30 to 40 percent. For example, a programmer may estimate that there is a 50/50 chance that he can complete an activity in six days. However, to ensure success and to protect against potential problems, he adds three days of safety time and reports that it will take nine days to complete the task. In this case the median (50/50) time is overestimated by approximately 50 percent. He now has a 50/50 chance of completing the project three days ahead of the schedule. If this hidden contingency is pervasive across a project, then most activities in theory should be completed ahead of schedule.

Not only do workers add safety, but project managers like to add safety to ensure that they will be able to bring the project in ahead of schedule. They will add a month to a nine-month project to cover any delays or risks that might spring up. This situation raises an interesting paradox:

Why, if there is a tendency to overestimate activity durations, and add safety to the end of a project, do so many projects come in behind schedule?

Critical-Chain Project Management (CCPM) offers several explanations:

- *Parkinson's law:* Work fills the time available. Why hustle to complete a task today when it isn't due until tomorrow? Not only will the pace of work be dictated by deadline, but workers will take advantage of perceived free time to catch up on other things. This is especially true in matrix environments where workers will use this time to clear work backlog on other projects and duties.

- *Self-protection:* Participants fail to report early finishes out of fear that management will adjust their future standards and demand more next time. For example, if a team member estimates that

---

[1] E. Goldratt, *The Goal* (Great Barrington, MA: North River Press, 1997).

a task will take seven days and delivers it in five, the next time he is asked for an estimate, the project manager may want to trim the estimate based on past performance. Peer pressure may also be a factor here: to avoid being labeled a "rate buster," members may not report early finishes.

- *Dropped baton:* Goldratt uses the metaphor of project as relay race to illustrate the impact of poor coordination. Just as a runner's time is lost if the next runner is not ready to receive the baton, so is the time gained from completing a task early lost if the next group of people are not ready to receive the project work. Poor communication and inflexible resource schedules prevent progress from occurring.
- *Excessive multitasking:* The norm in most organizations is to have project personnel work on several projects, activities, or assignments at the same time. This leads to costly interruptions and excessive task splitting. As pointed out on p. 268, this adds time to each activity. When looked at in isolation the time loss may seem minimal, but when taken as a whole the transition costs can be staggering.
- *Resource bottlenecks:* In multiproject organizations projects are frequently delayed because test equipment or other necessary resources are tied up on other project work.
- *Student syndrome (procrastination):* Goldratt asserts that just as students delay writing a term paper until the last minute, workers delay starting tasks when they perceive that they have more than enough time to complete the task. The problem with delaying the start of a task is that obstacles are often not detected until the task is under way. By postponing the start of the task, the opportunity to cope with these obstacles and complete the task on time is compromised.

CRITICAL-CHAIN IN ACTION

CCPM's solution to reducing project time overruns is to insist on people using the "true 50/50" activity time estimates (rather than estimates which have an 80 to 90 percent chance of being completed before the estimated time); the 50/50 estimates result in a project duration about one-half the low risk of 80 to 90 percent estimates. This requires a corporate culture which values accurate estimates and refrains from blaming people for not meeting deadlines. According to CCPM, using 50/50 estimates will discourage Parkinson's law, the student syndrome, and self-protection from coming into play because there is less "free time" available. Productivity will be increased as individuals try to meet tighter deadlines. Similarly, the compressed time schedule reduces the likelihood of the dropped baton effect.

CCPM recommends inserting time buffers into the schedule to act as "shock absorbers" to protect the project completion date against task durations taking longer than the 50/50 estimate. The rationale is that by using 50/50 estimates you are in essence taking out all of the "safety" in individual tasks. CCPM also recommends using portions of this collective safety strategically by inserting time buffers where potential problems are likely to occur. There are three kinds of buffers in CCPM:

- *Project buffer:* First, since all activities along the critical chain have inherent *uncertainty* that is difficult to predict, project duration is uncertain. Therefore, a project time buffer is added to the expected *project duration*. CCPM recommends using roughly 50 percent of the aggregate safety. For example, if the modified schedule reduces the project duration by 20 days from 50 to 30, then a 10-day project buffer would be used.
- *Feeder buffers:* Buffers are added to the network where noncritical paths merge with the critical chain. These buffers protect the critical chain from being delayed.
- *Resource buffers:* Time buffers are inserted where scarce resources are needed for an activity. Resource time buffers come in at least two forms. One form is a time buffer attached to a critical resource to ensure that the resource is on call and available when needed. This preserves

In the past Spirit Aero Systems, manufacturer of airplane parts, were forced to delay product development projects as a result of missing parts for assemblies. Spirit management cycled through several approaches, such as lean, value chain, cycle time reduction, knowledge based engineering, to reduce the problem. Although each yielded minor improvements, the impacts were not substantial. Rework, overtime, delay costs, and vendor expediting costs continued to have significant impact on costs, meeting commitments, and reputation. Spirit turned to critical chain management methodology in a pilot project.

Joseph Zenisek, the critical chain manager, said the choice of critical chain was "a game changer for us." Spirit applied the critical chain approach to assembly of newly designed pylons (brackets) used for failure destruction testing of casings for a jet engine project. Zenisek credited success to three key factors:

- Creating a rule to never start a work package until all parts and staff are available.
- Ensuring part buffers to cover work packages by vigilantly monitoring assembly parts that use a large number of parts or where rate or number used is high.
- Developing a small engineering team to manage vendors and buffers to ensure that delivery of over 300 parts arrived on time.

The critical chain program led to impressive results. The parts and staffing rule cut down on late deliveries and rework on partially completed work packages caused by missing parts. The result was a reduction of 50 percent in overtime. Reducing delays reduced assembly cycle time by 18 percent. Work in process and work packages were also reduced since availability of buffer parts avoided delays. The critical chain method led to better resource management and reduced stress.

Given the success of the critical chain program, Spirit intends to expand the application of the critical chain method to new product development projects for their clients.

*Peter Fretty, "E Is in the Air," *PMNetwork,* February 2012, Vol. 26, No. 2, pp. 50–56.

the relay race. The second form of time buffer is added to activities preceding the work of a scarce resource. This kind of buffer protects against resource bottlenecks by increasing the likelihood that the preceding activity will be completed when the resource is available.

All buffers reduce the risk of the project duration being late and increase the chance of early project completion.[2] See Snapshot from Practice: Critical Chain Applied to Airplane Part Arrivals.

CRITICAL-CHAIN VERSUS TRADITIONAL SCHEDULING APPROACH

To illustrate how CCPM affects scheduling let's compare it with the traditional approach to project scheduling. We will first resolve resource problems the way described in Chapter 8 and then the CCPM method. Figure A8.1A shows the *planned* Air Control project network without any concern for resources. That is, activities are assumed to be independent and resources will be made available and/or are interchangeable.

---

[2] For more information on buffers see: L. P. Leach, "Critical Chain Project Management Improves Project Performance," *Project Management Journal,* 30 (2) 1999, pp. 39–51.

FIGURE A8.1A   *Air Control Project: Time Plan without Resources*

Figure A8.1B depicts the bar chart for the project. The dark blue bars represent the durations of critical activities; the light blue bars represent the durations of noncritical activities; the gray bars represent slack. Note that the duration is 45 days and the critical path is represented by activities 1, 4, 6, 7, and 8.

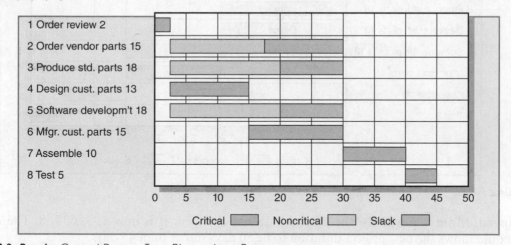

FIGURE A8.1B   *Air Control Project: Time Plan without Resources*

Parallel activities hold potential for resource conflicts. This is the case in this project. Ryan is the resource for activities 3 and 6. If you insert Ryan in the bar chart in Figure A8.1B for activities 3 and 6, you can see activity 3 overlaps activity 6 by five days—an impossible situation. Because Ryan cannot work two activities simultaneously and no other person can take his place, a resource dependency exists. The result is that two activities (3 and 6) that were assumed to be independent now become dependent. Something has to give! Figure A8.2A shows the Air Control project network with the resources included. A pseudo-dashed arrow has been added to the network to indicate the resource dependency. The bar chart in Figure A8.2B reflects the revised schedule resolving the overallocation of Ryan. Given the new schedule, slack for some activities has

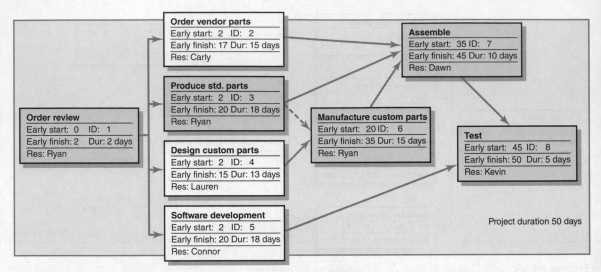

FIGURE A8.2A *Air Control Project: Schedule with Resources Limited*

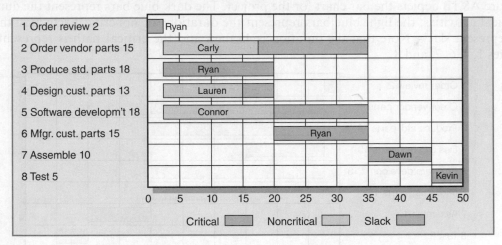

FIGURE A8.2B *Air Control Project: Schedule with Resources Limited*

changed. More importantly, the critical path has changed. It is now 1, 3, 6, 7, 8. The resource schedule shows the new project duration to be 50 days rather than 45 days.

Now let's apply the CCPM approach to the Air Control project. Figure A8.3 details many of the changes. First, notice that task estimates now represent approximations of the 50/50 rule. Second, observe that not all of the activities on the critical chain are technically linked. Manufacture custom parts is included because of previously defined resource dependency. Third, a project time buffer is added at the end of schedule. Finally, feeder buffers are inserted at each point where a noncritical activity merges with the critical chain.

The impact the CCPM approach has on the project schedule can best be seen in the Gantt chart presented in Figure A8.4. Notice first the late start times for each of the three noncritical activities. For example, under the critical path method, order vendor parts and software development would be scheduled to begin immediately after the order review. Instead they are scheduled later in the

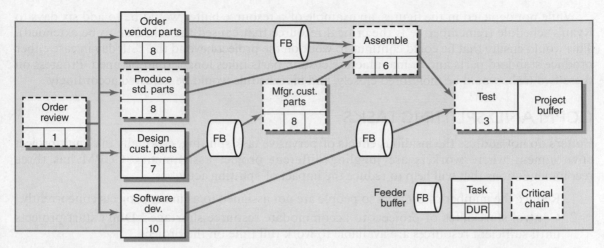

FIGURE A8.3 *Air Control Project: CCPM Network*

Activity	DUR	LS	LF	Buffer
1. Order review	1	0	1	0
2. Order vendor parts	8	7	15	3
3. Produce std. parts	8	1	9	0
4. Design cust. parts	7	1	8	3
5. Software dev.	10	11	21	3
6. Mfgr. cust. parts	8	11	19	0
7. Assemble	6	18	24	0
8. Test	3	24	27	12

FIGURE A8.4 *Air Control Project Gantt Chart: CCPM Network*

project. Three-day feeder buffers have been added to each of these activities to absorb any delays that might occur in these activities. Finally, instead of taking 50 days the project is now estimated to take only 27 days with a 10-day project buffer!

This example provides an opportunity for explaining the differences between buffers and slack. Slack is spare time inherent in the schedule of noncritical activities and can be determined by differences between the early start and late start of a specific activity. Buffers, on the other hand, are dedicated time blocks reserved to cover most likely contingencies and are monitored closely so, if they are not needed, subsequent activities can proceed on schedule. Buffers are needed in part because the estimates are based on 50/50 approximations, and therefore roughly half of the activities will take longer than planned. To protect against these extended activity durations, buffers are inserted to minimize the impact on the schedule. Buffers are not part of the project schedule and are used only when sound management dictates it.

While not depicted in the figures, an example of a resource buffer would be to add six days to Ryan's schedule (remember he is the critical resource that caused the schedule to be extended). This would ensure that he could continue to work on the project beyond the 18th day in case either produce standard parts and/or manufacture custom parts takes longer than planned. Progress on these two tasks would be monitored closely, and his schedule would be adjusted accordingly.

CCPM AND SPLITTING TASKS

Buffers do not address the insidious effects of pervasive task splitting, especially in a multiproject environment where workers are juggling different project assignments. CCPM has three recommendations that will help to reduce the impact of splitting activities:

1. Reduce the number of projects so people are not assigned to as many projects concurrently.
2. Control start dates of projects to accommodate resource shortages. Don't start projects until sufficient resources are available to work full time on the project.
3. Contract (lock in) for resources *before* the project begins.

MONITORING PROJECT PERFORMANCE

The CCPM method uses buffers to monitor project time performance. Remember that as shown in Figure A8.3 a project buffer is used to insulate the project against delays along the critical chain. For monitoring purposes, this buffer is typically divided into three zones—OK, Watch and Plan, and Act, respectively (see Figure A8.5). As the buffer begins to decrease and moves into the second zone, alarms are set off to seek corrective action. To be truly effective, buffer management requires comparing buffer usage with actual progress on the project. For example, if the project

FIGURE A8.5 *Project Control— Buffer Management*

is 75 percent complete and you have only used 50 percent of the project buffer, then the project is in pretty good shape. Conversely, if the project is only 25 percent complete and 50 percent of the buffer has already been used, you are in trouble and corrective action is needed. A method for estimating percentage complete is described in Chapter 13.

THE CCPM METHOD TODAY

CCPM has generated considerable debate within the project management community. While sound in theory, support at this time is limited but growing. For example, Harris Semiconductor was able to build a new automated wafer fabrication facility within 13 months using CCPM methods when the industry standard for such a facility is 26–36 months. The Israeli aircraft industry has used CCPM techniques to reduce average maintenance work on aircraft from two months to two weeks. The U.S. Air Force and Navy as well as Boeing, Lucent Technologies, Intel, GM, and 3M are applying critical-chain principles to their multi-project environments.[3]

[3] Cited in materials developed by the Eliyahu Goldratt Institute (New Haven, CT) for a workshop attended by one of the authors entitled, "Project Management the TOC Way," 1998.

CCPM is not without critics. First, CCPM does not address the biggest cause of project delays, which is an ill-defined and unstable project scope. Second, some critics challenge Goldratt's assumptions about human behavior. They question the tendency of experts to pad estimates and that employees act deliberately against the organization for their own interest and benefit. Critics also object to the insinuation that trained professionals would exhibit the student syndrome habits (Zalmanson, 2001). Third, evidence of success is almost exclusively anecdotal and based on single case studies or on computer modeling.[4] The lack of systematic evidence raises questions about generalizability of application. CCPM may prove to work best for only certain kinds of projects.

One of the keys to implementing CCPM is the culture of the organization. If the organization honors noble efforts that fail to meet estimates as it does efforts that do meet estimates, then greater acceptance will occur. Conversely, if management treats honest failure differently from success, then resistance will be high. Organizations adopting the CCPM approach have to invest significant energy to obtaining "buy-in" on the part of all participants to its core principles and allaying the fears that this system may generate.

APPENDIX SUMMARY

Regardless of where one stands in the debate, the CCPM approach deserves credit for bringing resource dependency to the forefront, highlighting the modern ills of multitasking, and forcing us to rethink conventional methods of project scheduling.

APPENDIX REVIEW QUESTIONS

1. Explain how time is wasted in management of projects.
2. Distinguish between project and feeder buffers.
3. Buffers are not the same as slack. Explain.

APPENDIX EXERCISES

1. Check out the Goldratt Institute's homepage at *http://www.goldratt.com* for current information on the application of critical-chain techniques to project management.
2. Apply critical-chain scheduling principles to the Print Software, Inc., project presented in Chapter 6 on pages 191–192. Revise the estimated time durations by 50 percent except round up the odd time durations (i.e., 3 becomes 4). Draw a CCPM network diagram similar to the one contained in Figure A8.3 for the Print Software project as well as a Gantt chart similar to Figure A8.4. How would these diagrams differ from the ones generated using the traditional scheduling technique?

APPENDIX REFERENCES

Budd, C. S., and M. J. Cooper, "Improving On-time Service Delivery: The Case of Project as Product," *Human Systems Management,* 24 (1) 2005, pp. 67–81.

Goldratt, *Critical Chain* (Great Barrington, MA: North River Press, 1997).

Herroelen, W., R. Leus, and E. Demeulemeester, "Critical Chain Project Scheduling: Do Not Oversimplify," *Project Management Journal,* Vol. 33 (4) 2002, pp. 48–60.

Leach, L. P., "Critical Chain Project Management," *Proceedings of 29th Annual Project Management Institute, 1998, Seminars and Symposium* (Newtown, PA: Project Management Institute, 1998), pp. 1239–44.

Levine, H. A., "Shared Contingency: Exploring the Critical Chain," *PM Network,* October 1999, pp. 35–38.

Newbold, R. C., *Project Management in the Fast Lane: Applying the Theory of Constraints* (Boca Raton, FL: St. Lucie Press, 1998).

Noreen, E., D. Smith, and J. Mackey, *The Theory of Constraints and Its Implication for Management Accounting* (Great Barrington, MA: North River Press, 1995).

Raz, T., R. Barnes, and D. Dvir, "A Critical Look at Critical Chain Project Management," *Project Management Journal,* December 2003, pp. 24–32.

Sood, S., "Taming Uncertainty: Critical-Chain Buffer Management Helps Minimize Risk in the Project Equation," *PM Network,* March 2003, pp. 57–59.

Zalmanson, E., "Readers Feedback," *PM Network,* Vol. 15 (1) 2001, p. 4.

CASE 8.1

Power Train, Ltd.

We have smashing systems for reporting, tracking, and controlling costs on design projects. Our planning of projects is better than any I have seen at other companies. Our scheduling seemed to serve us well when we were small and we had only a few projects. Now that we have many more projects and schedule using multiproject software, there are too many occasions when the right people are not assigned to the projects deemed important to our success. This situation is costing us big money, headaches, and stress!

Claude Jones, VP, Design and Operations

HISTORY

Power Train, Ltd. (PT), was founded in 1970 by Daniel Gage, a skilled mechanical engineer and machinist. Prior to founding PT he worked for three years as design engineer for a company that designed and built transmissions for military tanks and trucks. It was a natural transition for Dan to start a company designing and building power trains for farm tractor companies. Today, Dan is no longer active in the management of PT but is still revered as its founder. He and his family still own 25 percent of the company, which went public in 1998. PT has been growing at a 6 percent clip for the last five years but expects industry growth to level off as supply exceeds demand.

Today, PT continues its proud tradition of designing and building the best-quality power trains for manufacturers of farm tractors and equipment. The company employs 178 design engineers and has about 1,800 production and support staff. Contract design projects for tractor manufacturers represent a major portion of PT's revenue. At any given time, about 45 to 60 design projects are going on concurrently. A small portion of their design work is for military vehicles. PT only accepts military contracts that involve very advanced, new technology and are cost plus.

A new phenomenon has attracted management of PT to look into a larger market. Last year a large Swedish truck manufacturer approached PT to consider designing power trains for its trucks. As the industry consolidates, the opportunities for PT should increase because these large firms are moving to more outsourcing to cut infrastructure costs and stay very flexible. Only last week a PT design engineer spoke to a German truck manufacturing manager at a conference. The German manager was already exploring outsourcing of drive trains to Porsche and was very pleased to be reminded of PT's expertise in the area. A meeting is set up for next month.

CLAUDE JONES

Claude Jones joined PT in 1999 as a new MBA from the University of Edinburgh. He worked as a mechanical engineer for U.K. Hydraulics for five years prior to returning to school for the MBA. "I just wanted to be part of the management team and where the action is." Jones moved quickly through the ranks. Today he is the vice president of design and operations. Sitting at his desk, Jones is pondering the conflicts and confusion that seem to be increasing in scheduling people to projects. He gets a real rush at the thought of designing power trains for large trucks; however, given their current project scheduling problems, a large increase in business would only compound their problems. Somehow these conflicts in scheduling have to be resolved before any serious thought can be given to expanding into design of power transmissions for truck manufacturers.

Jones is thinking of the problems PT had in the last year. The MF project is the first to come to mind. The project was not terribly complex and did not require their best design engineers. Unfortunately, the scheduling software assigned one of the most creative and expensive engineers to the MF project. A similar situation, but reversed, happened on the Deer project. This project involved a big customer and new hydrostatic technology for small tractors. In this project the scheduling software assigned engineers who were not familiar with small tractor transmissions. Somehow, thinks Jones, the right people need to be scheduled to the right projects. Upon reflection, this problem with scheduling has been increasing since PT went to multiproject scheduling. Maybe a project office is needed to keep on top of these problems.

A meeting with the information technology team and software vendors was positive but not very helpful because these people are not really into detailed scheduling problems. The vendors provided all sorts of evidence suggesting the heuristics used—least slack, shortest duration, and identification number—are absolutely efficient in scheduling people and minimizing project delays. One project software vendor, Lauren, kept saying their software would allow PT to customize the scheduling of projects and people to almost any variation selected. Lauren repeated over and over, "If the standard heuristics do not meet your requirements, create your own heuristics that do." Lauren even volunteered to assist in setting up the system. But she is not willing to spend time on the problem until PT can describe to her exactly what criteria will be used (and their sequence) to select and schedule people to projects.

WHAT NEXT?

Potential expansion into the truck power train business is not feasible until the confusion in project scheduling is solved or reduced significantly. Jones is ready to tackle this problem, but he is not sure where to start.

CASE 8.2

The CCPM Dilemma

Pinyarat worked in the IT department of a diversified IT firm. She was describing the firm's early encounters with critical chain scheduling to a friend in another IT firm.

Three years ago management decided to add 10 percent time to all activity estimates because almost all projects were coming in late. One thought was people were simply working too hard and needed some relief. This approach did not work! Projects still came in late. Next, management decided to take away the extra time for activities and add 10 percent for project estimates to ensure project durations would be met. Again, nothing improved and projects continued to come in late. Recently, the firm hired a consultant who promoted critical chain scheduling, which was implemented for all projects in her division. Almost all failed to perform.

Pinyarat explained, "The estimates were basically impossible. The activity durations got squeezed down to less than the 50 percent guideline. We were late on nearly every task. In addition, I was not allowed to put in a big enough project buffer, which only added to projects being late. One colleague who was working on six projects gave up and quit; he said he was killing himself and saw no hope of things getting better. My projects are not the only ones having big problems. Some people had no idea why anyone would use CCPM scheduling. To quote one of my best programmers: 'They ask for an estimate and then they cut it 50 percent or more.' What kind of game is this? Apparently they don't trust us."

A week later, to Pinyarat's surprise, she was called to the IT manager's office. Pinyarat imagined numerous bad scenarios of how the meeting would go—even to the remote possibility of being fired! The manager wanted the division to straighten out their project management practices and stop this business of nearly all IT projects being late. There are rumors of cleaning house or outsourcing IT work.

The manager believed Pinyarat, who passed the PMP exam, had the best chance of turning things around. He said, "Pinyarat, I'm nearing the desperate level; top management is reaching the end of the rope with our division. We need to turn this around for both our sakes. Give me a plan that I can sponsor within the week."

Pinyarat explained to her friend a few of her ideas—like squeezing estimates too far. But she said she would take any ideas she can get from anyone.

Give Pinyarat a report that identifies the key problems and a plan of action she can present to her sponsor. Limit your report to 800 words or less.

9

REDUCING PROJECT DURATION

In skating over thin ice our safety is in our speed.

—*Ralph Waldo Emerson*

Imagine the following scenarios:

— After finalizing your project schedule, you realize the estimated completion date is two months beyond what your boss publicly promised an important customer.

— Five months into the project, you realize that you are already three weeks behind the drop-dead date for the project.

— Four months into a project top management changes its priorities and now tells you that money is not an issue. Complete the project ASAP!

What do you do?

This chapter addresses strategies for reducing project duration either prior to setting the baseline for the project or in the midst of project execution. Choice of options is based on the constraints surrounding the project. Here the project priority matrix introduced in Chapter 4 comes into play. For example, there are many more options available for reducing project time if you are not resource constrained than if you cannot spend more than your original budget. We will begin first by examining the reasons for reducing project duration followed by a discussion of different options for accelerating project completion. The chapter will conclude with the classic time-cost framework for selecting which activities to "crash." Crash is a term that has emerged in the Project Management lexicon for shortening the duration of an activity or project beyond when it can be normally done.

RATIONALE FOR REDUCING PROJECT DURATION

There are many good reasons for attempting to reduce the duration of a project. One of the more important reasons today is time to market. Intense global competition and rapid technological advances have made speed a competitive advantage. To succeed, companies have to spot new opportunities, launch project teams, and bring new products or services to the marketplace in a flash. Perhaps in no industry does speed matter as much as in the electronics industry. For example, a rule of thumb for moderate- to high-technology firms is that a six-month delay in bringing a product to market can result in a loss of market share of about 35 percent. In these cases, high-technology firms typically assume that the time savings and avoidance of lost profits are worth any additional costs to reduce time without any formal analysis. See the Snapshot from Practice: Smartphone Wars for more on this.

Business survival depends not only upon rapid innovation but also adaptability. Global recession and energy crises have stunned the business world, and those companies that survive will be those that can quickly adapt to new challenges. This requires speedy project management! For example, the fate of U.S. auto industry depends in part on how quickly they shift their efforts to develop fuel efficient, alternative forms of transportation.

Another common reason for reducing project time occurs when unforeseen delays—for example, adverse weather, design flaws, and equipment breakdown—cause substantial delays midway in the project. Getting back on schedule usually requires compressing the time on some of the remaining critical activities. The additional costs of getting back on schedule need to be compared with the consequences of being late. This is especially true when time is a top priority.

Incentive contracts can make reduction of project time rewarding—usually for both the project contractor and owner. For example, a contractor finished a bridge across a lake 18 months early and received more than $6 million for the early completion. The availability of the bridge to the

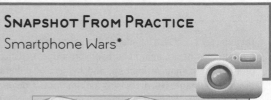

SNAPSHOT FROM PRACTICE
Smartphone Wars*

Speed has been critical in business ever since the California Gold Rush. The smartphone industry is a good example of an intensely competitive business that places a premium on speed and innovation. During the first week of September 2012, both Nokia and Motorola-mobile released new versions of their smartphones. The Nokia Lumina 920, which is considered crucial for the company's regaining prominence, featured puremotion +HD as well as many other new features. Motorola's RazrM featured a bigger screen and faster performance and updated Android OS. Both phones were in response to Apple's iPhone 5, which was revealed 10 days later. The new iPhone 5 featured a bigger screen and a faster interface.

   In order to survive, RIM, Samsung, Apple, and other smartphone manufacturers have become masters at project management. They have been able to cut the market release time of new phones from 12–18 months to 6–9 months. What is at stake is over $1 billion in forecasted sales of new smartphones.

* J. Garside, "Smartphone sales to hit 1bn a year for the first time in 2013," *The Guardian,* www.guardian.co.uk/2013/jan/06/smartphone.

Rex Features via AP Images

surrounding community 18 months early to reduce traffic gridlock made the incentive cost to the community seem small to users. In another example, in a continuous improvement arrangement, the joint effort of the owner and contractor resulted in early completion of a river lock and a 50/50 split of the savings to the owner and contractor. See Snapshot from Practice: Northridge Earthquake for a situation in which a contractor went to great lengths to complete a project as quickly as possible.

   "Imposed deadlines" is another reason for accelerating project completion. For example, a politician makes a public statement that a new law building will be available in two years. Or the president of a software company remarks in a speech that new advanced software will be available in one year. Such statements too often become imposed project duration dates—without any consideration of the problems or cost of meeting such a date. The project duration time is set while the project is in its "concept" phase before or without any detailed scheduling of all the activities in the project. This phenomenon occurs very frequently in practice! Unfortunately, this practice almost always leads to a higher cost project than one that is planned using low-cost and detailed planning. In addition, quality is sometimes compromised to meet deadlines. More important, these increased costs of imposed duration dates are seldom recognized or noted by project participants.

On January 17, 1994, a 6.8-magnitude earthquake struck the Los Angeles basin, near suburban Northridge, causing 60 deaths, thousands of injuries, and billions of dollars in property damage. Nowhere was the destructive power of nature more evident than in the collapsed sections of the freeway system that disrupted the daily commute of an estimated 1 million Los Angelenos. The Northridge earthquake posed one of the greatest challenges to the California Department of Transportation (CalTrans) in its nearly 100-year history. To expedite the recovery process, Governor Pete Wilson signed an emergency declaration allowing CalTrans to streamline contracting procedures and offer attractive incentives for completing work ahead of schedule. For each day that the schedule was beaten, a sizable bonus was to be awarded. Conversely, for each day over the deadline, the contractor would

© David Butow/Corbis SABA

be penalized the same amount. The amount ($50,000 to $200,000) varied depending on the importance of the work.

The incentive scheme proved to be a powerful motivator for the freeway reconstruction contractors. C. C. Myers, Inc., of Rancho Cordova, California, won the contract for the reconstruction of the Interstate 10 bridges. Myers pulled out all stops to finish the project in a blistering 66 days—a whopping 74 days ahead of schedule—and earning a $14.8 million bonus! Myers took every opportunity to save time and streamline operations. They greatly expanded the workforce. For example, 134 ironworkers were employed instead of the normal 15. Special lighting equipment was set up so that work could be performed around the clock. Likewise, the sites were prepared and special materials were used so that work could continue despite inclement weather that would normally shut down construction. The work was scheduled much like an assembly line so that critical activities were followed by the next critical activity. A generous incentive scheme was devised to reward teamwork and reach milestones early. Carpenters and iron-workers competed as teams against each other to see who could finish first.

Although C. C. Myers received a substantial bonus for finishing early, they spent a lot of money on overtime, bonuses, special equipment, and other premiums to keep the job rolling along. CalTrans supported Myers's efforts. With reconstruction work going on 24 hours a day, including jackhammering and pile-driving, CalTrans temporarily housed many families in local motels. CalTrans even erected a temporary plastic soundwall to help reduce the construction noise traveling to a nearby apartment complex. The double-layer curtain, 450 feet long and 20 feet high, was designed to reduce construction noise by 10 decibels.

Despite the difficulties and expense incurred by around-the-clock freeway building, most of Los Angeles cheered CalTrans's quake recovery efforts. The Governor's Office of Planning and Research issued a report concluding that for every day the Santa Monica Freeway was closed, it cost the local economy more than $1 million.

* Jerry B. Baxter, "Responding to the Northridge Earthquake," *PM Network* (November 1994), pp. 13–22.

Sometimes very high overhead costs are recognized before the project begins. For example, it may cost $80,000 per day to simply house and feed a construction crew in the farthest reaches of Northern Alaska. In these cases it is prudent to examine the direct costs of shortening the critical path versus the overhead cost savings. Usually there are opportunities to shorten a few critical activities at less than the daily overhead rate. Under specific conditions (which are not rare), huge savings are possible with little risk.

Finally there are times when it is important to reassign key equipment and/or people to new projects. Under these circumstances, the cost of compressing the project can be compared with the opportunity costs of not releasing key equipment or people.

OPTIONS FOR ACCELERATING PROJECT COMPLETION

Managers have several effective methods for crashing specific project activities when resources are not constrained. Several of these are summarized below.

Options When Resources Are Not Constrained

Adding Resources

The most common method for shortening project time is to assign additional staff and equipment to activities. There are limits, however, as to how much speed can be gained by adding staff. Doubling the size of the workforce will not necessarily reduce completion time by half. The relationship would be correct only when tasks can be partitioned so minimal communication is needed between workers, as in harvesting a crop by hand or repaving a highway. Most projects are not set up that way; additional workers increase the communication requirements to coordinate their efforts. For example, doubling a team by adding two workers requires six times as much pairwise intercommunication than is required in the original two-person team. Not only is more time needed to coordinate and manage a larger team; there is the additional delay of training the new people and getting them up to speed on the project. The end result is captured in Brooks's law: *Adding manpower to a late software project makes it later.*[1]

Frederick Brooks formulated this principle based on his experience as a project manager for IBM's System/360 software project during the early 1960s. While subsequent research confirmed Brooks's prediction, it also discovered that adding more people to a late project does not always cause the project to be later.[2] The key is whether the new staff is added early so there is sufficient time to make up for lost ground once the new members have been fully assimilated.

Outsourcing Project Work

A common method for shortening the project time is to subcontract an activity. The subcontractor may have access to superior technology or expertise that will accelerate the completion of the activity. For example, contracting for a backhoe can accomplish in two hours what it can take a team of laborers two days to do. Likewise, by hiring a consulting firm that specializes in ADSI programming, a firm may be able to cut in half the time it would take for less experienced, internal programmers to do the work. Subcontracting also frees up resources that can be assigned to a critical activity and will ideally result in a shorter project duration. See Snapshot from Practice: Outsourcing Bio-Tech. Outsourcing will be addressed more fully in Chapter 12.

Scheduling Overtime

The easiest way to add more labor to a project is not to add more people, but to schedule overtime. If a team works 50 hours a week instead of 40, it might accomplish 20 percent more. By scheduling

---

[1] Brooks's *The Mythical Man-Month* (Reading, MA: Addison-Wesley, 1994) is considered a classic on software project management.

[2] R. L. Gordon and J. C. Lamb, "A Close Look at Brooks' Law," *Datamation,* June 1977, pp. 81–86.

overtime you avoid the additional costs of coordination and communication encountered when new people are added. If people involved are salaried workers, there may be no real additional cost for the extra work. Another advantage is that there are fewer distractions when people work outside normal hours.

Overtime has disadvantages. First, hourly workers are typically paid time and a half for overtime and double time for weekends and holidays. Sustained overtime work by salaried employees may incur intangible costs such as divorce, burnout, and turnover. The latter is a key organizational concern when there is a shortage of workers. Furthermore, it is an oversimplification to assume that, over an extended period of time, a person is as productive during his or her eleventh hour at work as during his or her third hour of work. There are natural limits to what is humanly possible, and extended overtime may actually lead to an overall decline in productivity when fatigue sets in (DeMarco, 2002).

Overtime and working longer hours is the preferred choice for accelerating project completion, especially when the project team is salaried. The key is to use overtime judiciously. Remember a project is a marathon not a sprint! You do not want to run out of energy before the finish line.

Establish a Core Project Team

As discussed in Chapter 3, one of the advantages of creating a dedicated core team to complete a project is speed. Assigning professionals full time to a project avoids the hidden cost of multitasking in which people are forced to juggle the demands of multiple projects. Professionals are allowed to devote their undivided attention to a specific project. This singular focus creates a shared goal that can bind a diverse set of professionals into a highly cohesive team capable of accelerating project completion. Factors that contribute to the emergence of high-performing project teams will be discussed in detail in Chapter 11.

Do It Twice—Fast and Correctly

If you are in a hurry, try building a "quick and dirty" short-term solution, then go back and do it the right way. For example, pontoon bridges are used as temporary solutions to damaged bridges in combat. In business, software companies are notorious for releasing version 1.0 of products that are not completely finished and tested. Subsequent versions 1.1 . . . x correct bugs and add intended functionality to the product. The additional costs of doing it twice are often more than compensated for by the benefits of satisfying the deadline.

Options When Resources Are Constrained

A project manager has fewer options for accelerating project completion when additional resources are either not available or the budget is severely constrained. This is especially true once the schedule has been established. Below are some of these options, which are also available when resources are not constrained.

Fast-Tracking

Sometimes it is possible to rearrange the logic of the project network so that critical activities are done in parallel (concurrently) rather than sequentially. This alternative is a good one if the project situation is right. When this alternative is given serious attention, it is amazing to observe how creative project team members can be in finding ways to restructure sequential activities in parallel. As noted in Chapter 6, one of the most common methods for restructuring activities is to change a finish-to-start relationship to a start-to-start relationship. For example, instead of waiting for the final design to be approved, manufacturing engineers can begin building the production line as soon as key specifications have been established. Changing activities from sequential to parallel is not without risk. Late design changes can produce wasted effort and rework. Fast tracking requires close coordination among those responsible for the activities affected and confidence in the work that has been completed.

Critical-Chain

Critical-chain project management (CCPM) is designed to accelerate project completion. As discussed in Appendix 8.1, it would be difficult to apply CCPM midstream in a project. CCPM requires considerable training and a shift in habits and perspectives that take time to adopt. Although there have been reports of immediate gains, especially in terms of completion times, a long-term management commitment is probably necessary to reap full benefits. See the Snapshot from Practice: The Fastest House in the World for an extreme example of CCPM application.

Reducing Project Scope

Probably the most common response for meeting unattainable deadlines is to reduce or scale back the scope of the project. This invariably leads to a reduction in the functionality of the project. For example, the new car will average only 25 mpg instead of 30, or the software product will have fewer features than originally planned. While scaling back the scope of the project can lead to big savings in both time and money, it may come at a cost of reducing the value of the project. If the car gets lower gas mileage, will it stand up to competitive models? Will customers still want the software minus the features?

December 17, 2002—After revving up their power tools and lining up volunteers, Shelby County Habitat for Humanity broke the world record for the fastest house ever built, clocking in at 3 hours, 26 minutes, and 34 seconds. Former record holder New Zealand's Habitat Affiliate Mannakau held the record for three years at 3 hours, 44 minutes, and 59 seconds. The Alabama project beat the New Zealand record by 18 minutes.

"This was different than any construction project that I've ever been a part of," said Project Manager Chad Calhoun. "The minute-by-minute schedule, the planning of each precise movement, the organization of all the teams and materials, could not have gone more smoothly on build day. All the long hours of planning definitely paid off."

In preparation for the build, Habitat volunteers put the foundation in place and constructed prefabricated wall panels. Once the whistle blew at 11:00

AP Photo/Rogelio Solis

A.M. on December 17th, the exterior wall panels were raised into place, followed by the interior panel, which took only 16 minutes. Special color coded teams of workers connected the wiring and plumbing, put in insulation, installed appliances, laid carpet and tile, installed light fixtures, painted the house inside, applied vinyl siding outside, and attached assembled front and back porches.

At the same time, the roof was constructed on the ground next to the house. Once the roof was completed—approximately 1½ hours later—a Steel City crane lifted the 14,000–pound roof assembly into place. Crews attached the roof while others completed the interior work. There was even time to lay sod, plant shrubbery, and decorate a Christmas tree in the front yard—all within the official build time of 3 hours, 26 minutes, and 34 seconds.

The recipient of this wonderful holiday gift was Bonnie Lilly, a single mother and nursing technician who had applied to Habitat for Humanity three times before she was selected to receive the three-bedroom, two-bath home. "It's amazing," Lilly said. "Who am I to have this happen for me? A world record, hundreds of people coming together to build my house—I still can't believe it."

Habitat for Humanity is an international charitable organization that builds simple, affordable houses and sells them on a no-interest, no-profit basis to needy families.

* "The house that love built, really FAST—and just in time for Christmas kicker: Habitat for Humanity breaks world record set by New Zealand," Erin Drummond, www.csre.com. "Shelby County, Ala. Builds fastest Habitat House in three and a half hours," www.habitat.org/newsroom/2002archive.

The key to reducing a project scope without reducing value is to reassess the true specifications of the project. Often requirements are added under best-case, blue-sky scenarios and represent desirables, but not essentials. Here it is important to talk to the customer and/or project sponsors and explain the situation—you can get it your way but not until February. This may force them to accept an extension or to add money to expedite the project. If not, then a healthy discussion of what the essential requirements are and what items can be compromised in order to meet the deadline needs to take place. More intense reexamination of requirements may actually improve the value of the project by getting it done more quickly and for a lower cost.

Calculating the savings of reduced project scope begins with the work breakdown structure. Reducing functionality means certain tasks, deliverables, or requirements can be reduced or even eliminated. These tasks need to be found and the schedule adjusted. Focus should be on changes in activities on the critical path.

Compromise Quality

Reducing quality is always an option, but it is rarely acceptable or used. If quality is sacrificed, it may be possible to reduce the time of an activity on the critical path.

In practice the methods most commonly used to crash projects are scheduling overtime, outsourcing, and adding resources. Each of these maintains the essence of the original plan. Options that depart from the original project plan include do it twice and fast-tracking. Rethinking of project scope, customer needs, and timing become major considerations for these techniques.

PROJECT COST-DURATION GRAPH

Nothing on the horizon suggests that the need to shorten project time will change. In fact, if anything the pressure to get projects done quicker and sooner is likely to increase in importance. The challenge for the project manager is to use a quick, logical method to compare the benefits of reducing project time with the cost. When sound, logical methods are absent, it is difficult to isolate those activities that will have the greatest impact on reducing project time at least cost. This section describes a procedure for identifying the costs of reducing project time so that comparisons can be made with the benefits of getting the project completed sooner. The method requires gathering direct and indirect costs for specific project durations. Critical activities are searched to find the lowest direct-cost activities that will shorten the project duration. Total cost for specific project durations are computed and then compared with the benefits of reducing project time— before the project begins or while it is in progress.

Explanation of Project Costs

The general nature of project costs is illustrated in Figure 9.1, **Project Cost–Duration Graph.** The total cost for each duration is the sum of the indirect and direct costs. Indirect costs continue for the life of the project. Hence, any reduction in project duration means a reduction in indirect costs. Direct costs on the graph grow at an increasing rate as the project duration is

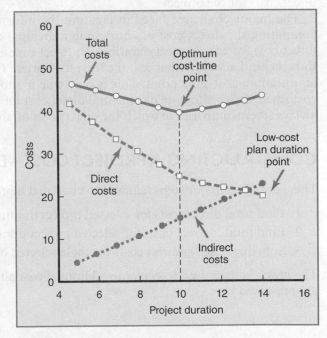

FIGURE 9.1   *Project Cost–Duration Graph*

reduced from its original planned duration. With the information from a graph such as this for a project, managers can quickly judge any alternative such as meeting a time-to-market deadline. Further discussion of indirect and direct costs is necessary before demonstrating a procedure for developing the information for a graph similar to the one depicted in Figure 9.1.

Project Indirect Costs

Indirect costs generally represent overhead costs such as supervision, administration, consultants, and interest. Indirect costs cannot be associated with any particular work package or activity, hence the term. Indirect costs vary directly with time. That is, any reduction in time should result in a reduction of indirect costs. For example, if the daily costs of supervision, administration, and consultants are $2,000, any reduction in project duration would represent a savings of $2,000 per day. If indirect costs are a significant percentage of total project costs, reductions in project time can represent very real savings (assuming the indirect resources can be utilized elsewhere).

Project Direct Costs

Direct costs commonly represent labor, materials, equipment, and sometimes subcontractors. Direct costs are assigned directly to a work package and activity, hence the term. The ideal assumption is that direct costs for an activity time represent normal costs, which typically mean low-cost, efficient methods for a normal time. When project durations are imposed, direct costs may no longer represent low-cost, efficient methods. Costs for the imposed duration date will be higher than for a project duration developed from ideal normal times for activities. Because direct costs are assumed to be developed from normal methods and time, any reduction in activity time should add to the costs of the activity. The sum of the costs of all the work packages or activities represents the total direct costs for the project.

The major challenge faced in creating the information for a graph similar to Figure 9.1 is computing the direct cost of shortening individual critical activities and then finding the total direct cost for each project duration as project time is compressed; the process requires selecting those critical activities that cost the least to shorten. (Note: The graph implies that there is always an optimum cost-time point. This is only true if shortening a schedule has incremental indirect cost savings exceeding the incremental direct cost incurred. However, in practice there are almost always several activities in which the direct costs of shortening are less than the indirect costs.)

CONSTRUCTING A PROJECT COST–DURATION GRAPH

There are three major steps required to construct a project cost–duration graph:

1. Find total direct costs for selected project durations.
2. Find total indirect costs for selected project durations.
3. Sum direct and indirect costs for these selected durations.

The graph is then used to compare additional cost alternatives for benefits. Details of these steps are presented here.

Determining the Activities to Shorten

The most difficult task in constructing a cost–duration graph is finding the total direct costs for specific project durations over a relevant range. The central concern is to decide which activities to shorten and how far to carry the shortening process. Basically, managers need to look for critical activities that can be shortened with the *smallest increase in cost per unit of time.* The rationale for selecting critical activities depends on identifying the activity's normal and crash times and corresponding costs. *Normal time* for an activity represents low-cost, realistic, efficient methods for completing the activity under normal conditions. Shortening an activity is called **crashing.** The shortest possible time an activity can realistically be completed in is called its **crash time.** The direct

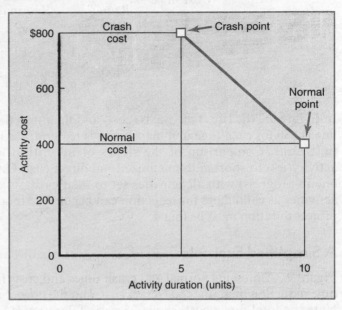

FIGURE 9.2 *Activity Graph*

cost for completing an activity in its crash time is called *crash cost.* Both normal and crash times and costs are collected from personnel most familiar with completing the activity. Figure 9.2 depicts a hypothetical cost–duration graph for an activity.

The normal time for the activity is 10 time units, and the corresponding cost is $400. The crash time for the activity is five time units and $800. The intersection of the normal time and cost represents the original low-cost, early-start schedule. The **crash point** represents the maximum time an activity can be compressed. The heavy line connecting the normal and crash points represents the slope, which assumes the cost of reducing the time of the activity is constant *per unit of time.* The assumptions underlying the use of this graph are as follows:

1. The cost-time relationship is linear.
2. Normal time assumes low-cost, efficient methods to complete the activity.
3. Crash time represents a limit—the greatest time reduction possible under realistic conditions.
4. Slope represents cost per unit of time.
5. All accelerations must occur within the normal and crash times.

Knowing the slope of activities allows managers to compare which critical activities to shorten. The less steep the cost slope of an activity, the less it costs to shorten one time period; a steeper slope means it will cost more to shorten one time unit. The cost per unit of time or slope for any activity is computed by the following equation:

$$\text{Cost slope} = \frac{\text{Rise}}{\text{Run}} = \frac{\text{Crash cost} - \text{Normal cost}}{\text{Normal time} - \text{Crash time}}$$

$$= \frac{CC - NC}{NT - CT} = \frac{\$800 - \$400}{10 - 5}$$

$$= \frac{\$400}{5} = \$80 \text{ per unit of time}$$

In Figure 9.2 the rise is the y axis (cost) and the run is the x axis (duration). The slope of the cost line is $80 for each time unit the activity is reduced; the limit reduction of the activity time is five time units. Comparison of the slopes of all critical activities allows us to determine which activity(ies) to shorten to minimize total direct cost. Given the preliminary project schedule (or one in progress) with all activities set to their early-start times, the process of searching critical activities as candidates for reduction can begin. The total direct cost for each specific compressed project duration must be found.

A Simplified Example

Figure 9.3A presents normal and crash times and costs for each activity, the computed slope and time reduction limit, the total direct cost, and the project network with a duration of 25 time units. Note the total direct cost for the 25-period duration is $450. This is an anchor point to begin the procedure of shortening the critical path(s) and finding the total direct costs for each specific duration less than 25 time units. The maximum time reduction of an activity is simply the difference between the normal and crash times for an activity. For example, activity D can be reduced from a normal time of 11 time units to a crash time of 7 time units, or a maximum of 4 time units. The positive slope for activity D is computed as follows:

$$\text{Slope} = \frac{\text{Crash cost} - \text{Normal cost}}{\text{Normal time} - \text{Crash time}} = \frac{\$150 - \$50}{11 - 7}$$

$$= \frac{\$100}{4} = \$25 \text{ per period reduced}$$

The network shows the critical path to be activities A, D, F, G. Because it is impossible to shorten activity G ("x" is used to indicate this), activity A is circled because it is the least-cost candidate; that is, its slope ($20) is less than the slopes for activities D and F ($25 and $30). Reducing activity A one time unit cuts the project duration to 24 time units but increases the total direct costs to $470 ($450 + $20 = $470). Figure 9.3B reflects these changes. The duration of activity A has been reduced to two time units; the "x" indicates the activity cannot be reduced any further. Activity D is circled because it costs the least ($25) to shorten the project to 23 time units. Compare the cost of activity F. The total direct cost for a project duration of 23 time units is $495 (see Figure 9.4A).

Observe that the project network in Figure 9.4A now has two critical paths—A, C, F, G and A, D, F, G. Reducing the project to 22 time units will require that activity F be reduced; thus, it is circled. This change is reflected in Figure 9.4B. The total direct cost for 22 time units is $525. This reduction has created a third critical path—A, B, E, G; all activities are critical. The least-cost method for reducing the project duration to 21 time units is the combination of the circled activities

Activity ID	Slope	Maximum crash time	Direct costs			
			Normal		Crash	
			Time	Cost	Time	Cost
A	$20	1	3	$50	2	$70
B	40	2	6	80	4	160
C	30	1	10	60	9	90
D	25	4	11	50	7	150
E	30	2	8	100	6	160
F	30	1	5	40	4	70
G	0	0	6	70	6	70

Total direct cost $450

FIGURE 9.3 *Cost–Duration Trade-off Example*

C, D, E which cost $30, $25, $30, respectively, and increase total direct costs to $610. The results of these changes are depicted in Figure 9.4C. Although some activities can still be reduced (those without the "x" next to the activity time), no activity or combination of activities will result in a reduction in the project duration.

With the total direct costs for the array of specific project durations found, the next step is to collect the indirect costs for these same durations. These costs are typically a rate per day and are easily obtained from the accounting department. Figure 9.5 presents the total direct costs, total indirect costs, and total project costs. These same costs are plotted in Figure 9.6. This graph shows that the optimum cost-time duration is 22 time units and $775. Assuming the project will actually

Time _23_

Total direct cost $ _495_

Activities changed
_D_
$25

(A)

Time _22_

Total direct cost $ _525_

Activities changed
_F_
$30

(B)

Time _21_

Total direct cost $ _610_

Activities changed
_C_   _D_   _E_
$30 $25 $30

(C)

FIGURE 9.4 *Cost–Duration Trade-off Example (continued)*

materialize as planned, any movement away from this time duration will increase project costs. The movement from 25 to 22 time units occurs because, in this range, the absolute slopes of the indirect costs are greater than the direct cost slopes.

PRACTICAL CONSIDERATIONS

Using the Project Cost–Duration Graph

This graph, as presented in Figures 9.1 and 9.6, is valuable to compare any proposed alternative or change with the optimum cost and time. More importantly, the creation of such a graph keeps the

FIGURE 9.5 *Summary Costs by Duration*

Project duration	Direct costs	+	Indirect costs	=	Total costs
25	450		400		$850
24	470		350		820
23	495		300		795
22	525		250		775
21	610		200		810

FIGURE 9.6 *Project Cost–Duration Graph*

importance of indirect costs in the forefront of decision making. Indirect costs are frequently forgotten in the field when the pressure for action is intense. Finally, such a graph can be used before the project begins or while the project is in progress. Creating the graph in the preproject planning phase without an imposed duration is the first choice because normal time is more meaningful. Creating the graph in the project planning phase with an imposed duration is less desirable because normal time is made to fit the imposed date and is probably not low cost. Creating the graph after the project has started is the least desirable because some alternatives may be ruled out of the decision process. Managers may choose not to use the formal procedure demonstrated. However, regardless of the method used, the principles and concepts inherent in the formal procedure are highly applicable in practice and should be considered in any cost–duration trade-off decision.

Crash Times

Collecting crash times for even a moderate-size project can be difficult. The meaning of crash time is difficult to communicate. What is meant when you define crash time as "the shortest time you can realistically complete an activity"? Crash time is open to different interpretations and judgments. Some estimators feel very uncomfortable providing crash times. Regardless of the comfort level, the accuracy of crash times and costs is frequently rough at best, when compared with normal time and cost.

Linearity Assumption

Because the accuracy of compressed activity times and costs is questionable, the concern of some theorists—that the relationship between cost and time is not linear but curvilinear—is seldom a concern for practicing managers. Reasonable, quick comparisons can be made using the linear assumption.[3] The simple approach is adequate for most projects. There are rare situations in which activities cannot be crashed by single time units. Instead, crashing is "all or nothing." For example, activity A will take 10 days (for say $1,000) or it will take 7 days (for say $1,500), but no options

---

[3] Linearity assumes that the cost for crashing each day is constant.

exist in which activity A will take 8 or 9 days to complete. In a few rare cases of very large, complex, long-duration projects, the use of present value techniques may be useful; such techniques are beyond the scope of this text.

Choice of Activities to Crash Revisited

The cost–time crashing method relies on choosing the cheapest method for reducing the duration of the project. There are other factors that should be assessed beyond simply cost. First, the inherent risks involved in crashing particular activities need to be considered. Some activities are riskier to crash than others. For example, accelerating the completion of a software design code may not be wise if it increases the likelihood of errors surfacing downstream. Conversely, crashing a more expensive activity may be wise if fewer inherent risks are involved.

Second, the timing of activities needs to be considered. Crashing an early activity may be prudent if there is concern that subsequent activities are likely to be delayed, and absorb the time gained. Then the manager would still have the option of crashing final activities to get back on schedule.

Third, crashing frequently results in overallocation of resources. The resources required to accelerate a cheaper activity may suddenly not be available. Resource availability, not cost, may dictate which activities are crashed.

Finally, the impact crashing would have on the morale and motivation of the project team needs to be assessed. If the least-cost method repeatedly signals a subgroup to accelerate progress, fatigue and resentment may set in. Conversely, if overtime pay is involved, other team members may resent not having access to this benefit. This situation can lead to tension within the entire project team. Good project managers gauge the response that crashing activities will have on the entire project team. See Snapshot from Practice: I'll Bet You . . . for a novel approach to motivating employees to work faster.

Time Reduction Decisions and Sensitivity

Should the project owner or project manager go for the optimum cost-time? The answer is, "It depends." Risk must be considered. Recall from our example that the optimum project time point represented a reduced project cost and was less than the original normal project time (review Figure 9.6). The project direct-cost line near the normal point is usually relatively flat. Because indirect costs for the project are usually greater in the same range, the optimum cost-time point is less than the normal time point. Logic of the cost-time procedure suggests managers should reduce the project duration to the lowest total cost point and duration.

How far to reduce the project time from the normal time toward the optimum depends on the *sensitivity* of the project network. A network is sensitive if it has several critical or near-critical paths. In our example project movement toward the optimum time requires spending money to reduce critical activities, resulting in slack reduction and/or more critical paths and activities. Slack reduction in a project with several near-critical paths increases the risk of being late. The practical outcome can be a higher total project cost if some near-critical activities are delayed and become critical; the money spent reducing activities on the original critical path would be wasted. Sensitive networks require careful analysis. The bottom line is that compression of projects with several near-critical paths reduces scheduling flexibility and increases the risk of delaying the project. The outcome of such analysis will probably suggest only a partial movement from the normal time toward the optimum time.

The focus of this chapter has been on how project managers crash activities by typically assigning additional manpower and equipment to cut significant time off of scheduled tasks. Project managers often encounter situations in which they need to motivate individuals to accelerate the completion of a specific, critical task. Imagine the following scenario.

Brue Young just received a priority assignment from corporate headquarters. The preliminary engineering sketches that were due tomorrow need to be e-mailed to the West Coast by 4:00 PM today so that the model shop can begin construction of a prototype to present to top management. He approaches Danny Whitten, the draftsman responsible for the task, whose initial response is, "That's impossible!" While he agrees that it would be very difficult he does not believe that it is as impossible as Danny suggests or that Danny truly believes that. What should he do?

He tells Danny that he knows this is going to be a rush job, but he is confident that he can do it. When Danny balks, he responds, "I tell you what, I'll make a bet with you. If you are able to finish the design by 4:00, I'll make sure you get two of the company's tickets to tomorrow night's Celtics–Knicks basketball game." Danny accepts the challenge, works feverishly to complete the assignment, and is able to take his daughter to her first professional basketball game.

Conversations with project managers reveal that many use bets like this one to motivate extraordinary performance. These bets range from tickets to sporting and entertainment events to gift certificates at high-class restaurants to a well-deserved afternoon off. For bets to work they need to adhere to the principles of expectancy theory of motivation.* Boiled down to simple terms, expectancy theory rests on three key questions:

1. Can I do it (Is it possible to meet the challenge)?
2. Will I get it (Can I demonstrate that I met the challenge and can I trust the project manager will deliver his/her end of the bargain)?
3. Is it worth it (Is the payoff of sufficient personal value to warrant the risk and extra effort)?

If in the mind of the participant the answer to any of these three questions is no, then the person is unlikely to accept the challenge. However, when the answers are affirmative, then the individual is likely to accept the bet and be motivated to meet the challenge.

Bets can be effective motivational tools and add an element of excitement and fun to project work. But, the following practical advice should be heeded:

1. The bet has greater significance if it also benefits family members or significant others. Being able to take a son or daughter to a professional basketball game allows that individual to "score points" at home through work. These bets also recognize and reward the support project members receive from their families and reinforces the importance of their work to loved ones.
2. Bets should be used sparingly; otherwise everything can become negotiable. They should be used only under special circumstances that require extraordinary effort.
3. Individual bets should involve clearly recognizable individual effort, otherwise others may become jealous and discord may occur within a group. As long as others see it as requiring truly remarkable, "beyond the call of duty" effort, they will consider it fair and warranted.

* Expectancy Theory is considered one of the major theories of human motivation and was first developed by V. H. Vroom, *Work and Motivation* (New York: John Wiley & Sons, 1964).

There is a positive situation where moving toward the optimum time can result in very real, large savings—this occurs when the network is *insensitive*. A project network is insensitive if it has a dominant critical path, that is, no near-critical paths. In this project circumstance, movement from the normal time point toward the optimum time will *not* create new or near-critical activities. The bottom line here is that the reduction of the slack of noncritical activities increases the risk of their becoming critical only slightly when compared with the effect in a sensitive network. Insensitive networks hold the greatest potential for real, sometimes large, savings in total project costs with a minimum risk of noncritical activities becoming critical.

Insensitive networks are not a rarity in practice; they occur in perhaps 25 percent of all projects. For example, a light rail project team observed from their network a dominant critical path and relatively high indirect costs. It soon became clear that by spending some dollars on a few critical activities, very large savings of indirect costs could be realized. Savings of several million dollars were spent extending the rail line and adding another station. The logic found in this example is just as applicable to small projects as large ones. Insensitive networks with high indirect costs can produce large savings.

Ultimately, deciding if and which activities to crash is a judgment call requiring careful consideration of the options available, the costs and risks involved, and the importance of meeting a deadline.

WHAT IF COST, NOT TIME, IS THE ISSUE?

In today's fast-paced world, there appears to be a greater emphasis on getting things done quickly. Still, organizations are always looking for ways to get things done cheaply. This is especially true for fixed-bid projects, where profit margin is derived from the difference between the bid and actual cost of the project. Every dollar saved is a dollar in your pocket. Sometimes, in order to secure a contract, bids are tight, which puts added pressure on cost containment. In other cases, there are financial incentives tied to cost containment.

Even in situations where cost is transferred to customers there is pressure to reduce cost. Cost overruns make for unhappy customers and can damage future business opportunities. Budgets can be fixed or cut, and when contingency funds are exhausted, then cost overruns have to be made up with remaining activities.

As discussed earlier, shortening project duration may come at the expense of overtime, adding additional personnel, and using more expensive equipment and/or materials. Conversely, sometimes cost savings can be generated by extending the duration of a project. This may allow for a smaller workforce, less-skilled (expensive) labor, and even cheaper equipment and materials to be used. Below are some of the more commonly used options for cutting costs.

Reduce Project Scope

Just as scaling back the scope of the project can gain time, delivering less than what was originally planned also produces significant savings. Again, calculating the savings of a reduced project scope begins with the work breakdown structure. However, since time is not the issue, you do not need to focus on critical activities. For example, on over-budget movie projects it is not uncommon to replace location shots with stock footage to cut costs.

Have Owner Take on More Responsibility

One way of reducing project costs is identifying tasks that customers can do themselves. Homeowners frequently use this method to reduce costs on home improvement projects. For example, to reduce the cost of a bathroom remodel, a homeowner may agree to paint the room instead of paying the contractor to do it. On IS projects, a customer may agree to take on some of the responsibility for testing equipment or providing in-house training. Naturally, this arrangement is best negotiated before the project begins. Customers are less receptive to this idea if you suddenly spring it on them. An advantage of this method is that, while costs are lowered, the original scope is retained. Clearly this option is limited to areas in which the customer has expertise and the capability to pick up the tasks.

Outsourcing Project Activities or Even the Entire Project

When estimates exceed budget, it not only makes sense to re-examine the scope but also search for cheaper ways to complete the project. Perhaps instead of relying on internal resources, it would be more cost effective to outsource segments or even the entire project, opening up work to external price competition. Specialized subcontractors often enjoy unique advantages, such as material discounts for large quantities, as well as equipment that not only gets the work done more quickly but also less expensively. They may have lower overhead and labor costs. For example, to reduce costs of software projects, many American firms outsource work to firms overseas where the salary of a software engineer is one-third that of an American software engineer. However, outsourcing means you have less control over the project and will need to have clearly definable deliverables.

Brainstorming Cost Savings Options

Just as project team members can be a rich source of ideas for accelerating project activities, they can offer tangible ways for reducing project costs. For example, one project manager reported that his team was able to come up with over $75,000 worth of cost saving suggestions without jeopardizing the scope of the project. Project managers should not underestimate the value of simply asking if there is a cheaper, better way.

Summary

The need for reducing the project duration occurs for many reasons such as imposed duration dates, time-to-market considerations, incentive contracts, key resource needs, high overhead costs, or simply unforeseen delays. These situations are very common in practice and are known as cost-time trade-off decisions. This chapter presented a logical, formal process for assessing the implications of situations that involve shortening the project duration. Crashing the project duration increases the *risk* of being late. How far to reduce the project duration from the normal time toward the optimum depends on the *sensitivity* of the project network. A sensitive network is one that has several critical or near-critical paths. Great care should be taken when shortening sensitive networks to avoid increasing project risks. Conversely, insensitive networks represent opportunities for potentially large project cost savings by eliminating some overhead costs with little downside risk.

Alternative strategies for reducing project time were discussed within the context of whether or not the project is resource limited. Project acceleration typically comes at a cost of either spending money for more resources or compromising the scope of the project. If the latter is the case, then it is essential that all relevant stakeholders be consulted so that everyone accepts the changes that have to be made. One other key point is the difference in implementing time-reducing activities in the midst of project execution versus incorporating them into the project plan. You typically have far fewer options once the project is underway than before it begins. This is especially true if you want to take advantage of the new scheduling methodologies such as fast-tracking and critical-chain. Time spent up front considering alternatives and developing contingency plans will lead to time savings in the end.

Key Terms

Crashing	Direct costs	Outsourcing
Crash point	Fast-tracking	Project cost–duration graph
Crash time	Indirect costs	

Review Questions

1. What are five common reasons for crashing a project?
2. What are the advantages and disadvantages of reducing project scope to accelerate a project? What can be done to reduce the disadvantages?
3. Why is scheduling overtime a popular choice for getting projects back on schedule? What are the potential problems for relying on this option?
4. Identify four indirect costs you might find on a moderately complex project. Why are these costs classified as indirect?
5. How can a cost-duration graph be used by the project manager? Explain.
6. Reducing the project duration increases the risk of being late. Explain.
7. It is possible to shorten the critical path and save money. Explain how.

Exercises

1. Draw a project network from the following information.

Activity	Predecessor	Duration
A	None	2
B	A	4
C	A	3
D	A	2
E	B	3
F	C	6
G	C, D	5
H	E, F	6
I	G	5
J	H, I	5

Activities B and H can be shortened to a minimum of 2 weeks. Which activity would you shorten to reduce the project duration by 2 weeks? Why?

2.* Use the information contained below to compress one time unit per move using the least cost method. Reduce the schedule until you reach the crash point of the network. For each move identify what activity(s) was crashed the adjusted total cost.

Act.	Crash Cost (Slope)	Maximum Crash Time	Normal Time	Normal Cost
A	0	0	1	100
B	100	2	3	150
C	50	1	4	200
D	60	1	3	200
E	70	2	4	200
F	90	1	3	150

Initial project duration *12*

Total direct cost $ ____

3. Assume the network and data that follow. Compute the total direct cost for each project duration. If the indirect costs for each project duration are $400 (19 time units), $350 (18), $300 (17), and $250 (16), compute the total project cost for each duration. Plot the total direct, indirect, and project costs for each of these durations on a cost-time graph. What is the optimum cost-time schedule for the project? What is this cost?

Act.	Crash Cost (Slope)	Maximum Crash Time	Normal Time	Normal Cost
A	20	1	3	50
B	60	2	5	60
C	40	1	3	70
D	0	0	10	50
E	50	3	6	100
F	100	3	7	90
G	70	1	5	50
				$470

4. Given the data and information that follow, compute the total direct cost for each project duration. If the indirect costs for each project duration are $90 (15 time units), $70 (14), $50 (13), $40 (12), and $30 (11), compute the total project cost for each duration. What is the optimum cost-time schedule for the project? What is this cost?

Act.	Crash Cost (Slope)	Maximum Crash Time	Normal Time	Normal Cost
A	20	1	5	50
B	60	2	3	60
C	0	0	4	70
D	10	1	2	50
E	60	3	5	100
F	100	1	2	90
G	30	1	5	50
H	40	0	2	60
I	200	1	3	200
				$730

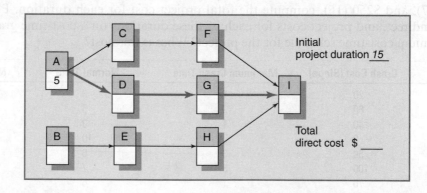

5. If the indirect costs for each duration are $1,200 for 16 weeks, $1,130 for 15 weeks, $1,000 for 14 weeks, $900 for 13 weeks, $860 for 12 weeks, $820 for 11 weeks, and $790 for 10 weeks, compute the total costs for each duration. Plot these costs on a graph. What is the optimum cost-time schedule?

Act.	Crash Cost (Slope)	Maximum Crash Time	Normal Time	Normal Cost
A	10	1	4	30
B	70	2	7	60
C	0	0	1	80
D	20	2	4	40
E	50	3	5	110
F	200	3	5	90
G	30	1	2	60
H	40	1	2	70
I	0	0	2	140
				$680

Time unit = 1 week

6. If the indirect costs for each duration are $300 for 27 weeks, $240 for 26 weeks, $180 for 25 weeks, $120 for 24 weeks, $60 for 23 weeks, and $50 for 22 weeks, compute the direct, indirect and total costs for each duration. What is the optimum cost-time schedule? The customer offers you $10 for every week you shorten the project from your original network. Would you take it? If so for how many weeks?

Act.	Crash Cost (Slope)	Maximum Crash Time	Normal Time	Normal Cost
A	80	2	10	40
B	30	3	8	10
C	40	1	5	80
D	50	2	11	50
E	100	4	15	100
F	30	1	6	20
				$300

Time unit = 1 week

7. Use the information contained below to compress one time unit per move using the least cost method. Reduce the schedule until you reach the crash point of the network. For each move identify what activity(s) was crashed, the adjusted total cost, and explain your choice if you have to choose between activities that cost the same.

Note: Crash point of the network is the point in which the duration cannot be reduced any further.

Activity ID	Crash Cost (Slope)	Maximum Crash Time	Normal Time	Normal Cost
A	—	0	4	$50
B	$40	3	5	70
C	40	1	5	80
D	40	2	4	40
E	40	2	5	60
F	40	1	5	50
G	30	1	4	70
H	30	1	4	80
I	—	0	3	50

Total direct normal costs—$550

Completion time: _21_   Total cost $ _550_

8.* Use the information contained below to compress one time unit per move using the least cost method. Reduce the schedule until you reach the crash point of the network. For each move identify what activity(s) was crashed, the adjusted total cost, and explain your choice if you have to choose between activities that cost the same.

If the indirect cost for each duration are $1,500 for 17 weeks, $1,450 for 16 weeks, $1,400 for 15 weeks, $1,350 for 14 weeks, $1,300 for 13 weeks, $1,250 for 12 weeks, $1,200 for 11 weeks, and $1,150 for 10 weeks, what is the optimum cost-time schedule for the project? What is the cost?

Act.	Crash Cost (Slope)	Maximum Crash Time	Normal Time	Normal Cost
A	0	0	3	150
B	100	1	4	200
C	60	1	3	250
D	40	1	4	200
E	0	0	2	250
F	30	2	3	200
G	20	1	2	250
H	60	2	4	300
I	200	1	2	200

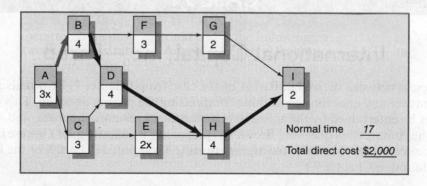

Normal time _17_

Total direct cost _$2,000_

---

* The solution to this exercise can be found in Appendix One.

References

Abdel-Hamid, T., and S. Madnick, *Software Project Dynamics: An Integrated Approach* (Englewood Cliffs, NJ: Prentice Hall, 1991).

Baker, B. M., "Cost/Time Trade-off Analysis for the Critical Path Method," *Journal of the Operational Research Society,* 48 (12) 1997, pp. 1241–44.

Brooks, F. P., Jr., *The Mythical Man-Month: Essays on Software Engineering Anniversary Edition* (Reading, MA: Addison-Wesley Longman, Inc., 1994), pp. 15–26.

DeMarco, T., *Slack: Getting Past Burnout, Busywork, and the Myth of Total Efficiency* (New York: Broadway, 2002).

Gordon, R. I. and J. C. Lamb, "A Closer Look at Brooke's Law," *Datamation,* June, 1977, pp. 81–86.

Ibbs, C. W., S. A. Lee, and M. I. Li, "Fast-Tracking's Impact on Project Change," *Project Management Journal,* 29 (4) 1998, pp. 35–42.

Khang, D. B., and M.Yin, "Time, Cost, and Quality Tradeoff in Project Management," *International Journal of Project Management,* 17 (4) 1999, pp. 249–56.

Perrow, L. A., *Finding Time: How Corporations, Individuals, and Families Can Benefit From New Work Practices* (Ithaca, NY: Cornell University Press, 1997).

Roemer, T. R., R. Ahmadi, and R. Wang, "Time-Cost Trade-offs in Overlapped Product Development," *Operations Research,* 48 (6) 2000, pp. 858–65.

Smith, P. G., and D. G. Reinersten, *Developing Products in Half the Time* (New York: Van Nostrand Reinhold, 1995).

Verzuh, E., *The Fast Forward MBA in Project Management,* 4th ed. (New York: John Wiley, 2012).

Vroom, V. H., *Work and Motivation* (New York: John Wiley & Sons, 1964).

CASE 9.1

International Capital, Inc.—Part B

Given the project network derived in Part A of the case from Chapter 7, Brown also wants to be prepared to answer any questions concerning compressing the project duration. This question will almost always be entertained by the accounting department, review committee, and the client. To be ready for the compression question, Brown has prepared the following data in case it is necessary to crash the project. (Use your weighted average times (t_e) computed in Part A of the International Capital case found in Chapter 7.)

Activity	Normal Cost	Maximum Crash Time	Crash Cost/Day
A	$ 3,000	3	$ 500
B	5,000	2	1000
C	6,000	0	—
D	20,000	3	3,000
E	10,000	2	1,000
F	7,000	1	1,000
G	20,000	2	3,000
H	8,000	1	2,000
I	5,000	1	2,000
J	7,000	1	1,000
K	12,000	6	1,000
Total normal costs = $103,000			

Using the data provided, determine the activity crashing decisions and best-time cost project duration. Given the information you have developed, what suggestions would you give Brown to ensure she is well prepared for the project review committee? Assume the overhead costs for this project are $700 per workday. Will this alter your suggestions?

CASE 9.2

Whitbread World Sailboat Race

Each year countries enter their sailing vessels in the nine-month Round the World Whitbread Sailboat Race. In recent years, about 14 countries entered sailboats in the race. Each year's sailboat entries represent the latest technologies and human skills each country can muster.

Bjorn Ericksen has been selected as a project manager because of his past experience as a master helmsman and because of his recent fame as the "best designer of racing sailboats in the world." Bjorn is pleased and proud to have the opportunity to design, build, test, and train the crew for next year's Whitbread entry for his country. Bjorn has picked Karin Knutsen (as chief design engineer) and Trygve Wallvik (as master helmsman) to be team leaders responsible for getting next year's entry ready for the traditional parade of all entries on the Thames River in the United Kingdom, which signals the start of the race.

As Bjorn begins to think of a project plan, he sees two parallel paths running through the project—design and construction and crew training. Last year's boat will be used for training until the new entry can have the crew on board to learn maintenance tasks. Bjorn calls Karin and Trygve together to develop a project plan. All three agree the major goal is to have a winning boat and crew ready to compete in next year's competition at a cost of $3.2 million. A check of Bjorn's calendar indicates he has 45 weeks before next year's vessel must leave port for the United Kingdom to start the race.

THE KICKOFF MEETING

Bjorn asks Karin to begin by describing the major activities and the sequence required to design, construct, and test the boat. Karin starts by noting that design of the hull, deck, mast, and accessories should only take six weeks—given the design prints from past race entries and a few prints from other countries' entries. After the design is complete, the hull can be constructed, the mast ordered, sails ordered, and accessories ordered. The hull will require 12 weeks to complete. The mast can be ordered and will require a lead time of eight weeks; the seven sails can be ordered and will take six weeks to get; accessories can be ordered and will take 15 weeks to receive. As soon as the hull is finished, the ballast tanks can be installed, requiring two weeks. Then the deck can be built, which will require five weeks. Concurrently, the hull can be treated with special sealant and friction-resistance coating, taking three weeks. When the deck is completed and mast and accessories received, the mast and sails can be installed, requiring two weeks; the accessories can be installed, which will take six weeks. When all of these activities have been completed, the ship can be sea-tested, which should take five weeks. Karin believes she can have firm cost estimates for the boat in about two weeks.

Trygve believes he can start selecting the 12-man or woman crew and securing their housing immediately. He believes it will take six weeks to get a committed crew on-site and three weeks to secure housing for the crew members. Trygve reminds Bjorn that last year's vessel must be ready to use for training the moment the crew is on-site until the new vessel is ready for testing. Keeping the old vessel operating will cost $4,000 per week as long as it is used. Once the crew is on-site and housed, they can develop and implement a routine sailing and maintenance training program, which will take 15 weeks (using the old vessel). Also, once the crew is selected and on-site, crew equipment can be selected, taking only two weeks. Then crew equipment can be ordered; it will take five weeks to arrive. When the crew equipment and maintenance training program are complete, crew maintenance on the new vessel can begin; this should take 10 weeks. But crew maintenance on the new vessel cannot begin until the deck is complete and the mast, sails, and accessories have arrived. Once crew maintenance on the new vessel begins, the new vessel will cost $6,000 per week until sea training is complete. After the new ship maintenance is complete and while the boat is being tested, initial sailing training can be implemented; training should take seven weeks. Finally, after the boat is tested and initial training is complete, regular sea training can be implemented—weather permitting; regular sea training requires eight weeks. Trygve believes he can put the cost estimates together in a week, given last year's expenses.

Bjorn is pleased with the expertise displayed by his team leaders. But he believes they need to have someone develop one of those critical path networks to see if they can safely meet the start deadline for the race. Karin and Trygve agree. Karin suggests the cost estimates should also include crash costs for any activities that can be compressed and the resultant costs for crashing. Karin also suggests the team complete the following priority matrix for project decision making (See Fig. C9.1).

FIGURE C9.1 *Project Priority Matrix: Whitbread Project*

TWO WEEKS LATER

Karin and Trygve submit the following cost estimates for each activity and corresponding crash costs to Bjorn (costs are in thousands of dollars):

	Activity	Normal Time	Normal Cost	Crash Time	Crash Cost
A	Design	6	$ 40	2	$ —
B	Build hull	12	1,000	2	—
C	Install ballast tanks	2	100	0	—
D	Order mast	8	100	1	200
E	Order sails	6	40	0	—
F	Order accessories	15	600	2	100
G	Build deck	5	200	0	—
H	Coat hull	3	40	0	—
I	Install accessories	6	300	1	100
J	Install mast and sails	2	40	1	40
K	Test	5	60	1	40
L	Sea trials	8	200	1	250
M	Select crew	6	10	1	10
N	Secure housing	3	30	0	—
O	Select crew equipment	2	10	0	—
P	Order crew equipment	5	30	0	—
Q	Routine sail/maintenance	15	40	3	30
R	Crew maintenance training	10	100	1	240
S	Initial sail training	7	50	2	150
	Total direct cost		$2,990		

Bjorn reviews the materials and wonders if the project will come in within the budget of $3.2 million and in 45 weeks. Advise the Whitbread team of their situation.

CASE 9.3

Nightingale Project—A

You are the assistant project manager to Rassy Brown, who is in charge of the Nightingale project. Nightingale was the code name given to the development of a handheld electronic medical reference guide. Nightingale would be designed for emergency medical technicians and paramedics who need a quick reference guide to use in emergency situations.

Rassy and her project team were developing a project plan aimed at producing 30 working models in time for MedCON, the biggest medical equipment trade show each year. Meeting the MedCON October 25 deadline was critical to success. All the major medical equipment manufacturers demonstrated and took orders for new products at MedCON. Rassy had also heard rumors that competitors were considering developing a similar product, and she knew that being first to market would have a significant sales advantage. Besides, top management made funding contingent upon developing a workable plan for meeting the MedCON deadline.

The project team spent the morning working on the schedule for Nightingale. They started with the WBS and developed the information for a network, adding activities when needed. Then the team added the time estimates they had collected for each activity. Following is the preliminary information for activities with duration time and predecessors:

Activity	Description	Duration	Predecessor
1	Architectural decisions	10	None
2	Internal specifications	20	1
3	External specifications	18	1
4	Feature specifications	15	1
5	Voice recognition	15	2,3
6	Case	4	2,3
7	Screen	2	2,3
8	Speaker output jacks	2	2,3
9	Tape mechanism	2	2,3
10	Database	40	4
11	Microphone/soundcard	5	4
12	Pager	4	4
13	Barcode reader	3	4
14	Alarm clock	4	4
15	Computer I/O	5	4
16	Review design	10	5,6,7,8,9,10,11,12,13,14,15
17	Price components	5	5,6,7,8,9,10,11,12,13,14,15
18	Integration	15	16,17
19	Document design	35	16
20	Procure prototype components	20	18
21	Assemble prototypes	10	20
22	Lab test prototypes	20	21
23	Field test prototypes	20	19,22
24	Adjust design	20	23
25	Order stock parts	15	24
26	Order custom parts	2	24
27	Assemble first production unit	10	25, FS—8 time units 26, FS—13 time units
28	Test unit	10	27
29	Produce 30 units	15	28
30	Train sales representatives	10	29

Use any project network computer program available to you to develop the schedule for activities (see Case Appendix for further instructions)—noting late and early times, the critical path, and estimated completion for the project.

Prepare a short memo that addresses the following questions:

1. Will the project as planned meet the October 25th deadline?
2. What activities lie on the critical path?
3. How sensitive is this network?

CASE 9.4

Nightingale Project—B

Rassy and the team were concerned with the results of your analysis. They spent the afternoon brainstorming alternative ways for shortening the project duration. They rejected outsourcing activities because most of the work was developmental in nature and could only be done in-house. They considered altering the scope of the project by eliminating some of the proposed product features. After much debate, they felt they could not compromise any of the core features and be successful in the marketplace. They then turned their attention to accelerating the completion of activities through overtime and adding additional technical manpower. Rassy had built into her proposal a discretionary fund of $200,000. She was willing to invest up to half of this fund to accelerate the project, but wanted to hold onto at least $100,000 to deal with unexpected problems. After a lengthy discussion, her team concluded that the following activities could be reduced at the specified cost:

- Development of voice recognition system could be reduced from 15 days to 10 days at a cost of $15,000.
- Creation of database could be reduced from 40 days to 35 days at a cost of $35,000.
- Document design could be reduced from 35 days to 30 days at a cost of $25,000.
- External specifications could be reduced from 18 days to 12 days at a cost of $20,000.
- Procure prototype components could be reduced from 20 days to 15 days at a cost of $30,000.
- Order stock parts could be reduced from 15 days to 10 days at a cost of $20,000.

Ken Clark, a development engineer, pointed out that the network contained only finish-to-start relationships and that it might be possible to reduce project duration by creating start-to-start lags. For example, he said that his people would not have to wait for all of the field tests to be completed to begin making final adjustments in the design. They could start making adjustments after the first 15 days of testing. The project team spent the remainder of the day analyzing how they could introduce lags into the network to hopefully shorten the project. They concluded that the following finish-to-start relationships could be converted into lags:

- Document design could begin 5 days after the start of the review design.
- Adjust design could begin 15 days after the start of field test prototypes.
- Order stock parts could begin 5 days after the start of adjust design.
- Order custom parts could begin 5 days after the start of adjust design.
- Training sales representatives could begin 5 days after the start of test unit and completed 5 days after the production of 30 units.

As the meeting adjourns, Rassy turns to you and tells you to assess the options presented and try to develop a schedule that will meet the October 25th deadline. You are to prepare a report to be presented to the project team that answers the following questions:

1. Is it possible to meet the deadline?
2. If so, how would you recommend changing the original schedule (Part A) and why? Assess the relative impact of crashing activities versus introducing lags to shorten project duration.

3. What would the new schedule look like?
4. What other factors should be considered before finalizing the schedule?

CASE 9.4 APPENDIX: TECHNICAL DETAILS

Create your project schedule and assess your options based on the following information:

1. The project will begin the first working day in January, 2010.
2. The following holidays are observed: January 1, Memorial Day (last Monday in May), July 4, Labor Day (first Monday in September), Thanksgiving Day (fourth Thursday in November), December 25 and 26.
3. If a holiday falls on a Saturday, then Friday will be given as an extra day off; if it falls on a Sunday, then Monday will be given as a day off.
4. The project team works Monday through Friday, 8 hour days.
5. If you choose to reduce the duration of any one of the activities mentioned, then it must be for the specified time and cost (i.e., you cannot choose to reduce database to 37 days at a reduced cost; you can only reduce it to 35 days at a cost of $35,000).
6. You can only spend up to $100,000 to reduce project activities; lags do not contain any additional costs.

CASE 9.5

The "Now" Wedding—Part A*

On December 31 of last year, Lauren burst into the family living room and announced that she and Connor (her college boyfriend) were going to be married. After recovering from the shock, her mother hugged her and asked, "When?" The following conversation resulted:

Lauren: January 21.
Mom: What?
Dad: The Now Wedding will be the social hit of the year. Wait a minute. Why so soon?
Lauren: Because on January 30 Connor, who is in the National Guard, will be shipping out overseas. We want a week for a honeymoon.
Mom: But Honey, we can't possibly finish all the things that need to be done by then. Remember all the details that were involved in your sister's wedding? Even if we start tomorrow, it takes a day to reserve the church and reception hall, and they need at least 14 days' notice. That has to be done before we can start decorating, which takes 3 days. An extra $200 on Sunday would probably cut that 14 day notice to 7 days, though.
Dad: Oh, boy!

_____
* This case was adapted from a case originally written by Professor D. Clay Whybark, University of North Carolina, Chapel Hill, N.C.

Lauren: I want Jane Summers to be my maid of honor.

Dad: But she's in the Peace Corps in Guatemala, isn't she? It would take her 10 days to get ready and drive up here.

Lauren: But we could fly her up in 2 days and it would only cost $1,000.

Dad: Oh, boy!

Mom: And catering! It takes 2 days to choose the cake and decorations, and Jack's Catering wants at least 5 days' notice. Besides, we'd have to have those things before we could start decorating.

Lauren: Can I wear your wedding dress, Mom?

Mom: Well, we'd have to replace some lace, but you could wear it, yes. We could order the lace from New York when we order the material for the bridesmaids' dresses. It takes 8 days to order and receive the material. The pattern needs to be chosen first, and that would take 3 days.

Dad: We could get the material here in 5 days if we paid an extra $20 to airfreight it. Oh, boy!

Lauren: I want Mrs. Jacks to work on the dresses.

Mom: But she charges $48 a day.

Dad: Oh, boy!

Mom: If we did all the sewing we could finish the dresses in 11 days. If Mrs. Jacks helped we could cut that down to 6 days at a cost of $48 for each day less than 11 days. She is very good too.

Lauren: I don't want anyone but her.

Mom: It would take another 2 days to do the final fitting and 2 more days to clean and press the dresses. They would have to be ready by rehearsal night. We must have rehearsal the night before the wedding.

Dad: Everything should be ready rehearsal night.

Mom: We've forgotten something. The invitations!

Dad: We should order the invitations from Bob's Printing Shop, and that usually takes 7 days. I'll bet he would do it in 6 days if we slipped him an extra $20!

Mom: It would take us 2 days to choose the invitation style before we could order them and we want the envelopes printed with our return address.

Lauren: Oh! That will be elegant.

Mom: The invitations should go out at least 10 days before the wedding. If we let them go any later, some of the relatives would get theirs too late to come and that would make them mad. I'll bet that if we didn't get them out until 8 days before the wedding, Aunt Ethel couldn't make it and she would reduce her wedding gift by $200.

Dad: Oh, boy!!

Mom: We'll have to take them to the Post Office to mail them and that takes a day. Addressing would take 3 days unless we hired some part-time girls and we can't start until the printer is finished. If we hired the girls we could probably save 2 days by spending $40 for each day saved.

Lauren: We need to get gifts for the bridesmaids. I could spend a day and do that.

Mom: Before we can even start to write out those invitations we need a guest list. Heavens, that will take 4 days to get in order and only I can understand our address file.

Lauren: Oh, Mom, I'm so excited. We can start each of the relatives on a different job.

Mom: Honey, I don't see how we can do it. Why, I've got to choose the invitations and patterns and reserve the church and . . .

Dad: Why don't you just take $3,000 and elope. Your sister's wedding cost me $2,400 and she didn't have to fly people up from Guatemala, hire extra girls and Mrs. Jacks, use airfreight, or anything like that.

1. Using a yellow sticky approach (see p. 153), develop a project network for the "Now" Wedding.
2. Create a schedule for the wedding using MS Project. Can you reach the deadline of January 21 for the "Now" Wedding? If you cannot, what would it cost to make the January 21 deadline and which activities would you change?

CASE 9.6

The "Now" Wedding—Part B

Several complications arose during the course of trying to meet the deadline of January 20 for the "Now" Wedding rehearsal. Since Lauren was adamant on having the wedding on January 21 (as was Connor for obvious reasons), the implications of each of these complications had to be assessed.

1. On January 1 the chairman of the Vestry Committee of the church was left unimpressed by the added donation and said he wouldn't reduce the notice period from 14 to 7 days.
2. Mother comes down with the three-day flu as she starts work on the guest list January 2.
3. Bob's Printing Shop press was down for one day on January 5 in order to replace faulty brushes in the electric motor.
4. The lace and dress material are lost in transit. Notice of the loss is received on January 10.

Can the wedding still take place on January 21? If not, what options are available?

10

LEADERSHIP: BEING AN EFFECTIVE PROJECT MANAGER

I couldn't wait to be the manager of my own project and run the project the way I thought it should be done. Boy, did I have a lot to learn!

—*first-time project manager*

This chapter is based on the premise that one of the keys to being an effective project manager is building cooperative relationships among different groups of people to complete projects. Project success does not just depend on the performance of the project team. Success or failure often depends on the contributions of top management, functional managers, customers, suppliers, contractors, and others.

The chapter begins with a brief discussion of the differences between leading and managing a project. The importance of managing project stakeholders is then introduced. Managers require a broad influence base to be effective in this area. Different sources of influence are discussed and are used to describe how project managers build social capital. This management style necessitates constant interacting with different groups of people whom project managers depend on. Special attention is devoted to managing the critical relationship with top management and the importance of leading by example. The importance of gaining cooperation in ways that build and sustain the trust of others is emphasized. The chapter concludes by identifying personal attributes associated with being an effective project manager. Subsequent chapters will expand on these ideas in a discussion of managing the project team and working with people outside the organization.

MANAGING VERSUS LEADING A PROJECT

In a perfect world, the project manager would simply implement the project plan and the project would be completed. The project manager would work with others to formulate a schedule, organize a project team, keep track of progress, and announce what needs to be done next, and then everyone would charge along. Of course no one lives in a perfect world, and rarely does everything go according to plan. Project participants get testy; they fail to complement each other; other departments are unable to fulfill their commitments; technical glitches arise; work takes longer than expected. The project manager's job is to get the project back on track. A manager expedites certain activities; figures out ways to solve technical problems; serves as peacemaker when tensions rise; and makes appropriate trade-offs among time, cost, and scope of the project.

However, project managers do more than put out fires and keep the project on track. They also innovate and adapt to ever-changing circumstances. They often have to deviate from what was planned and introduce significant changes in the project scope and schedule to respond to unforeseen threats or opportunities. For example, customers' needs may change, requiring significant design changes midway through the project. Competitors may release new products that dictate crashing project deadlines. Working relationships among project participants may break down, requiring a reformulation of the project team. Ultimately, what was planned or expected in the beginning may be very different from what was accomplished by the end of the project.

Project managers are responsible for integrating assigned resources to complete the project according to plan. At the same time they need to initiate changes in plans and schedules as persistent problems make plans unworkable. In other words, managers want to keep the project going while making necessary adjustments along the way. According to Kotter (1990) these two different activities represent the distinction between management and leadership. Management is about coping with complexity, while leadership is about coping with change.

Good management brings about order and stability by formulating plans and objectives, designing structures and procedures, monitoring results against plans, and taking corrective action when necessary. Leadership involves recognizing and articulating the need to significantly alter the direction and operation of the project, aligning people to the new direction, and motivating them to work together to overcome hurdles produced by the change and to realize new objectives.

Strong leadership, while usually desirable, is not always necessary to successfully complete a project. Well-defined projects that encounter no significant surprises require little leadership, as might be the case in constructing a conventional apartment building in which the project manager simply administrates the project plan. Conversely, the higher the degree of uncertainty encountered on a project—whether in terms of changes in project scope, technological stalemates, breakdowns in coordination between people, and so forth—the more leadership is required. For example, strong leadership would be needed for a software development project in which the parameters are always changing to meet developments in the industry.

It takes a special person to perform both roles well. Some individuals are great visionaries who are good at exciting people about change. Too often though, these same people lack the discipline or patience to deal with the day-to-day drudgeries of managing. Likewise, there are other individuals who are very well organized and methodical but lack the ability to inspire others.

Strong leaders can compensate for their managerial weaknesses by having trusted assistants who oversee and manage the details of the project. Conversely, a weak leader can complement his or her strengths by having assistants who are good at sensing the need to change and rallying project participants. Still, one of the things that make good project managers so valuable to an organization is that they have the ability to both manage and lead a project. In doing so they recognize the need to manage project interfaces and build a social network that allows them to find out what needs to be done and obtain the cooperation necessary to achieve it.

MANAGING PROJECT STAKEHOLDERS

First-time project managers are eager to implement their own ideas and manage their people to successfully complete their project. What they soon find out is that project success depends on the cooperation of a wide range of individuals, many of whom do not directly report to them. For example, during the course of a system integration project, a project manager was surprised by how much time she was spending negotiating and working with vendors, consultants, technical specialists, and other functional managers:

> Instead of working with my people to complete the project, I found myself being constantly pulled and tugged by demands of different groups of people who were not directly involved in the project but had a vested interest in the outcome.

Too often when new project managers do find time to work directly on the project, they adopt a hands-on approach to managing the project. They choose this style not because they are power-hungry egomaniacs but because they are eager to achieve results. They become quickly frustrated by how slowly things operate, the number of people that have to be brought on board, and the difficulty of gaining cooperation. Unfortunately, as this frustration builds, the natural temptation is to exert more pressure and get more heavily involved in the project. These project managers quickly earn the reputation of "micro managing" and begin to lose sight of the real role they play on guiding a project.

Some new managers never break out of this vicious cycle. Others soon realize that authority does not equal influence and that being an effective project manager involves managing a much more complex and expansive set of interfaces than they had previously anticipated. They encounter a web of relationships that requires a much broader spectrum of influence than they felt was necessary or even possible.

For example, a significant project, whether it involves renovating a bridge, creating a new product, or installing a new information system, will likely involve in one way or another working with a number of different groups of stakeholders. First, there is the core group of specialists assigned to complete the project. This group is likely to be supplemented at different times by professionals who work on specific segments of the project. Second, there are the groups of people within the performing organization who are either directly or indirectly involved with the project. The most notable is top management, to whom the project manager is accountable. There are also other managers who provide resources and/or may be responsible for specific segments of the project, and administrative support services such as human resources, finance, etc. Depending on the nature of the project, there are a number of different groups outside the organization that influence the success of the project; the most important is the customer for which the project is designed (see Figure 10.1).

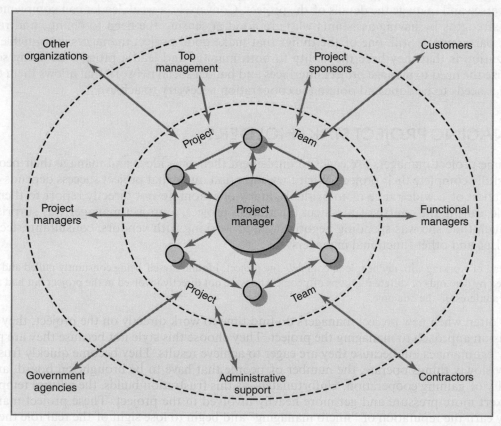

FIGURE 10.1 *Network of Stakeholders*

Each of these groups of stakeholders brings different expertise, standards, priorities, and agendas to the project. **Stakeholders** are people and organizations that are actively involved in the project, or whose interests may be positively or negatively affected by the project (PMBOK, 2013). The sheer breadth and complexity of stakeholder relationships distinguish project management from regular management. To be effective, a project manager must understand how stakeholders can affect the project and develop methods for managing the dependency. The nature of these dependencies is identified here:

- The **project team** manages and completes project work. Most participants want to do a good job, but they are also concerned with their other obligations and how their involvement on the project will contribute to their personal goals and aspirations.

- **Project managers** naturally compete with each other for resources and the support of top management. At the same time they often have to share resources and exchange information.

- **Administrative support** groups, such as human resources, information systems, purchasing agents, and maintenance, provide valuable support services. At the same time they impose constraints and requirements on the project such as the documentation of expenditures and the timely and accurate delivery of information.

- **Functional managers,** depending on how the project is organized, can play a minor or major role toward project success. In matrix arrangements, they may be responsible for assigning project personnel, resolving technical dilemmas, and overseeing the completion of significant segments of the project work. Even in dedicated project teams, the technical input from functional managers may be useful, and acceptance of completed project work may be critical to in-house projects. Functional managers want to cooperate up to a point, but only up to a certain point. They are also concerned with preserving their status within the organization and minimizing the disruptions the project may have on their own operations.

- **Top management** approves funding of the project and establishes priorities within the organization. They define success and adjudicate rewards for accomplishments. Significant adjustments in budget, scope, and schedule typically need their approval. They have a natural vested interest in the success of the project, but at the same time have to be responsive to what is best for the entire organization.

- **Project sponsors** champion the project and use their influence to gain approval of the project. Their reputation is tied to the success of the project, and they need to be kept informed of any major developments. They defend the project when it comes under attack and are a key project ally.

- **Contractors** may do all the actual work, in some cases, with the project team merely coordinating their contributions. In other cases, they are responsible for ancillary segments of the project scope. Poor work and schedule slips can affect work of the core project team. While contractors' reputations rest with doing good work, they must balance their contributions with their own profit margins and their commitments to other clients.

- **Government agencies** place constraints on project work. Permits need to be secured. Construction work has to be built to code. New drugs have to pass a rigorous battery of U.S. Food and Drug Administration tests. Other products have to meet safety standards, for example, Occupational Safety and Health Administration standards.

- **Other organizations,** depending on the nature of the project, may directly or indirectly affect the project. For example, suppliers provide necessary resources for completion of the project work. Delays, shortages, and poor quality can bring a project to a standstill. Public interest groups may apply pressure on government agencies. Customers often hire consultants and auditors to protect their interests on a project.

- **Customers** define the scope of the project, and ultimate project success rests in their satisfaction. Project managers need to be responsive to changing customer needs and requirements and to meeting their expectations. Customers are primarily concerned with getting a *good deal* and, as will be elaborated in Chapter 11, this naturally breeds tension with the project team.

These relationships are interdependent in that a project manager's ability to work effectively with one group will affect her ability to manage other groups. For example, functional managers are likely to be less cooperative if they perceive that top management's commitment to the project is waning. Conversely, the ability of the project manager to buffer the team from excessive interference from a client is likely to increase her standing with the project team.

The project management structure being used will influence the number and degree of external dependencies that will need to be managed. One advantage of creating a dedicated project team is that it reduces dependencies, especially within the organization, because most of the resources are assigned to the project. Conversely, a functional matrix structure increases dependencies, with the result that the project manager is much more reliant upon functional colleagues for work and staff.

The old-fashioned view of managing projects emphasized directing and controlling subordinates; the new perspective emphasizes managing project stakeholders and anticipating change as the most important jobs. Project managers need to be able to assuage concerns of customers, sustain support for the project at higher levels of the organization, quickly identify problems that threaten project work, while at the same time defend the integrity of the project and the interests of the project participants.[1]

Within this web of relationships, the project manager must find out what needs to be done to achieve the goals of the project and build a cooperative network to accomplish it. Project managers must do so without the requisite authority to expect or demand cooperation. Doing so requires sound communication skills, political savvy, and a broad influence base. See the Snapshot from Practice: The Project Manager as Conductor for more on what makes project managers special.

INFLUENCE AS EXCHANGE

To successfully manage a project, a manager must adroitly build a cooperative network among divergent allies. Networks are mutually beneficial alliances that are generally governed by the **law of reciprocity** (Kaplan, 1984; Grant, 2013). The basic principle is that "one good deed deserves another, and likewise, one bad deed deserves another." The primary way to gain cooperation is to provide resources and services for others in exchange for future resources and services. This is the age-old maxim: "Quid pro quo (something for something)." Or in today's vernacular: "You scratch my back, I'll scratch yours."

Cohen and Bradford (1990) described the exchange view of influence as "currencies." If you want to do business in a given country, you have to be prepared to use the appropriate currency,

---

[1] For a systematic treatise on stakeholder management, see: Lynda Bourne, *Stakeholder Relationship Management* (Farnham, England: Gower Publishing Ltd., 2009).

SNAPSHOT FROM PRACTICE

The Project Manager as
Conductor

Metaphors convey meaning beyond words. For example, a meeting can be described as being difficult or "like wading through molasses." A popular metaphor for the role of a project manager is that of *conductor*. The conductor of an orchestra integrates the divergent sounds of different instruments to perform a given composition and make beautiful music. Similarly, the project manager integrates the talents and contributions of different specialists to complete the project. Both have to be good at understanding how the different players contribute to the performance of the whole. Both are almost entirely dependent upon the expertise and know-how of the players. The conductor does not have command of all the musical instruments. Likewise, the project manager usually possesses only a small proportion of the technical knowledge to make decisions. As such, the conductor and project manager both facilitate the performance of others rather than actually perform.

Conductors use their arms, baton, and other nonverbal gestures to influence the pace, intensity, and involvement of different musicians. Likewise, project managers orchestrate the completion of the project by managing the involvement and attention of project members. Project managers balance time and process and induce participants to make the right decisions at the right time just as the conductor induces the wind instruments to perform at the right moment in a movement. Each controls the rhythm and intensity of work by managing the tempo and involvement of the players. Finally, each has a vision that transcends the music score or project plan. To be successful they must both earn the confidence, respect, and trust of their players.

and the exchange rates can change over time as conditions change. In the same way, what is valued by a marketing manager may be different from what is valued by a veteran project engineer, and you are likely to need to use different influence currency to obtain the cooperation of each individual. Although this analogy is a bit of an oversimplification, the key premise holds true that in the long run, "debit" and "credit" accounts must be balanced for cooperative relationships to work. Table 10.1 presents the commonly traded organizational currencies identified by Cohen and Bradford; they are then discussed in more detail in the following sections.

Task-Related Currencies

This form of influence comes directly from the project manager's ability to contribute to others' accomplishing their work. Probably the most significant form of this currency is the ability to respond to subordinates' requests for additional manpower, money, or time to complete a segment of a project. This kind of currency is also evident in sharing resources with another project manager who is in need. At a more personal level, it may simply mean providing direct assistance to a colleague in solving a technical problem.

Providing a good word for a colleague's proposal or recommendation is another form of this currency. Because most work of significance is likely to generate some form of opposition, the person who is trying to gain approval for a plan or proposal can be greatly aided by having a "friend in court."

Another form of this currency includes extraordinary effort. For example, fulfilling an emergency request to complete a design document in two days instead of the normal four days is likely to engender gratitude. Finally, sharing valuable information that would be useful to other managers is another form of this currency.

TABLE 10.1 •
Commonly Traded Organizational Currencies

Task-related currencies	
Resources	Lending or giving money, budget increases, personnel, etc.
Assistance	Helping with existing projects or undertaking unwanted tasks.
Cooperation	Giving task support, providing quicker response time, or aiding implementation.
Information	Providing organizational as well as technical knowledge.
Position-related currencies	
Advancement	Giving a task or assignment that can result in promotion.
Recognition	Acknowledging effort, accomplishments, or abilities.
Visibility	Providing a chance to be known by higher-ups or significant others in the organization.
Network/contacts	Providing opportunities for linking with others.
Inspiration-related currencies	
Vision	Being involved in a task that has larger significance for the unit, organization, customer, or society.
Excellence	Having a chance to do important things really well.
Ethical correctness	Doing what is "right" by a higher standard than efficiency.
Relationship-related currencies	
Acceptance	Providing closeness and friendship.
Personal support	Giving personal and emotional backing.
Understanding	Listening to others' concerns and issues.
Personal-related currencies	
Challenge/learning	Sharing tasks that increase skills and abilities.
Ownership/involvement	Letting others have ownership and influence.
Gratitude	Expressing appreciation.

Source: Adapted from A. R. Cohen and David L. Bradford, *Influence without Authority* (New York: John Wiley & Sons, 1990). Reprinted by permission of John Wiley & Sons, Inc.

Position–Related Currencies

This form of influence stems from the manager's ability to enhance others' positions within their organization. A project manager can do this by giving someone a challenging assignment that can aid their advancement by developing their skills and abilities. Being given a chance to prove yourself naturally generates a strong sense of gratitude. Sharing the glory and bringing to the attention of higher-ups the efforts and accomplishments of others generate goodwill.

Project managers confide that a useful strategy for gaining the cooperation of professionals in other departments/organizations is figuring out how to make these people look good to their bosses. For example, a project manager worked with a subcontractor whose organization was heavily committed to total quality management (TQM). The project manager made it a point in top-level briefing meetings to point out how quality improvement processes initiated by the contractor contributed to cost control and problem prevention.

Another variation of recognition is enhancing the reputation of others within the firm. "Good press" can pave the way for lots of opportunities, while "bad press" can quickly shut a person off and make it difficult to perform. This currency is also evident in helping to preserve someone's reputation by coming to the defense of someone unjustly blamed for project setbacks.

Finally, one of the strongest forms of this currency is sharing contacts with other people. Helping individuals expand their own networks by introducing them to key people naturally engenders gratitude. For example, suggesting to a functional manager that he should contact Sally X if he wants to find out what is really going on in that department or to get a request expedited is likely to engender a sense of indebtedness.

Inspiration–Related Currencies

Perhaps the most powerful form of influence is based on inspiration. Most sources of inspiration derive from people's burning desire to make a difference and add meaning to their lives. Creating an exciting, bold vision for a project can elicit extraordinary commitment. For example, many of the technological breakthroughs associated with the introduction of the original Macintosh computer were attributed to the feeling that the project members had a chance to change the way people approached computers. A variant form of vision is providing an opportunity to do something really well. Being able to take pride in your work often drives many people.

Often the very nature of the project provides a source of inspiration. Discovering a cure for a devastating disease, introducing a new social program that will help those in need, or simply building a bridge that will reduce a major traffic bottleneck can provide opportunities for people to feel good about what they are doing and that they are making a difference. Inspiration operates as a magnet—pulling people as opposed to pushing people toward doing something.

Relationship–Related Currencies

These currencies have more to do with strengthening the relationship with someone than directly accomplishing the project tasks. The essence of this form of influence is forming a relationship that transcends normal professional boundaries and extends into the realm of friendship. Such relationships develop by giving personal and emotional backing. Picking people up when they are feeling down, boosting their confidence, and providing encouragement naturally breed goodwill. Sharing a sense of humor and making difficult times fun is another form of this currency. Similarly, engaging in non-work-related activities such as sports and family outings is another way relationships are naturally enhanced.

Perhaps the most basic form of this currency is simply listening to other people. Psychologists suggest that most people have a strong desire to be understood and that relationships break down because the parties stop listening to each other. Sharing personal secrets/ambitions and being a wise confidant also creates a special bond between individuals.

Personal–Related Currencies

This last form of currency deals with individual needs and an overriding sense of self-esteem. Some argue that self-esteem is a primary psychological need; the extent to which we can help others feel a sense of importance and personal worth will naturally generate goodwill. A project manager can enhance a colleague's sense of worth by sharing tasks that increase skills and abilities, delegating authority over work so that others experience ownership, and allowing individuals to feel comfortable stretching their abilities. This form of currency can also be seen in sincere expressions of gratitude for the contributions of others. Care, though, must be exercised in expressing gratitude since it is easily devalued when overused. That is, the first *thank you* is likely to be more valued than the twentieth.

The bottom line is that a project manager will be influential only insofar as she can offer something that others value. Furthermore, given the diverse cast of people a project manager depends on, it is important that she be able to acquire and exercise different influence currencies. The ability to do so will be constrained in part by the nature of the project and how it is organized. For example, a project manager who is in charge of a dedicated team has considerably more to offer team members than a manager who is given the responsibility of coordinating the activities of different professionals across different departments and organizations. In such cases, that manager will probably have to rely more heavily on personal and relational bases of influence to gain the cooperation of others.

SOCIAL NETWORK BUILDING

Mapping Dependencies

The first step to building a **social network** is identifying those stakeholders on whom the project depends for success. The project manager and his or her key assistants need to ask the following questions:

- Whose cooperation will we need?
- Whose agreement or approval will we need?
- Whose opposition would keep us from accomplishing the project?

Many project managers find it helpful to draw a map of these dependencies. For example, Figure 10.2 contains the dependencies identified by a project manager responsible for installing a new financial software system in her company.

It is always better to overestimate rather than underestimate dependencies. All too often, otherwise talented and successful project managers have been derailed because they were blindsided by someone whose position or power they had not anticipated. After identifying the stakeholders associated with your project, it is important to assess their significance. Here the power/interest matrix introduced in Chapter 3 becomes useful. Those individuals with the most power over and interest in the project are the most significant stakeholders and deserve the greatest attention. In particular, you need to "step into their shoes" and see the project from their perspective:

- What differences exist between myself and the people on whom I depend (goals, values, pressures, working styles, risks)?
- How do these different people view the project (supporters, indifferents, antagonists)?
- What is the current status of the relationship I have with the people I depend on?
- What sources of influence do I have relative to those on whom I depend?

Once you start this analysis you can begin to appreciate what others value and what currencies you might have to offer as a basis on which to build a working relationship. You begin to realize where potential problems lie—relationships in which you have a current debit or no convertible currency. Furthermore, diagnosing another's point of view as well as the basis for their positions will help you anticipate their reactions and feelings about your decisions and actions. This information is vital for selecting the appropriate influence strategy and tactics and conducting win/win negotiations.

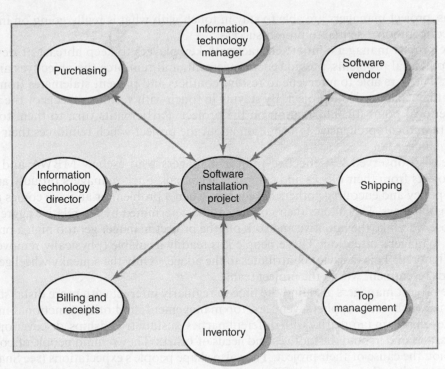

FIGURE 10.2 *Dependencies for Financial Software Installation Project*

For example, after mapping her dependency network, the project manager who was in charge of installing the software system realized that she was likely to have serious problems with the manager of the receipts department, who would be one of the primary users of the software. She had no previous history of working with this individual but had heard through the grapevine that the manager was upset with the choice of software and that he considered this project to be another unnecessary disruption of his department's operation. Prior to project initiation the project manager arranged to have lunch with the manager, where she sat patiently and listened to his concerns. She invested additional time and attention to educate him and his staff about the benefits of the new software. She tried to minimize the disruptions the transition would cause in his department. She altered the implementation schedule to accommodate his preferences as to when the actual software would be installed and the subsequent training would occur. In turn, the receipts manager and his people were much more accepting of the change, and the transition to the new software went more smoothly than anticipated.

Management by Wandering Around (MBWA)

The preceding example illustrates the next step in building a supportive social network. Once you have established who the key players are that will determine success, then you initiate contact and begin to build a relationship with those players. Building this relationship requires a management style employees at Hewlett-Packard refer to as **"management by wandering around" (MBWA)** to reflect that managers spend the majority of their time outside their offices. MBWA is somewhat of a misnomer in that there is a purpose/pattern behind the "wandering." Through face-to-face interactions, project managers are able to stay in touch with what is really going on in the project and build cooperation essential to project success.

Effective project managers initiate contact with key players to keep abreast of developments, anticipate potential problems, provide encouragement, and reinforce the objectives and vision of the project. They are able to intervene to resolve conflicts and prevent stalemates from occurring. In essence, they "manage" the project. By staying in touch with various aspects of the project they become the focal point for information on the project. Participants turn to them to obtain the most current and comprehensive information about the project which reinforces their central role as project manager.

We have also observed less-effective project managers who eschew MBWA and attempt to manage projects from their offices and computer terminals. Such managers proudly announce an open-door policy and encourage others to see them when a problem or an issue comes up. To them no news is good news. This allows their contacts to be determined by the relative aggressiveness of others. Those who take the initiative and seek out the project manager get too high a proportion of the project manager's attention. Those people less readily available (physically removed) or more passive get ignored. This behavior contributes to the adage, "Only the squeaky wheel gets greased," which breeds resentment within the project team.

Effective project managers also find the time to regularly interact with more distal stakeholders. They keep in touch with suppliers, vendors, top management, and other functional managers. In doing so they maintain familiarity with different parties, sustain friendships, discover opportunities to do favors, and understand the motives and needs of others. They remind people of commitments and champion the cause of their project. They also shape people's expectations (see Snapshot from Practice: Managing Expectations). Through frequent communication they alleviate people's concerns about the project, dispel rumors, warn people of potential problems, and lay the groundwork for dealing with setbacks in a more effective manner.

Unless project managers take the initiative to build a network of supportive relationships, they are likely to see a manager (or other stakeholder) only when there is bad news or when they need a favor (e.g., they don't have the data they promised or the project has slipped behind schedule). Without prior, frequent, easy give-and-take interactions around nondecisive issues, the encounter prompted by the problem is likely to provoke excess tension. The parties are more likely to act defensively, interrupt each other, and lose sight of the common problem.

Experienced project managers recognize the need to build relationships before they need them. They initiate contact with the key stakeholders at times when there are no outstanding issues or problems and therefore no anxieties and suspicions. On these social occasions, they engage in small talk and responsive banter. They respond to others' requests for aid, provide supportive counsel, and exchange information. In doing so they establish credit in that relationship, which will allow them to deal with more serious problems down the road. When one person views another as pleasant, credible, and helpful based on past contact, he or she is much more likely to be responsive to requests for help and less confrontational when problems arise.[2]

Managing Upward Relations

Research consistently points out that project success is strongly affected by the degree to which a project has the support of top management.[3] Such support is reflected in an appropriate budget,

---

[2] This discussion is based on Leonard R. Sayles, *Leadership: Managing in Real Organizations* (New York: McGraw-Hill, 1989) pp. 70–78.

[3] See, for example: J. L. Pinto and S. K. Mantel, "The Causes of Project Failure," *IEEE Transactions in Engineering Management,* Vol. 37, No. 4 (1990), pp. 269–76.

SNAPSHOT FROM PRACTICE
Managing Expectations*

Dorothy Kirk, a project management consultant and program manager with Financial Solutions Group of Mynd, offers several keen insights about the art of managing stakeholder expectations:

... expectations are hardy. All they need to take root is the absence of evidence to the contrary. Once rooted, the unspoken word encourages growth. They can develop and thrive without being grounded in reality. For this reason, project managers do daily battle with unrealistic expectations.

She goes on to offer several tips for managing expectations:

- The way you present information can either clarify or muddy expectations. For example, if you estimate that a task will take 317 hours, you are setting high expectations by your precision. The stakeholder is likely to be unhappy if it takes 323 hours. The stakeholder will not be unhappy with 323 hours if you quoted an estimate of 300–325 hours.

- Recognize that it is only human nature to interpret a situation in one's best interest. For example, if you tell someone it will be done by January, you are inclined to interpret it to your advantage and assume you have to the end of January, while the other person believes it will be done January 1st.

- Seize every opportunity to realign expectations with reality. Too often we avoid opportunities to adjust expectations because we hold onto a false hope that things will somehow work out.

- Do not ask for stakeholder suggestions for improvement if you do not intend to do something with their input. Asking for their input raises expectations.

- State the obvious. What is obvious to you may be obscure to others.

- Don't avoid delivering bad news. Communicate openly and in person. Expect some anger and frustration. Do not get defensive in return. Be prepared to explain the impact of the problems. For example, never say the project is going to be late without being able to give a new date. Explain what you are doing to see that this does not continue to happen.

All stakeholders have expectations about the schedule, cost, and project benefits. Project managers need to listen for, understand, and manage these expectations.

* D. Kirk, "Managing Expectations," *PM Network,* August 2000, pp. 59–62.

responsiveness to unexpected needs, and a clear signal to others in the organization of the importance of cooperation.

Visible top management support is not only critical for securing the support of other managers within an organization, but it also is a key factor in the project manager's ability to motivate the project team. Nothing establishes a manager's right to lead more than her ability to defend. To win the loyalty of team members, project managers have to be effective advocates for their projects. They have to be able to get top management to rescind unreasonable demands, provide additional resources, and recognize the accomplishments of team members. This is more easily said than done.

Working relationships with upper management is a common source of consternation. Laments like the following are often made by project managers about upper management:

They don't know how much it sets us back losing Neil to another project.

I would like to see them get this project done with the budget they gave us.

I just wish they would make up their minds as to what is really important.

While it may seem counterintuitive for a subordinate to "manage" a superior, smart project managers devote considerable time and attention to influencing and garnering the support of top management. Project managers have to accept profound differences in perspective and become skilled at the art of persuading superiors.

Many of the tensions that arise between upper management and project managers are a result of differences in perspective. Project managers become naturally absorbed with what is best for their project. To them the most important thing in the world is their project. Top management should have a different set of priorities. They are concerned with what is best for the entire organization. It is only natural for these two interests to conflict at times. For example, a project manager may lobby intensively for additional personnel only to be turned down because top management believes that the other departments cannot afford a reduction in staff. Although frequent communication can minimize differences, the project manager has to accept the fact that top management is inevitably going to see the world differently.

Once project managers accept that disagreements with superiors are more a question of perspective than substance, they can focus more of their energy on the art of persuading upper management. But before they can persuade superiors, they must first prove loyalty.[4] Loyalty in this context simply means that most of the time project managers have to show that they consistently follow through on requests and adhere to the parameters established by top management without a great deal of grumbling or fuss. Once managers have proven loyalty to upper management, senior management is much more receptive to their challenges and requests.

Project managers have to cultivate strong ties with upper managers who are sponsoring the project. As noted earlier, these are high-ranking officials who championed approval and funding of the project; as such, their reputations are aligned with the project. Sponsors are also the ones who defend the project when it is under attack in upper circles of management. They shelter the project from excessive interference (see Figure 10.3). Project managers should *always* keep such people informed of any problems that may cause embarrassment or disappointment. For example, if costs are beginning to outrun the budget or a technical glitch is threatening to delay the completion of the project, managers make sure that the sponsors are the first to know.

FIGURE 10.3 *The Significance of a Project Sponsor*

Timing is everything. Asking for additional budget the day after disappointing third-quarter earnings are reported is going to be much more difficult than making a similar request four weeks later. Good project managers pick the optimum time to appeal to top management. They enlist their project sponsors to lobby their cause. They also realize there are limits to top management's accommodations. Here, the Lone Ranger analogy is appropriate—you have only so many silver bullets, so use them wisely.

Project managers need to adapt their communication pattern to that of the senior group. For example, one project manager recognized that top management had a tendency to use sports metaphors to describe business situations, so she framed a recent slip in schedule by admitting that "we lost five yards, but we still have two plays to make a first down." Smart project managers learn the language of top management and use it to their advantage.

---

[4] Sayles, *Leadership*, pp. 136–45.

Research Highlight

IMPROVING THE PERFORMANCE OF NEW-PRODUCT TEAMS*

Ancona and Caldwell studied the performance of 45 new-product teams in five high-technology compa- nies and produced some startling results. The most significant was that internal team dynamics were not related to performance. That is, high-performance teams were not distinguished by clearer goals, smoother workflow among members, or greater ability to satisfy the individual goals of team members. What related to team performance were level and intensity of external interactions between the project team and the rest of the organization. Ancona and Caldwell identified four key patterns of activity which contribute to creating a high-performance team:

1. *Ambassador* activities are aimed at representing the team to others and protecting the team from interference. The project manager typically takes on this responsibility, which involves buffering the team from political pressures and building support for the project within the hierarchy of the company.

2. *Task coordinator* activities are aimed at coordinating the team's efforts with other units and organizations. Un- like the ambassador role, which is focused upward, these are more lateral activities and involve negotiating and interacting with interested parties within the organization.

3. *Scouts* act as a scout on an expedition; that is, they go out from the team to bring back information about what is going on elsewhere in the organization. This is a much less focused task than task coordinator.

4. *Guard* activities differ from the other activities in that they are intended to keep information and resources in- side the team, preventing drainage out of the group. A key guard activity is keeping necessary information se- cret until it is appropriate to share it.

Ancona and Caldwell found that the importance of these activities varies during the product development life cycle if the project team is to be successful. For example, scouting activities are more critical during the creation phase, when the product idea is being formulated and the team is being developed. Ambassador activities are especially critical during the development phase, when product specifications have been agreed upon and the major task is developing a prototype.

Ancona and Caldwell caution that their findings do not mean that teamwork and the internal operations of a project team are not important to project success. Effective team dynamics are necessary to successfully inte- grate information from outside sources and coordinate activities across groups. Their research supports the adage that problems and opportunities often lie at the borders of projects, and that one of the primary jobs of a project manager is to manage the interface between his or her team and the rest of the organization.

* D. G. Ancona and D. Caldwell, "Improving the Performance of New-Product Teams," *Research Technology Management,* Vol. 33, No. 2 (March–April 1990), pp. 25–29.

Finally, a few project managers admit ignoring chains of command. If they are confident that top management will reject an important request and that what they want to do will benefit the project, they do it without asking permission. While acknowledging that this is very risky, they claim that bosses typically won't argue with success.

Leading by Example

A highly visible, interactive management style is not only essential to building and sustaining cooperative relationships, it also allows project managers to utilize their most powerful leadership tool—their own behavior (Peters, 1988; Kouznes & Posner, 2012). Often, when faced with uncertainty, people look to others for cues as to how to respond and demonstrate a propensity to mimic the behavior of superiors. A project manager's behavior symbolizes how other people should work on the project. Through her behavior a project manager can influence how others act and respond to a variety of issues related to the project. (See Snapshot from Practice: Leading at the Edge for a dramatic example of this.)

SNAPSHOT FROM PRACTICE
Leading at the Edge*

In 1914, the intrepid explorer Ernest Shackleton embarked on the *Endurance* with his team of seamen and scientists, intent upon crossing the unexplored Antarctic continent. What happened in the two years between their departure and their ultimate incredible rescue has rarely been matched in the annals of survival: a ship crushed by expanding ice pack . . . a crew stranded on the floes of the frozen Weddell Sea . . . two perilous treks in open boats across a raging Southern Ocean . . . a team marooned on the wild, forlorn Elephant Island, stretched to the limits of human endurance.

This adventure provided the basis for the book *Leading at the Edge: Leadership Lessons from the Extraordinary Saga of Shackleton's Antarctic Expedition* written by Dennis Perkins. Perkins provides numerous incidents of how Shackleton's personal example influenced the behavior of his beleaguered crew. For example, from the beginning of the Trans-Atlantic expedition to its end Shackleton consistently encouraged behavior that emphasized caring and respect:

After the destruction of the *Endurance* Shackleton heated hot milk for the crew and went from tent to tent with the "life giving" drink. After the sail to the island of South Georgia, when the exhausted crew had landed, Shackleton took the first watch, which he kept for three hours instead of the usual one.

© Topham/The Image Works

Crew members emulated the caring behaviors that Shackleton modeled. A good example of this occurred during one of the most dramatic moments in the *Endurance* saga. The food supply had dwindled to perilously low levels. Less than a week's supply remained, and the tiny ration of seal steak usually served at breakfast was eliminated. The waste meat generally used to feed the dogs was inspected for edible scraps.

Under these wretched conditions, and after a wet sleepless night, an argument broke out among some of the team members. Caught in the middle, one crew member (Greenstreet) spilled his tiny ration of powdered milk and shouted at the biologist (Clark). Alfred Lansing described what happened next:

Greenstreet paused to get his breath, and in that instant his anger was spent and he suddenly fell silent. Everyone else in the tent became quiet, too, and looked at Greenstreet, shaggy-haired, bearded, and filthy with blubber soot, holding his empty mug in his hand and looking helplessly down into the snow that had thirstily soaked up his precious milk. The loss was so tragic he seemed almost on the point of weeping. Without speaking, Clark reached out and poured some milk into Greenstreet's mug. Then Worsely, then Macklin, and Rickerson and Kerr, Orde-Lees, and finally Blackborrow. They finished in silence.

* Adapted from Dennis N. T. Perkins, *Leading at the Edge: Leadership Lessons from the Extraordinary Saga of Shackleton's Antarctica Expedition* (New York: AMACOM Press, 2000), pp. 94–95; and Alfred Lansing, *Endurance: Shackleton's Incredible Voyage* (New York: Carroll & Graf, 1998), p. 127.

To be effective, project managers must "walk the talk" (see Figure 10.4). Six aspects of leading by example are discussed next.

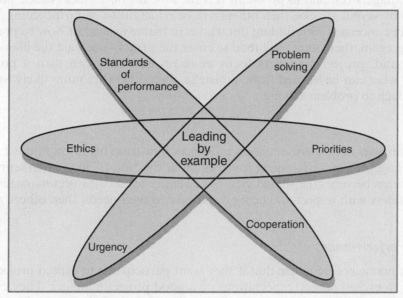

FIGURE 10.4 *Leading by Example*

Priorities

Actions speak louder than words. Subordinates and others discern project managers' priorities by how they spend their time. If a project manager claims that this project is critical and then is perceived as devoting more time to other projects, then all his verbal reassurances are likely to fall on deaf ears. Conversely, a project manager who takes the time to observe a critical test instead of simply waiting for a report affirms the importance of the testers and their work. Likewise, the types of questions project managers pose communicate priorities. By repeatedly asking how specific issues relate to satisfying the customer, a project manager can reinforce the importance of customer satisfaction.

Urgency

Through their actions project managers can convey a sense of urgency, which can permeate project activities. This urgency in part can be conveyed through stringent deadlines, frequent status report meetings, and aggressive solutions for expediting the project. The project manager uses these tools like a metronome to pick up the beat of the project. At the same time, such devices will be ineffective if there is not also a corresponding change in the project manager's behavior. If they want others to work faster and solve problems quicker, then they need to work faster. They need to hasten the pace of their own behavior. They should accelerate the frequency of their interactions, talk and walk more quickly, get to work sooner, and leave work later. By simply increasing the pace of their daily interaction patterns, project managers can reinforce a sense of urgency in others.

Problem Solving

How project managers respond to problems sets the tone for how others tackle problems. If bad news is greeted by verbal attacks, then others will be reluctant to be forthcoming.[5] If the project manager is more concerned with finding out who is to blame instead of how to prevent problems from happening again, then others will tend to cover their tracks and cast the blame elsewhere. If, on the other hand, project managers focus more on how they can turn a problem into an opportunity or what can be learned from a mistake, then others are more likely to adopt a more proactive approach to problem solving.

Cooperation

How project managers act toward outsiders influences how team members interact with outsiders. If a project manager makes disparaging remarks about the "idiots" in the marketing department, then this oftentimes becomes the shared view of the entire team. If project managers set the norm of treating outsiders with respect and being responsive to their needs, then others will more likely follow suit.

Standards of Performance

Veteran project managers recognize that if they want participants to exceed project expectations then they have to exceed others' expectations of a good project manager. They establish a high standard for project performance through the quality of their daily interactions. They respond quickly to the needs of others, carefully prepare and run crisp meetings, stay on top of all the critical issues, facilitate effective problem solving, and stand firm on important matters.

Ethics

How others respond to ethical dilemmas that arise in the course of a project will be influenced by how the project manager has responded to similar dilemmas. In many cases, team members base their actions on how they think the project manager would respond. If project managers deliberately distort or withhold vital information from customers or top management, then they are signaling to others that this kind of behavior is acceptable. Project management invariably creates a variety of ethical dilemmas; this would be an appropriate time to delve into this topic in more detail.

ETHICS AND PROJECT MANAGEMENT

Questions of ethics have already arisen in previous chapters that discussed padding of cost and time estimations, exaggerating pay-offs of project proposals, and so forth. Ethical dilemmas involve situations where it is difficult to determine whether conduct is right or wrong. Is it acceptable to falsely assure customers that everything is on track when, in reality, you are only doing so to prevent them from panicking and making matters worse?

---

[5] This is the classic "kill the messenger" syndrome. This and other forces that contribute to distorting information can be found in Erik Larson and Jon King "The Systemic Distortion of Information: An On-going Management Challenge," *Organizational Dynamics*, Winter 1996, pp. 49–62.

In a survey of project managers, 81 percent reported that they encounter ethical issues in their work.[6] These dilemmas range from being pressured to alter status reports, backdate signatures, or shade documentation to mask the reality of project progress to falsifying cost accounts, compromising safety standards to accelerate progress, and approving shoddy work.

Project management is complicated work, and, as such, ethics invariably involve gray areas of judgment and interpretation. For example, it is difficult to distinguish deliberate falsification of estimates from genuine mistakes or the willful exaggeration of project payoffs from genuine optimism. It becomes problematic to determine whether unfulfilled promises were deliberate deception or an appropriate response to changing circumstances.

To provide greater clarity to business ethics, many companies and professional groups publish a code of conduct. Cynics see these documents as simply window dressing, while advocates argue that they are important, albeit limited, first steps. In practice, personal ethics do not lie in formal statutes but at the intersection of one's work, family, education, profession, religious beliefs, and daily interactions. Most project managers report that they rely on their own private sense of right and wrong—what one project manager called his "internal compass." One common rule of thumb for testing whether a response is ethical is to ask, "Imagine that whatever you did was going to be reported on the front page of your local newspaper. How would you like that? Would you be comfortable?"

Unfortunately, scandals at Enron, Worldcom, and Arthur Andersen have demonstrated the willingness of highly trained professionals to abdicate personal responsibility for illegal actions and to obey the directives of superiors (see Snapshot from Practice: The Collapse of Arthur Andersen). Top management and the culture of an organization play a decisive role in shaping members' beliefs of what is right and wrong. Many organizations encourage ethical transgressions by creating a "win at all cost" mentality. The pressures to succeed obscure consideration of whether the ends justify the means. Other organizations place a premium on "fair play" and command a market position by virtue of being trustworthy and reliable.[7]

Many project managers claim that ethical behavior is its own reward. By following your own internal compass your behavior expresses your personal values. Others suggest that ethical behavior is doubly rewarding. You not only are able to fall asleep at night but you also develop a sound and admirable reputation. As will be explored in the next section, such a reputation is essential to establishing the trust necessary to exercise influence effectively.

BUILDING TRUST: THE KEY TO EXERCISING INFLUENCE

We all know people who have influence but whom we do not trust; these individuals are often referred to as "political animals" or "jungle fighters." While these individuals are often very successful in the short run, the prevalent sense of mistrust prohibits long-term efficacy. Successful project managers not only need to be influential, they also need to exercise influence in a manner that builds and sustains the trust of others.

The significance of trust can be discerned by its absence. Imagine how different a working relationship is when you distrust the other party as opposed to trusting them. When people distrust

---

[6] While this survey is a bit old, our conversations with project managers suggest that the results hold true today (J. Cabanis, "A Question of Ethics: The Issues Project Managers Face and How They Resolve Them," *PM Network,* December 1995, pp. 8–28).

[7] For a more in-depth discussion of ethics, see: L. Trevino and K. Nelson, *Managing Business Ethics: Straight Talk about How to Do It Right,* 5th ed. (Hoboken, NJ: John Wiley & Sons, 2011).

SNAPSHOT FROM PRACTICE
The Collapse of Arthur Andersen*

AP Photo/Stephen J. Carrera

"Think straight and talk straight" was the principle on which Arthur E. Andersen built his accounting firm in the early 1900s. It was a phrase his mother taught him and became the firm's motto. The commitment to integrity and a systematic, planned approach to work were instrumental in Arthur Andersen becoming one of the largest and best-known accounting firms in the world.

> Working for Arthur Andersen was not for everyone. It could be a tough culture. It was much too hierarchical and top down for the more free spirited. Many people left after less than two years, believing the rewards did not warrant the demands that were made on them. Others learned to play by the rules and some even thrived. To remain in the firm, staff members were expected to work hard, respect authority of rank, and maintain a high level of conformity. In return they were rewarded with support, promotion, and the possibility of making partner. Those individuals who made a career with the firm grew old together, professionally and personally, and most had never worked anywhere else. To these survivors, Andersen was their second family, and they developed strong loyalties to the firm and its culture. (p. 133)

On October 23, 2001, David Duncan told his Enron project team that they needed to start complying with Andersen's new policy on handling audit documents. The policy had been instituted to make sure that the firm's extraneous paperwork could not be used in court cases. Although the document retention policy required that papers supporting the firm's opinions and audit be retained, it allowed a broad category of secondary documents to be destroyed. The team reacted with stunned silence to Duncan's directive. Then everyone got up and began racing to do what they had been told to do. No one asked Duncan to explain further. None asked whether what they were doing was wrong. No one questioned whether what he or she were doing might be illegal. Andersen's Houston staff just reacted, following orders without question.

On November 9, 2001, the day after the Securities Exchange Commission (SEC) issued a subpoena to Andersen, the shredding stopped. More than one ton of documents had been destroyed and 30,000 e-mails and Enron-related computer files erased. According to Andersen's legal defense team, the shredding was business as usual. The lawyers claimed that the shredding was standard practice for eliminating unnecessary files. To the SEC, it appeared to be the start of a deep cover-up operation. Subsequently one of the most respected accounting firms in the world closed its doors.

* Susan E. Squires, Cynthia J. Smith, Lorna McDougall, and William R. Yeak, *Inside Arthur Andersen: Shifting Values, Unexpected Consequences* (Upper Saddle River, NJ: Prentice Hall, 2004).

each other, they often spend inordinate amounts of time and energy attempting to discern hidden agendas and the true meaning of communications and then securing guarantees to promises. They are much more cautious with each other and hesitant to cooperate. Here is what one line manager had to say about how he reacted to a project manager he did not trust:

> Whenever Jim approached me about something, I found myself trying to read between the lines to figure what was really going on. When he made a request, my initial reaction was "no" until he proved it.

Conversely, trust is the "lubricant" that maintains smooth and efficient interactions. When you trust, people are more likely to take your actions and intentions at face value when circumstances are ambiguous. For example, here is what a functional manager had to say about how he dealt with a project manager he trusted:

> If Sally said she needed something, no questions were asked. I knew it was important or she wouldn't have asked.

Trust is an elusive concept. It is hard to nail down in precise terms why some project managers are trusted and others are not. One popular way to understand trust is to see it as a function of character and competence. Character focuses on personal motives (i.e., does he or she want to do the right thing?), while competence focuses on skills necessary to realize motives (i.e., does he or she know the right things to do?).

Stephen Covey resurrected the significance of character in leadership literature in his best-selling *Seven Habits of Highly Effective People*. Covey criticized popular management literature as focusing too much on shallow human relations skills and manipulative techniques, which he labeled the personality ethic. He argues that at the core of highly effective people is a character ethic that is deeply rooted in personal values and principles such as dignity, service, fairness, the pursuit of truth, and respect.

One of the distinguishing traits of character is consistency. When people are guided by a core set of principles, they are naturally more predictable because their actions are consistent with these principles. Another feature of character is openness. When people have a clear sense of who they are and what they value, they are more receptive to others. This trait provides them with the capacity to empathize and the talent to build consensus among divergent people. Finally, another quality of character is a sense of purpose. Managers with character are driven not only by personal ambitions but also for the common good. Their primary concern is what is best for their organization and the project, not what is best for themselves. This willingness to subordinate personal interests to a higher purpose garners the respect, loyalty, and trust of others.

The significance of character is summarized by the comments made by two team members about two very different project managers.

> At first everyone liked Joe and was excited about the project. But after a while, people became suspicious of his motives. He had a tendency to say different things to different people. People began to feel manipulated. He spent too much time with top management. People began to believe that he was only looking out for himself. It was HIS project. When the project began to slip he jumped ship and left someone else holding the bag. I'll never work for that guy again.
>
> My first impression of Jack was nothing special. He had a quiet, unassuming management style. Over time I learned to respect his judgment and his ability to get people to work together. When you went to him with a problem or a request, he always listened carefully. If he couldn't do what you wanted him to do, he would take the time to explain why. When disagreements arose he always thought of what was

best for the project. He treated everyone by the same rules; no one got special treatment. I'd jump at the opportunity to work on a project with him again.

Character alone will not engender trust. We must also have confidence in the competency of individuals before we really trust them (Kanter, 1979). We all know well-intended managers whom we like but do not trust because they have a history of coming up short on their promises. Although we may befriend these managers, we don't like to work with or for them.

Competence is reflected at a number of different levels. First, there is task-related knowledge and skills reflected in the ability to answer questions, solve technical problems, and excel in certain kinds of work. Second, there is competence at an interpersonal level demonstrated in being able to listen effectively, communicate clearly, resolve arguments, provide encouragement, and so forth. Finally, there is organizational competence. This includes being able to run effective meetings, set meaningful objectives, reduce inefficiencies, and build a social network. Too often there is a tendency for young engineers and other professionals to place too much value on task or technical competence. They underestimate the significance of organizational skills. Veteran professionals, on the other hand, recognize the importance of management and place a greater value on organizational and interpersonal skills.

One problem new project managers experience is that it takes time to establish a sense of character and competency. Character and competency are often demonstrated when they are tested, such as when a tough call has to be made or when difficult problems have to be solved. Veteran project managers have the advantage of reputation and an established track record of success. Although endorsements from credible sponsors can help a young project manager create a favorable first impression, ultimately he or she will have to demonstrate character and competence during the course of dealings with others in order to gain their trust.

So far this chapter has addressed the importance of building a network of relationships to complete the project based on trust and reciprocity. The next section examines the nature of project management work and the personal qualities needed to excel at it.

QUALITIES OF AN EFFECTIVE PROJECT MANAGER

Project management is, at first glance, a misleading discipline in that there is an inherent logic in the progression from formulating a project scope statement, creating a WBS, developing a network, adding resources, finalizing a plan, and reaching milestones. However, when it comes to actually implementing and completing projects, this logic quickly disappears, and project managers encounter a much messier world, filled with inconsistencies and paradoxes. Effective project managers have to be able to deal with the contradictory nature of their work. Some of those contradictions are listed here:

- **Innovate and maintain stability.** Project managers have to put out fires, restore order, and get the project back on track. At the same time they need to be innovative and develop new, better ways of doing things. Innovations unravel stable routines and spark new disturbances that have to be dealt with.

- **See the big picture while getting your hands dirty.** Project managers have to see the big picture and how their project fits within the larger strategy of their firm. There are also times when they must get deeply involved in project work and technology. If they don't worry about the details, who will?

- **Encourage individuals but stress the team.** Project managers have to motivate, cajole, and entice individual performers while at the same time maintaining teamwork. They have to be careful that they are considered fair and consistent in their treatment of team members while at the same time treating each member as a special individual.

- **Hands-off/Hands-on.** Project managers have to intervene, resolve stalemates, solve technical problems, and insist on different approaches. At the same time they have to recognize when it is appropriate to sit on the sidelines and let other people figure out what to do.

- **Flexible but firm.** Project managers have to be adaptable and responsive to events and outcomes that occur on the project. At the same time they have to hold the line at times and tough it out when everyone else wants to give up.

- **Team versus organizational loyalties.** Project managers need to forge a unified project team whose members stimulate one another to extraordinary performance. But at the same time they have to counter the excesses of cohesion and the team's resistance to outside ideas. They have to cultivate loyalties to both the team and the parent organization.

Managing these and other contradictions requires finesse and balance. Finesse involves the skillful movement back and forth between opposing behavioral patterns (Sayles, 1989). For example, most of the time project managers actively involve others, move by increment, and seek consensus. There are other times when project managers must act as autocrats and take decisive, unilateral action. Balance involves recognizing the danger of extremes and that too much of a good thing invariably becomes harmful. For example, many managers have a tendency to always delegate the most stressful, difficult assignments to their best team members. This habit often breeds resentment among those chosen ("why am I always the one who gets the tough work?") and never allows the weaker members to develop their talents further.

There is no one management style or formula for being an effective project manager. The world of project management is too complicated for formulas. Successful project managers have a knack for adapting styles to specific circumstances of the situation.

So, what should one look for in an effective project manager? Many authors have addressed this question and have generated list after list of skills and attributes associated with being an effective manager (Posner, 1987; Shenhar and Nofziner, 1997; Turner and Müller, 2005). When reviewing these lists, one sometimes gets the impression that to be a successful project manager requires someone with superhuman powers. While we agree that not everyone has the right stuff to be an effective project manager, there are some core traits and skills that can be developed to successfully perform the job. Eight of these traits are noted below.

1. **Systems thinker.** Project managers must be able to take a holistic rather than a reductionist approach to projects. Instead of breaking up a project into individual pieces (planning, budget) and managing it by understanding each part, a systems perspective focuses on trying to understand how relevant project factors collectively interact to produce project outcomes. The key to success then becomes managing the interaction between different parts and not the parts themselves.[8]

2. **Personal integrity.** Before you can lead and manage others, you have to be able to lead and manage yourself (Bennis, 1989). Begin by establishing a firm sense of who you are, what you stand for, and how you should behave. This inner strength provides the buoyancy to endure

---

[8] For a practical elaboration on what it means to be a systems thinker, see: Peter M. Senge, *The Fifth Discipline* (New York: Doubleday, 1990).

the ups and downs of the project life cycle and the credibility essential to sustaining the trust of others.

3. **Proactive.** Good project managers take action before it is needed to prevent small concerns from escalating into major problems. They spend the majority of their time working within their sphere of influence to solve problems and not dwelling on things they have little control over. Project managers can't be whiners.[9]

4. **High emotional intelligence (EQ).** Project management is not for the meek. Project managers have to have command of their emotions and be able to respond constructively to others when things get a bit out of control. See the Research Highlight: Emotional Intelligence to read more about this quality.

5. **General business perspective.** Because the primary role of a project manager is to integrate the contributions of different business and technical disciplines, it is important that a manager have

Research Highlight

EMOTIONAL INTELLIGENCE*

Emotional intelligence (EQ) describes the ability or skill to perceive, assess, and manage the emotions of one's self and others. Although the notion of EQ emerged in the 1920s, it was not until Daniel Goleman published his book *Emotional Intelligence* that the concept captured the attention of business people and public alike.

Goleman divided EQ into the following five emotional competences:

- **Self-awareness**—knowing your emotions, recognizing feelings as they occur, and understanding the link between your emotions and your behavior. Self-awareness is reflected in confidence, realistic assessment of personal strengths/weaknesses, and ability to make fun of oneself.

- **Self-regulation**—being able to control disruptive impulses and moods and respond appropriately to situations. Self-regulation is reflected in trustworthiness and openness to change.

- **Self-motivation**—being able to gather up your feelings and pursue goals with energy, passion, and persistence. The hallmarks of self-motivation include a strong desire to achieve and internal optimism.

- **Empathy**—being able to recognize the feelings of others and tuning into their verbal and nonverbal cues. Empathy is reflected in the ability to sustain relationships and in cross-cultural sensitivity.

- **Social skills**—being able to build social networks and rapport with different kinds of people. Social skills include being able to lead change, resolve conflicts, and build effective teams.

Not much imagination is needed to see how EQ would contribute to being an effective project manager.

In Goleman's view, these competences build on each other in a hierarchy. At the bottom of his hierarchy is self-awareness. Some level of self-awareness is needed to move to self-regulation. Ultimately, social skills requires all four of the other competences in order to begin to be proficient at leading others. Experts believe that most people can learn to significantly increase their EQ. Numerous training programs and materials have emerged to help individuals realize their EQ potential.

* T. Bradberry, and J. Graves, *The Emotional Intelligence Quick Book: How to Put Your EQ to Work* (New York: Simon & Schuster, 2005); J. Cabanis-Brewin, "The Human Task of a Project Leader: Daniel Goleman on the Value of High EQ," *PM Network*, November 1999, pp. 38–42.

---

[9] For a more extensive discussion of the habit of being proactive, see Stephen Covey, *The Seven Habits of Highly Effective People* (New York: Simon & Schuster, 1989), pp. 65–94.

a general grasp of business fundamentals and how the different functional disciplines interact to contribute to a successful business.

6. **Effective time management.** Time is a manager's scarcest resource. Project managers have to be able to budget their time wisely and quickly adjust their priorities. They need to balance their interactions so no one feels ignored.

7. **Skillful politician.** Project managers have to be able to deal effectively with a wide range of people and win their support and endorsement of their project. They need to be able to sell the virtues of their project without compromising the truth.

8. **Optimist.** Project managers have to display a can-do attitude. They have to be able to find rays of sunlight in a dismal day and keep people's attention positive. A good sense of humor and a playful attitude are often a project manager's greatest strength.

So how does one develop these traits? Workshops, self-study, and courses can upgrade one's general business perspective and capacity for systems thinking. Training programs can improve emotional intelligence and political skills. People can also be taught stress and time management techniques. However, we know of no workshop or magic potion that can transform a pessimist into an optimist or provide a sense of purpose when there is not one. These qualities get at the very soul or being of a person. Optimism, integrity, and even being proactive are not easily developed if there is not already a predisposition to display them.

Summary

To be successful, project managers must build a cooperative network among a diverse set of allies. They begin by identifying who the key stakeholders on a project are, followed by a diagnosis of the nature of the relationships, and the basis for exercising influence. Effective project managers are skilled at acquiring and exercising a wide range of influence. They use this influence and a highly interactive management style to monitor project performance and initiate appropriate changes in project plans and direction. They do so in a manner that generates trust, which is ultimately based on others' perceptions of their character and competence.

Project managers are encouraged to keep in mind the following suggestions:

- *Build relationships before you need them.* Identify key players and what you can do to help them before you need their assistance. It is always easier to receive a favor after you have granted one. This requires the project manager to see the project in systems terms and to appreciate how it affects other activities and agendas inside and outside the organization. From this perspective they can identify opportunities to do good deeds and garner the support of others.

- *Trust is sustained through frequent face-to-face contact.* Trust withers through neglect. This is particularly true under conditions of rapid change and uncertainty that naturally engender doubt, suspicion, and even momentary bouts of paranoia. Project managers must maintain frequent contact with key stakeholders to keep abreast of developments, assuage concerns, engage in reality testing, and focus attention on the project. Frequent face-to-face interactions affirm mutual respect and trust in each other.

Ultimately, exercising influence in an effective and ethical manner begins and ends with how you view the other parties. Do you view them as potential partners or obstacles to your goals? If obstacles, then you wield your influence to manipulate and gain compliance and cooperation. If partners, you exercise influence to gain their commitment and support. People who view social network building as building partnerships see every interaction with two goals: resolving the immediate problem/ concern and improving the working relationship so that next time it will be even more effective. Experienced project managers realize that "what goes around comes around" and try at all cost to avoid antagonizing players for quick success.

Key Terms

Emotional intelligence (EQ)
Inspiration-related currencies
Law of reciprocity
Leading by example
Management by wandering
  around (MBWA)

Personal-related currencies
Position-related currencies
Proactive
Relationship-related
  currencies
Social network building

Stakeholder
Systems thinking
Task-related currencies

Review Questions

1. What is the difference between leading and managing a project?
2. Why is a conductor of an orchestra an appropriate metaphor for being a project manager? What aspects of project managing are not reflected by this metaphor? Can you think of other metaphors that would be appropriate?
3. What does the exchange model of influence suggest you do to build cooperative relationships to complete a project?
4. What differences would you expect to see between the kinds of influence currencies that a project manager in a functional matrix would use and the influence a project manager of a dedicated project team would use?
5. Why is it important to build a relationship before you need it?
6. Why is it critical to keep the project sponsor informed?
7. Why is trust a function of both character and competence?
8. Which of the eight traits/skills associated with being an effective project manager is the most important? The least important? Why?

Exercises

1. Do an Internet search for the Keirsey Temperament Sorter Questionnaire and find a site that appears to have a reputable self-assessment questionnaire. Respond to the questionnaire to

identify your temperament type. Read supportive documents associated with your type. What does this material suggest are the kinds of projects that would best suit you? What does it suggest your strengths and weaknesses are as a project manager? How can you compensate for your weaknesses?

2. Access the Project Management Institute Web site and review the standards contained in PMI Member Ethical Standards section. How useful is the information for helping someone decide what behavior is appropriate and inappropriate?

3. You are organizing an AIDS benefit concert in your hometown that will feature local heavy metal rock groups and guest speakers. Draw a dependency map identifying the major groups of people that are likely to affect the success of this project. Who do you think will be most cooperative? Who do you think will be the least cooperative? Why?

4. You are the project manager responsible for the overall construction of a new international airport. Draw a dependency map identifying the major groups of people that are likely to affect the success of this project. Who do you think will be most cooperative? Who do you think will be the least cooperative? Why?

5. Identify an important relationship (co-worker, boss, friend) in which you are having trouble gaining cooperation. Assess this relationship in terms of the influence currency model. What kinds of influence currency have you been exchanging in this relationship? Is the "bank account" for this relationship in the "red" or the "black"? What kinds of influence would be appropriate for building a stronger relationship with that person?

6. Each of the following seven mini-case scenarios involve ethical dilemmas associated with project management. How would you respond to each situation, and why?

Jack Nietzche

You returned from a project staffing meeting in which future project assignments were finalized. Despite your best efforts, you were unable to persuade the director of project management to promote one of your best assistants, Jack Nietzche, to a project manager position. You feel a bit guilty because you dangled the prospect of this promotion to motivate Jack. Jack responded by putting in extra hours to ensure that his segments of the project were completed on time. You wonder how Jack will react to this disappointment. More importantly, you wonder how his reaction might affect your project. You have five days remaining to meet a critical deadline for a very important customer. While it won't be easy, you believed you would be able to complete the project on time. Now you're not so sure. Jack is halfway through completing the documentation phase, which is the last critical activity. Jack can be pretty emotional at times, and you are worried that he will blow up once he finds he didn't get the promotion. As you return to your office, you wonder what you should do. Should you tell Jack that he isn't going to be promoted? What should you say if he asks about whether the new assignments were made?

Seaburst Construction Project

You are the project manager for the Seaburst construction project. So far the project is progressing ahead of schedule and below budget. You attribute this in part to the good working relationship you have with the carpenters, plumbers, electricians, and machine operators who work for your organization. More than once you have asked them to give 110 percent, and they have responded.

One Sunday afternoon you decide to drive by the site and show it to your son. As you point out various parts of the project to your son, you discover that several pieces of valuable equipment are missing from the storage shed. When you start work again on Monday you are about to discuss this matter with a supervisor when you realize that all the missing equipment is back in the shed. What should you do? Why?

The Project Status Report Meeting

You are driving to a project status report meeting with your client. You encountered a significant technical problem on the project that has put your project behind schedule. This is not good news because completion time is the number one priority for the project. You are confident that your team can solve the problem if they are free to give their undivided attention to it and that with hard work you can get back on schedule. You also believe if you tell the client about the problem, she will demand a meeting with your team to discuss the implications of the problem. You can also expect her to send some of her personnel to oversee the solution to the problem. These interruptions will likely further delay the project. What should you tell your client about the current status of the project?

Gold Star LAN project

You work for a large consulting firm and were assigned to the Gold Star LAN project. Work on the project is nearly completed and your clients at Gold Star appear to be pleased with your performance. During the course of the project, changes in the original scope had to be made to accommodate specific needs of managers at Gold Star. The costs of these changes were documented as well as overhead and submitted to the centralized accounting department. They processed the information and submitted a change order bill for your signature. You are surprised to see the bill is 10 percent higher than what you submitted. You contact Jim Messina in the accounting office and ask if a mistake has been made. He curtly replies that no mistake was made and that management adjusted the bill. He recommends that you sign the document. You talk to another project manager about this and she tells you off the record that overcharging clients on change orders is common practice in your firm. Would you sign the document? Why? Why not?

Cape Town Bio-Tech

You are responsible for installing the new Double E production line. Your team has collected estimates and used the WBS to generate a project schedule. You have confidence in the schedule and the work your team has done. You report to top management that you believe that the project will take 110 days and be completed by March 5. The news is greeted positively. In fact, the project sponsor confides that orders do not have to be shipped until April 1. You leave the meeting wondering whether you should share this information with the project team or not.

Ryman Pharmaceuticals

You are a test engineer on the Bridge project at Ryman Pharmaceuticals in Nashville, Tennessee. You have just completed conductivity tests of a new electrochemical compound. The results exceeded expectations. This new compound should revolutionize the industry.

You are wondering whether to call your stockbroker and ask her to buy $20,000 worth of Ryman stock before everyone else finds out about the results. What would you do and why?

Princeton Landing

You are managing the renovation of the Old Princeton Landing Bar and Grill. The project is on schedule despite receiving a late shipment of paint. The paint was supposed to arrive on 1/30, but instead arrived on 2/1. The assistant store manager apologizes profusely for the delay and asks if you would be willing to sign the acceptance form and backdate it to 1/30. He says he won't qualify for a bonus that he has worked hard to meet for the past month if the shipment is reported late. He promises to make it up to you on future projects. What would you do and why?

References

Abrashoff, D. M., *It's Your Ship* (New York: Business Plus, 2002).

Ancona, D. G., and D. Caldwell, "Improving the Performance of New-Product Teams," *Research Technology Management,* 33 (2) March-April 1990, pp. 25–29.

Anand, V., B. E. Ashforth, and M. Joshi, "Business as Usual: The Acceptance and Perpetuation of Corruption in Organizations," *Academy of Management Executive,* 19 (4) 2005, pp. 9–23.

Badaracco, J. L., Jr., and A. P. Webb, "Business Ethics: A View from the Trenches," *California Management Review,* 37 (2) Winter 1995, pp. 8–28.

Baker, B., "Leadership and the Project Manager," *PM Network,* December 2002, p. 20.

Baker, W. E., *Network Smart: How to Build Relationships for Personal and Organizational Success* (New York: McGraw-Hill, 1994).

Bennis, W., *On Becoming a Leader* (Reading, MA: Addison-Wesley, 1989).

Bradberry, T., and J. Graves, *The Emotional Intelligence Quick Book: How to Put Your EQ to Work* (New York: Simon & Schuster, 2005).

Bourne, L., *Stakeholder Relationship Management* (Farnham, England: Gower Publishing Ltd., 2009).

Cabanis, J., "A Question of Ethics: The Issues Project Managers Face and How They Resolve Them," *PM Network,* December 1996, pp. 19–24.

Cabanis-Brewin, J., "The Human Task of a Project Leader: Daniel Goleman on the Value of High EQ," *PM Network,* November 1999, pp. 38–42.

Cohen, A. R., and D. L. Bradford, *Influence Without Authority* (New York: John Wiley & Sons, 1990).

Covey, S. R., *The Seven Habits of Highly Effective People* (New York: Simon & Schuster, 1989).

Dinsmore, P. C., "Will the Real Stakeholders Please Stand Up?" *PM Network,* December 1995, pp. 9–10.

Einsiedel, A. A., "Profile of Effective Project Managers," *Project Management Journal,* 31 (3) 1987, pp. 51–56.

Ferrazzi, K., *Never Eat Alone and Other Secrets to Success One Relationship at a Time* (Crown Publishers, 2005).

Gabarro, S. J., *The Dynamics of Taking Charge* (Boston: Harvard Business School Press, 1987).

Grant, A., *Give and Take: A revolutionary Approach to Success,* (New York: Viking Press, 2013).

Hill, L. A., *Becoming a Manager: Mastery of a New Identity* (Boston: Harvard Business School Press, 1992).

Kanter, R. M., "Power Failures in Management Circuits," *Harvard Business review*, July–August, 1979, pp. 65–79.

Kaplan, R. E., "Trade Routes: The Manager's Network of Relationships," *Organizational Dynamics,* 12 (4) Spring 1984, pp. 37–52.

Kirk, D., "Managing Expectations," *PM Network,* August 2000, pp. 59–62.

Kotter, J. P., "What Leaders Really Do," *Harvard Business Review,* 68 (3) May–June 1990, pp. 103–11.

Kouzes, J. M., and B. Z. Posner, *The Leadership Challenge 5th edt.,* (San Francisco: Jossey-Bass, 2012).

Kouzes, J. M., and B. Z. Posner, *Credibility: How Leaders Gain and Lose It. Why People Demand It* (San Francisco: Jossey-Bass, 1993).

Larson, E. W., and J. B. King, "The Systemic Distortion of Information: An Ongoing Management Challenge," *Organizational Dynamics,* 24 (3) Winter 1996, pp. 49–62.

Lewis, M. W., M. A. Welsh, G. E. Dehler, and S. G. Green, "Product Development Tensions: Exploring Contrasting Styles of Project Management," *Academy of Management Journal,* 45 (3) 2002, pp. 546–64.

Peters, L. H., "A Good Man in a Storm: An Interview with Tom West," *Academy of Management Executive,* 16 (4) 2002, pp. 53–63.

Peters, L. H., "Soulful Ramblings: An Interview with Tracy Kidder," *Academy of Management Executive,* 16 (4) 2002, pp. 45–52.

Peters, T., *Thriving on Chaos: Handbook for a Management Revolution* (New York: Alfred A. Knopf, 1988).

Pinto, J. K., and S. K. Mantel, "The Causes of Project Failure," *IEEE Transactions in Engineering Management,* 37 (4) 1990, pp. 269–76.

Pinto, J. K., and D. P. Sleven, "Critical Success Factors in Successful Project Implementation," *IEEE Transactions in Engineering Management,* 34 (1) 1987, pp. 22–27.

Project Management Institute, *PMBOK Guide 5th edt.,* (Newtown Sq., PA: Project Management Institute, 2013).

Posner, B. Z., "What It Takes to Be an Effective Project Manager," *Project Management Journal,* March 1987, pp. 51–55.

Project Management Institute, *Leadership in Project Management Annual* (Newton Square, PA: PMI Publishing, 2006).

Robb, D. J., "Ethics in Project Management: Issues, Practice, and Motive," *PM Network,* December 1996, pp. 13–18.

Sayles, L. R., *Leadership: Managing in Real Organizations* (New York: McGraw-Hill, 1989), pp. 70–78.

Sayles, L. R., *The Working Leader* (New York: Free Press, 1993).

Senge, P. M., *The Fifth Discipline* (New York: Doubleday, 1990).

Shenhar, A. J., and B. Nofziner, "A New Model for Training Project Managers," *Proceedings of the 28th Annual Project Management Institute Symposium,* 1997, pp. 301–6.

Shtub, A., J. F. Bard, and S. Globerson, *Project Management: Engineering, Technology, and Implementation* (Englewood Cliffs, NJ: Prentice Hall, 1994).

Trevino, L. K., and K. A. Nelson, *Managing Business Ethics: Straight Talk about How to Do It Right,* 5th ed. (Hoboken, NJ: John Wiley & Sons, 2011).

Turner, J. R., and R. Müller, "The Project Manager Leadership Style as a Success Factor on Projects: A Literature Review," *Project Management Journal,* 36 (2) 2005, pp. 49–61.

APPENDIX 10.1

Project Stakeholder Management

1. AN OVERVIEW OF PROJECT STAKEHOLDER MANAGEMENT

Project Stakeholder Management includes processes required:

- To identify the project stakeholders (viz. people, groups or organizations, that could impact or be impacted by the project),
- To analyze their expectations and impact on the project, and
- To develop appropriate management strategies for engaging stakeholders in project decisions and executions.

(PMBOK® Guide, 5th Edition)

This group of project management processes is introduced as a separate project management knowledge area for the first time in the PMBOK® Guide, 5th Edition. For this purpose, the processes 'Identify Stakeholders' and ' Manage Stakeholder Expectations' were moved out from the Project Communications Management knowledge area in PMBOK® Guide, 4th Edition, to this newly created knowledge area in 5th Edition along with some corresponding changes in the name of processes, inputs, tools & techniques, and outputs.

1.1 Importance of Project Stakeholder Management

All successful project managers have always understood the importance of managing key stakeholders. Basically, projects are temporary endeavours to create a product, service or result but in reality key stakeholders are behind originating or proposing the project and supporting it throughout the project life cycle. In case of projects performed for other organization on a contract basis, these key stakeholders may be customer or his representatives and in case of internal projects, the key stakeholders are project sponsors and/or senior management. *Therefore, maintaining effective communications with all stakeholders – key stakeholders as well as stakeholders with peripheral interest and impact – for ensuring their support (or at least negotiating and overcoming the resistance to project objectives) by continuous engagement throughout the project life cycle is one of the very important roles of a project manager.* This is easier said than done; for often, the different stakeholders have different and conflicting interests and expectations. To resolve the issues arising out of this conflicting stakeholder interests and carrying all of them along to support the main project objectives requires on part of the project manager in charge of a major project excellent communications, interpersonal skills, and maturity acquired from successful general management experience.

2. PROJECT STAKEHOLDER MANAGEMENT PROCESSES

PMBOK® Guide, 5th Edition, proposes four processes in this knowledge area:

- Identify Stakeholders (Initiating Process Group)
- Plan Stakeholder Management (Planning Process Group)
- Manage Stakeholder Engagement (Executing Process Group), and
- Control Stakeholder Engagement (Monitoring and Controlling Process Group)

The inputs, tools and techniques, and outputs of each process are briefly described below.

2.1 Identify Stakeholders (Initiating Process Group)

Identify Stakeholders is the process of

- Identifying the people, groups, or organizations that could impact or be impacted by a decision, activity or outcome of the project.
- Analyzing and documenting their interests, involvements, interdependencies, influence and potential impact on project success. (PMBOK® Guide, 5th Edition)

According to the definition, the project stakeholders may be customer(s), project sponsor, project performing organization, project manager and his team, general public, people around the project site impacted by the project activities or outcome, government agencies and regulators, suppliers, and consultants. Of course all stakeholders are not equally important from the viewpoint of their interest, influence or impact on the project success. Mimicking George Orwell, we can say, "All stakeholders are equal, but some are *more equal* than others." The project manager has to be able to identify and analyze these *key stakeholders* and manage engagement with them in a manner, which would support the project success. The Inputs, tools and techniques and outputs are described below.

Inputs

Project Charter – Documents the internal and external parties related to the project, viz., project sponsor(s), customer(s), project manager and key project team members, groups or departments of the performing organization, and other organizations or general public around the project site and government agencies or regulators.

Procurement Documents – Suppliers and contractors for major project work packages may be important stakeholders.

Enterprise Environmental Factors – Particularly the organization structure and organization culture, governmental agencies, industry practices and standards.

Organizational Process Assets – Include lessons learned from similar earlier projects and stakeholders analysis templates.

Tools and Techniques

Expert Judgment – For a major project, the expertise based on earlier similar project execution, maturity and skill in interpersonal relationships are critical in identifying and analyzing key stakeholders.

Stakeholders Analysis – The stakeholders analysis is the principal and very important part of the Identify Stakeholders Process. Generally, it would be a sequence of activities consisting of:

- *Data Collection:* Identifying and listing all stakeholders and noting down the name, organizational affiliation and position, location, role in a project and contact information (postal address, telephone, e-mail ID, etc.)
- *Analysis*: Assess the potential impact, interest and expectations and influence in directing project objectives; based on this, the stakeholders could be classified into key stakeholders and other stakeholders.
- *Assessment for Managing Engagement*: Based on interests and expectations, how these stakeholders would react to individual project objectives, what would be their information needs and planning general strategy for engagement.

Meetings with Key Stakeholders – After identifying and classifying the stakeholders, meetings are often held with them to assess their interest, expectations and general preferences.

Outputs

Stakeholder Register – This is the principal, and single, output from the process. It documents the data collection, analyses data for assessing their importance and impact on the project, and classifies them into key stakeholders and other stakeholders. The sequential steps in stakeholders Analysis activity are formally and systematically recorded in this document. Stakeholder Register is one of the component plans of the Project Management Plan and offers inputs to several other project management processes.

2.2 Plan Stakeholder Management (Planning Process Group)

Plan Stakeholder Management is the process of developing appropriate management strategies to effectively engage stakeholders throughout the project life cycle, based on their needs, interests and potential impact on project success. (PMBOK® Guide, 5th Edition)

This is the next logical step in the process group for this knowledge area. Once the stakeholders are identified and the stakeholder register with analysis (which includes the key stakeholders, their interest and potential impact) is available, project manager considers the available option of engaging them on an individual basis for ensuring their support to the project. This would include communication needs of the key stakeholders for project status (content, the level of details, frequency, issue log, etc.) and the plan for engagement with them, which would set up and maintain a relationship of mutual trust between the stakeholder and project manager and his team.

Inputs

Stakeholder Register – This basic document provides the necessary background details of individual stakeholders and detailed analysis of key stakeholders. It is an important starting input.

Project Management Plan – How the project work is to be done during the entire Project Life Cycle, and how each stakeholder would impact the project progress and different component plans (human resources management plan, scope, time and cost baselines, and *particularly communications management plan*) provide important inputs.

Enterprise Environmental – *Factors* and *Organizational Process Assets* also provide inputs.

Tools and Techniques

Expert Judgment – For a major project, the expertise based on earlier similar project execution, maturity and skill in interpersonal relationships is the only reliable technique.

Meetings with Experts and Stakeholders – This is another input.

Analytical Techniques – The actual engagement level of any specific set of stakeholders and its comparison with the desired level of engagement would help to develop Stakeholder Engagement Assessment Matrix. The engagement levels could be varying from Unaware, Resistant, Neutral, Supportive and Leading Interest. Based on this analysis, engagement strategy could be modified suitably.

Outputs

Stakeholder Management Plan – This is the main output of the process. All information and analysis presented in stakeholders register, and strategy developed from available options are distilled into formulation of this plan. Its contents might include:

- Analysis of current engagement level with stakeholders and its comparison with the planned desired levels.
- Stakeholder communication requirement and setting up communication procedures to meet them.
- Issues raised by key stakeholders, approved change requests resulting from them and the progress on each suggested change.

2.3 Manage Stakeholder Engagement (Executing Process Group)

Manage Stakeholder Engagement is the process of communicating and working with stakeholders to meet their needs and expectations, address issues as they occur, and foster appropriate stakeholder engagement in project activities throughout the project life cycle. (PMBOK® Guide, 5th Edition)

The process is meant for the project manager to proactively increase the support and minimize the resistance to project. Such proactive activities would include:

- managing stakeholders' communication and addressing their concerns,
- resolving issues as they arise during the project life cycle, and
- managing their expectations and interests as far as practicable by resolving the conflicts between the interests and expectations of different stakeholder groups

Inputs

Stakeholder Management Plan – This plan lays down the overall strategy and approach for engaging stakeholders; hence it is logically the first and most important input.

Communications Management Plan – Effective communication is one of the core aspects of engaging stakeholders, and hence, the guidelines and strategies included in the project communications plan is an important input.

Changes Log – The impacts on cost, schedule and scope of the project due to approved changes incorporated in the project should be communicated to the project stakeholders.

Tools and Techniques

Interpersonal Skills (for communications, overcoming resistance and building mutual trust) and *Management Skills* (Ability to influence people, negotiate effectively and facilitate consensus) are the basic tools and techniques.

Outputs

While managing the stakeholders' engagement, two specific outputs would be generated. Both outputs have their roots in proactive activities carried out for effective engagement with the stakeholders:

Issues Log – This log would record the issues, which arise during engagement with the stakeholders and the status/progress in resolving these issues.

Change Requests – It might be necessary to originate and get approval for change requests to address the crucial concerns of the stakeholders.

2.4 Control Stakeholder Engagement (Monitoring and Controlling Process Group)

Control Stakeholder Engagement is the process of monitoring overall project stakeholder relationships and adjusting strategies and plans for engaging stakeholders. (PMBOK® Guide, 5th Edition)

The purpose of this process is to monitor the effectiveness of stakeholder engagement and maintain or increase its effectiveness. Like all monitoring and controlling processes, it works on the principle of feedback loop, which compares the actual performance with the planned or standard for the metric and takes corrective action to put the process back on track. With this perspective, we briefly review the inputs, tools and techniques and the outputs of the process.

Inputs

Project Management Plan (that includes as its component plan, *Project Stakeholder Management,* which is overarching the strategy and approach for all stakeholder management processes) provides the planned performance metrics.

Issue Logs and *Work Performance Data* provide the actual performance results obtained.

Hence these two are the basic inputs for the process. In addition to these three primary inputs, some secondary inputs from other *Project Documents* (Stakeholder Register, Project Schedule, Issue Logs and Change Logs) could be helpful.

Tools and Techniques

Expert Judgment (essentially the same kind of expertise, which is necessary during the execution of stakeholder engagement) and *Project Management Information System* (part of the project communications management tools) complemented by *Project Meetings* are the tools and techniques employed for this process.

Outputs

Work Performance Information (The distilled summaries of various control processes and the trends emerging from them is the content of *Work Performance Information*) This output is circulated through the project communications network to the stakeholders according to their interest and functional needs.

Change Requests – Some changes are originated for addressing the stakeholders' concerns, which surface while interacting during the stakeholder engagement processes; they are incorporated into the project plan through approved change requests.

Updates in Project Management Plan (in essence all project plan components like scope, schedule, cost, risk, quality, and communications management) and *Updates in Project Documents* (Stakeholder Register, Issue Logs, Baselines for scope, schedule and cost, etc.) are secondary outputs of the process.

CASE 10.1

The Blue Sky Project*

Garth Hudson was a 29-year-old graduate of Eastern State University (ESU) with a B.S. degree in management information systems. After graduation he worked for seven years at Bluegrass Systems in Louisville, Kentucky. While at ESU he worked part time for an oceanography professor, Ahmet Green, creating a customized database for a research project he was conducting. Green was recently appointed director of Eastern Oceanography Institute (EOI), and Hudson was confident that this prior experience was instrumental in his getting the job as information services (IS) director at the Institute. Although he took a significant pay cut, he jumped at the opportunity to return to his alma mater. His job at Bluegrass Systems had been very demanding. The long hours and extensive traveling had created tension in his marriage. He was looking forward to a normal job with reasonable hours. Besides, Jenna, his wife, would be busy pursuing her MBA at Eastern State University. While at Bluegrass, Hudson worked on a wide range of IS projects. He was confident that he had the requisite technical expertise to excel at his new job.

Eastern Oceanography Institute was an independently funded research facility aligned with Eastern State University. Approximately 50 full- and part-time staff worked at the Institute. They

---

* Prepared by Erik Larson and V. T. Raja, senior instructor at the College of Business, Oregon State University.

worked on research grants funded by the National Science Foundation (NSF) and the United Nations (UN), as well as research financed by private industry. There were typically 7 to 9 major research projects under way at any one time as well as 20 to 25 smaller projects. One-third of the Institute's scientists had part-time teaching assignments at ESU and used the Institute to conduct their own basic research.

FIRST YEAR AT EOI

Hudson made a point of introducing himself to the various groups of people upon his arrival at the Institute. Still, his contact with the staff had been limited. He spent most of his time becoming familiar with EOI's information system, training his staff, responding to unexpected problems, and working on various projects. Hudson suffered from food allergies and refrained from informal staff lunches at nearby restaurants. He stopped regularly attending the biweekly staff meetings in order to devote more time to his work. He now only attended the meetings when there was a specific agenda item regarding his operation.

The IS staff at EOI consisted of two full-time assistants, Tom Jackson and Grant Hill. They were supported by five part-time student assistants from the computer science department. Grant Hill was assigned full-time to a large five-year NSF grant aimed at creating a virtual library of oceanographic research. Hill worked out of the project leader's office and had very little interaction with Hudson or Jackson. Hudson's relationship with Jackson was awkward from the start. He found out, after the fact, that Jackson thought he would get the job as director. They never talked about it, but he sensed tension the first couple of months on the job. One of the problems was that he and Jackson were totally different personalities. Jackson was gregarious and very talkative. He had a habit of after lunch walking around the Institute talking to different scientists and researchers. Often this would lead to useful information. Hudson, on the other hand, preferred to stay in his office working on various assignments and ventured out only when called upon. While Hudson felt Jackson was not on top of the latest developments as he was, he respected Jackson's work.

Last month the system was corrupted by a virus introduced over the Internet. Hudson devoted an entire weekend to restoring the system to operation. A recurring headache was one of the servers, code-named "Poncho," that would occasionally shut down for no apparent reason. Instead of replacing it, he decided to nurse Poncho along until it could be replaced. His work was frequently interrupted by frantic calls from staff researchers who needed immediate help on a variety of computer-related problems. He was shocked at how computer illiterate some of the researchers were and how he had to guide them through some of the basics of e-mail management and database configuration. He did find time to help Assistant Professor Amanda Johnson on a project. Johnson was the only researcher to respond to Hudson's e-mail announcing that the IS staff was available to help on projects. Hudson created a virtual project office on the Internet so that Johnson could collaborate with colleagues from institutes in Italy and Thailand on a UN research grant. He looked forward to the day when he could spend more time on fun projects like that.

THE BLUE SKY CONVERSION PROJECT

The "Blue Sky" conversion project began in earnest four month ago. Ahmet Green returned from Washington, D.C., with grim news. The economic downturn was going to lead to a dramatic reduction in funding. He anticipated as much as a 25% reduction in annual budget over the next three to five years. This would lead to staff reductions and cutting operating costs. One cost-cutting measure was moving IT operations to the "cloud." Green had first proposed the idea to Hudson after attending a meeting with several directors of other institutes who faced similar financial challenges.

The basic strategy was to move all of the Institute's databases, software, and even hardware to a "private cloud." Staff would use their current PCs to simply access more powerful machines over the Internet. These powerful machines could be partitioned and configured differently as per the needs of research staff, giving each staff their own virtual machine (VM). Staff could also access, use, and share virtual servers over the Internet as needed. Hudson worked with the Institute's accountant on a cost/benefit analysis. From their standpoint it made perfect sense. First, the Institute would not have to replace or upgrade aging computers and servers. Second, the Institute would enjoy significant IT savings since they would pay for only IT resources actually used. They would not have to make any major IT capital expenditures. Third, cloud computing would provide scientists greater flexibility by accessing desired resources or software from anywhere at any time. And finally, once the system was up and running, the Institute would no longer need the services of at least one full-time IT worker. Green decided to name the project "Blue Sky" to put a positive spin on the conversion.

At first the associate directors balked at the idea. Some had a hard time conceptualizing what cloud computing meant. Others were worried about security and reliability. In the end they reluctantly signed off on the project when given alternative cost cutting initiatives. Hudson assured them that cloud computing was the wave of the future and setting-up or accessing virtual machines on the "cloud" was as simple as setting up or accessing their g-mail account.

The conversion project would be completed in stages. The first stage was selecting a provider. The next stage was migrating non–mission critical information to the cloud. The next stages would entail migrating each of the six big grant projects in waves to the cloud. The final stage would focus on the remaining smaller projects. Training would be an integral part of each stage. The Institute would maintain a back-up for all the data until 6 months after complete conversion. After that the cloud service provider would be responsible for backing up the data.

At first Jackson was excited about the project. He was savvy enough to realize that this was the future of computing and he was intrigued with how the whole system would work. His feelings soon changed when he started thinking about the potential ramifications for his job. He asked Hudson more than once what the department would look like after the conversion. Hudson replied vaguely that they would figure it out once the system was up and running.

A task force was formed, headed by Hudson, to select a cloud service provider. Hudson was surprised by how many choices there were. Plans and cost structures varied considerably. After much deliberation the committee narrowed the choices to three. The first two were among the bigger providers in the industry, VMWARE and Microsoft. The third choice was a relatively new company, OpenRange, which offered a cheaper solution. Jackson argued that even though the bigger providers would cost more, they were a much safer bet. Hudson responded that he had confidence in OpenRange and cutting costs was the primary goal behind the project. In the end, Hudson persuaded the committee to choose OpenRange. Not only would cost be significantly cheaper, but OpenRange would help in the training of the personnel. Hudson liked this idea; training was not his strength, and he wasn't looking forward to holding senior scientists' hands through the process.

It took Hudson and Jackson six weeks to identify non-critical data. Hudson worked on the back end while Jackson met with staff to identify non-critical information. The motto was when in doubt, leave it out. The actual migration only took a couple of days. Training proved to be more problematic. The staff sent by OpenRange appeared to be straight out of college. While enthusiastic, they were inexperienced in the art of getting older staff to accept and use new technology. Many trainers had the habit of simply doing things for the staff instead of showing them how to do it themselves. It all came to a head when a power outage at the OpenRange storage system shut down and disrupted operations at the Institute for 36 hours.

Ahmet held an emergency meeting. Hudson reported that the power outage occurred in North East India and that OpenRange was expanding their back-up systems. Several members argued that the Institute should switch to one of the bigger providers. When this came up Hudson looked at Jackson and was relieved when he remained silent. In the end, Ahmet announced that it would be too costly to switch providers and Hudson and his staff would have to make the conversion work. Jackson stepped forward and volunteered to manage the training. Everyone agreed that the Institute should hire 3 more part-time assistants to help the staff with the transition.

Hudson worked behind the scenes, coordinating with his counterparts at OpenRange and planning the conversion of the next segment of the project. Jackson worked closely with the OpenRange trainers and refocused their attention on teaching. Resistance was pretty high at first. Jackson used his personal contacts within the Institute to rally support for the change. He persuaded Hudson to change the conversion schedule to begin with those projects in which the leads were most supportive of the change. Training improved and Jackson created some useful training materials, including short videos on how to access the virtual machines.

One problem that occurred early in the process involved a graduate research assistant who mistakenly hit the wrong commands and terminated her virtual machine instead of logging off. This resulted in complete loss of that machine's data in the cloud. Fortunately, the Institute still had back-up and Jackson was able recover the work. Collaborating with some programmers at OpenRange, Jackson wrote a program that triggered a pop-up message on the screen warning users not to terminate their virtual machine when logging off.

CLOSING OUT THE BLUE SKY PROJECT

It took almost a year to complete the Blue Sky project. After the rocky beginning things went relatively smoothly. Acceptance was slow, but Jackson and his staff worked with the staff to demonstrate how the new system would make their work easier. Two student assistants were always on call to address any problem or question. Hudson spent most of his time interacting with the OpenRange counterparts and rarely ventured out of his office. He had his student assistants collect information from staff so he could configure the new virtual machines to exactly match staff needs. He put in long hours so that customized databases would work in the new environment. This proved to be a very difficult task and he was quite pleased with his work. Twice OpenRange experienced momentary power shortages at their server facility which disrupted work at the Institute. Hudson was happy to report that OpenRange was breaking ground on an alternative server system in Ukraine.

When the Institute conducted a retrospective (project review) on the Blue Sky project, some still questioned the choice of OpenRange as a cloud service provider, but praised Jackson's work on helping the staff make the transition. Despite the criticism over the choice of OpenRange, Hudson felt good about the project. The system was up and running and the staff was beginning to enjoy the flexibility it provided. Besides, the Institute would achieve real savings from the new system.

Soon after the retrospective, Hudson was surprised when Ahmet walked into his office and closed the door. Ahmet began by thanking Hudson for his work on the project. He then cleared his throat and said, "You know, Garth, one of the consequences of Blue Sky is reducing our IT staff. Grant Hill is needed for the data library project. So it comes down to you or Jackson. Frankly there is general agreement among the Associate Directors that Jackson is essential to the Institute. I know this might come as a surprise to you, and before I make a decision I want to give you a chance to change my mind."

1. If you were Hudson, how would you respond to the director?
2. What mistakes did Hudson make?
3. What are the lessons to be learned from this case?

CASE 10.2

Tom Bray

Tom Bray was mulling over today's work schedule as he looked across the bay at the storm that was rolling in. It was the second official day of the Pegasus project and now the real work was about to begin.

Pegasus was a two-month renovation project for AtlantiCorp, a major financial institution headquartered in Boston, Massachusetts. Tom's group was responsible for installing the furniture and equipment in the newly renovated accounts receivable department on the third floor. The Pegasus project was a dedicated project team formed out of AtlantiCorp facilities department with Tom as the project lead.

Tom was excited because this was his first *major league* project and he was looking forward to practicing a new management style—MBWA, aka management by wandering around. He had been exposed to MBWA in a business class in college, but it wasn't until he attended an AtlantiCorp leadership training seminar that he decided to change how he managed people. The trainer was devout MBWA champion ("You can't manage people from a computer!"). Furthermore, the testimonies from his peers reinforced the difference that MBWA can make when it comes to working on projects.

Tom had joined the facilities group at AtlantiCorp five years earlier after working for EDS for six years. He quickly demonstrated technical competences and good work habits. He was encouraged to take all the internal project management workshops offered by AtlantiCorp. On his last two projects he served as assistant project manager responsible for procurement and contract management.

He had read books about the soft side of project management and MBWA made sense—after all, people not tools get projects done. His boss had told him he needed to refine his people skills and work on developing rapport with team members. MBWA seemed like a perfect solution.

Tom reviewed the list of team member names; some of the foreign names were real tongue twisters. For example, one of his better workers was from Thailand and her name was Pinyarat Sirisomboonsuk. He practiced saying "Pin-ya-răt See-rē-som-boon-sook." He got up, tucked in his shirt, and walked out of his office and down to the floor where his team was busy unloading equipment.

Tom said "Hi" to the first few workers he met until he encountered Jack and three other workers. Jack was busy pulling hardware out of a box while his teammates were standing around talking. Tom blurted, "Come on guys, we've got work to do." They quickly separated and began unloading boxes.

The rest of the visit seemed to go well. He helped Shari unload a heavy box and managed to get an appreciative grin from Pinyarat when he almost correctly pronounced her name. Satisfied, Tom went back up to his office thinking that MBWA wouldn't be that tough to do.

After responding to e-mail and calling some vendors, Tom ventured back out to see how things were going downstairs. When he got there, the floor was weirdly quiet. People were busy doing their work and his attempts at generating conversation elicited stiff responses. He left thinking that maybe MBWA is going to be tougher than he thought.

1. What do you think is going on at the end of this case?
2. What should Tom do next and why?
3. What can be learned from this case?

CASE 10.3

Cerberus Corporation*

Cerberus is a successful producer of specialty chemicals. It operates nine large campus sites in the United States, with a number of different business units on each site. These business units operate independently, with direct reporting to corporate headquarters. Site functions such as safety, environmental, and facilities management report to a host organization—typically the business unit that is the largest user of their services.

SUSAN STEELE

Susan Steele has worked in the Facilities group at the Cerberus Richmond site for the last two years. The Facilities manager, Tom Stern, reports to the General Manager of the largest business unit on site, the highly profitable Adhesives and Sealants Division. Susan started with Cerberus when she graduated with her business degree from Awsum University. She was excited about her new assignment—leading a project for the first time. She remembered Tom saying, "We've got office furniture dating back to the 80s. There are those ugly green-top desks that look like they came from military surplus! I'm especially concerned about computer workstation ergonomics— it's a major issue that we absolutely must fix! I want you to lead a project to transition our office furniture to the new corporate standard."

Susan assembled her project team: Jeff, the site safety/ergonomics engineer; Gretchen, the space planner; Cindy, the move coordinator; and Kari, the accounting liaison for Facilities. At their first meeting, everyone agreed that ergonomics was the most urgent concern. All five business units responded to a workstation survey that identified injury-causing ergonomics. The team was developing a plan to replace old desks with new, ergo-adjustable furniture by the end of the year.

* Courtesy of John Sloan, Oregon State University.

Susan asked Kari about the budget, and Kari responded, "Facilities should not pay for this. We want the individual business units to pay so that the costs will show where they are incurred."

Gretchen spoke up: "You know, we've got lots of department moves going on constantly. Everybody is always jockeying for space and location as their business needs change. Besides the ergonomics, could we say that only corporate standard furniture gets moved? That would force changing some of the stuff that's just plain ugly." Everyone agreed that this was a great idea.

Susan presented the project plan to Tom and got a green light to proceed.

JON WOOD

Jon Wood is a planning manager, with 22 years experience at Cerberus. His business unit, Photographic Chemicals Division (PCD), is losing money. Digital photography is continuing to reduce the size of the market, and PCD is having trouble matching the competition's relentless price-cutting. Jon recently transferred to Richmond from corporate headquarters, where he ran the economic forecasting group. He is considered a new broom, and he is determined to sweep clean.

One of Jon's early actions was to negotiate with his general manager for a department move. Money was tight, and the site facilities function charged an arm and a leg for moves (covering all their fixed overhead, the operations people groused). However, Jon felt it was important to move from Building 4, where they were next to Production, to Building 6, where they could be close to Marketing, Forecasting, and Accounting. His General Manager agreed, and there was lots of excitement in his team about their upcoming move. Jon assigned one of his planners, Richard, to work with the Facilities team on the layout and move plan for the group. Things seemed to be going fine—Jon saw Richard sitting down with the move coordinator, and they seemed to be on track.

The day before the move, Jon hung up the phone from a particularly tense teleconference with a Canadian subcontractor. Production was not going well, and product availability would be tight for the rest of the quarter. Clustered around his desk were Richard, Cindy, and a person he hadn't met yet, Susan. After hurried introductions, Susan told Jon that his filing cabinets could not be moved. The cabinets are large lateral files, five feet wide and two feet deep, a combination of both filing cabinets and bookshelves. Jon brought them with him from Corporate because he thought they looked nice with their dark grey steel sides and wood veneer tops. Susan told him that he would have to replace them with new corporate standard cabinets, virtually the same size. Jon said, "You mean you want me to throw away perfectly good filing cabinets and spend another $2,000 on new ones, just so they match? I won't do it!"

Susan replied, "Then I won't authorize the movement of the old cabinets."

Jon said, "You're joking—these cabinets are grey, the new ones are grey—the only difference is the wood top! You'd throw away $2,000 for nothing?"

Susan replied stiffly, "I'm sorry, that's the policy."

Jon said, "I don't care what the policy is. If I have to move them myself, those cabinets are not going to the dump. My division is losing money and I'm not going to throw money away. If you don't like it, you're going to have to get your general manager to convince my general manager to make me do it. Now would you please leave so I can get some work done."

1. If you were Susan, what would you do?
2. What, if anything, could Susan have done differently to avoid this problem?
3. What could the management of Cerberus do to more effectively manage situations like this?

CASE 10.4

Temples and Towers
(Case Illustrating Stakeholders Management)

Abstract

While authorizing projects, the organizations commit their resources to achieve the objectives reflecting the business leader's vision or strategic policy. Though, the need may be clearly felt, sometimes, its articulation may not be precise enough for its translation into project scope and key deliverables. For true project success, the project manager must start with understanding the real needs, refining them for optimal solution and incorporating them into technical and performance specifications. At this stage of formulating and defining the scope, the effective project manager needs to give due consideration to managing the key project stakeholders, and particularly, the conceptual requirements of the project originator and project champions. The case study focuses on this aspect of scope management.

CASE TEXT

It was a rather late Friday evening and Rajani Shah was just collecting his briefcase to start for home, when Kapasi rushed into his cabin almost breathless. "Sir, we have to send these drawings by courier service to Prachi Chemicals today for final approval and then ask Bhuva to visit the site and discuss with the contractor on Tuesday. You need to put in the final approval signature on the tracing for getting the prints to be dispatched." Kapasi completed in a hurry and lowered himself in the chair – almost half-ready to get up and leave as soon as this formality of approval signature would be over.

Rajani was the Chief Engineer of the Indian Projects Consultants, a medium-size project consultancy company specializing in detailed engineering and project construction for industrial projects. He had joined this organization only six months back and with his background of a long career in a much more open and participative type of organizational structure, he personally strongly disapproved rigid hierarchy and old-fashioned procedures – one of which required the Chief Engineer to sign approval on every drawing to be finally released for construction.

Rajani was visibly annoyed and just casually shot a question without looking up while reaching out for a pencil and getting ready to sign the tracing of the drawing, "It is about that temple construction in the industrial complex, right? Then, why this unseemly hurry to send the drawings before weekend and sending Bhuva for a site visit immediately?" Then as Rajani shot a rapid glance at the tracing, he realized it to be a drawing of a large steel tower structure. Rajani looked up and asked. "Why do they want this power transmission tower at the temple site?"

"Sir, Chairman Nayana Devi wants to inaugurate the temple on Mahashivaratri Day and there is only 6-week time in-between for us to get this tower up. You know how particular she is about these temples projects that's why this hurry. And to answer your other question: this drawing is not of a power transmission tower; it is the support for the lightning protection rod to be erected on its top."

Kapasi's reply shook Rajani like a thunderbolt itself!

"What? This 120-feet tall tower just to support the lightning arrestor? Is there no other suitable tall structure nearby?"

"No, sir. This temple site is half a kilometer away from all the industrial plant structures. During our first project meeting, in fact, we had a brief meeting with Nayana Devi and I personally showed her a sketch of a small steel lightning protection rod to be installed on the side of the temple dome, and the routing plan for the usual 40 mm x 6 mm steel earthing strip. But she just flared up and told me," Mr. Kapasi, get this straight. We could very well have done ourselves installation of a lightning conductor and the steel-earthing strip. We want you to come up with an innovative technical solution and install a proper lightning arrestor to protect my temples. I can't allow this steel lightning protector and steel plate earthing connection anywhere inside the temple surrounding. Do you know, I have got the entire temple grounds dug up and the soil sifted through magnetic screens to remove even a trace of a steel nail or stray iron? I have been told that presence of even a small piece of iron in this temple premises is a very bad omen indeed. And you come up with such proposals of hundreds of kilograms of steel lightning rods and steel earthing strip?"

After a pause, Kapasi added, "Technically, silver, copper or gold would be acceptable materials as earthing connection materials, though very costly, and Nayana Devi probably would not mind these materials inside the complex, but there is another problem. She does not want any electrical conductor seen outside the temple's marble sculptures. So, we have no option except constructing a steel tower outside and that's what we are proposing as an alternative here. The tower would be just outside the temple area and of adequate height to extend the protection from lightning to the temple structures. According to the code of practice for lightning conductors and its installation published by the Indian Standards Bureau, Specification No. IS-2309, the 45 degrees cone of protection from the tip of the lightning arrestor should cover the temple domes and our drawing accomplishes this by .... "

"Wait, Kapasi, wait; you are going too fast." Rajani interrupted the communication express train of Kapasi and asked, "Your solution may be technically sound, and may be also economical. But is it in harmony with the vision of the whole project? Can't we think of anything better than this grotesque looking steel tower near the beautifully carved marble temples? People tell me, that when they will be complete, they will be probably the most beautiful temples in the hundred miles vicinity. Your steel towers would spoil the entire show! Surely, we have to make one more try to think of something out of the box." Then he added, as an afterthought, "Nayana Devi had asked me to visit the site on two other occasions. They say these temples are beautiful. And not too far is the famous Mandu fort – Rani Rupamati and Baj Bahadur story about Mandu fort, you must have read about in your school days. We could also take a look at it the next afternoon. Why not you and I personally go there for a visit next weekend? "

Kapasi saw the twinkle in Rajani's eyes and he did not hesitate for a second to welcome the proposal. Not that he expected any miraculous technical solution to emerge from the visit, but at least his head would not be now on the block, if the client is somehow unhappy with the design and progress in construction.

The airline announced a delay of 2 hours for the flight to Indore, when Rajani and Kapasi reached the airport the next weekend. Kapasi and Rajani sat waiting in the cafeteria over a cup of coffee,

"So, how is your Executive MBA program coming up?" Rajani asked. Kapasi had enrolled for a part-time evening classes program for an Executive MBA degree.

"It is going on well–still two more terms to go. The last contact sessions were for my elective of Project Management" Kapasi replied.

"Oh, come on. You don't need to learn anything from the schools for project management; you can very well teach all they may want to learn" Rajani smiled and remarked.

"Yes, that is almost true but now and then I do get some new angle on the approach or new insight into the procedure routinely followed without much thought. It is like this. We may be incanting some mantra in a religious ceremony for years and when some one knowing Sanskrit explains the full meaning, we kind of get a new insight into the entire ceremonial rite."

"So, tell me if you learnt any new meaning of your project management practice Mantras", Rajani continued with his light-hearted ribbing.

"For one thing, in scope management, we have good control procedures to prevent unintended project scope creep – the Change Request Form to be filled by the client, working out at our end the changes in Work Breakdown Structure (WBS) and project network associated with the proposed change request; their cost and time impacts and finally the client's authorization signature of accepting the cost and time impacts on the project, etc. Honestly, they looked to me like a boring chore earlier; now they have assumed new importance for me. All these are very helpful in preventing the scope creep and getting paid well if scope changes do occur.

On the other hand, we often do not question to what extent the original scope of project would meet the client's needs. The book says that at the start of the project planning, a comprehensive review of the main stakeholders' needs should be done. Not only that, the project team should also endeavor to optimize the process of refinement of these ambiguously expressed needs into precise project requirements and technical specifications. I understand that major software companies do adopt this practice – the first part of the software project being to collect and analyze the client's requirements. I believe that we should also adopt this practice and start doing something on this line. When this is missed out, the project sponsor or a key stakeholder is sometimes likely to express dissatisfaction halfway through the project."

Then after a short pause he added, "We also learnt an integrated approach to project cost and schedule control using the Earned Value Management technique, supposed to be one of the newest effective techniques for project cost control, and …."

The conversation suddenly ended as the announcement for the flight came over the public address system and they started towards the departure gate.

Rajani and Kapasi reached the site of Prachi Chemicals in the early part of morning. Nayana Devi used to spend the afternoon at the plant office and an appointment was taken for meeting her in the afternoon. It was Rajani's first visit to the site. They met the Works Manager there, who accompanied them through a short tour of the plant. It was a well laid out plant, maintained well and with a standard of cleanliness much higher than in similar chemicals production plants. He also introduced them to Bhagavan Lal, the architect-cum-site engineer in charge of the temple project. Bhagavan Lal led Rajani and Kapasi to the temple area.

A little away from the plant complex, they could see the temples from a distance. Though it was a common enclosure, the temples were set apart with a small separate compound around them. The area around the temples was covered with flowerbeds, with suitably spaced Champa trees with their beautiful white flowers and leaves clusters forming canopies. Indeed a lovingly planned beautiful landscape was developed around. Though the work was far from complete, the promise was great. The temple group was constructed on a raised platform, with the frieze of the platform sides having the carvings of 108 marble sculptured trees appearing as if they held up the platform. The construction of four temples appeared to be in almost the last completion stages; the front pillars and ornamental arch for the fifth one were being sculpted. About 12 carvers, sitting under the shade of the trees, were patiently absorbed in their work. When Rajani, Kapasi and Bhagavan Lal approached them, the head sculptor got up and came to them. Rajani asked him about his native place and where he learnt this art and so on. The head sculptor was a bit hesitant in talking in the beginning, but soon he felt easy after some light conversation and started opening up.

"And how do you make such huge sculptures? If there were just one wrong hammer blow, the marble would chip. All your days of work would come to a naught." Rajani wondered. He repeated for emphasis, "Just a single wrong blow and waste of days of painstakingly created art!"

"It is indeed a great risk," replied the sculptor and then after a pause he added, "But let me ask you, do these pillar and arch carvings look to you like single piece structures?"

"But of course, are they not?" asked Rajani.

"No, they are not", replied the head sculptor with the natural pride of an artisan, "Come here, look closely. You see this hairline crack?"

"Where is the crack?" Kapasi and Rajani exclaimed.

"Right here." sculptor pointed out and added, "It is not really a crack. It is a joint. We sculpt these pillars and arches in pieces and then join them. The interface must be so clean that you should not be able to spot it even if you watch very closely. That is the art; it is the hard part; and we learn it from years of learning it at the feet of our fathers."

Rajani and Kapasi were awestruck with the finish and beauty of the joint and the carving.

Rajani remembered his visit to Belur and Halebid temples. Looking the beauty of these fresh sculptures, he wondered, how heavenly the sight must have been when they were first created! They closely watched the pillars and figurines carved on those statuettes for a few minutes. Then suddenly an idea flashed through Rajani's mind and he asked the head sculptor, " Do you mean to say that you could actually join these sculpted stones so cleanly that you could hide something behind the exposed face and no body can spot it?"

"Not, if it is not bigger than this – all along the length" the sculptor showed about an inch wide slot size.

Rajani's mind was racing now. He turned to Kapasi and asked, "Would not a 3/8 inches diameter silver wire serve as an adequate connection from the lightning protector? What does your Indian Standard so and so specify for silver conductors? "

"Surely, you are joking! I have not checked, but from my electrical engineering knowledge and experience, I am almost sure that it should suffice. At the guesthouse, I will check out using the Indian Bureau's Standard IS 2309 and run some conductivity calculations. But you do realize that it would cost a small fortune!"

Bhagavan Lal, Rajani and Kapasi reached Nayana Devi's office 15 minutes before the appointment – Bhagavan Lal pestered them to make sure that they did! It was a very simple office for a chairman of a prosperous company like Prachi Chemicals. Except for two beautiful calligraphies showing shlokas of Bhagvad Geeta and a large portrait of the company's founder (Nayana Devi's father), the walls were starkly blank. Rajani was absorbed in thinking what inner drives propel these industrialists for such single-minded commitment and devotion to work to build grand enterprises, when Nayana Devi's secretary came and woke him up from his daydream, "Nayana Devi would see you now."

Nayana Devi sat behind a large uncluttered desk. Dressed very simply in off-white clothes and yet she had an impressive presence. She welcomed the visitors and asked if their travel and guesthouse arrangements were comfortable. Then she asked a few questions about the progress of other on-going projects in the plant and finally came to the subject nearer to her heart. "Mr. Shah, I am told you spent a good part of the morning at the temples. How did you find our temples? We want to inaugurate them for worship on Mahashivaratri day. How did you find the progress? Last week, Mr. Kapasi was to send some scheme and drawings for lightning protection. I suppose you have brought them with you?"

"Nayana Devi, some people who visited these temples had admired the way the temples are designed and coming up. Frankly, one of the uppermost thoughts in my mind was not to visit just the chemicals plant but to see these temples also. They are indeed beautiful."

"I am glad that you think so. I try to give it as much personal attention as I can. Everyday afternoon, after I finish my work here, I visit the temples in the company of Bhagavanbhai and see for myself how things are going."

"In fact, the reason we did not send the lightning protection scheme drawings last week was that it occurred to me that the tower supporting the lightning conductor would look very incongruent in this environment. We like it or not, but anyone, who would come to visit the temples, would first notice these tall ugly towers in the background, and then the temples. So, we decided to take a fresh look at the problem." Rajani responded.

"I was also concerned about those steel towers, but then what else can we do? I don't want the temples to get damaged by lightning – and in this region, the thunderstorms are quite frequent. Also, I just cannot allow the steel structure within the temples area and they tell me that the top of the lightning protection must be high enough if the tower is located outside the temple area. So they have to be tall. Have you got any different ideas for lightning protection now after looking at the site today?"

"Well, just while talking with the sculptors and visiting the temple site, an idea has struck me. Kapasi here tells me that it is technically acceptable but it would cost almost 60 % more than the steel tower outside the temple area."

"Just that much more? The beauty of the temples is my first concern, Mr. Shah. Do you have any idea how much money – most of it my own personal money – is spent for constructing these temples? If you can suggest something aesthetically more pleasing and yet effective in protecting the temples, the cost is just of no consequence to me."

"I thought of using a silver connecting wire to be used as an earthing conductor and connected to the arrestor – both of them located right inside the temple area – in fact the pointed top of the arrestor would be a part of the flag flying atop the temple!" Rajani explained his proposal.

Nayana Devi and Bhagavan Lal, both were amazed by such unusual suggestion. After a silence of over a minute, Nayana Devi asked, "What will be the size of silver wire? Would it show over the marble carvings? I just cannot allow any wire over the marble carvings- even if it were a silver wire."

"Well our first calculations suggest that it would be of 3/8th inch in diameter, "Rajani explained, "Say about the size of my finger", and then added smilingly, "rather your finger, Madam. The head sculptor at the temple assured me that he can hide the silver wire of this size threading behind the carvings face so that it would not be visible at all from outside"

Nayana Devi looked inquiringly at Bhagavan Lal. He replied, "Yes Madam. Vireshvar explained Mr. Shah the method of sculpture jointing they use and it would be possible for his team to thread the earthing connection through the center of the pillar. The lightning arrestor can be on the top of the temple dome and, as Mr. Shah suggested, it would also not be conspicuous, as we can use it by wrapping around it the saffron flag on top of the temple."

This lightning protection and tall ugly towers had bothered Nayana Devi for the last few weeks and this neat solution pleased her immensely. A deep relief visbly appeared on her face, as she heard Bhagavan Lal confirming the technical feasibility of the solution.

"Well then, it is all settled", Nayana Devi was prompt in making the decision, "Mr. Shah, please work out the full details and send these to us as soon as you can. You know our Mahashivaratri deadline for inauguration."

"Refining the project sponsor's real needs into optimal solutions for developing technical specifications for project scope" Kapasi began to whisper to himself. Nayana Devi saw his lip movement and felt that he was trying to say something. "Yes, Mr. Kapasi, you wanted to add anything?"

"No Madam, we will work out the scheme and send it to you by the next week end."

Questions for Discussion

1. The 5th Edition of PMBOK® Guide has introduced a new project management knowledge area: Project Stakeholders Management. Discuss the importance of the focus on stakeholders management for ensuring that the project scope is properly aligned to the stakeholders' real needs – even unspoken or ambiguously expressed needs. In what industry or applications, this need to check and recheck the real needs of the client while planning the project is particularly more important?

2. In general, what are the key issues in project stakeholders management and how are they addressed in the policies and procedures used in your organization.

11

MANAGING PROJECT TEAMS

Coming together is a beginning. Keeping together is progress. Working together is success.

—Henry Ford

The magic and power of teams is captured in the term "synergy," which is derived from the Greek word *sunergos:* "working together." There is positive and negative synergy. The essence of positive **synergy** can be found in the phrase "The whole is greater than the sum of the parts." Conversely, negative synergy occurs when the whole is less than the sum of the parts. Mathematically, these two states can be symbolized by the following equations:

$$\text{Positive Synergy } 1 + 1 + 1 + 1 + 1 = 10$$
$$\text{Negative Synergy } 1 + 1 + 1 + 1 + 1 = 2 \text{ (or even } -2)$$

Synergy perhaps can best be seen on a basketball court, a soccer pitch, or a football field where teammates play as one to defeat a superior foe (see Snapshot from Practice: The 2008 Olympic Redeem Team). Although less visible than in team sports, positive and negative synergy can also be observed and felt in the daily operations of project teams. Here is a description from one team member we interviewed:

> Instead of operating as one big team we fractionalized into a series of subgroups. The marketing people stuck together as well as the systems guys. A lot of time was wasted gossiping and complaining about each other. When the project started slipping behind schedule, everyone started covering their tracks and trying to pass the blame on to others. After a while we avoided direct conversation and resorted to e-mail. Management finally pulled the plug and brought in another team to salvage the project. It was one of the worst project management experiences in my life.

This same individual fortunately was also able to recount a more positive experience:

> There was a contagious excitement within the team. Sure we had our share of problems and setbacks, but we dealt with them straight on and, at times, were able to do the impossible. We all cared about the project and looked out for each other. At the same time we challenged each other to do better. It was one of the most exciting times in my life.

The following is a set of characteristics commonly associated with high-performing teams that exhibit **positive synergy:**[1]

1. The team shares a sense of common purpose, and each member is willing to work toward achieving project objectives.
2. The team identifies individual talents and expertise and uses them, depending on the project's needs at any given time. At these times, the team willingly accepts the influence and leadership of the members whose skills are relevant to the immediate task.
3. Roles are balanced and shared to facilitate both the accomplishment of tasks and feelings of group cohesion and morale.
4. The team exerts energy toward problem solving rather than allowing itself to be drained by interpersonal issues or competitive struggles.
5. Differences of opinion are encouraged and freely expressed.
6. To encourage risk taking and creativity, mistakes are treated as opportunities for learning rather than reasons for punishment.
7. Members set high personal standards of performance and encourage each other to realize the objectives of the project.
8. Members identify with the team and consider it an important source of both professional and personal growth.

---

[1] See E. H. Schein, *Process Consultation*, 2nd ed. (Reading, MA: Addison-Wesley, 1988), pp. 42–43; and R. Likert, *New Patterns of Management* (New York: McGraw-Hill, 1961), pp. 162–77.

In the 2004 Olympics in Athens, twelve years after Magic Johnson and Michael Jordon led the U.S. Dream Team to Olympic gold in Barcelona, the U.S. Basketball Team composed of NBA stars lost not once but three times to international competition. For the first time in Olympic history the U.S. settled for a bronze medal in men's basketball. Basketball was no longer America's game.

An autopsy of the debacle in Athens turned up a severe case of negative synergy. The causes were many. The team featured only three holdovers from the group that had qualified the previous summer. Seven of the original invitees withdrew. In the end some 14 players turned down Uncle Sam, invoking excuses from family obligations to nagging injuries to the security situation in Greece. As a result, coach Larry Brown took charge of a team with an average age of 23 years, and it showed. Behind the scenes, problems of dress and punctuality festered and on the eve of the games Brown wanted to send several players home. The million dollar players were overconfident,

AP Photo/Dusan Vranic

and assumed that their individual brilliance would prevail. An over reliance on one-on-one basketball and poor team defense doomed them as they lost games to Puerto Rico, Lithuania, and Argentina.

Enter Jerry Colangelo, 68, former coach, player, and president of the Phoenix Suns. "The way they conducted themselves left a lot to be desired," he says of the 2004 team. "Watching and listening to how people reacted to our players, I knew we'd hit bottom." Colangelo told NBA commissioner David Stern that he would only assume duties as managing director if he was given complete control. As a measure of how abysmal the situation was, he immediately got what he asked for.

In 2005 Colangelo met face-to-face with every prospective national player, to hear in their own words why they wanted to represent their country. The few good men to set things right wouldn't be paid or guaranteed playing time, much less a starting spot. A key recruit was superstar LeBron James who had been tagged "LeBronze" after his performance on the disappointing 2004 team. Colangelo says, "I got buy-in. Halfway through my talk with him, LeBron said, I'm in." Kobe Bryant soon followed and all but two of the 30 top NBA stars turned Colangelo down.

Mike Kryzewski, the college coach at Duke, was hired with one project objective in mind—win the gold medal. To do so he had to change the attitude of team USA. They had to subordinate their superstar egos and buy-in to the concept of team ball. A blessing in disguise was being knocked out of the 2006 world championship by a Greek team. The players came away from that disappointment committed to team ball as extra passes became the staple in practices. The change in attitude was evident in more subtle ways. The USA on the uniforms was bright red, while the players' names were muted blue. The players no longer referred to hoops as "our game" and spoke about how it had become the world's game. Even the team's official slogan (United we rise) and unofficial nickname (the Redeem Team) implied room for improvement.

The team bought into a common objective. Team USA marched to the final gold medal game by beating opponents by an average margin of 30+ points. Experts marveled not so much by the victory margin, but by how well they played as a team. "Our goal is to win a gold medal and be humble about it," says Jason Kidd, six time all-pro point guard, "and if we do it by 50, to make sure it's because we're playing the right way." Nothing exemplified the right way more than a moment in the final, in which flawless ball movement from the Redeemers for 16 seconds, without a dribble being taken, culminated with Dwight Howard receiving a perfect pass for an uncontested dunk.

In the end, they didn't dominate the gold medal game. Spain proved to be inspired opponents. They simply closed the game out and for the first time since NBA players have come to the Olympics the USA played as a team rather than showboating individuals.

* Wolff, Alexander, "The Redeem Team: New nickname, new outlook for U.S. at Olympics," http://sportsillustrated.cnn.com/2008/writers/alexander_wolff/07/22/redeem.team0728/index.html

Varkonyi, Greg, "The Redeem Team played like a dream in the Olympic basketball final," http://www.sportingo.com/olympic-games/basketball/a10072_redeem-team-played-like-dream-olympic-basketball-final

High-performing teams become champions, create breakthrough products, exceed customer expectations, and get projects done ahead of schedule and under budget. They are bonded together by mutual interdependency and a common goal or vision. They trust each other and exhibit a high level of collaboration.

THE FIVE-STAGE TEAM DEVELOPMENT MODEL

Just as infants develop in certain ways during their first months of life, many experts argue that groups develop in a predictable manner. One of the most popular models identifies five stages (see Figure 11.1) through which groups develop into effective teams (Tuchman, 1965; Tuchman and Jensen, 1977):

1. **Forming.** During this initial stage the members get acquainted with each other and understand the scope of the project. They begin to establish ground rules by trying to find out what behaviors are acceptable with respect to both the project (what role they will play, what performance expectations are) and interpersonal relations (who's really in charge). This stage is completed once members begin to think of themselves as part of a group.

2. **Storming.** As the name suggests, this stage is marked by a high degree of internal conflict. Members accept that they are part of a project group but resist the constraints that the project and group put on their individuality. There is conflict over who will control the group and how decisions will be made. As these conflicts are resolved, the project manager's leadership becomes accepted, and the group moves to the next stage.

3. **Norming.** The third stage is one in which close relationships develop and the group demonstrates cohesiveness. Feelings of camaraderie and shared responsibility for the project

FIGURE 11.1 *The Five-Stage Team Development Model*

are heightened. The norming phase is complete when the group structure solidifies and the group establishes a common set of expectations about how members should work together.

4. **Performing.** The team operating structure at this point is fully functional and accepted. Group energy has moved from getting to know each other and how the group will work together to accomplishing the project goals.

5. **Adjourning.** For conventional work groups, performing is the last stage of their development. However, for project teams, there is a completion phase. During this stage, the team prepares for its own disbandment. High performance is no longer a top priority. Instead attention is devoted to wrapping up the project. Responses of members vary in this stage. Some members are upbeat, basking in the project team's accomplishments. Others may be depressed over loss of camaraderie and friendships gained during the project's life.

This model has several implications for those working on project teams. The first is that the model provides a framework for the group to understand its own development. Project managers have found it useful to share the model with their teams. It helps members accept the tensions of the storming phase, and it directs their focus to moving toward the more productive phases. Another implication is that it stresses the importance of the norming phase, which contributes significantly to the level of productivity experienced during the performing phase. Project managers, as we shall see, have to take an active role in shaping group norms that will contribute to ultimate project success. For an alternative model of group development see the Punctuated Equilibrium Research Highlight.

Research Highlight

THE PUNCTUATED EQUILIBRIUM MODEL OF GROUP DEVELOPMENT*

Gersick's research suggests that groups don't develop in a universal sequence of stages as suggested by the five-phase model. Her research, which is based on the systems concept of *punctuated equilibrium,* found that the *timing* of when groups form and actually change the way they work is highly consistent. What makes this research appealing is that it is based on studies of more than a dozen field and laboratory task forces assigned to complete a specific project. This research reveals that each group begins with a unique approach to accomplishing its project that is set in its first meeting and includes the behavior and roles that dominate phase I. Phase I continues until one-half of the allotted time for project completion has expired (regardless of actual amount of time). At this midpoint, a major transition occurs that includes the dropping of the group's old norms and behavior patterns and the emergence of new behavior and working relationships that contribute to increased progress toward completing the project. The last meeting is marked by accelerated activity to complete the project. These findings are summarized in Figure 11.2.

The remarkable discovery in these studies was that each group experienced its transition at the same point in its calendar—roughly halfway between the first meeting and the completion deadline—despite the fact that some groups spent as little as an hour on their project while others spent six months. It was as if the groups universally experienced a midlife crisis at this point. The midpoint appeared to work like an alarm clock, heightening members' awareness that time was limited and they needed to get moving. Within the context of the five-stage model, it suggests that groups begin by combining the forming and norming stages, then go through a period of low performing, followed by storming, then a period of high performing, and finally adjourning.

Gersick's findings suggest that there are natural transition points during the life of teams in which the group is receptive to change and that such a moment naturally occurs at the midpoint of a project. However, a manager does not want to have to wait 6 months on a complicated 12-month project for a team to get its act together! Here

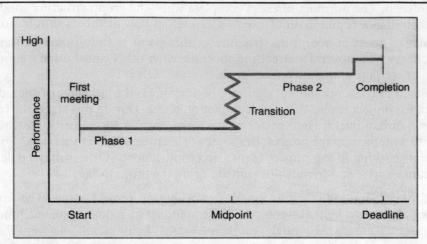

Figure 11.2 *The Punctuated Equilibrium Model of Group Development*

it is important to note that Gersick's groups were working on relatively small-scale projects, i.e., a 4-person bank task force in charge of designing a new bank account in one month and a 12-person medical task force in charge of reorganizing two units of a treatment facility. In most cases no formal project plan was established. If anything, the results point to the importance of good project management and the need to establish deadlines and milestones. By imposing a series of deadlines associated with important milestones, it is possible to create multiple transition points for natural group development. For example, a 12-month construction project can be broken down into six to eight significant milestones with the challenge of meeting each deadline producing the prerequisite tension for elevating team performance.

* Connie J. Gersick, "Time and Transition in Work Teams: Toward a New Model of Group Development," *Academy of Management Journal,* Vol. 31, No. 1 (March 1988), pp. 9–41; and Connie J. Gersick, "Making Time Predictable Transitions in Task Groups," *Academy of Management Journal,* Vol. 32, No. 2 (June 1989), pp. 274–309.

SITUATIONAL FACTORS AFFECTING TEAM DEVELOPMENT

Experience and research indicate that high-performance project teams are much more likely to develop under the following conditions:[2]

- There are 10 or fewer members per team.
- Members volunteer to serve on the project team.
- Members serve on the project from beginning to end.
- Members are assigned to the project full time.
- Members are part of an organization culture that fosters cooperation and trust.

---

[2] See, for example: G. C. Homans, *Social Behavior: Its Elementary Forms* (New York: Harcourt Brace Jovanovich, 1961); Sherif, M., *Group Conflict and Cooperation: Their Social Psychology* (Chicago: Aldine, 1967); Seta, J. J., P. B. Paulus, and J. Schkade, "Effects of Group Size and Proximity under Cooperative and Competitive Conditions," *Journal of Personality and Social Psychology,* 98 (2) 1976, pp. 47–53; and A. Zander, *Making Groups Effective* (San Francisco: Jossey-Bass, 1994).

- Members report solely to the project manager.
- All relevant functional areas are represented on the team.
- The project involves a compelling objective.
- Members are located within conversational distance of each other.

In reality, it is rare that a project manager is assigned a project that meets all of these conditions. For example, many projects' requirements dictate the active involvement of more than 10 members and may consist of a complex set of interlocking teams comprising more than 100 professionals. In many organizations, functional managers or central manpower offices assign project members with little input from the project manager. To optimize resource utilization, team member involvement may be part time, and/or participants may move in and out of the project team on an as-needed basis. In the case of ad hoc task forces, no member of the team works full time on the project. In many corporations an NIH (not invented here) culture exists that discourages collaboration across functional boundaries.

Team members often report to different managers, and, in some cases, the project manager will have no direct input over performance appraisals and advancement opportunities of team members. Key functional areas may not be represented during the entire duration of the project but may only be involved in a sequential manner. Not all projects have a compelling objective. It can be hard to get members excited about mundane projects such as a simple product extension or a conventional apartment complex. Finally, team members are often scattered across different corporate offices and buildings or, in the case of a virtual project, across the entire globe.

It is important for project managers and team members to recognize the situational constraints they are operating under and do the best they can. It would be naive to believe that every project team has the same potential to evolve into a high-performance team. Under less-than-ideal conditions, it may be a struggle just to meet project objectives. Ingenuity, discipline, and sensitivity to team dynamics are essential to maximizing the performance of a project team.

BUILDING HIGH-PERFORMANCE PROJECT TEAMS

Project managers play a key role in developing high-performance project teams. They recruit members, conduct meetings, establish a team identity, create a common sense of purpose or a shared vision, manage a reward system that encourages teamwork, orchestrate decision making, resolve conflicts that emerge within the team, and rejuvenate the team when energy wanes (see Figure 11.3). Project managers take advantage of situational factors that naturally contribute to team development while improvising around those factors that inhibit team development. In doing so they exhibit a highly interactive management style that exemplifies teamwork and, as discussed in the previous chapter, manage the interface between the team and the rest of the organization.

Recruiting Project Members

The process of selecting and recruiting project members will vary across organizations. Two important factors affecting recruitment are the importance of the project and the management structure being used to complete the project. Often for high-priority projects that are critical to the future of the organization, the project manager will be given virtual carte blanche to select whomever he or she deems necessary. For less significant projects, the project manager will have to persuade personnel from other areas within the organization to join the team.

FIGURE 11.3 *Creating a High–Performance Project Team*

In many matrix structures, the functional manager controls who is assigned to the project; the project manager will have to work with the functional manager to obtain necessary personnel. Even in a project team where members are selected and assigned full time to the project, the project manager has to be sensitive to the needs of others. There is no better way to create enemies within an organization than to be perceived as unnecessarily robbing other departments of essential personnel.

Experienced project managers stress the importance of asking for volunteers. However, this desirable step oftentimes is outside the manager's control. Still, the value of having team members volunteer for the project as opposed to being assigned cannot be overlooked. Agreeing to work on the project is the first step toward building personal commitment to the project. Such commitment will be essential to maintain motivation when the project hits hard times and extra effort is required.

When selecting and recruiting team members, project managers naturally look for individuals with the necessary experience and knowledge/technical skills critical for project completion. At the same time, there are less obvious considerations that need to be factored into the recruitment process:

- *Problem-solving ability.* If the project is complex and fuzzy, then a manager wants people who are good at working under uncertainty and have strong problem identification and solving skills. These same people are likely to be bored and less productive working on straightforward projects that go by the book.
- *Availability.* Sometimes the people who are most available are not the ones wanted for the team. Conversely, if members recruited are already overcommitted, they may not be able to offer much.
- *Technological expertise.* Managers should be wary of people who know too much about a specific technology. They may be technology buffs who like to study but have a hard time settling down and doing the work.
- *Credibility.* The credibility of the project is enhanced by the reputation of the people involved in the project. Recruiting a sufficient number of "winners" lends confidence to the project.

- *Political connections.* Managers are wise to recruit individuals who already have a good working relationship with key stakeholders. This is particularly true for projects operating in a matrix environment in which a significant portion of the work will be under the domain of a specific functional department and not the core project team.
- *Ambition, initiative, and energy.* These qualities can make up for a lot of shortcomings in other areas and should not be underestimated.
- *Familiarity.* Research suggests repeat collaboration stifles creativity and innovation. On challenging, breakthrough projects it is wise to interject the team with experts who have little previous working experience with others (Skilton and Dooley, 2010).

See the Managing Martians snapshot for further advice on recruiting team members.

After reviewing needed skills, the manager should try and find out through the corporate grapevine who is good, who is available, and who might want to work on the project. Some organizations may allow direct interviews. Often a manager will have to expend political capital to get highly prized people assigned to the project.

In matrix environments, the project manager will have to request appointments with functional managers to discuss project requirements for staffing. The following documents should be available at these discussions: an overall project scope statement, endorsements of top management, and a description of the tasks and general schedule that pertain to the people from their departments. Managers need to be precise as to what attributes they are seeking and why they are important.

SNAPSHOT FROM PRACTICE
Managing Martians*

Donna Shirley's 35-year career as aerospace engineer reached a pinnacle in July 1997 when Sojourner—the solar-powered, self-guided, microwave-oven-sized rover—was seen exploring the Martian landscape in Pathfinder's spectacular images from the surface of the red planet. The event marked a milestone in space exploration: No vehicle had ever before roamed the surface of another planet. Shirley, a manager at the Jet Propulsion Laboratory's Mars Exploration Program, headed the mostly male team that designed and built Sojourner. In her insightful memoir, *Managing Martians,* written with Danelle Morton, she makes the following observation about managing creative teams:

Courtesy of NASA.

When you are managing really brilliant, creative people, at some point you find it's impossible to command or control them because you can't understand what they are doing. Once they have gone beyond your ability to understand them, you have a choice to make as a manager. You can limit them and the project by your intelligence, which I think is the wrong way to do it. Or you can trust them and use your management skills to keep them focused on the goal.

A lot of bad managers get threatened when their "subordinates" know more than they do. They either hire people who are inferior to them so they can always feel in control or they bottleneck people who know something they don't so they can maintain control. The whole project suffers from the manager's insecurities.

* Donna Shirley and Danelle Morton, *Managing Martians* (New York: Broadway Books, 1998), pp. 88–89.

Conducting Project Meetings

The First Project Team Meeting

Research on team development confirms what we have heard from project managers: The first **project kick-off meeting** is critical to the early functioning of the project team. According to one veteran project manager:

> The first team meeting sets the tone for how the team will work together. If it is disorganized, or becomes bogged down with little sense of closure, then this can often become a self-fulfilling prophecy for subsequent group work. On the other hand, if it is crisply run, focusing on real issues and concerns in an honest and straightforward manner, members come away excited about being part of the project team.

There are typically three objectives project managers try to achieve during the first meeting of the project team. The first is to provide an overview of the project, including the scope and objectives, the general schedule, method, and procedures. The second is to begin to address some of the interpersonal concerns captured in the team development model: Who are the other team members? How will I fit in? Will I be able to work with these people? The third and most important objective is to begin to model how the team is going to work together to complete the project. The project manager must recognize that first impressions are important; her behavior will be carefully monitored and interpreted by team members. This meeting should serve as an exemplary role model for subsequent meetings and reflect the leader's style.

The meeting itself comes in a variety of shapes and forms. It is not uncommon in major projects for the kick-off meeting to involve one or two days, often at a remote site away from interruptions. This retreat provides sufficient time for preliminary introduction, to begin to establish ground rules, and to define the structure of the project. One advantage of off-site kick-off meetings is that they provide ample opportunity for informal interaction among members during breaks, meals, and evening activities; such informal interactions are critical to forming relationships.

However, many organizations do not have the luxury of holding elaborate retreats. In other cases the scope of project does not warrant such an investment of time. In these cases, the key operating principle should be KISS (keep it simple stupid!). Too often when constrained by time, project managers try to accomplish too much during the first meeting; in doing so, issues do not get fully resolved, and members come away with an information headache.

The project manager needs to remember that the primary goal is to run a productive meeting, and objectives should be realistic given the time available. If the meeting is only one hour, then the project manager should simply review the scope of the project, discuss how the team was formed, and provide an opportunity for members to introduce themselves to the team.

Establishing Ground Rules

Whether as part of an elaborate first meeting or during follow-up meetings, the project manager must quickly begin to establish operational ground rules for how the team will work together. These ground rules involve not only organizational and procedural issues but also normative issues on how the team will interact with each other. Although specific procedures will vary across organizations and projects, some of the major issues that need to be addressed include the following:

Planning Decisions

- How will the project plan be developed?

- Will a specific project management software package be used? If so, which one?
- What are the specific roles and responsibilities of all the participants?
- Who needs to be informed of decisions? How will they be kept informed?
- What are the relative importance of cost, time, and performance?
- What are the deliverables of the project planning process?
- Who will approve and sign off at the completion of each deliverable?
- Who receives each deliverable?

Tracking Decisions

- How will progress be assessed?
- At what level of detail will the project be tracked?
- How will team members get data from each other?
- How often will they get this data?
- Who will generate and distribute reports?
- Who needs to be kept informed about project progress, and how will they be informed?
- What content/format is appropriate for each audience?
- Meetings
  - Where will meetings be located?
  - What kind of meetings will be held?
  - Who will "run" these meetings?
  - How will agendas be produced?
  - How will information be recorded?

Managing Change Decisions

- How will changes be instituted?
- Who will have change approval authority?
- How will plan changes be documented and evaluated?

Relationship Decisions

- What department or organizations will the team need to interact with during the project?
- What are the roles and responsibilities of each organization (reviewer, approver, creator, user)?
- How will all involved parties be kept informed of deliverables, schedule dates, expectations, etc.?
- How will the team members communicate among themselves?
- What information will and won't be exchanged?

Checklists like these are only a guide; items should be added or deleted as needed. Many of these procedures will have already been established by precedent and will only have to be briefly reviewed. For example, *Microsoft Project* or *Primavera* may be the standard software tool for planning and tracking. Likewise, a specific firm is likely to have an established format for reporting status information. How to deal with other issues will have to be determined by the project team. When appropriate, the project manager should actively solicit input from the project team members and draw upon their experience and preferred work habits. This process also contributes to their buying into the operational decisions. Decisions should be recorded and circulated to all members.

During the course of establishing these operational procedures, the project manager, through word and deed, should begin working with members to establish the norms for team interaction. Below are examples of some of the norms researchers have found associated with high-performance teams.[3]

- Confidentiality is maintained; no information is shared outside the team unless all agree to it.
- It is acceptable to be in trouble, but it is not acceptable to surprise others. Tell others immediately when deadlines or milestones will not be reached.
- There is zero tolerance for bulling a way through a problem or an issue.
- Agree to disagree, but when a decision has been made, regardless of personal feelings, move forward.
- Respect outsiders, and do not flaunt one's position on the project team.
- Hard work does not get in the way of having fun.

One way of making these norms more tangible is by creating a team charter that goes beyond the scope statement of the project and states in explicit terms the norms and values of the team. This charter should be a collaborative effort on the part of the core team. Project managers can lead by proposing certain tenets, but they need to be open to suggestions from the team. Once there is general agreement to the rules of conduct, each member signs the final document to symbolize commitment to the principles it contains.

Unfortunately, in some cases charters become a meaningless ritual because the charter is signed and filed away, never to be discussed again. To have a lasting effect, the charter has to be a legitimate part of the project monitoring system. Just as the team reviews progress toward project objectives, the team assesses the extent to which members are adhering to the principles in the charter.

Project managers play a major role in establishing team norms through personal example. If they freely admit mistakes and share what they have learned from them, other team members will begin to do the same. At the same time, project managers need to intervene when they believe such norms are being violated. They should talk to offenders privately and clearly state their expectations. The amazing thing about groups is that once a group is cohesive, with well-established norms, the members will police themselves so that the manager doesn't have to be the heavy. For example, one project manager confided that his team had a practice of having a small bean bag present at every meeting. If any one member felt that a colleague was shooting hot air or shading the truth, he or she was obligated to toss the bean bag at the speaker. See the Snapshot: Putting Ford on Fast Forward for examples of norms that encourage innovation.

Managing Subsequent Project Meetings

The project kick-off meeting is one of several kinds of meetings required to complete a project. Other meetings include status report meetings, problem-solving meetings, and audit meetings.

---

[3] See Katzenbach, J. R., and D. K. Smith, *The Wisdom of Teams* (Boston: Harvard Business School Press, 1993); Bolman, L. G. and T. E. Deal, "What Makes Teams Work," *Organizational Dynamics*, vol. 21 (2), pp. 34–45; Katz, R., "How a Team at Digital Equipment Designed the 'Alpha' Chips," *The Human Side of Managing Technological Innovation*, R. Katz, Editor (New York: Oxford Press, 1997) pp. 137–148.

SNAPSHOT FROM PRACTICE

Putting Ford on Fast
Forward*

Adam Gryglak was given mission impossible: deliver an all new Ford diesel engine in less than 36 months. The challenge was all the more daunting in that in the past Ford had outsourced design and manufacture of diesel engines to Navistar. Not only did he have to meet a ridiculous deadline, but he also had to build an in-house engine from scratch. Gryglak, the chief diesel engineer, knew that success depended on short-circuiting the design process at Ford. So he put together a team of hungry engineers, moved offsite, and shielded the team from anxious top management. He called the project Scorpion after the heavy metal band the Scorpions.

Progress was immediate. Specialists who were used to working only with their own kind became familiar with what the other engineers were up to. "We saved months by knowing hourly what the others guys were thinking and what their problems were," says Pat Morgan, a veteran Ford engineer. "The result was that the engine fit into the truck perfectly the first time, and that almost never happens."

Gryglak also realized that engineers work harder and smarter when they are having fun. To relieve pressure the engineers played jokes on each other, building full-size snowmen decorated with machine parts on each other's desks. Gryglak encouraged friendly competition. After hitting a critical design milestone the team organized a Pinewood Derby contest. Pinewood Derby is a famous Cub Scout event where young boys whittle toy cars out of wood and race them down a ramp. These were engineers not Cub Scouts, so instead of wooden cars, the engineers milled cars out of aluminum. Some of the cars even had remote controls and engines.

The new Ford diesel engine was completed on time to critical acclaim. The engine was the first of its kind to use state-of-the-art antipollution technology that meets new federal standards. It also had the best fuel economy in its category and won't need significant maintenance for 300,000 miles. The engine is featured in the best selling F-150 line of trucks and is considered one of the keys to Ford's comeback.

* "Putting Ford Fast Forward," *Businessweek,* October 26, 2009, pp. 58–59.

Issues unique to these meetings will be discussed in subsequent chapters. For now, here are some general guidelines for running effective meetings. They speak directly to the person chairing the meeting:

- Start meetings on time regardless of whether everyone is present.
- Prepare and distribute an agenda prior to the meeting.
- Identify an adjournment time.
- Periodically take time to review how effective previous meetings have been.
- Solicit recommendations and implement changes.
- Assign good recordkeeping.
- Review the agenda before beginning, and tentatively allocate time for each item.
- Prioritize issues so that adjustments can be made given time constraints.
- Encourage active participation of all members by asking questions instead of making statements.
- Summarize decisions, and review assignments for the next meeting.
- Prepare and distribute a summary of the meeting to appropriate people.
- Recognize accomplishments and positive behavior.

Meetings are often considered an anathema to productivity, but this does not have to be the case. The most common complaint is that meetings last too long. Establishing an agenda and adjournment time helps participants budget discussion time and provides a basis for expediting the proceedings. Recordkeeping can be an unwelcome, tedious task. Utilizing laptop computers to record decisions and information in real time can facilitate the communication process. Careful preparation and consistent application of these guidelines can make meetings a vital part of projects.

Establishing a Team Identity

One of the challenges project managers often face in building a team is the lack of full-time involvement of team members. Specialists work on different phases of the project and spend the majority of their time and energy elsewhere. They are often members of multiple teams, each competing for their time and allegiance. Project expert David Frame (1995) points out that for many of these specialists a specific project is an abstraction; as a consequence their level of motivation suffers. Project managers need to try to make the project team as tangible as possible to the participants by developing a unique team identity to which participants can become emotionally attached. Team meetings, co-location of team members, team names, and team rituals are common vehicles for doing so.

- *Effective use of meetings.* Periodic project team meetings provide an important forum for communicating project information. A less obvious function of project meetings is to help establish a concrete team identity. During project meetings, members see that they are not working alone. They are part of a larger project team, and project success depends on the collective efforts of all the team members. Timely gatherings of all the project participants help define team membership and reinforce a collective identity.

- *Co-location of team members.* The most obvious way to make the project team tangible is to have members work together in a common space. This is not always possible in matrix environments where involvement is part time and members are working on other projects and activities. A worthwhile substitute for co-location is the creation of a project office, sometimes referred to as the project war room or clubhouse. Such rooms are the common meeting place and contain the most significant project documentation. Frequently, their walls are covered with Gantt charts, cost graphs, and other output associated with project planning and control. These rooms serve as a tangible sign of project effort.

- *Creation of project team name.* The development of a team name such as the "A-Team" or "Casey's Crusaders" is a common device for making a team more tangible. Frequently an associated team logo is also created. Again the project manager should rely on the collective ingenuity of the team to come up with the appropriate name and logo. Such symbols then can be affixed to stationery, T-shirts, coffee mugs, etc., to help signify team membership.

- *Get the team to build or do something together early on.* Nothing reinforces a sense of a team more than working on something together. In the case of one international project, the manager simply hosted a potluck dinner where each member brought a dish his or her country was famous for.

- *Team rituals.* Just as corporate rituals help establish the unique identity of a firm, similar symbolic actions at the project level can contribute to a unique team subculture. For example, on one project members were given ties with stripes that corresponded to the number of milestones on the project. After reaching each milestone, members would gather and cut the next stripe off their ties to signify progress.[4] Ralph Katz (2004) reports it was common practice for Digital Equipment's alpha chip design team to recognize people who found a bug in the design by giving them a phosphorescent toy roach. The bigger the bug that was discovered, the bigger the toy roach received. Such rituals help set project work apart from mainstream operations and reinforce a special status.

Creating a Shared Vision

Unlike project scope statements, which include specific cost, completion dates, and performance requirements, a **vision** involves the less tangible aspects of project performance. It refers to an image a project team holds in common about how the project will look upon completion, how they will work together, and/or how customers will accept the project. At its simplest level, a shared vision is the answer to the question, "What do we want to create?" Not everyone will have the same vision, but the images should be similar. Visions come in a variety of shapes and forms; they can be captured in a slogan or a symbol or can be written as a formal vision statement.

What a vision is, is not as important as what it does. A vision inspires members to give their best effort. (See A Good Man in a Storm Snapshot.) Moreover, a shared vision unites professionals with different backgrounds and agendas to a common aspiration. It helps motivate members to subordinate their individual agendas and do what is best for the project. As psychologist Robert Fritz puts it, "In the presence of greatness, pettiness disappears."[5] Visions also provide focus and help communicate less tangible priorities, helping members make appropriate judgment calls. Finally, a shared vision for a project fosters commitment to the long term and discourages expedient responses that collectively dilute the quality of the project.

Visions can be surprisingly simple. For example, the vision for a new car could be expressed as a "pocket rocket." Compare this vision with the more traditional product description—"a sports car in the midprice range." The "pocket rocket" vision provides a much clearer picture of what the final product should be. Design engineers would immediately understand that the car will be both small and fast and that the car should be quick at the getaway, nimble in the turns, and very fast in the straightaways (Bowen et al., 1994). Alternatively, visions can be more concrete:

"The Helpdesk Automated Site (HASS) Version 4.5 will address the top 10 customer complaints across the university without any negative impact on average performance, reliability or response time across the system."[6]

There appear to be four essential qualities of an effective vision (see Figure 11.4). First, its essential qualities must be able to be communicated. A vision

FIGURE 11.4   *Requirements for an Effective Project Vision*

[4] This anecdote was provided by Dr. Frances Hartman, University of Calgary, Alberta.

[5] Quoted in P. Senge, *The Fifth Discipline* (New York, Doubleday, 1990) p. 209.

[6] S. Berkun, *The Art of Project Management* (Sebastopol. CA: O'Reilly, 2005), p. 79.

Once upon a time, back in 1976, Data General Corporation needed to come up quickly with a fast, reasonably priced 32-bit mini-computer to compete with Digital Equipment Corporation's VAX. Data General CEO Edson de Castro launched the Fountainhead Project and gave it the best people and ample resources to complete the 32-bit initiative. As a back-up to the Fountainhead project, Data General created the Eagle project within the Eclipse group under the leadership of Tom West. Work on both projects began in 1978.

In 1980 Data General announced its new computer, featuring simplicity, power, and low cost. This computer was not the Fountainhead from the well-funded "best" DG group but the Eagle from Tom West's under-funded Eclipse team. Tracy Kidder saw all this happen and told the story in *The Soul of a New Machine,* which won a Pulitzer Prize in 1982. This book, which Kidder thought might be of interest to a handful of computer scientists, has become a project management classic.

In the beginning of his book, Kidder introduces the readers to the book's protagonist Tom West by telling the story of him sailing a yacht across rough seas off the coast of New England. Kidder's title for the prologue was "A Good Man in a Storm."

Twenty years after Kidder's book was published Tom West was interviewed by Lawrence Peters for the *Academy of Management Executive.* Below are some excerpts that capture Tom's views on managing innovative projects:

On selecting team members:

You explain to a guy what the challenge was, and then see if his eyes light up.

On motivating team members:

. . . Challenge was everything. People, especially creative technical people who really want to make a difference, will do whatever is possible or whatever is necessary. I've done this more than once, and I've repeated it over and over. It seems to work.

On the importance of having a vision:

. . . you've got to find a rallying cry. You need to have something that can be described very simply and has that sort of ring of truth to an engineer that says "yes that's the thing to be doing right now." Otherwise you're going to be rolling rocks up hill all the time.

On the role of being a project manager:

You have to act as a cheerleader. You have to act as the instructor. You have to constantly bring to mind what the purpose is and what's moving the ball towards the goal post, and what's running sideways, and you have to take up a lot of battles for them. I mean you really don't want your design engineer arguing with the guy in the drafting shop about why he ought to do it the designer's way. I can do that, and I can pull rank too, and sometimes I did just that.

* Tracy Kidder, *The Soul of a New Machine* (New York: Avon Books, 1981); Lawrence H. Peters, "'A Good Man in a Storm': An Interview with Tom West," *Academy of Management Executive,* Vol. 16, No. 4, 2002, pp. 53–60.

is worthless if it only resides in someone's head. Second, visions have to be challenging but also realistic. For example, a task force directed at overhauling the curriculum at the college of business at a state university is likely to roll its eyes if the dean announces that their vision is to compete against the Harvard Business School. Conversely, developing the best undergraduate business program in that state may be a realistic vision for that task force. Third, the project manager has to believe in the vision. Passion for the vision is an essential element of an effective vision. Finally, it should be a source of inspiration to others.

Once a project manager accepts the importance of building a shared vision, the next question is how to get a vision for a particular project. First, project managers don't get visions. They act as catalysts and midwives for the formation of a shared vision of a project team (Smith, 1994). In many cases visions are inherent in the scope and objectives of the project. People get naturally excited about being the first ones to bring a new technology to the market or solving a problem that is threatening their organization. Even with mundane projects, there are often ample opportunities for establishing a compelling vision. One way is to talk to various people involved in the project and find out early on what gets them excited about the project. For some it may be doing a better job than on the last project or the satisfaction in the eyes of the customers when the project is over. Many visions evolve reactively in response to competition. For example, the Kodak team responsible for developing the single-use FunSaver camera was driven by the vision of beating a similar effort by Fuji to the market (Bowen et al., 1994).

Some experts advocate engaging in formal vision-building meetings. These meetings generally involve several steps, beginning with members identifying different aspects of the project and generating ideal scenarios for each aspect. For example, on a construction project the scenarios may include "no accidents," "no lawsuits," "winning a prize," or "how we are going to spend our bonus for completing the project ahead of schedule." The group reviews and chooses the scenarios that are most appealing and translates them into vision statements for the project. The next step is to identify strategies for achieving the vision statements. For example, if one of the vision statements is that there will be no lawsuits, members will identify how they will have to work with the owner and subcontractors to avoid litigation. Next, members volunteer to be the keeper of the flame for each statement. The vision, strategies, and the name of the responsible team member are published and distributed to relevant stakeholders.

In more cases than not, shared visions emerge informally. Project managers collect information about what excites participants about the project. They test bits of their working vision in their conversations with team members to gauge the level of excitement the early ideas elicit in others. To some extent they engage in basic market research. They seize opportunities to galvanize the team, such as a disparaging remark by an executive that the project will never get done on time or the threat of a competing firm launching a similar project. Consensus in the beginning is not essential. What is essential is a core group of at least one-third of the project team that is genuinely committed to the vision. They will provide the critical mass to draw others aboard. Once the language has been formulated to communicate the vision, then the statement needs to be a staple part of every working agenda, and the project manager should be prepared to deliver a "stump" speech at a moment's notice. When problems or disagreements emerge, all responses should be consistent with the vision.

Much has been written about visions and leadership. Critics argue that vision is a glorified substitute for shared goals. Others argue that it is one of the things that separate leaders from managers. The key is discovering what excites people about a project, being able to articulate this source of excitement in an appealing manner, and finally protecting and nurturing this source of excitement throughout the duration of the project.

Managing Project Reward Systems

Project managers are responsible for managing the reward system that encourages team performance and extra effort. One advantage they have is that often project work is inherently satisfying, whether it is manifested in an inspiring vision or simple sense of accomplishment. Projects provide participants with a change in scenery, a chance to learn new skills, and an opportunity to break out of their departmental cocoon. Another inherent reward is what was referred to in Tracy Kidder, *The Soul of a New Machine* as "pinball"—project success typically gives team members an option to play another exciting game.[7]

Still, many projects are underappreciated, boring, interfere with other more significant priorities, and are considered an extra burden. In some of these cases, the biggest reward is finishing the project so that team members can go back to what they really enjoy doing and what will yield the biggest personal payoffs. Unfortunately, when this attitude is the primary incentive, project quality is likely to suffer. In these circumstances, external rewards play a more important role in motivating team performance.

Most project managers we talk to advocate the use of group rewards. Because most project work is a collaborative effort, it only makes sense that the reward system would encourage teamwork. Recognizing individual members regardless of their accomplishments can distract from team unity. Project work is highly interdependent, so it can become problematic to distinguish who truly deserves additional credit. Cash bonuses and incentives need to be linked to project priorities. It makes no sense to reward a team for completing their work early if controlling cost was the number one priority.

One of the limitations of lump-sum cash bonuses is that all too often they are consumed by the household budget to pay the dentist or mechanic. To have more value, rewards need to have lasting significance (Preston & Reinertsen, 1995). Many companies convert cash into vacation rewards, sometimes with corresponding time off. For example, there is one firm that rewarded a project team for getting the job done ahead of schedule with a four-day, all-expenses-paid trip to Walt Disney World for the members' entire families. That vacation not only will be remembered for years, but it also recognizes spouses and children who, in a sense, also contributed to the project's success. Similarly, other firms have been known to give members home computers and entertainment centers. Wise project managers negotiate a discretionary budget so that they can reward teams surpassing milestones with gift certificates to popular restaurants or tickets to sporting events. Impromptu pizza parties and barbecues are also used to celebrate key accomplishments.

Sometimes project managers have to use negative reinforcement to motivate project performance. For example, Ritti and Levy recounts the story of one project manager who was in charge of the construction of a new, state-of-the-art manufacturing plant. His project team was working with a number of different contracting firms. The project was slipping behind schedule, mostly because of a lack of cooperation among the different players. The project manager did not have direct authority over many key people, especially the contractors from the other companies. He did, however, have the freedom to convene meetings at his convenience. So the project manager instituted daily "coordination meetings," which were required of all the principals involved, at 6:00 A.M. The meetings continued for about two weeks until the project got back on schedule. At that time the project manager announced that the next meeting was canceled, and no further sunrise meetings were ever scheduled.[8]

While project managers tend to focus on group rewards, there are times when they need to reward individual performance. This is done not only to compensate extraordinary effort but also

---

[7] T. Kidder, *The Soul of a New Machine* (New York: Avon Books, 1981), pp. 221–22.

[8] R. R. Ritti and S. L. Levy, *Ropes to Skip and Ropes to Know: Studies in Organizational Theory and Behavior* (New York: Wiley, 2009) pp. 93–94.

to signal to the others what exemplary behavior is. More specifically, among the rewards they use to motivate and recognize individual contributions are the following:

- **Letters of commendation.** While project managers may not have responsibility for their team members' performance appraisals, they can write letters commending their project performance. These letters can be sent to the workers' supervisors to be placed in their personnel files.
- **Public recognition for outstanding work.** Superlative workers should be publicly recognized for their efforts. Some project managers begin each status review meeting with a brief mention of project workers who have exceeded their project goals.
- **Job assignments.** Good project managers recognize that, while they may not have much budgetary authority, they do have substantial control over who does what, with whom, when, and where. Good work should be rewarded with desirable job assignments. Managers should be aware of member preferences and, when appropriate, accommodate them.
- **Flexibility.** Being willing to make exceptions to rules, if done judiciously, can be a powerful reward. Allowing members to work at home when a child is sick or excusing a minor discretion can engender long-lasting loyalty.

Individual rewards should be used judiciously, and under extraordinary circumstances. Nothing undermines the cohesiveness of a team more than members beginning to feel that others are getting special treatment or that they are being treated unfairly. Camaraderie and collaboration can quickly vanish only to be replaced by bickering and obsessive preoccupation with group politics. Such distractions can absorb energy that otherwise would be directed toward completing the project. Individual rewards typically should be used only when everyone in the team recognizes that a member is deserving of special recognition.

Orchestrating the Decision-Making Process

Most decisions on a project do not require a formal meeting to discuss alternatives and determine solutions. Instead decisions are made in real time as part of the daily interactions between project managers, stakeholders, and team members. For example, as a result of a routine "how's it going?" question, a project manager discovers that a mechanical engineer is stuck trying to meet the performance criteria for a prototype he is responsible for building. The project manager and engineer go down the hallway to talk to the designers, explain the problem, and ask what, if anything, can be done. The designers distinguish which criteria are essential and which ones they think can be compromised. The project manager then checks with the marketing group to make sure the modifications are acceptable. They agree with all but two of the modifications. The project manager goes back to the mechanical engineer and asks whether the proposed changes would help solve the problem. The engineer agrees. Before authorizing the changes he calls the project sponsor, reviews the events, and gets the sponsor to sign off on the changes. This is an example of how, by practicing MBWA (management by wandering around), project managers consult team members, solicit ideas, determine optimum solutions, and create a sense of involvement that builds trust and commitment to decisions.

Still, projects encounter problems and decisions that require the collective wisdom of team members as well as relevant stakeholders. Group decision making should be used when it will improve the quality of important decisions (Vroom and Jago, 1988). This is often the case with complex problems that require the input of a variety of different specialists. Group decision making should also be used when strong commitment to the decision is needed and there is a low probability of acceptance if only one person makes the decision. Participation is used to reduce resistance and secure support for the decision. Guidelines for managing group decision making are provided below.

Facilitating Group Decision Making

Project managers play a pivotal role in guiding the group decision-making process. They must remind themselves that their job is not to make a decision but to facilitate the discussion within the group so that the team reaches a consensus on the best possible solution. Consensus within this context does not mean that everyone supports the decision 100 percent, but that they all agree what the best solution is under the circumstances. Facilitating group decision making essentially involves four major steps. Each step is briefly described next with suggestions for how to manage the process.[9]

1. **Problem identification.** The project manager needs to be careful not to state the problem in terms of choices (e.g., should we do X or Y?). Rather the project manager should identify the underlying problem to which these alternatives and probably others are potential solutions. This allows group members to generate alternatives, not just choose among them. One useful way of defining problems is to consider the gap between where a project is (i.e., the present state) and where it should be (desired state). For example, the project may be four days behind schedule or the prototype weighs two pounds more than the specifications. Whether the gap is small or large, the purpose is to eliminate it. The group must find one or more courses of action that will change the existing state into the desired one.

   If one detects defensive posturing during the problem identification discussion, then it may be wise to postpone the problem-solving step if possible. This allows for emotions to subside and members to gain a fresh perspective on the issues involved.

2. **Generating alternatives.** Once there is general agreement as to the nature of the problem(s), then the next step is to generate alternative solutions. If the problem requires creativity, then **brainstorming** is commonly recommended. Here the team generates a list of possible solutions on a flipchart or blackboard. During that time the project manager establishes a moratorium on criticizing or evaluating ideas. Members are encouraged to "piggyback" on other's ideas by extending them or combining ideas into a new idea. The object is to create as many alternatives as possible no matter how outlandish they may appear to be. Some project managers report that for really tough problems they have found it beneficial to conduct such sessions away from the normal work environment; the change in scenery stimulates creativity.

3. **Reaching a decision.** The next step is to evaluate and assess the merits of alternative solutions. During this phase it is useful to have a set of criteria for evaluating the merits of different solutions. In many cases the project manager can draw upon the priorities for the project and have the group assess each alternative in terms of its impact on cost, schedule, and performance as well as reducing the problem gap. For example, if time is critical, then the solution that solves the problem as quickly as possible would be chosen.

   During the course of the discussion the project manager attempts to build consensus among the group. This can be a complicated process. Project managers need to provide periodic summaries to help the group keep track of its progress. They must protect those

---

[9] This discussion is based on the classic work of N. R. F. Maier, *Problem-Solving Discussion and Conferences* (New York: McGraw-Hill, 1963); and *Problem Solving and Creativity in Individuals and Groups* (Belmont, CA: Brooks-Cole, 1970).

members who represent the minority view and ensure that such views get a fair hearing. They need to guarantee that everyone has an opportunity to share opinions and no one individual or group dominates the conversation. It may be useful to bring a two-minute timer to regulate the use of air time. When conflicts occur, managers need to apply some of the ideas and techniques discussed in the next section.

Project managers need to engage in consensus testing to determine what points the group agrees on and what are still sources of contention. They are careful not to interpret silence as agreement; they confirm agreement by asking questions. Ultimately, through thoughtful interaction, the team reaches a "meeting of the minds" as to what solution is best for the project.

4. **Follow-up.** Once the decision has been made and implemented, it is important for the team to find the time to evaluate the effectiveness of the decision. If the decision failed to provide the anticipated solution, then the reasons should be explored and the lessons learned added to the collective memory bank of the project team.

Managing Conflict within the Project

Disagreements and conflicts naturally emerge within a project team during the life of the project. Participants will disagree over priorities, allocation of resources, the quality of specific work, solutions to discovered problems, and so forth. Some conflicts support the goals of the group and improve project performance. For example, two members may be locked in a debate over a design trade-off decision involving different features of a product. They argue that their preferred feature is what the primary customer truly wants. This disagreement may force them to talk to or get more information from the customer, with the result that they realize neither feature is highly valued, but instead the customer wants something else. On the other hand, conflicts can also hinder group performance. Initial disagreements can escalate into heated arguments with both parties storming out of the room and refusing to work together.

Sources of conflict are likely to change as projects progress along the project life cycle (Thamhain and Wilemon, 1975; Posner, 1986; Adams and Brandt, 1988). Figure 11.5 summarizes the major sources of conflict in each phase.

FIGURE 11.5   *Sources of Conflict over the Project Life Cycle*

So far the discussion of team building has been directed primarily to significant projects that command the attention and involvement of assigned members. But what about projects that have low priority for team members: The perfunctory task forces that members begrudgingly join? The committee work people get assigned to do? The part-time projects that pull members away from the critical work they would rather be doing? Projects that cause members to privately question why they are doing this?

There is no magic wand available that transforms mildly interested, part-time project teams into high-performance teams. We interviewed several project managers about such project scenarios. They all agreed that these can be very difficult and frustrating assignments and that there are limits to what is possible. Still, they offered tips and advice for making the best of the situation. Most of these tips focus on building commitment to the project when it does not naturally exist.

One project manager advocated orchestrating a large "time" investment upfront on such projects—either in the form of a lengthy meeting or a significant early assignment. He viewed this as a form of down payment that members would forfeit if they didn't carry the project to completion.

Others emphasize interjecting as much fun into activities as possible. Here rituals discussed under building team identity come into play. People become committed because they enjoy working together on the project. One project manager even confided that the perfect attendance at her project meetings was due primarily to the quality of the doughnuts she provided.

Another strategy is to make the benefits of the project as real to the team members as possible. One project manager escalated commitment to a mandated accidents prevention task force by bringing accident victims to a project meeting. Another project manager brought the high-ranking project sponsor to recharge the team by reinforcing the importance of the project to the company.

Most project managers emphasized the importance of building a strong personal relationship with each of the team members. When this connection occurs, members work hard not so much because they really care about the project but because they don't want to let the project manager down. Although not couched in influence currency terms, these managers talked about getting to know each member, sharing contacts, offering encouragement, and extending a helping hand when needed.

Finally, all project managers cautioned that nothing should be taken for granted on low-priority projects. They recommend reminding people about meetings and bringing extra copies of materials to meetings for those who have forgotten them or can't find them. Project managers should remain in frequent contact with team members and remind them of their assignments. One manager summed it up best when he said, "Sometimes it all boils down to just being a good nag."

During project definition, the most significant sources of conflict are priorities, administrative procedures, and schedule. Disputes occur over the relative importance of the project compared with other activities, which project management structure to use (especially how much control the project manager should have), the personnel to be assigned, and the scheduling of the project into existing workloads.

During the planning phase, the chief source of conflict remains priorities, followed by schedules, procedures, and technical requirements. This is the phase where the project moves from a general concept to a detailed set of plans. The relative importance of the project is still trying to be established as well as project priorities (time, cost, scope). Disagreements often emerge over the final schedule, the assignment of resources, communication and decision making procedures, and technical requirements for the project.

During the execution phase, friction arises over schedule slippage, technical problems, and staff issues. Milestones become more difficult to meet because of accumulating schedule slippages. This leads to tension within the team as delays prevent others from starting or completing their work. Managing the trade-offs between time, cost, and performance becomes paramount. Project managers must decide between letting the schedule slip, investing additional funds to get back on track, or scaling back the scope of the project in order to save time. Technical problems involve finding solutions to unexpected problems and integrating the contributions of different people. The strain of the project may be expressed in interpersonal conflicts as well as pressures to use resources more effectively.

During the delivery phase, the level of conflict tends to subside. On troubled projects schedules continue to be the biggest source of conflict as schedule slippages make it more difficult to meet target completion dates. Pressures to meet objectives coupled with growing anxiety over future assignments increases interpersonal tensions. Technical problems are rare since most of them have been worked out during the earlier phases.

Encouraging Functional Conflict

The demarcation between **functional** and **dysfunctional conflict** is neither clear nor precise. In one team, members may exchange a diatribe of four-letter expletives and eventually resolve their differences. Yet in another project team, such behavior would create irreconcilable divisions and would prohibit the parties from ever working together productively again. The distinguishing criterion is how the conflict affects project performance, not how individuals feel. Members can be upset and dissatisfied with the interchange, but as long as the disagreement furthers the objectives of the project, then the conflict is functional. Project managers should recognize that conflict is an inevitable and even a desirable part of project work; the key is to encourage functional conflict and manage dysfunctional conflict.

A shared vision can transcend the incongruities of a project and establish a common purpose to channel debate in a constructive manner. Without shared goals there is no common ground for working out differences. In the previous example involving the design trade-off decision, when both parties agreed that the primary goal was to satisfy the customer, there was a basis for more objectively resolving the dispute. Therefore, agreeing in advance which priority is most important—cost, schedule, or scope—can help a project team decide what response is most appropriate.

Sometimes it's not the presence of conflict, but the absence of conflict that is the problem. Oftentimes as a result of compressed time pressures, self-doubt, and the desire to preserve team harmony, members are reluctant to voice objections. This hesitation robs the team of useful information that might lead to better solutions and the avoidance of critical mistakes. Project managers need to encourage healthy dissent in order to improve problem solving and innovation. They can demonstrate this process by asking tough questions and challenging the rationale behind recommendations. They can also orchestrate healthy conflict by bringing in people with different points of view to critical meetings.

Project managers can legitimize dissent within the team by designating someone to play the role of devil's advocate or by asking the group to take 15 minutes to come up with all the reasons the team should not pursue a course of action. Functional conflict plays a critical role in obtaining a deeper understanding of the issues and coming up with the best decisions possible.

One of the most important things project managers can do is model an appropriate response when someone disagrees or challenges their ideas. They need to avoid acting defensively and instead encourage critical debate. They should exhibit effective listening skills and summarize the key issues before responding. They should check to see if others agree with the opposing point of view. Finally, project managers should value and protect dissenters. Organizations have a tendency to create too many yes-men, and the emperor needs to be told when he doesn't have any clothes on.

Managing Dysfunctional Conflict

Managing dysfunctional conflict is a much more challenging task than encouraging functional conflict. First, dysfunctional conflict is hard to identify. A manager might have two highly talented professionals who hate each other's guts, but in the heat of competition they produce meritorious results. Is this a pleasant situation? No. Is it functional? Yes, as long as it contributes to project performance. Conversely, sometimes functional conflict degenerates into dysfunctional conflict. This change occurs when technical disagreements evolve into irrational personality clashes or when failure to resolve an issue causes unnecessary delays in critical project work.

The second major difficulty managers face is that there is often no easy solution to dysfunctional conflict. Project managers have to decide among a number of different strategies to manage it; here are five possibilities:

1. **Mediate the conflict.** The manager intervenes and tries to negotiate a resolution by using reasoning and persuasion, suggesting alternatives and the like. One of the keys is trying to find common ground. In some cases the project manager can make the argument that the win/lose interchange has escalated to the point that it has become lose/lose for everyone and now is the time to make concessions.

2. **Arbitrate the conflict.** The manager imposes a solution to the conflict after listening to each party. The goal is not to decide who wins but to have the project win. In doing so, it is important to seek a solution that allows each party to save face; otherwise the decision may provide only momentary relief. One project manager admits that she has had great success using a King Solomon approach to resolving conflict. She confided she announces a solution that neither party will like and gives the opponents two hours to come up with a better solution they can both agree on.

3. **Control the conflict.** Reducing the intensity of the conflict by smoothing over differences or interjecting humor is an effective strategy. If feelings are escalating, the manager can adjourn the interaction and hope cooler heads prevail the next day. If the conflict continues to escalate, project assignments may need to be rearranged if possible so that two parties don't have to work together.

4. **Accept it.** In some cases the conflict will outlive the life of the project and, though a distraction, it is one the manager has to live with.

5. **Eliminate the conflict.** Sometimes the conflict has escalated to the point that it is no longer tolerable. If there is a clear villain then only he or she should be removed. If, as is often the case, both parties are at fault, then it would be wise if possible to eliminate both individuals. Their removal would give a clear signal to the others on the team that this kind of behavior is unacceptable.

In summary, project managers establish the foundation for functional conflict by establishing clear roles and responsibilities, developing common goals or a shared vision, and using group incentives that reward collaboration. Project managers have to be adroit at reading body language to identify unspoken disagreement. They also have to keep in touch with what is going on in a project to identify small problems that might escalate into big conflicts. Well-timed humor and redirecting the focus to what is best for the project can alleviate the interpersonal tensions that are likely to flare up on a project team.

Rejuvenating the Project Team

Over the course of a long project, a team sometimes drifts off course and loses momentum. The project manager needs to swing into action to realign the team with the project objectives and step on the pedal. There are both formal and informal ways of doing this. Informally, the project manager can institute new rituals like the "toy roaches" to reenergize a team. On one project that was experiencing rough going, the project manager stopped work and took the team bowling to relieve frustrations. On another project, a manager showed her team the movie *The Shawshank Redemption* to rekindle hope and commitment to success.

Another option is to have the project sponsor give a pep talk to the "troops." In other cases, a friendly challenge can reinvigorate a team. For example, one project sponsor offered to cook a five-course meal if the project got back on track and hit the next milestone.

Sometimes more formal action needs to be taken. The project manager may recognize the need for a team-building session devoted to improving the work processes of the team. This meeting is particularly appropriate if she senses that the team is approaching a transition point in its development. The goal of such a session is to improve the project team's effectiveness through better management of project demands and group processes. It is an inward look by the team at its own performance, behavior, and culture for the purpose of eliminating dysfunctional behaviors and strengthening functional ones. The project team critiques its performance, analyzes its way of doing things, and attempts to develop strategies to improve its operation.

Oftentimes an external consultant is hired, or an internal staff specialist is assigned to facilitate the session. This process brings a more objective, outside perspective to the table, frees the project manager to be part of the process, and provides a specialist trained in group dynamics. Furthermore, if preliminary information is to be collected, team members may be more candid and open to an outsider.

One caveat about using outside consultants is that too often managers resort to this as a method for dealing with a problem that they have been unable or unwilling to deal with. The marching order to the consultant is "fix my team for me." What the managers fail to recognize is that one of the keys to fixing the team is improving the working relationship between themselves and the remainder of the team. For such sessions to be effective, project managers have to be willing to have their own role scrutinized and be receptive to changing their own behavior and work habits based on the comments and suggestions of the project team.

Consultants use a wide variety of **team-building** techniques to elevate team performance. Here is a brief description of one of the more common approaches. The first step is to gather information and make a preliminary diagnosis of team performance. Whether through individual interviews or in a group forum, the consultant asks general questions about the project team performance, that is, what obstacles are getting in the way of the team being able to perform better? This information is summarized in terms of themes. When everyone has understood the themes, the group ranks them in terms of both their importance and the extent the team has ownership over them. This last dimension is critical. *Ownership* refers to whether the team has direct influence over the issue. For example, a team probably has little influence over delivery of contracted supplies, but team members do control how quickly they inform each other of sudden changes in plans.

If the group becomes preoccupied with issues outside its control, the meeting can quickly evolve into a demoralizing gripe session. Therefore, the most important issues they have direct control over become the subjects of the agenda. During the course of the meeting, much interpersonal and group process information will be generated, and that is examined too. Thus, the group works on two sets of items: the agenda items and the items that emerge from the interaction of the participants. This is where the expertise of the external facilitator becomes critical for identifying interaction patterns and their implications for team performance.

As important problems are discussed, alternatives for action are developed. The team-building session concludes by deciding on specific action steps for remedying problems and setting target dates for who will do what, when. These assignments can be reviewed at project status meetings or at a special follow-up session.

It has become fashionable to link team-building activities with outdoor experiences. The outdoor experience—whether it is whitewater rafting down the Rogue River in Oregon or rock climbing in Colorado—places group members in a variety of physically challenging situations that must be mastered through teamwork, not individual effort. By having to work together to overcome difficult obstacles, team members are supposed to experience increased self-confidence, more respect for another's capabilities, and a greater commitment to teamwork. No empirical data are available to support such exotic endeavors other than the enthusiastic support of the participants. Such activities are likely to provide an intense common experience that may accelerate the social development of the team. Such an investment of time and money communicates the importance of teamwork and is considered by some a perk for being on the project. At the same time, unless the lessons from these experiences can be immediately transferred to actual project work, their significance is likely to vanish.

MANAGING VIRTUAL PROJECT TEAMS

Building a high-performance project team among a mixture of part-time and full-time members is a challenging task. Consider how much more challenging it is to build a team when members cannot engage in face-to-face interactions. Such would be the case for a **virtual project team** in which the team members are geographically situated so that they may seldom, if ever, meet face-to-face as a team. For example, Hewlett-Packard's integrated circuit business headquarters and a portion of the R&D facilities are located in Palo Alto, California; the two wafer fabrication operations are located in Corvallis, Oregon, and Fort Collins, Colorado; and the packaging assembly process is primarily in Singapore and Korea. It is not uncommon for professionals at each of these locations to be involved in the same project. When team members are spread across different time zones and continents, the opportunity for direct communication is severely limited. Electronic communication such as the Internet, e-mail, and teleconferencing takes on much more importance in virtual projects because this is the primary means of communication. See Snapshot from Practice: Managing Virtual Global Teams for an example of how this works.

SNAPSHOT FROM PRACTICE
Managing Virtual Global
Teams*

Carl A. Singer, a senior program manager at IBM Global Services, described how global time zones were used to complete a time intensive project. The project required subject matter experts (SMEs) to document existing best practices in maintenance domain and to port these into a knowledge management tool. The most proficient SMEs available were on opposite sides of the globe—Australia and Scotland. Review and control of the project was from the United States.

Management realized that just working harder and smarter was not going to meet the time and quality targets. For this project they used the dimension of time to their benefit. Applying sound management principles as well as taking advantage of electronic communication systems, the team was able to create a virtual 24-hour workday for quick responses and accelerated reviews.

Each team consisted of veteran professionals familiar with the rigors of time-pressured consulting projects. A local point person was identified for each team and mutually agreed-upon targets, terminology, and processes were established.

An all-hands kick-off meeting was organized in which participants were able to socialize, understand local and projectwide constraints, and finalize an agreed-upon plan. The meeting was held at a corporate hotel with dining accommodations. The facility was considered an "assisted living community for IBM consultants." This hastened recovery from jet lag and provided an interruption-free work environment.

Upon returning to their home bases, each team created the majority of their deliverables independently with periodic three-way conference calls to maintain coordination. A project control book was established electronically so that all participants had access to the latest project documents.

The final phase of the project required intense interfacing and reviews between the teams. These reviews necessitated changes to deal with concerns, differences among subprojects, and other issues. It was here that the worldwide nature of the project was leveraged. Using a "dry cleaning approach" (in by 5 P.M. out by 9 A.M.) team members in Australia and Scotland were able to address issues generated during the U.S.-based external reviews and provide concrete responses by the beginning of the next business day. Conference calls at 6:00 A.M. (U.S. EST) were used to coordinate responses and resolve issues. Conference calls at the end of the U.S. workday were used to finalize issues and assignments. Figure 11.6 depicts the 24-hour clock used to align communication schedules.

Telephone conferencing was used instead of videoconferencing due to the setup lead time and because it would force participants to leave their offices. E-mail was used extensively for general communication. An electronic repository of project work was used to coordinate global involvement. In practice, a participant could draft a document and deposit it electronically only to wake up the next day to find the document annotated with suggested revisions. Likewise, one could start the day by checking an in-basket populated with documents to review and issues to address. Over time, "G'day" and "Cheers" crept into the U.S. speech—a clear indicator of team cohesion.

Singer identified a number of lessons learned from the project. These included:

- The all-hands kick-off meeting was critical for establishing goals and procedures as well as "rules of courtesy."
- Loosen the reins—establish clear deliverables and then step out of the way and let the professionals do their work.
- Establish and enforce agreed-upon quality standards and deliverable templates.
- Maintain a regular schedule of conference calls, even if only to say "Hello, we have nothing to talk about today." Conference calls should be guided by pre-established agendas, note-taking procedures, and reviews.

* Carl A. Singer, "Leveraging a Worldwide Project Team," *PM Network,* April 2001, pp. 36–40.

United States (East Coast)	Australia	Scotland	Comments
12 midnight	2 PM	5 AM	
1 AM	3 PM	6 AM	
2 AM	4 PM	7 AM	
3 AM	5 PM	8 AM	
4 AM	6 PM	9 AM	Australia handoff for off-shift review
5 AM	7 PM	10 AM	
6 AM	8 PM	11 AM	3-way conferencing window (primary)
7 AM	9 PM	12 noon	3-way conferencing window (primary)
8 AM	10 PM	1 PM	3-way conferencing window (primary)
9 AM	11 PM	2 PM	
10 AM	12 midnight	3 PM	
11AM	1 AM	4 PM	
12 noon	2 AM	5 PM	Scotland handoff for off-shift review
1 PM	3 AM	6 PM	
2 PM	4 AM	7 PM	
3 PM	5 AM	8 PM	
4 PM	6 AM	9 PM	3-way conferencing window (secondary)
5 PM	7 AM	10 PM	3-way conferencing window (secondary)
6 PM	8 AM	11 PM	U.S. handoff for off-shift review
7 PM	9 AM	12 midnight	
8 PM	10 AM	1 AM	
9 PM	11 AM	2 AM	
10 PM	12 noon	3 AM	
11 PM	1 PM	4 AM	
12 midnight	2PM	5 AM	

☐ Prime time   ☐ Secondary time   ■ Downtime

FIGURE 11.6   *24–Hour Global Clock*

Two of the biggest challenges involved in managing a virtual project team are developing trust and effective patterns of communication (Lipsinger and DeRosa, 2010). Trust is difficult to establish in virtual project management. Unlike working as a traditional team, where members can see whether someone has done what they say they have done, virtual team members depend on the word of distant members. At the same time, it can be difficult to trust someone whom you may have met only one or two times or not at all. Geographical separation also prohibits the informal social interactions that are often essential to building camaraderie among team members. As one virtual team member put it, "You can't have a beer together over the Internet."

So how can a project manager facilitate the development of trust within a virtual team? First, if it is impossible to hold a face-to-face meeting in the beginning, managers need to orchestrate the exchange of social information—who everyone is and some personal background information during the initial electronic interchange. Second, they need to set clear roles for each team member. Ideally, specific tasks should be assigned to each member so that they can make an immediate contribution to the project. Trust in virtual projects grows through team member reliability, consistency, and responsiveness (Coutu, 1998). Finally, the project manager must consistently display enthusiasm and an action orientation in all messages; this spirit will hopefully spread to other team members.

The second major challenge for managing a virtual project team is to establish effective patterns of communication. E-mail and faxes are great for communicating facts—but not the feelings behind the facts; nor do they allow for real-time communication. Conference calls and project chat rooms can help, but they also have their limitations. Videoconferencing is a significant improvement over nonvisual electronic forms of communication. Still, it is a very expensive medium, and real-time interaction is available on only the most advanced and expensive systems. The maxim is match technology to the communication need. Here are some guidelines developed by 3M for use on their distributed projects:[10]

- *When to e-mail.* To distribute important information and news in a one-to-one or one-to-many frame of reference.
- *When to use electronic bulletin boards.* To encourage discussion and flush out diversity of opinion on issues.
- *When to videoconference.* Videoconference when you need to see each other's face and expressions. This is important during the early phases of a project, when you are building relationships and developing a common understanding of what needs to be done. Use, again, when working on critical decisions and/or contentious issues.
- *When to use conference calls.* When people in different locations are working with common documents, presentations, sketches, and models. Use for status report meetings and to sustain social camaraderie.
- *When to fly.* Fly to build or repair trust. Use travel budget to get all key players together early on to instill commitment to the goals of the project and engage in team-building activities.

Even with the best communication system, managers have to overcome the problem of time zone differences, cultural nuances, and finding a convenient time for people to conference.

Below are some additional tips for alleviating communication problems and enhancing the performance of virtual teams:

1. **Keep team members informed on how the overall project is going.** Use shareware or develop a central access point such as either a Web site or LAN account to provide members with updated project schedules. Team members need to know where they fit in the big picture.
2. **Don't let team members vanish.** Virtual teams often experience problems getting in touch with each other. Use an Internet scheduling software to store members' calendars.
3. **Establish a code of conduct to avoid delays.** Team members need to agree not only on what, when, and how information will be shared but also on how and when they will respond to it.

---

[10] "3M Meeting Network," from www.3M.com/meetings, accessed 6/6/2002.

Develop a priority system to distinguish messages that require immediate response from those with longer time frames.

4. **Establish clear norms and protocols for surfacing assumptions and conflicts.** Because most communication is nonvisual, project managers cannot watch body language and facial expressions to develop a sense of what is going on. They need to probe deeper when communicating to force members to explain their viewpoints, actions, and concerns more clearly; they must double-check comprehension.

5. **Share the pain.** Do not require everyone to conform to your time zone and preferences. Rotate meeting times so that all team members have a turn working according to their clock.

To some extent managing a virtual project team is no different from managing a regular project team. The key is working within the constraints of the situation to develop effective ways for team members to interact and combine their talents to complete the project.

PROJECT TEAM PITFALLS

High-performance project teams can produce dramatic results. However, like any good thing, there is a dark side to project teams that managers need to be aware of. In this section we examine in more detail some of the pathologies that high-performance project teams can succumb to and highlight what project managers can do to reduce the likelihood of these problems occurring.

Groupthink

Janis (1982) first identified *groupthink* as a factor that influenced the misguided 1961 Bay of Pigs invasion of Cuba. His term refers to the tendency of members in highly cohesive groups to lose their critical evaluative capabilities. This malady appears when pressures for conformity are combined with an illusion of invincibility to suspend critical discussion of decisions. As a result decisions are made quickly with little consideration of alternatives; often the practice leads to fiascoes that, after the fact, appear totally improbable. Some of the symptoms of groupthink include the following:

- *Illusion of invulnerability.* The team feels invincible. It is marked by a high degree of esprit de corps, an implicit faith in its own wisdom, and an inordinate optimism that allows group members to feel complacent about the quality of their decisions.

- *Whitewash of critical thinking.* The group members discuss only a few solutions, ignoring alternatives; they fail to examine the adverse consequences that could follow their preferred course of action; and they too quickly dismiss any alternatives that, on the surface, appear to be unsatisfactory.

- *Negative stereotypes of outsiders.* "Good guy/bad guy" stereotypes emerge in which the group considers any outsiders who oppose their decisions as the bad guys, who are perceived as incompetent and malicious and whose points are unworthy of serious consideration.

- *Direct pressure.* When a team member does speak out or question the direction in which the team is headed, direct pressure is applied to the dissenter. He or she is reminded that speed is important and that the aim is agreement, not argument.

Bureaucratic Bypass Syndrome

Project teams are often licensed to get things done without having to go through normal protocols of the parent organization. Bypassing bureaucratic channels is appealing and invigorating. However, if bypassing becomes a way of life, it results in the rejection of bureaucratic policies and procedures, which provide the glue for the overall organization. A team that operates outside the organization may alienate other workers who are constrained by the norms and procedures of the organization; eventually, these outside bureaucrats will find ways to put up roadblocks and thwart the project team (Johansen et al., 1991).

Team Spirit Becomes Team Infatuation

High-performance project teams can be a tremendous source of personal satisfaction. The excitement, chaos, and joy generated by working on a challenging project can be an invigorating experience. Leavitt and Lipman-Blumen (1995) even go so far as to say that team members behave like people in love. They become infatuated with the challenge of the project and the talent around them. This total preoccupation with the project and the project team, while contributing greatly to the remarkable success of the project, can leave in its wake a string of broken professional and personal relationships that contribute to burnout and disorientation upon completion of the project.

Going Native

Going native is a phrase first used by the British Foreign Service during colonial times to describe agents who assumed the customs, values, and prerogatives of their foreign country assignment.[11] They did so to the point that they were no longer representing the best interests of the British government but rather those of the natives. This same phenomenon can occur within project teams working abroad or in those who become closely identified with their customers. In essence, the customer's interests take precedence over the parent organization's interests. This change in viewpoint can lead to excessive scope creep and open defiance of corporate policy and interests.

Dealing with these maladies is problematic because, in most cases, they are a distortion of a good thing, rather than a simple evil. Awareness is the first step for prevention. The next step is to take preemptive action to reduce the likelihood of these pitfalls occurring. For example, managers can reduce the isolation of the project team by creating work-related connections outside the project team. These interactions naturally occur in a matrix environment where members work on multiple projects and maintain ties to their home department. Likewise, the isolation of dedicated project teams can be reduced by the timely involvement of external specialists. In either case, the active involvement of relevant members of the parent organization at project status meetings can help maintain the link between the project and the rest of the organization. If the team appears to be suffering from groupthink, then the project manager can encourage functional conflict by playing a devil's advocate role to encourage dissent or using a structured problem-solving approach like the nominal group technique (see Snapshot). Finally, formal team-building sessions may reveal dysfunctional norms and refocus the attention of the team on project objectives.

---

[11] Recent movie examples of this include *Avatar* (2010) and *The Sleeping Dictionary* (2003).

SNAPSHOT FROM PRACTICE

Nominal Group
Technique*

GE Appliances, U.S. West, Marriott Corp., and Hewlett-Packard are among the many firms that use **nominal group technique (NGT)** to guide decisions on projects. The NGT begins by gathering project team members and/or stakeholders around a table and identifying the project problem at hand. Each member then writes his or her solutions. Next, each member presents his or her solution to the group, and the leader writes these solutions on a chart. No criticism is allowed. This process continues until all of the ideas have been expressed. Each solution then is discussed and clarified by the group. After all the ideas have been discussed, the group members privately rank-order their preferred solutions. The balloting is tallied to create a rank-ordering of each solution. These steps are repeated if necessary to refine the list further in order to get the most preferred solution.

NGT provides an orderly process for dealing with potentially inflammatory problems. It also prevents groupthink from occurring. NGT discourages any pressure to conform to the wishes of a high-status, powerful group member since all ideas are discussed and all preferences are expressed privately. Creativity should be enhanced since members are able to offer a solution based on their expertise and viewpoint. Finally, important decisions can be made in a relatively timely manner. NGT works best when there is a well-defined problem.

* Andrew Delbeeq, Andrew H. Van de Ven, and D. H. Gustafson, *Group Techniques for Program Planning* (Glenview, Il: Scott Foresman, 1975).

Summary

Project managers often work under less-than-ideal conditions to develop a cohesive team committed to working together and completing the project to the best of their abilities. They have to recruit personnel from other departments and manage the temporary involvement of team members. They have to bring strangers together and quickly establish a set of operational procedures that unite their efforts and contributions. They have to be skilled at managing meetings so that they do not become a burden but rather a vehicle for progress. Project managers need to forge a team identity and a shared vision, that command the attention and allegiance of participants. They need to use group incentives to encourage teamwork while recognizing when it is appropriate to single out individuals for special recognition. Project managers have to encourage functional conflict that contributes to superior solutions while being on guard against dysfunctional conflict that can break a team apart. In doing these things, they have to be careful not to do too good a job and avoid the pitfalls of excessive group cohesion.

While agendas, charters, visions, rewards, and so forth are important tools and techniques, it has been emphasized both in this chapter and in Chapter 10 that the most important tool a project manager has to build an effective project team is his or her own behavior. Just as the founding members of an organization shape the culture of the organization, the project manager shapes and influences the internal culture of the project team. A positive example can define how team members respond to changes, how they handle new tasks, and how they relate to one another and the rest of the organization. There is no easy way to lead by example. It requires personal conviction, discipline, sensitivity to team dynamics, and a constant awareness of how personal actions are perceived by others.

Key Terms

Brainstorming
Dysfunctional conflict
Functional conflict
Groupthink

Nominal group technique
 (NGT)
Positive synergy
Project kick-off meeting

Project vision
Team building
Team rituals
Virtual project team

Review Questions

1. What are the differences between the five-stage model of team development and the punctuated equilibrium model?
2. What are the elements of an effective project vision? Why are they important?
3. Why should a project manager emphasize group rewards over individual rewards?
4. What is the difference between functional and dysfunctional conflict on a project?
5. When would it be appropriate to hold a formal team-building session on a project?
6. What are the unique challenges to managing a virtual project team?
7. What can a project manager do to avoid some of the pitfalls of a highly cohesive project team?

Exercises

1. The following activities are based on a recently completed group project that you have been involved in. This project may have been a student project, a work project, or an extracurricular project.
   a. Analyze the development of the team in terms of the five-phase model and the punctuated equilibrium model. Which model does the best job of describing how the team evolved?
   b. Analyze the group in terms of the nine situational factors that influence team development. What factors positively contributed to group performance? What factors negatively contributed to group performance? How did the group try to overcome the negative factors? What could you have done differently to overcome these negative factors?

c. Analyze how effectively the group managed meetings. What did the group do well? What didn't the group do well? If the group were formed again, what specific recommendations would you make about how the group should manage meetings?

2. Assume that you have the following decision-making options: (1) make the decision on your own with available information, (2) consult others before making a decision, and (3) call a meeting and reach a consensus, seeking to arrive at a final decision everyone can agree on. Which approach would you use to make each of the following decisions and why?

a. You are the project leader for Casino Night on campus, a charitable event organized by your group to raise money for the homeless. The event was a big success, garnering a net profit of $3,500. Before the event your team researched nearby organizations that support the homeless and to whom the money could be given. You narrowed the choices to the "Chunk of Coal House" and "St. Mary's Soup Kitchen." Eventually your group decided that the funds be given to Chunk of Coal. You are about to write a check to its director when you read in the local newspaper that the Chunk of Coal House has terminated operations. What should you do with the money?

b. You are a golf course designer hired by Trysting Tree Golf Club to renovate their golf course. You have worked closely with the board of directors of the club to develop a new layout that is both challenging and aesthetically pleasing. Everyone is excited about the changes. The project is nearly 75 percent complete when you encounter problems on the 13th hole. The 13th hole at Trysting Tree is a 125-yard par three in which golfers have to hit their tee shots over a lake to a modulated green. During the construction of the new tee box, workers discovered that an underground spring runs beneath the box to the lake. You inspected the site and agreed with the construction supervisor that this could create serious problems, especially during the rainy winter months. After surveying the area, you believe the only viable option would be to extend the hole to 170 yards and create elevated tees on the adjacent hillside.

c. You are the leader of a new product development project. Your team has worked hard on developing a third-generation product that incorporates new technology and meets customer demands. The project is roughly 50 percent complete. You have just received a report from the marketing department detailing a similar product that is about to be released by a competitor. The product appears to utilize radical new design principles that expand the functionality of the product. This poses a serious threat to the success of your project. Top management is considering canceling your project and starting over again. They want you to make a recommendation.

3. The following activities are based on a current or recently completed group project that you have been involved in. This project may be a student project, a work project, or an extracurricular project.

a. How strong is the team identity on this project and why?

b. What could participants do to strengthen team identity?

c. What kind of informal activities could be used to rejuvenate the team? Why would these activities work?

References

Adams, J. R., and S. E. Brandt, "Behavioral Implications of the Project Lifecyle," *Project Management Handbook,* 2nd ed., D. I. Cleland and W. R. King (eds.), (New York: Van Nostrand Reinhold, 1988), pp. 206–30.

Berkun, S., *The Art of Project Management* (Sebastopol, CA: O'Reilly, 2005).

Cleland, D. I., "Team Building: The New Strategic Weapon," *PM Network,* Vol. 11 (1) 1997.

Bowen, K. H., K. B. Clark, C. A. Holloway, and S. C. Wheelwright, *The Perpetual Enterprise Machine,* (New York: Oxford Press, 1994).

Bolman, D. G., and T. E. Deal, What Makes Teams Work," *Organizational Dynamics,* vol. 21 (2), 1992, pp. 34–45.

Coutu, D. L., "Organization Trust in Virtual Teams," *Harvard Business Review,* Vol. 76 (3) 1998, pp. 20–21.

DeMarco, T., and T. Lister, *Peopleware: Productive Projects and Teams,* 2nd ed. (New York: Dorsett House, 1999).

Ericksen, J., and L. Dyer, "Right from the Start: Exploring the Effects of Early Team Events on Subsequent Project Team Performance," *Administrative Science Quarterly*, 49 (3) 2004, pp. 438–71.

Frame, J. D., *Managing Projects in Organizations* (San Francisco: Jossey-Bass, 1995).

Hackman, J. R., *Leading Teams: Setting the Stage for Great Performances* (Cambridge, MA: Harvard Business School Press, 2002).

Homans, G. C., *Social Behavior: Its Elementary Forms* (New York: Harcourt Brace Jovanovich, 1961).

Janis, I. L., *Groupthink* (Boston: Houghton Mifflin, 1982).

Johansen, R., D. Sibbett, S. Benson, A. Martin, R. Mittman, and P. Saffo, *Leading Business Teams: How Teams can use Technology and Group Process Tools to Enhance Performance* (Reading, MA: Addison-Wesley, 1991).

Katz, R., "How a Team at Digital Equipment Designed the 'Alpha' Chip," *The Human Side of Managing Technological Innovation,* 2nd ed. Ed. Ralph Katz (New York: Oxford University Press, 2004), pp. 121–33.

Katzenbach, J. R., and D. K. Smith, *The Wisdom of Teams* (Boston: Harvard Business School Press, 1993).

Kidder, T., *The Soul of a New Machine* (New York: Avon Books, 1981).

Kirkman, B. L., B. Rosen, C. B. Gibson, P. E. Tesluk, and S. O. McPherson, "Five Challenges to Virtual Team Success: Lessons From Sabre, INC.," *Academy of Management Executive,* 16 (2) 2002, pp. 67–79.

Leavitt, H. J., and J. Lipman-Blumen, "Hot Groups," *Harvard Business Review,* Vol. 73 1995, pp. 109–16.

Likert, R., *New Patterns in Management,* (New York: McGraw-Hill, 1961).

Linetz, B. P., and K. P. Rea, *Project Management for the 21st Century* (San Diego: Academic Press, 2001).

Lipsinger, R., and DeRosa D., *Virtual Team Success: A Practical Guide for Working and Leading from a Distance* (San Francisco: Jossey-Bass, 2010).

Maier, N. R. F., *Problem Solving and Creativity in Individuals and Groups* (Belmont, CA: Brooks-Cole, 1970).

Maier, N. R. F., *Problem-Solving Discussion and Conference,* (New York: McGraw-Hill, 1963).

Malhotra, A., A. Majchrzak, and B. Rosen, "Leading Virtual Teams," *Academy of Management Perspectives*, 21 (1) 2007, pp. 60–70.

Maznevski, M. L., and K. M. Chudoba, "Bridging Space over Time: Global Virtual Team Dynamics and Effectiveness," *Organization Science,* Vol. 11 (5), September–October 2000, pp. 473–92.

Posner, B. Z., "What's All the Fighting About? Conflicts in Project Management," *IEEE Transactions in Engineering Management*, EM-33, 1986, pp. 207–211.

Peters, T., *Thriving on Chaos: Handbook for a Management Revolution* (New York: Knopf, 1988).

Ritti, R. R., and S. L. Levy, *The Ropes to Skip and the Ropes to Know: Studies in Organizational Behavior* (New York: Wiley, 2009).

Senge, P. M., *The Fifth Discipline* (New York: Doubleday, 1990).

Seta, J. J., P. B. Paulus, and J. Schkade, "Effects of Group Size and Proximity under Cooperative and Competitive Conditions," *Journal of Personality and Social Psychology,* 98 (2) 1976, pp. 47–53.

Sherif, M., *Group Conflict and Cooperation: Their Social Psychology* (Chicago: Aldine, 1967).

Siebdrat, F., M. Hoegl, and H. Ernst, "How to Manage Virtual Teams," *MIT Sloan Management Review,* http://sloanreview.mit.edu/the-maazine/2009-summer/50412/ how-to manage-virtual teams/2009.

Skilton, P. F., and K. J. Dooley, "The Effects of Repeat Collaboration on Creative Abrasion," *Academy of Management Review,* 35 (1) 2010, pp. 118–34.

Smith, B. J., "Buiolding Shared Visions: How to Begin," *The Fifth Discipline Fieldbook: Strategies and Tools for Building a Learning Organization,* eds. P. M. Senge, C. Roberts, R. B. Ross, B. J. Smith, and A. Kleiner (New York: Doubleday, 1994), pp. 312–327.

Smith, P. G., and D. G. Reinertsen, *Developing Products in Half the Time* (New York: Van Nostrand Reinhold, 1995).

Thamhain, H. J., and D. L. Wilemon, "Conflict Management in Project Life Cycle," *Sloan Management Review,* Vol. 16 (3) 1975, pp. 31–41.

Thoms, P., "Creating a Shared Vision with a Project Team," *PM Network,* January 1997, pp. 33–35.

3M, "Leading a Distributed Team," *www.3m.com/meetingnetwork/readingroom/ meetingguide_distribteam.html.* Accessed June 6, 2006.

Tuchman, B. W., "Development Sequence of Small Groups," *Psychological Bulletin,* vol. 63 (1965), pp. 384–399.

Tuchman, B. W., and M. C. Jensen, "Stages of Small Group Development Revisited," *Group and Organizational Studies,* Vol. 2 1977, pp. 419–27.

Vroom, V. H., and A. G. Jago, *The New Leadership* (Englewood Cliffs, NJ: Prentice Hall, 1988).

Zander, A., *Making Groups Effective* (San Francisco: Jossey-Bass, 1994).

APPENDIX 11.1

Project Human Resource Management

1. INTRODUCTION

In the final analysis, some aspects of human association are inevitable in any group of activities – whether primarily industrial, economic, political, social, or cultural in nature. Project management is no exception. Therefore, proficiency in understanding the human behavior and making skillful use of the knowledge and techniques for managing the group of human resources contribute immensely to success in project management.

Human behavior is highly complex in nature and no simple theories for understanding human behaviour or techniques for successfully managing them for achieving specific objectives have been established so far. Indeed, some general principles for setting up and maintaining effective relationships in an industrial or commercial organization are in practice, but there is probably more art than science to it. In this backdrop the discussion on human relation aspect in project management should be approached.

The approach of PMBOK® Guide for project human resources management is focused specifically on four aspects:

1. *Different types of organizational structures* for project management and the impact of the organization structure on effectiveness in managing project and efficient use of human resources.
2. *Professional and ethical behavior* of the project manager and project team.
3. *Project manager's leadership qualities in building and managing high performance project teams* with judicious use of ways to:
   * motivate the team,
   * influence the behavior of team members through forms of sources for power as well as leading by setting an example, and
   * negotiate effectively and manage the conflict within the team.
4. *Four processes for project human relations management*, which embody generally recognized good practices for successful project management and aim to organize, manage and lead the project team.

In the following text, we shall take up brief discussion of the above four topics.

1.1 Different Forms of Organizational Structures

All organizational structures serve two purposes:

* Division of labour of the tasks required to be performed for effective functioning of organization as a unit.
* Formal structuring of the roles, responsibilities, and reporting relationships necessary for coordinating the activities of all members of the organization.

Projects are performed within the ambits of the organization. The nature of the organization structure as a whole, and particularly, the organization of the project management team within the organization play a very important part in how the projects are managed. The organization structure of the entire organization and the place of project management in it have a great influence on the project manager's role, his authority or influencing power and the availability of resources at his command for managing the project. It is, therefore, a very important enterprise environmental factor influencing the project success. Organization adopts the organization structure for project management depending on the strategic importance of the project in the organization's overall performance.

Depending on the power or position of the project manager and his reporting relationship to the higher management on one hand and the roles and reporting relationships of the project team members with the project manager on the other, the project organizations can be classified into three distinct types:

• *Functional Organization*
• *Projectized Organization (Organizing Projects as Dedicated Teams), and*
• *Matrix Organizations (Weak, Balanced and Strong Matrix Organizations)*

In Chapter 3, 'Organization: Structure and Culture', the three types mentioned above as well as several other variations of different project management organization structures are described and the advantages and disadvantages associated with each structure have been discussed in detail. The interested readers should revisit that part at this point for a review on project organization structures and their relevance to effective and efficient project management. For the sake of comprehensive coverage of topic, the following very brief review is presented below.

(*a*) *Functional Organization:* In the organizations with a very strong emphasis on routine operations and where the focus on the projects is diffused, project management is organized as a part of the existing functional organization. Each manager from the group of functional managers plans, schedules and manages the part of project work related to his functional department and the manager having the maximum work part for the project carries out project coordination. Project manager plays a small part time role and has little or no overall authority for the way the project is managed or the resources are allocated. The merit of such organization structure is that the project are managed with the existing organizational set-up without any major change and the quality of project work carried out by professionals under the functional organization's hierarchy is relatively superior.

(*b*) *Projectized Organization:* In the organizations, where innovation and expansion of diversity and size in its operating activities is very important or in the organizations performing projects for other organization on a contractual basis (essentially construction industry and other contracted project work); the project management plays a major part in the company's overall success. In a projectized organization, though there may be certain functional departments, the major work force of the company is organized under separate different project managers in charge of their individual projects. The staff working for the project manager is entirely devoted to that particular project work. Project manager is a full time manager committed and devoted to that particular project managed by him and has full authority to plan and schedule work, prepare and control budget, and deploy manpower. In this set-up, the project manager has a major role to play, full time assignment, and complete responsibility for project management. He has a better availability of resources and superior communication channels including access to top management. The need for reshuffling the organization every time a new major project is taken up, duplication of efforts for executing similar work packages, and inefficiency in deployment of manpower, are some of the downside features.

(c) *Matrix Organizations:* In between the above two extremes are matrix organizations devised from different blends of the functional and projectized organizations. Depending on the degree of authority and managing role assigned to the project manager and committed resources made available to him, the organizations may be classified as strong, weak or balanced matrix organizations. Weak matrix organizations are closest to functional organizations and strong matrix organizations are closest to the projectized organization. When organizations adopt matrix pattern for organization pattern, most organizations develop their own special version of matrix organization.

1.2 Code of Ethics for the Project Management Profession

PMI ® has all along laid heavy stress on this aspect of the project management profession. A code of ethics for the project management profession was created at PMI 1982 Symposium on Project Management, updated and approved in 1989, and again in 1995. Since 1998, when the code was adopted, many dramatic changes have occurred within PMI and the business world. PMI membership has grown significantly. A great deal of growth has also occurred in regions outside North America. In the business world, ethics scandals have caused the downfall of global corporations and not-for-profit organizations, caused public outrage and sparked increased government regulations. In 2005, the Board commissioned the Ethics Standards Development Committee to deliver the reviewed code by the end of 2006. This Code of Ethics and Professional Development was approved by the PMI Board of Directors in October 2006.

The result of this effort is a Code of Ethics and Professional Conduct that not only describes the ethical values to which the global project management community aspires, but also addresses the specific conduct that is mandatory for every individual bound by this Code. This code affirms four values as its foundation, which the global project management community defined as most important: responsibility, respect, fairness, and honesty.

The full text of the code is accessible from PMI®'s website; interested persons should go to the original PMI®'s site and also see other details about the organization.

1.3 Project Manager's Leadership Qualities: Building and Managing High Performance Project Teams

1.3.1 *Project Manager's Role*

Organization appoints a project manager for looking after or managing the project and achieving the objectives for which the project is authorized. Therefore the first and foremost task for a project manager is to discharge this duty. His role is different from other managers in the functional area, who look after some specific areas of the organization's operation (like a specific production, maintenance or quality control department in a manufacturing plant, accounts or finance function, marketing, sales, human relations management, etc.). Just as the project is a 'temporary endeavor for creating a unique product or service', the project manager is a manager assigned for managing just that specific task – the project. So, what is project manager expected to bring to the table to discharge his duty satisfactorily? The chances for a project manager to succeed in this role and successfully completing the project would depend on to what extent or degree his background includes the following three:

(i) Project management knowledge and skills: The project manager should be familiar with generally accepted good project management practices – knowledge, skills, tools & techniques- for planning and managing a project.

He should, therefore, have knowledge of the project management process groups for initiating, planning, executing, controlling and closing the project. He should also be conversant with the project management processes in different knowledge areas: managing project's scope, time, cost, quality, communication, human relations, risk, procurement and stakeholders. More importantly, he should be able to take a holistic view of these different component plans and requirements and unify and integrate them into a whole cohesive project plan. This would require him to balance the conflicting requirements of different stakeholders and project objectives, make suitable trade-offs and proactively manage the project risk.

(ii) Domain expertise: Of the next importance in the project manager's background would be his domain expertise. The project manager for a chemical manufacture plant should know chemical engineering and preferably also the specific chemical; project manger for a marketing campaign should be a seasoned professional in the marketing; project manger for a banking project should know about the general nature of banking operations. A strong domain expertise is very helpful in empowering the project manager to take the decision of coordinating or trade-off nature about some crucial issue in project management.

(iii) General management experience: Finally, as explained at the start of this appendix, the project manager has to proactively manage relationship with a large number of different interest groups: sponsors and stakeholders, members of project team, client, vendors and contractors, officials of statutory regulation agencies and special public interest groups. The project manager for a major project should be a mature individual, having years of experience in working with people and organizations. He should have developed during this working experience skills for communication, negotiation, and conflict resolution and ability to handle unexpected situations coming up during project planning and execution.

1.3.2 Leadership, Management Style, and Professional Ethics

The personal leadership style and ability to build and manage a motivated high performance project team would greatly improve the chance for project success. The project manager would need to employ the leadership style in the situational context of the nature of the industry, the project and the project phase. For execution phase of very traditional industrial projects, a directive and controlling style might suit better, while for initiating or planning phases of new product or research and development projects, a collaborative and consultative approach would be more helpful. A judicious mixture of both basic management styles (described by McGregor in his famous theory as 'Theory X' and 'Theory Y') is very necessary for all project management situations. Above all, his personal conduct should provide a role model for the team members to follow and at all times it should be above board and fully complying with the professional ethics for project management profession.

Chapter 10, 'Leadership: Being an Effective Project Manager', offers discussion on the issues related to project leadership, management style and professional ethics in somewhat more details:

- Managing versus leading a project
- Managing project stakeholders
- Exercising power and use of influence as an exchange
- Building trust: the key to exercising influence
- Social network building
- Ethics and project management, and
- Qualities of an effective project manager

2.0 Project Human Resource Management Processes

Project Human Resource Management include the processes that organize, manage, and lead project team. (PMBOK® Guide, 5th Edition)

Project human resource management involves preparing a plan for the human resources for the project and building and managing a high performance project management team. This in turn would involve acquiring the project team, training and developing the team members and managing the team to be able to function at desired high performance level to ensure project success. This aspect of building and managing a team would require influencing the project team (motivation, conflict resolution and negotiation) and ensuring ethical and professional behavior of all project team members.

PMBOK® Guide, 5th Edition, includes 4 processes in the project human resource management knowledge area:

- Plan Human Resource Management   (Planning Process Group),
- Acquire Project Team   (Executing Process Group),
- Develop Project Team   (Executing Process Group), and
- Manage Project Team   (Executing Process Group).

We will briefly overview the processes and the inputs, tools and techniques and outputs associated with them.

2.1 Plan Human Resource Management (Planning Process Group)

Plan Human Resource Management is the process of identifying and documenting project roles, responsibilities, required skills, reporting relationships and creating a staffing management plan. (PMBOK® Guide, 5th Edition.)

The basic idea underlying the process is to make sure that a plan is developed for assigning a person or a group of persons to each and every task or activity of the project. In the case of an outsourced product or service, the vendor and the project tem member assigned to supervise the vendor's work should be identified and the role should be accordingly assigned. The process involves identifying and documenting the project roles, responsibilities and reporting relationships and creating a plan for project staffing. In some cases, when the available personnel in the organization require some specific supplementary training, identifying the need and planning for such training is also a part of this process.

Inputs

Project Management Plan – The Project management plan would include the project life cycle, deliverables and how the work would be carried out, baselines for scope, time and cost, type of activities and necessary skills and training in technology. These data would enable the project manager to make a broad high-level plan for the human resources required for managing the project.

Activity Resources Requirements – How many and what skill level persons are required for all project activities is the starting point input for detailed planning. The output of the activity resource requirement process would provide these details.

Enterprise Environmental Factor – The availability of the required people within the organization and the organization's recruitment or training policies and procedures is the next input for this process; it is classified as one of the Enterprise Environmental Factors.

Organizational Process Assets – This refers to the experience of creating the project teams and organization structures for similar earlier projects and the historical information and templates available for use in the organization's archives.

Tools and Techniques

Organization Chart – The technique to be used for the process is construction of organization charts, which would show roles, responsibilities and reporting relationships. Depending on the basic characteristic of the project organization, the organization chart could be presented according to one of the following types:

- *Hierarchical Type Organization Chart – In* case of pure projectized, pure functional form or in some weak matrix based organization structures, organization structure would be Hierarchical Type.
- *Responsibility Assignment Matrix* – It is the usual way of showing the role or responsibility of the person for any specific project activity in balanced or strong matrix organizations.
- *Text Oriented Formats or Position Descriptions* – This mode requires spelling out in text fully the Qualifications, competencies and skills for holding the staff position, responsibilities and authorities.

Expert Judgment – For developing a good project management organization structure, expertise developed by some high level managerial experience is very useful.

Meetings – The meetings are particularly helpful for planning human resources requirements for special technology or special industry projects, where collective experience of the team members, particularly of those members, who had earlier exposure to similar projects in those industries holds a key factor contributing to success.

Outputs

The output of the process is a comprehensive *Human Resource Plan.*

Contents of Human Resource Plan

Human Resource Plan should contain:

- *The roles and responsibilities* of required project team – The role would be like a job description, identifying the main activity for which a person would be accountable. The responsibility would describe the specific work he would be responsible to complete for the project. Along with this, the person's authority for normal working and the competence or skill required to do the job are also included to make the plan comprehensive.

- *Project Organization Chart* – This would include the inter-relationship between the different members of the project organization showing the reporting relationship and extended responsibility and accountability of the function.
- *Staffing Management Plan* – Need for people is different during the different phases and activities of the project. The exact staffing requirement, resource calendar and expected requirement and release dates for staff, and general staff management policies for recruitment, remuneration, training, leave, recognition and reward, etc. are also a part of staffing management plan.

2.2   Acquire Project Team (Executing Process Group)

Acquire Project Team is the process of confirming human resources availability and obtaining the team necessary to complete project activities.

(PMBOK® Guide, 5th Edition)

The human resource planning needs to ensure that the required team member or resource would be available at the time scheduled for carrying out the necessary project activity. The emphasis is usually on claiming and reserving rare resources from the organization's pool. The project manager's detailed planning and communicating & negotiating skills play an important role in effectiveness in this process.

Inputs

Human Resource Management Plan, the output of the earlier process, is the main input for this process. In effect, the human resources, which the project manager planned to include in his team for carrying out the project activities, are acquired either as fulltime team members or according to the resource calendar for activities.

Enterprise Environmental Factors – The availability in the existing organization of human resources with the skills, knowledge or training desired for various project management activities, organization's policies for recruitment and training new personnel, and existing organization structure are important inputs to this process from enterprise environmental factors.

Organizational Process Assets – Organization's personnel policies, particularly for inter-departmental transfers, training, compensatory allowances for special assignments, etc. are inputs based on Organizational Process Assets.

Tools and Techniques

Pre-assignment – The easiest and surest way to acquire project team would be to get the key team members pre-assigned at the very beginning of the project life cycle – say, at the time of designating the project manager at the project charter award stage. The importance of the project in the organization's strategic plan and the project manager's negotiating skills play a crucial role in employment of this technique.

Negotiation – Project manager's negotiating skills and power or influencing play a major role in securing the scarce resources for project team.

Acquisition of Team Members from Outsourcing – Sometimes, the organization does not have , or cannot spare for a particular project certain subject matter experts necessary for project management, e.g. technologists, construction supervisors, security personnel, inspectors, legal experts, project management staff, etc. In these cases, the external agencies or project consultancy organizations can be approached to acquire these resources.

Virtual Teams – In case of multinational organizations, and particularly for a project requiring inputs from consideration of international aspects, virtual teams are constituted. The members of these teams are physically located in different countries (or different places in the same country), but they work on a specific project assignment allotted to them with good mutual coordination. Excellent communication skills and access to modern electronic communication technologies (like e-mails, international dedicated telephone network, facilities for video conferences, effective project management information systems backed by excellent project management software, etc.) are of prime importance for successful working of such teams.

Criteria for Selection of a New Member in the Project Team – For selecting a new additional member to a project team, specific criteria may be set up. These would include the prospective new employee's knowledge, skills, qualifications, experience, expected compensation and its conformity to existing compensation for other members, attitude, and cultural characteristics for easy assimilation in the existing team.

Outputs

Project Staff Assignments – Full time project staff or project team members are assigned specific role, responsibility and reporting relationships in the formal project management organization and the project team organization chart.

Resource Calendars – These documents cover the planning and record of the persons who are going to work for a short specific time or specific activities during the project life cycle. Responsibility Assignment Matrix (RAM) is the tool employed for developing resource calendars.

The above two components of project team, complemented as necessary by procurement from external agencies, constitute the complete project team.

2.3 Develop Project Team (Executing Process Group)

Develop Project Team is the process of improving the technical competencies, team member interaction and overall team environment to enhance project performance.

(PMBOK® Guide, 5th Edition)

For any medium to large size project, the project manager has to depend on a fairly large group of project team members. Project manager's success in managing the project, therefore, depends to a great extent on his in ability to manage the project team – building and maintaining a cohesive, motivated group committed to achieve project objectives. Excellent teamwork is predominantly contributing factor for success and the responsibility of building such a team rests with the project manager. Project manager is responsible for creating an environment for committed cooperative efforts, open and clear communications, smooth conflict resolutions and fair and unbiased treatment of individual team members. Mentoring the junior team members in general managerial practices and arranging for special technical or skills training are also a part of project manager's responsibility.

Inputs

Completion of the project team (through staff assignments, pre-assignments or resource calendars) is the starting point for the team development process. Accordingly the logical inputs for the process are:

Human Resource Management Plan – This plan provides organization charts, staffing management plan, and methodology (policies and procedures) for acquiring, developing (technical training) and managing the staff.

Resource Calendars – and Project *Staff Assignments*, the outputs of the Acquire Project Team process, provide details of the specific persons or groups assigned to the project and become a part of the project team.

Tools and Techniques

In this process, tools and techniques assume much more importance than the inputs.

- *Training* – For removing the specific technical deficiencies related to project tasks is the simpler and explicit form of team development.
- *Team Building Activities* – This is the more difficult part and it puts to test the leadership and general management skills of the project manager. The general principles of good team building are: unambiguous task assignments, clear description of authority and reporting relationships, and fairness in treatment of rewards and recognitions (without favouritism) and transparent communication on project status. *All this is easier said than done and the great project managers and average ones have distinctly different levels of performance in this area.*

The organization behavior (OB) theories have identified five stages for building high performance teams and dismantling them painlessly and fairly after the task completion:

- *Forming* – In this phase, the induction of project team members and their becoming familiar with the project tasks, project team organization and other team members takes place.
- *Storming* – The interaction between the members (and sometimes conflicts between the members) takes place in this phase. Project manager's communication, negotiation and conflict resolution skills are called for here for effective team building.
- *Norming* – The conflicts having been resolved and rough edges honed for collaborative work, the team members work for the project goals.
- *Performing* – The team members strive to attain project goals; the project manager's influencing skills, inspiring the team members with his vision, and leading by personal example would be the norms here.
- *Adjourning* – The team completes the work and the team members are reassigned other tasks in the organization. It is project manager's professional responsibility to facilitate the rehabilitation of the members.

A major part of this Chapter 11: 'Managing Project Teams' is devoted to discussion on developing and managing the project team:

- *The five-stage team development model*
- *Situational factors affecting team development*
- *Building high performance teams*
  - Recruiting suitable project members
  - Conducting project meetings
  - Establishing a team identity
  - Creating a shared vision
  - Managing project reward system

- ▪ Orchestrating decision making process, and
- ▪ Managing conflicts within the project
- *Managing Virtual teams* – (effect of spread of organization across the country and globalization)
- *Dysfunctional teams* – diagnosis and recommendations for revitalization.
- *Co-location* – In cross-functional teams far flung over different geographical areas or seated in distant unconnected places, the development of close bond between the team members is inhibited. Co-location, when possible, is considered an effective way in building high performance teams.

(The interested readers should revisit the corresponding part in this chapter at this point.)

Output

Effectively and cohesively working high performance team and the records of training and team development for lessons learned are the output.

2.4   Manage Project Team (Executing Process Group)

This process is for tracking team member performance, providing feedback, resolving issues, and managing team changes to optimize project performance.   (PMBOK® Guide, 5th Edition)

The process involves the following activities:

- Tracking performance of individual members and facilitating for optimum performance
- Providing transparent and unbiased feedback in the capacity of a mentor
- Resolving issues and smoothen out conflicts
- Providing transparent communication about project activities
- Ensuring that general environment would encourage personal best contributions in project work

Inputs

Like all performance review processes, this process also requires on one hand the work planned for each team member and compare it with the actual performance carried out to measure the performance. Accordingly, *Human Resource Management Plan,* (output of Plan Human Resources Management process), *Project Staff Assignments* (output of Acquire Project Team process), and *Organization Charts*) or *Responsibility Assignment matrix* (*in* case of matrix organizations) are logical inputs for planned work. *Team Performance Assessment* is an input providing a measure of actual performance. *Performance Reports* is one more metric for the results achieved. The comparison of planned versus actual performance gives basis for assessment and feedback for individual team member's performance.

Tools and Techniques

The techniques called for managing the project team effectively and empowering it to give high performance are:

- Creation of a culture for cooperation and collaboration between the team members
- Influencing the team members with the shared vision for project objectives

These techniques are:

Managing the conflict between the team members (to improve collaboration and cooperation between the team members),

Performance appraisals (to provide feedback and guidance for improved performance),

Leadership and influencing skills (to share the project vision and strive for higher performance level),

Delegating tasks and democratic decision-making process (to allow sense of accomplishment and ownership of tasks).

As mentioned earlier, these techniques are discussed in detail in the main body of this chapter and, therefore, not repeated here.

Outputs

The monitoring and *feedback of the performance to the team members on* one hand and sending the record for *organizational performance appraisal* system are two main outputs. Staffing changes may be found from the performance reviews and they in turn could require *change requests for project team.*

CASE 11.1

Kerzner Office Equipment

Amber Briggs looked nervously at her watch as she sat at the front of a large table in the cafeteria at Kerzner Office Equipment. It was now 10 minutes after 3:00 and only 10 of the 14 members had arrived for the first meeting of the Kerzner anniversary task force. Just then two more members hurriedly sat down and mumbled apologies for being late. Briggs cleared her throat and started the meeting.

KERZNER OFFICE EQUIPMENT

Kerzner Office Equipment is located in Charleston, South Carolina. It specializes in the manufacture and sales of high-end office furniture and equipment. Kerzner enjoyed steady growth during its first five years of existence with a high-water employment mark of more than 1,400 workers. Then a national recession struck, forcing Kerzner to lay off 25 percent of its employees. This was a traumatic period for the company. Justin Tubbs was brought in as the new CEO, and things began to slowly turn around. Tubbs was committed to employee participation and redesigned operations around the concept of self-managing teams. The company soon introduced an innovative line of ergonomic furniture designed to reduce back strain and carpal tunnel. This line of equipment proved to be a resounding success, and Kerzner became known as a leader in the industry. The company currently employs 1,100 workers and has just been selected for the second straight time by the *Charleston Post and Courier* as one of the 10 best local firms to work for in South Carolina.

AMBER BRIGGS

Amber Briggs is a 42-year-old human resource specialist who has worked for Kerzner for the past five years. During this time she has performed a variety of activities involving recruitment, training, compensation, and team building. David Brown, vice president of human resources, assigned Briggs the responsibility for organizing Kerzner's 10th anniversary celebration. She was excited about the project because she would report directly to top management.

CEO Tubbs briefed her as to the purpose and objectives of the celebration. Tubbs stressed that this should be a memorable event and that it was important to celebrate Kerzner's success since the dark days of the layoffs. Moreover, he confided that he had just read a book on corporate cultures and believed that such events were important for conveying the values at Kerzner. He went on to say that he wanted this to be an employee celebration—not a celebration conjured up by top management. As such, she would be assigned a task force of 14 employees from each of the major departments to organize and plan the event. Her team was to present a preliminary plan and budget for the event to top management within three months. When discussing budgets, Tubbs revealed that he felt the total cost should be somewhere in the $150,000 range. He concluded the meeting by offering to help Briggs in any way he could to make the event a success.

Soon thereafter Briggs received the list of the names of the task force members, and she contacted them either by phone or e-mail to arrange today's meeting. She had to scramble to find a meeting place. Her cubicle in human resources was too small to accommodate such a group, and all the meeting rooms at Kerzner were booked or being refurbished. She settled on the cafeteria because it was usually deserted in the late afternoon. Prior to the meeting she posted the agenda on a flipchart (see Figure C11.1) adjacent to the table. Given everyone's busy schedules, the meeting was limited to just one hour.

Agenda	
3:00	Introductions
3:15	Project overview
3:30	Ground rules
3:45	Meeting times
4:00	Adjourn

FIGURE C11.1
Celebration Task Force

THE FIRST MEETING

Briggs began the meeting by saying, "Greetings. For those who don't know me, I'm Amber Briggs from human resources and I've been assigned to manage the 10th anniversary celebration at Kerzner. Top management wants this to be a special event—at the same time they want it to be our event. This is why you are here. Each of you represents one of the major departments, and together our job is to plan and organize the celebration." She then reviewed the agenda and asked each member to introduce him/herself. The tall, red-haired woman to the right of Briggs broke the momentary silence by saying, "Hi, I'm Cara Miller from Plastics. I guess my boss picked me for this task force because I have a reputation for throwing great parties."

In turn each member followed suit. Below is a sampling of their introductions:

"Hi, I'm Mike Wales from maintenance. I'm not sure why I'm here. Things have been a little slow in our department, so my boss told me to come to this meeting."

"I'm Megan Plinski from domestic sales. I actually volunteered for this assignment. I think it will be a lot of fun to plan a big party."

"Yo, my name is Nick Psias from accounting. My boss said one of us had to join this task force, and I guess it was my turn."

"Hi, I'm Rick Fennah. I'm the only one from purchasing who has been here since the beginning. We've been through some rough times, and I think it is important to take time and celebrate what we've accomplished."

"Hi, I'm Ingrid Hedstrom from international sales. I think this is a great idea, but I should warn you that I will be out of the country for most of the next month."

"I'm Abby Bell from engineering. Sorry for being late, but things are a bit crazy in my department."

Briggs circled the names of the two people who were absent and circulated a roster so that everyone could check to see if their phone numbers and e-mail addresses were correct. She then summarized her meeting with Tubbs and told the group that he expected them to make a formal presentation to top management within 10 weeks. She acknowledged that they were all busy people and that it was her job to manage the project as efficiently as possible. At the same time, she reiterated the importance of the project and that this would be a very public event: "If we screw up, everyone will know about it."

Briggs went over the ground rules and emphasized that from now on meetings would start on time and that she expected to be notified in advance if someone was going to be absent. She summarized the first part of the project as centering on five key questions: when, where, what, who, and how much? She created a stir in the group when she responded to a question about cost by informing them that top management was willing to pay up to $150,000 for the event. Megan quipped, "This is going to be one hell of a party."

Briggs then turned the group's attention to identifying a common meeting time. After jousting for 15 minutes, she terminated the discussion by requesting that each member submit a schedule of free time over the next month by Friday. She would use this information and a new planning software to identify optimal times. She ended the meeting by thanking the members for coming and asking them to begin soliciting ideas from co-workers about how this event should be celebrated. She announced that she would meet individually with each of them to discuss their role on the project. The meeting was adjourned at 4:00 P.M.

1. Critique Briggs's management of the first meeting. What, if anything, should she have done differently?
2. What barriers is she likely to encounter in completing this project?
3. What can she do to overcome these barriers?
4. What should she do between now and the next meeting?

CASE 11.2

Ajax Project

Tran was taking his dog Callie on her evening walk as the sun began to set over the coastal range. He looked forward to this time of the day. It was an opportunity to enjoy some peace and quiet. It was also a time to review events on the Ajax project and plot his next moves.

Ajax is the code name given by CEBEX for a high-tech security system project funded by the U.S. Department of Defense (DOD). Tran is the project manager and his core team consisted of 30 full-time hardware and software engineers.

Tran and his family fled Cambodia when he was four years old. He joined the U.S. Air Force when he was 18 and used the education stipend to attend Washington State University. He joined CEBEX upon graduating with a dual degree in mechanical and electrical engineering. After working on a variety of projects for 10 years Tran decided he wanted to enter management. He went to night school at the University of Washington to earn an MBA.

Tran became a project manager for the money. He also thought he was good at it. He enjoyed working with people and making the right things happen. This was his fifth project and up to now he was batting .500, with half of his projects coming ahead of schedule. Tran was proud that he could now afford to send his oldest child to Stanford University.

Ajax was one of many defense projects the CEBEX Corporation had under contract with DOD. CEBEX is a huge defense company with annual sales in excess of $30 billion and more than 120,000 employees worldwide. CEBEX's five major business areas are Aeronautics, Electronic Systems, Information & Technology Services, Integrated Systems & Solutions, and Space Systems. Ajax was one of several new projects sponsored by the Integrated Systems & Solutions division aimed at the homeland security business. CEBEX was confident that it could leverage its technical expertise and political connections to become a major player in this growing market. Ajax was one of several projects directed at designing, developing, and installing a security system at an important government installation.

Tran had two major concerns when he started the Ajax project. The first was the technical risks inherent in the project. In theory the design principles made sense and the project used proven technology. Still the technology had never been applied in the field in this matter. From past experience, Tran knew there was a big difference between the laboratory and the real world. He also knew that integrating the audio, optical, tactile, and laser subsystems would test the patience and ingenuity of his team.

The second concern involved his team. The team was pretty much split down the middle between hardware and electrical engineers. Not only did these engineers have different skill sets and tend to look at problems differently, but generational differences between the two groups were evident as well. The hardware engineers were almost all former military, family men with conservative attire and beliefs. The electrical engineers were a much motlier crew. They tended to be young, single, and at times very cocky. While the hardware engineers talked about the Seattle Mariners, raising teenagers, and going to Palm Desert to play golf, the software engineers talked about Vapor, the latest concert at the Gorge amphitheater, and going mountain biking in Peru.

To make matters worse, tension between these two groups within CEBEX festered around salary issues. Electrical engineers were at a premium, and the hardware engineers resented the new hires' salary packages, which were comparable to what they were earning after 20 years of working for CEBEX. Still the real money was to be made from the incentives associated with project performance. These were all contingent on meeting project milestones and the final completion date.

Before actual work started on the project, Tran arranged a two-day team-building retreat at a lodge on the Olympic peninsula for his entire team as well as key staff from the government installation. He used this time to go over the major objectives of the project and unveil the basic project plan. An internal consultant facilitated several team-building activities that made light of cross-generational issues. Tran felt a real sense of camaraderie within the team.

The good feelings generated from the retreat carried over to the beginning of the project. The entire team bought into the mission of the project and technical challenges it represented. Hardware and electrical engineers worked side by side to solve problems and build subsystems.

The project plan was built around a series of five tests, with each test being a more rigorous verification of total system performance. Passing each test represented a key milestone for the project. The team was excited about conducting the first Alpha test one week early—only to be disappointed by a series of minor technical glitches that took two weeks of problem solving to resolve. The team worked extra hard to make up for the lost time. Tran was proud of the team and how hard members had worked together.

The Alpha II test was conducted on schedule, but once again the system failed to perform. This time three weeks of debugging was needed before the team received the green light to move to the next phase of the project. By this time, team goodwill had been tested, and emotions were a bit frayed. A cloud of disappointment descended over the team as hopes of bonuses disappeared with the project falling further behind schedule. This was augmented by cynics who felt that the original schedule was unfair and the deadlines were impossible to begin with.

Tran responded by starting each day with a status meeting where the team reviewed what they accomplished the previous day and set new objectives for that day. He believed these meetings were helpful in establishing positive momentum and reinforcing a team identity among the engineers. He also went out of his way to spend more time with the "troops," helping them solve problems, offering encouragement, and a sincere pat on the back when one was deserved.

He was cautiously optimistic when the time came to conduct the Alpha III test. It was the end of the day when the switch was turned on, but nothing happened. Within minutes the entire team heard the news. Screams could be heard down the hallway. Perhaps the most telling moment was when Tran looked down at the company's parking lot and saw most of his project team walking by themselves to their cars.

As Callie chased some wild bunnies, Tran pondered what he should do next.

1. How effective has Tran been as a project manager? Explain.
2. What problem(s) does Tran face?
3. How would you go about solving them? Why?

CASE 11.3

Franklin Equipment, Ltd.*

Franklin Equipment, Ltd. (FEL), with headquarters and main fabrication facilities in Saint John, New Brunswick, was founded 75 years ago to fabricate custom-designed large machines for construction businesses in the Maritime Provinces. Over the years its product lines became strategically focused on creating rock-crushing equipment for dam and highway construction and for a few other markets that require the processing of aggregate. FEL now designs, fabricates, and assembles stationary and portable rock-crushing plants and services its own products and those of its competitors.

In the 1970s, FEL began to expand its market from the Maritime Provinces to the rest of Canada. FEL currently has several offices and fabrication facilities throughout the country. More recently, FEL has made a concerted effort to market its products internationally.

---

* Courtesy of John A. Drexler Jr., Oregon State University.

Last month, FEL signed a contract to design and fabricate a rock-crushing plant for a Middle East construction project, called Project Abu Dhabi. Charles Gatenby secured this contract and has been assigned as project manager. This project is viewed as a coup because FEL has wanted to open up markets in this area for a long time and has had difficulty getting prospective customers to realize that FEL is a Canadian firm and not from the United States. Somehow these customers view all North American vendors as the same and are reluctant to employ any of them because of international political considerations.

A project of this scope typically starts with the selection of a team of managers responsible for various aspects of the design, fabrication, delivery, and installation of the product. Manager selection is important because the product design and fabrication vary with the unique needs of each customer. For example, the terrain, rock characteristics, weather conditions, and logistical concerns create special problems for all phases of plant design and operations. In addition, environmental concerns and labor conditions vary from customer to customer and from region to region.

In addition to the project manager, all projects include a design engineer; an operations manager, who oversees fabrication and on-site assembly; and a cost accountant, who oversees all project financial and cost reporting matters. Each of these people must work closely together if a well-running plant is to be delivered on time and within cost constraints. Because international contracts often require FEL to employ host nationals for plant assembly and to train them for operations, a human resource manager is also assigned to the project team. In such cases, the human resource manager needs to understand the particulars of the plant specifications and then use this knowledge to design selection procedures and assess particular training needs. The human resource manager also needs to learn the relevant labor laws of the customer's country.

FEL assigns managers to project teams based on their expertise and their availability to work on a particular project given their other commitments. This typically means that managers without heavy current project commitments will be assigned to new projects. For instance, a manager finishing one project will likely be assigned a management position on a new project team. The project manager typically has little to say about who is assigned to his or her team.

Because he secured Project Abu Dhabi and has established positive working relationships with the Abu Dhabi customer, Gatenby was assigned to be project manager. Gatenby has successfully managed similar projects. The other managers assigned to Project Abu Dhabi are Bill Rankins, a brilliant design engineer, Rob Perry, operations manager with responsibility for fabrication and installation, Elaine Bruder, finance and cost accounting manager, and Sam Stonebreaker, human resource manager. Each of these managers has worked together on numerous past projects.

A few years ago, FEL began contracting for team facilitator services from several consulting firms to help new project teams operate effectively. Last month, FEL recruited Carl Jobe from one of these consulting firms to be a full-time internal consultant. A number of managers, including Gatenby, were so impressed with Jobe's skills that they convinced FEL top management of the need to hire a permanent internal facilitator; Jobe was the obvious choice.

Because Gatenby was instrumental in hiring Jobe at FEL, he was excited at the prospect of using Jobe to facilitate team building among Project Abu Dhabi team members. Gatenby was very proud of having secured this project and had expected to be appointed project manager. He knew that this project's success would be instrumental in advancing his own career.

Gatenby told Jobe, "This project is really important to FEL and to me personally. I really need for you to help us develop into a team that works well together to achieve the project's goals within budget. I've observed your success in developing teams on other projects, and I expect you'll do the same for Project Abu Dhabi. I'll take care of you if you help me make this work."

Jobe outlined for Gatenby how he would proceed. Jobe would begin by interviewing team members individually to learn their perceptions of each other and of the promises and pitfalls of being involved in this project. Meetings of the entire team would follow these interviews using the information he collected to help establish a team identity and a shared vision.

Jobe interviewed Bruder first. She expressed skepticism about whether the project could succeed. During the interview, Bruder appeared to be distant, and Jobe could not figure out why he had not established good rapport with her. Bruder intimated that she expected a lot of cost overruns and a lot of missed production deadlines. But not knowing Jobe well, Bruder was reluctant to identify any specific barriers to the project's success. While she would not directly say so, it was clear to Jobe that Bruder did not want to be a part of Project Abu Dhabi. Jobe left this interview confused and wondering what was going on.

Jobe's next interview was with Perry, the operations manager. Perry has worked at FEL for 15 years, and he immediately came to the point: "This project is not going to work. I cannot understand why upper management keeps assigning me to work on projects with Rankins. We simply cannot work together, and we don't get along. I've disliked him from day one. He keeps dropping the fact that he has earned all these advanced degrees from Purdue. And he keeps telling us how things are done there. I know he's better educated than I am, and he's really smart. But I'm smart too and am good at what I do. There's no need for Rankins to make me feel like an idiot because I don't have a degree. Jobe, I'll be honest with you. Rankins has only been here for five years, but I hold him personally responsible for my problem with alcohol, and for its resulting effect on my marriage. I got divorced last year, and it's Rankins's fault."

Jobe next talked with Rankins, who said, "I don't care what you do. Perry and I simply can't work closely together for the nine months it will take to get it done. One of us will kill the other. Ever since I arrived at FEL, Perry has hated my guts and does everything he can to sabotage my designs. We usually worry about customers creating change orders; here it's the fabrication and operations manager who is responsible for them. Perry second-guesses everything I do and makes design changes on his own, and these are always bad decisions. He is out of control. I swear he stays awake at nights thinking up ways to ruin my designs. I don't have this problem with any other manager."

Jobe left these interviews thoroughly discouraged and could not imagine what would come up in his interview with Stonebreaker. But Stonebreaker was quite positive: "I enjoy these international projects where I get to travel abroad and learn about different cultures. I can't wait to get started on this."

Jobe asked Stonebreaker about the ability of various team members to work together. Stonebreaker replied, "No problem! We've all worked together before and have had no problems. Sure, there have been ruffled feathers and hurt feelings between Rankins and Perry. Rankins can be arrogant and Perry stubborn, but it's never been anything that we can't work around. Besides, both of them are good at what they do—both professionals. They'll keep their heads on straight."

Jobe was even more bewildered. Gatenby says this project's success rides on Jobe's facilitation skills. The finance manager appears to want off this project team. The design engineer and operations manager admit they detest each other and cannot work together. And the human resources manager, having worked on projects with Perry and Rankins before, expects a rosy working relationship and anticipates no problems.

Jobe had a second meeting with Gatenby. Before discussing the design of the team-building sessions, he asked questions to learn what Gatenby thought about the ability of team members to work together. Gatenby admitted that there has been very bad blood between Perry and Rankins, but added, "That's why we hired you. It's your job to make sure that the history between those two doesn't interfere with Project Abu Dhabi's success. It's your job to get them to work well together. Get it done."

Their dialogue toward the end of this meeting progressed as follows:

> **Jobe:** "Why do you expect Rankins and Perry to work well together, given their history? What incentives do they have to do so?"
>
> **Gatenby:** "As you should know, FEL requires formal goal setting between project managers and functional managers at the beginning of each project. I've already done this with Bruder, Stonebreaker, Perry, and Rankins. Perry and Rankins have explicit goals stating they must work well together and cooperate with each other."
>
> **Jobe:** "What happens if they do not meet these goals?"
>
> **Gatenby:** "I've already discussed this with top management. If it appears to me after two months that things are not working out between Perry and Rankins, FEL will fire Rankins."
>
> **Jobe:** "Does Perry know this?"
>
> **Gatenby:** "Yes."

1. Evaluate the criteria FEL uses to assign managers to project teams. What efficiencies do these criteria create? What are the resulting problems?
2. Why is it even more important that project team members work well together on international projects such as Project Abu Dhabi?
3. Discuss the dilemma that Jobe now faces.
4. What should Jobe recommend to Gatenby?

CASE 11.4

Kalpataru Team

(Building and Managing a High Performance Project Team)

Abstract

As a leader of the project team, the role of a project manager is to ensure that the entire project team works effectively and efficiently as a coherent unit for project success. Therefore, it is as much important for him to pay attention to managing human relation aspects of the team as focusing on the project related specific major issues. The project manager has to pay close attention to selection of key team members with complimentary skills and mutual compatibility in day-to-day working, excellent communication- listening and persuading, developing empathetic relationship with the team members, and inspiring them with the project vision which would lead them to subordinate personal agenda in favour of project objectives. Above all, he should be able to lead by his own example and project himself as a true leader of his team. The case study describes the formation and working of a project team in an engineering consultancy organization and in the process highlights the relevance of these issues to the project success.

CASE TEXT

The Task

The heat and sultry atmosphere of late October in a non-air conditioned office in Mumbai was sufficient to make most people uncomfortable and uneasy, but Hitesh Mehta had some more reasons to feel depressed. Mr Mehta had come back to India after a stint of 12 years in the US after his Masters in mechanical engineering and working with the prestigious Flour Corporation office as a senior design team leader. He had to come back at a very short notice, about 4 months back, after learning about his father's heart attack and hospitalization. His father was now back home and recuperating and he could feel the sense of relief seen on his mother's and father's faces seeing him around. Being a bachelor, Hitesh had no problems of adjustment of other family members during his stay in India. At first, he had thought of his stay in India as just temporary to tide over the emergency of his father's sickness. He had planned that once his father recovers, he would be able to persuade his parents to join him in the US. As an afterthought, he decided to stay over in India for about a year or so. It was in that context, that he took up the offer of Synergy Engineering Consultants (Synergy) to head their special projects section. Synergy had hoped that while handling some special projects, Hitesh would be able to incorporate into the group some improved practices in handling the engineering design assignments. Five weeks on the job, and Hitesh had begun having serious doubts about the wisdom of his decision to stay back longer and particularly his decision to take up a temporary job with Synergy in the meantime.

The ringing of his intercom broke his chain of thoughts. It was a call from the Chairman Ramesh Lal calling him for a discussion in his office. When Hitesh reached Mr. Lal's office, Arun Desai, HR Director and B.K. Sarkar, Director Finance, were already there. As soon as Raman Patel, Director Engineering, joined the group, Mr. Lal opened the discussion on the special agenda for which this meeting was called.

"We have finally won the tender for preparing the detailed mechanical engineering drawings for the Nuclear Power Corporation, for which we had bid two months back. This is the kind of breakthrough I was looking for. Once we perform creditably on two or three such prestigious assignments, we can move ahead as a leading premium quality engineering consultant", Mr. Lal introduced the agenda for discussion.

"The entire utilities and off sites piping?" inquired Raman Patel.

"No, they have split the order. We got the cooling water, process water and DM water piping. The total work is not large at all – may be around 6,000 man-hours: eighteen or twenty piping layouts and sections, about 400 piping isometrics, some piping supports drawings, and bill of materials summary. We have done many much larger and more complex jobs, I know. It is not the size or complexity of the job, and let me confide: the way we had bid aggressively to beat the competition and get this order, we will probably not make any money on the job either. The reason I want all of us to treat it as an important assignment is only for our strategy to be able to add the name of Nuclear Power Corporation (NPC) to our clients' list. The name adds prestige; so we must do it well and definitely strive to secure from the client a letter of appreciation for work well done.

That's the crux of the situation. After all, who would know what actual detailed engineering we did for them?"

There was a brief silence, while the group digested the information. Then Raman Patel broke the silence and asked, "When are we expected to start and what is the deadline for final completion?"

"By the end of the next week, we should get formal delivery of the relevant details of the basic engineering package to start our work – the equipment layout plans and sections, utility requirements of the process equipment, the equipment drawings and the piping specifications which they want us to follow for the cooling water, process water and DM water services. But it is the usual stuff from the prime engineering contractor, United Engineers India, and I have here with me a set of the draft on which the final version is based. We would have about 3 months to complete our job. Say, we would need to organize a group of about 8-10 engineers and draftsmen to work on the job and, of course, a lot of overtime." Ramesh Lal summed up the situation.

There was a prolonged silence for a few seconds.

"The timing ... The timing is a bit problematical." whispered Raman Patel, " Our contract with the union is up for renewal in the next month and the union workers have already started to put pressure on all members to work to rules, refuse overtime, sort of slow down. The design engineers, though they are not a part of the union, look the other way when these things go on; after all they would have to work with these draftsmen on an hour-to-hour basis once this struggle for the contract renewal is over. So, the job, which could have been done with no sweat at all, is likely to test our managerial ability."

"So, what do you suggest? It would be indeed very difficult to back out at this stage, but bad as it would be, it would be much preferable to our attempting and failing on the job."

"No.... ", Raman hesitated and then continued, "Not back out, but, I think we should handle it differently from our regular jobs. May be as a special project?" And then he looked around the table and smiled at Hitesh.

That is how, after some further discussion, Hitesh got his special project assignment for Nuclear Power Corporation piping detailed engineering.

Kalpataru Team

Heading the Special Projects Cell, Hitesh was not a line manager and the only staffs directly reporting to him was a management trainee engineer Pushpakant and the secretary Geeta. He were to coordinate with the other functional line managers: the heads of different engineering departments, procurement head and three site construction managers and get services of the engineers, draftsmen, site supervisors and other technical personnel to get his special projects planned and executed.

Returning to his office, Hitesh called Pushpakant and briefed him on the meeting's proceedings and the new special project assigned to him. Pushpakant was a mechanical engineering graduate – not too bright academically but quite skillful in interpersonal relations. He had joined as a management trainee, only about a year ago; however, in that relatively short time, he had built up friendly working relationships most people in the office. So, he was quite up-to-date with the undercurrents of corporate politics and could feel the pulse of the middle managers and lower level workers.

On learning about the next special project assignment, he sensed the problems lurking ahead. "Is it the Kalpakam Nuclear Power plant, which is so much in the news every day? It would be a very prestigious assignment, sir; something we would be able to talk with our friends with pride",

Pushpakant started with enthusiasm and then slipped in the caveat, "But, we will have a very difficult time, sir. In this project, the emphasis will be mostly on detailed engineering drafting – layouts, sections and isometric drawings – and not on engineering designs or calculations. The draftsmen and junior engineers' union is just getting ready to intensify their struggle for negotiating the next three years' agreement. They would like to put pressure on the management by putting as many roadblocks in operations as possible for forcing the management to accept the terms in the union's demands. And what better target they would want than this type of prestigious project?"

Hitesh considered this and the realities of the situation started gradually to sink in. Then in a measured tone, he went ahead explaining the plan he had in mind. "I had not thought about this union situation to be so serious. I had just thought that we would form a small team of about 10 or 12 piping draftsmen and two group leaders. The group leaders would help in preparing the master plan, feeding the junior draftsmen with the details necessary to prepare the piping isometrics and keep an eye on the overall accuracy of the work. One good piping engineer can spot-check the layouts and isometrics for improving the accuracy and keeping a tab on the total workflow. Now, I see that we will indeed have difficult times because mostly we would have to get the drawings out from draftsmen. Anyway, the jobs are in our lap and let's try to do the best we can. I am personally determined to make it a success. A work of national importance – building a nuclear power plant of this capacity; I would feel deeply hurt if our group would fail in making our small personal contributions to this national cause. So let us start. Who would you suggest to take in our team as group leaders for the drafting team?"

"We want the top talent on this, right? Then, my personal choice would be Sudhakar Joshi. He is the person you should take as a group leader for this job. He has over 10 years of experience in piping and some earlier work also in mechanical equipment drawings. He is very meticulous and thorough. The only problem, I am afraid, is that he will not agree to work as a group leader for this job, for he is one of the three union leaders and you don't expect that he would cooperate to make things easy for the management at the time of intensified struggle."

"From what you say, he appears to be *the right person* to work as group leader for this job. Then, let me ask you, do you feel that he will not take up this assignment willingly or that he might sabotage the work if we make him accept it?"

"No, he would never sabotage the work. He is that way a straightforward and principled man. But he will just not accept", Pushpakant responded.

"In that case I would at least want to try to persuade him to take this job. I hope to win him over and build the team around him", Hitesh mused.

"Well, in our Hindu mythology, there is a concept of a tree, Kalpataru. If a person would be sitting under such a tree, all wishes of the person would be answered. Sir, if you succeed in winning him over, you would have a winning team – let me call it the 'Kalpataru Team.' The name Kalpataru is also suggestive of Kalpakam Project," Pushpakant chuckled.

"OK, let us try to build the 'Kalpataru Team'. I will talk with Sudhakar tomorrow morning. In the meanwhile, take a look at this draft specification to check if there are any surprises."

Inducting the Key Team Member

The next morning, Hitesh invited Sudhakar in his cabin for a talk. Hitesh had met Sudhakar earlier, but had noticed nothing particularly remarkable about him. Now Hitesh started observing closely and making notes in his mind. He saw that Sudhakar was a medium height, lean man, neatly dressed and wearing glasses. He spoke rather slowly and with a typical Maharashtrian accent, but he talked in a focused manner and he could articulate well what he wanted to convey.

Hitesh explained to him the background of the project and the engineering design and drafting work involved. He stressed the prestigious nature of the assignment, national importance of the Kalpakam Project and the prominent position of National Nuclear Power Corporation in the Indian scene. He explained the urgency in completing the assignment in 3 months time – even if meeting that schedule required doing a lot of overtime. Finally, Hitesh told him that he wanted to take him as the group leader for this project.

Hitesh found Sudhakar quite quick on grasping the nature of the work. His eyes sparkled with interest while grasping the technical details of the work. Then he appeared to be deeply engrossed in thinking out his response. Finally he slowly started to reply, "Sir, this is indeed a very nice project and I feel good that you want to take me up as a group leader for this job. But, in the interest of this important work, I should suggest that you take as a group leader some one else this time."

"But why, another person? I am told *you are just the right person* in our company to work as a group leader for this job."

"Well, I am happy if you have heard good reports about me. But there is a special reason that I should not work as a group leader for this job now. Since you joined the company only a few weeks back, you may not be aware, but I am one of the three leaders of the junior engineers and draftsmen's union. As a part of our strategy to intensify struggle to force management to accept our demands – and they are very fair demands, sir, I assure you, – we are going to ask all draftsmen to work to rules. Not to take any initiatives themselves - just to make design sketches or drawings strictly according to instructions only. If any major changes are required, insist on written instructions from design engineers or supervisors. If a minor detail is missing, just wait at the board until the supervisor comes around and clears that up before drawing the next line. No volunteering of information for improvement. *No overtime – strictly no overtime.* I have been working as a piping draftsman for over 10 years and I know if any one should know, that no group of ten or twelve draftsmen would complete this job in 3 months, unless they take initiatives in preparing drawings and actively cooperate. And the kind of deadline for completion you mention will require full cooperation and very heavy overtime – almost the entire group to be working on the job for 3-4 hours overtime each day. Just take the overtime issue. Now, on one hand, how do I go about my work as a conscientious group leader without asking people to do overtime? And on the other hand how should I ask them to disregard the policy of our union, which I myself advocate to them as a union leader? Some other time, I would have been happy and proud to accept the assignment. But, not now. I cannot refuse to accept the assignment, if you decide to give it to me; but I must make my position clear that in that case, you would not have an effective group leader in your team; like everybody else, I would have to work to rules. Please consider farming this out to some other smaller drafting agency."

There was a silence for a moment, till Hitesh recovered from the impact. Then he stared, "Sudhakar, I am so glad that you put the position so transparently. In fact, your approach makes me more sure of project success now with you as the group leader than I had earlier thought. But, I would respect your feeling and position and not force you to accept the assignment. I too wish that the job had not come at such a time to our company. But then, we have to take things as they come. You know our company and the jobs we got so far. Do you recall any past jobs, which were so prestigious or important? The western world is bent on making the progress of our nuclear development as tough as possible. Waiving aside the tempting rewards and recognition in overseas job offers, some dedicated scientists, who have chosen to work for our atomic energy program, are trying to build the peaceful nuclear power plant in face of such express hostility of the western world. Kalpakam Power Project is one of the challenges our nation has accepted – whether the Indian scientists and engineers rise to meet the challenge of self-reliance of engineering in nuclear energy field. It is the duty of every Indian, who would be in a position to work on and actively contribute towards success of this effort, to do his best. I will share with you my personal feelings and views on this. May be I might not continue working in India – or for that matter, for Synergy Consultants – and I might return to my Flour Corporation job in USA in the next few months. But I imagine, whatever course I might happen to choose a few months from now, if this job is done well, then when I would look back on my professional career years later, I would surely remember with pride my own contribution to this national project – though I do realize that it is indeed a very small contribution." Hitesh stopped to reflect and then added, "Sudhakar, I understand your feelings and position. If you do not want to take up the Group Leader's position now, then I would not pressurize or force you. But, I have one suggestion. Think coolly on what we discussed and come back and tell me about your decision the first thing next week Monday morning."

Sudhakar knocked on Hitesh's cabin door late Monday afternoon – almost just before quitting time. Hitesh waved him in. "Sir, I had a hard thinking to do for the last two days and finally I have decided to accept your suggestion to join as a group leader of the Kalpakam Project Team", Sudhakar said without any preface taking his seat on a chair," And I have also talked about it with our other union brothers. Sir, we all also understand the overall bigger picture and we have decided that our union struggle would not to come in the way of this national effort. I have resigned as the joint secretary of the union, so no personal conflict of interest. As a special exception, the union would not object to our taking up in our team 3-4 senior and competent draftsmen and their doing overtime if necessary, but we would have to make – do for the rest of help from the trainee draftsmen's pool only. The union's struggle would remain as intense as ever as far as other projects are concerned; in fact, it may turn more intense."

Hitesh just offered his hand for handshake and added, "I am happy about your decision and feel proud of the commitment you have shown. We will make this project like a showpiece work. I have just one question. Do you think the trainee draftsmen would be able to give the right quality of work?"

"Sir, don't worry on that score. Since major part of the work is preparing piping isometrics, all that is required for preparing those drawings is for the draftsmen to properly sketch out and enter the details prepared by senior draftsmen. There is no problem with the draftsmanship quality as such with these trainee draftsmen; they just cannot be depended to work out the details independently. We will make sure that they get all details and we will check the drawings prepared by them rather more thoroughly."

Forming the Project Team and Project Launch

Hitesh asked Pushpakant the next day morning to sit down with Sudhakar and finalize the list of the project team members. "If Sudhakar has agreed to take up this assignment as a group leader, we have succeeded in making a right start." Pushpakant was enthusiastic. "Well, then let Sudhakar, you and I meet today afternoon and review the list."

That afternoon, after the list was reviewed in the meeting, Hitesh suggested, "OK, I will take this list and clear it with Raman Patel to check if any of the proposed team members are not working on some other urgent projects, so that they can be immediately released for our work. Once our list is final, then tomorrow afternoon, we will have our first project team meeting."

"Meeting?" Sudhakar was a bit taken back, but he quickly checked himself and said, "Sure, we will be ready."

Raman Patel cleared the list except for one senior draftsman, who was working on another urgent assignment and could not be spared. Sudhakar replaced him with another draftsman of comparable experience.

Hitesh took Ramesh Lal's appointment and explained to him the developments so far. He explained that some special arrangements might be necessary to facilitate the group to work during regular hours and especially for overtime work. Hitesh told him, that for a start, he envisaged the need for the draftsmen in his group for special transport arrangement in the evening and availability of canteen facilities after office hours. He added that as and when he ran into a wall, he might want to come back to Mr. Lal to get his support. Mr. Lal assured Hitesh full support of the management on all reasonable issues.

In the meeting held in the canteen, Hitesh explained the nature of the project work, the types of drawings to be prepared and the tight schedule for completing the drawings. He stressed the importance of the project in context of national development and the also the prestige it would bring to the company, if the job was well done. "Two things are very important for this project: each of our drawings must be entirely free from errors or slips. So if you have any doubts, check and recheck or ask Sudhakar or Pushpakant or me. Secondly, we have to complete this job on a very tight time deadline and so, not only that we would have to work sincerely during the regular time, we would also have to be ready to put in overtime of up to 2- 3 hours every working day if necessary. You would not be able to avail the regular staff bus ride back, when you work overtime; we would make special arrangement for all people who stay back to reach the nearest suburban railway station. Our canteen does not serve tea or snacks after regular office hours. I would talk to the canteen contractor and ask him to make arrangements for serving tea and snacks after office hours. I believe, our good work will bring satisfaction and prestige to all of us and the company. Any questions?" Hitesh posed, but there were no questions. Then Hitesh continued, "So, all of you are ready to start from tomorrow for next 3 months of hard work?" There rose from the group a quiet hum indicating the group's acceptance.

The Kalptaru Team Camp

The list of drawings and the plan for completing them was prepared in the next two days and the selected senior draftsmen started working on he piping plans and sections assigned to them. It was easy to spot who worked on the Kalpataru team in this rather large spread out hall: the drafting tables, over which the lights were on after the office hours till late evening!

After a week, Pushpakant suggested, "Sir, rather than having these draftsmen working on Kalpataru Team scattered all over the hall, why don't we get them together in a small group in a small hall?"

"A good idea, but where is that 'small hall'?"

"In the back side of the records room, there is a space to accommodate 10-12 drafting tables. It will be little cramped, but close working of the group would be helpful"

Hitesh liked the idea and got it done in the next 2 days. Now at the back of the records room was the camp of Kalpataru Team – a group of about 12 draftsmen closely working together for the whole day and doing overtime till about 9:00 PM practically every day. At 5 PM, as all regular workforces closed the shop and left, snacks and tea were ordered and served and the Kalpataru Team camp would turn into a mini-canteen!

After two weeks, the group started working with firm commitment to their tasks. Every one knew the overall plan of work and their own share in the group efforts. There was a strong peer pressure if someone appeared to be not up to the task. If someone had a difficulty, his peers would help him out. The identity of the team became so strong that it was felt even by other engineers and draftsmen in the company, who started referring to the group by the name christened by Pushpakant: "Kalpataru Team". The overtime became such a common practice that if some table was unoccupied after the office hours, it became conspicuous. Hitesh and Pushpakant also started doing overtime and working out some engineering details, re-checking the finished drawings or planning the next week's work. More than anything else, Hitesh wanted the team members to know and feel that as a team leader he was also ready to work as hard as other team members and subordinate his own personal agenda for the group's greater objectives. Not that, there was no friction whatsoever, the differences of opinion and spirited arguments did take place now and then. Under intense work pressure, all people become more edgy. But they never allowed this small friction to come in the way of overall group's work plan.

The team members started knowing other members more closely – not just the names, where they lived and what other family members were. But also some special details like whose children were studying what, if there was any major sickness in the family, who likes hockey and who played cricket in the school team.

So, Hitesh was surprised to see Kumaram working after regular office hours that day. "Isn't today your two-year old son's birthday party? I thought you would leave today on regular time" Hitesh observed. "Yes, it is Viren's birthday, and I would have left on regular time if I could have completed this piping section as I thought I would before the close of the day. But I need some more time. The isometrics of three draftsmen will be held up till I complete it. So I decided to complete it and go – may be I would be an hour and a half late. I called my wife and explained it."

When Kumaram was finally ready to leave for the day, Hitesh came over to his table and slipped in a small package. "A toy car set for your son on his birthday. Appreciate your staying back on your own. Have good celebrations and don't forget to bring a piece of birthday cake for our group!". Kumaram could not say much except muttering a sincere "Thank you, sir."

Mid-term Review

Mid-term project review was scheduled after 5 weeks in the conference room. The senior managers of the company attended such review meetings.

Two days before the meeting, Hitesh discussed with Sudhakar and Pushpakant the type of data and information, which should be available for the mid-term review and asked them to prepare it. The next day, he reviewed it with them, polished it a bit, and finally told them, "O.K., this is fine. Now be ready to present it to the review meeting to-morrow afternoon." This took Pushpakant and Sudhakar by surprise; they did not expect to attend the high-level project review meeting. Hitesh understood the expression on their face and responded, "Well, you are far more familiar with the fine details, so you may as well present them and answer any queries if our senior managers have".

For Pushpakant and Sudhakar, it was a new and first experience to meet the top managers of the company in such a review meeting. They prepared well for the presentation – the drawings, which were completed; the drawings, which were scheduled and the time they would take, the technical queries pending clarification from the client, and so on. At the meeting, Hitesh gave a brief overview of the project indicating that the project was going so far well and that further details would be presented by his assistants. He introduced Pushpakant and Sudhakar to the group, and they gave the detailed presentation.

After the meeting, when they were alone, Raman Patel remarked to Mr. Lal, "The project is doing fine. Hitesh is really fortunate to get hold of good assistants and draftsmen to work on this job". Mr. Lal did not miss the subtle undertone in Raman Patel's remark of belittling of Hitesh's own personal contribution to the project success. Ordinarily, he might have ignored such petty rivalry. This time, though, he was so impressed by exemplary work done by a new man on his managerial team that he felt necessary to go to his rescue with a smiling repartee, "Yes, Raman, but they have been here all this time!"

Eleven weeks passed and the just two days before the set deadline, all drawings were completed. The whole day was spent in preparing the sets and arranging them in the proper order for packing and couriering. The entire team assembled at the end of the day – but this time just for celebration of a job well done and sharing a few snacks and cold drinks. The success of the Kalpataru Team had by this time become a common talk in the company and every one associated with it started feeling the pride of belonging to this team.

Ramesh Lal called Hitesh to his office and said, "I want to talk to your Kalpataru Team before you disband it. Just remind me to drop in by the day end."

"I am very happy with the way you have worked together to make this project a success. In fact, you have shown all of us in this company a new pathway", Ramesh Lal told the team, "Let me share with you that the negotiations with the union are almost in the final stage. We have agreed on certain increases in basic wages, overtime compensation and amenities. I was not sure in the beginning if we could afford this higher burden, but now I am convinced that we would be able to do well with the good name and marketing push this success might give. Though technically, the union agreement would be signed and come into force from the first of the next month, I have decided to make the new agreement on overtime payment rates applicable retroactively to the overtime work you did for this project." This announcement was greeted by the team with spontaneous enthusiasm.

"And something else, which I am sure you all would be happy to hear", Ramesh Lal continued, "We have decided to promote Hitesh to be the Deputy Director- Engineering". Ramesh Lal's announcement caught everyone, including Hitesh, by surprise. The announcement started to draw great applause, when Hitesh intervened and said, "I feel so deeply satisfied that we all made a success of this project. All of you in the project team deserve credit and particularly Pushpakant and Sudhakar deserve great credit. At the same time, the visibility of the project in the organization and the support of the top management – from Mr. Lal and from all other top managers – also played a major role in the project success. So, it is a combination of all these that has culminated in success. I feel happy and proud that the company has considered rewarding me with a promotion. However, I must now share with you all, and you Mr. Lal, particularly, a closely guarded personal secret. My ex-boss at Flour Corporation had asked me four weeks back to return to USA and join back there. He gave me an offer that was like the proverbial 'offer you cannot refuse'. I told him that I needed a month more to honour my current commitments and wind up if he could wait that long. He has graciously extended my joining time and in the long-term interest of my professional career, I have decided to accept that offer. My parents will join me there as soon as visa formalities are taken care of. I was just waiting to bring this common effort of ours to a winning close before I left the company."

In the silence that fell, even scratching of a 2-B pencil on a drawing paper would have been audible!

Questions for Discussion

1. In this chapter, 'Five-Stage Team development Model' and 'Situational Factors Affecting Team development' are described. Explain how the description in that model and the identified factors conform or otherwise with the case details.

2. The chapter highlights a few hints on 'Building High-Performance Project Teams':
   - Recruiting Project Members
   - Conducting Project Meetings
   - Establishing a Team Identity
   - Creating a Shared Vision
   - Managing Project Rewards System,
   - Orchestrating the Decision-Making Process,
   - Managing Conflict within the Project', and
   - Rejuvenating the Project Team

   In the light of the details given in the case, discuss how relevant these techniques or hints appear for building a high-performance team.

3. The earlier chapter, 'Leadership: Being an Effective Project Manager', focused on the role played by the leadership qualities of the project manager in building successful project teams. Discuss the background, general managerial approach and personal character (professional ethics and empathy with the team members) of Hitesh in his role as a project manager in context of that chapter.

4. Notice the professional ethics observed by the principal characters of this project team: Sudhakar Joshi and Hitesh Mehta.

12

OUTSOURCING: MANAGING INTERORGANIZATIONAL RELATIONS

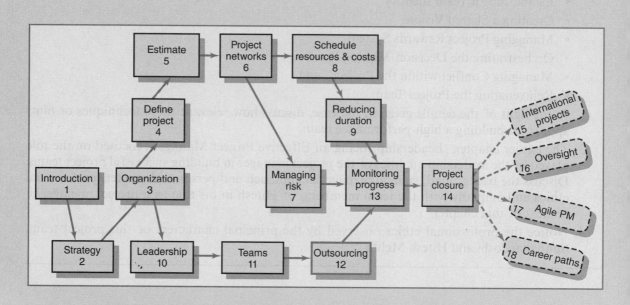

Estimate 5	Project networks 6
Define project 4	Schedule resources & costs 8
Introduction 1	Reducing duration 9
Organization 3	Managing risk 7
Strategy 2	Monitoring progress 13
Leadership 10	Project closure 14
Teams 11	International projects 15
Outsourcing 12	Oversight 16
	Agile PM 17
	Career paths 18

OUTSOURCING: MANAGING INTERORGANIZATIONAL RELATIONS

... being a good partner has become a key corporate asset. I call it a company's
collaborative advantage. In the global economy, a well-developed ability to create
and sustain fruitful collaborations gives companies a significant competitive leg up.

—*Rosabeth Moss Kanter, Harvard Business School professor*

It is rare in today's flat world to find important projects that are being completed totally in-house. Outsourcing or contracting significant segments of project work to other companies is commonplace. For example, nine states attempting to unify the accounting of all their state agencies did not have the internal resources to implement such a large project. Hence, project teams were formed consisting of personnel from software, hardware, and accounting firms to implement the projects. Small high-tech firms outsource research to determine what features customers value in new products they are developing. Even industry giants such as Microsoft and Intel commonly hire independent firms to test new products they are developing.

Contracting project work has long been the norm in the construction industry, where firms hire general contractors who, in turn, hire and manage cadres of subcontractors to create new buildings and structures. For example, the Chunnel project, which created a transportation tunnel between France and England, involved more than 250 organizations. Contracting is not limited to large projects. For example, an insurance company worked with an outside contractor to develop an answering service that directs customers to specific departments and employees. The trend for the future suggests that more and more projects will involve working with people from different organizations.

This chapter extends the previous two chapters' discussion of building and managing relations by focusing specifically on issues surrounding working with people from other organizations to complete a project. First, the advantages and disadvantages of outsourcing project work are introduced. This is followed by a discussion of *best practices* used by firms to outsource and collaborate with each other on projects. The focus then shifts to the art of negotiating, which is at the heart of effective collaboration. Negotiating skills and techniques for resolving disagreements and reaching optimal solutions are then presented. The chapter closes with a brief, but important, note on managing customer relations. In addition, an appendix on contract management is included to augment our discussion of how organizations work together on projects.

OUTSOURCING PROJECT WORK

The term **outsourcing** has traditionally been applied to the transferring of business functions or processes (e.g., customer support, IT, accounting) to other, often foreign companies. For example, when you call your Internet provider to solve a technical problem you are likely to talk to a technician in Bangalore, India, or Bucharest, Romania. Outsourcing is now being applied to contracting significant chunks of project work. For example, Apple and Motorola work closely with manufacturers in China to develop next-generation smartphones. Toyota and DaimlerChrysler collaborate with suppliers to develop new automobile platforms.

The shift toward outsourcing is readily apparent in the film industry. During the golden era of Hollywood, huge, vertically integrated corporations made movies. Studios such as MGM, Warner Brothers, and 20th Century–Fox owned large movie lots and employed thousands of full-time specialists—set designers, camera people, film editors, and directors. Star actors like Humphrey

Bogart and Marilyn Monroe were signed to exclusive studio contracts for a set number of films (e.g., six films over three years). Today, most movies are made by a collection of individuals and small companies who come together to make films project-by-project. This structure allows each project to be staffed with the talent most suited to its demands rather than choosing from only those people the studio employs. This same approach is being applied to the creation of new products and services. For example, see Figure 12.1.

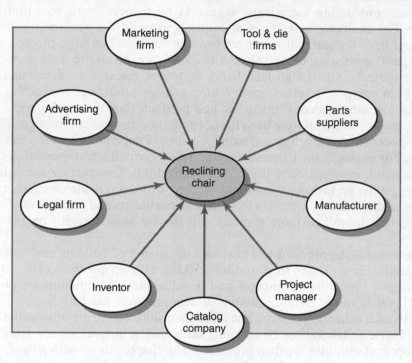

FIGURE 12.1 *Reclining Chair Project*

Figure 12.1 depicts a situation in which a zero-gravity reclining chair is being developed. The genesis for the chair comes from a mechanical engineer who developed the idea in her garage. The inventor negotiates a contract with a catalog firm to develop and manufacture the chair. The catalog company in turn creates a project team of manufacturers, suppliers, and marketing firms to create the new chair. Each participant adds requisite expertise to the project. The catalog firm brings its brand name and distribution channels to the project. Tool and die firms provide customized parts which are delivered to a manufacturing firm that will produce the chair. Marketing firms refine the design, develop packaging, and test market potential names. A project manager is assigned by the catalog firm to work with the inventor and the other parties to complete the project.

Many outsourced projects operate in a virtual environment in which people are linked by computers, faxes, computer-aided design systems, and video teleconferencing. They rarely, if ever, see one another face-to-face. On other projects, participants from different organizations work closely together, for example, at a construction site or in shared office space. In either case, people come and go as services are needed, much as in a matrix structure, but they are not formal members of one organization, just technical experts who form a temporary alliance with an organization, fulfill their contractual obligations, and then move on to the next project.

The advantages of outsourcing project work are many:

1. *Cost reduction.* Companies can secure competitive prices for contracted services, especially if the work can be outsourced offshore. Furthermore, overhead costs are dramatically cut since the company no longer has to internally maintain the contracted services.

2. *Faster project completion.* Not only can work be done more cheaply, but it can also be done faster. Competitive pricing means more resources for the dollar. For example, you can hire three Indian software engineers for the price of one American software engineer. Furthermore, outsourcing can provide access to equipment that can accelerate completion of project tasks. For example, by contracting a backhoe operater you are able to accomplish in four hours what it would take a landscaping crew four days to complete.

3. *High level of expertise.* A high level of expertise and technology can be brought to bear on the project. A company no longer has to keep up with technological advances. Instead, it can focus on developing its core competencies and hire firms with the know-how to work on relevant segments of the project.

4. *Flexibility.* Organizations are no longer constrained by their own resources but can pursue a wide range of projects by combining their resources with talents of other companies. Small companies can instantly go global by working with foreign partners.

The disadvantages of outsourcing project work are less well documented:

1. *Coordination breakdowns.* Coordination of professionals from different organizations can be challenging, especially if the project work requires close collaboration and mutual adjustment. Breakdowns are exacerbated by physical separation with people working in different buildings, different cities, if not different countries.

2. *Loss of control.* There is potential loss of control over the project. The core team depends on other organizations that they have no direct authority over. While long-term survival of participating organizations depends on performance, a project may falter when one partner fails to deliver.

3. *Conflict.* Projects are more prone to interpersonal conflict since the different participants do not share the same values, priorities, and culture. Trust, which is essential to project success, can be difficult to forge when interactions are limited and people come from different organizations.

4. *Security issues.* Depending on the nature of the project, trade and business secrets may be revealed. This can be problematic if the contractor also works for your competitor. Confidentiality is another concern and companies have to be very careful when outsourcing processes like payroll, medical transcriptions, and insurance information.

5. *Political hot potato.* Foreign outsourcing of work is perceived as a major cause of underemployment and U.S. companies are under increased pressure to keep jobs local. Furthermore, companies like Apple have been criticized for the oppressive labor practices of some of their suppliers in China.

Few people disagree that reducing costs is the primary motive behind outsourcing project work. However, there are limits to outsourcing (see Snapshot from Practice: Boeing 787 Dreamliner), and

BACKGROUND

In 2002 the basic design and plans for Boeing's 787 Dreamliner were accepted and given the charter to "Go." The Dreamliner boasts the latest design and revolutionary technology in the history of commercial air travel. But the project met bumpy weather. The first 787 aircraft, scheduled to be tested in July 2007, was delayed until December 2009. Orders for the advanced 787 grew quickly to over 800 planes. This rosy picture presented Boeing with a giant-sized headache. For various reasons (such as design, outsourcing, and labor issues) delivery dates slipped behind three years or more and costs ballooned to several billion dollars. Many analysts blame outsourcing work to foreign suppliers for a majority of the cost and schedule overruns.

KEY FACTORS INFLUENCING OUTSOURCING DECISION

The Dreamliner outsourcing decision that gave 70 percent of plane content to outside suppliers included 30 percent to foreign suppliers. These percentages are greater than any previous commercial plane built by Boeing. Boeing's outsourcing rationale was based on typical economic considerations of cost, sales, and risk. In Boeing's case this meant:

Kyodo via AP Images

Cost. Establishing partnerships with suppliers to lower risks and development costs, along with gaining some valuable expertise and process innovation.

Sales. Farming out numerous designs and component to foreign countries (e.g., Sweden, Italy, South Korea, and China) with the expectation that these countries will buy planes from Boeing in the future.

Risk. Recognizing the need to balance risk of outsourcing at the organizational and operational levels is crucial. The different levels are co-dependent. Taking gigantic steps away from successful outsourcing small amounts of past aircraft to foreign suppliers increases risk. The complexities in coordinating new technology and advance capabilities are daunting.

Clearly, the outsourcing decision ricocheted. Costs are over budget, some sales have been rescinded, customers are seeking compensation for delays, and potential ROI is reduced.

IMPACTS

Boeing's brand has been seriously tarnished by delays and mismanagement. The process to manage the logistics of outsourcing was not able to handle the volume of logistical problems and change management issues. Chronic delays of a few nonperforming partners induced Boeing to buy out or support partners and consumed cash. Wall Street estimates cost overruns range between 12 and 18 billion dollars over the original planned investment of $5 billion. Lessons learned from outsourcing of the 787 Dreamliner can point the way to bring back the shine to Boeing's reputation as the leader in design, technology, and integration.

LESSONS LEARNED

The lessons learned in the Dreamliner launch have been well documented. A few obvious relevant lessons are noted in suggestion form here:

- Identify and analyze all risks of outsourcing at organization *and* component levels. For example, assess the risks and implications of farming out large portions (30 percent) of the design and manufacture of crucial components to foreign suppliers. Outsourcing tends to work better in non-core areas.

- Thoroughly investigate partnership capabilities and resources. Due diligence reduces problems.

- Develop processes for quickly addressing issues and problems. Increase liaison and supervision of supply chain logistics with outsource partners.

- Reconsider seriously the implications of farming out key expertise. This runs the risk of becoming fully reliant on suppliers and transferring unique intellectual property. Partners get risk free technical knowhow, high margin markets for component parts over the life of the plane, and perhaps the future ability to become a future competitor.

- The risk of outsourcing complex, high technology components carries the burden of careful coordination and liaison.

Boeing executives have acknowledged the problems associated with outsourcing large portions of the 787 Dreamliner. For example, Boeing's Commercial Airplanes Chief, Jim Albaugh, expressed to students at Seattle University, "We spent a lot more money in trying to recover [the project] than we ever would have spent if we'd tried to keep the key technologies closer to home. The pendulum swung too far." He added that, in part, chasing the financial measure of return on assets led Boeing astray. Boeing CEO Jim McNerney noted that the 787 game plan may have been overly ambitious, incorporating too many firsts all at once.

THE FUTURE

Although Boeing's 787 outsourcing experience was very costly, outsourcing will continue and evolve. Lessons learned will prompt aircraft builders to reevaluate future outsourcing and move on. Expect to see emphasis on risk- and cost-sharing partnerships.

The major short-term challenge for Boeing is to ramp up production to satisfy the hundreds of waiting orders. Boeing can recoup by adjusting their integrative outsourcing and logistics model as a top priority.

---

* http://seattletimes.nwsource.com/html/sundaybuzz/2014125414_sundaybuzz06.html; http://atwonline.com/aircraft-engines-components/news/boeing-commercial-airplanes-ceo-concedes-787-outsourcing-backfired. Accessed: 1/12/2013.

there appears to be a shift away from simply nailing the best low-cost deal to securing services from companies that provide the best value in terms of both cost and performance. Performance is not limited to simply the quality of specific work but also ability to collaborate and work together. Companies are doing their homework to determine "Can we work with these people?"

BEST PRACTICES IN OUTSOURCING PROJECT WORK

This section describes some of the best practices we have observed being used by firms that excel in project management (see Figure 12.2). Although the list is by no means comprehensive, it reflects strategies used by organizations with extensive outsourcing experience. These practices reveal an underlying theme in how firms approach contracted work on projects.

> - Well-defined requirements and procedures.
> - Extensive training and team-building activities.
> - Well-established conflict management processes in place.
> - Frequent review and status updates.
> - Co-location when needed.
> - Fair and incentive-laden contracts.
> - Long-term outsourcing relationships.

FIGURE 12.2 *Best Practices in Outsourcing Project Work*

Instead of the traditional master–slave relationship between owner and provider or buyer and seller, all parties work together as partners sharing the ultimate goal of a successful project.

Differences between the traditional approach and the partnering approach to managing contracted relationships are summarized in Table 12.1.[1] Partnering requires more than a simple hand-shake. It typically entails a significant commitment of time and energy to forge and sustain

TABLE 12.1 ....

Key Differences Between Partnering and Traditional Approaches to Managing Contracted Relationships

Partnering Approach	Traditional Approach
Mutual trust forms the basis for strong working relationships.	Suspicion and distrust; each party is wary of the motives for actions by the other.
Shared goals and objectives ensure common direction.	Each party's goals and objectives, while similar, are geared to what is best for them.
Joint project team exists with high level of interaction.	Independent project teams; teams are spatially separated with managed interactions.
Open communications avoid misdirection and bolster effective working relationships.	Communications are structured and guarded.
Long-term commitment provides the opportunity to attain continuous improvement.	Single project contracting is normal.
Objective critique is geared to candid assessment of performance.	Objectivity is limited due to fear of reprisal and lack of continuous improvement opportunity.
Access to each other's organization resources is available.	Access is limited with structured procedures and self-preservation taking priority over total optimization.
Total company involvement requires commitment from CEO to team members.	Involvement is normally limited to project-level personnel.
Integration of administrative systems equipment takes place.	Duplication and/or translation takes place with attendant costs and delays.
Risk is shared jointly among the partners, which encourages innovation and continuous improvement.	Risk is transferred to the other party.

[1] C. Cowan, C. F. Gray, and E. W. Larson, "Project Partnering," *Project Management Journal,* 12 (4) December 1992, pp. 5–15.

collaborative relations among all parties. This commitment is reflected in the seven best practices which will be discussed next.

Well-Defined Requirements and Procedures

Convincing people from different professions, organizations, and cultures to work together is difficult. If expectations and requirements are fuzzy or open to debate, this is even harder. Successful firms are very careful in selecting the work to be outsourced. They often choose to contract only work with clearly defined deliverables with measurable outcomes. For example, contractors hire electric firms to install heating and air-conditioning systems, electronic firms use design firms to fabricate enclosures for their products, and software development teams outsource the testing of versions of their programs. In all of these cases, the technical requirements are spelled out in detail. Even so, communicating requirements can be troublesome, especially with foreign providers (see the Snapshot from Practice: Four Strategies for Communicating with Outsourcers), and extra care has to be taken to ensure that expectations are understood.

Not only do requirements have to be spelled out, but the different firms' project management systems need to be integrated. Common procedures and terminology need to be established so that different parties can work together. This can be problematic when you have firms with more advanced project management systems working with less developed organizations. Surprisingly, this often is the case when U.S. firms outsource software work to India. We have heard reports that Indian providers are shocked at how unsystematic their U.S. counterparts are in their approach to managing software projects.

The best companies address this issue up front instead of waiting for problems to emerge. First they assess "fit" between providers' project management methods and their own project management system. This is a prime consideration in choosing vendors. Work requirements and deliverables are spelled out in detail in the procurement process. They invest significant time and energy to establishing project communication systems to support effective collaboration.

Finally, whenever you work with other organizations on projects, security is an important issue. Security extends beyond competitive secrets and technology to include access to information systems. Firms have to establish robust safeguards to prevent information access and the introduction of viruses due to less secure provider systems. Information technology security is an additional cost and risk that needs to be addressed up front before outsourcing project work.

Extensive Training and Team-Building Activities

Too often managers become preoccupied with the plans and technical challenges of the project and assume that people issues will work themselves out over time. Smart firms recognize that people issues are as important, if not more important than technical issues. They train their personnel to work effectively with people from other organizations and countries. This training is pervasive. It is not limited to management but involves all the people, at all levels, who interact with and are dependent upon outsourcers. Whether in a general class on negotiation or a specific one on working with Chinese programmers, team members are provided with a theoretical understanding of the barriers to collaboration as well as the skills and procedures to be successful.

The training is augmented by interorganizational team-building sessions designed to forge healthy relationships before the project begins. Team-building workshops involve the key players

SNAPSHOT FROM PRACTICE

Four Strategies for Communicating with Outsourcers*

Dr. Adam Kolawa offers four strategies for overcoming poor communication with offshore project partners.

STRATEGY 1: RECOGNIZE CULTURAL DIFFERENCES

Realize that not everyone you communicate with shares your assumptions. What is obvious to you is not necessarily obvious to your partner. This is especially true with foreign outsourcers. As an American, you likely assume that laws are generally obeyed. Believe it or not, that's generally not true in most of the world, where laws are guidelines that are not necessarily followed. This can lead to major communication problems! You think if you write a contract, everybody is going to adhere to it. For many people, a contract is merely a suggestion.

STRATEGY 2: CHOOSE THE RIGHT WORDS

When you explain your requirements to an outsourcer, word choice is critical. For many outsourcers, English is still a foreign language—even in India, where both outsourcing and the English language are common. No matter how prevalent English has become, your outsourcer might have a basic understanding of each word you utter yet be not completely clear on the exact meaning of the message you're trying to convey. This is why you should speak in a direct manner using short sentences made of basic, simple words.

STRATEGY 3: CONFIRM YOUR REQUIREMENTS

You should take the following steps to confirm that the outsourcer thoroughly understands your requirements:

1. *Document your requirements.* Follow up your conversations in writing. Commit your requirements to paper for the outsourcer. Many people understand written language better than spoken language, probably because they have more time to process the message.

2. *Insist your outsourcer re-document your requirements.* Leave nothing to chance. Require outsourcers to write the requirements in their own words. If outsourcers cannot relay to you what you explained to them, then they didn't understand.

3. *Request a prototype.* After the requirements are written, ask the outsourcer to create a prototype for you. This is a safety net to ensure that your wants and needs are positively understood. Ask the provider to sketch what you want your final product to look like or build a quick, simple program that reflects how the final product will look.

STRATEGY 4: SET DEADLINES

Another important cultural difference relates to schedules and deadlines. To most Americans, a deadline is a set completion date. In many other cultures, a deadline is a suggestion that maybe something will be finished by that indicated date. To ensure that outsourced work is completed on time it is imperative to add a penalty clause to your contract or enforce late fees.

Although these strategies were directed toward working with foreign outsourcers, you would be surprised to find how many project managers use them when working with their American counterparts!

* Adam Kolawa, "Four Strategies for Communicating with Outsourcers," *Enterprise Systems Journal* at www.esj.com, accessed September 13, 2005.

from the different firms, for example, engineers, architects, lawyers, specialists, and other staff. In many cases, firms find it useful to hire an outside consultant to design and facilitate the sessions. Such a consultant is typically well-versed in interorganizational team building and can provide an impartial perspective to the workshop.

The length and design of the team-building sessions will depend on the experience, commitment, and skill level of the participants. For example, one project, in which the owner and the contractors were relatively inexperienced at working together, utilized a two-day workshop. The first day was devoted to ice-breaking activities and establishing the rationale behind partnering. The conceptual foundation was supported by exercises and minilectures on teamwork, synergy, win/win, and constructive feedback. The second day began by examining the problems and barriers that prevented collaboration in the past. Representatives from the different organizations were separated and each asked the following:

- What actions do the other groups engage in that create problems for us?
- What actions do we engage in that we think create problems for them?
- What recommendations would we make to improve the situation?

The groups shared their responses and asked questions on points needing clarification. Agreements and disparities in the lists were noted and specific problems were identified. Once problem areas were noted, each group was assigned the task of identifying its specific interests and goals for the project. Goals were shared across groups, and special attention was devoted to establishing what goals they had in common. Recognition of shared goals is critical for transforming the different groups into a cohesive team.

The team-building sessions often culminate with the creation of a **partnering charter** signed by all of the participants. This charter states their common goals for the project as well as the procedures that will be used to achieve these goals (see Figure 12.3 for an example of the first page of a project charter).

Well-Established Conflict Management Processes in Place

Conflict is inevitable on a project and, as pointed out in the previous chapter, disagreements handled effectively can elevate performance. Dysfunctional conflict, however, can catch fire and severely undermine project success. Outsourced projects are susceptible to conflicts since people are unaccustomed to working together and have different values and perspectives. Successful firms invest significant time and energy up front in establishing the "rules of engagement" so that disagreements are handled constructively.

Escalation is the primary control mechanism for dealing with and resolving problems. The basic principle is that problems should be resolved at the lowest level within a set time limit (say, 24 hours), or they are "escalated" to the next level of management. If so, the principals have the same time limit to resolve the problem, or it gets passed on to the next higher level. No action is not an option. Nor can one participant force concessions from the other by simply delaying the decision. There is no shame in pushing significant problems up the hierarchy; at the same time, managers should be quick to point out to subordinates those problems or questions that they should have been able to resolve on their own.

If possible, key personnel from the respective organizations are brought together to discuss potential problems and responses. This is usually part of a coordinated series of team-building activities discussed earlier. Particular attention is devoted to establishing the change management control system where problems often erupt. People who are dependent on each other try to identify potential problems that may occur and agree in advance how they should be resolved. See the Snapshot from Practice: "Partnering" a Flu Shot for Projects for the benefits of doing this.

Partnering Charter

Edwards AFB – F-22 Fighter Building 1870

U.S. Air Force F-22 CTF, 411 FLTS • Edwards AFB Civil Engineers
Computer Science Corporation • Lockheed Martin • Telecom Solutions
U.S. Army Corps of Engineers • Valenzuela Engineering, Inc • VRR & Associates

We, the partners of the F-22 design and construction team, recognizing the unique nature of this project, commit to creating an environment of trust and communication to design and build a quality project, which meets or exceeds the customer's requirements. We commit to maintaining a positive and optimistic work environment in which all partners goals can be achieved.

- **Quality Project**
  - Meet program requirements for F-22 Support Systems.
- Complete on schedule and within cost constraints.
- Incorporate lessons learned from other F-22 projects.
- Create an environment for a fair and reasonable profit.
- Create an enjoyable work environment.

- **Safe Project**
  - Provide a safe environment.
  - With no lost-time accidents.
- Maintain positive, cooperative relationships
  - Clear and open communications through appropriate channels.
  - No surprises.
  - No hidden agendas.
  - Minimum delays of paperwork.
  - Resolve problems quickly at the lowest level.

The Partnering concept is a team relationship that promotes the achievement of mutually beneficial goals. This Partnering Charter does not create any legally enforceable rights or duties. Any changes to the contracts must be made by the contracting officers under the terms of the written contracts.

FIGURE 12.3   Project Partnering Charter

SNAPSHOT FROM PRACTICE

"Partnering" a Flu Shot for Projects*

Before starting a bond-financed school construction project, Ohio does what a theater company does before opening night—it holds a dress rehearsal. Led by Cleveland-based Project Management Consultants, state and local school officials, construction managers, and architects get together before building begins to figure out how to talk to each other and how to handle problems. Each party discusses problems that have occurred in the past and collectively they problem solve ways for preventing them from occurring on the current project. Consultants help participants develop a set of guidelines for working together.

Just as a theatrical dress rehearsal can allow a company to find and fix glitches before they ruin a show, preconstruction partnering can find early solutions to problems before they become lawsuits. For example, during the discussions it becomes apparent that different parties are interpreting a key requirement differently. Instead of waiting for this difference to escalate into a major problem, the parties reach a shared understanding before work begins.

"This works because traditionally everyone does their own work on a project, behind their own walls," said Jeffrey Applebaum, a construction lawyer and managing director of Project Management Consultants, a wholly owned subsidiary of the law firm of Thompson, Hine, & Flory. "We're taking down the walls. This is more efficient."

"We couldn't be more pleased with this process," said Randy Fischer, executive director of the Ohio School Facilities Commission, which distributes state money to school construction projects. "We are currently administering $3 billion of construction, and we don't have any major disputes."

Crystal Canan, chief of contract administration for the commission, offered a medical metaphor, comparing partnering to a "flu shot" that will prevent the debilitating effects of litigation, work stoppages, and communication breakdowns. "Every building construction project is a candidate for the flu," Canan said. "We see partnering as a vaccination."

* Mary Wisneiski, "Partnering Used to Curb Costs in Ohio School Construction," *Bond Buyer,* 11/22/2000, 334 (31023) 3/4p, 2bw.

Finally, principled negotiation is the norm for resolving problems and reaching agreements. This approach, which emphasizes collaborative problem solving, is discussed in detail later in this chapter.

Frequent Review and Status Updates

Project managers and other key personnel from all involved organizations meet on a regular basis to review and assess project performance. Collaborating as partners is considered a legitimate project priority which is assessed along with time, cost, and performance. Teamwork, communication, and timely problem resolution are evaluated. This provides a forum for identifying problems not only with the project but also with working relationships so that they can be resolved quickly and appropriately.

More and more companies are using online surveys to collect data from all project participants about the quality of working relations (see Figure 12.4 for a partial example). With this data one can gauge the "pulse" of the project and identify issues that need to be addressed. Comparison of survey responses period by period permits tracking areas of improvement and potential problems. In some cases, follow-up team-building sessions are used to focus on specific problems and recharge collaboration.

FIGURE 12.4 *Sample Online Survey*

Evaluation of partnering process: attitudes, teamwork, process.
(Collected separately from owner and contractor participants, compared, and aggregated.)

1. Communications between the owner/contractor personnel are

1	2	3	4	5
Difficult, guarded				Easy, open, up front

2. Top management support of partnering process is

1	2	3	4	5
Not evident or inconsistent				Obvious and consistent

3. Problems, issues, or concerns are

1	2	3	4	5
Ignored				Attacked promptly

4. Cooperation between owner and contractor personnel is

1	2	3	4	5
Cool, detached, unresponsive, removed				Genuine, unreserved, complete

5. Responses to problems, issues, or concerns frequently become

1	2	3	4	5
Personal issues				Treated as project problems

Finally, when the time to celebrate a significant milestone arrives, no matter who is responsible, all parties gather if possible to celebrate the success. This reinforces a common purpose and project identity. It also establishes positive momentum going into the next phase of the project.

Co-Location When Needed

One of the best ways to overcome interorganizational friction is to have people from each organization working side by side on the project. Smart companies rent or make available the necessary accommodations so that all key project personnel can work collectively together. This allows the high degree of face-to-face interaction needed to coordinate activities, solve difficult problems, and form a common bond. This is especially relevant for complex projects in which close collaboration from different parties is required to be successful. For example, the U.S government provides housing and common office space for all key contractors responsible for developing disaster response plans.

Our experience tells us that co-location is critical and well worth the added expense and inconvenience. When creating this is not practically possible, the travel budget for the project should contain ample funds to support timely travel to different organizations.

Co-location is less relevant for independent work that does not require ongoing coordination between professionals from different organizations. This would be the case if you are outsourcing discrete, independent deliverables like beta testing or a marketing campaign. Here normal channels of communication can handle the coordination issues.

Fair and Incentive-Laden Contracts

When negotiating contracts the goal is to reach a fair deal for all involved. Managers recognize that cohesion and cooperation is undermined if one party feels he or she is being unfairly treated by others. They also realize that negotiating the best deal in terms of price can come back to haunt them with shoddy work and change order gouging.

Performance-based contracts, in which significant incentives are established based on priorities of the project, are becoming increasingly popular. For example, if time is critical, then contractors accrue payoffs for beating deadlines; if scope is critical, then bonuses are issued for exceeding performance expectations. At the same time contractors are held accountable with penalty clauses for failure to perform up to standard, meet deadlines, and/or control costs. More specific information about different types of contracts is presented in this chapter's appendix on contract management.

Companies recognize that contracts can discourage continuous improvement and innovation. Instead of trying some new, promising technique that may reduce costs, contractors will avoid the risks and apply tried and true methods to meet contracted requirements. Companies that treat contractors as partners consider continuous improvement as a joint effort to eliminate waste and pursue opportunities for cost savings. Risks as well as benefits are typically shared 50/50 between the principals, with the owner adhering to a fast-track review of proposed changes.

How the U.S. Department of Defense reaps the benefits of continuous improvement through value engineering is highlighted in the Snapshot from Practice: Value Engineering Awards.

Long-Term Outsourcing Relationships

Many companies recognize that major benefits can be enjoyed when outsourcing arrangements extend across multiple projects and are long term. For example, Corning and Toyota are among the many firms that have forged a network of long-term strategic partnerships with their suppliers. The average large corporation is involved in around 30 alliances today versus fewer than 3 in the early 1990s. Among the many advantages for establishing a long-term partnership are the following:

- **Reduced administrative costs**—The costs associated with bidding and selecting a contractor are eliminated. Contract administration costs are reduced as partners become knowledgeable of their counterpart's legal concerns.
- **More efficient utilization of resources**—Contractors have a known forecast of work while owners are able to concentrate their workforce on core businesses and avoid the demanding swings of project support.
- **Improved communication**—As partners gain experience with each other, they develop a common language and perspective, which reduces misunderstanding and enhances collaboration.

As part of an effort to cut costs the United States Department of Defense (DoD) issues annual Value Engineering Awards. Value engineering is a systematic process to analyze functions to identify actions to reduce cost, increase quality, and improve mission capabilities across the entire spectrum of DoD systems, processes, and organizations. The Value Engineering Awards Program is an acknowledgment of outstanding achievements and encourages additional projects to improve in-house and contractor productivity.

In 2012, 48 different individuals and project teams received recognition with the DoD, reporting over $4 billion in savings.

One team that received an award was the Defense Intelligence Agency (DIA) Hosted Server Computing (HSC) Virtualization Team. This team was recognized for planning, engineering, implementing and deploying the new HSC Virtual Infrastructure for the DoD Intelligence Information System enterprise and virtualizing more than 300 existing servers and applications residing on

Photo by Sgt. Ken Hammond, U.S. Air Force

those servers. These efforts ensure 100 percent failover and disaster-recovery capability for more than 175 applications critical to the support of the DoD intelligence mission. Additionally, this initiative provides service to customers and mission enablers throughout the intelligence community.

The HSC team also provided a platform service to enable both internal- and external-solution hosting for DIA and its mission partners. Every intelligence business and infrastructure is, or will be, processed by 5,000 virtual servers that this service integrates, tests, deploys and maintains. The platform guarantees resources for tenants, increases agility and operational efficiency, shortens time to market, and provides greater automation and self-service when possible. The HSC service has demonstrated compelling value by increasing capability to customers and end users by more than 40 percent.

* http://www.dia.mil/public-affairs/news/2012-08-06.html. Accessed: 12/2/2012.

- **Improved innovation**—The partners are able to discuss innovation and associated risks in a more open manner and share risks and rewards fairly.
- **Improved performance**—Over time partners become more familiar with each other's standards and expectations and are able to apply lessons learned from previous projects to current projects.

Working as partners is a conscious effort on the part of management to form collaborative relationships with personnel from different organizations to complete a project. For outsourcing to work, the individuals involved need to be effective negotiators capable of merging interests and discovering solutions to problems that contribute to the project. The next section addresses some of the key skills and techniques associated with effective negotiation.

THE ART OF NEGOTIATING

Effective negotiating is critical to successful collaboration. All it takes is one key problem to explode to convert a sense of "we" into "us versus them." At the same time, negotiating is pervasive through all aspects of project management work. Project managers must negotiate support and funding from top management. They must negotiate staff and technical input from functional managers. They must coordinate with other project managers and negotiate project priorities and commitments. They must negotiate within their project team to determine assignments, deadlines, standards, and priorities. Project managers must negotiate prices and standards with vendors and suppliers. A firm understanding of the negotiating process, skills, and tactics is essential to project success.

Many people approach negotiating as if it is a competitive contest. Each negotiator is out to win as much as he or she can for his or her side. Success is measured by how much is gained compared with the other party. While this may be applicable when negotiating the sale of a house, it is not true for project management. *Project management is not a contest!* First, the people working on the project, whether they represent different companies or departments within the same organization, are not enemies or competitors but rather allies or partners. They have formed a temporary alliance to complete a project. For this alliance to work requires a certain degree of trust, cooperation, and honesty. Second, if conflicts escalate to the point where negotiations break down and the project comes to a halt, then everyone loses. Third, unlike bartering with a street vendor, the people involved on project work have to continue to work together. Therefore, it behooves them to resolve disagreements in a way that contributes to healthy working relationships. Finally, as pointed out in the previous chapter, conflict on a project can be good. When dealt with effectively it can lead to innovation, better decisions, and more creative problem solving.

Project managers accept this noncompetitive view of negotiation and realize that negotiation is essentially a two-part process: The first part deals with reaching an agreement; the second part is the implementation of that agreement. It is the implementation phase, not the agreement itself, that determines the success of negotiations. All too often, managers reach an agreement with someone only to find out later that they failed to do what they agreed to do or that their actual response fell far short of expectations. Experienced project managers recognize that implementation is based on satisfaction not only with the outcome but also with the process by which the agreement was reached. If someone feels bullied or tricked into doing something, this feeling will invariably be reflected by halfhearted performance.

Veteran project managers do the best they can to merge individual interests with what is best for the project and come up with effective solutions to problems. Fisher and Ury from the Harvard Negotiation Project champion an approach to negotiating that embodies these goals.[2] It emphasizes developing win/win solutions while protecting yourself against those who would take advantage of your forthrightness. Their approach is called **principled negotiation** and is based on four key points listed in Table 12.2 and discussed in the following sections.

TABLE 12.2 ······························
Principled Negotiation

1. Separate the people from the problem
2. Focus on interests, not positions
3. Invent options for mutual gain
4. When possible, use objective criteria

---

[2] R. Fisher and W. Ury, *Getting to Yes: Negotiating Agreement without Giving In,* 2nd ed. (New York: Penguin Books, 1991).

1. Separate the People from the Problem

Too often personal relations become entangled with the substantive issues under consideration. Instead of attacking the problem(s), people attack each other. Once people feel attacked or threatened their energy naturally goes to defending themselves, and not to solving the problem. The key, then, is to focus on the problem—not the other person—during the negotiation. Avoid personalizing the negotiation and framing the negotiation as a contest. Instead, try to keep the focus on the problem to be resolved. In Fisher and Ury's words: *Be hard on the problem, soft on the people.*

By keeping the focus on the issues and not the personalities, negotiators are better able to let the other person blow off steam. On important problems it is not uncommon for people to become upset, frustrated, and angry. However, one angry attack produces an angry counterattack, and the discussion quickly escalates into a heated argument, an emotional chain reaction.

In some cases people use anger as a means of intimidating and forcing concessions because the other person wishes to preserve the relationship. When people become emotional, negotiators should keep a cool head and remember the old German proverb, "Let anger fly out the window."[3] In other words, in the face of an emotional outburst, imagine opening a window and letting the heat of the anger out the window. Avoid taking things personally, and redirect personal attacks back to the question at hand. Don't react to the emotional outburst, but try to find the issues that triggered it. Skilled negotiators keep their cool under stressful times and, at the same time, build a bond with others by empathizing and acknowledging common sources of frustration and anger.

While it is important to separate the people from the problem during actual negotiations, it is beneficial to have a friendly rapport with the other person prior to negotiating. Friendly rapport is consistent with the social network tenet introduced in Chapter 10 of building a relationship before you need it. If, in the past, the relationship has been marked by healthy give-and-take, in which both parties have demonstrated a willingness to accommodate the interests of the other, then neither individual is likely to adopt an immediate win/lose perspective. Furthermore, a positive relationship adds a common interest beyond the specific points of contention. Not only do both parties want to reach an agreement that suits their individual interests, but they also want to do so in a manner that preserves their relationship. Each is therefore more likely to seek solutions that are mutually beneficial.

2. Focus on Interests, Not Positions

Negotiations often stall when people focus on positions:

I'm willing to pay $10,000. No, it will cost $15,000.

I need it done by Monday. That's impossible, we can't have it ready until Wednesday.

While such interchanges are common during preliminary discussions, managers must prevent this initial posturing from becoming polarized. When such positions are stated, attacked, and then defended, each party figuratively begins to draw a line he or she will not cross. This line creates a win/lose scenario in which someone has to lose by crossing the line in order to reach an agreement. As such, the negotiations can become a war of wills, with concessions being seen as a loss of face.

---

[3] Ibid.

The key is to focus on the interests behind your positions (what you are trying to achieve) and separate these goals from your ego as best you can. Not only should you be driven by your interests, but you should try to identify the interests of the other party. Ask why it will cost so much or why it can't be done by Monday. At the same time, make your own interests come alive. Don't just say that it is critical that it be done by Monday; explain what will happen if it isn't done by Monday.

Sometimes when the true interests of both parties are revealed, there is no basis for conflict. Take, for example, the Monday versus Wednesday argument. This argument could apply to a scenario involving a project manager and the production manager of a small, local firm that was contracted to produce prototypes of a new generation of computer mouse. The project manager needs the prototypes on Monday to demonstrate to a users' focus group. The production manager said it would be impossible. The project manager said this would be embarrassing because marketing had spent a lot of time and effort setting up this demonstration. The production manager again denied the request and added that he already had to schedule overtime to meet the Wednesday delivery date. However, when the project manager revealed that the purpose of the focus group was to gauge consumers' reactions to the color and shape of the new devices, not the finished product, the conflict disappeared. The production manager told the project manager that she could pick up the samples today if she wanted because production had an excess supply of shells.

When focusing on interests, it is important to practice the communication habit: *Seek first to understand, then to be understood.* This involves what Stephen Covey calls empathetic listening, which allows a person to fully understand another person's frame of reference—not only what that person is saying but also how he or she feels. Covey asserts that people have an inherent need to be understood. He goes on to observe that satisfied needs do not motivate human behavior, only unsatisfied needs do. People try to go to sleep when they are tired, not when they are rested. The key point is that until people believe they are being understood, they will repeat their points and reformulate their arguments.[4] If, on the other hand, you satisfy this need by seeking first to understand, then the other party is free to understand your interests and focus directly on the issues at hand. Seeking to understand requires discipline and compassion. Instead of responding to the other person by asserting your agenda, respond by summarizing both the facts and feelings behind what the other person has said and checking the accuracy of comprehension.

3. Invent Options for Mutual Gain

Once the individuals involved have identified their interests, then they can explore options for mutual gain. This is not easy. Stressful negotiations inhibit creativity and free exchange. What is required is collaborative brainstorming in which people work together to solve the problem in a way that will lead to a win/win scenario. The key to brainstorming is separating the inventing from the deciding. Begin by taking 15 minutes to generate as many options as possible. No matter how outlandish any option is, it should not be subject to criticism or immediate rejection. People should feed off the ideas of others to generate new ideas. When all the possible options are exhausted, then sort through the ideas that were generated to focus on those with the greatest possibilities.

Clarifying interests and exploring mutual options create the opportunity for dovetailing interests. Dovetailing means one person identifies options that are of low cost to them but of high interest to the other party. This is only possible if each party knows what the other's needs are. For example, in

[4] S. R. Covey, *The Seven Habits of Highly Effective People* (New York: Simon and Schuster, 1990).

negotiating price with a parts supplier, a project manager learned from the discussion that the supplier was in a cash flow squeeze after purchasing a very expensive fabrication machine. Needed cash was the primary reason the supplier had taken such a rigid position on price. During the brainstorming session, one of the options presented was to prepay for the order instead of the usual payment on delivery arrangement. Both parties seized on this option and reached an amicable agreement in which the project manager would pay the supplier for the entire job in advance in exchange for a faster turnaround time and a significant price reduction. Such opportunities for win/win agreements are often overlooked because the negotiators become fixated on solving their problems and not on opportunities to solve the other person's problems.

4. When Possible, Use Objective Criteria

Most established industries and professions have developed standards and rules to help deal with common areas of dispute. Both buyers and sellers rely on the blue book to establish price parameters for a used car. The construction industry has building codes and fair practice policies to resolve proof of quality and safe work procedures. The legal profession uses precedents to adjudicate claims of wrongdoing.

Whenever possible, you should insist on using external, objective criteria to settle disagreements. For example, a disagreement arose between a regional airlines firm and the independent accounting team entrusted with preparing the annual financial statement. The airline firm had made a significant investment by leasing several used airplanes from a larger airline. The dispute involved whether this lease should be classified as an operating or capital lease. This was important to the airline because if the purchase was classified as an operating lease, then the associated debt would not have to be recorded in the financial statement. However, if the purchase was classified as a capital lease, then the debt would be factored into the financial statement and the debt/equity ratio would be much less attractive to stockholders and would-be investors. The two parties resolved this dispute by deferring to formulas established by the Financial Accounting Standards Board. As it turns out the accounting team was correct, but, by deferring to objective standards, they were able to deflect the disappointment of the airline managers away from the accounting team and preserve a professional relationship with that firm.

Dealing with Unreasonable People

Most people working on projects realize that in the long run it is beneficial to work toward mutually satisfying solutions. Still, occasionally you encounter someone who has a dominant win/lose attitude about life and will be difficult to deal with. Fisher and Ury recommend that you use negotiation jujitsu when dealing with such a person. That is, when the other person begins to push, don't push back. As in the martial arts, avoid pitting your strengths against another's directly; instead use your skill to step aside and turn that person's strength to your ends. When someone adamantly sets forth a position, neither reject it nor accept it. Treat it as a possible option and then look for the interests behind it. Instead of defending your ideas, invite criticism and advice. Ask why it's a bad idea and discover the other's underlying interest.

Those who use negotiation jujitsu rely on two primary weapons. They ask questions instead of making statements. Questions allow for interests to surface and do not provide the opponent with something to attack. The second weapon is silence. If the other person makes an unreasonable proposal or attacks you personally, just sit there and don't say a word. Wait for the other party to break the stalemate by answering your question or coming up with a new suggestion.

The best defense against unreasonable, win/lose negotiators is having what Fisher and Ury call a strong **BATNA (best alternative to a negotiated agreement).** They point out that people try to reach an agreement to produce something better than the result of not negotiating with that person. What those results would be the true benchmark for determining whether you should accept an agreement. A strong BATNA gives you the power to walk away and say, "No deal unless we work toward a win/win scenario."

Your BATNA reflects how dependent you are on the other party. If you are negotiating price and delivery dates and can choose from a number of reputable suppliers, then you have a strong BATNA. If on the other hand there is only one vendor who can supply you with specific, critical material on time, then you have a weak BATNA. Under these circumstances you may be forced to concede to the vendor's demands. At the same time, you should begin to explore ways of increasing your BATNA for future negotiations. This can be done by reducing your dependency on that supplier. Begin to find substitutable material or negotiate better lead times with other vendors.

Negotiating is an art. There are many intangibles involved. This section has reviewed some time-tested principles of effective negotiating based on the groundbreaking work of Fisher and Ury. Given the significance of negotiating, you are encouraged to read their book as well as others on negotiating. In addition, attending training workshops can provide an opportunity to practice these skills. You should also take advantage of day-to-day interactions to sharpen negotiating acumen.

A NOTE ON MANAGING CUSTOMER RELATIONS

In Chapter 4 it was emphasized that ultimate success is not determined by whether the project was completed on time, within budget, or according to specifications, but whether the customer is satisfied with what has been accomplished. Customer satisfaction is the bottom line. Bad news travels faster and farther than good news. For every happy customer who shares his satisfaction regarding a particular product or service with another person, a dissatisfied customer is likely to share her dissatisfaction with eight other people. Project managers need to cultivate positive working relations with clients to preserve their reputations.

Customer satisfaction is a complex phenomenon. One simple but useful way of viewing customer satisfaction is in terms of **met expectations.** According to this model, customer satisfaction is a function of the extent to which perceived performance (or outcome) exceeds expectations. Mathematically, this relationship can be represented as the ratio between perceived performance and expected performance (see Figure 12.5). When performance falls short of expectations (ratio < 1), the customer is dissatisfied. If the performance matches expectations (ratio = 1), the customer is satisfied. If the performance exceeds expectations (ratio > 1), the customer is very satisfied or even delighted.

$$\underset{\text{Dissatisfied}}{0.90} = \frac{\text{Perceived performance}}{\text{Expected performance}} = \underset{\text{Very satisfied}}{1.10}$$

FIGURE 12.5 *The Met–Expectations Model of Customer Satisfaction*

High customer satisfaction is the goal of most projects. However, profitability is another major concern. Exceeding expectations typically entails additional costs. For example, completing a construction project two weeks ahead of schedule may involve significant overtime expenses. Similarly, exceeding reliability requirements for a new electronic component may involve considerably more design and debugging effort. Under most circumstances, the most profitable arrangement occurs when the customer's expectations are only slightly exceeded. Returning to the mathematical model, with all other things being equal, one should strive for a satisfaction ratio of 1.05, not 1.5!

The met-expectations model of customer satisfaction highlights the point that whether a client is dissatisfied or delighted with a project is not based on hard facts and objective data but on perceptions and expectations. For example, a customer may be dissatisfied with a project that was completed ahead of schedule and under budget if he thought the work was poor quality and that his fears and concerns were not adequately addressed. Conversely, a customer may be very satisfied with a project that was over budget and behind schedule if she felt the project team protected her interests and did the best job possible under adverse circumstances.

Project managers must be skilled at managing customer expectations and perceptions. Too often they deal with these expectations after the fact when they try to alleviate a client's dissatisfaction by carefully explaining why the project cost more or took longer than planned. A more proactive approach is to begin to shape the proper expectations up front and accept that this is an ongoing process throughout the life of a project. Project managers need to direct their attention both to the customer's base expectations, the standard by which perceived performance will be evaluated, and to the customer's perceptions of actual performance. The ultimate goal is to educate clients so that they can make a valid judgment as to project performance.

Managing customer expectations begins during the preliminary project approval phase of negotiations. It is important to avoid the temptation to oversell the virtues of a project to win approval because this may create unrealistic expectations that may be too difficult, if not impossible, to achieve. At the same time, project proponents have been known to lower customer expectations by underselling projects. If the estimated completion time is 10 to 12 weeks, they will promise to have the project completed within 12 to 14 weeks, therefore increasing the chances of exceeding customer expectations by getting the project completed early.

Once the project is authorized, the project manager and team need to work closely with the client organization to develop a well-defined project scope statement that clearly states the objectives, parameters, and limits of the project work. The project scope statement is essential to establishing customer expectations regarding the project. It is critical that all parties are in agreement as to what is to be accomplished and that people are reading as best they can from the same page. It is also important to share significant risks that might disrupt project execution. Customers do not like surprises, and if they are aware in advance of potential problems they are much more likely to be accepting of the consequences.

Once the project is initiated it is important to keep customers abreast of project progress. The days when you would simply take orders from customers and tell them to return when the project is done are over. More and more organizations and their project managers are treating their customers as de facto members of the project team and are actively involving them in key aspects of project work. In the case of consulting assignments project managers sometimes *morph* into a member of the client organization (see Research Highlight: IT Project Managers).

Project managers need to keep customers informed of project developments so that customers can make adjustments in their own plans. When circumstances dictate changing the scope or priorities of the project, project managers need to be quick to spell out as best they can the implications of these changes to the customers so that they can make an informed choice. Active customer involvement

Research Highlight

IT PROJECT MANAGERS DOUBLING AS CLIENT ACCOUNT EXECUTIVES*

Webber and Torti studied the multiple roles project managers play on IT projects. Based on a comprehensive set of interviews with project managers and clients in three different information-technology service organizations, they identified five key roles critical to successfully implement IT projects in client organizations: entrepreneur, politician, friend, marketer, and coach. They are described in part in Table 12.3.

TABLE 12.3 ·
Project Roles, Challenges, and Strategies

Project Manager Roles	Challenges	Strategies
Entrepreneur	Navigate unfamiliar surroundings	Use persuasion to influence others
Politician	Understand two diverse cultures (parent and client organization)	Align with the powerful individuals
Friend	Determine the important relationships to build and sustain outside the team itself	Identify common interests and experiences to bridge a friendship with the client
Marketer	Understand the strategic objectives of the client organization	Align new ideas/proposals with the strategic objectives of the client organization
Coach	Motivate client team members without formal authority	Provide challenging tasks to build the skills of the team members

Webber and Torti observed that instead of maintaining a clearly defined relationship with the client, project managers become part of the client organization. They report that project managers attempt to "dress like the client, act like the client, and participate in the client organization's activities (i.e., social gatherings, blood drives, etc.)." They become such an integral part of their existence that many client employees, over the course of time, forget that the project manager is not an employee of the client organization. This helps establish a degree of trust essential to effective collaboration.

* S. S. Webber, and M. T. Torti, "Project Managers Doubling as Client Account Executives," *Academy of Management Executive,* Vol. 18, No. 1, pp. 60–71, 2004.

allows customers to naturally adjust their expectations in accordance with the decisions and events that transpire on a project, while at the same time, the customer's presence keeps the project team focused on the customer's objectives for the project.

Active customer involvement also provides a firmer basis for assessing project performance. The customer not only sees the results of the project but also acquires glimpses of the effort and actions that produced those results. Naturally project managers want to make sure these glimpses reflect favorably on their project teams, so they exercise extra care that customer interactions are handled in a competent and professional manner. In some respects, customer perceptions of performance are shaped more by how well the project team deals with adversity than by actual performance. Project managers can impress customers with how diligently they deal with unexpected problems and setbacks. Likewise, industry analysts have noted that customer dissatisfaction can be transformed into customer satisfaction by quickly correcting mistakes and being extremely responsive to customer concerns.

Managing customer relations on a project is a broad topic; we have only highlighted some of the central issues involved. This brief segment concludes with two words of advice passed on by veteran project managers:

Speak with one voice. Nothing erodes confidence in a project more than for a customer to receive conflicting messages from different project members. The project manager should remind team members of this fact and work with them to ensure that appropriate information is shared with customers.

Speak the language of the customer. Too often project members respond to customer inquiries with technical jargon that exceeds the customer's vocabulary. Project managers and members need to describe problems, trade-offs, and solutions in ways that the customer can understand.

Summary

Outsourcing has become an integral part of project management. More and more companies are collaborating with each other on projects to compete in today's business world. The advantages of outsourcing include cost reduction, quicker completion times, greater flexibility, and higher level of expertise. Disadvantages include coordination problems, loss of control, conflicts, security issues and political fallout.

A number of proactive best practices have emerged among firms that have mastered the outsourcing process. These practices include establishing well-defined requirements and procedures and utilizing fair and incentive-laden contracts. Team-building sessions are held before the project begins to forge relationships between personnel from different organizations. Escalation guidelines for resolving conflicts are established, as are provisions for process improvement and risk sharing. On highly critical work, arrangements are made so that key personnel work together, face to face. Joint assessments of how well people are collaborating is the norm during status report briefings. Finally, many companies are realizing the benefits of forming long-term alliances with each other on projects. The ultimate goal is to work together as partners.

Effective negotiating skills are essential to working on projects as partners. People need to resolve differences at the lowest level possible in order to keep the project on track. Veteran project managers realize that negotiating is not a competitive game and work toward collaborative solutions to problems. They accomplish this by separating people from the problem, focusing on interests and not positions, inventing options for mutual gain, and relying on objective criteria whenever possible to resolve disagreements. They also recognize the importance of developing a strong BATNA, which provides them with the leverage necessary to seek collaborative solutions.

Customer satisfaction is the litmus test for project success. Project managers need to take a proactive approach to managing customer expectations and perceptions. They need to actively involve customers in key decisions and keep them abreast of important developments. Active customer involvement keeps the project team focused on the objectives of the project and reduces misunderstandings and dissatisfaction.

Key Terms

Best alternative to a
negotiated agreement
(BATNA)

Co-location
Escalation
Met-expectations model

Outsourcing
Partnering charter
Principled negotiation

Review Questions

1. Why do firms outsource project work?
2. What are the best practices used by firms to outsource project work?
3. What does the term "escalate" refer to, and why is it essential to project success?
4. Why is the principled negotiation approach recommended for negotiating agreements on projects?
5. What does the acronym BATNA refer to, and why is it important to being a successful negotiator?
6. How can a project manager influence customer expectations and perceptions?

Exercises

1. Break into groups of four to five students. Assign half of the groups the role of Owner and the other half the role of Contractor.

Owners: After saving for many years you are about to hire a contractor to build your "dream home." What are your objectives for this project? What concerns or issues do you have about working with a general contractor to build your home?

Contractors: You specialize in building customized homes. You are about to meet with prospective owners to begin to negotiate a contract for building their "dream home." What are your objectives for this project? What concerns or issues do you have about working with the owners to build their home?

Each Owner group meets with another Contractor group and shares their objectives, concerns, and issues.

Identify what objectives, issues, and concerns you have in common and which ones are unique. Discuss how you could work together to realize your objectives. What would be the keys to working as partners on this project?

2. Enter "outsourcing" in an Internet search engine and browse different Web sites. Who appears to be interested in outsourcing? What are the advantages of outsourcing? What are the disadvantages? Does outsourcing mean the same thing to different people? What are future trends in outsourcing?

3. Break into four groups and review the instructions for "Get the most you can" exercise provided by your teacher. Complete the exercise. What was your initial strategy? Did it

change? If so, why? What does this exercise tell you about our ability to collaborate with each other?

References

Cowan, C., C. F. Gray, and E. W. Larson, "Project Partnering," *Project Management Journal,* Vol. 12, No. 4, December 1992, pp. 5–15.

Covey, S. R., *The Seven Habits of Highly Effective People* (New York: Simon and Schuster, 1990).

DiDonato, L. S., "Contract Disputes: Alternatives for Dispute Resolution (Part 1)," *PM Network,* May 1993, pp. 19–23.

Drexler, J. A., and E. W. Larson, "Partnering: Why Project Owner-Contractor Relationships Change," *Journal of Construction Engineering and Management,* Vol. 126, No. 4, July/August 2000, pp. 293–397.

Dyer, S., *Partner Your Project* (Warwickshire, UK: Pendulum Pub., 1997).

Economy, P., *Business Negotiating Basics* (Burr Ridge, IL: Irwin Professional Publishing, 1994).

Fisher, R., and W. Ury, *Getting to Yes: Negotiating Agreement without Giving In,* 2nd ed. (New York: Penguin Books, 1991).

Hedberg, B., G. Dahlgren, J. Hansson, and N. Olve, *Virtual Organizations and Beyond* (New York: Wiley, 1997).

Hoang, H., and F. T. Rothaermel, "The Effect of General and Partner-Specific Alliance Experience on Joint R&D Project Performance," *Academy of Management Journal,* Vol. 48, No. 2, 2005, pp. 332–45.

Kanter, R. M., "Collaborative Advantage: The Art of Alliances," *Harvard Business Review,* July–August 1994, pp. 92–113.

Kezsbom, D. S., D. L. Schilling, and K. A. Edward, *Dynamic Project Management* (New York: Wiley, 1989).

Larson, E. W., "Project Partnering: Results of a Study of 280 Construction Projects," *Journal of Management Engineering,* Vol. 11, No. 2, March/April 1995, pp. 30–35.

Larson, E. W., "Partnering on Construction Projects: A Study of the Relationship between Partnering Activities and Project Success," *IEEE Transactions in Engineering Management,* Vol. 44, No. 2, May 1997, pp. 188–95.

Larson, E. W., and J. A. Drexler, "Barriers to Project Partnering: Report from the Firing Line," *Project Management Journal,* Vol. 28, No. 1, March 1997, pp. 46–52.

Magenau, J. M., and J. K. Pinto, "Power, Influence, and Negotiation in Project Management," in *The Wiley Guide to Managing Projects*, P. W. G. Morris and J. K. Pinto (Eds.), (New York: Wiley, 2004), pp. 1033–60.

Maurer, I., "How to Build Trust in Inter-organizational Projects: The Impact of Project Staffing and Project Rewards on the Formation of Trust, Knowledge Acquisition, and Product Innovation," *International Journal of Project Management*, Vol. 28 (7), 2010, pp. 629–37.

Nambisan, S., "Designing Virtual Customer Environments for New Product Development: Toward a Theory," *Academy of Management Review,* Vol. 27, No. 3, 2002, pp. 392–413.

Nissen, M. E., "Procurement: Process Overview and Emerging Project Management Techniques," in *The Wiley Guide to Managing Projects*, P. W. G. Morris and J. K. Pinto (Eds.), (New York: Wiley, 2004), pp. 643–54.

Quinn, R. E., S. R. Faerman, M. P. Thompson, and M. R. McGrath, *Becoming a Master Manager: A Competency Framework* (New York: Wiley, 1990).

Schultzel, H. J., and V. P. Unruh, *Successful Partnering: Fundamentals for Project Owners and Contractors* (New York: Wiley, 1996).

Shell, G. R., *Bargaining for Advantage: Negotiation Strategies for Reasonable People* (New York: Penguin, 2000).

APPENDIX 12.1

Contract Management

Since most outsourced work on projects is contractual in nature, this appendix discusses the different kinds of contracts that are used, their strengths and weaknesses, and how contracts shape the motives and expectations of different participants. Contract management is a key element of any project procurement management system. It is beyond the scope of this book to describe this system. However, the basic processes are listed here to put contract management and related topics like Request for Proposal (RFP) (see Appendix 2.1) in perspective. Six main steps comprise procurement management:

- **Planning purchases and acquisitions** involves determining what to procure, when, and how. This entails the classic build-versus-buy analysis as well as determination of the type of contract to use.
- **Planning contracting** involves describing the requirements for products or services desired from outsourcing and identifying potential suppliers or sellers. Outputs include procurement documents such as a RFP as well as selection criteria.
- **Requesting seller responses** involves obtaining information, quotes, bids, or proposals from sellers and providers. The main outputs of this process include a qualified sellers list and specific proposals.
- **Selecting sellers** involves choosing from potential suppliers through a process of evaluating potential providers and negotiating a contract.
- **Administering the contract** involves managing the relationship with the selected seller or provider.
- **Closing the contract** involves completion and settlement of the contract.

Most companies have purchasing departments that specialize in procurement. Often purchasing agents will be assigned to project teams and they work with other team members to come up with optimum solutions for the project. Even if project teams are not directly involved in contract negotiations and the decision to outsource project work, it is important that the team understand the procurement process and the nature of different kinds of contracts.

CONTRACTS

A contract is a formal agreement between two parties wherein one party (the contractor) obligates itself to perform a service and the other party (the client) obligates itself to do something in return, usually in the form of a payment to the contractor. For example, an insurance firm contracted with a consulting firm to reprogram segments of their information system to conform to Windows 8.

A contract is more than just an agreement between parties. A contract is a codification of the private law, which governs the relationship between the parties to it. It defines the responsibilities, spells out the conditions of its operations, defines the rights of the parties in relationship to each other, and grants remedies to a party if the other party breaches its obligations. A contract attempts to spell out in specific terms the transactional obligations of the parties involved as well as contingencies associated with the execution of the contract. An ambiguous or inconsistent contract is difficult to understand and enforce.

There are essentially two different kinds of contracts. The first is the "fixed-price" contract in which a price is agreed upon in advance and remains fixed as long as there are no changes to scope or provisions of the agreement. The second is a "cost-plus" contract in which the contractor is reimbursed for all or some of the expenses incurred during the performance of the contract. Unlike the fixed-price contract, the final price is not known until the project is completed. Within these two types of contracts, several variations exist.

FIXED-PRICE CONTRACTS

Under a fixed-price (FP) or lump-sum agreement, the contractor agrees to perform all work specified in the contract at a fixed price. Clients are able to get a minimum price by putting out the contract to competitive bid. Advertising an invitation for bid (IFB) that lists customer requirements usually results in low bids. Prospective contractors can obtain IFB notices through various channels. In the case of large business organizations and government agencies, potential contractors can request to be included on the bidder's list in the area of interest. In other cases, IFBs can be found by scanning appropriate industry media such as newspapers, trade journals, and Web sites. In many cases, the owner can put restrictions on potential bidders, such as requiring that they be ISO 9000 certified.

With fixed-price contract bids, the contractor has to be very careful in estimating target cost and completion schedule because once agreed upon, the price cannot be adjusted. If contractors overestimate the target cost in the bidding stage, they may lose the contract to a lower-priced competitor; if the estimate is too low, they may win the job but make little or no profit.

Fixed-price contracts are preferred by both owners and contractors when the scope of the project is well defined with predictable costs and low implementation risks. Such might be the case for producing parts or components to specifications, executing training programs, or orchestrating a banquet. With fixed-price contracts, clients do not have to be concerned with project costs and can focus on monitoring work progress and performance specifications. Likewise, contractors prefer fixed-price contracts because the client is less likely to request changes or additions to the contract. Fewer potential changes reduce project uncertainty and allow the contractors to more efficiently manage their resources across multiple projects.

The disadvantage of a fixed-price contract for owners is that it is more difficult and more costly to prepare. To be effective, design specifications need to be spelled out in sufficient detail to leave little doubt as to what is to be achieved. Because the contractor's profit is determined by the difference between the bid and the actual costs, there is some incentive for contractors to use cheaper quality materials, perform marginal workmanship, or extend the completion date to reduce costs. The client can counteract these by stipulating rigid end-item specifications and completion date and by supervising work. In many cases, the client will hire a consultant who is an expert in the field to oversee the contractor's work and protect the client's interest.

The primary disadvantage of a fixed-price contract for contractors is that they run the risk of underestimating. If the project gets into serious trouble, cost overruns may make the project unprofitable, and, in some cases, may lead to bankruptcy. To avoid this, contractors have to invest significant time and money to ensure that their estimates are accurate.

Contracts with long lead times such as construction and production projects may include escalation provisions that protect the contractor against external cost increases in materials, labor rates, or overhead expenses. For example, the price may be tied to an inflation index, so it can be adjusted to sudden increases in labor and material prices, or it may be redetermined as costs become known. A variety of redetermination contracts are used. Some establish a ceiling price for a contract and permit only downward adjustments, others permit upward and downward adjustments; some establish one readjustment period at the end of the project, others use more than one period. Redetermination contracts are appropriate where engineering and design efforts are difficult to estimate or when final price cannot be estimated for lack of accurate cost data.

While, in principle, redetermination contracts are used to make appropriate adjustments in cost uncertainties, they are prone to abuse. A contractor may win an initial low bid contract, initiate the contracted work, and then "discover" that the costs are much higher than expected. The contractor can take advantage of redetermination provisions and a client's ignorance to justify increasing the actual cost of the contract. The contract evolves into a cost-plus contract.

To alleviate some of the disadvantages of a fixed-price contract while maintaining some certainty as to final cost, many fixed-price contracts contain incentive clauses designed to motivate contractors to reduce costs and improve efficiency. For example, a contractor negotiates to perform the work for a target price based on a target cost and a target profit. A maximum price and maximum profit are also established. If the total cost ends up being less than the target cost, the contractor makes a higher profit up to the profit maximum. If there is a cost overrun, the contractor absorbs some of the overrun until a profit floor is reached.

Profit is determined according to a formula based on a cost-sharing ratio (CSR). A CSR of 75/25, for example, indicates that for every dollar spent above target costs, the client pays 75 cents and the contractor pays 25 cents. This provision motivates contractors to keep costs low since they pay 25 cents on every dollar spent above the expected cost and earn 25 cents more on every dollar saved below the expected cost. Fixed-price incentive contracts tend to be used for long-duration projects with fairly predictable cost estimates. The key is being able to negotiate a reasonable target cost estimate. Unscrupulous contractors have been known to take advantage of the ignorance of the client to negotiate an unrealistically high target cost and use performance incentives to achieve excessive profits.

COST-PLUS CONTRACTS

Under a cost-plus contract the contractor is reimbursed for all direct allowable costs (materials, labor, travel) plus an additional fee to cover overhead and profit. This fee is negotiated in advance and usually involves a percentage of the total costs. On small projects this kind of contract comes under the rubric "time and materials contract" in which the client agrees to reimburse the contractor for labor cost and materials. Labor costs are based on an hourly or daily rate, which includes direct and indirect costs as well as profit. The contractor is responsible for documenting labor and materials costs.

Unlike fixed-price contracts, cost-plus contracts put the burden of risk on the client. The contract does not indicate what the project is going to cost until the end of the project. Contractors are supposed to make the best effort to fulfill the specific technical requirements of the contract but cannot be held liable, in spite of their best efforts, if the work is not produced within the estimated cost and time frame. These contracts are often criticized because there is little formal incentive for the contractors to control costs or finish on time because they get paid regardless of the final cost. The major factor motivating contractors to control costs and schedule is the effect overruns have on their reputation and their ability to secure future business.

The inherent weakness of cost-plus contracts has been compensated for by a variety of incentive clauses directed at providing incentives to contractors to control costs, maintain performance, and avoid schedule overruns. Contractors are reimbursed for costs, but instead of the fee being fixed, it is based on an incentive formula and subject to additional provisions. This is very similar to fixed-price incentive contracts, but instead of being based on a target cost, the fee is based on actual cost, using a cost-sharing formula.

Most contracts are concerned with the negotiated cost of the project. However, given the importance of speed and timing in today's business world, more and more contracts involve clauses concerning completion dates. To some extent schedule incentives provide some cost-control measures because schedule slippage typically but not always involves cost overruns. Schedule incentives/penalties are stipulated depending on the significance of time to completion for the owner. For example, the contract involving the construction of a new baseball stadium is likely to contain stiff penalties if the stadium is not ready for opening day of the season. Conversely, time-constrained projects in which the number one priority is getting the project completed as soon as possible are likely to include attractive incentives for completing the project early.

A good example of this can be seen in the Northridge Earthquake Snapshot from Practice (Chapter 9) in which the construction firm pulled out all the stops to restore the damaged highway system 74 days ahead of schedule. The firm received a $14.8 million bonus for these efforts!

Figure A12.1 summarizes the spectrum of risk to the buyer and supplier for different kinds of contracts. Buyers have the lowest risk with firm fixed-price contracts because they know exactly what they will need to pay the supplier. Buyers have the most risk with cost-plus percentage of cost contracts because they do not know in advance what the suppliers' costs will be and suppliers may be motivated to increase costs. From the suppliers' perspective, the cost-plus contract offers the least risk and the firm fixed-price contract entails the most risk.

CONTRACT CHANGE CONTROL SYSTEM

A contract change control system defines the process by which the contract may be modified. It includes the paperwork, tracking systems, dispute resolution procedures, and approval levels necessary for authorizing changes. There are a number of reasons a contract may need to be changed. Clients may wish to alter the original design or scope of the project once the project is initiated. This is quite common as the project moves from concept to reality. For example, an

FIGURE A12.1   *Contract Type versus Risk*

owner may wish to add windows after inspecting the partially completed homesite. Market changes may dictate adding new features or increasing the performance requirements of equipment. Declining financial resources may dictate that the owner cut back on the scope of the project. The contractor may initiate changes in the contract in response to unforeseen legitimate problems. A building contractor may need to renegotiate the contract in the face of excessive groundwater or the lack of availability of specified materials. In some cases, external forces may dictate contract changes, such as a need to comply with new safety standards mandated by the federal government.

There need to be formal, agreed-upon procedures for initiating changes in the original contract. Contract change orders are subject to abuse. Contractors sometimes take advantage of owners' ignorance to inflate the costs of changes to recoup profit lost from a low bid. Conversely, owners have been known to "get back" at contractors by delaying approval of contract changes, thus delaying project work and increasing the costs to the contractor. All parties need to agree upon the rules and procedures for initiating and making changes in the original terms of the contract in advance.

CONTRACT MANAGEMENT IN PERSPECTIVE

Contract management is not an exact science. For decades, the federal government has been trying to develop a more effective contract administration system. Despite their best efforts, abuses are repeatedly exposed in the news media. The situation is similar to trying to take a wrinkle out of an Oriental rug. Efforts to eliminate a wrinkle in one part of the rug invariably create a wrinkle in another part. Likewise, each new revision in government procurement procedures appears to generate a new loophole that can be exploited. There is no perfect contract management system. Given the inherent uncertainty involved in most project work, no contract can handle all the issues that emerge. Formal contracts cannot replace or eliminate the need to develop effective working relationships between the parties involved that are based on mutual goals, trust, and cooperation. For this reason, the earlier discussion of best practices in outsourcing and effective negotiating is very important.

APPENDIX REVIEW QUESTIONS

1. What are the fundamental differences between fixed-price and cost-plus contracts?
2. For what kinds of projects would you recommend that a fixed-price contract be used? For what kinds of projects would you recommend that a cost-plus contract be used?

APPENDIX 12.1: REFERENCES

Angus, R. B., N. A. Gundersen, and T. P. Cullinane, *Planning, Performing, and Controlling Projects* (Upper Saddle River, NJ: Prentice Hall, 2003).

Cavendish, J., and M. Martin, *Negotiating and Contracting for Project Management* (Upper Darby, PA: Project Management Institute, 1982).

Fleming, Q. W., *Project Procurement Management: Contracting, Subcontracting, Teaming* (Tustin, CA: FMC Press, 2003).

Fraser, J., *Professional Project Proposals* (Aldershot, U.K.: Gower/Ashgate, 1995).

Lowe, D., "Contract Management" in *The Wiley Guide to Managing Projects,* P. W. G. Morris and J. K. Pinto (Eds.), (New York: Wiley, 2004), pp. 678–707.

Schwalbe, K., *Information Technology Project Management,* 4th ed. (Boston: Thomson Course Technology, 2006).

Worthington, M. M., and L. P. Goldsman, *Contracting with the Federal Government,* 4th ed. (New York: Wiley, 1998).

APPENDIX 12.2

Project Procurement Management

1. AN OVERVIEW OF PROJECT PROCUREMENT FUNCTION

In the modern global context and major projects, most organizations need to outsource some part of the project work to an external agency 'to provide a product, service or result', which would form a part of the project-in-hand. In major construction projects, it is a well-accepted tradition to outsource contracts for special construction work to specialized agencies (agencies or contractors for civil construction, electrical installation, piping and mechanical erection and even further sub-specialization in each of them for specialty in piping or mechanical installation). But such outsourcing is also necessary for several high technology or essentially knowledge-based work.

In this introductory part, we shall take up discussion on:

i. Necessity for outsourcing and the benefits of procurement.
ii. Difference between the project procurement and procurement for routine operations.
iii. Good practices for project procurement.

iv. Different types of project contracts, their special advantages and limitations, selecting the type of contract most suitable for different types of project.

In the later part of this appendix, we shall discuss the approach to procurement management outlined in the PMBOK® Guide, 5th Edition and how it relates to the good procurement practices.

1.1 Necessity for Outsourcing – Benefits and Limitations of Project Procurement

As mentioned earlier, it may be necessary for most organizations outsource project work. When an organization just does not have capability to complete a part of the project work, it needs to outsource that particular work to an external agency. Even when the organization may have the basic capability to execute a particular task, make versus buy analysis might indicate the outsourcing to be a better option.

A more comprehensive list of reasons for an organization to procure products or project services from external agencies is presented below:

- Supplementing its own capacity for the outsourced work for faster project schedule.
- Contracting out the work to a specialized agency, which can offer lower cost product or services than what the organization can manage.
- Ensuring higher quality of workmanship or product features from a specialized agency.
- Availing technology or expertise, which the organization does not have.
- Transferring the overall risk for delivering the product or service of acceptable quality standard as per project schedule to the supplier at some cost premium.
- Increasing the capability for accepting project of larger scope by outsourcing the work for which the organization does not have capability. For bidding on mega projects, it is a very common practice to form a consortium of several organizations, which combine to offer the project delivery.

Of course, subcontracting project work to external agencies is not an unmixed blessing. The organization has to be vigilant about the issues of reduced control during execution, necessity of close coordination, arranging for stage-wise inspection of work to ensure quality workmanship and delivery, sharing the business or technology data with outsiders and related confidentiality issues, and assuming the risk of the contracting agency's lapses on project outcomes, among others. The project manager has to weigh these factors and decide on the basis of *costs versus benefits analysis*, what and how much of the project product or services should be procured from outside.

1.2 Difference between Project Procurement and Operating Procurement

The main differences between the project and operation procurements are rooted in the transient and temporary nature of project work compared to operation and the necessity of delivering the project objectives under cost and schedule constraints. In case of operating purchases, the suppliers are established over a period and the cost, quality and delivery issues are sorted out over a period. While for project work, the organization may not have sufficient experience of dealing with the suppliers and thus may not be aware of the pitfalls to be avoided in contracting the specialized work. Ordinarily, the organization's procurement departments can help out the project procurement by providing the data on suppliers, the price levels and availability of products and services in the market, the standard procurement terms or contracts, and the expertise in the process of technical and commercial negotiations. All the same, it would be worthwhile to keep in mind the following points for efficient project procurement:

i.   *Precision in formulating technical & performance specifications:* Technical and performance specifications should be unambiguous and applicable quality standards to meet quality requirements should be included. The contract should include a clause for stage-wise inspection, if necessary, for ensuring quality conformance and delivery schedule.

ii. *Precision in negotiating the scope of supply*: The scope of supply should be unambiguous and the inclusions and exclusions from the contracted product should be clearly mentioned to effectively manage the interface of the contracted work with other project work or work in scope of other contractors.

iii. *Selection of the type of contract*: The project contracts can be of different type and each type has some benefits and some limitations. Choice of the type of contract to suit the nature of project work to be contracted should be based on careful analysis of the technical and performance requirements of the product or service and the project need for minimizing cost or ensuring quality and timely delivery.

iv. *Selection of the vendor:* The processes of vendor qualification and evaluation of technical bids should precede the short-listed contractors for commercial negotiations.

v.   *Contract drafting:* The contract should very clearly spell-out the critical issues related to supply, whether it is the quality of the product or services or delivery at a specific time. The contract should include clauses for proper emphasis on the critical issues (delivery penalty clause and stage-wise inspection and release of payment for ensuring promised delivery and stage-wise inspection of raw materials, production process validation (say, welding) and inspection routines for ensuring quality of delivered product or service).

vi. *Contract Administration:* The project manager should always pay attention to the following three important aspects for contract administration:

   - Close follow-up on quality of work and whether the pace of working is adequate for meeting the desired delivery: Project meetings and periodic reviews for site contract work and visits to the supplier's plant to check progress in case of delivery of a complete product or system would ensure conformance to contracted quality and delivery.

   - Payment Terms: The contractor should be paid no more than the completed contract work. At the same time, the certification of completed contracted work should be prompt.

   - Maintaining relationship: It should be borne in mind that maintaining a pleasant and efficient working relationship with a vendor and his key personnel is as much in project interest as in the vendor's interest. Sometimes, the project organization's team members assume overbearing and somewhat unreasonable posture towards contractors and their employees. This would often give rise to problems at critical project stage.

1.3   Good Procurement Management Practices

i. *Review all major work packages and decide which products or services should be considered for outsourcing*: The preliminary screening should ensure whether the:

   - organization has captive spare capability for delivering the product or service;

- outsourcing agency can provide desired quality of the product on desired delivery schedule;
- outsourcing would cede control over delivery of a critical item;
- outsourcing would make it necessary to share some closely guarded business or technical secrets;
- cost of outsourced product or service would equal or exceed the cost if organization delivered the service departmentally (essentially 'Make versus Buy' analysis).

ii. *Prepare for outsourcing the products or services to be procured*
   (a) Prepare Statement of Work (SOW) for the contract. It should include

   - Detailed performance requirement and technical specifications
   - Drawings for size, lay-outs or termination points for battery limits
   - Applicable quality standards or tests
   - Unambiguous scope of supply – specifying clearly the boundaries of scope of supply (inclusions and exclusion)
   - Delivery requirements

   (b) Prepare a list of pre-qualified suppliers (or review the list of qualified vendors from organization's procurement group and select).
   (c) Decide on the type of contract most suitable from scope of supply, quality, delivery, and cost or the product or service required and draft the contract terms (or select the suitable template and modify it by including the special contract terms for inclusion).
   (d) Review the nature of work under contract and try to envisage the changes likely in the quantity of required items, quality standards, unspecified new items, etc. Include the clauses for change management. Decide the terms of payment and specify the milestones to be reached for specific payments. Include clauses for termination of contract and arbitration.
   (e) Prepare independent estimate of the cost of supply of the product or service, which would serve as a benchmark for preliminary screening the vendor offers and price negotiations with the short-listed suppliers.

iii. *Select vendor for product or service and place order*
   (a) Invite bids for quotations, requests for proposals or tenders for contracts.
   (b) Offer explanations where necessary and get all bids, offers, or tender offers on equal technical footing.
   (c) Prepare technical bid analysis and shortlist the vendors whose offers are acceptable.
   (d) Prepare commercial evaluations and shortlist vendors for final negotiations
   (e) Negotiate with the prospective vendors for the supply and place order with the successful bidder.

iv. *Administer contract*
   (a) Periodic performance review for quality and work progress.
   (b) Certification of contracted work against agreed milestones in the contract payment terms and facilitating the payment for certified work.
   (c) Administer change control clauses of the contract certifying the changes as they occur and certifying the corresponding incremental payments for the certified changes.

(d) Maintain records of technical work (quantity measurements, any change in specifications of supply or as-built drawings) for project archives.

The section 'Best Practices in Outsourcing Project Work' in the chapter gives an elaborate account of this topic. The recap of the subject above is merely for providing the continuity and connection in the discussion of the good procurement practices and how the procurement processes described in PMBOK® Guide ensure those practices.

1.4 Different Types of Contracts

Appendix 12.1 describes the different types of contracts, their suitability for specific types of project works and their advantage and limitations. It is, therefore, not repeated here.

2. PROJECT PROCUREMENT PROCESSES

With the above overview of the key issues in project procurement, we shall proceed to how PMBOK® Guide, 5th Edition aims to address these issues and ensure good project procurement practices.

PMBOK® Guide lists four processes managing project procurement – one each in the planning, executing, monitoring & controlling and closing process groups as follows:

2.1 Plan Procurement Management	(Planning Process Group)
2.2 Conduct Procurements	(Executing Process Group).
2.3 Control Procurements	(Monitoring & Controlling Process Group), and
2.4 Close Procurements	(Closing Process Group)

We shall briefly review the inputs, tools and techniques and outputs of these processes.

2.1 Plan Procurement Management (Planning Process Group)

Plan Procurement Management is the process of documenting project procurement decisions, specifying the approach, and identifying potential sellers. (PMBOK® Guide, 5th Edition)

The process involves reviewing the products and services required for completing the work packages for all project deliverables and deciding which products or services should be outsourced and how. The process would have to come up with all decisions, procedures and policies for project procurement. It would include:

- Review of all project work and list make versus buy decisions for all project purchases.
- Prepare detailed Statement of Works (SOW) for the work decided to be outsourced (narrative description of work to be performed accompanied by technical specifications, overall assembly or lay-out drawings, performance specifications and acceptance testing).
- Prepare procurement documents
  - The nature of procurement process [whether procurement should be based on request for Information (RFI), invitation for bids (Bids), request for proposals (RFP) or notice and floating of tenders (Tender)]
  - The type of contract [some form of firm fixed price (FFP) contract, cost reimbursable (CR) contract, or time and materials contract (T & M)].
  - Templates for purchase orders or tenders.

- Applicable quality standards and technical and performance specifications to ensure quality.
- Payment terms and their linkage to milestones in supply of contracted work (advance with orders, raw materials acquisition, stage-wise processing and reaching milestones in work completion stages, etc.)
- Criteria for selecting the vendors and their prequalification if necessary.
- Procedures for change management and risk management.

Inputs

Understandably, procurement planning needs review of the work packages for deliverables of the entire project and assessment of the impact of the outsourcing on project scope, quality, cost and schedule. The list of inputs is, therefore, quite exhaustive. PMBOK® Guide lists the following inputs, most of which follow from common sense and logic. Some special inputs are treated at the end of the list.

- *Scope Baseline* – (scope statement, WBS and WBS Dictionary).
- *Requirements Documentation* – Focusing on all project requirements and especially legal, IPR or contractual and operational safety and health requirements.
- *Risk Register*
- *Risk Related Contract Decisions* – Especially concerned with what risks for quality, cost or schedule the organization wants to transfer to the outsourcing agency and at what cost premium if any.
- *Project Schedule* – The organization may have capability to complete all project work, but not adequate capacity to meet the schedule and, therefore, outsourcing is mandated to augment capacity.
- *Activity Resources requirements* – *Some* activities may require resources, which the organization does not have, e.g. technology, equipment, skilled manpower, etc.
- *Activity Cost Estimates* and *Cost Baseline*
- *Stakeholder Register*
- *Enterprise Environmental factors* – Price and availability of products and services in the market, typical terms and conditions for contracted work in the industry and within the organization.
- *Organizational Process Assets* – This would include all assistance which the project procurement can get from organization's group for routine procurement operation and the information on procurements for earlier similar projects. Policies, procedures and templates for different types of contracts is one of the an organizational process assets.
- *Teaming or Collaboration Agreements* – This input requires special mention and discussion. When the project is organized as a consortium or when the outsourced work content is a very large part of the total project in terms of scope and cost, the relationship between the collaborators is based on some common collaboration agreement and all terms are included in the agreement. The technical collaboration, licensing of specific technologies, technical and financial collaboration agreement for project work – all these relationships fall in this category. For such outsourcing work the project manager has to take extra care in observing the terms of the collaboration and maintain pleasant and efficient working relationship.

Tools and Techniques

Tools and techniques essentially involve what to buy, how to buy and from whom to buy. PMBOK® lists the following tools and techniques:

- *Analysis for Make-or-Buy Decisions* – It includes decision regarding what to outsource and what to produce departmentally. The criteria for buying from outside or producing departmentally would depend **on** whether the organization has the capacity to complete the project activity on its own or not. Often, though, the organization may have inherent capability to complete the project activity on its own, the constraints on cost or schedule might favour outsourcing the specific work package.
- *Contract Types* – (How to buy once the decision to outsource is made) Project manager and project team key members must have good conceptual background, working knowledge of contract work practices, and pitfalls and advantages of different types of contracts. The types of contracts have been described in detail in Appendix 12.1: 'Contract Management' and a brief summary are given in the table elsewhere in this appendix. So they are not repeated here.
- *Expert Judgment* – Judgment may be desirable to deal with special inputs from consultants on technology-related issues, legal advice for collaboration agreements or major contractual work, procurement practices and procurement negotiations for some product or services, etc.
- *Meetings with Potential Sellers* – This is a very important tool and procurements for almost all projects involve meetings with some vendors.

Outputs

The process outputs are *Procurement Management Plan, Procurement Statement of Works (SOW), Procurement Documents*, Make *versus Buy Decisions* and *Source Selection Criteria*. In this process discussion, we have already referred elsewhere to outputs other than procurement management plan, which is briefly described below.

Procurement Management Plan: It summarizes the decisions reached from the use of tools and techniques on the overall project management on all inputs for planning project procurement. *It outlines how the procurement management will be carried out throughout the procurement step or project life cycle phase cycle for all outsourced products or services.* With this omnibus scope for contents, it could include:

- The types of contracts to be used
- Risk management issues
- Managing interface between operating procurement set up and project procurement set up
- Standard purchase order or tender templates to be used
- Whether independent estimates for cost will be made and how they will be made
- How the prospective sellers' bids will be evaluated and negotiated
- Procedures for pre-qualification of suppliers, and so on
- Procurement metrics to be used for managing contracts and evaluate sellers

Procurement Management Plan essentially deals with the methods and procedures to be used for the rest of the project procurement processes. When an organization has several projects going on for over a period, the methodology for procurement processes is likely to be well set. In such a situation, there may be no need for a formal procurement management plan and some important points jotted down informally for reference might serve the purpose of a procurement management plan.

2.2 Conduct Procurements (Executing Process Group)

Conduct Procurements is the process of obtaining seller responses, selecting a seller, and awarding the contract. (PMBOK® Guide, 5th Edition)

This process, belonging to execution process group, is concerned with actually managing the outsourcing of products and services according to the planning for procurement set down in the earlier process. *It would, therefore, include all activities necessary for completing the procurement processes till the orders are placed for all items planned to be outsourced:*

- Floating Bids, Requests for Proposals (RFPs) or Tenders, preferably to the pre-qualified vendors list, availing the Statement of Works (SOW) and type of contract decided in procurement planning.
- Evaluating the bids, proposals or tenders received from technical and commercial aspects.
- Requesting and availing special guidance for technology related, legal or other contractual issues from consultants or experts.
- Negotiating with the short-listed vendors and placing the order or contract on the selected vendor.

Once the purchase orders or tender contracts are issued, the monitoring and controlling process, 'Administer Procurement', takes over.

Inputs

Essentially, the inputs for conducting procurements are the project management plan and all documents prepared for procurement planning in the earlier process. Most of the inputs, based on the common sense and understanding the basic outsourcing process, do not require elaborate explanation. PMBOK® Guide mentions these inputs to come up with a following comprehensive list:

Project Management Plan: The requirements and impacts of the component plans of the overall project plan (scope baseline, cost management plan, project schedule, risk register, communication management plan and so forth) need to be taken into account while conducting procurements.

Procurement Management Plan, and especially its following outputs, viz. *Procurement Documents, Source Selection Criteria, Qualified Sellers List, Make versus Buy Decisions, Procurement Statement of Works (SOW), Organizational Process Assets* (List of pre-qualified sellers or current sellers for some products to the operating group), *Teaming or Collaboration Agreements*. All of these are outputs of Plan Procurements Process or data collected as input for that process.

Tools and Techniques

PMBOK ® Guide lists the following tools and techniques, and again, they are also more or less self-evident once the basic nature of the process and what it aims to accomplish are grasped.

- *List of Qualified Sellers: Placing Advertisements for the Requirements, Reviewing Industry Magazines for Identifying Leading Suppliers, Internet Information* and *Organizational Process Assets* (vendors known to the organization for earlier projects) could be useful for preparing a list of qualified sellers

- *Bidder's Conferences*: They involve the meetings with individual parties or a common conference with all prospective suppliers to ensure that all suppliers are brought to a common base of understanding the total scope of supply – technical specifications and contractual requirements for applicable quality standards and delivery schedule. This is a very important part of conducting the procurements.
- *Techniques for evaluation of proposal* from technical and commercial aspects.
- Negotiations with Short-listed Vendors.
- *Expert Judgment* (availing advice from technology or industry experts within the organization or external consultants, legal and contractual issues and other experts).

Outputs

The list of selected sellers for outsourcing and *the award of purchase orders or specific contracts* for product services are the primary outputs. Secondary outputs include *Change Requests* (changes found necessary after issue of contract order, agreed with the seller, and accepted as part of modified contract), *Updates of Project Management Plans* (updates of scope, cost, and schedule baselines and procurement management plan based on the actual orders placed or contracts negotiated during the conducting procurement), *Updates of Project Documents* (updates in Risk Register, Requirements Documentation, etc.), and *Resource Calendars* (taking into account the schedule negotiated with the suppliers while placing contracts).

Some parts of Appendix 12.1 include brief discussions and references to issues involved in drafting, negotiating and awarding contracts. Effective and efficient contracting is at the heart of the procurement management. To describe the intricacies of the subject is beyond the scope of this appendix, which is meant only as reference for mapping the procurement management processes described in PMBOK® Guide with the overall project procurement activities. The interested readers could read some additional books, which provide elaborate exclusive discussion on this subject, and get a perspective of the issues and intricacies.

2.3 Control Procurements (Monitoring & Controlling Process Group)

Control Procurements is the process of managing procurement relationships, monitoring contract performance, and making changes and corrections as appropriate. (PMBOK® Guide, 5th Edition)

The process involves monitoring and controlling the contract during its execution and managing the changes along the course as necessary, so that the product or service is delivered according to contracted scope, specified quality standard, agreed schedule and agreed cost budget. Over and above, the supply of contracted product or service by the seller and the payment for it according to agreed payment schedule by the buyer, the legal aspect of the contract must always remain in the view-scope of the project manager and his team. Accordingly, Control Procurement process requires the project manager and his team to maintain as close as necessary contact with the supplier and interact effectively for mutually satisfactory results. This would involve:

- Developing a common understanding and acceptance of the contract for discharging the duties for mutual satisfaction.
- Seller's preparation of drawings and detailed specifications for tailoring the product or service to precise contracted requirements and their review and approval by the buyer.
- Periodic review of the progress of the work to meet the delivery schedule and prompt certification of the agreed milestones for release of payments to the seller.

- Inspection, testing and quality audits during the contract period– stage-wise inspection when necessary.
- Managing the change during contract execution – record of the change and the mutually agreed impacts on the cost or schedule revision.
- Acceptance tests before closing the contract – performance tests and verifying technical specifications.
- Hand-over of technical documentation for project archives (design drawings, as-built drawings, operation and maintenance manuals, technical specifications and other details of bought out components incorporated into his product by the seller, recommended spare parts lists, etc.)

Inputs

One set of inputs specify what the contract should deliver. They include:

- *Project Management Plan* (its Procurement Management Plan part)
- *Procurement Documents* (SOW and other technical and contractual documents), and
- *Contract* – Contract is the agreement legally binding both parties and reflecting the understanding of both parties of responsibilities taken by both parties to the agreement. This is the most important of inputs for the process.

The other set of inputs include the report of work performance and corrective actions taken

- *Performance Reports* (the status reports of work completed and milestones achieved).
- *Work Performance Information* – Quality audit or other inspection and testing results, cost and payment records, etc.
- *Records of Approved Change Requests* – Record of agreed changes in the contracted work scope and agreed impacts in the project quality, schedule and cost.

Tools and Techniques

Controlling the procurements would require a close liaison with the supplier for assuring the performance of the contract on mutually beneficial terms. The tools and techniques to accomplish this aim include:

- *Performance Reviews*: This would include a comprehensive review of the seller's performance for work progress for completing the deliverables in the contract scope to agreed quality standards, at budgeted cost, and agreed schedule. The performance reviews of major contracts would be an important part of project status review report.
- *Inspection and Audit Reports:* The audits and inspection by the buyer of the seller's work in progress would be helpful for assessing the compliance to quality standards as well as the work progress to meet the agreed schedule. Suitable corrective action can be taken based on these inspection reports.
- *Contract Change Control System:* This is a very important tool for administering procurements. The system should include:
  - Procedures and authorities for initiating changes.
  - Procedures and authority levels for assessment of impacts of proposed changes on the cost, quality and schedule.
  - The authority levels and procedures for approval of changes.

- Incorporation of approved changes in the project work and updating the project plans and project documents.

The procurement change control system should be apart of the integrated change control procedures for the entire project.

- *Payments Schedule*: The project team should promptly certify the work as soon as seller reports its completion and submits the request for authorization of payment.
- *Contract Administration Records:* The project team should maintain a proper record of all-important details of the contract. This would include a copy of the original contract, periodic performance review and inspection reports, change requests and their evaluation reports, payment records, correspondence and technical details useful for operating the product of the project.
- *Dispute Settlement and Claims Administration:* One problematic issue in administering contracts is settling the disputes, more often about the changes and their effects on contract work, and resolving the claim. Mutually accommodating negotiations would be a preferred method for resolving such issues but in rare cases it might be necessary to take recourse to provision in the contract for settling the disputes by third part arbitration.

Outputs

- *Procurement Documentation:* The procurement documentation should include a proper record of the important contract stages. The original contract, the record of requested and approved changes, the inspection and testing reports, status reports submitted by seller, correspondence, the periodically submitted bills and accompanying data, certification papers and actual payment records, issue log, material technical changes, final technical and performance testing reports before acceptance and other useful technical and contractual details.
- *Change Requests:* Though change requests form the part of overall procurement documentation, this special mention is to emphasize its importance in procurement administration. The record of change requests by the seller (or buyer), assessment of the change impact on cost and schedule, and rejected change requests, approved requests, should be documented.
- *Updates of Project Management Plan:* Procurement Management Plan, Schedule Baseline, and cost baselines should be updated based on the actual contract performance data.

2.4 Close Procurements (Closing Process Group)

This is the last of the procurement management processes and involves bringing to an orderly and formal close all project procurements.

A large part of the activities in this phase of procurements is administrative in nature. The activities in closing procurements might be:

- Carrying out final check of all deliverables and preparing a checklist of inadequately completed or defective items and getting them executed or repaired by the seller.
- Carrying out final performance testing of the product for acceptance and closing the contract.
- Final certification of all contract work and authorizing payments.
- Collecting technical details for maintenance and operation.
- Settling unresolved disputes and claims.

In some instances, it may be necessary to terminate the contract before its normal completion. In such case, the contract's termination clause comes into operation and the additional work of buyer and seller's representatives, making joint records of work executed till the termination and authorization of payment, also becomes necessary.

Inputs

Procurement Management Plan (component of Project Management Plan) and *Procurement Documentation* for individual contract are the inputs for the process.

Tools and Techniques

Inspection and Testing for final acceptance, *Negotiated Settlements* and *Procurement Records System* are the tools and techniques for the process.

Outputs

The main output of the process is essentially a *Closed Contract or Procurement*.

Update of Organizational Process: The secondary outputs from the process are the project records, which serve as project archives and are useful for the operation and maintenance of the contract's product or service and addition to the knowledge-base of the organization for similar projects in future.

CASE 12.1

Shell Case Fabricators

BACKGROUND

Shell Case Fabricators (SCF) designs and builds shell casings that enclose electronic products such as calculators, cell phones, modems. Typically the cases are plastic or plastic compounds. SCF has six different production lines that cover different types of product. For example, the largest high volume production line for modems can produce three different colors and two models (vertical and flat). Air Connection Links (ACL) is the biggest customer that buys product from this line. This high output line now runs at full capacity on an eight-hour shift. The other five lines run smaller quantities and tend to meet the needs of other specialty products manufactured by different smaller firms.

Ninety-five percent of SCF's product casings line is designed by the original hardware manufacturer. Getting a casing to the production stage requires a great deal of collaboration and interaction between the original hardware and case design manufacturer (e.g., ACL) and SCF's shell design engineers and production department. The latest new product of ACL is a modem designed to be used for monitoring water activity in bays, e.g., ship traffic, pollution, floating debris. Because of the product's high functionality and low cost, potential demand for the new product is out of sight. It seems every country with small bays used for shipping wants enough underwater modems to cover their respective bays.

THE UNDERWATER MODEM PROJECT

At SCF each new product is assigned a project manager to coordinate and manage the shell design, budgets, and manufacturing startup. Songsee is SCF's star project manager and is the project manager of the shell for the new short-range, underwater acoustical modem. The shell casing for the underwater modem required special design, materials, custom equipment, and a seal to withstand pressure to 50 meters. Air Connection Links, the product owner, needs sixty thousand modems in 91 days (next January 15) for the Estuary Control Institute meeting in Hong Kong.

Client Change Request

Songsee has felt the project was moving along smoothly, with the exception of being two weeks behind schedule. She feels she can "lean on" the design department to put the project on top priority and make up the two weeks. Yesterday, ACL's project manager, Sabin, came in with a "*simple* change." Change the outer shell shape from rectangular to dome shape; it will improve performance 2 percent. Songsee couldn't believe Sabin. He knows better. He knows the engineering implications, and it is NOT simple! Yet Sabin tells Songsee, "It shouldn't cost much." Songsee imagined a sharp retort, but she counted to five and aborted. At this late stage of the game, changes and schedule compression cost big money! Songsee said she would get together with her team and start on a new time and cost estimate today. She told Sabin he would have to give her a written change request of the new requirements by tomorrow. Sabin appeared disappointed. "Why don't we just add €100,000 to the price and get on with it? We have been doing business with SCF for six years. With expected demand out of sight, SCF will break even quickly and have a great profit on the production side." Songsee sighed. "Let's proceed with the change order process. I will bring your request to the change order governance committee."

Songsee's meeting with her team about the change went about as expected. Every department moaned about changing at this late date. The guesstimate cost and time estimates were over triple Sabin's idea of €100,000. For example, designing a new seal for a dome style modem will require a new custom water sealing approach, possibly an untested different sealant, and new molds. Has ACL frozen the design of the new style modem? Songsee asked the team to come in with a more detailed estimate by tomorrow afternoon, before her meeting with the change order governance committee.

The Next Day (Friday)

Sabin called from ACL at midmorning the next day. "Our senior management is upset that we have to be so formal for such a small change. They just want to get on with the project and meet the time to market launch date. €100,000 seems like a fair price. They believe you need to talk to your management. They want a response by Monday."

The team estimates came close to yesterday's guesstimate (€391,000). Not good news. Songsee knew the answer of the change committee would be to hold for the full amount. She was right. The change committee believed the costs are there and need to be covered to meet the launch date. The committee was also concerned that priorities and resource scheduling would have to change for

SCF's design and production departments. In three hours she would meet with senior management to decide to accept the client's request at their price or come up with an alternate plan. Songsee realized she should have several options for senior management to consider, along with a recommendation.

1. Should SCF accept or reject ACL's request? Which option would you select? What risks are involved?
2. How should SCF negotiate with ACL? How can SCF and ACL develop a positive, long-range relationship? Give some specifics.

CASE 12.2

The Accounting Software Installation Project

Sitting in her office, Karin Chung is reviewing the past four months of the large corporate accounting software installation project she has been managing. Everything seemed so well planned before the project started. Each company division had a task force that provided input into the proposed installation along with potential problems. All the different divisions had been trained and briefed on exactly how their division would interface and use the forthcoming accounting software. All six contractors, which included one of the Big Five consulting companies, assisted in developing the work breakdown structure—costs, specifications, time.

Karin hired a consultant to conduct a one-day "partnering" workshop attended by the major accounting heads, a member of each task force group, and key representatives from each of the contractors. During the workshop, several different team-building exercises were used to illustrate the importance of collaboration and effective communication. Everyone laughed when Karin fell into an imaginary acid pit during a human bridge-building exercise. The workshop ended on an upbeat note with everyone signing a partnering charter that expressed their commitment to working together as partners to complete the project.

TWO MONTHS LATER

One task force member came to Karin to complain that the contractor dealing with billing would not listen to his concerns about problems that could occur in the Virginia division when billings are consolidated. The contractor had told him, the task force member, he had bigger problems than consolidation of billing in the Virginia division. Karin replied, "You can settle the problem with the contractor. Go to him and explain how serious your problem is and that it will have to be settled before the project is completed."

Later in the week in the lunchroom she overheard one consulting contractor bad-mouthing the work of another—"never on time, interface coding not tested." In the hallway the same day an accounting department supervisor told her that tests showed the new software will never be compatible with the Georgia division's accounting practices.

While concerned, Karin considered these problems typical of the kind she had encountered on other smaller software projects.

FOUR MONTHS LATER

The project seemed to be falling apart. What happened to the positive attitude fostered at the team-building workshop? One contractor wrote a formal letter complaining that another contractor was sitting on a coding decision that was delaying their work. The letter went on: "We cannot be held responsible or liable for delays caused by others." The project was already two months behind, so problems were becoming very real and serious. Karin finally decided to call a meeting of all parties to the project and partnering agreement.

She began by asking for problems people were encountering while working on the project. Although participants were reluctant to be first for fear of being perceived as a complainer, it was not long before accusations and tempers flared out of control. It was always some group complaining about another group. Several participants complained that others were sitting on decisions that resulted in their work being held up. One consultant said, "It is impossible to tell who's in charge of what." Another participant complained that although the group met separately on small problems, it never met as a total group to assess new risk situations that developed.

Karin felt the meeting had degenerated into an unrecoverable situation. Commitment to the project and partnering appeared to be waning. She quickly decided to stop the meeting and cool things down. She spoke to the project stakeholders: "It is clear that we have some serious problems, and the project is in jeopardy. The project must get back on track, and the backbiting must stop. I want each of us to come to a meeting Friday morning with concrete suggestions of what it will take to get the project back on track and specific actions of how we can make it happen. We need to recognize our mutual interdependence and bring our relationships with each other back to a win/win environment. When we do get things back on track, we need to figure out how to stay on track."

1. Why does this attempt at project partnering appear to be failing?
2. If you were Karin, what would you do to get this project back on track?
3. What action would you take to keep the project on track?

CASE 12.3

Buxton Hall

Chad Cromwell, head of university housing, gazed up at the tower at Buxton Hall and smiled as he walked toward the landmark building.

Buxton Hall was built in 1927 as a residential complex for over 350 students at Pacifica State University. At the time Buxton was the tallest building on campus, and its tower had a panoramic view of the athletic fields and coastal range. Buxton quickly became a focal point at Pacifica State. Students perched on the tower dominated the campus during the annual spring water fight with their huge slingshots and catapults. The first intranet on the Pacific coast was created at Buxton that linked students' computers and allowed them to share printers. Around the 1970s, some student artists began the tradition of painting their room doors. Whether a Rolling Stones logo or Bugs Bunny on a skateboard, these colorful doors were an artistic legacy that caught the attention of students and faculty.

Buxton Hall served as a residence hall for the university for many years, but time was not kind to the stately building. Leaks destroyed plaster in the interior. Wiring and plumbing became outdated and so dangerous that the building was deemed unsafe. Buxton Hall's doors were closed to students and windows boarded up at the end of the 1996 spring quarter. For 10 years Buxton sat silent and over time became a symbol of the general decline of Pacifica State. Now thanks to state bonds and generous contributions, Buxton Hall was about to be reopened after a $20 million renovation.

18 MONTHS AGO

Chad and key representatives from university facilities were engaged in the second of a two-day partnering workshop. Also in attendance were managers from Crawford Construction, the chief contractor for the Buxton renovation project, as well as several key subcontractors and architects from the firm of Legacy West. During the first day a consultant ran them through a series of team-building and communication exercises that accentuated the importance of open communication, principle negotiation, and win/win thinking. The second day began with the "project from hell" exercise, with each group describing the worst project they had ever worked on. Chad was surprised that the people from Crawford and Legacy West descriptions were very similar to his own. For example, each group talked about how frustrating it was when changes were made without proper consultation or costs were hidden until it was too late to do anything about them. This was followed by a discussion of the best project they had ever worked on. The consultant then asked the groups which of the two they wanted the Buxton project to be. A genuine sense of common purpose emerged, and everyone became actively engaged in spelling out in specific terms how they wanted to work together. The session concluded with all of the participants signing a partnering charter followed by a picnic and a friendly softball game.

12 MONTHS AGO

Chad was on his way, with Nick Bolas, to meet Dat Nguyen, the Crawford Project Manager, on the third floor at Buxton tower. Dat had contacted him to discuss a problem with the tile work in one of the communal bathrooms. Dat's people had completed the work, but Nick, who was a Pacifica facilities manager, refused to sign off on it claiming that it was not up to spec. After a 24-hour impasse, the Crawford foreman exercised the escalation clause in partnering agreement and passed the issue up to management's level to be resolved. Dat and Chad inspected the work. While both agreed that the job could have been prettier, it did meet specification and Chad told Nick to sign off on it.

Chad met Dat again later in the day at the weekly Buxton status report meeting. The meeting kicked off with a brief review of what had been accomplished during the past week. Discussion centered on the removal of elm trees. Alternative strategies for dealing with the city inspector, who had a reputation of being a stickler for details, were considered. The project was two weeks behind schedule, which is an important issue since it was imperative that the building be ready for students to move in at the 2008 fall term. The project was also on a very tight budget, and the management reserve had to be carefully administered. Renovation of existing buildings was always a bit of a gamble, since you never knew what you would find once you began tearing down walls. Fortunately, only small amounts of asbestos were found, but rot was much more severe than anticipated.

The meeting included a partnering assessment. The results of a Web survey filled out by all the principals were distributed. The results revealed a dip in the ratings between the Crawford foremen and university officials regarding timely collaboration and effective problem solving. One of Chad's people said that the primary source of frustration was Crawford foremen failing to respond to e-mail and telephone messages. Dat asked for the names of his people and said he would talk to each of them. The Crawford foremen complained that the university officials were being too nit-picky. "We don't have the time or money to do A+ work on everything," argued a foreman. Chad told Dat and his people that he would talk to facilities guys and ask them to focus on what is really important.

6 MONTHS AGO

The project status report meeting started on time. Crawford had been able to make up for lost time, and it now looked like the building would open on time. Chad was glad to see that the partnering assessment had been positive and steady over the past month. The big issue was the surge in costs consuming all but $50,000 of management reserve. With six months to go everyone knew that this would not cover all the change orders needed to have the building ready. After all, there was already $24,000 worth of change orders pending.

Chad looked across the table and saw nothing but grim faces. Then one of the Crawford foremen proposed postponing treating all of the exterior walls. "Instead of cleaning and preserving the entire brick building, let's only do the front entrance and the North and South walls that the public sees. We can just refurbish the interior court walls as well as the West side. This would be adequate for at least eight years, in which time money should be available to complete the job."

At first Chad didn't like this idea, but eventually he realized that this was the only way they could have the building ready for the students. Friendly arguments broke out over which exterior segments needed the full treatment and which ones didn't. The whole team ended up touring the outside of the building identifying what kind of work needed to be done. In the end, only 70 percent of exterior brick walls were reconditioned according to plan with a savings of over $250,000. While this boost to the reserve would still make things tight everyone felt that they now had a fighting chance to complete the project on time.

TODAY

As Chad mingled with a glass of champagne, no one talked about the walls that still needed to be refurbished—tonight was a night to celebrate. All of the major participants and their spouses were at the party, and the university was hosting a five-course meal at the top of the tower. During the toasts, jokes were exchanged and stories told about the ghosts in the west wing and the discovery of a dead skunk in the south basement. Everyone talked about how proud they felt about bringing back to life the grand old building. More than one person mentioned that this was much more satisfying than tearing down an old relic and constructing a new building. The president of the university concluded the festivities by thanking everyone for their hard work and proclaiming that Buxton would become a bright, shining icon for Pacifica State.

1. How successful was this project?
2. What best practices were evident in the case? How did they contribute to project objectives?

CASE 12.4

Goldrush Electronics Negotiation Exercise

OBJECTIVE

The purpose of this case is to provide you with an opportunity to practice negotiations.

PROCEDURE

STEP 1

The class is divided into four groups, each comprising the project management group for one of four projects at Goldrush Electronics.

STEP 2

Read the Goldrush Electronics "Background Information" section given below. Then read the instructions for the project you represent. Soon you will meet with the management of the other projects to exchange personnel. Plan how you want to conduct those meetings.

BACKGROUND INFORMATION

Goldrush Electronics (GE) produces a range of electronic products. GE has a strong commitment to project management. GE operates as a projectized organization with each project organized as a fully dedicated team. The compensation system is based on a 40 + 30 + 30 formula. Forty percent is based on your base salary, 30 percent on your project performance, and 30 percent on overall performance of the firm.

Four new product development projects have been authorized. They are code named: Alpha, Beta, Theta, and Zeta. The preliminary assignment of personnel is listed below. You are assigned to represent the management of one of these projects.

The policy at GE is that once preliminary assignments are made project managers are free to exchange personnel as long as both parties agree to the transaction. You will have the opportunity to adjust your team by negotiating with other project managers.

Alpha Project		
Software Engineer	**Hardware Engineer**	**Design Engineer**
Jill	Cameron	Mitch
John	Chandra	Marsha

Beta Project		
Software Engineer	**Hardware Engineer**	**Design Engineer**
Jake	Casey	Mike
Jennifer	Craig	Maria

Theta Project		
Software Engineer	**Hardware Engineer**	**Design Engineer**
Jack	Chuck	Monika
Johan	Cheryl	Mark

Zeta Project		
Software Engineer	**Hardware Engineer**	**Design Engineer**
Jeff	Carlos	Max
Juwoo	Chad	Maile

Personnel may be traded for one or more other personnel.

STEP 3

Meet and negotiate with the other project managers.

STEP 4

Individual project scores are totaled and posted.

STEP 5

Discussion Questions

1. What was your initial strategy before starting the actual negotiations? How did you view the other groups?
2. Did your initial strategy change once negotiations began? If so, how and why?
3. What could top management at GE have done to make it easier to reach agreement with the other groups?

13

PROGRESS AND PERFORMANCE MEASUREMENT AND EVALUATION

How does a project get one year late?
. . . One day at a time.

—Frederick P. Brooks, *The Mythical Man Month, p. 153*

Evaluation and control are part of every project manager's job. Control by "wandering around" and/or "involvement" can overcome most problems in small projects. But large projects need some form of formal control. Control holds people accountable, prevents small problems from mushrooming into large problems, and keeps focus. Except for accounting controls, project control is not performed well in most organizations. Control is one of the most neglected areas of project management. Unfortunately, it is not uncommon to find resistance to control processes. In essence, those who minimize the importance of control are passing up a great opportunity to be effective managers and, perhaps, allow the organization to gain a competitive edge. Neglecting control in organizations with multiple projects is even more serious. For effective control, the project manager needs a single information system to collect data and report progress on cost, schedule, and specifications. The general structure of such a system is discussed next.

STRUCTURE OF A PROJECT MONITORING INFORMATION SYSTEM

A project monitoring system involves *determining what* data to collect; *how, when,* and *who* will collect the data; *analysis* of the data; and *reporting* current progress.

What Data Are Collected?   Data collected are determined by *which* metrics will be used for project control. Typical key data collected are actual activity duration times, resource usage and rates, and actual costs, which are compared against planned times, resources, and budgets. Since a major portion of the monitoring system focuses on cost/schedule concerns, it is crucial to provide the project manager and stakeholders with data to answer questions such as:

- What is the current status of the project in terms of schedule and cost?
- How much will it cost to complete the project?
- When will the project be completed?
- Are there potential problems that need to be addressed now?
- What, who, and where are the causes for cost or schedule overruns?
- What did we get for the dollars spent?
- If there is a cost overrun midway in the project, can we forecast the overrun at completion?

The performance metrics you need to collect should support answering these questions. Examples of specific metrics and tools for collecting data will be discussed in detail later in this chapter.

Collecting Data and Analysis   With the determination of what data are collected, the next step is to establish who, when, and how the data will be assembled. Will the data be collected by the project team, contractor, independent cost engineers, project manager? Or will the data be derived electronically from some form of surrogate data such as cash flow, machine hours, labor hours, or materials in place? Should the reporting period be one hour, one day, one week, or what? Is there a central repository for the data collected and is someone responsible for its dissemination?

Electronic means of collecting data have vastly improved data assembly, analysis, and dissemination. Numerous software vendors have programs and tools to analyze your customized collected data and present it in a form that facilitates monitoring the project, identifying sources of problems, and updating your plan.

Reports and Reporting First, who gets the progress reports? We have already suggested that different stakeholders and levels of management need different kinds of project information. Senior management's major interests are usually, "Are we on time and within budget? If not, what corrective action is taking place?" Likewise, an IT manager working on the project is concerned primarily about her deliverable and specific work packages. The reports should be designed for the right audience.

Typically, project progress reports are designed and communicated in written or oral form. A common topic format for progress reports follows:

- Progress since last report
- Current status of project
  1. Schedule
  2. Cost
  3. Scope
- Cumulative trends
- Problems and issues since last report
  1. Actions and resolution of earlier problems
  2. New variances and problems identified
- Corrective action planned

Given the structure of your information system and the nature of its outputs, we can use the system to interface and facilitate the project control process. These interfaces need to be relevant and seamless if control is to be effective.

THE PROJECT CONTROL PROCESS

Control is the process of comparing actual performance against plan to identify deviations, evaluate possible alternative courses of actions, and take appropriate corrective action. The project control steps for measuring and evaluating project performance are presented below.

1. Setting a baseline plan.
2. Measuring progress and performance.
3. Comparing plan against actual.
4. Taking action.

Each of the control steps is described in the following paragraphs.

Step 1: Setting a Baseline Plan

The baseline plan provides us with the elements for measuring performance. The baseline is derived from the cost and duration information found in the work breakdown structure (WBS) database and time-sequence data from the network and resource scheduling decisions. From the WBS the project resource schedule is used to time-phase all work, resources, and budgets into a baseline plan. See Chapter 8.

Step 2: Measuring Progress and Performance

Time and budgets are quantitative measures of performance that readily fit into the integrated information system. Qualitative measures such as meeting customer technical specifications and product function are most frequently determined by on-site inspection or actual use. This chapter is limited to quantitative measures of time and budget. Measurement of time performance is relatively easy and obvious. That is, is the critical path early, on schedule, or late; is the slack of near-critical paths decreasing to cause new critical activities? Measuring performance against budget (e.g., money, units in place, labor hours) is more difficult and is *not* simply a case of comparing actual versus budget. Earned value is necessary to provide a realistic estimate of performance against a time-phased budget. **Earned value** (EV) is defined as the budgeted cost of the work performed.

Step 3: Comparing Plan against Actual

Because plans seldom materialize as expected, it becomes imperative to measure deviations from plan to determine if action is necessary. Periodic monitoring and measuring the status of the project allow for comparisons of actual versus expected plans. It is crucial that the timing of status reports be frequent enough to allow for early detection of variations from plan and early correction of causes. Usually status reports should take place every one to four weeks to be useful and allow for proactive correction.

Step 4: Taking Action

If deviations from plans are significant, corrective action will be needed to bring the project back in line with the original or revised plan. In some cases, conditions or scope can change, which, in turn, will require a change in the baseline plan to recognize new information.

The remainder of this chapter describes and illustrates monitoring systems, tools, and components to support managing and controlling projects. Several of the tools you developed in the planning and scheduling chapters now serve as input to your information system for monitoring performance. Monitoring time performance is discussed first, followed by cost performance.

MONITORING TIME PERFORMANCE

A major goal of progress reporting is to catch any negative variances from plan as early as possible to determine if corrective action is necessary. Fortunately, monitoring schedule performance is relatively easy. The project network schedule, derived from the WBS/OBS, serves as the baseline to compare against actual performance.

Gantt charts (bar charts) and control charts are the typical tools used for communicating project schedule status. As suggested in Chapter 6, the Gantt chart is the most favored, used, and understandable. This kind of chart is commonly referred to as a tracking Gantt chart. Gantt and control charts serve well as a means for tracking and trending schedule performance. Their easy-to-understand visual formats make them favorite tools for communicating project schedule status—especially to top management, who do not usually have time for details. Adding actual and revised time estimates to the Gantt chart gives a quick overview of project status on the report date.

Tracking Gantt Chart

Figure 13.1 presents a baseline Gantt chart and a tracking Gantt chart for a project at the end of period 6. The solid bar below the original schedule bar represents the actual start and finish times for completed activities or any portion of an activity completed (see activities A, B, C, D, and E). For example, the actual start time for activity C is period 2; the actual finish time is period 5; the actual duration is three time units, rather than four scheduled time periods. Activities in process show the actual start time; the extended bar represents the expected remaining duration (see activities D and E). The remaining duration for activities D and E are shown with the hatched bar. Activity F, which has not started, shows a revised estimated actual start (9) and finish time (13).

Note how activities can have durations that differ from the original schedule, as in activities C, D, and E. Either the activity is complete and the actual is known, or new information suggests the estimate of time be revised and reflected in the status report. Activity D's revised duration results in an expected delay in the start of activity F. The project is now estimated to be completed one period later than planned. Although sometimes the Gantt chart does not show dependencies, when it is used with a network, the dependencies are easily identified if tracing is needed.

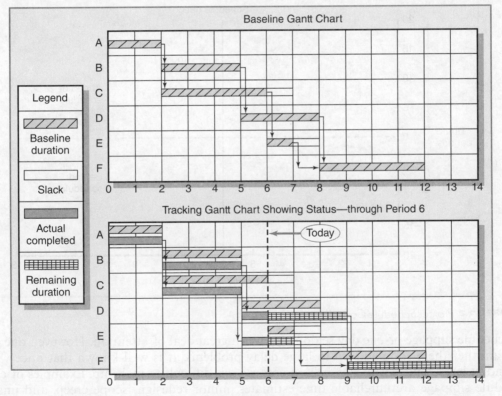

FIGURE 13.1 *Baseline Gantt Chart*

Control Chart

This chart is another tool used to monitor past project schedule performance and current performance and to estimate future schedule trends. Figure 13.2 depicts a project control chart.

The chart is used to plot the difference between the scheduled time on the critical path at the report date with the actual point on the critical path. Although Figure 13.2 shows the project was behind early in the project, the plot suggests corrective action brought the project back on track. If the trend is sustained, the project will come in ahead of schedule. Because the activity scheduled times represent average durations, four observations trending in one direction indicate there is a very high probability that there is an identifiable cause. The cause should be located and action taken if necessary. Control chart trends are very useful for giving warning of potential problems so appropriate action can be taken if necessary.

Control charts are also frequently used to monitor progress toward milestones, which mark events and as such have zero duration. Milestones are significant project events that mark major accomplishments. To be effective, milestones need to be concrete, specific, measurable events. Milestones must be easily identifiable by all project stakeholders—for example, product testing complete. Critical merge activities are good candidates for milestones. Control charts very similar to the example shown in Figure 13.2 are often used to record and communicate project progress toward a milestone.

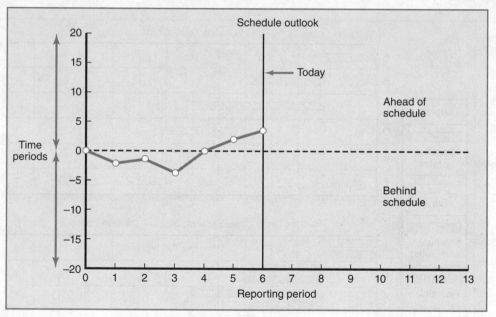

FIGURE 13.2 *Project Schedule Control Chart*

Schedule slippage of one day seldom receives a great deal of attention. However, one day here and another there soon add up to large delay problems. It is well known that once work gets behind, it has a tendency to stay behind because it is difficult to make up. Examples of causes of schedule slippage are unreliable time estimates, minor redesign, scope creep, and unavailable resources. Using slack early in a path may create a problem for someone responsible for a later activity; flexibility and potential opportunities are reduced. For these reasons, having frequent and clearly defined monitoring points for work packages can significantly improve the chances of catching schedule slippage early. Early detection reduces the chance of small delays growing to large ones and thereby reducing opportunities for corrective action to get back on schedule. See Snapshot from Practice: Status Reports at Microsoft.

When Bill Gates was in charge of Microsoft, project teams sent reports each month to top executives, as well as to the managers of all related projects. The status reports were brief and had a standard format. Gates read most of them quickly, and spotted potential delays, or changes he did not want. He especially looked for schedule slips, cutting too many product features, or the need to change a specification. Gates usually responded to the relevant managers or developers directly by electronic mail. Status reports are an important mechanism for communicating between top management and projects. As Gates explained:

"I get all the status reports. Right now there might be a hundred active projects...
. [The status reports] contain the schedule, including milestones dates, and any change in spec, and any comments about 'Hey, we can't hire enough people,' or 'Jeez, if this OLE (Object Linking and Embedding) 2 Mac release isn't done, we're just going to have to totally slip.' ... They know [their report] goes up to all the people who manage all the other groups that they have dependencies with. So if they don't raise it in the status report and then two months later they say something, that's a breakdown in communication. ... The internal group is totally copied on those things, so it's sort of the consensus of the group."

AP Photo/Keystone,
Alessandro della Valle

* From *Microsoft Secrets: The World's Most Powerful Software Company Creates Technology.*
Copyright © 1995 by Michael A. Cusumano
and Richard W. Selby.

DEVELOPMENT OF AN EARNED VALUE COST/SCHEDULE SYSTEM

Earned value is not new; although its initial use was in military contracts, in recent years the private sector has come to depend on the system for managing multiple and large projects.

The original earned value cost/schedule system was pioneered by the U.S. Department of Defense (DoD) in the 1960s. It is probably safe to say project managers in every major country are using some form of the system. The system is being used on internal projects in the manufacturing, pharmaceutical, and high-tech industries. For example, organizations such as EDS, NCR, Levi Strauss, Tektronics, and Disney have used earned value systems to track projects. The basic framework of the earned value system is withstanding the test of time. Most project management software includes the original framework; many systems have added industry-specific variations to more precisely track progress and costs. This chapter presents the "generic" core of an integrated cost/schedule information system.[1]

The earned value system starts with the time-phased costs that provide the project budget *baseline*, which is called the planned budgeted value of the work scheduled (PV). Given this time-phased baseline, comparisons are made with actual and planned schedule and costs using earned value. The earned value approach provides the missing links not found in conventional cost-budget systems. At any point in time, a status report can be developed for the project.

---

1 See Fleming and Koppelman for a more complete earned value description.

TABLE 13.1 ···
Glossary of Terms

EV	Earned value for a task is simply the percent complete times its original budget. Stated differently, EV is the percent of the original budget that has been earned by actual work completed. [The older acronym for this value was BCWP—budgeted cost of the work performed.]
PV	The planned time-phased baseline of the value of the work scheduled. An approved cost estimate of the resources scheduled in a time-phased cumulative baseline [BCWS—budgeted cost of the work scheduled].
AC	Actual cost of the work completed. The sum of the costs incurred in accomplishing work [ACWP—actual cost of the work performed].
CV	Cost variance is the difference between the earned value and the actual costs for the work completed to date where CV = EV − AC.
SV	Schedule variance is the difference between the earned value and the baseline line to date where SV = EV − PV.
BAC	Budgeted cost at completion. The total budgeted cost of the baseline or project cost accounts.
EAC	Estimated cost at completion.
ETC	Estimated cost to complete remaining work.
VAC	Cost variance at completion. VAC indicates expected actual over- or underrun cost at completion.

The earned value cost/schedule system uses several acronyms and equations for analysis. Table 13.1 presents a glossary of these acronyms. You will need this glossary as a reference. In recent years acronyms have been shortened to be more phonetically friendly. This movement is reflected in material from the Project Management Institute, in project management software, and by most practitioners. This text edition follows the recent trend. The acronyms found in brackets represent the older acronyms, which are often found in software programs. To the uninitiated, the terms used in practice appear horrendous and intimidating. However, once a few basic terms are understood, the intimidation index will evaporate.

Following five careful steps ensures that the cost/schedule system is integrated. These steps are outlined here. Steps 1, 2, and 3 are accomplished in the planning stage. Steps 4 and 5 are sequentially accomplished during the execution stage of the project.

1. Define the work using a WBS. This step involves developing documents that include the following information (see Chapters 4 and 5):
   a. Scope.
   b. Work packages.
   c. Deliverables.
   d. Organization units.
   e. Resources.
   f. Budgets for each work package.
2. Develop work and resource schedule.
   a. Schedule resources to activities (see Chapter 8).
   b. Time-phase work packages into a network.

3. Develop a time-phase budget using work packages included in an activity. The cumulative values of these budgets will become the baseline and will be called the planned budgeted cost of the work scheduled (PV). The sum should equal the budgeted amounts for all the work packages in the cost accounts (see Chapter 8).

4. At the work package level, collect the actual costs for the work performed. These costs will be called the actual cost of the work completed (AC). Collect percent complete and multiply this times the original budget amount for the value of the work actually completed. These values will be called earned value (EV).

5. Compute the schedule variance (SV = EV − PV) and cost variance (CV = EV − AC). Prepare hierarchical status reports for each level of management—from work package manager to customer or project manager. The reports should also include project rollups by organization unit and deliverables. In addition, actual time performance should be checked against the project network schedule.

Figure 13.3 presents a schematic overview of the integrated information system, which includes the techniques and systems presented in earlier chapters. Those who have tenaciously labored through the early chapters can smile! Steps 1 and 2 are already carefully developed. Observe that control data can be traced backward to specific deliverables and organization unit responsible.

The major reasons for creating a baseline are to monitor and report progress and to estimate cash flow. Therefore, it is crucial to integrate the baseline with the performance measurement system. Costs are placed (time-phased) in the baseline exactly as managers expect them to be "earned." This approach facilitates tracking costs to their point of origin. In practice, the integration is accomplished by using the same rules in assigning costs to the baseline as those used to measure

FIGURE 13.3 *Project Management Information System Overview*

progress using earned value. You may find several rules in practice, but percent complete is the workhorse most commonly used. Someone familiar with each task estimates what percent of the task has been completed or how much of the task remains.

Percent Complete Rule

This rule is the heart of any earned value system. The best method for assigning costs to the baseline under this rule is to establish frequent checkpoints over the duration of the work package and assign completion percentages in dollar terms. For example, units completed could be used to assign baseline costs and later to measure progress. Units might be lines of code, hours, drawings completed, cubic yards of concrete in place, workdays, prototypes complete, etc. This approach to percent complete adds "objectivity" to the subjective observation approaches often used. When measuring percent complete in the monitoring phase of the project, it is common to limit the amount earned to 80 or 90 percent until the work package is 100 percent complete.

What Costs Are Included in Baselines?

The baseline (PV) is the sum of the cost accounts, and each cost account is the sum of the work packages in the cost account. Three direct costs are typically included in baselines—labor, equipment, and materials. The reason: these are direct costs the project manager can control. Overhead costs and profit are typically added later by accounting processes. Most work packages should be discrete, of short time span, and have measurable outputs. If materials and/or equipment are a significant portion of the cost of work packages, they can be budgeted in separate work packages and cost accounts.

Methods of Variance Analysis

Generally the method for measuring accomplishments centers on two key computations:

1. Comparing earned value with the expected schedule value.
2. Comparing earned value with the actual costs.

These comparisons can be made at the project level or down to the cost account level. Project status can be determined for the latest period, all periods to date, and estimated to the end of the project.

Assessing the current status of a project using the earned value cost/schedule system requires three data elements—planned cost of the work scheduled (PV), budgeted cost of the work completed (EV), and actual cost of the work completed (AC). From these data the schedule variance (SV) and cost variance (CV) are computed each reporting period. *A positive variance indicates a desirable condition, while a negative variance suggests problems or changes that have taken place.*

Cost variance tells us if the work accomplished costs more or less than was planned at any point over the life of the project. If labor and materials have not been separated, cost variance should be reviewed carefully to isolate the cause to either labor or materials—or to both.

Schedule variance presents an overall assessment of *all* work packages in the project scheduled to date. It is important to note schedule variance contains *no* critical path information. Schedule variance measures progress in dollars rather than time units. Therefore, it is unlikely that any translation of dollars to time will yield accurate information telling if any milestone or critical path is early, on time, or late (even if the project occurs exactly as planned). *The only accurate method for determining the true time progress of the project is to compare the project network schedule against the actual network schedule to measure if the project is on time* (refer to Figure 13.1). However, SV is very useful in assessing the direction all the work in the project is taking—after 20 or more percent of the project has been completed.

Figure 13.4 presents a sample cost/schedule graph with variances identified for a project at the current status report date. Note the graph also focuses on what remains to be accomplished and any favorable or unfavorable trends. The "today" label marks the report date (time period 25) of where the project has been and where it is going. Because our system is hierarchical, graphs of the same form can be developed for different levels of management. In Figure 13.4 the top line represents the actual costs (AC) incurred for the project work to date. The middle line is the baseline (PV) and ends at the scheduled project duration (45). The bottom line is the budgeted value of the work actually completed to date (EV) or the earned value. The dotted line extending the actual costs from the report date to the new estimated completion date represents revised estimates of *expected* actual costs; that is, additional information suggests the costs at completion of the project will differ from what was planned. Note that the project duration has been extended and the variance at completion (VAC) is negative (BAC − EAC).

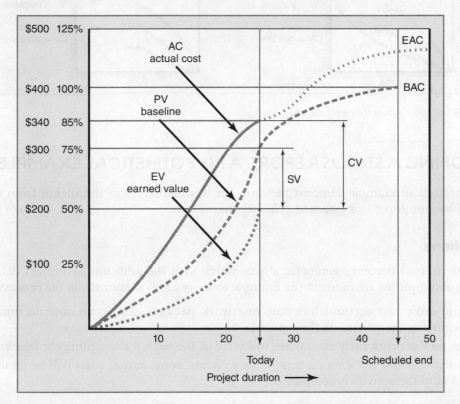

FIGURE 13.4 *Cost/Schedule Graph*

Another interpretation of the graph uses percentages. At the end of period 25, 75 percent of the work was scheduled to be accomplished. At the end of period 25, the value of the work accomplished is 50 percent. The actual cost of the work completed to date is $340, or 85 percent of the total project budget. The graph suggests the project will have about a 18 percent cost overrun and be five time units late. The current status of the project shows the cost variance (CV) to be over budget by $140 (EV − AC = 200 − 340 = −140). The schedule variance (SV) is negative $100 (EV − PV = 200 − 300 = −100), which suggests the project is behind schedule. Before moving to an example, consult Figure 13.5 to practice interpreting the outcomes of cost/schedule graphs. Remember, PV is your baseline and anchor point.

FIGURE 13.5 *Earned–Value Review Exercise*

DEVELOPING A STATUS REPORT: A HYPOTHETICAL EXAMPLE

Working through an example demonstrates how the baseline serves as the anchor from which the project can be monitored using earned value techniques.

Assumptions

Because the process becomes geometrically complex with the addition of project detail, some simplifying assumptions are made in the example to more easily demonstrate the process:

1. Assume each cost account has only one work package, and each cost account will be represented as an activity on the network.
2. The project network early start times will serve as the basis for assigning the baseline values.
3. From the moment work on an activity task begins, some actual costs will be incurred each period until the activity is completed.

Baseline Development

Figure 13.6 (Work Breakdown Structure with Cost Accounts) depicts a simple work breakdown structure (WBS/OBS) for the Digital Camera example. There are six deliverables (Design Specifications, Shell & Power, Memory/Software, Zoom System, Assemble, and Test), and five

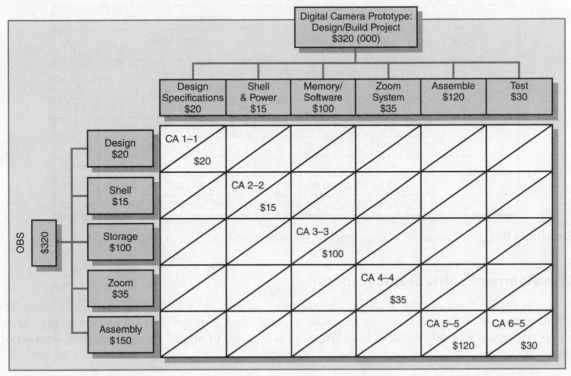

FIGURE 13.6   **Work Breakdown Structure with Cost Accounts**

responsible departments (Design, Shell, Storage, Zoom, and Assembly). The total for all the cost accounts (CA) is $320,000, which represents the total project cost. Figure 13.7, derived from the WBS, presents a planning Gantt chart for the Digital Camera project. The planned project duration is 11 time units. This project information is used to time-phase the project budget baseline. Figure 13.8 **(Project Baseline Budget)** presents a worksheet with an early start baseline developed with costs assigned. They are assigned "exactly" as managers plan to monitor and measure schedule and cost performance.

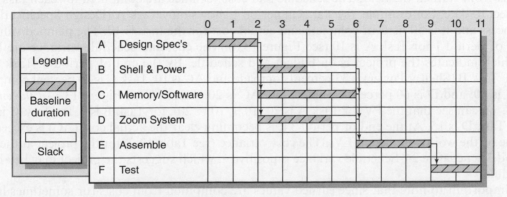

FIGURE 13.7 *Digital Camera Prototype Project Baseline Gantt Chart*

Schedule information						Baseline budget needs												
ACT/ WP	DUR	ES	LF	SL	Total PV	Time period												
						0	1	2	3	4	5	6	7	8	9	10	11	
A	2	0	2	0	20	10	10											
B	2	2	6	2	15				5	10								
C	4	2	6	0	100				20	30	30	20						
D	3	2	6	1	35				15	10	10							
E	3	6	9	0	120								30	40	50			
F	2	9	11	0	30											10	20	
Total PV by period						10	10	40	50	40	20	30	40	50	10	20		
Cumulative PV by period						10	20	60	110	150	170	200	240	290	300	320		

FIGURE 13.8 *Digital Camera Prototype Project Baseline Budget ($000)*

Development of the Status Report

A status report is analogous to a camera snapshot of a project at a specific point in time. The status report uses earned value to measure schedule and cost performance. Measuring earned value begins at the work package level. Work packages are in one of three conditions on a report date:

1. Not yet started.
2. Finished.
3. In-process or partially complete.

Earned values for the first two conditions present no difficulties. Work packages that are not yet started earn zero percent of the PV (budget). Packages that are completed earn 100 percent of their PV. In-process packages apply the percent complete rule to the PV baseline to measure earned value (EV). In our camera example we will only use the percent complete rule to measure progress.

Table 13.2 presents the completed, separate status reports of the Digital Camera Prototype project for periods 1 through 7. Each period percent complete and actual cost were gathered for each task from staff in the field. The schedule and cost variance are computed for each task and the project to date. For example, the status in period 1 shows only Task A (Design Specifications) is in process and it is 50 percent complete and actual cost for the task is 10. The planned value at the end of period 1 for Task A is 10 (see Figure 13.8). The cost and schedule variance are both zero, which indicates the project is on budget and schedule. By the end of period 3, Task A is finished. Task B (Shell & Power) is 33 percent complete and AC is 10; Task C is 20 percent complete and AC is 30; and D is 60 percent complete and AC is 20. Again, from Figure 13.8 *at the end of period 3,* we can see that the PV for Task A is 20 (10 + 10 = 20), for Task B is 5, for Task C is 20, and for Task D is 15. At the end of period 3 it is becoming clear the actual cost (AC) is exceeding the value of the work completed (EV). The cost variance (see Table 13.2) for the project at the end of period 3 is negative 24. Schedule variance is positive 6, which suggests the project may be ahead of schedule.

It is important to note that since earned values are computed from costs (or sometimes labor

TABLE 13.2 ···
Digital Camera Prototype Status Reports: Periods 1–7

Cost Variance		CV = EV − AC				
Schedule Variance		SV = EV − PV				
Status Report: Ending Period 1						
Task	**%Complete**	**EV**	**AC**	**PV**	**CV**	**SV**
A	50%	10	10	10	0	0
Cumulative Totals		**10**	**10**	**10**	**0**	**0**
Status Report: Ending Period 2						
Task	**%Complete**	**EV**	**AC**	**PV**	**CV**	**SV**
A	Finished	20	30	20	−10	0
Cumulative Totals		**20**	**30**	**20**	**−10**	**0**
Status Report: Ending Period 3						
Task	**%Complete**	**EV**	**AC**	**PV**	**CV**	**SV**
A	Finished	20	30	20	−10	0
B	33%	5	10	5	−5	0
C	20%	20	30	20	−10	0
D	60%	21	20	15	+1	+6
Cumulative Totals		**66**	**90**	**60**	**−24**	**+6**
Status Report: Ending Period 4						
Task	**%Complete**	**EV**	**AC**	**PV**	**CV**	**SV**
A	Finished	20	30	20	−10	0
B	Finished	15	20	15	−5	0
C	50%	50	70	50	−20	0
D	80%	28	30	25	−2	+3
Comulative Totals		**113**	**150**	**110**	**−37**	**+3**
Status Report: Ending Period 5						
Task	**%Complete**	**EV**	**AC**	**PV**	**CV**	**SV**
A	Finished	20	30	20	−10	0
B	Finished	15	20	15	−5	0
C	60%	60	100	80	−40	−20
D	80%	28	50	35	−22	−7
Cumulative Totals		**123**	**200**	**150**	**−77**	**−27**
Status Report: Ending Period 6						
Task	**%Complete**	**EV**	**AC**	**PV**	**CV**	**SV**
A	Finished	20	30	20	−10	0
B	Finished	15	20	15	−5	0
C	80%	80	110	100	−30	−20
D	Finished	35	60	35	−25	0
Cumulative Totals		**150**	**220**	**170**	**−70**	**−20**
Status Report: Ending Period 7						
Task	**%Complete**	**EV**	**AC**	**PV**	**CV**	**SV**
A	Finished	20	30	20	−10	0
B	Finished	15	20	15	−5	0
C	90%	90	120	100	−30	−10
D	Finished	35	60	35	−25	0
E	0%	0	0	30	0	−30
F	0%	0	0	0	0	0
Cumulative Totals		**160**	**230**	**200**	**−70**	**−40**

hours or other metrics), the relationship of costs to time is not one-for-one. For example, it is possible to have a negative SV variance when the project is actually ahead on the critical path. Therefore, it is important to remember, SV is in dollars and is not an accurate measure of time; however, it is a fairly good indicator of the status of the whole project in terms of being ahead or behind schedule after the project is over 20 percent complete. Only the project network, or Tracking Gantt chart, and actual work completed can give an accurate assessment of schedule performance down to the work package level.

By studying the separate status reports for periods 5 through 7, you can see the project will be over budget and behind schedule. By period 7 Tasks A, B, and D are finished, but all are over budget—negative 10, 5, and 25. Task C (Memory/Software) is 90 percent complete. Task E is late and hasn't started because Task C is not yet completed. The result is that, at the end of period 7, the digital camera project is over budget $70,000, with a schedule budget over $40,000.

Figure 13.9 shows the graphed results of all the status reports through period 7. This graph represents the data from Table 13.2. The cumulative actual costs (AC) to date and the earned value budgeted costs to date (EV) are plotted against the original project baseline (PV). The cumulative AC to date is $230; the cumulative EV to date is $160. Given these cumulative values, the cost variance (CV = EV − AC) is negative $70 (160 − 230 = −70). The schedule variance (SV = EV − PV) is negative $40 (160 − 200 = −40). Again, recall that only the project network or Tracking Gantt chart can give an accurate assessment of schedule performance down to the work package level.

A Tracking Gantt bar chart for the Digital Camera Prototype is shown in Figure 13.10. From

FIGURE 13.9 *Digital Camera Prototype Summary Graph ($000)*

this figure you can see Task C (Memory/Software), which had an original duration of 4 time units, now is expected to require 6 time units. This delay of 2 time units for Task C will also delay Tasks E and F two time units and result in the project being late 2 time periods.

Figure 13.11 shows an oversimplified project rollup at the end of period 7. The rollup is by deliverables and organization units. For example, the Memory/Software deliverable has an SV of $−10 and a CV of −30. The responsible "Storage" department should have an explanation for these

FIGURE 13.10   *Digital Camera Project–Tracking Gantt Chart Showing Status—Through Period 7*

variances. Similarly, the assembly department, which is responsible for the Assemble and Test deliverables, has an SV of $ −30 due to the delay of Task C (see Figure 13.10). Most deliverables look unfavorable on schedule and cost variance.

In more complex projects, the crosstabs of cost accounts by deliverables and organization units can be very revealing and more profound. This example contains the basics for developing a status report, baseline development, and measuring schedule and cost variance. In our example, performance analysis had only one level above the cost account level. Because all data are derived from the detailed database, it is relatively easy to determine progress status at all levels of the work and organization breakdown structures. Fortunately, this same current database can provide additional views of the current status of the project and forecast costs at the completion of the project. Approaches for deriving additional information from the database are presented next.

To the uninitiated, a caveat is in order. In practice budgets may not be expressed in total dollars for an activity. Frequently, budgets are time-phased for materials and labor separately for more effective control over costs. Another common approach used in practice is to use labor hours in place of dollars in the earned value system. Later, labor hours are converted to dollars. The use of labor hours in the earned value system is the *modus operandi* for most construction work. Labor hours are easy to understand and are often the way many time and cost estimates are developed. Most earned value software easily accommodates the use of labor hours for development of cost estimates.

INDEXES TO MONITOR PROGRESS

Practitioners sometimes prefer to use schedule and cost indexes over the absolute values of SV and CV, because indexes can be considered efficiency ratios. Graphed indexes over the project life cycle can be very illuminating and useful. The trends are easily identified for deliverables and the whole project.

Indexes are typically used at the cost account level and above. In practice, the database is also

FIGURE 13.11 *Project Rollup End Period 7 ($000)*

used to develop indexes that allow the project manager and customer to view progress from several angles. An index of 1.00 (100 percent) indicates progress is as planned. An index greater than 1.00 shows progress is better than expected. An index less than 1.00 suggests progress is poorer than planned and deserves attention. Table 13.3 presents the interpretation of the indexes.

TABLE 13.3 ••
Interpretation of Indexes

Index	Cost (CPI)	Schedule (SPI)
>1.00	Under cost	Ahead of schedule
=1.00	On cost	On schedule
<1.00	Over cost	Behind schedule

Performance Indexes

There are two indexes of performance efficiency. The first index measures *cost* efficiency of the work accomplished to date: (Data from Table 13.2)

$$\text{Cost performance index (CPI)} = EV/AC = 160/230 = .696 \text{ or } .70$$

The CPI of .696 shows that $.70 worth of work planned to date has been completed for each $1.00 actually spent—an unfavorable situation indeed. The CPI is the most accepted and used index. It has been tested over time and found to be the most accurate, reliable, and stable. For example, U.S. government studies have shown that the CPI is stable from the 20 percent completion point regardless of contract type, program, or service. The CPI can provide an "early warning signal" as to cost overruns so that adjustments can be made to the budget or scope of a project.[2]

The second index is a measure of scheduling efficiency to date:

$$\text{Scheduling performance index (SPI)} = EV/PV = 160/200 = .80$$

The schedule index indicates $.80 worth of work has been accomplished for each $1.00 worth of scheduled work to date. Figure 13.12 shows the indexes plotted for our example project through period 7. This figure is another example of graphs used in practice.

FIGURE 13.12 *Indexes Periods 1–7*

[2]Cited by Q. W. Fleming and J. M. Koppleman, *Earned Value Project Management* (Newton Square, PA: Project Management Institute, 2010), pp. 39–42.

Project Percent Complete Indexes

Two project percent complete indexes are used, depending on your judgment of which one is most representative of your project. The first index assumes the original budget of work complete is the most reliable information to measure project percent complete. The second index assumes the actual costs-to-date and expected cost at completion are the most reliable for measuring project percent complete. These indexes compare the to-date progress to the end of the project. The implications underlying use of these indexes are that conditions will not change, no improvement or action will be taken, and the information in the database is accurate. The first index looks at percent complete in terms of *budget* amounts:

$$\text{Percent complete index PCIB} = \text{EV/BAC} = 160/320 = .50 \ (50\%)$$

This PCIB indicates the work accomplished represents 50 percent of the total budgeted (BAC) dollars to date. Observe that this calculation does not include actual costs incurred. Because actual dollars spent do not guarantee project progress, this index is favored by many project managers when there is a high level of confidence in the original budget estimates.

The second index views percent complete in terms of *actual* dollars spent to accomplish the work to date and the actual expected dollars for the completed project (EAC). For example, at the end of period 7 the staff re-estimates that the EAC will be 575 instead of 320. The application of this view is written as

$$\text{Percent complete index PCIC} = \text{AC/EAC} = 230/575 = .40 \ (40\%)$$

Some managers favor this index because it contains actual and revised estimates that include newer, more complete information.

These two views of percent complete present alternative views of the "real" percent complete. These percents may be quite different as shown above. (Note: The PCIC index was not plotted in Figure 13.12. The new figures for EAC would be derived each period by estimators in the field.)

Technical Performance Measurement

Measuring technical performance is as important as measuring schedule and cost performance. Although technical performance is often assumed, the opposite can be true. The ramifications of poor technical performance frequently are more profound—something works or it doesn't if technical specifications are not adhered to.

Assessing technical performance of a system, facility, or product is often accomplished by examining the documents found in the scope statement and/or work package documentation. These documents should specify criteria and tolerance limits against which performance can be measured. For example, the technical performance of a software project suffered because the feature of "drag and drop" was deleted in the final product. Conversely, the prototype of an experimental car exceeded the miles per gallon technical specification and, thus, its technical performance. Frequently tests are conducted on different performance dimensions. These tests become an integral part of the project schedule.

It is very difficult to specify how to measure technical performance because it depends on the nature of the project. Suffice it to say, measuring technical performance must be done. Technical performance is frequently where quality control processes are needed and used. Project managers must be creative in finding ways to control this very important area.

Software for Project Cost/Schedule Systems

Software developers have created sophisticated schedule/cost systems for projects that track and report budget, actual, earned, committed, and index values. These values can be labor hours, materials, and/or dollars. This information supports cost and schedule progress, performance measurements, and cash flow management. Recall from Chapter 5 that budget, actual, and committed dollars usually run in different time frames (see Figure 5.6). A typical computer-generated status report includes the following information outputs:

1. Schedule variance (EV − PV) by cost account and WBS and OBS.
2. Cost variance (EV − AC) by cost account and WBS and OBS.
3. Indexes—total percent complete and performance index.
4. Cumulative actual total cost to date (AC).
5. Expected costs at completion (EAC).
6. Paid and unpaid commitments.

The variety of software packages, with their features and constant updating, is too extensive for inclusion in this text. Software developers and vendors have done a superb job of providing software to meet the information needs of most project managers. Differences among software in the last decade have centered on improving "friendliness" and output that is clear and easy to understand. Anyone who understands the concepts and tools presented in Chapters 4, 5, 6, 8, and 13 should have little trouble understanding the output of any of the popular project management software packages.

Additional Earned Value Rules

Although the percent complete rule is the most-used method of assigning budgets to baselines and for cost control, there are additional rules that are very useful for reducing the overhead costs of collecting detailed data on percent complete of individual work packages. (An additional advantage of these rules, of course, is that they remove the often subjective judgments of the contractors or estimators as to how much work has actually been completed.) The first two rules are typically used for short-duration activities and/or small-cost activities. The third rule uses gates before the total budgeted value of an activity can be claimed.

- **0/100 rule.** This rule assumes credit is earned for having performed the work once it is completed. Hence, 100 percent of the budget is earned when the work package is completed. This rule is used for work packages having very short durations.
- **50/50 rule.** This approach allows 50 percent of the value of the work package budget to be earned when it is started and 50 percent to be earned when the package is completed. This rule is popular for work packages of short duration and small total costs.
- **Percent complete with weighted monitoring gates.** This more recent rule uses subjective estimated percent complete in combination with hard, tangible monitoring points. This method works well on long-duration activities that can be broken into short, discrete work packages of no more than one or two report periods. These discrete packages limit the

subjective estimated values. For example, assume a long-duration activity with a total budget of $500. The activity is cut into three sequentially discrete packages with monitoring gates representing 30, 50, and 100 percent of the total budget. The earned amount at each monitoring gate cannot exceed $150, $250, and $500. These hard monitoring points serve as a check on overly optimistic estimates.

Notice the only information needed for the first two rules is that the work package has started and the package has been completed. For those who wish to explore the application of these two rules, or who are studying for certification, Appendix 13.1 presents two exercises that apply these rules along with the percent complete rule.

The third rule is frequently used to authorize progress payments to contractors. This rule supports careful tracking and control of payments; it discourages payment to contractors for work not yet completed.

FORECASTING FINAL PROJECT COST

There are basically two methods used to revise estimates of future project costs. In many cases both methods are used on specific segments of the project. The result is confusion of terms in texts, in software, and among practitioners in the field. We have chosen to note the differences between the methods.

The first method allows experts in the field to change original baseline durations and costs because new information tells them the original estimates are not accurate. We have used EAC_{re} to represent revisions made by experts and practitioners associated with the project. The revisions from project experts are almost always used on smaller projects.

The equation for calculating revised estimated cost at completion (EAC_{re}) is as follows:

$$EAC_{re} = AC + ETC_{re}$$

where
EAC_{re} = revised estimated cost at completion.
AC = cumulative actual cost of work completed to date.
ETC_{re} = revised estimated cost to complete remaining work.

A second method is used in large projects where the original budget is less reliable. This method uses the actual costs to date plus an efficiency index (CPI = EV/AC) applied to the remaining project work. When the estimate for completion uses the CPI as the basis for forecasting cost at completion, we use the acronym **EAC_f**. The equation is presented here.

The equation for this forecasting model (EAC_f) is as follows:

$$EAC_f = ETC + AC$$

$$ETC = \frac{\text{Work remaining}}{CPI} = \frac{BAC - EV}{EV/AC}$$

where
EAC_f = estimated total cost at completion.
ETC = estimated cost to complete remaining work.
AC = cumulative actual cost of work completed to date.

CPI = cumulative cost index to date.

BAC = total budget of the baseline.

EV = cumulative budgeted cost of work completed to date.

The following information is available from our earlier example; the estimate cost at completion (EAC_f) is computed as follows:

Total baseline budget (BAC) for the project	$320
Cumulative earned value (EV) to date	$160
Cumulative actual cost (AC) to date	$230

$$EAC_f = \frac{320 - 160}{160/230} + 230 = \frac{160}{.7} + 230 = 229 + 230$$

$$EAC_f = 459$$

The final project projected cost forecast is $459,000 versus $320,000 originally planned.

Another popular index is the **To Complete Performance Index** (TCPI), which is useful as a supplement to the estimate at complete (EAC_f) computation. This ratio measures the amount of value each *remaining* dollar in the budget must earn to stay within the budget. The index is computed for the Digital Camera project at the end of period 7.

$$TCPI = \frac{BAC - EV}{BAC - AC} = \frac{320 - 160}{320 - 230} = \frac{160}{90} = 1.78$$

The index of 1.78 indicates that each remaining dollar in the budget must earn $1.78 in value. There is more work to be done than there is budget left. Clearly, it would be tough to increase productivity that much to make budget. The work to be done will have to be reduced or you will have to accept running over budget. If the TCPI is less than 1.00, you should be able to complete the project without using all of the remaining budget. A ratio of less than 1.00 opens the possibility of other opportunities such as improving quality, increasing profit, or expanding scope.

Research data indicate that on large projects that are more than 15 percent complete, the model performs well with an error of less than 10 percent (Fleming and Koppleman, 2010; Christensen, 1998). This model can also be used for WBS and OBS cost accounts that have been used to forecast remaining and total costs. It is important to note that this model assumes conditions will not change, the cost database is reliable, EV and AC are cumulative, and past project progress is representative of future progress. This objective forecast represents a good starting point or benchmark that management can use to compare other forecasts that include other conditions and subjective judgments.

Exhibit 13.1 presents an abridged monthly status report similar to one used by a project organization. The form is used for all projects in their project portfolio. (Note that the schedule variance of −$22,176 does not translate directly to days. The 25 days were derived from the network schedule.)

Another summary report is shown in the Snapshot from Practice: Trojan Decommissioning Project. Compare the differences in format.

EXHIBIT 13.1 ···
Monthly Status Report

Project number: 163					Project manager: Connor Gage

Project priority now: 4
Status as of: April 1
Earned value figures:

PV	EV	AC	SV	CV	BAC
588,240	566,064	596,800	−22,176	−30,736	1,051,200
EAC	**VAC**	**EAC$_f$**	**CPI**	**PCIB**	**PCIC**
1,090,640	−39,440	1,107,469	.95	.538	.547

Project description: A computer-controlled conveyor belt that will move and position items on the belt with accuracy of less than one millimeter.

Status summary: The project is approximately 25 days behind schedule. The project has a cost variance of ($30,736).

Explanations: The schedule variance has moved from noncritical activities to those on the critical path. Integration first phase, scheduled to start 3/26, is now expected to start 4/19, which means it is approximately 25 days behind schedule. This delay is traced to the loss of the second design team which made it impossible to start utilities documentation on 2/27 as planned. This loss illustrates the effect of losing valuable resources on the project. The cost variance to date is largely due to a design change that cost $21,000.

Major changes since last report: The major change was loss of one design team to the project.
Total cost of approved design changes: $21,000. Most of this amount is attributed to the improved design of the serial I/O drivers.

Projected cost at completion: EAC$_f$ is estimated to be $1,107,469. This represents an overrun of $56,269, given a CPI of .95. The CPI of .95 causes the forecast to be greater than the VAC −$39,440.

Risk watch: Nothing suggests the risk level of any segments has changed.

SNAPSHOT FROM PRACTICE
Trojan Decommissioning Project

Portland General Electric Company has been charged with decommissioning the Trojan Nuclear Plant. This is a long and complex project extending over two decades. The first segment of the project of moving the used reactors to a storage location is complete and was awarded the Project of the Year, 2000, by the Project Management Institute (PMI). The remainder of the project—decontamination of the remaining structures and waste—is ongoing.

Exhibit 13.2 shows their earned value status report. This report measures schedule and cost performance for monitoring the project. The report also serves as a basis for funding for rate filings with the Public Utilities Commission.

The SPI (0.94) suggests the project schedule is falling behind. Resolving issues with a major vendor and solutions for technical problems should solve these delay problems. The CPI (1.14) for the project is positive. Some of this good cost performance is attributed to partnering and incentive arrangements with vendors and labor unions.

AP Photo/Don Ryan

Interview with Michael B. Lackey, general manager, Trojan, PGE.

EXHIBIT 13.2

Cost/Budget Performance — Portland General Electric Co.-Trojan Nuclear Plant
Report Run: 23-Jan-01 — Report Number: DECT005 — Page: 1 of 1

Description	PV	EV	AC	PV	EV	AC	PV	YTD Variance EV-AC	PV (Nominal Year)	CPI EV/AC	SPI EV/PV
ISFSI	193,014	182,573	162,579	3,655,677	3,586,411	3,263,995	3,655,677	322,416	3,655,677	1.10	0.98
RVAIR	0	0	0	0	0	399	0	(399)	0	0.00	0.00
Equip removal—AB/FB	79,083	79,649	73,899	497,197	504,975	308,461	497,197	196,514	497,197	1.64	1.02
Equip removal—other	0	0	0	0	(36,822)	519	0	(37,341)	0	0.00	0.00
Embed piping—AB/FB	3,884	0	2,118	532,275	540,232	515,235	532,275	24,997	532,275	1.05	1.01
Embed piping—other	0	0	3,439	175,401	210,875	79,235	175,401	131,640	175,401	2.66	1.20
Surface decon—AB/FB	29,935	23,274	21,456	1,266,685	1,293,315	1,171,712	1,266,665	121,603	1,266,665	1.10	1.02
Surface decon—other	2,875	2	11,005	308,085	199,853	251,265	308,085	(51,412)	308,085	0.80	0.65
Surface decon—containment	680,502	435,657	474,427	5,271,889	4,950,528	4,823,338	5,271,889	127,190	5,271,889	1.03	0.94
Radwaste disposal	884,873	453,032	(28,675)	10,680,118	8,276,616	10,807,916	10,880,118	(2,531,300)	10,880,118	0.77	0.77
Final survey	58,238	57,985	27,091	780,990	780,990	700,942	780,990	80,048	780,990	1.11	1.00
Nonradiological areas	92,837	91,956	58,538	2,471,281	2,376,123	834,643	2,471,281	1,541,480	2,471,281	2.85	0.96
Staffing	714,806	714,509	468,858	9,947,775	9,947,775	8,241,383	9,947,775	1,706,392	9,947,775	1.21	1.00
ISFSI—Long-term ops	85,026	85,028	19,173	2,004,398	2,004,398	337,206	2,004,398	1,667,192	2,004,398	5.94	1.00
Labor loadings	258,289	258,289	240,229	3,216,194	3,216,194	2,755,604	3,216,194	460,590	3,216,194	1.17	1.00
Material loadings	17,910	17,910	(95,128)	211,454	211,454	136,973	211,454	74,481	211,454	1.54	1.00
Corporate governance	153,689	228,499	228,521	1,814,523	1,814,523	1,814,520	1,814,523	3	1,814,523	1.00	1.00
Undistributable costs	431,840	401,720	242,724	5,541,679	5,575,879	4,007,732	5,541,679	1,567,947	5,541,679	1.39	1.01
Total decommissioning	3,688,481	3,008,081	1,905,084	48,375,399	45,453,119	40,051,079	48,375,399	5,402,040	48,375,399	1.13	0.94
Total (less ISFSI and RVAIR)	3,493,467	2,845,508	1,743,485	44,719,720	41,886,710	36,788,680	44,719,720	5,080,024	44,719,720	1.14	0.94

OTHER CONTROL ISSUES

Scope Creep

Large changes in scope are easily identified. It is the "minor refinements" that eventually build to be major scope changes that can cause problems. These small refinements are known in the field as **scope creep.** For example, the customer of a software developer requested small changes in the development of a custom accounting software package. After several minor refinements, it became apparent the changes represented a significant enlargement of the original project scope. The result was an unhappy customer and a development firm that lost money and reputation.

Although scope changes are usually viewed negatively, there are situations when scope changes result in positive rewards. Scope changes can represent significant opportunities.[3] In product development environments, adding a small feature to a product can result in a huge competitive advantage. A small change in the production process may get the product to market one month early or reduce product cost.

Scope creep is common early in projects—especially in new-product development projects. Customer requirements for additional features, new technology, poor design assumptions, etc., all manifest pressures for scope changes. Frequently these changes are small and go unnoticed until time delays or cost overruns are observed. Scope creep affects the organization, project team, and project suppliers. Scope changes alter the organization's cash flow requirements in the form of fewer or additional resources, which may also affect other projects. Frequent changes eventually wear down team motivation and cohesiveness. Clear team goals are altered, become less focused, and cease being the focal point for team action. Starting over again is annoying and demoralizing to the project team because it disrupts project rhythm and lowers productivity. Project suppliers resent frequent changes because they represent higher costs and have the same effect on their team as on the project team.

The key to managing scope creep is change management. One project manager of an architectural firm related that scope creep was the biggest risk his firm faced in projects. The best defense against scope creep is a well-defined scope statement. Poor scope statements are one of the major causes of scope creep.

A second defense against scope creep is stating what the project is not, which can avoid misinterpretations later. (Chapter 7 discusses the process. See Figure 7.9 to review key variables to document in project changes.) First, the original baseline must be well defined and agreed upon with the project customer. Before the project begins, it is imperative that clear procedures be in place for authorizing and documenting scope changes by the customer or project team. If a scope change is necessary, the impact on the baseline should be clearly documented—for example, cost, time, dependencies, specifications, responsibilities, etc. Finally, the scope change must be quickly added to the original baseline to reflect the change in budget and schedule; these changes and their impacts need to be communicated to all project stakeholders.

Baseline Changes

Changes during the life cycle of projects are inevitable and will occur. Some changes can be very beneficial to project outcomes; changes having a negative impact are the ones we wish to avoid. Careful project definition can minimize the need for changes. The price for poor project definition

[3]See S. Keifer, "Scope Creep ... Not Necessarily a Bad Thing," *PM Network,* 10 (5), 1996, pp. 33–35.

can be changes that result in cost overruns, late schedules, low morale, and loss of control. Change comes from external sources or from within. Externally, for example, the customer may request changes that were not included in the original scope statement and that will require significant changes to the project and thus to the baseline. Or the government may render requirements that were not a part of the original plan and that require a revision of the project scope. Internally, stakeholders may identify unforeseen problems or improvements that change the scope of the project. In rare cases scope changes can come from several sources. For example, the Denver International Airport automatic baggage handling system was an afterthought supported by several project stakeholders that included the Denver city government, consultants, and at least one airline customer. The additional $2 billion in costs were staggering, and the airport opening was delayed 16 months. If this automatic baggage scope change had been in the original plan, costs would have been only a fraction of the overrun costs, and delays would have been reduced significantly. Any changes in scope or the baseline should be recorded by the change management system that was set in place during risk control planning. (See Chapter 7.)

Generally, project managers monitor scope changes very carefully. They should allow scope changes only if it is clear that the project will fail without the change, the project will be improved significantly with the change, or the customer wants it and will pay for it. This statement is an exaggeration, but it sets the tone for approaching baseline changes. The effect of the change on the scope and baseline should be accepted and signed off by the project customer. Figure 13.13 depicts the cost impact of a scope change on the baseline at a point in time—"today." Line A represents a scope change that results in an increase in cost. Line B represents a scope change that decreases cost. Quickly recording scope changes to the baseline keeps the computed earned values valid. Failure to do so results in misleading cost and schedule variances.

Care should be taken to not use baseline changes to disguise poor performance on past or current work. A common signal of this type of baseline change is a constantly revised baseline that seems to match results. Practitioners call this a "rubber baseline" because it stretches to match

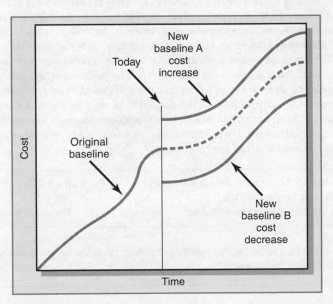

FIGURE 13.13 *Scope Changes to a Baseline*

results. Most changes will not result in serious scope changes and should be absorbed as positive or negative variances. Retroactive changes for work already accomplished should not be allowed. Transfer of money among cost accounts should not be allowed after the work is complete. Unforeseen changes can be handled through the contingency reserve. The project manager typically makes this decision. In some large projects, a partnering "change review team," made up of members of the project and customer teams, makes all decisions on project changes.

The Costs and Problems of Data Acquisition

Data acquisition is time consuming and costly. The Snapshot from Practice: A Pseudo-Earned Value Percent Complete Approach captures some of the frequent issues surrounding resistance to data collection of percent complete for earned value systems. Similar pseudo-percent complete systems have been used by others. Such pseudo-percent complete approaches appear to work well in multiproject environments that include several small and medium-sized projects. Assuming a one-week reporting period, care needs to be taken to develop work packages with a duration of about one week long so problems are identified quickly. For large projects, there is no substitute for using a percent complete system that depends on data collected through observation at clearly defined monitoring points.

SNAPSHOT FROM PRACTICE

A Pseudo–Earned Value
Percent Complete Approach

A consultant for the U.S. Forest Service suggested the use of earned value to monitor the 50-plus timber sale projects taking place concurrently in the district. As projects were completed, new ones were started. Earned value was tried for approximately nine months. After a nine-month trial, the process was to be reviewed by a task force. The task force concluded the earned value system provided good information for monitoring and forecasting project progress; however, the costs and problems of collecting timely percent complete data were unacceptable because there were no funds available to collect such data.

The level of detail dilemma was discussed, but no suggestions satisfied the problem. The discussion recognized that too little data fail to offer good control, while excessive reporting requires paperwork and people, which are costly. The task force concluded progress and performance could be measured using a pseudo-version of percent complete while not giving up much accuracy for the total project. This modified approach to percent complete required that very large work packages (about 3 to 5 percent of all work packages in a project) be divided into smaller work packages for closer control and identification of problems sooner. It was decided work packages of about a week's duration would be ideal. The pseudo-version required only a telephone call and "yes/no" answers to one of the following questions to assign percent complete:

Has work on the work package started?	No = 0%
Working on the package?	Yes = 50%
Is the work package completed?	Yes = 100%

Data for the pseudo-earned value percent complete system was collected for all 50-plus projects by an intern working fewer than eight hours each week.

In some cases data exist but are not sent to the stakeholders who need information relating to project progress. Clearly, if the information does not reach the right people in a timely manner, you can expect serious problems. Your communication plan developed in the project planning stage can greatly mitigate this problem by mapping out the flow of information and keeping stakeholders informed on all aspects of project progress and issues. See Figure 13.14 for an internal communication plan for a WiFi Project. The information developed in this chapter contributes significant data to support your communication plan and ensures correct dissemination of the data.

What Information	When?	Mode?	Responsible?	Recipient?
Milestone report	Bimonthly	E-mail	Project office	Senior management
Time/cost report	Weekly	E-mail	Project office	Staff and customer
Risk report	Weekly	E-mail	Project office	Staff and customer
Issues	Weekly	E-mail	Anyone	Staff and customer
Team meeting times	Weekly	Meeting	Project manager	Staff and customer
Outsourcing performance	Bimonthly	Meeting	Project manager	Project office, staff, and customer
Change requests	Anytime	Document	Project manager, customer, design	Project office, staff, and customer
Stage gate decisions	Monthly	Meeting	Project office	Senior management

FIGURE 13.14 *Conference Center WiFi Project Communication Plan*

Summary

The best information system does not result in good control. Control requires the project manager to *use* information to steer the project through rough waters. Control and Gantt charts are useful vehicles for monitoring time performance. The cost/schedule system allows the manager to have a positive influence on cost and schedule in a timely manner. The ability to influence cost decreases with time; therefore, timely reports identifying adverse cost trends can greatly assist the project manager in getting back on budget and schedule. The integrated cost/schedule model provides the project manager and other stakeholders with a snapshot of the current and future status of the project. The benefits of the cost/schedule model are as follows:

1. Measures accomplishments against plan and deliverables.
2. Provides a method for tracking directly to a problem work package and organization unit responsible.
3. Alerts all stakeholders to early identification of problems, and allows for quick, proactive corrective action.
4. Improves communication because all stakeholders are using the same database.
5. Keeps customer informed of progress, and encourages customer confidence that the money spent is resulting in the expected progress.

6. Provides for accountability over individual portions of the overall budget for each organizational unit.

With your information system in place, you need to use your communication plan to keep stakeholders informed so timely decisions can be made to ensure the project is managed effectively.

Key Terms

Baseline budget
Budget at completion (BAC)
Control chart
Cost performance index (CPI)
Cost variance (CV)
Earned value (EV)
Estimated cost at completion—Forecasted (EAC$_f$)

Estimated cost at completion—Revised estimates (EAC$_{re}$)
Percent complete index—budget costs (PCIB)
Percent complete index—actual costs (PCIC)
Schedule performance index (SPI)

Schedule variance (SV)
Scope creep
To complete performace index (TCPI)
Tracking Gantt chart
Variance at completion (VAC)

Review Questions

1. How does a Tracking Gantt chart help communicate project progress?
2. How does earned value give a clearer picture of project schedule and cost status than a simple plan versus actual system?
3. Schedule variance (SV) is in dollars and does not directly represent time. Why is it still useful?
4. How would a project manager use the CPI?
5. What are the differences between BAC and EAC?
6. Why is it important for project managers to resist changes to the project baseline? Under what conditions would a project manager make changes to a baseline? When would a project manager not allow changes to a baseline?

Exercises

1. In month 9 the following project information is available: actual cost is $2,000, earned value is $2,100, and planned cost is $2,400. Compute the SV and CV for the project.
2. On day 51 a project has an earned value of $600, an actual cost of $650, and a planned cost of $560. Compute the SV, CV, and CPI for the project. What is your assessment of the project on day 51?
3. Given the project network and baseline information below, complete the form to develop a status report for the project at the end of period 4 and the end of period 8. From the data you

have collected and computed for periods 4 and 8, what information are you prepared to tell the customer about the status of the project at the end of period 8?

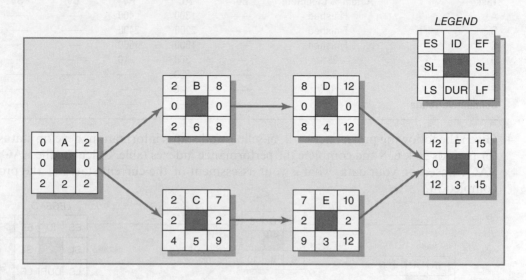

				Project baseline (PV) (in $)																
Task	DUR	ES	LF	SL	Budget (PV)	0	1	2	3	4	5	6	7	8	9	10	11	12	13	14	15
A	2	0	2	0	400	200	200														
B	6	2	8	0	2400			200	600	200	600	200	600								
C	5	2	9	2	1500			200	400	500	100	300									
D	4	8	12	0	1600									400	400	400	400				
E	3	7	12	2	900								300	400	200						
F	3	12	15	0	600														200	100	300
			Period PV total			200	200	400	1000	700	700	500	900	800	600	400	400	200	100	300
			Cumulative PV total			200	400	800	1800	2500	3200	3700	4600	5400	6000	6400	6800	7000	7100	7400

End of Period 4

Task	Actual % Complete	EV	AC	PV	CV	SV
A	Finished	—	300	400	—	—
B	50%	—	1000	800	—	—
C	33%	—	500	600	—	—
D	0%	—	0	—	—	—
E	0%	—	—	—	—	—
Cumulative Totals		—	—	—	—	—

End of Period 8

Task	Actual % Complete	EV	AC	PV	CV	SV
A	Finished	——	300	400	——	——
B	Finished	——	2200	2400	——	——
C	Finished	——	1500	1500	——	——
D	25%	——	300	0	——	——
E	33%	——	300	——	——	——
F	0%	——	0	——	——	——
Cumulative Totals		——	——	——	——	——

4. Given the following project network, baseline, and status information, develop status reports for periods 2, 4, 6, 8 and complete the performance indexes table. Calculate the EAC_f and the VAC_f. Based on your data, what is your assessment of the current status of the project? At completion?

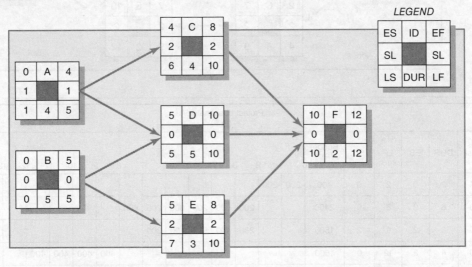

Status Report: Ending Period 2 ($000)

Task	% Complete	EV	AC	PV	CV	SV
A	75%	——	25	——	——	——
B	50%	——	12	——	——	——
Cumulative Totals		——	**37**	——	——	——

Status Report: Ending Period 4 ($000)

Task	% Complete	EV	AC	PV	CV	SV
A	100%	——	35	——	——	——
B	100%	——	24	——	——	——
Cumulative Totals		——	**59**	——	——	——

Status Report: Ending Period 6 ($000)

Task	% Complete	EV	AC	PV	CV	SV
A	100%	——	35	——	——	——
B	100%	——	24	——	——	——
C	75%	——	24	——	——	——
D	0%	——	0	——	——	——
E	50%	——	10	——	——	——
Cumulative Totals		——	**93**	——	——	——

Status Report: Ending Period 8 ($000)

Task	% Complete	EV	AC	PV	CV	SV
A	100%	——	35	——	——	——
B	100%	——	24	——	——	——
C	100%	——	32	——	——	——
D	33%	——	20	——	——	——
E	100%	——	20	——	——	——
Cumulative Totals		——	**131**	——	——	——

Performance Indexes Summary

Period	EV	AC	PV	SPI	CPI	PCI-B
2	——	——	——	——	——	——
4	——	——	——	——	——	——
6	——	——	——	——	——	——
8	——	——	——	——	——	——

$EAC_f =$ _____ $VAC_f =$ _____

5. Given the following project network, baseline, and status information, develop status reports for periods 1–4 and complete the project summary graph (or a similar one). Report the final SV, CV, CPI, and PCIB. Based on your data, what is your assessment of the current status of the project? At completion?

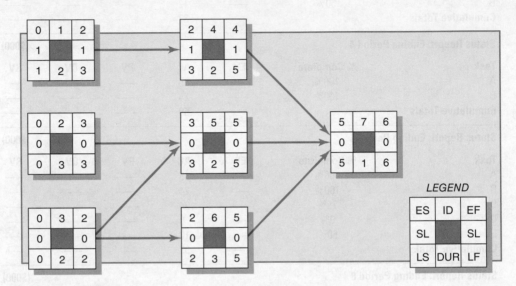

Schedule information					Baseline budget needs ($ 000)							
ACT/WP	DUR	ES	LF	SL	Total PV	Time period						
						0	1	2	3	4	5	6
1	2	0	3	1	12	4	8					
2	3	0	3	0	15	3	7	5				
3	2	0	2	0	8	4	4					
4	2	2	5	1	6			3	3			
5	2	3	5	0	10				6	4		
6	3	2	5	0	9			3	3	3		
7	1	5	6	0	5							5
			Total PV by period			11	19	11	12	7	5	
			Cumulative PV by period			11	30	41	53	60	65	

Status Report: Ending Period 1 ($000)

Task	%Complete	EV	AC	PV	CV	SV
1	50%	—	6	4	—	—
2	40%	—	8	3	—	—
3	25%	—	3		—	—
Cumulative Totals		—	**17**	—	—	—

Status Report: Ending Period 2 | | | | | ($000)

Task	%Complete	EV	AC	PV	CV	SV
1	Finished	——	13	——	——	——
2	80%	——	14	——	——	——
3	75%	——	8	——	——	——
Cumulative Totals		——	**35**	——	——	——

Status Report: Ending Period 3 | | | | | ($000)

Task	%Complete	EV	AC	PV	CV	SV
1	Finished	12	13	——	——	——
2	80%	——	15	——	——	——
3	Finished	——	10	——	——	——
4	50%	——	4	——	——	——
5	0%	——	0	——	——	——
6	33.3%	——	4	——	——	——
Cumulative Totals		——	——	——	——	——

Status Report: Ending Period 4 | | | | | ($000)

Task	%Complete	EV	AC	PV	CV	SV
1	Finished	12	13	——	——	——
2	Finished	15	18	——	——	——
3	Finished	——	10	——	——	——
4	Finished	——	8	——	——	——
5	30%	——	3	——	——	——
6	66.7%	——	8	——	——	——
7	0%	——	0	——	——	——
Cumulative Totals		——	——	——	——	——

Summary Graph

6. The following labor hours data have been collected for a nanotechnology project for periods 1 through 6. Compute the SV, CV, SPI, and CPI for each period. Plot the EV and the AC on the summary graph provided (or a similar one). Plot the SPI, CPI, and PCIB on the index graph provided (or a similar one). What is your assessment of the project at the end of period 6?

Legend

ES	ID	EF
SL		SL
LS	DUR	LF

	Schedule information					Baseline budget needs–labor hours (00)														
ACT/WP	DUR	ES	LF	SL	Total PV	Time period														
						0	1	2	3	4	5	6	7	8	9	10	11	12	13	14
1	2	0	2	0	20	10	10													
2	2	2	7	3	24			16	8											
3	6	2	11	3	30			5	5	10	3	2	5							
4	5	2	7	0	25			10	10	2	2	1								
5	4	4	11	3	16					4	4	4	4							
6	4	7	11	0	20							5	5	6	4					
7	2	11	13	0	10													5	5	
Total PV by period						10	10	31	23	16	9	7	14	5	6	4	5	5		
Cumulative PV by period						10	20	51	74	90	99	106	120	125	131	135	140	145		

Status Report: Ending Period 1

Task	%Complete	EV	AC	PV	CV	SV
1	50%	——	500	1000	——	——
Cumulative Totals		——	**500**	**1000**	——	——

Status Report: Ending Period 2

Task	%Complete	EV	AC	PV	CV	SV
1	Finished	——	1500	2000	——	——
Cumulative Totals		——	**1500**	**2000**	——	——

Status Report: Ending Period 3

Task	%Complete	EV	AC	PV	CV	SV
1	Finished	2000	1500	2000	——	——
2	0%	——	0	——	——	——
3	10%	——	200	——	——	——
4	20%	——	500	——	——	——
Cumulative Totals		——	**2200**	——	——	——

Status Report: Ending Period 4

Task	%Complete	EV	AC	PV	CV	SV
1	Finished	2000	1500	2000	——	——
2	50%	——	1000	——	——	——
3	30%	——	800	——	——	——
4	40%	——	1500	——	——	——
Cumulative Totals		——	**4800**	——	——	——

Status Report: Ending Period 5

Task	%Complete	EV	AC	PV	CV	SV
1	Finished	2000	1500	2000	——	——
2	Finished	——	2000	——	——	——
3	50%	——	800	——	——	——
4	60%	——	1500	——	——	——
5	25%	——	400	——	——	——
Cumulative Totals		——	**6200**	——	——	——

Status Report: Ending Period 6

Task	%Complete	EV	AC	PV	CV	SV
1	Finished	2000	1500	2000	——	——
2	Finished	——	2000	——	——	——
3	80%	——	2100	——	——	——
4	80%	——	1800	——	——	——
5	50%	——	600	——	——	——
Cumulative Totals		——	**8000**	——	——	——

Period	SPI	CPI	PCIB
1	——	——	——
2	——	——	——
3	——	——	——
4	——	——	——
5	——	——	——
6	——	——	——

$$SPI = EV/PV$$
$$CPI = EV/AC$$
$$PCIB = EV/BAC$$

Summary Graph

Indexes Periods 1–6

7. The following data have been collected for a British health care IT project for two-week reporting periods 2 through 12. Compute the SV, CV, SPI, and CPI for each period. Plot the EV and the AC on the summary graph provided. Plot the SPI, CPI, and PCIB on the index graph provided. (You may use your own graphs.) What is your assessment of the project at the end of period 12?

					Baseline (PV) ($00)												
Task	DUR	ES	LF	SL	PV ($00)	0	2	4	6	8	10	12	14	16	18	20	22
1	4	0	4	0	8	4	4										
2	8	4	14	2	40				10	10	10	10					
3	6	4	10	0	30				10	15	5						
4	4	4	10	2	20				10	10							
5	4	10	14	0	40							20	20				
6	8	8	18	2	60						20	20	10	10			
7	4	14	18	0	20									10	10		
8	4	18	22	0	30											20	10
Period PV total						4	4	30	35	35	50	30	20	10	20	10	
Cumulative PV total						4	8	38	73	108	158	188	208	218	238	248	

Status Report: Ending Period 2   **($00)**

Task	%Complete	EV	AC	PV	CV	SV
1	50%	——	4	——	——	——
Cumulative Totals		——	**4**	——	——	——

Status Report: Ending Period 4   **($00)**

Task	%Complete	EV	AC	PV	CV	SV
1	Finished	——	10	——	——	——
Cumulative Totals		——	**10**	——	——	——

Status Report: Ending Period 6   ($00)

Task	%Complete	EV	AC	PV	CV	SV
1	Finished	——	10	——	——	——
2	25%	——	15	——	——	——
3	33%	——	12	——	——	——
4	0%	——	0	——	——	——
Cumulative Totals		——	**37**	——	——	——

Status Report: Ending Period 8   ($00)

Task	%Complete	EV	AC	PV	CV	SV
1	Finished	——	10	——	——	——
2	30%	——	20	——	——	——
3	60%	——	25	——	——	——
4	0%	——	0	——	——	——
Cumulative Totals		——	**55**	——	——	——

Status Report: Ending Period 10   ($00)

Task	%Complete	EV	AC	PV	CV	SV
1	Finished	——	10	——	——	——
2	60%	——	30	——	——	——
3	Finished	——	40	——	——	——
4	50%	——	20	——	——	——
5	0%	——	0	——	——	——
6	30%	——	24	——	——	——
Cumulative Totals		——	**124**	——	——	——

Status Report: Ending Period 12   ($00)

Task	%Complete	EV	AC	PV	CV	SV
1	Finished	——	10	——	——	——
2	Finished	——	50	——	——	——
3	Finished	——	40	——	——	——
4	Finished	——	40	——	——	——
5	50%	——	30	——	——	——
6	50%	——	40	——	——	——
Cumulative Totals		——	**210**	——	——	——

Period	SPI	CPI	PCIB
2	——	——	——
4	——	——	——
6	——	——	——
8	——	——	——
10	——	——	——
12	——	——	——

SPI = EV/PV
CPI = EV/AC
PCIB = EV/BAC

8.*Part A. You are in charge of the Aurora Project. Given the following project network, baseline, and status information, develop status reports for periods 1–8 and complete the performance indexes table. Calculate the EAC$_f$ and VAC$_f$. Based on your data, what is the current status of the project? At completion?

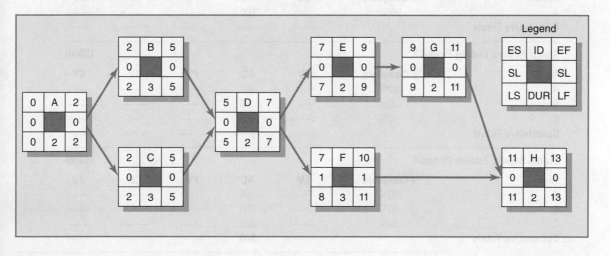

* The solution to this exercise can be found in Appendix 1.

ID	Budget ($000)	0	1	2	3	4	5	6	7	8	9	10	11	12	13
A	100		50	50											
B	250				100	50	100								
C	450				150	150	150								
D	200							100	100						
E	300									200	100				
F	300									100	50	150			
G	200											150	50		
H	200													100	100
Total	2000		50	50	250	200	250	100	100	300	150	300	50	100	100
Cumulative			50	100	350	550	800	900	1000	1300	1450	1750	1800	1900	2000

Status Report: Ending Period 1 ($000)

Task	% Complete	EV	AC	PV	CV	SV
A	25%	——	50	——	——	——
Cumulative Totals		——	**50**	——	——	——

Status Report: Ending Period 2 ($000)

Task	% Complete	EV	AC	PV	CV	SV
A	50%	——	100	——	——	——
Cumulative Totals		——	——	——	——	——

Status Report: Ending Period 3 ($000)

Task	% Complete	EV	AC	PV	CV	SV
A	100%	——	200	——	——	——
B	0%	——	0	——	——	——
C	0%	——	0	——	——	——
Cumulative Totals		——	——	——	——	——

Status Report: Ending Period 4 ($000)

Task	% Complete	EV	AC	PV	CV	SV
A	100%	——	200	——	——	——
B	60%	——	100	——	——	——
C	50%	——	200	——	——	——
Cumulative Totals		——	**500**	——	——	——

Status Report: Ending Period 5   ($000)

Task	% Complete	EV	AC	PV	CV	SV
A	100%	——	200	——	——	——
B	100%	——	200	——	——	——
C	100%	——	400	——	——	——
Cumulative Totals		——	**800**	——	——	——

Status Report: Ending Period 6   ($000)

Task	% Complete	EV	AC	PV	CV	SV
A	100%	——	200	——	——	——
B	100%	——	200	——	——	——
C	100%	——	400	——	——	——
D	75%	——	100	——	——	——
Cumulative Totals		——	**900**	——	——	——

Status Report: Ending Period 7   ($000)

Task	% Complete	EV	AC	PV	CV	SV
A	100%	——	200	——	——	——
B	100%	——	200	——	——	——
C	100%	——	400	——	——	——
D	100%	——	150	——	——	——
E	20%	——	100	——	——	——
F	5%	——	50	——	——	——
Cumulative Totals		——	**1100**	——	——	——

Status Report: Ending Period 8   ($000)

Task	% Complete	EV	AC	PV	CV	SV
A	100%	——	200	——	——	——
B	100%	——	200	——	——	——
C	100%	——	400	——	——	——
D	100%	——	150	——	——	——
E	100%	——	350	——	——	——
F	10%	——	100	——	——	——
Cumulative Totals		——	**1400**	——	——	——

Performance Indexes Summary

Period	EV	AC	PV	SPI	CPI	PCI-B
1	——	——	——	——	——	——
2	——	——	——	——	——	——
3	——	——	——	——	——	——
4	——	——	——	——	——	——
5	——	——	——	——	——	——
6	——	——	——	——	——	——
7	——	——	——	——	——	——
8	——	——	——	——	——	——

$EAC_f =$ _____ $VAC_f =$ _____

Part B. You have met with your Aurora project team and they have provided you with the following revised estimates for the remainder of the project:

- Activity F will be completed at the end of period 12 at a total cost of 500.
- Activity G will be completed at the end of period 10 at a total cost of 150.
  - Activity H will be completed at the end of period 14 at a total cost of 200.

Calculate the EAC_{re} and VAC_{re}. Based on the revised estimates, what is the expected status of the project in terms of cost and schedule? Between the VAC_f and the VAC_{re}, which one would you have the greatest confidence in?

$EAC_{re} = $ _____ $VAC_{re} = $ _____

References

Abramovici, A., "Controlling Scope Creep," *PM Network,* Vol. 14, No. 1, January 2000, pp. 44–48.

Anbari, F. T., "Earned Value Project Management Method and Extensions," *Project Management Journal,* Vol. 34, No. 4, December 2003, pp. 12–22.

Brandon, D. M., Jr., "Implementing Earned Value Easily and Effectively," *Project Management Journal,* Vol. 29, No. 3, June 1998, pp. 11–17.

Bowles, M. "Keeping Score," *PMNetwork,* May 2011, pp. 50–59.

Christensen, D. S., and S. Heise, "Cost Performance Index Stability," *National Contract Management Association Journal,* 25, 1993, pp. 7–15.

Christensen, D. S., "The Cost and Benefits of the Earned Value Management Process," *Acquisition Review Quarterly,* 5 (1998), pp. 373–86.

Fleming, Q., and Joel M. Koppelman, *Earned Value Project Management,* 4th ed. (Newton Square, PA: Project Management Institute, 2010).

Kerzner, H., "Strategic Planning for a Project Office," *Project Management Journal,* Vol. 34, No. 2, June 2003, pp. 13–25.

Kim, E. H., W. G. Wells, and M. R. Duffey, "A Model for Effective Implementation of Earned Value Methodology," *International Journal of Project Management,* 21 (5), 2003, pp. 375–82.

Naeni, L., S. Shadrokh, and A. Salehipour, "A Fuzzy Approach to the Earned Value Management," *International Journal of Project Management,* 9 (6), 2011, pp. 764–72.

Webb, A., *Using Earned Value: A Project Manager's Guide* (Aldershot, UK: Gower Publishing Co., 2003).

APPENDIX 13.1

The Application of Additional Earned Value Rules

The following example and exercises are designed to provide practice in applying the following three earned value rules:

- Percent complete rule
- 0/100 rule
- 50/50 rule

See the chapter for an explanation of each of these rules.

Electroscan, Inc. 555 Acorn Street, Suite 5 Boston, Massachusetts				29 In-store Scanner Project (thousands of dollars) Actual Progress as of January 1				
Name	PV	EV	AC	SV	CV	BAC	EAC$_f$	
Scanner project	420	395	476	−25	−81	915	1103	
H 1.0 Hardware	92	88	72	−4	16	260	213	
H 1.1 Hardware specifications (DS)	20	20	15	0	5	20	15	
H 1.2 Hardware design (DS)	30	30	25	0	5	30	25	
H 1.3 Hardware documentation (DOC)	10	6	5	−4	1	10	8	
H 1.4 Prototypes (PD)	2	2	2	0	0	40	40	
H 1.5 Test prototypes (T)	0	0	0	0	0	30	30	
H 1.6 Order circuit boards (PD)	30	30	25	0	5	30	25	
H 1.7 Preproduction models (PD)	0	0	0	0	0	100	100	
OP 1.0 Operating system	195	150	196	−45	−46	330	431	
OP 1.1 Kernel specifications (DS)	20	20	15	0	5	20	15	
OP 1.2 Drivers	45	55	76	10	−21	70	97	
OP 1.2.1 Disk drivers (DEV)	25	30	45	5	−15	40	60	
OP 1.2.2 I/O drivers (DEV)	20	25	31	5	−6	30	37	
OP 1.3 Code software	130	75	105	−55	−30	240	336	
OP 1.3.1 Code software (C)	30	20	40	−10	−20	100	200	
OP 1.3.2 Document software (DOC)	45	30	25	−15	5	50	42	
OP 1.3.3 Code interfaces (C)	55	25	40	−30	−15	60	96	
OP 1.3.4 Beta test software (T)	0	0	0	0	0	30	30	
U 1.0 Utilities	87	108	148	21	−40	200	274	
U 1.1 Utilities specifications (DS)	20	20	15	0	5	20	15	
U 1.2 Routine utilities (DEV)	20	20	35	0	−15	20	35	
U 1.3 Complex utilities (DEV)	30	60	90	30	−30	100	150	
U 1.4 Utilities documentation (DOC)	17	8	8	−9	0	20	20	
U 1.5 Beta test utilities (T)	0	0	0	0	0	40	40	
S 1.0 System integration	46	49	60	3	−11	125	153	
S 1.1 Architecture decisions (DS)	9	9	7	0	2	10	8	
S 1.2 Integration hard/soft (DEV)	25	30	45	5	−15	50	75	
S 1.3 System hard/software test (T)	0	0	0	0	0	20	20	
S 1.4 Project documentation (DOC)	12	10	8	−2	2	15	12	
S 1.5 Integration acceptance testing (T)	0	0	0	0	0	30	30	

SIMPLIFYING ASSUMPTIONS

The same simplifying assumptions used for the chapter example and exercises will also be used here.

1. Assume each cost account has only one work package, and each cost account will be represented as an activity on the network.
2. The project network early start times will serve as the basis for assigning the baseline values.
3. Except when the 0/100 rule or 50/50 rule is used, baseline values will be assigned linearly, unless stated differently. (Note: In practice estimated costs should be applied "exactly" as they are expected to occur so measures of schedule and cost performance are useful and reliable.)
4. For purposes of demonstrating the examples, from the moment work on an activity begins, some actual costs will be incurred each period until the activity is completed.
5. When the 0/100 rule is used, the total cost for the activity is placed in the baseline on the early finish date.
6. When the 50/50 rule is used, 50 percent of the total cost is placed in the baseline on the early start date and 50 percent on the early finish date.

APPENDIX EXERCISES

1. Given the information provided for development of a product warranty project for periods 1 through 7, compute the SV, CV, SPI, and CPI for each period. Plot the EV and the AC on the PV graph provided. Explain to the owner your assessment of the project at the end of period 7 and the future expected status of the project at completion. Figure A13.1A presents the project network. Figure A13.1B presents the project baseline noting those activities using the 0/100 (rule 3) and 50/50 (rule 2) rules. For example, activity 1 uses rule 3, the 0/100 rule. Although the early start time is period 0, the budget is not placed in the time-phased baseline until period 2 when the activity is planned to be finished (EF). This same procedure has been used to assign costs for activities 2 and 7. Activities 2 and 7 use the 50/50 rule. Thus, 50 percent of the budget for each activity is assigned on its respective early start date (time period 2 for activity 2 and period 11 for activity 7) and 50 percent for their respective finish dates. Remember, when assigning earned value as the project is being implemented, if an activity actually starts early or late, the earned values must shift with the actual times. For example, if activity 7 actually starts in period 12 rather than 11, the 50 percent is not earned until period 12.

Status Report: Ending Period 1

Task	%Complete	EV	AC	PV	CV	SV
1	0%	——	3	0	——	——
Cumulative Totals		——	3	0	——	——

Status Report: Ending Period 2

Task	%Complete	EV	AC	PV	CV	SV
1	Finished	6	5	——	——	——
Cumulative Totals		6	5	——	——	——

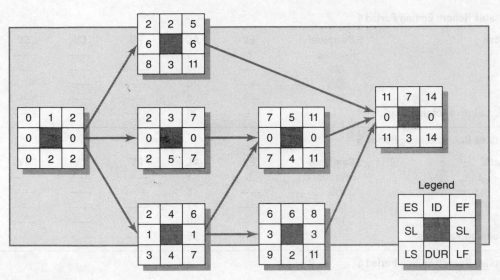

FIGURE A13.1A

EV Rule	ACT/WP	DUR	ES	LF	SL	Total PV	0	1	2	3	4	5	6	7	8	9	10	11	12	13	14
3	1	2	0	2	0	6		6													
2	2	3	2	11	6	20			10		10										
1	3	5	2	7	0	30			9	6	6	6	3								
1	4	4	2	7	1	20			8	2	5	5									
1	5	4	7	11	0	16								4	4	4	4				
1	6	2	6	11	3	18							9	9							
2	7	3	11	14	0	8												4		4	

Schedule information / Baseline budget needs — Time period

Rule: 1 = %complete; 2 = 50/50; 3 = 0/100

| Total PV by period | | | | | | | 0 | 6 | 27 | 8 | 21 | 11 | 12 | 13 | 4 | 4 | 4 | 4 | 0 | 4 | |
| Cumulative PV by period | | | | | | | 0 | 6 | 33 | 41 | 62 | 73 | 85 | 98 | 102 | 106 | 110 | 114 | 114 | 118 | |

FIGURE A13.1B

Status Report: Ending Period 3

Task	%Complete	EV	AC	PV	CV	SV
1	Finished	6	5	——	——	——
2	0%	——	5	——	——	——
3	30%	——	7	——	——	——
4	25%	——	5	——	——	——
Cumulative Totals		——	**22**	——	——	——

Status Report: Ending Period 4

Task	%Complete	EV	AC	PV	CV	SV
1	Finished	6	5	___	___	___
2	0%	___	7	___	___	___
3	50%	___	10	___	___	___
4	50%	___	8	___	___	___
Cumulative Totals		___	**30**	___	___	___

Status Report: Ending Period 5

Task	%Complete	EV	AC	PV	CV	SV
1	Finished	6	5	___	___	___
2	50%	___	8	___	___	___
3	60%	___	12	___	___	___
4	70%	___	10	___	___	___
Cumulative Totals		___	**35**	___	___	___

Status Report: Ending Period 6

Task	%Complete	EV	AC	PV	CV	SV
1	Finished	6	5	___	___	___
2	50%	___	10	___	___	___
3	80%	___	16	___	___	___
4	Finished	___	15	___	___	___
Cumulative Totals		___	**46**	___	___	___

Status Report: Ending Period 7

Task	%Complete	EV	AC	PV	CV	SV
1	Finished	6	5	___	___	___
2	Finished	___	14	___	___	___
3	Finished	___	20	___	___	___
4	Finished	___	15	___	___	___
5	0%	___	0	___	___	___
6	50%	___	9	___	___	___
Cumulative Totals		___	**63**	___	___	___

Period	SPI	CPI	PCIB
1	___	___	___
2	___	___	___
3	___	___	___
4	___	___	___
5	___	___	___
6	___	___	___
7	___	___	___

SPI = EV/PV
CPI = EV/AC
PCIB = EV/BAC

FIGURE A13.1C

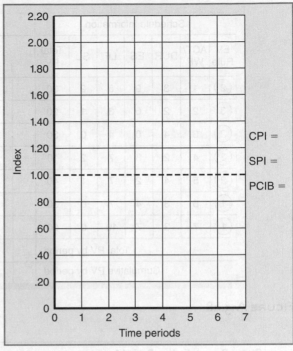

FIGURE A13.1D

2. Given the information provided for development of a catalog product return process for periods 1 through 5, assign the PV values (using the rules) to develop a baseline for the project. Compute the SV, CV, SPI, and CPI for each period. Explain to the owner your assessment of the project at the end of period 5 and the future expected status of the project at the completion.

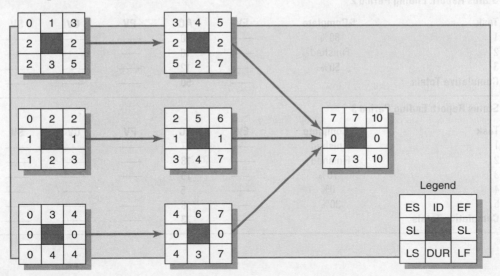

FIGURE A13.2A

EV Rule	ACT/WP	DUR	ES	LF	SL	Total PV	\multicolumn{12}{c}{Baseline budget needs — Time period}

Schedule information | Baseline budget needs

EV Rule	ACT/WP	DUR	ES	LF	SL	Total PV	0	1	2	3	4	5	6	7	8	9	10
②	1	3	0	5	2	30											
③	2	2	0	3	1	20											
②	3	4	0	4	0	30											
③	4	2	3	7	2	10											
②	5	4	2	7	1	40											
①	6	3	4	7	0	30											
①	7	3	7	10	0	60											

Rule
1 = %complete
2 = 50/50
3 = 0/100

Total PV by period

Cumulative PV by period

FIGURE A13.2B

Status Report: Ending Period 1

Task	%Complete	EV	AC	PV	CV	SV
1	40%		8			
2	0%		12			
3	30%		10			
Cumulative Totals			**30**			

Status Report: Ending Period 2

Task	%Complete	EV	AC	PV	CV	SV
1	80%		20			
2	Finished		18			
3	50%		12			
Cumulative Totals			**50**			

Status Report: Ending Period 3

Task	%Complete	EV	AC	PV	CV	SV
1	Finished		27			
2	Finished		18			
3	70%		15			
4	0%		5			
5	30%		8			
Cumulative Totals			**73**			

Status Report: Ending Period 4

Task	%Complete	EV	AC	PV	CV	SV
1	Finished	——	27	——	——	——
2	Finished	——	18	——	——	——
3	Finished	——	22	——	——	——
4	0%	——	7	——	——	——
5	60%	——	22	——	——	——
Cumulative Totals		——	**96**	——	——	——

Status Report: Ending Period 5

Task	%Complete	EV	AC	PV	CV	SV
1	Finished	——	27	——	——	——
2	Finished	——	18	——	——	——
3	Finished	——	22	——	——	——
4	Finished	——	8	——	——	——
5	70%	——	24	——	——	——
6	30%	——	10	——	——	——
Cumulative Totals		——	**109**	——	——	——

FIGURE A13.2C

Period	SPI	CPI	PCIB
1	——	——	——
2	——	——	——
3	——	——	——
4	——	——	——
5	——	——	——

SPI = EV/PV
CPI = EV/AC
PCIB = EV/BAC

APPENDIX 13.2

Obtaining Project Performance Information from MS Project 2010[4]

The objective of this appendix is to illustrate how one can obtain the performance information discussed in Chapter 13 from MS Project 2010. One of the great strengths of MS Project is its flexibility. The software provides numerous options for entering, calculating, and presenting project information. Flexibility is also the software's greatest weakness in that there are so many options that working with the software can be frustrating and confusing. The intent here is to keep it simple and present basic steps for obtaining performance information. Students with more ambitious agendas are advised to work with the software tutorial or consult one of many instructional books on the market.

For purposes of this exercise we will use the Digital Camera project, which was introduced in Chapter 13. In this scenario the project started as planned on March 1 and today's date is March 7. We have received the following information on the work completed to date:

Design Spec.s took 2 days to complete at a total cost of $20.

Shell & Power took 3 days to complete at a total cost of $25.

Memory/Software is in progress with 4 days completed and two days remaining. Cost to date is $100.

Zoom System took 2 days to complete at a cost of $25.

All tasks started on time.

STEP 1 ENTERING PROGRESS INFORMATION

We enter this progress information in the TRACKING TABLE from the GANTT CHART VIEW ► VIEW ► TABLES ► TRACKING:

TABLE A13.2A ···
Tracking Table

ID	Task Name	Act. Start	Act. Finish	% Comp.	Act. Dur.	Rem. Dur.	Act. Cost	Act. Work
1	**Digital Camera Prototype**	3/1	NA	61%	6.72 days	4.28 days	$170.00	272 hrs
2	Design Spec.s	3/1	3/2	100%	2 days	0 days	$20.00	32 hrs
3	Shell & Power	3/3	3/7	100%	3 days	0 days	$25.00	40 hrs
4	Memory/Software	3/3	NA	67%	4 days	2 days	$100.00	160 hrs
5	Zoom System	3/3	3/4	100%	2 days	0 days	$25.00	40 hrs
6	Assemble	NA	NA	0%	0 days	3 days	$0.00	0 hrs
7	Test	NA	NA	0%	0 days	2 days	$0.00	0 hrs

---

[4] For MS Project 2007 users the instructions are very similar except you can access the Tables option directly from Gantt View.

Note that the software automatically calculates the percent complete and actual finish, cost, and work. In some cases you will have to override these calculations if they are inconsistent with what actually happened. **Be sure to check** to make sure the information in this table is displayed the way you want it to be.

The final step is to enter the current status date (March 7). You do so by clicking PROJECT ▶ PROJECT INFORMATION and inserting the date into the status date window.

STEP 2 ACCESSING PROGRESS INFORMATION

MS Project provides a number of different options for obtaining progress information. The most basic information can be obtained from PROJECT ▶ REPORTS ▶ COSTS ▶ EARNED VALUE. You can also obtain this information from GANTT CHART view. Click VIEW ▶ TABLE ▶ MORE TABLES ▶ EARNED VALUE.

TABLE A13.2B
Earned Value Table

ID	Task Name	PV	EV	AC	SV	CV	EAC	BAC	VAC
2	Design Spec.s	$20.00	$20.00	$20.00	$0.00	$0.00	$20.00	$20.00	$0.00
3	Shell & Power	$15.00	$15.00	$25.00	$0.00	($10.00)	$25.00	$15.00	($10.00)
4	Memory/Software	$100.00	$70.00	$100.00	($30.00)	($30.00)	$153.85	$100.00	($53.85)
5	Zoom System	$35.00	$35.00	$25.00	$0.00	$10.00	$25.00	$35.00	$10.00
6	Assemble	$0.00	$0.00	$0.00	$0.00	$0.00	$120.00	$120.00	$0.00
7	Test	$0.00	$0.00	$0.00	$0.00	$0.00	$30.00	$30.00	$0.00
		$170.00	$140.00	$170.00	($30.00)	($30.00)	$373.85	$320.00	($53.85)

When you scale this table to 80 percent you can obtain all the basic CV, SV and VAC information on one convenient page.

Note: Older versions of MS Project use the old acronyms:

BCWS = PV

BCWP = EV

ACWP = AC

and the EAC is calculated using the CPI and is what the text refers to as EAC_f.

STEP 3 ACCESSING CPI INFORMATION

To obtain additional cost information such as CPI and TCPI click from the GANTT CHART view click VIEW ▶ TABLE ▶ MORE TABLES ▶ EARNED VALUE COST INDICATORS, which will display the following information:

Table A13.2C
Earned Value Cost Indicators Table

ID	Task Name	PV	EV	CV	CV%	CPI	BAC	EAC	VAC	TCPI
1	**Digital Camera Prototype**	$170.00	$140.00	($30.00)	−21%	0.82	$320.00	$373.85	($53.85)	1.2
2	Design Spec.s	$20.00	$20.00	$0.00	0%	1	$20.00	$20.00	$0.00	
3	Shell & Power	$15.00	$15.00	($10.00)	−66%	0.6	$15.00	$25.00	($10.00)	
4	Memory/Software	$100.00	$70.00	($30.00)	−42%	0.7	$100.00	$153.85	($53.85)	
5	Zoom System	$35.00	$35.00	$10.00	28%	1.4	$35.00	$25.00	$10.00	
6	Assemble	$0.00	$0.00	$0.00	0%	0	$120.00	$120.00	$0.00	
7	Test	$0.00	$0.00	$0.00	0%	0	$30.00	$30.00	$0.00	

Note: For MS Project 2007 users the instructions are very similar except you can access the Tables option directly from Gantt View.

STEP 4 ACCESSING SPI INFORMATION

To obtain additional schedule information such as SPI from the GANTT CHART view, click VIEW ▶ TABLE ▶ MORE TABLES ▶ EARNED VALUE SCHEDULE INDICATORS, which will display the following information:

TABLE A13.2D
Earned Value Schedule Indicators Table

ID	Task Name	PV	EV	SV	SV%	SPI
1	**Digital Camera Prototype**	$170.00	$140.00	($30.00)	−18%	0.82
2	Design Spec.s	$20.00	$20.00	$0.00	0%	1
3	Shell & Power	$15.00	$15.00	$0.00	0%	1
4	Memory/Software	$100.00	$70.00	($30.00)	−30%	0.7
5	Zoom System	$35.00	$35.00	$0.00	0%	1
6	Assemble	$0.00	$0.00	$0.00	0%	0
7	Test	$0.00	$0.00	$0.00	0%	0

STEP 5 CREATING A TRACKING GANTT CHART

You can create a Tracking Gantt Chart like the one presented on page 460 by simply clicking TASK ▶ GANTT CHART (upper left hand corner) ▶ TRACKING GANTT ▶ TRACKING GANTT.

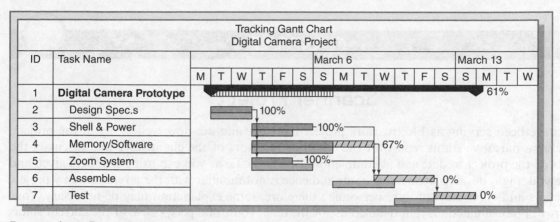

ID	Task Name																	

Tracking Gantt Chart
Digital Camera Project

March 6 — March 13

M T W T F S S M T W T F S S M T W

1 **Digital Camera Prototype** — 61%
2 Design Spec.s — 100%
3 Shell & Power — 100%
4 Memory/Software — 67%
5 Zoom System — 100%
6 Assemble — 0%
7 Test — 0%

FIGURE A13.2E   **Tracking Gantt Chart**

CASE 13.1

Tree Trimming Project

Wil Fence is a large timber and Christmas tree farmer who is attending a project management class in the fall, his off season. When the class topic came to earned value, he was perplexed. Isn't he using EV?

Each summer Wil hires crews to shear fields of Christmas trees for the coming Holiday season. Shearing entails having a worker use a large machete to shear the branches of the tree into a nice, cone shaped tree.

Will describes his business as follows:

A. I count the number of Douglas Fir Christmas trees in the field (24,000).

B. Next, I agree on a contract lump sum for shearing with a crew boss for the whole field ($30,000).

C. When partial payment for work completed arrives (5 days later), I count or estimate the actual number sheared (6,000 trees). I take the actual as a percent of the total to be sheared, multiply the percent complete by total contract amount for the partial payment [(6,000/$30,000 = 25%), (.25 × $30,000 = $7500)].

1. Is Wil over, on, or below cost and schedule? Is Wil using earned value?

2. How can Wil set up a scheduling variance?

CASE 13.2

Scanner Project

You have been serving as Electroscan's project manager and are now well along in the project. Develop a narrative status report for the board of directors of the chain store that discusses the status of the project to date and at completion. Be as specific as you can using numbers given and those you might develop. Remember, your audience is not familiar with the jargon used by project managers and computer software personnel; therefore, some explanation may be necessary. Your report will be evaluated on your detailed use of the data, your total perspective of the current status and future status of the project, and your recommended changes (if any).

CASE 13.3

Project Quality: A Dialogue with the Zen Master
(An Overview of Project Quality Management Processes)

Abstract

The case presents the basic concepts on project quality management generally following the guidelines and processes suggested by Project Management Institute (PMI), U.S.A. At the same time, the main thrust of teachings of Quality Gurus like Joseph Juran, Philip Crosby and Edward Deming are also included in the passing. To make the presentation interesting and easy to follow, the case is written as an imaginary scenario of a dialogue on this subject between a Zen Master and his disciples. Notice that the Zen Master helps the disciples to explore the subject and bring out the learning using Socratic technique of asking the right questions without himself preaching a word.

CASE TEXT

The Zen master sat under the banyan tree in a lotus-seating pose with the eyes closed. He had a very lean body and shaved head and wore a saffron robe. Written all over his face was peace – the kind of all-encompassing peace, which could be expected to be found only on the face of a Zen master. The disciples started flowing in and quietly taking their seats without a word.

After a while, the master opened his eyes. The silence continued to rule the place for another 10 minutes. Then one of the disciples slowly spoke in a hushed voice, 'Master, we want to learn today something about quality and how to improve the quality of construction projects we are managing". The question was not incorrectly aimed. This Zen master was a modern Guru; he had read a lot, understood and experienced life in many facets and was capable of counseling about many things –including project quality.

After a pregnant silence of a few seconds, the master slowly spoke, "And, what is quality?"

"*Fitness for use*", one disciple offered.

"Yes, which is how Joseph Juran put it" replied the master, "Can you elaborate?"

"Well, it means that customers' or stakeholders' expectations are fully met or even exceeded. The product or service fully conforms to the specifications – the spoken or unspoken needs of the clients. Meaning the product or service provides all that the customer expected it to do at the time of acquiring it and meets the real needs …"

Another interrupted, "The totality of characteristics of an entity that bear on its ability to satisfy (customer's) stated or implied needs; that's the way ISO 8400, 1994: Quality Management & Quality Assurance defines it".

"There should be 'zero defect', as we heard Quality Guru Philip Crosby recommend it" offered the third one.

"All of that's true." said the master, "So you all know what quality means in general and how quality gurus define it. Now, how do you perceive the quality management defined in the context of your construction projects?"

One of the groups offered, "I look at the quality of project management as meeting two distinct criteria:

- First, the quality of the project construction should be up to the planned level and meeting the requirements set down by the organization.
- Secondly, the project management must ensure that the thresholds set down on the cost, time and resource values for the project are achieved."

"Very well said." said the master encouragingly, "The distinction you made is very important. Project quality management touches both these aspects – the quality of the product of the project as well as the quality of how the project is managed; and not many keep this distinction in mind. Now, let us leave out, for a while, the aspect of quality of managing the project – that is, managing the project within approved budget and on time; you all are getting training for this at a business school. Let's focus for the moment on the first aspect of quality you mentioned. How would you proceed to go about systematically for meeting the objectives for the quality of construction – the quality of the product created by the project?"

"First we must go through the quality planning process" said one.

And how would you go about doing that?" the master asked.

Several disciples started replying.

"We need to have the rules, standards, and guidelines set down by the government, industry associations or common industry practice – the so-called environmental factors for the enterprise enveloping the organization as well as the project."

"We need to have the policies, procedure and the guidelines for quality management in the organization's operations and other projects."

"The project scope statement should provide the key inputs. It should document the overall project objectives, the project deliverables and what standards they should meet. It should state the measurable objective criteria for stakeholders' satisfaction – the criteria for acceptance of the product by the clients or stakeholders for accepting the project deliverables."

"All of you are correct", the master encouraged, "All successful journeys start with the clear idea of the destination to reach. We must first know the destination we want to reach in our quality journey and that is what a quality management plan would serve as. Now, how will you translate this planning into concrete actionable documents?"

Again, there was a cacophony of voices.

"The quality plan should describe how the project management team would implement the organization's quality policy. It should ensure that the concepts, designs and the vision included in the project brief are actually incorporated into the detailed project planning and followed during the project construction by quality assurance and closely monitored and controlled by quality control."

"The plan should state the quality metrics – the specific characteristic of the product or deliverable and how precisely it would be measured and evaluated."

"I have found the quality check lists very useful for this purpose. They are helpful in a systematic and comprehensive review of all important characteristics, which we might otherwise miss out in the midst of project rush." "Great", the master responded, "Those documents would surely help to serve as the basic tools for quality management plan – the first step in the project quality management. Now that the first process for project quality management would be properly in place, what would you need to ensure during the execution so that the quality plan is implemented and all those quality metrics, checklists and standards are satisfied? In other words, how would you carry out quality assurance during actual project execution phase?"

"We will have to start with the overall plan, metrics and the checklists for quality, we talked about. Then, of course, we need the feedback on how exactly the work is being carried out: we would need to carry out inspection of the construction at the site during the process of construction and the site inspection reports with their records. If the inspection reports show that construction methods or the outcome of construction activities is not up to the standards set in the plan, we have to willy-nilly order corrective action to enforce the quality edict. That's how we assure quality", one disciple offered.

"Include with the general inspection, the quality control measurements – like the sand analysis, the bricks strength, the quality of cement the strengths of the cast test cubes, the size and spacing of reinforcing bars and all that stuff. Quite routine quality control tests, nothing glamorous about them, but they form the backbone of quality assurance for construction."

"Very true", the master supported." The great Michael Angelo once said, 'Attention to trifles make perfection, but perfection is no trifle'. Though it would be too much to expect any one to strive for the kind of perfection Michael Angelo tried to achieve in his master sculpture Pieta; attention to details is indeed the key to high quality."

"For large projects, you can also have periodic quality audits. Some one, preferably outside the project team, should carry out quality audit at some pre-determined time frames or project phase end. Such quality audits by outsiders from the project team ensure objectivity and blind spots of the members of the project team are compensated." a lean man in a corner added.

"Your father was a chartered accountant?" the Zen master asked smilingly and the whole group burst out laughing.

After a pause for laughter to subside, another disciple ventured, "If the problem appears to be generic, then it would be wise to carry out the root-cause analysis of the construction problem linking the underlying cause to the quality problem persisting - what they call Ishikawa Diagrams."

"That's very important" another supported. "Quality must be built in and not inspected into – the basic premise of modern effective quality management. Root-cause analysis would point a direction for consistently carrying out high quality work."

"And let me mention another Japanese buzz word in quality management discussions – what the Japanese call the Kaizen Approach. Continuous efforts for improvement for quality – a people-centered approach with getting not only the entire project team but even the contractor's workers committed to quality improvement."

"Good ... Good", approved the master, "And when you mentioned quality control process, did you have in mind any techniques or tools specifically to monitor and improve the quality?"

"There are many tools and techniques", responded one, "statistical process control (with the control charts and the mean value and upper and lower control limits). This could be systematically applied to all RCC or structural steel construction ..."

"Acceptance sampling based on acceptable quality level (AQL), if we need to inspect far too many samples for a given activity ..." added another.

"Flow-charting – to improve the work process flow and understand how successive steps are linked to quality is another such tool. This is similar to Ishikawa diagram except that chronological relationship is taken into account here", a third disciple ventured.

"For concentrating on the most acute problem first, we can use Pareto Diagrams – a sort of frequency distribution diagram linking the type or category of identified cause with the number of defects or quality deficiency it generated. It is a sort of 80/20 rule: A few important causes account for a vast majority of effects; identify and take corrective action on them and your majority of defect problems will be taken care of."

One disciple, who had not uttered a word so far, intervened somewhat authoritatively "Let's not talk theory. We all know it or can learn from the books. Let us learn from the master, how we can apply in practice these quality management aspects in our green field construction projects."

"Well, what are your views?" the master turned to him and asked. The Zen master hardly ever preached directly. He was adept at the Socratic method of asking the questions and leading the discussion to bring out the learning.

"Well the first thing which comes to my mind is that though every project team member should be vigilant about the quality aspect and insist on the work performance to meet the quality standards, it is the management, which bears a major responsibility in delivering quality. If the infrastructure or resources provided, the materials and worker skills made available are not up to what the quality output would need, there is hardly anything that the project team member can accomplish."

"You are echoing Edwards Deming", the master responded, "Indeed, no organization can turn out a high quality product unless the top management is committed to provide the resources needed to achieve quality. But I know your organization – it is in the forefront of executing the prestigious mega projects. I presume that they would provide you with the necessary infrastructure, men, materials and technology. So the question is only how you should go about it systematically. Tell me what thoughts occur to you."

"I have several thoughts rushing into my mind and I will blurt them out as they occur without trying to evaluate them. Like brainstorming", the disciple replied, and then in almost a single breath, he continued:

- Firstly we do not have detailed technical specifications of the deliverables for the project. We any way do not make a formal work breakdown structure; the work contents or work packages are just listed. I believe we should have those specs set down for all critical or important work packages; in effect, quality metrics should be clearly set.

- Second, quality checklists should be continually up-dated in light of quality audits and made available to all project teams in the organization.

- Third, many of our clients may be familiar with and accustomed to international levels of infrastructure; we should constantly keep on benchmarking our infrastructure facilities with such international standards and attempt to upgrade our facilities. This is particularly important for our organization, which is one of the national leaders in construction projects.

- Fourth, the quality function deployment techniques should be employed to translate vague observations by site visitors into concrete actionable specifications.

And one very important necessary condition for all this to happen: the strong management support for the project team in whatever reasonable time or cost is necessary to achieve quality – yes I realize I keep coming back to the Edward Deming point of view I started with. But I feel it is very important. In the rush of finishing the project and the inevitable over-runs likely, the project team is under great pressure to take shortcuts on quality to meet cost and schedule objectives. Project team would need the top management's support...." here he stopped for catching his breath.

The master intervened before he could start again, "Well, well; that is enough. So you know practically all that you need to know about quality in project management. There is really nothing much more on this in the whole project management book of knowledge. You have made a very good start in thinking through what you need to do to achieve the highest quality standards in construction. But remember, it is just a start. Contemplate... contemplate more. All that you need to know will reveal itself to you. Just contemplate what you need to do and then ... just do it ".

After a brief silence, he added, "And I would go back to do what I need to do: meditation."

Soon, the master closed his eyes and started breathing deeply and peacefully. The silence reigned supreme for a while and then one by one all disciples left.

Questions for Discussion

1. Compare the formal description of the quality management processes given in PMBOK® Guide, 5th Edition, with the informal descriptions given here.
2. Similarly, identify and compare informal presentation of the inputs and tools and techniques given in this with the corresponding formal presentation.

CASE 13.4

Comfortable Homes

Abstract

Earned Value Management, control system described in this chapter, has become very popular as an integrated system for control of scope, cost and schedule performance of the project. The technique, originally developed for integrated monitoring and control of scope, cost and schedule of huge defense projects has started finding more support among the project management professionals. The case below illustrates an interesting application of the Earned Value Management technique for a construction project.

CASE TEXT

Madhav Prasad Jhunjhunwala was the Chairman and Managing Director of Comfortable Homes, a development and construction company specialized in constructing residential buildings. Starting from a very humble position, Madhav Prasad had built his industrial empire by sheer hard work, risk-taking capacity and vision. Now that he had enough able and sincere assistants to run around, he could relax a bit. Most trusted among them was turning out to be his daughter Gauravi.

After a degree in science, Gauravi had secured an MBA degree from a very prestigious management school with extra electives taken in the field of project management. Her choice of electives was good, for she expected to be in a position to put the knowledge and skills learnt in the business school to practical use in industry. She was constantly prodding her father to adopt new managerial approaches in running the family business. Most of the time, her father's response was a condescending smile.

Looking at the letter in his incoming file folder set by his secretary, Madhav Prasad leafed through the papers. Then he stopped to look closely at a letter and then while continuing to scan other papers in the folder, he pressed an intercom buzzer. In a few seconds Gauravi rushed to Madhav Prasad's cabin. Without knocking, she entered, sat down in the chair opposite to him and asked, "You called me Daddy?"

"Yes Dear", Madhav Prasad looked up from the folder and said, "All along you have been talking about using modern management techniques in our projects. Now, I have a job for you. We won the tender for constructing the factory complex for Aditya Textiles at Panvel. It is not a very big job – a firm fixed price contract for rupees nine crore, with bonus and penalty for early/late construction completion thrown in. There will be a 1 % bonus for every week or part thereof if the project is completed earlier than the contract date, subject to 10% maximum. There will also be a penalty of 1 % for delay of every week, but the maximum limit of penalty will be 12.5 %. I want to see how you manage it." Then he added teasingly, "Don't loose more than a few lakhs on the job; with my methods, which you call 'archaic', I would have earned at least about a crore of rupees."

"Daddy, I will show you! I had two special sessions on Earned Value Management (EVM) controlling technique at my business school. That is the method American Defense Department uses for controlling projects costing billions of dollars."

"All that theory is fine. In actual construction project, you have to watch, watch and again watch costs. And watch, watch and again watch how fast the work is going on and push. That is the secret; but you try your hand on this in your own way with your methods."

"Daddy, what you mentioned in your plain simple words is what Earned Value Management is all about. – EVM is a system for an integrated control of cost and schedule of a project ..." Before she could complete, her father lovingly waved her away, "Don't lecture me, just go and do your work!"

Gauravi rushed back to her cabin. She called Samir, a bright civil engineer, who had been with company for over two years. With his MBA degree background, Gauravi and Samir had established good working relationship. "Samir, we have landed the Aditya Textiles job. I want you to work with me on that project. Look at all the papers, we prepared for the tender, and go to the site one day. Then work out the major work packages and preliminary cost estimate for them. Then we will take a look at how to proceed early next week."

Samir worked hard for the rest of the week and prepared the documents. Gauravi and Samir rechecked those work packages and cost estimates prepared by Samir. "O.K. this looks fine. Now, let us construct the project network using these WBS and find the critical path and the expected completion date. The tender calls for ten months, but there is an early completion bonus of 1% per week and I want to earn that bonus – full 10 % if things go our way! We are here on June 4. Let us target the construction to be completed in eight months flat – say by January 31, 2005. If our preliminary network does not indicate that target to be achieved in our routine construction ways, we should plan for some overtime on the project activities, which we can expedite to crash the project schedule to our target. So first let us have the WBS based on work packages with estimated costs." For the next four days, again Samir was furiously busy with decomposing the project into basic work packages and sub-packages suitable for coming up with cost estimates. Gauravi had pointed out that the work packages and sub-packages should have clear identifiable milestones for beginning and end of the work package activities.

What Samir came up with the next week was a 1-page summary of the project (Exhibit 1), which listed:

* Construction activities identified by logically designed work packages
* Estimated time duration and cost for each work package
* Mandatory dependency of activities (preceding/ following activities) for creating the preliminary network

EXHIBIT 1 ....

Work Packages for Aditya Textile Project Construction

Control Account Plan (CAPs)	Construction Activity	Work package	Estimated Time (weeks)	Estimated Cost (Rs '000)	Preceding Activity/ Work Package	Following Activity/ Work Package
CAP: 1 (Earth work)	Site Preparation & Leveling	A	5	7,000	START	B, C, D
CAP:2 (Electrical)	Electrical substation & feeder cables	B	7	9,000	A	E
	Internal wiring & electrical fittings	E	10	12,000	B	I
CAP-3 (Water Services)	Overhead and underground water tanks and headers	C	8	10,000	A	F
	Water & drainage piping within the buildings	F	2	3,000	C	I
CAP 4 (Civil/ Structural)	Civil Foundations	D	5	6,000	A	G
	RCC Superstructure (Columns, Plinth Beams, Lintels, Beams and Slabs)	G	7	9,000	D	H
	Brickwork, windows, plaster	H	4	5,000	G	I
Cap-5 (A.C & Finishing)	Air Conditioning system and ductwork	I	6	8,000	E, F, H	J
	Flooring, finishing, and false ceiling and painting	J	4	6,000	I	END
	Total Cost			75,000		

- Control account plan (CAP), which assigned the control account to each work package depending on the nature of construction activity (earth work, RCC work, electrical work, water storage and plumbing, etc.) and likely mode of contracting.

Gauravi sat down with Samir and reviewed the summaries and the background papers. "I am impressed, Samir; this is just what we needed to start our EVM Control System. I was going to suggest that the next thing we need to do is to set up the Control Account Plan (CAP) for collection and analysis of project costs. But you have pre-empted my suggestion and already included them!", said Gauravi very pleased with the work of her capable colleague.

"I have already done some preliminary work and passed on the papers to Accounts Department." Samir responded, "In the next two days I expect them to get back with their response."

After half an hour, Gauravi's phone rang.

"Madam, I want to talk to you."

"Yes Ramanbhai, what is it? Something urgent? You sound a bit upset."

"No Madam, no question of being upset, but I do have something urgent to report. Samirbhai has told an accountant in my department to record the Aditya Textile project accounts in a particular way. It is all so different from the way we have been keeping records all these years…If you have some time, I will drop by in the afternoon and discuss with you."

Ramanlal Shah was a trusted accountant of Comfortable Homes. In his late 40s, he had worked for over 10 years with the company. His competence, and more importantly his trustworthiness, had won him the position of The Chief Accountant.

When Ramanlal dropped in, he explained that their regular practice of keeping project accounts was to record the expense only after the payment was actually made after full checking and certification of the contractor's bill by the site engineer – not when contract order was issued. But Samir had asked to book the project cost as soon as any particular item of the contracted work was reported as completed by the site.

"Ramanbhai, you continue to keep project account records for Aditya Textile exactly the same way as you have done all these years. I want only one small additional report for better project cost control. In this special project cost report for me, you include the expenses for any item completed according to the contract as soon as the site engineer reports that activity as completed. We are contractually committed to pay the amount due as per rate contract once our site engineer reports the status and the interim bill is raised by the contractor – a few thousand rupees this way or other depending on actual certification. You know, many times, we get the project's actual costs report only 4 to 6 months after it is already over. By that time, there is no corrective action to be taken if we are off the track on cost or schedule. One more thing. We should collect these project costs not by some buildings or facilities but by the contractor involved and the major work package contracted to him. Will this be too much additional work?"

"No Madam, not a big job if that is all you want. Actually we pick usually five or six contractors from our approved pool to work on any project and all of them have given their rate contracts for all construction items. So, if the contractor selected for Aditya Textiles and the work packages contracted to him are given, we can give back your special report within three days of the completion of the month – not a day more. It is not a big job. Ramanlal was happy that his apple cart of years of accounting tradition would not be upset after all by these new MBA up-starts and he left the cabin smiling.

Madhav Prasad dropped in after three weeks, "What are you busy with? Just shuffling papers and files? I hope the weight of your papers won't be more than the concrete we will pour at the site!"

"Daddy, we have already presented three alternative architect's sketches with the client and Aditya Textile management has selected one and suggested some minor changes in the selected version. In the next two days, we would have our reworked architectural plans ready to present to the client and get his formal approval. In the meanwhile, the contour survey at the site is already in progress – may be in a day, we will get contour maps to plan accurately detailed excavation and earthwork leveling quantities. So we should be all set to start excavations and leveling by middle of next week."

Then she added, "I know, you hate a lot of paper work, but let me assure you, that as far as the paper work for EVM is concerned, there will be only three simple computer files. See here..." and she proudly displayed to her father the file structure for EVM controls. Madhav Prasad just glanced at it, smiled and walked away.

For the next two months, the activities at the site picked up rapidly. There were over 200 workers employed by different contractors working at the site. The site engineer, Daya Shanker, was an experienced hand and quite conscientious. Samir explained to him the need of keeping a close watch on the site construction activities and keep him at the head office informed of all site progress and developments. Daya Shanker used to call Samir almost every second day and update him on the site activities. He also used to send some e-mails periodically on issues which he felt like to be on record. Exhibit 2 contains the excerpts of some of the e-mails sent by the site engineer to the head office.

At the head office, Samir and Gauravi studied all reports and kept watch on the site work progress compared to the planned progress and particularly the milestones for the work packages. They also took prompt corrective actions in the form of authorizing overtime (and consequent additional cost) when the work progress appeared to fall behind the planned schedule, promptly taking decisions on unexpected issues which came up from time to time and visiting the site every two weeks to make the site contractors aware of the top management's watchful eye on their work.

At the end of the first month, the only work package which had any progress was earthwork, leveling and site preparation. The second month onward, the work started on several fronts simultaneously and Daya Shanker submitted the site progress reports formally in the format set up by Samir. Exhibit 3 gives the site work progress reports sent by Daya Shanker to Samir at the head office at the end of the first, second and the third month respectively.

Gauravi and Samir carried out Earned Value Analysis of the data in the progress reports and used them to forecast the project completion date and the total cost at project completion.

It was a rather late evening around three months later – the end of the first week of September. Seeing the cabin lights on, Madhav Prasad stepped into Gauravi's cabin. She was so engrossed studying the papers that she did not even notice. The father fondly looked at the daughter and hesitantly broke the silence, "my daughter, you know our quarterly project review meeting is on September 12th. I want you to make a presentation of Aditya Textile Project and the new method you are using. I hope you and Samir would finish this project better than my expectations."

"Daddy, look at these figures...." Gauravi started with enthusiasm.

"No, not now Gauravi", Madhav Prasad waved his hand, "Tell us all about it in the board room meeting next week" and he left the room.

Taking into account the actually completed work, the performance reports and their corresponding CAP summary reports for the 2nd and 3rd month, Gauravi and Samir sat down to work out the metrics for EVM Controls at the 2-month and 3-month period and the projections from them to present at the next quarterly project review meeting.

EXHIBIT 2 ••

The extracts from some of the site engineer's e-mails for the progress of construction work at the site

June 12, 2004

"The contour survey has been started at the site. Because of heavy rains, there was a delay in starting the work; trying to push the contractor to make up for the delay ..."

June 22, 2004

"The architect had come to the site and marked the lay-out. The excavation contractor reported to the site yesterday, but he could not start work. From to-morrow the excavation at the site for foundations will start and it will be in full swing by the end of the week. He feels the excavations, leveling and other earthwork will take longer than five weeks shown in your plan, but he would definitely complete all excavation before July 24, i.e., 10 days before the end of the second month."

July 7, 2004

"The contractor's electrical engineer visited the site. He would be bringing along the MSEB's engineer to fix the location of the electrical substation tomorrow... The RCC contractor has also mobilized to the site. He had shipped the first batch of re-bars to the site a week back. He would be starting with bar bending from tomorrow. He plans to start pouring the first set of column foundations from July 12th... The overhead water tank contractor will come tomorrow; he showed his design for the tank structure. It is not my job, but I must point out that the design looks kind of too fancy. I think our architect has gone overboard and we will end up spending a lot more money than we should...We need to get a better canteen contractor; so many workers are the site and the canteen man just can't cope up with ...."

July 16, 2004

"The excavation contractor's men and RCC contractor's men had some quarrel. There was a total work stoppage for 4 hours. I had a hard time in getting them to stop quarreling and get on with the work. But with my experience, somehow, I managed..."

July 26, 2004

"The earthwork contractor has completed all the excavations required for RCC foundations – three days late but it has not delayed the RCC contractor's work. He would be able to complete the leveling work, which is relatively easy in the next four days.... The small substation building in the corner with simple steel structure columns and AC sheet roofing construction is almost ready. He has started laying out the routing for feeder cables ... Deep foundations for the overhead storage tanks took a bit longer than expected because of a small rock at four-feet depth. But now all the excavation problems are over for him and he will start pouring the column foundations and plinth beams from next week... "

August 2, 2004

"Remarkable way the overhead storage tank contractor has speeded up. He confided to me that the rates for this contract have an additional early completion bonus ..."

August 4, 2004

"One old Peepal tree in the corner of the plot was worshipped by the tribal people all these years before the land was requisitioned for this project. It was possible to save the tree if the cooling tower location was shifted by 10 feet on one side. I have checked with the architect and Aditya's representative and they did not mind this minor location shift. So I have shifted the cooling tower location and informed the water system contractor accordingly."

Exhibit 3 •••
Monthly Site Work Progress Report

(The First Month)

(All figures in ₹'000)

Control Account Plan & Work Package	Construction Activity	Value of Budgeted Work Planned For the Month	Value of Budgeted Work completed during the Month	Cost of Work completed during the Month	Cumulative Value of Budgeted Work planned Till to-date	Cumulative Value of Budgeted Work completed Till to-date	Cumulative Cost of Work completed Till to-date
CAP: 1 Wk Pk A	Earthwork, excavation and leveling	5600	5550	5800	5600	5550	5800
CAP:2 Wk Pk B	Electrical substation & feeder cables	-					
CAP:2 Wk Pk E	Internal wiring & electrical fittings						
CAP:3 Wk Pk C	Overhead & underground water storage tanks						
CAP:3 Wk Pk F	Water & drainage piping						
CAP:4 Wk Pk D	Civil foundations						
CAP:4 Wk Pk G	RCC superstructures						
CAP:4 Wk Pk H	Brickwork, windows and plaster						
CAP:5 Wk Pk I	Air-conditioning system & ductwork						
CAP:5 Wk Pk J	Flooring, finishing and false ceiling						
Total		5600	5550	5800	5600	5550	5800

(Contd.)

(The Second Month)

All figures in ₹'000)

Control Account Plan &Work Package	Construction Activity	Value of Budgeted Work Planned for the Month	Value of Budgeted Work Completed During the Month	Cost of Work Completed During the Month	Cumulative Value of Budgeted Work Planned Till to-date	Cumulative Value of Budgeted Work Completed Till to-date	Cumulative Cost of Work Completed Till to-date
CAP: 1 Wk Pk A	Earthwork, excavation and leveling	1400	1450	1900	7000	7000	7700
CAP: 2 Wk Pk B	Electrical substation & Feeder cables	3857	3240	3270	3857	3240	3270
CAP: 2 Wk Pk E	Internal wiring & electrical fittings	—	—	—	—	—	—
CAP: 3 Wk Pk C	Overhead & underground water storage tanks	3750	3800	3825	3750	3800	3825
CAP: 3 Wk Pk F	Water & drainage piping	—	—	—	—	—	—
CAP: 4 Wk Pk D	Civil foundations	3600	3600	3872	3600	3600	3872
CAP:4 Wk Pk G	RCC superstructures	—	—	—	—	—	—
CAP: 4 Wk Pk H	Brickwork, windows and plaster	—	—	—	—	—	—
CAP:5 Wk Pk I	Air-conditioning system & ductwork	—	—	—	—	—	—
CAP:5 Wk Pk J	Flooring, finishing and false ceiling	—	—	—	—	—	—
	Total	12607	12090	12667	18207	17640	18667

(Contd.)

(The Third Month)

(All figures in ₹'000)

Control Account Plan & Work Package	Construction Activity	Value of Budgeted Work Planned for the Month	Value of Budgeted Work Completed During the Month	Cost of Work Completed During the Month	Cumulative Value of Budgeted Work Planned Till to-date	Cumulative Value of Budgeted Work Completed Till to-date	Cumulative Cost of Work Completed Till to-date
CAP: 1 Wk Pk A	Earthwork, excavation and leveling	—	—	—	7000	7000	7700
CAP: 2 Wk Pk B	Electrical substation & feeder cables	5143	4910	5100	9000	8150	8370
CAP: 2 Wk Pk E	Internal wiring & electrical fittings	—	—	—	—	—	
CAP: 3 Wk Pk C	Overhead & underground water storage tanks	5000	4700	5300	8750	8500	9125
CAP: 3 Wk Pk F	Water & drainage piping	—	—	—	—	—	—
CAP: 4 Wk Pk D	Civil foundations	2400	2300	2628	6000	5900	6500
CAP: 4 Wk Pk G	RCC superstructures	2571	2200	2450	2571	2200	2450
CAP: 4 Wk Pk H	Brickwork, windows and plaster	—	—	—	—	—	
CAP: 5 Wk Pk I	Air-conditioning system & ductwork	—	—	—	—	—	
CAP: 5 Wk Pk J	Flooring, finishing and false ceiling	—	—	—	—	—	
	Total	15114	14110	15478	33321	31750	34145

Questions for Discussion and Working Exercise

1. **Setting up Project Budget and Cost Baseline**

   Prepare the network diagram for the project

   Map it to the project calendar and prepare the month-wise project budget (using the worksheet provided), and Prepare the cost baseline for project cost

2. **Earned value Analysis from the progress report at the end of the second month**

   From the Monthly Progress Report No.2 (Exhibit 3, The Second Month), work out the metrics for EVM control: viz., schedule and cost variances, earned value and the cost and schedule performance indices. Forecast the estimated completion date and estimated completion project cost. Use the worksheet provided for the exercise.

3. **Earned value Analysis from the progress report at the end of the third month**

   From the Monthly Progress Report No.3 (Exhibit 3, The Third Month), work out the metrics for EVM control: viz., schedule and cost variances, earned value and the cost and schedule performance indices. Forecast the estimated completion date and estimated completion project cost. Use the worksheet provided for the exercise.

4. **Forecasts for project completion**

   Based on your forecast for the project completion schedule and total project cost, will Gauravi and Samir's team earn early completion bonus? Will they earn more money from the project contract than Madhav Prasad would have earned in ordinary course?

14

PROJECT CLOSURE

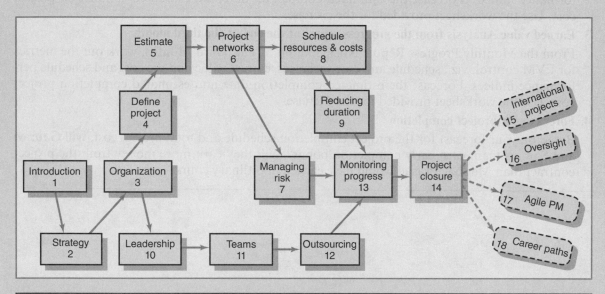

Estimate
5

Project
networks
6

Schedule
resources & costs
8

Define
project
4

Reducing
duration
9

International
projects
15

Introduction
1

Organization
3

Managing
risk
7

Monitoring
progress
13

Project
closure
14

Oversight
16

17 Agile PM

Strategy
2

Leadership
10

Teams
11

Outsourcing
12

18 Career paths

PROJECT CLOSURE

Those who cannot remember the past are condemned to relive it.

—*George Santayana, 1863–1952*

Every project comes to an end eventually. But how many project participants get excited about closing out a project? The deliverables are complete. Ownership is ready to be transferred. Everyone's focus is what's next—hopefully a new, exciting project. Carefully managing the closure phase is as important as any other phase of the project. Observation tells us that organizations that manage closure and review well prosper. Those who don't tend to have projects that drag on forever and repeat the same mistakes over and over.

Closing out a project includes a daunting number of tasks. In the past and on small projects the project manager was responsible for seeing all tasks and loose ends were completed and signed off. This is no longer true. In today's project-driven organizations that have many projects occurring simultaneously, the responsibility for completing closure tasks has been parsed among the project manager, project teams, project office, an oversight "review committee," and an independent retrospective facilitator. Many tasks overlap, occur simultaneously, and require coordination and cooperation among these stakeholders.

The three major deliverables for **project closure** are described below (see Figure 14.1):

1. *Wrapping up the project.* The major wrap-up task is to ensure the project is approved and accepted by the customer. Other wrap-up activities include closing accounts, paying bills, reassigning equipment and personnel, finding new opportunities for project staff, closing facilities, and the final report. Checklists are used extensively to ensure tasks are not overlooked. In many organizations, the lion's share of closure tasks are largely done by the project office in coordination with the project manager. The final report writing is usually assigned to one project office staff member, who assembles input from all stakeholders. In smaller organizations and projects, these closure activities are left to the project manager and team.

2. *Evaluation of performance and management of the project.* Evaluation includes team, individual team members, and project manager performance. Vendors and the customer may provide external input. Evaluation of the major players provides important information for the future.

3. *Retrospectives.* Retrospectives of lessons learned are designed to improve performance on current and future projects. Today, most retrospectives are the responsibility of an independent facilitator. The facilitator also provides major input to the closure report that will include lessons learned. These post-project reviews should be held with the team to catch any missing issues or gaps.

This chapter begins with the recognition that projects are shut down for many reasons. Not all projects end with a clear "Finished" and are turned over to a customer. Regardless of the

FIGURE 14.1 *Project Closure and Review Deliverables*

conditions for ending a project, the general process of closure is similar, though the endings may differ significantly. Wrap-up closure tasks are noted first. These tasks represent all the tasks that must be "cleaned up" before the project is terminated. Evaluation of project performance is next. Finally, lessons learned or retrospective methods are examined in detail.

TYPES OF PROJECT CLOSURE

On some projects the end may not be as clear as would be hoped. Although the scope statement may define a clear ending for a project, the actual ending may or may not correspond. Fortunately, a majority of projects are blessed with a well-defined ending. Regular project reviews will identify projects having endings different from plans. The different types of closure are identified here:

Normal   The most common circumstance for project closure is simply a completed project. For many development projects, the end involves handing off the final design to production and the creation of a new product or service line. For other internal IT projects, such as system upgrades or creation of new inventory control systems, the end occurs when the output is incorporated into ongoing operations. Some modifications in scope, cost, and schedule probably occurred during implementation.

Premature   For a few projects, the project may be completed early with some parts of the project eliminated. For example, in a new product development project, a marketing manager may insist on production models before testing:

> Give the new product to me now, the way it is. Early entry into the market will mean big profits! I know we can sell a bazillion of these. If we don't do it now, the opportunity is lost!

The pressure is on to finish the project and send it to production. Before succumbing to this form of pressure, the implications and risks associated with this decision should be carefully reviewed and assessed by senior management and all stakeholders. Too frequently, the benefits are illusory, dangerous, and carry large risks.

Perpetual   Some projects never seem to end. The major characteristic of this kind of project is constant "add-ons," suggesting a poorly conceived project scope. At some point the review group should recommend methods for bringing final closure to this type of project or the initiation of another project. For example, adding a new feature to an old project could replace a segment of a project that appears to be perpetual.

Failed Project   Failed projects are usually easy to identify and easy for a review group to close down. However, every effort should be made to communicate the technical (or other) reasons for termination of the project; in any event project participants should not be left with an embarrassing stigma of working on a project that failed. Many projects will fail because of circumstances beyond the control of the project team. See Snapshot from Practice: Project Canceled.

Changed Priority   Organizations' priorities often change and strategy shifts directions. For example, during the 2008–10 financial crisis organizations shifted their focus from money-making projects to cost savings projects. The oversight group continually revises project selection priorities to reflect changes in organizational direction. Projects in process may need to be altered or canceled. Thus, a project may start with a high priority but see its rank erode or crash during its

SNAPSHOT FROM PRACTICE

Project Canceled*

Germany is the major crossroad for Europe's international commercial trucks. The German government felt the need to have international trucks (over 12 tons) using their road infrastructure assist in paying for the road maintenance and additional new infrastructure. The project objectives were clear—a new electronic truck toll-collection system that ensures accurate charges and easy fee collection across German, Swiss, and Austrian highways by August 31, 2003. The technology relied on global positioning systems (GPS), telecommunications, and software to record miles and charges, without using toll booths along the highways.

Several problems sabotaged the project. Time-to-market deadlines were impossible to meet. Delayed launch dates were caused by technical problems with truck tracking units and software that failed to function as expected. Interface communication with public and private stakeholders failed. As a result, the August 2003 deadline was never met. The revised November 2003 deadline was not met. Finally, in March 2004 the German government pulled the plug and canceled the project.

The cancellation of the project had serious impacts on other governmental programs. The shortfall of not receiving the revenue from the new toll system is estimated at $1.6 billion. Some of those revenues were destined for a high-speed maglev train in Munich and other infrastructure projects.

Lessons learned reveal that lack of project management knowledge was evident. More importantly, failure to identify and assess the impact of schedule and complex technology risks resulted in the death of the project. Perhaps a simpler, cheaper microwave system recommended by the Swiss and Austrians to be operational by 2005 would have sufficed. See http://www.toll-collect.de/frontend/HomepageVP.do: Jsessionid-F840E12142D.

* "Case Analysis: Taking a Toll," *PM Network,* Vol. 18, No. 3, March, 2004, p. 1.

project life cycle as conditions change. When priorities change, projects in process may need to be altered or canceled.

Different types of project termination present unique issues. Some adjustments to generic closure processes may be necessary to accommodate the type of project termination you face.

WRAP-UP CLOSURE ACTIVITIES

The major challenges for the project manager and team members are over. Getting the project manager and project participants to wrap up the odds and ends necessary to fully complete a project is often difficult. It's like the party is over—now who wants to help clean up? Much of work is mundane and tedious. Motivation can be the chief challenge. For example, accounting for equipment and completing final reports are perceived as dull administrative tasks by project professionals who are action-oriented individuals. The project manager's challenge is to keep the project team focused on the remaining project activities and delivery to the customer until the project is complete. Communicating a closure and review plan and schedule early allows the project team to (1) accept the psychological fact the project will end and (2) prepare to move on. The ideal scenario is to have the team member's next assignment ready when project completion is announced. Project managers need to be careful to maintain their enthusiasm for completing the project and hold people accountable to deadlines, which are prone to slip during the waning stages of the project.

Implementing the closure process includes several wrap-up activities. Many organizations develop lengthy lists for closing projects as they gain experience. These are very helpful and ensure nothing is overlooked. Implementing closedown includes the following six major activities:

1. Getting delivery acceptance from the customer.
2. Shutting down resources and releasing to new uses.
3. Reassigning project team members.
4. Closing accounts and seeing all bills are paid.
5. Delivering the project to the customer.
6. Creating a final report.

Administering the details of closing out a project can be intimidating. Some organizations have checklists of over 100 wrap-up tasks! These checklists deal with closure details such as facilities, teams, staff, customer, vendors, and the project itself. A partial administrative closure checklist is shown below in Table 14.1.

TABLE 14.1
Wrap-up Closure Checklist

	Task	Completed? Yes/No
	Team	
1	Has a schedule for reducing project staff been developed and accepted?	
2	Has staff been released or notified of new assignments?	
3	Have performance reviews for team members been conducted?	
4	Has staff been offered outplacement services and career counseling activities?	
	Vendors/contractors	
5	Have performance reviews for all vendors been conducted?	
6	Have project accounts been finalized and all billing closed?	
	Customer/Users	
7	Has the customer signed-off on the delivered product?	
8	Has an in-depth project review and evaluation interview with the customer been conducted?	
9	Have the users been interviewed to assess their satisfaction with the deliverables? With the project team? With vendors? With training? With support? With maintenance?	
	Equipment and facilities	
10	Have project resources been transferred to other projects?	
11	Have rental or lease equipment agreements been closed out?	
12	Has the date for the closure review been set and stakeholders notified?	
	Attach comments or links on any tasks you feel need explanation.	

Getting delivery acceptance by the customer is a major and critical closure activity. Delivery of some projects to the customer is straightforward. Others are more complex and difficult. Ideally there should be no surprises. This requires a well-defined scope and an effective change management system with active customer involvement. User involvement is critical to acceptance (see Snapshot from Practice: New Ball Goes Flat in the NBA).

SNAPSHOT FROM PRACTICE
New Ball Goes Flat in the NBA*

On October 31, 2006, the National Basketball Association (NBA) opened its 57th season with new official game balls. The new ball, manufactured by Spalding, featured a new design and a new material that together was believed to offer better grip, feel, and consistency than the previous leather ball. The material is microfiber composite with moisture management that provides superior grip and feel throughout the course of a game. Additionally, the new composite material eliminates the need for a break-in period, which is necessary for the current leather ball, and achieves consistency from ball to ball.

The NBA and Spalding subjected the ball to a rigorous evaluation process that included laboratory and on-court testing process. Every NBA team received the new ball and had the opportunity to use it in practice. The ball was also tested in the NBA summer development league.

At the press conference announcing the shift from leather to microfiber balls, NBA commissioner David Stern pronounced "The advancement that Spalding has made to the new game ball ensures that the best basketball players in the world will be playing with the best basketball in the world."

Animal rights advocates applauded the shift from leather to microfiber. Such was not the case for the players who would actually use the new ball. Grumblings emerged immediately when training camps opened in October. Washington Wizards guard Gilbert Arenas said the new basketball gets slippery when it comes in contact even with small amounts of sweat. Then Miami Heat center Shaquille O'Neil said "it feels like one of those cheap balls that you buy at a toy store."

Some players, including league MVP Steve Nash, began complaining that the new ball was producing small cuts on their hands, "It's awful, (the friction burns) its like an irritant . . . sometimes I even have to tape my fingers in practice." Perhaps LeBron James from the Cleveland Cavaliers best summed up the players attitudes toward the NBA's introduction of the new ball when he said "You can change the dress code, you can make our shorts shorter, but when you take our basketball away from us, that not a transition we handle."

On December 1, 2006, four weeks into the season the NBA players union filed an unfair labor practice suit because the league management switched to the new ball without consulting the players. Ten days later, the NBA announced that they would revert back to the old leather ball beginning January 1st 2007. In a terse statement, Commissioner David Stern said "Our player's response to this particular composite ball has been overwhelmingly negative and we are acting accordingly."

The failure to check with the players (the end-users) and get buy-in for the new basketball was loudly criticized by the press. "How they could actually even get it that far and not have run it by the players is just an amazing, amazing exercise in ineptitude," Rob Frankel, a Los Angeles–based branding expert told Bloomberg News.

* "NBA Introduces New Game Ball", www.nba.com/news, posted 6-28-2006; Howard Bloom, "The NBA- uneventful 2006 II," *Sports Business News, www.sportsbixnews.blogspot.com.* 12-30-2006.

The conditions for completing and transferring the project should be set before the project begins. A completed software program is a good example of the need to work out the details in advance. If the user has problems using the software, will the customer withhold final payments? Who is responsible for supporting and training the user? If these conditions are not clearly defined up front, getting delivery acceptance can be troublesome.

Another delivery tactic (briefly mentioned in Chapter 7) for a project that has been outsourced is known as build, own, operate, and transfer (BOOT). In this type of project the contractor builds, owns, and operates the project deliverable for a set period of time. For example, Haliburton will operate a hydro-electric plant for six months before turning over operations to their Indian counterparts. During this time all the bugs are worked out and conditions for delivery are satisfied. Again, note the delivery conditions need to be carefully set up before the project begins; if not, wrap-up activities can develop a life of their own.

Releasing the project team typically occurs gradually during the closure phase. For some people, termination of their responsible activities ends before the project is delivered to the customer or user. Reassignment for these participants needs to take place well before the final finish date. For the remaining team members (full or part time), termination may result in a new project or returning to their functional job. Sometimes, on product development efforts, team members will be assigned to operations positions and play an active role in the production of the new product. For contract people it may mean the end of their assignment to this project; in some cases there may be follow-up work or user support possibilities. A small number of part-time participants may be recommended to the user organization to train or operate new equipment or systems.

Since many work invoices are not submitted until after the project is officially over, closing out contracts is often messy and filled with untied ends. For example, it is improbable all invoices have been finalized, billed, and paid. Further, when contractors are used, there is a need to verify that all the contracted work has been done. Keeping contract records, such as progress reports, invoices, change records, and payment records, is important should a compliance or lawsuit occur. Too often in the haste to meet deadlines, paperwork and record keeping gets short changed, only to create major headaches when it comes time for final documentation.

There are many more wrap-up activities; it is important to complete all of them. Experience has proved time and again that not doing all the little cleanup tasks well will create problems later. Two other examples of closure checklists are shown in this chapter: Appendix 14.1 presents an example used by the state of Virginia and Appendix 14.2 presents an abridged closure checklist for the Euro Conversion project. The final wrap-up activity of closure that provides a clear signal that the project is truly over is submission of the final project report.

Creating the Final Report

The final project report summarizes project performance and provides useful information for continuous improvement. Although the final report will be customized to your project and organization, the content of the final report typically includes the following topics: executive summary, review and analysis, recommendations, lessons learned, and appendix.

Executive Summary   This summary simply highlights the key findings and facts relating to the project implementation. For example, the project goals for the customer were met, or not. Are stakeholders satisfied that their strategic intents have been met? What has been user reaction to quality of the deliverables? Are the project deliverables being used as intended and providing the expected benefits? Final time, cost, and scope performances are listed. Any major problems encountered and addressed are noted. Key lessons learned are identified.

Review and Analysis   Data are collected to record the project history, management performance, and lessons learned to improve future projects. Analysis examines in detail the underlying causes of problems, issues, and successes. The analysis section includes succinct, factual review statements of the project—for example, project mission and objectives, procedures and systems used, and organizational resources used. It is common to collect data from the organizational view and from the team view. The project office or closure facilitators often use questionnaires and surveys to pick up on issues and events that need to be examined further. For example, "Was the organizational culture supportive and correct for this type of project? Why? Why not?" Or, "Did the team have adequate access to organizational resources—people, budget, support groups, equipment?" The project office also provides project schedules, cost comparisons, scope data, and other needed data to tell the story of performance. This information is used to create a final project report.

Recommendations   Usually, review recommendations represent major improvement actions that should take place. They are often technical in nature and focus on solutions to problems that surfaced. For example, to avoid rework, the report for a construction project recommended shifting to more resilient building material. In other cases, they may include terminating or sustaining vendor or contractor relationships.

Lessons Learned   Perhaps lessons learned are the most valuable contribution of the closure process. Given the process evaluation and input from the stakeholder meetings, lessons learned should be succinctly and clearly set out. Stress the need to help others in future projects. In practice, new project teams studying past project reports similar to the project they are about to start have found past review reports very useful. Team members will frequently remark later, "The recommendations were good, but the 'lessons learned' section really helped us avoid many pitfalls and made our project implementation smoother." It is for precisely this reason that lessons learned in the form of project retrospectives have taken on greater prominence in the field and warrant an extended discussion at the end of this chapter. See Snapshot from Practice: Lessons Learned from Katrina.

SNAPSHOT FROM PRACTICE
Lessons Learned from Katrina*

On August 25, 2005, winds of 145 miles per hour and rains covered 80 percent of New Orleans with some areas under 20 feet of water. Hurricane Katrina dispersed havoc on every corner of New Orleans. In its trail it left over 1,300 people dead in Louisiana and Mississippi. Katrina will long be remembered as the costliest and most deadly hurricane ever recorded in the United States.

Response came from many different groups from within the country and from other countries. Katrina also drew the largest response of The National Guard to a national emergency in history. Governors from every state sent National Guard troops to support and assist the state of Mississippi. By September 8, 51,000 troops were responding to the emergency. Many other nonprofit groups offered help in a variety of ways—food, shelter, financial, health care, and transportation. Groups that contributed support have reviewed their efforts to see what lessons learned can be used to improve future emergency efforts. The results of the review of The National Guard efforts follow here:

Three of the key lessons from The National Guard retrospective are described.

- *Lack of equipment was one of the biggest problems—especially communication equipment. Ability to communicate among the many different support groups (e.g., civilian and military) was thwarted by incompatible systems or simple lack of availability.*

  Action Item: $1.3 billion has been authorized for new equipment that is compatible across major emergency groups.

> - *Lack of protocols and standardization of reports, graphics, and communication caused delays and poor coordination among the many support groups.*
>   *Action Item:* A single standard protocol for all states is now being applied.
> - *The National Guard is under state control. Guard troops integrated quickly into the host-state command structures and cooperation ensued.*
>   *Action Item:* Maintain status quo.
>
> Because Guard soldiers are controlled by the states, they were empowered to enforce civil laws, something federal troops are prohibited from doing, except under the provisions of the insurrection laws. Fortunately, coordination and cooperation among state and federal troop command work reasonably well. However, the federal agencies (e.g., Homeland Security) need to incorporate the Guard into planning and preparation for the federal response to catastrophic disasters.
>
> Lessons learned from the Katrina disaster are not limited to the military. Almost every agency and support group, such as individuals, communities, churches, and other groups, have developed lessons learned from their project response experience. For example, the Red Cross and state guard have better plans for handling thousands of people problems involving shelter, evacuation, and medical assistance. These lessons learned from Katrina are ready to go and should be enormously helpful in future hurricane situations.
>
> ---
>
> * Les A. Melnyk, "Katrina Lessons Learned," *Soldiers Magazine*, June 20, 2006 and "Lessons Learned from Katrina: Preparing Your Institution for a Catastrophic Event." Federal Deposit Insurance Corporation is the source of this information. 1/20/08

Appendix The appendix may include backup data or details of analysis that would allow others to follow up if they wished. It should not be a dumping ground used for filler; only critical pertinent information should be attached.

POST-IMPLEMENTATION EVALUATION

The purpose of **project evaluation** is to assess how well the project team, team members, and project manager performed.

Team Evaluation

Evaluation of performance is essential to encourage changes in behavior and to support individual career development and continuous improvement through organizational learning. Evaluation implies measurement against specific criteria. Experience corroborates that before commencement of a project, the stage must be set so expectations, standards, supportive organizational culture, and constraints are in place; if not, the effectiveness of the evaluation process will suffer.

In a macro sense, the evidence today suggests that performance evaluation is not done well. See Research Highlight: Measures of Team Performance. The major reasons cited by practitioners are twofold:

1. Evaluations of individuals are still left to supervisors of the team member's home department.
2. Typical measures of team performance center on time, cost, and specifications.

Research Highlight

MEASURES OF TEAM PERFORMANCE*

If team evaluation is not done well in practice, how bad is it? Joseph Fusco surveyed 1,667 project managers representing 134 different projects. Fifty-two percent of the respondents indicated their team received no collective evaluation of their team performance. Of the 22 percent who indicated their team was evaluated, further probing found their evaluation was informal, lasting little more than 20 minutes. This apparent lack of team evaluation practices may be sending the wrong signal. Individual team members can slough off poor team performance by relying on the old saying, "I did my job." Strong team evaluation practices need to emphasize team members are "in this together," while minimizing individual performance. Nearly every company in Fusco's survey lacked an effective project management reward system.

* Joseph Fusco, "Better Policies Provide the Key to Implementing Project Management," *Project Management Journal,* Vol. 28, No. 3, September 1997, p. 38.

Most organizations do not go beyond these measures, although they are important and critical. Organizations should consider evaluating the team-building process, effectiveness of group decision and problem-solving processes, group cohesion, trust among team members, and quality of information exchanged. Measurement of customer and user satisfaction with project deliverables (i.e., the project results) is often missed completely. Yet, project success depends significantly on satisfying these two very important groups. The quality of the deliverables is the responsibility of the team.

Before an evaluation of the project team can be effective and useful, a minimum core of conditions needs to be in place before the project begins (see Chapter 11). Some typical conditions are listed here in the form of questions:

1. Do standards for measuring performance exist? (You can't manage what you can't measure.) Are the goals clear for the team and individuals? Challenging? Attainable? Lead to positive consequences?
2. Are individual and team responsibilities and performance standards known by all team members?
3. Are team rewards adequate? Do they send a clear signal that senior management believes that the synergy of teams is important?
4. Is a clear career path for successful project managers in place?
5. Is the team empowered to manage short-term difficulties?
6. Is there a relatively high level of trust emanating from the organizational culture?
7. Team evaluation should go beyond time, cost, and specifications. Are there criteria beyond the constraint criteria? Creation of project deliverables would be a good place to start. The "characteristics of highly effective teams" from Chapter 11 can easily be adapted as measurements of team performance.

The "in-place conditions" will support any evaluation approach for teams and their members.

In practice, the actual team evaluation process takes many forms—especially when evaluation goes beyond time, budget, and specifications. The typical mechanism for evaluation of teams is a survey administered by a consultant, a staff member from the human resources department, or through computer e-mail. The survey is normally restricted to team members, but in some cases, other project stakeholders interacting with the team may be included in the survey. An example of a partial survey is found in Table 14.2. After the results are tabulated, the team meets with the facilitator and/or senior management, and the results are reviewed.

This session is comparable to the team-building sessions described in Chapter 11, except that the focus is on using the survey results to assess the development of the team, its strengths and weaknesses, and the lessons that can be applied to future project work. The results of team evaluation surveys are helpful in changing behavior to better support team communication, the team approach, and continuous improvement of team performance.

TABLE 14.2 ....

Sample Team Evaluation and Feedback Survey

	Disagree				Agree
Using the scale below, assess each statement.					
1. The team shared a sense of common purpose, and each member was willing to work toward achieving project objectives.	1	2	3	4	5
2. Respect was shown for other points of view. Differences of opinion were encouraged and freely expressed.	1	2	3	4	5
3. All interaction among team members occurred in a comfortable, supportive atmosphere.	1	2	3	4	5

Individual, Team Member, and Project Manager Performance Reviews

Organizations vary in the extent to which their project managers are actively involved in the appraisal process of team members. In organizations where projects are managed within a functional organization, the team member's area manager, not the project manager, is responsible for assessing performance. The area manager may solicit the project manager's opinion of the individual's performance on a specific project; this will be factored into the individual's overall performance. In a balanced matrix, the project manager and the area manager jointly evaluate an individual's performance. In project matrix and project organizations in which the lion's share of the individual's work is project related, the project manager is responsible for appraising individual performance. One process that appears to be gaining wider acceptance is the multi-rater appraisal or "360-degree feedback," which involves soliciting feedback concerning team members' performance from all the people their work affects. This would include not only project and area managers, but also peers, subordinates, and even customers. See Snapshot from Practice: The 360-Degree Feedback.

Performance appraisals generally fulfill two important functions. The first is developmental in nature: the focus is on identifying individual strengths and weaknesses and developing action plans for improving performance. The second is evaluative and involves assessing how well the person has performed in order to determine salary or merit adjustments. These two functions are not compatible. Employees, in their eagerness to find out how much pay they will receive, tend to tune out constructive feedback on how they can improve their performance. Likewise, managers tend to be more concerned with justifying their decision than engaging in a meaningful discussion on how the employee can improve his or her performance. It is difficult to be both a coach and a judge. As a result, several experts on performance appraisal systems recommend that organizations separate performance reviews, which focus on individual improvement, and pay reviews, which allocate the distribution of rewards (cf., Romanoff, 1989; Latham and Wexley, 2003).

In some matrix organizations, project managers conduct the performance reviews, while area managers are responsible for pay reviews. In other cases, performance reviews are part of the project closure process, and pay reviews are the primary objective of the annual performance appraisal. Other organizations avoid this dilemma by allocating only group rewards for project work and providing annual awards for individual performance. The remaining discussion is directed at reviews designed to improve performance because pay reviews are often outside the jurisdiction of the project manager.

Individual Reviews

Organizations employ a wide range of methods to review individual performance on a project. In general, review methods of individual performance center on the technical and social skills brought to the project and team. Some organizations rely simply on an informal discussion between the project manager and the project member. Other organizations require project managers to submit written evaluations that describe and assess an individual's performance on a project. Many organizations use rating scales similar to the team evaluation survey in which the project manager rates the individual according to a certain scale (i.e., from 1 to 5) on a number of relevant performance dimensions (i.e., teamwork, customer relations). Some organizations augment these rating schemes with behaviorally anchored descriptions of what constitutes a 1 rating, a 2 rating, and so forth. Each method has its strengths and weaknesses, and, unfortunately, in many organizations the appraisal systems were designed to support mainstream operations and not unique project work. The bottom line is that project managers have to use as best they can the performance review system mandated by their organization.

Regardless of the method, the project manager needs to sit down with each team member and discuss his or her performance. Here are some general tips for conducting performance reviews:

- Always begin the process by asking the individual to evaluate his or her contributions to the project. First, this approach may yield valuable information that you were not aware of. Second, the approach may provide an early warning for situations in which there is disparity in assessments. Finally, this method reduces the judgmental nature of the discussion.

- Avoid, when possible, drawing comparisons with other team members; rather, assess the individual in terms of established standards and expectations. Comparisons tend to undermine cohesion and divert attention away from what the individual needs to do to improve performance.

- When you have to be critical, focus the criticism on specific examples of behavior rather than on the individual personally. Describe in specific terms how the behavior affected the project.

- Be consistent and fair in your treatment of all team members. Nothing breeds resentment more than if, through the grapevine, individuals feel they are being held to a different standard than are other project members.

- Treat the review as only one point in an ongoing process. Use it to reach an agreement as to how the individual can improve his or her performance.

Both managers and subordinates may dread a formal performance review. Neither side feels comfortable with the evaluative nature of the discussion and the potential for misunderstanding and hurt feelings. Much of this anxiety can be alleviated if the project manager is doing her job well. Project managers should be constantly giving team members feedback throughout the project so that individual team members can have a pretty good idea how well they have performed and how the manager feels before the formal meeting. Post-project angst can be avoided if pre-project expectations are discussed before the project and regularly reenforced during project performance.

While in many cases the same process that is applied to reviewing the performance of team members is applied to evaluating the project manager, many organizations augment this process, given the importance of the position to their organization. This is where conducting the **360-degree review** is becoming more popular. In project-driven organizations, the project office typically will be responsible for collecting information on a specific project manager from customers, vendors, team members, peers, and other managers. This approach has tremendous promise for developing more effective project managers (Cochran, 2000).

In addition to performance reviews, data are collected for project retrospectives, which can present situations that may influence performance. In these situations performance evaluations should recognize and note the unusual situation.

RETROSPECTIVES

Why Retrospectives?

Lessons learned represent *an analysis carried out during and shortly after the project life cycle; they attempt to capture positive and negative project learning.* That is, "what worked and what didn't?" Lessons learned (postmortems, post-project review, or whatever name you choose to use) have long been part of project management. Peter Senge's *The Fifth Discipline: The Art and Practice of the Learning Organization* (1990) drew attention to institutionalizing organizational learning.

Although the past processes have been useful for closure and lessons learned, sadly their real value has not been exploited. Large, multinational companies with projects spread across the globe have been disappointed in their failure to effectively mine lessons learned. Smaller organizations observed, they too were not reaping the golden rewards of lessons learned. The same mistakes continue year after year. In the words of one executive: "Lessons learned are worth their weight in gold. I do not understand why we don't do a better job nurturing, dispersing, and implementing lessons learned." The processes for capturing lessons learned continue to evolve, but there are still many barriers to effectively mining the lessons learned that have been identified by practitioners. A few of the most ubiquitous barriers are noted here.

* The most common reason given for not creating lessons learned is lack of time.
* Most lessons learned are captured when the project is complete; teams get little direction or support after the lessons are reported.
* Lessons learned often degenerate into blame sessions that became emotionally damaging.
* Lessons learned are not being used across different locations.
* Lessons learned while implementing the project are seldom used to improve the remaining work in the project.
* Too often the lessons learned are not used in future projects because the organizational culture fails to recognize the value of learning.

What is needed to overcome these barriers is a methodology and management philosophy to ensure lessons learned are identified, utilized, and become a significant part of the project management organizational culture. The keys are to turn lessons learned into actions taken and to have someone own the lesson. One effort that appears to address the barriers and offer a solution is retrospectives. The military has long used retrospectives to improve their operations (e.g., after each maneuver). Retrospectives have emerged as a strong process and management philosophy used by project-driven organizations around the world to mine the gold that lessons learned can provide. Retrospectives are championed by Norman Kerth in his text *Project Retrospectives* (2001).

> *A **retrospective** is a methodology that analyzes a past project event to determine what worked and what didn't, develops lessons learned, and creates an action plan that ensures lessons learned are used to improve management of future projects.*

The major goals of retrospectives are to reuse solutions and stop repetitive mistakes across the organization.

Retrospectives methodology has several embedded, distinguishing characteristics to ensure its effectiveness and value:

* Uses an independent facilitator.

- Includes a minimum of three in-process learning gates during the project life cycle.
- Has an owner.
- Develops a repository that is easy to use.
- Mandates a discipline that ensures retrospectives are used.

Initiating the Retrospective Review

The review process depends primarily on organization size and project size. Every effort should be made to make the project review a normal process rather than a surprise notice. In small organizations and projects where face-to-face contact at all levels is prevalent, the closure may be informal and only represent another staff meeting. But even in these environments the content of a formal project review should be examined and covered with notes made of the lessons learned. In some organizations, review initiation comes from a formal project review group or can be automatic. For example, in the latter case, all projects are reviewed at specific stages in the project life cycle—perhaps when a project is 10 to 20 percent complete in time or money, 50 percent complete, and after completion. In most other multiproject organizations, reviews (called stage gates) are planned for the completion of major milestones. The review is not linked to percent complete. Milestones are binary; either you have reached requirements completion or you have not. Regardless of how reviews are set up, they should be set up in the project planning stage—before the project begins.

Use of an Independent Facilitator

The retrospective methodology uses an independent **facilitator** to collect and implement lessons learned to improve management of current and future projects. *A project facilitator is a guide who leads the project team through an analysis of project activities that went well, what needs improvement, and development of a follow-up action plan with goals and accountability.*

Selection of a Facilitator

Characteristics of a Facilitator

Any project review starts with staffing. That is, who will facilitate the review and be accountable for conducting it? Perhaps nothing influences the success of project review more than the selection of the closure facilitator. Selection of the facilitator should not be a random selection from the project office! The key requirement in selection of the facilitator is *independence*. It is imperative that the closure facilitator possess the following characteristics, at a minimum:

1. No direct involvement or direct interest in the project.
2. Perceived as impartial and fair.
3. Respect of senior management and other project stakeholders.
4. Willingness to listen.
5. Independence and authority to report review results without fear of recriminations from special interests.
6. Perceived as having the best interests of the organization in making decisions.
7. Broad-based experience in the organization or industry.

Other review participants should have similar characteristics even if they are selected for their special expertise.

Roles of a Facilitator

There are good reasons for using an independent facilitator. Lessons learned exercises can have negative consequences. The exercise can degenerate into a griping session that places blame. Word of the negative consequences travels fast and results in poor, guarded participation. The focus fails to stay on causes and improving future performance. The facilitator needs to be careful to avoid blame and allow stakeholders to feel safe to provide input.

A trained independent facilitator is often capable of gleaning information that would not be forthcoming to the project manager. Project participants report they are far more willing to attend and contribute to a lessons learned session run by an *independent* facilitator who can eliminate most political aspects in gathering lessons learned. The facilitator can deliver bad news to the project sponsor or senior management without recriminations. For example, since it is never pleasant for the project manager to deliver bad or potentially bad news to senior management or the project owner, many people wait until it is too late. In one project the facilitator received information and was able to give senior management a heads-up that there was a better than 60 percent risk of a delay of new, self-controlled, diesel railcars from a vendor having financial difficulties. Action was taken and money was loaned to the railcar company to avoid delay.

In the words of one project manager, "The facilitator takes the monkey off my back." For this and other reasons, many organizations use an independent retrospective facilitator to manage the retrospective process. Team members may be intimidated when the project manager or senior management attends team meetings. A recognized facilitator can elicit a 360-degree view/input from all stakeholders to create a richer, fuller picture of project issues and successes. The key criterion for selecting a project facilitator is that the facilitator has an independent and unbiased relationship to the project. Nike, Intel, Portland General Electric, Conway trucking, and various state governments use trained independent facilitators for lessons learned on large projects.

Managing a Retrospective

Having a facilitator available at the start of a project is preferred. The retrospective approach stresses gathering lessons learned during project execution and using them to change remaining work. Experience tells us memories fade as time passes; people leave the project. If lessons learned are not captured early, they may be lost. Catching lessons midway in the project life cycle allows for changing the way the remaining work is performed. (Some practitioners call this process "correcting course while the project is in flight.") Most retrospective methods use a minimum of three gates during the project life cycle to collect lessons learned that can be used to self correct the remainder of project execution. See Figure 14.2 for a flow chart of the collection of lessons learned.

It is critical to have a separate repository or library where reports and lessons learned are accessible and easy to retrieve. Your authors have encountered more than one organization that does a nice job of creating a closure report, but the report is placed in someone's bottom drawer or file cabinet, never to be seen again. This is truly a big mistake! The lessons learned are often the single best information a project manager or team can use in planning a future project. Repeatedly, project managers tell stories of how lessons learned "saved their lives" by allowing them to avoid a pitfall. Presentations at organization meetings or conferences encourage others to use and develop

FIGURE 14.2 *Retrospectives Process*

lessons learned. It also provides a chance to shine. The responsibility for maintaining a repository for lessons learned and encouraging its use is normally the responsibility of the project office or oversight committee. See Research Highlight: CHAOS: Software Projects.

Research Highlight

CHAOS: SOFTWARE PROJECTS*

The Standish Group International is a market research and advisory firm specializing in mission-critical software and electronic commerce. They have conducted and published extensive research on the success and failure of software development/application projects. Their research, code name "CHAOS," shows that a staggering 31 percent of software projects will be canceled before they are ever completed. In addition, 53 percent of projects will cost 189 percent of their original estimates. In terms of success, on the average only 16 percent of software projects are completed on time and within budget. In larger companies, the success rate is much worse—9 percent. The Standish Group estimated that in 1995 American companies and government agencies spent $81 billion for canceled software projects.

The CHAOS research is based on "key findings" from research surveys and personal interviews. The respondents were information technology (IT) executive managers. The sample included large, medium, and small companies across major industry segments, for example, banking; securities; manufacturing; retail; wholesale; health care; insurance service; and local, state, and federal organizations. The total sample size was 365 respondents and represented 8,380 projects.

Based on an in-depth comparison of successful versus unsuccessful software projects, the Standish Group created a success potential chart that identifies key factors associated with project success. The success criteria were weighted based on the input from the surveyed IT managers. The most important criterion, "user involvement," was given 19 success points, while the least important, "hard-working, focused staff," was given 3 success points. The following chart lists the criteria in order of importance:

* Used by permission of the Standish Group International, Inc., 196 Old Town House Rd., West Yarmouth, MA 02673. The CHAOS report was updated in 2001 and 2009. Although improvement was noted (e.g., cost overruns were reduced to 145 percent), the magnitude of the core problems remains the same.

Success Criteria	Points
1. User involvement	19
2. Executive management support	16
3. Clear statement of requirements	15
4. Proper planning	11
5. Realistic expectations	10
6. Smaller project milestones	9
7. Competent staff	8
8. Project team ownership	6
9. Clear vision and objectives	3
10. Hard-working, focused staff	3
Total	100

Overseeing a Post–Project Retrospective

In the past, lessons learned were primarily collected from a post-project survey. Someone reviewed the answers, summarized the results, and filed the document. In retrospective methodology, the facilitator uses several questionnaires as a starting point to conduct the post-project retrospective. These surveys often offer clues to unrecognized deeper problems. A facilitator relates that clues to areas needing improvement are often found by checking the changes running through the project's change management system. For example, change management in multiple design changes might suggest poor freeze rules for design. These hard data can point directly to areas that hold potential for improvement. In some cases the data direct the facilitator to the area where a problem was solved.

Process and Methods Review

Process review begins with a review of the strategic intent of the project, selection criteria, project charter, project objectives, project scope, and acceptance criteria. This starting point reinforces and clarifies the business case for the project and the final project deliverables. Additional data gathering for process review is initiated through a questionnaire that is distributed to all major project stakeholders for responses. Some typical questions used are shown in Table 14.3. Although this questionnaire has some areas of omission, it can be used to initiate developing a questionnaire for your project.

Organizational Review

One of the themes of this text is that project performance is strongly influenced by organizational culture. It is therefore important to assess what fundamental organizational culture properties affect project successes and failures or become a hindrance to project teams. Again, survey questionnaires are easy, quick, and inexpensive to develop and collect data. Table 14.4, Organizational Culture Review, shows a partial organizational survey found in practice.

TABLE 14.3
Project Process Review Questionnaire

	Item	Comments
1.	Were the project objectives and strategic intent of the project clearly and explicitly communicated?	
2.	Were the objectives and strategy in alignment?	
3.	Were the stakeholders identified and included in the planning?	
4.	Were project resources adequate for this project?	
5.	Were people with the right skill sets assigned to this project?	
6.	Were time estimates reasonable and achievable?	
7.	Were the risks for the project appropriately identified and assessed before the project started?	
8.	Were the processes and practices appropriate for this type of project? Should projects of similar size and type use these systems? Why/why not?	
9.	Did outside contractors perform as expected? Explain.	
10.	Were communication methods appropriate and adequate among all stakeholders? Explain.	
11.	Is the customer satisfied with the project product?	
12.	Are the customers using the project deliverables as intended? Are they satisfied?	
13.	Were the project objectives met?	
14.	Are the stakeholders satisfied their strategic intents have been met?	
15.	Has the customer or sponsor accepted a formal statement that the terms of the project charter and scope have been met?	
16.	Were schedule, budget, and scope standards met?	
17.	Is there any one important area that needs to be reviewed and improved upon? Can you identify the cause?	

TABLE 14.4
Organizational Culture Review Questionnaire

	Item	Comments
1.	Was the organizational culture supportive for this type of project?	
2.	Was senior management support adequate?	
3.	Were people with the right skills assigned to this project?	
4.	Did the project office help or hinder management of the project? Explain.	
5.	Did the team have access to organizational resources (people, funds, equipment)?	
6.	Was training for this project adequate? Explain.	
7.	Were lessons learned from earlier projects useful? Why? Where?	
8.	Did the project have a clear link to organizational objectives? Explain.	
9.	Was project staff properly reassigned?	
10.	Was the Human Resources Office helpful in finding new assignments? Comment.	

It is rare that important problems or successes will not show up in answers to a well-developed questionnaire.

With survey information in hand, the facilitator then visits one-on-one with project team members, the project manager, and other stakeholders to dive deeper into cause-effect impacts. Fundamentally, the attempt is to isolate "the lack of x resulted in y." It is important to stay with the big lessons. For example, the facilitator might ask team members, "What was the biggest pain point in the project?" From these discussions the facilitator synthesizes collective wisdom.

Armed with the information gleaned from one-on-one sessions and other sources, the facilitator leads a team retrospective session. This session first reviews the facilitator's report and attempts to add key information. In fact, one of the roles of the facilitator is to lead the team in exploring new ways for solving a problem. Once the team reaches consensus of the key retrospective(s), the team develops and documents an action plan for improving future projects. Each retrospective should have at least one lesson that will improve current or future projects. One person needs to be assigned "owner" of the lesson learned and serve as the go-to person for more information. If possible, the facilitator should get senior management's commitment to implement the lesson.

An additional task of a facilitator is a review of the archived lessons to identify any trends across similar projects. For example, are there affinities between problems and successes among many projects? Have resources been inadequate? Has senior management visibly supported mining lessons learned? What fundamental organizational culture dimensions affect project successes and failures or become a hindrance to project teams?

In a conversation with one project office manager, she related that a facilitator found that the same problem across most multicountry projects had been occurring for over four years! It is difficult to believe no one picked up on such an obvious problem on so many projects. In this organization, U.S. managers were too focused on schedules, performance, and the bottom line; they neglected to establish a personal relationship with their foreign counterparts—e.g., the counterpart's key interests, family, holiday celebrations, and many other cultural aspects. Relationships were often strained and performance suffered. The result was that the project participants in each country are now required to attend a culture awareness class of the country of their counterparts to learn of customs, culture, and mores. Results improved dramatically.

Utilization of Retrospectives

Each retrospective is assigned an owner, typically a team member who is very interested in and familiar with the retrospective. This team member/owner will serve as the contact point for anyone needing information (expertise, contacts, templates, etc.) relating to the retrospective.

Another task of the retrospective facilitator is to guarantee there is a clear process to ensure retrospectives are used to improve management of future projects. Where retrospective methodology is used, some organizations mandate that the team of a new project review the retrospectives of similar projects. This mandate is one tactic that ensures that the most significant lessons are institutionalized. There is no excuse for not using past best practices and avoiding past mistakes. If the project managers before your project had completed retrospectives more effectively, your project might have avoided many mistakes. Of course, a requirement is archiving the lessons in a repository/library. But beyond a retrospective lessons learned library, a simple, easy to use, consistent format is necessary to ensure that information is easily found, used, and updated over time. A blog can be used to receive user comments on how helpful the retrospective is in improving a process or product.

Archiving Retrospectives

If retrospectives are to be used, it is critical to have a repository where reports and retrospective/lessons learned are accessible and easily retrieved. This is usually done using a Web site or other electronic means. For example, a round table of project office directors estimated that among their group of companies, 60–70 percent of their projects are global and virtual; all use some version of a Web-based system to collaborate and archive learning (e.g., Basecamp, SharePoint, Net Meeting, Voice Over IP). The responsibility for maintaining a repository for retrospectives and encouraging their use is normally the responsibility of the project office or oversight committee. Encouraging use of the repository depends on the ease of searching for information that is relevant to your project. Utilizing the information is defeated if information is difficult to find. For example, one project manager reported to your authors, "There are so many lessons learned items in the retrospectives library, I can't find information that applies to my project." This manager either wasn't interested in learning from others or the archive was poorly arranged.

At a minimum the repository should classify projects by type or characteristics. Each project review is categorized because there are differences in the way projects with different characteristics are managed and handled in an organization. A prospective project manager of a software coding project will have little interest in the construction of a clean room or recycling of inkjet reservoirs for printers. A prospective project manager of a small project will not be as interested in a computer project planning and control system as a project manager who is going to manage a very large project. The classification of projects by characteristics allows prospective readers, teams, and project managers to be selective in the search and use of report content.

One repository search engine uses the following classification scheme to allow prospective project stakeholders to start their search for information related to their prospective project:

- Project type—e.g., development, marketing, systems, construction.
- Size—monetary.
- Number of staff.
- Technology level—low, medium, high, new.
- Strategic or support.

Other classifications relevant to the organization could be included to drill further in search of projects that match the features of the prospective project. For example, another classification system indexes retrospectives by issues and problems.

Celebration   A final wrap-up activity for the facilitator is the project closure celebration. An upbeat, festive celebration brings closure to the enjoyable experiences everyone has had and the need to say good-bye. Celebration is an opportunity to recognize the effort project stakeholders contributed. Even if the project did not reach its objectives, recognize the effort and goals that were achieved. If the project was a success, invite everyone who in some way contributed to project success. Thank the team and each one individually. The spirit of the celebration should be one in which the stakeholders are thanked for a job well done and leave with a good feeling of accomplishment and success.

Concluding Retrospective Notes

The retrospective methodology is more inclusive and disciplined than past lessons learned approaches. The impetus for its success has been accompanied by greater recognition of the real value of lessons learned in improving the management of projects. For example, Intel, which has project teams dispersed over 290 locations in 45 countries, has found using trained facilitators to be highly effective in mining and using retrospectives. Intel continues to train 15 new facilitators each year. Retrospective methodology is now standard operating procedure in many project-driven organizations. The lessons learned are often the single best source of information a project manager or team can use in planning their next project. Retrospectives are a main change agent for developing best project-management practices across the organization. Retrospective methodology is one positive step toward ensuring lessons learned are developed and implemented.

Summary

The goals of project closure are to complete the project and to improve performance of future projects. Implementing closure and review has three major closure deliverables: wrap-up, evaluation, and retrospectives. Wrap-up closure activities include delivering the final project deliverable, closing accounts, finding new opportunities for project staff, closing facilities, and creating the final report. Project evaluation verifies and documents project performance. The retrospectives methodology promises lessons learned are identified and used. Too often we spend massive dollars planning a project and little to nothing learning from the experience of completing the project. Failure to review, assess, and record successes and failures has consistently proven to be a costly waste. Retrospective methodology addresses this waste.

Key Terms

Lessons learned	Project evaluation	Team evaluation
Performance review	Project facilitator	360-degree review
Project closure	Retrospective	

Review Questions

1. How does the project closure review differ from the performance measurement control system discussed in Chapter 13?
2. What major information would you expect to find in a project review?
3. Why is it difficult to perform a truly independent, objective review?

4. Comment on the following statement: "We cannot afford to terminate the project now. We have already spent more than 50 percent of the project budget."
5. Why should you separate performance reviews from pay reviews? How do you do this?
6. Advocates of retrospective methodology claim there are distinguishing characteristics that increase its value over past lessons learned methods. What are they? How does each characteristic enhance project closure and review?

Exercises

1. Consider a course that you recently completed. Perform a review of the course (the course represents a project and the course syllabus represents the project plan).
2. Imagine you are conducting a review of the International Space Station project. Research press coverage and the Internet to collect information on the current status of the project. What are the successes and failures to date? What forecasts would you make about the completion of the project, and why? What recommendations would you make to top management of the program, and why?
3. Interview a project manager who works for an organization that implements multiple projects. Ask the manager what kind of closure procedures are used to complete a project and whether lessons learned are used.
4. What are some of the lessons learned from a recent project in your organization? Was a retrospective done? What action plans were generated to improve processes as a result of the project?

References

Anonymous, "Annual Survey of Business Improvement Architects," Toronto, Canada, in *PM Network,* "Deliverables," Vol. 21, No. 4, April 2007, p. 18.

Cochran, D., "Finally, a Way to Completely Measure Project Manager Performance," *PM Network,* September 2000, pp. 75–80.

Cooke-Davies, T., "Project Management Closeout Management: More than Simply Saying Good Bye and Moving On," in J. Knutson (Ed.), *Project Management for Business Processionals* (Indianapolis, IN: John Wiley and Sons, 2001), pp. 200–14.

Fretty, P., "Why Do Projects Really Fail?" *PM Network,* March 2006, pp. 45–48.

Gobeli, D., and E. W. Larson, "Barriers Affecting Project Success," in *1986 Proceedings Project Management Institute: Measuring Success* (Upper Darby, PA: Project Management Institute, 1986), pp. 22–29.

Hoffman, R., "Ten Reasons You Should Be Using 360 Degree Feedback," *HR Magazine,* April 1995, pp. 82–85.

Jedd, Marcia, "Standing Guard," *PM Network,* Vol. 21, No. 1, January 2007, pp. 73–77.

Kendrick, Tom, *Identifying and Managing Project Risk,* 2nd ed. ANACOM, New York, NY 2009.

Kerth, Norman L., *Project Retrospectives: A Handbook for Team Reviews* (New York: Dorset House, 2001).

Kwak, Y. H., and C. W. Ibbs, "Calculating Project Management's Return on Investment," *Project Management Journal,* Vol. 31, No. 2, March 2000, pp. 38–47.

Ladika, S., "By Focusing on Lessons Learned, Project Managers Can Avoid Repeating the Same Old Mistakes," *PM Network,* Vol. 22, No. 2, February 2008, pp. 75–77.

Lavell, Debra, and Russ Martinelli, "Program and Project Retrospectives: An Introduction," *PM World Today,* Vol. 10, No. 1, January 2008, p. 1.

Latham, G. P., and K. N. Wexley, *Increasing Productivity through Performance Appraisal,* 2nd ed. (Reading, MA: Addison-Wesley, 1994).

Marlin, Mark, "Implementing an Effective Lessons Learned Process in a Global Project Environment," *PM World Today,* Vol. 10, No. 11, November 2008, pp. 1–6.

Nelson, Ryan R., "Project Retrospectives: Evaluating Project Success, Failure, and Everything in Between," *MIS Quarterly Executive,* Vol. 4, No. 3, September 2005, p. 372.

Pippett, D. D., and J. F. Peters, "Team Building and Project Management: How Are We Doing?" *Project Management Journal,* Vol. 26, No. 4, December 1995, pp. 29–37.

Romanoff, T. K., "The Ten Commandments of Performance Management," *Personnel,* Vol. 66, No. 1, 1989, pp. 24–26.

Royer, I., "Why Bad Projects Are So Hard to Kill," *Harvard Business Review,* February 2003, pp. 49–56.

Senge, P., *The Fifth Discipline: The Art and Practice of the Learning Organization* (New York: Doubleday, 1990).

Sheperd, D. A., H. Patzelt, and M. Wolfe, "Moving Forward from Project Failure: Negative Emotions, Affective Commitment, and Learning from the Experience," *Academy of Management Journal,* Vol. 54, No. 6, 2011, pp. 1229–60.

Staw, Berry M., and Jerry Ross, "Knowing When to Pull the Plug," *Harvard Business Review,* March-April 1987, pp. 68–74.

Wheatly, M., "Over the Bar," *PM Network,* Vol. 17, No. 1, January 2003, pp. 40–45.

Yates, J. K., and S. Aniftos, "ISO 9000 Series of Quality Standards and the E/C Industry," *Project Management Journal,* Vol. 28, No. 2, June 1997, pp. 21–31.

Zaitz, Les, "Rail Car Deal Snags Tri Met for Millions," *Oregonian,* December 14, 2008, p. 1, and January 7, 2009, p. D4.

APPENDIX 14.1

Project Closeout Checklist

Section 5: Project Closeout

Project Closeout Transition Checklist

Provide basic information about the project including: Project Title—The proper name used to identify this project; Project Working Title—The working name or acronym that will be used for the project; Proponent Secretary—The Secretary to whom the proponent agency is assigned or the Secretary that is sponsoring an enterprise project; Proponent Agency—The agency that will be responsible for the management of the project; Prepared by—The person(s) preparing this document; Date/Control Number—The date the checklist is finalized and the change or configuration item control number assigned.

Project Title: _____   Project Working Title: _____
Proponent Secretary: _____   Proponent Agency: _____
Prepared by : _____   Date/Control Number: _____

Complete the Status and Comments columns. In the Status column indicate: Yes, if the item has been addressed and completed; No, if the item has not been addressed, or is incomplete; N/A, if the item is not applicable to this project. Provide comments or describe the plan to resolve the item in the last column.

	Item	Status	Comments/Plan to Resolve
1	Have all the product or service deliverables been accepted by the customer?		
1.1	Are there contingencies or conditions related to the acceptance? If so, describe in the Comments.		
2	Has the project been evaluated against each performance goal established in the project performance plan?		
3	Has the actual cost of the project been tallied and compared to the approved cost baseline?		
3.1	Have all approved changes to the cost baseline been identified and their impact on the project documented?		
4	Have the actual milestone completion dates been compared to the approved schedule?		

(Continued)

	Item	Status	Comments/Plan to Resolve
4.1	Have all approved changes to the schedule baseline been identified and their impact on the project documented?		
5	Have all approved changes to the project scope been identified and their impact on the performance, cost, and schedule baselines documented?		
6	Has operations management formally accepted responsibility for operating and maintaining the product(s) or service(s) delivered by the project?		
6.1	Has the documentation relating to operation and maintenance of the product(s) or service(s) been delivered to, and accepted by, operations management?		
6.2	Has training and knowledge transfer of the operations organization been completed?		
6.3	Does the projected annual cost to operate and maintain the product(s) or service(s) differ from the estimate provided in the project proposal? If so, note and explain the difference in the Comments column.		
7	Have the resources used by the project been transferred to other units within the organization?		
8	Has the project documentation been archived or otherwise disposed as described in the project plan?		
9	Have the lessons learned been documented in accordance with the Commonwealth Project Management guideline?		
10	Has the date for the post-implementation review been set?		
10.1	Has the person or unit responsible for conducting the post-implementation review been identified?		

Signatures

The signatures of the people below relay an understanding that the key elements within the Closeout Phase section are complete and the project has been formally closed.

Position/Title	Name	Date	Phone Number

Source: http://www.vita.virginia.gov/projects/cpm/cpmDocs/CPMG-SEC5-Final.pdf

APPENDIX 14.2

Euro Conversion—Project Closure Checklist

Project _____ Euro Conversion _____   Customer _____ Finance Department _____

Project manager _____ Hans Kramer _____   Completion date _____ 12 December XX _____

	Due date	Person responsible	Notes
1. Document finance department acceptance	16/12	Hans	
2. Customer training in Euro software	28/12	Joan	Train all departments before conversion
3. Archive all			
Schedules/actuals	31/12	Maeyke	
Budgets/actual costs	31/12	Maeyke	
Changes	31/12	Maeyke	
4. Close out all accounts with vendors	31/12	Guido	
5. Close out all work orders	31/12	Mayo	
6. Close out partner accounts	31/12	Guido	
7. Reassign project staff	16/12	Sophie	
8. Evaluation of			
Vendors	31/12	Mayo	Use standard questionnaire for vendors
Staff members	31/12	Sophie	Have HR department develop and administer
9. Final report and lessons learned meeting	4/1	Hans	Send notice to all stakeholders
10. Lessons learned archive to database	10/1	Maeyke	Contact IS department
...tribute awards		Sophie	Notify all stakeholders

APPENDIX 14.3

Project Quality Management

1. INTRODUCTION

1.1 Definitions of Quality

Quality is a word in very common usage in day-to-day language and, therefore, everybody has formed some very personal concept of what quality should mean. Moreover, in the past few decades, considerable thought and work have been invested in working out systems that should address the issue of improving and sustaining the quality of activities of the commercial enterprises and industrial organizations. The specific definitions of quality provided in these systems introduce another element of ambiguity in the meaning of the word. Therefore, for a start, we would review the essence of definitions provided in some of the better-known quality management systems and how they relate to the definition and approach used in PMBOK® Guide, 5th Edition.

Juran's definition emphasizes 'Fitness (of product) for use'.

Phillip Crosby's emphasis is on 'conformance to requirements'.

Edward Deming sees three cornerstones for quality: the characteristics of the product itself, how the users interact and use the product and instructions for use.

ISO 9000 (published by ISO, International Organization for Standardization) defines quality as 'the degree to which a set of inherent characteristics fulfills requirements.'

The approach to project quality management presented in the *PMBOK® Guide* is generally compatible with the ISO definition of quality: "the totality of characteristics of an entity that bear on its ability to satisfy the client's stated or implied needs" (ISO 8400, 1994). In the context of project management, the project stakeholders are the clients and, hence, satisfactory project quality management should meet the project objectives set down by all stakeholders of the project.

1.2 Definitions of Project Quality Management

One school of thought regards project quality, 'the inherent characteristics which fulfill requirements', to be an integral part and parcel of the basic project objectives and the project deliverables based on them. This approach holds that the project work to be completed is invariably stipulated to be performed to meet certain quality standards or performance criteria, and, hence, managing quality of the product of the project is often not treated as a separate issue, but only as a part of the project scope management. This is the approach taken in Chapter 4, 'Defining the Project.'

PMI offers a different approach and discusses quality management as a separate knowledge area for project management. According to this departure in approach, project quality management includes the processes and the activities of the performing organization that determine quality policies, objectives and responsibilities so that the project will satisfy the needs for which it was undertaken.

We describe below the framework presented by PMBOK® GUIDE, which treats project quality management as a separate knowledge area.

1.3 Approach to Project Quality Management

Since definition of quality given in PMBOK® Guide is aligned with ISO, the project quality is judged according to its ability to satisfy the needs of the project stakeholders. The project stakeholders can be visualized to be of two distinct categories:

- *The project sponsors:* These stakeholders are involved in financing the project or with the management of the project performing organization committed to delivering the project results. Their focus is on the effectiveness and efficiency of how the project is managed with emphasis on whether the project is completed within budget and on time, how project communication or procurement was managed, and so on.
- *The actual users of the product of the project:* These stakeholders are interested in the long-term quality aspects during the product's lifetime. Their focus would be on how the product of the project meets the technical specifications or performance requirements.

For example, for a project for a large-scale development of a residential area, the project sponsor would be the project construction or development organization and its management. From the sponsor's point of view, expectation from the project management is that all construction envisaged for the project is completed on schedule and within the budgeted cost. The actual users of the residential complex would be the people who buy and live in these homes. Their expectations concern certain functional and aesthetic aspects of the building like the building lay-out plans, architectural features, quality of construction for long life, quality of materials and finishes used in construction, maintainability and low maintenance costs, etc.

The first category of stakeholders is concerned with the quality of project management, while the second category of the stakeholders is concerned with the product resulting from the project. The project quality management, therefore, must address the issues of both the management of the project as well as the product of the project. In other words, project quality management should ensure the following:

- Efficient and effective project management in terms of meeting the scope, cost and schedule objectives.
- Incorporating into the product of the project the quality desired by the end users during the product's lifetime.

1.4 PMBOK® Guide, 5th Edition, Alignment with Paradigms of Modern Quality Management Systems

In the recent years, quality management for operations has come into limelight in management literature. New insights in the subject have been attained and several quality management systems and quality improvement movements incorporating these insights have been proposed. PMBOK® GUIDE recognizes the importance of these approaches and supports the concepts advocated by eminent quality movement leaders summarized below:

1. *Customer Satisfaction:* Quality of the product of the project must meet the customer's requirement (*"Fitness for Use" as enunciated by Joseph Juran*). This would involve

understanding the customer's requirements, define and evaluate them, manage them by formulating a proper quality plan, and delivering accordingly.

2. *Prevention over Inspection:* "The quality is planned, designed and built into the product and not inspected in."

3. *Continuous Improvement:* Initiatives are undertaken for continuous improvement of the product quality. Adopt "Plan-Do-Check-Act cycle (recommended by Schewhart and Deming).

4. *Management Responsibility:* The final responsibility for building the quality into a product lies with the management. Without strong support of the management, the project team would not be able to muster the resources necessary for building quality in the product (recommended by Edward Deming).

5. *Ishikawa's seven and techniques for quality control based on statistical analysis:* Cause-and-effects diagrams (Fishbone diagrams), Control Charts, Flowcharting, Histograms, Pareto Charts, Run Charts and Scatter Diagrams (for regression analysis).

6. *The Subtle Distinction in the Connotations of the Commonly Used Other Quality Terms.*

Quality and Grade

Grades refer to the categories assigned to products for same general functional service but different technical specifications or characteristics. So the product with different features and technical characteristics would have different grades. A car may be available in a basic model just for serving transportation function or it may have a number of additional features. The grade has nothing to do with the quality. A high-grade product with many technical attributes and features may have poor quality (frequent failures, high maintenance cost, etc.). On the other hand, a low-grade product, with few basic functional features, may have high quality (high reliability, accuracy in basic service, etc.)

Precision and Accuracy

Accuracy refers to how far the measured value may be from the true value. Precision concerns the repeatability of the performance – the size of scatter or spread between different measurements of the same true value. A product can have high accuracy and low precision; for a product giving readings 103,100 and 97 for a true value of 100, the accuracy is high (– the mean of three readings is exactly the true value), but the individual readings have high spread +/– 3%, i.e. the precision is low. On the other hand, a low accuracy and high precision product might give the values 102,103, and 104; here the spread is just +/– 1 %, but the mean of three readings is 3 % far from the true value – fairly inaccurate performance.

Standards and Regulations

The standards are meant to convey general good practice; they have no legal or compulsion associated with it. On the other hand, the regulations are formal legal instruments and it is mandatory to follow them.

1.5 Key Issues in Project Quality Management

In the light of above background, the focus should be essentially on building into the product the quality, which will meet the satisfaction criteria for the deliverables of the project. This approach recognizes processes for planning the quality, testing and inspection as on-going processes for quality assurance and quality control activities.

As discussed earlier, the key issues in project quality management revolve around a balanced trade-off between:

- effectiveness and efficiency of how the project is managed – reflecting the viewpoints of project sponsors and project performing organization's management, and
- long-term quality aspects during the product's lifetime – reflecting the viewpoint of the actual users of the product of the project.

2.0 Project Quality Management Processes

PMBOK® GUIDE, 5th Edition, identifies three processes to address the key issues of project quality management:

Plan Quality Management   (Planning Process Group)

Perform Quality Assurance   (Executing Process Group)

Control Quality   (Monitoring and Controlling Process Group)

Let us look at these three processes in more detail – focusing on the inputs, tools and techniques and the outputs from the processes.

2.1 Plan Quality Management

Plan Quality Management is the process of identifying quality requirements and/or standards for the project and the deliverables, and documenting how the project will demonstrate compliance with relevant quality requirements. (PMBOK® Guide, 5th Edition)

Inputs

Project Management Plan – Three component plans of the project plan are major inputs:

- Scope Baseline (Project Scope Statement, WBS and WBS Dictionary) – These documents set standards or acceptance criteria for the deliverables or quality of the project's product.
- Cost Baseline (project budget) – This document provides the standard for cost performance of the project.
- Schedule Baseline (project schedule and milestones for major deliverables) – This document provides the standard for schedule cost performance of the project.

Stakeholder Register – Input for stakeholder's interest and its impact on quality.

Risk Register – Input for threats and opportunities, which would impact quality.

Requirements Documentation – Input useful for assessing what requirements the project's product must meet and their impact on quality management.

Enterprise Environmental Factors – Government rules and regulations and industry standards and practices for product.

Organizational Process Assets – Organization's quality policies, procedures and guidelines and lessons *learned on* earlier similar projects (from the organization's project records and written as well as unwritten traditions for quality management).

Tools and Techniques

Quality management has developed into a major management attention area and quality-planning process could use a number of the tools and techniques borrowing from the organization's quality management practices as well as techniques described in the literature. General familiarity with these techniques and their application in the Plan Quality Processes are expected from the PMP certification aspirants. Hence, these tools and techniques are listed below and described very briefly; their detailed description would have to be obtained from specific quality management literature for those interested in details.

Cost-Benefit Analysis – An economic analysis of cost of achieving a particular quality level and the benefit of cost savings from avoiding rework due to quality achievement.

Cost of Quality – This tool aims to analyze the cost of providing a particular quality level. This concept requires some elaboration. The cost of quality is the total of the cost for achieving the conformance of the product to the desired quality and the penalty costs on account of the non-performance of the product to desired quality standards.

- *The cost of conformance* – This consists of cost for building a quality product (*Prevention Costs* – costs for training, documentation, and specific equipment) and the cost to Inspect and assess the quality (*Appraisal Costs*- Testing and Inspection costs).

- *The cost of non-conformance* – This consists of *internal failure costs* (failures found in the project, which require reworking and scrap) and *external failure costs* (costs related to product liability, warranties and lost business opportunities).

Seven Basic Quality Tools (Known as 7QC in Industry)

Seven techniques described below based on Ishikawa's statistical analysis are useful in analyzing and focusing on the relationship between various causes and the corresponding quality issues or defects. *They form together a more or less comprehensive set of techniques for preventing defects or building in the quality in the product of the project.*

1. *Cause–Effect or Fishbone Diagrams:* They give diagrammatic representation between various potential sources of defective work and defects. The analysis based on this presentation (asking "Why?–Why? Or How?-How?") can be helpful in getting at the root causes of the quality problems and improving the quality by addressing the issues involved.

2. *Flowcharting:* Flowcharts present in a sequential nature project activities. From a critical analysis of this chart, the sources for quality problems can be anticipated and accordingly decision points based on suitable testing could be included. Quality Plan would include such testing at critical points decided by flowchart analysis.

3. *Check Sheets:* Useful for preparing and using checklists, they include list of quality checks to be applied.

4. *Pareto Charts:* These are specific types of histograms, where the bars of the chart are ordered according to the frequency of occurrence, which immediately brings attention to the most serious of the quality issues. This type of presentation, used first by Pareto, shows that typically a very small number of causes account for a major portion of the quality issues or defects – say, only 20 % of all causes account for 80 % of the defects. Hence, it is also referred to as 80/20 principle.

5. *Histogram:* This technique involves creating a bar chart with the causes of or quality plotted on X-axis and the frequency of the occurrence of that condition on Y-axis. Histogram gives a graphical presentation and provides a focus on the most important of quality issues immediately.

6. *Control Charts:* The process control charts are tools for control of quality from repetitive processes used during project activities. They are based on the statistical analysis of the process performance to determine whether a project activity is based on a process, which is stable and has a predictable performance or not. Ordinarily, three standard deviation limits about the mean are stipulated as upper and lower process limits. When the inspection and testing reveal the performance of the process to lie beyond the upper or lower limit, or if seven consecutive points lie on the same side of the process mean, the process is assessed to be out of control and suitable adjustments are made to bring it back under control. Generally, the upper and lower control limits, which represent the natural limits for a stable process in control, are taken into account while setting the tolerance for acceptance for quality plan.

7. *Scatter Diagram:* This is merely a plot of the points corresponding to two specific variables for a particular observation point. The points might show a scatter, but might also show a trend line, which presents the general nature of relationship between the two variables. This relationship is called the regression line and if it is a straight line, it is called linear regression.

Benchmarking
Benchmarking involves comparing the planned or actual performance of the project on hand with the similar characteristics from another project (another company or competitor or another department of the same organization) in order to set an improved standard and method of measuring it. The idea is based on the reference levels used in civil engineering surveys. It can be used as a tool for setting the quality standard during preparation of Quality Plan.

Design of Experiments
It is a statistical method for developing an optimized design for how the experiments should be planned for identifying which factors would influence the desired characteristic and to what extent. Ordinarily, an optimized combination of factors could be obtained from this experimental analysis, which would permit much greater variation or tolerance in the input factors without sacrificing the impact on the desired characteristic. Tagucci's Robust Design technique is based on this and the statistical analysis is known as 'Analysis of Variance' ('ANOVA'). The technique has wider application in routine operations and manufacture than for project work, but it could be helpful in some large number of repetitive project tasks, like welding for structural components, RCC work, etc.

Statistical Sampling
Statistical sampling can be used to minimize the cost of inspection and testing in case of project activities requiring a large number of repetitive works. The published sampling tables provide the size of the sample for a population from which it is drawn; this could provide the basis for the quantum of testing or inspection to be carried out for a project and permit to estimate the cost of quality.

Outputs

Quality Management Plan – This would form a component of the comprehensive project plan and provide overarching description of how the organization's quality management policy will be implemented, what quality standards and quality related operating procedures will be enforced and how the rest of quality management planning, executing and controlling processes will be carried out.

Process Improvement Plan – A component plan of the Project Management Plan, it would provide the road map for how the current processes used in project execution can be improved by analysis of their existing status and tools for process improvement.

Quality Metrics – Quality metrics are specific measurable attributes of the project's product and determines how the quality control process will measure them and the applicable standards for acceptance in terms of precise tolerances.

Quality Checklists – These tools, based on lessons learnt from earlier projects, systematically summarize the attributes or characteristics of a particular component or work package result, which the project team should check to ensure the desired quality level.

2. PERFORM QUALITY ASSURANCE (PROJECT EXECUTING GROUP)

Perform Quality Assurance is the process of auditing the equality requirements and the results from quality control measurements to ensure that appropriate quality standards and operational definitions are used. (PMBOK® Guide, 5th Edition)

The process involves carrying out all work related to achieving the quality planned in the earlier process during project execution. Essentially, it would involve carrying out physical inspection, testing, and performance evaluation of the deliverables. If any deficiencies are spotted during inspection and testing, corrective actions are recommended and taken. If any change in the planning or execution would contribute towards higher quality, such changes are also recommended.

Distinction between Perform Quality Assurance and Perform Quality Control processes
There is a close similarity between the Perform Quality Assurance and Perform Quality Control processes. Both use similar or common procedures used for inspection and testing; however, reporting and analysis in case of quality assurance is just to be sure that the right procedures are used in operation and convince the stakeholders about the quality built into the product of the project. The analysis and reporting in case of quality control is to determine the cause and effect relationship and measure and control the project activity to make it conform to quality plan standards. Quality Assurance is concerned with process being stable and defects being prevented, while Quality Control is concerned with detecting the defects and repair of defective project work.

Inputs

The nature of the process being to assure that project work under execution conforms to Quality Plan. Most of the outputs of the Plan Quality process are inputs for this process. These inputs are:
Quality Management Plan, Process Improvement Plan, Quality Checklists, and *Quality Metrics. The Work Performance Data*, from test and inspection results and cost and schedule status reports, provides the actual performance data. The comparison of the work performance with the quality plan and quality metrics gives the quality assurance data.

Tools and Techniques

Most of the tools and techniques used for Plan Quality and Perform Quality Control process are applicable. One important additional tool, Quality Audits, is described below.

Quality Audits – Quality Audit is a systematic independent and documented process for obtaining evidence and evaluating it to determine as to what extent the project activities comply with the policies, procedures and process steps followed in the organization. The degree of independence depends on the real purpose of the Quality Audit; it could be an outside independent agency or an independent authority unit from the same organization.

Outputs

Process Documentation – The reports confirming that proper policies and procedures have been used for building in the quality are the main output.

Change Requests – They are originated to prevent defects or request for rework or repair of defective works are other outputs.

Quality Audit Reports – They have more credibility and are better relied on as instruments for quality assurance.

Updates in Organizational Process Assets – Lessons learned during application of the process are useful in updating the organizational process assets.

3. CONTROL QUALITY (A PROCESS IN THE MONITORING & CONTROLLING GROUP)

Control Quality is the process of monitoring and recording results of executing the quality activities to assess performance and recommend necessary changes.   (PMBOK® Guide, 5th Edition)

Essentially, the process includes activities in monitoring specific project performance and comparing it with quality standard, laid down to check if the work complies with it. While the nature of quality assurance process is merely collecting the information concerning the quality and to have documentary evidence of having followed all procedures necessary to maintain quality. Control quality process is more actively involved in carrying out controlled actions for achieving quality – viz., not only monitoring and recording the results of quality activities for assessing the performance but also recommend corrective actions to bring the quality on track. The project team involved with quality control activities should be able to distinguish between the following terms.

Prevention and Inspection – Building the quality in the product by doing the right thing the first time is prevention of defective quality product and it is the preferred mode of quality control. Removing the defectives from reaching the customer by inspection is a less-preferred mode of quality control, but it is helpful to an extent that byt preventing the defective product reaching the customer or clients it helps to maintain the reputation of the brand equity.

Attribute sampling and variables sampling – The assessment of quality based on selection of a representative sample of the product from the population and their test results is a cost-effective way of keeping a check on quality of products. The success of the acceptance sampling for quality control depends on the homogeneity of the population and the unbiased selection of the sample selected for test. There are two techniques in applying sampling test technique. In attribute sampling, the samples are assessed for either meeting or not meeting the standard — like 'Go-Not-Go' Gauge for acceptance. A continuous scale for the degree of conformance of the products in the selected sample to relevant quality standard is used for variable sampling.

Tolerance and Control Limits – Tolerance is based on acceptability of the work result and is independent of the natural process variations; if the tolerance is stricter than the natural process variation limits, the inspection is used to weed out unacceptable specimens. Control Limits indicate the limits based on the variations, which would occur in the process naturally. In a statistical process control, the standard deviation calculated from the measurements of the randomly occurring variations is used for setting the control limits. The Upper Control Limit (UCL) is set at mean plus 3 standard deviations and Lower Control Limit (LCL) is set at mean minus 3 standard deviations. When the process is stable and in control, 99.73 % of the population is expected to fall within the UCL and LCL.)

Inputs

The Quality Management Plan (One of the component plans of Project Management Plan), *Quality Metrics* and *Quality Checklists* are one set of inputs and serve to provide the quality standards for comparison. *Work Performance Data*, obtained by inspection and testing, reflect the actual results achieved. Comparing the planned versus actual performance for technical attributes, schedule and cost and metrics provide another set of inputs.

In addition to these obvious logical inputs, *quality related clauses in the contracts* or agreement, impact on quality of *approved change requests* and a fresh look at the acceptability criteria of *deliverables* are other inputs for the process mentioned in the PMBOK® Guide.

Tools and Techniques

The primary tools for Control Quality process are the *seven basic quality tools* summarized by Ishikava (sometimes referred to as 7QC) and discussed in details during discussion of inputs for Plan Quality Management Process.

Two more techniques for improving quality rely not just on building the quality into the product, but on preventing the defective project work to reach the customer. They are *inspection* and *statistical sampling* variation of the technique for inspection, which have been briefly discussed above.

Outputs

The outputs of this process are *quality control measurements* (documented data of test results), *validated deliverables* (from documented tests and accompanying analysis), and *organizational process assets* (Up-dated checklists, improved quality metrics and improved processes – with preventive and defects corrective procedures).

CASE 14.1

Maximum Megahertz Project

Olaf Gundersen, the CEO of Wireless Telecom Company, is in a quandary. Last year he accepted the Maximum Megahertz Project suggested by six up-and-coming young R&D corporate stars. Although Olaf did not truly understand the technical importance of the project, the creators of the project needed only $600,000, so it seemed like a good risk. Now the group is asking for $800,000 more and a six-month extension on a project that is already four months behind. However, the team feels confident they can turn things around. The project manager and project team feel that if they hang in there a little longer they will be able to overcome the roadblocks they are encountering—especially those that reduce power, increase speed, and use a new technology battery. Other managers familiar with the project hint that the power pack problem might be solved, but "the battery problem will never be solved." Olaf believes he is locked into this project; his gut feeling tells him the project will never materialize, and he should get out. John, his human resource manager, suggested bringing in a consultant to axe the project.

Olaf decided to call his friend Dawn O'Connor, the CEO of an accounting software company. He asked her, "What do you do when project costs and deadlines escalate drastically? How do you handle doubtful projects?" Her response was, "Let another project manager look at the project. Ask: 'If you took over this project tomorrow, could you achieve the required results, given the extended time and additional money?' If the answer is no, I call my top management team together and have them review the doubtful project in relation to other projects in our project portfolio." Olaf feels this is good advice.

Unfortunately, the Maximum Megahertz Project is not an isolated example. Over the last five years there have been three projects that were never completed. "We just seemed to pour more money into them, even though we had a pretty good idea the projects were dying. The cost of those projects was high; those resources could have been better used on other projects." Olaf wonders, "Do we ever learn from our mistakes? How can we develop a process that catches errant projects early? More importantly, how do we ease a project manager and team off an errant project without embarrassment?" Olaf certainly does not want to lose the six bright stars on the Maximum Megahertz Project.

Olaf is contemplating how his growing telecommunications company should deal with the problem of identifying projects that should be terminated early, how to allow good managers to make mistakes without public embarrassment, and how they all can learn from their mistakes.

Give Olaf a plan of action for the future that attacks the problem. Be specific and provide examples that relate to Wireless Telecom Company.

CASE 14.2

At the Close of the Jharkhand Project
(An Overview of Issues at the Project Closing Phase)

Abstract

Bringing the project to an orderly close is a very important part of project management. "Close a Project" is often crucial and a very significant part of project integration management, but rarely, it receives from the project manager or the project team the kind of attention it deserves. The case describes the issues faced by the project manager at the closing phase of a project.

CASE TEXT

Ajay sat leaning in front of the computer in his makeshift project construction site office in a remote town in Jharkhand holding in his hand a letter. The letter was from his home. His wife Smita's complaint was understandable: "It is over two months that you wrote that the plant is erected; the trial runs have been started and shortly you would be returning home. So, what is holding you up till now?"

"Yes, what is holding me up now here in this place in the middle of no-where?", he wondered and fell into a sort of trance dreaming of reuniting with the family – Smita and daughter Nidhi. Nidhi was going to be one year old next month. The last time he saw her six months back, she had just learnt to sit up for a few seconds before rolling over. Smita wrote that she could now stand up with the support of a chair and kept on prattling all day and making meaningless noises. Smita wrote, "she has become very possessive and demanding and though she cannot utter a word she makes it clear that she wants to sit in my lap (pointing at the lap and making a sound which Smita interpreted as 'Godi mein')". Ajay reached in his daydream his Borivali flat and was just getting ready to talk to Smita and Nidhi.

But he was not lucky to remain in this trance for long. His assistant knocked and said, "Sir, all seventeen items in the punch-list for civil construction are over. They have handed over another list with eight items. They are all very minor – really silly – issues, but . . ." There was no need to complete; both Ajay and his assistant Nilesh knew what it meant – they would have to slog over those "silly issues" here for another four days at least.

"We have to work out the rate for new item in the piping contractor's bill and certify." Sudhir mentioned in the passing as he put two files with contractor's measurements and certification papers on his desk; he left as hurriedly as he had come. Ajay picked up the files and got up to put them with the pile of other pending work. Sudhir had become very impatient and restless – now that the main project work was over. He was offered another assignment in a new and challenging project at one notch higher position and he was very impatient to leave this site and make a new beginning elsewhere. But why Sudhir alone? His entire team had now become very impatient and everybody had lost interest in whatever loose ends of the project needed to be tied. Everybody wanted to leave the site and make a new start somewhere else.

He just sat there. He was dead tired. Without any real thought, he picked up the letter from home to read it once again – the fifth time to be precise. But Nilesh once again entered. This time he had a slip of the fax message from the head office – fax from Director of Projects, Sanjay Saha. It was marked "Most Urgent". Sanjay informed Ajay that based on the industry news of our success in this Jharkhand project; the company was likely to land a very lucrative similar project. Sanjay wanted Ajay to summarize the highlights of the just completed project and the key issues which should be kept in mind while bidding for and planning this new project. "How can I make Smita understand what is holding me up here…?" muttered Ajay to himself while pulling out a file from the drawer to start the "most urgent" assignment.

Points for Discussion

From the case and from your own experience

- Summarize the general nature of activities in closing the project.
- Bring out the importance of recapitulating the lessons learnt during the closing phase of a project in knowledge management and innovation capability of an organization.

EPILOGUE

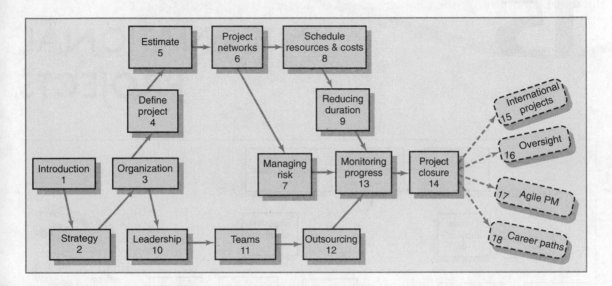

With Chapter 14 the project life cycle is complete. You have been exposed to the core elements of project management. We have consciously tried to incorporate a blend of socialcultural and process practices required to successfully manage any project. These best practices are transferable across industries. Your understanding of these chapters should enhance your ability to make a positive contribution in any project environment.

The supplemental chapters that follow expand on the core by covering international project management, oversight, and Agile methods.

- Chapter 15. Explores different international environments in which you may have to manage a project. In large high technology firms we estimate that 60–90 percent of their projects are virtual and across many cultures. If you find yourself new in this environment, the international chapter is an excellent primer on the types of conditions and issues you may encounter in an international project.

- Chapter 16. Oversight of managing projects is growing and evolving. Depending on the degree of oversight, oversight will set the operating environment in which you manage your project.

- Chapter 17. Agile methodology is used in complex projects (e.g., software and new innovation products) where the final design requirements are not known and evolve as the project is implemented. The methodology breaks requirements into small functional pieces that allow rapid response to change. Agile embraces flexibility, change, small teams, and owner involvement.

Familiarity and understanding these different operating environments should give you confidence to enter and manage your project. We encourage you to read these chapters to increase your overall understanding of project management.

Chapter 18 presents thoughts on career paths. You may find them useful as you consider your future.

15

INTERNATIONAL PROJECTS

> *The principal benefit of living abroad is that it enables us to get glimpses of ourselves as others see us and to realize that others' views are more accurate than ours. Progress begins with grasping the truth about ourselves, however unpleasant it may be.*
>
> —*Russel Ackoff, The Wharton School, University of Pennsylvania*

Projects are frequently classified as domestic, overseas, foreign, or global. A domestic project is one performed in its native country for a resident firm (a construction firm building a bridge in its state). An overseas project is one executed in a foreign country for a native firm (a Swedish company building a truck factory in the United States for their native company). A foreign project is executed in a foreign country for a foreign firm (a U.S. firm developing an information system in Malaysia for Malaysian banks). A global project consists of teams formed from professionals spanning multiple countries, continents, and cultures with their work integrated for the entire enterprise (e.g., multinational enterprise developing a global distribution system). Global teams are a crisscross of functions, work locale, markets, culture, and products. Today, these distinctions become blurred as the world economy and organizations become more integrated.

This chapter targets the international project manager who must resettle in a foreign environment to manage the project. The chapter also includes useful information for project professionals working overseas as well as those working on virtual projects involving colleagues from different countries.

There is no generally accepted framework or road map for project managers given international assignments. These project managers typically face a difficult set of problems—for example, absence from home, friends, and sometimes family; personal risks; missed career opportunities; foreign language, culture, and laws; adverse conditions. Of course there are positives—for example, increased income, increased responsibilities, career opportunities, foreign travel, new lifetime friends. How the international project manager adapts and approaches problems encountered in the host country often determines the success or failure of a project.

This chapter focuses on four major issues surrounding the management of international projects. First, major environmental factors that impact project selection and implementation are briefly highlighted. Second, an example of how organizations decide where to expand globally is provided. Third, the challenge of working in a strange and foreign culture is addressed. Finally, how companies select and train professionals for international projects is discussed. Although by no means comprehensive, this chapter attempts to provide a solid understanding of the major issues and challenges confronting the international project manager.

ENVIRONMENTAL FACTORS

The major challenge international project managers face is the reality that what works at home may not work in a foreign environment. Too often project managers impose practices, assumed to be superior, from their home country on host-country nationals without questioning applicability to the new environment. Although there are similarities between domestic and international projects, it is a fact that good management practices vary across nations and cultures. It is these differences that can turn an international project into a nightmare. If potential international project managers have a keen awareness of differences in the host country's environment from their own domestic environment, dangers and obstacles of the global project can be reduced or avoided. There are several basic factors in the host country's environment that may alter how projects will be implemented: legal/political, security, geographical, economic, infrastructure, and culture (see Figure 15.1).

Legal/Political

Expatriate project managers should operate within the laws and regulations of the host country. Political stability and local laws strongly influence how projects will be implemented. Typically, these laws favor protection of local workers, suppliers, and environment. For example, how much

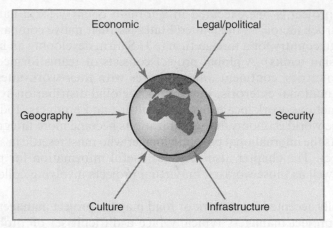

FIGURE 15.1 *Environmental Factors Affecting International Projects*

control will be imposed from government agencies? What is the attitude of federal and state bureaucracies toward regulations and approval policies that can cause project delays? How much government interference or support can one expect? For example, some governments interpret regulations arbitrarily, depending upon personal interests.

The constraints imposed by national and local laws need to be identified and adhered to. Are local ecological laws restrictive? Will manufacturing a new product in a computer chip plant require exporting toxic waste materials? What are the pollution standards? How will labor laws affect the use of indigenous workers to complete the project? Given laws that affect business vary widely across countries, qualified legal assistance is essential.

Government corruption is a very real part of international business. In China various forms of obligatory "profit sharing" with city officials in the Hainan province have been reported. Employment of relatives, donations, and other "favors" are an expected cost of doing business in that region. Likewise, *Bloomberg BusinessWeek* reported that in Russia the threat of being targeted for abuse by government officials—sometimes operating in league with Russian businesses—is the primary reason that country has attracted less than one-fifth of the foreign investment in Brazil (Cahill, 2010).

Political stability is another key factor in deciding to implement a project in a foreign country. What are the chances that there will be a change in the party in power during the project? Are the tax provisions and government regulations stable or subject to change with the winds of political change? How are laws made, and what is the past record of fairness? How are labor unions treated in the political realm? Does labor unrest exist? Is there a chance for a coup d'état? Contingency plans need to be established to respond to emergencies.

Security

International terrorism is a fact of life in today's world. Tim Daniel, chief operating officer of International SOS Assistance, Inc., reported that the number of his firm's clients doubled after September 11th. SOS is a security firm that specializes in evacuating expatriates from dangerous situations around the world. The company cites PricewaterhouseCoopers, Nortel Networks Corp., and Citigroup among its clients (Scown, 1993).

While the 9/11 attacks magnified the fact that Americans are vulnerable to terrorism at home, they also heightened security concerns for working abroad. For example, after September 11th, several American firms canceled or scaled back projects in potential hotspots such as Somalia and the Philippines. Others reported increased pressures from expatriates who wanted to return home with their families. On May 7, 2009, the Nobel Peace Prize-winning relief agency *Médecins Sans Frontières* (Doctors Without Borders) reduced emergency projects in northwest Pakistan due to clashes between government forces and Taliban fighters.[1]

Crime is another factor. The growing presence of the Russian Mafia has discouraged many foreign firms from setting up operations in the former Soviet Union. Kidnapping of American professionals is also a very real threat in many parts of the world.

Security nationally involves the capacity of a country's military and police forces to prevent and respond to attacks. In many foreign countries, American firms will have to augment the countries' security system. For example, it is common practice to hire tribal bodyguards in such places as Angola and Uzbekistan.

Another real cost associated with international terrorism is the ease of commerce across borders. Heightened security measures have created border congestions that have expanded the time and cost of moving personnel, materials, and equipment across countries. These constraints need to be factored into the budget and schedule of projects.

Risk management is always a vital part of project management. It plays an even bigger role in managing projects overseas. For example, Strohl Systems Group, a global leader in recovery-planning software and services, includes the following among the questions it uses to evaluate vulnerability to terrorism: Have you included possible terrorist targets (facilities and personnel) in your hazard and vulnerability analysis? Have you conducted a counterterrorism exercise complete with law enforcement, fire, medical, and emergency management participation? What should your organization's policy be on negotiating with a person threatening a terrorist act?[2]

Managing projects in a dangerous world is a tough assignment. Security precautions are major cost considerations not only in dollars and cents, but also in the psychological well-being of personnel sent abroad. Effective risk management is critical to success.

Geography

One factor that is often underestimated until project personnel actually arrive at a foreign destination is the geography of the country. Imagine what it is like to deplane from a modern aircraft and encounter the 105- degree heat and 90 percent humidity of Jakarta, Indonesia, or three feet of fresh snow and −22 degree temperatures in Kokkla, Finland. Whether it is the wind, the rain, the heat, the jungle, or the desert, more than one project manager has asserted that their greatest challenge was overcoming the "elements." Mother Nature cannot be ignored.

The planning and implementation of a project must take into account the impact the country's geography will have on the project. For example, a salvage operation off the coast of Greenland can only be scheduled one month out of the year because the waterway is frozen over during the remainder of the year. Construction projects in Southeast Asia have to accommodate the monsoon season when rainfall can be as high as 50 inches per month. Geography does not just affect outdoor projects. It can have an indirect effect on "indoor" projects. For example, one information systems

[1] www.doctorswithoutborders.org/press/release, June 2009.

[2] Contingency Planning and Management.com, "Strohl Systems Offers Terrorism Readiness Questionnaire," September 24, 2001.

specialist reported that his performance on a project in northern Sweden declined due to sleep deprivation. He attributed his problems to the 20 hours of daylight this part of the world experiences during summer months. Finally, extreme weather conditions can make extraordinary demands on equipment. Projects can grind to a halt because of equipment breakdown under the brunt of the elements. Working under extreme conditions typically requires special equipment, which increases the costs and complexity of the project.

Before beginning a project in a foreign land, project planners and managers need to study carefully the unique characteristics of the geography of that country. They need to factor into project plans and schedules such items as climate, seasons, altitude, and natural geographical obstacles. See the Snapshot from Practice: The Filming of *Apocalypse Now* for an example of a poorly planned endeavor in the Philippines.

Economic

Basic economic factors in foreign countries and regions influence choices of site selection and project success. The gross domestic product (GDP) of a country suggests the level of development of a country. A faltering economy may indicate fewer sources of capital funding. Changes in

---

SNAPSHOT FROM PRACTICE
The Filming of *Apocalypse Now**

In February 1976, Francis Ford Coppola took his Hollywood film crew to the Philippines to shoot *Apocalypse Now,* a film adaptation of Joseph Conrad's *Heart of Darkness* within the context of the Vietnam conflict. The Philippines was chosen because the terrain was similar to Vietnam's, and the government was willing to rent its helicopter force for the movie. At the time, the U.S. military was unwilling to cooperate on a film about Vietnam. An additional advantage was cheap labor. Coppola was able to hire more than 300 laborers at $1 to $3 per day to construct elaborate production sets, including an impressive Cambodian temple. *Apocalypse Now* was scheduled for 16 weeks of shooting at a budget of $12 to $14 million.

Months earlier, George Lucas, of *Star Wars* fame, warned Coppola against filming the movie in the Philippines. He said, "It's one thing to go over there for three weeks with five people and scrounge some footage with the Filipino Army, but if you go over there with a big Hollywood production, the longer you stay the more in danger you are of getting sucked into the swamp." His words turned out to be prophetic.

A civil war was going on between government forces and communist rebels. Shooting was repeatedly interrupted because the Philippine military ordered their helicopter pilots to leave the set and fly to the mountains to fight the rebels.

In May 1976, a typhoon struck the Philippine Islands, destroying most of the movie sets. The film team was forced to shut down production and returned to the United States for two months.

The lead character was played by Martin Sheen, who suffered a serious heart attack under the stress and heat of the filming and had to return to the United States. Coppola scrambled to film the scenes that did not require Sheen, but eventually production came to a standstill until Sheen's return nine weeks later.

The entire project proved to be a traumatic experience for Coppola, who had enjoyed Academy Award success with his previous *Godfather* movies. "There were times when I thought I was going to die, literally, from the inability to move the problems I had. I would go to bed at four in the morning in a cold sweat."

Film production ended in May 1977 after more than 200 days of shooting. The final cost was about $30 million. To date, *Apocalypse Now* has earned more than $150 million throughout the world.

* *Hearts of Darkness: A Filmmaker's Apocalypse* (Paramount Pictures, 1991).

protectionist strategies of a host country, such as import quotas and tariffs, can quickly alter the viability of projects. Other factors such as balance of payments, taxation, labor laws, safety regulations, and market size can influence project choices and operations.

Skills, educational level, and labor supply prevalent in a host country can determine the choice of a project site. Is project selection driven by low wage levels or availability of technically skilled talent? For example, you can hire three computer programmers in Ukraine for the price of one programmer in the United States. Conversely, many high-tech companies are willing to endure the additional expense of setting up joint projects in Switzerland and Germany to take advantage of their engineering prowess.

Financial exposure is a significant risk for many international projects. Let's look first at the potential impact of currency fluctuations on project success. For example, a U.S. contractor agrees to build a customized product for a German client. The product will be built in the United States. The contractor estimates that the project will cost $925,000, and, in order to earn a nice profit, prices the project at $1,000,000. To accommodate the German buyer the price is converted to euros. Suppose at the time of the contract, the exchange rate is $1.15 per Euro, and the price specified in the contract is €869,566.

Ten months later the project is completed as expected, with work costing the estimated $925,000 and the customer pays the agreed upon price of €869,566. However the exchange rate has changed; it is now $1.05 per Euro. That being the case, the payment equates to €869,566 × 1.05 = $913,044. Instead of reaping a nice profit the contractor suffers a $(913,044 − 925,000) = $−11,956 loss!

A company can protect against adverse currency fluctuations in a number of related ways. First, they can *hedge* against this risk by having all parties agree to finalize the deal and make payments at a specified future date. Finance people call this a *forward exchange* or *contract*. Second, they can stipulate in the contract certain conditions based on exchange rates to insure their profit margin. Finally, many multinational companies who do business in the client country avoid currency exchange and simply use local currency to manage operations in that country. Financiers refer to this as a *natural hedge* (Moffet et al., 2012).

Inflation is another significant risk. One of the greatest strengths of the U.S. economy is its relatively low inflation rate (below 3 percent from 1990–2012). Other countries, especially underdeveloped countries, do not enjoy such stability. Rapid inflation can strike at any time and have profound impact on project costs and profits. For example, a European contractor successfully wins the bid to build a bridge for the Tanzanian government in East Africa. Work started in 2010 and will be completed by the end of 2011. In 2010 the Tanzanian inflation ratio was less than 6 percent with an average inflation rate of 6.7 over the past decade. The contractor used what she considered a conservative inflation rate of 9 percent when estimating the costs of the project at 1,800,000 schillings (Tanzanian currency). In order to win the bid and enjoy a solid profit the agreed upon price is 2,000,000 schillings.

Early in 2011 Tanzania experiences a sporadic rainfall which, coupled with increased oil prices, causes the inflation rate to jump to over 20 percent! Suddenly costs of certain elements of the project increase dramatically and instead of garnering a nice profit the contractor barely breaks even. Companies can protect against inflation by tying costs to a strong currency such as the U.S. dollar, British pound, or euro and/or negotiating cost-plus contracts (see Chapter 12 Appendix) with the client.

Bartering is a form of compensation that is still used by some countries and organizations. For example, one project in Africa was paid in goat skins. The goat skins were eventually sold to an Italian manufacturer of gloves. Another project along the Caspian Sea was paid for in oil. There is a small group of firms that specialize in bartering for project contractors. These intermediaries charge a commission to sell the bartered goods (e.g., oil, diamonds, wheat) for the contractor. However, dealing with commodities can be a risky enterprise.

Infrastructure

Infrastructure refers to a country or community's ability to provide the services required for a project. Infrastructure needs for a project could be communication, transportation, power, technology, and education systems. Power outages are common in many parts of the world. For example, India's burgeoning economy came to a halt during the 2012 summer when over 670 million people were without power for more than two days. If reliable power is not sufficient, other alternatives need to be considered. For example, construction firms often rely on heavy diesel generators as backups on their projects. Software projects across borders are common today; however, they depend on reliable telecommunication networks. These networks simplify and facilitate project coordination and management among project stakeholders in different locations. If the project depends on a high ratio of vendor suppliers, good roads, and other transportation modes such as air and seaports, a good infrastructure will be imperative.

An example of a project that failed to take into account the needs and infrastructure of the host nation involved a U.S. company that was awarded the contract for building a hospital in an African nation. The local African officials wanted a "low-tech" health care facility that would take local traditions into consideration. Because their relatives generally accompanied patients, space had to be provided for them, too. Electricity was not reliably supplied, and it was doubtful whether well-educated doctors would want to spend careers away from the city. Therefore, the locals wanted a hospital for basic care with minimum technology. The construction company doing the building, on the other hand, had a preconceived notion of what a hospital should be and was not going to be accused of building a second-rate facility. It built a modern hospital that could have stood in any U.S. city. The building was completed; however, even after several years it was not used because the electricity was not sufficient, the air-conditioning could not be used, and doctors refused to live in the rural area (Adler and Gunderson, 2007).

Organizations need to consider the needs of the families of personnel they send overseas. Will the facilities and living conditions for the expatriate families place an undue hardship on families? Will schooling for children be available? The welfare and comfort of expatriate families play an important role in retaining good project managers and promoting their peak performance.

Culture

Visiting project managers must accept and respect the customs, values, philosophies, and social standards of their host country. Global managers recognize that if the customs and social cultural dimensions of the host country are not accommodated, projects will not succeed. Too many project audits and final reports of international projects reflect challenges and problems linked to cultural differences.

For most project managers, the biggest difference in managing an international project is operating in a national culture where things are done differently. For example, most developed nations use the same project management techniques (CPM, risk analysis, trade-off analysis). However, how activity work is performed can be very different in the host country.

Will English be the operating language, or will the project manager need to be fluent in the foreign language? Will translation services be available and sufficient? Communication problems—because of language differences—often become a major problem in carrying out even simple tasks. Although the use of translators can help tremendously, their use does not solve the communication problem completely because something is lost in translation. For example, consider the disastrous consequences of differences in interpretations and expectations between the Brazilians and Americans highlighted in the Snapshot from Practice: River of Doubt.

After his crushing election defeat in 1912 as a third-party candidate, former president Theodore ("Teddy") Roosevelt set his sights on a grand adventure, the first descent of an unmapped rapids-choked tributary of the Amazon aptly titled the "River of Doubt." Together with Brazil's most famous explorer, Candido Mariano da Silva Rondon, Roosevelt accomplished a feat that belongs in the annals of great expeditions.

Along the way, Roosevelt and his men faced an unbelievable series of hardships, losing their canoes and supplies to crushing whitewater rapids, and enduring starvation, Indian attacks, disease, drowning, and even murder within their ranks. Candice Millard brings alive these extraordinary events in her nonfiction thriller *The River of Doubt*. While her account details the ill-fated journey it also reveals insights into international project management as it describes the collaboration between the American and Brazilian cohorts. While each party ultimately earned the respect and admiration of the other, friction between the two parties simmered from the outset.

One source of consternation was the amount of supplies and luggage that the Americans required for the journey. Warned that the luggage requirements of the former president and his party would be extensive, the Brazilian commodore Rondon ordered 110 mules and 17 pack oxen to be used for the expedition's overland journey across

© Fotomas/Topham/The Image Works

the Brazilian highland to the great river. Surely, he felt, this would be more than necessary for such a trip.

The Brazilians were astounded by the sheer volume of baggage that was unloaded from Roosevelt's ship, the *Vandycks*. There were mountains of crates: guns and ammunition, chairs and tables, tents and cots, equipment for collecting and preserving specimens, surveying the river, and cooking meals. An exhausted stevedore elicited a roar of laughter from the onlooking crowd when he announced, "Nothing lacking but the piano!"

Rather than risk embarrassment by telling Roosevelt that they were not prepared to take so much luggage, Rondon scrambled to find additional animals. Extra oxen and mules were located, but they were far from tame. Loaded with supplies, the oxen would buck and throw off the packs. The expedition was delayed as gauchos (South American cowboys) endeavored to "break" the animals as quickly as possible.

Within days of finally setting off across the vast highlands, Roosevelt and his men began to experience the harsh realities that were to plague the expedition. After crossing a bone-strewn graveyard of oxen and mules that had starved to death or been eaten during previous expeditions, they were stunned by the sight of unopened supply crates, all clearly marked "Roosevelt South American Expedition." The pack animals, still making their weary away across the plateau ahead of the them, had begun bucking off their heavy loads!

As the officers rode slowly past the boxes, they wondered what they were leaving behind and how precious it might become in the months ahead. Little did they know how true those fears would be.

* Candice Millard, *The River of Doubt* (New York: Doubleday), 2005.

Will religious factors influence the project? For example, religious factors touched the spouse of a Scandinavian project manager responsible for building a water desalination plant from sea water in a Middle East country. She was restricted to the living compound for families of foreign guest workers. Going outside the compound to a nearby city meant covering her head, arms, and legs and being accompanied by another woman or, preferably, a man. A physical altercation in the city concerning her clothing was traumatic for her. She left the country and returned home. Her husband requested a transfer back home three months later. The loss of the original project manager from the project required the assigned project manager to establish relationships with the project team and host country's nationals to get the project moving smoothly again.

Not only do project managers have to adapt to the culture of the host country, but often times overseas projects require working with people from different countries. For example, on a light rail project in the Philippines, an American firm was hired to oversee the interests of local real estate companies who were funding the project. The American project manager had to work with Czech representatives who were providing the rail equipment, Japanese engineers responsible for building the rail, Australian bankers who were providing additional financing, an Indian firm that were the principal architects, as well as the native Filipinos.

Of all the factors, working within a multicultural environment is most often the greatest challenge for project managers. It will be dealt with in detail later in this chapter.

PROJECT SITE SELECTION

As the project manager studies the factors contributing to site selection, he will see that inherent in all of these factors is the risk level senior management and directors are willing to accept for the potential rewards of a successful international project. One approach for the project manager to digest, clarify, and understand the factors leading to the selection of a specific project is to use a risk matrix similar to those found in Chapter 7. The major difference lies in the selection of the risk factors for different project sites.

Figure 15.2 presents a truncated matrix for project site selection of the construction of a laser printer factory in Singapore, India, or Ireland. In this example, political stability, worker skill and

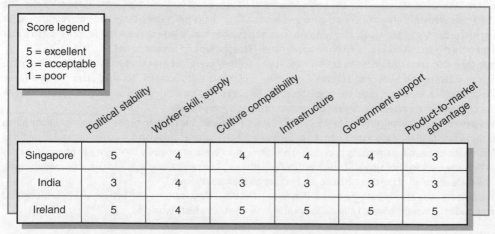

	Political stability	Worker skill, supply	Culture compatibility	Infrastructure	Government support	Product-to-market advantage
Singapore	5	4	4	4	4	3
India	3	4	3	3	3	3
Ireland	5	4	5	5	5	5

Score legend

5 = excellent
3 = acceptable
1 = poor

FIGURE 15.2   *Assessment Matrix Project Site Selection*

supply, culture compatibility, infrastructure, government support, and product-to-market advantage were the major assessment factors. Each project site is compared against each factor. Figure 15.3 depicts a further breakdown of the infrastructure evaluation factor. In this example, transportation, educated workforce, utilities, telecommunications, and vendor suppliers are considered important to evaluating the infrastructure for each site. The scores given in Figure 15.3 are used to assign values to the infrastructure factor of the assessment matrix, Figure 15.2. In this project, Ireland was the choice. Clearly, Singapore and Ireland were very close in terms of infrastructure and several other factors. However, the major assessment factor of using Ireland to access the EEC (product-to-market advantage) turned the decision.

Score legend

5 = excellent
3 = acceptable
1 = poor

	Transportation	Educated workforce	Utilities	Telecommunications	Vendor suppliers
Singapore	5	4	5	5	4
India	3	4	4	4	2
Ireland	5	4	5	5	5

FIGURE 15.3 *Evaluation Matrix Breakdown for Infrastructure*

Given the macro economic factors, the firm's strategic posture toward global projects, and the major considerations for selecting this project, it is imperative the project manager quickly become sensitized to the foreign cultural factors that can spell project success or failure.

CROSS-CULTURAL CONSIDERATIONS: A CLOSER LOOK

The concept of culture was introduced in Chapter 3 as referring to the unique personality of a particular firm. More specifically, culture was defined as a system of shared norms, beliefs, values, and customs that bind people together, creating shared meaning and a unique identity. *Culture* is a concept created for descriptive purposes and depends on the group that is the focus of attention. For example, within a global context culture can refer to certain regions (i.e., Europeans, Arabs), to specific nations (i.e., French, Thai), or to certain ethnic or religious groups (i.e., Kurds, African-Americans). This chapter looks at national cultures; we freely recognize that many cultural characteristics are borderless and that there is considerable variation within any one country. Still, national cultures provide a useful anchor for understanding different habits, customs, and values around the world.

Right or wrong, Americans have a reputation for not being able to work effectively in foreign cultures. (When we use the term "American," we are referring to people from the United States; we apologize to our friends in Canada and Central and South America.) In the 1960s, the term "Ugly

American" encapsulated the apparent indifference of Americans to native cultures when working or traveling abroad. Americans are often criticized for being parochial; that is, they view the world solely through their own eyes and perspectives. People with a parochial perspective do not recognize that other people have different ways of living and working effectively. American parochial attitudes probably reflect the huge domestic market of the United States, the geographic isolation of the United States, and the reality that English is becoming the international business language in many parts of the world.

It is important that Americans working on international projects anticipate cultural differences. Take, for example, a project manager from a large North American construction company who was given responsibility to select a site for the design and construction of a large fish-processing plant in a West African country. The manager assessed potential sites according to the availability of reliable power, closeness to transportation, nearness to the river for access of fishing boats from the Atlantic Ocean, proximity to main markets, and availability of housing and people for employment. After evaluating alternative sites, the project manager chose the optimum location. Just prior to requesting bids from local contractors for some of the site preparation, the manager discovered, in talking to the contractors, that the site was located on ground considered sacred by the local people, who believed this site was the place where their gods resided. None of the local people upon whom the project manager was depending for staff would ever consider working there! The project manager quickly revised his choice and relocated the site. In this case, he was lucky that the cultural gaffe was discovered prior to construction. Too often these errors are realized only after a project is completed.[3]

Some argue that Americans have become less parochial. International travel, immigration, movies, and the popularity of such international events as the Olympics have made more Americans sensitive to cultural differences. While Americans may be more worldly, there is still a tendency for them to believe that American cultural values and ways of doing things are superior to all others. This ethnocentric perspective is reflected in wanting to conduct business only on their terms and stereotyping other countries as lazy, corrupt, or inefficient. Americans need to make a serious effort to appreciate other ways of approaching work and problems in other countries.

Finally, American project managers have earned a reputation abroad for being very good at understanding technology but not good at understanding people. As one Indonesian engineer put it, "Americans are great at solving technical problems, but they tend to ignore the people factor." For example, Americans tend to underestimate the importance that relationship building plays in conducting business in other countries. Americans have a tendency to want to get down to work and let friendships evolve in the course of their work. In most other cultures just the opposite is true. Before a foreigner works with you, he wants to get to know you as a person. Trust is not established by credentials but rather evolves from personal interaction. Business deals often require a lengthy and elaborate courtship (Arms and Lucas, 1978; Chen and Miller, 2010). For example, it may take five to eight meetings before Arab managers are even willing to discuss business details.

Adjustments

Two of the biggest adjustments Americans typically have to make in working abroad are adapting to the general pace of life and the punctuality of people. In America "time is money," and a

---

[3] This incident was cited in H. W. Lane and J. J. DiStefano, *International Project Management,* 2nd ed. (Boston: PWS-Kent, 1992), p. 27.

premium is placed on working quickly. Other cultures do not share Americans' sense of urgency and are accustomed to a much slower pace of life. They can't understand why Americans are always in such a hurry. Punctuality varies across cultures. For example, Americans will generally tolerate someone being 5 to 10 minutes late. In contrast, among Peruvians, the period before an apology or explanation for being late is expected might be 45 minutes to an hour!

While working on multicultural projects, managers sometimes encounter ethical dilemmas that are culturally bound. For example, the 1999 Olympic site selection scandal featured the sordid details of committee members peddling their votes for a wide range of gifts (i.e., university scholarships for their children, extravagant trips). In many societies such "bribes" or "tributes" are expected and the only way to conduct meaningful business. Moreover, many cultures will not grant a female project manager the same respect they will a male project manager. Should U.S. management increase project risk or violate its own sex-discrimination policy?

These cultural differences are just the tip of the iceberg. There are numerous "How to Do Business in . . ." books written by people who have traveled and worked abroad. Although these books may lack rigor, they typically do a good job of identifying local customs and common mistakes made by outsiders. On the other hand, anthropologists have made significant contributions to our understanding of why and how the cultures of societies are different (see the accompanying Research Highlights). Students of international project management are encouraged to study these works to gain a deeper understanding of the root causes of cultural diversity.

So what can be said to prepare people to work on international projects? The world is too diverse to do justice in one chapter to all the cultural variations managers are likely to encounter when working on international projects. Instead, a sample of some of these differences will be highlighted by discussing working on projects in four different countries: Mexico, France, Saudi Arabia, and China. We apologize to our readers outside the United States because briefings are presented from the viewpoint of a U.S. project manager working in these countries. Still, in an effort not to be too ethnocentric, we present a fifth scenario for foreign project managers assigned to working in the United States. Although by no means exhaustive, these briefings provide a taste of what it is like to work in and with people from these countries.

Working in Mexico

America developed historically in an environment where it was important for strangers to be able to get along, interact, and do business. On the American frontier almost everyone was a stranger, and people had to both cooperate and keep their distance. The New England Yankee sentiment that "Good fences make good neighbors" expresses this American cultural value well. Conversely, Mexico developed historically in an environment where the only people to trust were family and close friends—and by extension, people who were known to those whom you knew well. As a consequence, personal relationships dominate all aspects of Mexican business. While Americans are generally taught not to do business with friends, Mexicans and other Latin Americans are taught to do business with no one but friends.

The significance of personal relationships has created a *compadre* system in which Mexicans are obligated to give preference to relatives and friends when hiring, contracting, procuring, and sharing business opportunities. North Americans often complain that such practices contribute to inefficiency in Mexican firms. While this may or may not be the case, efficiency is prized by Americans, while Mexicans place a higher value on friendship.

Research Highlight

CROSS-CULTURAL ORIENTATIONS*

Anthropologists Kluckhohn and Strodtbeck assert that cultural variations reflect how different societies have responded to common issues or problems throughout time (see Figure 15.4). Five of the issues featured in their comparative framework are discussed here.

- *Relationship to nature*—This issue reflects how people relate to the natural world around them and to the supernatural. Should people dominate their environment, live in harmony with it, or be subjugated to it? North Americans generally strive to harness nature's forces and change them as they need. Other societies, as in India, strive to live in harmony with nature. Still other societies see themselves at the mercy of physical forces and/or subject to the will of a supreme being. Life in this context is viewed as predetermined, preordained, or an exercise in chance.

- *Time orientation*—Does the culture focus on the past, present, or future? For example, many European countries focus on the past and emphasize maintaining tradition. North Americans, on the other hand, are less concerned with tradition and tend to focus on the present and near future. Paradoxically, Japanese society, while rich with tradition, has a much longer time horizon.

- *Activity orientation*—This issue refers to a desirable focus of behavior. Some cultures emphasize "being" or living in the moment.

Cultural issue	Variations		
Relationship to nature	Domination	Harmony	Subjugation
Time orientation	Past	Present	Future
Activity orientation	Being	Doing	Controlling
Nature of people	Good	Evil	Mixed
Relationships among people	Individualist	Group	Hierarchical

FIGURE 15.4 *Kluckhohn–Strodtbeck's Cross-Cultural Framework*

Note: The line indicates where the United States tends to fall along these issues.

This orientation stresses experiencing life and seeking immediate gratification. Other cultures emphasize "doing" and emphasize postponing immediate gratification for greater accomplishment. A third alternative is the "control" orientation, where people restrain their desires by detaching themselves from objects. The activity dimension affects how people approach work and leisure and the extent to which work-related concerns pervade their lives. It is reflected in the age-old question, "Do we live to work or work to live?"

- *Basic nature of people*—Does a culture view people as good, evil, or some mix of these two? In many Third World countries, people see themselves as basically honest and trustworthy. Conversely, some Mediterranean cultures have been characterized as taking a rather evil view of human nature. North Americans are somewhere in between. They see people as basically good but stay on guard so as not to be taken advantage of.

- *Relationships among people*—This issue concerns the responsibility one has for others. Americans, for instance, tend to be highly individualistic and believe everyone should take care of him- or herself. In contrast, many Asian societies emphasize concern for the group or community he or she is a member of. A third variation is hierarchical, which is similar to the group except that in these societies groups are hierarchically ranked, and membership is essentially stable over time. This is a characteristic of aristocratic societies and caste systems.

The Kluckhohn and Strodtbeck framework provides a basis for a deeper understanding of cultural differences. At the same time, they warn that not all members of a culture practice the same behavior all the time, and, as in the United States, there is likely to be considerable variation within a given culture.

* F. Kluckhohn and F. L. Strodtbeck, *Variations in Value Orientations* (Evanston, IL: Row, Peterson, 1961).

Research Highlight

HOFSTEDE FRAMEWORK*

The Hofstede framework grew from a study of 88,000 people working in IBM subsidiaries in 50 countries and 3 multicountry regions. Based on responses to a 32-item questionnaire, Dutch social scientist Geert Hofstede developed different dimensions for examining cultures:

1. Individualism versus collectivism. Identifies whether a culture holds individuals or the group responsible for each member's welfare.
2. Power distance. Describes the degree to which a culture accepts status and power differences among its members.
3. Uncertainty avoidance. Identifies a culture's willingness to accept uncertainty and ambiguity about the future.
4. Masculinity-femininity. Describes the degree to which the culture emphasizes competitive and achievement-oriented behavior or displays concerns for relationships.

Figure 15.5 shows how he ranked selected countries according to collectivism-individualism and power distance. Wealth appears to influence both factors. Power distance is correlated with income inequality in a country while individualism is correlated with national wealth (Per Capita Gross National Product). As a result high power distance and collectivism are often found together, as are low power distance and individualism. This can affect decision making on project teams. For example, while the high collectivism may lead a project team in Thailand to operate consensually, the high power distance may cause decisions to be heavily influenced by the desires of the project manager. Conversely, a similar team operating in more individualistic and low power distance such as Great Britain or America might make decisions with more open debate including challenging the preferences of the project manager.

Collectivism		Colombia, Peru, Thailand, Singapore, Mexico, Turkey, Indonesia
Individualism	Israel, Finland, Germany, Ireland, New Zealand, Canada, Great Britain, United States	Spain, South Africa, France, Italy, Belgium
	Low power distance	High power distance

FIGURE 15.5 *Sample Country Clusters on Hofstede's Dimensions of Individualism–Collectivism and Power Distance*

* G. Hofstede, *Culture's Consequences: Comparing Values, Behaviors, Institutions and Organizations Across Nations,* 2nd Edition (Thousand Oaks, CA: Sage Publications, 2001). http://www.geerthofstede.nl

Mexicans tend to perceive Americans as being "cold." They also believe that most Americans look down on them. Among the most effective things an American can do to prevent being seen as a typical *Gringo* is to take the time and effort in the beginning of a working relationship to really get to know Mexican counterparts. Because family is all-important to Mexicans, a good way for developing a personal relationship is exchanging information about each other's family. Mexicans will often gauge people's trustworthiness by the loyalty and attention they devote to their family.

The *mañana* syndrome reflects another cultural difference between Americans and Mexicans. Mexicans have a different concept of time than Americans do. Mexicans feel confined and pressured when given deadlines; they prefer open-ended schedules. They generally consider individuals to be more important than sticking to a schedule. If a friend drops in at work, most Mexicans will stop and talk, regardless of how long it takes, and even if chatting makes their work late. This sometimes contributes to the erroneous perception that Mexicans lack a work ethic. Quite the contrary; given a minimal incentive, Mexicans can be quite industrious and ambitious.

Finally, as in many other cultures, Mexicans do not share Americans' confidence that they control their own destiny. While Americans are taught, "When the going gets tough, the tough get going," Mexicans are taught, "Taking action without knowing what is expected or wanted can have dangerous consequences." Mexicans tend to be more cautious and want to spend more time discussing risks and potential problems that Americans might dismiss as improbable or irrelevant.

Other useful guidelines for working with Mexicans on projects include the following:

1. Americans tend to be impersonal and practical when making arguments; Mexicans can be very passionate and emotional when arguing. They enjoy a lively debate.
2. Where Americans tend to use meetings as the place to work things out publicly, Mexicans tend to see meetings as the place where persons with authority ratify what has been decided during informal private discussions.
3. While Mexicans can be emotional, they tend to shy away from any sort of direct confrontation or criticism. A long silence often indicates displeasure or disagreement.
4. Speech in Mexico is often indirect. People rarely say no directly but are more likely to respond by saying maybe *(quizas),* or by saying "I will think about it" or changing the subject. Yes *(si)* is more likely to mean "I understand you" than "yes."
5. Titles are extremely important in Mexico and are always used when a person is introducing him- or herself or being introduced. Pay as much attention to remembering a person's title as to remembering his or her name.

Today, with NAFTA and increased international business activity in Mexico, old traditions are disappearing. American managers report that cultural differences are less evident in northern Mexico where many multinational firms operate. Here *hora americana* (American time) rather than *hora mexicana* tends to be used when dealing with foreigners. Project managers should devote up-front effort to understanding how much older mores of Mexican culture apply to their project.[4]

Working in France

Some Americans consider the French the most difficult to work with among Europeans. This feeling probably stems from a reflection of the French culture, which is quite different from that in the United States.

In France, one's social class is very important. Social interactions are constrained by class standing, and during their lifetimes most French people do not encounter much change in social status. Unlike an American, who through hard work and success can move from the lowest economic stratum to the highest, a successful French person might, at best, climb one or two rungs up the social ladder. Additionally, the French are very status conscious and like to provide signs of this status, such as knowledge of literature and arts; a well-designed, tastefully decorated house; and a high level of education.

---

[4] Adapted from E. Kras, *Management in Two Cultures: Bridging the Gap between U.S. and Mexican Managers,* rev. ed. (Yarmouth, ME: Intercultural Press, 1995); L. W. Tuller, *An American's Guide to Doing Business in Latin America* (Avon, MA: Adams Business, 2008).

The French tend to admire or be fascinated with people who disagree with them; in contrast, Americans are more attracted to those who agree with them. As a result, the French are accustomed to conflict and, during negotiations, accept the fact that some positions are irreconcilable and must be accepted as such. Americans, on the other hand, tend to believe that conflicts can be resolved if both parties make an extra effort and are willing to compromise. Also, the French often determine a person's trustworthiness based on their first-hand, personal evaluation of the individual's character. Americans, in contrast, tend to evaluate a person's trustworthiness on the basis of past achievements and other people's evaluations.

The French are often accused of lacking an intense work ethic. For example, many French workers frown on overtime and on average they have one of the longest vacations in the world (four to five weeks annually). On the other hand, the French enjoy a reputation for productive work, a result of the French tradition of craftsmanship. This tradition places a greater premium on quality rather than on getting things accomplished quickly.

Most French organizations tend to be highly centralized with rigid structures. As a result, it usually takes longer to carry out decisions. Because this arrangement is quite different from the more decentralized organizations in the United States, many U.S. project managers find the bureaucratic red tape a source of considerable frustration.

In countries like the United States, a great deal of motivation is derived from professional accomplishments. The French do not tend to share this same view of work. While they admire American industriousness, they believe that quality of life is what really matters. As a result they attach much greater importance to leisure time, and many are unwilling to sacrifice the enjoyment of life for a dedication to project work.

Cautions to remember with the French include these:

1. The French value punctuality. It is very important to be on time for meetings and social occasions.
2. Great importance is placed on neatness and taste. When interacting with French businesspeople, pay close attention to your own professional appearance and appear cultured and sophisticated.
3. The French can be very difficult to negotiate with. Often, they ignore facts, no matter how convincing they may be. They can be quite secretive about their position. It is difficult to obtain information from them, even in support for their position. Patience is essential for negotiating with them.
4. French managers tend to see their work as an intellectual exercise. They do not share the American view of management as an interpersonally demanding exercise, where plans have to be constantly "sold" upward and downward using personal skills.
5. The French generally consider managers to be experts. They expect managers to give precise answers to work-related questions. To preserve their reputation, some French managers act as if they know the answers to questions even when they don't.[5]

[5] Adapted from R. Hallowell, D. Bowen, and C. I. Knoop, "Four Seasons Goes to Paris," *Academy of Management Executive,* 16 (4) November 2002, pp. 7–24; J. Hooker, *Working across Cultures* (Stanford, CA: Stanford Business Books, 2003); T. Morrison and W. A. Conaway, *Kiss, Bow, or Shake Hands (The Bestselling Guide to Doing Business in More than 60 Countries)*, 2nd ed. (New York: Adams Media, 2006).

Working in Saudi Arabia

Project management has a long tradition in Saudi Arabia and other Arab countries. Financed by oil money, European and American firms have contributed greatly to the modernization of Arab countries. Despite this tradition, foreigners often find it very hard to work on projects in Saudi Arabia. A number of cultural differences can be cited for this difficulty.

One is the Arabian view of time. In North America, it is common to use the cliché, "The early bird gets the worm." In Saudi Arabia, a favorite expression is, "Bukra insha Allah," which means, "Tomorrow if God wills," an expression that reflects the Saudis' approach to time. Unlike Westerners, who believe they control their own time, Arabs believe that Allah controls time. As a result, when Saudis commit themselves to a date in the future and fail to show up, there is no guilt or concern on their part because they have no control over time in the first place. In planning future events with Arabs, it pays to hold lead time to a week or less, because other factors may intervene or take precedence.

An associated cultural belief is that destiny depends more on the will of a supreme being than on the behavior of individuals. A higher power dictates the outcome of important events, so individual action is of little consequence. As a result, progress or the lack of progress on a project is considered more a question of fate than effort. This leads Saudis to rely less on detailed plans and schedules to complete projects than Americans do.

Another important cultural contrast between Saudi Arabians and Americans is emotion and logic. Saudis often act on the basis of emotion; in contrast, those in an Anglo culture are taught to act on logic. During negotiations, it is important not only to share the facts but also to make emotional appeals that demonstrate your suggestion is the right thing to do.

Saudis also make use of elaborate and ritualized forms of greetings and leave-takings. A businessperson may wait far past the assigned meeting time before being admitted to a Saudi office. Once there, the individual may find a host of others present; one-on-one meetings are rare. Moreover, during the meeting there may be continuous interruptions. Visitors arrive and begin talking to the host, and messengers may come in and go out on a regular basis. The businessperson is expected to take all this activity as perfectly normal and to remain composed and ready to continue discussions as soon as the host is prepared to do so.

Initial meetings are typically used to get to know the other party. Business-related discussions may not occur until the third or fourth meeting. Business meetings typically conclude with an offer of coffee or tea. This is a sign that the meeting is over and that future meetings, if there are to be any, should now be arranged.

Saudis attach a great deal of importance to status and rank. When meeting with them, defer to the senior person. It is also important never to criticize or berate anyone publicly. This causes the individual to lose face; the same is true for the person who makes these comments. Mutual respect is expected at all times.

Other useful guidelines for working in an Arab culture such as Saudi Arabia include the following:

1. It is important never to display feelings of superiority because this makes the other party feel inferior. No matter how well someone does something, the individual should let the action speak for itself and not brag or draw attention to himself.
2. A lot of what gets done is a result of going through administrative channels in the country. It is often difficult to sidestep a lot of this red tape, and efforts to do so can be regarded as disrespect for legal and governmental institutions.

3. Connections are extremely important in conducting business. More important people get fast service from less important people. Close relatives take absolute priority; non-relatives are kept waiting.

4. Patience is critical to the success of business negotiations. Time for deliberations should be built into all negotiations to prevent a person from giving away too much in an effort to reach a quick settlement.

5. Important decisions are usually made in person and not by correspondence or telephone. While Saudis seek counsel from many people, the ultimate power to make a decision rests with the person at the top, and this individual relies heavily on personal impressions, trust, and rapport.[6]

Working in China

In recent years the People's Republic of China (PRC, or China, for short) has moved away from isolation to encourage more business with the rest of the world. While China holds tremendous promise, many Western firms have found working on projects in China to be a long, grueling process that often results in failure. One of the primary reasons for problems is the failure to appreciate Chinese culture.

Chinese society, like those of Japan and Korea, is influenced by the teachings of Confucius (551–478 B.C.). Unlike America, which relies on legal institutions to regulate behavior, in Confucian societies the primary deterrent against improper or illegal behavior is shame or loss of face. Face is more than simply reputation. There is a Chinese saying that, "Face is like the bark of a tree; without its bark, the tree dies." Loss of face not only brings shame to individuals but also to family members. A member's actions can cause shame for the entire family, hampering that family from working effectively in Chinese society.

In China, "whom you know is more important than what you know." The term *guanxi* refers to personal connections with appropriate authorities or individuals. China observers argue that *guanxi* is critical for working with the Chinese. Chinese are raised to distrust strangers, especially foreigners. Trust is transmitted via *guanxi.* That is, a trusted business associate of yours must pass you along to his trusted business associates. Many outsiders criticize *guanxi,* considering it to be like nepotism where decisions are made regarding contracts or problems based on family ties or connections instead of an objective assessment of ability.

Many believe that the quickest way to build *guanxi* relationships is through tendering favors. Gift-giving, entertainment at lavish banquets, questionable payments, and overseas trips are common. While Westerners see this as nothing short of bribery, the Chinese consider it essential for good business. Another common method for outsiders to acquire *guanxi* is by hiring local intermediaries, who use their connections to create contacts with Chinese officials and businesspeople.

In dealing with the Chinese, you must realize they are a collective society in which people pride themselves on being a member of a group. For this reason, you should never single out a Chinese for specific praise because this is likely to embarrass the individual in front of his peers. At the same time, you should avoid the use of "I" because it conveys that the speaker is drawing attention to himself or herself.

---

[6] Adapted from R. T. Moran, P. R. Harris, and S. V. Moran, *Managing Cultural Differences,* 5th ed. (Houston, TX: Gulf Publishing, 2010); and J. Hooker, *Working across Cultures* (Stanford, CA: Stanford Business Books, 2003).

Chinese do not appreciate loud, boisterous behavior, and when speaking to each other they maintain a greater physical distance than is typical in America. Other cautions include the following:

1. Once the Chinese decide who and what is best, they tend to stick to their decisions. So while they may be slow in formulating a plan, once they get started they make good progress.
2. Reciprocity is important in negotiations. If Chinese give concessions, they expect some in return.
3. The Chinese tend to be less animated than Americans. They avoid open displays of affection and physical contact; they are more reticent and reserved than Americans.
4. The Chinese place less value on the significance of time and often get Americans to concede concessions by stalling.
5. In Confucian societies those in position of power and authority are obligated to assist the disadvantaged. In return they gain face and a good reputation.[7]

For more insights on Chinese culture see the Snapshot from Practice: Project Management X-Files.

Working in the United States

In the world of international projects, professionals from other countries will come to the United States to manage projects. To them, the United States is a foreign assignment. They will have to adapt their management style to the new environment they find in the States.

Immigration has made the United States a melting pot of diverse cultures. While many are quick to point out the differences between North and South, Silicon Valley and Wall Street, social anthropologists have identified certain cultural characteristics that shape how many Americans conduct business and manage projects.

Mainstream Americans are motivated by achievement and accomplishment. Their identity and, to a certain extent, their self-worth are measured by what they have achieved. Foreigners are often astounded by the material wealth accumulated by Americans and the modern conveniences most Americans enjoy. They are also quick to point out that Americans appear too busy to truly enjoy what they have achieved.

Americans tend to idolize the self-made person who rises from poverty and adversity to become rich and successful. Most Americans have a strong belief that they can influence and create their future, that with hard work and initiative, they can achieve whatever they set out to do. Self-determination and pragmatism dominate their approach to business.

Although Americans like to set precise objectives, they view planning as a means and not an end. They value flexibility and are willing to deviate from plans and improvise if they believe change will lead to accomplishment. Obstacles on a project are to be overcome, not worked around. Americans think they can accomplish just about anything, given time, money, and technology.

Americans fought a revolution and subsequent wars to preserve their concept of democracy, so they resent too much control or interference, especially by governments. While more an ideal than practice, there is deep-rooted belief in American management philosophy that those people who

---

[7] Adapted from J. L. Graham and N. M. Lam, "The Chinese Negotiation," *Harvard Business Review,* October 1, 2003, pp. 82–91; I. Yeung and R. L. Tung, "Achieving Business Success in Confucian Societies: The Importance of Guanxi (Connections)," *Organizational Dynamics,* 25 (2) Autumn 1996, pp. 54–65; and Hooker, *Working across Cultures.*

Americans tend to discount the significance of luck and believe that good fortune is generally a result of hard work. In other cultures, luck takes on greater significance and has supernatural ramifications. For example, in many Asian cultures certain numbers are considered lucky, while others are unlucky. In Hong Kong the numbers 7, 3, and especially 8 (which sounds like the word for prosperity) are considered lucky, while the number 4 is considered unlucky (because it is pronounced like the word "death"). Hong Kong businesspeople go to great lengths to avoid the number 4. For example, there is no fourth floor in office and hotel buildings. Business executives have been known to reject ideal sites in heavily congested Hong Kong because the address would contain the number 4. They pay premium prices for suitable sites containing addresses with the lucky numbers. Likewise, Hong Kong business managers avoid scheduling important events on the fourth day of each month and prefer to arrange critical meetings on the eighth day.

Hong Kong is also a place where the ancient art of *Feng shui* (literally "wind water") is practiced. This involves making sure a site and buildings are aligned in harmony with the earth's energy forces so that the location will be propitious. Feng shui practitioners are often called in on construction projects to make sure that the building is aligned correctly on the site. In some cases, the technical design of the building is changed to conform to the recommendations of such experts. Similarly, Feng shui experts have been known to be called

© Rob Brimson/Taxi/Getty Images

in when projects are experiencing problems. Their recommendations may include repositioning the project manager's desk or hanging up mirrors to deflect the flow of unharmonious influences away from the building or site of the project.

In cultures where luck is believed to play a role in business, people who discount luck may not only insult the luck seekers, they may risk being thought negligent in not paying enough attention to what is viewed as a legitimate business concern.

will be affected by decisions should be involved in making decisions. Many foreign businesspeople are surprised at the amount of autonomy and decision-making authority granted to subordinates. Foreign personnel have to learn to interact with American professionals below their rank in their own organizations.

Businesspeople from different African, Asian, and Latin American countries are amazed and often somewhat distressed at the rapid pace of America. "Getting things done" is an American characteristic. Americans are very time-conscious and efficient. They expect meetings to start on time. They tinker with gadgets and technological systems, always searching for easier, better, more efficient ways of accomplishing things. American professionals are often relentless in pursuing project objectives and expect that behavior of others also.

Americans in play or business generally are quite competitive, reflecting their desire to achieve and succeed. Although the American culture contains contradictory messages about the importance of success (i.e., "It's not whether you win or lose but how you play the game" versus "nice guys finish last"), winning and being number one are clearly valued in American society. Foreigners are often surprised at how aggressively Americans approach business with adversarial attitudes toward competitors and a desire to not just meet but to exceed project goals and objectives.

Other guidelines and cautions for working with Americans on projects include:

1. More than half of U.S. women work outside the home; females have considerable opportunity for personal and professional growth, guaranteed by law. It is not uncommon to find women in key project positions. Female professionals expect to be treated as equals. Behavior tolerated in other countries would be subject to harassment laws in the States.

2. In the United States, gifts are rarely brought by visitors in a business situation.

3. Americans tend to be quite friendly and open when first meeting someone. Foreigners often mistake this strong "come-on" for the beginning of a strong reciprocal friendship. This is in contrast to many other cultures where there is more initial reserve in interpersonal relations, especially with strangers. For many foreigners, the American comes on too strong, too soon, and then fails to follow up with the implicitly promised friendship.

4. Although in comparison to the rest of the world Americans tend to be informal in greeting and dress, they are a noncontact culture (e.g., they avoid embracing in public usually) and Americans maintain certain physical/psychological distance with others (e.g., about two feet) in conversations.

5. American decision making is results oriented. Decisions tend to be based on facts and expected outcomes, not social impact.[8]

Summary Comments about Working in Different Cultures

These briefings underscore the complexity of working on international projects. It is common practice to rely on intermediaries—often natives who are foreign educated—to bridge the gap between cultures. These intermediaries perform a variety of functions. They act as translators. They use their social connections to expedite transactions and protect the project against undue interference. They are used to sidestep the touchy bribery/gift dilemma (see the Dealing with Customs Snapshot from Practice). They serve as cultural guides, helping outsiders understand and interpret the foreign culture. In today's world, there are a growing number of consulting firms that perform these functions by helping foreign clients work on projects in their country.

The international briefings also highlight the importance of project managers doing their homework and becoming familiar with the customs and habits of the host country they are going to be working in. As far as possible, the project should be managed in such a way that local-country norms and customs are honored. However, there are limits to the extent to which you should accommodate foreign cultures. *Going native* is generally not an alternative. After all, it took a Russian his entire life to learn how to be a Russian. It would be foolish to think an outsider could learn to be one in six months, two years, or perhaps ever.

---

[8] Adapted from Moran et al., *Managing Cultural Differences;* and D. Z. Milosevic, "Echoes of the Silent Language of Project Management," *Project Management Journal,* 30 (1) March 1999, pp. 27–39.

SNAPSHOT FROM PRACTICE
Dealing with Customs

Will corruption influence the project? Bribes are illegal in the United States, but in some countries they are the usual way to do business. For example, one American project manager in a foreign country requested that a shipment of critical project equipment be sent "overnight rush." Two days later, inquiries to the sender confirmed the materials had been delivered to the nearby airport. Further inquiries to the port found the shipment "waiting to pass customs." Locals quickly informed the American that money paid to the chief customs inspector would expedite clearance. The American project manager's response was, "I will not be held hostage. Bribes are illegal!" Two more days of calling government officials did not move the shipment from customs. The manager related his problem to a friendly businessman of the host nation at a social affair. The local businessman said he would see if he could help. The shipment arrived the next morning at 10:00 A.M. The American called his local business friend and thanked him profusely. "I owe you one." "No," replied the local. "You owe me a $50 dinner when I visit you in the States." The use of an intermediary in such situations may be the only avenue available to a manager to reduce the stress and personal conflict with the U.S. value system.

The remainder of this chapter focuses on the selection and training of project personnel for international projects. But before these issues are discussed, this section concludes with a discussion of the phenomenon of culture shock, which can have a profound effect on a foreigner's performance on a project in a strange culture.

Culture Shock

My first few weeks in Chiang Mai [Thailand] were filled with excitement. I was excited about the challenge of building a waste treatment plant in a foreign country. I was fascinated with Thai customs and traditions, the smells and sights of the night market. Soon I noticed a distinct change in my attitude and behavior. I started having problems sleeping and lacked energy. I became irritable at work, frustrated by how long things took to accomplish, and how I couldn't seem to get anything accomplished. I started staying up late at night watching CNN in my hotel room.

This engineer is experiencing what many would call "culture shock." *Culture shock* is a natural psychological disorientation that most people suffer when they move into a culture different from their own. The culture shock cycle has four stages (see Figure 15.6):

1. *Honeymoon*—You start your overseas assignment with a sense of excitement. The new and the unusual are welcomed. At first it is amusing not to understand or be understood. Soon a sense of frustration begins to set in.

2. *Irritability and hostility*—Your initial enthusiasm is exhausted, and you begin to notice that differences are greater than you first imagined. You become frustrated by your inability to get things done as you are accustomed to. You begin to lose confidence in your abilities to communicate and work effectively in the different culture.

3. *Gradual adjustment*—You begin to overcome your sense of isolation and figure out how to get things done in the new culture. You acquire a new perspective of what is possible and regain confidence in your ability to work in the culture.

4. *Adaptation*—You recover from your sense of psychological disorientation and begin to function and communicate in the new culture.

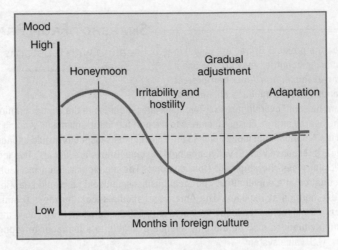

FIGURE 15.6 *Culture Shock Cycle*

Culture shock is not a disease but a natural response to immersing yourself in a new environment. Culture shock results from a breakdown in your selective perception and effective interpretation system. At a subliminal level, your senses are being bombarded by a wide variety of strange sounds, sights, and smells. At the same time, the normal assumptions you are accustomed to using in your home culture to interpret perceptions and to communicate intentions no longer apply. When this happens, whether in a business context or in normal attempts to socialize, confusion and frustration set in. The natives' behavior does not seem to make sense, and, even more importantly, your behavior does not produce expected results. Frustration occurs because you are used to being competent in such situations and now find you are unable to operate effectively.

Culture shock is generally considered a positive sign that the professional is becoming involved in the new culture instead of remaining isolated in an expatriate ghetto. The significant question is how best to manage culture shock, not how to avoid it. The key appears to be managing the stress associated with culture shock.

Stress-related culture shock takes many forms: disappointment, frustration, withdrawal, anxiety, and physiological responses such as fatigue, sleeplessness, and headaches. Stress is induced by the senses being overwhelmed by foreign stimuli and the inability to function effectively in a strange land. Stress is exacerbated when one encounters disturbing situations that, as a foreigner, are neither understood nor condoned. For example, many North Americans are appalled by the poverty and hunger in many underdeveloped countries.

Coping with Culture Shock

There are a wide range of stress management techniques for coping with culture shock. One method does not necessarily work any better than another; success depends on the particular individual and situation involved. Some people engage in regular physical exercise programs, some practice meditation and relaxation exercises, and others find it healthy to keep a journal.

Many effective international managers create "stability zones." They spend most of their time immersed in the foreign culture but then briefly retreat into an environment—a stability zone—that closely recreates home. For example, when one of the authors was living in Kraków, Poland, with his family, they would routinely go to the Polish movie houses to see American movies with Polish subtitles. The two hours spent hearing English and seeing a familiar environment on the screen had a soothing effect on everyone.

On the project, managers can reduce the stress caused by culture shock by recognizing it and modifying their expectations and behavior accordingly. They can redefine priorities and develop more realistic expectations as to what is possible. They can focus their limited energy on only the most important tasks and relish small accomplishments.

After three to six months, depending on the individual and assignment, most people come up from their culture shock "low" and begin living a more normal life in the foreign country. They talk to acquaintances from the host country and experienced outsiders from their own culture to find out how to behave and what to expect. Little by little they learn how to make sense of the new environment. They figure out when "yes" means "yes" and when it means "maybe" and when it means "no." They begin to master the language so that they can make themselves understood in day-to-day conversations. See the Snapshot from Practice: Project X—Namibia, Africa, for further insights on coping with culture shock.

The vast majority of people eventually make the adjustment, although for some people it can take much longer than three to six months. A smaller number never recover, and their international

SNAPSHOT FROM PRACTICE
Project X—Namibia, Africa*

While U.S. reality TV shows focus on finding love, outwitting opponents, and garnering audience support, a Norwegian TV show shone a light on project management under extreme conditions. The plot was deceptively simple: send 10 Scandinavian volunteers 6,000 miles away from home to the dry sub-tropics of southern Africa and charge them with building a school for orphans and poor children in less than 30 days. Not only would they be forced to adjust to vastly different language, climate, and cuisines, but only one of the 10 had previous construction experience. The team's trials and tribulations were aired over Norwegian TV in 2009. The marketing blitz for the show, titled *Project X,* played up the drama with the tagline: "Can they achieve the mission?"

The team was enthusiastic at the outset, but discontent began as soon as they arrived at the small mining town of Tsumeb in Namibia. The team immediately experienced culture shock—all the while the TV crew followed them, sticking cameras in their faces and asking how they felt.

The sweltering heat, slumlike conditions, and limited cuisine immediately elicited complaints: "I can't sleep." "The food is awful." "Where are the toilets?"

One of the biggest mistakes the volunteers made was applying a Eurocentric sense of time and planning. "I brought my Danish mindset that 'On Friday we will do this and on Saturday we will do that,'" reported Merete Lange, one of the volunteers. "Then I came to understand African time, and that was the biggest surprise."

Hoping to secure local buy-in, Ms. Lange arranged for a local carpenter to build desks and tables. A few days before the furniture was needed, she discovered work hadn't even begun.

"I got pretty stressed and tried to be my best at being diplomatic," Ms. Lange recalls. "I asked, 'When do you think you will be ready with the furniture?'" The carpenter responded, "Time is unpredictable. I will call you."

Over time, Ms. Lange and her teammates were able to adapt to the elements and figure out ways to work with the locals to successfully build the school within 30 days. "The trick is reflecting upon 'where people were coming from, how to meet them there, and how to create a win-win situation that would satisfy both parties.'"

* B. G. Yovovich, "Worlds Apart," *PMNetwork,* October 2010, pp. 24–29.

experience turns into a nightmare. Some exhibit severe stress symptoms (e.g., alcoholism, drug abuse, nervous breakdown) and must return home before finishing their assignment.

Professionals can use project work as a bridge until they adjust to their new environment. Unfortunately, spouses who do not work do not have this advantage. When spouses are left to cope with the strange environment on their own, they often have a much more difficult time overcoming culture shock. The effect on spouses cannot be underestimated. The number one reason expatriate managers return home is that their spouses failed to adjust to the new environment (Tung, 1987).

Project professionals working overseas accept that they are in a difficult situation and that they will not act as effectively as they did at home, especially in the initial stages. They recognize the need for good stress management techniques, including stability zones. They also recognize that it is not an individual problem and invest extra time and energy to help their spouses and families manage the transition. At the same time, they appreciate that their colleagues are experiencing similar problems and are sensitive to their needs. They work together to manage the stress and pull out of a culture shock low as quickly as possible.

It is somewhat ironic, but people who work on projects overseas experience culture shock twice. Many professionals experience the same kind of disorientation and stress when they return home, although it is usually less severe. For some, their current job has less responsibility and is boring compared with the challenge of their overseas assignment. For others, they have problems adjusting to changes made in the home organization while they were gone. This can be compounded by financial shock when the salary and fringe benefits they became accustomed to in the foreign assignment are now lost, and adjusting to a lower standard of living is difficult. It typically takes six months to a year before managers operate again at full effectiveness after a lengthy foreign assignment (Adler and Gunderson, 2007).

SELECTION AND TRAINING FOR INTERNATIONAL PROJECTS

When professionals are selected for overseas projects and they do not work out, the overall costs can be staggering. Not only does the project experience a serious setback, but the reputation of the firm is damaged in the region. This is why many firms have developed formal screening procedures to help ensure the careful selection of personnel for international projects. Organizations examine a number of characteristics to determine whether an individual is suitable for overseas work. They may look for work experience with cultures other than one's own, previous overseas travel, good physical and emotional health, a knowledge of a host nation's language, and even recent immigration background or heritage. Prospective candidates and their family members are often interviewed by trained psychologists, who assess their ability to adapt and function in the new culture.

While there is growing appreciation for screening people for foreign assignments, the number one reason for selection is that the personnel assigned are the best people available for the technical challenges of the project (Mendenhall et al., 1987). Technical know-how takes precedence over cross-cultural sensitivity or experience. As a consequence, training is critical to fill in the cultural gaps and prepare individuals to work in a foreign land.

Training varies widely, depending on the individual, company, nature of the project, and cultures to work with. Project professionals assigned to foreign countries should have a minimal understanding of the following areas:

- Religion.
- Dress codes.

- Education system.
- Holidays—national and religious.
- Daily eating patterns.
- Family life.
- Business protocols.
- Social etiquette.
- Equal opportunity.

An example of a short-term training program is the one developed by Underwriter Laboratories, Inc., to train staff who travel to Japan to work with clients on projects. The program is designed around a series of mini-lectures that cover topics ranging from how to handle introductions to the proper way to exchange gifts to the correct way of interpreting Japanese social and business behavior. The two-day program consists of lectures, case studies, role plays, language practice, and a short test on cultural terminology; it concludes with a 90-minute question-and-answer period. At the end of the program, participants have a fundamental understanding of how to communicate with the Japanese. More importantly, they know the types of information they lack and how to go about learning more to become effective intercultural communicators.

Other training programs are more extensive. For example, Peace Corps volunteers undergo an intense two- to four-month training program in their country of service. The training includes classes on the history and traditions of the country, intensive language instruction, and cross-cultural training as well as home-stays with local families. Many companies outsource training to one of the many firms specializing in overseas and intercultural training.

Figure 15.7 attempts to link the length and type of training with the cultural fluency required to successfully complete the project. Three different learning approaches are highlighted (Mendenhall et al., 1987):

1. The "information-giving" approach—the learning of information or skills from a lecture-type orientation.
2. The "affective" approach—the learning of information/skills that raise the affective responses on the part of the trainee and result in cultural insights.
3. The "behavioral/experiential" approach—variant of the affective approach technique that provides the trainee with realistic simulations or scenarios.

According to this framework, the length and level of training would depend on the degree of cultural fluency required to be successful. In general, the longer the person is expected to work in the foreign country, the more intensive the training should be. Length of stay should not be the only consideration; high levels of cultural fluency, and therefore more extensive training, may be required to perform short-term, intense projects. In addition, location is important. Working in Australia will likely require less cultural fluency than working on a project in Pakistan.

While English is rapidly becoming the international language for business in many parts of the world, you should not underestimate the value of being able to speak the language of the host country. At a minimum you should be able to exchange basic pleasantries in the native tongue. Most foreigners consider this a sign of respect, and even if you stumble they appreciate the effort.

In many situations translators are used to facilitate communication. While time-consuming, this is the only way to communicate with non-English-speaking personnel. Be careful in the selection of translators, and do not just assume they are competent. For example, one of the authors enlisted

FIGURE 15.7 *Relationship between Length and Rigor of Training and Cultural Fluency Required*

the help of a Polish translator to conduct a meeting with some Polish managers. After the meeting the translator, who taught English at a local university, asked if the author "had good time." I responded that I felt things went well. The translator repeated her question. Puzzled, I reaffirmed that I felt things went well. After the interchange was repeated several times, the translator finally grabbed my wrist, pointed at my watch, and asked again if I "had good time?" Doubts arose concerning the accuracy of the meeting translation!

Summary

The number of international projects continues to increase, and nothing on the horizon suggests things will change in the new millennium. More and more project managers will be needed to implement international projects. There are few guidelines for the fledgling international project manager. Preparing for international projects can be enhanced through training. As a general background, potential international project managers can benefit from a basic international business course that sensitizes them to the forces of change in the global economy and to cultural differences. Learning a foreign language is also strongly recommended.

Further training specific to the host country is a very useful preproject endeavor. The length and type of training usually depend on the duration of the project manager's assignment. Review Figure 15.7. Still, self-learning, on-the-job training, and experience are the best teachers for international project managers.

Preparing for a specific international project requires serious preproject homework. Understanding the motivation of the firm in selecting the project and its site provides important insights. What basic political, geographic, economic, and infrastructure factors were key considerations? How will they impact the implementation of the project?

Finally, preparation and understanding the cultural differences of the host country go a long way toward making positive first impressions with the nationals and managing the project. International projects have distinct personalities. All people are not the same. Differences within and among countries and cultures are numerous and complex. Project managers need to accept these differences and treat them as real—or live with the consequences. What works at home may not work in the foreign country. Americans are regarded as friendly by our neighbors in the global village, but Americans are also noted to be insensitive to differences in local cultures and customs and awkward in our use of languages other than English. Although most attention in foreign projects is focused on technical efforts and their cost, the project must be carried out within the environment of the country's social customs, work practices, government controls, and religious beliefs. In most cultures, sincerity and flexibility will pay off.

Key Terms

Cross-cultural
orientations

Culture
Culture shock

Infrastructure

Review Questions

1. How do environmental factors affect project implementation?
2. What role do local intermediaries play in helping an outsider complete a project?
3. Why is it important to honor the customs and traditions of a country when working on an international project?
4. What is culture shock? What can you do to reduce the negative effects of culture shock?
5. How should you go about preparing yourself for an international project?

Exercises

1. Interview someone who has worked or lived in a foreign country for more than six months.
   a. What was his experience with culture shock?
   b. What did he learn about the culture of the country he lived in?

    c. What advice would he give to someone who would be working on a project in that country?

2. Try as best you can to apply the Kluckhohn-Strodtbeck cross-cultural framework to the four countries discussed in this chapter: Mexico, France, Saudi Arabia, and China. Where do you think these countries lie on each of the cultural issues?

3. Place in order the following countries in terms of what you would think would be the least to most corrupt:

    United States, Denmark, Saudi Arabia, Russia, Australia, Hong Kong, Nepal, China, Kenya, Indonesia, Botswana, Greece, Chile.

Use an Internet search engine to find the most recent International Corruptions Perceptions Index (CPI) released by the Berlin-based organization Transparency International.

    a. Check your predictions with the Index.

    b. How well did you do? What countries surprised you? Why?

4. Safety is a major concern when working on projects abroad. Select a country that you would consider dangerous to work in and look up the travel advisory provided for that country by the U.S. State Department (http://travel.state.gov/). How safe is it to work in that country?

References

Ackoff, R. L., *Ackoff's Fables: Irreverent Reflections on Business and Bureaucracy* (New York: Wiley, 1991), p. 221.

Adler, N., and A. Gunderson, *International Dimensions of Organizational Behavior,* 5th ed. (Mason, OH: Thomson Publishing, 2007).

Arms, P. B. and E, Lucas, "How do Foreign Clients Really See American Project Managers?," *Proceedings of the 1978 Annual Seminar/Symposium on Project Management* (Newtown, PA: Project Management Institute, 1978), pp. 11K 1–7.

Borsuk, R., "In Indonesia, a Twist on Spreading the Wealth: Decentralization of Power Multiplies Opportunities for Bribery, Corruption," *The Wall Street Journal,* January 29, 2003, p. A16.

Cahill, T., "Deadly Business in Moscow," *Bloomberg Businessweek,* March 1, 2010, pp. 22–23.

Chen, M., and D. Miller, "West Meets East: Toward an Ambicultural Approach to Management," *The Academy of Management Perspectives,* 24 (4) November 2010, pp. 17–24.

Contingency Planning and Management.com, "Strohl Systems Offers Terrorism Readiness Questionnaire," September 24, 2001.

Deneire, M., and M. Segalla, "Mr. Christian Pierret, Secretary of State for Industry (1997–2002), on French Perspectives on Organizational Leadership and Management," *Academy of Management Executive,* 16 (4) November 2002, pp. 25–30.

Doh, J. P., P. Rodriguez, K. Uhlenbruck, J. Collins, and L. Eden, "Coping with Corruption in Foreign Markets," *Academy of Management Executive,* 17 (3) August 2003, pp. 114–27.

Graham, J. L., and N. M. Lam, "The Chinese Negotiation," *Harvard Business Review,* October 1, 2003, pp. 82–91.

Hallowell, R., D. Bowen, and C. I. Knoop, "Four Seasons Goes to Paris," *Academy of Management Executive,* 16 (4) November 2002, pp. 7–24.

Hodgetts, R. M., and F. Luthans, *International Management: Culture, Strategy, and Behavior,* 5th ed. (Boston: McGraw-Hill/Irwin, 2003).

Hofstede, G., *Cultures Consequences: International Difference in Work-Related Values* (Beverly Hills, CA: Sage Publishing, 1980).

Hooker, J., *Working across Cultures* (Stanford, CA: Stanford Business Books, 2003).

Kluckhohn, F., and F. L. Strodtbeck, *Variations in Value Orientations* (Evanston, IL: Row, Peterson, 1961).

Krane, J., "Intelligence Companies Help Overseas Business Travelers," *The Cincinnati Enquirer,* April 2, 2002, website.

Kras, E., *Management in Two Cultures: Bridging the Gap between U.S. and Mexican Managers,* rev. ed. (Yarmouth, ME: Intercultural Press, 1995).

Lane, H. W., and J. J. DiStefano, *International Project Management,* 2nd ed. (Boston: PWS-Kent, 1992).

Lieberthal, K., and G. Lieberthal, "The Great Transition," *Harvard Business Review,* October 1, 2003, pp. 71–81.

Mendenhall, M. E., E. Dunbar, and G. R. Oddou, "Expatriate Selection, Training, and Career-Pathing: A Review and Critique," *Human Resource Management,* 26 (3) Fall 1987, pp. 331–45.

Milosevic, D. Z., "Echoes of the Silent Language of Project Management," *Project Management Journal,* 30 (1) March 1999, pp. 27–39.

Moffett, M. H., I. Stonehill, and D. K. Eiteman, *Fundamentals of Multinational Finance* (Boston: Pearson, 2012).

Moran, R. T., P. R. Harris, and S. V. Moran, *Managing Cultural Differences,* 5th ed. (Houston, TX: Gulf Publishing, 2010).

Morrison, T., and W. A. Conaway, *Kiss, Bow, or Shake Hands (The Bestselling Guide to Doing Business in More than 60 Countries),* 2nd ed. (New York: Adams Media, 2006).

Ricks, D. A., *Blunders in International Business* (London: Blackwell, 2000).

Saunders, C., C. Van Slyke, and D. R. Vogel "My Time or Yours? Managing Time Visions in Global Virtual Teams," *Academy of Management Executive,* 18 (1) 2004, pp. 19–31.

Scown, M. J., "Managers Journal: Barstool Advice for the Vietnam Investor," *Asian Wall Street Journal,* July 15, 1993.

Tung, R. L., "Expatriate Assignments: Enhancing Success and Minimizing Failure," *Academy of Management Executive,* 1 (2) 1987, pp. 117–26.

Yeung, I., and R. L. Tung, "Achieving Business Success in Confucian Societies: The Importance of Guanxi (Connections)," *Organizational Dynamics,* 25 (2) Autumn 1996, pp. 54–65.

CASE 15.1

AMEX, Hungary

Michael Thomas shouted, "Sasha, Tor-Tor, we've got to go! Our driver is waiting for us." Thomas's two daughters were fighting over who would get the last orange for lunch that day. Victoria ("Tor-Tor") prevailed as she grabbed the orange and ran out the door to the Mercedes Benz waiting for them. The fighting continued in the back seat as they drove toward the city of Budapest, Hungary. Thomas finally turned around and grabbed the orange and proclaimed that he would have it for lunch. The back seat became deadly silent as they made their way to the American International School of Budapest.

After dropping the girls off at the school, Thomas was driven to his office in the Belvéros area of Budapest. Thomas worked for AMEX Petroleum and had been sent to Budapest four months earlier to set up business operations in central Hungary. His job was to establish 10 to 14 gas stations in the region by purchasing existing stations, building new ones, or negotiating franchise arrangements with existing owners of stations. Thomas jumped at this project. He realized that his career at AMEX was going nowhere in the United States, and if he were going to realize his ambitions, it would be in the "wild, wild east" of the former Soviet empire. Besides, Thomas's mother was Hungarian, and he could speak the language. At least he thought he could until he arrived in Budapest and realized that he had greatly exaggerated his competence.

As he entered the partially refurbished offices of AMEX, he noticed that only three of his staff were present. No one knew where Miklos was, while Margit reported that she would not be at work today because she had to stay at home to take care of her sick mother. Thomas asked Béla why the workmen weren't present to work on finishing the office. Béla informed him that the work had to be halted until they received approval from the city historian. Budapest, anxious to preserve its historical heritage, required that all building renovations be approved by the city historian. When Thomas asked Béla how long it would take, Béla responded, "Who knows—days, weeks, maybe even months." Thomas muttered "great" to himself and turned his attention to the morning business. He was scheduled to interview prospective employees who would act as station managers and staff personnel.

The interview with Ferenc Erkel was typical of the many interviews he held that morning. Erkel was a neatly dressed, 42-year-old, unemployed professional who could speak limited English. He had a masters degree in international economics and had worked for 12 years in the state-owned Institute for Foreign Trade. Since being laid off two years ago, he has been working as a taxicab driver. When asked about his work at the Institute, Erkel smiled sheepishly and said that he pushed paper and spent most of the time playing cards with his colleagues.

To date Thomas had hired 16 employees. Four quit within three days on the job, and six were let go after a trial period for being absent from work, failing to perform duties, or showing a lack of initiative. Thomas thought that at this rate it would take him over a year just to hire his staff.

Thomas took a break from the interview schedule to scan the *Budapest Business Journal,* an English newspaper that covered business news in Hungary. Two items caught his eye. One article was on the growing threat of the Ukrainian Mafia in Hungary, which detailed extortion attempts in Budapest. The second story was that inflation had risen to 32 percent. This last item disturbed Thomas because at the time only one out of every five Hungarian families owned a car. AMEX's strategy in Hungary depended on a boom in first-time car owners.

Thomas collected his things and popped a few aspirin for the headache he was developing. He walked several blocks to the Kispipa restaurant where he had a supper meeting with Hungarian businessman Zoltán Kodaly. He had met Kodaly briefly at a reception sponsored by the U.S. consulate for American and Hungarian businesspeople. Kodaly reportedly owned three gas stations that Thomas was interested in.

Thomas waited, sipping bottled water for 25 minutes. Kodaly appeared with a young lady who could not have been older than 19. As it turned out Kodaly had brought his daughter Annia, who was a university student, to act as translator. While Thomas made an attempt to speak in Hungarian at first, Kodaly insisted that they use Annia to translate.

After ordering the house specialty, *szekelygulas,* Thomas immediately got down to business. He told Kodaly that AMEX was willing to make two offers to him. They would like to either purchase two of his stations at a price of $150,000 each, or they could work out a franchise agreement. Thomas said AMEX was not interested in the third station located near Klinikak because it would be too expensive to modernize the equipment. Annia translated, and as far as Thomas could tell she was doing a pretty good job. At first Kodaly did not respond and simply engaged in side conversations with Annia and exchanged pleasantries with people who came by. Thomas became frustrated and reiterated his offer. Eventually Kodaly asked what he meant by franchising, and Thomas tried to use the local McDonald's as an example of how it worked. He mentioned that Kodaly would still own the stations, but he would have to pay a franchisee fee, share profits with AMEX, and adhere to AMEX procedures and practices. In exchange, AMEX would provide petroleum and funds to renovate the stations to meet AMEX standards.

Toward the end of the meal Kodaly asked what would happen to the people who worked at the stations. Thomas asserted that according to his calculation the stations were over-staffed by 70 percent and that to make a profit, at least 15 workers would have to be let go. This statement was greeted with silence. Kodaly then turned the conversation to soccer and asked Thomas if it was true that in America girls play "football." Thomas said that both of his daughters played AYSO soccer in America and hoped to play in Hungary. Kodaly said girls don't play football in Hungary and that Annia was an accomplished volleyball player. Thomas pressed Kodaly for a response to his offer, but Kodaly rose and thanked Thomas for the meal. He said he would think about his offer and get back in touch with him.

Thomas left the Kispipa wondering if he would ever see Kodaly again. He returned to his office where an urgent message was waiting from Tibor. Tibor was responsible for retrofitting the first station Thomas had purchased for AMEX. The new tanks had not arrived from Vienna, and the construction crew had spent the day doing nothing. After several phone calls he found out that the tanks were being held at the border by customs. This irritated him because he had been assured by local officials that everything had been taken care of. He asked his secretary to schedule an appointment with the Hungarian trade office as soon as possible.

At the end of the day he checked his e-mail from the States. There was a message from headquarters asking about the status of the project. By this time he had hoped to have his office staffed and up and running and at least three stations secured. So far he had only one-third of his staff, his office was in shambles, and only one station was being retrofitted. Thomas decided to wait until tomorrow to respond to the e-mail.

Before returning home Thomas stopped off at the English Pub, a favorite hangout for expats in Budapest. There he met Jan Krovert, who worked for a Dutch company that was building a large discount retail store on the outskirts of Badapest. Thomas and Krovert often talked about being "strangers in a strange land" at the pub. Thomas talked about the interviews and how he could just see in their eyes that they didn't have the drive or initiative to be successful. Krovert responded that Hungary has high unemployment but a shortage of motivated workers. Krovert confided that he no longer interviewed anyone over the age of 30, claiming that what fire they had in their bellies was burned out after years of working in state-run companies.

1. What are the issues confronting Thomas in this case?
2. How well is Thomas dealing with these issues?
3. What suggestions would you have for Thomas in managing this project?

CASE 15.2

Phuket A

On December 26, 2004, an earthquake reaching 9.1 on the Richter scale triggered a series of devastating tsunamis off the coast of Indonesia. They spread throughout the Indian Ocean, killing large numbers of people and inundating coastal communities across South and Southeast Asia, including parts of Indonesia, Sri Lanka, India, and Thailand. The 2004 Asian tsunami was one of the deadliest catastrophes in modern history, with more than 220,000 lives lost.

Nils Lofgrin, who had managed several construction projects in Australia and New Guinea, was sent by his construction firm to restore a five-star resort along the Andaman coast in southern Thailand that had been ravaged by this tsunami. Casualties at the resort included 12 staff and 37 guests. This was Nils's first assignment in Thailand.

Nils flew down and toured the site. His assessment of the damage was that it was not as severe as feared. The basic infrastructure was intact but debris needed to be cleared and the resort refurbished. He reported back to headquarters that with a bit of luck he should have the resort up and running in a matter of months. Little did he realize how soon he would regret making such a promise.

The problems began immediately when he was unable to recruit workers to help clean up the mess at the resort. Burmese migrant workers comprised a significant portion of the workforce in the region. The heavy government presence caused them to flee into the hills out of growing fears of being arrested and deported. Even when he offered double wages he was not able to recruit many Thais.

1. Why do you think Nils is unable to recruit Thai workers for his project?

16 OVERSIGHT

*Without continual growth and progress, such words as achievement and success have
no meaning.*

—*Benjamin Franklin*

PROJECT OVERSIGHT

In the recent years the paradigm shift to project oversight/governance has been profound. **Project
oversight** can be defined as *a set of principles and processes to guide and improve the management of
projects.* The intent is to ensure projects meet the needs of the *organization* through standards,
procedures, accountability, efficient allocation of resources, and continuous improvement in the

management of projects. A second purpose is to support the project manager. We estimate over 95 percent of project-driven organizations have been implementing some form of oversight for several years. Progress has been rapid and steady. The typical activities of project oversight cover two dimensions: organization and project. Here are some of the major oversight activities used in practice:

At the Organization Level

- Project selection.
- Portfolio management.
- Improving the way all projects are managed over time.
- Assessing and elevating the maturity level of the organization's project management system.
- Using the balanced scorecard approach to review progress on strategic priorities.

At the Project Level

- Review projects' objectives.
- Decide on issues raised by the project manager such as resource needs and escalation.
- Track and assist the project to resolve bottlenecks.
- Review status reports from the project manager.
- Audit and review lessons learned.
- Authorize any major deviations from the original scope.
- Cancel the project.

All of these activities are designed to bring consistency, structure, accountability, and improvement to the management of projects. Today, project oversight, through an executive committee, oversight team, or a project office, covers every aspect of managing projects in the organization.

Importance of Oversight to the Project Manager

What does this solid paradigm shift mean to a project manager who is normally in charge of only one or two projects? Four things. First, in almost all cases oversight is interested in supporting and helping the project manager where needed. This is an improvement over the past. Second, the oversight function determines the environment in which the project manager will implement his or her project. This can affect the management of a project in a positive or negative manner. Third, depending on the size and complexity of the project, methods used to hold the project manager responsible and accountable will influence how performance is measured. Finally, the project manager, who is responsible for day-to-day management, will probably be reporting to this oversight group at predetermined phases in the project. In short, project oversight supports project management at the organization and project levels.

As a project manager you need to be aware of how these oversight activities can and will influence management of your projects. A short description of two significant organizational oversight structures of these oversight activities follows.

Portfolio Project Management

Portfolio project management is the centralized oversight of projects ensuring that allocation of resources to projects is directed toward projects that contribute the greatest value to organization goals. Portfolio management is becoming more common and important in project organizations. A PMI global survey of over 1,000 project practitioners and leaders over a variety of industries found that 72 percent of high-performing organizations use portfolio management compared to only 39 percent of low performers.[1]

A senior executive oversight committee ensures the project portfolio includes a balance of projects to best utilize the organization's resources and competencies and represent the organization's risk tolerance level. Managing the organization project portfolio includes several key responsibilities:

- Review project options available by type (new, operational, compliance)
- Confirm business case and linkage to organizational strategy
- Select, prioritize, and balance risk of all organizational projects
- Ensure availability of resources
- *Set macro time, cost, and requirements
- *Review gating outcomes (see next section on "Gating")

Bringing these responsibilities of portfolio management under one umbrella provides benefits not available from managing them individually. Some responsibilities of portfolio project management are often delegated to the project management office—especially the last two responsibilities marked with an asterisk.

Project Office

A PMI study found 65 percent of project organizations have a project office.[2] The project office is used as the vehicle to support and manage oversight activities. Here is one definition:

> The *project office (PO)* is the unit responsible for the continued support of consistent application of selection criteria, standards, and processes; training of and general assistance to project managers; and continued improvement and use of best practices.

The project office frequently includes project portfolio management. Project portfolios and project offices both result in an integration function for planning and control. The PO also supports the integration of the processes of managing projects within the social/cultural environment of the organization. High-tech firms such as Hewlett-Packard (HP), International Business Machines (IBM), and Dell all use project offices to coordinate projects and to ensure best practices are being used to manage projects.[3] For example, HP has project offices in Europe/Middle East, Americas, Asia Pacific, and Japan with several others planned. Because projects are used to implement strategy, HP has created a new position—vice president of project offices. Project offices ensure a consistent approach to all projects in all locations. See Snapshot from Practice: The Project Office.

Figures 16.1 and 16.2 provide an example of a report the project office provides senior management of an international organization. Note that such a report requires a standard format for all projects. Figure 16.1 depicts a project portfolio cost summary report developed for top management. Figure 16.2 presents the same summary for project schedules. Additional detailed information for any

---

[1] "PMI's Pulse of the Profession," March 2012, *Project Management Institute Report*, p. 7, www.pmi.org.

[2] Ibid.

[3] D. Kingsberry and Jake Steward, "Implementing a Global Program Management Office," PMI Global Conference, 2003.

As more and more companies embrace project management as a critical vehicle for realizing corporate objectives, they are creating centralized project offices (POs) to oversee and improve the management of projects. PO functions vary widely by organization and need. In some cases, they serve as a simple clearinghouse for project management information. In other cases, they recruit, train, and assign managers to specific projects. As POs mature and evolve over time, they become full-service providers of project management expertise within a firm. The different services POs may provide include the following:

© Cliff Gray

- Creating and maintaining the internal project management information system.

- Recruiting and selecting project managers both within and outside the organization.

- Establishing standardized project planning and reporting methodologies.

- Training personnel in project management techniques and tools.

- Auditing ongoing and recently completed projects.

- Developing comprehensive risk management programs.

- Providing in-house project management consulting and mentoring services.

- Maintaining an internal project management library containing critical documents, including project plans, funding papers, test plans, audit reports, and so forth.

- Establishing and benchmarking best practices in project management.

- Maintaining and tracking the portfolio of projects within an organization.

A good example of how project offices evolve is the global project office (GPO) at Citibank's Global Corporate Bank. GPO originated at the grassroots level within the small world of Operations and Technology for Global Cash Management. Committed to bringing order to the chaos of managing projects, GPO instituted training programs and professional project management practices on a very small scale. Soon the success of GPO-supported projects caught the eye of upper management. Within three years the department was expanded to offer a full range of PO services across Citibank's entire banking operation. GPO's mission is to establish project management as a core competency throughout the entire Citibank organization.

* T. R. Block and J. D. Frame, "Today's Project Office: Gauging Attitudes," *PM Network,* August 2001; W. Gradante and D. Gardner, "Managing Projects from the Future, Not from the Past," *Proceedings of the 29th Annual Project Management Institute 1998 Seminars and Symposium* (Newtown Square, PA: Project Management Institute, 1998), pp. 289–94.

specific highlighted project—such as the project schedule, cost status report, project team—is only a double click away. For example, the Smart Card project in the European Economic Community (EEC) appears to be behind schedule. The cause can be identified by "drilling down" to the project schedule, WBS, resources, or issues. Standard project formats such as these provide a wealth of information in multiproject organizations.

	Location	Project ID	Description	PV	EV	AC	CPI	SPI	PCIB	BAC	EAC	VAC
Net Services, Inc. View Cost ▼			Project Portfolio Cost Summary ($ 000)								Date:	▲
	Summary	All	Portfolio							$18,120		
Gantt	United States									$10,500		
	○	01-003	Digitize Fingerprints-FBI	3,000	3,500	3,230	1.08	1.17	97.2%	3,600	3,322	278
	◑	01-011	Encryption	270	250	250	1.00	0.93	71.4%	350	350	0
	◑	01-002	Internet Protocol--CIA						0.0%	950		
Network	◑	01-009	Supply Chain Partners	90	90	90	1.00	1.00	16.7%	540	540	0
		01-012	Bonus Mileage Awards						0.0%	630		
	●	01-005	E-sales Claims	150	140	150	0.93	0.93	35.0%	400	429	-29
	●	01-011	Procurement Net	400	340	380	0.89	0.85	27.6%	1,230	1,375	-145
Resource	○	01-008	Smart Tag Tracking	850	900	900	1.00	1.06	32.1%	2,800	2,800	0
	Asia/Pacific									$2,800		
	◑	02-007	Currency Conversion	125	120	120	1.00	0.96	80.0%	150	150	0
	◑	02-002	Billing System	280	280	280	1.00	1.00	70.0%	400	400	0
Status	○	02-005	Web-Based Cash Flow	210	220	200	1.10	1.05	73.3%	300	273	27
		02-004	Olympic Simulation						0.0%	1,950		
WBS	EEC									$4,820		
Sponsor Team	●	03-008	Smart Card	145	110	140	0.79	0.76	18.3%	600	764	-164
Priority		03-003	Warranty						0.0%	70		
Issues		03-004	Simulation--ESA						0.0%	800		
	●	03-005	Air Reservation Net	510	490	520	0.94	0.96	35.0%	1,400	1,486	-86
	●	03-007	Pilot Internet Log Syst.	540	490	550	0.89	0.91	57.6%	850	954	-104
LEGEND	◑	03-006	Internet Telephone Syst.	850	850	860	0.99	1.00	77.3%	1,100	1,113	-13

○ Under Budget
◑ On Budget
● Over Budget

FIGURE 16.1 *Project Portfolio Cost Summary Report for Top Management*

Project offices are known to result in positive benefits such as the following:

- They serve as a bridge between senior management and project managers.
- They support integration of all project management processes from selection through project closure and lessons learned.
- Through training they support the movement of the organization to a higher level of project management maturity.

The growth in the application of portfolio project management and project offices will continue. Portfolio management and project offices strongly influence how a project manager will manage his or her respective project. A more recent oversight activity has been the quick implementation of phase gate reviews.

Phase Gate Methodology

Phase gates provide an in-depth review of individual projects at *specific phases* in the project life cycle. These reviews cover assessments to continue or kill the project, reassess resource allocation, reassess prioritization, and evaluate execution progress, as well as strategic alignment decisions. The phase review process serves the organization by having gatekeepers (usually selected from

	Location	Project ID	Description	Project Manager	Start Date	Finish Date	SPI	A M J J A S O N D J F M
	Summary	All	Portfolio					
	United States							
○		01-003	Digitize Fingerprints-FBI	Beth Gage	11/15	8/15	1.17	
●		01-011	Encryption	Alfonso Buco	1/1	9/25	0.93	
○		01-002	Internet Protocol--CIA		10/1	6/1		
○		01-009	Supply chain partners	Mike Chow	6/5	11/16	1.00	
○		01-012	Bonus Mileage Awards	Sally Peters	8/1	2/12		
●		01-005	E-sales Claims	Kevin Lee	2/4	11/15	0.93	
●		01-011	Procurement Net	Tzvi Jafarri	5/5	12/30	0.85	
○		01-008	Smart Tag Tracking	Jan Snyder	3/1	12/4	1.06	
	Asia/Pacific							
○		02-007	Currency Conversion	Jeff Bush	2/1	7/10	0.96	
○		02-002	Billing System	Kia Wong	10/7	10/5	1.00	
○		02-005	Web-Based Cash Flow	Naoki Oshima	2/15	9/15	1.05	
○		02-004	Olympic Simulation		7/12	2/10		
	EEC							
●		03-008	Smart Card	Ido Alons	4/16	9/15	0.76	
○		03-003	Warranty	Connor Gage	8/11	12/12		
○		03-004	Simulation--ESA	Ib Ericson	9/15	2/13		
○		03-005	Air Reservation Net	Dragan Milosovik	3/22	1/12	0.96	
●		03-007	Pilot Internet Log Syst.	Ken Thompson	3/1	10/3	0.91	
○		03-006	Internet Telephone Syst	Ann McGraddy	8/10	9/29	1.00	

Net Services, Inc. | View | Schedule | Project Portfolio Schedule Summary | Date:

Side toolbar: Gantt, Network, Resource, Status, WBS, Sponsor, Team, Priority, Issues

LEGEND
○ Ahead of schedule
○ On schedule
● Behind schedule

FIGURE 16.2 *Project Portfolio Schedule Summary Report for Project Schedules*

several areas of the firm) perform the review. The phase gate process is also designed to support the project manager on decisions and other issues such as escalation and resource needs. The idea of phase gate methodology fits effortlessly into the oversight function of the project office. Phase gate methodology was originally developed for product development, but the application of the methodology has grown beyond new product development to include all projects in the portfolio. One study by Morris and Jamieson showed 85 percent of those surveyed use phase review gates, while 85 percent who did not thought they should.

The original *Stage-Gate™* model was pioneered by Robert G. Cooper (2000) several decades ago to improve management of new product development. The original model incorporates five stages: preliminary investigation, detailed investigation, development, testing and validation, and full production and market launch. Stages precede gates and represent information developed to enable gatekeepers to make the right decision at the next gate. These decision points at each gate are known as go, kill, hold, or recycle decisions. Given the information developed for each stage, the gatekeepers (the oversight team) can decide to continue with the project, abort the project, or revise/recycle.

Today, variations of the original model are being used across all industries to help manage project portfolios. These variations are not limited to new product development. The number of stages and gates varies. But the idea of oversight review several times throughout the project life cycle appears in all models. Each gate check will always, at a minimum, check the project against alignment with current strategic goals.

Phase gate methodology has appeal because it provides a clean-cut, structured process that can be consistently applied across all projects in the portfolio. Distinct review stages and go/kill gates comprise this oversight function. The major goals for phase gating are to ensure oversight and support for the project manager and the project team, to direct organization resources toward strategic goals, and to reduce the number of projects that do not support the forward direction of the organization. A multiproject organization having employees spread across many time zones that does not use some form of phase review methodology is rare. For example, companies such as 3M, General Motors, Northern Telecom, DuPont, Intel, Hewlett-Packard, and Dell all use some form of phase gating to manage projects.

The **phase gate** review process can be defined as a *structured process to review, evaluate, and document outcomes in each project phase and to provide management with information to guide resource deployment toward strategic goals.* This oversight activity begins with project selection and tracking the project life cycle through closure and lessons learned. Phase gates need to occur at consistent points in the project life cycle so each project encounters similar gates at predefined authorization points.

The phase review process may appear similar to the project audit discussed in an earlier chapter. Some overlap does occur, but the focus here is more integrated and holistic. Individual projects are reviewed as part of a total portfolio. For example, have strategic priorities changed the importance of the project? If the priorities of the organization have changed, a project that is executing on time, on budget, and meeting the project goals may have to be "killed." Phase review takes place at each phase from project selection through lessons learned as opposed to the audit, which often takes place at the end of the project. Phase gating provides a larger perspective to managing multiple projects in a project portfolio. Gatekeepers first focus on organization needs, with individual project needs second.

Figure 16.3 is a flow diagram of an abridged, generic variation of phase gate methodology that has application across all types of projects. Another practice used during the implementation phase is to create gates at significant milestones.

The decision gates focus on go/kill decisions based on major questions such as those shown in Gates 1 and 2 below. At a minimum each gate should include three components:

1. Required deliverables (e.g., project goals, progress, variances).
2. Gate criteria and specific outputs (e.g., adjusting project scope, schedule).
3. A clear yes/no decision on whether to go ahead.

The criteria for all of the gates during the project are selected *before* the start of the project.

The value of phase gating methods rests firmly on having enough information to support the gate decision. Significant amounts of support data must be gathered to answer critical gate questions. Using the best practices shown in earlier chapters will prepare you to easily answer critical gate questions. Frequent questions from practice for each gate are presented here.

Gate 1: Proposal Decision

- What business problem does the proposed project solve?
- Does this project align with our strategic direction?
- What type of project is this? Strategic, organization maintenance, "must," etc.?
- Should the project be considered?

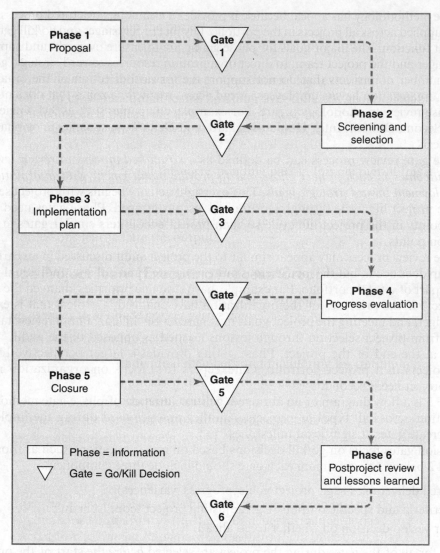

FIGURE 16.3 *Abridged Generic Phase Gate Process Diagram*

This *proposal* phase answers a fundamental question: Is the project a good idea and does it solve a business problem or issue? Basically, anyone can propose a project. However, the proposal should provide enough key information to allow an oversight team to decide if the proposal should be considered further. For example, the information might include the business problem the proposed project will solve, the urgency of the project, and clear, relevant project objectives. Gate 1 provides information at a minimal expenditure of cost and resources and in a short time, so the project can be reevaluated more thoroughly if it is perceived to have merits.

Gate 2: Screening and Selection Decision

- Is the sponsor identified and supportive?
- Should this project be selected and implemented?
- How does the project support the organization strategy and goals?
- Is it important to implement this project now? Why?
- What is the impact or risk of not doing this project?
- What are the project's ROI and/or nonfinancial benefits?
- How does the project fit our skills and culture?
- What metrics will be used to measure progress? Success?
- What are the major risks for this project?
- Will this project be implemented internally or outsourced?
- Will our business culture support this project?
- How long and how large is this project?

The *screening and selection* review includes a thorough analysis based on selection criteria. The gating group uses weighted scoring model criteria, which typically include project risks, costs, resource needs, urgency, financial analysis, benefits, identified sponsor, and other criteria found in selection models. Many information requirements for Gate 2 are discussed in detail in Chapter 2 (see project selection section) and should answer most of the decision criteria for this phase review.

Gate 3: Implementation Plan Decision

- Are the project scope, tasks, milestones and deliverables, and gates established and acceptable?
- Are the resources needed identified and available?
- Are tasks sequenced and is a time-phased budget established?
- Are appropriate performance metrics in place for tracking the project?
- Are project risks identified and is how they will be managed clearly stated?
- Are all stakeholders identified?
- Is the stakeholder communication plan complete and appropriate?
- Is a formal change management system in place?
- Are accountability metrics in place and is responsibility assigned?

The *implementation plan* review information should include the planning document developed in earlier chapters. For example, what are the specific goals for the project and what are the major deliverables (scope)? What tasks will be performed to complete the deliverables (WBS)? How are tasks sequenced (network)? When will the tasks be performed (schedule)? What resources are needed to complete the tasks (resource schedule)? What are the estimated costs for the tasks (time-phased budget)? What and how will performance be measured (variance metrics)? How will information be collected and distributed (communication plan)? What and how will project risks be identified and handled (risk plan)? What vendors will be used for procurement?

Gate 4: Progress Evaluation Decision

- Is the project still aligned with business requirements?
- Are activities completed according to the project plan?
- Are the technical requirements of the project being met?
- Are contractors meeting defined performance requirements?
- Are there urgent corrective actions that must be done quickly?
- Are time, costs, and scope performances within acceptable limits?
- Have the project objectives changed?
- What risks can be retired?

Your *progress evaluation* review covers the control activities of tracking progress, identifying variances from your plan, and taking corrective action. A major chunk of the data requirements for the phase review are simply measures against the project plan. Tracking progress and identifying variances against scope, time, budget, and control of changes and identified risks are easily accomplished using available software (see Chapters 7 and 13). For example, if the project is not going according to plan, your risk assessment plan may help you decide an action to be taken. Beyond these quantitative measures, there are always "issues" that deserve attention. Moreover, project priority must be checked against strategy to determine whether this measure is still valid. If not, a change in scope or killing the project may be necessary. Don Kingsberry, director of HP's Global Program Management Office, describes HP's progress phase review succinctly: "We have 42 health checks on current projects. We look at risks, issues, critical path analysis, resource analysis, sponsorship, alignment with strategy, earned value metrics, dependency, and other factors impacting the triple constraints of project management: time, cost, and scope." (See Boyer [2003] for more on HP's efforts.)

Gate 5: Closure

- Did the project deliver the business outcomes? Were the metrics and benefits used to justify the project met?
- Were project scope objectives met?
- Were project cost and schedule met?
- Are contracts closed out?
- Are the end users satisfied?
- Have staff been recognized and reassigned?
- Was the organization culture right for this type of project?
- Was senior management support adequate?
- Were the right people assigned to the project?
- Were project risks identified and assessed realistically?
- Did technology overextend our competencies?
- How will the project be delivered?

The *closure* and lessons learned activities closely follow the closure activities found in the audit chapter. Some organizations have wrapped phases 5 and 6—closure, post project review and lessons learned—into a single gate.

Gate 6: Post Project Review and Lessons Learned

- Have we identified what went wrong and what contributed to success?
- Have changes to improve delivery of future projects been communicated and archived?
- Has an owner of each retrospective been identified?
- What hindered or contributed to delivering the expected ROI or business outcomes?
- Can others learn from this experience?
- What changes in scope or quality were made?
- Who will be responsible for archiving the lessons learned?

The questions shown above for each phase only touch the surface of those found in practice. Some are formalized, others very porous and less structured, but all phase review models are designed to check management of a project from selection to lessons learned. Key benefits of using phase gating are:

- Provides excellent training for functional staff who serve on oversight review groups.
- Encourages a larger perspective and role of projects within the organization.
- Is a clear-cut process, easily understood, and applicable to all projects in a portfolio.
- Provides a structured process for a project office to follow on all projects.
- Eliminates poor value projects.
- Supports faster decision making with predefined deliverables for each gate.

See Snapshot from Practice: Phase Gate Side Benefits for a project manager's opinion on the benefits of phase gating.

Another key oversight function is benchmarking your project management maturity against others in your industry.

Snapshot From Practice
Phase Gate Side Benefits

One manager from a high-tech firm related to your authors that "phase-gating is the best thing that has ever happened to [his] firm—better than apple pie. We rotate middle managers to serve on the project oversight committee to give them as much exposure as possible." Serving on the oversight committee has great rewards for the organization and individual. The following relates the core of his conversation:

First, the process itself gets everyone on the same menu. Everyone is constantly reminded of the strategic vision of the firm and how the project supports the vision. Second, serving on a review or oversight committee provides a more holistic insight that creates more understanding and tolerance of changes that need to occur. Serving on the oversight committee is the cheapest, most rewarding training vehicle we have ever had. Best of all, the training lasts and the learned holistic view is transferred to others. The cost of serving on the oversight committee is near zero. Members are more likely to support and help see a project through to a speedy, successful completion. Next, using the phased approach limits scope creep, which has been a constant issue in all our projects. Finally, the bottom line is that the number of useless projects has practically disappeared—pet projects are out in the open, resources are used more efficiently, and most projects come in on time and within budget. Phase gating has changed the whole culture of our firm and the way projects are managed.

ORGANIZATION PROJECT MANAGEMENT IN THE LONG RUN

Organization Project Management Maturity

Individual audits and phase gate reviews can yield valuable lessons that team members can apply to future project work. A more encompassing look, from an organizationwide point of view, uses a project maturity model that strives for a never-ending goal to continuously improve the management of projects. It is well established that project-driven companies with higher maturity levels are more successful in managing projects than those lacking project maturity programs. Project maturity has become a competitive edge. Companies are increasingly using outsourcing or external contractors and RFPs (Request for proposals) to look for contractors that have reached high maturity levels. Harold Kerzner, a project management consultant and professor, eloquently states why a company should pursue maturity:

> Given the fact that many executives today view their company as a stream of projects, project management
> permeates the entire organization, mandating that maturity is necessary. So only those companies that
> want to stay in business and remain competitive should pursue maturity. The alternative is rather unpleas-
> ant. (Quoted in Mueller, 2005)

The purposes of all maturity models, and many are available, are to enable organizations to assess their progress in implementing the best practices in their industry and continuously move to improvement. It is important to understand that the model does not ensure success; it serves only as a measuring stick and an indicator of progress.

The term *maturity model* was coined in the late 1980s from a research study by the United States government and the Software Engineering Institute (SEI) at Carnegie Mellon University. The government wanted a tool to predict successful software development by contractors. The outcome of this research was the Capability Maturity Model (CMMI). The model focuses on guiding and assessing organizations in implementing concrete best practices of managing software development projects. Since its development, the model is used across all industries.

CMMI was retired and in 2004 replaced with, the Project Management Institute (PMI) version of the Organizational Project Management Maturity Model. The latest version is called OPM3 (See *www.pmi.org/opm3*). Typically, these models are divided into a continuum of growth layers: initial, repeatable, defined, managed, and optimized. Figure 16.4 presents our version, which borrows liberally from other models.

Level 1: Ad Hoc Project Management No consistent project management process is in place. How a project is managed depends upon the individuals involved. Characteristics of this level include:

* No formal project selection system exists—projects are done because people decide to use them or because a high-ranking manager orders them done.
* How any one project is managed varies by individual and thus is unpredictable.
* No investment is made in project management training.
* Working on projects is a struggle because it goes against the grain of established policies and procedures.

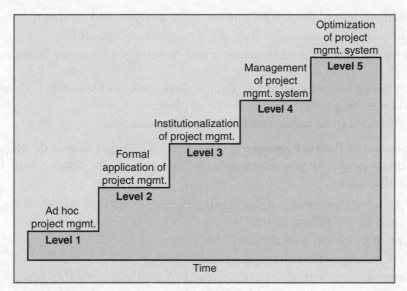

FIGURE 16.4 *Project Management Maturity Model*

Level 2: Formal Application of Project Management The organization applies established project management procedures and techniques. This level is often marked by tension between project managers and line managers who need to redefine their roles. Features of this level include:

- Standard approaches to managing projects, including scope statements, WBS, and activity lists, are used.
- Quality emphasis is on the product or outcome of the project and is inspected instead of built in.
- The organization is moving in the direction of a stronger matrix with project managers and line managers working out their respective roles.
- Recognition of the need for cost control, not just scope and time management, is growing.
- No formal project priority selection system is established.
- Limited training in project management is provided.

Level 3: Institutionalization of Project Management An organizationwide project management system, tailored to specific needs of the organization with the flexibility to adapt the process to unique characteristics of the project, is established. Characteristics of this level include:

- An established process for managing projects is evident by planning templates, status report systems, and checklists for each stage of the project life cycle.
- Formal criteria are used to select projects.
- Project management is integrated with quality management and concurrent engineering.
- Project teams try to build in quality, not simply inspect it.
- The organization is moving toward a team-based reward system to recognize project execution.

- Risk assessment derived from WBS and technical analyses and customer input is in place.
- The organization offers expanded training in project management.
- Time-phased budgets are used to measure and monitor performance based on earned value analysis.
- A specific change control system for requirements, cost, and schedule is developed for each project, and a work authorization system is in place.
- Project audits tend to be performed only when a project fails.

Level 4: Management of Project Management System   The organization develops a system for managing multiple projects that are aligned with strategic goals of the organization. Characteristics of this level include:

- Portfolio project management is practiced; projects are selected based on resource capacity and contribution to strategic goals.
- A project priority system is established.
- Project work is integrated with ongoing operations.
- Quality improvement initiatives are designed to improve both the quality of the project management process and the quality of specific products and services.
- Benchmarking is used to identify opportunities for improvement.
- The organization has established a Project Management Office or Center for Excellence.
- Project audits are performed on all significant projects and lessons learned are recorded and used on subsequent projects.
- An integrative information system is established for tracking resource usage and performance of all significant projects.

Level 5: Optimization of Project Management System   The focus is on continuous improvement through incremental advancements of existing practices and by innovations using new technologies and methods. Features include:

- A project management information system is fine-tuned; specific and aggregate information is provided to different stakeholders.
- An informal culture that values improvement drives the organization, not policies and procedures.
- There is greater flexibility in adapting the project management process to demands of a specific project.

Progress from one level to the next will not occur overnight. The Software Engineering Institute estimates the following median times for movement:

- Maturity level 1 to 2 is 22 months.
- Maturity level 2 to 3 is 29 months.
- Maturity level 3 to 4 is 25 months.
- Maturity level 4 to 5 is 13 months.

Why does it take so long? One reason is simply organizational inertia. It is difficult for social organizations to institute significant changes while at the same time maintaining business efficacy. "How do we find time to change when we are so busy just keeping our heads above water?"

A second significant reason is that one cannot leapfrog past any one level. Just as a child cannot avoid the trials and tribulations of being a teenager, people within an organization have to work through the unique challenges and problems of each level to get to the next level. Learning of this magnitude naturally takes time and cannot be avoided by using quick fixes or simple remedies.

Our best-guess estimates are that most companies are in the throes of moving from level 2 to level 3 and that fewer than 10 percent of those firms that actively practice project management are at either level 4 or 5. Remember, project maturity is not an end; project maturity is a never-ending process of continuous improvement. An additional view of the success of the projects you have selected over time is discussed next.

The Balanced Scorecard Model

Project priority selection models select which actions (projects) best support organizational strategy. The balanced scorecard model differs from selection models by reviewing projects over a longer horizon—5 to 10 years after the project is implemented. It is more "macro" in perspective than project selection models. This model measures the results of major activities taken to support the overall vision, mission, and goals of the organization. It helps answer two questions: Did we select the right projects? Did the projects contribute to long-range strategic direction of the firm? American Express, the U.S. Department of Transportation, ExxonMobil, Kaiser Permanente, National Semiconductor, and others are known to be using their own customized models of the balanced scorecard. (See Kaplan and Norton, 1992.)

The scorecard model limits measures of performance to goals in four main areas: *customer, internal, innovation and learning,* and *financial measures.* For example, a performance measure for a customer might be industry ranking for sales, quality, or on-time projects. Internal measures that influence employees' actions could mean time to market or reduction of design time to final product. Innovation and learning measures frequently deal with process and product innovation and improvement. For example, the percentage of sales or profit from new products is often used as a performance goal and measure. Project improvement savings from partnering agreements are another example of an innovation and learning measure. Finally, financial measures such as ROI, cash flow, and projects on budget reflect improvement and actions that contribute value to the bottom line.

These four perspectives and performance measures keep vision and strategy at the forefront of employees' actions. The basic assumption underlying the balanced scorecard model is that people will take the necessary actions to improve the performance of the organization on the given measures and goals. The balanced scorecard model and priority selection models should never conflict with each other. If a conflict exists, both models should be reviewed and conflicts eliminated. When both models are used in project-driven organizations, focus on vision, strategy, and implementation are reinforced. Both models encourage employees to determine the actions needed to improve performance.

Summary

Oversight practices are directed to improving the way the organization manages all projects. Oversight or governance in multiproject organizations supports the trend of integration over the last three decades. Centralization of project management activities became imperative as projects became more numerous and became the means to implement organization strategy. Project portfolios and project offices serve to gain centralized control over all projects in the organization. The multiproject environment also assists as an impetus for phase gate checks at several points over the project life cycle. Benchmarking your project management maturity quickly surfaced as large organizations realized the amount of organization resources devoted to projects and the importance of projects to meeting competition. The need for assessing the long-run value of selected projects over several years continues to increase each year. The balance score card methodology appears to be meeting this need. Succinctly, the major goals of project oversight are to ensure the effective allocation of organization resources and to improve the management of projects. Oversight activities continue to be adopted by most organizations participating in the global economy. Oversight activities are not limited to only large organizations; oversight activities continue to move down the size ladder to smaller organizations where successful project management can be a significant competitive edge.

How projects are managed in your organization will depend heavily on the level of project oversight and maturity. As oversight continues to evolve, you will need to view your job as a project manager from a broader, top-down view of project management in your organization and even in the total field of project management.

Key Terms

Balanced scorecard	Phase gating	Project management maturity
Oversight	Portfolio management	Project office (PO)

Review Questions

1. What are the major economic forces that serve as an impetus for using oversight/ governance tools and processes?
2. The Super Web Design president asked you to justify present and future oversight activities. Answer her request.
3. What are the three major advantages to an organization using a maturity model?
4. "We aren't big enough to have a project office, but we need the discipline of project management methods and standards." What advice would you give the CEO of this organization? Justify.

5. Explain to a fellow student the major benefits of project management oversight to the organization.

Exercise

1. Reread the "Day in a Life" case in Chapter 1. How would you assess her effectiveness now that you have studied project management? What part of Rachel's experience contributes to her success?

References

Archibald, Russell D., "The Interfaces between Strategic Management of an Enterprise and Project Portfolio Management within the Enterprise," *Proceedings of 22nd IPMA World Congress,* "Project Management to Run," Rome, Italy, November 2008, pp. 9–11.

Archibald, Russell D., "Five Decades of Modern Project Management: Where It Came From— Where It's Going," *PM World Today,* Vol. XI, Issue X, October 2009.

Baker, B., "The Nominees Are . . . ," *PM Network,* Vol. 18, No. 6, June 2004, p. 23.

Boyer, C., "Make Profit Your Priority," *PM Network,* Vol. 17, No. 10, October 2003, p. 40.

Cooper, R. G., *Product Leadership: Creating and Launching Superior New Products* (Cambridge, MA: Perseus Publishing, 2000).

Cooper, R. G., S. J. Edgett, and E. J. Kleinschmidt, *Portfolio Management for New Products* (Reading, MA: Addison-Wesley, 1998).

Ibbs, C. W., and Y. H. Kwak, "Assessing Project Maturity," *Project Management Journal,* Vol. 31, No. 1, March 2000, pp. 32–43.

Jafari, Ali, "Bridging the Gap," *The Project Manager (The Magazine of the Australian Institute of Project Management),* Vol. 29, No. 4, June/July 2010, pp. 24–26.

Kaplan, R. S., and D. Norton, "The Balanced Scorecard—Measures that Drive Performance," *Harvard Business Review,* January–February 1992, pp. 73–79. Note: A CD simulation is available from Harvard Customer Service, Product 8387. This interactive simulation provides hands-on experience for learning more about the method.

Morris, P. W., and A. Jamieson, "Moving from Corporate Strategy to Project Strategy," *Project Management Journal,* Vol. 36, No. 4, December 2005, pp. 5–18.

Mueller, E., "Maturity, Do or Die?" *PM Network,* Vol. 20, No. 2, February 2006, p. 32.

Norrie, J., and D. H. T. Walker, "A Balanced Scorecard Approach to Project Management Leadership," *Project Management Journal,* Vol. 35, No. 4, December 2004, pp. 47–56. "Pull the Plug," *PM Network,* Vol. 20, No. 6, June 2006, pp. 39–42.

PMI Report, "PMI's Pulse of the Profession," March 2012, Project Management Institute, p. 7.

Rover, I., "Why Bad Projects Are So Hard to Kill," *Harvard Business Review,* February 2003, pp. 49–56.

Stewart, W. E., "Balanced Scorecard for Projects," *Project Management Journal,* Vol. 32, No. 1, March 2001, pp. 38–47. (2000 International Student Paper Award Winner.)

CASE 16.1

Don't Tell Me What You Have Done. Tell Me What You Are Going to Do

The firm has been merged with a larger firm carrying a similar product line of information technology consumer and industry products. One major goal of the merger was to save costs by eliminating duplication and improving management. Weeks before the merger, Lauren (not her real name) had just been promoted to project office director of the smaller firm. She assumed her position would be absorbed into the project office of the large firm. Mentally, Lauren was prepared to start job hunting. Maybe she should change careers and go back to a job that used her bachelor's degree in political science. Two weeks after the merger was finalized, others, including herself, received a letter to report for an interview with the new company senior management "conversion" vice president. Lauren spent three days gathering materials to substantiate all of her past accomplishments, to demonstrate her management skills, and to show her potential value to the new firm. When the big day came, Lauren entered the office of the interviewer with approximately nine inches of substantiating material. She was prepared!

The first few minutes were spent explaining her past roles in the firm, the new project office, and other niceties. She explained to the VP she had all of the materials with her to back up her statements and he could take them if he wished. He replied, "I am not as interested in your past accomplishments as I am in your possible future accomplishments. Here is the need. Projects eat up about 40 percent of our yearly expenses. We need to cut 10 million off those expenses. In five minutes tell me how you will do it and how it will be verified."

Her last statement at the end of four minutes was: "I can give you five million within the next year. Ten million is too big a stretch."

His retort was, "Lauren, can you get five in six months?"

(Gulp.) "I'm pretty sure I can."

"Congratulations, Lauren, you are now the new project office director of this continental division."

In 500 words or less, write what you believe Lauren could have used as key points to get the position.

17

AN INTRODUCTION TO AGILE PROJECT MANAGEMENT

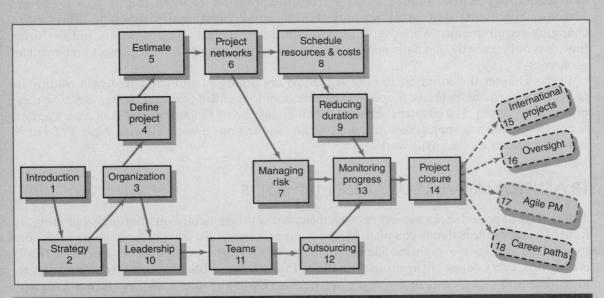

We know less about the project today than at any time in the future.

—*Chet Hendrickson*

As project management entered the new millennium, many professionals recognized that one-size fits all project management methods did not meet their needs. This recognition was especially true for those working on software and product development projects in which the end product is not well defined and evolves over time. This project environment requires flexibility and the ability to manage changes as more information and learning take place. Enter **Agile Project Management** (Agile PM). Instead of attempting to plan the entire project up front, Agile PM relies on incremental, iterative development cycles to complete projects.

Ken Schwaber uses the analogy of building a house to explain the difference between incremental, iterative development and traditional project management.[1] The traditional approach would be that the buyers could not move into the house until the entire house is completed. The iterative approach would build the house room by room. The plumbing, electrical, and infrastructure would be built for the most important room (i.e., kitchen) first and then extended to each room as it was constructed. Each time a room is completed, the builders and the buyers would assess progress and make adjustments. In some cases, the buyers would realize that they didn't need that extra room they felt they had to have. In other cases, they would add features they didn't realize they needed to have. Ultimately the house is built to fit the customer's wishes.

Agile PM is ideal for exploratory projects in which requirements need to be discovered and new technology tested. It focuses on active collaboration between the project team and customer representatives, breaking projects into small functional pieces, and adapting to changing requirements. While iterative development principles have been around for some time, it is only recently that agile methodologies have taken root within the project management profession.

In this chapter the core principles of Agile PM are discussed and compared with traditional project management methods. A specific agile methodology called Scrum is used to describe these principles in action. The chapter concludes with a discussion of limitations and concerns. The goal is not to provide a comprehensive account of all the methods associated with Agile PM but to provide a primer on how agile works.

TRADITIONAL VERSUS AGILE METHODS

Traditional approaches to project management concentrate firmly on thorough planning up front. The rationale is that if you plan, execute your plan, and take corrective action on deviations from plan, you have a high probability of success. Once the project scope has been firmly established, every detail of the project is defined through the WBS. Most problems and risks are identified and assessed before the project begins. Estimates are made, resources assigned, adjustments made, and ultimately a baseline schedule and budget are created. Control of the project is a comparison of plan versus actual and corrective action to get back on plan.

Traditional project management requires a fairly high degree of predictability to be effective. For plans to be useful managers have to have a firm idea on what is to be accomplished and how to do it. For example, when it comes to building a bridge across a river, engineers can draw upon proven technology and design principles to plan and execute the project. Not all projects enjoy such certainty. Figure 17.1 speaks to this issue and is often used to support the use of Agile PM.

Project uncertainty varies according to the extent the project scope is known and stable and the technology to be used is known and proven. Many projects, like the bridge example, as well as other construction projects, events, product extensions, marketing campaigns, and so forth have

---

[1] Schwaber, K., *Agile Project Management with Scrum,* (Seattle: Microsoft, 2004) p. xviii.

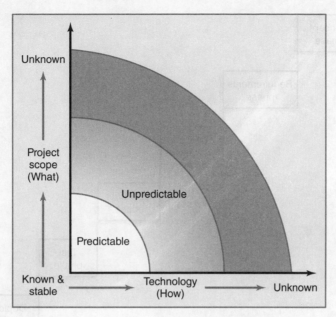

FIGURE 17.1 *Project Uncertainty*

well-established scopes and use proven technology that provides a degree of predictability for effective planning. However, when the project scope and/or technology are not fully known, things become much less predictable and plan-driven methods suffer.

For example, before agile, software development projects relied on a "waterfall" approach to software development. The waterfall method features a series of logical phases in which progress flows from one phase to the next (see Figure 17.2). The key assumption is that essential requirements can be defined upfront so the software can be designed, built, and tested. Software projects typically involve many different customers with different needs. These needs frequently change and are often difficult to articulate. In many cases, customers only begin to understand what they actually desire when they are provided with someone's impression of what they want. Under these conditions it would be difficult if not futile to develop a detailed list of scope requirements at project launch. This is one of the major reasons why software projects utilizing the waterfall approach have a history of coming in late and/or being canceled.

Technology can be another source of unpredictability. For example, a development team charged with designing the next generation electric car may know they are to build a car that seats four adults comfortably and travels over 200 miles before being charged, but they may not know if the battery technology exists to power such a vehicle. Again it would be very difficult to develop a reliable schedule when such questions exist.

The key point is that traditional PM techniques were developed to operate in the predictable zone where the scope of the project is fairly well defined and technology to be used is established. Agile lives in the unpredictable zone. Agile PM represents a fundamental shift away from the traditional plan-driven project management approach by adopting a more experimental and adaptive approach to managing projects. Projects evolve rather than are executed. Some of the differences between Agile PM and traditional project management are displayed in Table 17.1.

FIGURE 17.2 *The Waterfall Approach to Software Development*

TABLE 17.1 ···
Traditional Project Management versus Agile Project Management

Traditional	Agile
Design up front	Continuous design
Fixed scope	Flexible scope
Deliverables	Features/requirements
Freeze design as early as possible	Freeze design as late as possible
Low uncertainty	High uncertainty
Avoid change	Embrace change
Low customer interaction	High customer interaction
Conventional project teams	Self-organized project teams

AGILE PM

Fundamentally, Agile PM is related to the rolling wave planning and scheduling project methodology (see Chapter 5). That is, the final project design is not known in great detail and is continuously developed through a series of incremental iterations over time. Iterations are short time frames ("time boxes") that typically last from one to four weeks. The goal of each iteration is to develop a workable product that satisfies one or more desired product features to demonstrate to the customer and other key stakeholders. At the end of each iteration, stakeholders and customers review progress and re-evaluate priorities to ensure alignment with customer needs and company goals. Adjustments are

IDEO, headquartered in Palo Alto, California, is one of the premier design firms in the world. They are responsible for a wide range of product innovations including the first Apple mouse, Head's Airflow Tennis Racket, Zyliss Salad Spinner, and Nokia N-Gage Smartphones. IDEO's many clients include Pepsi-Cola, 3M, Logitech, Nike, and HBO. IDEO has won more of the *BusinessWeek/IDSA Industrial Design Excellence Awards* than any other firm.

IDEO's approach to product design relies heavily on an iterative development process in which product prototypes are used to explore and further refine product ideas. CEO Tim Brown states that the goal of prototyping "is to learn about the strengths and weaknesses of the idea and identify new directions that the prototype might take."

For example, IDEO worked with Procter and Gamble to develop a new Crest toothpaste tube. The challenge was to improve the traditional screw-on cap, which always gets gunked up with toothpaste. IDEO's first

© Mark Richards/PhotoEdit

solution was a pop-on, pop-off cap. However, when designers created rough prototypes and watched people use them, they quickly noticed that users kept trying to unscrew the cap even though they were told how it worked. The designers concluded that the action was a well-ingrained habit that would probably be impossible to break. So they came up with a hybrid: a twist-off cap that had a short thread but would still be easy to clean.

Focused prototyping resolves critical problems one by one. Brown recommends that prototypes should only take as much time and effort needed to generate useful feedback and evolve an idea.

For example, IDEO was working on a chair for Vecta, a high-end office furniture manufacturer. The project had evolved to the point where the height adjustment lever that tilted with the chair became critical. The team didn't build the whole chair or even the tilt mechanism. They just built the little lever and its interface with the tilt mechanism. It took only a couple of hours. When finished the prototype quickly demonstrated that the principle would work.

"It doesn't matter how clever you are, your first idea about something is never right," Brown says, "so the great value of prototyping—and prototyping quickly and inexpensively—is that you learn about the idea and make it better."

* J. M. Pethokoukis, "The Deans of Design: From the Computer Mouse to the Newest Swiffer, IDEO is the Firm behind the Scenes," *U.S. News & World Report,* Posted 9-24-2008; T. Brown, "Design Thinking," *Harvard Business Review,* June 2008, pp. 84–95.

made and a different iterative cycle begins. Each new iteration subsumes the work of the previous iterations and adds new capabilities to the evolving product (see Figure 17.3) to produce a next, expanded version of the product. See the Snapshot from Practice: IDEO for an example of iterative development in action.

Iterative development processes provide the following important advantages:

- Continuous integration, verification, and validation of the evolving product.
- Frequent demonstration of progress to increase the likelihood that the end product will satisfy customer needs.
- Early detection of defects and problems.

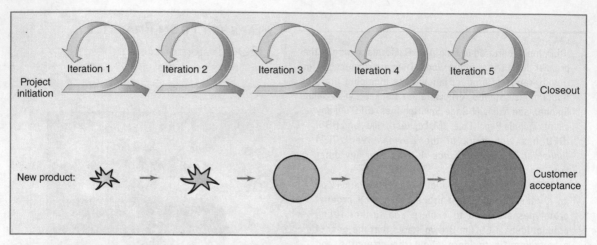

FIGURE 17.3 *Iterative, Incremental Product Development*

There is growing evidence that iterative and evolutionary development is superior to traditional plan-driven project management when it comes to creating new products. (See Research Highlight: Product Development Practices That Work.)

It should be noted that Agile PM is not one set method, but a family of methods designed to respond to the challenges of unpredictable projects. A few of the more popular ones are listed here:

Scrum	RUP (Rational Unified Process)
Extreme Programming (XP)	Crystal Clear
Agile Modeling	Dynamic Systems Development Method (DSDM)
Lean Development	Rapid Product Development (RPD)

While each of these methods has unique elements and applications, most are based on the following Agile principles:

- Focus on customer value—Employ business-driven prioritizations of requirements and features.
- Iterative and incremental delivery—Create a flow of value to customers by "chunking" project delivery into small, functioning increments.
- Experimentation and adaptation—Test assumptions early and build working prototypes to solicit customer feedback and refine product requirements.
- Self-organization—Team members decide amongst themselves who and what should be done.
- Continuous improvement—Teams reflect, learn, and adapt to change; work informs the plan.

The Agile methodology known as "Scrum" will be used to illustrate how these core principles are put into action.

Research Highlight

PRODUCT DEVELOPMENT PRACTICES THAT WORK*

Alan MacCormack and his colleagues at Harvard Business School conducted a two-year in-depth study of 29 software projects to answer the question: "Does evolutionary development, rather than the waterfall model, result in better success?" The waterfall model is the name used in the software industry for the traditional approach to project management in which a process breakdown structure (PBS) is used to first define all the requirements up front and then initiate a design, build, test, deploy sequence. Conversely, evolutionary development is the term they use to describe an Agile approach in which customers test early versions of the software and requirements emerge and are refined after each demonstration.

The results of the study overwhelmingly favored the iterative, Agile approach to software development. Several key practices now associated with Agile Project Management were found to be statistically correlated with the most successful projects:

1. An iterative life cycle with early release of the evolving product to stakeholders for review and feedback.
2. Daily incorporation of new software and rapid feedback on design changes.
3. A flexible product architecture that is both modular and scaleable.

MacCormack asserts that uncertainty on software projects dictates short "microprojects"—down to level of features. This is not limited to just software projects but to any new product endeavor where uncertainty is high and the need for customer feedback and refinement is critical to success.

* A. MacCormack, "Product-Development Practices that Work: How Internet Companies Build Software," *MIT Sloan Management Review*, 42(2), 2001, pp. 75–84.

AGILE PM IN ACTION: SCRUM

Scrum can be traced back to the work of Hirotaka Takeuchi and Ikujiro Nonaka who in 1986 described a new holistic approach in new commercial product development efforts. They compare this approach of a cross-functional team collaborating to develop a new product to rugby, where the whole team "tries to go the distance as a unit, passing the ball back and forth." The scrum metaphor has been expanded and refined into a fairly prescriptive framework that has enjoyed success on high-tech and software development projects (see Snapshot from Practice: Soul Searching).

Scrum, like other Agile methods, begins with a high-level scope definition and ballpark time and cost estimates for the project. The scope and cost estimates should be complete enough that management is comfortable with the estimates. The theory is that since requirements evolve over time, detailed up-front planning will be wasted. In place of a product WBS, Scrum uses product *features* as deliverables. *A* **feature** *is defined as a piece of a product that delivers some useful functionality to a customer*. In the case of a software project, a feature may be a bank customer being able to change her PIN. In the case of a high-tech product, it may be 3G wireless access. Features are prioritized by their perceived highest value. The project team tackles the highest, feasible priority features first. Priorities are re-evaluated after each iteration. Iterations are called sprints and should last no longer than four weeks. The goal of each sprint is to produce fully functional features. This forces the team to tackle tough decisions early in order to create a workable demo.

Over 2,792 lives were lost in the collapse of the World Trade Center (WTC) on September 11, 2001. While rescuers labored night and day to recover the bodies, a small team of Michigan software engineers set about salvaging their identities.

New York City hired Gene Codes, the Ann Arbor, Michigan, bioinformatics company, to reinvent the science of DNA mass identification by creating software that would inventory and match the victims' remains and reunite them with their families. They were to do so as soon as possible with no errors. Experts predicted that the violence of the collapse and the intense heat of the fires meant that at best 25 percent of the victims would be identified.

Gene Codes hired William Wake, an independent software coach, to work with their team of eight software engineers on the project. Wake introduced the team to Agile PM. Under Wake's guidance an environment of intense interaction and communication was created within the programming team by scheduling frequent releases, tempered by constant testing, and feedback from its users. Testing was done, before, during, and after the code was written to ensure the same bugs (errors) didn't surface twice.

At the end of each week's iteration, the staff held a retrospective. They listed things that worked well and what needed improvement on fluorescent pink, green, and yellow Post-It notes, transforming the entire wall into a case of art imitating life. Under "Worked Well," a note said, "Figured out how to use debug form on a wrapped test class." One square under the "Needs Improvement" category merely read, "I'm tired."

Whether out of patriotism or professionalism, the team routinely arrived each day at 7:00 A.M. and worked till midnight. Engineers like Dave Relyea just wanted to help. "We thought about the victims, the families, and the people at the Office of the Chief Medical Examiner working around the clock. What they were going through made us feel like we could never work hard enough."

The product of their labor was the Mass Fatality Identification System (M-FISys) that contained more than 164,000 lines of code. M-FISys linked all the information in the identification project: 11,641 swab samples from 7,166 family members; 7,681 personal effects (i.e., toothbrushes, hair brushes) and the results of the three types of DNA tests; and nearly 20,000 human remains. The chance of false match was less than 1 in 3.58 million.

In the end, with the help of M-FISys, the New York Medical examiner was able to identify 1,521 of the 2,792 people who perished in the WTC disaster.

* Melissa Krause, "Soul Searching" *Bio-ITworld*. Accessed on 3/10/2008 at http://www.bio-itworld.com/archive/091103/soul.html.

Specific features are created according to four distinct phases: analysis, design, build, and test (see Figure 17.4). Each feature can be thought of as a mini-project. The first phase is analysis and review of functional requirements that will be needed to complete the feature. The team commits to meet these requirements. The second phase is the development of a design that meets the requirements of the feature. The third phase is to build the feature so that it is functional. Finally, the feature is tested and documented. At the end of each sprint, features are demonstrated. Within this sprint framework, Scrum relies on specific roles, meetings, and documents/logs to manage the project.

Roles and Responsibilities

There are three key roles to the scrum process: Product owner, development team, and scrum master.

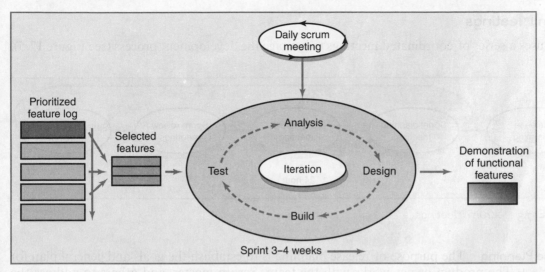

FIGURE 17.4   *Scrum Development Process*

Product Owner   This person acts on behalf of customers/end users to represent their interests. For commercial development projects the product owner may be the product manager. For internal projects, the product owner could be the manager of the business group that will benefit from the software. In other cases, the product owner could be a representative of the client organization. They are responsible for ensuring that the development team focuses their efforts on developing a product that will fulfill the business objective of the project.

The product owner in consultation with others establishes the initial list of product requirements and prioritizes them in the product backlog. Owners often work with the development team to refine features through stories and end user cases (e.g., when the user clicks the F2 key an option drop down window appears). The product owners negotiate sprint goals and backlog items with the development team. Owners have the option to change features and priorities at the end of each sprint if desired. *However, no changes should be made once a sprint has started*. Product owners are the final arbiter on requirements questions and are empowered to accept or reject each product increment. They ultimately decide whether the project is completed. Product owners are the keeper of the product vision and the watchdog on project cost.

Development Team   The team is responsible for delivering the product. A team is typically made up of five to nine people with cross-functional skill sets. There are no designated roles or titles; people take on different responsibilities depending on the nature of the work. The team is **self organizing** in the sense they decide both who and how the work is to be accomplished. Team members should be co-located so that intense face-to-face collaboration occurs. They are responsible for the achieving commitments they make at the sprint planning and sprint review meetings.

Scrum Master (aka Project Manager)   The Scrum master facilitates the scrum process and resolves impediments at the team and organization level. The Scrum master is not the leader of the team (the team leads itself!) but acts as a buffer between the team and outside interference. They have no formal authority. Instead, they are responsible for making sure that the Scrum process is adhered to. They help the product owner with planning and try to keep the team energized. The Scrum master serves more as a coach than a manager.

Scrum Meetings

Scrum uses a series of coordinated meetings to manage the development process (see Figure 17.5).

FIGURE 17.5   *Scrum Meetings*

Release Planning   The purpose of release planning is to establish the goals and general plan for the project. The product owner works with the team, Scrum master, and others to address the question on how the project can meet or exceed the desired customer expectations and return on investment. Outcomes of this meeting include establishing highest priority product backlog, the major risks, and the overall features and functionality that the released product will contain. The meeting also produces a probable delivery date and initial cost estimates if nothing changes. Management can then monitor progress and make changes to the release plan on a sprint-by-sprint basis.

Sprint Planning   At the start of each sprint, the product owner and development team negotiate which product backlog items the team will attempt this sprint. The product owner is responsible for identifying which features are most important, and the team is responsible for determining what is possible within the sprint. If it is impossible to complete a certain key item within four weeks, the team works with the product owner to break the feature down into doable pieces. All committed items are recorded in a product backlog. The team uses this backlog to prioritize specific work to be done and assign initial responsibilities. These tasks are recorded in the sprint backlog. Once the meeting has adjourned the goals for the sprint cannot be changed.

Daily Scrum   The heartbeat of an Agile project is the daily meetings which are commonly referred to as the "Scrum." Each work day at the same time and place, team members stand in a circle and take turns answering the following key questions:

1. What have you done since the last Scrum?
2. What will you do between now and the next Scrum?
3. What is getting in the way (blocks) you from performing your work as effectively as possible?

The Scrum, which typically lasts 15 minutes, is held next to a whiteboard, at which time all tasks and blocks are recorded. The Scrum master erases blocks once they have been removed.

The meetings must start on time. A late fine (e.g., $1) collected by the Scrum master and donated to charity, is a popular rule. The meeting is limited to just those three core questions. Members stand to create a sense of urgency. Immediately afterwards, specific members may meet to resolve issues that surfaced.

The value of the Scrum is that it creates a daily mechanism to quickly inform the team about the state of the project. It sustains a sense of team identity that encourages openness and resolution of problems in real time. Having everyone report what they plan to do for that day generates a social promise to the group, thereby building accountability.

Notice again that the team is self-managed. The Scrum master does not assign daily tasks to team members; the team decides amongst themselves. The Scrum master role is to see that the Scrum is running correctly. They are not "master" of the team but rather "master" of the process.

Sprint Review   At the end of each sprint, the team demonstrates the actual work product increments they have built to the product owner and other relevant stakeholders. Feedback is solicited from the product owner and other relevant stakeholders. The product owner declares which items are "done" and which items need further work and are returned to the product backlog. The team can take this opportunity to suggest improvements and new features for the product owner to accept or reject. The sprint review meeting is an opportunity to examine and adapt the product as it emerges and iteratively refine key requirements. Such refinements will be the subject of the next sprint planning meeting.

Sprint Retrospective   The purpose of the retrospective meeting is to reflect on how well the previous sprint went and identify specific actions that can improve future sprints. The Scrum master typically facilitates this meeting and the team decides which changes will be made in how they work together for the next sprint. The retrospective reflects Scrum's commitment to continuous improvement and the value it places on improving not only products but team interactions.

Product and Sprint Backlogs

Each project has a product backlog and a sprint backlog. The product owner controls the product backlog and the team controls the sprint backlog. The **product backlog** is the customer's prioritized list of key features desired when the project is completed. The product backlog usually defines each feature and estimates of time, cost, and work remaining. See Figure 17.6 for a partial product backlog for a software project.

	A	B	C	D	E	F	G
1	**Phone-In Prescription Software Project**						
2		**Product Backlog**					
3							
4	**ID**	**Product**	**Priority**	**Status**	**Estimate**	**Actual**	
5					**Hours**	**Hours**	
6							
7	1	Customer Information	2	Complete	100	90	
8	2	Insurance Information	1	Complete	160	180	
9	3	Drug Information	3	Started	80		
10	4	Doctor Information	5	Not started	40		
11	5	Inventory status	4	Started	120		
12							

FIGURE 17.6   *Partial Product Backlog*

The **sprint backlog** is developed and controlled by the team. It represents the amount of work the team commits to complete during the next sprint. The sprint backlog lists the tasks (activities) that must be completed to deliver a functional feature or segment of a feature. The sprint backlog also serves as a status document by listing the person responsible for each task, remaining hours of work, and recording the task as *finished, in process*, or *not yet started*. See Figure 17.7 for a partial example of a sprint backlog.

	A	B	C	D	E	F	G	H	I
1		Phone-In Prescription Software Project							
2		Sprint Backlog							
3									
4	Sprint Description	Responsible	Actual Hours	Remaining Hours	Defined	In Progress	Tested	Accepted	
5									
6									
7	Drug categories	RT	16	0	X	X	X	✅	
8	Generics	CG	32	0	X	X	X	✅	
9	Branded	AL	24	8	X	X	X		
10									
11									
12	Design drug inventory system	EL	40	0	X	X	X	✅	
13	Code inventory availability	CE		32					
14	Code manufacture order	MC		32					
15	Integrate all inventory systems	LE	4	16	X				
16									

FIGURE 17.7 *Partial Sprint Backlog*

Scrum does not use any of the conventional project management tools like Gantt charts or network diagrams. Instead it relies on the daily scrums and the active involvement of the product owner to manage work flow. Risk is mitigated by short developmental cycles and rigorous testing.

Sprint and Release Burndown Charts

Scrum uses "burndown" charts which focus on the work remaining are used to track progress. **Sprint Burndown Charts** are used to track progress on a daily basis (See Figure 17.8). The axis on the left shows the remaining effort required to complete the sprint backlog and the axis on the bottom contains the number days until the sprint is completed. The remaining effort is calculated by summing the time estimates for incomplete tasks recording in the sprint backlog. These estimates are updated on a daily basis.

In Figure 17.8 the solid line shows the ideal scenario if the sprint progresses as predicted by the initial task estimates and the dotted line shows the actual performance. Ideally the dotted line should be very close to the solid line. When it is above the solid line the team is behind schedule and when it is below the solid line, the team is ahead of schedule. If the actual remaining line is above the ideal line for an extended period of time, then this signals that adjustments need to be made to the project. This could mean dropping a task, assigning additional resources, or working late. None of these are pleasant, but because of the burndown chart, the team can respond sooner than just before the sprint deadline.

The **Release Burndown chart** is used to monitor progress towards completion of the project (see Figure 17.8). This chart displays the amount of work remaining across time. Before the start of each sprint completion estimates are revised in the Product Backlog and totaled in the Release burndown chart. Over time the chart becomes an excellent method for visualizing the relationship

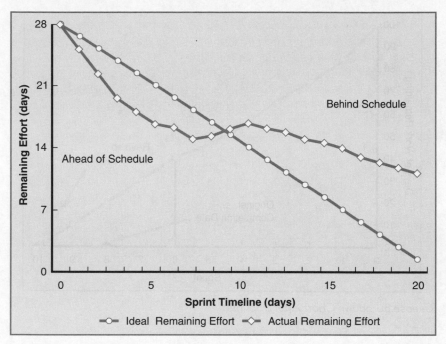

FIGURE 17.8 *Sprint Burn Down Chart*

between amount of work remaining and the rate at which team is reducing this work. Also the intersection of the trend line for work remaining and the horizontal time line can be used to estimate probable completion date. The Product owner and team use this information to "what if" the project by removing or adding functionality from the release to achieve a specific completion date or extend the date to include more functionality.

In Figure 17.9 work remaining is recorded for the first six sprints and a trend line is used to revise the expected completion date. Note that in this example the project is expected to be completed later than planned. Does this mean the team is underperforming? No, not necessarily! Remember the product backlog is dynamic and at the end of each sprint the backlog is revised. Features are added, modified, or deleted. Work estimates are increased or decreased. There is no established baseline in Agile PM.

APPLYING AGILE PM TO LARGE PROJECTS

Scrum and most other Agile methods are ideally suited for distinct projects that can be completed by a small, five to nine person team. Agile methods can be used on larger scale projects in which several teams are working on different features at the same time. In practice this condition is called "**scaling.**" The chief challenge with scaling is integration—making sure that the different features being created work in harmony with each other.

There are no easy solutions to the integration challenge. Significant up-front planning is required to manage the interdependences of different features that will be developed. This is called "staging" and often is the subject of the first development iteration. Here protocols and roles for

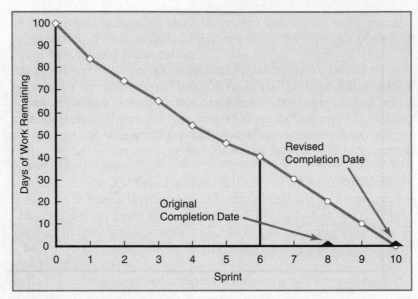

FIGURE 17.9 *Release Burndown Chart After 6 Sprints*

coordinating efforts and assuring compatibility are established. This is supported by establishing a clear product vision so that trade-off decisions are consistent at the local team level.

Agile advocates recommend creating a hub structure (see Figure 17.10) with overlapping roles and responsibilities to manage large projects. There are several feature development teams. A separate integration and build team is formed consisting of part-time members of each feature team. This team tackles the sticky integration issue through testing and establishing requirements for the feature teams. To coordinate the multiteam structure a central project team is created consisting of a higher level project manager, a product manager (who represents the interests of the customer), and the leads ("project managers") from the feature development teams. The project management team provides coordination and facilitates project decision making. Their role is to steer rather than command the other teams. Teams may be real, virtual, or a combination. The entire system requires a spirit of collaboration to work.

LIMITATIONS AND CONCERNS

Agile methods in the software industry grew at a grass roots level. Many engineers saw traditional plan-driven project management as stifling effective development with too much emphasis on processes and documentation and not enough on creativity and experimentation. Early on there was a rebellious tone to the Agile movement, so much so, that several of the key founders published an *Agile Manifesto* (see Snapshot from Practice on Agile Alliance). The manifesto affirmed a different set of values than those currently being applied by management to projects they were working on.

The revolutionary nature of Agile is reflected in the story one IT manager told the authors about her efforts several years ago at using Agile PM. She worked for a large, multinational high-tech firm that had spent five years rigidly institutionalizing a set of traditional project management policies

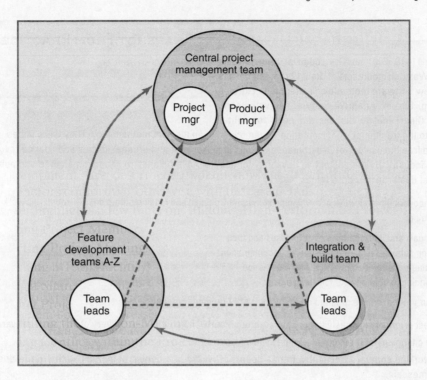

FIGURE 17.10   *Hub Project Management Structure*

and procedures. Despite their best efforts, her department consistently completed projects behind schedule with several cancellations. Out of desperation she started secretly using Agile methods to complete software projects. By using Agile PM her project teams were able to not only meet but beat project schedules—a rarity within her company. When top management confronted her for not conforming to procedure, she pointed to her recent success rate to defend being left alone. Ultimately management couldn't argue with success, and she was allowed to expand her efforts.

The repeated success and improvement in software development projects have led to key elements of Agile PM being incorporated in the Project Management Body of Knowledge (PMBOK). In 2011 the Project Management Institute began offering a certification in Agile PM along with the traditional Project Management Professional (PMP).

Agile PM does not satisfy top management's need for budget, scope, and schedule control. Remember the new house analogy. The buyers got exactly what they wanted but did not know how much it would cost. Nor did they know how long it would take or even what it would look like when it was done. While ballpark estimates are provided, Agile methods by their very nature do not provide the detail estimates of time and costs that management likes. No matter how realistic "it depends" is, management as well as customers are accustomed to working with a greater level of certainty than Agile provides. In response to the financial concerns, many organizations establish "ceilings," which is the maximum budget that should not be exceeded in the development of a given product or service.

Even if management totally buys into the value of Agile PM, one cannot simply install it into an organization over night, it needs to evolve over time. Many of the Agile principles, including

On February 11–13, 2001, at The Lodge at Snowbird ski resort in the Wasatch mountains of Utah, 17 representatives of various new software methodologies (such as Extreme Programming, Scrum, Adaptive Software Development, and Crystal Clear) met to discuss the need for lighter alternatives to the traditional, documentation-driven project management methodology. They were united by a desire to free themselves of Dilbert manifestations of make-work and arcane policies and spark a revolution in the software industry. By the end of two days they formed the Agile Alliance to champion change and published a manifesto that declared four core values.

> We are uncovering better ways of developing software by doing it and helping others do it. Through this work we have come to value:
>
> > Individuals and interactions over processes and tools
> > Working software over comprehensive documentation
> > Customer collaboration over contract negotiation
> > Responding to change over following a plan
>
> These four values were expanded upon by a set of 12 guiding principles.

1. Our highest priority is to satisfy the customer through early and continuous delivery of valuable software.
2. Welcome changing requirements, even late in development.
3. Deliver working software frequently, from a couple of weeks to a couple of months, with a preference to the shorter timescale.
4. Businesspeople and developers must work together daily throughout the project.
5. Build projects around motivated individuals. Give them the environment and support they need, and trust them to get the job done.
6. The most efficient and effective method of conveying information to and within a development team is face-to-face conversation.
7. Working software is the primary measure of progress.
8. Agile processes promote sustainable development.
9. Continuous attention to technical excellence and good design enhances agility.
10. Simplicity—the art of maximizing the amount of work not done—is essential.
11. The best architectures, requirements, and designs emerge from self-organizing teams.
12. At regular intervals, the team reflects on how to become more effective, then turns and adjusts its behavior accordingly.

To find a wealth of information on Agile PM, log onto the Agile Alliance website at: http://www.agilealliance.org/.

self-organizing teams and intense collaboration, are incompatible with corporate cultures. For example, the principle of self-organizing teams, in which members decide who should do what, regardless of rank or title, contradicts command and control structures. Likewise, intense collaboration is not for everyone. One Agile manager confessed that she had to let several of her top engineers go because their lone-wolf personalities were not compatible with collaboration. Most companies report gradual introduction of Agile project management. For example, Siemens Medical Systems started with one Scrum team in 2004, then 10 Scrum teams in 2005, 70 teams in 2006, and over 97 teams in 2007.

As noted earlier, Agile methods appear to work best on small projects that require only five to nine dedicated team members to complete the work. Here face-to-face communication replaces time-consuming documentation and informal coordination supplants top-down control.

Although some companies have successfully applied Agile PM to large projects, others have struggled with the scaling challenge. Too often coordination requirements undermine the adaptability of small teams, which is a chief strength of Agile PM. This has led many companies to use hybrid models that combine Agile and waterfall methods. For example, IPC Media, a subsidiary of Time Inc., uses an iterative waterfall approach in which large projects are broken down into subprojects performed by different teams in parallel. Short sprints and additional check points are used within a structured planned process. A recent survey of more than 800 software engineers reported that 40 percent were using a hybrid approach on their projects.[2]

Companies that enjoy success on large projects tend to have had a strong history of using Agile on smaller projects, and Agile principles are part of their product development culture.

Agile requires active customer involvement. Involvement comes in different shapes and forms. Designating an internal person to act as a product owner to represent the interests of customers is relatively easy. Soliciting the active participation of external customers can be more problematic. Even though there is consistent evidence that customer participation enhances project success, not all customers want to be that actively involved. Many are simply too busy. Others believe that they hired the project team so they would not have to be involved. Securing the cooperation of customers to devote the requisite time to support Agile PM is a common source of frustration in the field.

Agile PM frameworks, like Scrum, are used exclusively to complete software development projects from beginning to end. Other companies are using Agile PM only during the early exploratory phase of a project. Agile PM is used to develop critical breakthrough technology or define essential features. Once the features and technology are known then traditional project management is applied to complete the project.

Summary

Agile project management has emerged as a response to the challenges of managing projects with loosely defined scopes and high levels of uncertainty. Agile relies on an iterative development process in which the scope of the project evolves over time. Development teams create feature-driven working products at the end of each development cycle. Active customer involvement is used to guide this process. Here are some of the key advantages of Agile methods:

- Work is divided into smaller and smaller chunks that are more easily scheduled and controlled.
- Collaboration between the customer and designers is increased leading to solid change control.
- Methods demand that features be tested and functional when completed.

[2] http://www.jamasoftware.com/media/documents/State_of_Requirements_Management_2011.pdf.

Agile PM is still evolving. While much of the attention in this chapter has been devoted to software development, Agile PM is being successfully applied to a wide range of unpredictable projects. New methods and approaches will continue to be developed and adapted to meet the specific needs of projects. Stay tuned.

Key Terms

Agile PM	Product owner	Self-organizing team
Feature	Release burndown chart	Sprint backlog
Iterative incremental	Scaling	Sprint burndown chart
development (IID)	Scrum master	
Product backlog	Scrum meeting	

Review Questions

1. Why is the traditional project management approach less effective when project scope and technology are not well known?
2. What is iterative incremental development? Why is it useful for developing new products?
3. What are the advantages of Agile PM? What are the disadvantages of Agile PM?
4. What similarities and differences exist between a traditional project manager and a Scrum master?
5. What are the differences between a self-organizing team and a conventional project team?
6. Why is it difficult to apply Agile PM to large scale projects?

Exercises

1. Break into small groups and identify at least two real-life examples of projects in which:
   a. The scope and technology are well known.
   b. The scope is well known but the technology is less well known.
   c. The scope is not well known but the technology is known.
   d. Neither the scope nor the technology is well known.
2. Break into small groups and discuss the following question:
   What organizational, group, individual, and project factors do you think would promote the successful adoption of Agile PM methodologies like Scrum? Why?
3. Use a project you are currently working on to hold a Scrum meeting according to the guidelines on page 599. Designate one member to act as the Scrum master and hold a standing meeting that lasts no longer than 15 minutes. Assess the value of such meetings.
4. Below are four mini-cases from practice. Break into small groups and (1) analyze the case and (2) provide five recommendations for the IT department.

Project A

You've just taken over a project from another project manager and have come back from a very uncomfortable meeting with your business sponsor. In the meeting, the sponsor told you how dissatisfied he is with the project's performance to date and that he's getting ready to pull the plug on the project entirely. Deadlines keep slipping, the application isn't complete, and the sponsor feels like he can't get in touch with anyone to give him an update on the project's status and progress.

From conversations with your project team, you learn that requirements still haven't been finalized, and the team is waiting for input before being able to proceed on several key parts of the application. Despite that, they've been able to push forward in other areas, and are quite proud of the work they've done. However, they haven't had a chance to show it to the sponsor.

To complicate matters further, your boss has made it clear that this project must be completed on schedule, because he needs the resources for another project.

What do you do? What impact do your decisions have on the project's cost, schedule, and performance?

Project B

Your project team has finished gathering the requirements and developing the solution design. Your team is broken into two main groups: The first group consists of the project manager, business analysts, and management and is located in the United States. The second group consists of the development and QA teams and they are located in India.

The WBS was developed based on estimates from the teams in India. The development team agreed to provide daily updates to you about progress against the WBS to make sure that the project's milestones are going to be met.

However, by the time the development team got close to the first milestone, it became obvious that they were behind even though their daily updates indicated that they are on track. In addition, the team adopted a different design approach than the one agreed upon at the beginning of the project.

The lack of meaningful updates from the development team along with a different design track has jeopardized the whole project by rendering the whole plan obsolete. Your team is now at risk of not delivering the project.

What do you do? What is the impact to cost, schedule, and performance?

Project C

You have just taken over as the program manager of a large program with multiple tracks and a go-live scheduled in three months. At the first meeting with the project sponsors and key stakeholders, you find out that the business requirements are not complete and in some cases not started, project scope is not realistic to meet the upcoming go-live and overall the project teams are confused due to lack of communication and understanding of priorities.

What do you do? What impact do your decisions have on the project's cost, schedule, and performance?

Project D

You've just been assigned to take over a new project from an outgoing project manager. The project is a high-visibility project that is using a development methodology that is new to you and to your company. In your transition meetings with the outgoing project manager, he assures you that development is complete, and all you have to do is shepherd the project through acceptance testing and release. As a result, several project team members were released as scheduled.

The acceptance testing does not go as smoothly as planned. The application has more defects than anticipated, and some core functionality is not able to be tested. The project team doesn't feel like they are getting the direction they need to continue moving forward, and the business sponsor has asked you when he can expect to test application functionality you didn't know is in scope. In addition, your project's deadline is rapidly approaching, and interproject dependencies make it unlikely that you will be able to push your launch date.

What do you do? What impact do your decisions have on cost, schedule, and performance?

References

Boulter, M., *Smart Client Architecture and Design Guide* (Seattle: Microsoft Press, 2004).

Decarlo, D., *eXtreme Project Management* (Jossey-Bass, 2004).

Faris, R., and I. Abdelshafi, "Project Management and Agile: Perfect Fit," 2006 PMI Global Congress Proceedings, Seattle, Washington.

Griffiths, M., *Using Agile Principles Alongside: A Guide to the Project Management Body of Knowledge,* PMI Global Proceedings, Anaheim, California, 2004.

Highsmith, J., *Agile Project Management* (Boston: Addison Wesley, 2004).

Hildebrand, C., *Full Speed Ahead, PM Network,* Vol. 21, No. 10, October 2007. pp. 36–41.

Jackson, M. B., "Step by Step," *PM Network,* 26 (6), June 2012, pp. 57–61.

James, M., "Scrum" (Download PDF @ *http://refcardz.dzone.com/* on 5/18/2009), 2009.

Jonasson, Hans, *Determining Project Requirements* (Boca Raton, FL: Auerback Publications, 2008).

Kruchten, P., *The Rational Unified Process: An Introduction,* Third Edition. (Upper Saddle River, NJ: Pearson Education, 2004).

Larman, C., *Agile & Iterative Development: A Manager's Guide* (Boston: Addison-Wesley, 2004).

McConnel, S., *Rapid Development: Taming Wild Software Schedules* (Redmond, WA: Microsoft Press, 1996).

Schwaber, K., *Agile Project Management with Scrum* (Redmond, WA: Microsoft Press, 2004).

Takeuchi, H., and I. Nonaka, "The New Product Development Game," *Harvard Business Review,* January–February 1986.

Vanderjack, B., "21 Methods to Engage and Retain Your Product Owner in an Agile Project," www.pmworldjournal.net, Vol. 1, No. 4, November 2012, pp. 1–6.

Worthen, B., "Try Software on Workers First, Fix It Later," *The Wall Street Journal,* September 25, 2007, pp. B1 and B4.

CASE 17.1

Introducing Scrum at P2P

PART A

Kendra Hua had worked for six years as a software engineer in the IT department at Point 2 Point (P2P), a large freight moving company. She liked her job and the people she worked with. While she did some maintenance work, she worked primarily on projects, usually full time. Her work covered a wide range of projects including system upgrades, inventory control, GPS tracking, billing, and customer databases. These projects were typically able to meet project requirements but were consistently late. Within the IT department it was common practice for a betting pool to emerge regarding completion dates. The rule of thumb was to take the original schedule and multiply it by 1.5 and start guessing from then on.

Management decided to try to turn things around by changing the way P2P completed IT projects. Instead of the traditional waterfall approach in which all the requirements were defined upfront, the IT department was to start using Agile project management, and more specifically Scrum, to complete their projects.

Kendra had just been assigned to the Big Foot project, which involved developing a system for monitoring P2P's carbon footprint. To prepare for this project, Kendra and her entire team of software engineers would attend a two-day Scrum workshop.

Everyone was given a book on Scrum to prepare themselves for the workshop. At first Kendra was overwhelmed by terminology—Scrum master, sprints, product manager, sprint logs, and so forth. She questioned the rugby metaphor, since the only thing she knew about the sport was that one of her ex-boyfriends in college would come back to the dorm inebriated and bloodied after a match. And why was the project manager called a master? It seemed demeaning to her. Still, she had heard some good things about Scrum from a friend who was using it in another company. He claimed it gave programmers more freedom to do their work, and work at a faster pace. So she approached the two-day workshop with an open mind.

The workshop was facilitated by a trainer who was well versed in the world of software development. Participants included her other five team members as well as Prem Gupta, a veteran project manager who would now assume the role of Scrum master, and Isaac Smith, who would act as the product manager representing the interests of the customers. At first everyone gave Prem a hard time, by bowing to him, pleading "master, master, master . . ." The facilitator quickly corrected them by saying he was not their master but rather master of the Scrum process. The facilitator went on to emphasize that they would work as a self-organizing team. Kendra wasn't exactly sure what that meant, but she felt it had something to do with the team managing itself, not Prem.

The workshop covered all the basic Scrum tools, concepts, and roles. Everyone got to practice the process by completing a simulated project involving the creation of a new board game. Kendra liked the idea of the standing Scrum meeting, since most of her meetings at P2P took way too long. She also liked having the product manager who was the ultimate decider on features and when work was completed. Everyone laughed at the "only one neck to wring" analogy that the facilitator used to describe this role. Overall she thought the process had promise and she was excited about trying it out on the Big Foot project. The Big Foot project was estimated to be completed after five sprints with each sprint lasting four weeks.

THE FIRST SPRINT

The first sprint planning meeting went pretty much by the book. Isaac had done his homework and came to the meeting with a comprehensive list of features the software needed to provide. There was healthy discussion, and Isaac amended the list to include some features that the team felt was necessary. The afternoon session featured Isaac, the product owner, prioritizing the features in the product backlog with feedback from the team. The final segment was devoted to the team deciding among themselves which high priority features they would commit to build within the four-week sprint. Prem did a good job of reminding the team that they were expected to build a fully functional feature. This tempered the team's enthusiasm, and in the end a challenging but doable set of features was assigned to the sprint backlog for the first sprint.

The first couple of daily Scrum meetings were a bit awkward as members were careful not to step on each others' toes. One of the first impediments identified was not having a shared understanding of how a self-organizing team worked. Prem kept emphasizing that it was up to the team to decide who does what and when. Then one morning it just suddenly clicked and members came forward claiming work they felt needed to be done. After that the daily scrums took on a life of their own, interrupted only when a member had to do five push-ups for every minute late. The pace of work picked up, and there was a shared enthusiasm as tasks and ultimately functional features were completed in rapid fashion. Kendra worked side by side with the other software engineers to solve problems and share what they had learned. Occasionally Isaac would be called into the project room to answer questions about specific features and be shown work in progress.

By the time of the first sprint review meeting, the team was able to demonstrate all but one of the designated features to Isaac and even three more that were not on the initial hit list. The team got some useful feedback not only from Isaac but also from a couple of the end users he brought with him. Eighty percent of the features were proclaimed done by Isaac while the others needed only slight modifications. Everyone agreed that the next Sprint review would even be more successful.

The sprint retrospective meeting was refreshing as members spoke candidly about both the good and the bad. Everyone agreed that the team needed to do a better job at documentation. Issues regarding fairness and spreading both the fun work and the tough work among the entire team was brought to the surface. Kendra was impressed by how everyone focused on what was best for the project not just themselves.

THE SECOND SPRINT

The second sprint meeting went well. The features that needed rework after the first sprint review meeting were at the top of the backlog and Isaac made appropriate adjustments in priorities and a couple of new features that were discovered during the sprint review meeting were added. The meeting convened with the team confident that they would be able to complete the work they had committed to.

Project work progressed quickly over the next week. Kendra felt pressure to accomplish what she said she would at the daily Scrum. At the same time, she felt a tremendous amount of satisfaction reporting work done. The entire team seemed energized. Then one day everything came to a standstill over a sticky integration problem. The team struggled over the next three days trying to solve the problem until at the next Scrum, Prem stepped forward saying "I think you should do this . . ." He then proceeded to outline a specific method for solving the problem, even assigning specific tasks to each team member. During the next two days Prem went back and forth between team members coordinating their work and solving problems. While there was some grumbling within the team, his solution worked, and Kendra was grateful to get back on track.

From then on Prem took a more active role in daily Scrum meetings, often having the final say as to the work agenda for that day. The meetings took on a different tone as members waited for Prem to speak first. Isaac was absent from the project room during this time as he was visiting sites that would be using the new software. Still features were being completed and Kendra was happy with its progress. Then one day Isaac showed up at the morning Scrum meeting. He had just gotten back and had fresh information he wanted to introduce into the project. He had rewritten the product log and added several new, high priority features and eliminated a few of the features that the team had been working on. He wanted the team to shift their efforts and complete the new features by the end of the sprint.

The team was shocked because one of the principles they had been taught is that you don't change course midway through a sprint. Prem did his best to explain this to Isaac, but he was insistent. He kept saying that these changes had to be made, otherwise much of the sprint output would be a waste of time. He kept repeating that the team needed to be flexible, "After all isn't that what the Agile approach is all about." The meeting came to an impasse until Prem came forward with a compromise. The team would agree to do the new work, but the sprint needed to be extended by two weeks. Everyone agreed and Kendra went back to work.

Up till the end of the second sprint, Prem continued to direct project work. When it came for the sprint review meeting four of the five new features were completed as well as most of the original features. However, the feature demonstrations did not go well. Isaac and several of the end users that were present were critical of the user friendliness of several of the completed features. Kendra and other team members defended their work by saying, "Why didn't you tell us you wanted it to perform that way?" Prem did his best to keep the meeting under control, but the team had little to say when an important feature simply did not work. In the end, only half of the features were accepted as being done.

Kendra walked out of the sprint review discouraged. Tomorrow morning was the sprint retrospective meeting. She had a lot on her mind, but wasn't sure what she should say or how to say it at the meeting.

1. How well is Scrum working?
2. What are the issues confronting the Big Foot project?
3. Assume you are Kendra. What would you want to say at the retrospective? How would you say it?
4. What improvements or changes need to be made?

PART B

Prem opened the retrospective by saying he had gotten a call from his boss and she was not happy with the progress. Prem said that he and the team were under the gun to get back on track. The list of things that went well during the second sprint was short and when it came time to discuss improvements there was an awkward silence. Kendra spoke up and began by saying she had gone back and reviewed the Scrum book. She went on to say that she thought the whole idea behind Scrum was that the team was to work to solve their own problems and it wasn't Prem's role to play task master. A couple of other team members murmured agreement. Prem became defensive and said if he had not intervened it would have taken days for the team to solve the problem.

Another member said he thought it was a mistake allowing Isaac to change the sprint commitments. Prem agreed that in principle that was true, but said sometimes you have to bend the rules to do what is right. He admonished the team by saying that they had to practice being more agile. The retrospective ended with few specific recommendations other than that in order to get back on track, Prem felt he would have to get even more involved in the execution of the project.

The subsequent sprint 3 planning meeting was more of a formality. Isaac updated the product backlog with revised priorities and Prem signed off for the team as to what they would commit to. There was little interaction between the team and Isaac except seeking clarification on performance requirements for specific features.

The team met under Prem's leadership for their daily Scrums. Sometimes the Scrums went beyond the normal 15 minutes as Prem reviewed progress and described in detail what needed to be done that day. Isaac would occasionally show up, change priorities, review work and answer questions. Kendra worked hard on her assignments and often received praise from Prem for work well done.

One evening when the team got together for a few beers and sushi, one of the team members pulled out a spreadsheet and asked who wanted to make the first bet on when they thought the project would be done.

After several sprints, Isaac finally signed off on the last feature and declared the project completed. A collective "yahoo" sprang from the team. After the meeting Kendra went around collecting money from each of her teammates—she had predicted that the project would take 12 weeks longer than planned.

1. How would you assess P2P effort at introducing Scrum?
2. What challenges does an organization face when adopting an Agile approach like Scrum?
3. What could P2P have done to enhance success?

18

PROJECT MANAGEMENT CAREER PATHS

Eighty percent of success is showing up.

—*Woody Allen*

This chapter discusses basic issues regarding a career in project management. One point to remember is that pursuing a career in project management does not necessarily mean you will ever have the title of project manager. Yes, there are growing numbers of fields in which project manager is a career path, but there are many more jobs in which project management is not a title but a job requirement. This underscores a major advantage to being good at managing projects; and that is the basic project management methodology you have been exposed to in this text is transferable across most businesses and professions. Think back to the Snapshots from Practice contained in the different chapters. They were not limited to one or two industries or professions, but rather entailed a smorgasbord of industries and professions! So, whether you are interested in a formal career in project management or just see managing projects as being important for your aspirations, this chapter provides advice for further developing your project management skills and know-how.

SNAPSHOT FROM PRACTICE
Rod Gwinn

1988–2002	Information Technology Professional
2002–2006	B.S. Business Administration–Oregon State University
2005–2006	Project Management Intern–Symantec Inc.
2006–2008	IT Manager–ECOS Consulting
2008–Pres	IT Project Manager–State of Oregon

Over the years I have worked on, and managed, many technology projects. Some of these went well, others did not. In retrospect, I see that the projects that went smoothly were the ones that were well organized and had some sort of a plan to follow. I did not realize at the time how much project management played a role in even the smallest IT project.

After working in the IT field for almost 20 years, I decided it was time to head back to college to finish my elusive degree. In my junior year, our MIS class took on a project to assist Symantec Corporation with a small development project. This allowed me to directly utilize the skills I had acquired during my early career, plus my learning experiences from the College of Business. One of the outcomes of this project was that the representative from Symantec mentioned an intern program that may be of interest to us.

As we were nearing our summer break, I pursued the opportunity at Symantec. I started as an intern shortly before the end of my junior year, and worked with them through the end of 2005. This proved to be a tremendous opportunity. I was directly working on IT projects for one of the largest software organizations in the world. I was exposed to their very formal process for project management and had the chance to apply my recent classroom experience in a meaningful way.

After graduation, I accepted a position at ECOS, a small environmental consulting company, where I applied my newly developed skills to help shape their technology strategic plan. I continued to explore opportunities in project management and was made aware of a position with the state of Oregon that seemed to be a very good fit for my experience and education. In April 2008, I accepted the position of enhancement project manager. My primary responsibility was to oversee the enhancement phase (Version 1.5) of the new MMIS (Medicaid Management Information System). I am very satisfied to have a new career path, as an IT project manager, which allows me to utilize both my past experiences and my recent education. One of the things I enjoy most about this type of work is the sense of accomplishment in delivering a project that is useful, usable, and meets, or even exceeds, expectations.

CAREER PATHS

There is no set career path for becoming a project manager. Career avenues vary from industry to industry, organization to organization, and from profession to profession. What can be said is that advancement occurs incrementally. You don't simply graduate and become a project manager. As in other careers, you have to work your way up to the position. For example, in project-based organizations such as construction firms, you may begin by working on several projects as an assistant engineer, then take an assignment as a project analyst. From there you are promoted to principal engineer, advance to assistant project manager, assume the role of project manager over a small project, and then continue to bigger, riskier projects. In other organizations, project management careers run parallel with functional advancement with many crossovers. For example, at Intel a management information systems (MIS) specialist might start his career as a designer, then take an assignment as a project specialist, later work as a project manager, and then return to a functional position as head of a department or as a product manager. See the Rod Gwinn Snapshot from Practice for an example of how a former student launched a career in project management.

Other people find that their project management responsibilities expand as they move up the organization's hierarchy. For example, a former marketing student began her career as an assistant buyer for a large retail company. She then became area sales manager at a specific store and became involved on a part-time basis in a series of projects, acting as a facilitator of focus groups. She was promoted to buyer and eventually became a store manager. In her current position, she coordinates a variety of projects ranging from improving the sales acumen of her salesforce to altering the physical layout of the store. Although the title of project manager does not appear in her job description, almost 50 percent of her work involves managing projects.

One aspect of project managing that is unique is the temporary nature of assignments. With line appointments, promotions are for the most part permanent and there is a natural, hierarchical progression to positions with greater authority and responsibility. In the example of the former marketing student, she progressed from assistant buyer to sales manager to buyer to store manager. Only under very unusual circumstances would she regress to being a buyer. Conversely, tenure is rarely granted to project managers. Once the project is completed, the manager may return to his previous department, even to a lesser position. Or, depending on the projects available, he may be assigned to manage a more or less significant project. Future work depends on what projects are available at the time the individual is available and how well the last project went. See the Ron Parker Snapshot for another example of a former student who leveraged his ability to manage projects into a successful career in the glass products industry.

PURSUING A CAREER

Students often complain that employers are only looking for candidates with experience, but how can they get experience unless someone takes a chance and hires them? While there is some truth to this Catch 22, a university or college can provide an amazing playground to acquire project management skills and experience. Whether it is organizing a fund-raising event for your living group, managing an intramural sports tournament, or leading a student government task force, project management opportunities abound on most campuses. By the time they graduate students with initiative can have a robust portfolio of projects that signal to employers that they can get the

1986	B.S. Business Administration–Oregon State University
1986–1990	Food Products Manufacturing
1990–1994	Wood Products Manufacturing
1994–Current	Glass Products Manufacturing

Upon completion of my business degree at OSU, I was recruited by a Fortune 100 food products company for a first line production supervisor position. In that role, an opportunity came up for me to manage a project that involved rolling out a new statistical package-weight-control program throughout the factory. Successfully completing that project was instrumental in accelerating my career within the company, advancing from supervisor to product manager in less than three years.

After four years in food products I accepted an offer to join a wood products manufacturing company. Initially my role in this company was Human Resources Manager. My HR responsibilities included managing several projects to improve safety and employee retention. Successful completion of these projects led to a promotion to Plant Manager. In the Plant Manager role, I was tasked with building and managing a new wood door manufacturing factory. After successfully taking that factory to full production, I was promoted again to Corporate Manager of Continuous Improvement. This "culture change" project involved implementing Total Quality Management throughout 13 different manufacturing factories as well as all the indirect and support functions within the corporation. Shortly after we successfully ingrained this new culture in the company, the owner passed away, leading me to look for other employment.

I was able to leverage my previous experience and success to convince the owner of a struggling glass fabrication company to hire me. In this new role as General Manager, I was tasked with turning the company around. This was my largest project yet. Turning a company around involves a myriad of smaller improvement projects spanning from facilities and equipment improvements to product line additions and deletions to sales and marketing strategy and everything in between. In four years, we successfully turned the company around to the extent that the owner was able to sell the company and comfortably retire.

Successfully turning that glass company around got the attention of a much larger competitor of ours, resulting in an offer of employment. This new offer involved the start-up of a $30M high-tech glass manufacturing facility in another state. We were able to take that facility from a dirt field to the highest volume manufacturing facility of its kind in the world in just three years. After building and operating this factory at a world-class benchmark level for 8 years, I came across a new and exciting opportunity to help expand a strong glass fabrication company in Canada. I spent four years successfully transitioning this Canadian company from a medium size glass fabrication facility to one of the largest and most successful of its kind in North America.

After tiring of the "Great White North," I found an opportunity to tackle the largest and most impactful project of my career. I'm currently VP of Operations in a venture-funded high-tech start-up company. In this role, I'm overseeing the construction and start-up of the first full-scale, high-volume electrochromic glass fabrication factory in the world. This new project involves building a company from the ground up and taking an exciting new technology from the lab to full-scale commercialization. Success in this role, although still far from being certain, will eventually revolutionize the glass industry through the introduction of a product that dramatically improves the energy efficiency and occupant comfort of buildings around the world.

Looking back on my career, it is apparent that my degree of success has largely been the result of taking on and successfully completing successively larger and increasingly impactful projects.

There's a saying that's always resonated with me: "If your only tool is a hammer, all your problems look like nails." Good tools are hard to come by and heavy to carry around. I like my tool bag filled with generalist tools; things like communication skills, leadership, common sense, judgment, reasoning, logic and a strong sense of urgency. I often wonder how much more I could have accomplished had I actually studied project management and had more of that toolset in my bag. With a bag full of strong generalist tools, you can tackle any problem in any business. Project management is clearly one of those skills where the better you are at it, the higher your chances of success in any business environment. Having the tools is only part of the equation though. To be successful, you must also be willing to run at problems/opportunities when everyone else is running away from them.

things done right. For example, one former student, after graduating in four years, was able to list on his resume:

- Organized a bowling event that raised over $2,500 for local Boys and Girls Club.
- Launched a Go Green project that lead to a 220 percent increase in recyclable materials across five student dorms.
- Co-chaired a student government task force that produced seven approved recommendations for improving interaction between American and International students.
- Organized a speaker series for the Management Club that brought nine prominent business professionals on campus to talk to students about career opportunities and essential management skills.

During very tough economic times he was able to land a plum job with Nike despite having just a 3.2 GPA.

When interviewing for potential jobs related to project management, you can impress interviewers by asking them questions about how their firm manages projects:

- What kinds of projects does the firm conduct? What are the opportunities to be a part of these projects?
- What is the project management structure of the organization? Is it projectized, functional, or matrix?
- How does the organization monitor project progress? Does it use an earned value system?
- What software do they use on projects? Microsoft Project? Excel? Primavera?
- How does the organization determine whether a project is a success? What is most important: time, dollars, scope, customer satisfaction?

These questions not only are likely to impress the interviewer, but yield valuable information to help you make a choice. In particular they should give you a glimpse of the organizational culture and whether you're a good fit. They also reveal how mature project management processes are within the organization. Organizations with established project management procedures and processes provide great learning grounds.

If you are considering a career in project management, you should first find out what specific project job opportunities exist in your company. You should talk to people in project management positions and find out how they got to where they are and what advice they can give you. Because career paths, as noted earlier, vary from organization to organization, you need to be attuned to the unique pathways within your company. For example, retail companies naturally assign marketing managers to projects. Electronics firms, on the other hand, typically assign engineers to be project leads.

Once you have concluded that you wish to pursue a career in project management, or see project management as an avenue for advancement, you need to share your aspirations with your immediate superior. Your superior can champion your ambitions, sanction additional training in project management, and assign immediate work that will contribute to your project skill base.

PROFESSIONAL TRAINING AND CERTIFICATION

Most project managers have never received formal training in project management. They mastered the job through on-the-job training, buttressed by occasional workshops on specific project topics such as project scheduling or negotiating contracts. It wasn't until recently that universities started offering courses on project management outside of schools of engineering; to date there are only a handful of degree programs in project management. Regardless of your level of training you will likely need to supplement your education. Many large companies have in-house training programs on project management. For example, at one time, Hewlett-Packard had more than 32 training modules in its project management curriculum, which is organized around five levels of experience: project team, new project manager, project manager, experienced project manager, and manager of project managers. Take advantage of professional workshops, which can cover a range of specific project management tools and topics. Continued education should not be restricted to project management. Many technical professionals return to universities to complete an MBA or take night classes in management to expand their general business background.

Many professionals find it beneficial to join the Project Management Institute (PMI). Membership entitles you to subscriptions to PMI publications including the academic *Project Management Journal* and the *PM Network,* a trade magazine. PMI sponsors workshops and national forums on project management. When you join PMI you also become a member of one of the more than 400 local chapters across North America. PMI also has local chapters in over 60 countries across the globe. These chapters meet on a monthly basis and provide project professionals with opportunities to network and learn from each other.

In addition, PMI, as part of its effort to advance the profession, certifies mastery of project manager competencies through a formal examination that covers the entire body of knowledge of project management. Two of the most popular certifications are Certified Associate in Project Management **(CAPM)** and Project Management Professional **(PMP).** The CAPM is designed for young professionals getting started in the field while PMP is restricted to seasoned veterans with significant project management experience (see Table 18.1).

Most students, by taking a formal class in project management at the university level, qualify to sit for the CAPM exam. Both the CAPM and PMP exams are based on the official Project Management Body of Knowledge (PMBOK) published by PMI. There are several "prep" books available to assist students in taking the examinations. These books provide useful tips as well as practice exams.

Passing the exam and being certified as either a CAPM or PMP is a clearly visible way to signal your competence and interest. See the Ginger Butler Snapshot from Practice for an example of how one former student used the CAPM to launch a career in project management.

TABLE 18.1 •••

PMI Certification Requirements

	CAPM	PMP
Full Name:	Certified Associate in Project Management	Project Management Professional
Project Role:	Contributes to project team	Leads and directs project teams
Eligibility Requirements:	High school diploma/global equivalent **AND** 1,500 hours experience **OR** 23 hours project management education	High school diploma/global equivalent **5** years project management experience **35** hours project management education **OR** Bachelor's degree/global equivalent **3** years project management experience **35** hours project management education
Exam Information:	3 hours; 150 multiple-choice questions	4 hours; 200 multiple-choice questions

SNAPSHOT FROM PRACTICE
Ginger Butler

2000	B.S. Business Administration
2000-07	Software Analyst
2007	Master Business Administration (MBA) CAPM PMI Project Management Certification
2007	Project Manager
2008	Director Project Management Office
2009	Vice President, Products & Operations

After 10 years of bookkeeping, I decided to return to college to complete a bachelor's degree in business administration–management information systems. It was in my junior year that I took a project management (PM) course. I was impressed with how PM methods can break down the most complicated projects into steps that could then be turned into processes that would likely result in successful projects. The next seven years were spent as a software analyst. Time and time again, I could see the need for effective PM in our software development shop. Slowly, I started to apply what I had learned and began to realize how useful project management tools and techniques were to getting things done.

I knew that I needed to learn more. I was contemplating whether to take a project management course to acquire PM certification or make a bolder move and earn an MBA. I made the decision to earn the MBA and, once again, had the opportunity to take an advanced course in PM. Before I graduated, I orchestrated a PM certification prep course in which I and 11 other graduate students ultimately earned their certification.

One week after graduation, I took a project management position at Avant Assessment. PM certification was a requirement for the job. Avant Assessment (founded in 2001) designs, develops, and delivers four-skill language proficiency assessments that are standards-based, validated, and delivered in a Web environment. The company embraced the science of PM and provided an amazing opportunity for me to make a significant impact as a project manager. Within two years, I was promoted to director of our PM office. From there I was able to create cohesive and effective processes in our production department and have repeated the process development successes in our products department.

Recently, I was promoted to director of operations. This is a direct result of what I have been able to accomplish with the education and continued learning about project management. By coupling the MBA with PM, I was prepared to take on significant challenges and produce tactical, operational, and strategic improvements within and across departments. Granted, I was in the right place at the right time to get such a great opportunity at Avant Assessment. This company is an innovative thinking, action-oriented company that has been very rewarding to work for. Avant recognizes and encourages personal and professional growth and development. Thanks to the spark of interest found years ago in project management, and to Avant Assessment for igniting a passion for improvment, my career has skyrocketed.

More on Certification

The benefit of earning certification lies in adding value to your degree. You may find being certified opens a door to an interview. Levinson reports that certified project managers may have greater access to jobs and higher salaries. According to the Seventh Edition of the PMI Project Management Salary Survey, individuals with certain credentials like the PMP earn at least $10,000 more than those without. IBM reports that some of their customers request a certified project manager. However, Steve DelGrosso, director of IBM's Project Management Center of Excellence, points out: "Being a certified project manager doesn't necessarily make you better than any other project manager. It just indicates that you have a certain level of knowledge and expertise, and that you can work proficiently in a project environment." If seven of ten projects fail, customers may believe a certified manager will bring a project in on time and on budget. However, many factors affect the success of a project. The best that can be said is that hiring a certified project manager may increase the odds of success (Levinson, 2010).

Interviews of IT executives show that many of the so-called "soft" skills of leadership, communication skills (oral and writing), and ability to deal with ambiguity and change are more valuable than certification (Stevenson and Starkweather, 2010). PMI certification indicates that you have learned the processes of project management along with the common terms used in the field (e.g., scope, requirements, work breakdown structure, project network, risk, earned value, critical chain, agile). On the inside front cover of this text, you can find a chart that correlates sections of the text to the accrediting exam. In summary, PMI certification exams are very process oriented and may help you pass a hiring filter.

GAINING VISIBILITY

As you accumulate knowledge and techniques, you need to apply them to your immediate job situation. Most people's jobs entail some form of project work, whether realizing a mandated objective or simply figuring out ways to improve the quality of performance. Gantt charts, responsibility matrixes, CPM networks, and other project management tools can be used to plan and implement these endeavors. It may also be wise to look outside the workplace for opportunities to develop project management skills. Active involvement in your local community can provide numerous opportunities to manage projects. Organizing a local soccer tournament, managing a charitable fund-raising event, or coordinating the renovation of the neighborhood park can allow you to practice project management. Furthermore, given the volunteer nature of most of these projects, they can provide you with an excellent training ground to sharpen your ability to exercise influence without formal authority.

Regardless of how competent and worthy you are, your project management skills must be visible to others for them to be recognized. Many project managers' careers began by volunteering for task forces and small projects. Ideally you should select task forces and projects that allow you access to higher-ups and other departments within your organization, providing you with opportunities to develop contacts.

This was certainly true for a former student of ours named Bob who escaped the trenches of a large corporation by volunteering to lead the organization's annual United Way campaign. While an important cause, directing the United Way campaign was generally given to someone who was expendable. This was true for Bob whose career had bottomed out. Bob took advantage of the United Way task force to show off his project management skills. Through recruiting key participants, establishing a shared vision, managing milestones, and contagious enthusiasm the campaign was a resounding success shattering previous records. Bob's efforts caught the attention of top management, and he was rewarded with more project work.

MENTORS

In pursuing your ambition you should continually be on the lookout for a mentor. Most fast-track managers acknowledge that mentors played a significant role in their advancement. **Mentors** are typically superiors who take a special interest in you and your career. They use their clout to champion your ambitions and act as a personal coach, teaching you "the ropes to skip and the ropes to know." This special treatment does not come without a price. Mentors typically require fervent loyalty and superior performance; after all, the mentor's reputation rests on your performance. How do you find a mentor? Most people say it just happens. But it doesn't happen to everyone. Mentors typically seek A+ workers, not C workers, and you must make your abilities known to others.

Many organizations have instituted formal mentoring programs in which experienced project managers are assigned to promising young managers (see Snapshot: Grooming the Next Generation at Intel). Although the relationship may not evolve to the personal level experienced with an informal mentor, designated mentors play a very similar role in coaching and championing one's professional progress. You should take advantage of this opportunity to learn as much as you can from these seasoned veterans.

Since much project work is temporary and contractual in nature, it is important to develop professional contacts that may lead to future work. Attending conferences, trade fairs, and workshops provides good opportunities to "network" and develop social connections that might precipitate project assignments. These social/professional networks can provide a safety net for project work during times of downsizing and layoffs.

SNAPSHOT FROM PRACTICE

Grooming the Next
Generation at Intel*

"Mentoring is how we groom the next generation of talent," asserts Jeff Hodgkinson, senior program manager at IT giant Intel. A 30-year Intel veteran, he has mentored dozens of people across the corporation—from new recruits to project managers looking for help as they transition to new roles.

"I had great mentors and managers over the years, and now I'm at the age where I feel obligated to pass the knowledge on to the next generation," Mr. Hodgkinson says. "Besides I want to make sure the next generation of Intel employees keep our stock up and keep putting out good products."

Even seasoned professionals can benefit from mentoring. Hodgkinson was assigned to be a mentor for Bill Crider, a senior program manager in the engineering computing program office at Intel in Austin, Texas. Crider was in the midst of managing a massive five-year IT upgrade project that involved 48 sub-teams, more than 85,000 computers, and 24 project managers who reported to him.

"There were many times on that project where I felt completely in over my head," Crider admits.

Mentoring helped Crider improve his project management style, teaching him to focus on the big picture and delegate more of the daily tasks. "I was heading toward a classic burnout situation. I was working 12-hour days, but I couldn't complain to anyone over or under me," Crider says, "Jeff helped me see that I was taking too much on and how to worry less about the little things."

Crider now mentors and coaches about 15 project managers. He admits mentoring takes time, but he says it's worth the effort—both to the mentee and to the organization. "You need to mentor because it's wrong not pass on what you know," he says.

For Hodgkinson, mentoring has expanded his social network and established him as a project management go-to guy. "When you mentor other people, you earn respect," he says. "They come to you for help, which establishes your reputation as an expert."

* S. F. Gale, "Building Leaders," *PM Network*, October 2010, pp. 34–37.

SUCCESS IN KEY PROJECTS

Ultimately your goal is to accumulate a portfolio of project management experiences that broaden your skill base and reputation. Early on you should choose, when possible, projects with the greatest learning opportunities. Pick projects more for the quality of the people working on them than for the scope of the projects. There is no better way to learn how to be an effective project manager than by watching one at work. Keep a diary of your observations and review and refine lessons learned. Later, as your confidence and competency grow, you should try to get involved in projects that will enhance your reputation within the firm. Remember the comments about customer satisfaction. You want to exceed your superior's expectations. Avoid run-of-the-mill projects or assignments. Seek high-profile projects that have some risks and tangible payoffs. At the same time, be careful to be involved in projects commensurate with your abilities.

Finally, despite your efforts you may find that you are not making satisfactory progress toward your career goals. If this is your appraisal, you may wish to seriously consider moving to a different company or even a different industry that might provide more project management opportunities. Hopefully, you have managed to accumulate sufficient project management experience to aid in your job search. One advantage of project work over general management is that it is typically easier to highlight and "sell" your accomplishments.

Summary

It is rare to find a job or a career path that would not benefit from being good at managing projects. Students starting their careers should take advantage of every opportunity to continue to develop and expand their project management skills. They should volunteer to work on task forces, take advantage of training opportunities, and apply project management tools and techniques to their work. They should signal to their superiors their interest in project management and garner project assignments. Over time they should accumulate a portfolio of project management experiences that establishes their skill base and reputation as someone who gets things done quickly and done right.

As you pursue your career we leave you two suggestions as a project manager:

1. Maintain a sense of the big picture. Engage regularly in what some have called "helicopter management," which means expand your perspective beyond immediate concerns and assess how the project fits in the larger scheme of things. Project managers need to constantly assess how the project fulfills the mission and strategy of the firm, how the project is affecting the rest of the organization, whether the expectations of stakeholders are changing, and what key project interfaces have to be managed.

2. Remember that successful project management is essentially a balancing act. Project managers need to balance the soft (people) side of project management with the hard (technical) side, the demands of top management with the needs of team members, short-term gain with long-term need, and so forth.

Key Terms

CAPM   Mentor   PMP

Review Questions

1. Why are project management knowledge and skills transferable across industries? Professions?
2. Is there a set career path in project management? Explain.
3. How can a mentor help someone pursue a career in project management?

Exercises

1. Interview someone who has worked as a project manager or project management professional.
   a. How did they get started in the field?
   b. How has their career progressed?
   c. What advice would they give someone wishing to pursue a career in project management?
2. Interview someone who works in a field you are interested in pursuing.
   a. How did they get started in the field?
   b. How important is project management in the field? In their current job?
   c. What advice would they give someone wishing to pursue a career in their field?
3. Use an Internet job search engine (e.g., Monster.com) and search for jobs in the field of project management. What did this search reveal about
   a. the demand for project managers?
   b. the importance of certification?
   c. different industries looking for project managers?

References

Ferrazzi, K., and T. Rhaz, *Never Eat Alone: And Other Secrets to Success, One Relationship at a Time* (New York: Broadway Business, 2005).

Gray, C., "Accelerating Management Maturity in Project-Oriented Organizations," *PM World Today,* May 2011, pp. 1–4.

Lientz, B. P., and K. P. Rea, *Project Management for the 21st Century* (San Diego: Academic Press, 1995).

Hölzle, K., "Designing and Implementing a Career Path for Project Managers," *International Journal of Project Management,* 28 (8), 2010, pp. 779–786.

Levinson, M., "Why Project Management Certifications Matter," *Networkworld.com* (retrieved November 17, 2010).

Martin, P., and K. Tate, *Getting Started in Project Management* (New York: Wiley, 2004).

Pant, L., and B. Baroudi, "Project Management Education: The Human Skills Imperative," *International Journal of Project Management,* Vol. 26, 2008, pp. 124–128.

Project Management Institute, *Project Management Salary Survey, 7th ed.* (Newton Sq., PA: PMI Publications, 2012).

Stevenson, D. H., and Jo A. Starkweather, "IT Critical Competency Index: IT Execs Prefer Soft Skills," *International Journal of Project Management,* Vol. 7, October 2010, pp. 663–671.

1

SOLUTIONS TO SELECTED EXERCISES

Chapter 2

2-2. Payback = Investment/Annual Savings
Project Alpha: $150,000/$40,000 = 3.75 years
Project Beta: $200,000/$50,000 = 4.0 years
Project Alpha is the better payback.

2-5. The only project SIMSOX should consider is **Voyagers.** Each of the other two projects would not satisfy the high rate of return SIMSOX expects from its projects.

Project: **Dust Devils**

Year	Inflows	Outflows	Net flow	Discount Factor	NPV
0		500,000	(500,000)	1.00	(500,000)
1	50,000		50,000	0.81	40,500
2	250,000		250,000	0.66	165,000
3	350,000		350,000	0.54	189,000

Total: $(105,500)

If calculated in EXCEL: $(106,020)

Project: **Ospry**

Year	Inflows	Outflows	Net flow	Discount Factor	NPV
0		250,000	(250,000)	1.00	(250,000)
1	75,000		75,000	0.81	60,750
2	75,000		75,000	0.66	49,500
3	75,000		75,000	0.54	40,500
4	50,000		50,000	0.44	22,000

Total: $(77,250)

If calculated in EXCEL: $(77,302)

Project: **Voyagers**

Year	Inflows	Outflows	Net flow	Discount Factor	NPV
0		75,000	(75,000)	1.00	(75,000)
1	15,000		15,000	0.81	12,150
2	25,000		25,000	0.66	16,500
3	50,000		50,000	0.54	27,000
4	50,000		50,000	0.44	22,000
5	150,000		150,000	0.36	54,000

Total: $(56,650)

If calculated in EXCEL: $(55,714)

Chapter 6

6-3. Activity C is a burst activity. Activity G is a merge activity.

6-11.

6-13.

6-20.

The only activities that have the start or finish on the critical path are E and K.

Chapter 8

8-4.

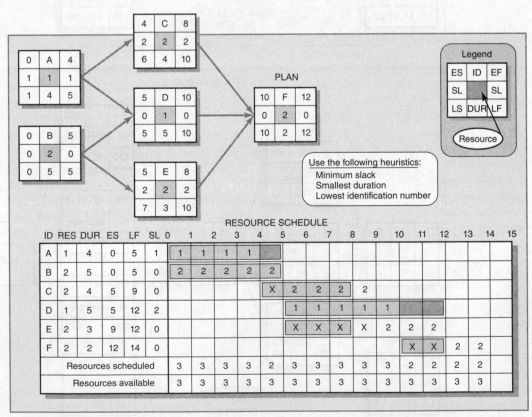

8-7. You should not spend time planning how you are going to spend your bonus. The schedule will take 16 days.

Use the following heuristics:
 Minimum slack
 Smallest duration
 Lowest identification number

Legend

ES	ID	EF
SL		SL
LS	DUR	LF

Resource

RESOURCE SCHEDULE

ID	RES	DUR	ES	LF	SL	0	1	2	3	4	5	6	7	8	9	10	11	12	13	14	15	16	17	18
A	2	2	0	2	0	2	2																	
B	2	1	5	6	0							2												
C	2	3	2	5	0			2	2	2														
D	2	1	6	7	0								2											
E	2	2	7	9	0									2	2									
F	1	3	9	12	0											1	1	1						
G	2	2	12	14	0												2	2						
H	2	2	14	16	0														2	2				
Resources scheduled						2	2	2	2	2	2	2	2	2	1	1	1	2	2	2	2			
Resources available						2	2	2	2	2	2	2	2	2	2	2	2	2	2	2	2			

8-10.

Legend:

ES	ID	EF
SL		SL
LS	DUR	LF

ID	Budget	0	1	2	3	4	5	6	7	8	9	10	11	12
A	40	10	10	10	10									
B	32	8	4	8	4	8								
C	48					12	12	12	12					
D	18						6	2	2	2	6			
E	28						8	8	12					
F	40											20	20	
Total	206	18	14	18	14	20	26	22	26	2	6	20	20	
Cumulative		18	32	50	64	84	110	132	158	160	166	186	206	

Cost by Week

A	10	10	10	10	
B	8	4	8	4	8
C	12	12	12	12	
D	6	2	2	2	6
E	8	8	12		
F	20	20			

Chapter 9

9-2.

Activity	Normal Time	Normal Cost	Maximum Crash Time	Crash Cost
A	1	100	0	0
B	3	150	2	100
C	4	200	1	50
D	3	200	1	60
E	4	200	2	70
F	3	150	1	90

9-8.

Activity	Normal Time	Normal Cost	Maximum Crash Time	Crash Cost
A	3	150	0	0
B	4	200	1	100
C	3	250	1	60
D	4	200	1	40
E	2	250	0	0
F	3	200	2	30
G	2	250	1	20
H	4	300	2	60
I	2	200	1	200

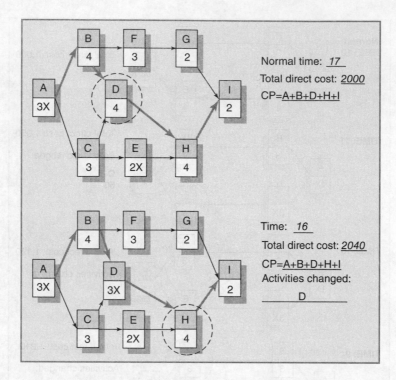

Normal time: _17_
Total direct cost: _2000_
CP=A+B+D+H+I

Time: _16_
Total direct cost: _2040_
CP=A+B+D+H+I
Activities changed:
D

Time: _15_
Total direct cost: _2100_
CP=A+B+D+H+I
Activities changed:
H

Time: _14_
Total direct cost: _2160_
CP=A+B+D+H+I
A+B+F+G+I
Activities changed:
H

Duration	Direct Cost	Indirect Cost	Total Cost
17	2000	1500	3500
16	2040	1450	3490
15	2100	1400	3500
14	2160	1350	3510
13	2260	1300	3560
12	2460	1250	3710

The optimum time cost schedule would be 16 weeks at a cost of $3490.

Chapter 13

13-4.

Status Report: **Ending Period 2** ($000)

Task	% Complete	EV	AC	PV	CV	SV
A	75%	30	25	20	5	10
B	50%	16	12	12	4	4
Cumulative Totals		46	37	32	9	14

Status Report: **Ending Period 4** ($000)

Task	% Complete	EV	AC	PV	CV	SV
A	100%	40	35	40	5	0
B	100%	32	24	24	8	8
Cumulative Totals		72	59	64	13	8

Status Report: **Ending Period 6** ($000)

Task	% Complete	EV	AC	PV	CV	SV
A	100%	40	35	40	5	0
B	100%	32	24	32	8	0
C	75%	36	24	24	12	12
D	0%	0	0	6	0	−6
E	50%	14	10	8	4	6
Cumulative Totals		122	93	110	29	12

Status Report: **Ending Period 8** ($000)

Task	% Complete	EV	AC	PV	CV	SV
A	100%	40	35	40	5	0
B	100%	32	24	32	8	0
C	100%	48	32	48	16	0
D	33%	6	20	10	−14	−4
E	100%	28	20	28	8	0
Cumulative Totals		154	131	158	23	−4

Performance Indexes Summary ($000)

Period	EV	AC	PV	SPI	CPI	PCIB
2	46	37	32	1.44	1.24	22%
4	72	59	64	1.13	1.22	35%
6	122	93	110	1.11	1.31	59%
8	154	131	158	.97	1.18	75%

Forecast Costs at Completion

$$\text{EAC}_f = \frac{(\text{BAC} - \text{EV})}{(\text{EV/AC})} + \text{AC}$$

$$= \frac{(206 - 154)}{(154/131)} + 131$$

$$= 175$$

$$\text{VAC}_f = \text{BAC} - \text{EAC}_f$$

$$\text{VAC}_f = 206 - 175$$

$$\text{VAC}_f = 31$$

At the end of the 8th period, three-quarters of the project has been completed at a savings of $23,000. If the project continues to get $1.18 worth of work for each dollar spent the project will be $31,000 under budget at completion. The project appears to be slightly behind of schedule.

13-8. Part A

Status Report: **Ending Period 1**						($000)
Task	**% Complete**	**EV**	**AC**	**PV**	**CV**	**SV**
A	25%	25	50	50	−25	−25
Cumulative Totals		25	50	50	−25	−25

Status Report: **Ending Period 2**						($000)
Task	**% Complete**	**EV**	**AC**	**PV**	**CV**	**SV**
A	50%	50	100	100	−50	−50
Cumulative Totals		50	100	100	−50	−50

Status Report: **Ending Period 3**						($000)
Task	**% Complete**	**EV**	**AC**	**PV**	**CV**	**SV**
A	100%	100	200	100	−100	0
B	0%	0	0	100	0	−100
C	0%	0	0	150	0	−150
Cumulative Totals		100	200	350	−100	−250

Status Report: **Ending Period 4**						($000)
Task	**% Complete**	**EV**	**AC**	**PV**	**CV**	**SV**
A	100%	100	200	100	−100	0
B	60%	150	100	150	50	0
C	50%	225	200	300	25	−75
Cumulative Totals		475	500	550	−25	−75

Status Report: **Ending Period 5**						($000)
Task	**% Complete**	**EV**	**AC**	**PV**	**CV**	**SV**
A	100%	100	200	100	−100	0
B	100%	250	200	250	50	0
C	100%	450	400	450	50	0
Cumulative Totals		800	800	800	0	0

Status Report: **Ending Period 6** ($000)

Task	% Complete	EV	AC	PV	CV	SV
A	100%	100	200	100	−100	0
B	100%	250	200	250	50	0
C	100%	450	400	450	50	0
D	75%	150	100	100	50	50
Cumulative Totals		950	900	900	50	50

Status Report: **Ending Period 7** ($000)

Task	% Complete	EV	AC	PV	CV	SV
A	100%	100	200	100	−100	0
B	100%	250	200	250	50	0
C	100%	450	400	450	50	0
D	100%	200	150	200	50	0
E	20%	60	100	0	−40	60
F	5%	15	50	0	−35	15
Cumulative Totals		1075	1100	1000	−25	75

Status Report: **Ending Period 8** ($000)

Task	% Complete	EV	AC	PV	CV	SV
A	100%	100	200	100	−100	0
B	100%	250	200	250	50	0
C	100%	450	400	450	50	0
D	100%	200	150	200	50	0
E	100%	300	350	200	−50	100
F	10%	30	100	100	−70	−70
Cumulative Totals		1330	1400	1300	−70	30

Performance Indexes Summary ($000)

Period	EV	AC	PV	SPI	CPI	PCIB
1	25	50	50	.50	.50	2%
2	50	100	100	.50	.50	3%
3	100	200	350	.29	.50	5%
4	475	500	550	.86	.95	24%
5	800	800	800	1.00	1.00	40%
6	950	900	900	1.06	1.06	48%
7	1075	1100	1000	1.08	.98	54%
8	1330	1400	1300	1.02	.95	67%

$$EAC_f = \frac{(BAC - EV)}{(EV/AC)} + AC \qquad\qquad VAC_f = BAC - EAC_f$$

$$2105 = \frac{(2000 - 1330)}{(1330/1400)} + 1400 \qquad\qquad -105 = 2000 - 2105$$

With two-thirds of the project completed the forecast is that the project will be $105,000 over budget at completion.

13-8 Part B.

Revised Estimates: **Ending Period 14**

Task	% Complete	EV	AC	PV	CV	SV
A	100%	100	200	100	−100	0
B	100%	250	200	250	50	0
C	100%	450	400	450	50	0
D	100%	200	150	200	50	0
E	100%	300	350	300	−50	0
F	100%	300	500	300	−200	0
G	100%	200	150	200	50	0
H	100%	200	200	200	0	0
Cumulative Totals		2000	2150	2000	−150	0

$$EAC_{re} = AC + ETC_{re} \qquad\qquad 2150 = 1400 + 750$$
$$VAC_{re} = BAC - EAC_{re} \qquad\qquad -150 = 2000 - 2150$$

Revised estimates indicate that the project will be one period behind schedule and $150,000 over budget.

2

COMPUTER PROJECT EXERCISES

In developing the exercises, trade-offs had to be made to enrich the learning experience. One of the major problems students initially encounter is data and detail overload. This reduces their ability to identify project and data problems and to compare alternatives. Although the project found in the exercises is real, it has been reduced and detail has been eliminated many times to concentrate on applying project management principles and understanding linkages. In addition, other simplifying assumptions have been made so that students and instructors can trace problems and discuss outcomes. These assumptions detract from reality, but they keep the focus on the objectives of the exercises and reduce student frustration with software intricacies. Moving from these exercises to real projects is primarily one of increasing detail. The simplifying assumptions are given below (make sure they are included in "default," "preferences," and/or "options" sections of the software used):

THE POM+ PROJECT*

Big Kola Company has been concerned that specialized fruit drinks have been eroding their cola market. The CEO mandates that "If you can't beat them, join them." Grape juice was the first product that was successful after an advertising blitz claiming the antitoxin benefits. Lately, competition is compressing grape juice margins and profits. Months of additional market surveys and focus groups have resulted in three potential high-margin drinks: cranberry, blueberry, and pomegranate. All these choices represent antitoxins. The decision is to produce the pomegranate drink that has many health claims. For example, the relative ability of these juices to eliminate harmful free radicals (antitoxins) is 71 percent for pomegranate, 33 percent for blueberry, and 20 percent for cranberry (Technion Institute of Technology). The market potential appears very attractive and should have a higher profit margin than the other potential juice products. Another appeal for pomegranate juice is its familiarity in the Middle East and Asia.

---

* Cliff Gray, Erik Larson, & Pinyarat Sirisomboonsuk, doctoral candidate at Rawls College of Business, Texas Tech University.

The Priority Matrix for the POM+ Project is:

	Time	Scope	Cost
Constrain			X
Enhance		X	
Accept	X		

Connor Gage, the project manager, has formed his project team and the members have come up with the following work breakdown structure.

1.0 POM+Project
1.1 R&D product development
    1.1.1 Need survey
    1.1.2 Set product specs
    1.1.3 Shelf life report
    1.1.4 Nutrition report
1.2 Secure fruit suppliers
1.3 Initial Production
    1.3.1 Equipment rehab
    1.3.2 Production trials
    1.3.3 Quality trials
    1.3.4 Quality metrics
    1.3.5 Quality training
1.4 Distribution
    1.4.1 Market testing
    1.4.2 Package design
    1.4.3 Select distributors
1.5 Legal
    1.5.1 Complete FDA certification
    1.5.2 Register trademark
1.6 Prepare product launch

Part 1

1. Develop the WBS outline using the software available (save your file).
2. Use this file and the information provided below to create a project schedule.
3. The following holidays are observed: January 1, Martin Luther King Day (third Monday in January), Memorial Day (last Monday in May), July 4th, Labor Day (first Monday in September), Thanksgiving Day (4th Thursday in November), December 25 and 26.
4. If a holiday falls on a Saturday then Friday will be given as an extra day off, and if it falls on a Sunday then Monday will be given off.
5. The project team works eight-hour days, Monday through Friday.
6. The project will begin on January 3, 2012.

7. Based on this schedule, submit a memo that answers the following questions:
   a. When is the project estimated to be completed? How many working days will it take?
   b. What is the critical path?
   c. Which activity has the most total slack?
   d. How sensitive is this network?
   e. Identify two sensible milestones and explain your choice.

Include the following (one page) printouts:

- A Gantt chart.
- A network diagram highlighting the critical path.
- A schedule table reporting ES, LS, EF, LF, and slack for each activity.

Hints: Change the timescale to months and weeks. The estimated duration of the project is 135 days.

Remember: Save your files for future exercises!

The following information has been derived from the WBS. *Note* that the activity number is what appears in the software with the complete WBS entered.

#*	Activity	Duration	Predecessor(s)
3	Need survey	20	None
4	Set product specs	15	3
5	Shelf life report	10	4
6	Nutrition report	5	4
7	Select fruit suppliers	20	5, 6
9	Equipment rehab	30	4
10	Production trials	15	7, 9
11	Quality trials	20	10
12	Quality metrics	5	11
13	Quality training	15	12
15	Market testing	30	5, 6
16	Package design	15	15
17	Select distributors	25	5, 6
19	Complete FDA certification	15	7, 15
20	Register trademark	5	7, 15
21	Prepare product launch	15	13, 16, 17, 19FS + 25 days, 20FS + 15 days

FS = Finish to Start lag

Part 2

Remember the old saying, "A project plan is not a schedule until resources are committed." This exercise illustrates this sometime subtle, but important point.

Using your files from Part 1, input resources and their costs if you have not already done so. All information is found in Tables A2.1 and A2.2.

TABLE A2.1
Resource Assignments

Activity	Resources
Need survey	MRKT (500%)
Set product specs	R&D (400%), MRKT (200%)
Shelf life report	R&D (300%)
Nutrition report	R&D (300%)
Select fruit suppliers	PURCH (100%)
Equipment rehab	ENG (1,000%), PROD (2,000%)
Production trials	PROD (1,500%), PURCH (100%), ENG (1,000%)
Quality trials	QUAL (300%), PROD (500%)
Quality metrics	QUAL (300%), PROD (100%)
Quality training	QUAL (300%), PROD (1,500%)
Market testing	MRKT (500%)
Package design	DESIGN (300%), MRKT (100%)
Select distributors	MRKT (500%)
Complete FDA certification	LEGAL (300%)
Register trademark	LEGAL (300%)
Prepare product launch	QUAL (300%), PURCH (200%), PROD (1,500%), MRKT (500%), ENG (500%), R&D (100%)

TABLE A2.2
Resources Availability and Pay Rates

Resource	Abbrev	Available	Hourly rate
Marketing staff	MRKT	5	$ 80/hr
R&D	R&D	5	$ 80/hr
Engineering	ENG	10	$100/hr
Purchasing	PURCH	2	$ 60/hr
Quality engineers	QUAL	3	$ 80/hr
Designers	DESIGN	3	$ 60/hr
Legal staff	LEGAL	3	$120/hr
Production	PROD	20	$ 60/hr

Prepare a memo that addresses the following questions:

1. Which if any of the resources are overallocated?
2. Assume that the project is time constrained and try to resolve any overallocation problems by leveling within slack. What happens?
3. What is the impact of leveling within slack on the sensitivity of the network?

Include a Gantt chart with the schedule table after leveling within slack.

4. Assume the project is resource constrained and resolve any overallocation problems by leveling outside of slack. What happens?

Include a Gantt chart with the schedule table after leveling outside of slack.

Note: No splitting of activities is allowed.

Note: No partial assignments (e.g., 50 percent). All resources must be assigned 100 percent.

Part 3

Top management has accepted the July 19th completion schedule created at the end of Part 2. Prepare a brief memo that addresses the following questions:

1. How much will the project cost? What is the most expensive activity?
2. What does the cash flow statement tell you about how costs are distributed over the life span of the project?

Include a monthly cash flow for the project.

Once you are confident that you have the final schedule, save the file as a baseline. **Hint:** Save a backup file just in case without baseline!

Part 4 A

Assume that today is March 31, 2012, and Table A2.3 contains the tracking information for the project up till now. Enter this information into your saved baseline file and prepare a status report for the first three months of the POM+ project.

TABLE A2.3 ....
Status Report March 31, 2012

Activity	Actual Start	Actual Finish	Actual Duration	Remaining Duration
Need survey	1/3/12	2/2/12	22	0
Set product specs	2/3/12	2/28/12	18	0
Shelf life report	2/29/12	3/13/12	10	0
Nutrition report	3/14/12	3/19/12	4	0
Equipment rehab	2/29/12		23	12

Your status report should also address the following questions:

1. How is the project progressing in terms of cost and schedule?
2. What activities have gone well? What activities have not gone well?
3. What do the PCIB and PCIC indicate in terms of how much of the project has been accomplished to date?
4. What is the forecasted cost at completion (EAC_f)? What is the predicted VAC_f?
5. Report and interpret the TCPI for the project at this point in time.
6. What is the estimated date of completion?
7. How well is the project doing in terms of its priorities?

Try to present the above information in a form worthy of consideration by top management.

Include an Earned Value table and a Tracking Gantt Chart.

Note: Insert March 31, 2012, as the status date in the Project Information box.

Part 4 B

Assume that today is May 31, 2012, and Table A2.4 contains the tracking information for the project up till now. Enter this information into your saved baseline file and prepare a status report for the POM+ project.

TABLE A2.4 ··
Status Report May 31, 2012

Activity	Actual Start	Actual Finish	Actual Duration	Remaining Duration
Need survey	1/3/12	2/2/12	22	0
Set product specs	2/3/12	2/28/12	18	0
Shelf life report	2/29/12	3/13/12	10	0
Nutrition report	3/14/12	3/19/12	4	0
Select fruit suppliers	4/3/12	4/30/12	20	0
Equipment rehab	2/29/12	4/11/12	31	0
Production trials	4/17/12	5/4/12	14	0
Quality trials	5/7/12	5/31/12	18	0
Market testing	4/4/12	5/9/12	26	0
Package design	5/10/12	5/25/12	12	0
Select distributors	5/28/12		4	18
Complete FDA certification	5/11/12	5/31/12	14	0

Your status report should address the following questions:

1. How is the project progressing in terms of cost and schedule?
2. What activities have gone well? What activities have not gone well?
3. What do the PCIB and PCIC indicate in terms of how much of the project has been accomplished to date?
4. What is the forecasted cost at completion (EAC_f)? What is the predicted VAC_f?
5. Report and interpret the TCPI for the project at this point in time.
6. What is the estimated date of completion?
7. How well is the project doing in terms of its priorities?

Try to present the above information in a form worthy of consideration by top management.

Include an Earned Value table and a Tracking Gantt Chart.

Note: Insert May 31, 2012, as the status date in the Project Information box.

RED ZUMA PROJECT

The ARC Company specializes in developing and selling a wide range of high-quality scooters. Sales representatives report that there is a growing demand for racing scooters. ARC's president, Robin Lane, is excited about the possibilities and predicts that one day these kinds of razor scooters will be featured in X-Game events. ARC is a small company and uses a strong matrix to optimally utilize limited manpower.

The Project Priority Matrix for the Red Zuma Project is:

	Time	Scope	Cost
Constrain		X	
Enhance	X		
Accept			X

Part 1

You are a member of a project team assigned to develop the new razor scooter code named "Red Zuma." Table A2.5 contains the information necessary to create a project schedule. For the purpose of this case assume the following:

1. The project begins January 2, 2015.
2. The following holidays are observed: January 1, Martin Luther King Day (third Monday in January), Memorial Day (last Monday in May), July 4th, Labor Day (first Monday in September), Thanksgiving Day (4th Thursday in November), December 25.
3. If a holiday falls on a Saturday, then Friday will be given as an extra day off, and if it falls on a Sunday, then Monday will be given as a day off. If December 25th falls on a Friday then Monday will not be given a day off.
4. The project team works eight-hour days, Monday through Friday.

TABLE A2.5 ··

Red Zuma: Project Schedule

ID	Task Name	Duration	Predecessors
1	**1 Red Zuma Project**	260 days	
2	1.1 Market Analysis	25 days	
3	1.2 Product Design	30 days	2
4	1.3 Manufacturing Study	20 days	2
5	1.4 Product Design Selection	10 days	3, 4
6	1.5 Detailed Marketing Plan	15 days	5
7	1.6 Manufacturing Process	30 days	5
8	1.7 Detailed Product Design	45 days	5
9	1.8 Build Prototypes	25 days	8
10	1.9 Lab Test Prototypes	10 days	9
11	1.10 Field Test Prototypes	15 days	9
12	1.11 Finalized Product Design	20 days	7,10,11
13	1.12 Final Manufacturing Process	10 days	12
14	1.13 Order Components	7 days	12
15	1.14 Order Production Equipment	14 days	13
16	1.15 Install Production Equipment	35 days	14FS + 20 days,15FS + 30 days
17	1.16 Celebrate	1 days	6, 16

Note: FS refers to a Finish-to-Start lag.

Construct a network schedule for this project and prepare a memo that answers the following questions:

1. When is the project estimated to be completed? How long will the project take?
2. What is the critical path for the project?
3. Which activity has the greatest amount of slack?
4. How sensitive is this network?
5. Identify two sensible milestones and explain your choices.

Include the following printouts:

- A Gantt chart.
- A network diagram highlighting the critical path.
- A schedule table reporting ES, LS, EF, LF, and slack for each activity.

Part 2

The following personnel have been assigned full-time to the Red Zuma project team:

4 marketing specialists
4 design engineers
4 development engineers
4 industrial engineers
4 test riders
2 purchasing agent

Use the file from Part 1 and the information contained in Tables A2.6 and A2.7 to assign resources to the project schedule.

Part A

Prepare a memo that addresses the following questions:

1. Which if any of the resources are overallocated?

TABLE A2.6 ···
Red Zuma Project Resources

	$	Number available
Marketing specialist	$80,000/yr	4
Design engineer	$125,000/yr	4
Development engineer	$110,000/yr	4
Industrial engineer	$100,000/yr	4
Purchasing agent	$75,000/yr	2
Test rider	$70/hr	4

Note: MS Project considers resources in terms of percentages with one full-time worker being 100%.

TABLE A2.7 ··
Red Zuma Resource Assignments

Task Name	Resource Names
Red Zuma Project	
Market Analysis	Marketing Specialist [400%]
Product Design	Marketing Specialist, Design Engineer [400%], Development Engineer [200%], Industrial Engineer, Purchasing Agent
Manufacturing Study	Industrial Engineer [400%], Development Engineer [200%]
Product Design Selection	Marketing Specialist [200%], Design Engineer [300%], Development Engineer [200%], Industrial Engineer [200%], Purchasing Agent [25%]
Detailed Marketing Plan	Marketing Specialist [400%]
Manufacturing Process	Design Engineer, Development Engineer [200%], Industrial Engineer [300%]
Detailed Product Design	Marketing Specialist [200%], Design Engineer [400%], Development Engineer [200%], Industrial Engineer [200%], Purchasing Agent [25%]
Build Prototypes	Design Engineer [200%], Development Engineer [200%], Industrial Engineer [400%]
Lab Test Prototypes	Design Engineer [200%], Development Engineer [200%], Test Rider
Field Tests	Marketing Specialist, Design Engineer [200%], Development Engineer, Industrial Engineer, Test Rider [300%]
Finalized Product Design	Marketing Specialist [200%], Design Engineer [300%], Development Engineer [300%], Industrial Engineer [200%], Purchasing Agent [25%]
Final Manufacturing Process	Industrial Engineer [300%], Design Engineer, Purchasing Agent [25%]
Order Components	Purchasing Agent
Order Production Equipment	Purchasing Agent
Install Production Equipment	Design Engineer, Development Engineer [300%], Industrial Engineer [400%]
Celebration	Design Engineer [400%], Development Engineer [400%], Industrial Engineer [400%], Marketing Specialist [400%], Purchasing Agent [200%]

Note: Resource assignments without brackets is 100%.

2. Assume that the project is time constrained and try to resolve any overallocation problems by leveling within slack. What happens?
3. What is the impact of leveling within slack on the sensitivity of the network?

Include a Gantt chart with the schedule table after leveling within slack.

4. Assume that the project is resource constrained and no additional personnel are available. How long will the project take given the resources assigned? (Hint: Undo leveling performed in Part A before answering this question.)

Note: No splitting of activities is allowed.

5. How does the new duration compare with the estimated completion date generated from Part 1? What does this tell you about the impact resources can have on a schedule?

Include a Gantt chart with a schedule table displaying free and total slack depicting the resource-constrained schedule.

Part B

Top management is not happy with the resource-constrained schedule. Robin Lane, the president, has promised retailers that ARC will begin production in time for the major trade show in Las Vegas on January 22, 2016, which means the project needs to be completed by January 17, 2016. She has authorized working the first available Saturday of each month to help the project get completed sooner. She realizes that this will only reduce the project duration by 12–13 days.

After talking to the engineers, everyone agrees that they do not have to wait for the Detailed Product Design to be 100% completed before starting to build the prototype. The consensus is that Building the Prototype can start 30 days after the start of the Detailed Product Design. Likewise the Final Manufacturing Process can start 15 days after the start of Finalized Product Design.

Dewey Martin, director of product development, is also willing to add personnel to the project. He is willing to make available at least one more Development, Design, and/or Industrial Engineer to the project as well as Marketing Specialist. Since there is an acute shortage of personnel at ARC he requests that you only use additional manpower that will help meet the deadline. Your objective is to develop a schedule which will satisfy the deadline with minimum additional resource usage.

Prepare a memo that addresses the following questions:

1. What was the impact of introducing Start-to-Start lags to the schedule and budget?
2. Which, if any additional personnel assignments, would you choose to complete the project before the January 17th deadline? Explain your choices as well as the reasons for not choosing other options.
3. How have these changes affected the sensitivity of the network and the critical path?

Include a Gantt chart with a schedule table displaying free and total slack for the new schedule.

Note: Do not assign new personnel to specific tasks, simply add them to the Resource Sheet. All new personnel are available full time (100%).

> At first glance—this appears to be a very complicated, difficult assignment, but if you enter the information correctly, the computer is able to generate the answers with a few simple clicks.

Part 3

Top management has accepted the schedule created at the end of Part 2. Prepare a brief memo that addresses the following questions:

1. How much will the project cost? What is the most expensive activity?
2. What does the cash flow statement tell you about how costs are distributed over the life span of the project?

Include a monthly cash flow for the project.

Once you are confident that you have the final schedule, save the file as a baseline. **Hint:** Save a backup file just in case without baseline!

Part 4

Part A

Today's date is July 8, 2015, the milestone date for the completion of the Prototype. You are charged with preparing a status report for top management. Table A2.8 summarizes progress on the Red Zuma project:

Submit a professional status report to Robin Lane that addresses the following questions:

1. How is the project progressing in terms of cost and schedule?
2. What activities have gone well? What activities have not gone well?
3. How much of the project has been accomplished (PCIB)?
4. What is the forecasted cost at completion (EAC$_f$)?
5. What is the estimated completion date?
6. How is the project doing in terms of priorities (see Part 1)?

Report and interpret relevant Earned Value metrics in your report.

Include a Tracking Gantt chart as well as an Earned Value Table with your memo.

TABLE A2.8 ....
Red Zuma Project Update

	Task Name	Act. Start	Act. Finish	% Comp.	Phys. % Comp.	Act. Dur.	Rem. Dur.
1	**1 Red Zuma**	**Fri 1/9/15**	**NA**	**46%**	**0%**	**125.85 days**	**146.4 days**
2	1.1 Market Analysis	Fri 1/9/15	Thu 2/12/15	100%	0%	25 days	0 days
3	1.2 Product Design	Fri 2/13/15	Wed 4/1/15	100%	0%	35 days	0 days
4	1.3 Manufacturing Study	Fri 2/13/15	Fri 3/6/15	100%	0%	16 days	0 days
5	1.4 Product Design Selection	Thu 4/2/15	Fri 4/17/15	100%	0%	13 days	0 days
6	1.5 Detailed Marketing Plan	NA	NA	0%	0%	0 days	15 days
7	1.6 Manufacturing Process	NA	NA	0%	0%	0 days	30 days
8	1.7 Detailed Product Design	Mon 4/20/15	Wed 6/24/15	100%	0%	49 days	0 days
9	1.8 Build Prototypes	Wed 6/10/15	NA	39%	0%	9 days	14 days
10	1.9 Lab Test Prototypes	NA	NA	0%	0%	0 days	10 days
11	1.10 Field Test Prototypes	NA	NA	0%	0%	0 days	15 days
12	1.11 Finalized Product Design	NA	NA	0%	0%	0 days	20 days
13	1.12 Final Manufacturing Process	NA	NA	0%	0%	0 days	10 days
14	1.13 Order Components	NA	NA	0%	0%	0 days	7 days
15	1.14 Order Production Equipment	NA	NA	0%	0%	0 days	14 days
16	1.15 Install Production Equipment	NA	NA	0%	0%	0 days	35 days
17	1.16 Celebrate	NA	NA	0%	0%	0 days	1 days

Part B

You have told Robin Lane that based on what you know now you need to revise the estimates for some of the remaining activities. Detailed Product Design is expected to take 3 days longer than planned. Build Prototypes is expected to take 2 days less than planned and Finalized Product Design is expected to take 3 days longer than planned. Final Manufacturing Process is expected to take 2 days less than planned, while Install Production Equipment is now expected to take only

30 days. You also report that Detailed Marketing plan will be completed before the end of the New Year. She is insisting that the project be completed by January 17th in order to be ready for the Las Vegas show. She is willing to spend $50,000 from Management Reserves to expedite shipping if necessary. $25,000 would reduce the shipping of components by 5 days and/or $25,000 would reduce the shipping of manufacturing parts by 5 days (Hint: Adjust lag). Prepare a memo to Robin that addresses the following questions:

1. What is the impact of the revised estimates for Finalized Product Design and Install Production Equipment on the project schedule and cost?
2. Would you recommend authorizing the expenditure of $50,000? Explain.
3. What, if any other recommendations, would you make so that the project can achieve Robin's deadline? Justify your recommendations.

Include a Tracking Gantt chart with variance schedule that depicts your final recommendations and revised schedule.

Hint: After adjusting the Installation of Production Equipment and Finalized Product Design, level outside of slack to eliminate any resource over allocation problems.

CONVEYOR BELT PROJECT

Part 1

Project Description

The new computer-controlled conveyor belt is an exciting project that moves and positions items on the conveyor belt within <1 millimeter. The project will produce a new system for future installations, and for replacement of those in the field, at a low cost. The computer-controlled conveyor belt has the potential to be a critical unit in 30 percent of the systems installed in factories. The new system is also easier to update with future technologies.

The Project Priority Matrix for the Conveyor Belt Project (CBP) is:

	Time	Scope	Cost
Constrain	X		
Enhance		X	
Accept			X

Table A2.9 has been developed for you to use in completing the project exercises.

Assignment

Develop the WBS outline using the software available to you.

Question

Does this information (WBS) allow you to define any milestones of the project? Why or why not? What are they?

Remember: Save your file for future exercises!

TABLE A2.9 ·······························
Conveyor Belt Project; WBS

Conveyor Belt Project	
Hardware	Hardware specifications
	Hardware design
	Hardware documentation
	Prototypes
	Order circuit boards
	Assemble preproduction models
Operating system	Kernel specifications
	Drivers
	Disk drivers
	Serial I/O drivers
	Memory management
	Operating system documentation
	Network interface
Utilities	Utilities specifications
	Routine utilities
	Complex utilities
	Utilities documentation
	Shell
System integration	Architectural decisions
	Integration first phase
	System hard/software test
	Project documentation
	Integration acceptance testing

Part 2

Use your file from Part 1 and the information provided below to complete this exercise. (See Table A2.10.)

1. Each work package will represent an activity.
2. The project begins January 4, 2010.
3. The following holidays are observed: January 1, Memorial Day (last Monday in May), July 4th, Labor Day (first Monday in September), Thanksgiving Day (4th Thursday in November), December 25 and 26.
4. If a holiday falls on a Saturday then Friday will be given as an extra day off, and if it falls on a Sunday, then Monday will be given as a day off.
5. The project teams work eight-hour days, Monday through Friday.

Warning: Experience has taught students to frequently make separate backup files for each exercise. The software is never as friendly as users expect!

Construct a network schedule for the conveyor belt project and prepare a memo that addresses the following questions:

1. When is the project estimated to be completed? How long will the project take?

TABLE A2.10 ••
Conveyor Belt Project; Schedule

Activity	Description	Resource	Duration (days)	Preceding Activity
1	Architectural decisions	Design	25	—
2	Hardware specifications	Development, design	50	1
3	Kernel specifications	Design	20	1
4	Utilities specifications	Development, design	15	1
5	Hardware design	Design, development	70	2
6	Disk drivers	Assembly, development	100	3
7	Memory management	Development	90	3
8	Operating system documentation	Design, documentation	25	3
9	Routine utilities	Development	60	4
10	Complex utilities	Development	80	4
11	Utilities documentation	Documentation, design	20	4
12	Hardware documentation	Documentation, design	30	5
13	Integration first phase	Assembly, development	50	6,7,8,9,10,11,12
14	Prototypes	Assembly, development	80	13
15	Serial I/O drivers	Development	130	13
16	System hard/software test	Assembly	25	14,15
17	Order circuit boards	Purchasing	5	16
18	Network interface	Development	90	16
19	Shell	Development	60	16
20	Project documentation	Documentation, development	50	16
21	Assemble preproduction models	Assembly, development	30	17F-S, lag 50 days
22	Integrated acceptance testing	Assembly, development	60	18,19,20,21

Note: F-S refers to a Finish-to-Start lag.

2. What is the critical path(s) for the project?
3. Which activity has the greatest amount of slack?
4. How sensitive is this network?
5. Identify two sensible milestones and explain your choices.
6. Compare the advantages/disadvantages of displaying the schedule as a network versus a Gantt chart.

Include the following printouts:

- A Gantt chart.
- A network diagram highlighting the critical path.
- A schedule table reporting. ES, LS, EF, LF, and slack for each activity.

Hint: the project should be completed in 530 days.
Remember: Save your file for future exercises!

Part 3

Remember the old saying, "A project plan is not a schedule until resources are committed." This exercise illustrates this subtle, but very important, difference.

Part A

Using your files from Part 2 input resources and their costs if you have not already done so. All information is found in Tables A2.10 and A2.11.

TABLE A2.11 ··
Organization Resources

Name	Group	Cost ($/hr)
Design	R&D (2 teams)	$100
Development	R&D (2 teams)	70
Documentation	R&D (1 team)	60
Assembly/test	R&D (1 team)	70
Purchasing	Procurement (1 team)	40

Prepare a memo that addresses the following questions:

1. Which if any of the resources are overallocated?
2. Assume that the project is time constrained and try to resolve any overallocation problems by leveling within slack. What happens?
3. What is the impact of leveling within slack on the sensitivity of the network?

Include a Gantt chart with the schedule table after leveling within slack.

4. Assume the project is resource constrained and resolve any overallocation problems by leveling outside of slack. What happens? What are the managerial implications?
5. What options are available at this point in time?

Include a Gantt chart with the schedule table after leveling outside of slack.

Note: No splitting of activities is allowed.
Note: No partial assignments (e.g., 50 percent). All resources must be assigned 100 percent.

Part B

When you show the resource-constrained network to top management, they are visibly shaken. After some explanation and negotiation they make the following compromise with you:

- The project must be completed no later than February 2, 2012 (530 days).
- You may assign two additional development teams.
- If this does not suffice, you may hire other development teams from the outside. Hire as few external teams as possible because they cost $50 more per hour than your inside development people.

Internal Development

Add as many development units (teams) as needed to stay within the 530 days. If you need more than two internal development units, then hire as few external teams as necessary. Select the cheapest possibility! Change as few activities as possible. It is recommended you keep work packages which require cooperation of several organizational units inside your company. You decide how best to do this.

Hint: Undo leveling prior to adding new resources.

Once you have obtained a schedule that meets the time and resource constraints, prepare a memo that addresses the following questions:

1. What changes did you make and why?
2. How long will the project take?
3. How did these changes affect the sensitivity of the network?

Include a Gantt chart with a schedule table presenting the new schedule.

Part 4

Based on the file created at the end of Part 3, prepare a memo that addresses the following questions:

1. How much will the project cost?
2. What does the cash flow statement tell you about how costs are distributed over the life span of the project?

Include a monthly cash flow and a cost table for the project.

Once you are confident that you have the final schedule, save the file as a baseline.

Hint: Save a backup file just in case without baseline!

Part 5

Prepare status reports for each of the first four quarters of the project given the information provided here. This requires saving your resource schedule as a baseline and inserting the appropriate status report date in the program. Assume that no work has been completed on the day of the status report.

Your status report should include a table containing the PV, EV, AC, BAC, EAC, SV, CV, and CPI for each activity and the whole project. The report should also address the following questions:

1. How is the project progressing in terms of cost and schedule?
2. What activities have gone well? What activities have not gone well?
3. What do the PCIB and PCIC indicate in terms of how much of the project has been accomplished to date?
4. What is the forecasted cost at completion (EAC_f)? What is the predicted VAC_f?
5. Report and interpret the TCPI for the project at this point in time.
6. What is the estimated date of completion?
7. How well is the project doing in terms of its priorities?

Try to present the above information in a form worthy of consideration by top management.

Include a Tracking Gantt chart with each report.

First Quarter, April 1, 2010

Table A2.12 summarizes the information regarding activities accomplished to date.
Be sure to save your file after each quarterly report and use it to build the next report!

TABLE A2.12 ••
April 1, 2010

Activity	Start Date	Finish Date	Actual Duration	Remaining Duration
Hardware specifications	2/9/10		37	8
Kernel specifications	2/8/10	3/12/10	25	0
Disk drivers	3/15/10		13	87
Memory management	3/15/10		13	77
Op. systems documentation	3/15/10		13	7
Utilities specifications	3/8/10	3/29/10	16	0
Complex utilities	3/30/10		2	85
Architectural decisions	1/4/10	2/5/10	25	0

Second Quarter, July 1, 2010

Table A2.13 summarizes the information regarding activities accomplished since the last report.

TABLE A2.13 ••
July 1, 2010

Activity	Start Date	Finish Date	Actual Duration	Remaining Duration
Hardware specifications	2/9/10	4/12/10	45	0
Hardware design	4/13/10		56	11
Kernel specifications	2/8/10	3/12/10	25	0
Disk drivers	3/15/10		77	33
Memory management	3/15/10		77	19
Op. systems documentation	3/15/10	4/16/10	25	0
Utilities specifications	3/8/10	3/29/10	16	0
Routine utilities*	4/26/10		47	18
Complex utilities	3/30/10		66	25
Utilities documentation	5/3/10	6/2/10	22	0
Architectural decisions	1/4/10	2/5/10	25	0

* The project manager for the external development team that was hired to perform routine utilities reported that due to commitments to other clients they would be able to start on that activity 4/26/10.

Third Quarter, October 1, 2010

Table A2.14 summarizes the information regarding activities accomplished since the last report.

TABLE A2.14
October 1, 2010

Activity	Start Date	Finish Date	Actual Duration	Remaining Duration
Hardware specifications	2/9/10	4/12/10	45	0
Hardware design	4/13/10	7/16/10	67	0
Hardware documentation	7/19/10	8/24/10	27	0
Kernel specifications	2/8/10	3/12/10	25	0
Disk drivers	3/15/10	8/17/10	110	0
Memory management	3/15/10	7/30/10	98	0
Op. systems documentation	3/15/10	4/16/10	25	0
Utilities specifications	3/8/10	3/29/10	16	0
Routine utilities	4/26/10	7/27/10	65	0
Complex utilities	3/30/10	8/11/10	95	0
Utilities documentation	5/3/10	6/2/10	22	0
Architectural decisions	1/4/10	2/5/10	25	0
Integration 1st phase	8/25/10		26	24

Fourth Quarter, January 1, 2011

Table A2.15 summarizes the information regarding activities accomplished since the last report.

TABLE A2.15
January 1, 2011

Activity	Start Date	Finish Date	Actual Duration	Remaining Duration
Hardware specifications	2/9/10	4/12/10	45	0
Hardware design	4/13/10	7/16/10	67	0
Hardware documentation	7/19/10	8/24/10	27	0
Prototypes	11/11/10		34	44
Kernel specifications	2/8/10	3/12/10	25	0
Disk drivers	3/15/10	8/17/10	110	0
Serial I/O drivers	11/11/10		34	119
Memory management	3/15/10	7/30/10	98	0
Op. systems documentation	3/15/10	4/16/10	25	0
Utilities specifications	3/8/10	3/29/10	16	0
Routine utilities	4/26/10	7/27/10	65	0
Complex utilities	3/30/10	8/11/10	95	0
Utilities documentation	5/3/10	6/2/10	22	0
Architectural decisions	1/4/10	2/5/10	25	0
Integration 1st phase	8/25/10	11/10/10	55	0

Part 6

You have received revised estimates for the remaining activities at the end of the fourth quarter:

- Prototypes will be completed on 3/8/11.
- Serial I/O drivers will be completed on 6/30/11.
- System hardware/software test will start on 7/1/11 and take 25 days.
- Order circuit boards will start on 8/8/11 and take 5 days.
- Assemble preproduction model will begin on 10/14/11 and take 18 days.
- Project documentation is expected to start on 8/8/11 and will take 55 days.
- Network interface is expected to start on 8/8/11 and will take 99 days.
- Shell is expected to start on 8/8/11 and will take 55 days.
- Integrated acceptance testing is expected to start on 12/29/11 and will take 54 days.

Prepare a memo that addresses the following questions:

1. What is the new EAC for the project? How long should the project take given these revised estimates?
2. How happy will top management be with these forecasts given the priorities of the project?
3. What recommendations would you make?

Include a revised schedule, a Tracking Gantt chart, and cost table with your memo.

ACRONYMS

AC	Actual cost of work completed		**FF**	Free float
ACWP	Actual cost of work performed		**IFB**	Invitation for bid
AOA	Activity-on-arrow		**KISS**	Keep it simple, stupid
AON	Activity-on-node		**LF**	Late finish
BAC	Budget at completion		**LS**	Late start
BATNA	Best alternative to a negotiated agreement		**MBWA**	Management by wandering around
			NIH	Not invented here
BCWP	Budgeted cost of work performed		**NPV**	Net present value
BCWS	Budgeted cost of work scheduled		**OBS**	Organization breakdown structure
BOOT	Build-own-operate-transfer		**PCI**	Percent complete index
CAPM	Certified Associate in Project Management		**PCIB**	Percent complete index—budget costs
			PCIC	Percent complete index—actual costs
CCPM	Critical-chain approach to project planning and management		**PDM**	Precedence diagramming method
CPI	Cost performance index		**PERT**	Project evaluation review technique
CPM	Critical path method		**PMP**	Project Management Professional
CV	Cost variance		**PO**	Project office
DUR	Duration		**PV**	Planned value of work scheduled
EAC	Estimate at completion (with revised cost estimates)		**RBS**	Risk breakdown structure
			RM	Responsibility matrix
EF	Early finish		**SL**	Slack
EQ	Emotional intelligence		**SPI**	Schedule performance index
ES	Early start		**SV**	Schedule variance
ETC	Estimate to complete		**TCPI**	To complete performance index
EV	Earned value		**VAC**	Variance at completion
FAC	Forecast at completion		**WBS**	Work breakdown structure

PROJECT MANAGEMENT EQUATIONS

$$PCIB = \frac{EV}{BAC}$$

$$CV = EV - AC$$

$$CPI = \frac{EV}{AC}$$

$$EAC_f = \frac{(BAC - EV)}{\left(\frac{EV}{AC}\right)} + AC$$

$$EAC_{re} = AC + ETC_{re}$$

$$t_e = \frac{a + 4m + b}{6}$$

$$\sigma_{t_e} = \left(\frac{b - a}{6}\right)$$

$$TCPI = \frac{(BAC - EV)}{(BAC - AC)}$$

$$PCIC = \frac{AC}{EAC}$$

$$SV = EV - PV$$

$$SPI = \frac{EV}{PV}$$

$$VAC_f = BAC - EAC_f$$

$$VAC_{re} = BAC - EAC_{re}$$

$$\sigma_{T_E} = \sqrt{\Sigma \sigma_{t_e}^2}$$

$$Z = \frac{T_S - T_E}{\sqrt{\Sigma \sigma_{t_e}^2}}$$

INDEX

Note: Page numbers followed by n indicate material in source notes and footnotes.